Do the Right Thing

The Jones and Bartlett Series in Philosophy

Robert Ginsberg, General Editor

Ayer, A. J., *Metaphysics and Common Sense*, 1994 reissue with corrections and new introduction by Thomas Magnell, Drew University

Beckwith, Francis J., University of Nevada, Las Vegas, Editor, *Do the Right Thing: A Philosophical Dialogue on the Moral and Social Issues of Our Time*

Bishop, Anne H., and John R. Scudder, Jr., Lynchburg College, *Nursing Ethics: Therapeutic Caring Presence*

Caws, Peter, The George Washington University, *Ethics from Experience*

DeMarco, Joseph P., Cleveland State University, *Moral Theory: A Contemporary Overview*

Gert, Bernard, et al., Dartmouth College, *Morality and the New Genetics: A Guide for Students and Health Care Providers*

Gorr, Michael, Illinois State University, and Sterling Harwood, San Jose State University, Editors, *Crime and Punishment: Philosophic Explorations*

Haber, Joram Graf, Bergen Community College, Interviewer, *Ethics in the '90s*, a 26-part Video Series

Harwood, Sterling, San Jose State University, Editor, *Business as Ethical and Business as Usual: Text, Readings, and Cases*

Heil, John, Davidson College, *First-Order Logic: A Concise Introduction*

Jason, Gary, San Diego State University, *Introduction to Logic*

Minogue, Brendan, Youngstown State University, *Bioethics: A Committee Approach*

Moriarty, Marilyn, Hollins College, *Writing Science through Critical Thinking*

Pauling, Linus, and Daisaku, Ikeda, *A Lifelong Quest for Peace, A Dialogue*, Translator and Editor, Richard L. Gage

Pojman, Louis P., The University of Mississippi, and Francis Beckwith, University of Nevada, Las Vegas, Editors, *The Abortion Controversy: A Reader*

Pojman, Louis P., The University of Mississippi, Editor, *Environmental Ethics: Readings in Theory and Application*

Pojman, Louis P., The University of Mississippi, *Life and Death: Grappling with the Moral Dilemmas of Our Time*

Pojman, Louis P., The University of Mississippi, Editor, *Life and Death: A Reader in Moral Problems*

Rolston III, Holmes, Colorado State University, Editor, *Biology, Ethics, and the Origins of Life*

Townsend, Dabney, The University of Texas at Arlington, Editor, *Aesthetics: Classic Readings from the Western Tradition*

Veatch, Robert M., The Kennedy Institute of Ethics, Georgetown University, Editor, *Cross-Cultural Perspectives in Medical Ethics: Readings*

Veatch, Robert M., The Kennedy Institute of Ethics, Georgetown University, Editor, *Medical Ethics, Second Edition*

Verene, D. P., Emory University, Editor, *Sexual Love and Western Morality: A Philosophical Anthology, Second Edition*

Williams, Clifford, Trinity University, Illinois, Editor, *On Love and Friendship: Philosophical Readings*

Do the Right Thing

*A Philosophical Dialogue on the
Moral and Social Issues of Our Time*

Francis J. Beckwith
University of Nevada, Las Vegas

Jones and Bartlett Publishers
Sudbury, Massachusetts

Boston   London   Singapore

Editorial, Sales, and Customer Service Offices
Jones and Bartlett Publishers
40 Tall Pine Drive
Sudbury, MA 01776
508-443-5000
1-800-832-0034

Jones and Bartlett Publishers International
7 Melrose Terrace
London W6 7RL
England

Library of Congress Cataloging-in-Publication Data
Do the right thing : a philosophical dialogue on the moral and social
    issues of our time / edited by Francis J. Beckwith
        p.   cm. -- (The Jones and Bartlett series in philosophy)
    Includes bibliographical references and index.
    ISBN 0-86720-972-0
    1. Applied ethics.   2. Ethical problems.   3. United States--Moral
conditions.   I. Beckwith, Francis.   II. Series.
BJ1031.D6   1995
170--dc20   95-41391
                                                    CIP

Acquisitions Editors: Arthur C. Bartlett and Nancy E. Bartlett
Production Administrator: Anne S. Noonan
Manufacturing Buyer: Dana L. Cerrito
Editorial Production Service: Seahorse Prepress/Book 1
Typesetting: Seahorse Prepress/Book 1
Printing and Binding: Hamilton Printing Company
Cover Printing: New England Book Components, Inc.
Cover Designer: Hannus Design Associates

Printed in the United States of America
99 98 97   10 9 8 7 6 5 4 3 2

To my brothers James and Patrick and my sister, Elizabeth Ann,
the first three pages in our parents' book of virtues.

CONTENTS

PREFACE

Moral discussion rules the day. Best-selling books and political celebrities are calling for greater virtue in the public square, while at the same time the nastiness of our public discourse is at an all-time high. Appeals to justice, fairness, rights, decency, and equality dominate the way we argue about issues such as abortion, euthanasia, affirmative action, homosexuality, and family values. And yet the temptation to dismiss our opponent without rationally critiquing his or her arguments is overwhelming in our media-driven soundbite culture.

The purpose of this book is to provide a text for applied ethics, applied social philosophy, and social issues courses for use by instructors who are deeply committed to raising the level of public discourse.

Do the Right Thing is an anthology with 63 selections covering 11 moral issues under eight general headings, two discussions on moral practice and ethical theory, and one section covering the role of moral education in elementary and secondary education. It is thoroughly pedagogical, containing a general introduction to the text, an introduction to each of the 11 sections (including introductions under the four general headings), study questions after each entry, and a bibliography after each section.

Although this text deals with the issues usually discussed in others, such as abortion, euthanasia, and affirmative action, it also addresses issues not found in most texts yet that are currently of great interest to many students and instructors: "family values and sex roles," "speech codes on college campuses," "multiculturalism and justice," "fetal tissue research," and "homosexuals in the military."

My goal in putting together this anthology is to provide both instructors and students with a user-friendly product that contains the most representative and articulate defenses of the positions covered.

This book would not have been possible if not for the enthusiasm, encouragement, and patience of the publishers, Nancy and Art Bartlett. It is deeply gratifying to work with people who truly care about providing university professors with outstanding texts. I would like to also thank the following readers who provided insightful comments that resulted in a number of key changes in the text before it went to press: Louis P. Pojman (U.S. Military Academy, West Point), Dianne N. Irving (DeSales School of Theology), Henry R. West (Macalester College), Caroline J. Simon (Hope College), Joseph DeMarco (Cleveland State University), Marina Oshana (California State University, Sacramento), and Linda Bomstad (California State Polytechnic University, Pomona). Finally, I am eternally grateful to my wife, Frankie R. D. Beckwith, who has served for nearly a decade as my business manager, booking agent, best friend, lover, and conscience.

INTRODUCTION

It seems that people everywhere and in every place agree that we should all strive to do the right thing, that is, to do what is morally appropriate or obligatory in a given situation or circumstance. Where people disagree, however, is over the question of *what exactly* is the right thing to do. In some cases there is little or no disagreement. For example, it is uncontroversial to claim that Mother Teresa is morally superior to Adolf Hitler, that torturing three-year-olds for fun is evil, that giving 10 percent of one's financial surplus to an invalid is praiseworthy, that raping a woman is morally wicked, and that providing food and shelter for one's spouse and children is a good thing. But why do we make these moral judgments rather than their opposites? And why is it that on some issues—such as abortion, euthanasia, affirmative action, and homosexuality—there is impassioned disagreement? The purpose of this text is to guide the student through some of the great moral ideas and great moral debates of the present day so that he or she can arrive at a reasoned answer to these and other questions.

In October 1992 I participated in a panel discussion entitled "Sex, Laws, and Videotapes: Morality in the Media," sponsored by the Clark County Bar Association in Southern Nevada. Its purpose was to discuss the issue of the moral responsibility of the media, focusing for the most part on sex, violence, and obscenity. The participants represented a potpourri of interests and professions: two radio shock jocks, two attorneys, the owner of a phone sex line, the general manager of a local television station, a home-school mom, a Christian radio disk jockey, a television reporter, and me, a philosopher. The moderator was the incoming president of the bar association, a David Letterman wannabe who was very entertaining and quite fair. Throughout the discussion I agreed with most of the participants that government censorship was not the answer to our problems. However, I did say that this does not preclude the media from morally evaluating the content of their programming and being concerned about how such programming may influence young people and society as a whole. At that point, a young woman in the audience raised her hand and asked me the question, "Who are you to judge?" This was a rhetorical question, not really meant to be answered. (She was really making the *claim*: Beckwith, you have no right to make moral judgments about society.) But I answered it anyway: "I am a rational human person who is aware of certain fundamental principles of logical and moral reasoning. I think I'm qualified." This response absolutely shocked her. I went on to say, "Your claim that I have no right to make judgments is itself a judgment about me. Your claim, therefore, is self-refuting." Although our exchange brought the audience to laughter, the young woman's question was a very serious one that is raised by many people in our contemporary culture. It is a question that apparently assumes that when it comes to the discussion of moral issues there are no right or wrong answers and no inappropriate or appropriate judgments, no reasonable or rational way to make moral distinctions. There are only subjective opinions, no different from opinions about one's favorite ice cream flavor, football team, or movie star.

But the young woman in the audience did not fully comprehend the scope of her denial. For to deny that one can make moral distinctions one must deny the legitimacy of the uncontroversial moral judgments listed above. That is, one must admit that Mother Teresa is no more or less moral than Adolf Hitler, torturing three-year-olds for fun is neither good nor evil, giving 10 percent of one's financial surplus to an invalid is neither praiseworthy nor not praiseworthy, raping a woman is not right or wrong, and providing food and shelter for one's spouse and children is neither a good thing nor a bad thing.

When people deny that we can reason about moral matters, they give up much more than they ever imagined. Consider the following example. In the following paraphrase of a tape-recorded conversation with one of his victims, serial murderer Ted Bundy attempts to justify the murder of his victim:

> Then I learned that all moral judgments are "value judgments," that all value judgments are subjective, and that none can be proved to be either "right" or "wrong." I even read somewhere that the Chief Justice of the United States had written that the American Constitution expressed nothing more than collective value judgments. Believe it or not, I figured out for myself—what apparently the Chief Justice couldn't figure out for himself—that if the rationality of one value judgment was zero, multiplying it by millions would not make it one whit more rational. Nor is there any "reason" to obey the law for anyone, like myself, who has the boldness and daring—the strength of character—to throw off its shackles. . . . I discovered that to become truly free, truly unfettered, I had to become truly uninhibited. And I quickly discovered that the greatest obstacle to my freedom, the greatest block and limitation to it, consisted in the insupportable "value judgment" that I was bound to respect the rights of others. I asked myself, who were these "others"? Other human beings, with human rights? . . . Surely, you would not, in this age of scientific enlightenment, declare that God or nature has marked some pleasures as "moral" or "good" and others as "immoral" or "bad"? In any case, let me assure you, my dear young lady, that there is absolutely no comparison between the pleasure I might take in eating ham, and the pleasure I anticipate in raping and murdering you. That is the honest conclusion to which my education has led me—after the most conscientious examination of my spontaneous and uninhibited self.[1]

After a sharp scream, the tape clicks off. Although no rational person will condone Ted Bundy's behavior, the unthoughtful slogans we hear in the public square (e.g., "Who are you to judge?") may unwittingly abet it. It is no secret that people disagree, sometimes vehemently, over a variety of moral and social issues, just as do the contributors to this text. But many of us, including all the contributors to this volume (no matter how differently they approach the subject), agree on at least one thing: we can reason about moral matters.

Approaches to the Study of Morality and Ethics

Four different approaches to the study of morality and ethics have dominated the literature. They are outlined in the following diagram.[2]

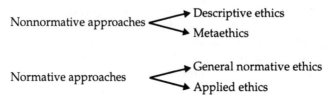

The first two approaches are called *nonnormative approaches* because they examine morality without concern for making judgments as to what is morally right or wrong; that is, they take no moral positions. The second two are called *normative approaches* because they concern making judgments as to what is morally right or wrong; that is, they take moral positions. When a person makes a *normative* moral judgment, she is saying that a particular act, rule, principle, law, behavior, or person is right or wrong, appropriate or inappropriate, in some sense in violation of or in accordance with particular ethical principles, rules, intuitions, or examples of morality. For instance, if David were to say, "Frank is wrong in not helping the homeless," he would be making a normative moral judgment. In contrast, a nonnormative analysis of morality and ethics would be quite different; it would not involve a moral judgment of rightness or wrongness, but it might entail an evaluation of moral terms (e.g., "What does David mean when he says that Frank is wrong in not helping the homeless?") or a nonjudgmental description of moral activity (e.g., "David says that Frank is wrong in not helping the homeless."). Let us look at each of these types of approaches in greater detail.

1. Nonnormative Approaches

There are two nonnormative approaches: descriptive ethics and metaethics. *Descriptive ethics* concerns what sociologists, anthropologists, and historians often do in their study and research: describe and sometimes try to explain the moral and ethical practices and beliefs of certain societies and cultures. In their descriptions and explanations, the sociologist, the anthropologist, and the historian do not make judgments about the morality of the practices and beliefs. For example, the observation that a particular culture may sanction infanticide (the killing of infants) because it does not believe that children are human persons is not a moral judgment; it is simply a description and an explanation of the practice.

Metaethics (which literally means "above ethics") focuses on the analysis of the meanings of the central terms used in ethical reasoning and decision-making, such as "good," "bad," "duty," and "right." Like descriptive ethics, it does not involve the making of normative moral judgments. Metaethical inquiries attempt to answer questions of meaning, such as the following: What do people mean when they say some action or behavior is morally wrong? Do they mean "society disapproves" or do they mean "it violates somebody's fundamental rights"? When people make a moral claim, such as "helping the homeless is good," do they mean that the act itself has the moral property of "goodness," which is just as real as a physical property such as the homeless person's property of "height"?

Although nonnormative issues in ethics are important and are in fact raised in some places in this text (especially in Part I), the chief focus of this book is on normative ethics.

2. Normative Approaches

There are two normative approaches to ethics: general normative ethics and applied ethics. *General normative ethics* is concerned with ethical theory and the study of moral systems. It is not so much concerned with discovering whether a particular act is right or wrong (e.g., "What position on affirmative action is the most ethical?"), but rather with discovering the moral theory or moral system that best establishes and/or confirms our moral intuitions about certain actions, such as the wrongness of murder and thievery. The two most prominent categories of ethical theories are *deontological* and *utilitarian*. Tom Beauchamp broadly characterizes utilitarian theories:

> Some philosophers have argued that there is one and only one fundamental principle determining right action. It is, roughly, the following: An action is morally right if, and only if, it produces at least as great a balance of value over disvalue as any available alternative action. This principle is known as the "principle of utility," and philosophers who subscribe to it are referred to as "utilitarians."[3]

Although there are many different versions of utilitarianism,[4] all versions judge the moral rightness or wrongness of an act or moral rule by its nonmoral results; for example, whether it results in more pleasure than pain or more benefit than harm.

Nonutilitarians, though not dismissing the importance of results, stress the intrinsic moral rightness or wrongness of a particular act, motive, virtue, habit, or moral rule. Beauchamp writes:

> Nonutilitarians claim that one or more fundamental principles of ethics differ from the principle of utility. These are usually principles of strict obligation, such as "Never treat another person merely as a means to your own goals." This principle means that it is immoral, for example, to deceive, coerce, or fail to consult with others merely in order to promote your goals. Many philosophers who accept a nonutilitarian account of principles of moral obligation are referred to as "deontologists."[5]

There are many different versions of deontological ethics,[6] though all seem to agree that what makes an act, motive, habit, or moral rule intrinsically right or wrong is not its results but whether it is consistent with fundamental moral duties, prima facie obligations, a universal moral principle (e.g., the golden rule, or Kant's categorical imperative), and/or natural moral law.

Thus, both the utilitarian and the deontologist may agree that in general killing human persons is wrong, but for entirely different reasons. The utilitarian may decry homicide because it denies a human person, in most instances, a future of possible happiness and/or pleasure. The deontologist, on the other hand, may condemn homicide because human persons have an intrinsic right to life that cannot be violated except when a higher moral duty is demanded (e.g., a just war, self-defense).

Although ethical theory will be covered in Part I of this text, our primary focus is on *applied ethics*, the area of study that focuses on specific moral and social issues such as abortion, euthanasia, affirmative action, and homosexuality. It will become evident as we study each one of these issues that the disputants in defending their cases appeal to particular moral principles, rules, virtues, etc. Thus, ethical theory plays an integral part in the study of applied ethics.

Wrong Ways Students Look at Moral Issues

Often when students first begin to study ethics and contemporary moral issues, they become overwhelmed by the disagreements and the level of sophistication of the disputants. This causes many students to throw up their hands and say, "There are no answers to be found. Morality is just subjective." I believe that this frustration occurs because of at least three reasons: (1) students overrate the amount of disagreement; (2) students ignore values disputants have in common, including the far greater number of issues on which people agree and the many past moral problems that have been "solved"; and (3) students erroneously appeal to personal autonomy as an "easy way out."

1. Students overrate the amount of disagreement.   Although it is evident that people disagree about certain moral issues, the number of legitimate options per issue is very limited. That is to say, it does not follow from disagreement that "anything goes." For example, on the issue of preferential treatment in hiring (which comes under the broader issue of "affirmative action"), some people who support this position argue that a less, though adequately, qualified candidate ought to be hired for a job over more qualified candidates if the less qualified candidate is part of a minority group whose members have suffered discrimination in the past (e.g., blacks, women, Hispanics, Native Americans). On the other hand, some opponents of this view argue that preferential treatment is unfair because it penalizes someone (e.g., a white male) who most likely never engaged in discrimination against anyone let alone the minority person receiving the preferential treatment.

Notice that neither says that fairness, justice, equality, and merit have no bearing on this issue. Neither side is saying that it is morally justified for an employer to choose an employee solely on the basis of his or her race. Rather, each side appeals to the values of fairness, justice, equality, and merit but applies them differently. For example, each side believes that merit is important in evaluating potential employees (i.e., they should be minimally qualified), but the supporters of preferential treatment believe that considerations of past injustice and unfairness against the group to which the potential employee belongs demands that he or she be hired in the interest of equality. On the other hand, the opponents of preferential treatment believe that group membership is irrelevant to the question of whether an applicant is the best qualified candidate in *a particular case* (merit), because it is the individual and not the group who is being hired. And in the interest of fairness and justice, it would be morally wrong to deny someone (e.g., a white male) a job when he is the most qualified for it, for to engage in a practice that denies someone what he deserves and to give that desert to someone who does not deserve it is to deny the wronged applicant equal treatment.

What is interesting here is that the values of fairness, justice, equality, and merit limit the number of different positions one can take on the issue of preferential treatment. There are roughly two major positions on this issue and a couple of minor viewpoints. But certainly it does not follow from this that "anything goes." Common values and facts are the parameters within which disputants debate this issue.

This is true of other issues as well. Concerning abortion, capital punishment, and euthanasia there are roughly three or four major positions on each issue. Consequently, the student should not infer from impassioned disagreement that any position is as good as any other. In other words, anarchic moral relativism does not follow from disagreement on certain moral issues.

2. Students ignore values disputants have in common, including the far greater number of issues on which people agree and the many past moral problems that have been "solved."   By focusing only on different viewpoints on moral issues, the student is sometimes given the mistaken impression that all moral conflicts are in some sense insoluble. In discussing moral conflicts in the United States we tend to focus our attention on contemporary issues, such as abortion, euthanasia, and affirmative action, over which there is obviously wide and impassioned disagreement. However, we ignore the fact that disputants in these moral debates hold a number of values in common, as we saw above on the issue of preferential treatment. Take for example the two main positions taken in the debate over abortion: pro life and pro choice.

First, each side believes that all human persons possess certain inalienable rights regardless of whether their governments protect these rights. That is why both sides appeal to what each believes is a fundamental right. The pro-life advocate appeals to "life" whereas the pro-choice advocate appeals to "liberty" (or "choice").

Second, each side believes that its position best exemplifies its opponent's fundamental value. The abortion-rights advocate does not deny that "life" is a value, but argues that his position's appeal to human liberty is a necessary ingredient by which an individual can pursue the fullest and most complete life possible. Furthermore, more sophisticated pro-choice advocates argue that the unborn are not human persons. And for this reason, the unborn do not have a right to life if their life hinders the liberty of a being who is a person (i.e., the pregnant woman). Others argue that even if the unborn entity is a human person, it has no right to use the body of another against that person's will, since such a usage of another's body demands of that person great risk and sacrifice that goes beyond any ordinary moral obligation. Hence, since a pregnant woman is not morally obligated to put herself at great risk and to make a significant sacrifice for another, she is morally justified in removing her unborn offspring even if such a removal results in its death.

On the other hand, the pro-life advocate does not eschew "liberty." She believes that all human liberty is limited by another human person's right to life. For example, one has a right to freely pursue any goal one believes is consistent with one's happiness, such as attending a Boston Celtics basketball game. However, one has no right to freely pursue this goal at the expense of another's life or liberty, such as running over pedestrians with one's car so that one can get to the game on time. And, of course, the pro-life advocate argues that the unborn are persons with a full right to life. And because the act of abortion typically results in the death of the unborn, abortion is not morally justified unless the mother's life is in danger (because it is a prima facie greater good that one person should live rather than two die).

It is apparent then that the main dispute in the abortion debate does not involve differing values, but disagreement about both the application of these values and the truth of certain facts. The pro-choice advocate does not deny that human persons have a right to life. He just believes that this right to life is not extended to the unborn because they are not human persons and/or their existence demands that another (the pregnant woman) is asked to make significant nonobligatory sacrifices. The pro-life advocate does not deny that human persons have the liberty to make choices that they believe are in their best interests. She believes that this liberty does not entail the right to choose abortion because such a choice conflicts with the life, liberty, and interests of another human person (the fetus), which is defenseless, weak, and vulnerable, and has a natural claim upon its parents' care, both pre- and postnatally.

Because there is a common ground between two moral positions that are often depicted as absolutely polarized, we can coherently reason and argue about the issue of abortion. And since there is a common ground of values, the question as to which position is correct rests on which one is best established by the facts and is consistent with our common values.

We also sometimes ignore the fact that there are a great number of issues on which almost all Americans agree (e.g., it is wrong to torture babies for fun, it is wrong to molest six-year-old children, rape is morally wrong) and that a number of past moral conflicts have been solved (e.g., slavery, women's suffrage, forced segregation). Thus, by focusing our attention on disagreements, our perception is skewed. James Rachels points out how such a mistaken focus can also be applied to other disciplines:

> If we think of questions like *this* [e.g., abortion, euthanasia, affirmative action], it is easy to believe that "proof" in ethics is impossible. The same can be said of the sciences. There are many complicated matters that physicists cannot agree on; and if we focused our attention entirely on *them* we might conclude that there is no "proof" in physics. But of course, many simpler matters in physics *can* be proven, and about those all competent physicists agree. Similarly, in ethics there are many matters far simpler than abortion, about which all reasonable people must agree.[7]

3. Students erroneously appeal to personal autonomy as an "easy way out." Instead of actually wrestling with arguments for and against a particular moral position, students give in to the temptation to reduce the dispute to a question of "personal preference" or "subjective opinion." Take for example the issue of whether certain interest groups have a right to boycott products that are advertised on television programs these groups find to be morally inappropriate, especially for children. The usual argument in response to these groups is the following: "If you don't like a particular program, you don't have to watch it. You can always change the channel." But is this response really compelling? After all, these groups are not *merely* saying that they personally find these programs offensive. Rather, they are saying something a bit more subtle and profound: that these programs convey messages and create a moral climate that will affect others, especially children, in a way that is adverse to the public good. Hence, what bothers these groups is that *you* and *your children* will not change the channel. Furthermore, it bothers these people that there is probably somewhere in America an unsupervised ten-year-old watching on MTV the rock group Aerosmith sing about the virtues of oral sex on an elevator (in the song "Love on an Elevator"). Most of these people fear that their ten-year-olds may have to socially interact with, and possibly date in the near future, the unsupervised MTV-watching ten-year-old. Frankly, there are many well-educated reasonable people who do not believe that such a parental concern is totally unjustified, especially in light of what we know about how certain forms of entertainment and media affect people. Therefore, the question cannot be relegated to a question of one's personal preference or autonomy. The appropriate question is what sort of social action is permissible and would best serve the public good.

Some have suggested that as long as these groups do not advocate state censorship, but merely apply social and economic pressures to private corporations and businesses (which civil rights and feminist groups have done for quite some time), a balance of freedoms is achieved. All are free to pursue their interests within the confines of constitutional protection, although all must be willing to suffer the social and economic consequences for their actions. This, according to some, best serves the public good. Notice that this response does not resort to "personal autonomy" or "personal preference," but takes seriously the values of freedom of expression, the public good, and individual rights, and attempts to uphold these values in a way that is believed to be consistent and fair.

Consider one more example. In the debate over abortion rights, many people who support these rights are fond of telling those who oppose abortion, "Don't like abortion? Then don't have one." This request reduces the abortion debate to one of subjective preference, which is clearly a mistake, because those who oppose abortion do so because they believe that the fetus during most, if not all, of a woman's pregnancy is a human person with a right to life. This is why when the pro-lifer hears the pro-choicer tell her that if she doesn't like abortion she doesn't have to have one, it sounds as if the pro-choicer is saying, "Don't like murder? Then don't kill any innocent persons." Understandably, the pro-lifer is not persuaded by such rhetoric.

Certainly the pro-lifer's arguments may be flawed, but the pro-choice advocate does not attack those flawed arguments when he reduces the debate to one of subjective preference. In any disagreement over such a serious issue as abortion, it is incumbent on those on all sides to present *reasons* for their views rather than merely appealing to personal autonomy, especially when the issue in dispute is whether it is permissible for people to exercise personal autonomy, i.e., "Should women have the right to abort their fetuses?"

Organization of Text

This text is divided into three major parts: (I) Ethical Theory, Ethical Practice, and Moral Education; (II) Life and Death Issues; and (III) Issues of Social Justice and Personal Liberty.

Part I, Ethical Theory, Ethical Practice, and Moral Education, covers theoretical and practical issues some philosophers believe are necessary in order to be able to discuss the moral and social issues of Parts II and III. This part contains articles that address three issues: Relativism versus Objectivism (Section A), Ethical Theory (Section B), and Values Clarification and Moral Education (Section C). Section A deals with the question of whether or not moral judgments are merely culturally relative. Section B contains an assessment of leading ethical theories (deontology and utilitarianism), an essay on the relationship between personal virtue and public policy, and a discussion of ethical egoism. Section C concerns moral education and the important question of how to appropriately impart morality in public schools. A focus of this section will be values clarification, the controversial program of teaching moral education in primary and secondary schools, which continues to be the most influential model of moral education in the United States.

Part II, Life and Death Issues, covers issues that surround the questions of what is a human life and when, if ever, it is morally justified to take such a life. This part will focus on three issues: Abortion (Section A), Euthanasia (Section B), and Fetal Tissue Transplantation and Embryo Research (Section C).

Part III, Issues of Social Justice and Personal Liberty, deals with issues that do not involve life and death but that have wide-ranging ramifications for the future of our society and how we are to define and apply such concepts as liberty, justice, and equality. The issues covered in Part III are among the most politically volatile of our time: Affirmative Action (Section A), Economic and Social Justice (Section B), Freedom of Expression (Section C), Homosexuality (Section D), and Family Values and Sex Roles (Section E).

Three sections in Part III concern more than one topic. Section B contains two discussions, one on Distributive Justice (1) and another on Multiculturalism and Justice (2). Two discussions are also contained in Section B: Law, Morality, and the Censorship of Pornography (1) and Speech Codes on College Campuses (2). In addition to a brief section on the law, Section D includes articles concerning two debates: Social Policy, Morality, and Homosexual Rights (2) and Homosexuals in the Military (3).

In sum, this text contains discussions on twelve moral and social issues, including a section on moral education, as well as two sections on ethical theory. It concludes with an appendix on how to write philosophical essays.

In addition to the general introduction to the text, I have written a substantial introduction for each of the sections, including brief introductions for the three major parts, discussion questions after each article, and a list for further reading after each section. Although this text deals with the usual issues discussed in other texts (e.g., abortion, euthanasia, and affirmative action), it also deals with issues that are for some strange reason ignored by others yet seem to be of interest to many students and instructors (e.g., family values and sex roles, speech codes on college campuses, multiculturalism and justice, fetal tissue research, and homosexuals in the military).

It is no accident that the subtitle of this text is *A Philosophical Dialogue on the Moral and Social Issues of Our Time.* It is structured so that each entry presents a different perspective on the issue (though not always an *opposite* perspective). It is not a pro/con anthology, because many of these issues do not lend themselves to such false dichotomies. Rather, it is framed as a philosophical dialogue, a polite interaction between the proponents of differing views. As the editor, I have striven to present a text that presents a balanced approach to each of these issues.

Notes

1. As paraphrased and rewritten by Harry V. Jaffa in his *Homosexuality and the Natural Law* (Claremont, Calif: The Claremont Institute for the Study of Statesmanship and Political Philosophy, 1990), 3–4.

2. This diagram is taken from Tom L. Beauchamp, *Philosophical Ethics: An Introduction to Moral Philosophy,* 2nd. ed. (New York: McGraw-Hill, 1991), 33. Professor Beauchamp's work in this area is state of the art.

3. Ibid., 35.

4. See Louis Pojman, *Ethics: Discovering Right and Wrong* (Belmont, Calif.: Wadsworth, 1990), chapter 6.

5. Beauchamp, *Philosophical Ethics,* 35.

6. See Pojman, *Ethics,* Chapter 5.

7. James Rachels, "Some Basic Points about Arguments," in *The Right Thing to Do: Basic Readings in Moral Philosophy,* ed. James Rachels (New York: Random House, 1989), 40.

PART I

Ethical Theory, Ethical Practice, and Moral Education

General Introduction

If your neighbor calls you at 3 a.m. telling you that he is stranded 20 miles away with a flat tire and needs a lift home, do you have a moral obligation to pick him up? If you are a non-Jew in Nazi Germany and you are hiding in your home Jews who are going to be sent to a concentration camp, is it right to tell the Nazi soldiers, when they come to your door inquiring, that you are not hiding Jews in your home? Is this falsehood morally justified? Are we our brothers' keepers? What is the scope of our moral responsibility to others? Do we have a right, and possibly an obligation, to prevent practices in other cultures that we perceive as violating fundamental human rights? These and other questions are answered within the framework of an ethical theory together with our intuitions about ethical practice on both a social and personal level.

Consequently, before we can deal with *applied ethics* we must first confront the issue of *ethical theory* and how we can put these *theories* into practice, that is, apply them to the particular issues covered in this text. In this section we will cover a number of important topics relating to ethical theory and ethical practice. One topic that is essential to confront is the issue of ethical relativism. It is fashionable in contemporary North America to be an ethical relativist. We hear it in the rhetorical question, "Who are you to judge? Most people who espouse this view assume (usually without argument) that ethical relativism is more tolerant, open-minded, and consistent with our observations about the world than its chief rival, ethical objectivism, which is perceived to breed intolerance, narrow-mindedness, and moral imperialism. Section A of this part, which deals with the issue of ethical relativism vs. ethical objectivism, contains two essays and a fictional dialogue.

Section B of this part concerns the issue of ethical theory. Throughout the history of philosophy a number of philosophers have put forth ethical theories in order to better explain how we come to the moral conclusions we do about such things as killing, lying, sexuality, obligation, and rights. Philosophers have also been concerned about how these theories influence how we make ethical decisions. This section contains one article that deals with these issues. The remaining articles address questions of personal morality, the scope of our moral obligations to others, and the philosophical foundation of moral duty.

Section C concerns the important public policy issue of how to appropriately impart morality in public schools as well as the controversial program for teaching moral education in primary and secondary schools, values clarification, which "has been and still is the most influential model of moral education in the United States in recent years." [1]

Notes

1. Paul Vitz, *Psychology as Religion,* 2nd ed. (Grand Rapids, Mich.: Eerdmans, 1994), 68.

For Further Reading

Hadley Arkes, *First Things: An Inquiry into the First Principles of Morals and Justice* (Princeton, N.J.: Princeton University Press, 1986).

Tom L. Beauchamp, *Philosophical Ethics: An Introduction to Moral Philosophy,* 2nd ed. (New York: McGraw-Hill, 1991).

Alasdair MacIntyre, *A Short History of Ethics* (New York: Macmillan, 1966).

_____, *After Virtue* (Notre Dame, Ind.: University of Notre Dame Press, 1981).

_____, *Whose Justice? Which Rationality?* (Notre Dame, Ind.: University of Notre Dame Press, 1988).

J. P. Moreland, *Scaling the Secular City* (Grand Rapids, Mich.: Baker Book House, 1987), Chapter 4.

Kai Nielsen, *Ethics without God,* rev. ed. (Buffalo, N.Y.: Prometheus, 1989).

Christina Hoff Sommers and Fred Sommers, eds. *Vice and Virtue in Everyday Life: Introductory Readings in Ethics,* 3rd ed. (New York: Harcourt Brace Jovanovich, 1993).

Andrew Varga, *The Main Issues in Bioethics,* rev. ed. (New York: Paulist Press, 1984).

Bernard Williams, *Morality: An Introduction to Ethics* (New York: Harper & Row, 1972).

SECTION A

Relativism versus Objectivism

Moral relativism is the view that there are no objective moral norms or values that transcend either culture or the individual. Moral claims are merely opinions, personal preferences, cultural rules, and/or emotive exclamations. This seems to be borne out by the findings of anthropology, sociology, and history as well as by our personal experience. For example, many people who live in India do not eat cows whereas many Americans eat beef; some people think that homosexuality is morally correct while others do not; some cultures practice polygamy while many practice monogamy; there is enormous disagreement about the morality of abortion, euthanasia, and social justice; many people are morally offended by hardcore pornography while others consume it on a regular basis with no apparent moral offense.

Moral objectivism is the view that there are objective moral norms and values that transcend both culture and the individual. The Declaration of Independence presupposes this view when it says that "we hold these truths to be self-evident, that all men are created equal, that they are endowed by their Creator with certain unalienable rights, that among these are life, liberty and the pursuit of happiness."[1] That is to say, any culture or nation that violates any of these unalienable rights is morally wrong. Just like moral relativism, moral objectivism seems to be consistent with our observations and intuitions. For example, it seems obvious that Mother Teresa is objectively a better person than Adolf Hitler; providing food and shelter for one's spouse and children is a good thing; torturing babies for fun is morally wrong; some cultural practices are inherently wicked (e.g., Nazi Holocaust, racial apartheid, rape); helping those less fortunate than ourselves is virtuous; there can exist real moral reformers, such as Martin Luther King, Jr., and the prophets of the Jewish Tanuch (the Christian Old Testament), who serve as prophetic voices to reprimand their cultures for having drifted from a true moral practice based on fundamental human values.

The moral objectivist is usually stereotyped as narrow-minded, intolerant, and dogmatic, since she believes that there is only one set of objectively true moral values, whereas the moral relativist is usually portrayed as open-minded, tolerant, and nondogmatic, since he believes that there are a diverse number of alternative moral systems each of which is valid for the person, culture, or nation that embraces it. But these stereotypes are far from accurate—in addition to being irrelevant to the question of each view's *plausibility*, because it is the views' defenders that are being described rather than the views' merits. For example, the author of the bestseller, *The Closing of the American Mind*, Allan Bloom, observed that "there is one thing a professor can be absolutely certain of: almost every student entering the university believes, or says he believes, that truth is relative. . . . The students, of course, cannot defend their opinion. It is something with which they have been indoctrinated."[2] Bloom called this "a closing of the American mind" because by dogmatically asserting that there is no moral truth, the student has closed his or her mind to the possibility of knowing moral truth if in fact it does exist.

Of course, the sophisticated moral relativist does not believe he is close-minded; in fact, he has looked at the findings of anthropologists, sociologists, and historians and has concluded that cultures, nations, and individuals have strikingly different views of morality. For this reason, he is skeptical that there is such a thing as moral truth.

This section contains three pieces: two essays and a dialogue. The first ("A Defense of Moral Relativism") is by anthropologist Ruth Benedict, who argues from anthropological data that moral relativism is the correct view and that moral objectivism conflicts with the evidence. Louis P. Pojman, in this section's second piece ("The Case for Moral Objectivism"), challenges Benedict's position by showing what he believes are the shortcomings of moral relativism as well as the positive case for moral objectivism. The third piece is a fictional dialogue authored by Peter Kreeft ("On Objective Values: A Dialogue"), in which a 20th century Socrates argues for objective values in response to seven arguments for moral subjectivism (a version of moral relativism) presented to him by Felicia Flake.

Notes

1. "The Declaration of Independence (1776)" in *The Constitution of the United States and Related Documents*, ed. Martin Shapiro (Northbrook, Ill.: AHM Publishing, 1973), 78.
2. Allan Bloom, *The Closing of the American Mind* (New York: Simon & Schuster, 1987), 25.

For Further Reading

Francis J. Beckwith, *Politically Correct Death: Answering the Arguments for Abortion Rights* (Grand Rapids, Mich.: Baker Book House, 1993), Chapter 1.

Ruth Benedict, *Patterns of Culture* (New York: Houghton Mifflin, 1934).

"The Declaration of Independence (1776)" in *The Constitution of the United States and Related Documents*, ed. Martin Shapiro (Northbrook, Ill.: AHM Publishing, 1973), 78.

Michael Krausz and Jack W. Meiland, eds. *Relativism: Cognitive and Moral* (Notre Dame, Ind.: University of Notre Dame Press, 1982).

John Ladd, ed. *Ethical Relativism* (Belmont, Calif.: Wadsworth, 1973).

J. L. Mackie, *Ethics: Inventing Right and Wrong* (New York: Penguin, 1977).

John Warwick Montgomery, *Human Rights & Human Dignity* (Grand Rapids, Mich.: Zondervan, 1986).

J. P. Moreland, *Scaling the Secular City* (Grand Rapids, Mich.: Baker Book House, 1987), 105–132, 240–248.

James Rachels, "Some Basic Points about Arguments," in *The Right Thing to Do: Basic Readings in Moral Philosophy*, ed. James Rachels (New York: Random House, 1989).

David B. Wong, *Moral Relativity* (Berkeley: University of California, 1984).

1

A Defense of Moral Relativism

Ruth Benedict

Ruth Benedict (1887–1948) taught at Columbia University and was one of the foremost American anthropologists. She was the author of numerous scholarly articles. Among her published books is *Patterns of Culture* (1934).

Professor Benedict argues that morality is merely conventional, that is, morality is a useful term to indicate socially approved customs, nothing more and nothing less. For Professor Benedict, there are no transcultural objective moral principles to which all people everywhere and in every place are obligated to subscribe; morality is culturally relative. Like styles of clothing and rules of etiquette, moral rules and moral values differ from culture to culture. For example, in the southern United States there was a time when slavery was considered moral whereas today it is looked upon as an evil institution; some cultures approve of homosexual behavior whereas other cultures do not; in India it is considered immoral by many to eat cattle whereas in the United States people devour hamburgers and steaks without a second thought. What is considered "normalcy" in one society may be considered "abnormalcy" in another. Since there are no universal objective moral norms and morality is the result of a culture's evolution, Professor Benedict maintains that "modern civilization, from this point of view, becomes not a necessary pinnacle of human achievement but one entry in a long series of possible adjustments." Thus, no culture can be said to be morally better than any other.

Reprinted by permission from *Journal of General Psychology* 10 (1934): 59–82.

Modern social anthropology has become more and more a study of the varieties and common elements of cultural environment and the consequences of these in human behavior. For such a study of diverse social orders primitive peoples fortunately provide a laboratory not yet entirely vitiated by the spread of a standardized worldwide civilization. Dyaks and Hopis, Fijians and Yakuts are significant for psychological and sociological study because only among these simpler peoples has there been sufficient isolation to give opportunity for the development of localized social forms. In the higher cultures the standardization of custom and belief over a couple of continents has given a false sense of the inevitability of the particular forms that have gained currency, and we need to turn to a wider survey in order to check the conclusions we hastily base upon this near-universality of familiar customs. Most of the simpler cultures did not gain the wide currency of the one which, out of our experience, we identify with human nature, but this was for various historical reasons, and certainly not for any that gives us as its carriers a monopoly of social good or of social sanity. Modern civilization, from this point of view, becomes not a necessary pinnacle of human achievement but one entry in a long series of possible adjustments.

These adjustments, whether they are in mannerisms like the ways of showing anger, or joy, or grief in any society, or in major human drives like those of sex, prove to be far more variable than experience in any one culture would suggest. In certain fields, such as that of religion or of formal marriage arrangements, these wide limits of variability are well known and can be fairly described. In others it is not yet possible to give a generalized account, but that does not absolve us of the task of indicating the significance of the work that has been done and of the problems that have arisen.

One of these problems relates to the customary modern normal-abnormal categories and our conclusions regarding them. In how far are such categories culturally determined, or in how far can we with assurance regard them as absolute? In how far can we regard inability to function socially as diagnostic of abnormality, or in how far is it necessary to regard this as a function of the culture?

As a matter of fact, one of the most striking facts that emerge from a study of widely varying cultures is the ease with which our abnormals function in other cultures. It does not matter what kind of "abnormality" we choose for illustration, those which indicate extreme instability, or those which are more in the nature of character traits like sadism or delusions of grandeur or of persecution, there are well-described cultures in which these abnormals function at ease and with honor, and apparently without danger or difficulty to the society. . . .

The most notorious of these is trance and catalepsy. Even a very mild mystic is aberrant in our culture. But most peoples have regarded even extreme psychic manifestations not only as normal and desirable, but even as characteristic of highly valued and gifted individuals. This was true even in our own cultural background in that period when Catholicism made the ecstatic experience the mark of sainthood. It is hard for us, born and brought up in a culture that makes no use of the experience, to realize how important a role it may play and how many individuals are capable of it, once it has been given an honorable place in any society. . . .

Cataleptic and trance phenomena are, of course, only one illustration of the fact that those whom we regard as abnormals may function adequately in other cultures. Many of our culturally discarded traits are selected for elaboration in different societies. Homosexuality is an excellent example, for in this case our attention is not constantly diverted, as in the consideration of trance, to the interruption of routine activity which it implies. Homosexuality poses the problem very simply. A tendency toward this trait in our culture exposes an individual to all the conflicts to which all aberrants are always exposed, and we tend to identify the consequences of this conflict with homosexuality. But these consequences are obviously local and cultural. Homosexuals in many societies are not incompetent, but they may be such if the culture asks adjustments of them that would strain any man's vitality. Wherever homosexuality has been given an honorable place in any society, those to whom it is congenial have filled adequately the honorable roles society assigns to them. Plato's *Republic* is, of course, the most convincing statement of such a reading of homosexuality. It is presented as one of the major means to the good life, and it was generally so regarded in Greece at that time.

The cultural attitude toward homosexuals has not always been on such a high ethical plane, but it has been very varied. Among many American Indian tribes there exists the institution of the berdache, as the French called them. These men-women were men who at puberty or thereafter took the dress and the occupations of women. Sometimes they married other men and lived with them. Sometimes they were

men with no inversion, persons of weak sexual endowment who chose this role to avoid the jeers of the women. The berdaches were never regarded as of first-rate supernatural power, as similar men-women were in Siberia, but rather as leaders in women's occupations, good healers in certain diseases, or, among certain tribes, as the genial organizers of social affairs. In any case, they were socially placed. They were not left exposed to the conflicts that visit the deviant who is excluded from participation in the recognized patterns of his society.

The most spectacular illustrations of the extent to which normality may be culturally defined are those cultures where an abnormality of our culture is the cornerstone of their social structure. It is not possible to do justice to these possibilities in a short discussion. A recent study of an island of northwest Melanesia by Fortune describes a society built upon traits which we regard as beyond the border of paranoia. In this tribe the exogamic groups look upon each other as prime manipulators of black magic, so that one marries always into an enemy group which remains for life one's deadly and unappeasable foes. They look upon a good garden crop as a confession of theft, for everyone is engaged in making magic to induce into his garden the productiveness of his neighbors'; therefore no secrecy in the island is so rigidly insisted upon as the secrecy of a man's harvesting of his yams. Their polite phrase at the acceptance of a gift is, "And if you now poison me, how shall I repay you this present?" Their preoccupation with poisoning is constant; no woman ever leaves her cooking pot for a moment untended. Even the great affinal economic exchanges that are characteristic of this Melanesian culture area are quite altered in Dobu since they are incompatible with this fear and distrust that pervades the culture. They go farther and people the whole world outside their own quarters with such malignant spirits that all-night feasts and ceremonials simply do not occur here. They have even rigorous religiously enforced customs that forbid the sharing of seed even in one family group. Anyone else's food is deadly poison to you, so that communality of stores is out of the question. For some months before harvest the whole society is on the verge of starvation, but if one falls to the temptation and eats up one's seed yams, one is an outcast and a beachcomber for life. There is no coming back. It involves, as a matter of course, divorce and the breaking of all social ties.

Now in this society where no one may work with another and no one may share with another, Fortune describes the individual who was regarded by all his fellows as crazy. He was not one of those who periodically ran amok and, beside himself and frothing at the mouth, fell with a knife upon anyone he could reach. Such behavior they did not regard as putting anyone outside the pale. They did not even put the individuals who were known to be liable to these attacks under any kind of control. They merely fled when they saw the attack coming on and kept out of the way. "He would be all right tomorrow." But there was one man of sunny, kindly disposition who liked work and liked to be helpful. The compulsion was too strong for him to repress it in favor of the opposite tendencies of his culture. Men and women never spoke of him without laughing; he was silly and simple and definitely crazy. Nevertheless, to the ethnologist used to a culture that has, in Christianity, made his type the model of all virtue, he seemed a pleasant fellow. . . .

. . . Among the Kwakiutl it did not matter whether a relative had died in bed of disease, or by the hand of an enemy, in either case death was an affront to be wiped out by the death of another person. The fact that one had been caused to mourn was proof that one had been put upon. A chief's sister and her daughter had gone up to Victoria, and either because they drank bad whiskey or because their boat capsized they never came back. The chief called together his warriors, "Now I ask you, tribes, who shall wail? Shall I do it or shall another?" The spokesman answered, of course, "Not you, Chief. Let some other of the tribes." Immediately they set up the war pole to announce their intention of wiping out the injury, and gathered a war party. They set out, and found seven men and two children asleep and killed them. "Then they felt good when they arrived at Sebaa in the evening."

The point which is of interest to us is that in our society those who on that occasion would feel good when they arrived at Sebaa that evening would be the definitely abnormal. There would be some, even in our society, but it is not a recognized and approved mood under the circumstances. On the Northwest Coast those are favored and fortunate to whom that mood under those circumstances is congenial and those to whom it is repugnant are unlucky. This latter minority can register in their own culture only by doing violence to their congenial responses and acquiring others that are difficult for them. The person, for instance, who, like a Plains Indian whose wife has been taken from him, is too proud to fight, can deal with the Northwest Coast civilization only by

ignoring its strongest bents. If he cannot achieve it, he is the deviant in that culture, their instance of abnormality.

This headhunting that takes place on the Northwest Coast after a death is no matter of blood revenge or of organized vengeance. There is no effort to tie up the subsequent killing with any responsibility on the part of the victim for the death of the person who is being mourned. A chief whose son has died goes visiting wherever his fancy dictates, and he says to his host, "My prince has died today, and you go with him." Then he kills him. In this, according to their interpretation, he acts nobly because he has not been downed. He has thrust back in return. The whole procedure is meaningless without the fundamental paranoid reading of bereavement. Death, like all the other untoward accidents of existence, confounds man's pride and can only be handled in the category of insults.

Behavior honored upon the Northwest Coast is one which is recognized as abnormal in our civilization, and yet it is sufficiently close to the attitudes of our own culture to be intelligible to us and to have a definite vocabulary with which we may discuss it. The megalomaniac paranoid trend is a definite danger in our society. It is encouraged by some of our major preoccupations, and it confronts us with a choice of two possible attitudes. One is to brand it as abnormal and reprehensible, and is the attitude we have chosen in our civilization. The other is to make it an essential attribute of ideal man, and this is the solution in the culture of the Northwest Coast.

These illustrations, which it has been possible to indicate only in the briefest manner, force upon us the fact that normality is culturally defined. An adult shaped to the drives and standards of either of these cultures, if he were transported into our civilization, would fall into our categories of abnormality. He would be faced with the psychic dilemmas of the socially unavailable. In his own culture, however, he is the pillar of society, the end result of socially inculcated mores, and the problem of personal instability in his case simply does not arise.

No one civilization can possibly utilize in its mores the whole potential range of human behavior. Just as there are great numbers of possible phonetic articulations, and the possibility of language depends on a selection and standardization of a few of these in order that speech communication may be possible at all, so the possibility of organized behavior of every sort, from the fashions of local dress and houses to the dicta of a people's ethics and religion, depends upon a similar selection among the possible behavior traits. In the field of recognized economic obligations or sex tabus this selection is as nonrational and subconscious a process as it is in the field of phonetics. It is a process which goes on in the group for long periods of time and is historically conditioned by innumerable accidents of isolation or of contact of peoples. In any comprehensive study of psychology, the selection that different cultures have made in the course of history within the great circumference of potential behavior is of great significance.

Every society, beginning with some slight inclination in one direction or another, carries its preference farther and farther, integrating itself more and more completely upon its chosen basis, and discarding those types of behavior that are uncongenial. Most of those organizations of personality that seem to us most incontrovertibly abnormal have been used by different civilizations in the very foundations of their institutional life. Conversely the most valued traits of our normal individuals have been looked on in differently organized cultures as aberrant. Normality, in short, within a very wide range, is culturally defined. It is primarily a term for the socially elaborated segment of human behavior in any culture; and abnormality, a term for the segment that that particular civilization does not use. The very eyes with which we see the problem are conditioned by the long traditional habits of our own society.

It is a point that has been made more often in relation to ethics than in relation to psychiatry. We do not any longer make the mistake of deriving the morality of our locality and decade directly from the inevitable constitution of human nature. We do not elevate it to the dignity of a first principle. We recognize that morality differs in every society, and is a convenient term for socially approved habits. Mankind has always preferred to say, "It is morally good," rather than "It is habitual," and the fact of this preference is matter enough for a critical science of ethics. But historically the two phrases are synonymous.

The concept of the normal is properly a variant of the concept of the good. It is that which society has approved. A normal action is one which falls well within the limits of expected behavior for a particular society. Its variability among different peoples is essentially a function of the variability of the behavior patterns that different societies have created for themselves, and can never be wholly divorced from a consideration of culturally institutionalized types of behavior.

Each culture is a more or less elaborate working-out of the potentialities of the segment it has chosen. In so far as a civilization is well integrated and consistent within itself, it will tend to carry farther and farther, according to its nature, its initial impulse toward a particular type of action, and from the point of view of any other culture those elaborations will include more and more extreme and aberrant traits.

Each of these traits, in proportion as it reinforces the chosen behavior patterns of that culture, is for that culture normal. Those individuals to whom it is congenial either congenitally, or as the result of childhood sets, are accorded prestige in that culture, and are not visited with the social contempt or disapproval which their traits would call down upon them in a society that was differently organized. On the other hand, those individuals whose characteristics are not congenial to the selected type of human behavior in that community are the deviants, no matter how valued their personality traits may be in a contrasted civilization.

The Dobuan who is not easily susceptible to fear of treachery, who enjoys work and likes to be helpful, is their neurotic and regarded as silly.

On the Northwest Coast the person who finds it difficult to read life in terms of an insult contest will be the person upon whom fall all the difficulties of the culturally unprovided for. The person who does not find it easy to humiliate a neighbor, nor to see humiliation in his own experience, who is genial and loving, may, of course, find some unstandardized way of achieving satisfactions in his society, but not in the major patterned responses that his culture requires of him. If he is born to play an important role in a family with many hereditary privileges, he can succeed only by doing violence to his whole personality. If he does not succeed, he has betrayed his culture; that is, he is abnormal.

I have spoken of individuals as having sets toward certain types of behavior, and of these sets as running sometimes counter to the types of behavior which are institutionalized in the culture to which they belong. From all that we know of contrasting cultures it seems clear that differences of temperament occur in every society. The matter has never been made the subject of investigation, but from the available material it would appear that these temperament types are very likely of universal recurrence. That is, there is an ascertainable range of human behavior that is found wherever a sufficiently large series of individuals is observed. But the proportion in which behavior types stand to one another in different societies is not universal. The vast majority of individuals in any group are shaped to the fashion of that culture. In other words, most individuals are plastic to the molding force of the society into which they are born. In a society that values trance, as in India, they will have supernormal experience. In a society that institutionalizes homosexuality, they will be homosexual. In a society that sets the gathering of possessions as the chief human objective, they will amass property. The deviants, whatever the type of behavior the culture has institutionalized, will remain few in number, and there seems no more difficulty in molding the vast malleable majority to the "normality" of what we consider an aberrant trait, such as delusions of reference, than to the normality of such accepted behavior patterns as acquisitiveness. The small proportion of the number of the deviants in any culture is not a function of the sure instinct with which that society has built itself upon the fundamental sanities, but of the universal fact that, happily, the majority of mankind quite readily take any shape that is presented to them. . . .

Discussion Questions

1. Present and explain Professor Benedict's defense of ethical relativism. How does Professor Benedict account for the existence of morality in any particular culture?

2. Since according to Professor Benedict no culture can be said to be morally better than any other, is she able to condemn apartheid in South Africa, slavery in the world and throughout history, and the Holocaust, all of which were or are morally acceptable to the society that practiced or practice them?

3. Professor Benedict maintains that cultural diversity proves ethical relativism. Do you agree with this position? Explain and defend your answer.

2

The Case for Moral Objectivism

Louis P. Pojman

Louis P. Pojman is Professor of Philosophy at the U.S. Military Academy at West Point, N.Y. He has published widely in the areas of philosophy of religion, epistemology, and ethics. Among his many books are *Ethical Theory: Classical and Contemporary Readings* (1989), *Ethics: Discovering Right and Wrong* (1990), and *The Abortion Controversy: A Reader* (1994).

In this essay Professor Pojman defends moral objectivism—the view that there are universally valid moral values or principles—against moral relativism—the view that there are no universally valid moral values or principles. He first analyzes the structure of moral relativism, pointing out that it consists of two theses: (1) a diversity thesis, the claim "that what is considered morally right and wrong varies from society to society, so that there are no moral principles accepted by all societies," and (2) a dependency thesis, the claim "that all moral principles derive their validity from cultural acceptance." Professor Pojman then critically evaluates two types of moral relativism: (1) subjectivism, the view that individual choice determines a moral principle's validity, and (2) conventionalism, the view that moral principles are relative to society or culture. He concludes that both are riddled with serious philosophical problems. He then presents a case for moral objectivism and concludes with some observations about the attraction of moral relativism.

Reprinted by permission of the author from *Philosophy: The Quest for Truth*, 2nd ed., ed. Louis P. Pojman (Belmont, Calif.: Wadsworth, 1992), 314–324.

"Who's to judge what's right or wrong?"
—A common question asked by students

In the nineteenth century Christian missionaries sometimes used coercion to change the customs of pagan tribal people in parts of Africa and the Pacific Islands. Appalled by the customs of public nakedness, polygamy, working on the Sabbath, and infanticide, they paternalistically went about reforming the "poor pagans." They clothed them, separated wives from their husbands in order to create monogamous households, made the Sabbath a day of rest, and ended infanticide. In the process they sometimes created social malaise, causing the estranged women to despair and their children to be orphaned. The natives often did not understand the new religion, but accepted it in deference to the white man's power. The white people had guns and medicine.

Since the nineteenth century we have made progress in understanding cultural diversity and realize that the social dissonance caused by do-gooders was a bad thing. In the last century or so, anthropology has exposed our penchant for ethnocentricism, the prejudicial view that interprets all of reality through the eyes of our cultural beliefs and values. We have come to see enormous variety in social practices throughout the world.

Eskimos allow their elderly to die by starvation; we believe that this is morally wrong. The Spartans of ancient Greece and the Dobu of New Guinea believe that stealing is morally right; we believe it is wrong. Many cultures, past and present, have practiced or still practice infanticide (a tribe in East Africa once threw deformed infants to hippopotamuses); our society condemns such acts. Sexual practices vary over time and clime. Some cultures permit, while others condemn, homosexual behavior. Some cultures, including Moslem societies, practice polygamy, while most Christian cultures view it as immoral. Ruth Benedict describes a tribe in Melanesia which views cooperation and kindness as vices, and Colin Turnbull has documented that the Ik in Northern Uganda have no sense of duty towards their children or parents. There are societies which make it a duty for children to kill (sometimes strangle) their aging parents.

The ancient Greek historian, Herodotus (485–430 B.C.) tells the story of how Darius, the king of Persia, once brought together some Callatians (Asian tribal people) and some Greeks. He asked the Callatians how they disposed of their deceased parents. They told how they ate the bodies of their dead parents. The Greeks, who cremated their parents, were horrified at such barbarous behavior. No amount of money could tempt them to do such an irreverent thing. Then Darius asked the Callatians what he should give them "to burn the bodies of their fathers at their decease." The Callatians were utterly horrified at such barbarous behavior and begged Darius to cease from such irreverent discourse. Herodotus concludes, "Custom is the king o'er all."[1]

Today we condemn ethnocentricism, the uncritical belief in the inherent superiority of one's own culture, as tantamount to racism and sexism. What is right in one culture may be wrong in another; what is good east of the river may be bad west of the river; what is a virtue in one nation may be a vice in another—so it behooves us not to judge others but to tolerate diversity.

This rejection of ethnocentricism in the West has contributed to a shift in public opinion about morality, and for a growing number of Westerners, consciousness-raising about the validity of other ways of life has led to an erosion of belief in moral *objectivism*, the view that there are universal moral principles, valid for all people at all times and in all climes. In polls taken in my ethics and introduction to philosophy classes over the past several years (in universities in three different areas of the country) students affirmed by a two to one ratio a version of *moral relativism* over *moral absolutism*, with hardly three percent seeing something between these two opposites. I am not suggesting that all these students had a clear understanding of what is entailed by relativism, for many of those who said that they were ethical relativists also stated, on the same questionnaire, that "abortion except to save the mother's life is always wrong," that "capital punishment is always morally wrong," or that "suicide is never morally permissible." The (apparent) contradictions signal an (apparent) confusion on the matter.

I want to argue that ethical relativism is a mistaken theory and that the cultural differences do not demonstrate that all ways of life are equally valid from a moral perspective. Indeed, ethical relativism, were it true, would spell the death of ethics. In spite of cultural divergences there is a *universally* valid core morality. I call this core morality "moral objectivism," to distinguish it from both "moral absolutism" and "moral relativism."

An Analysis of Relativism

Ethical relativism is the theory that there are no universally valid moral principles; that all moral principles are valid relative to *culture* or *individual choice*. That is, there are two types of relativism: *conventionalism*, which holds that moral principles are relative to the culture or society, and *subjectivism*, which holds that it is the individual choice that determines the validity of a moral principle. We'll start with conventionalism. Philosopher John Ladd, of Brown University, defines *conventional ethical relativism* this way:

> Ethical relativism is the doctrine that the moral rightness and wrongness of actions varies from society to society and that there are no absolute universal moral standards binding on all men at all times. Accordingly, it holds that whether or not it is right for an individual to act in a certain way depends on or is relative to the society to which he belongs (John Ladd, *Ethical Relativism*, Wadsworth, 1973).

According to Ladd, ethical relativism consists of two theses: a *Diversity Thesis*, which specifies that what is considered morally right and wrong varies from society to society, so that there are no moral principles accepted by all societies, and a *Dependency Thesis*, which specifies that all moral principles derive their validity from cultural acceptance. From these two ideas he concludes that there are no universally valid moral principles, objective standards which apply to all people everywhere and at all times.

The first thesis, the *Diversity Thesis*, or what may simply be called *cultural relativism*, is an anthropological thesis, which registers the fact that moral rules differ from society to society. As we noted at the beginning of this essay, there is enormous variety in what may count as a moral principle in a given society. The human condition is malleable in the extreme, allowing any number of folkways or moral codes. Ruth Benedict has written:

> The cultural pattern of any civilization makes use of a certain segment of the great arc of potential human purposes and motivations, just as we have seen . . . that any culture makes use of certain selected material techniques or cultural traits. The great arc along which all the possible human behaviors are distributed is far too immense and too full of contradictions for any one culture to utilize even any considerable portion of it. Selection is the first requirement. [*Patterns of Culture*, New York, 1934, p. 219]

The second thesis, the *Dependency Thesis*, asserts that individual acts are right or wrong depending on the nature of the society from which they emanate. What is considered morally right or wrong must be seen in a context, depending on the goals, wants, beliefs, history, and environment of the society in question. As William Graham Sumner says, "We learn the [morals] as unconsciously as we learn to walk and hear and breathe, and we never know any reason why the [morals] are what they are. The justification of them is that when we wake to consciousness of life we find them facts which already hold us in the bonds of tradition, custom, and habit."[2] Trying to see things from an independent, noncultural point of view would be like taking out our eyes in order to examine their contours and qualities. We are simply culturally determined beings.

In a sense, we all live in radically different worlds. Each person has a different set of beliefs and experiences, a particular perspective that colors all of his or her perceptions. Do the farmer, the real estate dealer, and the artist, looking at the same spatiotemporal field, see the same field? Not likely. Their different orientations, values, and expectations govern their perceptions, so that different aspects of the field are highlighted and some features are missed. Even as our individual values arise from personal experience, social values are grounded in the peculiar history of the community. Morality, then, is just the set of common rules, habits, and customs which have won social approval over time, so that they seem part of the nature of things, as facts. There is nothing mysterious or transcendent about these codes of behavior. They are the outcomes of our social history.

The conclusion that there are no absolute or objective moral standards binding on all people follows from the first two propositions. Cultural relativism (the Diversity Thesis) plus the Dependency Thesis yields ethical relativism in its classic form. If there are different moral principles from culture to culture and if all morality is rooted in culture, it follows that there are no universal moral principles valid for all cultures and people at all times.

Subjective Ethical Relativism (Subjectivism)

Some people think that even this conclusion is too tame and maintain that morality is not dependent on the society but on the individual. As students sometimes maintain, "Morality is in the eye of the beholder." Ernest Hemingway wrote, "So far, about morals, I know only that what is moral is what you feel good after and what is immoral is what you feel bad after and judged by these moral standards, which

I do not defend, the bullfight is very moral to me because I feel very fine while it is going on and have a feeling of life and death and mortality and immortality, and after it is over I feel very sad but very fine."[3]

This form of moral subjectivism has the sorry consequence that it makes morality a useless concept, for, on its premises, little or no interpersonal criticism or judgment is logically possible. Hemingway may feel good about the killing of bulls in a bullfight, while Albert Schweitzer or Mother Teresa may feel the opposite. No argument about the matter is possible. The only basis for judging Hemingway or anyone else wrong would be if he failed to live up to his own principles, but, of course, one of Hemingway's principles could be that hypocrisy is morally permissible (he feels good about it), so that it would be impossible for him to do wrong. For Hemingway, hypocrisy and nonhypocrisy could both be morally permissible. On the basis of Subjectivism it could very easily turn out that Adolf Hitler is as moral as Gandhi, so long as each believes he is living by his chosen principles. Notions of moral good and bad, right or wrong cease to have interpersonal evaluative meaning.

Once, Columbia University Professor Sidney Morgenbesser taught a philosophy class in which the students argued vehemently for subjectivism. When a test was taken, Morgenbesser returned all the tests marked "F" even though his comments showed that most of the tests were of a very high quality. When the students expressed outrage at this injustice, Morgenbesser answered that he had accepted the notion of Subjectivism for purposes of marking the exams in which case the principle of justice had no objective validity.

Absurd consequences follow from subjective ethical relativism. If it is correct, then morality is reduced to aesthetic tastes over which there can be no argument or interpersonal judgment. Although many people say that they hold this position, there seems to be a conflict between it and other of their moral views (e.g., that Hitler is really morally bad or that capital punishment is always wrong). There seems to be a contradiction between subjectivism and the very concept of morality, which it is supposed to characterize, for morality has to do with "proper" resolution of interpersonal conflict and the amelioration of the human predicament. As Thomas Hobbes pointed out, whatever else it does, morality aims at preventing a state of chaos where life is "solitary, poor, nasty, brutish, and short." But if so, Subjectivism is no help at all in doing this, for it doesn't rest on social *agreement* of principle (as the conventionalist maintains) or on an objectively independent set of norms that bind all people for the common good.

Subjectivism treats individuals as billiard balls on a societal pool table where they meet only in radical collisions, each aiming for its own goal and striving to do in the other fellow before he does it to you. This atomistic view of personality is belied by the fact that we develop in families and mutually dependent communities, in which we share a common language, common institutions, and habits, and that we often feel each other's joys and sorrows. As John Donne said, "No man is an island, entire of itself; every man is a piece of the continent."

Radical individualistic relativism seems incoherent. If so, it follows that the only plausible view of ethical relativism must be one that grounds morality in the group or culture. This form of relativism is called conventionalism, which we looked at earlier and to which we now return.

Conventional Ethical Relativism (Conventionalism)

Conventional ethical relativism, the view that there are no objective moral principles but that all valid moral principles are justified by virtue of their cultural acceptance, recognizes the social nature of morality. That is precisely its power and virtue. It does not seem subject to the same absurd consequences that plague Subjectivism. Recognizing the importance of our social environment in generating customs and beliefs, many people suppose that ethical relativism is the correct ethical theory. They are further drawn to it for its liberal philosophical stance. It seems to be an enlightened response to the "sin of ethnocentricity," and it seems to entail or strongly imply an attitude of tolerance towards other cultures. As Benedict says, in recognizing ethical relativity "we shall arrive at a more realistic social faith, accepting as grounds of hope and as new bases for tolerance the coexisting and equally valid patterns of life which mankind has created for itself from the raw materials of existence."[4] The most famous of those holding this position is the anthropologist Melville Herskovits, who argues even more explicitly than Benedict that ethical relativism entails intercultural tolerance.[5]

The view contains a contradiction. If no moral principles are universally valid, how can tolerance be universally valid? Whence comes its validity? If morality is simply relative to each culture and if the culture does not have a principle of tolerance, its members have no obligation to be tolerant. Herskovits seems to be treating the *principle of tolerance* as the one exception to his relativism—as an absolute moral principle. But from a relativistic point of view, there is no more reason to be tolerant than to be intolerant and neither stance is objectively morally better than the other.

Not only do relativists fail to offer a basis for criticizing those who are intolerant, but they cannot rationally *criticize* anyone who espouses what they might regard as a heinous principle. If, as seems to be the case, valid criticism supposes an objective or impartial standard, relativists cannot morally criticize anyone outside their own culture. Adolf Hitler's genocidal actions, so long as they are culturally accepted, are as morally legitimate as Mother Teresa's works of mercy. If conventional relativism is accepted, racism, genocide, oppression of the poor, slavery, and even the advocacy of war for its own sake are as moral as their opposites. And if a subculture within our own culture decided that starting a nuclear war was somehow morally acceptable, we could not morally criticize the members of that subculture.

Any moral system, whatever its content, is as valid as every other, as well as more valid than ideal moralities, since the latter aren't adhered to by any culture.

There are other disturbing consequences of ethical relativism. It seems to entail that reformers are always (morally) wrong since they go against the tide of cultural standards. William Wilberforce was wrong in the eighteenth century to oppose slavery, the British were immoral in opposing suttee (the burning of widows) in India. The early Christians were wrong in refusing to serve in the Roman army or to bow down to Caesar, acts which the majority in the Roman Empire believed to be moral duties. And Jesus was immoral in breaking the law of his day by healing on the Sabbath and by preaching the Sermon on the Mount, since few in his time (as in ours) accepted its principles.

Yet most of us normally feel just the opposite: that the reformer is the courageous innovator who is right, who has the truth—and that the mindless majority is wrong. Sometimes the individual must stand alone with the truth, risking social censure and persecution. As Dr. Stockman says in Ibsen's *Enemy of the People,* after he loses the battle to declare his town's profitable polluted tourist spa unsanitary, "The most dangerous enemy of the truth and freedom among us—is the compact majority. Yes, the damned, compact and liberal majority. The majority has *might*—unfortunately—but *right* it is not. Right—are I and a few others." Yet if relativism is correct, the opposite is necessarily the case. Truth is with the crowd and error with the individual.

An even more basic problem with the conventionalist view that morality is dependent on cultural acceptance for its validity is that the concept of a culture or society is notoriously difficult to define. This is especially so in a pluralistic society like our own, where the notion seems to be vague, to have unclear boundary lines. One person may belong to several subcultures, each with different value emphases and arrangements of principles. A person may belong to the nation as a single society, with its values of patriotism, honor, and courage, and its laws (including some that are controversial but have majority acceptance, such as the law on abortion). But he or she may also belong to a church that opposes some of the laws of the State. He may also be a member of a socially mixed community where different principles hold sway, and he may belong to clubs and a family with still other rules. Relativism seems to tell us that where he is a member of societies with conflicting moralities he must be judged both wrong and not-wrong, whatever he does. For example, if Mary is a citizen of the United States and a member of the Roman Catholic Church, she is wrong (qua Catholic) if she chooses to have an abortion and not-wrong (qua citizen of the United States) if she acts against the teaching of her church on abortion. As a member of a racist organization (say the Ku Klux Klan) John has no obligation to treat his fellow black citizens as equals, but as a member of the university community itself (where the principle of equal rights is accepted) he does have the obligation; but as a member of the surrounding community (which may reject the principle of equal rights) he again has no such obligation; but then again as a member of the nation at large (which accepts the principle) he is obligated to treat his fellow with respect. What is the morally right thing for John to do? The question no longer makes much sense in this moral Babel. It has lost its action-guiding function.

Perhaps the relativist would say that in such cases the individual may choose which group to belong to as primary. If Mary chooses to have an abortion, she

is choosing to belong to the larger society relative to that issue. If John acts as a racist, he is choosing against belonging to the university and the nation on that issue. The trouble with this option is that it seems to lead back to counterintuitive results. If Gangland Gus of Murder, Incorporated, feels like killing bank president Ortcutt and wants to feel good about it, he identifies with the Murder, Incorporated, society rather than with the general public morality. Does this justify the killing? In fact, couldn't one justify anything simply by forming a small subculture that approved of it? Charles Manson would be moral in killing innocents simply by virtue of forming a coterie. How large must the group be to be a legitimate subculture or society? Does it need ten people or fifteen? How about just three? Come to think about it, why can't my partner in burglary and I found our own society with a morality of its own? Of course, if my partner dies, I could still claim that I was acting from an originally social set of norms. Finally, why can't I dispense with interpersonal agreements altogether and invent my own morality, since morality, on this view, is only an invention anyway? Conventionalist relativism seems to reduce to subjectivism. And subjectivism leads, as we have seen, to the demise of morality altogether.

The Case for Ethical Objectivism

Where does the relativist go wrong? I think the relativist makes an unwarranted slide from the observation that different cultures have different rules to the conclusion that no culture's set of rules is better than any other culture's set of rules, or even an ideal set of rules. Some sets of rules are better than other sets relative to the purposes of morality. As I have argued elsewhere, the purposes of moral rules are the survival of the society, the alleviation of suffering, human flourishing, and the just resolution of conflicts of interest.[6] These purposes will yield a set of common principles that may actually underlie some of the cultural differences reported by anthropologists. In the eighteenth century, David Hume noted that human nature was fundamentally similar throughout time and clime; more recently, the sociobiologist E. O. Wilson has identified over a score of universal features. The anthropologist Clyde Kluckhohn sums up his findings on common cultural features:

> Every culture has a concept of murder distinguishing this from execution killing in war and

other "justifiable homicides." The notions of incest and other regulations upon sexual behavior, the prohibitions upon untruth under defined circumstances, of restitution and reciprocity, of mutual obligations between parents and children—these and many other moral concepts are altogether universal ["Ethical Relativity: Sic et Non," *Journal of Philosophy*, LII (1955)].

Colin Turnbull, whose description of the sadistic, semidisplaced Ik in Northern Uganda was cited as evidence of a people without principles of kindness and cooperation, has produced evidence that, underneath the surface of this dying society, there is a deeper moral code from a time when the tribe flourished, and that this occasionally surfaces and shows its nobler face.

The nonrelativist can accept a certain relativity in the way moral principles are *applied* in different cultures, depending on each culture's beliefs, history, and environment. For example, a raw environment with scarce natural resources may justify the Eskimos' brand of euthanasia to the objectivist, who in another environment would consistently reject that practice. The Greeks and the Callatians disposed of their parents differently, but that does not prove that conventionalism is correct. Both groups seem to adhere to a common principle of showing respect to one's elders. Why can't there be latitude in how that respect is shown?

The members of a tribe in East Africa throw their deformed children into the river because of their belief that such infants *belong* to the hippopotamus, the god of the river. We believe that they have a false belief about this, but the same principles—of respect for property and respect for human life—operate in both societies. They differ with us only in belief, not in substantive moral principle. This is an illustration of how nonmoral beliefs (e.g., deformed children belong to the hippopotamus) when applied to common moral principles (e.g., give to each his due) generate different actions in different cultures. In our culture the difference in belief about the status of a fetus (is it a person or only a potential person?) generates opposite moral prescriptions. Both the pro-choice movement and the anti-abortionists agree that it is wrong to kill innocent persons, but they disagree as to a fact (not the principle) of whether a fetus is a *person* (a being with a right to life). Roman Catholics believe that the fetus is a person because—they say—it has a soul; most liberal Protestants and secularists deny this. Abortion is a serious moral issue, but what divides many of us is not a moral principle but how that principle should be applied. Antiabortionists believe that the principle of not killing innocent persons applies to fetuses whereas pro-choicers do not. But the two sides do not disagree on the fundamental principle.

The relativist, responding to this point may argue that even if we do *often* share deep principles, we don't *always* share them. Some people may not value life at all. How can we prove them wrong? "Who's to say which culture is right and which is wrong?" This response is of dubious merit. We can reason and perform thought experiments in order to make a case for one system over another. We may not be able to *know* with certainty that our moral beliefs are closer to the truth than those of another culture (or those of others within our own culture), but we may be *justified* in believing that they are. If we can be closer to the truth regarding factual or scientific matters, why can't we be closer to the truth on moral matters? Why can't a culture simply be confused or wrong about its moral perceptions? Why can't we say that a society like the Ik, which sees nothing wrong with enjoying watching its children fall into fires, is less moral in that regard than the culture that cherishes children and grants them protection and equal rights? To take such a stand is not to commit the fallacy of ethnocentricism, for we are seeking to derive principles through critical reason, not simply uncritical acceptance of one's own mores.

The Positive Case for a Core Morality

The discussion heretofore has been largely negative, against relativism. Now I want to make a case for a core set of moral principles that are necessary to the good society and the good life.

First, I must make it clear that I am distinguishing moral *absolutism* from moral *objectivism*. The absolutist believes that there are non-overridable moral principles which ought never to be violated. Kant's system is a good example of this. One ought never break a promise or tell a lie, no matter what. An objectivist need not posit any non-overridable principles, at least not in unqualified general form, and so need not be an absolutist. As Renford Barmbrough put it,

> To suggest that there is a *right* answer to a moral problem is at once to be accused of or credited with a belief in moral absolutes. But it is no more necessary to believe in moral absolutes in order

to believe in moral objectivity than it is to believe in the existence of absolute space or absolute time in order to believe in the objectivity of temporal and spatial relations and of judgments about them. [*Moral Skepticism and Moral Knowledge*, RKP, p. 33]

In the objectivist's account, moral principles are what the Oxford University philosopher William Ross (1877–1971) refers to as prima facie principles—valid rules of action that should generally be adhered to, but that may be overridden by another moral principle in cases of moral conflict.[7] For example, while a principle of justice may generally outweigh a principle of benevolence, there are times when enormous good could be done by sacrificing a small amount of justice, so that an objectivist would be inclined to act according to the principle of benevolence. There may be some absolute or nonoverridable principles (indeed the next principle I mention is probably one), but there need not be any or many for objectivism to be true.

If we can establish or show that it is reasonable to believe that there is at least one objective moral principle which is binding on all people everywhere in some ideal sense, we shall have shown that relativism is probably false and that a limited objectivism is true. Actually, I believe that there are many qualified general ethical principles which are binding on all rational beings, but one will suffice to refute relativism. I will call the principle I've chosen "A":

A: It is morally wrong to torture people for the fun of it.

I claim that this principle is binding on all rational agents, so that if agent S rejects A, we should not let that affect our intuition that A is a true principle but rather try to explain S's behavior as perverse, ignorant, or irrational. Suppose Adolf Hitler doesn't accept A, should that affect our confidence in the truth of A? Is it not more reasonable to infer that Hitler is morally deficient, morally blind, ignorant, or irrational than to suppose that his noncompliance is evidence against the truth of A?

Suppose further that there is a tribe of Hitlerites somewhere who enjoy torturing people. The whole culture accepts torturing others for the fun of it. Suppose that Mother Teresa or Gandhi tries unsuccessfully to convince them that they should stop torturing people altogether, and they respond by torturing *them*. Should this affect our confidence in A? Would it not be more reasonable to look for some explanation of Hitlerite behavior? For example, we might hypothesize that this tribe lacked a developed sense of the sympathetic imagination necessary for the moral life. Or we might theorize that this tribe was on a lower evolutionary level than most *Homo sapiens*. Or we might simply conclude that the tribe was closer to a Hobbesian state of nature than most societies, and as such probably would not survive. But we need not know the correct answer as to why the tribe was in such bad shape in order to maintain our confidence in A as a moral principle. If A is a basic or core belief for us, we will be more likely to doubt the Hitlerites' sanity or ability to think morally than to doubt the validity of A.

We can perhaps produce other candidates for membership in our basic objective moral set. For example:

1. Do not kill innocent people.
2. Do not cause unnecessary pain or suffering.
3. Do not commit rape.
4. Keep your promises and contracts.
5. Do not deprive another person of his or her freedom.
6. Do justice, treating equals equally and unequals unequally.
7. Do not commit adultery.
8. Tell the truth.
9. Help other people.
10. Obey just laws.

These ten principles are examples of the core morality—principles necessary for the good life. Fortunately, the ten principles are not arbitrary, for we can give reasons why we believe that these rules will be necessary to any satisfactory social order. Principles like those formulated in the Ten Commandments and the Golden Rule, and the principle of justice—treat equals equally, tell the truth, keep promises, and the like—are central to the fluid progression of social interaction and the resolution of conflicts. These are what ethics is about (at least minimal morality is, even though there may be more to morality than simply these kinds of concerns). For example, language itself depends on a general and implicit commitment to the principle of truth-telling. Accuracy of expression is a primitive form of truthfulness. Hence, every time we use words correctly we are implicitly telling the truth. Without accurate speech, language wouldn't be possible. Likewise, without the recognition of a rule of promise-keeping, contracts are of no avail and cooperation is less likely to occur; without the recognition of rules to protect life and liberty, we could not secure other goals.

A morality would be adequate if it contained the principles of the core morality, but different (adequate) moralities would apply these principles differently. That is, there may be a certain relativity as to secondary principles (whether to opt for monogamy rather than polygamy, whether to include a principle of high altruism in the set of moral duties, whether to allocate more resources to medical care than to environmental concerns, whether to institute a law to drive on the left side of the road or the right side of the road), but in every morality a certain core will remain. The applications would differ because of differences in environment, belief, tradition, and the like.

The core moral rules are analogous to the set of vitamins necessary for a healthy diet. We need an adequate amount of each vitamin—some people needing more of one, some more of another—but in prescribing a nutritious diet we don't have to set forth recipes, specific foods, place settings, or culinary habits. Gourmets will meet the requirements in one way, ascetics and vegetarians in another, but all will receive the basic nutrients.

Imagine that you have been miraculously transported to the dark kingdom of hell, and there you get a glimpse of the sufferings of the damned. What is their punishment? Well, they have eternal back itches, which ebb and flow constantly, but they cannot scratch their backs, for their arms are paralyzed in front of their bodies. And so they writhe with itchiness through eternity. Just as you begin to feel the itch in your own back, you are transported to heaven. What do you see in the kingdom of the blessed? You see people with eternal back itches who cannot scratch their own backs—but they are all smiling instead of writhing. Why? Because everyone has his or her arms stretched out to scratch someone else's back, and, with people so arranged in one big circle, a hell of suffering is turned into a heaven of ecstasy.

If we can imagine some states of affairs or cultures that are better than others in a way that depends on human action, we can ask what are those characteristics that make them so. In our story, people in heaven, but not those in hell, cooperate for the amelioration of suffering and the production of pleasure. These are very primitive goods, not sufficient for a full-blown moral system, but they give us a hint as to the objectivity of morality. Moral goodness has something to do with the amelioration of suffering, the resolution of conflict, and the promotion of human flourishing. If cooperative heaven is really better than itchy hell, then whatever makes it so is constitutively related to moral rightness.

An Explanation of the Attraction of Ethical Relativism

Why, then, is there such a strong inclination toward ethical relativism? The reasons—there are three—have not, I think, been sufficiently talked about. One is that the options are usually presented as though absolutism and relativism were the only alternatives, so conventionalism wins out against an implausible competitor. My student questionnaire reads as follows: "Are there any ethical absolutes, moral duties binding on all persons at all times, or are moral duties relative to culture? Is there any alternative to these two positions?" Hardly three percent suggest a third position and very few of them identify objectivism. Granted it takes a little philosophical sophistication to make the crucial distinctions, and it is precisely for lack of this sophistication or reflection that relativism has procured its enormous prestige. But, as I have argued, one can have an objective morality without being absolutist.

The second reason is that our recent sensitivity to cultural relativism and the evils of ethnocentrism, which have plagued the relations of Europeans and Americans with people of other cultures, has made us conscious of the frailty of many aspects of our moral repertoire, so that there is a tendency to wonder "Who's to judge what's really right or wrong?" However, the move from a reasonable cultural relativism, which rightly causes us to rethink our moral systems, to an ethical relativism, which causes us to give up the heart of morality altogether, is an instance of the fallacy of confusing factual or descriptive statements with normative ones. Cultural relativism doesn't entail ethical relativism. The very reason that we are *against* ethnocentrism constitutes the basis for our being *for* an objective moral system: impartial reason draws us to both conclusions.

We may well agree that cultures differ and that we ought to be cautious in condemning what we don't understand, but this in no way implies that there are not better and worse ways of living. We can understand and excuse, to some degree at least, those who differ from our best notions of morality, without abdicating the notion that cultures without principles of justice, or of promise-keeping, or of protection of the innocent, are morally poor for these omissions.

The third reason, which has driven some to moral nihilism and others to relativism, is the decline of religion in Western society. As one of Dostoevsky's characters said, "If God is dead, all things are permitted." The person who has lost religious faith feels a deep vacuum and understandably may confuse it with living in a *moral* vacuum, or he or she finally resigns him- or herself to a form of secular conventionalism. Such people reason that if there is no God to guarantee the validity of the moral order, there must not be a universal moral order: There is just radical cultural diversity and death at the end. But even if there turns out to be no God and no immortality, we still will want to live happy, meaningful lives during our fourscore years on earth. If this is true, then it matters by which principles we live, and those principles that win out in the test of time will be objectively valid.

To sum up, there *are* moral truths, principles belonging to the core morality, without which society will not long survive and individuals will not flourish. Reason can discover these principles—and it is in our interest to promote them.

So "Who's to judge what's right or wrong?" We are. We are to do so on the basis of the best reasoning we can bring forth and with sympathy and understanding.

Discussion Questions

1. How, according to Professor Pojman, do ethical relativism and cultural relativism differ? What are some of the philosophical problems he sees in ethical relativism?

2. According to Professor Pojman, what is wrong with the relativist's claim that ethical relativism promotes tolerance of people who hold different views? Do you agree with his assessment? Why or why not?

3. How does Professor Pojman distinguish between ethical objectivism and ethical absolutism? What is his main argument for ethical objectivism? According to Professor Pojman, are some moralities better than others? Explain. Also, tell why you agree or disagree with his position.

4. Name some of the moral claims that Professor Pojman believes are objectively true. Do you disagree with any of the claims on his list? Explain and defend your answer.

Notes

1. *History of Herodotus*, book 3, ch. 38, translated by George Rawlinson (D. Appleton, 1859).

2. *Folkways*, New York, 1906, section 80. And Ruth Benedict indicates the depth of our cultural conditioning this way: "The very eyes with which we see the problem are conditioned in the long traditional habits of our own society." ["Anthropology and the Abnormal," in *The Journal of General Psychology* (1934), reprinted above as "A Defense of Moral Relativism."]

3. Ernest Hemingway, *Death in the Afternoon* (Scribner's, 1932), p. 4.

4. *Patterns of Culture*, p. 27.

5. Melville Herskovits, *Cultural Relativism* (Random House, 1972).

6. *Ethics: Discovering Right and Wrong* (Wadsworth, 1990), pp. 29–34.

7. W. D. Ross, *The Right and the Good* (Oxford, 1931).

3

On Objective Values: A Dialogue

Peter Kreeft

Peter Kreeft is Professor of Philosophy at Boston College. He is the author of numerous books, including *The Best Things in Life* (1984), *The Unaborted Socrates* (1981), and *Between Heaven and Hell* (1982). He is well known for his use of fictional dialogue to convey in an entertaining way important philosophical issues.

The following is a fictional dialogue between a moral subjectivist (and relativist), Felicia Flake, and a moral objectivist, Socrates. Felicia confronts Socrates with the following seven arguments for moral relativism: (1) "individuals and cultures *do* have different values, different moralities," (2) "we are [morally] conditioned by our society, differently conditioned by different societies," (3) "the consequence of [moral] subjectivism is tolerance; the consequence of objectivism intolerance and dogmatism," (4) "morality is a matter of the heart, motive, and that's obviously subjective," (5) "moral choices are conditioned by the situation, and that's relative to thousands of things," (6) "it makes no sense to call an objective act good or evil," for "we interpret the facts in terms of our feelings," (7) "objective values would mean we are not free," since we would not be able to freely create our own values. Using the Socratic method (asking questions in order to "box in" the truth) developed by the historical Socrates, Professor Kreeft's fictional Socrates responds to each one of Felicia's arguments and concludes that they all fail.

Reprinted by permission from Peter Kreeft, *The Best Things in Life* (Downers Grove, Ill.: InterVarsity Press, 1984), 158–187.

Socrates:	Well, Felicia, here we are again in our outdoor classroom in the groves of academe. Are you ready for your Oxford tutorial?
Felicia:	Yes, Socrates. You know, I'm still not sure who you are or how you got here, but I'm grateful for your free teaching.
Socrates:	How could I put a price on the priceless?
Felicia:	Desperate State University does. The tuition rises each year.
Socrates:	Indeed. How could my pupil Plato ever have foreseen that his great invention of the university would one day be in such a desperate state? Or that it would take twenty-four centuries for bread to become smorgasbord? But here—are you ready to read to me your paper, as we planned, defending the subjectivity of values?
Felicia:	Yes, Socrates, and I'm glad it's a warm and sunny morning, because I think this is going to take some time. My paper is quite short, but your method of cross-examination is usually very long.
Socrates:	That's because I think many errors take place through haste, and perhaps this is especially true about errors concerning values.
Felicia:	You know, maybe we can save ourselves a lot of sweat. Maybe neither of us is in error. Maybe values are whatever we think they are, so that if I think they're subjective, why then they're subjective to me, and if you think they're objective, well, then, they're objective—to you.
Socrates:	That is a statement of your position but not of mine. I do not believe values are objective *to me;* I believe they are objective. "Objective to me"—what possible sense could that make? Is that not the same sort of contradiction as "subjective in themselves"?
Felicia:	You mean "objective to me" equals "objective subjectively" and "subjec-

	tive in themselves" equals "subjective objectively"?
Socrates:	Something like that. I think we had better define our terms before we begin. For if we cannot meaningfully agree about the meaning of the terms *values, subjective* and *objective*, then we cannot meaningfully disagree about whether values are objective or subjective.
Felicia:	That was going to be the first point in my paper: defining my terms.
Socrates:	Excellent, Felicia. Excuse me for anticipating you. What are your definitions?
Felicia:	They're very simple. I mean by *values* simply "rightness and wrongness," by *objective* simply "independent of the human mind" and by *subjective* "dependent on the human mind." How's that?
Socrates:	I think those are fine definitions: they are simple and clear, and they are what people usually mean by those words. Now let us get to your arguments against the objectivity of values.
Felicia:	I found seven arguments, Socrates. Here they are.

The first argument is unanswerable because it is based on undeniable facts: the facts discovered by sociologists and anthropologists. The fact is simply that individuals and cultures *do* have very different values, different moralities. As Descartes says, you can't imagine any idea so strange that it hasn't been taught by some philosopher. And you can't imagine any morality so weird that it hasn't been taught by some society. Anyone who thinks values aren't relative to culture simply doesn't know much about other cultures.

Here's a second argument, also based on a fact. The fact is that we are conditioned by our society, differently conditioned by different societies. If I had been born in a Hindu society, I would have Hindu values today. We don't discover values as we discover planets; we *have* them as we have measles: we catch them from our society.

My third argument is practical, from the *consequences* of believing subjectivism or objectivism. The consequence of subjectivism is tolerance; the consequence of objectivism is intolerance and dogmatism and trying to impose your values on others because you think everyone ought to believe your way. If you believe values are only yours, you don't try to force people to believe in them, unless you want to force them to believe in *you*.

My fourth argument is the primacy of motive. To do the right thing for the wrong reason is wrong, but you can't blame someone for doing the wrong thing for the right reason, the right motive. Morality is a matter of the heart, motive, and that's obviously subjective.

My fifth argument is circumstances, or the situation. Moral choices are conditioned by the situation, and that's relative to thousands of things. There can't be the same rules for all situations. You can imagine an exception to every rule in some situation. For instance, it can be good to kill if you kill a homicidal aggressor, good to steal if you steal a weapon from a madman, good to lie if you're the Dutch lying to the Nazis about where the Jews are hiding. There's no absolute morality; it's always relative to the situation.

My sixth argument is that it makes no sense to call an objective act good or evil. When you see an evil deed, like a murder, you feel terrible; the morality is in our feelings, in how we feel about the act, not in the act itself. Where's the evil? In the gun? The arm? The trigger finger? The wound? Those are simply facts. We interpret the facts in terms of our feelings. We add value colors to the black and white world of physical facts.

My seventh argument is that objective values would mean we are not free. Either we are free to create our own values, or values are imposed on us as a hammer is imposed on a nail. To preserve human dignity we must preserve human freedom, and to preserve human freedom we must preserve our creativity, our ability to create our own values freely.

Well, there you are, Socrates. It was short, as I said, and I hope sweet too.

Socrates: There is no question about its being short, but I have a few questions about its sweetness.

Felicia: Somehow I thought you would.

Socrates: My first question is about your term "values."

Felicia: I thought you agreed with my definition of it.

Socrates: I do. But I wonder whether you mean by it the *law* of right and wrong, or just the *feeling* of right and wrong.

Felicia: The feeling of right and wrong.

Socrates: So you would rather talk about moral values than about moral law.

Felicia: Yes.

Socrates: That's what I was afraid of. I fear you beg the question in your terminology. As you use it, the very word "values" connotes something subjective rather than something objective: feelings rather than laws. So for you to speak of "objective values" would be as self-contradictory as for me to speak of "subjective laws." I think your reluctance to talk about moral laws really means you believe there *are* no moral laws.

Felicia: Of course there are moral laws. The Ten Commandments, for instance. But that's old familiar stuff. Everybody knows that.

Socrates: Could you recite the Ten Commandments, since they are so familiar?

Felicia: Well . . . thou shalt not steal, thou shalt not kill, thou shalt not commit adultery. . . .

Socrates: Yes?

Felicia: That's all I remember right now . . .

Socrates: Three out of ten. Perhaps it is an illusion that everyone knows that old familiar stuff. Or perhaps you are the only one who forgot the other seven?

Felicia: All right, so I'm not an expert in the moral laws. We're talking about moral values today, aren't we?

Socrates: About whether they are laws or feelings. If they are laws, then you are not an expert in moral values, since you are not an expert in moral laws.

Felicia: So I'm not an expert. Lesson One again. You've made your point.

Socrates: Perhaps not sufficiently, if you are so impatient to move beyond it so quickly.

Felicia: You really love to get in your favorite point, don't you?

Socrates: It is not my favorite point by any means; it is quite embarrassing, in fact. But it must be truly believed and fully realized; that is the one thing I know. The point with regard to knowledge is that there are only two kinds of people in the world: the foolish, who think they are wise, and the wise, who know they are foolish. The same point with regard to morality is that there are only two kinds of people: sinners, who think they are saints, and saints, who know they are sinners. I will never cease to teach this embarrassing truth because without it, I am convinced, there simply is no knowledge and no morality, only the deceptive appearances of them.

Felicia: Humility first, eh?

Socrates: Exactly. Do you know what St. Bernard answered when someone asked him what were the first four virtues?

Felicia: What?

Socrates: Humility, humility, humility and humility.

Felicia: He wasn't impatient to go beyond that, is that it?

Socrates:	Yes. And now you?
Felicia:	All right, Socrates. I'm a fool too.
Socrates:	Good. Then we belong together, we two. Now let us get back to your paper, since we know who we are.
Felicia:	All right. Remember, if you can't refute every one of my objections to objective values, I will have proved my thesis.
Socrates:	Agreed. Now then, your first argument was that scientists have discovered that different cultures have different moralities, isn't that correct?
Felicia:	Yes.
Socrates:	And you claimed this argument was unanswerable because it was based on a fact, isn't that right?
Felicia:	Yes.
Socrates:	So you presuppose that all arguments that are based on facts are unanswerable?
Felicia:	Yes.
Socrates:	But surely that is a mistake in logic?
Felicia:	What do you mean?
Socrates:	Can't you make a logically unwarranted inference from a fact?
Felicia:	Oh. Of course. But how do you think I did that?
Socrates:	By using your ambiguous term "values." Value-opinions or value-feelings are one thing; true, real, objective values would be another thing, wouldn't they?
Felicia:	Yes, if they existed. But now you're begging the question in assuming that they exist.
Socrates:	I am assuming nothing, merely clarifying two different meanings of a term.
Felicia:	So what's your point?
Socrates:	Though value-opinions may be relative to different cultures and subjective to individuals, that does not necessarily mean that real values are. For even if people's opinions about anything vary

with time or place or weather or digestion or the prejudices of teachers, that does not prove that the thing itself varies in these ways, does it?

Felicia:	But *this* thing is values, "right and wrong." But right and wrong are matters of opinion, or conviction. So when opinions or convictions vary, right and wrong vary.
Socrates:	Ah, but that is precisely the question at issue: are right and wrong just matters of opinion? You are begging the question, assuming exactly the conclusion you must prove: that right and wrong are matters of subjective opinion.
Felicia:	Oh.
Socrates:	Not only that, there is a second and even simpler mistake in your argument: it is not based on a fact.
Felicia:	What? Of course it is. Don't you know about different cultures?
Socrates:	Of course; I am from one myself. But scientists have not proved that values are relative or subjective for the simple reason that they have never observed values. Values cannot be measured by scientific instruments.
Felicia:	Value-opinions, then. They have gone to many different places and taken opinion polls, you know.
Socrates:	I know. And even there you are simply mistaken about the facts. Even value-opinions are not wholly relative to cultures or individuals.
Felicia:	What? Of course they are. Don't you know your social sciences? You're simply ignoring the facts.
Socrates:	Let us see who is ignoring the facts. Let's look closely at some of the facts you appeal to to prove your point. Could you give a few examples?
Felicia:	Certainly. Suicide, for instance, is honorable for an ancient Roman or in Japan, but not for a Jew or a Christian. Usury was wrong in the Middle Ages but right today. It's wrong to bare your

breasts in England, but not in the South Seas. Value-opinions vary tremendously. That's a fact.

Socrates: But not totally. And that is another fact. Doesn't every society have some code of honor, and justice, and modesty (to speak only of your three examples)?

Felicia: I think so . . .

Socrates: So those three value-opinions, at any rate, are universal. No society prizes dishonor above honor, or injustice above justice, or immodesty above modesty. And there are many more things like this. Perhaps we should call these things "principles"—I mean things like the law of fair play and courage and generosity and honesty and unselfishness. I know that the rules of behavior differ greatly, but different rules of behavior seem designed to differently apply or obey the same principles. For instance, both South Sea Island dress and English dress are for modesty as well as for beauty and perhaps for other things as well. No society feels the same way about the sexual organs as it feels about the other parts of the body, does it?

Felicia: I think not. So you're distinguishing the principles from the rules, and saying the values are in the principles rather than the rules, and that the principles are the same for everyone?

Socrates: Yes—even that opinions about principles are the same for everyone, or nearly everyone. Did you ever hear of anyone who valued dishonesty above honesty? Or a society that rewarded homicidal maniacs and punished life-saving surgeons?

Felicia: No. So what is the relation between principles and rules?

Socrates: I think it is rather like the relation between meaning and expression. The same meaning can be expressed differently, or in different languages. So the same value can be expressed in different codes of rules. If there were no common meaning, it would be impos-

sible to translate from one language to another. And if there were no common principles, we could not even argue about which set of rules was better, because we would have no common meaning to "better."

Felicia: You mean we couldn't even be doing what we're doing now, arguing about morality?

Socrates: Right. Now here's a fact: people do argue about morality. They nearly always assume the same principles, and each tries to prove he or she is right according to those principles. No one argues about whether it's better to be fair or unfair, loyal or disloyal, full of hate or full of love. They argue not about principles but applications.

Felicia: I see. That sounds like a very simple point, the distinction between principles and applications. How could so many of our leading thinkers have missed it?

Socrates: Perhaps because they were not "leading thinkers" at all, but following thinkers, sheep with their nose to the tail of the Zeitgeist.

Felicia: But don't you think older societies often absolutized their relativities and exalted their applications into principles? They had their nose to the tail of their Zeitgeist too.

Socrates: Yes, and your society relativizes absolutes, and demotes principles to the level of applications. Two wrongs don't make a right; and two mistakes don't make a truth. They are simply opposite errors.

Felicia: But Socrates, just because most societies so far have agreed about many values, that doesn't mean there can't be a society that comes up with a new value tomorrow.

Socrates: No society has ever invented a new value, Felicia. That would be like inventing a new sound, or a new color. All we can do is put the primary sounds or colors together in new ways.

Felicia:	Then what happened in Nazi Germany? Didn't they create new values?
Socrates:	Certainly not. They just denied old ones. The only radical novelty in values that any society has ever come up with has been negations. Just as an occasional individual shows up who is color blind, or tone deaf. But no one ever shows up who sees a color no one ever saw before, or hears a note no one ever heard before.
Felicia:	I wonder. Isn't an individual free to go by any rules at all?
Socrates:	Do you think you are?
Felicia:	Perhaps.
Socrates:	I think not, and I think I can show you that.
Felicia:	Go ahead.
Socrates:	Do you think I am also free to create wholly new values and live by them?
Felicia:	If I am, you are too.
Socrates:	Very well, then, let us experiment and test your theory.
Felicia:	How?
Socrates:	By my announcing my new value system. It is this: I have won the argument with you simply because I am much older than you are. I also have sharper eyesight. I do not need glasses, as you do. Therefore I am wiser than you.
Felicia:	That's silly, Socrates. You can't win an argument just because you're older and don't wear glasses.
Socrates:	Those are my values. If I were teaching a class and you were in it, you would pass my course only if you were one of the older students and needed no glasses.
Felicia:	That's not fair.
Socrates:	But what is "fair"? Fairness, or justice, is merely subjective and relative, remember? It is whatever I make it. How dare you now assume some objective and universal standard of

justice to which you expect me to conform? Why should I conform to your subjective standard of justice? What right do you have to impose your personal, subjective values on me? My subjective standard is just as valid as yours if there is no objective standard. And I say justice is age and sight. But to my arbitrary subjectivism you now reply with the old idea of a single objective justice or "fairness" that you expect me to know and obey. So the cat is out of the bag; you are an objectivist after all, in practice. Your subjectivism in theory was only a disguise.

Felicia:	All right, Socrates, you win round one. Let's go to round two, all right? How do you demolish my second objection?
Socrates:	Would you summarize it for me first, please?
Felicia:	Yes. Society conditions values in us. If I had been born into a Hindu society I would have Hindu values.
Socrates:	Once again that slippery word "values." We must bear in mind the distinction we agreed to. What society conditions in us, what we have, is opinions about values. But to identify these with values themselves is to beg the question once again, is it not?
Felicia:	But at least society determines those value opinions.
Socrates:	Determines or conditions?
Felicia:	What's the difference?
Socrates:	An artist's palette and brushes condition his painting, but they leave him free to choose within the bounds set by his conditioning. Parents condition their children not to steal, but the children are free to disobey. Conditioning leaves you free. Determining does not.
Felicia:	My sociology textbooks don't make that distinction.
Socrates:	That's because their writers are not philosophers.
Felicia:	I still think if I were born a Hindu I'd

have Hindu values.

Socrates: Has everyone who was born into a Hindu society grown up to accept Hindu values? Or are there rebels, nonconformists? Do some Hindus become Christians, or Marxists?

Felicia: Yes.

Socrates: Then they are only conditioned, not determined.

Felicia: All right, but they do condition us, at least. We do learn different values from different societies.

Socrates: Not wholly different values, as we have already seen. No society teaches us cowardice, or selfishness.

Felicia: Partially different values, then. But that, at least, is a fact.

Socrates: Let us look more closely at this fact. You speak of "society" as an agent. "Society" means teachers, does it not? Especially parents!

Felicia: Yes. Why do you have to say that?

Socrates: Because "society" sounds so abstract and ghostly, like the thing I could not defend myself against in my *Apology:* the Zeitgeist, or public opinion, or "what everyone knows." It is always helpful to be concrete. So let us substitute "teachers" for "society" in our argument. All right?

Felicia: All right.

Socrates: Would you say this is your argument then—that values are subjective because we learn them from our society, that is, our teachers?

Felicia: Yes.

Socrates: Do you see the hidden premise?

Felicia: Let's see . . . that what we learn from society is subjective?

Socrates: What we learn from teachers is subjective. Yes. Now is this true? Is everything we learn from teachers subjective?

Felicia: I don't know.

Socrates: Did you learn the laws of physics from teachers?

Felicia: Yes.

Socrates: Are they subjective?

Felicia: No.

Socrates: Then not everything we learn from teachers is subjective.

Felicia: But teachers disagree. We learn different things from different teachers. They can't all be objectively true. So they must be subjective.

Socrates: All of them?

Felicia: Yes.

Socrates: Why couldn't some be true and some false, just as in science? Different physics teachers teach you different things, too, on some issues; not everything is known and agreed on in physics, you know. But that does not prove that physics is merely subjective, does it?

Felicia: No.

Socrates: Then why does it prove that ethics is subjective?

Felicia: But physics is different.

Socrates: How?

Felicia: It's about the real world. Ethics is about our ideals.

Socrates: That is precisely the point at issue. You beg the question again in reducing "the real world" to the physical world and in assuming that ideals are not objectively real, that they are only "ours."

Felicia: But the fact remains that teachers of physics agree a whole lot more than do teachers of ethics.

Socrates: What follows from that, if we grant it to be a fact?

Felicia: That ethics is subjective, of course.

Socrates: Only if you assume another premise again. Do you see which one?

Felicia: Let's see—I'm catching on to this—teachers of ethics disagree, therefore

	ethics is subjective. That assumes that what teachers disagree about is subjective.
Socrates:	Correct. And do you claim that premise is true?
Felicia:	Yes. Why not?
Socrates:	Because there seem to be many exceptions. In physics, for instance.
Felicia:	But physics is different!
Socrates:	How?
Felicia:	It's about . . .
Socrates:	The real world?
Felicia:	Yes. I see. I'm begging the question again. And also my premise is not true. And also I used the term "values" ambiguously. What else can possibly go wrong with my argument?
Socrates:	One other thing. Your other premise is also false, it seems: ethical teachers do agree about many things, about basic values. And scientists do not wholly agree.
Felicia:	More than ethical teachers, at any rate.
Socrates:	Perhaps not even that. Many scientists in the past had very different opinions than most scientists today, didn't they?
Felicia:	Yes, but that's disagreement across time. The scientists of any one time largely agree across space.
Socrates:	That is true, but what follows from it? Ethical teachers agree across time, and scientists agree across space; do time or space determine truth?
Felicia:	I guess not. Well, you've pretty thoroughly demolished my second argument. What about the third one? Aren't you in favor of toleration?
Socrates:	I am, but I do not see how the subjectivity of values follows.
Felicia:	If you think your values are objective, you'll try to impose them on others.
Socrates:	But if they are *not* "my" values, but also real values, then I no more impose them on others than I impose gravity

or mathematics on others. They are simply there. Teaching them is like teaching mathematics. As one of your wise men has put it, it's not propaganda but propagation, like old birds teaching young birds to fly.

Felicia:	But won't you be much more tolerant if you think values are subjective, and less tolerant if you think they are objective?
Socrates:	I think not, and I think I can show you why. Tell me, what modern enterprise do you think has benefitted and progressed the most because of toleration and open-mindedness?
Felicia:	Science, I suppose.
Socrates:	I agree. Now then, does science believe its discoveries are only subjective?
Felicia:	No. But it's silly to impose them by force.
Socrates:	Yes it is, and it's just as silly to try to impose ethical values by force. The parallel holds.
Felicia:	But people tried to do just that in the past; the Inquisition burned heretics.
Socrates:	Yes, and other foolish people tried to impose scientific theories by force or threat: the Galileo case, for instance. The parallel still holds. Both fields have their fools.
Felicia:	Hmmm. The parallel seems to hold, all right. But maybe the parallel is that they're both subjective. Maybe we were wrong to think science deals with objective truth. Don't today's philosophers of science say that all scientific theories are only conceptual models or myths, relative to the human mind and radically inadequate to reality?
Socrates:	Models, yes. Inadequate, yes. Even myths, perhaps. But not subjective, not fantasies. Not humanly invented worlds, just humanly invented words, or word systems, or pictures. Our way of understanding the physical world is limited and inadequate. So is our way of understanding the spiritual world,

the world of values. But both worlds are equally real.

Felicia: Even though our minds are so inadequate?

Socrates: "Inadequate" does not mean "untrue," does it?

Felicia: I suppose not. It seems strange to say ethics deals with truth though, as science does.

Socrates: If we believed it didn't, if we thought no ethical teaching could be true, why would we pay attention to it? Values are important to us only if they are true values, isn't that so?

Felicia: I thought values were important to us because of our emotional investment in them. They are our cherished opinions.

Socrates: Opinions about what?

Felicia: What?

Socrates: That is my question, yes.

Felicia: I mean, what do you mean?

Socrates: Is there a reality about which to opine? A referent? If not, how can there be an opinion? An opinion is an opinion *about* something, and that something is the standard to judge one opinion as closer to it than another. Isn't this how we judge opinions?

Felicia: That would imply an objective truth outside the opinions.

Socrates: Precisely.

Felicia: But we only have opinions, so we don't know the truth.

Socrates: But we want to. The opinion intends the truth, aims at it. If it were not there, how could we aim at it?

Felicia: Oh. Well, then, I guess I don't mean to say that values are opinions but feelings.

Socrates: The objectivity of values, then, seems to you to be ridiculous because it means the objectivity of feelings, the objectivity of something that is by its essence subjective.

Felicia: Exactly. So you see it as I do after all.

Socrates: Not at all. To me, the *subjectivity* of values is ridiculous because it means the subjectivity of something that is by its essence objective: goods, real goods.

Felicia: How differently we use the same word! Well, then, it's just a matter of preference, of arbitrarily choosing one meaning or another. It's not a thing to argue about. It's subjective. Even your idea of the objectivity of values is just your subjective preference about the word. Neither of us can disprove the other.

Socrates: On the contrary, I think from your own starting point of value-feelings, we can be led to the doctrine of the objectivity of values.

Felicia: How?

Socrates: Consider: what are these value-feelings? Do you not feel called, challenged, "oughted," so to speak, by moral values?

Felicia: You could put it that way.

Socrates: Well, if these values were only subjective, how could they make such demands on you?

Felicia: They come from me. I bind myself by them.

Socrates: If you bind yourself, how are you really bound? You can just as easily loose yourself. Do you feel that you can? Can you be dishonest with a good conscience?

Felicia: No.

Socrates: If you disobey values, they continue to haunt you, to condemn you, to make you feel guilt, don't they?

Felicia: Yes.

Socrates: Now that doesn't feel like the rules of a manmade game, does it? If you change the rules of a game of tag, do you feel guilt?

Felicia:	No. But didn't Kant come up with some clever explanation of how we bind ourselves by morality?
Socrates:	He distinguished two aspects of the self. His "transcendental ego" posited the values for the "empirical ego" to obey. So it's not really binding yourself. You can't simply bind yourself, or obey yourself, or even have responsibilities to yourself. How can you split yourself in two like that?
Felicia:	But we always do say things like that.
Socrates:	And what do you think you mean by them?
Felicia:	I don't know. What do you think?
Socrates:	I think you must mean one of two things. Either you are doing what Kant did, and splitting yourself into two selves . . .
Felicia:	That can't be. I'm one self. And it's not part of me that insists on values; it's simply me.
Socrates:	Then it must be the second alternative: you are mistaken about the one to whom you are bound, or responsible.
Felicia:	You mean I'm putting myself in the place of God?
Socrates:	If the shoe fits . . .
Felicia:	Hmmm. I'll have to think more about that. Well, there goes my third argument down the tubes. I guess toleration doesn't prove subjectivity, does it?
Socrates:	Oh, it's much worse than that. It proves objectivity.
Felicia:	How?
Socrates:	Very simply. The real value of toleration presupposes real values. Do you say toleration is really valuable?
Felicia:	Suppose I don't? Suppose I just say it is my subjective preference to be tolerant?
Socrates:	Then suppose I say it is mine to be intolerant?
Felicia:	Well, then we differ, that's all.
Socrates:	Exactly: that's all. Then we can no longer argue, or even quarrel. We can only fight. It then becomes a contest of wills or weapons, not words, not minds. And then we really do try to "impose our values," as you put it, on each other. Do you choose to do that?
Felicia:	Certainly not. I choose to be tolerant.
Socrates:	And do you believe this choice of yours to be tolerant is really better than its opposite?
Felicia:	Oops. If I say yes . . .
Socrates:	Then there is a real "better."
Felicia:	And there can't be a real "better" without a real "good," so then there is a real good, an objective value. So I will have to say no, I do not believe my choice to be tolerant is really better than its opposite, intolerance.
Socrates:	Do you honestly believe that?
Felicia:	Well . . . no. I can't quite brazen that one out.
Socrates:	And here is another argument. If you think that toleration of all values and value systems is good, are you not then "imposing your values," your value system, which includes the value of toleration, on other people or other cultures, not all of whom agree that toleration is a value? Many traditional cultures see toleration as a weakness, as a disvalue. So for you to say that everyone ought to be tolerant is for you to say that your value system, with tolerance, is really better than others, without tolerance. Isn't that "imposing your values" on others?
Felicia:	I never thought of that.
Socrates:	Do so now, please.
Felicia:	I don't think that is imposing my values on them.
Socrates:	Neither do I.
Felicia:	What is it, then?

Socrates:	I think it is an insight into a real, objective, universal value: toleration. Some cultures and some individuals simply fail to see it. We make mistakes in values, you know, just as we make mistakes in anything else. Or did you think we were infallible in just this one area?
Felicia:	No . . .
Socrates:	Well, if you admit that, you admit objectivity.
Felicia:	How?
Socrates:	A mistake means a failure to know the truth. Where there is no truth, there is no error.
Felicia:	But we should tolerate error, not impose the truth.
Socrates:	Indeed. Notice what we tolerate: error, not truth. Evil, not good. Lesser evils, necessary evils. So the very word "toleration" presupposes real good and evil.
Felicia:	Oh, Socrates, you have tangled me up in my words again. How typically Socratic.
Socrates:	You know better than that by now, Felicia. You know the point of my method is not to win the argument but to win the truth, not to defeat the opponent but to defeat the error.
Felicia:	But you use language like a rapier, and your opponent always finds herself full of holes. It's an unfair fight.
Socrates:	But as I just said, it's not a fight. Or if it is, we're fighting on the same side. And it's not unfair because we are all equally in the web of words, in language, just as we are equally within the structures of logic. We live in them as we live in air or light or time. They are the same for all. They are not mine.
Felicia:	I understand, I think. I just don't like to be made a fool of.
Socrates:	The only fool is the one who refuses ever to be a fool.
Felicia:	Yes, I've learned that too. But what do you mean by saying that even
	language is objective? Surely we invent language.
Socrates:	Yes, but not language itself. "In the beginning was the Word." It's a nice parallel to morality, in fact: moralities are invented; morality is discovered. Mores are subjective; morals are objective. Positive law is posited by people; natural law is natural, given.
Felicia:	Socrates, I am astonished at your clear distinctions and definitions and arguments. I never thought ethics could be done with such clear and simple logic.
Socrates:	That was part of your culture's problem: separating the sciences and the humanities so much that logical thought was separated from values, and values from logical thought.
Felicia:	I know that the separation between the sciences and the humanities has harmed both.
Socrates:	Worse, it has harmed people, who thought about the most important questions in their lives vaguely, and even often praised this vagueness and demeaned logic as a kind of enemy of values, while they reserved clear and tough-minded thinking for the cave.
Felicia:	The cave?
Socrates:	Plato's cave. The world of the senses.
Felicia:	You mean that's all science is? In the cave?
Socrates:	Did you think science dealt with values?
Felicia:	You just said you wanted to do values logically.
Socrates:	You see? You are assuming an identity between science and logical thought, as if only science can use logic.
Felicia:	Oh. But you're insulting science by putting it down in the cave.
Socrates:	Not at all. It explores the cave very well. But not the larger world outside. You moderns think very clearly about the structure of the atom, but not about

the structure of Adam; about the heart of matter, but not about the heart of the matter, the heart of man. You are more rational about the life of fruit flies than about your own lives.

Felicia: I always thought morality couldn't be logical because it was a matter of subjective motive. And that's my fourth argument. Do you mean to say that motive isn't the most important thing in morality? Or that motive isn't mysterious?

Socrates: No, but I do mean to say that mysteries are to be explored, not ignored.

Felicia: So morality is a matter of motive. And motive is subjective. So morality is subjective. See? I can syllogize too.

Socrates: And I can distinguish. Morality is motive, but not only motive. Even if motive is primary, that does not exclude other, secondary aspects of morality—if indeed they are secondary.

Felicia: I don't know whether we need anything secondary after all. Love alone is enough, isn't it? And love is a motive.

Socrates: But is love only a motive? Is it not also a deed? And can you separate its motives from its deeds? Can you hate, or rape, or murder, or steal, or bear false witness out of love?

Felicia: No.

Socrates: Do you see? The commandments which specify good and evil acts are ways of specifying loving and unloving motives too. Love does not steal, love does not kill, and so on.

Felicia: Love seems to commit adultery.

Socrates: Not the kind the commandments command. Not faithful love, not unadulterated love.

Felicia: I see. But the motive is the primary thing, at least.

Socrates: Yes. But does the primacy of one thing discount second things? The soul is more important than the body, but isn't the body important too? Humanity is more important than nature, but isn't nature precious? You moderns seem to have this tendency to assume that the greater is somehow in competition with the lesser, and to think of only one thing at a time. You don't think of hierarchy and order and balance. Perhaps the Romantics are to blame, for romanticizing revolutionary extremism and scorning our old Greek wisdom of moderation.

Felicia: Moderation sounds so boring, Socrates.

Socrates: It is just the opposite. Extremism is boring. Did you ever meet a mono-maniac? Moderation is exciting because it is the principle of life itself. Life is a balancing act between dull and deathly extremes.

Felicia: What extremes?

Socrates: Physically, things like cold and heat, which threaten the body. Morally, things like cowardice and foolhardiness, which threaten the soul.

Felicia: So you think Aristotle was right about the Golden Mean?

Socrates: Yes, but he carried it to extremes. He was moderate to excess.

Felicia: I think I know at least one thing that doesn't fit moderation and the Golden Mean: love. How can you have too much love?

Socrates: If I love a stone as much as a man, isn't that too much?

Felicia: Yes, but how can you love a person too much?

Socrates: If I thought you were God and worshipped you, would that not be loving a person too much? The great rule is to love your neighbor *as yourself*, isn't it? Do you worship yourself?

Felicia: No. I don't even worship God. I mean, I don't know whether there is a God to worship or not. But I guess we'd bet-

	ter save that for another day. First things first. Let's finish our tutorial.
Socrates:	Second things first, you mean, in this case. Well, as you will. Let's look at your fourth argument. Could you summarize it briefly?
Felicia:	Yes. Situations are relative; morality is determined by situations; so, morality is relative. How's that for brief?
Socrates:	For brief, you get an A. For logic, perhaps a C. For one thing, it does not prove the thesis you are supposed to be arguing for.
Felicia:	Sure it does.
Socrates:	I thought you were supposed to be trying to prove that morality was subjective.
Felicia:	Yes.
Socrates:	But situations are objectively real, aren't they? So even if morality is determined by situations, it is still objective.
Felicia:	But it's relative, at least.
Socrates:	If it is wholly determined by situations. Once again, I think we must distinguish conditioning from determining. Do you think morality is wholly determined by situations, or only that situations *help* determine morality?
Felicia:	I don't know. I never thought of that.
Socrates:	Did you ever study Thomas Aquinas's moral philosophy?
Felicia:	Of course not. We read only up-to-date authors here.
Socrates:	You mean the ones that will become dated very soon. Yes, I see; that is a good part of your problem.
Felicia:	What does Aquinas say about situations?
Socrates:	Something moderate and reasonable, I think: that there are three things that make a human act good or evil, not just one: the nature of the act itself, the motive, and the situation or circumstances.

Felicia:	What's "the nature of the act itself"?
Socrates:	Well, whether it's an act of theft or payment, for instance, or whether it's an act of adultery or married love. The moral law specifies good and evil acts. That's the objective and absolute part of morality. The subjective part is the motive and the relative part is the situation. (But even that is not relative to us; it's objective.)
Felicia:	So all three have to be right for the act to be right?
Socrates:	Right. If I give money to a beggar just to show off, the act in itself is good but my motive is not, so it becomes a morally deficient act. Or if I make love to my wife in the wrong situation, for instance when it is medically dangerous, it becomes a morally deficient act.
Felicia:	What a sophisticated position! You say old Aquinas came up with this?
Socrates:	He is not so old, after all, compared with me. Actually this position is as old as Augustine. Are you surprised at that?
Felicia:	Yes.
Socrates:	Perhaps that's because you shared the modern myopia about the history of thought that one of your sages has called "chronological snobbery."
Felicia:	Don't you believe in progress?
Socrates:	Yes, and also in regress; don't you?
Felicia:	Do you think ethics has regressed?
Socrates:	In this area, yes.
Felicia:	Why?
Socrates:	Your three most popular modern ethical philosophies each seem childishly oversimplified. Each isolates and absolutizes one of the three parts of morality.
Felicia:	You mean legalism and subjectivism and situationism?
Socrates:	Precisely.

Felicia:	I don't want to defend childishness. But I think my strongest objection is my next one, because it's so simple. Where is the good or evil in the physical act itself? I just don't understand what that could mean. When I look at a physical act, all I see are facts, not values.
Socrates:	So you think the values are in your own feelings instead?
Felicia:	Yes. We project our feelings out onto things.
Socrates:	Surely you don't mean that literally?
Felicia:	Why not?
Socrates:	Because then you would be saying that when you see a murder, you feel evil and you project your evil feeling out onto the act.
Felicia:	Right.
Socrates:	But when you see a murder take place, you don't feel evil. You feel that the murder, or the murderer, is evil.
Felicia:	Yes, but the feeling is in me. So I find the evil in me.
Socrates:	I think you are confusing adjectives with adverbs.
Felicia:	Is this what they do at Oxford? Grammatical pettifoggery?
Socrates:	No, necessary distinctions. Let me try to explain. If "in me" is adjectival, it modifies the noun "evil," and then when you say "I find the evil in me," you mean that the evil itself is in you, that you are evil. You just admitted that you didn't feel that you were evil, but that the murder, or the murderer, was evil. So that can't be what you mean. The alternative is that "in me" is adverbial. Then it modifies the verb "find," and when you say, "I find the evil in me," you mean only that the act or process of finding the evil is in you, not the object found. But that's what I say too. The evil is objective, the process of finding it is subjective, just as physical facts are objective, but the process of our sensing them is subjective.
Felicia:	But where is the evil in the object, then? I just don't understand. How can a thing be evil? You apparently believe in God; didn't God make all things good? Is the maker of all things the maker of ill things?
Socrates:	Oh, all *things* are good all right. But *acts* are not *things*. We make acts, God makes things.
Felicia:	How can the act be evil, then? It's just a physical event.
Socrates:	Is it? You don't think the act of murder is a moral event?
Felicia:	No. The moral event is in me. What's out there is just the physical event. "There is nothing good or bad, but thinking makes it so."
Socrates:	I don't believe you really believe that. Do you think that if I murdered you and I didn't *think* that was an evil deed, then it wouldn't *be* an evil deed?
Felicia:	Not in your mind.
Socrates:	Would I be right or wrong in thinking that?
Felicia:	I think you would be wrong, but you'd think you were right.
Socrates:	That is not what I asked. I asked which of these two opinions, yours or mine, would be true.
Felicia:	Both.
Socrates:	But they are contradictories. How can contradictories both be true?
Felicia:	Neither, then.
Socrates:	But of two contradictories, one must be true and the other false.
Felicia:	Socrates, I can't answer your logic. But there's something more than formal logic involved here.
Socrates:	I agree. But not less. The law of non-contradiction is never abrogated.
Felicia:	I don't know about that.
Socrates:	Give me an example—real or imag-ined—of anything real violating the law of noncontradiction.

Felicia:	Paradoxes.
Socrates:	They are only *apparent* contradictions. Distinguish two meanings and they are resolved.
Felicia:	Mysteries, then.
Socrates:	Mysteries meaning the unknown?
Felicia:	Yes.
Socrates:	How can the unknown be *known* to be contradictory?
Felicia:	All right, so I can't escape your logic. But I still don't understand the reality. That's more important.
Socrates:	I agree. With all three statements.
Felicia:	When I look at the act, I see only physical things, squint as I will.
Socrates:	What do you look at the act with?
Felicia:	My eyes, of course.
Socrates:	Which ones?
Felicia:	Both of them, of course.
Socrates:	You mean you think you have only two?
Felicia:	What do you think I am, a monster?
Socrates:	No, a human being, but you apparently think you are only an animal. Do you not know you have an inner eye too?
Felicia:	What in the world is that?
Socrates:	Perhaps not something "in the world" at all. Or perhaps "in the world but not of the world". . .
Felicia:	Now you're really mystifying me.
Socrates:	Sorry. But you have surely heard of "conscience"?
Felicia:	Oh, *that*. But that's just my subjective feeling.
Socrates:	You don't see it as a *seeing*?
Felicia:	No. I see only feeling in conscience.
Socrates:	You see this feeling then? With your outer eyes?
Felicia:	No . . .

Socrates:	Then you do have an inner eye. You just haven't used it well. And you know what happens to any organ, inner or outer, when it is unused, don't you? It atrophies. You need exercise. You see, this is the reason why you did not believe in objective values: you did not see them.
Felicia:	That's right. That's what I've been trying to tell you.
Socrates:	And I'm trying to tell you that the reason you didn't see them is because you didn't look at them.
Felicia:	That's a departure from your Socratic method: telling me instead of questioning me.
Socrates:	That's because as you said, the point you need to see lies beyond the realm of merely formal logic. It's like opening your eyes rather than measuring the light.
Felicia	If you're right, it's very embarrassing—a very simple and a very big mistake, isn't it?
Socrates:	I think so. Why do you think so?
Felicia:	Because if goodness is objective, if there's a goodness outside us and above us that measures us, a standard, a norm, a real ideal, why then it must be God's goodness. Where else could this objective, absolute, universal goodness be? So then I've got to admit a God too.
Socrates:	Do you find it hard to follow the leading of the argument to that point?
Felicia:	Yes. In fact, my admitting this much to you is amazing. In effect, I'm confessing to you that I may have reduced the perfection of the Creator to the feelings of a creature, that I've been trying to take the place of God as the standard of goodness. That's not an easy thing to admit.
Socrates:	Perhaps the reason it's so threatening concerns your last reason for the subjectivity of values, the one you ended your paper with.

Felicia:	You're right. I found both God and objective goodness threatening to my freedom.
Socrates:	Then let us examine this last objection, by all means. Shall we try to formulate it first, as simply as possible?
Felicia:	All right. How's this—if values are objective, we are not free. We are free. Therefore values cannot be objective.
Socrates:	Fine. Now what do you mean by "free"? Free to do what?
Felicia:	To create values.
Socrates:	Then I agree with your first premise. If values are objective, we would not be free to create them. But then I disagree with your second premise: we are not free in this sense. We cannot create values.
Felicia:	What kind of freedom do you think we have, then?
Socrates:	The freedom to choose between good and evil.
Felicia:	Free will, you mean?
Socrates:	Yes. Do you believe we have this freedom or not?
Felicia:	I do.
Socrates:	But if there is no real, objective good and no real, objective evil, and no real, objective difference between the two, then we do not have the freedom to *choose* between these two gifts that are given, but only the freedom to *imagine* them, to make them up as fantasies, feelings or the rules of our little games.
Felicia:	I see. I have to choose between the two kinds of freedom.
Socrates:	Yes. Why did you want to create values?
Felicia:	I thought it was grander, and greater. But if the values we make aren't real, it's not so grand after all. In fact, it's pretty paltry. Perhaps that's why modern life is so paltry. Say! Maybe that's why I loved Tolkien's *Lord of the Rings* so much: it's got this assumed back-

	ground of real, strong, objective good and evil. Maybe I missed that in typical modern literature. But if I decide I was wrong and decide to believe in objective values, won't I miss the other thing, the freedom to create my own values?
Socrates:	Will you miss hell?
Felicia:	Hell?
Socrates:	Yes. In hell they create their own values.
Felicia:	How do you know that?
Socrates:	I will not tell you that now. But I will tell you more about hell. Everyone there wants to be God. That's why they went there in the first place. Did you think God would force anyone to go there if they didn't want to? No, they all chose it freely. They wouldn't have liked heaven. Too objectively real for them. Too threatening to their "freedom."
Felicia:	Ooh! My mistake was serious.
Socrates:	Yes. More than a logical fallacy. That is why I departed from my usual Socratic method to try to free you from it. You see, I put a high value on freedom too.
Felicia:	Don't you ever yearn for the other kind of freedom, the freedom to create new values?
Socrates:	Instead of answering that question directly, let me do it by asking you one. Do you know any group of people who never yearn for freedom but for bondage instead? Who wants not to be free but to be bound?
Felicia:	I don't know. What a silly thing to want! What silly people they must be! Who are they?
Socrates:	Lovers.
Felicia:	Oh! They *don't* talk about freedom, do they?
Socrates:	No. And do you know why?
Felicia:	No. Why?
Socrates:	Because they are already free.

Felicia:	It takes time getting used to this new way of seeing things, you know. A part of me still wants to create my own values.
Socrates:	Let's see whether we can use the light of logic again to educate that part of you. Those values you want to create, are they good ones or bad ones? Do you want to create good values?
Felicia:	Of course.
Socrates:	Then even when you want to create values, you are admitting objective values, a real standard of good and bad to which you want your manmade values to conform.
Felicia:	I guess I wasn't the thoroughgoing apostle of subjective values that I thought I was.
Socrates:	The thoroughgoing apostate? No.
Felicia:	Thank you for helping me to know my true self.
Socrates:	That is my mission, to others as to myself.
Felicia:	And thank you for going beyond your method of logical questioning for a while and giving me some answers.
Socrates:	It hasn't stopped your questioning, has it?
Felicia:	No, the answers have created many more questions. That's why I think I'm going to take some religion courses here, just as Peter Pragma decided to do.
Socrates:	You realize, of course, that religion is not a *course*?
Felicia:	What is it, then?
Socrates:	It's a relationship.
Felicia:	Something like my relationship with Peter? Oh, did I tell you, we're going out with each other now. We used to be the worst of enemies—he called me a jellyfish and I called him an icicle—and now we're the best of friends. It's like he supplies the bones and I supply the flesh for a single body. I think being in love helped me to understand

a lot of those things about God. Well, I've only begun—both relationships—and I've got a long way to go and a lot to learn.

Socrates: You have learned Lesson One very well, Felicia. And at the end of the road you are now beginning lies the realization of your name.

Outline of Arguments in the Dialog on "Objective Values"

Objections:

1. Values are relative to cultures.
2. Society conditions values in us.
3. Moral subjectivism produces toleration.
4. Morality is a matter of subjective motive.
5. Morality is a matter of relative situations.
6. We find no moral values in objects.
7. If we are free, we create values.

Replies:

to 1:
1. Distinguish value-opinions (which are culturally relative) from values (which are not).
2. Even value-opinions are not wholly relative to cultures; disagreement on applications presupposes agreement on principles.
3. Moral argumentation presupposes agreement on principles.
4. The ad hominem argument: even the subjectivist expects objective justice from the objectivist.

to 2:
1. Society conditions opinions but not values.
2. Not everything we learn from society (teachers) is subjective.
3. There is a parallel between ethics and physics, even regarding disagreement; disagreement does not prove subjectivity.

to 3:
1. The value of toleration does not logically entail subjectivism.
2. The value of toleration presupposes real values.
3. It is intolerant to refuse to tolerate intolerance.

4. We tolerate only evils, presupposing an objective standard.

to 4: 1. Motives are naturally connected with objective deeds.
2. The primacy of motive does not entail the absence of other moral determinants.

to 5: 1. Situations are objective, not subjective.
2. Situations are only one of three moral determinants.

to 6: We see values by the inner eye of conscience.

to 7. 1. We do not have freedom to create values.
2. Free will presupposes an objective good/evil distinction.
3. Freedom to create your own values is hellish, not heavenly.
4. Lovers yearn to be bound, not free; they are free.

Discussion Questions

1. What are Felicia's first three arguments for ethical subjectivism (or relativism)? Present and explain Socrates's response to each of them.

2. What are Felicia's final four arguments for ethical subjectivism (or relativism)? Present and explain Socrates's response to each of them.

3. Do you find Socrates's case against ethical subjectivism (or relativism) in this dialogue a good reason to be an ethical objectivist, or do you think his case should be supplemented in some way? Explain and defend your answer.

SECTION B

Ethical Theory

The field of ethics traditionally has been dominated by two types of ethical systems, that is, methods of reasoning that either tell us what is the correct moral decision to make in a given situation or explain why the moral judgment we have already made is either correct or incorrect. *Utilitarian* systems of ethics say that moral decisions ought to be made because of their nonmoral consequences (e.g., more pleasure than pain or more benefit than harm for the greatest number), resulting from either the act itself (act utilitarianism) or obeying a general rule (rule utilitarianism). Although agreeing that results may play a part in ethical decision-making, *deontological* systems of ethics say that moral decisions ought to be made on the basis of the intrinsic moral goodness or badness of the act in question. In order to better understand the two types of systems, Professor Louis P. Pojman provides the following story:

> Suppose that you are on an island with a dying millionaire. As he lies dying, he asks you for one final favor. He entreats you, "I've dedicated my whole life to baseball and have gotten endless pleasure (and some pain) rooting for the New York Yankees for 50 years. Now that I am dying, I want to give all of my assets, $2 million, to the Yankees. Would you take this money (he indicates a box containing the money in large bills) back to New York and give it to the Yankees' owner, George Steinbrenner?" You agree to carry out his wish, at which point a huge smile of relief and gratitude breaks out on his face as he expires in your arms. Now on traveling to New York you see a newspaper advertisement placed by the World Hunger Relief Organization (whose integrity you do not doubt), pleading for $2 million to be used to save 100,000 people dying of starvation in East Africa. Not only will the $2 million save their lives, but it will also enable the purchase of certain kinds of technology and the kinds of fertilizers necessary to build a sustainable economy. You begin to consider your promise to the dying Yankees fan in the light of this advertisement. What should you do with the money?[1]

If you decide to give the money to the World Hunger Relief Organization you are siding with the utilitarians (at least, the act utilitarians), since they would conclude that the greatest good for the greatest number is achieved by donating the money to charity and not following the millionaire's wishes (some rule utilitarians may not do this, since they may see a greater societal benefit in keeping a promise made to a dying person). On the other hand, if you decide to give the money to the Yankees' organization, you are siding with the deontologists, who maintain that truth-telling and promise-keeping are intrinsically good.

In Chapter 4 of this section ("Ethical Theories and Ethical Decision-Making"), Professors J. P. Moreland and Norman L. Geisler present an overview of the two major ethical systems, covering different versions of each category. They also go over each system's strengths and shortcomings and how the insights of each system figure in ethical decision-making. The authors of this essay do an excellent job of showing the relevancy of ethical theory to moral decision-making, which, unfortunately, is not always clearly articulated in many moral issues textbooks.

In Chapter 5 ("Minimalist Ethics") bioethicist Daniel Callahan claims that instead of asking the question "What would the virtuous person do?," there is a tendency in our society to frame ethical obligation in terms of what is the minimum one is required to do without being unethical.

In Chapters 6 and 7 we return to ethical theory in order to discuss the question of whether ethics can be reduced to self-interest. In Chapter 6, novelist and philosopher Ayn Rand defends *ethical egoism,* the view that one's only ethical obligation is to one's self. According to Rand, all true morality is grounded in ethical egoism. Chapter 7, penned by Professor James Rachels, is a critique of ethical egoism and includes a reply to Ms. Rand's position.

Notes

1. Louis P. Pojman, *Ethics: Discovering Right and Wrong* (Belmont, Calif.: Wadsworth, 1990), 73–74.

For Further Reading

Tom L. Beauchamp, *Philosophical Ethics: An Introduction to Moral Philosophy,* 2nd ed. (New York: McGraw-Hill, 1991)

David K. Clark and Robert V. Rakestraw, eds., *Readings in Christian Ethics, Volume 1: Theory and Method* (Grand Rapids, Mich.: Baker Book House, 1994).

William K. Frankena, *Ethics,* 2nd ed. (Englewood Cliffs, N.J.: Prentice-Hall, 1973).

Bernard Gert, *Morality: A New Justification of the Moral Rules,* 2nd ed. (Oxford: Oxford University Press, 1988).

Immanuel Kant, *Foundations of the Metaphysics of Morals,* trans. Lewis White Beck (Indianapolis, Ind.: Bobbs-Merrill, 1959).

John Stuart Mill, *Utilitarianism* (Indianapolis, Ind.: Bobbs-Merrill, 1957).

Kai Nielsen, *Ethics without God,* rev. ed. (Buffalo, N.Y.: Prometheus, 1989).

Louis P. Pojman, ed., *Ethical Theory: Classical and Contemporary Readings* (Belmont, Calif.: Wadsworth, 1989).

———, *Ethics: Discovering Right and Wrong* (Belmont, Calif.: Wadsworth, 1990).

Christina Hoff Sommers and Fred Sommers, eds. *Vice and Virtue in Everyday Life: Introductory Readings in Ethics,* 3rd ed. (New York: Harcourt Brace Jovanovich, 1993).

4

Ethical Theories and Ethical Decision-Making

J. P. Moreland
Norman L. Geisler

J. P. Moreland is Professor of Philosophy of Religion at Talbot School of Theology, Biola University. He has contributed to numerous scholarly journals, in addition to writing several books, including *Immortality* (1992) and *Scaling the Secular City* (1987). Norman L. Geisler is Dean of Southern Evangelical Seminary in Charlotte, North Carolina. He is the author and/or editor of over 40 books, including *Christian Ethics* (1989) and *Ethics: Alternatives and Issues* (1971). Moreland and Geisler coauthored *The Life and Death Debate: Moral Issues of Our Time* (1990).

In the first half of this essay Professors Moreland and Geisler present and explain the two major categories of ethical theories: utilitarianism and deontological ethics. They go over differing versions of each category, explaining their strengths and weaknesses. The second half of this essay concerns the issue of how to make ethical decisions. The authors explain how utilitarian and deontological theories contribute to the making of ethical judgments and decisions. Although they stress the primacy of deontological ethics, they maintain that results (the emphasis in utilitarianism) should play a part in making ethical decisions. Professors Moreland and Geisler deal with two other issues in the second half of this essay: how to discover basic ethical values, and why people disagree about moral issues.

When a person approaches specific issues in applied ethics, such as abortion, capital punishment, eutha-

Reprinted with permission from J. P. Moreland and Norman L. Geisler, *The Life and Death Debate: Moral Issues of Our Time* (New York: Praeger, 1990), 1–21, 143–154. This selection has been revised and edited for this anthology by the editor.

nasia, he or she brings to those issues a set of background beliefs about general ethical topics. This is the way it should be. In any field of study, specific debates are argued within the framework of broad theories which are relevant to those debates. For example, if two historians are going to discuss the causes for the decline of the Roman Empire, they will utilize arguments rooted in broader theories about history, civilizations, and so forth: Do historians create facts or discover them? Do we have good records about ancient Rome? How does one determine the relative importance for a civilization of economic factors compared to other factors? And so on. . . .

Before we examine different normative theories, our discussion . . . provides a fitting occasion to mention the role of intuitions in ethical theory. Princeton philosopher Saul Kripke once remarked that it was difficult to see what could be said more strongly for a view than that it squared with one's basic, reflective intuitions. Kripke's remark reminds us that in philosophy, ethical theory included, intuitions play an important role.

What is an intuition? The philosophical use of "intuition" does not mean a mere hunch or a prereflective expression of, say, a moral attitude. Nor is it a way of playing it safe, as when one says, "My intuition tells me that P is true but I really don't know, and if you choose to accept P, you do so at your own risk." While philosophers differ over a precise definition of intuitions, a common usage defines an intuition as an immediate, direct awareness or acquaintance with something. An intuition is a mode of awareness—sensory, intellectual, or otherwise—in which something seems or appears to be directly present to one's consciousness. For example, one can have a sensory intuition of a table or an intellectual intuition of a conceptual truth, for instance, that something cannot be red and green all over at the same time.

Intuitions are not infallible, but they are prima facie justified. That is, if one carefully reflects on something, and a certain viewpoint intuitively seems to be true, then one is justified in believing that viewpoint in the absence of overriding counterarguments (which will ultimately rely on alternative intuitions). Furthermore, an appeal to intuitions does not rule out the use of additional arguments which add further support to that appeal. One can claim to know a brown chair is present by appealing to a basic, sensory intuition of being appeared to in a brown, chairtype way. But one could also support the claim that there is a chair by further arguments, for example, the testimony of others or the fact that if we postulate a chair in the room, then we have an explanation for why people walk around a certain spatial location where the chair is postulated. Similarly, an appeal to intuitions in ethics is not a claim to infallibility or a substitute for further arguments.

In ethics, appeals to intuition occur in four main areas. First, there are specific cases or judgments (e.g., Dr. Jones ought not to lie to the patient in room 10 tomorrow morning). Second, there are moral rules and principles (e.g., promises should be kept, persons ought to be respected). Third, there are general, normative theories (e.g., deontological theories are to be preferred to utilitarian theories or vice versa). Finally, there are background philosophical or religious factual beliefs (e.g., a human has a property of intrinsic value). Again, such appeals to intuition claim prima facie justification and do not rule out further argumentation. Appeals to reflective, considered intuitions occur throughout one's intellectual life, and ethics is no exception.

[I.] Normative Theories of Right

Normative theories in ethics seek to provide an account of what actions are right and wrong and why. In current discussions of ethics, normative theories are usually grouped into two basic and mutually exclusive groups—*teleological* and *deontological*. Roughly, a teleological theory holds that the rightness or wrongness of an act is exclusively a function of the goodness or badness of the consequences of that act. Consequences are crucial. A deontological theory denies this claim and places limits on the relevance of teleological considerations. Deontologists claim that some acts are intrinsically right or wrong from a moral point of view. Utilitarianism is the major form of teleological theory; so in what follows we will compare, contrast, and evaluate utilitarianism and deontological approaches to ethics.[1] Let us begin by looking at three aspects of utilitarianism: utilitarian theories of value, different views of the principle of utility, and different forms of utilitarianism.

A. Utilitarianism

Utilitarians view the moral life in terms of means-to-ends reasoning. They are agreed that the rightness/wrongness of an act or moral rule is solely a matter of the nonmoral good produced directly or indirectly in the consequences of that act or rule. In clarifying the notion of nonmoral value, a utilitarian can correctly point out that a number of things can have intrinsic value without that value being moral. Good food, beautiful art, friendship, mathematical knowledge can possess value without that value being moral rightness. Utilitarians differ, however, regarding their views as to what values we should try to produce as consequences of our actions.

1. Utilitarian Theories of Value There are three major utilitarian views regarding value. First, there are *hedonistic* utilitarians who conceive of utility solely in terms of happiness or pleasure. All other things are valuable insofar as they are a means to gaining happiness or pleasure and avoiding unhappiness and pain. One of the earliest utilitarians, Jeremy Bentham (1748–1832), was a *quantitative hedonist*. According to Bentham, the amount of pleasure versus pain is what matters, and he tried to develop a hedonic calculus whereby one can calculate the total amount of pleasure versus pain likely to be produced by an act by considering things like the intensity and duration of pleasure an act will have as its consequences.

Another early utilitarian, John Stuart Mill (1806–73), rejected this approach. Mill pointed out that it is better to be a human being dissatisfied than a pig satisfied; better to be Socrates dissatisfied than a fool satisfied. In other words, Bentham failed to distinguish different kinds of pleasure and the fact that some kinds of pleasure are of more value than others, for example, intellectual pleasure versus a full stomach. It could also be pointed out that it is difficult to know how to calculate the duration and intensity of various pleasures as envisaged by Bentham. Mill embraced *qualitative hedonism* wherein it is still pleasure versus pain that constitutes utility, but room is made for different kinds of pleasure.

A second view, in opposition to hedonism, is called *pluralistic utilitarianism.* In this view, it is not merely pleasure and happiness that have nonmoral value, but a number of other things have intrinsic, nonmoral value as well, such as knowledge, friendship, love, beauty, health, freedom, courage, self-esteem, and so on. For example, according to pluralistic utilitarianism, it is not merely the pleasure produced by friendship that is of value, but friendship itself.

As with hedonism, a number of modern utilitarians have rejected pluralistic utilitarianism. The main problem they point out is this. The aforementioned values are relatively useless in determining what one should do. Widely different views exist about the relative merits of the items listed above, and no common scale seems to exist for comparing, say, friendship, including the various kinds of friendship that can take place, with aesthetic experience or courage. Further, there seem to be moral and immoral examples of many of the items listed above. For example, there are immoral and moral friendships. For these and other reasons, many contemporary utilitarians embrace a third theory of value—*subjective preference utilitarianism*.

Because it seems to many to be futile and presumptuous to attempt to develop a general theory of value, this theory holds that an act ought to maximize the satisfaction of individual desires and preferences. The goal of moral actions is the satisfaction of desires or wants which express individual preferences.

Unfortunately, this theory is very subjective and virtually collapses into a form of relativism when it is used as an action guide. Why? Because when one attempts to use the principle to determine what action to take, any act whatever can be justified just as long as it satisfies an individual's private preferences. If someone desires to be a child molester or to practice some form of self-deprecation, then in this view such an act is appropriate because it could maximize the satisfaction of individual desires. The simple fact is that people can have morally unacceptable preferences, such as the desire for genocide.

Utilitarians have responded to this charge in the following way. They supplement the principle with a condition of *rationality*. They claim that utilitarianism is not responsible for treating the problem of universal idiocy. In other words, the subjective preference view only takes into account rational preferences. Being a child molester or acts of self-deprecation are not rational, so they do not count as appropriate preferences.

But what is meant by rationality here? Let us distinguish between *prescriptive rationality* and *descriptive rationality*. Prescriptive rationality is the ability to "see" or have intellectual insight into what is intrinsically valuable. This type of rationality cannot be meant here, for such a rationality either implies pluralistic utilitarianism (the ability to truly see what has nonmoral value) or it is deontological (the ability to truly see what has intrinsic moral value).

The only type of rationality available to the subjective preference form of utilitarianism is descriptive rationality. This involves two things. First, the ability to use efficient means to accomplish certain ends, once those ends are posited. But this alone is not adequate to save subjective preference utilitarianism, for one could posit morally abhorrent ends and still be rational if one knew efficient means to accomplish those ends. So a second thing must be included in descriptive rationality: One is rational if and only if one desires what all psychologically normal people desire. If one is psychologically balanced, then one presumably will not choose to be a child molester.

But the question is why would a normal person not choose such a way of life? The answer cannot be because such acts are wrong, for that would be to argue in a circle for the subjective preference utilitarian. It could have turned out that psychologically "normal" (i.e., typical) people would prefer to have satisfied a number of highly immoral desires. No contradiction is involved in this claim. But if this were the case, the satisfaction of these desires would be morally appropriate in the subjective preference view. For this reason, such a view must be judged inadequate. Any view which even allows for the logical possibility that child molestation and a host of other immoral acts could be morally justified has a wrong conception of value.[2]

2. The Principle of Utility   Utilitarians differ over what value counts in defining utility. They also differ over the form of the principle of utility itself. According to utilitarianism, an act is right if and only if it

- produces only good consequences
- maximizes good consequences
- avoids all bad consequences
- minimizes bad consequences
- maximizes the average net balance per person of good versus bad consequences (i.e., good minus bad consequences or good divided by bad consequences)
- produces the greatest happiness for the greatest number[3]
- maximizes the net balance of good versus bad consequences

It is beyond the scope of our present discussion to analyze these alternative formulations of the principle of utility. If one spends time thinking about them, it should be possible to content oneself that each principle can come into conflict with each other principle; for instance, eating one piece of candy may have only good consequences, eating fifty pieces may have more good consequences but some bad ones as well, giving fifty pieces of candy to fifty people may maximize the greatest happiness for the greatest number but it may not maximize the net good versus bad consequences if twenty of those people hate candy and one of them was a real connoisseur (then it might produce a greater net amount of utility to give him twenty pieces and thirty others one piece each). Probably the most widely held of the principles listed above is the maximization of good versus bad consequences. But utilitarians do differ on this question.

3. Different Forms of Utilitarianism

Finally, there are two major versions of utilitarianism depending on the structure that utilitarianism takes: act utilitarianism and rule utilitarianism. The former focuses on the utility produced by particular concrete acts, and the latter focuses on the utility produced by adopting rules governing kinds of acts. Let us look at this distinction in more detail.

a. Act Utilitarianism According to act utilitarianism, an act is right if and only if no other act available to the agent maximizes utility more than the act in question. Here, each moral act is treated atomistically; that is, it is evaluated in complete isolation from other acts. General moral rules like "Don't steal," "Don't break promises," or "Don't punish innocent people" are mere rules of thumb, summaries of how people up to this moment have generally experienced the consequences of acts similar to the one under consideration. If I am considering the morality of an act of stealing, then the rule "Don't steal" reminds me that such acts usually do not maximize utility. But such rules have no intrinsic moral value, nor do they dictate to me how I must view the present act. They are mere rules of thumb.

A number of objections have been raised against act utilitarianism. First, act utilitarianism makes it possible to morally justify a number of acts which seem to be immoral. For example, if it would maximize utility to break a promise, for the police to punish a man they know to be innocent (perhaps to show the efficiency of the police and serve as a deterrent, provided of course that they keep this a secret to prevent social chaos resulting from a lowering of respect for the police), or for a few to be enslaved for the benefit of the majority, then there are no grounds within act utilitarianism to judge these acts as immoral. But any doctrine which treats these immoral acts as morally justifiable is wrong.

Second, these examples tend to show that act utilitarianism does not accord with our conviction that individuals have intrinsic value with individual rights and that persons are not merely bundles of social utility. In the cases cited above, people are treated as means to an end, sometimes on the grounds that doing so will have great social utility. But this fails to treat these persons as intrinsically valuable ends with individual rights. Put differently, it is difficult to derive a robust, intuitively acceptable principle of justice from a principle of utility.

Third, act utilitarianism turns trivial acts into moral acts. Consider the choice of what cereal to eat for breakfast. Suppose three cereals were available to you and that one of these would produce slightly more utility than the others if it were selected, perhaps because it is slightly better in flavor, texture, and so on. In this case, act utilitarianism would imply that you were morally obligated to eat this cereal because that act would maximize utility. But in spite of act utilitarian claims, such an act does not seem to be a moral act at all. Thus, act utilitarianism fails because it turns trivial acts like this into issues of moral obligation.

Other objections, which apply equally to act utilitarianism and rule utilitarianism, will be considered below. In light of the objections just mentioned, some utilitarians have formulated different versions of rule utilitarianism which they believe handle these objections in a way not possible within an act utilitarian framework.

b. Rule Utilitarianism According to rule utilitarianism, an act is right if and only if it falls under a correct moral rule which covers that generic type of act. And a rule is a correct moral rule if and only if everyone's acting on this rule would maximize utility compared to everyone's acting on an alternative rule.

Here acts are no longer evaluated in isolation from moral rules. The reason act utilitarianism failed was that one could sever a particular act of keeping a promise or punishing an innocent person from general moral rules ("Keep promises," "Punish only guilty people") and evaluate the utility produced by that particular act directly. In act utilitarianism, if breaking a promise does not weaken respect for the moral rule to keep promises (in which case chaos would result and bad utility would be produced), then the act can be justified. Rule utilitarians tighten the connection between rules and acts. An act is evaluated by reference to the correctness of a moral rule relevant to that act. Utility calculations enter into the process at the level of evaluating alternative rules. For example, if everyone followed the rule "Punish only guilty people," then this would lead to greater utility than if everyone followed the rule "Punish innocent people as well as guilty people."

Thus, rule utilitarianism cannot be used to justify the problematic acts cited against act utilitarianism. Further, it is claimed that it would not maximize utility if we treated trivial acts like what to eat for breakfast as moral issues. Utility is maximized if areas of individual freedom are maintained, or so say rule utilitarians.

But is it really the case that we do not treat choices of breakfast food as moral questions because doing so would fail to maximize utility? On the contrary, it seems that such acts are just not moral by their very nature. Further, act utilitarians argue that when faced with any moral situation, we should always follow this rule: When faced with a moral dilemma, then maximize utility. This is the correct moral rule for everyone to adopt, for if one does, then utility will be maximized and, thus, rule utilitarianism would entail the adoption of this particular rule. But, say act utilitarians, this rule is just another way of expressing act utilitarianism. So in reality rule utilitarianism collapses back into act utilitarianism. After all, act utilitarians claim that producing utility is what matters, and acts, not rules, produce utility in the concrete, actual world.

Two further objections have been raised against both rule and act utilitarianism. First, rule utilitarianism denies the existence of supererogatory acts whereas such acts do seem to exist. A supererogatory act is one which is not morally obligatory (one is not immoral for failing to do such an act) but which is morally praiseworthy if it is done. A supererogatory act is thus an act of moral heroism done above and beyond the call of moral duty. Examples would be giving half of one's income to the poor, throwing oneself on a bomb to save another person, and so on. In each of these cases one could either do the supererogatory act or fail to do it. Either option would produce a certain amount of utility, and the option which produced the greater utility would be morally obligatory according to rule (and act) utilitarianism. So supererogatory acts become impossible. But in spite of utilitarianism, such acts not only seem possible, they sometimes appear to happen.

Finally, rule (and act) utilitarianism is inadequate in its treatment of motives. We praise good motives and blame bad ones. But utilitarianism implies that motives have no intrinsic moral worth. All that matters from a moral point of view is the consequences of actions, not the motives for which they are done.

Utilitarians have a response to these last two criticisms which helps to clarify the nature of utilitarianism as a moral position. They argue that it maximizes utility if we allow areas of moral freedom (recall the breakfast example). Thus, any rule requiring that one must do supererogatory acts would not itself maximize utility. So supererogatory acts should be preserved because that would itself produce the best consequences. Similarly we should praise good motives and blame bad ones because such acts of praise and blame will maximize utility compared with praising bad motives and blaming good ones or failing to discuss motives altogether.

At this point, the real difficulty with utilitarianism seems obvious. Contrary to what utilitarianism implies, some acts just appear to be intrinsically good or bad (torturing babies for fun), some rules seem to be intrinsically good or bad (punishing only guilty people), some areas of life seem to be intrinsically trivial (what to eat for breakfast) or supererogatory (giving half your income to the poor) from a moral point of view, some motives are blamed or praised for what they are intrinsically and not because such acts of praise or blame produce utility, and humans seem to have intrinsic value and rights which ground what is just and unjust treatment regarding them. In our opinion, utilitarianism fails to adequately explain these features of the moral life. Let us turn to a more adequate normative theory which does account for these phenomena—deontological ethics.

B. Deontological Ethics

A deontological approach to normative ethics is to be preferred to utilitarianism, because as we have seen, the latter fails to account for our basic, considered intuitions about what a good moral theory must explain. Because the chapters which follow will treat topics from within a deontological framework, here we need only give a brief overview of the main features of such a framework.

Deontological ethics are sometimes associated with divine command theories of morality (what is right or wrong is a matter of what God commands) and with the moral theories of the philosopher

Immanuel Kant (1724–1804).[4] Thus, deontological theories can be theistic or nontheistic in nature.

The word "deontological" comes from the Greek word *deon* which means "binding duty." A deontological ethical theory has a number of features, but three are especially important.

1. Characteristics of Deontological Ethics

First, duty should be done for duty's sake. The rightness or wrongness of an act is, at least in part, a matter of the intrinsic moral features of that kind of act. For example, acts of lying, promise breaking, murder, and so on are intrinsically wrong when considered as such from a moral point of view. This does not mean consequences are not relevant for assessing the morality of an act. But consequences are not the only features that matter, and when consequences are taken into account they provide factual information for discovering what action is more in keeping with what is already our duty. For example, we may have a duty to benefit a patient, but alternative consequences may result from different actions. The action which benefits the patient most would, all things being equal, be our duty. We do not benefit a patient simply because such acts maximize utility. But as we do our duty to benefit him, consequences can help us discover what benefits the patient the most. Moral rules are intrinsically right or wrong, and certain kinds of acts considered as such are intrinsically right or wrong.

Second, as Immanuel Kant argued, people should be treated as members of the kingdom of ends. People are objects of intrinsic moral worth and should be treated as ends in themselves, never merely as mean to some other end. We often treat each other as means to an end—for instance, a student may treat a teacher as a means to gaining knowledge—but we ought not treat people *merely* as means. Such treatment dehumanizes persons by treating them as things. Persons are not bundles of pleasant or unpleasant mental states, nor are they merely valuable because of their social utility. A human being is a person with intrinsic value simply because that person is a member of the natural class "human being."

Third, a moral principle is a categorical imperative which must be universally applicable for everyone who is in the same moral context. Moral statements do not say, "If you want to maximize pleasure versus pain in this instance, then do such and such." Such a statement is a hypothetical indicative. It states a hypothetical "if, then" situation and indicates or describes the means to accomplish the hypothetical situation postulated in the antecedent. Rather, moral statements are imperatives or commands which hold for all examples of the type of act under consideration.

There are other features that characterize deontological ethics; for example, in contrast to utilitarianism a deontological ethical theory places emphasis on the past (if I promised in the past, that informs my present moral duty and I should not merely consider future consequences), it recognizes several different social relationships as relevant to morality and spells out special duties that follow from those relationships (e.g., parent/child, promiser/promisee, employer/employee, patient/physician), whereas utilitarianism tends to emphasize only one social relationship, namely benefactor/beneficiary, and deontological theories recognize the intrinsic moral worth of certain motives and virtues. These factors, together with the three mentioned earlier, constitute the basic understanding of the nature of moral obligation contained in a deontological approach to morality.[5]

Before we consider some objections to deontological theories, there is an important deontological distinction first expressed by W. D. Ross in his book titled *The Right and the Good* (1930). Ross distinguishes between a conditional or prima facie duty and an absolute duty. A prima facie duty is a duty which can be overridden by a more stringent duty, but when such a situation occurs, the prima facie duty does not disappear but still makes its presence felt. A prima facie duty is always to be acted upon unless it conflicts on a particular occasion with an equal or stronger duty. A duty is absolute if it cannot be overridden; that is, if it has the highest degree of incumbency possible.

An example may help illustrate the nature of a prima facie duty. Suppose an elderly man is in a nursing home and is engaging in certain forms of self-destructive behavior. He pulls out his feeding tube, tears off the bandages protecting his bed sores, and scratches them violently. A nurse has two duties to the man. First, there is the duty to benefit the patient and not harm him. Second, there is the duty to preserve the autonomy of the patient and preserve his individual liberty of action. In this case, the presence of self-destructive behavior seems to make the first duty more important than the second. The latter duty is overridden and it is morally justifiable to restrain the elderly man's liberty of action. But the duty to preserve autonomy, even though overridden, still makes its presence felt. How? We are not justified in constraining him in any way we wish (e.g., taping his mouth shut so he cannot talk). We are only justified in constraining him as little as is needed to protect him. Thus, the prima facie duty, though overridden, is still present to inform the situation.

Regardless of the specifics of this case, it illustrates an important point. When objective values appear to conflict, one of them may be more weighty than the other and the less weighty duty is a *prima facie* one. More will be said about conflicting situations. . . .

[2.] Some Objections to Deontological Ethics By now you should have a feeling for what a deontological approach to normative ethics is like. It is safe to say that such a view is embraced by most ethicists, but there are a number of utilitarians who reject a deontological approach. Two objections are prominent in their rejection. First, the claim is made that there simply are no intrinsically valid moral principles. This claim is sometimes, though not always, supported by the further claim that morality is a human invention and must respond to the needs, desires, and values of the human situation as those needs, desires, and values become embodied in the consequences of our moral rules and actions.

The best way to respond to this claim is twofold. First, one can repeat the problems with utilitarian approaches to ethics and hold that those problems are telling, and second, one can assert that, contrary to what utilitarians say, some moral rules are intrinsically valid from a moral point of view. Essentially, this dialectic means that one must sooner or later simply bring one's considered moral intuitions to bear on evaluating which picture of the nature of morality seems to be more reasonable and to comply with basic moral judgments.

A second objection is that deontological theories, especially those which embrace a number of different, fundamental prima facie duties . . . are too nonsystematic and provide no clear procedure (besides troublesome appeals to moral intuitions) for determining, in a particular case, what the right thing is.

Part of the response to this objection will be the adequacy of the deontological treatment of various issues considered in the chapters that follow. These issues will be approached from a deontological perspective, and the reader can judge for himself or herself whether or not the issues are treated in a systematic way. But it must be admitted that ethical issues are sometimes difficult to solve, and moral delibera-

tion is not always easy. However, this feature is more a property of ethics in general; it is not the special terrain of deontological theories. Utilitarian theories, especially pluralistic versions of utilitarianism, have the same difficulty as well as the difficulty of predicting the consequences of a given act before they occur. So this objection, even if successful, counts against both views. . . .[6]

[How to Make Ethical Decisions]

Ethical decisions are not made in a vacuum. However, many people are unaware of the atmosphere in which their decisions live and breathe. In this [section] we would like to make more explicit some of the context in which ethical decisions are made. Like anything else in life, ethical decisions flow from one's overall worldview and life-view.

Logically, ethical decisions are system dependent. Of course, not everyone is conscious of the system on which one's ethical decisions are dependent. It is part of our purpose here to make this more explicit. Basically, there are two broad categories into which ethical decisions fall: deontological and utilitarian.

I. Are Ethical Decisions Deontological or Utilitarian?

The first question that calls for answer is whether ethical decisions are to be made in a deontological or utilitarian context. Since the differences to these approaches have already been discussed . . . we will only summarize them here.

A. The Basic Differences

Deontological and utilitarian ethics are clearly different. A chart will be helpful in focusing these differences.

Deontological	Utilitarian
Rule-centered	Result-centered
Duty-focused	Destiny-focused
Command-oriented	Consequence-oriented
Rule determines result	Result determines rule

According to deontological ethics, the primary concern is with our ethical duty, whereas the utilitarian is focused on the results of our actions. For the deontologists the ethical rule determines the results. That is, our obligation is to follow the ethical rule whatever the consequences may be. The utilitarian, on the other hand, believes that one should make up the rule in view of the anticipated results. In this way the results determine the rules. In other words, an act is good only if it or the rule under which it falls brings good results. The deontologist, however, believes an act or rule is right in and of itself, even if it does not bring good results.

Embedded in the difference between these two ethical approaches is another crucial difference: Are ethical principles *discovered* or are they *created*? Obviously, the deontologist believes they are discovered, while the utilitarian holds they are invented. In making rationally explicit ethical decisions we will find it helpful to keep this in mind.

B. The Contribution of Each System

One way to compare and contrast deontological and utilitarian ethics is by examining some specific cases. Suppose someone is drowning and we fail in our attempt to rescue him. According to at least an unsophisticated version of utilitarianism, that attempt to rescue a drowning person was not a good act because it did not have a good result. The deontologists, however, claim that the mere *attempt* to rescue a drowning person is good, whether or not we succeed. More sophisticated utilitarians might argue that there were other intangibly good results from an unsuccessful rescue attempt, such as the model it sets for others, the appreciation of the family, and the good feeling it produced in the rescuer. However, even with this refined definition of "results" the act is considered good *only* because of the results, not because it is good in and of itself. Presumably, if no good result, tangible or intangible, occurred, then the attempted rescue would not be a good act.

The two views seem to be at an impasse, the deontologist holding that an act can be good regardless of the results, and the utilitarian insisting that it can be good only because of the results. However, on closer examination all is not as categorically opposed as it first seems. Notice, first of all, that the deontologist is also concerned about results. He is definitely concerned about near-view results, or else he would not have attempted the res-

cue. And, if interrogated, he would admit to a concern about the lost life of the drowned individual as well as his bereaved family and so on. So he too is concerned about results; he simply does not wish to make them the *basis* on which he acts.

Further, even the utilitarian is not concerned solely about results. One cannot make up *all* the rules on a purely utilitarian basis. Take, for example, his utilitarian rule that "we should act so as to maximize good and minimize evil." This rule itself is not based on results. Furthermore, the utilitarian must have some previous notion of what constitutes "good" and what does not; otherwise he could not act with a view to the greater good. Likewise, how would he know what to put in his fund of experience by which he designs guidelines for life, unless he had some standard or *basis* by which he determined what is good and what is not? Further, if he had no standard of value by which he judged what was "good" or bad, then he would not even know how to judge whether the realized results he had anticipated were good or not.

In brief, it would seem that it is not a matter of choosing between deontological and utilitarian ethics, but rather of synthesizing the contribution each makes to the overall ethical decision. For even the deontologist is concerned about results, and the utilitarian has an ethical basis on which he decides what is to be judged a "good" result.

Now that we have seen that our decision is not a purely either/or, let's try to synthesize the results into a meaningful basis for making ethical decisions. In what sense is ethics deontological and in what sense is it utilitarian? Ultimately, basic values are discovered, not created. Not everything can be willed for the sake of another; something has to be desired (or desirable) for its own sake. In short, it would seem that there must be some ultimate intrinsic value in terms of which right is defined; otherwise there would be no basis on which to evaluate any results—short range or long range.

1. The Wrong Use of Results Both intrinsic rules and results play an important part in making ethical decisions. However, there is a wrong use of both. The misuse of results takes place in several ways.

First, and foremost, the anticipated results should not be used to determine what is right. As deontologists rightly contend, the intrinsic character of good determines what is right. It is our obligation to obey the rules that accord with what is right; the results must not determine the rules. Right is right no matter how painful the consequences may be.

Second, anticipated results should not be the basis of an ethical action. The basis should be what is known to be intrinsically right. One may act *with a view to* bringing about the greatest good for the greatest number, but should not act simply *because* these results will probably follow from this activity.

Third, the results do not *make* an act right. Rightness is not conferred by consequence, but is inherent in the value represented by the ethical rule. An act of well-intended bravery or benevolence is right in and of itself, whether or not it brings desired results. At best the consequences only manifest the rightness of an act; they do not make the act right.

Fourth, the consideration of long-range results is not helpful for most ethical acts. Since we cannot really know what the long-range results will be, we must content ourselves with the short-range results. That is, the most that can be gained from contemplating results would be from results that can be foreseen. There is no immediate value whatsoever to results that cannot be predicted with some measure of success.

Fifth, results should never lead us to formulate, change, or break rules known to be based on intrinsic value. For instance, the long-range genetic results of mercy killing of handicapped persons may be good in that it relieves society of the great burden of caring for them. However, in this sense the end (a genetically more perfect world) does not thereby justify the means (violating human right to life). It is never right to break a good rule simply to obtain good results.

Sixth, there is the issue of justice in the distribution of goods. If we are concerned simply with the maximal increase in goods, then we could easily distribute them unfairly by taking away from the deserving and giving to the undeserving.

2. The Right Use of Results Despite the misuse of results by total utilitarians, there is a proper use of results in connection with a deontological ethic. The following suggestions will serve to illustrate the right use of results.

First of all, whereas results do not determine what is right, this does not mean they should be ignored in considering what is the right thing to do. If neither of two courses of action violates any moral duty, and if one of them is reasonably calculated to bring about a greater good, then at least it is not wrong to do the latter. Indeed, doing one's best or maximizing the good at hand may itself be viewed as a moral obligation. Thus, results can help me factually decide which option fulfills my intrinsic duty (e.g., to benefit) while the results do not *make* the option my duty by giving it value, as utilitarians claim. In this case, then, *not* to facilitate the achievement of the greatest anticipated future good would be a violation of one's present duty.

Second, action directed toward achieving the greatest good must always be *within* the bounds of intrinsic ethical norms, but never beyond them or against them. For example, most would agree that it is right to inoculate the masses in order to bring about the greatest good of better health; for inoculation as such (at least with informed consent) does not break any moral law. However, forced sterilization for the purpose of population control would seem to go beyond and against the moral principles of freedom and dignity.

Third, as has already been pointed out, in one sense all ethical decisions are made, or ought to be made, with *immediate* results in view. Doctors make such decisions regularly. "What will the probable prognosis be, and what should I do to prevent further harm to this body?" is the continual question before the physician, and rightly so. Indeed, anticipated results are a part of everyday life. "Shall I go to this school? Shall I take that job? Shall I go outside with a sore throat?" and the like are questions continually before us. Virtually everything we do should be done with a view to bringing about the best results possible (within the bounds of our ethical duties). The deontologists, however, should generally be content with acting for short-range results. Since we do not know the future, we should allow the long range to take care of itself.

Fourth, anticipated results should sometimes be used in a deontological ethic to help determine which ethical norm to apply. That is, intrinsic rules determine *what is* right, but circumstances (both present and anticipated) play a role in helping us to discover *which* of these good rules should be applied or which course of action is more in keeping with a rule. For example, whether one has the right to kill in self-defense will be discovered by anticipating whether one's life is actually being threatened or not. The anticipated results, however, do not determine the rule regarding self-defense; they simply help one to discover whether that rule applies to the situation at hand or whether another rule does. If the thief breaking into one's house, for example, is unarmed and not threatening anyone's life, then the killing in self-defense rule does not apply. But this can only be known by anticipating results, by asking, "Is this thief a danger to my life or not?"

Fifth, results do not *make* a thing right, but they often *manifest* what is right. By their fruits they shall be known. In other words, good results do not prove the act good, but we may reasonably presume that following good rules will bring good results. So right action will bring right results at least in the long run. Good results, however, are no assurance that the action was right, since we are sometimes blessed in spite of ourselves and good sometimes emerges in spite of evil.

II. How to Discover Basic Ethical Values

If basic human values are discovered, not created, then it is necessary to ask just how one goes about discovering them. After all, there seems to be serious disagreement about values. Which values are the right ones?

A. Moral Values as Manifest in Human Nature

Human values are found in the most readily accessible place for human beings—in their own heart. They are also manifest in a way everyone can read—intuitively. No lessons in language are necessary, and no books are needed. Values can be seen instinctively. These values are known by inclination even before they become known by cognition. We know what is right and wrong by our own natural intuitions. Our very nature predisposes us in that direction.

Being selfish creatures, we do not always desire to do what is right, but we do nonetheless desire that it be done to us. This is represented in most major ethical systems. Judaism's Torah declares, "Love your neighbor as yourself" (Leviticus 19:18). Likewise, Jesus said, "In everything do to others what you would have them do to you" (Matthew 7:12). Confucius recognized the same truth by general revelation when he said, "Never do to others what you would not like them to do to you."[7]

Basic ethical values are not hard to discover; they are just difficult to practice. We usually know how we want others to act toward us, even if we do not always want to act the same way toward them. Basic values, then, can be seen better in humans' *reactions* than in their *actions*. That is, one's real moral beliefs are manifest not so much in what a person does but in what he wants done to him. Some people may cheat, but no businessperson wants to be cheated. Others may be dishonest in their dealings, but none of them likes to be lied to in any of his deals.

B. Moral Values as Expressed in Human Reactions

Our moral *actions* are often contrary to our own moral *inclinations*. This is why our best understanding of the natural law comes not from seeing our actions but from observing our reactions. This is true because we know the moral law instinctively. We do not have to read it in any books; we know it intuitively since it is written on our own hearts. So when reading the moral law, we must be careful to read it from actions truly indicative of it. These are not necessarily the actions we do to others, but rather those that we desire to be done to us. Our moral inclinations are manifest in our reactions when others violate our rights. We do not see the moral law nearly as clearly when we violate others' rights. But again our failure is not found in our inability to know what the moral duty is but in our unwillingness to do it to others.

The kind of reactions that manifest the moral law were brought home forcefully when a professor we know graded a student's paper written in defense of moral relativity. After carefully reading his well-researched paper, the professor wrote: "'F.' I do not like blue folders." The student stormed into his office protesting, "That's not *fair*. That's not *just!*" The student's reaction to the injustice done to him revealed, contrary to what he wrote, that he truly believed in an objective moral principle of justice. The real measure of his morals was not what he had written in his paper but what was written on his heart. What he really believed was right manifested itself when he was wronged.

C. Moral Laws as Expressed in Writings

Contrary to popular belief, the great moral writings of the world do not manifest a total diversity of perspectives. On the contrary, there is a striking similarity among them. In fact, the similarity within writings expressing the natural law is just as great as that within writings on science. Few deny the objective existence of an external world simply because scientists have differed widely on how to interpret it. Likewise, we should not deny the objectivity of moral law simply because people have differed on how to interpret it.

C. S. Lewis has provided a noteworthy service in cataloging many of these expressions of the natural moral law in an extended appendix to his excellent book, *The Abolition of Man*. Of course there is diversity of ethical expression among the great cultures too. But this diversity no more negates their unanimity than diversity of belief among lawyers about the Constitution proves that there is no such objective statement about our civil rights. The general agreement of diverse ethical writers about general moral duties is manifest in the writings of the great cultures down through the centuries.[8]

III. Why People Disagree about Moral Issues

If moral values are so similar, then why do people disagree so much about moral issues? There are many reasons for this, the most important of which will be considered now.

A. Many Disagree about Facts, Not Values

Many moral disputes are not about values but are actually about facts. For example, some have argued that values have changed in America over the past two hundred years because we used to burn witches but no longer do. However, this is not really a difference in value. We still execute murderers. The real difference between now and the days of the Salem witch trials is that *as a matter of fact* we no longer believe that witches are murderers. If it could be proven *as fact* that a witch's incantations could kill someone today, then witches would still be subject to capital punishment, like any other capital criminal. The basic value has not changed: Murderers should be punished as murders. What has changed is the factual understanding of what witches can do.

Likewise, the great disagreements about the rightness or wrongness of the Vietnam War do not

necessarily reflect a difference in value. Most disputants on both sides agree to the basic *moral principle* that all unjust wars are wrong. Their disagreement was whether *as a matter of fact* this was a just involvement in war on our part. The same can be applied to most such disputes. They are really disagreements about *facts,* not about basic *values.*

B. Progress in Understanding Morality versus Progress in Morality

Often those who oppose the belief in timeless ethical values point to the fact that people actually change their ethical beliefs as they become more enlightened. Certainly, modern cultures are less barbaric than many ancient ones. The practice of torture, slavery, and oppression is frowned upon in civilized societies. However, at best this only indicates a change in human *understanding* of moral values, not a change in *moral values*. The fact that some societies are more just today does not prove that *justice* has changed; it simply shows that we *comprehend* (or apply) justice better. Likewise, the fact that one understands love better after being married for years does not mean that love has changed. What changed was his/her understanding of love.

C. Many Disagreements Are about Means, Not Ends

Many social clashes seem to be about *ends* (value) when in truth they are about *means* to attain that end. For example, most of the "liberal" versus "conservative" disputes fall into this category. Virtually everyone wants an adequate defense, because they believe in the *end* (value) of protecting innocent lives. The real arguments are about how much of the national budget is a necessary *means* of attaining that end (and about what it should be spent on).

Likewise, virtually everyone agrees that we should help the poor and oppressed in our society. The *end* is clear. What is less evident and what generates heated differences is the best *means* to attain this end. Is it government programs or private initiative? Just what laws should be passed to help accomplish this worthy goal? These are the kinds of means over which people argue.

D. A Confusion of Circumstances and Principles

The whole situation ethics debate spawned by Joseph Fletcher brought to focus the importance of clarifying the relation between circumstances and moral principles.[9] Fletcher argued that the circumstances determine what one should do. In some circumstances it is right to lie and in others it is not. In some it is right to commit adultery but in others it is not. Thus, he insisted, the situation, not moral laws, determines what is right. This is admittedly a utilitarian viewpoint. In fact, Fletcher says frankly, "Only the end justifies the means; nothing else."[10]

Let's take a closer look at the relation between moral principles and circumstances. Certainly both play an important part in ethical decision-making. The circumstances, however, do not really determine our values; they simply help us to discover which moral value should be applied in a particular case. In other words, circumstances don't determine *what* the value is; they simply help us find out *which* value should be followed. Circumstances, then, merely *condition* the ethical action, but they do not *cause* the ethical value. For example, a police officer does not study the circumstances of the homicide in order to determine whether murder is wrong but, rather, in order to discover who the murderer is. So circumstances do not determine what is right; they help us find out who did not do what is right.

IV. How to Go About Making Moral Decisions

Now that we have laid the basis for more decisions and cleared away some of the confusion, let's outline just how one should go about making a moral decision. Moral situations are often complex. They involve several considerations.

A. Identify Moral Principles Used in Ethical Decisions

Before we can make ethical evaluations we must have ethical values on which these e-*valuations* are made. There are a number of sources for moral values that should be considered.

First, *moral* laws and right reason should be sought. These are found in many of the great moral and ethical works, such as the Code of Hammurabi, Plato's *Laws,* Aristotle's *Nicomachaean Ethics,* and Cicero's *De Officiis.*

Second, these may include religious sources, such as the Analects of Confucius, Bible, Gita, or Koran.

Third, there are *professional* codes of conduct produced by the various professions, such as doctors, nurses, and lawyers. These are especially helpful in that they spell out duties in specific areas. Some of these come from the ancient world, such as the "Hippocratic Oath" for physicians. Others are more recent.

Fourth, *civil* law should be examined. Most laws, particularly in more democratic countries, represent an attempt at justice born out of experience. As such they reflect wisdom and value judgments that must be considered in making an ethical judgment.

B. Get a Clear Understanding of the Circumstances

When you are confronted with an ethical decision, the first thing you should try to do is get clear on all relevant facts involved in the dilemma. For example, if it is a medical decision, we must ask: What are the medical facts of the situation? What is the diagnosis/prognosis and how urgent is the case? Is there a need for further tests or a second opinion? What treatment options are available and what is the probable result of not treating the situation at all? What are the values of all the persons involved in the situation (the patient himself, the family members, the doctor or nursing staff)?

In addition, broader questions are relevant. Is life a gift or not? Does a human being have intrinsic value? What is the nature of medicine, and what metaphor best captures that nature?

C. Look at the Consequences of Each Decision

Finally, what are the consequences for each available option? What are the factual consequences? These can be medical consequences (e.g., what are the medical results of each alternative?). They can be economic consequences (e.g., are there less expensive alternatives that are morally acceptable?). And there can be social consequences (what impact will this option have on the family, the other members of the nursing home, the friends of the patient?). What are the moral consequences of each alternative? For example, will this alternative weaken respect for human life?

D. Discover Which Is the Overriding Moral Obligation

Sometimes there are two or more moral obligations in one situation. When this occurs, it is necessary to find a way out of the dilemma.

Some guidelines for dilemma solving include the following.

First, look for a way of fulfilling both obligations. Moral duties cannot be set aside at will. They are, by their very nature as universal moral duties, binding on us at all times and in all places.

Second, if two or more duties come into unavoidable conflict, then we must always follow the greater duty. For example, when a would-be murderer demands we return his gun we have borrowed so that he can kill his wife, then a dilemma results. We should of course try to talk him out of it. But if he demands it anyway, then we must choose between obeying the moral duty to return his property and the moral duty to preserve her life. The latter takes precedence over the former. In short, although a moral duty is universally binding as such, it can be overridden by another. W. D. Ross calls moral duties "prima facie."[11] A duty becomes one's actual duty when it is the only or overriding duty.

Some have referred to the preferred of conflicting duties as the "lesser evil." This, however, makes no sense if taken literally, since it is meaningless to claim one has a moral duty to do evil. One never has a *moral* duty to do what is not moral. Furthermore, it is contrary to the time-honored ethical principle that "ought implies can." For to claim that one should have done right when there was no possible right course of action in the circumstances is to say one should have done what was not possible to do. As Aristotle noted, the so-called lesser evil is really the greater good.

Others have held out the vain hope that there is always a "third alternative" which avoids all real moral conflicts. Reality, however, says otherwise. Sometimes no one will jump off an overcrowded lifeboat, and either all will sink or some must be pushed off. Sometimes either the mother will die (along with the baby), as in tubal pregnancies, or else action must be taken that will lead to the death of the unborn baby. There are times when either the would-

be murderer is killed or else his victim(s) will die.

Ideally, moral duties do not conflict, but this is not an ideal world. In the real world there are moral tragedies. In such cases, one has a moral duty to follow the higher moral principle. The innocent should be saved from aggressors. One can protect one's life in self-defense. And it would be better to hit an old man in the road than to crash into a bus loaded full of children, if there was no way to avoid both. And it would be wrong to return a borrowed gun to a madman who demands it in order to kill his daughter.

Conclusion

This decision-making procedure is not exhaustive, nor are we suggesting that one needs to go through every detail of this grid each time one faces a moral dilemma. But these questions and the grid of which they are a part can help you to order your thoughts, gather appropriate information, and clarify just what the issues are in making a good, rational moral decision. After all, moral issues are often a matter of life and death. Something this urgent needs careful consideration.

Discussion Questions

1. What in general are the differences between utilitarian and deontological ethics? Present and explain the different versions within each category. How do Professors Moreland and Geisler see each category of ethical theory functioning in ethical decision-making? Which ethical theory do you consider the most plausible? Explain and defend your answer.

2. How do Professors Moreland and Geisler believe one can discover basic ethical values? Can you come up with any objections to this approach? Explain and defend your answer. And why do the authors believe some people disagree about moral issues? Do you agree with their conclusions? Explain why or why not.

3. Briefly explain how Professors Moreland and Geisler suggest one go about making moral decisions. Can you come up with any objections to this approach? Explain and defend you answer.

4. Do you think that Professors Moreland and Geisler are correct when they claim that deontological

ethics trumps utilitarianism? How do they defend this perspective? If you think that they are incorrect, explain and defend your objection(s).

Notes

1. Two other teleological theories are ethical egoism, roughly the idea that the rightness or wrongness of an act is solely a matter of the consequences of that act for the agent himself, and ethical altruism, roughly the idea that the rightness or wrongness of an act is solely a matter of the consequences of that act for everyone else except the agent.

2. For more on the notion of rationality in ethics, see Panayot Butchvarov, *Skepticism in Ethics* (Bloomington: Indiana University Press, 1989), 5, 8–9, 36–39, 137–95.

3. Some utilitarians argue for the greatest good for *all* (not just *most*) persons. In this way they avoid some of the objections, though not all.

4. See Immanuel Kant, *Foundations of the Metaphysics of Morals,* trans. Lewis White Beck (Indianapolis: Bobbs-Merrill, 1959).

5. As with utilitarianism, there is a distinction between act and rule deontological theories. The former states that an individual on any particular occasion must grasp immediately what ought to be done without relying on rules. The latter emphasizes the fact that acts are right or wrong depending on their conformity/ nonconformity with intrinsically correct moral rules. Virtually all current deontologists are rule deontologists because of their view of the importance of rules for the moral life and because of the subjectivity inherent in act deontological theories.

6. Currently, there is a growing interest in *virtue ethics.* Generally speaking, virtue ethics begins with a vision of what the good life and good person ought to be by describing a set of habitually formed dispositions or character traits true of the virtuous person. Thus, virtue ethics places an emphasis on agents and not on principles or rules. There are four main models for integrating virtue ethics and a principles approach to ethics (e.g., deontological ethics): (1) Virtue ethics are basic and principles/duties are derivative (e.g., the principle of benevolence is obligatory because it is what a beneficent person would do): (2) Moral principles are basic and virtues are derivative (e.g., a beneficent person is one who naturally and habitually obeys the principle of benevolence): (3) Virtue ethics and moral principles are complementary, equally basic spheres of morality, the former focusing on the character traits of persons, the latter on principles: (4) Virtue ethics and moral principles are two different aspects of morality, the former specifying an ethics of supererogation for moral saints and heroes, the latter specifying an ethics of obligation for common morality. Virtue ethics will enter into the discussions of different issues in latter chapters, but we have chosen to emphasize the role of rules and principles in solving ethical dilemmas. For more on virtue ethics, see Peter A. French, Theodore E. Uehling, Jr., and Howard K. Wettstein, eds., *Ethical Theory; Character and Virtue,* Midwest Studies in Philosophy, vol. 13 (Notre Dame, Ind.: University of Notre Dame Press, 1988).

7. Confucius, *Analects of Confucius* 25.23, cf. 12:2.

8. C. S. Lewis, *The Abolition of Man* (New York: Macmillan, 1947), Appendix, 95–121.

9. Joseph Fletcher, *Situation Ethics* (Philadelphia: The Westminster Press, 1966), 26.

10. Fletcher, *Situation Ethics,* 120.

11. W. David Ross, *Foundations of Ethics* (Oxford: The Clarendon Press, 1951), Chapter 5.

5

Minimalist Ethics: On the Pacification of Morality

Daniel Callahan

Daniel Callahan, one of the foremost philosophical ethicists in the United States, is Director of the Hastings Center, a nonpartisan bioethics think-tank outside of New York City. He is the author and editor of numerous works, including *Abortion: Law, Morality, and Choice* (1970) and *Abortion: Understanding Differences* (1984).

In this essay Dr. Callahan maintains that the predominant way in which American culture looks at ethical obligation and duty is fundamentally flawed. He calls this flawed view *the minimalist ethic,* which can be stated in a simple proposition: *"One may morally act in any way one chooses so far as one does not harm others."* According to Dr. Callahan, there are certain consequences that follow from this ethic, among which are the following: (1) it tends to confuse principles of government and civil liberties with one's moral duties to oneself and one's community, (2) it misleads people into thinking that there is a sharp distinction between the private and public spheres, with different moral standards applying to each, (3) it is suspicious of attempts to answer deeply important philosophical questions about the nature and/or inherent or intrinsic goodness of human persons, and (4) it reduces moral questions of human sexuality and drug use to issues of preference arbitrated only by the informed consent of the adults involved. Dr. Callahan argues that the origin of the minimalist ethic can be found in the writings of John Stuart Mill, who, according to Dr. Callahan, is not read critically enough by the defenders of the

Reprinted by permission from *The Hastings Center Report* (October 1981). The article was supported by a grant to The Hastings Center from the Humanities Division of the Rockefeller Foundation.

minimalist ethic. He goes on to argue that the strict dichotomy between public and private morality, assumed in the minimalist ethic, is seriously flawed. He concludes with a recommendation for an antidote to the minimalist ethic.

The attraction of morality in affluent times is that not much of it seems needed. More choices are available and thus fewer harsh dilemmas arise. If they do arise, money can be used to buy out of or evade the consequences of choice. The "wages of sin" are offset by the cheapness of therapy, drugs, liquor, economy flights, and a career change. If all else fails, public confessions can profitably be produced as a miniseries. Vice is rewarded because everything is rewarded, even virtue.

Matters are otherwise in hard times. Options are fewer, choices nastier. Where forgiveness and therapeutic labels could once be afforded, blaming and denunciation become more congenial. If life is going poorly, someone obviously must be at fault—if not the government, then my neighbor, wife, or child. The warm, expansive self, indulgent of the foibles of others, gives way to the harsh, competitive self; enemies abound, foreign and domestic. It is not so much that the "least well off" cease to count (though they do), but that most people imagine that they are now in that category. Nastiness becomes the standard of civility, exposé the goal of journalism, a lawsuit the way friends, families, and colleagues reconcile their differences.

Meanwhile, in hard times, every would-be Jeremiah has plentiful material with which to work, and the moral panaceas may be just the opposite of the economic ones. Ethical conservatives want a fatter moral budget: more prayer in more schools, more bombs in more missiles, and more virtue in more hearts to keep more families together. Liberals want a leaner moral budget: less personal moral judgment, less social coercion, and less dominance by the military-industrial-multinational-pharmaceutical–technological expert–Political Action Committee complex.

What, then, is the problem to be diagnosed? Here is the question I want to ask, and attempt to address: as we move into what will most likely be chronically hard economic times, how can our society muster the moral resources necessary to endure as a valid human culture? Three assumptions underlie that question. The first is that economic strength and military power have no necessary ethical connection with the internal human and moral viability of a culture; they can only help assure its mere existence. The second is that the era of sustained economic growth is over, and with it the perennially optimistic psychology of affluence. The prospects are at best for a steady-state economy, one where the next generation can only hope that it will do as well as the previous generation; only that, no more, and probably less.

My third assumption is that the kind of morality that was able to flourish during affluent times will, if carried over unchanged into hard times, lead to moral chaos and maybe worse. That morality has stressed the transcendence of the individual over the community, the need to tolerate all moral viewpoints, the autonomy of the self as the highest human good, and the voluntary, informed consent contract as the model of human relationships. To be sure, in its "great society" phase, it was a morality sensitive to poverty and economic oppression, just as it more recently supported a quest for universal human rights. But its central agenda was always that of individual liberty, that of the self seeking a liberation from both economic and cultural restraints, free to find its own truth and its own way. What is that "truth" and what is the "way"? If you felt you had to ask yourself that question, you probably missed the whole point, failing to use your freedom creatively. If you went so far as to press that question with insistence upon others, you could be certain of some suspicion among those for whom the essential value of autonomy is its resistance to any universal content. Free choice is its own reward, and the philosophical road to hell, supposedly, is paved with teleological ends, ultimate purposes, and essentialist meanings.

Now all of that autonomy is doubtless fine, and lofty, and lovely. But to live that kind of life you need to have money at hand, good health, and a clinic full of psychological counselors at the ready. It is a good-time philosophy for comfortable people living in the most powerful, rich nation on earth. Will it work in hard times? Some doubt is in order. Hard times require self-sacrifice and altruism—but there is nothing in an ethic of moral autonomy to sustain or nourish those values. Hard times necessitate a sense of community and the common good—but the putative virtues of autonomy are primarily directed toward the cultivation of independent selfhood. Hard times demand restraint in the blaming of others for misfortune—but moral autonomy as an ideal makes more people blameworthy for the harms they supposedly do others. Hard times need a broad sense

of duty toward others, especially those out of sight—but an ethic of autonomy stresses responsibility only for one's freely chosen, consenting-adult relationships.

Whether suffering brings out the best or the worst in people is an old question, and the historical evidence is mixed. Yet a people's capacity to endure suffering without turning on each other is closely linked to the way they have envisioned, and earlier embodied, their relationship to each other. When one's perceived and culturally supported primary duty is to others rather than to self, to transcendent rather than private values, to future needs rather than to present attachments, then there can be a solid moral foundation to survive pain, turmoil, and evil. Naturally, that set of values can, and often does, have its dark side. Many nations and cultures serve as unhappy examples of communities that stifled and killed individuals. Tight families and kinfolk systems can run roughshod over liberty, and totalitarian states are all too ready to capitalize upon the willingness of their citizens to give their lives for some higher cause.

What we have not had, until recently, are cultures that have systematically tried to forswear communal goals; that have tried to replace ultimate ends with procedural safeguards; that have resolutely worked to banish the most profound questions of human meaning to the depths of hidden, private lives only; and that have strived to sanctify the morally autonomous agent as the cultural ideal. Can that kind of a culture survive hard times? Or better, if it is to survive—mere size and residual power may assure that much—can it do so without the wanton violence, moral indifference, and callous self-interest that are the growing pathologies of life in the United States? It would be foolish to give a flat answer to that question. Our cultural experiment is not over. Only now it is faced with a shift in those material circumstances that, as much or more than articulated values, made the culture possible in the first place. The changes will pose a severe test.

Defining the Minimalist Ethic

One set of moral values that emerged during our recent decades of affluence is peculiarly ill-suited, and even dangerous, for the hard times ahead. For lack of a more graceful term, I will call those values a "minimalistic ethic." I have already hinted at some of the features of that ethic, but will now try to be more specific. That ethic can be stated in a simple proposition: *One may morally act in any way one chooses so far as one does not do harm to others.* The accent and some of the substance of John Stuart Mill's "On Liberty" are familiar enough in that proposition. But something has gone awry in the way Mill's thinking has been appropriated by our culture. What he understood to be a principle that ought to govern only the relationship between the individual and the state has been wrongly construed to encompass the moral life itself.

I call this a "minimalistic ethic" because, put crudely, it seems to be saying that the sole test of the morality of an action, or of a whole way of life, is whether it avoids harm to others. If that minimal standard can be met, then there is no further basis for judging personal or communal moral goods and goals, for praising or blaming others, or for educating others about higher moral obligations to self or community. In the language of our day: the only judgment we are permitted on the way others make use of their moral autonomy is to assess whether they are doing harm to others. If we can discern no such harm, then we must suspend any further moral judgment. Should we fail to suspend that judgment, we are then guilty of a positive violation of their right to privacy and self-determination.

The pervasiveness of this ethic has had a number of general consequences.

First, a minimalist ethic has tended to confuse useful principles for government regulation and civil liberties with the broader requirements of the moral life, both individual and communal.

Second, it has misled many in our society into thinking that a sharp distinction can be drawn between the public and the private sphere, and that different standards of morality apply to each.

Third, it has given us a thin and shriveled notion of personal and public morality. We are obliged under the most generous reading of a minimalist ethic only to honor our voluntarily undertaken family obligations, to keep our promises, and to respect contracts freely entered into with other freely consenting adults. Beyond those minimal standards, we are free to do as we like, guided by nothing other than our private standards of good and evil. Altruism, beneficence, and self-sacrifice beyond that tight circle are in no sense moral obligations and, in any case, cannot be universally required. My neighbor can and will remain a moral stranger unless and until, as an exercise of my autonomy, I choose to enter into a contract with him; and I am bound to him by no more

than the letter of that contract. While l ought to treat my neighbor with justice, that is because I may otherwise do harm to him, or owe it to him as a way of discharging the debt of former injustices, or because it seems a rational idea to develop a social contract with others as a way of enhancing my own possibilities for greater liberty and the gaining of some primary goods.

Fourth, a minimalist ethic has deprived us of meaningful language to talk about our life together outside our contractual relationships. The only language that does seem common is that of "the public interest," a concept which for most translates into the aggregate total of individual desires and demands. The language of "rights" is common enough (though not of putatively archaic "natural" or "God-given" rights). But it is to be understood that the political and moral purpose of both negative and positive rights is to protect and advance individual autonomy. It is not the kind of language that can comfortably be used any longer to talk about communal life, shared values, and the common good.

Fifth, a minimalist ethic has made the ancient enterprise of trying to determine the inherent or intrinsic good of human beings a suspect, probably subversive activity. It assumes that no one can answer such lofty and vague questions, that attempts to try probably pose a threat to liberty, and that, in any event, any purported answers should be left resolutely private.

Sixth, unless I can demonstrate that the behavior of others poses some direct public harm, I am not allowed to question that behavior, much less to pass a public negative judgment on it. The culture of a minimalist ethic is one of rigid and rigorous toleration. Who am I to judge what is good for others? One is—maybe—entitled to personal moral opinions about the self-regarding conduct of others. But a public expression of those opinions would contribute to an atmosphere of moral suppression in the civil order, and of an anti-autonomous moral repression in the private psychological order. One question is taken to be the definitive response to anyone who should be so uncivil as to talk about ethics for its own sake: "But whose ethics?"

In some quarters, a minimalist ethic has gone a step further, to a de-listing of many behavioral choices as moral problems at all. Thus abortion becomes a "religious" rather than a moral issue, and it is well known that all religious issues are private, a-rational, and idiosyncratic; questions of sex, and most recently homosexuality, become matters of "alternative life styles" or "sexual preference"; and the use of pleasure-enhancing drugs becomes an amusing choice between two value-soaked (subjective) norms, "psychotropic hedonism" or "pharmacological Calvinism."[1]

Seventh, under the terms of a "minimalist ethic" only a few moral problems are worth bothering with at all. The issue of liberty versus justice is one, and that of autonomy versus paternalism is another. The former is important because distributive justice is required to finally enthrone a community of fully autonomous individuals. The latter is vital because it is well recognized that paternalism, even the beneficently motivated and kindly sort, poses the most direct threat to individual liberty. A lack of informed consent, decisions taken by experts, and a failure to observe due process will be high on the list of evils of a minimalist ethic. Anything less than a full egalitarianism—equal decisions made by equally autonomous moral agents—is seen as an eschatological failure.

I have drawn here an exaggerated picture of a minimalist ethic. It fits the views of no one person precisely and, to be sure, cannot be taken to represent any single, coherent, well-developed ethical theory. Not all those who favor a perfect egalitarianism would equally favor (or favor at all) a moral delisting of matters of sex and drugs. There is no necessary incompatibility between favoring a civil libertarian political ethic and affirming the value of close community ties, of seeking transcendent values and of recognizing duties over and above those of self-realization. Permutations of and exceptions to this general portrait are easy enough to find. Nonetheless, I believe it sufficiently accurate as a composite portrait of a mainstream set of values in American culture to take seriously—and to reject. A society heavily composed of those who aspire to, or unwittingly accept, a minimalistic ethic cannot be a valid human community. In times of stress, it could turn into a very nasty community.

Rereading Mill

I suggested above that a minimalistic ethic sounds very much like a close relative of John Stuart Mill's position in "On Liberty" (1859), but also that it presses that position beyond the limits he intended. Is that true? I think so, but it is instructive to look at the way Mill tried to find a good fit between principles of public morality, narrow and limited, and the demands of a broader private and communal morality. It is not easy to find that fit, and Mill's troubles in doing so foreshadow many of our own in trying to do likewise. While Mill is by no means responsible for what has transpired in Anglo-American culture since the nineteenth century, his thinking has remained powerful in civil libertarian thought, either as a foundation or as an important point of departure for revised theories.

Recall Mill's famous principle and point of departure in "On Liberty":

> . . . the sole end for which mankind are warranted, individual or collectively, in interfering with the liberty of action of any of their number, is self-protection. That the only purpose for which power can be rightfully exercised over any member of a civilized community, against his will, is to prevent harm to others.[2]

Mill goes on to reiterate and embellish that principle in a variety of ways, stressing not only that society ought to be solely concerned with individual conduct that "concerns others," but also that "over himself, over his own body and mind, the individual is sovereign."[3]

Nor is it sufficient that the individual be protected "against the tyranny of the magistrate." Protection is also needed

> against the tyranny of the prevailing opinion and feeling; against the tendency of society to impose, by other means than civil penalties, its own ideas and practices or rules of conduct on those who dissent from them. . . . There is a limit to the legitimate interference of collective opinion with individual independence: and to find that limit, and maintain it against encroachment, is as indispensable to a good condition of human affairs, as protection against human despotism.[4]

With an even more contemporary flavor, Mill wrote that

> the principle requires liberty of tastes and pursuits; of framing the plan of our life to suit our own character; of doing as we like, subject to such consequences as may follow: without impediment from our fellow creatures, as long as what we do does not harm them, even though they should think our conduct foolish, perverse, or wrong.[5]

Nevertheless, despite the firmness of those statements, Mill apparently had no desire to reduce all of morality to his "simple principle," as if the moral universe can solely be encompassed by the relationship between the individual and the state. As long as we do not compel anyone in those matters that concern himself only, there can be "good reasons for remonstrating with him, or persuading him, or entreating him . . . "[6] So, also, Mill states that

It would be a great misunderstanding of this doctrine to suppose that it is one of self indifference, which pretends that human beings have no business with each other's conduct in life, and that they should not concern themselves about the well-doing or well-being of one another, unless their own interest is involved. . . . Human beings owe to each other help to distinguish the better from the worse, and encouragement to choose the former and avoid the latter.[7]

Mill's intention, then, is not to promote a society of amoral atoms, each existing in undisturbed isolation from the moral community of others. There are standards of right and wrong, good and bad, in our self-regarding conduct and in our relationship with our fellow creatures—"cruelty of disposition," "malice," "envy," "pride," "egotism," "rashness," and "obstinacy" are all vices for Mill. Yet he is walking a delicate line. He wants to exclude legal pressures in that which concerns ourselves only, and exclude as well "the moral coercion of public opinion." Yet, he also agrees that so long as the individual is the final judge," considerations to aid his judgment, exhortations to strengthen his will, may be offered to him, even obtruded on him, by others. . . . "[8]

I find it difficult to see as sharp a distinction as Mill does between exhorting and obtruding upon others, and allowing them to be free of "the moral coercion of public opinion." It is just that exhortation by others that may and probably will represent public opinion. So what if I am allowed in the end to be my own moral judge? If others insist upon their right to harangue, bother, and even condemn me with their moral sentiments, my life is considerably less well off—on one reading of Mill—than if they would just let me alone.[9] Moreover, this is exactly what many say in our day: "It is not enough that you grant me the legal and civil liberty to act as I see fit. You must also grant me that private respect and equality that will lead you to stop judging altogether my moral actions."[10]

Much of what Mill says in "On Liberty" would seem to reject that latter extension of his "simple principle." For him, the problem of his day was not too much individuality, but too little. One can only read with a kind of wondrous bemusement a passage like the following:

. . . the danger which threatens human nature is not the excess, but the deficiency, of personal impulses and preferences. . . . In our times, from the highest class of society down to the lowest, everyone lives as under the eye of a hostile and dreadful censorship. . . . It does not occur to them to have any inclination, except for what is customary.[11]

If one worked at it, I suppose, one could still find many in our society who have no inclination except for what is customary. There are allegedly one or two people like that on my street and many more, I have been assured, living in the Sun Belt, Palm Springs, and Scarsdale. But how do we determine what counts as "customary" any longer in a society that allows any and all moral flowers to bloom?

Mill is not unaware of the possibility that the kind of liberty he seeks can lead to some undesirable outcomes:

I fully admit that the mischief which a person does to himself may seriously affect, both through their sympathies and their interests, those nearly connected with him and, in a minor degree, society at large.[12] . . . But with regard to the merely contingent, as it may be called, constructive injury which a person causes to society, by conduct which neither violates any specific duty to the public, nor occasions hurt to any assignable individual except himself: the inconvenience is one which society can afford to bear, for the sake of the greater good of human freedom.[13]

In another place, he writes that "mankind are greater gainers by suffering each other to live as seem good to themselves, than by compelling each to live as seems good to the rest."[14]

That may be too confident and optimistic a judgment. What societies did Mill have in mind when he came to that conclusion? Apparently not his own or any other extant society. In the passage quoted above, for instance, those societies were characterized as repressive and conformist. He must have been extrapolating from some parts, or circles, of his own social world to have reached such a universal judgment. Yet only in our day have we actually begun to see an approximation, on a mass scale, of the kind of society he had in mind. Lacking other historical examples, it is those we must judge. Whatever its other failings, Mill lived in a time and a culture that could take many if not most Western moral values for granted. He did not have to specify or defend the standards by which his countrymen should judge the self-regarding behavior of others, or the moral principles to be inculcated in children, or the norms on which the moral exhortation he countenanced was based.

Public and Private Morality

Increasingly, no such background—tacitly held and almost superfluous to state—can be assumed. Precisely because that is so, and because a minimalist ethic has been one outcome of the train of thought that Mill helped set in motion, we are forced to now reexamine the relationship between public and private morality. Can they, in the first place, sharply be distinguished, as Mill thought possible?

The evidence provided by the emergence of a minimalist ethic is hardly encouraging. Not only would it have us obsessively make such a distinction; it would have us go a step further and eschew moral judgment on the private lives of others as well. In response, I want to argue three points. First, the distinction between the private and the public is a cultural artifact only, varying with time and place. Second, only a thoroughly dulled (or self-interested) imagination could even pretend to think that there can be private acts with no public consequences. Third, the effort to sharply distinguish the two spheres can do harm to our general moral life.

What kind of human nature, and what kind of society, would be necessary to viably and sensibly separate the private and the public sphere? As for human nature, the individual would have to exist in total isolation from all others, dependent upon them for nothing at all, neither food, shelter, culture, nor language. If a universe existed that made possible that kind of individual, one might then speak of a wholly private, inward world. But the concept of a "public" world would then make no sense. There would be none of those interconnections and interdependencies, past, present, and future human relationships, that characterize what is ordinarily meant by "public." In such a universe, it would also be hard to make much sense of "human nature." It would lack those traits, language, and culture in particular, reasonably thought necessary to distinguish the "human" from other forms of nature.

If we leave that never-never universe, and ask what kind of society would have to be imagined to support a sharply separable private and public space,

our task might seem a bit easier. Do we not, after all, have our secret thoughts, and do things that others never hear about or see? Of course, but what does that prove? As Mill himself acknowledges, actions have their cause in internal dispositions,[15] precisely within the hidden self. While our behavior can belie our secret thoughts and feelings some of the time, it is difficult to imagine a constant discrepancy between the inner and the outer self. One way of coming to know our inner self, it often turns out, is by observing our outer self, that self which acts and responds in the company of others; it is normally impossible to say just where the one begins and the other ends. Aristotle's observation that virtue is a habit was not unperceptive, nor is it any the less consonant with general experience to suggest that our habits of private thought, our hidden feelings and dispositions toward others, have a direct bearing on observable conduct on our habits.

One need not turn to the complicated relationship between an inner and an outer self to wholly make the point. Our more recent historical experience indicates that the distinction between the public and the private is at the least a cultural artifact and quite possibly a matter of the sheerest ideology. I earlier pointed to a "de-listing" phenomenon in our society—the attempt to remove whole spheres of behavior from moral scrutiny and judgment. That point needs a complementary one: a number of activities once thought to be only private in their moral significance are now judged to be of public importance. For example, the common moral wisdom tells us—in a way it did not tell Mill's generation—that we have among other things: no right to pollute the water and the air; to knowingly procreate defective children or even to have too many healthy children; to utter slurs against females, ethnic, or racial groups; or to ignore the private domestic life of public officials. Family planning was, in the days of Margaret Sanger, an entirely public and proscribed matter. Then, with the triumph of the family planning movement, it became an issue of wholly private morality. With the perception of a world population explosion, it became once again a public matter. The frequenting of prostitutes was once legal in many places, and thought to be a concern of private morality only. Not many feminists, aware of the degradation of women that has been a part of prostitution, are likely to be impressed with a private-morality-consenting-adult rationale. They are hardly keen on pornography either, and for the same kind of reason.

If it is so hard to separate the private and the public, why does the idea continue to persist? One reason is that, on occasion, it can serve to buttress our personal predilections or ideologies. I know that I cannot make a good moral case to myself about why I continue to smoke in the face of all that distressing health evidence. Yet I do not have to try quite so hard when I can persuade myself that the issue is between myself and myself and is no one else's affair. (That others ordinarily believe it necessary to cite potential harm to others as the essence of their moral point against me only confirms the power of a minimalist ethic.) Think also how much more arduous it would be morally for the "pro-choice" group in the abortion debate to have to admit that abortion decisions are fully public in their direct implications, and then to be forced to make the case for the public benefits of abortion. The argument could perhaps be made in some cases—but it is much, much easier to relegate the whole issue to the private realm, where the standards of moral rigor are more accommodating.

There are other, less self-serving reasons for the persistence of the distinction. We need some language and concepts for finding a limit to the right of the government, or the populace, to intervene in our lives. That was Mill's concern and it is as legitimate now as it was in his day. In groping around for a solution, our legal system stumbled on a "right to privacy." That concept represents a latter-day reading of the Constitution, and has resisted efforts to give it a clear meaning. Even so, it has its heuristic uses and no better formulation has been proposed to get at some kinds of civil liberties issues. Yet to say that the concept is useful does not mean that we need to reify, as if it represented reality, a sharp distinction between private and public life. A loose, shifting, casual distinction, taken with a nice grain of salt, may be equally serviceable.

The problem we now face is twofold. Do those of us who want to protect civil liberties have the nerve to openly admit the possibility that our society is paying an increasingly high moral cost for isolating the "private" sphere from moral judgment? We have certainly gained a number of valuable civil liberties as a result. But there is growing evidence that the diffuse and general consequences of that gain have been as harmful as they have been beneficial—the multiple indignities of daily life in large cities, for example. Mill was prepared to recognize that a price could well be paid for the liberty he proposed. But without offering any specific evidence, he simply asserted that it was a price worth paying. We have

less reason to remain confident about that equation. He was not speaking about the realities of his own society but projecting one yet to be. Not until our own day have we seen, in actuality, what he had in mind. We can thus make a far better judgment than was possible for him. My own observation, however, is that defenders of his "simple principle" in its revised and extended "minimalist ethic" form are resolutely unwilling to look some unsavory reality straight in the face.

If that were done, we would be driven to grapple with the need to set some limits on those liberties which, in balance, produce an intolerable level of moral nihilism and relativism as a cultural outcome. It is not, and ought not to be, just the Moral Majority that worries about violence and more-tolerant-than-thou sex on television; or about children neglected by parental quests for greater psychological fulfillment; or about casual stealing, cheating, lying, and consenting-adult infidelity; or about rising assault and murder rates. Whatever the gain to liberty of the private standards and dispositions that tacitly support those developments, they all point to the emergence of an intolerable society, destructive as much to private as to public life. Any society can survive some degree of those vices, but life becomes much more fragile, and human relationships much less secure, when they are pervasive and inescapable. A legitimate respect for civil liberties does not require foregoing standards by which to judge private behavior any more than respect for freedom of speech requires suspending judgment on the contents of free speech.

Mill's problem was to find a "limit" to "the legitimate interference of collective opinion with individual independence . . . ."[16] While our task may not exactly be the opposite, the weight of inquiry may now have to shift. What ought to be the limits of liberty, and how can we identify those points at which "collective opinion" ought to hold sway against claims of private moral autonomy? To even ask that question implies that we must be prepared once again to judge the private lives of others and the way they use their liberty, and our standards ought to be more demanding than those required by a minimalist ethic.

Why should we believe that the sum total of private, self-interested acts that do no ostensible harm to others will add up to a favorable societal outcome? Those who would be the first to declaim against a pure economic market economy, guided by an "invisible hand," seem quite willing to tolerate a moral market economy, as if the result in the moral realm will be more favorable than in the economic. (There is an equal irony on the other side, of course: those who rage against a government-controlled economy seem quite prepared to accept a government-controlled morality.) There is equally no reason to believe that the good of the individual is necessarily the good of society, as if any free act is, by virtue of its freedom alone, a social contribution. That is especially true if the good is defined simply as moral autonomy and, to make matters worse, is combined with a systematic agnosticism about the morally proper uses of that autonomy. We are then deterred from passing a moral judgment on our neighbor (which he may well need and deserve) and, still more, harmed in our capacity as a society to determine what individual virtues, dispositions, and behaviors we want to promote and publicly support. Under a minimalist ethic that discussion cannot even begin. It is ruled out in principle.

The strong tendency in our society to confuse legal standards with moral principles has become a major part of the problem. When it is assumed that, under the aegis of liberty, moral judgment cannot be passed on private life, then the only general moral norms become those supplied by the law. On occasion, to be sure, the law can be a powerful and positive moral educator. The civil rights legislation of the 1960s gradually served to change moral attitudes as well as specific discriminatory practices, whatever the local bitterness it occasioned at the time. But just as frequently a change in the law—particularly a change that sees inhibitory laws removed from the books—can suggest that the matter has been removed from the moral order as well.

The proper relationship between law and morality is an old and difficult question. Yet it can only be fully meaningful when there are some generally accepted moral standards against which the law can be measured. If that is too strong a statement, then there must at least be an expectation that explicit limits will be recognized within the private moral order; put in the starkest terms, that behavior not controlled by statute will be controlled or modulated by the power of public opinion. And by "public opinion" I mean the direct and strong moral judgment of others. If (as I believe) the law should be minimal in publicly enforcing moral standards, that ought not mean a parallel shrinking of the moral realm. But that is precisely the conclusion a minimalist ethic entails. By default, law is left as the only standard by which to measure and reliably control behavior. It should thus be no surprise that,

when cries of moral decline are in the air, many will immediately rush to the law to fill the vacuum. What does a minimalist ethic offer in the place of law? Nothing, and that by definition.

An Antidote to the Minimalist Ethic?

Is there an antidote to a minimalist ethic, one that could avoid the moral anemia and casual ethical relativism that is its inevitable outcome, but avoid as well a reactionary reimposition of restrictions on hard-won civil liberties? I am not at all certain, and finding one will not be easy. Mill could make a strong case for his "simple principle" in the relationship between the individual and the state because he could assume a relatively stable body of moral conviction below the surface. Can we make a similar assumption? I think we must. There are no new and better values on the moral horizon than those we already possess: liberty, justice, human dignity, charity, benevolence, and kindness, and that is not a full list. A minimalist ethic cannot endure a serious attempt to deploy not just liberty and justice but all those values. Nor could it survive a new willingness to pass public judgment on conduct that the law may and should still permit.

Civil tolerance is hardly tolerance at all if one moral choice is in principle as good as another. It can only make sense, and show its full strength, when there are standards against which to measure behavior. Then, within limits, we can allow others to speak and act as they see fit. But we owe it both to them and to morality to let them know when we think they are behaving badly, whether to themselves or to others. We do not have to ban tawdry television programs, or publications, or obnoxious viewpoints. We just bring to bear all the private and public opinion we can against them. Will that work? It had better, for the next step will be far worse, and there are already many who would have the law do what ought to be the work of morality.

Discussion Questions

1. What does Dr. Callahan mean by the *minimalist ethic?* Provide a detailed definition, citing some examples.

2. Why does Dr. Callahan believe that the dichotomy between private and public morality is

flawed? Present and explain his position. Do you agree or disagree with him? Explain and defend your answer.

3. Dr. Callahan claims that a minimalist ethic "can serve to buttress our personal predilections or ideologies," without requiring that we actually *defend* our moral positions, since they are simply personal preferences. What does Dr. Callahan mean by this and why does he think it counts against the plausibility of a minimalist ethic?

4. What does Dr. Callahan recommend as an antidote to the minimalist ethic? Do you agree or disagree with his recommendation? Explain and defend your answer.

Notes

1. Gerald L. Klerman. "Psychotropic Hedonism vs. Pharmacological Calvinism," *Hastings Center Report* (September 1972), pp. 1–3.

2. John Stuart Mill, "On Liberty," in *John Stuart Mill: Selected Writings,* ed. Mary Warnock (New York: Meridian Books, 1962), p. 135.

3. *Ibid.*

4. *Ibid.*, p. 130.

5. *Ibid.*, p. 138.

6. *Ibid.*, p. 135.

7. *Ibid.*, p. 206.

8. *Ibid.*, p. 207.

9. Gerald Dworkin has pointed out to me that Mill did not consider moral condemnation, even of a very harsh kind, a form of doing harm to another. *Cf* the following passage from *On Liberty:* "There is a degree of folly, and a degree of what may be called (though the phrase is not unobjectionable) lowness or a deprivation of taste, which, though it cannot justify doing harm to the person who manifests it, renders him necessarily and properly a subject of distaste, or, in extreme cases, even of contempt . . ." *Ibid.*, p. 207.

10. Anonymous, circa 1980.

11. Mill, p. 190.

12. *Ibid.*, p. 212.

13. *Ibid.*, p. 213.

14. *Ibid.*, p. 138.

15. *Ibid.*, p. 209.

16. *Ibid.*, p. 130.

6

In Defense of Ethical Egoism

Ayn Rand

Ayn Rand, who died in 1982, is one of the most popular intellectual novelists of the 20th century. Her novels included *The Fountainhead* (1943), *We the Living* (1936), and *Atlas Shrugged* (1959), from which the following selection is taken.

In this essay, Ms. Rand argues for a form of ethical egoism which is called *objectivism*. According to this view, pursuit of one's self-interest and happiness is the only proper life for rational beings; self-sacrifice and altruism are inconsistent with rational morality. Ms. Rand supports this view by starting with what she believes is "the only one fundamental alternative in the universe: existence or nonexistence." She moves on from there to argue that "since life requires a specific course of action, any other course will destroy it. A being who does not hold his own life as the motive and goal of his actions, is acting on the motive and standard of *death.*" He is, in her words, a *metaphysical monstrosity.* Consequently, those who hold that morality ought to be altruistic—that is, meeting the needs of others so that they can be happy—propose a morality which is irrational and immoral. Ms. Rand is not saying that giving to others is morally wrong, just not morally obligatory. That is, she is arguing that giving to others is permissible if it is something the giver believes will lead to his happiness. Moreover, she is not arguing that anything chosen by the self is prudent or morally good. There could be situations when the self makes a choice—e.g., to steal, to murder, to lie—which may be in his short-term interests but violates his long-term interests, since his behavior contributes to the dissolution of social institutions which protect him from others' harm and he may wind up in jail and/or shunned by others.

Value Yourself

". . . Yes, this is an age of moral crisis. Yes, you *are* bearing punishment for your evil. But it is not man who is now on trial and it is not human nature that will take the blame. It is your moral code that's through, this time. Your moral code has reached its climax, the blind alley at the end of its course. And if you wish to go on living, what you now need is not to *return* to morality—you who have never known any—but to discover it.

"You have heard no concepts of morality but the mystical or the social. You have been taught that morality is a code of behavior imposed on you by whim, the whim of a supernatural power or the whim of society, to serve God's purpose or your neighbor's welfare, to please an authority beyond the grave or else next door—but not to serve *your* life or pleasure. Your pleasure, you have been taught, is to be found in immorality, your interests would best be served by evil, and any moral code must be designed not *for* you, but *against* you, not to further your life, but to drain it.

"For centuries, the battle of morality was fought between those who claimed that your life belongs to God and those who claimed that it belongs to your neighbors—between those who preached that the good is self-sacrifice for the sake of ghosts in heaven and those who preached that the good is self-sacrifice for the sake of incompetents on earth. And no one came to say that your life belongs to you and that the good is to live it.

"Both sides agreed that morality demands the surrender of your self-interest and of your mind, that the moral and the practical are opposites, that morality is not the province of reason, but the province of faith and force. Both sides agreed that no rational morality is possible, that there is no right or wrong in reason—that in reason there's no reason to be moral.

"Whatever else they fought about, it was against man's mind that all your moralists have stood united. It was man's mind that all their schemes and systems were intended to despoil and destroy. Now choose to perish or to learn that the anti-mind is the anti-life.

Reprinted by permission of the executor of the Estate of Ayn Rand from *Atlas Shrugged* (New York: Random House, 1959) by Ayn Rand.

"Man's mind is his basic tool of survival. Life is given to him, survival is not. His body is given to him, its sustenance is not. His mind is given to him, its content is not. To remain alive, he must act, and before he can act he must know the nature and purpose of his action. He cannot obtain his food without a knowledge of food and of the way to obtain it. He cannot dig a ditch—or build a cyclotron—without a knowledge of his aim and of the means to achieve it. To remain alive, he must think.

"But to think is an act of choice. The key to what you so recklessly call 'human nature,' the open secret you live with, yet dread to name, is the fact that *man is a being of volitional consciousness.* Reason does not work automatically; thinking is not a mechanical process; the connections of logic are not made by instinct. The function of your stomach, lungs, or heart is automatic; the function of your mind is not. In any hour and issue of your life, you are free to think or to evade that effort. But you are not free to escape from your nature, from the fact that *reason* is your means of survival—so that for *you*, who are a human being, the question 'to be or not to be' is the question 'to think or not to think.'

"A being of volitional consciousness has no automatic course of behavior. He needs a code of values to guide his actions. 'Value' is that which one acts to gain and keep, 'virtue' is the action by which one gains and keeps it. 'Value' presupposes an answer to the question: of value to whom and for what? 'Value' presupposes a standard, a purpose and the necessity of action in the fact of an alternative. Where there are no alternatives, no values are possible.

"There is only one fundamental alternative in the universe: existence or non-existence—and it pertains to a single class of entities: to living organisms. The existence of inanimate matter is unconditional, the existence of life is not: it depends on a specific course of action. Matter is indestructible, it changes its forms, but it cannot cease to exist. It is only a living organism that faces a constant alternative: the issue of life or death. Life is a process of self-sustaining and self-generated action. If an organism fails in that action, it dies; its chemical elements remain, but its life goes out of existence. It is only the concept of 'Life' that makes the concept of 'Value' possible. It is only to a living entity that things can be good or evil.

"A plant must feed itself in order to live; the sunlight, the water, the chemicals it needs are the values its nature has set it to pursue; its life is the standard of value directing its actions, but a plant has no choice of action; there are alternatives in the conditions it encounters, but there is no alternative in its function; it acts automatically to further its life, it cannot act for its own destruction.

"An animal is equipped for sustaining its life; its senses provide it with an automatic code of action, an automatic knowledge of what is good for it or evil. It has no power to extend its knowledge or to evade it. In conditions where its knowledge proves inadequate, it dies. But so long as it lives, it acts on its knowledge, with automatic safety and no power of choice, it is unable to ignore its own good, unable to decide to choose the evil and act as its own destroyer.

"Man has no automatic code of survival. His particular distinction from all other living species is the necessity to act in the face of alternatives by means of *volitional choice.* He has no automatic knowledge of what is good for him or evil, what values his life depends on, what course of action it requires. Are you prattling about an instinct of self-preservation? An *instinct* of self-preservation is precisely what man does not possess. An 'instinct' is an unerring and automatic form of knowledge. A desire is not an instinct. A desire to live does not give you the knowledge required for living. And even man's desire to live is not automatic: your secret evil today is that *that* is the desire you do not hold. Your fear of death is not a love for life and will not give you the knowledge needed to keep it. Man must obtain his knowledge and choose his actions by a process of thinking, which nature will not force him to perform. Man has the power to act as his own destroyer—and that is the way he has acted through most of his history.

"A living entity that regarded its means of survival as evil, would not survive. A plant that struggled to mangle its roots, a bird that fought to break its wings would not remain for long in the existence they affronted. But the history of man has been a struggle to deny and to destroy his mind.

"Man has been called a rational being, but rationality is a matter of choice—and the alternative his nature offers him is: rational being or suicidal animal. Man has to be man—by choice; he has to hold his life as a value—by choice; he has to learn to sustain it—by choice; he has to discover the values it requires and practice his virtues—by choice.

"A code of values accepted by choice is a code of morality.

"Whoever you are, you who are hearing me now, I am speaking to whatever living remnant is left uncorrupted within you, to the remnant of the human, to your *mind*, and I say: There *is* a morality of reason, a morality proper to man, and *Man's Life* is its standard of value.

"All that which is proper to the life of a rational being is the good; all that which destroys it is the evil.

"Man's life, as required by his nature, is not the life of a mindless brute, of a looting thug or a mooching mystic, but the life of a thinking being—not life by means of force or fraud, but life by means of achievement—not survival at any price, since there's only one price that pays for man's survival: reason.

"Man's life is the *standard* of morality, but your own life is its *purpose*. If existence on earth is your goal, you must choose your actions and values by the standard of that which is proper to man—for the purpose of preserving, fulfilling and enjoying the irreplaceable value which is your life.

"Since life requires a specific course of action, any other course will destroy it. A being who does not hold his own life as the motive and goal of his actions is acting on the motive and standard of *death*. Such a being is a metaphysical monstrosity, struggling to oppose, negate and contradict the fact of his own existence, running blindly amuck on a trail of destruction, capable of nothing but pain.

"Happiness is the successful state of life, pain is an agent of death. Happiness is that state of unconsciousness which proceeds from the achievement of one's values. A morality that dares to tell you to find happiness in the renunciation of your happiness—to value the failure of your values—is an insolent negation of morality. A doctrine that gives you, as an ideal, the role of a sacrificial animal seeking slaughter on the altars of others, is giving you *death* as your standard. By the grace of reality and the nature of life, man—every man—is an end in himself, he exists for his own sake, and the achievement of his own happiness is his highest moral purpose.

"But neither life nor happiness can be achieved by the pursuit of irrational whims. Just as man is free to attempt to survive in any random manner, but will perish unless he lives as his nature requires, so he is free to seek his happiness in any mindless fraud, but the torture of frustration is all he will find, unless he seeks the happiness proper to man. The purpose of morality is to teach you, not to suffer and die, but to enjoy yourself and live.

"Sweep aside those parasites of subsidized classrooms, who live on the profits of the mind of others and proclaim that man needs no morality, no values, no code of behavior. They, who pose as scientists and claim that man is only an animal, do not grant him inclusion in the law of existence they have granted to the lowest of insects. They recognize that every living species has a way of survival demanded by its nature, they do not claim that a fish can live out of water or that a dog can live without its sense of smell—but man, they claim, the most complex of beings, man can survive in any way whatever, man has no identity, no nature, and there's no practical reason why he cannot live with his means of survival destroyed, with his mind throttled and placed at the disposal of any orders *they* might care to issue.

"Sweep aside those hatred-eaten mystics who pose as friends of humanity and preach that the highest virtue man can practice is to hold his own life as of no value. Do they tell you that the purpose of morality is to curb man's instinct of self-preservation? It is for the purpose of self-preservation that man needs a code of morality. The only man who desires to be moral is the man who desires to live.

"No, you do not have to live; it is your basic act of choice; but if you choose to live, you must live as a man—by the work and the judgment of your mind.

"No, you do not have to live as a man: it is an act of moral choice. But you cannot live as anything else—and the alternative is that state of living death which you now see within you and around you, the state of a thing unfit for existence, no longer human and less than animal, a thing that knows nothing but pain and drags itself through its span of years in the agony of unthinking self-destruction.

"No, you do not have to think; it is an act of moral choice. But someone had to think to keep you alive; if you choose to default, you default on existence and you pass the deficit to some moral man, expecting him to sacrifice his good for the sake of letting you survive by your evil. . . .

"This much is true: the most *selfish* of all things is the independent mind that recognizes no authority higher than its own and no value higher than its judgment of truth. You are asked to sacrifice your intellectual integrity, your logic, your reason, your standard of truth—in favor of becoming a prostitute whose standard is the greatest good for the greatest number.

"If you search your code for guidance, for an answer to the question: 'What *is* the good?'—the only answer you will find is '*The good of others.*' The good is whatever others wish, whatever you feel they feel they wish, or whatever you feel they ought to feel. 'The good of others' is a magic formula that transforms anything into gold, a formula to be recited as a guarantee of moral glory and as a fumigator for any action, even the slaughter of a continent. Your standard of virtue is not an object, not an act, nor a principle, but an *intention*. You need no proof, no reasons, no success, you need not achieve *in fact* the good of others—all you need to know is that your motive was the good of others, *not* your own. Your only definition of the good is a negation: the good is the 'non-good for me.'

"Your code—which boasts that it upholds eternal, absolute, objective moral values and scorns the conditional, the relative and the subjective—your code hands out, as its version of the absolute, the following rule of moral conduct: If *you* wish it, it's evil; if others wish it, it's good; if the motive of your action is *your* welfare, don't do it; if the motive is the welfare of others, then anything goes.

"As this double-jointed, double-standard morality splits you in half, so it splits mankind into two enemy camps: one is you, the other is all the rest of humanity. You are the only outcast who has no right to wish or live. You are the only servant, the rest are the masters, you are the only giver, the rest are the takers, you are the eternal debtor, the rest are the creditors never to be paid off. You must not question their right to your sacrifice, or the nature of their wishes and their needs: their right is conferred upon them by a negative, by the fact that they are 'non-you.'

"For those of you who might ask questions, your code provides a consolation prize and booby trap: it is for your own happiness, it says, that you must serve the happiness of others, the only way to achieve your joy is to give it up to others, the only way to achieve your prosperity is to surrender your wealth to others, the only way to protect your life is to protect all men except yourself—and if you find no joy in this procedure, it is your own fault and the proof of your evil; if you were good, you would find your happiness in providing a banquet for others, and your dignity in existing on such crumbs as they might care to toss you.

"You who have no standard of self-esteem, accept the guilt and dare not ask the questions. But you know the unadmitted answer, refusing to acknowledge what you see, what hidden premise moves your world. You know it, not in honest statement, but as a dark uneasiness within you, while you flounder between guiltily cheating and grudgingly practicing a principle too vicious to name.

"I, who do not accept the unearned, neither in values nor in guilt, am here to ask the questions you evaded. Why is it moral to serve the happiness of others, but not your own? If enjoyment is a value, why is it moral when experienced by others, but immoral when experienced by you? If the sensation of eating a cake is a value, why is it an immoral indulgence in your stomach, but a moral goal for you to achieve in the stomach of others? Why is it immoral for you to desire, but moral for others to do so? Why is it immoral to produce a value and keep it, but moral to give it away? And if it is not moral for you to keep a value, why is immoral for others to accept it? If you are selfless and virtuous when you give it, are they not selfish and vicious when they take it? Does virtue consist of serving vice? Is the moral purpose of those who are good, self-immolation for the sake of those who are evil? . . .

"Under a morality of sacrifice, the first value you sacrifice is morality; the next is self-esteem. When need is the standard, every man is both victim and parasite. As a victim, he must labor to fill the needs of others, leaving himself in the position of a parasite whose needs must be filled by others. He cannot approach his fellow men except in one of two disgraceful roles: he is both a beggar and a sucker.

"You fear the man who has a dollar less than you, that dollar is rightfully his, he makes you feel like a moral defrauder. You hate the man who has a dollar more than you, that dollar is rightfully yours, he makes you feel that you are morally defrauded. The man below is a source of your guilt, the man above is a source of your frustration. You do not know what to surrender or demand, when to give and when to grab, what pleasure in life is rightfully yours and what debt is still unpaid to others—you struggle to evade, as 'theory,' the knowledge that by the moral standard you've accepted you are guilty every moment of your life, there is no mouthful of food you swallow that is not *needed* by someone somewhere on earth—and you give up the problem in blind resentment, you conclude that moral perfection is not to be achieved *or desired,* that you will muddle through by snatching as snatch can and by avoiding the eyes of the young, of those who look at you as if self-esteem were possible and they expected you to have it. Guilt is all that you retain within your soul—and so does every other man, as he goes past, avoiding *your* eyes. Do you wonder why your morality has not achieved brotherhood on earth or the good will of man to man?

"The justification of sacrifice, that your morality propounds, is more corrupt than the corruption it purports to justify. The motive of your sacrifice, it tells you, should be *love*—the love you ought to feel for every man. A morality that professes the belief that the values of the spirit are more precious than matter, a morality that teaches you to scorn a whore who gives her body indiscriminately to all men—this same morality demands that your surrender your soul to promiscuous love for all comers.

"As there can be no causeless wealth, so there can be no causeless love or any sort of causeless emotion. An emotion is a response to a fact of reality, an estimate dictated by your standards. To love is to *value.* The man who tells you that it is possible to value without values, to love those whom you appraise as worthless, is the man who tells you that it is possible to grow rich by consuming without producing and that paper money is as valuable as gold.

"Observe that he does not expect you to feel a causeless fear. When his kind get into power, they are expert at contriving means of terror, at giving you ample cause to feel the fear by which they desire to rule you. But when it comes to love, the highest of emotions, you permit them to shriek at you accusingly that you are a moral delinquent if you're incapable of feeling causeless love. When a man feels fear without reason, you call him to the attention of a psychiatrist; you are not so careful to protect the meaning, the nature and the dignity of love.

"Love is the expression of one's values, the greatest reward you can earn for the moral qualities you have achieved in your character and person, the emotional price paid by one man for the joy he receives from the virtues of another. Your morality demands that you divorce your love from values and hand it down to any vagrant, not as response to his worth, but as response to his *need*, not as reward, but as alms, not as a payment for virtues, but as a blank check on vices. Your morality tells you that the purpose of love is to set you free of the bonds of morality, that love is superior to moral judgment, that true love transcends, forgives and survives every manner of evil in its object, and the greater the love the greater the depravity it permits to be loved. To love a man for his virtues is paltry and human, it tells you; to love him for his flaws is divine. To love those who are worthy of it is self-interest; to love the unworthy is sacrifice. You owe your love to those who don't deserve it, the more love you owe them, the more loathsome the object, the nobler your love—

the more unfastidious your love, the greater your virtue—and if you can bring your soul to the state of a dump heap that welcomes anything on equal terms, if you can cease to value moral values, you have achieved the state of moral perfection.

"Such is your morality of sacrifice and such are the twin ideals it offers: to refashion the life of your body in the image of a human stockyards, and the life of your spirit in the image of a dump. . . .

"Since childhood, you have been hiding the guilty secret that you feel no desire to be moral, no desire to seek self-immolation, that you dread and hate your code, but dare not say it even to yourself, that you're devoid of those moral 'instincts' which others profess to feel. The less you felt, the louder you proclaimed your selfless love and servitude to others, in dread of ever letting them discover your own self, the self that you betrayed, the self that you kept in concealment, like a skeleton in the closet of your body. And they, who were at once your dupes and your deceivers, they listened and voiced their loud approval, in dread of ever letting you discover that they were harboring the same unspoken secret. Existence among you is a giant pretense, an act you all perform for one another, each feeling that he is the only guilty freak, each placing his moral authority in the unknowable known only to others, each faking the reality he feels they expect him to fake, none having the courage to break the vicious circle.

"No matter what dishonorable compromise you've made with your impracticable creed, no matter what miserable balance, half cynicism, half superstition, you now manage to maintain, you still preserve the root, the lethal tenet: the belief that the moral and the practical are opposites. Since childhood, you have been running from the terror of a choice you have never dared fully to identify: If the practical, whatever you must practice to exist, whatever works, succeeds, achieves your purpose, whatever brings you food and joy, whatever profits you is evil—and if the good, the moral is the *impractical*, whatever fails, destroys, frustrates, whatever injures you and brings you loss or pain—then your choice is to be moral or to live.

"The sole result of that murderous doctrine was to remove morality from life. You grew up to believe that moral laws bear no relation to the job of living, except as an impediment and threat, that man's existence is an amoral jungle where anything goes and anything works. And in that fog of switching definitions which descends upon a frozen mind, you have forgotten that the evils damned by your creed were the virtues required for living, and you have come to believe that actual evils are the *practical* means of existence. Forgetting that the impractical 'good' was self-sacrifice, you believe that self-esteem is impractical; forgetting that the practical 'evil' was production, you believe that robbery is practical. . . .

"Accept the fact that the achievement of your happiness is the only *moral* purpose of your life, and that *happiness*—not pain or mindless self-indulgence—is the proof of your moral integrity, since it is the proof and the result of your loyalty to the achievement of your values. Happiness was the responsibility you dreaded, it required the kind of rational discipline you did not value yourself enough to assume—and the anxious staleness of your days is the monument to your evasion of the knowledge that there is no moral substitute for happiness, that there is no more despicable coward than the man who deserted the battle for his joy, fearing to assert his right to existence, lacking the courage and the loyalty to life of a bird or a flower reaching for the sun. Discard the protective rags of that vice which you call a virtue: humility—learn to value yourself, which means: to fight for your happiness—and when you learn that *pride* is the sum of all virtues, you will learn to live like a man.

"As a basic step of self-esteem, learn to treat as the mark of a cannibal any man's *demand* for your help. To demand it is to claim that your life is *his* property—and loathsome as such claim might be, there's something still more loathsome: your agreement. Do you ask if it's ever proper to help another man? No—if he claims it as his right or as a moral duty that you owe him. Yes—if such is your own desire based on your own selfish pleasure in the value of his person and his struggle.

Discussion Questions

1. What philosophical argument does Ms. Rand employ to justify self-interest as the basis of morality? Do you think there are any flaws in her argument? Why or why not? Explain and defend your answer.

2. According to Ms. Rand, what is properly our higher moral purpose?

3. Conventional morality, according to Ms. Rand, has taught us how to live in a certain way, how to behave morally. What does Ms. Rand think conventional morality has taught us is immoral and evil? Do you agree with Ms. Rand's assessment of conventional morality? Why or why not? Explain and defend your answer.

4. Why should an ethical egoist, like Ms. Rand, try to persuade others to become ethical egoists, which she is evidently doing in her novel? After all, wouldn't an ethical egoist want everyone else to be altruistic while she remains an ethical egoist, since in that state of affairs she and everyone else would try to make her happy? If others were to become ethical egoists, there would be fewer people trying to make the ethical egoist happy. Wouldn't it follow then that the consistent ethical egoist ought not to persuade others of the "truth" of her doctrine, since to do so would violate her own self-interest and thus run counter to ethical egoism? How do you think the ethical egoist would respond to these questions?

7

A Critique of Ethical Egoism

James Rachels

James Rachels is Professor of Philosophy at the University of Alabama, Birmingham. He is the author of numerous scholarly articles in ethics and moral philosophy. Among his published books are *The End of Life: Euthanasia and Morality* (1986) and *The Right Thing to Do: Basic Readings in Moral Philosophy* (1989).

    In this essay Professor Rachels contends that ethical egoism fails as a moral theory. He begins by asking the question, "Is there a duty to contribute to famine relief?" He asks this question in order to bring out the moral challenge raised by ethical egoism: Do I have a moral duty to others? Professor Rachels then makes a distinction between psychological egoism and ethical egoism. The former is a theory of human nature that asserts that people do act in their self-interest even if they think or it appears to them and others that they are acting altruistically. The latter is a moral theory that claims that people ought to act in their self-interest. It is the latter view to which he is responding. Professor Rachels reviews and critiques three arguments used to support ethical egoism, including one set forth by Ayn Rand (author of the previous chapter). Although he thinks that they all fail, he believes that the last of the three is the "best try." He concludes by presenting three arguments against ethical egoism. He contends that the first two arguments come up short but that the third argument works. That last argument maintains that ethical egoism fails since it is based on preferring oneself over others, which is just as arbitrary (and thus irrational) as preferring one's racial or ethnic group over another's.

Reprinted by permission from James Rachels, *The Elements of Moral Philosophy* (New York: Random House, 1986).

Is There a Duty to Contribute for Famine Relief?

Each year millions of people die of malnutrition and related health problems. A common pattern among children in poor countries is death from dehydration caused by diarrhea brought on by malnutrition. The executive director of the United Nations Children's Fund (UNICEF) has estimated that about 15,000 children die in this way every *day*. That comes to 5,475,000 children annually. Even if this estimate is too high, the number that die is staggering.

    For those of us in the affluent countries, this poses an acute moral problem. We spend money on ourselves, not only for the necessities of life but for innumerable luxuries—for fine automobiles, fancy clothes, stereos, sports, movies, and so on. In our country, even people with modest incomes enjoy such things. The problem is that we *could* forgo our luxuries and give the money for famine relief instead. The fact that we don't suggests that we regard our luxuries as more important than feeding the hungry.

    Why do we allow people to starve to death when we could save them? Very few of us actually believe our luxuries are that important. Most of us, if asked the question directly, would probably be a bit embarrassed, and we would say that we probably should do more for famine relief. The explanation of why we do not is, at least in part, that we hardly ever think of the problem. Living our own comfortable lives, we are effectively insulated from it. The starving people are dying at some distance from us; we do not see them and we can avoid even thinking of them. When we do think of them, it is only abstractly, as bloodless statistics. Unfortunately for the starving, statistics do not have much power to motivate action.

    But leaving aside the question of *why* we behave as we do, what is our duty? What *should* we do? We might think of this as the "common-sense" view of the matter: morality requires that we balance our own interests against the interests of others. It is understandable, of course, that we look out for our own interests, and no one can be faulted for attending to his own basic needs. But at the same time the needs of others are also important, and when we can help others—especially at little cost to ourselves—we should do so. Suppose you are thinking of spending ten dollars on a trip to the movies, when you are reminded that ten dollars could buy food for a starving child. Thus you could do a great service for the child at little cost to yourself. Common-sense morality would say, then, that you should give the money for famine relief rather than spending it on the movies.

This way of thinking involves a general assumption about our moral duties: it is assumed that we have moral duties *to other people*—and not merely duties that we create, such as by making a promise or incurring a debt. We have "natural" duties to others *simply because they are people who could be helped or harmed by our actions*. If a certain action would benefit (or harm) other people, then that is a reason why we should (or should not) do that action. The common-sense assumption is that other people's interests *count,* for their own sakes, from a moral point of view.

But one person's common sense is another person's naive platitude. Some thinkers have maintained that, in fact, we have no "natural" duties to other people. *Ethical Egoism* is the idea that each person ought to pursue his or her own self-interest exclusively. It is different from Psychological Egoism, which is a theory of human nature concerned with how people *do* behave—Psychological Egoism says that people do in fact always pursue their own interests. Ethical Egoism, by contrast, is a normative theory—that is, a theory about how we *ought* to behave. Regardless of how we do behave, Ethical Egoism says we have no moral duty except to do what is best for ourselves.

It is a challenging theory. It contradicts some of our deepest moral beliefs—beliefs held by most of us, at any rate—but it is not easy to refute. We will examine the most important arguments for and against it. If it turns out to be true, then of course that is immensely important. But even if it turns out to be false, there is still much to be learned from examining it—we may, for example, gain some insight into the reasons why we *do* have obligations to other people.

But before looking at the arguments, we should be a little clearer about exactly what this theory says and what it does not say. In the first place, Ethical Egoism does not say that one should promote one's own interests *as well as* the interests of others. That would be an ordinary, unexceptional view. Ethical Egoism is the radical view that one's *only* duty is to promote one's own interests. According to Ethical Egoism, there is only one ultimate principle of conduct, the principle of self-interest, and this principle sums up *all* of one's natural duties and obligations.

However, Ethical Egoism does not say that you should *avoid* actions that help others, either. It may

very well be that in many instances your interests coincide with the interests of others, so that in helping yourself you will be aiding others willy-nilly. Or it may happen that aiding others is an effective *means* for creating some benefit for yourself. Ethical Egoism does not forbid such actions; in fact, it may demand them. The theory insists only that in such cases the benefit to others is not what makes the act right. What makes the act right is, rather, the fact that it is to one's own advantage.

Finally, Ethical Egoism does not imply that in pursuing one's interests one ought always to do what one wants to do, or what gives one the most pleasure in the short run. Someone may want to do something that is not good for himself or that will eventually cause himself more grief than pleasure—he may want to drink a lot or smoke cigarettes or take drugs or waste his best years at the race track. Ethical Egoism would frown on all this, regardless of the momentary pleasure it affords. It says that a person ought to do what *really is* to his or her own best advantage, *over the long run.* It endorses selfishness, but it doesn't endorse foolishness.

Three Arguments in Favor of Ethical Egoism

What reasons can be advanced to support this doctrine? Why should anyone think it is true? Unfortunately, the theory is asserted more often than it is argued for. Many of its supporters apparently think its truth is self-evident, so that arguments are not needed. When it *is* argued for, three lines of reasoning are most commonly used.

1. The first argument has several variations, each suggesting the same general point:

a. Each of us is intimately familiar with our own individual wants and needs. Moreover, each of us is uniquely placed to pursue those wants and needs effectively. At the same time, we know the desires and needs of other people only imperfectly, and we are not well situated to pursue them. Therefore, it is reasonable to believe that if we set out to be "our brother's keeper," we would often bungle the job and end up doing more mischief than good.

b. At the same time, the policy of "looking out for others" is an offensive intrusion into other people's privacy; it is essentially a policy of minding other people's business.

c. Making other people the object of one's "charity" is degrading to them; it robs them of their individual dignity and self-respect. The offer of charity says, in effect, that they are not competent to care for themselves; and the statement is self-fulfilling—they cease to be self-reliant and become passively dependent on others. That is why the recipients of "charity" are so often resentful rather than appreciative.

What this adds up to is that the policy of "looking out for others" is self-defeating. If we want to promote the best interests of everyone alike, we should *not* adopt so-called altruistic policies of behavior. On the contrary, if each person looks after his or her *own* interests, it is more likely that everyone will be better off, in terms of both physical and emotional well-being. Thus Robert G. Olson says in his book *The Morality of Self-Interest* (1965), "The individual is most likely to contribute to social betterment by rationally pursuing his own best long-range interests." Or as Alexander Pope said more poetically,

> Thus God and nature formed the general frame
> And bade self-love and social be the same.

It is possible to quarrel with this argument on a number of grounds. Of course no one favors bungling, butting in, or depriving people of their self-respect. But is this really what we are doing when we feed hungry children? Is the starving child in Ethiopia really harmed when we "intrude" into "her business" by supplying food? It hardly seems likely. Yet we can set this point aside, for considered as an argument for Ethical Egoism, this way of thinking has an even more serious defect.

The trouble is that it isn't really an argument for Ethical Egoism at all. The argument concludes that we should adopt certain policies of action; and on the surface they appear to be egoistic policies. However, the *reason* it is said we should adopt those policies is decidedly unegoistic. The reason is one that to an egoist shouldn't matter. It is said that we should adopt those policies because doing so will promote the "betterment of society"—but according to Ethical Egoism, that is something we should not be concerned about. Spelled out fully, with everything laid on the table, the argument says:

1. We ought to do whatever will promote the best interests of everyone alike.
2. The interests of everyone will best be promoted if each of us adopts the policy of pursuing our own interests exclusively.
3. Therefore, each of us should adopt the policy of pursuing our own interests exclusively.

If we accept this reasoning, then we are not ethical egoists at all. Even though we might end up *behaving* like egoists, our ultimate principle is one of beneficence—we are doing what we think will help everyone, not merely what we think will benefit ourselves. Rather than being egoists, we turn out to be altruists with a peculiar view of what in fact promotes the general welfare.

2. The second argument was put forward with some force by Ayn Rand, a writer little heeded by professional philosophers but who nevertheless was enormously popular on college campuses during the 1960s and 1970s. Ethical Egoism, in her view, is the only ethical philosophy that respects the integrity of the individual human life. She regarded the ethics of "altruism" as a totally destructive idea, both in society as a whole and in the lives of individuals taken in by it. Altruism, to her way of thinking, leads to a denial of the value of the individual. It says to a person: *your* life is merely something that may be sacrificed. "If a man accepts the ethics of altruism," she writes, "his first concern is not how to live his life, but how to sacrifice it." Moreover, those who would *promote* this idea are beneath contempt—they are parasites who, rather than working to build and sustain their own lives, leech off those who do. Again, she writes:

> Parasites, moochers, looters, brutes and thugs can be of no value to a human being—nor can he gain any benefit from living in a society geared to *their* needs, demands and protections, a society that treats him as a sacrificial animal and penalizes him for his virtues in order to reward *them* for their vices, which means: a society based on the ethics of altruism.

By "sacrificing one's life" Rand does not necessarily mean anything so dramatic as dying. A person's life consists (in part) of projects undertaken and goods earned and created. To demand that a person abandon his projects or give up his goods is also a clear effort to "sacrifice his life." Furthermore, throughout her writings Rand also suggests that there is a *metaphysical* basis for egoistic ethics. Somehow, it is the only ethics that takes seriously the *reality* of the individual person. She bemoans "the enormity of the extent to which altruism erodes men's capacity to grasp . . . the value of an individual life; it reveals a mind from which the reality of a human being has been wiped out."

What, then, of the starving people? It might be argued, in response, that Ethical Egoism "reveals a mind from which the reality of a human being has been wiped out"—namely, the human being who is starving. Rand quotes with approval the evasive answer given by one of her followers: "Once, when Barbara Brandon was asked by a student: 'What will happen to the poor . . .?'—she answered: 'If you want to help them, you will not be stopped.'"

All these remarks are, I think, part of one continuous argument that can be summarized like this:

1. A person has only one life to live. If we place any value on the individual—that is, if the individual has any moral worth—then we must agree that this life is of supreme importance. After all, it is all one has and all one is.
2. The ethics of altruism regards the life of the individual as something one must be ready to sacrifice for the good of others.
3. Therefore, the ethics of altruism does not take seriously the value of the human individual.
4. Ethical Egoism, which allows each person to view his or her own life as being of ultimate value, *does* take the human individual seriously—in fact, it is the only philosophy that does so.
5. Thus, Ethical Egoism is the philosophy that ought to be accepted.

The problem with this argument, as you may already have noticed, is that it relies on picturing the alternatives in such an extreme way. "The ethics of altruism" is taken to be such an extreme philosophy that *nobody*, with the possible exception of certain monks, would find it congenial. As Ayn Rand presents it, altruism implies that one's own interests have *no* value, and that *any* demand by others calls for sacrificing them. If that is the alternative, then any other view, including Ethical Egoism, will look good by comparison. But this is hardly a fair picture of the choices. What we called the common-sense view stands somewhere between the two extremes. It says that one's own interests and the interests of others are both important and must be balanced against one another. Sometimes, when the balancing is done, it will turn out that one should act in the interests of others; other times, it will turn out that one should take care of oneself. So even if the Randian argument refutes the extreme "ethics of altruism," it does not follow that one must accept the other extreme of Ethical Egoism.

3. The third line of reasoning takes a somewhat different approach. Ethical Egoism is usually presented as a *revisionist* moral philosophy, that is, as a philosophy that says our common-sense moral views are mistaken and need to be changed. It is possible, however, to interpret Ethical Egoism in a much less radical way, as a theory that *accepts* common-sense morality and offers a surprising account of its basis.

The less radical interpretation goes as follows. In everyday life, we assume that we are obliged to obey certain rules. We must avoid doing harm to others, speak the truth, keep our promises, and so on. At first glance, these duties appear to be very different from one another. They appear to have little in common. Yet from a theoretical point of view, we may wonder whether there is not some hidden *unity* underlying the hodgepodge of separate duties. Perhaps there is some small number of fundamental principles that explain all the rest, just as in physics there are basic principles that bring together and explain diverse phenomena. From a theoretical point of view, the smaller the number of basic principles, the better. Best of all would be *one* fundamental principle, from which all the rest could be derived. Ethical Egoism, then, would be the theory that all our duties are ultimately derived from the one fundamental principle of self-interest.

Taken in this way, Ethical Egoism is not such a radical doctrine. It does not challenge common-sense morality; it only tries to explain and systematize it. And it does a surprisingly successful job. It can provide plausible explanations of the duties mentioned above, and more:

a. If we make a habit of doing things that are harmful to other people, people will not be reluctant to do things that will harm us. We will be shunned and despised; others will not have us as friends and will not do us favors when we need them. If our offenses against others are serious enough, we may even end up in jail. Thus it is to our own advantage to avoid harming others.

b. If we lie to other people, we will suffer all the ill effects of a bad reputation. People will distrust us and avoid doing business with us. We will often need for people to be honest with us, but we can hardly expect them to feel much of an obligation to be honest with us if they know we have not been honest with them. Thus it is to our own advantage to be truthful.

c. It is to our own advantage to be able to enter into mutually beneficial arrangements with other people. To benefit from those arrangements, we need to be able to rely on others to keep their parts of the bargains we make with them—we need to be able to rely on them to keep their promises to us. But we can hardly expect others to keep their promises to us if we are not willing to keep our promises to them. Therefore, from the point of view of self-interest, we should keep our promises.

Pursuing this line of reasoning, Thomas Hobbes suggested that the principle of Ethical Egoism leads to nothing less than the Golden Rule: we should "do unto others" *because* if we do, others will be more likely to "do unto us."

Does this argument succeed in establishing Ethical Egoism as a viable theory of morality? It is, in my opinion at least, the best try. But there are two serious objections to it. In the first place, the argument does not prove quite as much as it needs to prove. At best, it shows only that *as a general rule* it is to one's own advantage to avoid harming others. It does not show that this is *always* so. And it could not show that, for even though it may usually be to one's advantage to avoid harming others, sometimes it is not. Sometimes one might even *gain* from treating another person badly. In that case, the obligation not to harm the other person could *not* be derived from the principle of Ethical Egoism. Thus it appears that not all our moral obligations can be explained as derivable from self-interest.

But set that point aside. There is still a more fundamental question to be asked about the proposed theory. Suppose it is true that, say, contributing money for famine relief is somehow to one's own advantage. It does not follow that this is the only reason, or even the most basic reason, why doing so is a morally good thing. (For example, the most basic reason might be *in order to help the starving people*. The fact that doing so is also to one's own advantage might be only a secondary, less important, consideration.) A demonstration that one could *derive* this duty from self-interest does not prove that self-interest is the *only reason* one has this duty. Only if you accept an additional proposition—namely, the proposition that there is no reason for giving *other than* self-interest—will you find Ethical Egoism a plausible theory.

Three Arguments against Ethical Egoism

Ethical Egoism has haunted twentieth-century moral philosophy. It has not been a popular doctrine; the most important philosophers have rejected it outright. But it has never been very far from their minds. Although no thinker of consequence has defended it, almost everyone has felt it necessary to explain why he was rejecting it—as though the very possibility that it might be correct was hanging in the air, threatening to smother their other ideas. As the merits of the various "refutations" have been debated, philosophers have returned to it again and again.

The following three arguments are typical of the refutations proposed by contemporary philosophers.

1. In his book *The Moral Point of View* (1958), Kurt Baier argues that Ethical Egoism cannot be correct because it cannot provide solutions for conflicts of interest. We need moral rules, he says, only because our interests sometimes come into conflict. (If they never conflicted, then there would be no problems to solve and hence no need for the kind of guidance that morality provides.) But Ethical Egoism does not help to resolve conflicts of interest; it only exacerbates them. Baier argues for this by introducing a fanciful example:

> Let B and K be candidates for the presidency of a certain country and let it be granted that it is in the interest of either to be elected, but that only one can succeed. It would then be in the interest of B but against the interest of K if B were elected, and vice versa, and therefore in the interest of B but against the interest of K if K were liquidated, and vice versa. But from this it would follow that B ought to liquidate K, that it is wrong for B not to do so, that B has not "done his duty" until he has liquidated K; and vice versa. Similarly K, knowing that his own liquidation is in the interest of B and therefore, anticipating B's attempts to secure it, ought to take steps to foil B's endeavors. It would be wrong for him not to do so. He would "not have done his duty" until he had made sure of stopping B. . . .
>
> This is obviously absurd. For morality is designed to apply in just such cases, namely, those where interests conflict. But if the point of view of morality were that of self-interest, then there could never be moral solutions of conflicts of interest.

Does this argument prove that Ethical Egoism is unacceptable? It does *if* the conception of morality to which it appeals is accepted. The argument assumes that an adequate morality must provide solutions for conflicts of interest in such a way that everyone concerned can live together harmoniously. The conflict between B and K, for example, should be resolved so that they would no longer be at odds with one another. (One would not then have a duty to do something that the other has a duty to prevent.) Ethical Egoism does not do that, and if you think an ethical theory should, then you will not find Ethical Egoism acceptable.

But a defender of Ethical Egoism might reply that *he* does not accept this conception of morality. For him, life is essentially a long series of conflicts in which each person is struggling to come out on top; and the principle he accepts—the principle of Ethical Egoism—simply urges each one to do his or her best to win. In his view, the moralist is not like a courtroom judge, who resolves disputes. Instead, he is like the Commissioner of Boxing, who urges each fighter to do his best. So the conflict between B and K will be "resolved" not by the application of an ethical theory but by one or the other of them winning the struggle. The egoist will not be embarrassed by this—on the contrary, he will think it no more than a realistic view of the nature of things.

2. Some philosophers, including Baier, have leveled an even more serious charge against Ethical Egoism. They have argued that it is a *logically inconsistent* doctrine—that is, they say it leads to logical contradictions. If this is true, then Ethical Egoism is indeed a mistaken theory, for no theory can be true if it is self-contradictory.

Consider B and K again. As Baier explains their predicament, it is in B's interest to kill K, and obviously it is in K's interest to prevent it. But, Baier says,

> if K prevents B from liquidating him, his act must be said to be both wrong and not wrong—wrong because it is the prevention of what B ought to do, his duty, and wrong for B not to do it; not wrong because it is what K ought to do, his duty, and wrong for K not to do it. But one and the same act (logically) cannot be both morally wrong and not morally wrong.

Now, does *this* argument prove that Ethical Egoism is unacceptable? At first glance it seems persuasive. However, it is a complicated argument, so we need to set it out with each step individually identified. Then we will be in a better position to evaluate it. Spelled out fully, it looks like this:

1. Suppose it is each person's duty to do what is in his own best interests.
2. It is in B's best interest to liquidate K.
3. It is in K's best interest to prevent B from liquidating him.
4. Therefore B's duty is to liquidate K, and K's duty is to prevent B from doing it.
5. But it is wrong to prevent someone from doing his duty.
6. Therefore it is wrong for K to prevent B from liquidating him.
7. Therefore it is both wrong and not wrong for K to prevent B from liquidating him.
8. But no act can be both wrong and not wrong—that is a self-contradiction.
9. Therefore the assumption with which we started—that it is each person's duty to do what is in his own best interests—cannot be true.

When the argument is set out in this way, we can see its hidden flaw. The logical contradiction—that it is both wrong and not wrong for K to prevent B from liquidating him—does *not* follow simply from the principle of Ethical Egoism. It follows from that principle *and* the additional premise expressed in step (5)—namely, "that it is wrong to prevent someone from doing his duty." Thus we are not compelled by the logic of the argument to reject Ethical Egoism. Instead, we could simply reject this additional premise, and the contradiction would be avoided. That is surely what the ethical egoist would want to do, for the ethical egoist would never say, without qualification, that it is always wrong to prevent someone from doing his duty. He would say, instead, that *whether one ought to prevent someone from doing his duty depends entirely on whether it would be to one's own advantage to do so.* Regardless of whether we think this is a correct view, it is, at the very least, a *consistent* view, and so this attempt to convict the egoist of self-contradiction fails.

3. Finally, we come to the argument that I think comes closest to an outright refutation of Ethical Egoism. It is also the most interesting of the arguments, because at the same time it provides the most insight into why the interests of other people *should* matter to a moral agent.

Before this argument is presented, we need to look briefly at a general point about moral values. So let us set Ethical Egoism aside for a moment and consider this related matter.

There is a whole family of moral views that have this in common: they all involve dividing people into groups and saying that the interests of some groups count for more than the interests of other groups. Racism is the most conspicuous example; it involves dividing people into groups according to race and assigning greater importance to the interests of one race than to others. The practical result is that members of the preferred race are to be *treated better* than the others. Anti-Semitism works the same way, and so can nationalism. People in the grip of such views will think, in effect: "*My* race counts for more," or "Those who believe in *my* religion count for more," or "*My* country counts for more," and so on.

Can such views be defended? Those who accept them are usually not much interested in argument—racists, for example, rarely try to offer rational grounds for their position. But suppose they did. What could they say?

There is a general principle that stands in the way of any such defense, namely: *We can justify treating people differently only if we can show that there is some factual difference between them that is relevant to justifying the difference in treatment.* For example, if one person is admitted to law school while another is rejected, this can be justified by pointing out that the first graduated from college with honors and scored well on the admissions test, while the second dropped out of college and never took the test. However, if *both* graduated with honors and did well on the entrance examination—in other words, if they are in all relevant respects equally well qualified—then it is merely arbitrary to admit one but not the other.

Can a racist point to any differences between, say, white people and black people that would justify treating them differently? In the past, racists have sometimes attempted to do this by picturing blacks as stupid, lacking in ambition, and the like. If this were true, then it might justify treating them differently, in at least some circumstances. (This is the deep purpose of racist stereotypes—to provide the "relevant differences" needed to justify differences in treatment.) But of course it is not true, and in fact there are no such general differences between the races. Thus racism is an *arbitrary* doctrine, in that it advocates treating some people differently even though there are no differences between them to justify it.

Ethical Egoism is a moral theory of the same type. It advocates that each of us divides the world into two categories of people—ourselves and all the rest—and that we regard the interests of those in the first group as more important than the interests of those in the second group. But each of us can ask, what is the difference between myself and others that justifies placing myself in this special category? Am I more intelligent? Do I enjoy my life more? Are my accomplishments greater? Do I have needs or abilities that are so different from the needs or abilities of others? *What is it that makes me so special?* Failing an answer, it turns out that Ethical Egoism is an arbitrary doc-

trine, in the same way that racism is arbitrary.

The argument, then, is this:

1. Any moral doctrine that assigns greater importance to the interests of one group than to those of another is unacceptably arbitrary unless there is some difference between the members of the groups that justifies treating them differently.
2. Ethical Egoism would have each person assign greater importance to his or her own interests than to the interests of others. *But there is no general difference between oneself and others, to which each person can appeal, that justifies this difference in treatment.*
3. Therefore, Ethical Egoism is unacceptably arbitrary.

And this, in addition to arguing against Ethical Egoism, also sheds some light on the question of why we should care about others.

We should care about the interests of other people *for the very same reason we care about our own interests;* for their needs and desires are comparable to our own. Consider, one last time, the starving people we could feed by giving up some of our luxuries. Why should we care about them? We care about ourselves, of course—if *we* were starving, we would go to almost any lengths to get food. But what is the difference between us and them? Does hunger affect them any less? Are they somehow less deserving than we? If we can find no relevant difference between us and them, then we must admit that if *our* needs should be met, so should *theirs*. It is this realization, that we are on a par with one another, that is the deepest reason why our morality must include some recognition of the needs of others, and why, then, Ethical Egoism fails as a moral theory.

Discussion Questions

1. According to Professor Rachels, what is the difference between psychological egoism and ethical egoism?

2. Professor Rachels provides three arguments for ethical egoism, all of which he critiques. Explain and present each of these arguments. Also, describe the weaknesses Professor Rachels contends that they have. Do you agree with his assessment of the arguments for ethical egoism? Why or why not? Explain and defend your answer.

3. Why does Professor Rachels believe that the third argument for ethical egoism is the "best try"?

4. Describe and explain the three arguments Professor Rachels presents against ethical egoism? Why does Professor Rachels believe that the first two arguments do not work while the last one does? What does Professor Rachels believe are the weaknesses of the first two arguments? Do you agree that the third argument succeeds? Why or why not? Explain and defend your answer.

5. Why does Professor Rachels believe that we do not do more to help starving people?

SECTION C

Values Clarification and Moral Education

There are not many issues on which liberals and conservatives agree. However, there seems to be a growing consensus that there is a moral crisis in America. For example, President Bill Clinton, in proposing his health care plan to the country, has been very vocal in calling on Americans to reflect upon their moral obligation to those less fortunate than themselves. Many have suggested that this crisis in our society requires that moral education be a part of the curriculum in our primary and secondary schools, where students during their formative years are socialized into a community of their peers.

Focusing on the public school system, former U.S. Secretary of Education William J. Bennett explains the moral crisis in that institution by contrasting the concerns of teachers in two different eras:

> Over the years teachers have been asked to identify the top problems in America's schools. In 1940 teachers identified them as talking out of turn; chewing gum; making noise; running in the hall; cutting in line; dress code infractions; and littering. When asked the same question in 1990, teachers identified drug abuse; alcohol abuse; pregnancy; suicide; rape; robbery; and assault.[1]

During the 30-year period, from 1960 to 1990, "there has been a 560 percent increase in violent crime; more than a 400 percent increase in illegitimate births; a quadrupling in divorces; a tripling of the percentage of children living in single-parent homes; more than a 200 percent increase in the teenage suicide rate; and a drop of 75 points in the average SAT scores of high school students."[2]

Many different ways to address these problems have been proposed. Some religious people have called for prayer in school as well as the teaching of explicitly theological lessons in public education, but the problem with that proposal is that it apparently violates the First Amendment's prohibition of establishing a religion. Others have suggested secular approaches that apparently give no preference to any particular value system. The most famous and influential example of this approach is *values clarification*. Developed in the 1960s by Louis Raths and Sidney Simon as well as other educators, this approach "is not concerned with the *content* of people's values, but the *process of valuing*." It is an approach that "tries to help young people answer some of these [moral] questions and build their own value system,"[3] rather than relying on their parents' moralizing. Chapter 8, written by Sidney B. Simon, Leland W. Howe, and Howard Kirschenbaum, is an essay that describes and defends this approach ("The Values Clarification Approach").

As you may guess, there are many educators who do not agree with values clarification. Many of these critics perceive it as philosophically incoherent, not established by empirical studies, morally harmful, and/or an invasion of a student's and his or her family's right to privacy. One of these critics, Professor Paul Vitz, is the author of the essay in Chapter 9 ("Why Values Clarification Must Be Rejected").

Some educators, although they do not agree with values clarification, see the danger of teaching one sectarian value system in public education. On the other hand, they recognize that there are a large number of values that must be presupposed in a free society and on which all reasonable people agree, e.g., honesty, integrity, hard work, fair play. These educators believe that public education should instill these common values in a nonsectarian manner. George Sher and William J. Bennett defend this viewpoint in Chapter 10 ("Moral Education and Indoctrination").

The essay in Chapter 11 ("Vision and Virtue"), by education professor William K. Kilpatrick, takes the position that the traditional way of teaching ethics and morality—reasoning from theories to principles and applying them to moral dilemmas—is highly contrived and artificial and should be supplemented, if not eclipsed, by virtue ethics (or character ethics), the instilling of ethics by studying the stories, lives, and example of virtuous people found in history, fiction, and mythology. This is a view championed by William J. Bennett, in his book *The Book of Virtues* (1993).

Notes

1. William J. Bennett, "Revolt against God: America's Spiritual Despair," *Policy Review* (Winter 1994): 20.
2. Ibid. These statistics are documented in William J. Bennett, *The Index of Leading Cultural Indicators* (Washington, D.C.: The Heritage Foundation, 1993).
3. Sidney B. Simon, Leland W. Howe, and Howard Kirschenbaum, *Values Clarification* (New York: Hart, 1972), 19, 18.

For Further Reading

Richard A. Baer, Jr., "Values Clarification as Indoctrination," *The Educational Forum* 41 (1977).
William J. Bennett and Ernst J. Delattre, "Moral Education in the Schools," *The Public Interest* 50 (1978).
Martin Eger, "The Conflict in Moral Education," *The Public Interest* 53 (Spring 1981).
William Kilpatrick, *Why Johnny Can't Tell Right from Wrong* (New York: Simon & Schuster, 1992).
Alan L. Lockwood, "The Effects of Values Clarification and Moral Development Curricula on School-Age Subjects: A Critical Review of Recent Research," *Review of Educational Research* 48 (1978).
_____ , "Values Education and the Right to Privacy," *Journal of Moral Education* 6 (1977).
Louis E. Raths, Merrill Harmin, and Sidney B. Simon, *Values and Teaching*, 2nd ed. (Columbus, Ohio: C. E. Merrill, 1978).
Donald Read, Sidney B. Simon, and Joel Goodman, *Health Education: The Search for Values* (Englewood Cliffs, N.J.: Prentice-Hall, 1977).
Sidney B. Simon, Leland W. Howe, and Howard Kirschenbaum, *Values Clarification*, rev. ed. (New York: Hart, 1978).
Paul Vitz, *Psychology as Religion*, 2nd ed. (Grand Rapids, Mich.: Eerdmans, 1994).

8

The Values Clarification Approach

Sidney B. Simon
Leland W. Howe
Howard Kirschenbaum

Sidney B. Simon, Leland W. Howe, and Howard Kirschenbaum have all served on the faculties of a number of universities. They have lectured and published widely in the areas of moral education and child psychology. Their book, *Values Clarification* (1972), was the standard in the field of moral education for over a decade. And although their approach has come under criticism, the values clarification approach to moral education is still very influential in the shaping of elementary and secondary education curricula. Professors Simon, Howe, and Kirschenbaum are also co-authors of *Values Clarification: A Handbook of Practical Strategies for Individuals, Families, and Groups* (1995).

In this essay the authors present and defend the employment of the values clarification approach as a program for moral education. At the beginning of this essay the authors defend the need for moral education, pointing out that students (in fact, all of us) often become confused about values and how to decide what is right or wrong. The authors reject two traditional approaches. The first, *inculcating*, is rejected because it denies people the opportunity to learn a process by which to select the best in competing value systems. For this reason, the authors claim that "inculcation cannot anticipate all choice situations or make some of life's most difficult choices much easier when the moment of truth arrives." The second approach,

Reprinted by permission from Sidney B. Simon, Leland W. Howe, and Howard Kirschenbaum, *Values Clarification: A Handbook of Practical Strategies for Individuals, Families, and Groups* (New York: Warner Books, 1995), pp. 3–12. For further information on workshops and publications on values clarification, write Values Realization Institute, Box 230, Hadley, MA 01035.

modeling, is considered flawed as well because "people are exposed to so many different models to emulate," including parents, politicians, friends, and movie stars. The authors suggest *values clarification* as the alternative to these defective approaches. Values clarification is concerned more with the *process of valuing* than the content of one's value judgments. This process is composed of seven subprocesses.

Every day, every one of us meets life situations that call for thought, decision making, and action. Some of these situations are familiar, some novel; some are casual, some are of extreme importance. Everything we do, every decision we make and course of action we take, is based on our consciously or unconsciously held beliefs, attitudes, and values.

Which car shall I buy—the stripped-down model for basic transportation or the snazzy version with all the extras?

Should Bill and I live together before marriage? Shouldn't we know if we're really compatible?

Just how much am I willing to modify my diet to reduce fat and cholesterol? How many extra weeks of living justify my giving up ice cream and chocolate cake?

What can I do to bring about political change these days?

How can I find greater spirituality? Does religion have meaning in my life, or is it simply a series of outmoded traditions and customs?

How important to me is my partner's physical appearance? How important is my own? Can I justify spending $200 on that item of clothing?

What can I do so that I don't spend my life like so many others who regret the jobs they go to every morning?

Why is it that at the end of every weekend I feel anxious and guilty about all I didn't do?

Shall I take early retirement?

Should I ask more of my children? Am I spoiling them?

What role shall I take in caring for my aging parent?

This is the only life I'm going to get. How can I make it more fun?

This is a confusing world to live in. At every turn we are forced to make choices about how to live our lives. Ideally, our choices will be made on the basis of the values we hold—the principles and priorities that are important to us. But frequently we are not clear about our own values, or we are not clear about how to translate them into daily living.

Some typical areas where we may experience confusion and conflict in values are:

politics	family
religion	friends
work	money
leisure time	aging, death
school	health
love and sex	multicultural issues
material possessions	culture (art, music, and so on)
personal tastes (clothes, hairstyle, and so on)	

All of us, young and old, often become confused about our values. Yet today we are confronted by many more choices that in previous generations. We are surrounded by a bewildering array of alternatives. Modern society has made us less provincial and more sophisticated, but the complexity of these times has made the act of choosing infinitely more difficult.

Traditionally, our values have been formed and influenced in a variety of ways. These include:

1. Inculcation

There are numerous ways that our parents, teachers, religious institutions, workplaces, and societies attempt to instill their values and to form and influence ours. By explanation, moralizing, rules, rewards, punishments, slogans, symbols, and many other methods, from birth to death, the world around us tries to pass on and perpetuate its values.

All this is appropriate and inevitable. Civilization has learned a great deal over the millennia about how to create a social order in which people can live peaceably together, secure in their persons and property, respectful of one another's liberty, working cooperatively for the common good. Although people often do not live up to those ideals, nevertheless, we hope that they will, and we know that we should, and therefore we want to pass these values on to our children and to one another. So we do our best, as Prov-

erbs suggests, "to train up the children in the way they should go," to pass on our most cherished values and beliefs to those whose lives we touch.

As important and inevitable as is the effort to inculcate the best values and the cultural wisdom we have developed, the approach of instilling values in others has certain limitations. One of these limitations is that there is so much diversity in the world around us. The direct inculcation of values works best when there is complete consistency about what constitutes "desirable" values. But consider the situation today. Parents offer one set of shoulds and should nots. The church often suggests another. The peer group offers a third view of values. Hollywood and the popular magazines, a fourth. The seventh-grade teacher, a fifth. The college professor, a sixth. The president of the United States, a seventh. The next president, an eighth. The spokespersons for the counterculture, a ninth, and on and on.

Bombarded by all these influences, we are ultimately left to make our own choices about whose advice or values to follow. Young people who have received effective inculcation of values will have some standards of value and right and wrong to apply in difficult choice situations, but inculcation cannot anticipate all choice situations or make some of life's most difficult choices much easier when the moment of truth arrives. And people who received little inculcation when they were young (e.g., their parents and other adults were absent, did not seem to care, or were ineffective) have an even tougher time of it. They have not learned a process for selecting the best and rejecting the worst elements contained in the various value systems that others have been urging them to follow. Thus, too often, the important choices in life are made on the basis of peer pressure, unthinking submission to authority, or the power of the mass media.

Another limitation with the direct inculcation of values is that it often results in a dichotomy between theory and practice; lip service is paid to the values of the authority or the culture, while behavior contradicts these values. Thus we have religious people who love their neighbors on the Sabbath and spend the rest of the week competing with them or downgrading them. And we have patriots who would deny freedom of speech to any dissenters whose concept of patriotism is different from theirs. And we have good, obedient students who sit quietly in class and wouldn't dare speak without raising their hands, but who freely interrupt their friends and parents in the middle of a sentence. Inculcation frequently influences only people's words and little else in their lives.

2. Modeling

The second major approach to transmitting values is modeling. The rationale here is: "I will present myself as an attractive model who lives by a certain set of values. The people with whom I come in contact will be duly impressed by me and by my values, and will want to adopt and emulate my attitudes and behavior."

Demonstrating something is almost always a more effective teaching method than simply talking about it. Modeling is so potent a means of value education because it presents a vivid example of values in action. Of course modeling operates whether we consciously work at being a model or not. We *do* notice how other people act and how they seem to negotiate life's many values choices. We also notice whether their behavior matches their stated beliefs. As positive models or negative ones, we each serve continually as models for one another. Young people in particular are hungry for role models and will find them among adults or their peers, for better or worse.

Modeling, like inculcation, is an important and inevitable form of values transmission, but like inculcation it also has its limitations. The main problem is that people are exposed to so many different models to emulate. Parents, teachers, politicians, movie and rock stars, friends, religious figures, literary characters, and others all present different models. How is a person to sort out all the pros and cons and achieve his or her own values? How can one tell a superficially attractive model from the model with true wisdom, morality, and happiness?

So young people and adults can benefit from good inculcation and good models. We all deserve to be exposed to responsible adults who care about our welfare, teach us the best wisdom and morality they and society have accumulated over the centuries, and model a zest and joy of living. Yet when it comes time to choose an occupation, a spouse, or a candidate, how does a person choose a course of action from among the many models and many moralizing lectures with which he or she has been bombarded? Where do we learn whether to stick to the old moral and value standards or try new ones? How

do we develop our own sense of identity? How do we learn to relate to people whose values differ from our own? What do we do when two important values are in conflict, and the more we choose one value the less we achieve of the other?

3. Values Clarification

The values-clarification approach tries to help people answer some of these questions and build their own value system. It is not a new approach. There have always been parents, teachers, and other educators dating at least back to Socrates who have sought ways to help people think through values issues for themselves. They have done this in many ways—by asking good questions, being a good listener, encouraging self-knowledge, and demonstrating trust in the seeker's ability to find the answer.

All these attitudes and techniques are part of the values-clarification process. However, the values-clarification approach utilized in this book is more systematic than more general techniques for encouraging introspection and personal decision making. It is based on the approach formulated by Louis Raths,[1] who in turn built upon the thinking of John Dewey. Unlike other theoretical approaches to values, Raths' special contribution was to focus on the *process of valuing*. His focus was on how people come to hold certain beliefs and establish certain behavior patterns.

Valuing, according to Raths, is composed of seven subprocesses:

PRIZING one's beliefs and behaviors
1. prizing and cherishing
2. publicly affirming, when appropriate

CHOOSING one's beliefs and behaviors
3. choosing from alternatives
4. choosing after consideration of consequences
5. choosing freely

ACTING on one's beliefs
6. acting
7. acting with a pattern, consistency, and repetition

In this framework, *a value* has three components—emotional, cognitive, and behavioral. Our values are based on our feelings. We don't just hold our stronger values; we care deeply and passionately about them. They are so important to us that we don't keep them hidden from the world, but in appropriate circumstances we are willing, even eager, to speak about them to others. At the same time our values are derived by a careful process of thought, in which we evaluate the pros and cons and consequences of various choices and positions, and we strive to make choices that are our own and not the result of undue peer or authority pressure. And finally, we act upon our values. We don't just say some things are important to us, but those beliefs or preferences are clearly and consistently discernible in how we live our lives.

Values, in this sense, are distinguishable from feelings, attitudes, goals, opinions, beliefs, habits, and other "value indicators." Values are those aspects of our lives that are so important and pervasive that they include feelings, thoughts, *and* behavior. By utilizing the seven processes of valuing, we are encouraged to elevate value indicators to values, that is, to begin to act on life goals that we have hitherto only wished for, to consider alternatives to behavior patterns that are perhaps no longer satisfying, to reexamine what we really prize and cherish and to act accordingly, in short, to achieve a fuller integration of our feelings, beliefs, and behavior. Thus the values-clarification approach helps people utilize the above seven processes of values in their own lives, to apply these valuing processes to already formed beliefs and behavior patterns and to those still emerging.

Because values clarification is all about developing and acting upon one's personal values, the question often arises: Is values clarification, then, a purely selfish and amoral approach to making life's decisions? Is it only about making choices to make ourselves happy and to hell with everyone else? No, for two reasons.

First, values clarification is only one part of a more comprehensive process of values formation. We don't just make decisions on our own. We are also influenced by the inculcation and modeling we have been exposed to. People are entitled to moral and caring inculcation and to wise and effective models. We are not suggesting that parents, teachers, employers, political leaders, and others do away with inculcation and modeling, but only that these traditional methods be augmented by a more conscious and deliberate approach for helping people make their own best decisions.

Second, attention to the needs and rights of others should always be a part of the values-clarification process. An essential part of examining the con-

sequences of any choice is to ask: What effect will this choice have on others around me? If there are moral issues involved, what is right or wrong? What is the ethical thing to do? If everyone followed my example, what kind of world would this become? If a person never had any inculcation about right and wrong and caring for others, he or she would be at a loss to answer such questions. This is why good inculcation and modeling are so important. Concepts of justice, ethics, and morality do not necessarily occur spontaneously; they must be instilled as well as discovered. So consideration of moral and ethical issues should be a part of the values-clarification process.

We believe that considerable empirical research and even greater practical experience in using the values-clarification approach over the past thirty years indicates that those who have utilized this approach in their lives have become less apathetic, less flighty, less conforming as well as less overdissenting. They are more zestful and energetic, more critical in their thinking, and are more likely to follow through on decisions. In the case of underachievers, values clarification has led to better success in school and on the job. And, as long as it is understood that the values-clarification process includes consideration of appropriate moral questions, values clarification leads not only to more personally satisfying choices in life but also to more socially constructive behavior.

Discussion Questions

1. What is values clarification and how does it differ from traditional approaches to moral education?

2. How do the authors defend values clarification as a moral program? Present and explain what you believe are their central reasons. Do you think there are any flaws in their case? Why or why not? Explain and defend your answer.

3. The authors claim that "the values clarification approach tries to help people . . . build their own value system." They say that one of the goals of this approach is that "by utilizing the seven processes of valuing, we are encouraged to elevate value indicators to values . . . to reexamine what we really prize and cherish and to act accordingly, in short, to achieve a fuller integration of our feelings, beliefs, and behavior. Thus the values-clarification approach helps people utilize the above seven processes of values in

their own lives, to apply these valuing processes to already formed beliefs and behavior patterns and to those still emerging." What are these seven processes? Do you think there are problems with them? Explain and defend your answer. Do you think that the authors are saying that schools should not instill any particular set of values? Explain and defend your answer.

Notes

1. Louis Raths, Louis E. Sidney B. Simon, and Merrill Harmin, *Values and Teaching* (Columbus, OH: Charles Merrill Publishing Co., 1966).

9

Why Values Clarification Must Be Rejected

Paul Vitz

Paul Vitz is Professor of Psychology at New York University. He is the author of many scholarly articles and books. Among his books are *Psychology as Religion,* 2nd ed. (1994) and *Sigmund Freud's Christian Unconscious* (1988).

In this essay Professor Vitz argues that values clarification is seriously flawed for several reasons. After presenting a brief overview of the controversial program, he first unpacks the program's philosophical assumptions, which he believes are rarely presented and never explicitly defended in the literature. Professor Vitz then goes on to point out that the two fundamental assumptions of values clarification, personal relativism and the nonexistence of objective values, entail a number of problems: (1) if there exist no objective values and all value judgments can be reduced to personal relativism, then why is values clarification *valuable* and *better* than its rivals? (2) moral relativism's basic absurdity; and (3) values clarification is a direct attack on traditional religious morality. Professor Vitz also critiques the procedures and strategies of the program: (1) it asks questions of students that presuppose without argument the social ideology of a tiny segment of American society (relativistic, very permissive, secular, openly antireligious, and generally ultraliberal); (2) it isolates the student as an individual separated from family and society and encourages the student to understand morality as self-gratification; and (3) it creates an environment in which students

with firm beliefs are made to feel uncomfortable. Professor Vitz provides two other critiques of values clarification: (1) research evaluating it has shown that it does not produce the effects its proponents claim for it; and (2) it violates the privacy rights of the student and his or her family. He concludes with a brief explanation of the popularity of values clarification as well as a call for educators to reject it. Keep in mind that Professor Vitz is critiquing the version of values clarification that was presented by the authors of Chapter 8 in 1972. However, since the authors of Chapter 8 (which was published in 1995) appeal to findings from "the past 30 years" as well as some of the same research that they appealed to in 1972 to defend their 1972 position, there is little doubt that values clarification has not undergone any essential change.

Values Clarification

This chapter presents a critical evaluation of what has been and still is the most influential model of moral education operating in the United States in recent years. That it is a self-based model should not be surprising. The specific approach, known as values clarification, was developed by Louis E. Raths and Sidney B. Simon in collaboration with several colleagues.[1] The model was first published in the 1960s, while its widespread use in the public school system came in the seventies and early eighties. But its influence is still prevalent today.

Very generally, values clarification is a set of related procedures

> designed to engage students and teachers in the active formulation and examination of values. It does not teach a particular set of values. There is no sermonizing or moralizing. The goal is to involve students in practical experiences, making them aware of *their own* feelings, *their own* ideas, *their own* beliefs, so that the choices and decisions they make are conscious and deliberate, based on *their own* value systems.[2]

As this passage demonstrates, the values clarification approach is contrasted with the traditional explicit praise of virtue and condemnation of wrongdoing (referred to pejoratively as "sermonizing"). Simon and Raths reject as hopelessly outdated any form of

Reprinted by permission from Paul Vitz, *Psychology as Religion,* 2nd ed. (Grand Rapids, Mich.: Eerdmans, 1994), Chapter 6.

"inculcation of the adults' values upon the young."[3] Direct teaching of values is outdated, they say, because today's complex society presents so many inconsistent sources of values. It is argued that "parents offer one set of should and should nots. The church often suggests another. The peer group offers a third view of values. Hollywood and the popular magazines, a fourth. . . . The spokesman for the new Left and the counterculture an eighth; and on and on."[4]

In the context of the confusing contemporary scene, the developers of values clarification reject teaching morality. They also reject indifference to the problem of values, since indifference just ignores the problem and leaves students vulnerable to unexamined influences from the popular culture. Instead, Raths and Simon and their colleagues argue that all students need to know is a process. By using this process, students will be able to select the best and reject the worst in terms of their own values and special circumstances.

To enable young people to "build their own values system," the Raths system focuses on what is conceived as the "valuing process."[5] Valuing, according to values clarification, is composed of three basic processes, each with subcategories, which are presented in the following order:

CHOOSING one's beliefs and behaviors
1. choosing from alternatives
2. choosing after consideration of consequences
3. choosing freely

PRIZING one's beliefs and behaviors
4. prizing and cherishing
5. publicly affirming, when appropriate

ACTING on one's beliefs
6. acting
7. acting with a pattern, consistency and repetition.[6]

Instead of teaching particular values, the goal is to help students apply the seven elements of valuing to beliefs and behavior patterns that are already formed and to those that are still emerging. The values clarification theorists propose classroom exercises designed to implement their process. The exercises, called "strategies," represent the major contribution of their recent writing.

Self Theory Again

Raths and his colleagues specifically note the similarity of their basic orientation to that of psychologist Carl Rogers—one of our major theorists committed to self-fulfillment and to the innate goodness of the self.[7] Additional evidence that values clarification theorists don't accept any tendency to do evil or harm others as a part of human nature is the very fact that they never even discuss the issue. Presumably, the problem of evil raises the issue of objective values, as well as the question of how to deal with the intrinsically flawed self— a self that is given absolute power in the values clarification model.

It is not just the previously discussed scientific evidence and theoretical reflection that discredit the "total intrinsic goodness" assumption. The growth of self-expression in our classrooms in the last two decades has not served to bring a glorious increase in student happiness and mental health. If anything, the great rise in student violence and the continued decline in student test scores are evidence that the opposite has occurred. In short, the assumption about the complete natural goodness of the self, which stands at the heart of the values clarification theory, is false. This weakness alone is enough to remove it as a sensible candidate for a theory of moral education.

The psychological and, one should add, educational assumptions of the values clarification theorists are rarely presented and to my knowledge never explicitly defended. But their premises are essential to the approach, and their basic assumptions about human nature and education can easily be inferred from the model. At the center of values clarification theory is the concept of the self, with a corresponding emphasis on self-expression and self-realization. The way in which this psychological notion of the self is related to the educational theory of the values clarification theorists has been nicely captured by philosopher Nicholas Wolterstorff. Here is his description:

> The fundamental theses are that each *self* comes with a variety of innate desires, interests, and motivations, that mental health and happiness will be achieved if these innate desires are allowed to find their satisfaction within the natural and social environment, and that an individual's mental health and happiness constitute his or her ultimate goal. [Such theorists characteristically stress the malleability of the natural and social environments. . . . What must be avoided at all

costs, though, is imposing the wishes and expectations of others onto the self. Down that road lie unhappiness and disease. . . .

The proper goal of the educator, then, is to provide the child with an environment which is *permissive*— in that there is no attempt to impose the wishes of others onto the child— and *nourishing*— in that it provides for the satisfaction of the child's desires and interests.

According to some, a permissive and nourishing school environment is all the child needs:

Others, however, argue that persons characteristically develop internal blockages or inhibitions of their natural desires and interests, with the result that they fall into mental disease and unhappiness. . . . [T]he school should not only provide a permissive nourishing environment, but also work to remove inhibitions on self-expression.[8]

The advocates of values clarification hold this latter view. Their procedures aim to remove any inhibitions in the realm of values (all inhibitions are negative) that students might have picked up from home, church, or elsewhere.

The view that the self is intrinsically good, that corruption comes only from one's parents and from society, arose at least in modern times with Rousseau, continued through the nineteenth century, and has culminated in the twentieth century, especially in the United States. In the recent past this self-expression or actualization theory of human nature has dominated much educational theory, even more than the field of psychology. From Rogerian therapy to Maslow's self-actualization to open classrooms to self-esteem programs and values clarification, "self theorists" as educators have sought to promote mental health and happiness through the magic door of "self-expression." If we develop unconditional trust among students (and between students and teachers), remove inhibitions, support moral relativism, and let each do his or her own thing, then all will be well. Unfortunately, such has not proven to be true.[9]

A Philosophical Critique

The actual moral position of values clarification is usually personal relativism: something is good or bad only for a given person. At other times the model seems to assume the still more drastic position that values don't actually exist—there are only things that one likes or dislikes. In both cases, it follows that blaming or praising anyone's values or behavior is to be avoided. The problem is that the relativist position involves values clarification in a number of very basic contradictions. Taken as a whole, these contradictions completely undermine the coherence of the system. The first basic contradiction is that, in spite of the personal relativity of all values, the theorists clearly believe that values clarification is good. That is, relativity aside, students should prize their model of how to clarify values. Raths and Simon attack the inculcation of traditional values by teachers. But they simultaneously urge teachers to inculcate values clarification. Indeed, when they argue for their system they moralize and sermonize like anyone else. They criticize traditional teaching of values as "selling," "pushing," and "forcing one's own pet values" on children. But when it comes to the value of their own position, relativism has conveniently disappeared, and they push their moral position with their own sermons.

The second major contradiction in values clarification derives from the basic absurdity of moral relativism. This is beautifully identified by Wolterstorff, whose analysis follows.

When values clarification brings up the question of whether children in the classroom should be allowed to choose anything they wish, the answer is "No." Teachers have the right to set some "choices" as off limits. But they have this right, not because the choices are wrong, but because certain choices would be *intolerable* to the teacher. As Wolterstorff cogently concludes, values clarification turns into arbitrary authority. This most disturbing "logic" is instructively portrayed by values clarification theorists themselves in the following example:

Teacher: So some of you think it is best to be honest on tests, is that right? (Some heads nod affirmatively.) And some of you think dishonesty is all right? (A few hesitant and slight nods.) And I guess some of you are not certain. (Heads nod.) . . .

Ginger: Does that mean that we can decide for ourselves whether we should be honest on tests here?

Teacher: No, that means that you can decide on the value. I personally value honesty; and although you may choose to be dishonest, I shall insist that we be honest on our tests here. In other areas of your life, you may have more freedom to be dishonest, but one can't do *anything any time,* and in this class I shall expect honesty on tests.

Ginger: But then how can we decide for ourselves? Aren't you telling us what to value?

Sam: Sure, you're telling us what we should do and believe in.

Teacher: Not exactly. I don't mean to tell you what you should value. That's up to you. But I do mean that in this class, not elsewhere necessarily, you have to be honest on tests or suffer certain consequences. I merely mean that I cannot give tests without the rule of honesty. All of you who choose dishonesty as a value may not practice it here, that's all I'm saying. Further questions anyone?[10]

From this startling example, we might suggest the following analogies: "You may steal in other stores, but I shall expect and insist on honesty in my store"; likewise, "You are not to be a racist—or a rapist—in my class, but elsewhere that is up to you." You may have "more freedom" somewhere else!

The only rationale for forbidding a particular choice in the classroom is that the teacher finds the choice personally offensive or inconvenient. And, of course, teachers (usually!) also have the power to enforce their will.

As previously mentioned, the values clarification theorists explicitly support the position that each student should choose and develop his or her own morality. That is, morality is relative to each individual. The advocates of values clarification should acknowledge—although they don't—that as a result their theory, their system, pushes and indoctrinates one particular interpretation of morality. Out of all the many different approaches to morality and to values, only theirs is singled out for approval.

A further major problem raised by a morality of personal relativism is that it explicitly rejects all absolute or nonrelativist interpretations of the moral life. In particular, values clarification represents a direct attack on traditional religious morality. For example, traditional Jews, Christians, Muslims, and Hindus would all reject values clarification. For that matter, the morality of Aristotle or any contemporary representative of such a "noble pagan" view is also

rejected by those advocating values clarification. There is a serious political issue here. The public schools in recent years have given values clarification much support, and in so doing the schools have given the morality of personal relativism a privileged position. That is, the public schools have used tax money systematically to attack the values of those students and parents who believe that certain values are true, especially those who have a traditional religious position. Such a policy is a serious injustice to those taxpayers who expect that in the public school classroom their values will be treated with respect or at least will be left alone.

A Critique of Procedures and Strategies

A major part of values clarification is comprised by the classroom exercises that exemplify the system in action. These exercises are called "strategies," and they are easily used vehicles for discussing and clarifying values within the framework of the values clarification philosophy. There are more than seventy strategies, and they have been a major reason for the popularity of the approach. Even those educators who are aware of the relativistic philosophy of values clarification have often used the exercises under the assumption that they are neutral tools with which to approach the topic of moral education.[11]

First, the strategies involve questions that are asked of the students, questions that embody the social ideology of a small segment of American society. The questions are reliably secular, relativistic, very permissive, openly antireligious, and generally ultraliberal. This is, of course, a perfectly legitimate position in American society—but it has no right to be accorded special status in our public schools.

In addition, the procedures always focus on the isolated individual, separated from family and society, making choices based on the clarity and personal appeal of each alternative value. Such a procedure, as Bennett and Delattre point out, strongly encourages the student to understand morality as self-gratification.

The common procedures of values clarification have other negative consequences. The procedural goal of having the teacher try to increase the number of alternative moral positions propounded by students on a given issue reinforces the idea that values are relative to each person. Each of the potential different values, for example, about premarital chastity is likely to be embodied by at least one of the students' peers. This makes it psychologically very hard to maintain a firm belief in any absolute value without experiencing painful peer rejection. It is very difficult even for adults to reject a belief without also seeming to reject the person who holds the belief.

Another type of bias in a values clarification strategy for use with adults is quoted from an article by Bennett and Delattre:

> In *Priorities*, Simon "asks you and your family at the dinner table, or your friends across the lunch table, to rank choices and to defend those choices in friendly discussion." One example of Simon's "delightful possibilities" for mealtime discussion is this:
>
> > Your husband or wife is a very attractive person. Your best friend is very attracted to him or her. How would you want them to behave?
> >
> > a. Maintain a clandestine relationship so you wouldn't know about it.
> > b. Be honest and accept the reality of the relationship.
> > c. Proceed with a divorce.
> >
> > In this exercise . . . [a]ll possibilities for self-restraint, fidelity, regard for others, or respect for mutual relationships and commitments are ignored.[12]

This example, with its biased and limited options, speaks for itself about the values clarification system.

Research Evaluating Values Clarification

In contrast to the clear negative side effects of values clarification just mentioned—for example, pushing a particular social ideology, encouraging self-indulgence, ignoring or rejecting parental values—the *direct*, intended effects of values clarification are very limited. Despite the high level of interest in and writing about this approach, only a small proportion of these writings represents focused, relatively rigorous research. In other words, much of the writing has been either of the how-to-do-it variety or general pleadings for the approach. There has been only modest attention to whether it actually does what its proponents say it should.

The advocates of values clarification have contended that their aim is not to change students' states of mind but their actual behavior. But when their definitions of behavior are articulated, we dis-

cover that the desired "behaviors" come close to states of mind. The proponents want students to overcome apathy, overconformity, flightiness, etc., and to acquire "purposeful, proud, positive and enthusiastic behavior patterns." (Note that all of these moderately positive traits can be directed toward either moral or immoral ends; for example, Hitler and Stalin were certainly purposeful, proud, and enthusiastic.) The practical fact is that most of the limited research on values clarification has been directed toward paper and pencil tests that evaluate students' states of mind. In these studies, some students were exposed to values clarification approaches, while other students were not. Then both groups of students were tested to see whether the experimental or control groups shifted their patterns of values toward becoming more positive, proud, and so on.

Leming has examined the relatively few good-quality studies of the values clarification approach.[13] He determined that these studies applied, among themselves, seventy separate tests of statistical significance to the data assembled (many studies applied two or more such tests). Of the seventy tests, only fifteen (twenty-one percent) showed that the experimental group moved significantly in the appropriate direction. In the other fifty-five tests, either there was no significant movement or the movement was in the wrong direction. Another thorough review of the research reported approximately similar negative conclusions about values clarification having any predicted effects.[14]

Thus it appears that, even in paper and pencil tests, values clarification does not typically produce the effects its supporters claim for it. This does not mean that values clarification has no effects; it only means that it does not appear to generate the effects its designers hoped to produce. Whether it promotes negative side effects on students and whether the effects it does produce are good or bad were not issues addressed in the evaluative research.

We must also, of course, be concerned with the question of whether the approach, if it does work, is a good idea in terms of its own assumptions. The obvious assumptions underlying the approach are (a) that it is important that people in general, and young persons in particular, believe strongly in whatever they value and (b) that the values they choose without adult intervention will be desirable or good. Neither common sense nor research supports these assumptions. Clearly, on many occasions, tentativeness and open-mindedness are normal and healthy characteristics—they suggest a willingness to learn or to consider both sides. In addition, when someone has a correct opinion and must carry it out in the face of resistance, then pride and certitude may be desirable. But under other circumstances, such characteristics can be associated with arrogance and dogmatism. As to the assumption that young people will usually choose good values without special instruction, as we noted above, this is a naive view of human nature. In fact, our opinions about important social issues are always largely shaped by the socializing environment around us. Thus, adolescent declarations to the contrary, young peoples' values are significantly affected by adult influences. If responsible adults, such as teachers, do not try to promote good values, then irresponsible sources—gangs, TV, or other media— may succeed in promoting bad ones, even if the youths who apply such values believe they are reaching their own conclusions.

A Violation of Privacy Critique

The techniques and strategies of values clarification often very seriously violate the privacy of the student and the student's family. In fact, parents disturbed by the loss of personal privacy have been some of the most vocal and effective critics of values clarification and related procedures used in the schools.[15] The exact nature of this important criticism has been spelled out by Professor Alan L. Lockwood,[16] and his analysis will be summarized here.

To begin with, for all Americans personal privacy is considered to be something of great value, and a general right to such privacy is assumed. Reasons for this are worth mentioning. Privacy protects us from public embarrassment or ridicule. "For example, consider the probability of hazing were it known that the captain of the football team slept with a tattered, old teddy bear. Similarly we could predict adverse social reaction were it known that a person, currently living in a racist community, were coming to believe in racial integration."[17]

Privacy also helps to maintain our psychological well-being. We need privacy to get rest from the pressures and demands of life. We need time to reflect privately about our life. It is hard to imagine how this reflection could function if we were under frequent pressure to reveal our feelings, thoughts, and plans—often when they are only tentative and partially formed. Even more crucial to psychological well-being is the very private inner core of beliefs, hopes, faith, and ultimate secrets that everyone has at the center of their personality. To be forced to expose these to the public view is for most people to threaten basic psychological integrity.

Lockwood also notes that "privacy is . . . essential for preserving liberties characteristic of a political democracy."[18] Secret ballots, the right to assembly, and many of our other liberties are only possible if social and government surveillance is limited and our privacy is maintained. The right to privacy is, Lockwood mentions, not an absolute right since there are many kinds of information that the state, the schools, and other public institutions need in order to function properly. Nevertheless, the right to privacy is a very important one, and invasions of it should never be allowed except when fully justified.

In order to maintain our privacy, we need to be able to control information about ourselves. This means that, when information is requested, one must be informed about what information is being requested and what it will be used for. That is, there must be *informed consent*. Certain ways of getting information undermine a person's informed consent. First, informed consent requires a mature judgment— something no child is likely to have. Second, the information being requested must be clearly specified. However, many psychological tests, such as projective tests, elicit information that the person doesn't know is being asked for—for example, when subjects are asked to respond to the Rorschach inkblots or when subjects are asked to complete sentences. In these situations people may reveal information about themselves of which they are quite unaware. Of course, if the person is doing this within the context of psychotherapy there is no violation of privacy, since the person has sought out psychological help and the therapist is trained in the use of such information and is legally bound to secrecy. But when a teacher, playing amateur psychologist, requests such information in a classroom setting, a violation of privacy is very likely.

Another way in which informed consent is violated occurs when the person giving the information is under strong group pressure to be especially open with personal information. (Again, if the individual in question has chosen to go into group therapy and knows this pressure is going to develop, there is normally no violation of the right to privacy.)

As Lockwood makes clear, many of the questions that are used in values clarification violate students' right to privacy. In particular, questions about the interpersonal dynamics of family life, about personal, emotional life, and about general world-views—all are almost certain to invade one's personal life. Lockwood notes the following questions from the values clarification handbook:

> *Family dynamics:* What does your mother do? Does she like it? Is she home a lot? What disturbs you most about your parents? Reveal who in your family brings you the greatest sadness, and why?
>
> *Personal behavior and emotions:* Recall the last ten times you have cried. What was each about? Is there something you once did that you are ashamed of? What do you dream at night? The subject I would be most reluctant to discuss here is . . .
>
> *General world view:* How many of you think that parents should teach their children to masturbate? If your parents were in constant conflict, which would you rather have them do: get divorced and your father leave home, stay together and hide their feelings for the sake of the children, get divorced and you stay with your father?[19]

Clearly, the above questions are likely to violate the privacy of the child or the parents or both. Keep in mind that there is strong group pressure in the classroom setting where the questions are asked, that the answers will often become public knowledge in the school and community, that the children are too young to give truly informed consent, that the teachers or facilitators are untrained in psychology, and that the students—still less, the parents—have never agreed to participate in such a process.

To undermine privacy even further, values clarification questions are often open-ended in a way that makes them a projective technique. Lockwood gives these examples of values clarification sentences that students are to complete:

> Secretly I wish . . .
>
> I'd like to tell my best friend . . .
>
> My parents are usually . . .
>
> I often find myself . . .[20]

Lockwood concludes from his analysis that "a substantial proportion of the content and methods of Values Clarification constitute a threat to the privacy rights of students and their families."[21] The strength and clarity of Lockwood's analysis should make it clear that this criticism alone is enough to reject the values clarification approach to morality in any school where informed student and parent consent has not been obtained.

Why Has Values Clarification Been So Popular?

Given the obvious serious problems with values clarification, a natural question arises: Why has it been so popular? And it has been very popular indeed. Values clarification theorists were enthusiastically received speakers at scores of education conferences. Their books sold hundreds of thousands of copies. Workshops showing teachers how to use values clarification in the classroom were common at countless national and regional meetings of teachers and educators. Tens of thousands of teachers were trained to use it. As a result, values clarification spread quickly throughout the country in the 1970s, and many aspects of it are still prevalent in school courses in the 1990s, especially those courses dealing with values or value-laden topics— for example, drug, health, and sex education programs.

The major reasons for the popularity of values clarification seem to be the following:

1. For the students, the many strategies required no prior preparation; they were easily grasped and led to spirited classroom discussion.
2. The teacher was only a facilitator—not a true teacher—since there was no actual knowledge to be passed on. As a result, little preparation was required of the teacher, and exams were usually unnecessary. After all, there were no right or wrong answers. The spirited and active discussions implied that the class had been a success.
3. The entire philosophy of letting each student pick his or her own values fitted in easily with our consumer society. People picked value systems rather like they picked a magazine to read, a movie to see, or a brand of soap to use.
4. The alternative seemed to be the direct teaching of particular values, and this seemed almost impossible to do. It seemed impossible because the reasons justifying

many values were no longer familiar to teachers or students and seemed easily rebutted. Teaching specific values required prior training and knowledge justifying particular values, but most teachers had never received this training or the appropriate knowledge. Finally, the only way to teach such values seemed to involve heavy doses of lecturing or sermonizing. This kind of teaching is hard to do and is often rightly unpopular with students.

5. Many teachers had come to believe that, in a pluralistic society, teaching any value might be illegal. That is, a parent might complain or even sue if a teacher taught a value that the parent rejected. Along with this fear was the belief— at least at first— that values clarification was value-free or neutral, as its proponents claimed.

Conclusion: Why Values Clarification Must Be Rejected

In spite of the immediate appeal of letting each student pick his or her own values (personal relativism), the values clarification approach must be firmly rejected. The major reasons for this are that individual relativism leads to social anarchy and that it flies in the face of simple common sense.

The issue of social anarchy may sound abstract and distant, but it is actually concrete and in each citizen's backyard. For example, racism is perfectly okay in the values clarification system. Remember that to hate people because of their race or religion or ethnic background is fine as long as the student chooses it. To reject school itself, to say "yes" to drugs, to cheat on exams, to steal from your schoolmates— all of these choices are okay if values are up to each person. These behaviors cannot be rejected by values clarification advocates.

Common sense tells us that certain values (or virtues) are regularly admired and accepted as obviously valid. Everywhere such traits as honesty, altruism, heroism, hard work, and loyalty are admired, and the liar, the thief, the coward, the lazy, the selfish, and the traitor are rejected. In short, there are cross-cultural values and character traits that go with them. Furthermore, the other criticisms mentioned put the final nails in the coffin of values clarification. Recall that values clarification takes as

a fundamental assumption that the self is entirely good, without the slightest tendency to harm or exploit others. In addition, the strategies and exercises used in values clarification often contain particular ideological biases, and the questions used often violate the privacy of the student and the student's family.

Very simply put, the contradictions and incoherence of values clarification demonstrate that it is a simple-minded, intellectually incompetent system. In schools throughout the country, primarily because of parental protest, values clarification has lost some of its acceptance; nevertheless, its widespread success reveals the disturbing prevalence of a confused moral relativism in much of American education.[22]

Unfortunately, this moral relativism based on the complete autonomy of the self remains, even today, a part of many programs. The name "values clarification" is gone—but the same self-oriented moral relativism, under other names, continues to undermine the moral life of our children. Be on your guard against programs that focus on "deciding," "choosing," "decision making," etc. Programs that emphasize the *process* of deciding, and ignore the *content* of what is chosen, are almost always relativistic.

Discussion Questions

1. Present and explain Professor Vitz's philosophical critique of values clarification. Do you think it succeeds? Why or why not? Explain and defend your case.

2. Present and explain Professor Vitz's critique of the strategies and procedures of values clarification. Do you think it succeeds? Why or why not? Explain and defend your case.

3. Professor Vitz claims that (1) research has shown that values clarification has failed, and (2) the program violates the privacy rights of students and their families. Present and explain his arguments for these two claims. Do you think they succeed? Why or why not? Explain and defend your case.

Notes

This chapter was supported by a contract from the Department of Education, "Toward a Psychology of Character Education," and by NIE Grant NIEG-84-0012 (Project No. 2-0099), "Equity in Values Education."

1. See L. E. Raths, M. Harmin, and S. B. Simon, *Values and Teaching*, 2d ed. (Columbus: C.E. Merrill, 1978); S. B. Simon, L. W. Howe, and H. Kirschenbaum, *Values Clarification*, rev. ed. (New York: Hart, 1978).

2. Simon, Howe, and Kirschenbaum, *Values Clarification*, back cover; also pp. 18–22. Italics in original.

3. Simon, Howe, and Kirschenbaum, *Values Clarification*, p. 15.

4. Simon, Howe, and Kirschenbaum, *Values Clarification*, p. 16.

5. Simon, Howe, and Kirschenbaum, *Values Clarification*, pp. 18–19.

6. The order choosing, prizing, acting is from Raths, Harmin, and Simon, *Values and Teaching*, p. 30. For reasons that are not clear, in their very popular book *Values Clarification*, Simon, Howe, and Kirschenbaum propose a different order: first prizing, then choosing, then acting. This order is no accident or error, since it is stated with emphasis on p. 9 and brought up later in connection with one of the strategies (p. 36). In that book, little attention is paid to where students get their initial values. The primary emphasis is on prizing already-existing values. Thus there is no concern with whether or not the values of these young students are *worth* prizing. (That would obviously raise the disturbing prospect of objective criteria for values.)

7. Raths, Harmin, and Simon, *Values and Teaching*, p. 9.

8. Nicholas Wolterstorff, *Educating for Responsible Action* (Grand Rapids: Eerdmans, 1980), pp. 17–18.

9. For a powerful critique of Carl Rogers's ideas as applied to education, see the remarks by William A. Coulson, a former associate of Rogers, as quoted extensively in Pearl Evans, *Hidden Danger in the Classroom* (Petaluma, CA: Small Helm Press, 1990). Coulson's revelations and analysis are required reading for anyone trying to evaluate Rogers's effects on education.

10. Wolterstorff, *Educating for Responsible Action*, pp. 127–29; see also Raths, Harmin, and Simon, *Values and Teaching*, pp. 114–15.

11. For strategies, see Simon, Howe, and Kirschenbaum, *Values Clarification*. For critiques of values clarification, see the following articles by Richard A. Baer, Jr.: "Values Clarification as Indoctrination," *The Educational Forum* 41 (1977): 155–65; "A Critique of the Use of Values Clarification in Environmental Education," *The Journal of Environmental Education* 12 (1980): 13–16; and "Teaching Values in the Schools," *Principal* (January 1982): 17–21, 36. See also William J. Bennett and Ernst J. Delattre, "Moral Education in the Schools," *Public Interest* 50 (1978): 81–98; and Paul C. Vitz, "Values Clarification in the Schools," *New Oxford Review* 48 (June 1981): 15–20.

12. Bennett and Delattre, "Moral Education in the Schools," pp. 81–98.

13. J. S. Leming, "Curricular Effectiveness in Moral Values Education: A Review of the Research," *Journal of Moral Education* 10 (1981): 147–84.

14. Alan L. Lockwood, "The Effects of Values Clarification and Moral Development Curricula on School-Age Subjects: A Critical Review of Recent Research," *Review of Educational Research* 48 (1978): 325–64.

15. See, e.g., Martin Eger, "The Conflict in Moral Education," *The Public Interest*, Spring 1981, pp. 62–80.

16. Alan L. Lockwood, "Values Education and the Right to Privacy," *Journal of Moral Education* 6 (1977): 9–26.

17. Lockwood, "Values Education," p. 10.

18. Lockwood, "Values Education," p. 11.

19. Lockwood, "Values Education," p. 18.

20. Lockwood, "Values Education," p. 19.

21. Lockwood, "Values Education," p. 19.

22. For a thoroughgoing analysis of the failure of moral education in today's schools, see W. Kirk Kilpatrick, *Why Johnny Can't Tell Right from Wrong* (New York: Simon and Schuster, 1992).

10

Moral Education and Indoctrination

George Sher
William J. Bennett

George Sher is Herbert S. Autrey Professor of Philosophy at Rice University (Houston, Texas). He is the author of many articles on metaphysics and moral philosophy, and has written the book *Desert* (1987). William J. Bennett, Distinguished Fellow in Cultural Policy Studies at the Heritage Foundation and co-director of Empower America, is the author of numerous articles and books on education, public policy, and ethics. Among his books are *The Book of Virtues* (1993) and *Devaluing America* (1992). As a member of President Ronald Reagan's administration, Dr. Bennett first served as chairman of the National Endowment for the Humanities, and then as Secretary of Education.

In this essay Professor Sher and Dr. Bennett defend directive moral education, the view that maintains that students ought to be explicitly encouraged to subscribe to certain core values (e.g., treating others as you would want them to treat you, respecting values that undergird our constitutional democracy) as morally correct and to develop certain virtues (e.g., courage, honesty, self-discipline) through reward, punishment, example, and classroom instruction. They respond to two objections to their view. The first is that directive moral education violates the child's autonomy. The authors respond by saying that what matters is the autonomy of the adult the child will become, and that the imparting of certain values and the cultivation of certain virtues contributes to creating a morally autonomous adult. The second objection is that directive moral education transgresses the

American ideals of pluralism and tolerance. They respond to this in two ways: (1) the pluralist, by proposing pluralism and tolerance as American ideals, is involved in directive moral education since she is saying that certain values must be inculcated in our youth, namely, pluralism and tolerance; and (2) although there is danger that fanatics could misuse the system, Professor Sher and Dr. Bennett argue that the problem can be circumvented if teachers are required to teach those values that meet "high standards of justification," such as honesty, fairness, and consideration of others.

It is now widely agreed that educators have no business inculcating moral views in the classroom. According to many philosophers and educational theorists, all attempts to influence students' moral behavior through exhortation and personal example are indoctrinative and should give way to more discursive afforts to guide children in developing their own values.[1] Yet although the nondirective approach to moral education has become the new orthodoxy, its philosophical underpinnings remain largely unexplored. In particular, the familiar charge that all directive moral education is indoctrinative has not been carefully defended. In this paper, we will argue that no plausible version of it *can* be defended and that adequate moral education must include both directive *and* discursive elements. Because the charge of indoctrination is so unclear, we will not confront it directly. Instead, we will address two closely related claims: that directive moral education (1) violates a student's autonomy, and (2) involves sectarian teaching inappropriate to a pluralistic society. If these complaints can be shown to lack substance, then the charge of indoctrination will carry little weight.

I

Before discussing the major objections to directive moral education, we must make clearer what such education involves. In particular, we must specify (a) the traits and principles to be taught, and (b) the relevant methods of teaching them, and (c) the positive reasons for adopting such methods.

The traits and principles we have in mind are best illustrated by example. In Talawanda, Ohio, the local school district recently took the position that

Reprinted by permission from *The Journal of Philosophy* (November 1982).

"the schools should help students realize the importance" of principles and traits including:

- Achieving self-discipline, defined as the strength to do what we believe we should do, even when we would rather not do it.
- Being trustworthy, so that when we say will or will not do something, we can be believed.
- Telling the truth, especially when it hurts us to do so.
- Having the courage to resist group pressures to do what we believe, when alone, that we should not do.
- Using honorable means, those that respect the rights of others, in seeking our individual and collective ends.
- Conducting ourselves, where significant moral behavior is involved, in a manner which does not fear exposure.
- Having the courage to say, "I'm sorry, I was wrong."
- Treating others as we would wish to be treated; recognizing that this principle applies to persons of every class, race, nationality, and religion.
- Doing work well, whatever that work may be.
- Respecting the democratic values of free speech, a free press, freedom of assembly, freedom of religion, and due process of law. Recognizing that this principle applies to speech we abhor, groups we dislike, persons we despise.

Later, we will discuss the degree to which the Talawanda list embodies moral or ideological bias. For now, it suffices to note that the items just listed are close to noncontroversial within our society. They illustrate, but do not exhaust, the traits and principles whose directive teaching we will discuss.

What, exactly, does such teaching involve? Although a full account is again impossible, certain elements stand out. Of these, perhaps the most important is a teacher or administrator's willingness to demonstrate that he himself endorses certain principles—that he accepts them as guides to his own conduct and expects his students to do likewise. This requires that he act as an intentional model of behavior in accordance with the favored principles. It also requires that he explicitly urge his students to develop habits of acting in similar ways and that he express his disapproval, both verbally and through punishment, when his expectations are not met. It is

often desirable to explain why one should act in the relevant ways, but efforts to influence behavior should not be confined to such explanations. Both encouragement and expressions of disapproval may persist when the proffered reasons are not grasped.

Why should morality be taught in these ways? Quite obviously, any rationale for adopting directive methods must be an instrumental one. The claim must be that, at elementary levels of development, such methods are effective ways of getting children to internalize desirable habits and behave in desirable ways and that, at more advanced levels, the previous application of these methods is necessary for the success of more discursive methods. We believe these claims are supported by recent studies of child and adolescent development and "moral psychology."[2] However, even if all empirical issues remained open, the permissibility of directive moral education would still be worth ascertaining. Even those who are not convinced that such methods work must be interested in learning whether we would be morally permitted to employ them if they did.

II

Consider, first, the objection that directive moral education violates autonomy. At the core of this objection is a distinction between actions produced by nonrational causes and actions motivated by an awareness of the reasons for performing them. When a child acts to imitate a respected model or in response to exhortation or threat, he is said to be motivated only in the former way. Even if there are good reasons for his action, the very same techniques that have motivated his act could just as well have been used to motivate behavior unsupported by such reasons. Thus, his behavior is evidently not produced simply by his appreciation of the reasons for it. Hence, it is said to be neither fully his own nor an appropriate object of moral appraisal.

There is plainly something right about this objection. On any plausible account, an adequate moral education must produce not only a tendency to act rightly, but also a tendency to do so for the right reasons. But, despite its superficial clarity, the objection as stated is both ambiguous and incomplete. It is ambiguous because it does not specify whether the person whose autonomy is violated is the child to whom directive education is administered or the adult whom the child will later become. It is incomplete because it does not explain *how* autonomy is violated in either case.

Whose autonomy is violated by directive moral education? Of the two possible answers, the more straightforward is "the child's." But to this answer, there is a quick rejoinder. However desirable it is to appeal to a person's appreciation of reasons, it surely need not be wrong to influence his behavior in other ways when he cannot respond to reasons alone. But this is manifestly true of young children. With them, appeals to principle simply fail. We must ascend the developmental scale quite far before such appeals promise much success. According to the leading proponent of nondirective moral education, Lawrence Kohlberg, the most common motive for moral action among 13-year-olds is still a desire to avoid disapproval and dislike by others.[3] In Kohlberg's typology, this motive is three full stages away from conscientious aversion to self-reproach. Moreover, in Kohlberg's view, one cannot reach a given stage of moral development without first traversing all the lower stages. Thus, even Kohlberg must acknowledge that, before middle adolescence, most children cannot respond to unadorned appeals to moral reasons. But if so, we do not violate their autonomy when we supplement such appeals with more efficacious influences.

This reply may appear inconclusive; for the opponent of directive moral education can respond by weakening his requirements for autonomy. Instead of contending that moral autonomy requires that one act from moral reasons, he can assert that it requires only that one's motives be those of the highest Kohlbergian level available to one. If so, even a child who acts to satisfy an impersonally construed authority (Kohlberg's level 4) may act significantly more autonomously than one who seeks to imitate a respected elder or to avoid punishment. However, considered by itself, such denatured "autonomy" has little value. Its main significance is pretty clearly to pave the way for further moral development. Thus, the response does not really save the claim that directive techniques violate a child's autonomy. If anything, it reinforces the claim that what is violated is the autonomy of the adult whom the child will become.

Put in this second form, the objection no longer presupposes an obviously impossible ideal of autonomy. Unlike children, mature adults often do seem to respond to moral reasons. But why should the previous application of directive techniques be thought to prevent this? It is true that directive techniques use nonrational means to produce desires and character traits that will eventually influence one's adult actions. However, even if an adult is motivated by a desire that was originally produced by nonrational means, it still seems possible for his action to be done for good moral reasons. In particular, this still seems possible if his nonrationally produced desire is precisely to act *in accordance with* such reasons. But it is surely just this desire which the sensitive practitioner of directive moral education seeks to instill.

If moral autonomy required only action in accordance with moral reasons, this response would be decisive. However, another strain of thought construes the requirements for autonomy more strictly. On this view, genuine moral autonomy requires not only that an agent act *in accordance with* moral reasons, but also that he be motivated by his awareness of them. In Kantian terms, the autonomous agent must be "self-legislating." On this expanded account the effectiveness of a past directive education may again seem threatening to current autonomy. If without his past directive education the agent would not now act as he does, then it is apparently just the desires produced by that education which supply the motivational energy for his current act. But if so, that motivational energy is evidently *not* supplied by his recognition of reasons themselves. His recognition of reasons may *trigger* the motivational energy for his act; but what is triggered is still energy with an independent source. Hence, the requirements for moral autonomy still seem unsatisfied.

With this refinement, we approach the heart of the objection that directive moral education violates autonomy. But although the refinement is familiar, the resulting argument is problematical. Most obviously, it rests on both the obscure metaphor of motivational energy and the undefended requirement that autonomous acts must draw such energy from reasons themselves. But the difficulty goes deeper. Even if its premises were both intelligible and defensible, the argument would be a non sequitur. Although it purports to demonstrate that directive moral education *violates* moral autonomy, it really shows only that such education does not *contribute* to moral autonomy. Far from establishing that directive techniques are pernicious, it at best establishes that they are morally neutral.

For why *should* desires produced by nonrational techniques be thought to prevent one from being motivated by an appreciation of reasons? Is the point merely that anyone subject to nonrationally produced desires would perform his act even if he were *not* motivated by an appreciation of the moral reasons for it? If so, then the most that follows is that his act is motivationally overdetermined. Since this does not negate the motivating force of his appreciation of reasons, it does not undermine his autonomy. Is the point rather that, if one's directively induced desires are required to produce one's action, then the motivation supplied by one's appreciation of reasons is too *weak* to produce it—that the latter motivation requires supplementation? If so, then, without his directive moral education, the agent would not have performed the act at all, and so *a fortiori;* would not have performed it autonomously. Here again, nothing suggests that his directive moral education has reduced or violated his autonomy.

Given these considerations, even the strengthened analysis of autonomy does not establish that directive moral education violates one's later autonomy. To show this, one would need two yet stronger premises: that (1) a single act cannot simultaneously be motivated by both the agent's recognition of reasons and a nonrationally induced desire, and (2) when motivation from both sources converges, the motivational energy supplied by the nonrationally induced desire always excludes that supplied by an appreciation of reasons. But although these premises would indeed save the argument, there is little independent basis for them. In ordinary contexts, energy from any number of sources can combine to produce a single result. Hence, given our working metaphor, we must also presume that *motivational* energy from different sources can combine. The presumption must be that the motivating force of reasons does *not* give way when other factors motivate the same act. Moreover, these presumptions are not defeated by any independent theoretical considerations; for no adequate theory of how reasons motivate has yet been proposed.

III

So far, we have argued that directive moral education need not violate anyone's present or future moral autonomy. This conclusion, if correct, suffices to rebut the first objection to directive education. But more can be said here. Even if autonomy does require motivation by moral reasons, one's past directive education may actually help such autonomy to develop and flourish.

To see how directive education can have this result, recall first that even if one's grasp of a moral reason does supply one with some impulse to do the right thing, that impulse may be too weak to issue in action. Because of this, its effect may depend on other factors. In particular, that effect may well be increased by one's past directive education. Of course, the desires produced by such education will not contribute to one's moral autonomy if they merely add their weight to the motivation supplied by one's appreciation of reasons. However, and crucially, a past directive education may also augment one's appreciation of reasons in another way. It may neutralize or eliminate what would otherwise be a competing motive, and so may enable one's appreciation of reasons to affect one more strongly. If directive education works this way, it will indeed render the agent more autonomous. Put in terms of our guiding metaphor, its function will be not to provide an additional source of motivational energy, but rather to clear away obstacles so that the energy supplied by reasons can suffice.

How likely is it that directive moral education actually does work in this way? It is not likely to do so always or exclusively. That directive education does not *always* work by eliminating obstacles to moral reasons is shown by the fact that it motivates even very young children and can motivate adults to act immorally. That it rarely works *only* by eliminating such obstacles is suggested by the fact that one's prerational desires seem likely to persist as one matures. But even if a past directive education often affects adults in ways that do not enhance their autonomy, it may simultaneously affect them in other ways as well. Thus, the question is not whether our model is exclusively correct, but only whether it accurately reflects one way in which directive moral education often works.

When the question is put this way, we think its answer is clearly yes. It is a psychological commonplace that one's ability to respond to any reason depends on various external considerations. Hunger, anxiety, pain, and fear can all reduce the effect of reasons by diminishing attention to them and by supplying other motives. Thus, eliminating these distractions plainly does increase the motivating force of reasons. But if so, then eliminating other distractions seems likely to serve a similar function. Two considerations which most often distract us from moral obligations are preoccupation with our own interests and concern for our own comfort. Hence, one very natural way of increasing the motivating force of moral reasons is to reduce the impact of such distractions. But how better to prevent someone from being unduly distracted by self-interest than by causing him to acquire settled habits of honesty, fair play, and concern for others? Given these habits, one will automatically discount one's selfish interests when they conflict with one's duty. Hence, one will attach proper weight to one's moral obligations as a matter of course. Moreover, how better to ensure that someone will follow his decisions through than by causing him to acquire further habits of diligence, perseverance, and conscientiousness? Given *these* habits, one will not be sidetracked by the blandishments of comfort or inertia. Hence, one's appreciation of reasons will again be rendered more effective.

Given all of this, the traditional content of directive moral education acquires new significance. As the Talawanda list suggests, such education has long aimed at producing the habits just mentioned. These habits are often criticized as poor substitutes for self-conscious and reasoned morality, but we can now see that this criticism misses the point. Far from being alternatives to self-conscious morality, the habits are best understood as indispensable auxiliaries to it. They increase the impact of moral reasons by reducing one's tendency to be diverted. When the habits exist in persons who do not appreciate moral reasons, they may be mere facsimiles of virtue. However, when they exist in conjunction with an appreciation of reasons, they surely do contribute to moral autonomy.

IV

Until now, we have considered only the objection that directive moral education violates the ideal of the morally autonomous agent. However, one may also argue that it violates a related *social* ideal. There is wide agreement that our society should be both tolerant and pluralistic. Instead of stifling disagreements, it should accept and encourage diversity of opinion and should protect unpopular attitudes and beliefs. But a society that officially practices directive moral education seems not to do this. Instead of encouraging diversity, it instills in all children a single "approved" set of values. Far from being neutral, it is unabashedly partisan. Thus, such education may seem flatly incompatible with pluralism and tolerance.

This argument is narrower in scope than its predecessor; for it tells only against the use of directive techniques in public schools. Still, it does seem to animate many charges of indoctrination, and so we must examine it. To see the problems it raises, consider first the premise that society should tolerate and protect diverse values. This premise may mean either that (1) society should not coerce or persecute those who already hold unorthodox values, or (2) society should not try to induce people to acquire (or prevent people from acquiring) any values they do not yet hold. Whenever society coerces or persecutes those with unpopular values, it provides a disincentive for others to acquire those values. Hence, any violation of (1) is likely to violate (2). However, society may tolerate dissenters while trying to prevent others from acquiring their values. Hence, a violation of (2) does not necessarily violate (1).

Directive moral education neither persecutes anyone nor coerces any adults. When its techniques include punishment, it may be said to coerce children. However, (1) is generally not taken to apply to children, and punishment is in any case theoretically dispensable. Thus, directive moral education need not violate (1). It does violate (2); but that counts against it only if (2) is a proper interpretation of the pluralistic ideal. At first glance, (2) may appear to follow from a more general requirement that unorthodox views should receive a fair hearing. However, this would imply that we owe fair treatment to values as well as persons; and, as John Rawls has noted, such an obligation is highly unlikely.[4] Thus, the more promising strategy is to defend (2) less directly. To do that, one might appeal either to a societal obligation to allow persons to choose their own values or else to the undesirable consequences of inculcating official values. We will argue that neither defense succeeds.

The claim that societal attempts to inculcate values would violate an obligation to allow people to choose their own values is inherently problematical. In standard cases, people's choices are guided by their values, but here it is precisely one's basic values that are said to *be* chosen. Hence, the relevant choices cannot be grounded in any deeper values. But how, then, *are* such choices grounded? Shall we say they have no grounding, but are simply arbitrary? If so, they hardly warrant society's protection. Are they grounded in considerations outside the agent's value system, such as his recognition of independent moral reasons? If so, the complaint against inculcating values must be that it prevents people from *responding* to such reasons. But we already know this is false.

The desires and habits produced by directive moral education need not diminish, but may actually enhance, the motivating force of moral reasons. Is the claim, finally, that societally induced desires and habits do allow rational choice of values when they coincide with moral reasons, but prevent it in cases of conflict? If so, the argument is not that it is wrong to inculcate values, but only that society may inculcate the wrong values. Thus construed, the argument appeals to consequences. Hence, having come this far, we may abandon the rubric of choice, and confront the consequentialist approach directly.

The *locus classicus* of consequentialist arguments for tolerance is John Stuart Mill's *On Liberty*.[5] It is true that Mill's main target is not the inculcation of values, but rather intolerance involving coercion and persecution. However, there are also passages where Mill suggests that his arguments *do* extend to education, and presumably *a fortiori* to directive education. Moreover, whatever Mill's own views, any convincing consequentialist argument for (2) is likely to rest on precisely the familiar claims that society is fallible, that genuine challenges to belief enhance understanding, and that diverse practices provide people with a variety of models and "experiments of living." Thus, it is essentially the Millian arguments that we must now consider. Do they show that society should refrain from using nonrational techniques to instill values in its citizens?

We think not. Mill is right to insist that neither anyone's subjective feeling of certainty nor the agreement of society can guarantee the truth of an opinion or the utility of its adoption. However, the warrant for accepting the values of fairness, honesty, and consideration of others is no mere feeling of conviction. Instead, there is good independent reason to believe that, if any moral propositions are true, propositions enjoining such behavior are among them. Moreover, if the issue turns on social utility, then the warrant for inculcating these values is still more obvious. There is of course a danger that, once any inculcation of values is admitted, dogmatists and fanatics will seek to inculcate values that are *not* well-grounded or useful. However, this danger, though real, is far from decisive. If we can avoid the slippery slope of insisting that no values be inculcated, then we can also do so by insisting that society inculcate only values that satisfy high standards of justifiability. This will of course require some exercise of judgment; but that seems unavoidable in any case. As Mill himself remarks, "there is no difficulty in proving any ethical standard whatever to work ill, if we suppose universal idiocy to be conjoined with it."[6]

In view of this, (2) cannot be supported by appealing to human fallibility. But the consequentialist arguments are no better. A person's comprehension of his beliefs and values may indeed be deepened by challenges posed by dissenters, but such challenges are generally not needed to promote either adequate comprehension or tenacious acceptance of moral values. The suggestion that they are is contradicted by common experience. Moreover, even if widespread challenges to moral values did bring real benefits, these would be trivial compared to the mischief done by large numbers of people uncommitted to honesty, integrity, or concern for others. Nor, similarly, is it likely that exposure to cruelty, dishonesty, and insensitivity will promote personal development or bring out traits beneficial to others.

These considerations show that directive moral education need not be condemned as incompatible with pluralism. But that point can also be made in another way. It would be self-defeating for pluralists to demand that society be completely neutral toward all values; for the general acceptance of some values is required by pluralism itself. This holds most obviously for the value of toleration, but it is no less true of other values on the Talawanda list. If people were not committed to fairness, cooperation, and trustworthiness, they could hardly maintain a framework within which the rights of the weak and unpopular were protected. This may or may not justify the coercive suppression of some views—intolerance in the name of tolerance remains a disputed question of liberalism—but it surely does call for something beyond mere neutrality. If we as a society value toleration, then we must also value the general acceptance of principles that support and further it. Hence, if there is an effective method of advancing such principles which is not otherwise objectionable, we must acknowledge a strong case for adopting it. But precisely this is true of directive moral education. Thus, at least some forms of it seem justified by our commitment to toleration itself.

V

We have now rejected several familiar arguments against directive moral education. However, in endorsing such education, we do not mean that it should be used to teach every widely accepted moral belief or that it should utilize every effective method of procuring assent. Despite the strong moral component in many issues of economic distribution, foreign policy, and religion, we believe that normative propositions about these matters should generally not be taught directively. And although we believe that fairness and honesty *should* be taught directively, we believe their teaching should not involve immoderate humiliation or pain. But if we are to make such distinctions, we face a difficult further question: why are some forms of directive moral education permissible but others not?

This question is too large for us to answer fully, but some considerations are obviously relevant. To warrant directive teaching, a moral principle must first be clearly and firmly grounded. In addition, it should be simple enough to be comprehended at an early developmental stage, general enough to apply in a variety of situations, and central rather than peripheral to our moral corpus. To be acceptable as a *method* of directive teaching, a practice must neither impair a child's later ability to respond to moral reasons nor violate his rights. In many instances, the satisfaction of these requirements is undisputed. However, if an otherwise eligible principle or method is unacceptable to a conscientious minority, then respect for that minority may itself dictate restraint in directive teaching.

With this we can confront a final objection. It is sometimes said that because directive moral education reflects the prevailing moral climate, it inevitably favors existing practices and institutions. Because it grows out of entrenched attitudes, it is said objectionably to perpetuate the status quo. But we can now see that such worries are overblown. If the principles and habits that are directively taught are strongly justified, central to our evaluative scheme, and of more than parochial application, they are not likely to ratify all aspects of the status quo. Instead, they may well generate considerable dissatisfaction with existing realities. If someone is fair, considers others' interests, and respects democratic values, then he will be highly critical of many existing practices. If he is unmoved by group pressures, he will press his criticism even when it is unpopular. If he respects the truth and disdains dishonorable means, he will abjure self-interested silence. All in all, such a person is unlikely to be passive and indiscriminately accepting. Instead, he is apt vigorously to oppose various existing practices.

This shows that directive moral education need not favor the status quo. But should it ever be used

to teach principles that *do* have this effect? To see the problem here, consider some further Talawanda entries:

- Practicing good sportsmanship. Recognizing that although the will to win is important, winning is not all-important.
- Showing respect for the property of others—school property, business property, government property, everyone's property.
- Abstaining from premature sexual experience and developing sexual attitudes compatible with the values of family life.

We believe there is much to be said for each of these. However, each is closely associated with a contested social institution. The first presupposes the legitimacy of competition, the second assumes an economic system which distributes wealth unequally, and the third overtly favors marriage and the family. Alternatives to each institution have been proposed. Does this imply that these principles should not be directively taught?

We believe this question has no simple answer. To decide whether association with an existing institution disqualifies a principle, one must first clarify the nature of the association. Does the principle merely apply *only in the context* of the institution? Or does it, in addition, require that one *accept* it? If acceptance of (say) property or the family is required, must one accept only some form of the institution, or all its current details? If the details need not be accepted, the argument amounts to little. But even if a principle does require full acceptance of an existing institution, the question of its directive teaching is not settled. The main reasons for not directively teaching such principles are to permit full evaluation of alternative institutions and to display respect for persons proposing them. However, despite their relevance, these factors are not always decisive. We saw above that a major determinant of whether a principle should be directively taught is its degree of justification. But if so, then when a principle requires acceptance of a contested institution, we cannot avoid asking how reasonable it is to oppose that institution and how plausible the alternatives are. If these questions are asked, their answers may tip the balance. Hence, directive teaching of principles favoring existing institutions cannot be ruled out.

This of course says little of substance. To evaluate directive teaching about property, sexual behavior, or other matters of controversy, one must say more about a whole range of issues. But that much more must be said is precisely our point. Where directive moral education is concerned, we begin to make progress only when we abandon as sterile the notion of indoctrination and its cognates.

Discussion Questions

1. Present and explain what Professor Sher and Dr. Bennett mean by *directive moral education.* Do you have any objection to this view? If you do, explain and defend your objections.

2. How do the authors respond to the charge that directive moral education violates a child's autonomy? Why do they believe that directive moral education actually *enhances* moral autonomy? Do you agree with the authors on these points? Explain and defend your answer.

3. Opponents of the authors' view claim that teachers should remain neutral about morality because we live in a pluralistic society in which we should be tolerant of other views. How do the authors respond to this charge. Do you agree with their response? Explain and defend your answer.

Notes

1. Thus, for example: "[I]t is . . . wrong to teach ethics by presenting and attempting to inculcate a number of rules or precepts of conduct so as to improve, or at least to alter character, dispositions, or responses. The most effective means for altering responses, and possibly character as well, are those of advertising, propaganda (is there any difference?), indoctrination, and brainwashing. These are all objectionable on moral grounds, so one cannot possibly improve character by these means" (Marcus Singer, "The Teaching of Introductory Ethics," *The Monist,* LVIII, 4 [October 1974], p. 617). "If moral education promotes a definite moral perspective, it tends to be toward indoctrination and the denial of moral autonomy. . . . The problem and the challenge of moral education in our age is to find a middle way which neither indoctrinates young people into one set of moral rules nor gives them the impression that decision making is all a matter of personal opinion" (Robert Hall, "Moral Education Today: Progress, Prospects, and Problems of a Field Come of Age," *The Humanist* [November/December 1978], p. 12).

2. See especially Norman T. Feather, "Values in Adolescence," and Martin L. Hoffman, "Moral Development in Adolescence," in Joseph Adelson, ed., *The Handbook of Adolescent Psychology* (New York: Wiley, 1980), pp. 247–344.

3. For elaboration, see Kohlberg, *The Philosophy of Moral Development* (New York: Harper & Row, 1981).

4. "Fairness to Goodness," *Philosophical Review,* LXXXIV, 4 (October 1975): p. 554.

5. *On Liberty* (Indianapolis: Hackett, 1978).

6. *Utilitarianism* (Indianapolis: Hackett, 1979), p. 23.

11

Vision and Virtue

William K. Kilpatrick

William K. Kilpatrick is Professor of Education at Boston College, where he teaches courses in human development and moral education. He is a frequent lecturer to parent and university audiences and the author of four books, including *Why Johnny Can't Tell Right from Wrong: Moral Literacy and the Case for Character Education* (1992).

In this essay Professor Kilpatrick argues that the traditional way of teaching ethics and morality—reasoning from theories to principles and applying them to moral dilemmas—is highly contrived and artificial and should be supplemented, if not eclipsed, by virtue ethics (or character ethics), the instilling of ethics by studying the stories, lives, and example of virtuous people found in history, fiction, and mythology. Why is it that we do not have to reason by way of ethical principles to conclude instantly that Mother Teresa is a virtuous person whereas Adolf Hitler was wicked and evil? Why do our eyes well up with tears when we see the character of George Bailey (in the film *It's a Wonderful Life)*, who sacrificed so much for the floundering Bailey Savings and Loan, accepting the generosity of countless friends on Christmas Eve only hours after he tried to take his own life? According to Professor Kilpatrick, it is because we recognize virtue, integrity, and character in others. Although ethical principles, ethical theories, and moral dilemmas have their place, the author believes that they are inadequate in teaching morality unless they are employed along with stories, myths, historical narratives, and tales that

teach us profound and important lessons of virtue and vice.

_____

One way to counter moral illiteracy is to acquaint youngsters with stories and histories that can give them a common reference point and supply them with a stock of good examples. One of the early calls for returning stories to the curriculum was made by William Bennett in a speech before the Manhattan Institute:

> Do we want our children to know what honesty means? Then we might teach them about Abe Lincoln walking three miles to return six cents and, conversely, about Aesop's shepherd boy who cried wolf.
>
> Do we want our children to know what courage means? Then we might teach them about Joan of Arc, Horatius at the Bridge, Harriet Tubman and the Underground Railroad.
>
> Do we want them to know about kindness and compassion, and their opposites? Then they should read *A Christmas Carol* and *The Diary of Anne Frank* and, later on, *King Lear.*

. . . Among the reasons Bennett puts forward in arguing for the primacy of stories are that "unlike courses in moral reasoning," they provide a stock of examples illustrating what we believe to be right and wrong," and that they "help anchor our children in their culture, its history and traditions. They give children a mooring." "This is necessary," he continues, "because morality, of course, is inextricably bound both to the individual conscience and the memory of society . . . We should teach these accounts of character to our children so that we may welcome them to a common world . . ."

Bennett is not liked in teachers colleges and schools of education. He wasn't liked when he was Secretary of Education, and the legacy he left makes him unpopular still. As education secretary he stood for all those things progressive educators thought they had gotten rid of once and for all. He wanted to reemphasize content—not just any content but the content of Western culture. And he wanted to return character education to the schools. His emphasis on stories of virtue and heroism was an affront to the . . . tradition that had dominated education for years. Furthermore, by slighting "moral reasoning," Bennett also managed to alienate the party of critical thinking. Educators reacted angrily. Bennett was accused of being simplistic, reactionary, and worst of all, dog-

Reprinted by permission from William K. Kilpatrick, *Why Johnny Can't Tell Right from Wrong: Moral Literacy and the Case for Character Education* (New York: Simon & Schuster, 1992), 129–143.

matic. William Damon of Brown University, himself the author of a book on moral development, wrote that "Bennett's aversion to conscious moral decision making is itself so misguided as to present a threat to the very democratic traditions that he professes to cherish. Habit without reflection is adaptive only in a totalitarian climate."

Yet Bennett's concern over character was not simply a conservative phenomenon. Liberals too were having second thoughts about a moral education that relied only on moral reasoning. In a 1988 speech that could easily have been mistaken for one of Bennett's, Derek Bok, the president of Harvard University, stated:

> Socrates sometimes talked as if knowledge alone would suffice to ensure virtuous behavior. He did not stress the value of early habituation, positive example and obedience to rules in giving students the desire and self-discipline to live up to their beliefs and to respect the basic norms of behavior essential to civilized communities.

Bok went on to call for "a broader effort to teach by habit, example and exhortation," and unlike Bennett, he was speaking not of the elementary or high school but of the university level.

Nevertheless, one still finds a resistance among educators toward the kind of stories Bennett recommends—stories that teach by example. I don't mean this in a conspiratorial sense. I find this reaction in student teachers who have never heard of Bennett. Moreover, as far as l know, no committee of educators ever came together to promulgate an antistory agenda. It has been more a matter of climate, and of what the climate would allow. In my conversations with teachers and would-be teachers, one of the most common themes I hear is their conviction that they simply don't have the right to tell students anything about right and wrong. Many have a similar attitude toward literature with a moral; they would also feel uneasy about letting a story do the telling for them. The most pejorative word in their vocabulary is "preach." But the loss of stories doesn't strike them as a serious loss. They seem to be convinced that whatever is of value in the old stories will be found out anyway. Some are Rousseauians and believe it will be found out through instinct; others subscribe to some version or other of critical thinking and believe it will be found out through reason.

The latter attitude is a legacy of the Enlightenment, but it is far more widespread now than it ever was in the eighteenth century. The argument then and now is as follows: Stories and myth may have been necessary to get the attention of ignorant farmers and fishermen, but intelligent people don't need to have their ethical principles wrapped in a pretty box; they are perfectly capable of grasping the essential point without being charmed by myths, and because they can reach their own conclusions, they are less susceptible to the harmful superstitions and narrow prejudices that may be embedded in stories. This attitude may be characterized as one of wanting to establish the moral of the story without the story. It does not intend to do away with morality but to make it more secure by disentangling it from a web of fictions. For example, during the Enlightenment the Bible came to be looked upon as an attempt to convey a set of advanced ethical ideas to primitive people who could understand them only if they were couched in story form. A man of the Enlightenment, however, could dispense with the stories and myths, mysteries and miracles, could dispense, for that matter, with a belief in God, and still retain the essence—the Christian ethic.

[Lawrence] Kohlberg's approach to moral education is in this tradition. His dilemmas are stories of a sort, but they are stories with the juice squeezed out of them. . . . They are simply there to present a dilemma. And this is the way Kohlberg wanted it. . . . The important thing is to understand the principles involved. Moreover, a real story with well-defined characters might play on a child's emotions and thus intrude on his or her thinking process.

But is it really possible to streamline morality in this way? Can we extract the ethical kernel and discard the rest? Or does something vital get lost in the process? As the noted short story writer Flannery O'Connor put it, "A story is a way to say something that can't be said any other way . . . You tell a story because a statement would be inadequate." In brief, can we have the moral of the story without the story? And if we can, how long can we hold it in our hands before it begins to dissolve?

The danger of such abstraction is that we quickly tend to forget the human element in morality. The utilitarian system of ethics that was a product of the English Enlightenment provides a good illustration of what can happen. It was a sort of debit-credit system of morality in which the rightness or wrongness of acts depended on their usefulness in maintaining a smoothly running social machine. Utilitarianism oiled the cogs of the Industrial Revolution by providing reasonable justifications for child labor, dangerous working conditions, long

hours and low wages. For the sake of an abstraction—
"the greatest happiness for the greatest number"—
utilitarianism was willing to ignore the real human
suffering created by the factory system.

Some of the most powerful attacks on that system
can be found in the novels of Charles Dickens.
Dickens brought home to his readers the human face
of child labor and debtor's prison. And he did it in a
way that was hard to ignore or shake off. Such graphic
"reminders" may come to us through reading or they
may come to us through personal experience, but
without them, even the most intelligent and best-
educated person will begin to lose sight of the fact
that moral issues are human issues.

I use the words "lose sight of" advisedly. There
is an important sense in which morality has a visual
base—or, if you want, a visible base. In other words,
there is a connection between virtue and vision. One
has to see correctly before one can act correctly. This
connection was taken quite seriously in the ancient
world. Plato's most famous parable—the parable of
the cave—explains moral confusion in terms of
simple misdirected vision: the men in the cave are
looking in the wrong direction. Likewise, the Bible
prophets regarded moral blindness not only as a sin
but as the root of a multitude of sins.

The reason why seeing is so important to the
moral life is that many of the moral facts of life are
apprehended through observation. Much of the
moral law consists of axioms or premises about
human beings and human conduct. And one does
not arrive at premises by reasoning. You either see
them or you don't. The Declaration of Independence's assertion that some truths are "self-evident"
is one example of this visual approach to right and
wrong. The word "evident" means "present and
plainly visible." Many of Abraham Lincoln's arguments were of the same order. When Southern slave
owners claimed the same right as Northerners to
bring their "property" into the new territories, Lincoln replied: "That is to say, inasmuch as you do not
object to my taking my hog to Nebraska, therefore I
must not object to your taking your slave. Now, I
admit this is perfectly logical, if there is no difference
between hogs and Negroes."

Lincoln's argument against slavery is not logical
but definitional. It is a matter of plain sight that
Negroes are persons. But even the most obvious
moral facts can be denied or explained away once
the imagination becomes captive to a distorted vision.
The point is illustrated by a recent Woody Allen film,

Crimes and Misdemeanors. The central character, Judah
Rosenthal, who is both an ophthalmologist and a
philanthropist, is faced with a dilemma: What should
he do about his mistress? She has become possessive
and neurotic and has started to do what mistresses
are never supposed to do: she has begun to make
phone calls to his office and to his home, thus
threatening to completely ruin his life, a life that in
many ways has been one of service. Judah seeks advice from two people: his brother Jack, who has ties
to the underworld, and a rabbi, who tries to call Judah
back to the vision of his childhood faith. The rabbi
(who is nearly blind) advises Judah to end the relationship, even if it means exposure, and to ask his
wife for forgiveness. Jack, on the other hand, having
ascertained the woman's potential for doing damage and her unwillingness to listen to reason, advises
Judah to "go on to the next [logical] step," and he
offers to have her "taken care of." The interesting
thing is that Jack's reasoning powers are just as good
as the rabbi's; and based on his vision of the world,
they make perfect sense. You simply don't take the
chance that a vindictive person will destroy your
marriage and your career. And indeed, Jack finally
wins the argument. In an imagined conversation,
Judah tells the rabbi, "You live in the Kingdom of
Heaven, Jack lives in the real world." The woman is
"taken care of."

Jack's reasoning may be taken as an example of
deranged rationality or—if you change your angle
of vision—as the only smart thing to do. Certain
moral principles make sense within the context of
certain visions of life, but from within the context of
other visions, they don't make much sense at all.
From within the vision provided by the rabbi's faith,
all lives are sacred; from Jack's viewpoint, some lives
don't count.

Many of the moral principles we subscribe to
seem reasonable to us only because they are
embedded within a vision or world-view we hold to
be true even though we might not think very often
about it. In the same way, a moral transformation is
often accompanied by a transformation of vision.
Many ordinary people describe their moral
improvement as the result of seeing things in a
different light or seeing them for the first time. "I was
blind but now I see" is more than a line from an old
hymn; it is the way a great many people explain their
moral growth.

If we can agree that morality is intimately bound
up with vision, then we can see why stories are so

important for our moral development, and why neglecting them is a serious mistake. This is because stories are one of the chief ways by which visions are conveyed (a vision, in turn, may be defined as a story about the way things are or the way the world works). Just as vision and morality are intimately connected, so are story and morality. Some contemporary philosophers of ethics—most notably, Alasdair MacIntyre—now maintain that the connection between narrative and morality is an essential one, not merely a useful one. The Ph.D. needs the story "part" just as much as the peasant. In other words, story and moral may be less separable than we have come to think. The question is not whether the moral principle needs to be sweetened with the sugar of the story but whether moral principles make any sense outside the human context of stories. For example, since I referred earlier to the Enlightenment habit of distilling out the Christian ethic from the Bible, consider how much sense the following principles make when they are forced to stand on their own:

· Do good to those that harm you.
· Turn the other cheek.
· Walk an extra mile.
· Blessed are the poor.
· Feed the hungry.

"Feed the hungry" seems to have the most compelling claim on us, but just how rational is it? Science doesn't tell us to feed the hungry. Moreover, feeding the hungry defeats the purpose of natural selection. Why not let them die and thus "decrease the surplus population" as Ebenezer Scrooge suggests? Fortunately, the storyteller in this case takes care to put the suggestion in the mouth of a disagreeable old man.

Of course, there are visions or stories or ways of looking at life other than the Christian one, from which these counsels would still make sense. On the other hand, from some points of view they are sheer nonsense. Nietzsche, one of the great geniuses of philosophy, had nothing but contempt for the Christian ethic.

In recent years a number of prominent psychologists and educators have turned their attention to stories. In *The Uses of Enchantment* (1975), child psychiatrist Bruno Bettelheim argued that fairy tales are a vital source of psychological and moral strength; their formative power, he said, had been seriously underestimated. Robert Coles of Harvard University followed in the 1980s with three books

(*The Moral Life of Children, The Spiritual Life of Children,* and *The Call of Stories*) which detailed the indispensable role of stories in the life of both children and adults. Another Harvard scholar, Jerome Bruner, whose earlier *The Process of Education* had helped stimulate interest in critical thinking, had, by the mid-eighties, begun to worry that "propositional thinking" had been emphasized at the expense of "narrative thinking"—literally, a way of thinking in stories. In *Actual Minds, Possible Worlds,* Bruner suggests that it is this narrative thought, much more than logical thought, that gives meaning to life.

A number of other psychologists had arrived at similar conclusions. Theodore Sarbin, Donald Spence, Paul Vitz, and others have emphasized the extent to which individuals interpret their own lives as stories or narratives. "Indeed," writes Vitz, "it is almost impossible not to think this way." According to these psychologists, it is such narrative plots more than anything else that guide our moral choices. Coles, in *The Moral Life of Children,* observes how the children he came to know through his work not only understood their own lives in a narrative way but were profoundly influenced in their decisions by the stories, often of a religious kind, they had learned.

By the mid-eighties a similar story had begun to unfold in the field of education. Under the leadership of Professor Kevin Ryan, Boston University's Center for the Advancement of Character and Ethics produced a number of position papers calling for a reemphasis on literature as a moral teacher and guide. Meanwhile, in *Teaching as Storytelling* and other books, Kieran Egan of Canada's Simon Fraser University was proposing that the foundations of all education are poetic and imaginative. Even logico-mathematical and rational forms of thinking grow out of imagination, and depend on It. Egan argues that storytelling should be the basic educational method because it corresponds with fundamental structures of the human mind. Like Paul Vitz, he suggests that it is nearly impossible not to think in story terms. "Most of the world's cultures and its great religions," he points out, "have at their sacred core a story, and we indeed have difficulty keeping our rational history from being constantly shaped into stories."

In short, scholars in several fields were belatedly discovering what Flannery O'Connor, with her writer's intuition, had noticed years before: "A story is a way to say something that can't be said any other way . . ."

This recent interest in stories should not, however, be interpreted as simply another Romantic reaction to rationalism. None of the people I have mentioned could be classified as Romanticists. Several of them (including Flannery O'Connor) freely acknowledge their indebtedness to Aristotle and Aquinas—to what might be called the "realist" tradition in philosophy. Although literature can be used as an escape, the best literature, as Jacques Barzun said, carries us back to reality. It involves us in the detail and particularity of other lives. And unlike the superficial encounters of the workaday world, a book shows us what other lives are like from the inside. Moral principles also take on a reality in stories that they lack in purely logical form. Stories restrain our tendency to indulge in abstract speculation about ethics. They make it a little harder for us to reduce people to factors in an equation.

I can illustrate the overall point by mentioning a recurrent phenomenon in my classes. I have noticed that when my students are presented with a Values Clarification strategy and then with a dramatic account of the same situation, they respond one way to the dilemma and another to the story. In the Values Clarification dilemma called "The Lifeboat Exercise," the class is asked to imagine that a ship has sunk and a lifeboat has been put out from it. The lifeboat is overcrowded and in danger of being swamped unless the load is lightened. The students are given a brief description of the passengers—a young couple and their child, an elderly brother and sister, a doctor, a bookkeeper, an athlete, an entertainer, and so on—and from this list they must decide whom to throw overboard. Consistent with current thinking, there are no right and wrong answers in this exercise. The idea is to generate discussion. And it works quite well. Students are typically excited by the lifeboat dilemma.

This scenario, of course, is similar to the situation that faced the crew and passengers of the *Titanic* when it struck an iceberg in the North Atlantic in 1912. But when the event is presented as a story rather than as a dilemma, the response evoked is not the same. For example, when students who have done the exercise are given the opportunity to view the film *A Night to Remember,* they react in a strikingly different way. I've watched classes struggle with the lifeboat dilemma, but the struggle is mainly an intellectual one like doing a crossword puzzle. The characters in the exercise, after all, are only hypothetical. They are counters to be moved around at will. We can't really identify with them, nor can we be inspired or repelled by them. They exist only for the sake of the exercise.

When they watch the film, however, these normally blasé college students behave differently. Many of them cry. They cry as quietly as possible, of course: even on the college level it is extremely important to maintain one's cool. But this is a fairly consistent reaction. I've observed it in several different classes over several years. They don't even have to see the whole film. About twenty minutes of excerpts will do the trick.

What does the story do that the exercise doesn't? Very simply, it moves them deeply and profoundly. This is what art is supposed to do.

If you have seen the film, you may recall some of the vivid sketches of the passengers on the dying ship as the situation becomes clear to them: Edith Evans, giving up a place on the last boat to Mrs. Brown, saying, "You go first; you have children waiting at home." Harvey Collyer pleading with his wife, "Go, Lottie! For God's sake, be brave and go! I'll get a seat in another boat." Mrs. Isidor Straus declining a place in the boats: "I've always stayed with my husband, so why should I leave him now?"

The story is full of scenes like this: Arthur Ryerson stripping off his life vest and giving it to his wife's maid; men struggling below-decks to keep the pumps going in the face of almost certain death; the ship's band playing ragtime and then hymns till the very end; the women in boat 6 insisting that it return to pick up survivors; the men clinging to the hull of an overturned boat, reciting the Lord's Prayer; the *Carpathia*, weaving in and out of ice floes, racing at breakneck speed to the rescue. But there are other images as well: the indolence and stupidity of the *California*'s crew who, only ten miles away, might have made all the difference, but did nothing; the man disguised in a woman's shawl; the panicked mob of men rushing a lifeboat; passengers in half-empty lifeboats refusing to go back to save the drowning.

The film doesn't leave the viewer much room for ethical maneuvering. It is quite clear who has acted well and who has not. And anyone who has seen it will come away hoping that if ever put to a similar test, he or she will be brave and not cowardly, will think of others rather than of self.

Not only does the film move us, it moves us in certain directions. It is definitive, not open-ended. We are not being asked to ponder a complex ethical dilemma; rather, we are being taught what is proper.

There are codes of conduct: women and children first; duty to others before self. If there is a dilemma in the film, it does not concern the code itself. The only dilemma is the perennial one that engages each soul: conscience versus cowardice, faith versus despair.

This is not to say that the film was produced as a moral fable. It is, after all, a true story and a gripping one, the type of thing that almost demands cinematic expression—hardly a case of didacticism. In fact, if we were to level a charge of didacticism, it would have to be against "The Lifeboat Exercise." It is quite obviously an artificially contrived teaching exercise. But this is didacticism with a difference. "The Lifeboat Exercise" belongs to the age of relativism, and consequently, it has nothing to teach. No code of conduct is being passed down; no models of good and bad behavior are shown. Whether it is actually a good or bad thing to throw someone overboard is up to the youngster to decide for himself. The exercise is designed to initiate the group into the world of "each man his own moral compass."

Of course, we are comparing two somewhat different things: a story, on the one hand, and a discussion exercise, on the other. The point is that the logic of relativism necessitates the second approach. The story of the *Titanic* was surely known to the developers of "The Lifeboat Exercise." Why didn't they use it? The most probable answer is the one we have alluded to: The story doesn't allow for the type of dialogue desired. It marshals its audience swiftly and powerfully to the side of certain values. We feel admiration for the radio operators who stay at their post. We feel pity and contempt for the handful of male passengers who sneak into lifeboats. There are not an infinite number of ways in which to respond to these scenes, as there might be to a piece of abstract art. Drama is not the right medium for creating a value-neutral climate. It exerts too much moral force.

Drama also forces us to see things afresh. We don't always notice the humanity of the person sitting next to us on the bus. It is often the case that human beings and human problems must be presented dramatically for us to see them truly. Robert Coles relates an interesting anecdote in this regard about Ruby Bridges, the child who first integrated the New Orleans schools. Ruby had seen A *Raisin in the Sun*, and expressed to Coles the wish that white people would see it: "If all the [white] people on the street [who were heckling her mercilessly] saw that movie, they might stop coming out to bother us." When

Coles asked her why she thought that, she answered, "Because the people in the movies would work on them, and maybe they'd listen." Ruby knew that whites who saw her every day didn't really see her. Maybe the movie would make them see.

Admittedly, I have been mixing media rather freely here, and this raises a question. Films obviously have to do with seeing, but how about books? The paradoxical answer is that the storyteller's craft is not only a matter of telling but also of showing. This is why writing is so often compared to painting, and why beginning writers are urged to visualize what they want to say. So, even when a writer has a moral theme, his work—if he is a good writer—is more like the work of an artist than a moralist. For example, C. S. Lewis's immensely popular children's books have strong moral and religious themes, but they were not conceived out of a moral intent. "All my seven Narnian books," Lewis wrote in 1960, "and my three science fiction books, began with seeing pictures in my head. At first they were not a story, just pictures. *The Lion [The Lion, the Witch and the Wardrobe]* all began with a picture of a faun carrying an umbrella and parcels in a snowy wood."

Stories are essentially moving pictures. That is why they are so readily adaptable to the screen. And a well-made film, in turn, needs surprisingly little dialogue to make its point. When, in A *Night to Remember*, the shawl is torn away from the man's head, we do not have to be told anything. We *see* that his behavior is shameful; it is written on his face.

On the simplest level the moral force of a story or film is the force of example. It shows us examples of men and women acting well or trying to act well, or acting badly. The story points to these people and says in effect, "Act like this; don't act like that." Except that, of course, nothing of the kind is actually stated. It is a matter of showing. There is, for instance, a scene in *Anna Karenina* in which Levin sits by the side of his dying brother and simply holds his hand for an hour, and then another hour. Tolstoy doesn't come out and say that this is what he ought to do, but the scene is presented in such a way that the reader knows that it is the right thing to do. It is, to use a phrase of Bruno Bettelheim's, "tangibly right."

"Do I have to draw you a picture?" That much used put-down implies that normally intelligent people can do without graphic illustration. But when it comes to moral matters, it may be that we do need the picture more than we think. The story suits our nature because we think more readily in pictures than in propositions. And when a proposition or principle has the power to move us to action it is often because it is backed up by a picture or image. Consider, for example, the enormous importance historians assign to a single book—*Uncle Tom's Cabin*—in galvanizing public sentiment against slavery. After the novel appeared, it was acted out on the stage in hundreds of cities. For the first time, vast numbers of Americans had a visible and dramatic image of the evils of slavery. Lincoln, on being introduced to author Harriet Beecher Stowe, greeted her with the words, "So this is the little lady who started the big war." In more recent times the nation's conscience has been quickened by photo images of civil rights workers marching arm in arm, kneeling in prayer, and under police attack. It is nice to think that moral progress is the result of better reasoning, but it is naive to ignore the role of the imagination in our moral life.

The more abstract our ethic, the less power it has to move us. Yet the progression of recent decades has been in the direction of increasing verbalization and abstraction, toward a reason dissociated from ordinary feelings and cut off from images that convey humanness to us. "At the core of every moral code," observed Walter Lippmann, "there is a picture of human nature." But the picture coming out of our schools increasingly resembles a blank canvas. The deep human sympathies—the kind we acquire from good literature—are missing.

Perhaps the best novelistic portrait of disconnected rationalism is that of Raskolnikov in *Crime and Punishment*. Raskolnikov has mastered the art of asking the question, "Why not?" What is wrong with killing a repulsive old woman? he asks himself. What is wrong with taking her money and using it for a worthy cause—namely, to pay for his own education? With that education, Raskolnikov eventually plans to bring his intellectual gifts to the service of mankind. It is good utilitarian logic.

In commenting on *Crime and Punishment*, William Barrett observes that in the days and weeks after the killing, "A single image breaks into this [Raskolnikov's] thinking." It is the image of his victim, and this image saves Raskolnikov's soul. Not an idea but an image. For Dostoevsky the value of each soul was a mystery that could never be calculated but only shown.

The same theme recurs in *The Brothers Karamazov*. At the very end of the book, Alyosha speaks to the youngsters who love him: "My dear children . . . You must know that there is nothing higher and stronger and more wholesome and useful for life in after years than some good memory, especially a memory connected with childhood, with home. People talk to you a great deal about your education, but some fine, sacred memory, preserved from childhood, is perhaps the best education. If a man carries many such memories with him into life, he is safe to the end of his days, and if we have only one good memory left in our hearts, even that may sometime be the means of saving us."

There is no point in trying to improve on this. Let us only observe that what Dostoevsky says of good memories is true also of good stories. Some of our "sacred" memories may find their source in stories.

We carry around in our heads many more of these images and memories than we realize. The picture of Narcissus by the pool is probably there for most of us; and the Prodigal Son and his forgiving father likely inhabit some corner of our imagination. Atticus Finch, Ebenezer Scrooge, Laura Ingalls Wilder, Anne Frank, David and Goliath, Abraham Lincoln, Peter and the servant girl: for most of us these names will call up an image, and the image will summon up a story. The story in turn may give us the power or resolve to struggle through a difficult situation or to overcome our own moral sluggishness. Or it may simply give us the power to see things clearly. Above all, the story allows us to make that human connection we are always in danger of forgetting.

Most cultures have recognized that morality, religion, story, and myth are bound together in some vital way, and that to sever the connection among them leaves us not with strong and independent ethical principles but with weak and unprotected ones. What "enlightened" thinkers in every age envision is some sort of progression from story to freestanding moral principles unencumbered by stories. But the actual progression never stops there. Once we lose sight of the human fact of principle, the way is clear for attacking the principles themselves as merely situational or relative. The final stage of the progression is moral nihilism and the appeal to raw self-interest. . . .

Discussion Questions

1. Why does Professor Kilpatrick believe that there is a danger in teaching moral principles abstractly by way of contrived dilemmas? What does he suggest we do to correct this problem?

2. What is the "Lifeboat Exercise" and why does Professor Kilpatrick think that it does not adequately

teach students about morality? How does he compare and contrast this exercise with the film *A Life to Remember?* What point is he trying to make with this comparison and contrast?

3. Professor Kilpatrick makes the claim that "much of the moral law consists of axioms and premises about human beings and human conduct. You either see them or you don't." What does he mean by this and what examples does he cite in order to make his point? Do you agree with Professor Kilpatrick's claim? Why or why not? Explain and defend your answer.

PART II

Life and Death Issues

General Introduction

When is it right to take one's own or another human being's life? Are there some human beings that are not human *persons*? Is experimentation on prenatal human beings morally justified? These and other questions will be discussed by the authors in this section, when they confront the following issues: Abortion (Section A), Euthanasia (Section B), and Fetal Tissue Transplantation and Embryo Experimentation (Section C).

The disputants in all these issues seem to presuppose a primary moral judgment: it is ordinarily wrong to kill a human person. Where they disagree is over two issues: (1) what constitute nonordinary circumstances that may justify the killing of a human person; (2) what is a human person. For instance, concerning (1), some ethicists argue that capital punishment is just retribution for the killing of another human person and others argue that killing persons in war is justified in order to defend one's nation against an unprovoked aggressor. On the issue of abortion, some pro-choice ethicists are willing to grant pro-lifers (those who oppose abortion) that the fetus is a human person, but they nevertheless argue that a pregnant woman still has a right to terminate her pregnancy, because the fetus has no right to use the pregnant woman's body against her will if she did not consent to the pregnancy, just as one has no claim upon a neighbor's kidney even if one needs it in order to live. Concerning (2), some ethicists argue that abortion is morally justified because the fetus whose death results in abortion, though a human being, is not a human *person*. Others argue that fetal tissue research is justified for precisely the same reason, because there is no person whose rights are being violated.

So, when reading and studying the issues and authors in this section, pay careful attention to the moral judgment on which they apparently agree and the reason (or reasons) why they disagree about the application of that moral judgment.

For Further Reading

Tom L. Beauchamp and James Childress, *Principles of Biomedical Ethics*, 4th ed. (New York: Oxford University Press, 1993).

Edwin R. Dubose, Ron Hamel, and Laurence J. O'Connell, eds., A *Matter of Principles?: Ferment in U.S. Bioethics* (Valley Forge, Pa.: Trinity Press International, 1994).

Stanley Hauerwaus, *Suffering Presence* (Notre Dame, Ind.: University of Notre Dame Press, 1986).

Louis P. Pojman, ed., *Life and Death: A Reader in Moral Problems*, the Jones and Bartlett Series in Philosophy (Boston: Jones and Bartlett, 1993).

Louis Pojman, *Life and Death: Grappling with the Moral Dilemmas of Our Time*, the Jones and

Bartlett Series in Philosophy (Boston: Jones and Bartlett, 1992).

President's Commission for the Study of Ethical Problems in Medicine and Biomedical and Behavioral Research, *Defining Death: Medical, Legal, and Ethical Issues in the Determination of Death* (Washington, D.C.: GPO, 1983).

J. P. Moreland and Norman L. Geisler, *The Life and Death Debate: Moral Issues of Our Time* (New York: Greenwood, 1990).

Thomas Regan, ed., *Matters of Life and Death: New Introductory Essays in Moral Philosophy*, 3rd ed. (New York: McGraw-Hill, 1993).

Andrew Varga, *The Main Issues in Bioethics*, rev. ed. (New York: Paulist Press, 1984).

Robert M. Veatch, *Medical Ethics*, the Jones and Bartlett Series in Philosophy (Boston: Jones and Bartlett, 1993).

SECTION A

Abortion

Introduction

Abortion is probably the most controversial and most often discussed moral issue in late 20th century America. The arguments for and against abortion rights are being put forth in the political arena with greater vigor and rhetorical hostility than ever before. However, in comparison to the way it is popularly portrayed, the abortion debate is approached quite differently by philosophers and ethicists. In fact, most of the popular arguments for and against abortion rights heard on television and radio talk programs are logically fallacious.

A. Flawed Pro-choice Arguments

One argument often presented goes like this: If abortion is made illegal, then women will once again be harmed by unsafe and illegal abortions performed by back-alley butchers. But there is a serious problem with this reasoning. If we are to accept the contention of *Roe v. Wade*'s author Justice Harry Blackmun, this argument turns out to beg the question, for Justice Blackmun argues that if the fetus is a person then abortion is homicide and cannot be a constitutional right.[1] In other words, the illegal abortion argument assumes without reason the very thing, if false, that would invalidate *Roe v. Wade*, namely, that the fetus is not a human person. That is to say, only by assuming that the fetus is not a human person does the argument work. For if the fetus is a human person, this pro-choice argument is tantamount to saying that because people die or are harmed while killing other people (i.e., preborn people), the government should make it safe for them to do so. Consequently, only by begging the question as to the status of the fetus does this pro-choice argument work. Even Professor Mary Anne Warren, an abortion rights supporter, clearly sees that the abortion rights position cannot use this argument for support unless it is first shown that the fetus is not a human person. Warren writes that "the fact that restricting access to abortion has tragic side effects does not, in itself, show that the restrictions are unjustified, since murder is wrong regardless of the consequences of prohibiting it."[2]

The same critique can be applied to most other popular abortion-rights arguments, such as those that appeal to the upsetting of the pregnant woman's career, the difficulty of child-rearing, or the mother's poverty. In none of these cases do we believe that the child's execution is justified *after* its birth. Thus, if we are to take Justice Blackmun seriously (as most supporters of abortion rights do), the status of the fetus is the issue that must be addressed, not these other issues.

The argument from fetal viability is another popular argument that is used to defend abortion rights in the first two trimesters of pregnancy. Viability is the time at which the fetus can live outside its mother's womb (with or without the assistance of artificial life support). Some abortion rights advocates have argued that since the fetus in the first two trimesters cannot survive independent of its mother, it is not a complete independent human life and hence not a human person. In arguing for increased state interest in fetal life after viability, Justice Blackmun makes use of the viability criterion in his dissenting opinion in *Webster v. Reproductive Health Services* (1989):

> The viability line reflects the biological facts and truths of fetal development; it marks the threshold moment prior to which a fetus cannot survive separate from the woman and cannot reasonably and objectively be regarded as a subject of rights or interests distinct from, or paramount to, those of the pregnant woman. At the same time, the viability standard takes account of the undeniable fact that as the fetus evolves into its postnatal form, and as it loses its dependence on the uterine environment, the State's interest in the fetus's potential human life, and in fostering a regard for human life in general, becomes compelling.[3]

Although some people employ this argument to defend fetal personhood at viability rather than merely a state's interest in potential human life as Blackmun argues, it nevertheless is a circular argument. Blackmun is claiming that the state has no interest in protecting fetal life before that life can live outside the womb. But why is this correct? Because, we are told, before it can live outside the womb the fetus has no interests or rights. But this is clearly a case of circular reasoning, for what Blackmun is assuming (that the fetus has no interests or rights prior to viability) is what he is trying to prove (that the fetus has no interests or rights prior to viability). This argument is no better than the one provided by the zealous Boston Celtics fan who argues that the Celtics are the best team because no team is better (which, of course, is the same as being the best team).[4]

B. Flawed Pro-life Arguments

In response to the abortion-rights argument that abortion is justified because there are too many unwanted children, some pro-life advocates cite statistics that they believe support the fact that there are a large number of childless couples wanting to adopt children.[5] There are several problems with this pro-life response. First, why should this point even matter? If there were no such couples, would abortion ipso facto become morally correct? If the unborn have an inherent right to life, a principle that is the foundation of the pro-life position, why should the absence or presence of a couple who wants a child make a difference? Second, a sophisticated pro-choice advocate would remain unconvinced, since according to his position a woman has a right to an abortion but has no obligation to make sure other people have the opportunity to adopt her child. Why should the pro-choice advocate accept pro-life assumptions? And third, it follows from these two points that the pro-life advocate's appeal to adoption puts him in the odd position of appearing to support the assumption of many pro-choice advocates that only if the fetus is wanted does it have value. This is a fatal concession for the pro-life cause.

Another popular pro-life argument can be put this way: Since the unborn is a human being from the moment of conception, and since it is morally wrong in almost all circumstances to kill human beings, therefore, abortion is morally wrong in almost all circumstances. Although the pro-life advocate is not incorrect in asserting that the unborn is a human being in the genetic sense from the moment of conception,[6] it is not clear from the biological facts alone, without philosophical reflection, that the unborn is a human *person* and possesses the rights that are entailed with that status. In this section, authors Mary Anne Warren ("On the Legal and Moral Status of Abortion"), Stephen D. Schwarz ("Human Personhood Begins at Conception"), and L. W. Sumner ("A Defense of the Moderate Position") wrestle with this issue.

Abortion and the Law

In addition to the fallacious arguments presented by proponents on both sides of the debate, the legal nature of the debate is often misunderstood. Arguing that the right to abortion is as constitutionally fundamental as freedom of religion or speech, Justice Blackmun, in *Roe v. Wade* (1973), divided pregnancy into three trimesters. Aside from normal procedural guidelines to ensure protection for the pregnant woman (e.g., an abortion must be safely performed by a licensed physician), Blackmun ruled that a state has no right to restrict abortion in the first six months of pregnancy (first two trimesters). Since, according to Blackmun, the state has a legitimate interest in prenatal life in the last trimester (after the fetus is viable), the state has a right—though no obligation—to restrict abortions to only those cases in which the mother's life or health is in danger. But this health exception for third trimester abortions, some have argued, is so broad in principle that *Roe* turns out to be a much more permissive decision than most people realize. In a decision *Doe v Bolton* that the Court considers a companion to *Roe*, the Court ruled that "health" must be taken in its broadest possible context, defined "in light of all factors—physical, emotional, psychological, familial, and the woman's age—relevant to the well being of the patient. All these factors relate to health."[7] This is why the U.S. Senate Judiciary Committee concluded in 1983 that "no significant legal barriers of any kind whatsoever exist today in the United States for a woman to obtain an abortion for any reason during any stage of her pregnancy."[8]

In *Webster v. Reproductive Health Services* (1989) the Court reversed a lower-court decision and upheld a Missouri statute that contains several provisions, one of which forbids physicians to perform abortions after the fetus is 20 weeks old, except when a pregnant woman's life is in imminent danger. The statute requires a physician, if he believes that his pregnant patient seeking an abortion may be 20 weeks pregnant, to have her undergo a test in order to determine the fetus's gestational age. *Webster* modified *Roe* in at least two significant ways. First, it rejected *Roe*'s trimester breakdown of pregnancy. Chief Justice William Rehnquist, who wrote the majority opinion in the 5 to 4 decision, argued that the trimester breakdown is not found in the Constitution and that the Court sees no reason why a state's interest in protecting the fetus should arrive at the point of viability. Second, the Court in *Webster* ruled as constitutional the portion of the Missouri statute that forbade the use of government funds and employees in performing and counseling for a nontherapeutic abortion. Although it chipped away at the foundation of *Roe*, *Webster* did not overturn it.

In *Planned Parenthood v. Casey* (1992) the Supreme Court was asked to consider the constitutionality of five provisions of the Pennsylvania Abortion Control Act of 1982. This act requires that (1) "a woman seeking an abortion give her informed consent prior to the procedure, and specifies that she be provided with certain information at least 24 hours before the abortion is performed." (2) The act "mandates the informed consent of one parent for a minor to obtain an abortion, but provides a judicial bypass procedure." (3) It also "commands that, unless certain exceptions apply, a married woman seeking an abortion must sign a statement indicating that she has notified her husband." (4) However, the act allows for "a 'medical emergency' that will excuse compliance with forgoing requirements." (5) The act also imposes "certain reporting requirements on facilities providing abortion services."[9]

The Court upheld as constitutional four of the five provisions, rejecting the third one based on what it calls the *undue burden* standard. This is a significant departure from *Roe. Roe* affirms abortion as a fundamental constitutional right and thus makes any possible restrictions subject to strict scrutiny. In other words, possible restrictions in order to be valid must be essential to meeting a compelling public need. For example, laws that forbid yelling "fire" in a crowded theater pass strict scrutiny when subject to the fundamental right of freedom of expression. But the *Casey* Court, by subscribing to the undue burden standard, does not support the right to abortion as fundamental. Therefore, the states may restrict abortion by passing laws that may not withstand strict scrutiny but nevertheless do not result in an undue burden for the pregnant woman.

The *Casey* Court upheld *Roe* as a precedent despite the fact that it rejected *Roe*'s trimester framework, a woman's right to abortion as fundamental, and *Roe*'s requirement that restrictions be subject to strict scrutiny. Perhaps this is why Chief Justice Rehnquist made the comment in his dissenting opinion in *Casey*: "*Roe* continues to exist, but only in the way a storefront on a western movie set exists: a mere façade to give the illusion of reality."[10]

Included in this text are abridged versions of the Supreme Court's two most important decisions on abortion rights, *Roe v. Wade* (Chapter 12) and *Planned Parenthood v. Casey* (Chapter 13). The former contains Justice Blackmun's majority opinion as well as Justice Rehnquist's dissent; the latter contains the plurality opinion of Justices O'Connor, Kennedy, and Souter as well as the dissenting opinion of Justice Scalia.

The Morality of Abortion

As alluded to above, philosophers and ethicists have argued for and against abortion rights in primarily two ways: (1) from the moral status of the fetus, or (2) from the bodily rights of the pregnant woman.

A. Arguments from the Moral Status of the Fetus

Scientifically there is no doubt that individual human life begins at conception and does not end until natural death. At the moment of conception, when sperm and ovum cease to exist as individual entities, a new being with its own genetic code comes into existence. No new genetic information is added to the individual from this moment until natural death. All that is needed for its development is food, water, air, and an environment conducive to its survival.

These facts are not denied by those who believe that abortion should be justified at some point during pregnancy. What they argue is that the unborn entity, though a human being from conception, is not a person until some decisive moment after conception. Some argue that personhood does not arrive until brain waves are detected (40 to 43 days). Others, such as Warren (Chapter 16), define a person as a being who can do certain things, such as have consciousness, solve complex problems, and communicate, which would put the arrival of personhood quite possibly *after birth*. Traditional pro-lifers, such as Schwarz (Chapter 17), present responses to these views, maintaining that there are good reasons to continue to accept and no good reason to deny that human personhood begins at conception. Still others, such as Sumner (Chapter 18), take a moderate position and argue that human personhood does not arrive until the fetus is sentient, which, according to Sumner, occurs possibly as early as the middle weeks of the second trimester of pregnancy and definitely by the end of the second trimester.

B. Arguments from the Bodily Rights of the Pregnant Woman

Some abortion-rights supporters, such as Judith Jarvis Thomson ("A Defense of Abortion"), disagree that the abortion debate hinges on the moral status of the fetus. They argue that even if the unborn is a human person from conception or sometime early on in pregnancy, abortion is still morally justified. Thomson argues that the fetus's physical dependence on the pregnant woman's body entails a conflict of rights if the pregnant woman did not consent to the pregnancy. Consequently, the fetus, regardless of whether it is a fully human person, cannot use another's body without her consent. Thus, a pregnant woman's removal of the fetus by abortion, though it will result in its death, is no more immoral than an adult person's refusal to donate her kidney to someone who needs one, though this refusal will probably result in the death of the person who needs a donated kidney. Thomson's essay defending this position is included in this section (Chapter 14). In response to Thomson's argument and two others is an essay by me ("Arguments from Bodily Rights: A Critical Analysis"—Chapter 15).

Notes

1. Blackmun writes: "If the suggestion of personhood [of the unborn] is established, the appellant's case, of course, collapses, for the fetus' right to life is then guaranteed specifically by the [Fourteenth Amendment]." (Justice Harry Blackmun, "Excerpts from Opinion in *Roe v. Wade*," in *The Problem of Abortion*, 2nd ed., ed. Joel Feinberg [Belmont, Calif.: Wadsworth, 1984], 195).

2. Mary Anne Warren, "On the Moral and Legal Status of Abortion," in *The Problem of Abortion*, 103.

3. Justice Harry Blackmun in *Webster v. Reproductive Health Services* (1989), as found in *The United States Law Week* 57, no. 50 (27 July 1989): 5040.

4. Other flaws in the viability argument have been pointed out elsewhere. See, for example, Francis J. Beckwith, *Politically Correct Death: Answering the Arguments for Abortion Rights* (Grand Rapids, Mich.: Baker Book House, 1993), 99–101; Stephen D. Schwarz, *The Moral Question of Abortion* (Chicago: Loyola University Press, 1990), 44–47; and Andrew Varga, *The Main Issues in Bioethics*, rev. ed. (New York: Paulist Press, 1984), 62–63.

5. See, for example, Dr. and Mrs. J. C. Willke, *Abortion: Questions and Answers*, rev. ed. (Cincinnati: Hayes Publishing, 1988), 305–313.

6. See Andre E. Hellegers, "Fetal Development," in *Biomedical Ethics*, ed. Thomas A. Mappes and Jane S. Zembaty (New York: McGraw-Hill, 1981), 405–409; and Beckwith, *Politically Correct Death*, 41–51.

7. *Doe v. Bolton* 410 U.S. 179, 192 (1973).

8. Report, Committee on the Judiciary, U.S. Senate, on Senate Resolution 3, 98th Congress, 98–149, 7 June 1983, 6.

9. *Planned Parenthood v. Casey*, nos. 91-744 and 91-902 (1992): I (Syllabus).

10. Ibid., 12 (Rehnquist, J., dissenting).

For Further Reading

Francis J. Beckwith, *Politically Correct Death: Answering the Arguments for Abortion Rights* (Grand Rapids, Mich.: Baker Book House, 1993).

Francis J. Beckwith and Louis P. Pojman, eds., *The Abortion Controversy: A Reader* (Boston: Jones and Bartlett, 1994).

Baruch Brody, *Abortion and the Sanctity of Human Life: A Philosophical View* (Cambridge: MIT Press, 1975).

Daniel Callahan, *Abortion: Law, Choice, and Morality* (New York: Macmillan, 1970).

Dan Drucker, *Abortion Decisions of the Supreme Court, 1973 through 1989: A Comprehensive Review and Historical Commentary* (Jefferson, N.C.: McFarland and Company, 1990).

Dennis J. Horan, Edward R. Grant, and Paige C. Cunningham, eds., *Abortion and the Constitution: Reversing* Roe v. Wade *through the Courts* (Washington, D.C.: Georgetown University Press, 1987).

Stephen D. Schwarz, *The Moral Question of Abortion* (Chicago: Loyola University Press, 1990).

Michael Tooley, *Abortion and Infanticide* (Oxford: Clarendon, 1983).

Laurence Tribe, *Abortion: The Clash of Absolutes* (New York: Norton, 1990).

Robert Wennberg, *Life in the Balance: Exploring the Abortion Controversy* (Grand Rapids, Mich.: Eerdmans, 1985).

Abortion and the Law

12

Roe v. Wade *(1973)*

U.S. Supreme Court

A resident of Texas, Jane Roe (a pseudonym for Norma McCorvey), claimed to have become pregnant after being gang-raped (which later was found to be a false charge). The law in Texas, which had been essentially unchanged since 1856, stated that a woman can have an abortion only if it is necessary to save her life. Roe sued the state of Texas, since her pregnancy was not life-threatening. The unmarried Roe, in 1970, filed a class action suit in federal court in Dallas. The court ruled that the Texas statute was over broad and constitutionally vague and infringed upon a woman's right to reproductive freedom. The case was appealed by the state of Texas to the U.S. Supreme Court. On January 22, 1973, the Court, in agreement with the federal court's opinion, ruled in *Roe v. Wade* that the Texas law was unconstitutional and that not only must all the states including Texas permit abortions in cases of rape but in all cases.

The following are excerpts from two opinions in *Roe*. The first is the Court's majority opinion, written by Justice Harry Blackmun. The second is a dissenting opinion, written by Justice William Rehnquist, who is presently the Court's Chief Justice.

Mr. Justice Blackmun delivered the opinion of the Court . . .

The principal thrust of appellant's attack on the Texas statutes is that they improperly invade a right, said to be possessed by the pregnant woman, to choose to terminate her pregnancy. Appellant would discover this right in the concept of personal "liberty" embodied in the Fourteenth Amendment's Due Process Clause; or in personal, marital, familial, and sexual privacy said to be protected by the Bill of Rights or its penumbras, see *Griswold v. Connecticut,* 381 U.S. 479 (1965); *Eisenstadt v. Baird,* 405 U.S. 438 (1972); *id.,* at 460 (White, J., concurring in result); or among those rights reserved to the people by the Ninth Amendment, *Griswold v. Connecticut,* 381 U.S., at 486 (Goldberg, J., concurring). Before addressing this claim, we feel it desirable briefly to survey, in several aspects, the history of abortion, for such insight as that history may afford us, and then to examine the state purposes and interests behind the criminal abortion laws.

It perhaps is not generally appreciated that the restrictive criminal abortion laws in effect in a majority of States today are of relatively recent vintage. Those laws, generally proscribing abortion or its attempt at any time during pregnancy except when necessary to preserve the pregnant woman's life, are not of ancient or even of common-law origin. Instead, they derive from statutory changes effected, for the most part, in the latter half of the 19th century.

Ancient Attitudes

These are not capable of precise determination. We are told that at the time of the Persian Empire abortifacients were known and that criminal abortions were severely punished. We are also told, however, that abortion was practiced in Greek times as well as in the Roman Era, and that "it was resorted to without scruple." The Ephesian, Soranos, often described as the greatest of the ancient gynecologists, appears to have been generally opposed to Rome's prevailing free abortion practices. He found it necessary to think first of the life of the mother, and he resorted to abortion when, upon this standard, he felt the procedure advisable. Greek and Roman law afforded little protection to the unborn. If abortion was prosecuted in some places, it seems to have been based on a concept of a violation of the father's right to his offspring. Ancient religion did not bar abortion.

The Hippocratic Oath

What then of the famous Oath that has stood so long as the ethical guide of the medical profession and that bears the name of the great Greek (460(?)-377(?) B.C.), who has been described as the Father of Medicine, the "wisest and the greatest practitioner of his art," and the "most important and most complete medical personality of antiquity," who dominated the medical schools of his time, and who typified the sum of the medical knowledge of the past? The Oath varies somewhat according to the particular translation, but in any translation the content is clear: "I will give no deadly medicine to anyone if asked, nor suggest any such counsel; and in like manner I will not give to a woman a pessary to produce abortion," or "I will neither give a deadly drug to anybody if asked for it, nor will I make a suggestion to this effect. Similarly, I will not give to a woman an abortive remedy."

Although the Oath is not mentioned in any of the principal briefs in this case or in *Doe v. Bolton, post,* p. 179, it represents the apex of the development of strict ethical concepts in medicine, and its influence endures to this day. Why did not the authority of Hippocrates dissuade abortion practice in his time and that of Rome? The late Dr. Edelstein provides us with a theory: The Oath was not uncontested even in Hippocrates' day; only the Pythagorean school of philosophers frowned upon the related act of suicide. Most Greek thinkers, on the other hand, commended abortion, at least prior to viability. See Plato, Republic, V, 461; Aristotle, Politics, VII, 1335b 25. For the Pythagoreans, however, it was a matter of dogma. For them the embryo was animate from the moment of conception, and abortion meant destruction of a living being. The abortion clause of the Oath, therefore, "echoes Pythagorean doctrines," and "[i]n no other stratum of Greek opinion were such views held or proposed in the same spirit of uncompromising austerity."

Dr. Edelstein then concludes that the Oath originated in a group representing only a small segment of Greek opinion and that it certainly was not accepted by all ancient physicians. He points out that medical writings down to Galen (A.D. 130–200) "give evidence of the violation of almost every one of its injunctions." But with the end of antiquity a decided change took place. Resistance against suicide and against abortion became common. The Oath came to be popular. The emerging teachings of Christianity were in agreement with the Pythagorean ethic. The Oath "became the nucleus of all medical ethics" and "was applauded as the embodiment of truth." Thus, suggests Dr. Edelstein, it is "a Pythagorean manifesto and not the expression of an absolute standard of medical conduct."

This, it seems to us, is a satisfactory and acceptable explanation of the Hippocratic Oath's apparent rigidity. It enables us to understand, in historical context, a long-accepted and revered statement of medical ethics.

The Common Law

It is undisputed that at common law, abortion performed before "quickening"—the first recognizable movement of the fetus in utero, appearing usually from the sixteenth to the eighteenth week of pregnancy—was not an indictable offense. The absence of a common-law crime for pre-quickening abortion appears to have developed from a confluence of earlier philosophical, theological, and civil and canon law concepts of when life begins. These disciplines variously approached the question in terms of the point at which the embryo or fetus became "formed" or recognizably human, or in terms of when a "person" came into being, that is, infused with a "soul" or "animated." A loose consensus evolved in early English law that these events occurred at some point between conception and live birth. This was "mediate animation" although Christian theology and the canon law came to fix the point of animation at 40 days for a male and 80 days for a female, a view that persisted until the 19th century, there was otherwise little agreement about the precise time of formation or animation. There was agreement, however, that prior to this point the fetus was to be regarded as part of the mother, and its destruction, therefore, was not homicide. Due to continued uncertainty about the precise time when animation occurred, to the lack of any empirical basis for the 40–80-day view, and perhaps to Aquinas' definition of movement as one of the first two principles of life, Brackton focused upon quickening as the critical point. The significance of quickening was echoed by later common-law scholars and found its way into the received common law in this country.

Whether abortion of a *quick* fetus was a felony at common law, or even a lesser crime, is still disputed. Brackton, writing early in the 13th century, thought it homicide. But the later and predominant view, following the great common-law scholars, has been that it was, at most, a lesser offense. In a frequently cited passage, Coke took the position that abortion of a woman "quick with childe" is "a great misprision and no murder." Blackstone followed, saying that while abortion after quickening had once been considered manslaughter (though not murder), "modern law" took a less severe view. A recent review of the common-law precedents argues, however, that those precedents contradict Coke and that even post-quickening abortion was never established as a common-law crime. This is of some importance because while most American courts ruled, in holding or dictum, that abortion of an unquickened fetus was not criminal under their received common law, others followed Coke in stating that abortion of a quick fetus was a "misprision," a term they translated to mean "misdemeanor." That their reliance on Coke on this aspect of the law was uncritical and, apparently in all reported cases dictum (due probably to the paucity of common-law prosecutions for post-quickening abortion), makes it now appear doubtful that abortion was ever firmly established as common-law crime even with respect to the destruction of a quick fetus.

. . .

The American Law

In this country, the law in effect in all but a few States until mid-19th century was the pre-existing English common law. Connecticut, the first State to enact abortion legislation, adopted in 1821 that part of Lord Ellenborough's Act that related to a woman "quick with child." The death penalty was not imposed. Abortion before quickening was made a crime in that State only in 1860. In 1828, New York enacted legislation that, in two respects, was to serve as a model for early antiabortion statutes. First, while barring destruction of an unquickened fetus as well as a quick fetus, it made the former only a misdemeanor, but the latter second-degree manslaughter. Second, it in-

corporated a concept of therapeutic abortion by providing that an abortion was excused if it "shall have been necessary to preserve the life of such mother or shall have been advised by two physicians to be necessary for such purpose." By 1840, when Texas had received the common law, only eight American States had statutes dealing with abortion. It was not until after the War Between the States that legislation began generally to replace the common law. Most of these initial statutes dealt severely with abortion after quickening but were lenient with it before quickening. Most punished attempts equally with completed abortions. While many statutes included the exception for an abortion thought by one or more physicians to be necessary to save the mother's life, that provision soon disappeared and the typical law required that the procedure actually be necessary for that purpose.

Gradually, in the middle and late 19th century, the quickening distinction disappeared from the statuatory law of most States and the degree of the offense and the penalties were increased. By the end of the 1950s, a large majority of the jurisdictions banned abortion, however and whenever performed, unless done to save or preserve the life of the mother. The exceptions, Alabama and the District of Columbia, permitted abortion to preserve the mother's health. Three States permitted abortions that were not "unlawfully" performed or that were not "without lawful justification," leaving interpretation of those standards to the courts. In the past several years, however, a trend toward liberalization of abortion statutes has resulted in adoption, by about one-third of the States, of less stringent laws, most of them patterned after the ALI Model Penal Code, §230.3.

It is thus apparent that at common law, at the time of the adoption of our Constitution, and throughout the major portion of the 19th century, abortion was viewed with less disfavor than under most American statutes currently in effect. Phrasing it another way, a woman enjoyed a substantially broader right to terminate a pregnancy than she does in most States today. At least with respect to the early stage of pregnancy and very possibly without such a limitation, the opportunity to make this choice was present in this country well into the 19th century. Even later the law continued for some time to treat less punitively an abortion procured in early pregnancy.

The Position of the American Medical Association

The antiabortion mood prevalent in this country in the late 19th century was shared by the medical profession. Indeed, the attitude of the profession may have played a significant role in the enactment of stringent criminal abortion legislation during that period.

An AMA Committee on Criminal Abortion was appointed in May 1857. It presented its report, 12 Trans. of the Am. Med. Assn. 73–78 (1859), to the Twelfth Annual Meeting. That report observed that the Committee had been appointed to investigate criminal abortion "with a view to its general suppression." It deplored abortion and its frequency and it listed three causes of "this general demoralization":

> "The first of these causes is a widespread popular ignorance of the true character of the crime—a belief, even among mothers themselves, that the foetus is not alive till after the period of quickening.
>
> "The second of the agents alluded to is the fact that the profession themselves are frequently supposed careless of foetal life. . . .
>
> "The third reason of the frightful extent of this crime is found in the grave defects of our laws, both common and statute, as regards the independent and actual existence of the child before birth, as a living being. These errors, which are sufficient in most instances to prevent conviction, are based, and only based, upon mistaken and exploded medical dogmas. With strange inconsistency, the law fully acknowledges the foetus in utero and its inherent rights, for civil purposes; while personally and as criminally affected, it fails to recognize it, and to its life as yet denies all protection." Id., at 75–76.

The Committee then offered, and the Association adopted, resolutions protesting "against such unwarrantable destruction of human life," calling upon state legislatures to revise their abortion laws, and requesting the cooperation of state medical societies "in pressing the subject." Id., at 28, 78.

In 1871 a long and vivid report was submitted by the Committee on Criminal Abortion. It ended with the observation, "We had to deal with human life. In a matter of less importance we could entertain no compromise. An honest judge on the bench would call things by their proper names. We could do no less." 22 Trans. of the Am. Med. Assn. 258 (1871). It proffered resolutions, adopted by the Association, id., at 38–39, recommending, among other things, that it "be unlawful and unprofessional for any physician to induce abortion or premature labor, without the concurrent opinion of at least one respectable consulting physician, and then always with a view to the safety of the child—if that be possible," and calling "the attention of the clergy of all denominations to the perverted views of morality entertained by a large class of females—aye, and men also, on this important question."

Except for periodic condemnation of the criminal abortionist, no further formal AMA action took place until 1967. In that year, the Committee on Human Reproduction urged the adoption of a stated policy of opposition to induced abortion, except when there is "documented medical evidence" of a threat to the health or life of the mother, or that the child "may be born with incapacitating physical deformity or mental deficiency," or that a pregnancy "resulting from legally established statutory or forcible rape or incest may constitute a threat to the mental or physical health of the patient," two other physicians "chosen because of their recognized professional competence have examined the patient and have concurred in writing," and the procedure "is performed in a hospital accredited by the Joint Commission on Accreditation of Hospitals." The providing of medical information by physicians to state legislatures in their consideration of legislation regarding therapeutic abortion was "to be considered consistent with the principles of ethics of the American Medical Association." This recommendation was adopted by the House of Delegates. Proceedings of the AMA House of Delegates 40–51 (June 1967).

In 1970, after the introduction of a variety of proposed resolutions, and of a report from its Board of Trustees, a reference committee noted "polarization of the medical professional on this controversial issue"; division among those who had testified; a difference of opinion among AMA councils and committees; "the remarkable shift in testimony" in six months felt to be influenced "by the rapid changes in state laws and by the judicial decisions which tend to make abortion more freely available" and a feeling "that this trend will continue." On June 25, 1970, the House of Delegates adopted preambles and most of the resolutions proposed by the reference committee. The preambles emphasized "the best interests of the patient," "sound clinical judgment," and "informed patient consent," in contrast to "mere acquiescence to the patient's demand." The resolutions asserted that abortion is a medical procedure that should be performed by a licensed physician in an accredited hospital only after consultation with two other physicians and in conformity with state law, and that no party to the procedure should be required to violate personally held moral principles. Proceedings of the AMA House of Delegates 220 (June 1970). The AMA Judicial Council rendered a complementary opinion.

The Position of the American Public Health Association

In October, 1970, the Executive Board of the APHA adopted Standards for Abortion Services. These were five in number:

"a. Rapid and simple abortion referral must be readily available through state and local public health departments, medical societies, or other nonprofit organizations.

"b. An important function of counseling should be to simplify and expedite the provision of abortion services; it should not delay the obtaining of these services.

"c. Psychiatric consultation should not be mandatory. As in the case of other specialized medical services, psychiatric consultation should be sought for definite indications and not on a routine basis.

"d. A wide range of individuals from appropriately trained, sympathetic volunteers to highly skilled physicians may qualify as abortion counselors.

"e. Contraception and/or sterilization should be discussed with each abortion patient." Recommended Standards for Abortion Services, 61 Am. J. Pub. Health 396 (1971).

Among factors pertinent to life and health risks associated with abortion were three that "are recognized as important":

"a. the skill of the physician,

"b. the environment in which the abortion is performed, and above all

"c. the duration of pregnancy, as determined by uterine size and confirmed by menstrual history." Id., at 397.

It was said that "a well-equipped hospital" offers more protection "to cope with unforeseen difficulties than an office or clinic without such resources. . . .

The factor of gestational age is of overriding importance." Thus, it was recommended that abortions in the second trimester and early abortions in the presence of existing medical complications be performed in hospitals as inpatient procedures. For pregnancies in the first trimester, abortion in the hospital with or without overnight stay "is probably the safest practice." An abortion in an extramural facility, however, is an acceptable alternative "provided arrangements exist in advance to admit patients promptly if unforeseen complications develop." Standards for an abortion facility were listed. It was said that at present abortions should be performed by physicians or osteopaths who are licensed to practice and who have "adequate training." . . .

Three reasons have been advanced to explain historically the enactment of criminal abortion laws in the 19th century and to justify their continued existence.

It has been argued occasionally that these laws were the product of a Victorian social concern to discourage illicit sexual conduct. Texas, however, does not advance this justification in the present case, and it appears that no court or commentator has taken the argument seriously. The appellants and *amici* contend, moreover, that this is not a proper state purpose at all and suggest that, if it were, the Texas statutes are overboard in protecting it since the law fails to distinguish between married and unwed mothers.

A second reason is concerned with abortion as a medical procedure. When most criminal abortion laws were first enacted, the procedure was a hazardous one for the woman. This was particularly true prior to the development of antisepsis. Antiseptic techniques, of course, were based on discoveries by Lister, Pasteur, and others first announced in 1867, but were not generally accepted and employed until about the turn of the century. Abortion mortality was high. Even after 1900, and perhaps until as late as the development of antibiotics in the 1940's, standard modern techniques such as dilation and curettage were not nearly so safe as they are today. Thus, it has been argued that a State's real concern in enacting a criminal abortion law was to protect the pregnant woman, that is, to restrain her from submitting to a procedure that placed her life in serious jeopardy.

Modern medical techniques have altered this situation. Appellants and various *amici* refer to medical data indicating that abortion in early pregnancy, that is, prior to the end of the first trimester, although not without its risk, is now relatively safe. Mortality rates for women undergoing early abortions, where the procedure is legal, appear to be as low as or lower than the rates for normal childbirth. Consequently, any interest of the State in protecting the woman from an inherently hazardous procedure, except when it would be equally dangerous for her to forgo it, has largely disappeared. Of course, important state interests in the areas of health and medical standards do remain. The State has a legitimate interest in seeing to it that abortion, like any other medical procedure, is performed under circumstances that insure maximum safety for the patient. This interest obviously extends at least to the performing physician and his staff, to the facilities involved, to the availability of aftercare, and to adequate provision for any complication or emergency that might arise. The prevalence of high mortality rates at illegal "abortion mills" strengthens, rather than weakens, the State's interest in regulating the conditions under which abortions are performed. Moreover, the risk to the woman increases as her pregnancy continues. Thus, the State retains a definite interest in protecting the woman's own health and safety when an abortion is proposed at a late stage of pregnancy.

The third reason is the State's interest—some phrase it in terms of duty—in protecting prenatal life. Some of the argument for this justification rests on the theory that a new human life is present from the moment of conception. The State's interest and general obligation to protect life then extends, it is argued, to prenatal life. Only when the life of the pregnant mother herself is at stake, balanced against the life she carries within her, should the interest of the embryo or fetus not prevail. Logically, of course, a legitimate state interest in this area need not stand or fall on acceptance of the belief that life begins at conception or at some other point prior to live birth. In assessing the State's interest recognition may be given to the less rigid claim that as long as at least *potential* life is involved, the State may assert interests beyond the protection of the pregnant woman alone.

Parties challenging state abortion laws have sharply disputed in some courts the contention that a purpose of these laws, when enacted, was to protect prenatal life. Pointing to the absence of legislative history to support the contention, they claim that most state laws were designed solely to protect the woman. Because medical advances have lessened this concern, at least with respect to abortion in early pregnancy, they argue that with respect to such abortions the laws can no longer be justified by any state interest. There is some scholarly support for this view of original purpose. The few state courts called upon to interpret their laws in the late 19th and early 20th centuries did focus on the State's interest in protecting the woman's health rather than in preserving the embryo and fetus. Proponents of this view point out that in many States, including Texas, by statute or judicial interpretation, the pregnant woman herself could not be prosecuted for self-abortion or for cooperating in an abortion performed upon her by another. They claim that adoption of the "quickening" distinction through received common law and state statutes tacitly recognizes the greater health hazards inherent in late abortion and impliedly repudiates the theory that life begins at conception.

It is with these interests, and the weight to be attached to them, that this case is concerned.

The Constitution does not explicitly mention any right of privacy. In a line of decisions, however, going back perhaps as far as *Union Pacific R. Co. v. Botsford*, 141 U.S. 250, 251 (1891), the Court has recognized that a right of personal privacy, or a guarantee of certain areas or zones of privacy, does exist under the Constitution. In carrying contexts, the Court or individual Justices have, indeed, found at least the roots of that right in the First Amendment, in the Fourth and Fifth Amendments, in the penumbras of the Bill of Rights, in the Ninth Amendment, or in the concept of liberty guaranteed by the first section of the Fourteenth Amendment. These decisions make it clear that only personal rights that can be deemed "fundamental" or "implicit in the concept of ordered liberty," are included in this guarantee of personal privacy. They also make it clear that the right has some extension to activities relating to marriage, procreation, contraception, family relationships, and child rearing and education.

This right of privacy, whether it be founded in the Fourteenth Amendment's concept of personal liberty and restrictions upon state action, as we feel it is, or, as the District Court determined, in the Ninth Amendment's reservation of rights to the people, is broad enough to encompass a woman's decision whether or not to terminate her pregnancy. The detriment that the State would impose upon the pregnant woman by denying this choice altogether is apparent. Specific and direct harm medically diagnosable even in early pregnancy may be involved. Maternity, or additional offspring, may force upon the woman a distressful life and future. Psychological harm may be imminent. Mental and physical health may be taxed by child care. There is also the distress, for all concerned, associated with the unwanted child, and there is the problem of bringing a child into a family already unable, psychologically and otherwise, to care for it. In other cases, as in this one, the additional difficulties and continuing stigma of unwed motherhood may be involved. All these are factors the woman and her responsible physician necessarily will consider in consultation.

On the basis of elements such as these, appellant and some *amici* argue that the woman's right is absolute and that she is entitled to terminate her pregnancy at whatever time, in whatever way, and for whatever reason she alone chooses. With this we do not agree. Appellant's arguments that Texas either has no valid interest at all in regulating the abortion decision, or no interest strong enough to support any limitation upon the woman's sole determination, are unpersuasive. The Court's decisions recognizing a right of privacy also acknowledge that some state regulation in areas protected by that right is appropriate. As noted above, a State may properly assert important interests in safeguarding health, in maintaining medical standards, and in protecting potential life. At some point in pregnancy, these respective interests become sufficiently compelling to sustain regulation of the factors that govern the abortion decision. The privacy right involved, therefore, cannot be said to be absolute. In fact, it is not clear to us that the claim asserted by some *amici* that one has an unlimited right to do with one's body as one pleases bears a close relationship to the right of privacy previously articulated in the Court's decisions. The Court has refused to recognize an unlimited right of this kind in the past.

We, therefore, conclude that the right of personal privacy includes the abortion decision, but that this right is not unqualified and must be considered against important state interests in regulation.

We note that those federal and state courts that have recently considered abortion law challenges have reached the same conclusion.

Although the results are divided, most of these courts have agreed that the right of privacy, however based, is broad enough to cover the abortion decision; that the right, nonetheless, is not absolute and is subject to some limitations; and that at some point the state interests as to protection of health, medical standards, and prenatal life, become dominant. We agree with this approach.

Where certain "fundamental rights" are involved, the Court has held that regulation limiting these rights may be justified only by a "compelling state interest," and that legislative enactments must be narrowly drawn to express only the legitimate state interests at stake.

In the recent abortion cases, cited above, courts have recognized these principles. Those striking down state laws have generally scrutinized the State's interests in protecting health and potential life, and have concluded that neither interest justified broad limitations on the reasons for which a physician and his pregnant patient might decide that she should have an abortion in the early stages of pregnancy. Courts sustaining state laws have held that the State's determinations to protect health or prenatal life are dominant and constitutionally justifiable.

The District Court held that the appellee failed to meet his burden demonstrating that the Texas statute's infringement upon Roe's rights was necessary to support a compelling state interest, and that, although the appellee presented "several compelling justifications for state presence in the area of abortions," the statutes outstripped these justifications and swept "far beyond any areas of compelling state interest." Appellant and appellee both contest that holding. Appellant, as has been indicated, claims an absolute right that bars any state imposition of criminal penalties in the area. Appellee argues that the State's determination to recognize and protect prenatal life from and after conception constitutes a compelling state interest. As noted above, we do not agree fully with either formulation.

A. The appellee and certain *amici* argue that the fetus is a "person" within the language and meaning of the Fourteenth Amendment. In support of this, they outline at length and in detail the well-known facts of fetal development. If this suggestion of personhood is established, the appellant's case, of course, collapses, for the fetus' right to life would then be guaranteed specifically by the Amendment. The appellant conceded as much on re-argument. On the other hand, the appellee conceded on re-argument that no case could be cited that holds that a fetus is a person within the meaning of the Fourteenth Amendment.

The Constitution does not define "person" in so many words. Section 1 of the Fourteenth Amendment contains three references to "person." In nearly all these instances, the use of the word is such that it has application only postnatally. None indicates, with any assurance, that it has any possible prenatal application.

All this, together with our observation, *supra*, that throughout the major portion of the 19th century prevailing legal abortion practices were far freer than they are today, persuades us that the word "person," as used in the Fourteenth Amendment, does not include the unborn. This is in accord with the results reached in those few cases where the issue has been squarely presented. Indeed, our decision in *United States v. Vuitch*, 402 U.S. 62 (1971), inferentially is to the same effect, for we there would not have indulged in statutory interpretation favorable to abortion in specified circumstances if the necessary consequence was the termination of life entitled to Fourteenth Amendment protection.

This conclusion, however, does not of itself fully answer the contentions raised by Texas, and we pass on to other considerations.

B. The pregnant woman cannot be isolated in her privacy. She carried an embryo and, later, a fetus, if one accepts the medical definitions of the developing young in the human uterus. See Dorland's Illustrated Medical Dictionary 478–479, 547 (24th ed. 1965). The situation therefore is inherently different from marital intimacy, or bedroom possession of obscene material, or marriage, or procreation, or education, with which *Eisenstadt* and *Griswold, Stanley, Loving, Skinner,* and *Pierce* and *Meyer* were respectively concerned. As we have intimated above, it is reasonable and appropriate for a State to decide that at some point in time another interest, that of health of the mother or that of potential human life, becomes significantly involved. The woman's privacy is no longer sole and any right of privacy she possesses must be measured accordingly.

Texas urges that, apart from the Fourteenth Amendment, life begins at conception and is present throughout pregnancy, and that, therefore, the State has a compelling interest in protecting that life from and after conception. We need not resolve the difficult question of when life begins. When those trained in the respective disciplines of medicine, philosophy, and theology are unable to arrive at any consensus, the judiciary, at this point in the development of man's knowledge, is not in a position to speculate as to the answer.

It should be sufficient to note briefly the wide divergence of thinking on this most sensitive and difficult question. There has always been strong support for the view that life does not begin until live birth. This was the belief of the Stoics. It appears to be the predominant, though not the unanimous, attitude of the Jewish faith. It may be taken to represent also the position of a large segment of the Protestant community, insofar as that can be ascertained; organized groups that have taken a formal position on the abortion issue have generally regarded abortion as a matter for the conscience of the individual and her family. As we have noted, the common law found greater significance in quickening. Physicians and their scientific colleagues have regarded that event with less interest and have tended to focus either upon conception, upon live birth, or upon the interim point at which the fetus becomes "viable," that is, potentially able to live outside the mother's womb, albeit with artificial aid. Viability is usually placed at about seven months (28 weeks) but may occur earlier, even at 24 weeks. The Aristotelian theory of "mediate animation," that held sway throughout the Middle Ages and the Renaissance in Europe, continued to be official Roman Catholic dogma until the 19th century, despite opposition to this "ensoulment" theory from those in the Church who would recognize the existence of life from the moment of conception. The latter is now, of course, the official belief of the Catholic Church. As one brief *amicus* discloses, this is a view strongly held by many non-Catholics as well, and by many physicians. Substantial problems for precise definition of this view are posed, however, by new embryological data that purport to indicate that conception is a "process" over time, rather than an event, and by new medical techniques such as menstrual extraction, the "morning-after" pill, implantation of embryos, artificial insemination, and even artificial wombs.

In areas other than criminal abortion, the law has been reluctant to endorse any theory that life, as we recognize it, begins before live birth or to accord legal rights to the unborn except in narrowly defined situations and except when the rights are contingent upon live birth. For example, the traditional rule of tort law denied recovery for prenatal injuries even though the child was born alive. That rule has been changed in almost every jurisdiction. In most States, recovery is said to be permitted only if the fetus was viable, or at least quick, when the injuries were sustained, though few courts have squarely so held. In a recent development, generally opposed by the commentators, some States permit the parents of a stillborn child to maintain an action for wrongful death because of prenatal injuries. Such an action, however, would appear to be one to vindicate the parents' interest and is thus consistent with the view that the fetus, at most, represents only the potentiality of life. Similarly, unborn children have been recognized as acquiring rights or interests by way of inheritance or other devolution of property, and have been represented by guardians *ad litem.* Perfection of the interests involved, again, has generally been contingent upon live birth. In short, the unborn have never been recognized in the law as persons in the whole sense.

In view of all this, we do not agree that, by adopting one theory of life, Texas may override the rights of the pregnant woman that are at stake. We repeat, however, that the State does have an important and legitimate interest in preserving and protecting the health of the pregnant woman, whether she be a resident of the State or a nonresident who seeks medical consultation and treatment there, and that it has still *another* important and legitimate interest in protecting the potentiality of human life. These interests are separate and distinct. Each grows in substantiality as the woman approaches term and, at a point during pregnancy, each becomes "compelling."

With respect to the State's important and legitimate interest in the health of the mother, the "compelling" point, in the light of present medical knowledge, is at approximately the end of the first trimester. This is so because of the now-established medical fact, referred to above, that until the end of the first trimester mortality in abortion may be less than mortality in normal childbirth. It follows that, from and after this point, a State may regulate the abortion procedure to the extent that the regulation reasonably relates to the preservation and protection of maternal health. Examples of permissible state regulation in this area are requirements as to the qualifications of the person who is to perform the abortion; as to the licensure of that person; as to the facility in which the procedure is to be performed, that is, whether it must be a hospital or may be a clinic or some other place of less-than-hospital status; as to the licensing of the facility; and the like.

This means, on the other hand, that, for the period of pregnancy prior to this "compelling" point, the attending physician, in consultation with his patient, is free to determine, without regulation by the State, that, in his medical judgment, the patient's pregnancy should be terminated. If that decision is reached, the judgment may be effectuated by an abortion free of interference by the State.

With respect to the State's important and legitimate interest in potential life, the "compelling" point is at viability. This is so because the fetus then presumably has the capability of meaningful life

outside the mother's womb. State regulation protective of fetal life after viability thus has both logical and biological justifications. If the State is interested in protecting fetal life after viability, it may go so far as to proscribe abortion during that period, except when it is necessary to preserve the life or health of the mother.

To summarize and to repeat:

1. A state criminal abortion statute of the current Texas type, that excepts from criminality only a *lifesaving* procedure on behalf of the mother, without regard to pregnancy stage and without recognition of the other interests involved, is violative of the Due Process Clause of the Fourteenth Amendment.

(a) For the stage prior to approximately the end of the first trimester, the abortion decision and its effectuation must be left to the medical judgment of the pregnant woman's attending physician.

(b) For the stage subsequent to approximately the end of the first trimester, the State, in promoting its interest in the health of the mother, may, if it chooses, regulate the abortion procedure in ways that are reasonably related to maternal health.

(c) For the stage subsequent to viability, the State in promoting its interest in the potentiality of human life may, if it chooses, regulate, and even proscribe, abortion except where it is necessary, in appropriate medical judgment, for the preservation of the life or health of the mother.

2. The State may define the term "physician" as it has been employed in the preceding paragraphs of this Part XI of this opinion, to mean only a physician currently licensed by the State, and may proscribe any abortion by a person who is not a physician as so defined.

In *Doe v. Bolton, post,* p. 179, procedural requirements contained in one of the modern abortion statutes are considered. That opinion and this one, of course, are to be read together.

This holding, we feel, is consistent with the relative weights of the respective interests involved, with the lessons and examples of medical and legal history, with the lenity of the common law, and with the demands of the profound problems of the present day. The decision leaves the State free to place increasing restrictions on abortion as the period of pregnancy lengthens, so long as those restrictions are tailored to the recognized state interests. The decision vindicates the right of the physician to administer medical treatment according to his professional judgment up to the points where important state interests provide compelling justifications for intervention. Up to those points, the abortion decision in all its aspects is inherently, and primarily, a medical decision, and basic responsibility for it must rest with the physician. If an individual practitioner abuses the privilege of exercising proper medical judgment, the usual remedies, judicial and intra-professional, are available.

Mr. Justice Rehnquist, dissenting.

The Court's opinion brings to the decision of this troubling question both extensive historical fact and a wealth of legal scholarship. While the opinion thus commands my respect, I find myself nonetheless in fundamental disagreement with those parts of it that invalidate the Texas statute in question, and therefore dissent.

The Court's opinion decides that a State may impose virtually no restriction on the performance of abortions during the first trimester of pregnancy. Our previous decisions indicate that a necessary predicate for such an opinion is a plaintiff who was in her first trimester of pregnancy at some time during the pendency of her lawsuit. While a party may vindicate his own constitutional rights, he may not seek vindication for the rights of others. The Court's statement of facts in this case makes clear, however, that the record in no way indicates the presence of such a plaintiff. We know only that plaintiff Roe at the time of filing her complaint was a pregnant woman; for aught that appears in this record, she may have been in her last trimester of pregnancy as of the date the complaint was filed.

Nothing in the Court's opinion indicates that Texas might not constitutionally apply its proscription of abortion as written to a woman in that stage of pregnancy. Nonetheless, the Court uses her complaint against the Texas statute as a fulcrum for deciding that States may impose virtually no restrictions on medical abortions performed during the *first* trimester of pregnancy. In deciding such a hypothetical lawsuit, the Court departs from the longstanding admonition that it should never "formulate a rule of constitutional law broader than is required by the precise facts to which it is to be applied." *Liverpool, New York & Philadelphia S.S. Co. v. Commissioners of Emigration*, 113 U.S. 33, 39 (1885).

Even if there were a plaintiff in this case capable of litigating the issue which the Court decides, I would reach a conclusion opposite to that reached by the Court. I have difficulty in concluding, as the Court does, that the right of "privacy" is involved in this case. Texas, by the statute here challenged, bars the performance of a medical abortion by a licensed physician on a plaintiff such as Roe. A transaction resulting in an operation such as this is not "private" in the ordinary usage of that word. Nor is the "privacy" that the Court finds here even a distant relative of the freedom from searches and seizures protected by the Fourth Amendment to the Constitution, which the Court has referred to as embodying a right to privacy. *Katz v. United States*, 389 U.S. 347 (1967).

If the Court means by the term "privacy" no more than that the claim of a person to be free from unwanted state regulation of consensual transactions may be a form of "liberty" protected by the Fourteenth Amendment, there is no doubt that similar claims have been upheld in our earlier decisions on the basis of that liberty. I agree with the statement of Mr. Justice Stewart in his concurring opinion that the "liberty," against deprivation of which without due process the Fourteenth Amendment protects, embraces more than the rights found in the Bill of Rights. But that liberty is not guaranteed absolutely against deprivation, only against deprivation without due process of law. The test traditionally applied in the area of social and economic legislation is whether or not a law such as that challenged has a rational relation to a valid state objective. The Due Process Clause of the Fourteenth Amendment undoubtedly does place a limit, albeit a broad one, on legislative power to enact laws such as this. If the Texas statute were to prohibit an abortion even where the mother's life is in jeopardy, I have little doubt that such a statute would lack a rational relation to a valid state objective under the test stated in *Williamson, supra*. But the Court's sweeping invalidation of any restrictions on abortion during the first trimester is impossible to justify under that standard, and the conscious weighing of competing factors that the Court's opinion apparently substitutes for the established test is far more appropriate to a legislative judgment than to a judicial one.

The Court eschews the history of the Fourteenth Amendment in its reliance on the "compelling state interest" test. But the Court adds a new wrinkle to this test by transposing it from the legal considerations associated with the Equal Protection Clause of the Fourteenth Amendment to this case arising under the Due Process Clause of the Fourteenth Amendment. Unless I misapprehend the consequences of this transplanting of the "compelling state interest test," the Court's opinion will accomplish the seemingly impossible feat of leaving this area of the law more confused than it found it.

While the Court's opinion quotes from the dissent of Mr. Justice Holmes in *Lochner v. New York*, 198 U.S. 45, 74 (1905), the result it reaches is more closely attuned to the majority opinion of Mr. Justice Peckham in that case. As in *Lochner* and similar cases applying substantive due process standards to economic and social welfare legislation, the adoption of the compelling state interest standard will inevitably require this Court to examine the legislative policies and pass on the wisdom of these policies in the very process of deciding whether a particular state interest put forward may or may not be "compelling." The decision here to break pregnancy into three distinct terms and to outline the permissible restrictions the State may impose in each one, for example, partakes more of judicial legislation than it does of a determination of the intent of the drafters of the Fourteenth Amendment.

The fact that a majority of the States reflecting, after all, the majority sentiment in those States, have had restrictions on abortions for at least a century is a strong indication, it seems to me, that the asserted right to an abortion is not "so rooted in the traditions and conscience of our people as to be ranked as fundamental," *Snyder v. Massachusetts*, 291 U.S. 97, 105 (1934). Even today, when society's views on abortion are changing the very existence of the debate is evidence that the "right" to an abortion is not so universally accepted as the appellant would have us believe.

To reach its result, the Court necessarily has had to find within the scope of the Fourteenth Amendment a right that was apparently completely unknown to the drafters of the Amendment. As early as 1821, the first state law dealing directly with abortion was enacted by the Connecticut Legislature. Conn. Stat., Tit. 22 §§ 14, 16. By the time of the adoption of the Fourteenth Amendment in 1868, there were at least 36 laws enacted by state or territorial legislatures limiting abortion. While many States have amended or updated their laws, 21 of the laws on the books in 1868 remain in effect today. Indeed, the Texas statute struck down today was, as the majority notes, first enacted in 1857 and "has remained substantially unchanged to the present time."

There apparently was no question concerning the validity of this provision or of any of the other state statutes when the Fourteenth Amendment was adopted. The only conclusion possible from this history is that the drafters did not intend to have the Fourteenth Amendment withdraw from the States the power to legislate with respect to this matter.

Discussion Questions

1. In *Roe*, on what basis did the U.S. Supreme Court reason that the right to abortion is a fundamental right? How did the Court's appeal to the history of abortion in Western law, especially American law, influence its decision?

2. The Court argued that since people are divided over the issue of fetal personhood, therefore, abortion should remain legal. Do you agree with this reasoning? If you do not, explain why. If you do, how would you respond to the pro-life reply that the Court's argument is an argument from ignorance? That is to say, if one *does not* know that one is killing a human person, isn't that a good reason *not to* proceed with the activity, just as it would be prudent to not blow up a building because you do not know whether or not someone is still inside it?

3. Briefly summarize Justice Rehnquist's dissent. Do you think that he adequately addresses Justice Blackmun's case? Why or why not?

13

Planned Parenthood v. Casey (1992)

U.S. Supreme Court

Planned Parenthood v. Casey (1992) is an important Supreme Court decision because, although it upheld *Roe* as a legal precedent, it rejected *Roe*'s trimester breakdown and its conclusion that abortion is a fundamental constitutional right. In *Casey* the Court was asked to consider the constitutionality of five provisions of the Pennsylvania Abortion Control Act of 1982: (1) a woman seeking an abortion must give her informed consent before the procedure and be provided with certain information at least 24 hours before the abortion is performed; (2) the informed consent of one parent must be obtained for a minor to undergo an abortion, but judicial bypass procedure is provided; (3) a married woman seeking an abortion must sign a statement indicating that she has notified her husband, unless certain exceptions apply (e.g., she is being abused by her husband); (4) a medical emergency will excuse compliance with the statute's requirements; and (5) abortion-providing facilities must fulfill certain reporting requirements. The Court upheld as constitutional four of the five provisions, rejecting the third one based on what it calls the "undue burden" standard. That is to say, does the provision constitute a "substantial obstacle" for the woman seeking an abortion?

The following are excerpts from two opinions in *Casey*. The first represents the Court's opinion. It is written by Justices Sandra Day O'Connor, David Souter, and Anthony Kennedy. The second is Justice Antonin Scalia's dissent.

Justice O'Connor, Justice Kennedy, and Justice Souter announced the judgment of the Court and delivered the opinion of the Court with respect to Parts I, II, III,

V-A, V-C, and VI, an opinion with respect to Part V-E, in which Justice Stevens joins, and an opinion with respect to Parts IV, V-B, and V-D.

I

Liberty finds no refuge in a jurisprudence of doubt. Yet 19 years after our holding that the Constitution protects a woman's right to terminate her pregnancy in its early stages, *Roe v. Wade*, 410 U.S. 113 (1973), the definition of liberty is still questioned. Joining the respondents as *amicus curiae*, the United States, as it has done in five other cases in the last decade, again asks us to overrule *Roe*. See Brief for Respondents 104–117; Brief for United States as *Amicus Curiae* 8.

At issue in these cases are five provisions of the Pennsylvania Abortion Control Act of 1982 as amended in 1988 and 1989. 18 Pa. Cons. Stat. §§3203–3220 (1990). Relevant portions of the Act are set forth in the appendix. *Infra*, at 60. The Act requires that a woman seeking an abortion give her informed consent prior to the abortion procedure, and specifies that she be provided with certain information at least 24 hours before the abortion is performed. §3205. For a minor to obtain an abortion, the Act requires the informed consent of one of her parents, but provides for a judicial bypass option if the minor does not wish to or cannot obtain a parent's consent. §3206. Another provision of the Act requires that, unless certain exceptions apply, a married woman seeking an abortion must sign a statement indicating that she has notified her husband of her intended abortion. §3209. The Act exempts compliance with these three requirements in the event of a "medical emergency," which is defined in §3203 of the Act. See §§3203, 3205(a), 3206(a), 3209(c). In addition to the above provisions regulating the performance of abortions, the Act imposes certain reporting requirements on facilities that provide abortion services. §§3207(b), 3214(a), 3214(f).

Before any of these provisions took effect, the petitioners, who are five abortion clinics and one physician representing himself as well as a class of physicians who provide abortion services, brought this suit seeking declaratory and injunctive relief. Each provision was challenged as unconstitutional on its face. The District Court entered a preliminary injunction against the enforcement of the regulations, and, after a 3-day bench trial, held all the provisions at issue here unconstitutional, entering a permanent injunction against Pennsylvania's enforcement of them. 744 F. Supp. 1323 (ED Pa. 1990). The Court of Appeals for the Third Circuit affirmed in part and reversed in part, upholding all of the regulations except for the husband notification requirement. 947 F. 2d 682 (1991). We granted certiorari. 502 U.S. ____ (1992).

The Court of Appeals found it necessary to follow an elaborate course of reasoning even to identify the first premise to use to determine whether the statute enacted by Pennsylvania meets constitutional standards. See 947 F. 2d, at 687–698. And at oral argument in this Court, the attorney for the parties challenging the statute took the position that none of the enactments can be upheld without overruling *Roe v. Wade.* Tr. of Oral Arg. 5–6. We disagree with that analysis; but we acknowledge that our decisions after *Roe* cast doubt upon the meaning and reach of its holding. Further, the Chief Justice admits that he would overrule the central holding of *Roe* and adopt the rational relationship test as the sole criterion of constitutionality. See *post,* at ____. State and federal courts as well as legislatures throughout the Union must have guidance as they seek to address this subject in conformance with the Constitution. Given these premises, we find it imperative to review once more the principles that define the rights of the woman and the legitimate authority of the State respecting the termination of pregnancies by abortion procedures.

After considering the fundamental constitutional questions resolved by *Roe,* principles of institutional integrity, and the rule of *stare decisis,* we are led to conclude this: the essential holding of *Roe v. Wade* should be retained and once again reaffirmed.

It must be stated at the outset and with clarity that *Roe*'s essential holding, the holding we affirm, has three parts. First is a recognition of the right of the woman to choose to have an abortion before viability and to obtain it without undue interference from the State. Before viability, the State's interests are not strong enough to support a prohibition of abortion or the imposition of a substantial obstacle to the woman's effective right to elect the procedure. Second is a confirmation of the State's power to restrict abortions after fetal viability, if the law contains exceptions for pregnancies which endanger a woman's life or health. And third is the principle that the State has legitimate interests from the outset of the pregnancy in protecting the health of the woman and the life of the fetus that may become a child. These principles do not contradict one another; and we adhere to each.

II

Constitutional protection of the woman's decision to terminate her pregnancy derives from the Due Process Clause of the Fourteenth Amendment. It declares that no State shall "deprive any person of life, liberty, or property, without due process of law." The controlling word in the case before us is "liberty." Although a literal reading of the Clause might suggest that it governs only the procedures by which a State may deprive persons of liberty, for at least 105 years, at least since *Mugler v. Kansas,* 123 U.S. 623, 660–661 (1887), the Clause has been understood to contain a substantive component as well, one "barring certain government actions regardless of the fairness of the procedures used to implement them." *Daniels v. Williams,* 474 U.S. 327, 331 (1986). As Justice Brandeis (joined by Justice Holmes) observed, "[d]espite arguments to the contrary which had seemed to me persuasive, it is settled that the due process clause of the Fourteenth Amendment applies to matters of substantive law as well as to matters of procedure. Thus all fundamental rights comprised within the term liberty are protected by the Federal Constitution from invasion by the States." *Whitney v. California,* 274 U.S. 357, 373 (1927) (Brandeis, J., concurring). "[T]he guaranties of due process, though having their roots in Magna Carta's *'per legem terrae'* and considered as procedural safeguards 'against executive usurpation and tyranny,' have in this country 'become bulwarks also against arbitrary legislation.'" *Poe v. Ullman,* 367 U.S. 497, 541 (1961).

The most familiar of the substantive liberties protected by the Fourteenth Amendment are those recognized by the Bill of Rights. We have held that the Due Process Clause of the Fourteenth Amendment incorporates most of the Bill of Rights against the States. See e.g.., *Duncan v. Louisiana,* 391 U.S. 145, 147–148 (1968). It is tempting, as a means of curbing the discretion of federal judges, to suppose that liberty encompasses no more than those rights already guaranteed to the individual against federal interference by the express provisions of the first eight amendments to the Constitution. See *Adamson v. California,* 332 U.S. 46, 68–92 (1947) (Black, J., dissenting). But of course this Court has never accepted that view.

It is also tempting, for the same reason, to suppose that the Due Process Clause protects only those practices, defined at the most specific level, that were protected against government interference by other rules of law when the Fourteenth Amendment was ratified. But such a view would be inconsistent with our law. It is a promise of the Constitution that there is a realm of personal liberty which the government may not enter. We have vindicated this principle before. Marriage is mentioned nowhere in the Bill of Rights and interracial marriage was illegal in most States in the 19th century, but the Court was no doubt correct in finding it to be an aspect of liberty protected against state interference by the substantive component of the Due Process Clause in *Loving v. Virginia*, 388 U.S. 1, 12 (1967) (relying, in an opinion for eight Justices, on the Due Process Clause). . . .

Neither the Bill of Rights nor the specific practices of States at the time of the adoption of the Fourteenth Amendment marks the outer limits of the substantive sphere of liberty which the Fourteenth Amendment protects. See U.S. Const., Amend. 9. As the second Justice Harlan recognized:

> "[T]he full scope of the liberty guaranteed by the Due Process Clause cannot be found in or limited by the precise terms of the specific guarantees elsewhere provided in the Constitution. This 'liberty' is not a series of isolated points pricked out in terms of the taking of property; the freedom of speech, press, and religion; the right to keep and bear arms; the freedom from unreasonable searches and seizures; and so on. It is a rational continuum which, broadly speaking, includes a freedom from all substantial arbitrary impositions and purposeless restraints, . . . and which also recognizes, what a reasonable and sensitive judgment must, that certain interests require particularly careful scrutiny of the state needs asserted to justify their abridgment." *Poe v. Ullman, supra*, at 543 (Harlan, J., dissenting from dismissal on jurisdictional grounds).

Justice Harlan wrote these words in addressing an issue the full Court did not reach in *Poe v. Ullman*, but the Court adopted his position four Terms later in *Griswold v. Connecticut, supra*. In Griswold, we held that the Constitution does not permit a State to forbid a married couple to use contraceptives. That same freedom was later guaranteed, under the Equal Protection Clause, for unmarried couples.

Constitutional protection was extended to the sale and distribution of contraceptives in *Carey v. Population Services International, supra*. It is settled now, as it was when the Court heard arguments in *Roe v. Wade*, that the Constitution places limits on a State's right to interfere with a person's most basic decisions about family and parenthood. . . .

The inescapable fact is that adjudication of substantive due process claims may call upon the Court in interpreting the Constitution to exercise that same capacity which by tradition courts always have exercised: reasoned judgment. Its boundaries are not susceptible of expression as a simple rule. That does not mean we are free to invalidate state policy choices with which we disagree; yet neither does it permit us to shrink from the duties of our office. As Justice Harlan observed:

> "Due process has not been reduced to any formula; its content cannot be determined by reference to any code. The best that can be said is that through the course of this Court's decisions it has represented the balance which our Nation, built upon postulates of respect for the liberty of the individual, has struck between that liberty and the demands of organized society. If the supplying of content to this Constitutional concept has of necessity been a rational process, it certainly has not been one where judges have felt free to roam where unguided speculation might take them. The balance of which I speak is the balance struck by this country, having regard to what history teaches are the traditions from which it developed as well as the traditions from which it broke. That tradition is a living thing. A decision of this Court which radically departs from it could not long survive, while a decision which builds on what has survived is likely to be sound. No formula could serve as a substitute, in this area, for judgment and restraint." *Poe v. Ullman*, 367 U.S., at 542 (Harlan, J., dissenting from dismissal on jurisdictional grounds).

Men and women of good conscience can disagree, and we suppose some always shall disagree, about the profound moral and spiritual implications of terminating a pregnancy, even in its earliest stage. Some of us as individuals find abortion offensive to our most basic principles of morality, but that cannot control our decision. Our obligation is to define the liberty of all, not to mandate our own moral code. The underlying constitutional issue is whether the State can resolve these philosophic questions in such a definitive way that a woman lacks all choice in the matter except perhaps in those rare circumstances in which the pregnancy is itself a danger to her own life or health, or is the result of rape or incest.

It is conventional constitutional doctrine that when reasonable people disagree the government can adopt one position or the other. That theorem, however, assumes a state of affairs in which the choice does not intrude upon a protected liberty. Thus, while some people might disagree about whether or not the flag should be saluted, or disagree about the proposition that it may not be defiled, we have ruled that a State may not compel or enforce one view or the other.

Our law affords constitutional protection to personal decisions relating to marriage, procreation, contraception, family relationships, child rearing, and education. Our cases recognize "the right of the individual, married or single, to be free from unwarranted governmental intrusion into matters so fundamentally affecting a person as the decision whether to bear or beget a child." *Eisenstadt v. Baird, supra*, at 453. Our precedents "have respected the private realm of family life which the state cannot enter." *Prince v. Massachusetts*, 321 U.S. 158, 166 (1944). These matters involving the most intimate and personal choices a person may make in a lifetime, choices central to personal dignity and autonomy, are central to the liberty protected by the Fourteenth Amendment. At the heart of liberty is the right to define one's own concept of existence, of meaning, of the universe, and of the mystery of human life. Beliefs about these matters could not define the attributes of personhood were they formed under compulsion of the State.

These considerations begin our analysis of the woman's interest in terminating her pregnancy but cannot end it, for this reason: though the abortion decision may originate within the zone of conscience and belief it is more than a philosophic exercise. Abortion is a unique act. It is an act fraught with consequences for others: for the woman who must live with the implications of her decision; for the persons who perform and assist in the procedure; for the spouse, family, and society which must confront the knowledge that these procedures exist, procedures some deem nothing short of an act of violence against innocent human life; and, depending on one's beliefs, for the life or potential life that is aborted. Though abortion is conduct, it does not follow that the State is entitled to proscribe it in all instances. That is because the liberty of the woman is at stake in a sense unique to the human condition and so unique to the law. The mother who carries a child to full term is subject to anxieties, to physical constraints, to pain that only she must bear. That these sacrifices have from the beginning of the human race been endured by woman with a pride that ennobles her in the eyes of others and gives to the infant a bond of love cannot alone be grounds for the State to insist she make the sacrifice. Her suffering is too intimate and personal for the State to insist, without more, upon its own vision of the woman's role, however dominant that vision has been in the course of our history and our culture. The destiny of the woman must be shaped to a large extent on her own conception of her spiritual imperatives and her place in society.

It should be recognized, moreover, that in some critical respects the abortion decision is of the same character as the decision to use contraception, to which *Griswold v. Connecticut, Eisenstadt v. Baird*, and *Carey v. Population Services International*, afford constitutional protection. We have no doubt as to the correctness of those decisions. They support the reasoning in *Roe* relating to the woman's liberty because they involve personal decisions concerning not only the meaning of procreation but also human responsibility and respect for it. As with abortion, reasonable people will have differences of opinion about these matters. One view is based on such reverence for the wonder of creation that any pregnancy ought to be welcomed and carried to full term no matter how difficult it will be to provide for the child and ensure its wellbeing. Another is that the inability to provide for the nurture and care of the infant is a cruelty to the child and an anguish to the parent. These are intimate views with infinite variations, and their deep, personal character underlay our decisions in *Griswold, Eisenstadt*, and *Carey*. The same concerns are present when the woman confronts the reality that, perhaps despite her attempts to avoid it, she has become pregnant.

It was this dimension of personal liberty that *Roe* sought to protect, and its holding invoked the reasoning and the tradition of the precedents we have discussed, granting protection to substantive liberties of the person. *Roe* was, of course, an extension of those cases and, as the decision itself indicated, the separate States could act in some degree to further their own legitimate interests in protecting prenatal life. The extent to which the legislatures of the States might act to outweigh the interests of the woman in choosing to terminate her pregnancy was a subject of debate both in *Roe* itself and in decisions following it.

While we appreciate the weight of the arguments made on behalf of the State in the case before us, arguments which in their ultimate formulation conclude that *Roe* should be overruled, the reservations any of us may have in reaffirming the central holding of *Roe* are outweighed by the explication of individual liberty we have given combined with the force of *stare decisis*. We turn now to that doctrine.

III

A

The obligation to follow precedent begins with necessity, and a contrary necessity marks its outer limit. With Cardozo, we recognize that no judicial system could do society's work if it eyed each issue afresh in every cases that raised it. See B. Cardozo, The Nature of the Judicial Process 149 (1921). Indeed, the very concept of the rule of law underlying our own Constitution requires such continuity over time that a respect for precedent is, by definition, indispensable. See Powell, Stare Decisis and Judicial Restraint, 1991 Journal of Supreme Court History 13, 16. At the other extreme, a different necessity would make itself felt if a prior judicial ruling should come to be seen so clearly as error that its enforcement was for that very reason doomed.

Even when the decision to overrule a prior case is not, as in the rare, latter instance, virtually foreordained, it is common wisdom that the rule of *stare decisis* is not an "inexorable command," and certainly it is not such in every constitutional case. . . . Rather, when this Court reexamines a prior holding, its judgment is customarily informed by a series of prudential and pragmatic considerations designed to test the consistency of overruling a prior decision with the ideal of the rule of law, and to gauge the respective costs of reaffirming and overruling a prior case. Thus, for example, we may ask whether the rule has proved to be intolerable simply in defying practical workability, *Swift & Co. v. Wickham*, 382 U.S. 111, 116 (1965); whether the rule is subject to a kind of reliance that would lend a special hardship to the consequences of overruling and add inequity to the cost of repudiation, e.g.., *United States v. Title Ins. & Trust Co.*, 265 U.S. 472, 486 (1924); whether related principles of law have so far developed as to have left the old rule no more than a remnant of abandoned doctrine, see *Patterson v. McLean Credit Union*, 491 U.S. 164, 173–174 (1989); or whether facts have so changed or come to be seen so differently, as to have robbed the old rule of significant application or justification.

So in this case we may inquire whether *Roe's* central rule has been found unworkable; whether the rule's limitation on state power could be removed without serious inequity to those who have relied upon it or significant damage to the stability of the society governed by the rule in question; whether the law's growth in the intervening years has left *Roe's* central rule a doctrinal anachronism discounted by society; and whether *Roe's* premises of fact have so far changed in the ensuing two decades as to render its central holding somehow irrelevant or unjustifiable in dealing with the issue it addressed.

1

Although *Roe* has engendered opposition, it has in no sense proven "unworkable," representing as it does a simple limitation beyond which a state law is unenforceable. While *Roe* has, of course, required judicial assessment of state laws affecting the exercise of the choice guaranteed against government infringement, and although the need for such review will remain as a consequence of today's decision, the required determinations fall within judicial competence.

2

The inquiry into reliance counts the cost of a rule's repudiation as it would fall on those who have relied reasonably on the rule's continued application. Since the classic case for weighing reliance heavily in favor of following the earlier rule occurs in the commercial context, see *Payne v. Tennessee, supra*, at ___ (slip op., at ___), where advance planning of great precision is most obviously a necessity, it is no cause for surprise that some would find no reliance worthy of consideration in support of *Roe*.

While neither respondents nor their *amici* in so many words deny that the abortion right invites some reliance prior to its actual exercise, one can readily imagine an argument stressing the dissimilarity of this case to one involving property or contract. Abortion is customarily chosen as an unplanned response to the consequence of unplanned activity or to the failure of conventional birth control, and except on the assumption that no intercourse would have occurred but for *Roe's* holding, such behavior may appear to justify no reliance claim. Even if reliance could be claimed on that unrealistic assumption, the argument might run, any reliance interest would be *de minimis*. This argument would be premised on the hypothesis that reproductive planning could take virtually immediate account of any sudden restoration of state authority to ban abortions.

To eliminate the issue of reliance that easily, however, one would need to limit cognizable reliance to specific instances of sexual activity. But to do this would be simply to refuse to face the fact that for two decades of economic and social developments, people have organized intimate relationships and made choices that define their views of themselves and their places in society, in reliance on the availability of abortion in the event that contraception should fail. The ability of women to participate equally in the economic and social life of the Nation has been facilitated by their ability to control their reproductive lives. See, *e.g.*, R. Petchesky, Abortion and Woman's Choice 109, 133, n. 7 (rev. ed. 1990). The Constitution serves human values, and while the effect of reliance on *Roe* cannot be exactly measured, neither can the certain cost of overruling *Roe* for people who have ordered their thinking and living around that case be dismissed.

3

No evolution of legal principle has left *Roe*'s doctrinal footings weaker than they were in 1973. No development of constitutional law since the case was decided has implicitly or explicitly left *Roe* behind as a mere survivor of obsolete constitutional thinking.

It will be recognized, of course, that *Roe* stands at an intersection of two lines of decisions, but in whichever doctrinal category one reads the case, the result for present purposes will be the same. The *Roe* Court itself placed its holding in the succession of cases most prominently exemplified by *Griswold v. Connecticut*, 381 U.S. 479 (1965), see *Roe*, 410 U.S., at 152-153. When it is so seen, *Roe* is clearly in no jeopardy, since subsequent constitutional developments have neither disturbed, nor do they threaten to diminish, the scope of recognized protection accorded to the liberty relating to intimate relationships, the family, and decisions about whether or not to beget or bear a child. . . .

Roe, however, may be seen not only as an exemplar of *Griswold* liberty but as a rule (whether or not mistaken) of personal autonomy and bodily integrity, with doctrinal affinity to cases recognizing limits on governmental power to mandate medical treatment or to bar its rejection. If so, our cases since *Roe* accord with *Roe*'s view that a State's interest in the protection of life falls short of justifying any plenary override of individual liberty claims. . . .

Finally, one could classify *Roe* as *sui generis*. If the case is so viewed then there clearly has been no erosion of its central determination. The original

holding resting on the concurrence of seven Members of the Court in 1973 was expressly affirmed by a majority of six in 1983, . . .

More recently, in *Webster v. Reproductive Health Services*, 492 U.S. 490 (1989), although two of the present authors questioned the trimester framework in a way consistent with our judgment today, see *id.*, at 518 (Rehnquist, C.J., joined by White, and Kennedy, JJ.) *id.*, at 529 (O'Connor, J., concurring in part and concurring in judgment), a majority of the Court either decided to reaffirm or declined to address the constitutional validity of the central holding of *Roe*. See *Webster*, 492 U.S., at 521 (Rehnquist, C.J., joined by White and Kennedy, JJ.); *id.*, at 525–526 (O'Connor, J., concurring in part and concurring in judgment); *id.*, 537, 553 (Blackmun, J. joined by Brennan and Marshall, JJ., concurring in part and dissenting in part); *id.*, at 561–563 (Stevens, J., concurring in part and dissenting in part).

Nor will courts building upon *Roe* be likely to hand down erroneous decisions as a consequence. Even on the assumption that the central holding of *Roe* was in error, that error would go only to the strength of the state interest in fetal protection, not to the recognition afforded by the Constitution to the woman's liberty. The latter aspect of the decision fits comfortably within the framework of the Court's prior decisions including *Skinner v. Oklahoma ex rel. Williamson*, 316 U.S. 535 (1942), *Griswold, supra*, *Loving v. Virginia*, 388 U.S. 1 (1967), and *Eisenstadt v. Baird*, 405 U.S. 438 (1972), the holdings of which are "not a series of isolated points," but mark a "rational continuum." *Poe v. Ullman*, 367 U.S. at 543 (1961) (Harlan, J., dissenting). As we described in *Carey v. Population Services International, supra*, the liberty which encompasses those decisions

> "includes 'the interest in independence in making certain kinds of important decisions.' While the outer limits of this aspect of [protected liberty] have not been marked by the Court, it is clear that among the decisions that an individual may make without unjustified government interference are personal decisions 'relating to marriage, procreation, contraception, family relationships, and child rearing and education.'" *Id.*, at 684–685 (citations omitted).

The soundness of this prong of the *Roe* analysis is apparent from a consideration of the alternative. If indeed the woman's interest in deciding whether to bear and beget a child had not been recognized as in *Roe* the State might as readily restrict a woman's right to choose to carry a pregnancy to term as to terminate it, to further asserted state interests in population control, or eugenics, for example. Yet *Roe* has been sensibly relied upon to counter any such suggestions. . . . In any event, because *Roe*'s scope is confined by the fact of its concern with post-conception potential life, a concern otherwise likely to be implicated only by some forms of contraception protected independently under *Griswold* and later cases, any error in *Roe* is unlikely to have serious ramifications in future cases.

4

We have seen how time has overtaken some of *Roe*'s factual assumptions: advances in maternal health care allow for abortions safe to the mother later in pregnancy than was true in 1973, and advances in neonatal care have advanced viability to a point somewhat earlier. . . . But these facts go only to the scheme of time limits on the realization of competing interests, and the divergences from the factual premises of 1973 have no bearing on the validity of *Roe*'s central holding, that viability marks the earliest point at which the State's interest in fetal life is constitutionally adequate to justify a legislative ban on nontherapeutic abortions. The soundness or unsoundness of that constitutional judgment in no sense turns on whether viability occurs at approximately 28 weeks, as was usual at the time of *Roe*, at 23 to 24 weeks, as it sometimes does today, or at some moment even slightly earlier in pregnancy, as it may if fetal respiratory capacity can somehow be enhanced in the future. Whenever it may occur, the attainment of viability may continue to serve as the critical fact, just as it has done since *Roe* was decided; which is to say that no change in *Roe*'s factual underpinning has left its central holding obsolete, and none supports an argument for overruling it.

5

The sum of the precedential inquiry to this point shows *Roe*'s underpinnings unweakened in any way affecting its central holding. While it has engendered disapproval, it has not been unworkable. An entire generation has come of age free to assume *Roe*'s concept of liberty in defining the capacity of women to act in society, and to make reproductive decisions, no erosion of principle going to liberty or personal autonomy has left *Roe*'s central holding a doctrinal

remnant; *Roe* portends no developments at odds with other precedent for the analysis of personal liberty; and no changes of fact have rendered viability more or less appropriate as the point at which the balance of interests tips. Within the bounds of normal *stare decisis* analysis, then, and subject to the considerations on which it customarily turns, the stronger argument is for affirming *Roe*'s central holding, with whatever degree of personal reluctance any of us may have, not for overruling it.

B

Overruling previous decisions by Sup. Ct. due to public controversy

In a less significant case, *stare decisis* analysis could, and would, stop at the point we have reached. But the sustained and widespread debate *Roe* has provoked calls for some comparison between that case and others of comparable dimension that have responded to national controversies and taken on the impress of the controversies addressed. Only two such decisional lines from the past century present themselves for examination, and in each instance the result reached by the Court accorded with the principles we apply today.

The first example is that line of cases identified with *Lochner v. New York*, 198 U.S. 45 (1905), which imposed substantive limitations on legislation limiting economic autonomy in favor of health and welfare regulation, adopting, in Justice Holmes' view, the theory of *laissez-faire*. *Id.*, at 75 (Holmes, J., dissenting). The *Lochner* decisions were exemplified by *Adkins v. Children's Hospital of D.C.*, 261 U.S. 525 (1923), in which this Court held it to be an infringement of constitutionally protected liberty of contract to require the employers of adult women to satisfy minimum wage standards. Fourteen years later, *West Coast Hotel Co. v. Parrish*, 300 U.S. 379 (1937), signaled the demise of *Lochner* by overruling *Adkins*. In the meantime, the Depression had come and, with it, the lesson that seemed unmistakable to most people by 1937, that the interpretation of contractual freedom protected in *Adkins* rested on fundamentally false factual assumptions about the capacity of a relatively unregulated market to satisfy minimal levels of human welfare. See *West Coast Hotel Co., supra*, at 399. As Justice Jackson wrote of the constitutional crisis of 1937 shortly before he came on the bench, "The older world of *laissez faire* was recognized everywhere outside the Court to be dead." R. Jackson, The Struggle for Judicial Supremacy 85 (1941). The facts upon which the earlier case had premised a constitutional resolution of social controversy had proved to be untrue, and history's demonstration of their untruth not only justified but required the new choice of constitutional principle that *West Coast Hotel* announced. Of course, it was true that the Court lost something by its misperception, or its lack of prescience, and the Court-packing crisis only magnified the loss; but the clear demonstration that the facts of economic life were different from those previously assumed warranted the repudiation of the old law.

The second comparison that 20th century history invites is with the cases employing the separate-but-equal rule for applying the Fourteenth Amendment's equal protection guarantee. They began with *Plessy v. Ferguson*, 163 U.S. 537 (1896), holding that legislatively mandated racial segregation in public transportation works no denial of equal protection, rejecting the argument that racial separation enforced by the legal machinery of American society treats the black race as inferior. The *Plessy* Court considered "the underlying fallacy of the plaintiff's argument to consist in the assumption that the enforced separation of the two races stamps the colored race with a badge of inferiority. If this be so, it is not by reason of anything found in the act, but solely because the colored race chooses to put that construction upon it." *Id.*, at 551. Whether, as a matter of historical fact, the Justices in the *Plessy* majority believed this or not, see *id.*, at 557, 562 (Harlan, J., dissenting), this understanding of the implication of segregation was the stated justification for the Court's opinion. But this understanding of the facts and the rule it was stated to justify were repudiated in *Brown v. Board of Education*, 347 U.S. 483 (1954). As one commentator observed, the question before the Court in *Brown* was "whether discrimination inheres in that segregation which is imposed by law in the twentieth century in certain specific states in the American Union. And that question has meaning and can find an answer only on the ground of history and of common knowledge about the facts of life in the times and places aforesaid." Black, The Lawfulness of the Segregation Decisions, 69 Yale L. J. 421, 427 (1960).

The Court in *Brown* addressed these facts of life by observing that whatever may have been the understanding in *Plessy*'s time of the power of segregation to stigmatize those who were segregated with a "badge of inferiority," it was clear by 1954 that legally sanctioned segregation had just such an effect, to the point that racially separate public educational facilities were deemed inherently unequal. 374 U.S., at 494–495. Society's understanding of the facts upon

which a constitutional ruling was sought in 1954 was thus fundamentally different from the basis claimed for the decision in 1896. While we think *Plessy* was wrong the day it was decided, see *Plessy, supra*, at 552–564 (Harlan, J., dissenting), we must also recognize that the *Plessy* Court's explanation for its decision was so clearly at odds with the facts apparent to the Court in 1954 that the decision to reexamine *Plessy* was on this ground alone not only justified but required.

West Coast Hotel and *Brown* each rested on facts, or an understanding of facts, changed from those which furnished the claimed justifications for the earlier constitutional resolutions. Each case was comprehensible as the Court's response to facts that the country could understand, or had come to understand already, but which the Court of an earlier day, as its own declarations disclosed, had not been able to perceive. As the decisions were thus comprehensible they were also defensible, not merely as the victories of one doctrinal school over another by dint of numbers (victories though they were), but as applications of constitutional principle to facts as they had not been seen by the Court before. In constitutional adjudication, as elsewhere in life, changed circumstances may impose new obligations, and the thoughtful part of the Nation could accept each decision to overrule a prior case as a response to the Court's constitutional duty.

Because the case before us presents no such occasion it could be seen as no such response. Because neither the factual underpinnings of *Roe*'s central holding nor our understanding of it has changed (and because no other indication of weakened precedent has been shown) the Court could not pretend to be reexamining the prior law with any justification beyond a present doctrinal disposition to come out differently from the Court of 1973. To overrule prior law for no other reason than that would run counter to the view repeated in our cases, that a decision to overrule should rest on some special reason over and above the belief that a prior case was wrongly decided. . . .

C

The examination of the conditions justifying the repudiation of *Adkins* by *West Coast Hotel* and *Plessy* by *Brown* is enough to suggest the terrible price that would have been paid if the Court had not overruled as it did. In the present case, however, as our analysis to this point makes clear, the terrible price would be paid for overruling. Our analysis would not be complete, however, without explaining why overruling *Roe*'s central holding would not only reach an unjustifiable result under principles of *stare decisis*, but would seriously weaken the Court's capacity to exercise the judicial power and to function as the Supreme Court of a Nation dedicated to the rule of law. To understand why this would be so it is necessary to understand the source of this Court's authority, the conditions necessary for its preservation, and its relationship to the country's understanding of itself as a constitutional Republic.

The root of American governmental power is revealed most clearly in the instance of the power conferred by the Constitution upon the Judiciary of the United States and specifically upon this Court. As Americans of each succeeding generation are rightly told, the Court cannot buy support for its decisions by spending money and, except to a minor degree, it cannot independently coerce obedience to its decrees. The Court's power lies, rather, in its legitimacy, a product of substance and perception that shows itself in the people's acceptance of the Judiciary as fit to determine what the Nation's law means and to declare what it demands.

The underlying substance of this legitimacy is of course the warrant for the Court's decisions in the Constitution and the lesser sources of legal principle on which the Court draws. That substance is expressed in the Court's opinions, and our contemporary understanding is such that a decision without principled justification would be no judicial act at all. But even when justification is furnished by apposite legal principle, something more is required. Because not every conscientious claim of principled justification will be accepted as such, the justification claimed must be beyond dispute. The Court must take care to speak and act in ways that allow people to accept its decisions on the terms the Court claims for them, as grounded truly in principle, not as compromises with social and political pressures having, as such, no bearing on the principled choices that the Court is obliged to make. Thus, the Court's legitimacy depends on making legally principled decisions under circumstances in which their principled character is sufficiently plausible to be accepted by the Nation.

The need for principled action to be perceived as such is implicated to some degree whenever this, or any other appellate court, overrules a prior case. This is not to say, of course, that this Court cannot give a perfectly satisfactory explanation in most cases. People understand that some of the Constitution's language is hard to fathom and that the Court's Justices are sometimes able to perceive significant facts or to understand principles of law that eluded their predecessors and that justify departures from existing decisions. However upsetting it may be to those most directly affected when one judicially derived rule replaces another, the country can accept some correction of error without necessarily questioning the legitimacy of the Court.

In two circumstances, however, the Court would almost certainly fail to receive the benefit of the doubt in overruling prior cases. There is, first, a point beyond which frequent overruling would overtax the country's belief in the Court's good faith. Despite the variety of reasons that may inform and justify a decision to overrule, we cannot forget that such a decision is usually perceived (and perceived correctly) as, at the least, a statement that a prior decision was wrong. There is a limit to the amount of error that can plausibly be imputed to prior courts. If that limit should be exceeded, disturbance of prior rulings would be taken as evidence that justifiable reexamination of principle had given way to drives for particular results in the short term. The legitimacy of the Court would fade with the frequency of its vacillation.

That first circumstance can be described as hypothetical; the second is to the point here and now. Where, in the performance of its judicial duties, the Court decides a case in such a way as to resolve the sort of intensely divisive controversy reflected in *Roe* and those rare, comparable cases, its decision has a dimension that the resolution of the normal case does not carry. It is the dimension present whenever the Court's interpretation of the Constitution calls the contending sides of a national controversy to end their national division by accepting a common mandate rooted in the Constitution.

The Court is not asked to do this very often, having thus addressed the Nation only twice in our lifetime, in the decisions of *Brown* and *Roe*. But when the Court does act in this way, its decision requires an equally rare precedential force to counter the inevitable efforts to overturn it and to thwart its implementation. Some of those efforts may be mere unprincipled emotional reactions; others may proceed from principles worthy of profound respect. But whatever the premises of opposition may be, only the most convincing justification under accepted standards of precedent could suffice to demonstrate that a later decision overruling the first was anything but a surrender to political pressure, and an unjustified repudiation of the principle on which the Court staked its authority in the first instance. So to overrule under fire in the absence of the most compelling reason to reexamine a watershed decision would subvert the Court's legitimacy beyond any serious question. . . .

The country's loss of confidence in the judiciary would be underscored by an equally certain and equally reasonable condemnation for another failing in overruling unnecessarily and under pressure. Some cost will be paid by anyone who approves or implements a constitutional decision where it is unpopular, or who refuses to work to undermine the decision or to force its reversal. The price may be criticism or ostracism or it may be violence. An extra price will be paid by those who themselves disapprove of the decision's results when viewed outside of constitutional terms, but who nevertheless struggle to accept it, because they respect the rule of law. To all those who will be so tested by following, the Court implicitly undertakes to remain steadfast, lest in the end a price be paid for nothing. The promise of constancy, once given, binds its maker for as long as the power to stand by the decision survives and the understanding of the issue has not changed so fundamentally as to render the commitment obsolete. From the obligation of this promise this Court cannot and should not assume any exemption when duty requires it to decide a case in conformance with the Constitution. A willing breach of it would be nothing less than a breach of faith, and no Court that broke its faith with the people could sensibly expect credit for principle in the decision by which it did that.

It is true that diminished legitimacy may be restored, but only slowly. Unlike the political branches, a Court thus weakened could not seek to regain its position with a new mandate from the voters, and even if the Court could somehow go to the polls, the loss of its principled character could not be retrieved by the casting of so many votes. Like the character of an individual, the legitimacy of the Court must be earned over time. So, indeed, must be the character of a Nation of people who aspire to live according to the rule of law. Their belief in themselves as such a people is not readily separable from their understanding of the Court invested with the authority to decide their constitutional cases and speak before all others for their constitutional ideals. If the Court's legitimacy should be undermined, then,

so would the country be in its very ability to see itself through its constitutional ideals. The Court's concern with legitimacy is not for the sake of the Court but for the sake of the Nation to which it is responsible.

The Court's duty in the present case is clear. In 1973, it confronted the already divisive issue of governmental power to limit personal choice to undergo abortion, for which it provided a new resolution based on the due process guaranteed by the Fourteenth Amendment. Whether or not a new social consensus is developing on that issue, its divisiveness is no less today than in 1973, and pressure to overrule the decision, like pressure to retain it, has grown only more intense. A decision to overrule *Roe*'s essential holding under the existing circumstances would address error, if error there was, at the cost of both profound and unnecessary damage to the Court's legitimacy, and to the Nation's commitment to the rule of law. It is therefore imperative to adhere to the essence of *Roe*'s original decision, and we do so today.

IV

From what we have said so far it follows that it is a constitutional liberty of the woman to have some freedom to terminate her pregnancy. We conclude that the basic decision in *Roe* was based on a constitutional analysis which we cannot now repudiate. The woman's liberty is not so unlimited, however, that from the outset the State cannot show its concern for the life of the unborn, and at a later point in fetal development the State's interest in life has sufficient force so that the right of the woman to terminate the pregnancy can be restricted.

That brings us, of course, to the point where much criticism has been directed at *Roe*, a criticism that always inheres when the Court draws a specific rule from what in the Constitution is but a general standard. We conclude, however, that the urgent claims of the woman to retain the ultimate control over her destiny and her body, claims implicit in the meaning of liberty, require us to perform that function. Liberty must not be extinguished for want of a line that is clear. And it falls to us to give some real substance to the woman's liberty to determine whether to carry her pregnancy to full term.

We conclude the line should be drawn at viability, so that before that time the woman has a right to choose to terminate her pregnancy. We adhere to this principle for two reasons. First, as we have said, is the doctrine of *stare decisis*. Any judicial act of line-drawing may seem somewhat arbitrary, but *Roe* was a reasoned statement, elaborated with great care. We have twice reaffirmed it in the face of great opposition. . . . Although we must overrule those parts of *Thornburgh* and *Akron I* which, in our view, are inconsistent with *Roe*'s statement that the State has a legitimate interest in promoting the life or potential life of the unborn, see *infra*, at ___, the central premise of those cases represents an unbroken commitment by this Court to the essential holding of *Roe*. It is that premise which we reaffirm today.

The second reason is that the concept of viability, as we noted in *Roe*, is the time at which there is a realistic possibility of maintaining and nourishing a life outside the womb, so that the independent existence of the second life can in reason and all fairness be the object of state protection that now overrides the rights of the woman. See *Roe v. Wade*, 410 U.S., at 163. Consistent with other constitutional norms, legislatures may draw lines which appear arbitrary without the necessity of offering a justification. But courts may not. We must justify the lines we draw. And there is no line other than viability which is more workable. To be sure, as we have said, there may be some medical developments that affect the precise point of viability, see *supra*, at ___, but this is an imprecision within tolerable limits given that the medical community and all those who must apply its discoveries will continue to explore the matter. The viability line also has, as a practical matter, an element of fairness. In some broad sense it might be said that a woman who fails to act before viability has consented to the State's intervention on behalf of the developing child.

The woman's right to terminate her pregnancy before viability is the most central principle of *Roe v. Wade*. It is a rule of law and a component of liberty we cannot renounce.

On the other side of the equation is the interest of the State in the protection of potential life. The *Roe* Court recognized the State's "important and legitimate interest in protecting the potentiality of human life." *Roe, supra*, at 162. The weight to be given this state interest, not the strength of the woman's interest, was the difficult question faced in *Roe*. We do not need to say whether each of us, had we been Members of the Court when the valuation of the State interest came before it as an original matter, would have concluded, as the *Roe* Court did, that its weight

is insufficient to justify a ban on abortions prior to viability even when it is subject to certain exceptions. The matter is not before us in the first instance, and coming as it does after nearly 20 years of litigation in *Roe*'s wake we are satisfied that the immediate question is not the soundness of *Roe*'s resolution of the issue, but the precedential force that must be accorded to its holding. And we have concluded that the essential holding of *Roe* should be reaffirmed.

Yet it must be remembered that *Roe v. Wade* speaks with clarity in establishing not only the woman's liberty but also the State's "important and legitimate interest in potential life." *Roe, supra*, at 163. That portion of the decision in *Roe* has been given too little acknowledgement and implementation by the Court in its subsequent cases. Those cases decided that any regulation touching upon the abortion decision must survive strict scrutiny, to be sustained only if drawn in narrow terms to further a compelling state interest. . . . Not all of the cases decided under that formulation can be reconciled with the holding in *Roe* itself that the State has legitimate interests in the health of the woman and in protecting the potential life within her. In resolving this tension, we choose to rely upon *Roe*, as against the later cases.

Roe established a trimester framework to govern abortion regulations. Under this elaborate but rigid construct, almost no regulation at all is permitted during the first trimester of pregnancy; regulations designed to protect the woman's health, but not to further the State's interest in potential life, are permitted during the second trimester and during the third trimester, when the fetus is viable, prohibitions are permitted provided the life or health of the mother is not at stake. *Roe v. Wade, supra*, at 163–166. Most of our cases since *Roe* have involved the application of rules derived from the trimester framework. . . .

The trimester framework no doubt was erected to ensure that the woman's right to choose not become so subordinate to the State's interest in promoting fetal life that her choice exists in theory but not in fact. We do not agree, however, that the trimester approach is necessary to accomplish this objective. A framework of this rigidity was unnecessary and in its later interpretation sometimes contradicted the State's permissible exercise of its powers.

Though the woman has a right to choose to terminate or continue her pregnancy before viability, it does not at all follow that the State is prohibited from taking steps to ensure that this choice is thoughtful and informed. Even in the earliest stages of pregnancy, the State may enact rules and regulations designed to encourage her to know that there are philosophic and social arguments of great weight that can be brought to bear in favor of continuing the pregnancy to full term and that there are procedures and institutions to allow adoption of unwanted children as well as a certain degree of state assistance if the mother chooses to raise the child herself. "'[T]he Constitution does not forbid a State or city, pursuant to democratic processes, from expressing a preference for normal childbirth.'" *Webster v. Reproductive Health Services*, 492 U.S., at 511 (opinion of the Court) (quoting *Poelker v. Doe*, 432 U.S. 519, 521 (1977). It follows that States are free to enact laws to provide a reasonable framework for a woman to make a decision that has such profound and lasting meaning. This, too, we find consistent with *Roe*'s central premises, and indeed the inevitable consequence of our holding that the State has an interest in protecting the life of the unborn.

We reject the trimester framework, which we do not consider to be part of the essential holding of *Roe*. See *Webster v. Reproductive Health Services, supra,* at 518 (opinion of Rehnquist, C.J.); *id.,* at 529 (O'Connor, J., concurring in part and concurring in judgment) (describing the trimester framework as "problematic"). Measures aimed at ensuring that a woman's choice contemplates the consequences for the fetus do not necessarily interfere with the right recognized in *Roe,* although those measures have been found to be inconsistent with the rigid trimester framework announced in that case. A logical reading of the central holding in *Roe* itself, and a necessary reconciliation of the liberty of the woman and the interest of the State in promoting prenatal life, require, in our view, that we abandon the trimester framework as a rigid prohibition on all previability regulation aimed at the protection of fetal life. The trimester framework suffers from these basic flaws: in its formulation it misconceives the nature of the pregnant woman's interest; and in practice it undervalues the State's interest in potential life, as recognized in *Roe*.

As our jurisprudence relating to all liberties save perhaps abortion has recognized, not every law which makes a right more difficult to exercise is *ipso facto*, an infringement of that right. An example clarifies the point. We have held that not every ballot access limitation amounts to an infringement of the right to vote. Rather, the States are granted substantial flexibility in establishing the framework within which voters choose the candidates for whom they wish to vote. *Anderson v. Celebrezze*, 460 U.S. 780, 788 (1983);

Norman v. Reed, 502 U.S. ___ (1992).

The abortion right is similar. Numerous forms of state regulation might have the incidental effect of increasing the cost or decreasing the availability of medical care, whether for abortion or any other medical procedure. The fact that a law which serves a valid purpose, one not designed to strike at the right itself, has the incidental effect of making it more difficult or more expensive to procure an abortion cannot be enough to invalidate it. Only where state regulation imposes an undue burden on a woman's ability to make this decision does the power of the State reach into the heart of the liberty protected by the Due Process Clause. . . .

For the most part, the Court's early abortion cases adhered to this view. In *Maher v. Roe,* 432 U.S. 464, 473–474 (1977), the Court explained: "*Roe* did not declare an unqualified 'constitutional right to an abortion,' as the District Court seemed to think. Rather, the right protects the woman from unduly burdensome interference with her freedom to decide whether to terminate her pregnancy." . . .

These considerations of the nature of the abortion right illustrate that it is an overstatement to describe it as a right to decide whether to have an abortion "without interference from the State," *Planned Parenthood of Central Mo. v. Danforth*, 428 U.S. 52, 61 (1976). All abortion regulations interfere to some degree with a woman's ability to decide whether to terminate her pregnancy. It is, as a consequence, not surprising that despite the protestations contained in the original *Roe* opinion to the effect that the Court was not recognizing an absolute right, 410 U.S., at 154–155, the Court's experience applying the trimester framework has led to the striking down of some abortion regulations which in no real sense deprived women of the ultimate decision. Those decisions went too far because the right recognized by *Roe* is a right "to be free from unwarranted governmental intrusion into matters so fundamentally affecting a person as the decision whether to bear or beget a child." *Eisenstadt v. Baird*, 405 U.S., at 453. Not all governmental intrusion is of necessity unwarranted; and that brings us to the other basic flaw in the trimester framework: even in *Roe*'s terms, in practice it undervalues the State's interest in the potential life within the woman.

Roe v. Wade was express in its recognition of the State's "important and legitimate interest[s] in preserving and protecting the health of the pregnant woman [and] in protecting the potentiality of human life." 410 U.S., at 162. The trimester framework, however, does not fulfill *Roe*'s own promise that the State has an interest in protecting fetal life or potential life. *Roe* began the contradiction by using the trimester framework to forbid any regulation of abortion designed to advance that interest before viability. *Id.*, at 163. Before viability, *Roe* and subsequent cases treat all governmental attempts to influence a woman's decision on behalf of the potential life within her as unwarranted. This treatment is, in our judgment, incompatible with the recognition that there is a substantial state interest in potential life throughout pregnancy. Cf. *Webster*, 492 U.S., at 519 (opinion of Rehnquist, C. J.); *Akron I, supra*, at 461 (O'Connor, J., dissenting).

The very notion that the State has a substantial interest in potential life leads to the conclusion that not all regulations must be deemed unwarranted. Not all burdens on the right to decide whether to terminate a pregnancy will be undue. In our view, the undue burden standard is the appropriate means of reconciling the State's interest with the woman's constitutionally protected liberty.

The concept of an undue burden has been utilized by the Court as well as individual members of the Court, including two of us, in ways that could be considered inconsistent. . . . Because we set forth a standard of general application to which we intend to adhere, it is important to clarify what is meant by an undue burden.

A finding of an undue burden is a shorthand for the conclusion that a state regulation has the purpose or effect of placing a substantial obstacle in the path of a woman seeking an abortion of a nonviable fetus. A statute with this purpose is invalid because the means chosen by the State to further the interest in potential life must be calculated to inform the woman's free choice, not hinder it. And a statute which, while furthering the interest in potential life or some other valid state interest, has the effect of placing a substantial obstacle in the path of a woman's choice cannot be considered a permissible means of serving its legitimate ends. To the extent that the opinions of the Court or of individual Justices use the undue burden standard in a manner that is inconsistent with this analysis, we set out what in our view should be the controlling standard. Cf. *McCleskey v. Zant*, 499 U.S. ____, ____ (1991) (slip op. at 20) (attempting to "define the doctrine of abuse of the writ with more precision" after acknowledging tension among earlier cases). In our considered judgment, an undue burden is an unconstitutional burden. See *Akron II, supra*, at ____ (opinion of Kennedy, J.) Understood another way, we answer the question, left open in previous opinions discussing the undue burden formulation, whether a law designed to further the State's interest in fetal life which imposes an undue burden on the woman's decision before fetal viability could be constitutional. See, *e.g., Akron I, supra*, at 462–463 (O'Connor, J., dissenting). The answer is no.

Some guiding principles should emerge. What is at stake is the women's right to make the ultimate decision, not a right to be insulated from all others in doing so. Regulations which do no more than create a structural mechanism by which the State, or the parent or guardian of a minor, may express profound respect for the life of the unborn are permitted, if they are not a substantial obstacle to the woman's exercise of the right to choose. See *infra*, at ____ (addressing Pennsylvania's parental consent requirement). Unless it has that effect on her right of choice, a state measure designed to persuade her to choose childbirth over abortion will be upheld if reasonably related to that goal. Regulations designed to foster the health of a woman seeking an abortion are valid if they do not constitute an undue burden.

Even when jurists reason from shared premises, some disagreement is inevitable. . . . That is to be expected in the application of any legal standard which must accommodate life's complexity. We do not expect it to be otherwise with respect to the undue burden standard. We give this summary:

(a) to protect the central right recognized by *Roe v. Wade* while at the same time accommodating the State's profound interest in potential life, we will employ the undue burden analysis as explained in this opinion. An undue burden exists, and therefore a provision of law is invalid, if its purpose or effect is to place a substantial obstacle in the path of a woman seeking an abortion before the fetus attains viability.

(b) We reject the rigid trimester framework of *Roe v. Wade*. To promote the State's profound interest in potential life, throughout pregnancy the State may take measures to ensure that the woman's choice is informed, and measures designed to advance this interest will not be invalidated as long as their purpose is to persuade the woman to choose childbirth over abortion. These measures must not be an undue burden on the right.

(c) As with any medical procedure, the State may enact regulations to further the health or safety of a woman seeking an abortion. Unnecessary health regulations that have the purpose or effect of presenting a substantial obstacle to a woman seeking an abortion impose an undue burden on the right.

(d) Our adoption of the undue burden analysis does not disturb the central holding of *Roe v. Wade*, and we reaffirm that holding. Regardless of whether exceptions are made for particular circumstances, a State may not prohibit any woman from making the ultimate decision to terminate her pregnancy before viability.

(e) We also reaffirm Roe's holding that "subsequent to viability, the State in promoting its interest in the potentiality of human life may, if it chooses, regulate, and even proscribe, abortion except where it is necessary, in appropriate medical judgment, for the preservation of the life or health of the mother." *Roe v. Wade*, 410 U.S., at 164–165. . . .

Justice Scalia, with whom the Chief Justice, Justice White, and Justice Thomas join, concurring in the judgment in part and dissenting in part.

My views on this matter are unchanged from those I set forth in my separate opinions in *Webster v. Reproductive Health Services*, 492 U.S. 490, 532 (1989) (Scalia, J., concurring in part and concurring in judgment) and *Ohio v. Akron Center for Reproductive Health*, 497 U.S. 502, 520 (1990) (*Akron II*) (Scalia, J., concurring). The States may, if they wish, permit abortion on demand, but the Constitution does not require them to do so. The permissibility of abortion, and the limitations upon it, are to be resolved like most important questions in our democracy: by citizens trying to persuade one another and then voting. As the Court acknowledges "where reasonable people disagree the government can adopt one position or the other." *Ante*, at 8. The Court is correct in adding the qualification that this "assumes a state of affairs in which the choice does not intrude upon a protected liberty," *ante*, at 9—but the crucial part of that qualification is the penultimate word. A State's choice between two positions on which reasonable people can disagree is constitutional even when (as is often the case) it intrudes upon a "liberty" in the absolute sense. Laws against bigamy, for example—which entire societies of reasonable people disagree with—intrude upon men and women's liberty to marry and live with one another. But bigamy happens not to be a liberty specially "protected" by the Constitution.

That is, quite simply, the issue in this case: not whether the power of a woman to abort her unborn child is a "liberty" in the absolute sense; or even whether it is a liberty of great importance to many women. Of course it is both. The issue is whether it is a liberty protected by the Constitution of the United States. I am sure it is not. I reach that conclusion not because of anything so exalted as my views concerning the "concept of existence, of meaning, of the universe, and of the mystery of human life." *Ibid.* Rather, I reach it for the same reason I reach the conclusion that bigamy is not constitutionally protected—because of two simple facts: (1) the Constitution says absolutely nothing about it, and (2) the long-standing traditions of American society have permitted it to be legally proscribed. *Akron II, supra*, at 520 (Scalia, J., concurring).

The Court destroys the proposition, evidently meant to represent my position, that "liberty" includes "only those practices, defined at the most specific level, that were protected against government interference by other rules of law when the Fourteenth Amendment was ratified," *ante*, at 5 (citing *Michael H. v. Gerald D.*, 491 U.S. 110, 127, n. 6 (1989) (opinion of Scalia, J.). That is not, however, what *Michael H.* says: it merely observes that, in defining a "liberty," we may not disregard a specific, "relevant tradition protecting, or denying protection to, the asserted right," 491 U.S., at 127, n. 6. But the Court does not wish to be fettered by any such limitations on its preferences. The Court's statement that it is "tempting" to acknowledge the authori-tativeness of tradition in order to "cur[b] the discretion of federal judges," *ante*, at 5, is of course rhetoric rather than reality; no government official is "tempted" to place restraints upon his own freedom of action, which is why Lord Acton did not say "Power tends to purify." The Court's temptation is in the quite opposite and more natural direction—towards systematically eliminating checks upon its own power; and it succumbs.

Beyond that brief summary of the essence of my position, I will not swell the United States Reports with repetition of what I have said before; and applying the rational basis test, I would uphold the Pennsylvania statute in its entirety. I must, however, respond to a few of the more outrageous arguments in today's opinion, which it is beyond human nature to leave unanswered. I shall discuss each of them under a quotation from the Court's opinion to which they pertain.

 "The inescapable fact is that adjudication of substantive due process claims may call upon the Court in interpreting the Constitution to exercise that same capacity which by tradition courts always have exercised: reasoned judgment." *Ante*, at 7.

Assuming that the question before us is to be resolved at such a level of philosophical abstraction, in such isolation from the traditions of American society, as by simply applying "reasoned judgment," I do not see how that could possibly have produced the answer the Court arrived at in *Roe* v. *Wade*, 410 U.S. 113 (1973). Today's opinion describes the methodology of *Roe,* quite accurately, as weighing against the woman's interest the State's "important and legitimate interest in protecting the potentiality of human life.'" *Ante,* at 28–29 (quoting *Roe, supra,* at 162). But "reasoned judgment" does not begin by begging the question, as *Roe* and subsequent cases unquestionably did by assuming that what the State is protecting is the mere "potentiality of human life." . . . The whole argument of abortion opponents is that what the Court calls the fetus and what others call the unborn child *is a human life.* Thus whatever answer *Roe* came up with after conducting its "balancing" is bound to be wrong, unless it is correct that the human fetus is in some critical sense merely potentially human. There is of course no way to determine that as a legal matter; it is in fact a value judgment. Some societies have considered newborn children not yet human, or the incompetent elderly no longer so.

The authors of the joint opinion, of course, do not squarely contend that *Roe* v. *Wade* was a *correct* application of "reasoned judgment"; merely that it must be followed, because of *stare decisis. Ante,* at 11, 18–19, 29. But in their exhaustive discussion of all the factors that go into the determination of when *stare decisis* should be observed and when disregarded, they never mention "how wrong was the decision on its face?" Surely, if "[t]he Court's power lies . . . in its legitimacy, a product of substance and perception," *ante,* at 23, the "substance" part of the equation demands that plain error be acknowledged and eliminated. *Roe* was plainly wrong—even on the Court's methodology of "reasoned judgment," and even more so (of course) if the proper criteria of text and tradition are applied.

The emptiness of the "reasoned judgment" that produced *Roe* is displayed in plain view by the fact that, after more than 19 years of effort by some of the brightest (and most determined) legal minds in the country, after more than 10 cases upholding abortion rights in this Court, and after dozens upon dozens of *amicus* briefs submitted in this and other cases, the best the Court can do to explain how it is that the word "liberty" *must* be thought to include the right to destroy human fetuses is to rattle off a collection of adjectives that simply decorate a value judgment and conceal a political choice. The right to abort, we are told, inheres in "liberty" because it is among "a person's most basic decisions" *ante,* at 7; it involves a "most intimate and personal choic[e]," *ante,* at 9; it is "central to personal dignity and autonomy," *ibid.;* it "originate[s] within the zone of conscience and belief," *ibid.;* it is "too intimate and personal" for state interference, *ante,* at 10; it reflects "intimate views" of a "deep, personal character," *ante,* at 11; it involves "intimate relationships," and notions of "personal autonomy and bodily integrity," *ante,* at 15; and it concerns a particularly "'important decisio[n]'" *ante,* at 16 (citation omitted). But it is obvious to anyone applying "reasoned judgment" that the same adjectives can be applied to many forms of conduct that this Court including one of the Justices in today's majority, see *Bowers* v. *Hardwick,* 478 U.S. 186 (1986) has held are *not* entitled to constitutional protection—because, like abortion, they are forms of conduct that have long been criminalized in American society. Those adjectives might be applied, for example, to homosexual sodomy, polygamy, adult incest, and suicide, all of which are equally "intimate" and "deep[ly] personal" decisions involving "personal autonomy and bodily integrity," and all of which can constitutionally be proscribed because it is our unquestionable constitutional tradition that they are proscribable. It is not reasoned judgment that supports the Court's decision; only personal predilection. Justice Curtis's warning is as timely today as it was 135 years ago:

> "[W]hen a strict interpretation of the Constitution, according to the fixed rules which govern the interpretation of laws, is abandoned, and the theoretical opinions of individuals are allowed to control its meaning, we have no longer a Constitution; we are under the government of individual men, who for the time being have power to declare what the Constitution is, according to their own views of what it ought to mean." *Dred Scott* v. *Sandford,* 19 How. 393, 621 (1857) (Curtis, J., dissenting).

"Liberty finds no refuge in a jurisprudence of doubt." *Ante,* at 1.

One might have feared to encounter this august and sonorous phrase in an opinion defending the real *Roe* v. *Wade,* rather than the revised version fabricated today by the authors of the joint opinion. The shortcomings of *Roe* did not include lack of clarity: Virtually all regulation of abortion before the third trimester was invalid. But to come across this phrase in the joint opinion—which calls upon federal district judges to apply an "undue burden" standard as doubtful in application as it is unprincipled in origin—is really more than one should have to bear.

The joint opinion frankly concedes that the amorphous concept of "undue burden" has been inconsistently applied by the Members of this Court in the few brief years since that "test" was first explicitly propounded by Justice O'Connor in her dissent in *Akron I, supra*. See *Ante*, at 34. Because the three Justices now wish to "set forth a standard of general application," the joint opinion announces that "it is important to clarify what is meant by an undue burden," *ibid.* I certainly agree with that, but I do not agree that the joint opinion succeeds in the announced endeavor. To the contrary, its efforts at clarification make clear only that the standard is inherently manipulable and will prove hopelessly unworkable in practice.

The joint opinion explains that a state regulation imposes an "undue burden" if it "has the purpose or effect of placing a substantial obstacle in the path of a woman seeking an abortion of a nonviable fetus." *Ibid.;* see also *ante,* at 35–36. An obstacle is "substantial," we are told, if it is "calculated[,] [not] to inform the woman's free choice, [but to] hinder it." *Ante,* at 34. This latter statement cannot possibly mean what it says. *Any* regulation of abortion that is intended to advance what the joint opinion concedes is the State's "substantial" interest in protecting unborn life will be "calculated [to] hinder" a decision to have an abortion. It thus seems more accurate to say that the joint opinion would uphold abortion regulations only if they do not *unduly* hinder the woman's decision. That, of course, brings us right back to square one: Defining an "undue burden" as an "undue hindrance" (or a "substantial obstacle") hardly "clarifies" the test. Consciously or not, the joint opinion's verbal shell game will conceal raw judicial policy choices concerning what is "appropriate" abortion legislation.

The ultimately standardless nature of the "undue burden" inquiry is a reflection of the underlying fact that the concept has no principled or coherent legal basis. As the Chief Justice points out, *Roe*'s strict scrutiny standard "at least had a recognized basis in constitutional law at the time *Roe* was decided," *ante,* at 22, while "[t]he same cannot be said for the 'undue burden' standard, which is created largely out of whole cloth by the authors of the joint opinion," *ibid.* The joint opinion is flatly wrong in asserting that "our jurisprudence relating to all liberties save perhaps abortion has recognized" the permissibility of laws that do not impose an "undue burden." *Ante,* at 31. It argues that the abortion right is similar to other rights in that a law "not designed to strike at the right itself, [but which] has the incidental effect of making it more difficult or more expensive to [exercise the right,]" is not invalid. *Ante,* at 31–32. I agree, indeed I have forcefully urged, that a law of general applicability which places only an incidental burden on a fundamental right does not infringe that right, see *R.A.V. v. St. Paul,* 505 U.S. ____, ____ (1992) (slip op. at 11); *Employment Division, Dept. of Human Resources of Ore. v. Smith,* 494 U.S. 872, 878–882 (1990), but that principle does not establish the quite different (and quite dangerous) proposition that a law which *directly* regulates a fundamental right will not be found to violate the Constitution unless it imposes an "undue burden." It is that, of course, which is at issue here: Pennsylvania has *consciously and directly* regulated conduct that our cases have held is constitutionally protected. The appropriate analogy, therefore, is that of a state law requiring purchasers of religious books to endure a 24-hour waiting period, or to pay a nominal additional tax of 1¢. The joint opinion cannot possibly be correct in suggesting that we would uphold such legislation on the ground that it does not impose a "substantial obstacle" to the exercise of First Amendment rights. The "undue burden" standard is not at all the generally applicable principle the joint opinion pretends it to be; rather, it is a unique concept created specially for this case, to preserve some judicial foothold in this ill-gotten territory. In claiming otherwise, the three Justices show their willingness to place all constitutional rights at risk in an effort to preserve what they deem the "central holding in *Roe*," *ante,* at 31.

The rootless nature of the "undue burden" standard, a phrase plucked out of context from our earlier abortion decisions, see n. 3, *supra*, is further reflected in the fact that the joint opinion finds it necessary expressly to repudiate the more narrow formulations used in Justice O'Connor's earlier opinions. *Ante,* at 35. Those opinions stated that a statute imposes an "undue burden" if it imposes *absolute* obstacles or *severe* limitations on the abortion decision," *Akron I,* 462 U.S., at 464. . . . Those strong adjectives are conspicuously missing from the joint opinion, whose authors have for some unexplained reason now determined that a burden is "undue" if it merely imposes a "substantial" obstacle to abortion decisions. See *e.g., ante,* at 53, 59. Justice O'Connor has also abandoned (again without explanation) the view she expressed in *Planned Parenthood Assn. of Kansas City, Mo., Inc. v. Ashcroft*, 462 U.S. 476 (1983) (dissenting opinion), that a medical regulation which imposes an "undue burden" could nevertheless be upheld if it "reasonably relate[s] to the preservation and protection of maternal health," *id.*, at 505 (citation and internal quotation marks omitted). In today's version, even health measures will be upheld only *"if they do not constitute an undue burden,"* ante, at 35 (emphasis added). Gone too is Justice O'Connor's statement that "the State possesses *compelling* interests in the protection of potential human life . . . throughout pregnancy," *Akron I, supra*, at 461 (emphasis added); see also *Ashcroft, supra*, at 505 (O'Connor, J., concurring in judgment in part and dissenting in part); instead, the state's interest in unborn human life is stealthily downgraded to a merely "substantial" or "profound" interest, *ante*, at 34, 36. (That had to be done, of course, since designating the interest as "compelling" throughout pregnancy would have been, shall we say, a "substantial obstacle" to the joint opinion's determined effort to reaffirm what it views as the "central holding" of *Roe*. . . . And "viability" is no longer the "arbitrary" dividing line previously decried by Justice O'Connor in *Akron I, id.*, at 461; the Court now announces that "the attainment of viability may continue to serve as the critical fact," *ante*, at 18. It is difficult to maintain the illusion that we are interpreting a Constitution rather than inventing one, when we amend its provisions so breezily.

Because the portion of the joint opinion adopting and describing the undue-burden test provides no more useful guidance than the empty phrases discussed above, one must turn to the 23 pages applying that standard to the present fads for further guidance. In evaluating Pennsylvania's abortion law, the joint opinion relies extensively on the factual findings of the District Court, and repeatedly qualifies its conclusions by noting that they are contingent upon the record developed in this case. Thus, the joint opinion would uphold the 24-hour waiting period contained in the Pennsylvania statute's informed consent provision, 18 Pa. Cons. Stat. §3205 (1990), because "the record evidence shows that in the vast majority of cases, a 24-hour delay does not create any appreciable health risk," *ante*, at 43. The three Justices therefore conclude that "on the record before us, . . . we are not convinced that the 24-hour waiting period constitutes an undue burden." *Ante*, at 44–45. The requirement that a doctor provide the information pertinent to informed consent would also be upheld because "there is no evidence on this record that [this requirement] would amount in practical terms to a substantial obstacle to a woman seeking an abortion," *ante*, at 42. Similarly, the joint opinion would uphold the reporting requirements of the Act, §§3207, 3214, because "there is no . . . showing on the record before us" that these requirements constitute a "substantial obstacle" to abortion decisions. *Ante*, at 59. But at the same time the opinion pointedly observes that these reporting requirements may increase the costs of abortions and that "at some point [that fact] could become a substantial obstacle," *ibid*. Most significantly, the joint opinion's conclusion that the spousal notice requirement of the Act, see §3209, imposes an "undue burden" is based in large measure on the District Court's "detailed findings of fact," which the joint opinion sets out at great length. *Ante*, at 45–49.

I do not, of course, have any objection to the notion that, in applying legal principles, one should rely only upon the facts that are contained in the record or that are properly subject to judicial notice. But what is remarkable about the joint opinion's fact-intensive analysis is that it does not result in any measurable clarification of the "undue burden" standard. Rather, the approach of the joint opinion is, for the most part, simply to highlight certain facts in the record that apparently strike the three Justices as particularly significant in establishing (or refuting) the existence of an undue burden; after describing these facts, the opinion then simply announces that the provision either does or does not impose a "substantial obstacle" or an "undue burden." . . . We do not know whether the same conclusions could have been reached on a different record, or in what respects the record would have had to differ before an opposite conclusion would have been appropriate. The inherently standardless nature of this inquiry invites the district judge to give effect to his personal preferences about abortion. By finding and relying upon the right facts, he can invalidate, it would seem, almost any abortion restriction that strikes him as "undue"—subject, of course, to the possibility of being reversed by a Circuit Court or Supreme Court that is as unconstrained in reviewing his decision as he was in making it.

To the extent I can discern *any* meaningful content in the "undue burden" standard as applied in the joint opinion, it appears to be that a State may not regulate abortion in such a way as to reduce significantly its incidence. The joint opinion repeatedly emphasizes that an important factor in the "undue burden" analysis is whether the regulation "prevent[s] a significant number of women from obtaining an abortion," ante, at 52; whether a "significant number of women . . . are likely to be deterred from procuring an abortion," ibid.; and whether the regulation often "deters" women from seeking abortions, ante, at 55–56. We are not told, however, what forms of "deterrence" are impermissible or what degree of success in deterrence is too much to be tolerated. If, for example, a State required a woman to read a pamphlet describing, with illustrations, the facts of fetal development before she could obtain an abortion, the effect of such legislation might be to "deter" a "significant number of women" from procuring abortions, thereby seemingly allowing a district judge to invalidate it as an undue burden. Thus, despite flowery rhetoric about the State's "substantial" and "profound" interest in "potential human life," and criticism of Roe for undervaluing that interest, the joint opinion permits the State to pursue that interest only so long as it is not too successful. As Justice Blackmun recognizes (with evident hope), ante, at 5, the "undue burden" standard may ultimately require the invalidation of each provision upheld today if it can be shown, on a better record, that the State is too effectively "express[ing] a preference for childbirth over abortion," ante, at 41. Reason finds no refuge in this jurisprudence of confusion.

> "While we appreciate the weight of the arguments . . . that Roe should be overruled, the reservations any of us may have in reaffirming the central holding of Roe are outweighed by the explication of individual liberty we have given combined with the force of stare decisis." Ante, at 11.

The Court's reliance upon stare decisis can best be described as contrived. It insists upon the necessity of adhering not to all of Roe, but only to what it calls the "central holding." It seems to me that stare decisis ought to be applied even to the doctrine of stare decisis, and I confess never to have heard of this new, keep-what-you-want-and-throw-away-the-rest version. I wonder whether, as applied to Marbury v. Madison, 1 Cranch 137 (1803), for example, the new version of stare decisis would be satisfied if we allowed courts to review the constitutionality of only those statutes that (like the one in Marbury) pertain to the jurisdiction of the courts.

I am certainly not in a good position to dispute that the Court has saved the "central holding" of Roe, since to do that effectively I would have to know what the Court has saved, which in turn would require me to understand (as I do not) what the "undue burden" test means. I must confess, however, that I have always thought, and I think a lot of other people have always thought, that the arbitrary trimester framework, which the Court today discards, was quite as central to Roe as the arbitrary viability test, which the Court today retains. It seems particularly ungrateful to carve the trimester framework out of the core of Roe, since its very rigidity (in sharp contrast to the utter indeterminability of the "undue burden" test) is probably the only reason the Court is able to say, in urging stare decisis, that Roe "has in no sense proven 'unworkable,'" ante, at 13. I suppose the Court is entitled to call a "central holding" whatever it wants to call a "central holding"—which is, come to think of it, perhaps one of the difficulties with this modified version of stare decisis. I thought I might note, however, that the following portions of Roe have not been saved:

- Under Roe, requiring that a woman seeking an abortion be provided truthful information about abortion before giving informed written consent is unconstitutional, if the information is designed to influence her choice, Thornburgh, 476 U.S., at 759–765; Akron I, 462 U.S., at 442–445. Under the joint opinion's "undue burden" regime (as applied today, at least) such a requirement is constitutional, ante, at 38–42.

- Under Roe, requiring that information be provided by a doctor, rather than by nonphysician counselors, is unconstitutional Akron I, supra, at 446–449. Under the "undue burden" regime (as applied today, at least) it is not, ante, at 42.

- Under Roe, requiring a 24-hour waiting period between the time the woman gives her informed consent and the time of the abortion is unconstitutional, Akron I, supra, at 449–451. Under the "undue burden" regime (as applied today, at least) it is not, ante, at 43–45.

- Under Roe, requiring detailed reports that include demographic data about each woman who seeks an abortion and various information about each abortion is unconstitutional, Thornburgh, supra, at 465–768. Under the "undue burden" regime (as applied today, at least) it generally is not, ante, at 58–59.

"Where, in the performance of its judicial duties, the Court decides a case in such a way as to resolve the sort of intensely divisive controversy reflected in *Roe* . . ., its decision has a dimension that the resolution of the normal case does not carry. It is the dimension present whenever the Court's interpretation of the Constitution calls the contending sides of a national controversy to end their national division by accepting a common mandate rooted in the Constitution." *Ante,* at 24.

The Court's description of the place of *Roe* in the social history of the United States is unrecognizable. Not only did Roe not, as the Court suggests, resolve the deeply divisive issue of abortion; it did more than anything else to nourish it, by elevating it to the national level where it is infinitely more difficult to resolve. National politics were not plagued by abortion protests, national abortion lobbying, or abortion marches on Congress, before *Roe v. Wade* was decided. Profound disagreement existed among our citizens over the issue—as it does over other issues, such as the death penalty—but that disagreement was being worked out at the state level. As with many other issues, the division of sentiment within each State was not as closely balanced as it was among the population of the Nation as a whole, meaning not only that more people would be satisfied with the results of state-by-state resolution, but also that those results would be more stable. Pre-*Roe,* moreover, political compromise was possible.

Roe's mandate for abortion on demand destroyed the compromises of the past, rendered compromise impossible for the future, and required the entire issue to be resolved uniformly, at the national level. At the same time, Roe created a vast new class of abortion consumers and abortion proponents by eliminating the moral opprobrium that had attached to the act. ("If the Constitution guarantees abortion, how can it be bad?"—not an accurate line of thought, but a natural one.) Many favor all of those developments, and it is not for me to say that they are wrong. But to portray *Roe* as the statesmanlike "settlement" of a divisive issue, a jurisprudential Peace of Westphalia that is worth preserving, is nothing less than Orwellian. *Roe* fanned into life an issue that has inflamed our national politics in general, and has obscured with its smoke the selection of Justices to this Court in particular, ever since. And by keeping us in the abortion-umpiring business, it is the perpetuation of that disruption, rather than of any *pax Roeana,* that the Court's new majority decrees.

"[T]o overrule under fire . . . would subvert the Court's legitimacy. . . .

"To all those who will be . . . tested by following, the Court implicitly undertakes to remain steadfast. . . . The promise of constancy, once given, binds its maker for as long as the power to stand by the decision survives and . . . the commitment [is not] obsolete. . . .

"[The American people's] belief in themselves as . . . a people [who aspire to live according to the rule of law] is not readily separable from their understanding of the Court invested with the authority to decide their constitutional cases and speak before all others for their constitutional ideals. If the Court's legitimacy should be undermined, then, so would the country be in its very ability to see itself through its constitutional ideals." *Ante,* at 25–26.

The Imperial Judiciary lives. It is instructive to compare this Nietzschean vision of us unelected, life-tenured judges—leading a Volk who will be "tested by following," and whose very "belief in themselves" is mystically bound up in their "understanding" of a Court that "speak[s] before all others for their constitutional ideals"—with the somewhat more modest role envisioned for these lawyers by the Founders.

> The judiciary . . . has . . . no direction either of the strength or of the wealth of the society, and can take no active resolution whatever. It may truly be said to have neither FORCE nor WILL but merely Judgment. . . ." The Federalist No. 78, pp. 393–394 (G. Wills ed. 1982).

Or, again, to compare this ecstasy of a Supreme Court in which there is, especially on controversial matters, no shadow of change or hint of alteration ("There is a limit to the amount of error that can plausibly be imputed to prior courts," *ante,* at 24), with the more democratic views of a more humble man:

> "[T]he candid citizen must confess that if the policy of the Government upon vital questions affecting the whole people is to be irrevocably fixed by decisions of the Supreme Court, . . . the people will have ceased to be their own rulers, having to that extent practically resigned their Government into the hands of that eminent tribunal." A. Lincoln, First Inaugural Address (Mar. 4, 1861), . . .

It is particularly difficult, in the circumstances of the present decision, to sit still for the Court's lengthy lecture upon the virtues of "constancy," *ante,* at 26, of "remain[ing] steadfast," *id.,* at 25, and adhering to "principle," *id., passim.* Among the five Justices who purportedly adhere to *Roe,* at most three agree upon the *principle* that constitutes adherence (the joint opinion's "undue burden" standard) and that principle is inconsistent with *Roe,* see 410 U.S., at 154–156. To make matters worse two of the three, in order thus to remain steadfast, had to abandon previously stated positions. See n. 4 *supra;* see *supra,* at 11–12. It is beyond me how the Court expects these accommodations to be accepted "as grounded truly in principle, not as compromises with social and political pressures having, as such, no bearing on the principled choices that the Court is obliged to make." *Ante,* at 23. The only principle the Court "adheres" to, it seems to me, is the principle that the Court must be seen as standing by *Roe.* That is not a principle of law (which is what I thought the Court was talking about), but a principle of *Realpolitik*—and a wrong one at that.

I cannot agree with, indeed I am appalled by, the Court's suggestion that the decision whether to stand by an erroneous constitutional decision must be strongly influenced—*against* overruling, no less—by the substantial and continuing public opposition the decision has generated. The Court's judgment that any other course would "subvert the Court's legitimacy" must be another consequence of reading the error-filled history book that described the deeply divided country brought together by *Roe.* In my history book, the Court was covered with dishonor and deprived of legitimacy by *Dred Scott v. Sandford,* 19 How. 393 (1857), an erroneous (and widely opposed) opinion that it did not abandon, rather than by *West Coast Hotel Co. v. Parrish,* 300 U.S. 379 (1937), which produced the famous "switch in time" from the Court's erroneous (and widely opposed) constitutional opposition to the social measures of the New Deal. (Both *Dred Scott* and one line of the cases resisting the New Deal rested upon the concept of "substantive due process" that the Court praises and employs today. Indeed, *Dred Scott* was "very possibly the first application of substantive due process in the Supreme Court, the original precedent for *Lochner v. New York* and *Roe v. Wade.*" D. Currie, The Constitution in the Supreme Court 271 (1985) (footnotes omitted).)

But whether it would "subvert the Court's legitimacy" or not, the notion that we would decide a case differently from the way we otherwise would have in order to show that we can stand firm against public disapproval is frightening. It is a bad enough idea, even in the head of someone like me, who believes that the text of the Constitution, and our traditions, say what they say and there is no fiddling with them. But when it is in the mind of a Court that believes the Constitution has an evolving meaning, see *ante,* at 6; that the Ninth Amendment's reference to "othe[r]" rights is not a disclaimer, but a charter for action, *ibid.;* and that the function of this Court is to "speak before all others for [the people's] constitutional ideals" unrestrained by meaningful text or tradition—then the notion that the Court must adhere to a decision for as long as the decision faces "great opposition" and the Court is "under fire" acquires a character of almost czarist arrogance. We are offended by these marchers who descend upon us, every year on the anniversary of *Roe,* to protest our saying that the Constitution requires what our society has never thought the Constitution requires. These people who refuse to be "tested by following" must be taught a lesson. We have no Cossacks, but at least we can stubbornly refuse to abandon an erroneous opinion that we might otherwise change—to show how little they intimidate us.

Of course, as the Chief Justice points out, we have been subjected to what the Court calls "political pressure" by *both* sides of this issue. *Ante,* at 21. Maybe today's decision not to overrule *Roe* will be seen as buckling to pressure from that direction. Instead of engaging in the hopeless task of predicting public perception—a job not for lawyers but for political campaign managers—the Justices should do what is legally right by asking two questions: (1) Was *Roe* correctly decided? (2) Has *Roe* succeeded in producing a settled body of law? If the answer to both questions is no, *Roe* should undoubtedly be overruled. In truth, I am as distressed as the Court is— and expressed my distress several years ago, see *Webster,* 492 U.S., at 535—about the "political pressure" directed to the Court: the marches, the mail, the protests aimed at inducing us to change our opinions. How upsetting it is, that so many of our citizens (good people, not lawless ones, on both sides of this abortion issue, and on various sides of other issues as well) think that we Justices should properly take into account their views, as though we were engaged not in ascertaining an objective law but in determining some kind of social consensus. The Court would profit, I think, from giving less attention to the *fact* of this distressing phenomenon, and more attention to the *cause of* it. That cause permeates today's opinion: a new mode of constitutional adjudication that relies not upon text and traditional practice to determine the law, but upon what the Court calls "reasoned judgment," *ante*, at 7, which turns out to be nothing but philosophical predilection and moral intuition. All manner of "liberties," the Court tells us, inhere in the Constitution and are enforceable by this Court—not just those mentioned in the text or established in the traditions of our society. *Ante*, at 56. Why even the Ninth Amend-ment—which says only that "[t]he enumeration in the Constitution of certain rights shall not be construed to deny or disparage others retained by the people"—is, despite our contrary understanding for almost 200 years, a literally boundless source of additional, unnamed, unhinted-at "rights," definable and enforceable by us, through "reasoned judgment." *Ante*, at 6–7.

What makes all this relevant to the bothersome application of "political pressure" against the Court are the twin facts that the American people love democracy and the American people are not fools. As long as the Court thought (and the people thought) that we Justices were doing essentially lawyers' work up here—reading text and discerning our society's traditional understanding of that text—the public pretty much left us alone. Texts and traditions are facts to study, not convictions to demonstrate about. But if in reality our process of constitutional adjudication consists primarily of making *value judgments*, if we can ignore a long and clear tradition clarifying an ambiguous text, as we did, for example, five days ago in declaring unconstitutional invocations and benedictions at public-high-school graduation ceremonies, *Lee v. Weisman*, 505 U.S. ___ (1992); if, as I say, our pronouncement of constitutional law rests primarily on value judgments, then a free and

intelligent people's attitude towards us can be expected to be (ought to be) quite different. The people know that their value judgments are quite as good as those taught in any law school—maybe better. If, indeed, the "liberties" protected by the Constitution are, as the Court says, undefined and unbounded, then the people *should* demonstrate, to protest that we do not implement *their* values instead of *ours*. Not only that, but confirmation hearings for new Justices should deteriorate into question-and-answer sessions in which Senators go through a list of their constituents' most favored and most disfavored alleged constitutional rights, and seek the nominee's commitment to support or oppose them. Value judgments, after all, should be voted on, not dictated; and if our Constitution has somehow accidentally committed them to the Supreme Court, at least we can have a sort of plebiscite each time a new nominee to that body is put forward.

Discussion Questions

1. In *Casey* Justices O'Connor, Kennedy, and Souter argue that *Roe* must be preserved as a precedent. On what bases do they draw this conclusion? *preserving of legit. by stare decisis*

2. According to the Court, a law that attempts to limit a fundamental right must be able to withstand *strict scrutiny* whereas a law which attempts to limit a liberty must not pose an *undue burden*. How does the Court distinguish the strict scrutiny standard from the undue burden standard? How does this distinction apply to *Casey*'s effect on *Roe*?

3. What is the basis of Justice Scalia's scathing dissent? Do you think his arguments are plausible? Why or why not?

The Morality of Abortion

14

A Defense of Abortion

Judith Jarvis Thomson

Judith Jarvis Thomson is Professor of Philosophy at Massachusetts Institute of Technology and the author of several books and articles in moral and political philosophy, including *Rights, Restitution, and Risk* (1986). She has served as a president of the American Philosophical Association.

In the following essay Professor Thomson argues that even if the fetus is a human person throughout or for most of a woman's pregnancy, a woman still has a right to an abortion. She employs a number of stories to make her point, including the case of the famous unconscious violinist who needs your kidneys for nine months. The Society of Music Lovers kidnaps you and then hooks you up to the violinist. Do you have the right to pull the plug on the violinist and withdraw your help even if it results in the violinist's death? Thomson answers yes. She argues from this fictional case that just as you have the right to unplug yourself from the violinist if you did not consent to have your kidneys used to preserve his life, the pregnant woman has a right to have an abortion if she did not consent to become pregnant and permit her body to be used to preserve the life of another (the fetus). However, Thomson does believe that there are times at which it would be a good thing for a woman not to have an abortion.

Reprinted by permission of Princeton University Press from *Philosophy and Public Affairs* 1, no. 1 (1971). Endnotes removed.

Most opposition to abortion relies on the premise that the fetus is a human being, a person, from the moment of conception. The premise is argued for, but, as I think, not well. Take, for example, the most common argument. We are asked to notice that the development of a human being from conception through birth into childhood is continuous; then it is said that to draw a line, to choose a point in this development and say "before this point the thing is not a person, after this point it is a person" is to make an arbitrary choice, a choice for which in the nature of things no good reason can be given. It is concluded that the fetus is, or anyway that we had better say it is, a person from the moment of conception. But this conclusion does not follow. Similar things might be said about the development of an acorn into an oak tree, and it does not follow that acorns are oak trees, or that we had better say they are. Arguments of this form are sometimes called "slippery slope arguments"—the phrase is perhaps self-explanatory—and it is dismaying that opponents of abortion rely on them so heavily and uncritically.

I am inclined to agree, however, that the prospects for "drawing a line" in the development of the fetus look dim. I am inclined to think also that we shall probably have to agree that the fetus has already become a human person well before birth. Indeed, it comes as a surprise when one first learns how early in its life it begins to acquire human characteristics. By the tenth week, for example, it already has a face, arms and legs, fingers and toes; it has internal organs, and brain activity is detectable. On the other hand, I think that the premise is false, that the fetus is not a person from the moment of conception. A newly fertilized ovum, a newly implanted clump of cells, is no more a person than an acorn is an oak tree. But I shall not discuss any of this. For it seems to me to be of great interest to ask what happens if, for the sake of argument, we allow the premise. How, precisely, are we supposed to get from there to the conclusion that abortion is morally impermissible? Opponents of abortion commonly spend most of their time establishing that the fetus is a person, and hardly any time explaining the step from there to the impermissibility of abortion.

Perhaps they think the step too simple and obvious to require much comment. Or perhaps instead they are simply being economical in argument. Many of those who defend abortion rely on the premise that the fetus is not a person, but only a bit of tissue that will become a person at birth; and why pay out more arguments than you have to? Whatever the explanation, I suggest that the step they take is neither easy nor obvious, that it calls for closer examination than it is commonly given, and that when we do give it this closer examination we shall feel inclined to reject it.

I propose, then, that we grant that the fetus is a person from the moment of conception. How does the argument go from here? Something like this, I take it. Every person has a right to life. So the fetus has a right to life. No doubt the mother has a right to decide what shall happen in and to her body; everyone would grant that. But surely a person's right to life is stronger and more stringent than the mother's right to decide what happens in and to her body, and so outweighs it. So the fetus may not be killed; an abortion may not be performed.

It sounds plausible. But now let me ask you to imagine this. You wake up in the morning and find yourself back to back in bed with an unconscious violinist. A famous unconscious violinist. He has been found to have a fatal kidney ailment, and the Society of Music Lovers has canvassed all the available medical records and found that you alone have the right blood type to help. They have therefore kidnapped you, and last night the violinist's circulatory system was plugged into yours, so that your kidneys can be used to extract poisons from his blood as well as your own. The director of the hospital now tells you, "Look, we're sorry the Society of Music Lovers did this to you—we would never have permitted it if we had known. But still, they did it, and the violinist is now plugged into you. To unplug you would be to kill him. But never mind, it's only for nine months. By then he will have recovered from his ailment, and can safely be unplugged from you." Is it morally incumbent on you to accede to this situation? No doubt it would be very nice of you if you did, a great kindness. But do you *have* to accede to it? What if it were not nine months, but nine years? Or longer still? What if the director of the hospital says, "Tough luck, I agree, but you've now got to stay in bed, with the violinist plugged into you, for the rest of your life. Because remember this. All persons have a right to life, and violinists are persons. Granted you have a right to decide what happens in and to

your body, but a person's right to life outweighs your right to decide what happens in and to your body. So you cannot ever be unplugged from him." I imagine you would regard this as outrageous, which suggests that something really is wrong with that plausible-sounding argument I mentioned a moment ago.

In this case, of course, you were kidnapped; you didn't volunteer for the operation that plugged the violinist into your kidneys. Can those who oppose abortion on the ground I mentioned make an exception for a pregnancy due to rape? Certainly. They can say that persons have a right to life only if they didn't come into existence because of rape; or they can say that all persons have a right to life, but that some have less of a right to life than others, in particular, that those who came into existence because of rape have less. But these statements have a rather unpleasant sound. Surely the question of whether you have a right to life at all, or how much of it you have, shouldn't turn on the question of whether or not you are the product of a rape. And in fact the people who oppose abortion on the ground I mentioned do not make this distinction, and hence do not make an exception in case of rape.

Nor do they make an exception for a case in which the mother has to spend the nine months of her pregnancy in bed. They would agree that would be a great pity, and hard on the mother, but all the same all persons have a right to life, the fetus is a person, and so on. I suspect, in fact, that they would not make an exception for a case in which, miraculously enough, the pregnancy went on for nine years, or even the rest of the mother's life.

Some won't even make an exception for a case in which continuation of the pregnancy is likely to shorten the mother's life; they regard abortion as impermissible even to save the mother's life. Such cases are nowadays very rare, and many opponents of abortion do not accept this extreme view. All the same, it is a good place to begin: a number of points of interest come out in respect to it.

1. Let us call the view that abortion is impermissible even to save the mother's life "the extreme view." I want to suggest first that it does not issue from the argument I mentioned earlier without the addition of some fairly powerful premises. Suppose a woman has become pregnant, and now learns that she has a cardiac condition such that she will die if she carries the baby to term. What may be done for her? The fetus—being a person—has a right to life, but as the mother is a person too, so has she a right to life. Presumably they have an equal right to life.

How is it supposed to come out that an abortion may not be performed? If mother and child have an equal right to life, shouldn't we perhaps flip a coin? Or should we add to the mother's right to life her right to decide what happens in and to her body, which everybody seems to be ready to grant—the sum of her rights now outweighing the fetus' right to life?

The most familiar argument here is the following. We are told that performing the abortion would be directly killing the child, whereas doing nothing would not be killing the mother, but only letting her die. Moreover, in killing the child, one would be killing an innocent person, for the child has committed no crime, and is not aiming at his mother's death. And then there are a variety of ways in which this might be continued. (1) But as directly killing an innocent person is always and absolutely impermissible, an abortion may not be performed. Or, (2) as directly killing an innocent person is murder, and murder is always and absolutely impermissible, an abortion may not be performed. Or, (3) as one's duty to refrain from directly killing an innocent person is more stringent than one's duty to keep a person from dying, an abortion may not be performed. Or, (4) if one's only options are directly killing an innocent person or letting a person die, one must prefer letting the person die, and thus an abortion may not be performed.

Some people seem to have thought that these are not further premises which must be added if the conclusion is to be reached, but that they follow from the very fact that an innocent person has a right to life. But this seems to me to be a mistake, and perhaps the simplest way to show this is to bring out that while we must certainly grant that innocent persons have a right to life, the theses in (1) through (4) are all false. Take (2), for example. If directly killing an innocent person is murder, and thus is impermissible, then the mother's directly killing the innocent person inside her is murder, and thus is impermissible. But it cannot seriously be thought to be murder if the mother performs an abortion on herself to save her life. It cannot seriously be said that she must refrain, that she must sit passively by and wait for her death. Let us look again at the case of you and the violinist. There you are, in bed with the violinist, and the director of the hospital says to you, "It's all most distressing, and I deeply sympathize, but you see this is putting an additional strain on your kidneys, and you'll be dead within the month. But you *have* to stay where you are all the same. Because unplugging you would be directly killing an innocent violinist, and

that's murder, and that's impermissible." If anything in the world is true, it is that you do not commit murder, you do not do what is impermissible, if you reach around your back and unplug yourself from that violinist to save your life.

The main focus of attention in writings on abortion has been on what a third party may or may not do in answer to a request from a woman for an abortion. This is in a way understandable. Things being as they are, there isn't much a woman can safely do to abort herself. So the question asked is what a third party may do, and what the mother may do, if it is mentioned at all, is deduced, almost as an afterthought, from what it is concluded that third parties may do. But it seems to me that to treat the matter in this way is to refuse to grant to the mother that very status of person which is so firmly insisted on for the fetus. For we cannot simply read off what a person may do from what a third party may do. Suppose you find yourself trapped in a tiny house with a growing child. I mean a very tiny house, and a rapidly growing child—you are already up against the wall of the house and in a few minutes you'll be crushed to death. The child on the other hand won't be crushed to death; if nothing is done to stop him from growing he'll be hurt, but in the end he'll simply burst open the house and walk out a free man. Now I could well understand it if a bystander were to say, "There's nothing we can do for you. We cannot choose between your life and his, we cannot be the ones to decide who is to live, we cannot intervene." But it cannot be concluded that you too can do nothing, that you cannot attack it to save your life. However innocent the child may be, you do not have to wait passively while it crushes you to death. Perhaps a pregnant woman is vaguely felt to have the status of house, to which we don't allow the right of self-defense. But if the woman houses the child, it should be remembered that she is a person who houses it.

I should perhaps stop to say explicitly that I am not claiming that people have a right to do anything whatever to save their lives. I think, rather, that there are drastic limits to the right of self-defense. If someone threatens you with death unless you torture someone else to death, I think you have not the right, even to save your life, to do so. But the case under consideration here is very different. In our case there are only two people involved, one whose life is threatened, and one who threatens it. Both are innocent: the one who is threatened is not threatened because of any fault, the one who threatens does not threaten because of any fault. For this reason we may feel that we bystanders cannot intervene. But the person threatened can.

In sum, a woman surely can defend her life against the threat to it posed by the unborn child, even if doing so involves its death. And this shows not merely that the theses in (1) through (4) are false; it shows also that the extreme view of abortion is false, and so we need not canvass any other possible ways of arriving at it from the argument I mentioned at the outset.

2. The extreme view could of course be weakened to say that while abortion is permissible to save the mother's life, it may not be performed by a third party, but only by the mother herself. But this cannot be right either. For what we have to keep in mind is that the mother and the unborn child are not like two tenants in a small house which has, by an unfortunate mistake, been rented to both: the mother *owns* the house. The fact that she does adds to the offensiveness of deducing that the mother can do nothing from the supposition that third parties can do nothing. But it does more than this: it casts a bright light on the supposition that third parties can do nothing. Certainly it lets us see that a third party who says "I cannot choose between you" is fooling himself if he thinks this is impartiality. If Jones has found and fastened on a certain coat, which he needs to keep him from freezing, but which Smith also needs to keep him from freezing, then it is not impartiality that says "I cannot choose between you" when Smith owns the coat. Women have said again and again "This body is *my* body!" and they have reason to feel angry, reason to feel that it has been like shouting into the wind. Smith, after all, is hardly likely to bless us if we say to him, "Of course it's your coat, anybody would grant that it is. But no one may choose between you and Jones who is to have it."

We should really ask what it is that says "no one may choose" in the face of the fact that the body that houses the child is the mother's body. It may be simply a failure to appreciate this fact. But it may be something more interesting, namely the sense that one has a right to refuse to lay hands on people, even where it would be just and fair to do so, even where justice seems to require that somebody do so. Thus justice might call for somebody to get Smith's coat back from Jones, and yet you have a right to refuse to be the one to lay hands on Jones, a right to refuse to do physical violence to him. This, I think, must be granted. But then what should be said is not "no one may choose," but only "*I* cannot choose," and indeed not even this, but "*I* will not *act*," leaving it open that

somebody else can or should, and in particular that anyone in a position of authority, with the job of securing people's rights, both can and should. So this is no difficulty. I have not been arguing that any given third party must accede to the mother's request that he perform an abortion to save her life, but only that he may.

I suppose that in some views of human life the mother's body is only on loan to her, the loan not being one which gives her any prior claim to it. One who held this view might well think it impartiality to say "I cannot choose." But I shall simply ignore this possibility. My own view is that if a human being has any just, prior claim to anything at all, he has a just, prior claim to his own body. And perhaps this needn't be argued for here anyway, since, as I mentioned, the arguments against abortion we are looking at do grant that the woman has a right to decide what happens in and to her body.

But although they do grant it, I have tried to show that they do not take seriously what is done in granting it. I suggest the same thing will reappear even more clearly when we turn away from cases in which the mother's life is at stake, and attend, as I propose we now do, to the vastly more common cases in which a woman wants an abortion for some less weighty reason than preserving her own life.

3. Where the mother's life is not at stake, the argument I mentioned at the outset seems to have a much stronger pull. "Everyone has a right to life, so the unborn person has a right to life." And isn't the child's right to life weightier than anything other than the mother's own right to life, which she might put forward as a ground for an abortion?

This argument treats the right to life as if it were unproblematic. It is not, and this seems to me to be precisely the source of the mistake.

For we should now, at long last, ask what it comes to, to have a right to life. In some views having a right to life includes having a right to be given at least the bare minimum one needs for continued life. But suppose that what in fact is the bare minimum a man needs for continued life is something he has no right at all to be given? If I am sick unto death, and the only thing that will save my life is the touch of Henry Fonda's cool hand on my fevered brow, then all the same, I have no right to be given the touch of Henry Fonda's cool hand on my fevered brow. It would be frightfully nice of him to fly in from the West Coast to provide it. It would be less nice, though no doubt well meant, if my friends flew out to the West Coast and carried Henry Fonda back with them.

But I have no right at all against anybody that he should do this for me. Or again, to return to the story I told earlier, the fact that for continued life that violinist needs the continued use of your kidneys does not establish that he has a right to be given the continuous use of your kidneys. He certainly has no right against you that *you* should give him continued use of your kidneys. For nobody has any right to use your kidneys unless you give him such a right; and nobody has the right against you that you shall give him this right— if you do allow him to go on using your kidneys this is a kindness on your part, and not something he can claim from you as his due. Nor has he any right against anybody else that *they* should give him continued use of your kidneys. Certainly he had no right against the Society of Music Lovers that they should plug him into you in the first place. And if you now start to unplug yourself, having learned that you will otherwise have to spend nine years in bed with him, there is nobody in the world who must try to prevent you, in order to see to it that he is given something he has a right to he given.

Some people are rather stricter about the right to life. In their view it does not include the right to be given anything, but amounts to, and only to, the right not to be killed by anybody. But here a related difficulty arises. If everybody is to refrain from killing that violinist, then everybody must refrain from doing a great many different sorts of things. Everybody must refrain from slitting his throat, everybody must refrain from shooting him—and everybody must refrain from unplugging you from him. But does he have a right against everybody that they shall refrain from unplugging you from him? To refrain from doing this is to allow him to use your kidneys. It could be argued that he has a right against us that *we* should allow him to continue to use your kidneys. That is, while he had no right against us that we should give him the use of your kidneys, it might be argued that he anyway has a right against us that we shall not now intervene and deprive him of the use of your kidneys. I shall come back to third-party interventions later. But certainly the violinist has no right against you that *you* shall allow him to continue to use your kidneys. As I said, if you do allow him to use them, it is a kindness on your part, and not something you owe him.

The difficulty I point to here is not peculiar to the right to life. It reappears in connection with all the other natural rights; and it is something which an adequate account of rights must deal with. For present purposes it is enough just to draw attention to it. But I would stress that I am not arguing that people do not have a right to life—quite to the contrary, it seems to me that the primary control we must place on the acceptability of an account of rights is that it should turn out in that account to be a truth that all persons have a right to life. I am arguing only that having a right to life does not guarantee having either a right to be given the use of or a right to be allowed continued use of another person's body— even if one needs it for life itself. So the right to life will not serve the opponents of abortion in the very simple and clear way in which they seem to have thought it would.

4. There is another way to bring out the difficulty. In the most ordinary sort of case, to deprive someone of what he has a right to is to treat him unjustly. Suppose a boy and his small brother are jointly given a box of chocolates for Christmas. If the older boy takes the box and refuses to give his brother any of the chocolates, he is unjust to him, for the brother has been given a right to half of them. But suppose that, having learned that otherwise it means nine years in bed with that violinist, you unplug yourself from him. You surely are not being unjust to him, for you gave him no right to use your kidneys, and no one else can have given him any such right. But we have to notice that in unplugging yourself, you are killing him; and violinists, like everybody else, have a right to life, and thus in the view we were considering just now, the right not to be killed. So here you do what he supposedly has a right you shall not do, but you do not act unjustly to him in doing it.

The emendation which may be made at this point is this: the right to life consists not in the right not to be killed, but rather in the right not to be killed unjustly. This runs a risk of circularity, but never mind: it would enable us to square the fact that the violinist has a right to life with the fact that you do not act unjustly toward him in unplugging yourself, thereby killing him. For if you do not kill him unjustly, you do not violate his right to life, and so it is no wonder you do him no injustice.

But if this emendation is accepted, the gap in the argument against abortion stares us plainly in the face: it is by no means enough to show that the fetus is a person, and to remind us that all persons have a right to life—we need to be shown also that killing the fetus violates its right to life, i.e., that abortion is unjust killing. And is it?

I suppose we may take it as a datum that in a case of pregnancy due to rape the mother has not given the unborn person a right to the use of her body for food and shelter. Indeed, in what pregnancy could it be supposed that the mother has given the unborn person such a right? It is not as if there were unborn persons drifting about the world, to whom a woman who wants a child says "I invite you in."

But it might be argued that there are other ways one can have acquired a right to the use of another person's body than by having been invited to use it by that person. Suppose a woman voluntarily indulges in intercourse, knowing of the chance it will issue in pregnancy, and then she does become pregnant; is she not in part responsible for the presence, in fact the very existence, of the unborn person inside her? No doubt she did not invite it in. But doesn't her partial responsibility for its being there itself give it a right to the use of her body? If so, then her aborting it would be more like the boy's taking away the chocolates, and less like your unplugging yourself from the violinist—doing so would be depriving it of what it does have a right to, and thus would be doing it an injustice.

And then, too, it might be asked whether or not she can kill it even to save her own life: If she voluntarily called it into existence, how can she now kill it, even in self-defense?

The first thing to be said about this is that it is something new. Opponents of abortion have been so concerned to make out the independence of the fetus, in order to establish that it has a right to life, just as its mother does, that they have tended to overlook the possible support they might gain from making out that the fetus is *dependent* on the mother, in order to establish that she has a special kind of responsibility for it, a responsibility that gives it rights against her which are not possessed by any independent person—such as an ailing violinist who is a stranger to her.

On the other hand, this argument would give the unborn person a right to its mother's body only if her pregnancy resulted from a voluntary act, undertaken in full knowledge of the chance a pregnancy might result from it. It would leave out entirely the unborn person whose existence is due to rape. Pending the availability of some further argument, then, we would be left with the conclusion that unborn persons whose existence is due to rape have no right to the use of their mothers' bodies, and thus that aborting them is not depriving them of anything that they have a right to and hence is not unjust killing.

And we should also notice that it is not at all plain that this argument really does go even as far as it purports to. For there are cases and cases, and the details make a difference. If the room is stuffy, and I therefore open a window to air it, and a burglar climbs in, it would be absurd to say, "Ah, now he can stay, she's given him a right to the use of her house—for she is partially responsible for his presence there, having voluntarily done what enabled him to get in, in full knowledge that there are such things as burglars, and that burglars burgle." It would be still more absurd to say this if I had had bars installed outside my windows, precisely to prevent burglars from getting in, and a burglar got in only because of a defect in the bars. It remains equally absurd if we imagine it is not a burglar who climbs in, but an innocent person who blunders or falls in. Again, suppose it were like this: people-seeds drift about in the air like pollen, and if you open your windows, one may drift in and take root in your carpets or upholstery. You don't want children, so you fix up your windows with fine mesh screens, the very best you can buy. As can happen, however, and on very, very rare occasions does happen, one of the screens is defective; and a seed drifts in and takes root. Does the person-plant who now develops have a right to the use of your house? Surely not—despite the fact that you voluntarily opened your windows, you knowingly kept carpets and upholstered furniture, and you knew that screens were sometimes defective. Someone may argue that you are responsible for its rooting, that it does have a right to your house, because after all you *could* have lived out your life with bare floors and furniture, or with sealed windows and doors. But this won't do—for by the same token anyone can avoid a pregnancy due to rape by having a hysterectomy, or anyway by never leaving home without a (reliable!) army.

It seems to me that the argument we are looking at can establish at most that there are some cases in which the unborn person has a right to the use of its mother's body, and therefore some cases in which abortion is unjust killing. There is room for much discussion and argument as to precisely which, if any. But I think she should sidestep this issue and leave it open, for at any rate the argument certainly does not establish that all abortion is unjust killing.

5. There is room for yet another argument here, however. We surely must all grant that there may be cases in which it would be morally indecent to detach a person from your body at the cost of his life. Suppose you learn that what the violinist needs is not nine years of your life, but only one hour: all you need do to save his life is to spend one hour in that

bed with him. Suppose also that letting him use your kidneys for that one hour would not affect your health in the slightest. Admittedly you were kidnapped. Admittedly you did not give anyone permission to plug him into you. Nevertheless it seems to me plain you *ought* to allow him to use your kidneys for that hour—that it would be indecent to refuse.

Again, suppose pregnancy lasted only an hour, and constituted no threat to life or health. And suppose that a woman becomes pregnant as a result of rape. Admittedly she did not voluntarily do anything to bring about the existence of a child. Admittedly she did nothing at all which would give the unborn person a right to the use of her body. All the same it might well be said, as in the newly emended violinist story, that she *ought* to allow it to remain for that hour—that it would be indecent in her to refuse.

Now some people are inclined to use the term "right" in such a way that it follows from the fact that you ought to allow a person to use your body for the hour he needs, that he has a right to use your body for the hour he needs, even though he has not been given that right by any person or act. They may say that it follows also that if you refuse, you act unjustly toward him. This use of the term is perhaps so common that it cannot be called wrong; nevertheless it seems to me to be an unfortunate loosening of what we would do better to keep a tight rein on. Suppose that box of chocolates I mentioned earlier had not been given to both boys jointly, but was given only to the older boy. There he sits, stolidly eating his way through the box, his small brother watching enviously. Here we are likely to say "You ought not to be so mean. You ought to give your brother some of those chocolates." My own view is that it just does not follow from the truth of this that the brother has any right to any of the chocolates. If the boy refuses to give his brother any, he is greedy, stingy, callous—but not unjust. I suppose that the people I have in mind will say it does follow that the brother has a right to some of the chocolates and that the boy does act unjustly if he refuses to give his brother any. But the effect of saying this is to obscure what should be kept distinct, namely the difference between the boy's refusal in this case and the boy's refusal in the earlier case, in which the box was given to both boys jointly, and in which the small brother thus had what was from any point of view clear title to half.

A further objection to so using the term "right" that from the fact that A ought to do a thing for B, it follows that B has a right against A that A do it for

him, is that it is going to make the question of whether or not a man has a right to a thing turn on how easy it is to provide him with it; and this seems not merely unfortunate, but morally unacceptable. Take the case of Henry Fonda again. I said earlier that I had no right to the touch of his cool hand on my fevered brow, even though I needed it to save my life. I said it would be frightfully nice of him to fly in from the West Coast to provide me with it, but that I had no right against him that he should do so. But suppose he isn't on the West Coast. Suppose he has only to walk across the room, place a hand briefly on my brow—and, lo, my life is saved. Then surely he ought to do it, it would be indecent to refuse. Is it to be said, "Ah, well, it follows that in this case she has a right to the touch of his hand on her brow, and so it would be an injustice in him to refuse"? So that I have a right to it when it is easy for him to provide it, though no right when it's hard? It's rather a shocking idea that anyone's rights should fade away and disappear as it gets harder and harder to accord them to him.

So my own view is that even though you ought to let the violinist use your kidneys for the one hour he needs, we should not conclude that he has a right to do so—we should say that if you refuse, you are, like the boy who owns all the chocolates and will give none away, self-centered and callous, indecent in fact, but not unjust. And similarly, that even supposing a case in which a woman pregnant due to rape ought to allow the unborn person to use her body for the hour he needs, we should not conclude that he has a right to do so; we should conclude that she is self-centered, callous, indecent, but not unjust, if she refuses. The complaints are no less grave; they are just different. However, there is no need to insist on this point. If anyone does wish to deduce "he has a right" from "you ought," then all the same he must surely grant that there are cases in which it is not morally required of you that you allow that violinist to use your kidneys, and in which he does not have a right to use them, and in which you do not do him an injustice if you refuse. And so also for mother and unborn child. Except in such cases as the unborn person has a right to demand it—and we were leaving open the possibility that there may be such cases—nobody is morally required to make large sacrifices, of health, of all other interests and concerns, of all other duties and commitments, for nine years, or even for nine months, in order to keep another person alive.

6. We have in fact to distinguish between two

kinds of Samaritan: the Good Samaritan and what we might call the Minimally Decent Samaritan. The story of the Good Samaritan, you will remember, goes like this:

> A certain man went down from Jerusalem to Jericho, and fell among thieves, which stripped him of his raiment, and wounded him, and departed, leaving him half dead.
>
> And by chance there came down a certain priest that way and when he saw him, he passed by on the other side.
>
> And likewise a Levite, when he was at the place, came and looked on him, and passed by on the other side.
>
> But a certain Samaritan, as he journeyed, came where he was; and when he saw him he had compassion on him.
>
> And went to him, and bound up his wounds, pouring in oil and wine, and set him on his own beast, and brought him to an inn, and took care of him.
>
> And on the morrow, when he departed, he took out two pence, and gave them to the host, and said unto him, "Take care of him; and whatsoever thou spendest more, when I come again, I will repay thee."   (Luke 10:30–35)

The Good Samaritan went out of his way, at some cost to himself, to help one in need of it. We are not told what the options were, that is, whether or not the priest and the Levite could have helped by doing less than the Good Samaritan did, but assuming they could have, then the fact they did nothing at all shows they were not even Minimally Decent Samaritans, not because they were not Samaritans, but because they were not even minimally decent.

These things are a matter of degree, of course, but there is a difference, and it comes out perhaps most clearly in the story of Kitty Genovese, who, as you will remember, was murdered while thirty-eight people watched or listened, and did nothing at all to help her. A Good Samaritan would have rushed out to give direct assistance against the murderer. Or perhaps we had better allow that it would have been a Splendid Samaritan who did this, on the ground that it would have involved a risk of death for himself. But the thirty-eight not only did not do this, they did not even trouble to pick up a phone to call the police. Minimally Decent Samaritanism would call for doing at least that, and their not having done it was monstrous.

After telling the story of the Good Samaritan, Jesus said, "Go, and do thou likewise." Perhaps he meant that we are morally required to act as the Good Samaritan did. Perhaps he was urging people to do more than is morally required of them. At all events it seems plain that it was not morally required of any of the thirty-eight that he rush out to give direct assistance at the risk of his own life, and that it is not morally required of anyone that he give long stretches of his life—nine years or nine months—to sustaining the life of a person who has no special right (we were leaving open the possibility of this) to demand it.

Indeed, with one rather striking class of exceptions, no one in any country in the world is *legally* required to do anywhere near as much as this for anyone else. The class of exceptions is obvious. My main concern here is not the state of the law in respect to abortion, but it is worth drawing attention to the fact that in no state in this country is any man compelled by law to be even a Minimally Decent Samaritan to any person; there is no law under which charges could be brought against the thirty-eight who stood by while Kitty Genovese died. By contrast, in most states in this country women are compelled by law to be not merely Minimally Decent Samaritans, but Good Samaritans to unborn persons inside them. This doesn't by itself settle anything one way or the other, because it may well be argued that there should be laws in this country—as there are in many European countries—compelling at least Minimally Decent Samaritanism. But it does show that there is a gross injustice in the existing state of the law and it shows also that the groups currently working against liberalization of abortion laws, in fact working toward having it declared unconstitutional for a state to permit abortion, had better start working for the adoption of Good Samaritan law generally, or earn the charge that they are acting in bad faith.

I should think, myself, that Minimally Decent Samaritan laws would be one thing, Good Samaritan laws quite another, and in fact highly improper. But we are not here concerned with the law. What we should ask is not whether anybody should be compelled by law to be a Good Samaritan, but whether we must accede to a situation in which somebody is being compelled—by nature, perhaps—to be a Good Samaritan. We have, in other words, to look now at third-party interventions. I have been arguing that no person is morally required to make large sacrifices to sustain the life of another who has no right to demand them, and this even where the sacrifices do not include life itself; we are not morally required to be Good Samaritans or anyway Very

Good Samaritans to one another. But what if a man cannot extricate himself from such a situation? What if he appeals to us to extricate him? It seems to me plain that there are cases in which we can, cases in which a Good Samaritan would extricate him. There you are, you were kidnapped, and nine years in bed with that violinist lie ahead of you. You have your own life to lead. You are sorry, but you simply cannot see giving up so much of your life to the sustaining of his. You cannot extricate yourself, and ask us to do so. I should have thought that—in light of his having no right to the use of your body—it was obvious that we do not have to accede to your being forced to give up so much. We can do what you ask. There is no injustice to the violinist in our doing so.

7. Following the thread of the opponents of abortion, I have throughout been speaking of the fetus merely as a person, and what I have been asking is whether or not the argument we began with, which proceeds only from the fetus' being a person, really does establish its conclusion. I have argued that it does not.

But of course there are arguments and arguments, and it may be said that I have simply fastened on the wrong one. It may be said that what is important is not merely the fact that the fetus is a person, but that it is a person for whom the woman has a special kind of responsibility issuing from the fact that she is its mother. And it might be argued that all my analogies are therefore irrelevant—for you do not have that special kind of responsibility for that violinist, Henry Fonda does not have that special kind of responsibility for me. And our attention might be drawn to the fact that men and women both are compelled by law to provide support for their children.

I have in effect dealt (briefly) with this argument in section 4 above; but a (still briefer) recapitulation now may be in order. Surely we do not have any such "special responsibility" for a person unless we have assumed it, explicitly or implicitly. If a set of parents do not try to prevent pregnancy, do not obtain an abortion, and then at the time of birth of the child do not put it out for adoption, but rather take it home with them, then they have assumed responsibility for it, they have given it rights, and they cannot now withdraw support from it at the cost of its life because they now find it difficult to go on providing for it. But if they have taken all reasonable precautions against having a child, they do not simply by virtue of their biological relationship to the child who comes

into existence have a special responsibility for it. They may wish to assume responsibility for it, or they may not wish to. And I am suggesting that if assuming responsibility for it would require large sacrifices, then they may refuse. A Good Samaritan would not refuse—or anyway, a Splendid Samaritan, if the sacrifices that had to be made were enormous. But then so would a Good Samaritan assume responsibility for that violinist; so would Henry Fonda, if he is a Good Samaritan, fly in from the West Coast and assume responsibility for me.

8. My argument will be found unsatisfactory on two counts by many of those who want to regard abortion as morally permissible. First, while I do argue that abortion is not impermissible, I do not argue that it is always permissible. There may well be cases in which carrying the child to term requires only Minimally Decent Samaritanism of the mother, and this is a standard we must not fall below. I am inclined to think it a merit of my account precisely that it does *not* give a general yes or a general no. It allows and supports our sense that, for example, a sick and desperately frightened fourteen-year-old schoolgirl, pregnant due to rape, may *of course* choose abortion, and that any law which rules this out is an insane law. And it also allows for and supports our sense that in other cases resort to abortion is even positively indecent. It would be indecent in the woman to request an abortion, and indecent in a doctor to perform it, if she is in her seventh month, and wants the abortion just to avoid the nuisance of postponing a trip abroad. The very fact that the arguments I have been drawing attention to treat all cases of abortion, or even all cases of abortion in which the mother's life is not at stake, as morally on a par ought to have made them suspect at the outset.

Secondly, while I am arguing for the permissibility of abortion in some cases, I am not arguing for the right to secure the death of the unborn child. It is easy to confuse these two things in that up to a certain point in the life of the fetus it is not able to survive outside the mother's body; hence removing it from her body guarantees its death. But they are importantly different. I have argued that you are not morally required to spend nine months in bed, sustaining the life of that violinist, but to say this is by no means to say that if, when you unplug yourself, there is a miracle and he survives, you then have a right to turn round and slit his throat. You may detach yourself even if this costs him his life; you have no right to be guaranteed his death, by some other means, if unplugging yourself does not kill him. There are some people who will feel dissatisfied by this feature of my argument. A woman may be utterly devastated by the thought of a child, a bit of herself, put out for adoption and never seen or heard of again. She may therefore want not merely that the child be detached from her, but more, that it die. Some opponents of abortion are inclined to regard this as beneath contempt—thereby showing insensitivity to what is surely a powerful source of despair. All the same, I agree that the desire for the child's death is not one which anybody may gratify, should it turn out to be possible to detach the child alive.

At this place, however, it should be remembered that we have only been pretending throughout that the fetus is a human being from the moment of conception. A very early abortion is surely not the killing of a person, and so is not dealt with by anything I have said here.

Discussion Questions

1. Present and explain Professor Thomson's argument for the permissibility of abortion. Do you think that she is correct in comparing the case of the violinist with pregnancy? What problems, if any, do you see with this analogy?

2. Some people, such as Harvard Law Professor Laurence Tribe, argue that the Supreme Court should have used Professor Thomson's argument in *Roe v. Wade*, rather than saying that the constitutional question of abortion hinged on fetal personhood. If you were a member of the Supreme Court, how would you incorporate Tribe's suggestion? And how would you address the question of fetal personhood in your rewritten decision?

3. Some people argue that Professor Thomson's argument seems applicable only to pregnancy resulting from rape, where the sex was not voluntary. If you do not agree because you believe it applies in other cases, explain and defend your position. If you agree that Thomson's argument does apply exclusively to cases of rape, why does it not apply to cases where sex is voluntary?

15

Arguments from Bodily Rights

Francis J. Beckwith

I am a Lecturer in Philosophy at the University of Nevada, Las Vegas, as well as Professor at Large, Simon Greenleaf University (Anaheim, California) and Senior Research Fellow, Nevada Policy Research Institute. My books include *Politically Correct Death: Answering the Arguments for Abortion Rights* (1993) and *The Abortion Controversy: A Reader* (1994).

In this essay I contend that Judith Jarvis Thomson's argument is flawed for several reasons: (1) it assumes that moral obligations must be voluntary in order to have moral weight, (2) it denies special obligations to family members, (3) it denies *prima facie* rights of children, including the unborn, to their parents' goods, (4) it ignores the distinction between killing and withholding treatment, (5) it does not take into consideration legal precedent, and (6) it seems in at least three ways inconsistent with the radical feminism espoused by many of the argument's proponents: (i) its use of the burden of pregnancy, (ii) its appeal to libertarian principles, and (iii) its macho view of bodily control. In addition to Professor Thomson's argument, I evaluate two popular arguments for abortion rights that appeal to bodily rights: (1) argument from a woman's right over her own body, and (2) argument from abortion being safer than childbirth. I argue that the first fails because it begs the question as to the fetus's personhood, and the second fails because it is based on a faulty comparison between the risks of abortion and childbirth as well as dubious statistics.

Reprinted by permission from Francis J. Beckwith, *Politically Correct Death: Answering the Arguments for Abortion Rights* (Grand Rapids, Mich.: Baker Book House, 1993), Chapter 7. Some notes and portions of the original text have been either revised or deleted for this anthology.

Some abortion-rights advocates do not see the status of the unborn as the decisive factor in whether or not abortion is morally justified. They argue that the unborn's presence in the pregnant woman's body entails a conflict of rights if the pregnant woman does not want to be pregnant. Therefore, the unborn, regardless of whether it is fully human and has a full right to life, cannot use the body of another against her will. Hence, a pregnant woman's removal of an unborn entity from her body, even though it will probably result in that entity's death, is no more immoral than an ordinary person's refusal to donate his kidney to another in need of one, even though this refusal will probably result in the death of the prospective recipient. In this essay we will discuss such arguments from rights.

The most famous and influential argument from rights is the one presented by philosopher Judith Jarvis Thomson. However, prior to analyzing that argument, I want to respond to two popular arguments that are much less sophisticated than Thomson's. These arguments, unlike Thomson's, do not assume for the sake of argument that the unborn is fully human, but ignore altogether the question of the unborn's humanness.

P124 of Polit Correct Death

Argument from a Woman's Right over Her Own Body

This argument asserts that because a woman has a right to control her own body, she therefore has a right to undergo an abortion for any reason she deems fit. Although it is not obvious that either the law or sound ethical reasoning supports such a strong view of personal autonomy (e.g., laws against prostitution and suicide), this abortion rights argument still fails logically even if we assume that such a strong view of personal autonomy is correct.

First, the unborn entity within the pregnant woman's body is not a part of her body, although many people (even very intelligent ones) seem unaware of this fact. Consider the comments of philosopher Mortimer Adler, who claims that prior to viability the life the unborn "has is as a part of the mother's body, in the same sense that an individual's arm or leg is a part of a living organism. An individual's decision to have an arm or leg amputated falls within the sphere of privacy—the freedom to do as one pleases in all matters that do not injure others or the public welfare."[1] Even someone as knowledgeable on the abortion issue as Laurence Tribe of the Harvard Law School writes that "although the fetus at some point develops an independent identity and even an independent consciousness, it begins as a living part of the woman's body."[2] Both Adler and Tribe are completely mistaken. For one thing, the conceptus is a genetically distinct entity with its own individual gender, blood type, bone structure, and genetic code. Although the unborn entity is attached to her mother, she is not part of her mother. To say that the unborn entity is part of her mother is to claim that the mother possesses four legs, two heads, two noses, and with the case of a male fetus, a penis and two testicles. Moreover, Bernard Nathanson points out "that the modern science of immunology has shown that the unborn child is not a part of a woman's body in the sense that her kidney or heart is."[3] This, of course, contradicts the claims of Adler and Tribe. Nathanson goes on to outline the scientific basis for this claim:

> Immunologic studies have demonstrated beyond cavil that when a pregnancy implants itself into the wall of the uterus at the eighth day following conception the defense mechanisms of the body, principally the white blood cells, sense that this creature now settling down for a lengthy stay is an intruder, an alien, and must be expelled. Therefore, an intense immunological attack is mounted on the pregnancy by the white blood cell elements, and through an ingenious and extraordinarily efficient defense system the unborn child succeeds in repelling the attack. In ten per cent or so of cases the defensive system fails and pregnancy is lost as a spontaneous abortion or miscarriage. Think how fundamental a lesson there is for us here: Even on the most minute microscopic scale the body has trained itself, or somehow in some inchoate way *knows*, how to recognize *self* from *nonself*.[4]

Furthermore, since scientists have been able to achieve conception in a petri dish (the "test-tube" baby), and this conceptus if it has white parents can be transferred to the body of a black woman and be born white, we know conclusively that the unborn is not part of the pregnant woman's body. Certainly a woman has a right to control her own body, but the unborn entity is not part of her body. Hence, abortion is not justified, since no one's right to personal autonomy is so strong that it permits the arbitrary execution of others.

Second, this abortion-rights argument is guilty of special pleading. The concept of a personal right over one's own body presupposes the existence of a person who possesses such a right. Such a right also presupposes that this right to personal autonomy should not interfere with another person's identical right. This is why smoking is being prohibited in more and more public places. Many studies have shown conclusively that a smoker's habit affects not only his own lungs, but also the lungs of others who choose not to smoke. The smoker's "secondary smoke" can cause the nonsmoker to be ill and quite possibly acquire lung cancer if he is exposed to such smoke over a long period of time. Since the nonsmoker has a personal right over his own body, and he chooses not to fill it with nicotine, the smoker's personal right to smoke and fill his own body with nicotine is limited by the nonsmoker's personal right to remain healthy. This is because in the process of smoking the smoker passes on harmful secondary smoke to the unwilling nonsmoker.

Suppose a smoker, in arguing against a prohibition of smoking in public places, continually appeals to his "personal right" to control his own body. And suppose he dismisses out of hand any counterargument that appeals to the possible existence of other persons (nonsmokers) whose rights his actions may obstruct. This sort of argumentation would be a case of *special pleading,* a fallacy that occurs when someone selects pieces of evidence that confirm his position (in this case, the smoker's legitimate right to personal autonomy) and ignores counterexamples that conflict with it (in this case, the nonsmoker's legitimate right to personal autonomy). Therefore, in terms of the abortion issue, when the abortion-rights advocate appeals to a woman's right to control her own body while ignoring the possibility that this control may entail the death of another, he is guilty of selecting principles that support his position (every person has a prima facie right to personal autonomy) while ignoring principles that conflict with it (every person has a prima facie obligation not to harm another). Thus the abortion-rights advocate is guilty of special pleading.

Of course, if the unborn entity is not fully human, this abortion-rights argument is successful. But this means that one begs the question when one argues for abortion rights from a woman's right to control her own body if one does not first show that the unborn entity is not fully human. Baruch Brody adds to this observation that although "it is surely true that one way in which women have been oppressed is by their being denied authority over their own bodies . . ., it seems to be that, as the struggle is carried on for meaningful amelioration of such oppression, it ought not to be carried so far that it violates the steady responsibilities all people have to one another." To cite a number of examples, "parents may not desert their children, one class may not oppress another, one race or nation may not exploit another. For parents, powerful groups in society, races or nations in ascendancy, there are penalties for refraining from these wrong actions, but those penalties can in no way be taken as the justification for such wrong actions. Similarly, if the fetus is a human being, the penalty of carrying it cannot, I believe, be used as justification for destroying it."[5]

Argument from Abortion Being Safer than Childbirth

This argument attempts to show that the pregnant woman has no moral obligation to carry her unborn offspring to term, regardless of whether or not it is fully human. The abortion-rights advocate argues that childbirth is an act that is not morally obligatory on the part of the pregnant woman, since an abortion is statistically safer than childbirth. The statistic often quoted to support this argument is one found in the most recent edition of the *American Medical Association Encyclopedia of Medicine:* "Mortality is less than one per 100,000 when abortion is performed before the 13th week, rising to three per 100,000 after the 13th week. (For comparison, maternal mortality for full-term pregnancy is nine per 100,000.)"[6] This argument can be outlined in the following way.

1. Among moral acts one is not morally obligated to perform are those that can endanger one's life (e.g., the man who dove into the Potomac in the middle of winter to save the survivors of a plane crash).
2. Childbirth is more life-threatening than having an abortion.
3. Therefore, childbirth is an act one is not morally obligated to perform.
4. Therefore, abortion is justified.

The problem with this argument lies in the inference from 2 to 3. First, assuming that childbirth is on the average more life-threatening than abortion, it does not follow that abortion is justified in every case. The fact that one act, A, is more life-threatening *on the average* than another act, B, does not mean that one is not justified or obligated to perform A in *specific*

situations where there is no prima facie reason to believe that A would result in death or severe physical impairment. To use an uncontroversial example, it is probably on the average less life-threatening to stay at home than to leave home and buy groceries (e.g., one can be killed in a car crash, purchase and take tainted Tylenol, or be murdered by a mugger), yet it seems foolish, not to mention counterintuitive, to always act in every instance on the basis of that average. This is a form of the informal *fallacy of division*, which occurs when someone erroneously argues that what is true of a whole (the average) must also be true of its parts (every individual situation). One would commit this fallacy if one argued that because Beverly Hills is wealthier than Barstow, every individual person who lives in Beverly Hills is wealthier than every individual person who lives in Barstow.

Second, one can also imagine a situation in which one is obligated to perform a particular moral action although there is statistically more risk in performing it than abstaining from it. That is to say, one can challenge the inference from 2 to 3 by pointing out that just because an act, X, is "more dangerous" relative to another act, Y, does not mean that one is not morally obligated to perform X. For example, it would be statistically more dangerous for me (a swimmer) to dive into a swimming pool to save my wife (a nonswimmer) from drowning than it would be for me to abstain from acting. Yet this does not mean that I am not morally obligated to save my wife's life. Sometimes my moral obligation is such that it outweighs the relatively insignificant chance of danger I avoid by not acting. One could then argue that although childbirth may be "more dangerous" than abortion, the special moral obligation one has to one's offspring far outweighs the relatively insignificant danger one avoids by not acting on that moral obligation (on the statistical insignificance between abortion and childbirth see below).

Of course, if a specific act, X, is significantly dangerous (i.e., there is a good chance that one will die or be severely harmed if one acts)—such as the act performed by that one man who dove into the freezing Potomac River to save the survivors of an airplane crash—then it would seem that an individual would not be obligated to perform X. However, if one had chosen to perform X, one would be performing an act of exceptional morality (what ethicists call a *supererogatory act*), although if one had refrained from X one would not be considered a bad or an evil person. In light of these observations, the abortion-rights argument in question can be strengthened if changed in the following way:

1. Among moral acts one is not morally obligated to perform are those that can endanger one's life.
2. A particular instance of childbirth, X, is more life-threatening to the pregnant woman than having an abortion.
3. Therefore, X is an act one is not morally obligated to perform.
4. Therefore, not-X via abortion is justified.

Although avoiding the pitfalls of the first argument, this one does not support the abortion-rights position. It is consistent with the pro-life assertion that abortion is justified if it is employed in order to save the life of the mother. Therefore, whether or not abortion is statistically safer than childbirth is irrelevant to whether or not abortion is justified in particular cases where sound medical diagnosis indicates that childbirth will pose virtually no threat to the mother's life.

Two other observations can be made about the argument from abortion being safer than childbirth. First, the AMA statistics are misused and do not really establish the abortion-rights position. The statistics claim that the mortality rate for a woman in childbirth is 9 per 100,000 while mortality is less than 1 per 100,000 when abortion is performed before the thirteenth week, increasing to 3 per 100,000 after the thirteenth week. This is why abortion-rights advocates often claim that a first trimester abortion is nine times safer than childbirth. Although this assertion is technically true if one assumes that the statistics are accurate, it is statistically insignificant. This becomes apparent when one converts the odds into percentages. If the mortality of childbirth is 9 per 100,000, then a woman has a 99.991 percent chance of surviving. If the mortality of a first-trimester abortion is 1 per 100,000, then a woman has a 99.999 percent chance of surviving. But the statistical difference between 99.991 percent and 99.999 percent (00.008 percent) is moot, especially if one considers the complex nature of both childbirth and abortion, as there are so many variables that may account for the small difference in the mortality rates.

Second, one can call into question the truth of the claim that abortion is safer than childbirth. David C. Reardon points out that claims that abortion is safer than childbirth are based on dubious statistical studies, simply because "accurate statistics are scarce because the reporting of complications is almost entirely at the option of abortion providers. In other words, abortionists are in the privileged position of being able to hide any information which might damage their reputation or trade." And since "federal court rulings have sheltered the practice of abortion in a 'zone of privacy,'" therefore "any laws which attempt to require that deaths and complications resulting from abortion are recorded, much less reported, are unconstitutional." This means that the "only information available on abortion complications is the result of data which is voluntarily reported."[7] From these and other factors,[8] Reardon concludes that

> complication records from outpatient clinics are virtually inaccessible, or nonexistent, even though these clinics provide the vast majority of all abortions. Even in Britain where reporting requirements are much better than in the United States, medical experts believe that less than 10 percent of abortion complications are actually reported to government health agencies.[9]

Reardon's study indicates that it may be more true to say that abortion is more dangerous than childbirth. His work deals with the physical risks as well as the psychological impact of abortion on women, in addition to the impact of abortion on later children. He concludes that the harm caused by abortion to the woman and her children is grossly understated by abortion-rights advocates.[10]

It should be noted that many scholars have disputed the claim of abortion-rights advocates that early abortions are safer than childbirth. These critics argue that the data used to draw this conclusion have been misinterpreted and/or are problematic. Consider the following example of how such a misinterpretation can occur. In a highly sophisticated study on the topic of abortion-related maternal mortality, Thomas W. Hilgers, M.D., a professor of obstetrics and gynecology at Creighton University, writes,

> Maternal mortality rates are generally expressed as the number of maternal deaths which occur—during the entire course of pregnancy and during the first three to six months following completion of the pregnancy—per 100,000 *live births*. The maternal mortality related to abortion, on the other hand, is expressed according to the type of procedure or the gestational age of the pregnancy per 100,000 *abortions*. In the latter case, the denominator is, in essence, the *number of cases* in which a particular procedure is carried out. With maternal mortality rates, this is not so. When the

denominator is live births, a number of cases of pregnancy are automatically excluded from the denominator, while their associated maternal deaths are included in the numerator. This automatically strains the traditional comparison between the maternal mortality in natural pregnancy and that in abortion. Such comparisons lack statistical accuracy.[11]

Taking into consideration this and other statistical problems, Hilgers draws among many conclusions the following: "In comparing the relative risk of natural pregnancy versus that of legal abortion, *natural pregnancy was found to be safer in both the first and second 20 weeks of pregnancy.*"[12]

Considering that the supposed fact that childbirth is not as safe as abortion played a substantial role in the U.S. Supreme Court opinions that made abortion legal, *Roe v. Wade* (410 U.S. 113 [1973]) and *Doe v. Bolton* (410 U.S. 179 [1973]), exposing the logical and factual flaws of this claim helps to undermine the foundation of the Court's opinions.

Argument from Unplugging the Violinist

Judith Jarvis Thomson presents a philosophically sophisticated version of the argument from a woman's right to control her body.[13] Thomson argues that even if the unborn entity is a person with a right to life, this does not mean that a woman must be forced to use her bodily organs to sustain its life. Just as one does not have a right to use another's kidney if one's kidney has failed, the unborn entity, although having a basic right to life, does not have a right to life so strong that it outweighs the pregnant woman's right to personal bodily autonomy.

Presentation of the Argument

This argument is called "the argument from unplugging the violinist" because of a story Thomson uses to illustrate her position:

> You wake up in the morning and find yourself back to back in bed with an unconscious violinist. A famous unconscious violinist. He has been found to have a fatal kidney ailment, and the Society of Music Lovers has canvassed all the available medical records and found that you alone

have the right blood type to help. They have therefore kidnapped you, and last night the violinist's circulatory system was plugged into yours, so that your kidneys can be used to extract poisons from his blood as well as your own. The director of the hospital now tells you, "Look, we're sorry the Society of Music Lovers did this to you—we would never have permitted it if we had known. But still, they did it, and the violinist now is plugged into you. To unplug you would be to kill him. But never mind, it's only for nine months. By then he will have recovered from his ailment, and can safely be unplugged from you." Is it morally incumbent on you to accede to this situation? No doubt it would be very nice of you if you did, a great kindness. But do you *have* to accede to it? What if it were not nine months, but nine years? Or still longer? What if the director of the hospital says, "Tough luck, I agree, but you've now got to stay in bed, with the violinist plugged into you, for the rest of your life. Because remember this. All persons have a right to life, and violinists are persons. Granted you have a right to decide what happens in and to your body, but a person's right to life outweighs your right to decide what happens in and to your body. So you cannot ever be unplugged from him." I imagine that you would regard this as outrageous."[14]

Thomson concludes that she is "only arguing that having a right to life does not guarantee having either a right to be given the use of or a right to be allowed continued use of another person's body even if one needs it for life itself."[15] Thomson anticipates several objections to her argument, and in the process of responding to them further clarifies it. It is not important, however, that we go over these clarifications now, for some are not germane to the pro-life position I am defending in this essay,[16] and the remaining will be dealt with in the following critique. In any event, it should not be ignored by the pro-life advocate that Thomson's argument makes some important observations which have gone virtually unnoticed by the pro-life movement. In defending the relevance of her story, Thomson points out that it is "of great interest to ask what happens if, for the sake of argument, we allow the premise [that the unborn are fully human or persons]. How, precisely, are we supposed to get from there to the conclusion that abortion is morally impermissible?" Thomson's argument poses a special difficulty because she believes that since pregnancy constitutes an infringement on the pregnant woman's personal rights by the unborn entity, the ordinary abortion, although it results in the death of an innocent human person, is not prima facie wrong.

A Critique of Thomson's Argument

There are at least nine problems with Thomson's argument. These problems can be put into three categories: ethical, legal, and ideological.

Ethical Problems with Thomson's Argument

1. Thomson assumes volunteerism. By using the story as a paradigm for all relationships, thus implying that moral obligations must be voluntarily accepted in order to have moral force, Thomson mistakenly infers that all true moral obligations to one's offspring are voluntary. But consider the following story. Suppose a couple has a sexual encounter that is fully protected by several forms of birth control short of surgical abortion (condom, the Pill, IUD), but nevertheless results in conception. Instead of getting an abortion, the mother of the conceptus decides to bring it to term, although the father is unaware of this decision. After the birth of the child, the mother pleads with the father for child support. Because he refuses, she takes legal action. Although he took every precaution to avoid fatherhood, thus showing that he did not wish to accept such a status, according to nearly all child-support laws in the United States he would still be obligated to pay support *precisely because* of his relationship to this child.[17] As Michael Levin points out, "All child-support laws make the parental body an indirect resource for the child. If the father is a construction worker, the state will intervene unless some of his calories he expends lifting equipment go to providing food for his children."[18]

But this obligatory relationship is not based strictly on biology, for this would make sperm donors morally responsible for children conceived by their seed. Rather, the father's responsibility for his offspring stems from the fact that he engaged in an act, sexual intercourse, that he fully realized could result in the creation of another human being, although he took every precaution to avoid such a result. This is not an unusual way to frame moral obligations, for we hold drunk people whose driving results in manslaughter responsible for their actions, even if they did not intend to kill someone prior

to becoming intoxicated. Such special obligations, although not directly undertaken voluntarily, are necessary in any civilized culture in order to preserve the rights of the vulnerable, the weak, and the young, who can offer very little in exchange for the rights bestowed upon them by the strong, the powerful, and the post-uterine in Thomson's moral universe of the social contract. Thus, Thomson is wrong, in addition to ignoring the *natural* relationship between sexual intercourse and human reproduction,[19] when she claims that if a couple has "taken all reasonable precautions against having a child, they do not by virtue of their biological relationship to the child who comes into existence have a special responsibility for it." "Surely we do not have any such 'special responsibility' for a person unless we have assumed it, explicitly or implicitly."[20] Hence, instead of providing reasons for rejecting any special responsibilities for one's offspring, Thomson simply dismisses the concept altogether.

2. Thomson's argument is fatal to family morality. It follows from the first criticism that Thomson's volunteerism is fatal to family morality which has as one of its central beliefs that an individual has special and filial obligations to his offspring and family that he does not have to other persons. Although Thomson may not consider such a fatality as being all that terrible, since she may accept the feminist dogma that the traditional family is "oppressive" to women, a great number of ordinary men and women, who have found joy, happiness, and love in family life, find Thomson's volunteerism to be counterintuitive. Philosopher Christina Sommers has come to a similar conclusion:

> For it [the volunteerist thesis] means that there is no such thing as filial duty per se, no such thing as the special duty of mother to child, and generally no such thing as morality of special family or kinship relations. All of which is contrary to what people think. For most people think that we do owe special debts to our parents even though we have not voluntarily assumed our obligations to them. Most people think that what we owe to our children does not have its origin in any voluntary undertaking, explicit or implicit, that we have made to them. And "preanalytically," many people believe that we owe special consideration to our siblings even at times when we may not *feel* very friendly to them. . . . The idea that to be committed to an individual is to have made a voluntarily implicit or explicit commitment to that individual is generally fatal to

family morality. For it looks upon the network of felt obligation and expectation that binds family members as a sociological phenomenon that is without presumptive moral force. The social critics who hold this view of family obligation usually are aware that promoting it in public policy must further the disintegration of the traditional family as an institution. But whether they deplore the disintegration or welcome it, they are bound in principle to abet it.[21]

3. A case can be made that the unborn does have a prima facie right to her mother's body. Assuming that there is such a thing as a special filial obligation, a principle that does not have to be voluntarily accepted in order to have moral force, it is not obvious that the unborn entity in ordinary circumstances (that is, with the exception of when the mother's life is in significant danger) does not have a natural prima facie claim to her mother's body. There are several reasons to suppose that the unborn entity does have such a natural claim.

a. Unlike Thomson's violinist, who is artificially attached to another person in order to save his life and is therefore not naturally dependent on any particular human being, the unborn entity is a human being who by her very nature is dependent on her mother, for this is how human beings are at this stage of their development.

b. This period of a human being's natural development occurs in the womb. This is the journey which we all must take and is a necessary condition for any human being's post-uterine existence. And this fact alone brings out the most glaring difference between the violinist and the unborn: the womb is the unborn's natural environment, whereas being artificially hooked up to a stranger is not the natural environment for the violinist. It would seem, then, that the unborn has a prima facie natural claim upon her mother's body.

c. This same entity, when she becomes a newborn, has a natural claim upon her parents to care for her, regardless of whether her parents wanted her (see the story of the irresponsible father). This is why we prosecute child abusers, people who throw their babies in trash cans, and parents who abandon their children. Although it should not be ignored that pregnancy and childbirth entail certain emotional, physical, and financial sacrifices on the part of the pregnant woman, these sacrifices are also endemic of parenthood in general (which ordinarily lasts much longer than nine months), and do not seem to justify the execution of troublesome infants and younger children whose existence entails a natural claim to certain financial and bodily goods that are under the ownership of their parents. If the unborn entity is fully human, as Thomson is willing to grant, why should the unborn's natural prima facie claim to her parents' goods differ before birth? Of course, a court will not force a parent to donate a kidney to her dying offspring, but this sort of dependence on the parent's body is highly unusual and is not part of the ordinary obligations associated with the natural process of human development, just as in the case of the violinist's artificial dependency on the reluctant music lover.

As Schwartz points out: "So, the very thing that makes it plausible to say that the person in bed with the violinist has no duty to sustain him, namely, that he is a stranger unnaturally hooked up to him, is precisely what is absent in the case of the mother and her child." That is to say, the mother "does have an obligation to take care of her child, to sustain her, to protect her, and especially, to let her live in the only place where she can now be protected, nourished, and allowed to grow, namely the womb."[22]

If Thomson responds to this argument by saying that birth is the threshold at which parents become fully responsible, then she has begged the question, for her argument was supposed to show us why there is no parental responsibility before birth. That is to say, Thomson cannot appeal to birth as the decisive moment at which parents become responsible in order to prove that birth is the time at which parents become responsible.

It is evident that Thomson's violinist illustration undermines the deep natural bond between mother and child by making it seem no different from that between two strangers artificially hooked up to each other so that one can "steal" the service of the other's kidneys. Never has something so human, so natural, so beautiful, and so wonderfully demanding of our human creativity and love been reduced to such a brutal caricature.

I am not saying that the unborn entity has an absolute natural claim to her mother's body, but simply that she has a prima facie natural claim. For one can easily imagine a situation in which this natural claim is outweighed by other important prima facie values, such as when a pregnancy significantly endangers the mother's life. Since the continuation of such a pregnancy would most likely entail the death of both mother and child, and since it is better that one human should live rather than two die, terminating such a pregnancy via abortion is morally justified.

Someone may respond to the three criticisms by agreeing that Thomson's illustration may not apply in cases of ordinary sexual intercourse, but only in cases in which pregnancy results from rape or incest, although it should be noted that Thomson herself does not press this argument. She writes: "Surely the question of whether you have a right to life at all, or how much of it you have, shouldn't turn on the question of whether or not you are the product of rape."[23]

But those who do press the rape argument may choose to argue in the following way. Just as the sperm donor is not responsible for how his sperm is used or what results from its use (e.g., it may be stolen, or an unmarried woman may purchase it, inseminate herself, and give birth to a child), the raped woman, who did not voluntarily engage in intercourse, cannot be held responsible for the unborn human who is living inside her.

But there is a problem with this analogy: The sperm donor's relinquishing of responsibility does not result in the death of a human person. The following story should help to illustrate the differences and similarities between these two cases.

Suppose that the sperm donated by the sperm donor was stolen by an unscrupulous physician and inseminated into a woman. Although he is not morally responsible for the child that results from such an insemination, the donor is nevertheless forced by an unjust court to pay a large monthly sum for child support, a sum so large that it may drive him into serious debt, maybe even bankruptcy. This would be similar to the woman who became pregnant as a result of rape. She was unjustly violated and is supporting a human being against her will at an emotional and financial cost. Is it morally right for the sperm donor to kill the child he is supporting in order to allegedly right the wrong that has been committed against him? Not at all, because such an act would be murder. Now if we assume, as does Thomson, that the raped woman is carrying a being who is fully human (or "a person"), her killing of the unborn entity by abortion, except if the pregnancy has a strong possibility of endangering her life, would be as unjust as the sperm donor killing the child he is unjustly forced to support. As the victimized man may rightly refuse to pay the child support, the raped woman may rightly refuse to bring up her child after the pregnancy has come to term. She can choose to put the child up for adoption. But in both cases,

the killing of the child is not morally justified. Although neither the sperm donor nor the rape victim may have the same special obligation to their biological offspring as does the couple who voluntarily engaged in intercourse with no direct intention to produce a child, it seems that the more general obligation not to directly kill another human person does apply.

4. Thomson ignores the fact that abortion is indeed killing and not merely the withholding of treatment. Thomson makes an excellent point: namely, there are times when withholding and/or withdrawing medical treatment is morally justified. For instance, I am not morally obligated to donate my kidney to Fred, my next-door neighbor, simply because he needs a kidney in order to live. In other words, I am not obligated to risk my life so that Fred may live a few years longer. Fred should not expect that of me. If, however, I donate one of my kidneys to Fred, I will have acted above and beyond the call of duty, since I will have performed a supererogatory moral act. But this case is not analogous to pregnancy and abortion.

Levin argues that there is an essential difference between abortion and the unplugging of the violinist. In the case of the violinist (as well as my relationship to Fred's welfare), the person who withdraws [or withholds] his assistance is not completely responsible for the dependency on him of the person who is about to die, while the mother is completely responsible for the dependency of her fetus on her. When one is completely responsible for dependence, refusal to continue to aid is indeed killing." For example, "if a woman brings a newborn home from the hospital, puts it in its crib and refuses to feed it until it has starved to death, it would be absurd to say that she simply refused to assist it and had done nothing for which she should be criminally liable."[24] In other words, just as the withholding of food kills the child after birth, in the case of abortion, the abortion kills the child. In neither case is there any ailment from which the child suffers and for which highly invasive medical treatment, with the cooperation of another's bodily organs, is necessary in order to cure this ailment and save the child's life.

Or consider the following case, which can be applied to the case of pregnancy resulting from rape or incest. Suppose a person returns home after work to find a baby at his doorstep. Suppose that no one else is able to take care of the child, but this person has only to take care of the child for nine months (after that time a couple will adopt the child). Imagine that this person, because of the child's presence, will have some bouts with morning sickness, water retention, and other minor ailments. If we assume with Thomson that the unborn child is as much a person as you or I, would "withholding treatment" from this child and its subsequent death be justified on the basis that the homeowner was only "withholding treatment" of a child he did not ask for in order to benefit himself? Is any person, born or unborn, obligated to sacrifice his life because his death would benefit another person? Consequently, there is no doubt that such "withholding" of treatment (and it seems totally false to call ordinary shelter and sustenance "treatment") is indeed murder.

But is it even accurate to refer to abortion as the "withholding of support or treatment"? Professors Schwarz and R. K. Tacelli make the important point that although "a woman who has an abortion is indeed 'withholding support' from her unborn child . . . abortion is far more than that. It is the active killing of a human person—by burning him, by crushing him, by dismembering him."[25] Euphemistically calling abortion the "withholding of support or treatment" makes about as much sense as calling suffocating someone with a pillow the withdrawing of oxygen.

In summary, I agree with Professor Brody when he concludes that "Thomson has not established the truth of her claim about abortion, primarily because she has not sufficiently attended to the distinction between our duty to save X's life and our duty not to take it." But "once one attends to that distinction, it would seem that the mother, in order to regain control over her body, has no right to abort the fetus from the point at which it becomes a human being."[26]

Legal Problems with Thomson's Argument

There are at least two legal problems with Thomson's argument: one has to do with tort law, and the other has to do with parental responsibility and child-welfare law.

1. Thomson's argument ignores tort law. Judge John T. Noonan of the U.S. Ninth Circuit Court of Appeals points out that "while Thomson focuses on this fantasy [the violinist story], she ignores a real case from which American tort law has generalized."[27]

On a January night in Minnesota, a cattle buyer, Orlando Depue, asked a family of farmers, the Flateaus, with whom he had dined, if he could remain overnight at their house. The Flateaus refused and, although Depue was sick and had fainted, put him out of the house into the cold night. Imposing liability on the Flateaus for Depue's loss of his frostbitten fingers, the court said: "In the case at bar defendants were under no contract obligation to minister to plaintiff in his distress; but humanity demanded they do so, if they understood and appreciated his condition. . . . The law as well as humanity required that he not be exposed in his helpless condition to the merciless elements." Depue was a guest for supper although not a guest after supper. The American Law Institute, generalizing, has said that it makes no difference whether the person is a guest or a trespasser. He has the privilege of staying. His host has the duty not to injure him or put him into an environment where he becomes nonviable. The obligation arises when one "understands and appreciates" the condition of the other.

Noonan concludes that "although the analogy is not exact, the case is much closer to the mother's situation than the case imagined by Thomson; and the emotional response of the Minnesota judges seems to be a truer reflection of what humanity requires."

2. Thomson's argument ignores family law. Thomson's argument is inconsistent with the body of well-established family law, which presupposes parental responsibility of a child's welfare. And, of course, assuming as Thomson does that the unborn are fully human, this body of law would also apply to parents' responsibility for their unborn children. According to legal scholars Dennis J. Horan and Burke J. Balche, "All 50 states, the District of Columbia, American Samoa, Guam, and the U.S. Virgin Islands have child abuse and neglect statutes which provide for the protection of a child who does not receive needed medical care." They further state that "a review of cases makes it clear that these statutes are properly applied to secure emergency medical treatment and sustenance (food or water, whether given orally or through intravenous or nasogastric tube) for children when parents, with or without the acquiescence of physicians, refuse to provide it."[28] Evidently, "pulling the plug" on a perfectly healthy unborn entity, assuming that it is a human person, would clearly violate these statutes.

For example, in a case in New York, the court ruled that the parents' actions constituted neglect when they failed to provide medical care to a child with leukemia: "The parent . . . may not deprive a child of life-saving treatment, however well-intentioned. Even when the parents' decision to decline necessary treatment is based on constitutional grounds, such as religious beliefs, it must yield to the State's interests, as parens patriae, in protecting the health and welfare of the child."[29] The fact of the matter is that the "courts have uniformly held that a parent has the legal responsibility of furnishing his dependent child with adequate food and medical care."[30]

It is evident then that child-protection laws reflect our deepest moral intuitions about parental responsibility and the utter helplessness of infants and small children. And without these moral scruples—which are undoubtedly undermined by "brave new notions" of a socially contracted "voluntaristic" family (Thomson's view)—the protection of children and the natural bonds and filial obligations that are an integral part of ordinary family life will become a thing of the past. This seems too high a price for bodily autonomy.

Ideological Problems with the Use of Thomson's Argument

There are at least three ideological problems in the use of Thomson's argument by others. The latter two problems are usually found in the books, speeches, articles, or papers, of those in the feminist and/or abortion-rights movements who sometimes uncritically use Thomson's argument or ones similar to it. In fact, Thomson may very well agree with most or all of the following critique.

1. Inconsistent use of the burden of pregnancy. Thomson has to paint pregnancy in the most horrific of terms in order to make her argument seem plausible. Dr. Bernard Nathanson, an obstetrician/gynecologist and former abortion provider, objects "strenuously to Thomson's portrayal of pregnancy as a nine-month involuntary imprisonment in bed. This casts an unfair and wrongheaded prejudice against the consideration of the state of pregnancy and skews the argument." Nathanson points out that "pregnancy is not a 'sickness.' Few pregnant women are bedridden and many, emotionally and physically, have never felt better. For these it is a stimulating

experience, even for mothers who originally did not 'want' to be pregnant." Unlike the person who is plugged into Thomson's violinist, "alpha [the unborn entity] does not hurt the mother by being 'plugged in,' . . . except in the case of well-defined medical indications." And "in those few cases where pregnancy *is* a medical penalty, it is a penalty lasting nine months."[31]

Compare and contrast Thomson's portrayal of pregnancy with the fact that researchers have recently discovered that many people believe that a pregnant woman cannot work as effectively as a nonpregnant woman who is employed to do the same job in the same workplace. This has upset a number of feminists, and rightfully so. They argue that a pregnant woman is not incapacitated or ill, but can work just as effectively as a nonpregnant woman.[32] But why then do feminists who use Thomson's argument argue, when it comes to abortion, that pregnancy is similar to being bedridden and hooked up to a violinist for nine months? When it comes to equality in the workplace (with which I agree with the feminists) there is no problem. But in the case of morally justifying abortion rights, pregnancy is painted in the most horrific of terms. Although not logically fatal to the abortion-rights position, this sort of double-mindedness is not conducive to good moral reasoning.

2. The libertarian principles underlying Thomson's case are inconsistent with the state-mandated agenda of radical feminism. If Thomson's illustration works at all, it works contrary to the statist principles of radical feminism (of course, a libertarian feminist need not be fazed by this objection). Levin points out that "while appeal to an absolute right to the disposition of one's body coheres well with other strongly libertarian positions (laissez-faire in the marketplace, parental autonomy in education of their children, freedom of private association), this appeal is most commonly made by feminists who are antilibertarian on just about every other issue." For example, "feminists who advocate state-mandated quotas, state-mandated comparable worth pay scales, the censorship of 'sexist' textbooks in the public schools, laws against 'sexually harassing speech' and legal limitations on private association excluding homosexuals, will go on to advocate abortion on the basis of an absolute libertarianism at odds with every one of those policies."[33] Although this criticism is ad hominem, as was the previous one, it serves to underscore the important political fad that many abortion-rights advocates are more than willing to hold and earnestly defend contrary principles for the sake of legally mandating their ideological agenda.

This sort of hypocrisy is evident in abortion-rights activity throughout the United States. In the state of Nevada, those who supported an abortion-rights referendum in November of 1990 told the voting public that they wanted to "get the government off of our backs and out of the bedrooms." But when the state legislature met in January these same abortion-rights supporters, under the auspices of the Nevada Women's Lobby, proposed legislation that asked for the taxpayers of the state to fund school-based sex clinics (which will refer teenage girls to abortion services and are euphemistically called health clinics) and assorted other programs. Forgetting that many of us keep our wallets in our back pockets and place them in the evening on our dressers in our bedrooms, the members of the Nevada Women's Lobby did not hesitate to do in January what they vehemently opposed in November: to get the government *on* our backs and *in* our bedrooms. The libertarians of November became the social engineers of March.

3. Thomson's argument implies a macho view of bodily control, a view inconsistent with true feminism. Some have pointed out that Thomson's argument and/or reasoning behind it is actually quite antifeminist.[34] In response to a similar argument from a woman's right to control her own body, one feminist publication asks, "What kind of control are we talking about? A control that allows for violence against another human being is a macho, oppressive kind of control. Women rightly object when others try to have that kind of control over them, and the movement for women's rights asserts the moral right of women to be free from the control of others." After all, "abortion involves violence against a small, weak and dependent child. It is macho control, the very kind the feminist movement most eloquently opposes in other contexts."[35]

Celia Wolf-Devine observes that "abortion has something . . . in common with the behavior ecofeminists and pacifist feminists take to be characteristically masculine; it shows a willingness to use violence in order to take control. The fetus is destroyed by being pulled apart by suction, cut in pieces, or poisoned." Wolf-Devine goes on to point out that "in terms of social thought . . . it is the masculine models which are most frequently employed in thinking about abortion. If masculine thought is

naturally hierarchical and oriented toward power and control, then the interests of the fetus (who has no power) would naturally be suppressed in favor of the interests of the mother. But to the extent that feminist social thought is egalitarian, the question must be raised of why the mother's interests should prevail over the child's. . . . Feminist thought about abortion has . . . been deeply pervaded by the individualism which they so ardently criticize."[36]

Discussion Questions

1. How does Professor Beckwith argue philosophically and legally against Professor Thomson's position? Do you think he is successful? Why or why not?

2. Professor Beckwith does not believe that Professor Thomson's argument applies to the case of the woman pregnant due to rape. Do you think that Professor Beckwith is correct in his assessment? Do you think the analogies he uses are successful when arguing for this position?

3. At what three points does Professor Beckwith believe that Professor Thomson's argument is inconsistent with radical feminism? How does he argue for this position? Do you think he is correct? Why or why not?

Notes

1. Mortimer J. Adler, *Haves Without Have-Nots: Essays for the 21st Century on Democracy and Socialism* (New York: Macmillan, 1991), 210.

2. Laurence H. Tribe, *Abortion: The Clash of Absolutes* (New York: Norton, 1990), 102.

3. Bernard N. Nathanson, M.D., *The Abortion Papers: Inside the Abortion Mentality* (New York: Frederick Fell, 1983), 150.

4. *Ibid.*, 150–51.

5. Baruch Brody, *Abortion and the Sanctity of Human Life: A Philosophical View* (Cambridge, Mass.: M.I.T. Press, 1975), 30.

6. *American Medical Association Encyclopedia of Medicine*, ed. Charles B. Clayman, M.D. (New York: Random House,1989), 58.

7. David C. Reardon, *Aborted Women: Silent No More* (Westchester, Ill.: Crossway, 1987), 90. Reardon cites a *Chicago Sun Times* piece ("The Abortion Profiteers," 12 November 1978), in which writers Pamela Zekman and Pamela Warrick "reveal how undercover investigators in abortion clinics found that clinic employees routinely checked 'no complications' before the abortion was even performed." (Reardon, *Aborted Women*, 343).

8. Some other reasons for underreporting could be the following: few outpatient clinics provide follow-up examinations; long-term complications may develop (e.g., sterility, incompetent uterus) that cannot be detected without prolonged surveillance; of the women who require emergency treatment after an outpatient abortion, more than 60 percent go to a local hospital rather than returning to the abortion clinic; some women who are receiving treatment for such long-term complications as infertility may either hide their abortion or not know that it is relevant (*Ibid.*, 91).

9. *Ibid.*

10. See *ibid.*, 89–160, 219–31.

11. Thomas W. Hilgers, M.D. and Dennis O'Hare, "Abortion Related Maternal Mortality: An In-Depth Analysis," in *New Perspectives on Human Abortion*, ed. Thomas W. Hilgers, M.D., Dennis J. Horan, and David Mall (Frederick, Md.: University Publications of America, 1981), pp 69–70. See also Robert Marshall and Charles Donovan, *Blessed Are the Barren: The Social Policy of Planned Parenthood* (San Francisco: Ignatius, 1991),187–210.

12. Hilgers and O'Hare, "Mortality," 90.

13. Judith Jarvis Thomson, "A Defense of Abortion," in *The Problem of Abortion*, 2d ed., ed. Joel Feinberg (Belmont, Calif.: Wadsworth, 1984), 173–87. This article was originally published in *Philosophy and Public Affairs* 1 (1971): 47–66.

14. Thomson, "Defense of Abortion," 174–75.

15. *Ibid.*, 180.

16. For example, in clarifying her own view, Thomson criticizes the absolutist position on abortion that it is morally impermissible to have an abortion even if the life of the mother is in significant danger. Needless to say, I agree with Thomson that this view is seriously flawed, and have spelled out my reasons for this in the introduction, Chap. 1 and Chap. 6 of *Politically Correct Death: Answering the Arguments for Abortion Rights* (Grand Rapids: Baker Book House, 1993).

17. See *In the Best Interest of the Child: A Guide to State Child Support and Paternity Laws*, ed. Carolyn Royce Kastner and Lawrence R. Young (n.p.: Child Support Enforcement Beneficial Laws Project, National Conference of State Legislatures, 1981).

18. Michael Levin, review of *Life in the Balance* by Robert Wennberg, *Constitutional Commentary* 3 (Summer 1986): 511.

19. The lengths to which Thomson will go in order to deny the natural relationship between sex, reproduction, and filial obligations is evident in her use of the following analogy: "If the room is stuffy, and I therefore open a window to air it, and a burglar climbs in, it would be absurd to say, 'Ah, now he can stay, she's given him a right to use her house—for she is partially responsible for his presence there, having voluntarily done what enabled him to get in, in full knowledge that there are such things as burglars, and that burglars burgle.'" (Thomson, "Defense of Abortion," 182). Since there is no natural dependency between burglar and homeowner, as there is between child and parent, Thomson's analogy is way off the mark. Burglars don't belong in other people's homes whereas preborn children belong in no other place *except* their mother's womb.

20. *Ibid.*, 186.

21. Sommers, "Philosophers Against the Family," 570 in this text (ch. 59).

22. Stephen D. Schwarz, *The Moral Question of Abortion* (Chicago: Loyola University Press, 1990), 118.

23. Thomson, "Defense of Abortion," 175.

24. Michael Levin, *Feminism and Freedom* (New Brunswick, N.J.: Transaction, 1987), 288–289.

25. Stephen D. Schwarz and R. K. Tacelli, "Abortion and Some Philosophers: A Critical Examination," *Public Affairs Quarterly* 3 (April 1989): 85.

26. Brody, *Abortion*, 30.

27. John T. Noonan, "How to Argue About Abortion," in *Morality in Practice*, 2d ed., ed. James P. Sterba (Belmont, Calif.: Wadsworth, 1988), 150.

28. Dennis J. Horan and Burke J. Balch, *Infant Doe and Baby Jane Doe: Medical Treatment of the Handicapped Newborn*, Studies in Law & Medicine Series (Chicago: Americans United for Life, 1985), 2.

29. *In re Storar*, 53 N.Y. 2d 363, 380–381, 420 N.E. 2d 64, 73, 438 N.Y.S. 2d 266, 275 (1981), as quoted in *ibid.*, 23.

30. Horan and Balch, *Infant Doe*, 3–4.

31. Bernard Nathanson, M.D., *Aborting America* (New York: Doubleday, 1979), 220.

32. Michelle Healy, "At Work: Maternity Bias," *USA Today* (30 July 1990): IA. Conducted by researcher Hal Grueual of State University of New York, Albany, this survey found that 41 percent of those interviewed (133 women and 122 men at eight businesses in the Northeast) said they think pregnancy "hurts a woman's job performance."

33. Levin, review of *Life in the Balance*, 507–8.

34. Although not dealing exclusively with Thomson's argument, Celia Wolf-Devine's article is quite helpful: "Abortion and the 'Feminine Voice,'" *Public Affairs Quarterly* 3 (July 1989): 181–97. See also Doris Gordon, "Abortion and Thomson's Violinist," a paper published by Libertarians for Life, 1991 (13424 Hathaway Drive, Wheaton, Md. 20906; 301-460-4141); Janet Smith, "Abortion as a Feminist Concern," in *The Zero People*, ed. Jeffe Lane Hensley (Ann Arbor, Mich.: Servant, 1983), 77–95; and John T. Wilcox, "Nature as Demonic in Thomson's Defense of Abortion," *The New Scholasticism* 63 (Autumn 1989): 463–84.

35. n.a. *Sound Advice for All Pro-life Activists and Candidates Who Wish to Include a Concern for Women's Rights in Their Pro-life Advocacy: Feminists for Life Debate Handbook* (Kansas City, Mo.: Feminists for Life of America, n.d.), 15–16.

36. Wolf-Devine, "Abortion," 86, 87.

16

On the Moral and Legal
Status of Abortion

Mary Anne Warren

Mary Anne Warren is Professor of Philosophy at San Francisco State University. She is the author of numerous works on moral philosophy, bioethics, and feminism, including two books, *Gendercide: The Implications of Sex Selection* (1985) and *The Nature of Woman* (1980).

In this article Professor Warren argues that though the fetus is a human being *in the genetic sense*, it is not a human being *in the moral sense*. That is to say, the fetus is a human being but not a human person. Professor Warren suggests five traits that are central to the concept of personhood. Although she admits a person may lack as many as two or even three of these traits, she does claim that any being that satisfies none of these traits is not a person: (1) consciousness of events and objects internal and/or external to one's being as well as the capacity to feel pain, (2) a developed capacity for reasoning, (3) self-motivated activity that is independent of complete external or genetic control, (4) the capacity to communicate, and (5) the presence of self-awareness and self-concepts.

The question which we must answer in order to produce a satisfactory solution to the problem of the moral status of abortion is this: How are we to define the moral community, the set of beings with full and equal moral rights, such that we can decide whether a human fetus is a member of this community or not? What sort of entity, exactly, has the inalienable rights to life, liberty, and the pursuit of happiness? Jefferson attributed these rights to all men,

Reprinted by permission from *The Monist* 57, no. 1 (1973).

and it may or may not be fair to suggest that he intended to attribute them *only* to men. Perhaps he ought to have attributed them to all human beings. If so, then we arrive, first, at [John T.] Noonan's problem of defining what makes a being human, and, second, at the equally vital question which Noonan does not consider, namely, What reason is there for identifying the moral community with the set of all human beings, in whatever way we have chosen to define that term?

1. On the Definition of "Human"

One reason why this vital second question is so frequently overlooked in the debate over the moral status of abortion is that the term "human" has two distinct, but not often distinguished, senses. This fact results in a slide of meaning, which serves to conceal the fallaciousness of the traditional argument that since (1) it is wrong to kill innocent human beings, and (2) fetuses are innocent human beings, then (3) it is wrong to kill fetuses. For if "human" is used in the same sense in both (1) and (2) then, whichever of the two senses is meant, one of these premises is question-begging. And if it is used in two different senses then of course the conclusion doesn't follow.

Thus, (1) is a self-evident moral truth,[1] and avoids begging the question about abortion, only if "human being" is used to mean something like "a full-fledged member of the moral community." (It may or may not also be meant to refer exclusively to members of the species *Homo sapiens*.) We may call this the *moral* sense of "human." It is not to be confused with what we will call the *genetic* sense, i.e., the sense in which *any* member of the species is a human being, and no member of any other species could be. If (1) is acceptable only if the moral sense is intended, (2) is non-question-begging only if what is intended is the genetic sense.

In "Deciding Who Is Human," Noonan argues for the classification of fetuses with human beings by pointing to the presence of the full genetic code, and the potential capacity for rational thought.[2] It is clear that what he needs to show, for his version of the traditional argument to be valid, is that fetuses are human in the moral sense, the sense in which it is analytically true that all human beings have full moral rights. But, in the absence of any argument showing that whatever is genetically human is also morally human, and he gives none, nothing more than genetic humanity can be demonstrated by the presence of the human genetic code. And, as we will see, the *potential* capacity for rational thought can at most show that an entity has the potential for *becoming* human in the moral sense.

2. Defining the Moral Community

Can it be established that genetic humanity is sufficient for moral humanity? I think that there are very good reasons for not defining the moral community in this way. I would like to suggest an alternative way of defining the moral community, which I will argue for only to the extent of explaining why it is, or should be, self-evident. The suggestion is simply that the moral community consists of all and only *people*, rather than all and only human beings;[3] and probably the best way of demonstrating its self-evidence is by considering the concept of personhood, to see what sorts of entity are and are not persons, and what the decision that a being is or is not a person implies about its moral rights.

What characteristics entitle an entity to be considered a person? This is obviously not the place to attempt a complete analysis of the concept of personhood, but we do not need such a fully adequate analysis just to determine whether and why a fetus is or isn't a person. All we need is a rough and approximate list of the most basic criteria of personhood, and some idea of which, or how many, of these an entity must satisfy in order to properly be considered a person.

In searching for such criteria, it is useful to look beyond the set of people with whom we are acquainted, and ask how we would decide whether a totally alien being was a person or not. (For we have no right to assume that genetic humanity is necessary for personhood.) Imagine a space traveler who lands on an unknown planet and encounters a race of beings utterly unlike any he has ever seen or heard of. If he wants to be sure of behaving morally toward these beings, he has to somehow decide whether they are people, and hence have full moral rights, or whether they are the sort of thing which he need not feel guilty about treating as, for example, a source of food.

How should he go about making this decision? If he has some anthropological background, he might look for such things as religion, art, and the manufacturing of tools, weapons, or shelters, since these factors have been used to distinguish our human from our prehuman ancestors, in what seems to be closer to the moral than the genetic sense of "human." And no doubt he would be right to consider the presence of such factors as good evidence that the alien beings were people, and morally human. It would, however, be overly anthropocentric of him to take the absence of these things as adequate evidence that they were not, since we can imagine people who have progressed beyond, or evolved without ever developing, these cultural characteristics.

I suggest that the traits which are most central to the concept of personhood, or humanity in the moral sense, are, very roughly, the following:

1. consciousness (of objects and events external and/or internal to the being), and in particular the capacity to feel pain;
2. reasoning (the *developed* capacity to solve new and relatively complex problems);
3. self-motivated activity (activity which is relatively independent of either genetic or direct external control);
4. the capacity to communicate, by whatever means, messages of an indefinite variety of types, that is, not just with an indefinite number of possible contents, but on indefinitely many possible topics;
5. the presence of self-concepts, and self-awareness, either individual or racial, or both.

Admittedly, there are apt to be a great many problems involved in formulating precise definitions of these criteria, let alone in developing universally valid behavioral criteria for deciding when they apply. But I will assume that both we and our explorer know approximately what (1)–(5) mean, and that he is also able to determine whether or not they apply. How, then, should he use his findings to decide whether or not the alien beings are people? We needn't suppose that an entity must have *all* of these attributes to be properly considered a person; (1) and (2) alone may well be sufficient for personhood, and quite probably (1)–(3) are sufficient. Neither do we need to insist that any one of these criteria is *necessary* for personhood, although once again (1) and (2) look like fairly good candidates for necessary conditions, as does (3), if "activity" is construed so as to include the activity of reasoning.

All we need to claim, to demonstrate that a fetus is not a person, is that any being which satisfies *none* of (1)–(5) is certainly not a person. I consider this claim to be so obvious that I think anyone who denied it, and claimed that a being which satisfied none of (1)–(5) was a person all the same, would thereby demonstrate that he had no notion at all of what a person is—perhaps because he had confused the concept of a person with that of genetic humanity. If the opponents of abortion were to deny the appropriateness of these five criteria, I do not know what further arguments would convince them. We would probably have to admit that our conceptual schemes were indeed irreconcilably different, and that our dispute could not be settled objectively.

I do not expect this to happen, however, since I think that the concept of a person is one which is very nearly universal (to people), and that it is common to both pro-abortionists and anti-abortionists, even though neither group has fully realized the relevance of this concept to the resolution of their dispute. Furthermore, I think that on reflection even the antiabortionists ought to agree not only that (1)–(5) are central to the concept of personhood, but also that it is a part of this concept that all and only people have full moral rights The concept of a person is in part a moral concept; once we have admitted that X is a person we have recognized, even if we have not agreed to respect, X's right to be treated as a member of the moral community. It is true that the claim that X is a *human being* is more commonly voiced as part of an appeal to treat X decently than is the claim that X is a person, but this is either because "human being" is here used in the sense which implies personhood, or because the genetic and moral senses of "human" have been confused.

Now if (1)–(5) are indeed the primary criteria of personhood, then it is clear that genetic humanity is neither necessary nor sufficient for establishing that an entity is a person. Some human beings are not people, and there may well be people who are not human beings. A man or woman whose consciousness has been permanently obliterated but who remains alive is a human being which is no longer a person; defective human beings, with no appreciable mental capacity, are not and presumably never will be people; and a fetus is a human being which is not yet a person, and which therefore cannot coherently be said to have full moral rights. Citizens of the next century should be prepared to recognize highly advanced, self-aware robots or computers, should such be developed, and intelligent inhabitants of other worlds, should such be found, as people in the fullest sense, and to respect their moral rights. But to ascribe full moral rights to an entity which is not a person is as absurd as to ascribe moral obligations and responsibilities to such an entity.

3. Fetal Development and the Right to Life

Two problems arise in the application of these suggestions for the definition of the moral community to the determination of the precise moral status of a human fetus. Given that the paradigm example of a person is a normal adult human being, then (1) How like this paradigm, in particular how far advanced since conception, does a human being need to be before it begins to have a right to life by virtue, not of being fully a person as of yet, but of being *like* a person? and (2) To what extent, if any, does the fact that a fetus has the *potential* for becoming a person endow it with some of the same rights? Each of these questions requires some comment.

In answering the first question, we need not attempt a detailed consideration of the moral rights of organisms which are not developed enough, aware enough, intelligent enough, etc., to be considered people, but which resemble people in some respects. It does seem reasonable to suggest that the more like a person, in the relevant respects, a being is, the stronger is the case for regarding it as having a right to life, and indeed the stronger its right to life is. Thus we ought to take seriously the suggestion that, insofar as "the human individual develops biologically in a continuous fashion . . . the rights of a human person might develop in the same way."[4] But we must keep in mind that the attributes which are relevant in determining whether or not an entity is enough like a person to be regarded as having some of the same moral rights are no different from those which are relevant to determining whether or not it is fully a person—i.e., are no different from (1)–(5)—and that being genetically human, or having recognizably human facial and other physical features, or detectable brain activity, or the capacity to survive outside the uterus, are simply not among these relevant attributes.

Thus it is clear that even though a seven- or eight-month fetus has features which make it apt to arouse in us almost the same powerful protective instinct as is commonly aroused by a small infant, nevertheless it is not significantly more person-like than is a very small embryo. It is *somewhat* more person-like; it can apparently feel and respond to pain, and it may even have a rudimentary form of consciousness, insofar as its brain is quite active. Nevertheless, it seems safe to say that it is not fully conscious, in the way that an infant of a few months is, and that it cannot reason, or communicate messages of indefinitely many sorts, does not engage in self-motivated activity, and has no self-awareness. Thus, in the *relevant* respects, a fetus, even a fully developed one, is considerably less person-like than is the average mature mammal, indeed the average fish. And I think that a rational person must conclude that if the right to life of a fetus is to be based upon its resemblance to a person, then it cannot be said to have any more right to life than, let us say, a newborn guppy (which also seems to be capable of feeling pain) and that a right of that magnitude could never override a woman's right to obtain an abortion, at any stage of her pregnancy.

There may, of course, be other arguments in favor of placing legal limits upon the stage of pregnancy in which an abortion may be performed. Given the relative safety of the new techniques of artificially inducing labor during the third trimester, the danger to the woman's life or health is no longer such an argument. Neither is the fact that people tend to respond to the thought of abortion in the later stages of pregnancy with emotional repulsion, since mere emotional responses cannot take the place of moral reasoning in determining what ought to be permitted. Nor, finally, is the frequently heard argument that legalizing abortion, especially late in the pregnancy, may erode the level of respect for human life, leading, perhaps, to an increase in unjustified euthanasia and other crimes. For this threat, if it is a threat, can be better met by educating people to the kinds of moral distinctions which we are making here than by limiting access to abortion (which limitation may, in its disregard for the rights of women, be just as damaging to the level of respect for human rights).

Thus, since the fact that even a fully developed fetus is not person-like enough to have any significant right to life on the basis of its person-likeness shows that no legal restrictions upon the stage of pregnancy in which an abortion may be performed can be justified on the grounds that we should protect the rights of the older fetus, and since there is no other apparent justification for such restrictions, we may conclude that they are entirely unjustified. Whether or not it would be *indecent* (whatever that means) for a

woman in her seventh month to obtain an abortion just to avoid having to postpone a trip to Europe, it would not, in itself, be *immoral* and therefore it ought to be permitted.

4. Potential Personhood and the Right to Life

We have seen that a fetus does not resemble a person in any way which can support the claim that it has even some of the same rights. But what about its *potential*, the fact that if nurtured and allowed to develop naturally it will very probably become a person? Doesn't that alone give it at least some right to life? It is hard to deny that the fact that an entity is a potential person is a strong prima facie reason for not destroying it; but we need not conclude from this that a potential person has a right to life, by virtue of that potential. It may be that our feeling that it is better, other things being equal, not to destroy a potential person is better explained by the fact that potential people are still (felt to be) an invaluable resource, not to be lightly squandered. Surely, if every speck of dust were a potential person, we would be much less apt to conclude that every potential person has a right to become actual.

Still, we do not need to insist that a potential person has no right to life whatever. There may well be something immoral, and not just imprudent, about wantonly destroying potential people, when doing so isn't necessary to protect anyone's rights. But even if a potential person does have some prima facie right to life, such a right could not possibly outweigh the right of a woman to obtain an abortion, since the rights of any actual person invariably outweigh those of any potential person, whenever the two conflict. Since this may not be immediately obvious in the case of a human fetus, let us look at another case.

Suppose that our space explorer falls into the hands of an alien culture, whose scientists decide to create a few hundred thousand or more human beings, by breaking his body into its component cells, and using these to create fully developed human beings, with, of course, his genetic code. We may imagine that each of these newly created men will have all of the original man's abilities, skills, knowledge, and so on, and also have an individual self-concept, in short that each of them will be a bona fide (though hardly unique) person. Imagine that the whole project will take only seconds, and that its chances of success are extremely high, and that our explorer knows all of this, and also knows that these people will be treated fairly. I maintain that in such a situation he would have every right to escape if he could, and thus to deprive all of these potential people of their potential lives; for his right to life outweighs all of theirs together, in spite of the fact that they are all genetically human, all innocent, and all have a very high probability of becoming people very soon, if only he refrains from acting.

Indeed, I think he would have a right to escape even if it were not his life which the alien scientists planned to take, but only a year of his freedom, or, indeed, only a day. Nor would he be obligated to stay if he had gotten captured (thus bringing all these people potentials into existence) because of his own carelessness, or even if he had done so deliberately, knowing the consequences. Regardless of how he got captured, he is not morally obligated to remain in captivity for *any* period of time for the sake of permitting any number of potential people to come into actuality, so great is the margin by which one actual person's right to liberty outweighs whatever right to life even a hundred thousand potential people have. And it seems reasonable to conclude that the rights of a woman will outweigh by a similar margin whatever right to life a fetus may have by virtue of its potential personhood.

Thus, neither a fetus's resemblance to a person, nor its potential for becoming a person provides any basis whatever for the claim that it has any significant right to life. Consequently, a woman's right to protect her health, happiness, freedom, and even her life, by terminating an unwanted pregnancy, will always override whatever right to life it may be appropriate to ascribe to a fetus, even a fully developed one. And thus, in the absence of any overwhelming social need for every possible child, the laws which restrict the right to obtain an abortion, or limit the period of pregnancy during which an abortion may be performed, are a wholly unjustified violation of a woman's most basic moral and constitutional rights.

Discussion Questions

1. Professor Warren claims that there are two senses to the term "human." What are they? How does she reason from these two senses to a justification of abortion? And what does she mean when she says that there could be persons who are not human beings?

2. Some have argued that Professor Warren's position supports the moral justification of infanticide (the killing of infants), since by her criteria newborns, it would seem, are not persons. How do you think she would respond to this observation?

3. Briefly describe Professor Warren's five-part criterion for personhood. One objection raised against this criterion is that some beings whom we clearly recognize as persons, such as the temporarily comatose, do not fulfill any part of the criterion. How do you think Professor Warren would respond to this objection?

Notes

1. Of course, the principle that it is (always) wrong to kill innocent human beings is in need of many other modifications, e.g., that it may be permissible to do so to save a greater number of other innocent human beings, but we may safely ignore these complications here.

2. John Noonan, "Deciding Who Is Human," *Natural Law Forum*, 13 (1968).

3. From here on, we will use "human" to mean genetically human, since the moral sense seems closely connected to, and perhaps derived from, the assumption that genetic humanity is sufficient for membership in the moral community.

4. Thomas L. Hayes, "A Biological View," *Commonweal*, 85 (March 17, 1967), 677–78; quoted by Daniel Callahan, in *Abortion: Law, Choice and Morality* (London: Macmillan & Co., 1970).

17

Personhood Begins at Conception

Stephen D. Schwarz

Stephen D. Schwarz is Professor of Philosophy at the University of Rhode Island. He has authored a number of works in philosophy of religion, metaphysics, and moral philosophy, including the book *The Moral Question of Abortion* (1990).

Professor Schwarz defends the traditional pro-life position on abortion: because abortion entails the intentional killing of an innocent human person who exists from the moment of conception, abortion is unjustified homicide, and, consequently, morally wrong, even if the pregnancy resulted from rape or incest. Although he believes that a woman has a right to terminate her pregnancy if continuing it will result in her death (what some call "the life of the mother" exception), he does not consider such termination an "abortion," because the intention is to save the life of the mother rather than to kill the fetus, although the procedure, if performed before fetal viability, will result in the fetus's death. In the following essay, Professor Schwarz responds to the position, defended by Mary Anne Warren (see Chapter 16), that the fetus is a human being but not a person. He argues that Professor Warren and others who defend similar arguments confuse *being a person* with *functioning as a person*. They mistakenly infer from the fetus's lack of certain personal functions that it is therefore not a person.

Reprinted by permission from Stephen D. Schwarz, *The Moral Question of Abortion* (Chicago: Loyola University Press, 1990), Chapter 7.

A Theory about Human Beings and Persons

Let us now examine a theory that defends abortion on the grounds that the child in the womb, though undoubtedly a human being, is not a person, and that it is only the killing of persons that is intrinsically and seriously wrong. The theory consists of two major theses: First, that killing human beings is not wrong; second, that the child (in the womb and for a time after birth) is human but not a person. I shall argue that both of these theses are mistaken.

This theory recognizes that abortion is the deliberate killing of an innocent human being, but it denies this is wrong because it denies that it is wrong to deliberately kill human beings. What is wrong is killing human beings who are persons. Now, of course, many human beings are persons, for example, normal adult human beings, and it is wrong to kill them because they are persons. But small infants, such as newborn babies or babies in the womb, though they are undoubtedly human, are not, according to this theory, persons. And so it is not intrinsically wrong to kill them. That is, it is not wrong in itself, though it may be wrong because of adverse consequences. A small child, therefore, has no right to life as a normal adult does, and if the child is unwanted, he may be killed.

Thus, the theory allows for abortion and infanticide alike. It rejects the typical pro-abortion lines, such as viability and birth. It agrees that there is no morally significant difference between "before" and "after." But instead of saying that killing a human being is *wrong* on both sides of such a line, it claims that it is *right* (or can be right) on both sides of the line.

Joseph Fletcher expresses this view when he remarks, "I would support the . . . position . . . that both abortion and infanticide can be justified if and when the good to be gained outweighs the evil—that neither abortion nor infanticide is as such immoral."[1]

Michael Tooley has an essay entitled, "A Defense of Abortion and Infanticide." If the idea that killing babies is morally right is shocking to most people, Tooley replies in his essay that this is merely an emotional response, not a reasoned one. "The response, rather than appealing to carefully formulated moral principles, is primarily visceral," he says. And, "It is reasonable to suspect that one is dealing with a taboo rather than with a rational prohibition."[2] His position is: "Since I do not believe human infants are persons, but only potential persons, and since I think that the destruction of potential persons is a morally neutral action, the correct conclusion seems to me to be that infanticide is in itself morally acceptable."[3]

I want to show that the theories held by Fletcher, Tooley, and others are absolutely wrong. Infanticide and abortion are both morally wrong, as wrong as the deliberate killing of an older child or an adult, and thus our emotional response of shock and horror at killing babies is completely grounded in reason and moral principles. I want to show that a small child, after birth or still in the womb, is a person, as much a person as the rest of us; that the notion of person as used by these writers is a special one, a narrower concept, and not the one that is crucial for morality. I want to make clear why the attempts to show that a small child is not a person are mistaken, and that all human beings as such are persons.

The Argument of Mary Ann Warren

In an argument for this theory, Mary Ann Warren examines "the traditional argument that since (1) it is wrong to kill innocent human beings, and (2) fetuses are innocent human beings, then (3) it is wrong to kill fetuses."[4] This argument, she claims, is "fallacious," because "the term 'human' has two distinct, but not often distinguished, senses."[5] In premise one, human means person, or full-fledged member of the moral community, a being whom it is wrong to kill. In premise two, on the other hand, the term human refers merely to a member of the biological species human, as opposed, say, to a rabbit or an eagle. Warren's claim is that mere membership in a biological species is morally irrelevant and thus does not confer on the being in question a right to life.[6]

"Yes, a fetus is biologically human (human in the genetic sense), but that does not make it the kind of being who has a right to life. It is only persons (those who are human in the moral sense) who have such a right. It is wrong to kill persons, and if a human being is not also a person he does not have a right to life, and it is, or often can be, morally right to destroy him." This, in essence, is Warren's argument.

Warren offers an analysis of what is a person, a full-fledged member of the moral community:

> I suggest that the traits which are most central to the concept of personhood, or humanity in the

moral sense, are, very roughly, the following:

> 1. consciousness (of objects and events external and/or internal to the being), and in particular the capacity to feel pain;
> 2. reasoning (the developed capacity to solve new and relatively complex problems);
> 3. self-motivated activity (activity which is relatively independent of either genetic or direct external control);
> 4. the capacity to communicate, by whatever means, messages of an indefinite variety of types, that is, not just with an indefinite number of possible contents, but on indefinitely many possible topics;
> 5. the presence of self-concepts, and self-awareness, either individual or racial, or both.[7]

This, she acknowledges, is not a full analysis of the concept of a person. It is not a list of necessary and sufficient conditions for being a person. But, she says, this does not matter.

> All we need to claim, to demonstrate that a fetus is not a person, is that any being which satisfies none of (1)–(5) is certainly not a person. I consider this claim to be so obvious that I think anyone who denied it, and claimed that a being which satisfied none of (1)–(5) was a person all the same, would thereby demonstrate that he had no notion at all of what a person is—perhaps because he had confused the concept of a person with that of genetic humanity.[8]

We can now see Warren's argument for abortion in its entirety. A fetus is human in the genetic sense; that is morally irrelevant. A fetus is not human in the moral sense; he is not a person since he satisfies none of the criteria she has outlined. Not being a person, he has no right to life, and abortion is morally permissible. The same applies to the child after birth. "Killing a newborn infant isn't murder."[9] Infanticide is wrong, according to Warren, only to the extent that the child is wanted, that there are couples who would like to adopt or keep him. "Thus, infanticide is wrong for reasons analogous to those which make it wrong to wantonly destroy natural resources, or great works of art."[10]

But destroying natural resources or works of art is not always wrong, and certainly not wrong in the sense in which murder is wrong. Warren acknowledges this when she says, "It follows from my argument that when an unwanted or defective infant is born into a society which I cannot afford and/or is not willing to care for it, then its destruction is permissible."[11]

Being a Person and *Functioning* as a Person

The failure of Warren's argument can be seen in light of the distinction between being a person and functioning as a person. Consider Warren's five characteristics of a person: consciousness, reasoning, self-motivated activity, the capacity to communicate, and the presence of self-concepts. Imagine a person in a deep, dreamless sleep. She is not conscious, she cannot reason, etc.; she lacks all five of these traits. She is not functioning as a person; that is part of what being asleep means. But of course she is a person; she retains fully her status of being a person, and killing her while asleep is just as wrong as killing her while she is awake and functioning as a person.

Functioning as a person refers to all the activities proper to persons as persons, to thinking in the broadest sense. It includes reasoning, deciding, imagining, talking, experiencing love and beauty, remembering, intending, and much more. The term *function* does not refer here to bodily functions, but rather to those of the mind, though certain bodily functions, especially those of the brain, are necessary conditions for functioning as a person.

When Warren points out that a fetus satisfies none of the five traits she mentions, she shows only that a fetus does not function as a person, not that it lacks the being of a person, which is the crucial thing.

At this point several objections are likely to be raised: First, the sleeping person will soon wake up and function as a person, while the being in the womb will not.

In reply, neither the sleeping person nor the being in the womb now displays the qualities of a functioning person. Both will display them. It is only a matter of time. Why should the one count as a real person because the time is short, while the other does not, simply because in her case the time is longer?

Second, the sleeping adult was already self-conscious, had already solved some problems. Therefore, she has a history of functioning as a person. The child in the womb has no such history. Thus Tooley argues that "an organism cannot have a serious right to life [be a person] unless it either now possesses, or did possess at some time in the past, the concept of a self . . . [what is required for functioning as a person]."[12] The human being sound asleep counts as a person because she once functioned as a person; the child never did, so she does not count as a person.

True, there is a difference with respect to past functioning, but the difference is not morally relevant. The reason the child never functioned as a person is because her capacity to do so is not yet sufficiently developed. It cannot be, for she is near the beginning of her existence, in the first phase of her life.

Imagine a case of two children. One is born comatose, and he will remain so until the age of nine. The other is healthy at birth, but as soon as she achieves the concept of a continuing self for a brief time, she, too, lapses into a coma, from which she will not emerge until she is nine. Can anyone seriously hold that the second child is a person with a right to life, while the first child is not? In one case, self-awareness will come only after nine years have elapsed, in the other, it will return. In both cases, self-awareness will grow and develop. Picture the two unconscious children lying side by side. Almost nine years have passed. Would it not be absurd to say that only one of them is a person, that there is some essential, morally relevant, difference between them? Imagine someone about to kill both of them. Consistent with his theory, Tooley would have to say: "You may kill the first, for he is not a person. He is human only in the genetic sense, since he has no history of functioning as a person. You may not kill the second, since she does have such a history." If this distinction is absurd when applied to the two born human beings, is it any less absurd when applied to two human beings, one born (asleep in a bed), the other preborn (sleeping in the womb)?

In short, when it comes to functioning as a person, there is no moral difference between "did, but does not" (the sleeping adult) and "does not, but will" (the small child).

Third, a sleeping person has the capacity to function as a person and therefore counts as being a person, even though this capacity is not now actualized. In contrast a child in the womb lacks this capacity, so he does not count as being a person.

This is the most fundamental objection, and probably underlies the preceding two objections. In considering it, compare the following beings:

A. A normal adult, sound asleep, not conscious.
B. An adult in a coma from which he will emerge in, say, six months and function normally as a person.
C. A normal newborn baby.
D. A normal baby soon to be born.

E. A normal "well proportioned small scale baby"in the womb at seven weeks.

F. A normal embryo or zygote.

Case A, the normal adult sound asleep, is someone who has the being of a person, who is not now functioning as a person, and who clearly has the capacity to function as a person. I want to show now that all the other cases are essentially similar to this one. That is, if case A is a person—a full-fledged member of the moral community, a being with a right to life, whose value lies in his own being and dignity, and not merely in his significance for others (like the natural resources and works of art), a being whose willful destruction is murder—each of the other cases is a person as well.

The objection claims that the being in the womb lacks the capacity to function as a person. True, it lacks what I shall call the *present immediate capacity* to function, where responses may be immediately elicited. Such a capacity means the capability of functioning, where such a capability varies enormously among people, and normally develops and grows (as a result of learning and other experiences).

The capability of functioning as a person is grounded in the *basic inherent capacity* to function. This is proper to the being of a person and it has a physical basis, typically the brain and nervous system. It is a capacity that grows and develops as the child grows and develops.

This basic inherent capacity may be fully accessible, as in a normal sleeping adult. It then exists in its present immediate form. It may also exist in other forms where it is latent, as in reversible coma. I shall call this the latent-1 capacity, where the basic inherent capacity is present but temporarily damaged or blocked. In a small child, the basic inherent capacity is there but insufficiently developed for the child to function in the manner of a normal adult. I shall call this the latent-2 capacity.

Let me turn to the actual refutation of this objection. I will begin with cases A through E (replies 1 and 2), then case F (3), then abnormal or handicapped human beings (4).

(1) The beings on our list, A through E, differ only with respect to their present immediate capacity to function. They are all essentially similar with respect to their basic inherent capacity, and through this, their being as persons.

Thus the adult in a coma, case B, is not essentially different from the sleeping person in case A.

Person B is in a deep, deep sleep; person A in a comparatively superficial sleep. Person B cannot be awakened easily; person A can be. Person B is in a very long sleep; person A is in a short sleep, say 8 hours. Both have the basic inherent capacity; in A it is present immediate; in B it is latent-1. That is certainly not a morally relevant difference. If the status of persons is to be viewed in terms of capacity to function as a person, then surely a latent-1 capacity (temporarily blocked—person B) qualifies as much as a non-latent capacity (present immediate—person A).

Consider now the newborn baby, case C. He too has the physical basis for functioning as a person (brain, nervous system, etc.). Only his overall development is insufficient for him to actually function on the level of the normal adult. He has a latent-2 capacity. Thus there is an essential similarity between cases B and C, the adult in a coma and the newborn baby. Neither has the present immediate capacity to function as a person. Both take longer than the sleeping adult (case A) to wake up from their slumber. But both have a latent capacity to function, because they both have the basic inherent capacity to function. In the case of B, the impossibility of eliciting an immediate response is due to an abnormality, which brought on the coma. In the other, case C, this is due to the fact that the being is not yet far enough along in his process of development. In both cases the basic inherent capacity is there, it is merely latent.

Cases C and D, babies just after birth and just before birth, are clearly the same in terms of their capacity to function as persons. Birth is, among other things, the beginning of vast new opportunities to develop the basic inherent capacity to function by seeing, hearing, touching, etc., a capacity that is equally present just before birth.

Case E, a baby at seven weeks, has "all the internal organs of the adult";[13] and "after the eighth week no further primordia will form; *everything* is already present that will be found in the full term baby."[14] It is these "internal organs" and "primordia" that constitute the physical base of the basic inherent capacity to function as a person. They are substantially present in both the very young preborn child, at seven and eight weeks (case E), and the older preborn child (case D). Thus the cases D and E are essentially similar with respect to their basic inherent capacity, and because of this, their being as persons.

In brief, cases A through E are essentially similar. Cases B through E are similar in themselves (each represents a latent capacity); and, taken together, in comparison with A (present immediate capacity). There is no essentially difference among cases B through E. If a person whose lack of present immediate capacity to function is due to a disorder (as in case B) should be respected as a person, then surely a being whose lack of this capacity to function is due to insufficient development (cases C through E) should also be respected as a person. Both are beings with the potential to function as a person; and this they can only have if they have the basis for it, that is, the being of a person. Case B represents a latent-1 capacity, cases C through E, a latent-2 capacity; both are forms of the basic inherent capacity to function, proper to the nature of a person. If a latent-1 capacity (B) is a mark of a person, then surely a latent-2 capacity (C through E) is also a mark of a person. Both B and C through E represent beings who will have the capability to function as persons, who lack this capability now because of the condition of the working basis of this capability (brain, nervous system, etc.). In one, that condition is one of disorder or blockage, in the other, the lack of development proper to the age of the being in question.

(2) The essential similarity among the beings A through E is also established if they are imagined as the same being: a being in the womb developing from seven weeks to birth (E to C), then lapsing into a coma (B), then recovering (A). Thus if there is a person at the end (A), there is also that same person at the beginning (E). It is the same person going through various stages, representing first a latent-2 capacity, then a latent-1 capacity, and finally a present immediate capacity.

I am now a being capable of functioning as a person (present immediate capacity). Many years ago I was a small newborn baby, and before that a smaller child in my mother's womb. My capabilities have changed, they have increased as my basic inherent capacity to function as a person has developed; but I remain always *the same person*, the same essential being, the being who has these growing capabilities. If I am essentially a person now, I was essentially a person then, when I was a baby. The fact that my capabilities to function as a person have changed and grown does not alter the absolute continuity of my essential being, that of a person. In fact, this variation in capabilities presupposes the continuity of my being as a person. It is *as a person* that I develop my capabilities to function as a person. It is because I am a person that I have these capabilities, to whatever degree.

And so the basic reality is being as a person. This is what entails your right to life, the wrongness of killing you, the necessity of respecting you as a person, and not just as a desired commodity like a natural resource.

(3) Let us turn now to case F, the zygote or embryo. There are three considerations that show the essential similarity between this case and cases A through E.

First: The continuum argument applies here as well. The adult now sleeping is the same being who was once an embryo and a zygote. There is a direct continuity between the zygote at F and the child at E, through to the adult at A. If the being at the later stages should be given the respect due to persons, then that same being should also be given this respect when he is at an earlier stage.

Second: It may be objected that the zygote lacks "a well-developed physical substratum of consciousness"[15]—that it lacks the actual physical basis (brain, nervous system, etc.) for the basic inherent capacity to function as a person. This is incorrect. The zygote does not lack this physical basis; it is merely that it is now in a primitive, undeveloped form. The zygote has the essential structure of this basis; a structure that will unfold, grow, develop, mature, which takes time. As Blechschmidt states, " . . . the fertilized ovum (zygote) is already a form of man. Indeed, it is already active. . . . All the organs of the developing organism are differentiation products of each unique (fertilized) human ovum."[16] That is, the organs that form the physical basis for the more developed basic inherent capacity to function as a person (at various stages, E to A) are "differentiation products" of what is already present in the zygote. Thus the zygote has, in primitive form, the physical basis of his basic inherent capacity to function as a person. In the adult this same basis exists in developed form.

The zygote actually has the basic inherent capacity to function as a person because he has the essential physical structure for this. This structure is merely undeveloped:

> The zygotic self cannot actually breathe, but he *actually has* the undeveloped capacity for breathing. Nor can this zygotic self actually think and love as an adult does, but he *actually has* the undeveloped capacity for thinking and loving. And the human zygote could not actually have such undeveloped capacities unless he actually IS the kind of being that *has* such capacities. Just as it is obviously true that only a human being can have

the *developed* capacities for thinking and loving, it should be obviously true that only a human being can have the *undeveloped* capacities for thinking and loving.[17]

Elsewhere, Robert Joyce remarks:

A person is not an individual with a *developed* capacity for reasoning, willing, desiring, and relating to others. A person is an individual with a *natural* capacity for these activities and relationships, whether this natural capacity is ever developed or not—i.e., whether he or she ever attains the functional capacity or not. Individuals of a rational, volitional, self-conscious nature may never attain or may lose the functional capacity for fulfilling this nature to any appreciable extent. But this inability to fulfill their nature does not negate or destroy the nature itself.[18]

A being at the beginning of his development cannot be expected to possess what only that development can provide for him. He is already the being who will later function as a person, given time. The sleeping person is also a being who will later function as a person, only he will do it much sooner. What they each have now—a fully developed brain in one case, and a potential brain, that which will grow into a developed brain, in the other—is a basis for their capacity to function as persons. It is the same essential basis, one undeveloped, the other developed. It is merely a matter of degree; there is no difference in kind.

One must already *be* a human being in order to develop the human brain necessary for the present and immediate capacity to function as a person. As we noted earlier, "*only a human being can develop a human brain, a human brain cannot develop before a human exists.*" "Human being" means of course "human person," the same being in different phases of his existence.

Third: Imagine a person J solving new and relatively complex problems (item 2 on Mary Ann Warren's list).

1. Person J *is doing* this.
2. Person K *has the capacity* to do this (like the sleeping person A on the list).
3. Person L *has the capacity to learn* to do this (to learn what is necessary for having this capacity; for example, a child in school).
4. Person M *has the capacity to acquire*, by natural development, what is necessary for the capacity to learn to do this.

What is true of person M applies to a newborn baby (C), or a baby about to be born (D), or a much younger baby, at seven weeks (E). It applies equally to that same being at a still earlier stage of her development, as a zygote (F).

There is a continuity here. If being a person is approached from the point of view of capacity to function as a person, then clearly persons K, L, and M are essentially alike. Each is removed by one or more steps from the person J, who is actually functioning as a person. None of these steps is of moral or metaphysical significance. In reverse order from M to J, there is, respectively, a capacity to acquire, a capacity to learn, and a capacity to do what the next being represents. If doing is to count for being a person, then surely the capacity to do, the capacity to learn to do, and the capacity to acquire what is needed to learn to do must also count.

This chain argument shows not only the essential similarity between the zygote (F) and the child at later stages (C through E) but also the essential similarity among the beings A through F.

We are now in a better position to understand the real significance of past functioning as a person, which is present in the adult (asleep or in a coma), and absent from the child. It is a sign that the being in question is a person. Because a certain being has functioned in the past, he must be a person. But if he has not, or we do not know it, it does not follow that he is not a person. Other indications must also be examined. In the case of a small baby, born or preborn, including the zygote stage of a baby's existence, there are three such indications.

One, the *continuum of being*, the identity of the person. The baby is now the same being, the same "self" that the child will be later on. "I was once a newborn baby and before that, a baby inside my mother." Since it is a human being's essential nature to be a person, this being—as a zygote, as a seven-week-old baby, as a newborn—is always a person.

Two, the *continuum of essential structure* for the basic inherent capacity to function as a person. The baby as a zygote has the essential physical structure that represents this capacity. Both in the primitive form of development and in all later stages of development, there exists the same essential structure.

Three, the *continuum of capacities*, to acquire, learn, and do. The zygote has the capacity to acquire what is needed to learn to function as a person.

If a being is not now functioning as a person, is he a person? Two perspectives can be used in answering this question: present to past and present to future. An affirmative answer in either case suffices to indicate that the being in question is a person. Present to past: yes, he is a person because he functioned as a person in the past. Present to future: yes, he is a person because he will function as a person in the future, based on the three-fold continuum. The mistake of writers such as Tooley is to ignore the second of these.

(4) Let us turn, finally, to the case of abnormal, or handicapped, human beings. Does the analysis offered here—that the beings A through F are essentially similar with respect to their being as persons—apply equally to abnormal, or handicapped, human beings?

It certainly does. A handicapped person (physically, mentally, or both) has the same being of a person as the rest of us who are fortunate enough not to be so afflicted. He has, with this, the same dignity, the same rights as the rest of us. We must "do unto him"as we would want others to "do unto us" if we were afflicted with a handicap. Just as there is no morally relevant difference between a normal functioning person and a small child who cannot yet function as a person because of his lack of development, there is also no morally relevant difference between the normal functioning person and one incapable, or less capable, of doing so. Any one of us who now has the present immediate capacity to function as a person may lose it through a severe illness or accident. If that happened to you, you would still have the same status of being a person, the same dignity and rights of a person.

Even a very severely abnormal or handicapped human being has the basic inherent capacity to function as a person, which is a sign that he is a person. The abnormality represents a hindrance to the actual working of this capacity, to its manifestation in actual functioning. It does not imply the absence of this capacity, as in a nonperson.

The normal adult and child were selected for this analysis because it is in them that the essence of functioning as a person, or its usual absence because of (normal) lack of development, can most easily be seen and understood. Once recognized there, it applies equally to all persons, regardless of the degree to which they are able to accomplish it.

To conclude this part of the main argument: would Mary Ann Warren admit the adult sound asleep to the status of person? If not, she is saying it is acceptable to kill people in their sleep. Suppose she admits sleeping person A. She must then admit sleeping person B, the one in a longer, deeper sleep. The only differences are the length and nature of the sleep. In each case there is a being with a capacity to function as a person, who will, if not killed, wake up to exercise it. Clearly there is no morally relevant difference between them. This proves decisively that present immediate capacity to function as a person is not necessary to being a person. This is plainly true of the newborn baby C. Having then admitted B as a person, Warren is forced to admit C as well, for the two cases are essentially the same; no present immediate capacity to function as a person, the presence of latent capacity, rooted in the basic inherent capacity.

With this, Warren's whole argument is destroyed. For she herself claims that, in terms of their intrinsic nature, their being (as persons or nonpersons), the newborn baby (C) and the preborn baby (D through F) are morally on a par. Neither (her argument shows) can now function as a person. Both, I have shown, have the basic inherent capacity to function as persons. In all of these cases, there is the same being, with the same essential structure of a person, differing only with respect to the degree of development of the capacity to function as a person.

Views like those of Warren and Tooley do not reach the crucial point: the fact that a human being functions as a person or has the present and immediate capacity to do so, is not the ground for his dignity, preciousness, and right to life; rather, that decisive ground is the fact of his *being* a person.

The Reality of the Person Seen through Love

Imagine a person you deeply love in a coma from which he will emerge in about thirty weeks, perfectly normal. Apply Warren's five criteria. He fails them all. He is not conscious, he cannot reason, he is incapable of self-motivated activity, he cannot communicate, he has no self-concepts or awareness of himself. This doesn't mean he is not a person; that he has no right to life of his own; that he could be killed if no one cared. He is just as real, just as precious, just as much a full person as if he were now capable of functioning as a person. It is just as important and necessary to respect him and care for him as if he were awake.

The child in the womb is in a comparable state, only his "sleep" is normal and is not preceded by a phase where he is able to function as a person. He is also unseen. But none of these makes a morally relevant difference. If one person in "deep sleep" (inability to function as a person) is to be respected and cared for, then the other person should be cared for and respected as well.

The Distinction Applied to Some Pro-Abortion Views

Given our understanding of the distinction between being a person and functioning as a person, we can now come to a better understanding of some of the things put forward by defenders of abortion.

1. *Drawing Lines.* We examined ten suggested places to draw the line between what is supposed to be merely a *preparation* for a person and the actual person. Every line proved false. In each case the same fully real person is clearly present in both sides of it. No line marks any real difference with regard to *being* a person; the person is there before as well as after. But many of these lines do have a bearing on *functioning* as a person. Thus a baby after birth interacts with others in a way not possible before birth. A baby who has reached sentience has developed an important dimension of his capacity to function as a person. And the presence of a functioning brain marks a significant milestone in the child's development as a functioning person. If these lines seem to have any plausibility, it is because one has in mind functioning as a person. But the plausibility evaporates when one realizes that the crucial thing is not functioning as a person, but being a person.

2. *The Agnostic Position.* Realizing that these lines do not work, some people say that it is simply not known when a human person begins to exist. What should be said is, rather, that it is not known when *functioning* as a person begins, for there is indeed no single place on the continuum of human life at which this begins. It is a gradual development. But the *being* of the person is there all along. And the development is what it is because the being of the person is there all the way through: it is the person's development. Agnosticism regarding functioning as a person should not lead to agnosticism regarding being a person.

3. *The Gradualist Position.* False when applied to the *being* of a person, the gradualist position is absolutely valid when applied to *functioning* as a person. That is indeed a matter of degree. We gradually develop our basic capacity to think and to communicate.

4. *The Notion of Potential Person.* False when applied to *being* a person, the notion of potential person has a validity when applied to *functioning* as a person. If by "person" we mean "functioning person," for example, a normal adult making a complex decision or reading a book, then clearly a child in the womb, or just born, or even at age one, is only potentially such a person. A baby is a potential functioning person; but he is that only because he has the actual being of a person.

Human Is Not Merely A Biological Category

The theory advanced by writers such as Fletcher, Tooley, and Warren holds that killing babies is permissible because they are not persons; whereas, in fact, they are nonfunctioning persons. A functioning person is one who either is now actually functioning as a person, or has the present immediate capacity to do so. What the theory holds is that only functioning persons (and those who were once such persons) are truly persons. It may, therefore, be called the *functioning-person theory.*[19]

Advocates of the functioning-person theory hold that it is not in itself wrong to kill human beings; that this can only be wrong when the being in question is a "person," as defined by the theory (one who has the present immediate capacity to function as a person, or has had it in the past). Such advocates hold that the single fact that a being is human does not constitute any reason for not deliberately killing it. Hence, they say, killing babies, born or preborn, is not in itself wrong. *If* it is ever wrong, it is so because these babies are wanted and would be missed by adults. The thesis, as Tooley puts it, is that "membership in a biological species is not morally significant *in itself.*"[20] In the words of Singer, "Whether a being is or is not a member of our species is, in itself no more relevant to the wrongness of killing it than whether it is or is not a member of our race."[21] Warren says that being human in the genetic sense does not give the being in question a right to life.

The thrust of this is to drive a wedge between two categories of beings —persons and human beings—and to hold that it is the former, not the latter, that is of moral significance. There are two fundamental and disastrous errors in this approach. The first concerns the category of persons, and consists in equating this term with functioning persons (present or past), thereby excluding babies who have not yet developed the present immediate capacity to function as persons. The second error, closely related to the first, is to dismiss the category of human being as not (in itself) morally significant.

Proponents of the functioning-person theory are quite right in maintaining that there is a distinction between persons and human beings. They point out that there could be persons who are not human beings, for example, creatures on distant planets who can think, make decisions, feel gratitude, and so forth. They would certainly be persons, without being human beings. In the Christian faith, angels are persons, but not human beings. So, not all persons are necessarily human beings. But, I shall maintain, all human beings are persons (though not necessarily functioning persons). Being human is not necessary to being a person (there could be others), but it is sufficient, for all human beings are persons.

The fundamental error here is the notion that human is a mere biological category,[22] that it designates simply one of many zoological species. If this were so, if the difference between human and other species were like the difference between, say, cats and dogs, or tigers and bears, then of course it would be morally irrelevant. But human—though it may be viewed as a zoological species, and compared to other species in the study of anatomy and physiology—is not simply a biological category. It is rather a mode of being a person.

Human designates, in its most significant meaning, a type of being whose nature it is to be a person. A person is a being who has the basic inherent capacity to function as a person, regardless of how developed this capacity is, or whether or not it is blocked, as in severe senility. We respect and value human beings, not because they are a certain biological species, but because they are persons; because it is the nature of a human being to be a person. All human beings are persons, even if they can no longer function as persons (severe senility), or cannot yet function as persons (small babies), or cannot now function as persons (sound asleep or under anesthesia or in a coma).

The theory is correct when it says that it is persons who are of moral significance; and that persons need not be human persons (they may be martians or angels). The error is to fail to recognize that humans are persons. Being human is a mode of existence of persons. So we should respect human beings—all human beings, regardless of race, degree of intelligence, degree of bodily health, degree of development as functioning persons—because they are persons.

"Do unto others as you would have them do unto you." Surely the class of others is not limited to functioning persons. It includes all human beings; perhaps others as well, but at least all human beings. "Do unto others" must include, very specifically, the lame, the retarded, the weak. It must include those no longer able to function as persons, as well as those not yet able to do so.

When we love another person, it is the *total human being* that we love, not just his or her rationality, or that which makes him or her capable of functioning as a person. We love their individual mode of being, expressed in many ways, such as gestures, facial features, tone of voice, expressions in the eyes, etc. These are, of course, in one respect, bodily features. This does not render them merely biological in the sense dismissed by Singer, Tooley, and others. They are dimensions of the total human person.

The present immediate capacity to function as a person is not essential to this fundamental reality, the total human being. When a loved one is under anesthesia, he is still fully that person, the total human being. More than that, part of the beauty, the charm, the lovableness of a small child is that he is *only a child*, not yet matured, not yet (fully) capable of functioning as a person. The total human being in such a case does not even require the present capacity to function as a person.

Warren, Tooley, and Singer fall into the trap of seeing "human" as a mere biological category because of an earlier, and more fundamental, error: confusing person and functioning person (present or past), indeed, grouping the two together. For if it is assumed that "person" equals "functioning person," and if a small child is not a (fully) functioning person, it follows that the child is not a person. If the child is not a human *person*, "human" can then refer only to a biological species. Once one strips the child of his status as a person (on the grounds that he cannot now function as a person), what is there left except his being a member of a biological species? Separated from the notion of person, the notion of "human" is indeed only a biological species, and as such morally irrelevant.

The fallacy is, then, the separation of human and person, the failure to see that humans are precisely *human persons.* Humans are human persons, where "persons" includes nonfunctioning persons as well as functioning persons.

The Notion of Potential Person

In arguing for this thesis that abortion is morally right, Tooley goes to great lengths to show that potential persons do not have a serious right to life. "There appears to be little hope of defending a conservative view [i.e., that abortion is wrong] unless it can be shown that the destruction of potential persons is intrinsically wrong, and seriously so."[23]

On the contrary, abortion is wrong because it destroys an actual person. The assumption that the being in the womb is merely a potential person is typical of the functioning-person theory. Thus Warren speaks of the "fetus" as a "potential person";[24] and of "its potential for becoming a person."[25] She denies that the latter "provides any basis whatever for the claims that it has any significant right to life."[26]

What is potential about the child in the womb is not her *being* as a person, but rather her *functioning* as a person. That functioning is potential in the sense that she now has only a latent capacity to function, and not yet a present immediate capacity, because her basic inherent capacity has not yet had a change to develop sufficiently.

The child in the womb is not, as the functioning-person theory maintains, a potential person, but rather a *potentially functioning actual person*. To be a potentially functioning person already ensures that the baby is a person, an actual, real, full person, for a potentially functioning person must necessarily be a person.

In the words of Joyce, "A one celled person at conception is not a potential person, but an actual person with great potential for development and self-expression. That single-celled individual is just as actually a person as you and I."[27]

I submit that there is no such thing as a potential person. The ovum and the sperm are preparations for a new person. Each of them is not that person in potential form, because it is not that person at all. There is a radical break between sperm/ovum and the new person in the zygotic state. The transition from "potential x" to "actual x" always involves a continuity. Thus a medical student is recognized as a potential doctor because when the student *becomes* a doctor this will have happened within a continuity involving the same person. In contrast, as Joyce puts it, "sperm and ovum . . . do not, even together, become a new human life, because they do not survive beyond conception."[28]

"The sperm and the ovum," Joyce says, "are not potential [personal] life; rather they are potential *causes* of individual human life."[29]

The Achievement View

The *functioning-person theory* implies a certain elitism, something that may be called the *achievement view*, namely, that only human beings who have achieved a certain degree of development of the present immediate capacity to function as persons count as real persons.[30] Thus Mary Ann Warren, Michael Tooley, and Peter Singer dismiss infants as nonpersons simply on the grounds that they have not yet achieved the status of functioning persons. But why hold that against them? That they have not achieved this status is perfectly normal, and could not be otherwise; for they have not yet reached that stage in their development over time when such a capacity is normal. The achievement view is a clear example of discrimination: "You don't count as a real person, for you have not yet achieved the degree of development necessary for the present immediate capacity to function as a person."

The functioning-person theory is presented as if it were the product of careful, rational, philosophical analysis, a contribution to clear thinking. It gains this appearance largely from the element of truth it contains: that the concepts of "person" and "human being" are not identical, for there could be nonhuman persons. This hides its true nature, that it is in fact a form of elitism, leading to discrimination of the worst sort. For the theory implies that only some persons count; those who have achieved the status of functioning persons.

"At what point in its development does a fetus become a person?" (Or, when does it become human, meaning a person, since it is obviously human in the biological sense all along.) This whole question is misplaced. For there is a person, a human being, all along. It is only a matter of degree of development of the basic inherent capacity to function as a person. What we can now see, with new clarity, is that this question assumes the achievement view, indeed expresses it, and would collapse without it. Translated, the question reads: "How much must a human being achieve in the way of attaining the capability of functioning as a person in order to count as a person, that is, a being whose life we must respect?" The answer is clear: nothing. No achievement is necessary, and to demand it is elitism and discrimination. What is required is *being*, not achievement: being a person, having the nature of a person, regardless of how far along the achievement scale one has progressed.

It is wrong for a white to demand that real persons be white in order to count as persons. Blacks are equally persons, though they are "different." So too, it is wrong for a functioning person to demand that real persons be capable of functioning as persons. Small babies, incapable of this—or less capable—are equally persons, though they are "different." Being white is not a special achievement that blacks have failed to reach. Having the capability of functioning as a person, while it is an achievement, is equally irrelevant, morally. To demand it as a condition for membership in the class of persons is equally unjust and discriminatory.

It is wrong to discriminate against anyone who has not yet achieved the status of a functioning person. It is equally wrong to discriminate against anyone who is *no longer* capable of functioning because of severe senility. Likewise, it is wrong to discriminate against anyone who cannot now function, whether or not he ever could function in the past and whether or not he will be able to function in the future.

In the present context, in which we are analyzing a theory that raises—as a serious issue—the question of which human beings may be killed and which may not, it is not a matter of discrimination in merely a general sense, but something very specific, and particularly odious: It is a discrimination that takes advantage of a person's inability to function as a person and uses that against them as a pretext for killing them. The effect of adopting the functioning-person theory would be to legitimize this taking advantage of a person's lack of ability. This is sheer "might over right," power and ability over frailty and (natural) disability. Those who have power and ability exercise it over those who do not—infants whom their theory can rule out as non-persons. I submit that, quite generally, it is wrong for those who have the advantage of power and ability to take advantage of it over those who do not and to discriminate against them on the basis of this advantage. Let me express

this in terms of the following moral principle:

It is always wrong for persons who have power and ability to take advantage of their status by discriminating against persons who are powerless, especially in order to kill them.

And, as a corollary: *it is always wrong to take advantage of anyone's inability to function as a person by acts of discrimination that would deny that individual the full respect that is due to every person.*

This principle and its corollary apply not only to actions but also to rules and theories that would legitimatize such actions. Any theory that calls for or allows such discrimination is itself an immoral theory. (This is not a moral judgment on those who propose the theory, but strictly a judgment on the theory itself, in terms of its content and its logical consequences.) The functioning-person theory legitimizes the deliberate killing of small babies merely because they have not reached a sufficient level of development as predetermined by the theory. This is immoral.

Multiple Definitions of Functioning Person

The *functioning-person theory* wants to divide humanity into two separate categories: "persons" and "mere human beings," who are nonpersons. I have argued that this is a false division, that all human beings are persons, and that "person" does not mean "functioning person" but includes those with a merely latent capacity to function.

The falsity of the view that "person" means "functioning person" can also be shown in another way—that is, by carefully examining the notion of functioning person with respect to the definition provided by the advocates of the functioning-person theory. What is this definition? What characteristics must a being have in order to be classified as a person? A survey of the current literature on this topic reveals a bewildering array of suggestions, some brief, some detailed, some at variance with others.[31] Let us look at some examples:

Mary Ann Warren proposes consciousness, reasoning, self-motivated activity, the capacity to communicate, the presence of self-concepts and self-awareness as the characteristics of a person.

Peter Singer offers a definition of "person" that "selects two crucial characteristics . . . as the core of the concept": rationality and self-consciousness.[32]

Joseph Fletcher proposes "a list of criteria or indicators" of "humanness" (by which he means personhood). They include minimum intelligence ("Any individual of the species *homo sapiens* who falls below an I.Q. grade of 40 . . . is questionably a person; below the mark of 20, not a person. . . . The *ratio* . . . is what makes a person of the *vita* [life]."), self-awareness, self-control, a sense of time, the capacity to relate to others, and curiosity.[33]

Michael Tooley, in his 1973 paper, "A Defense of Abortion and Infanticide," offers this list: (1) The capacity to envisage a future for oneself, and to have desires about one's future states. (2) The capacity to have a concept of a self, the concept of a continuing subject of experiences and other mental states. (3) Being a self. (4) Self-consciousness. (5) The capacity for self-consciousness.[34]

In his book *Abortion and Infanticide*, Tooley observes, "There is a very general agreement [among writers on this topic] that something is not a person unless it is, in some sense, capable of consciousness."[35] Further, that "many people . . . felt that mere consciousness is not itself sufficient to make something appear, and several proposals have been advanced as to what additional properties are required."[36] He then gives a list of some of "the more important suggestions" for these additional properties. Fifteen are mentioned, many of them similar to those listed above. Among the others are: (1) The capacity to experience pleasure and/or pain. (2) The capacity to have desires. (3) The capacity to use language.[37]

Tooley devotes a major portion of his book to his own proposal for defining a person. His perspective is that of "a right to continued existence." His thesis is, "An individual cannot have a right to continued existence unless there is at least one time at which it possesses the concept of a continuing self or mental substance."[38]

A few pages later he says "that some *psychological continuity* is required" for one to be a person; and that "there must also be *recognition of the continuity* by the enduring mental substance in question [the person]."[39] Putting them together, it seems that Tooley's criteria for being a person (as listed in his book) are: (1) being conscious, (2) possessing the concept of a continuing self or mental substance (at least at one time), (3) recognition of one's psychological continuity over time.[40]

Which of these definitions, or sets of indicators or criteria, or combinations of them, is the correct one for the concept of a person? Which features are necessary for being a person? Which ones are sufficient? Which ones are both necessary and sufficient? This problem is further complicated by the fact that the authors cited here offer conflicting views about the features to be used in defining the concept of person. Thus, *rationality* is affirmed by Warren and Singer, and denied by Tooley in his book.[41] It seems to be affirmed by Fletcher ("minimum intelligence"). *Self-consciousness* is affirmed by Warren, Singer, and Fletcher, and by Tooley in three of his articles.[42] It is later denied by Tooley in his book.[43] *Being an agent* or having self-control is affirmed by Fletcher ("control of existence"), denied by Tooley.[44]

Which criteria are to be employed is one problem. But there is another, equally serious problem. Given a criterion or feature that is to be employed in defining the concept of person, how much of it is necessary? How much is sufficient? Mary Ann Warren, for example, in listing reasoning as one of the features, says it must be "the *developed* capacity to solve new and relatively complex problems." That seems to be a tall order! Why wouldn't reasoning as the capacity to solve elementary problems be sufficient? In any case, how complex must the problems be? Or, more generally, what kinds of reasoning are to be required? And how extensive must the ability to reason be?

All, or virtually all, of these characteristics exist in degrees. Some people have more self-control, others less. Self-consciousness awakens gradually in a child. If it is to be counted as part of the definition of a person, how developed must it be? Parallel questions apply to the rest of the items on these lists.

There is still a further problem. Even if we knew which features were essential to being a person, and also how much development was necessary, even then we would have the problem of measuring the features and their degree of development. Given a small born baby, how do we know how much self consciousness the baby has? And suppose a child has a given feature but cannot display it? How are we to exclude such a possibility, so that we don't label the child a nonperson who is, in fact, a person? In a lengthy section of his book, Tooley tries to grapple with the problem of measurement, by examining a complexity of scientific evidence about "neuro-physical development."[45] But such evidence, even if it were adequate, could only be indirect, in that it measures the physical requirements for functioning as a person and not the functioning itself, for example, having self-consciousness. Needless to say, Tooley does not solve the problem.

The conclusion to be drawn from this is the following: There is no one correct definition of "person," in the sense of functioning person. It is not that there is a correct definition but no one has yet found it. There are many definitions, and a given being will be a person under one of them, and not under another. It is similar to the term *capable*. Is a given person capable? Yes, for some things, or to a certain degree; no, for other things, or to a greater degree. There are many definitions of capable, and the attempt to find the one true definition would obviously be misguided. If "person" is to be defined in terms of "capable of functioning," the same thing applies. There can be no one correct definition of person as a functioning person, because "functioning person" means precisely: one who has the present immediate capacity to function. And functioning as a person means a wide variety of things, each to varying degrees, as the above sample of proposals amply demonstrates.

This wide variety, representing the plurality and complexity of what it means to function as a person, involves two fundamental dimensions.

One is *gradual development*. The attainment of the status of functioning as a person is something that a human being develops gradually. During growth and development, both in the womb and after birth, the child gradually acquires more and more of the features discussed here, and each of them to greater and greater degrees. There is no one moment, or even a short period of time (such as a week), where one could draw a line and say, "Before that there is no functioning person, after that, there is." Thus even if we had an adequate definition, consisting of features A through Z, that makes someone a functioning person, it would still be impossible to divide humanity into two groups: human persons and human nonpersons. Whatever definition there is, a human being grows into the features that comprise it.

Consider self-consciousness: A human being is somewhat self-conscious at an early stage in life, a bit more later, still more at a later stage, and so on. The point is not that we do not know when these stages occur, or just what degree of self-consciousness is involved during each of them. The point is that self-consciousness is itself a matter of degree. And so a set of defining characteristics of the person, even if we had one, would have to be in terms of more or less. "Person" (in this context) means "functioning person," and a being that exemplifies more of A through Z, or exemplifies them to a greater degree, would have more capabilities of functioning as a person. There can be no definition of person that

picks out certain beings and excludes others; there can only be various features (such as self-consciousness) that different human beings exemplify to varying degrees.

The plurality and complexity of what it means to function as a person involves a second dimension, *relativity to context*; that is, how we construe the term person when it is used to designate "functioning person" varies from case to case. Suppose, for example, that in order to be legally binding, a document must be signed with two persons present as witnesses. Here a degree of functioning as a person is required that far exceeds the level attained by, say, a child of three. A three-year-old would hardly be an appropriate witness for the signing of a will. So the degree of attainment of present capacity to function as a person that we have in mind, and require, for someone to be called a person varies according to the situation, and is determined by our needs and interests.

There is no such thing as the definition of the term *functioning person* because the features that constitute any definition vary across the spectrum of gradual development, and the spectrum of context. Hence, the definition itself varies; there is no one meaning of functioning person. This shows that the whole attempt by Warren, Singer, Fletcher, Tooley, and others, to define the person is fundamentally misguided.

In her paper, "Abortion and the Concept of a Person," Jane English reaches what is in part the same conclusion: in part, because she fails to distinguish between being a person and functioning as a person. Her thesis is that there is no such thing as the correct definition of a person. She offers a refutation of the view that "the concept of a person can be captured in a straitjacket of necessary and/or sufficient conditions,"[46] which is what would be required for an adequate definition of a person. "Rather," she claims, "'person' is a cluster of features, of which rationality, having a self-concept . . . are only part."[47] Thus, "People typically exhibit rationality . . . but someone who was irrational would not thereby fail to qualify as a person."[48] Her conclusion, in the first part of her paper, is that "our concept of a person is not sharp or decisive enough to bear the weight of a solution to the abortion controversy. To use it to solve that problem is to clarify *obscurum peri obscurius* [the obscure by the more obscure]."[49]

When this is applied to the concept of functioning person, it is valid and of great significance. When, as in her paper, it is applied to the concept of being a person—and used as a reason for justifying some abortions—it is a serious mistake. The analysis offered by English is excellent, but she draws the wrong conclusion. What her analysis shows is that *functioning person* cannot be adequately defined. Nothing follows from this regarding *being a person*, especially not the conclusion that the being in the womb is not a person.

Practical Consequences

Consider again the fact that the meaning of *functioning person* is relative to context. When occasions such as validly witnessing the signing of legal documents arise, then a division of humanity into two groups is justified. Here the requirement of a particular level of achievement for functioning as a person is appropriate. But when it is a matter of deciding who will be respected as a real person, and who will be dismissed as a nonperson and treated as a being who may be killed, the requirement of a particular level of achievement for functioning as a person is another matter entirely. Specifically, if it is in the interests of some people to kill a certain class of human beings, they can simply define them as nonpersons, on the grounds that they have not attained [or no longer retain] a particular level of achievement as functioning persons. Abortion is an obvious example. When there is a strong predisposition on the part of some people to destroy a child, there is an interest that can obviously be used to draw a line in the scale of gradual development of the capacity to function as a person, designed specifically to exclude the child that one wants to get rid of. That line may come at birth, or it may come after birth, as in Tooley's analysis, which would justify infanticide as well.[50]

Since there is no one correct definition of person when that term designates "functioning person"; and since functioning as a person is something that develops gradually, any division of human beings into two classes, persons (who are to be respected) and nonpersons (who may be killed) must be based on a decision.[51] This will be a decision based on interests, and where the interest is "getting rid of," any person falling into that unlucky class can be labeled a nonperson and killed with impunity.

Preborn children are a striking example of this, but they are not alone. Parents who decide that their newborn child does not have a meaningful life because of a handicap, or who do not want to be burdened with the extra care that a child needs, can turn to the functioning-person theory, and use the achievement view inherent in it, to define their baby as a nonperson, in order to justify killing him.

When it is personal interests, utilizing the theory of the achievement view, rather than a person's inherent nature, that determines the morality of killing human beings, then ultimately no one is safe. For the functioning-person theory that underlies the achievement view can easily be formulated as excluding not only those who have not yet achieved functioning as a person (as in Tooley), but also those who no longer can function as persons in a particular, specified way. Thus if a person were to suffer a terrible accident that left him in a severely debilitated state, he could be classified as a nonperson and killed by those who wanted to get rid of him.

Ultimately, it would be a matter of power. Those in power could decide the level of achievement necessary for being counted as a person, and whether it would be only a matter of "not yet" or also a matter of "no longer." This is, of course, what we see in the case of abortion. Doctors kill babies, and not the other way around, because doctors have power, babies do not. This applies in an immediate and obvious way to the physical level. In general, the physically strong have the power to crush the physically weak. That is nothing new. What is new is the attempt to legitimize this by a theory: the functioning-person theory with its attendant achievement view. The effect of this is that those in power can decide who will, and who will not, count as a person, depending on whether or not the human being in question had attained (or retained) the requisite achievement.

"Might over right" is truly frightening. When it is raw physical might, with no pretense to moral legitimacy, it is frightening enough. When a claim to moral legitimacy is added, it becomes even more frightening. Murder is perpetrated without even being recognized as murder. The results of the functioning-person theory and achievement view is that, if adopted, they would provide precisely such a pretense of moral legitimacy to murder.

The Dignity of the Human Person

The true alternative to might over right is reverence for the dignity of each person as a person; because he or she has the being of a person.[52]

The important reality of the dignity of the human person can be seen, and taken seriously, in many ways, especially when that dignity is denied or under attack.[53] Slavery, child abuse, sexual molestation, and rape are among some of the more striking examples. Or, a person with a physical handicap is severely beaten by someone who takes advantage of that handicap. Another is the wrongness of taking advantage of a person's inability to function as a person, either because he is not now capable of doing so, or no longer capable, or not yet capable. This is perfectly parallel to the injustice of taking advantage of a person's physical inabilities. Persons are persons, they have the dignity of a person, whether they have these abilities or not. To take advantage of a person's inabilities is to affront his dignity. It is an antithesis to the reverence due to his dignity as a person.

It is wrong to kill a child in the womb, or a newborn baby, on the grounds that he has not yet reached a sufficient degree of functioning as a person. The same applies to a severely retarded child who probably never will achieve a certain normal level of functioning as a person. He has the same human nature, he is equally a person, he has the same dignity as a person fortunate enough to be normal. As always, it is his being as a person that counts, not his capabilities for functioning as a person.

It is the achievement view that constitutes the principal denial of this. In one case (the normal child), it denies his personhood, his dignity, because he has not yet achieved the required level of functioning as a person. In another case (the severely retarded child), it denies his personhood, his dignity, because he will never achieve the required level of functioning. But who says he must? Nobody has the right to set such standards, and impose them on others, especially at the price of their lives.

The normal person deserves our reverence, our respect for his dignity, not because he is normal, not because of actual or potential achievements in functioning as a person, but simply because he is a person. And the non-normal person is equally a person, and deserves equal reverence. If you were to become a victim of a disease or accident that left you severely retarded, incapacitated, you would want your dignity respected just as before. You would still be yourself, the same person, hence a person, hence a being with the dignity of a person. Exactly the same applies to the severely retarded child, and to the preborn child, who is in many respects similar in his capabilities.

Reverence is the most fundamental response due to another person in his dignity; it is not the whole of it. Love is the fulfillment and the highest form of this response. Each in its own way is an antithesis to using a person as a mere means, as in rape, enslavement, and other ways, and to the attitude of "get rid of it" so often displayed in the context of abortion. Each is also an antithesis to the achievement view and its odious discrimination between those who have achieved, and therefore count, and those who have not achieved, and therefore don't count, and thus may be destroyed.

The reality of love as the deepest response to another in his dignity manifests itself in the attitude and work of Mother Theresa of Calcutta. The story is told of a man whom she found abandoned in the gutter of a street. She picked him up, brought him to her home, cared for him in love for the few remaining days (or hours) of his life. He responded by saying, "I have lived like an animal in the street, but I will die like an angel, loved and cared for."[54]

Discussion Questions

1. Mary Anne Warren suggests a five-part criterion to distinguish human beings in the genetic sense from human beings in the moral sense. How does Professor Schwarz respond to this distinction? What does he mean when he says that Professor Warren and others confuse being a person with functioning as a person? Do you consider his argument compelling? Why or why not?

2. What imaginary story does Professor Schwarz tell in order to show that "when it comes to functioning as a person, there is no moral difference between 'did, but does not' (the sleeping adult) and 'does not, but will' (the small child)?" Do you consider the story an adequate argument to support Professor Schwarz's position? Why or why not?

3. One objection to Professor Schwarz's position goes something like this: if one's potential for personal function makes one a person (as his position appears to be saying), then could not a candidate for the U.S. Presidency (that is, a *potential* president) claim that he is an *actual* president because of his potential? How do you think Professor Schwarz would respond to this? Is it an accurate portrayal of his argument? Why or why not?

Notes

1. Fletcher (1979), p. 144.
2. Tooley (1973), p. 54. See also (1984), p. 122.
3. Tooley (1979), pp. 80–81.
4. Warren (1973), p. 43.
5. *Ibid.*
6. *Ibid.*, pp. 43–44.
7. *Ibid.*, p. 45
8. *Ibid.*
9. *Ibid.*, p. 50.
10. *Ibid.*
11. *Ibid.*, p. 51.
12. Tooley (1972), p. 82. Also (1983), p. 121 and (1984), p. 130. Essentially the same point is made by Engelhardt (1974), pp. 321–23.
13. *Amicus Curiae*, pp. 11–13.
14. *Ibid.*, pp. 13–14.
15. Engelhardt (1974), p. 322. He says this of the fetus in general. The context is a comparison of the fetus and a sleeping person.
16. Blechschmidt (1981), p. 8.
17. Joyce and Rosera (1970), p. 22.
18. Joyce (1981), p. 347.
19. The Functioning Person Theory, especially in its emphasis on the distinction between being "merely human" and being a "person" (meaning a functioning person), is held by a number of contemporary writers in different forms. See: Tooley (1972), pp. 55–69, *passim*; (1973), pp. 54–73, *passim.*; (1979), pp. 84–92; (1983), pp. 50–157, *passim*; (1984), *passim*. Warren (1973). Fletcher (1979), chapters 1, 10, 11. See also Engelhardt (1974). Speaking of a "fetus," he says "there may be merely human life present but not a person" (p. 321). Also Glover (1977), pp. 127, 138–40, and chapters 3, 9, 11 and 12, *passim*; Singer (1979a), chapter 4 and (1979b); Sumner (1981), pp. 90 ff. Finally, Kluge (1975), pp. 88–95, esp. 91, where the Theory is more restricted in scope than in authors such as Tooley, Singer and Warren.
20. Tooley (1983), p. 77. This is the conclusion he reaches in section 4.2, entitled "The Moral Irrelevance of Species Membership," pp. 61–77. See also (1979), p. 67, and (1972), p. 70.
21. Singer (1979a), p. 117. Also (1979b), p. 47.
22. Adherents of the Functioning Person Theory recognize that the term "human" may be used in a sense other than that of designating a mere biological category. It may mean, as the *Oxford English Dictionary* says, "of, belonging to, or characteristic of man," or "having or showing the qualities or attributes proper to or distinctive of man." [Singer (1979b), p. 48.]. The term "man" in this context is, of course, interpreted by adherents of the Functioning Person Theory as meaning "functioning person." It would then include only beings who had the (present immediate) capacity to function as persons; that is, who had "qualities or attributes we think characteristic of, proper to, or distinctive of man" [*Ibid.*], for example, the "characteristic . . . [of having] a capacity of self-awareness or self-consciousness" [*Ibid.* p. 49]. This would mean that "we will not count severely retarded infants as human beings even though they are clearly members of *homo sapiens* [the biological species human] (*Ibid.*)." Thus, the term "human" is taken by adherents of the theory to be ambiguous between "functioning person" and "member of the biological species 'human.'" See also Singer (1979a), pp. 74–76. In this connection, Tooley says that "the tendency to use expressions like 'person' and 'human being' interchangeably is an unfortunate one" (1972), p. 56. See also (1973), p. 56 and (1983), p. 50.

My criticism of the Functioning Person Theory in this section is therefore directed to it in so far as it uses the term "human" in one of the two meanings just described, namely, "member of the biological species 'human.'" It is in this sense that the term is claimed to be "a mere biological category."

23. Tooley (1983), p. 175; see also 193. See Marquis (1989) for another refutation of views such as those of Tooley that try to justify abortion by claiming that the "fetus" is not a person. Marquis argues that abortion is wrong because it denies the "fetus" a valuable future, regardless of whether "it" is a person.
24. Warren (1973), section 4, p. 48.
25. *Ibid.*, p. 49.
26. *Ibid.*
27. Joyce (1981), p. 351.
28. *Ibid.*, p. 350.
29. *Ibid.*
30. An explicit endorsement of the Achievement View is found in Sumner: "The future awaiting a human fetus is not relevant to its moral status; that status is based on what it has already achieved. The threshold [when "it" achieves moral status, namely at sentience] is a moral quantum leap, for it is the stage at which the fetus joins the class of beings whose rights are secured by our network of positive laws and conventional moral rules" [(1981), p. 227]. When Sumner says that "the paradigm bearer of moral standing is an adult human being with normal capacities of intellect, emotion, perception, sensation, decision, action, and the like" [(1984), p.74], he is expressing the Achievement View. The moral human adult has achieved these capacities, so he "counts" as a full moral being, a "paradigm bearer of moral standing." The "fetus" has not achieved them, at least not before sentience, so he lacks moral standing; or at least full moral standing. See also (1981), p. 10. Another explicit advocate of the Achievement View is Ashley Montagu. Devine tells us that "another possible account treats personhood, as Ashley Montagu once said, not as an endowment but as an achievement [Letter to the *New York Times*, March 9, 1967], an achievement (like the earning of a university degree) which confers a certain status on someone as long as he is" [(1978), p. 93]. See pp. 93–95 for

Devine's criticism of this view. See also Grisez (1972), pp. 278, 281, for a criticism.

31. Tooley acknowledges this. After listing fifteen "proposals [that] have been advanced as to what . . . properties are required" for being a "person," in addition to consciousness, he observes that "these alternatives, and various combinations of them, provide one with quite a bewildering selection of candidates for the properties that should enter into the definition of the concept of a person" [(1983), p. 90].

32. Singer (1979a), p. 76.

33. Fletcher (1979), pp. 12–15.

34. Tooley (1973), pp. 59–60.

35. Tooley (1983), p. 90.

36. *Ibid.*

37. *Ibid.*, pp. 90–91.

38. *Ibid.*, p. 121.

39. *Ibid.*, p. 132.

40. Tooley's discussion of the notion of a "person," in his book, is mainly in chapter 5, "The Concept of a Person" (pp. 87–164). See also chapters 4 and 6, "Persons and Human Beings" (pp. 50–86) and "Potential Persons" (pp. 165–241).

41. Warren, "reasoning"; Singer (1979a), p. 76; Tooley (1983), pp. 134–38 and 299.

42. Warren, "the presence of self-concepts and self-awareness." Singer (1979a), p. 76. Fletcher, "self-awareness." Tooley (1972), p. 59; (1973), pp. 59–60 and 72; (1979) p. 91, "at least . . . the *capacity* for self-consciousness."

43. Tooley (1983), pp. 144–46.

44. *Ibid.*, pp. 138–42. It is probably also affirmed by Warren, "self-motivated activity."

45. Section 11.54, "The Scientific Evidence: Human Neurophysiological Development," Tooley (1983), pp. 372–407.

46. English (1975), p. 152. All quotations are from Part I of her paper.

47. *Ibid.*

48. *Ibid.*, p. 153.

49. *Ibid.*, 154.

50. Where would Tooley "draw the line" after birth? In each of his three articles on abortion he says: "The practical moral problem can . . . be satisfactorily handled by choosing some short period of time, such as a week after birth, as the interval during which infanticide will be permitted" [(1972), p. 79; (1973), p. 91; (1984), p. 133]. In his book this period is considerably extended. "New-born humans are neither persons nor even quasi-persons [see sec. 11.6, pp. 407–12], and their destruction is in no way intrinsically wrong. At about the age of three months, . . . they probably acquire properties that are morally significant, and that make it to some extent intrinsically wrong to destroy them" [(1983), pp. 411–12]. Even at three months, the killing of a child is not as wrong as killing an adult, according to Tooley. The killing of infants, he says is only

"eventually . . . comparable in seriousness to the destruction of a normal adult human being" [*Ibid.*, p. 412].

51. This is reflected in Sumner's question: "To which creatures should we distribute (some degree of) moral standing?" [(1981), p. 128]. As if "moral standing," the right to be treated with respect as a person, were something we could distribute at will!

52. For a profound analysis of reverence, see von Hildebrand, "Reverence" [(1950), pp. 1–15; reprinted, (1967), pp. 1–9]. The dignity of a person is closely related to the intrinsic value of a person as person, which von Hildebrand calls the ontological value of the person. See his analysis, (1953), pp. 129–39.

53. For an analysis of the notion of the dignity of the human person, see Balduin Schwarz, "Von der Wurde des Menschen" (1984a).

54. *Ibid.*, p. 5638.

Works Cited

Amicus Curiae
1971   *Motion and Brief Amicus Curiae of Certain Physicians, Professors and Fellows of the American College of Obstetrics and Gynecology in Support of Appellees*, submitted to the Supreme Court of the United States, October Term, 1971, No. 70-18, Roe v. Wade and No. 70-40, Doe v. Bolton. Prepared by Dennis J. Horan, et. al. (The List of Amici contains the names of over 200 physicians.).

Blechschmidt, E., M.D.
1981   "Human Being from the Very First," in Hilgers, Horan and Mall (1981), pp. 6–28.

Cohen, et al. (eds.)
1974   Marshall Cohen, Thomas Nagel, and Thomas Scanlon (eds.), *The Rights and Wrongs of Abortion, a Philosophy and Public Affairs Reader*. Princeton, N.J.: Princeton University Press.

Devine, Philip
1978   *The Ethics of Homicide*. Ithaca and London: Cornell University Press.

Engelhardt, H. Tristan, Jr.
1974   "The Ontology of Abortion," in *Ethics* Vol. 84 (Fall), pp. 217–34. Reprinted in *Moral Problems in Medicine*, Samuel Gorovitz et al. (eds.), Englewood Cliffs, NJ: Prentice-Hall, 1976, pp. 318–34. References are to Gorovitz.

English, Jane
1975   "Abortion and the Concept of a Person," in *Canadian Journal of Philosophy*, Vol. 5., no. 2 (October). Reprinted in Feinberg (1984), pp. 151–60. References are to Feinberg.

Feinberg, Joel (ed.)
1973 *The Problem of Abortion*, 1st ed. Belmont, CA: Wadsworth Pub. Co.
1984 *The Problem of Abortion*, 2nd ed. Belmont, CA: Wadsworth Pub. Co.

Fletcher, Joseph
1979 *Humanhood: Essays in Biomedical Ethics*. Buffalo: Prometheus Books.

Glover, Jonathan
1977 *Causing Death and Saving Lives*. Harmondsworth, England and New York: Penguin Books.

Grisez, Germain
1972 *Abortion: the Myths, the Realities, and the Arguments*. New York: World Publishing Co., Corpus Books.

Hildebrand, Dietrich von
1950 *Fundamental Moral Attitudes*. New York, London, Toronto: Longmans Green
1953 *Ethics*. Chicago: Franciscan Herald Press.

Hildebrand and Hildebrand
1967 Dietrich and Alice von Hildebrand, *The Art of Living*. Chicago: Henry Regnery. Includes Hildebrand (1950).

Hilgers, Horan and Mall (eds.)
1981 Thomas W. Hilgers, M.D., Dennis J. Horan and David Mall (eds.), *New Perspectives on Human Abortion*. Frederick, MD: University Publications of America, Aletheia Books.

Joyce, Robert E.
1981 "When Does a Person Begin?" in Hilgers, Horan and Mall, (1981), pp. 345–56. An adaptation of an article in *The New Scholasticism* 52, no. 1 (Winter 1978), "Personhood and the Conception Event."

Joyce and Rosera
1970 Robert E. Joyce and Mary Rosera, *Let Us Be Born: The Inhumanity of Abortion*. Chicago: Franciscan Herald Press.

Kluge, Eike-Henner W.
1975 *The Practice of Death*. New Haven, CT and London: Yale University Press.

Ladd, John (ed.)
1979 *Ethical Issues Relating to Life and Death*. New York and Oxford: Oxford University Press.

Marquis, Don
1989 "Why Abortion Is Immoral," in *The Journal of Philosophy* Vol. 86, no. 4, pp. 183–202.

Schwarz, Balduin
1984a "Von der Wurde des Menschen," in *Theologisches*, no. 166 (February), pp. 5629–38.

Singer, Peter
1979a *Practical Ethics*. Cambridge, England: Cambridge University Press.
1979b "Unsanctifying Life," in Ladd (1979), pp. 41–61.

Sumner, L. W.
1981 *Abortion and Moral Theory*. Princeton, NJ: Princeton University Press.
1984 "A Third Way," in Feinberg (1984), pp. 71–93. A revised version of chap. 4, pp. 124–60, of Sumner (1981).

Tooley, Michael
1972 "Abortion and Infanticide," in *Philosophy and Public Affairs*, Vol. 2., no. 1 (Fall). Reprinted in Cohen (1974), pp. 52–84. References are to Cohen.
1973 "A Defense of Abortion and Infanticide," in Feinberg (1973), pp. 51–91.
1979 "Decisions to Terminate Life and the Concept of a Person," in Ladd (1979), pp. 62–93.
1983 *Abortion and Infanticide*. Oxford: Clarendon Press.
1984 "In Defense of Abortion and Infanticide," in Feinberg (1984), pp. 120–34.

Warren, Mary Ann
1973 "On the Moral and Legal Status of Abortion," in *The Monist*, Vol. 57, no. 1 (January). Reprinted in Wasserstrom (1979), pp. 35–51; "Postscript on Infanticide" was added especially for this volume. Also reprinted in Feinberg (1984). References are to Wasserstrom.

Wasserstrom, Richard A. (ed.)
1979 *Today's Moral Problems*, 2nd ed. New York: Macmillan; London: Collier Macmillan.

18

A Defense of the Moderate Position

L. W. Sumner

L. W. Sumner is Professor of Philosophy at the University of Toronto in Canada. He is the author of many philosophical works, including *Abortion and Moral Theory* (1981).

In this essay Professor Sumner puts forth a moderate position on the moral permissibility of abortion. He critiques both the liberal and conservative positions on abortion and maintains that these are inadequate in a number of places. Agreeing with both Warren (Chapter 16) and Schwarz (Chapter 17) that the morality of abortion is contingent upon the personhood of the fetus, Professor Sumner combines what he considers the best elements of the liberal and conservative views and contends that a fetus becomes a protectable human being when it becomes *sentient,* which may occur as early as the middle weeks of the second trimester of pregnancy and definitely by the end of the second trimester. Thus, he agrees with the liberals that early abortions are morally permissible but he also agrees with the conservatives that late abortions are not morally permissible. Professor Sumner argues that this moderate viewpoint coheres with our overall considered moral judgments better than its liberal and conservative competitors.

When confronted with a problem as complex as that of abortion, we have some initial reason to suspect simple solutions. . . . We need a view of abortion responsive to all of the elements whose conjunction renders the problem of abortion so perplexing and so divisive. Such a view cannot be a simple one.

Reprinted by permission from L. W. Sumner, *Abortion and Moral Theory* (Princeton, N.J.: Princeton University Press, 1981).

If an alternative to the established views is to be developed, three tasks must be successfully completed. The first is to construct this third way and to show how it is essentially different from both of the positions it supersedes. The indispensable ingredient at this stage is a a criterion of moral standing that will generate a view of the fetus and thus a view of abortion. . . . The second task is to defend this view on the intuitive level by showing that it coheres better than either of its predecessors with our considered moral judgments both on abortion itself and on cognate issues. Then finally, the view must be given a deep structure by grounding it in a moral theory. This chapter will undertake the first two tasks by outlining a position on the abortion problem and justifying it by appealing to moral intuitions. . . .

[1.] Specifications

The established views have failed in certain specific respects. Collating their points of weakness will provide us with guidelines for building a more satisfactory alternative. It will be convenient to divide these guidelines into two categories corresponding to the two ingredients that complicate the problem of abortion: the nature of the fetus and the implications of the mother/fetus relationship.

The conservative view, and also the more naive versions of the liberal view, select a precise point (conception, birth, etc.) as the threshold of moral standing, implying that the transition from no standing to full standing occurs abruptly. In doing so they rest more weight on these sudden events than they are capable of bearing. A view that avoids this defect will allow full moral standing to be acquired gradually. It will therefore attempt to locate not a threshold point, but a threshold period or stage.

Both of the established views attribute a uniform moral status to all fetuses, regardless of their dissimilarities. Each, for example, counts a newly conceived zygote for precisely as much (or as little) as a full-term fetus, despite the enormous differences between them. A view that avoids this defect will assign moral status differentially, so that the threshold stage occurs sometime during pregnancy.

A consequence of the uniform approach adopted by both of the established views is that neither can attach any significance to the development of the fetus during gestation.[1] Yet this development is the most obvious feature of gestation. A view that avoids this defect will base the (differential) moral standing of the fetus at least in part on its level of development. It will thus assign undeveloped fetuses a moral status akin to that of ova and spermatozoa, whereas it will assigned developed fetuses a moral status akin to that of infants.

So far, then, an adequate view of the fetus must be gradual, differential, and developmental. It must also be derived from a satisfactory criterion of moral standing. The conditions of adequacy for such a criterion [are] . . . it must be general (applicable to beings other than fetuses), it must connect moral standing with the empirical properties of such beings, and it must be morally relevant. Its moral relevance is partly testable by appeal to intuition, for arbitrary or shallow criteria will be vulnerable to counterexamples. But the final test of moral relevance is grounding in a moral theory.

An adequate view of the fetus promises a morally significant division between early abortions (before the threshold stage) and late abortions (after the threshold stage). It also promises borderline cases (during the threshold stage). Wherever that stage is located, abortions that precede it will be private matters, since the fetus will at that stage lack moral standing. Thus the provisions of the liberal view will apply to early abortions: they will be morally innocent (as long as the usual conditions of maternal consent, etc., are satisfied) and ought to be legally unregulated (except for rules equally applicable to all other medical procedures). Early abortion will have the same moral status as contraception.

Abortions that follow the threshold stage will be interpersonal matters, since the fetus will at that stage possess moral standing. The provisions of Thomson's argument will apply to late abortions: they must be assessed on a case-by-case basis and they ought to be legally permitted only on appropriate grounds. Late abortions will have the same moral status as infanticide, except for the difference made by the physical connection between fetus and mother.

A third way with abortion is thus a moderate and differential view, combining elements of the liberal view for early abortions with elements of (a weakened version of) the conservative view for late abortions. The policy that a moderate view will support is a moderate policy, permissive in the early stages of pregnancy and more restrictive (though not as restrictive as conservatives think appropriate) in the later stages. So far as the personal question of the moral evaluation of particular abortions is concerned, there is no pressing need to resolve the borderline cases around the threshold stage. But a workable abortion policy cannot tolerate this vagueness and will need to establish a definite time limit beyond which the stipulated grounds will come into play. Although the precise location of the time limit will unavoidably be somewhat arbitrary, it will be defensible as long as it falls somewhere within the threshold stage. Abortion on request up to the time limit and only for cause thereafter: these are the elements of a satisfactory abortion policy.

A number of moderate views may be possible, each of them satisfying all of the foregoing constraints. A particular view will be defined by selecting (a) a criterion of moral standing, (b) the natural characteristics whose gradual acquisition during normal fetal development carries with it the acquisition of moral standing, and (c) a threshold stage. Of these three steps, the first is the crucial one, since it determines both of the others.

[2.] A Criterion of Moral Standing

We have thus far assumed that for a creature to have moral standing is for it to have a right to life. Any such right imposes duties on moral agents; these duties may be either negative (not to deprive the creature of life) or positive (to support the creature's life). Possession of a right to life implies at least some immunity against attack by others, and possibly also some entitlement to the aid of others. As the duties may vary in strength, so may the corresponding rights. To have some moral standing is to have some right to life, whether or not it may be overridden by the rights of others. To have full moral standing is to have the strongest right to life possessed by anyone, the right to life of the paradigm person. Depending on one's moral theory, this right may or may not be inviolable and indefeasible and thus may or may not impose absolute duties on others.

Although this analysis of moral standing will later be broadened, it will still suffice for our present purposes. To which creatures should we distribute (some degree of) moral standing? On which criterion should we base this distribution? It may be easier to answer these questions if we begin with the clear case and work outward to the unclear ones. If we can determine why we ascribe full standing to the paradigm case, we may learn what to look for in other creatures when deciding whether or not to include them in the moral sphere.

The paradigm bearer of moral standing is an adult human being with normal capacities of intellect, emotion, perception, sensation, decision, action, and the like. If we think of such a person as a complex bundle of natural properties, then in principle we could employ as a criterion any of the properties common to all normal and mature members of our species. Selecting a particular property or set of properties will define a class of creatures with moral standing, namely, all (and only) those who share that property. The extension of that class will depend on how widely the property in question is distributed. Some putative criteria will be obviously frivolous and will immediately fail the tests of generality or moral relevance. But even after excluding the silly candidates, we are left with a number of serious ones. There are four that appear to be the most serious; we might attribute full moral standing to the paradigm person on the ground that he/she is (a) intrinsically valuable, (b) alive, (c) sentient, or (d) rational. An intuitive test of the adequacy of any of these candidates will involve first enumerating the class of beings to whom it will distribute moral standing and then determining whether that class either excludes creatures that upon careful reflection we believe ought to be included or includes creatures that we believe ought to be excluded. In the former case the criterion draws the boundary of the moral sphere too narrowly and fails as a necessary condition of moral standing. In the latter case the criterion draws the boundary too broadly and fails as a sufficient condition. (A given criterion may, of course, be defective in both respects.)

Beings may depart from the paradigm along several different dimensions, each of which presents us with unclear cases that a criterion must resolve. These cases may be divided into seven categories: (1) inanimate objects (natural and artificial); (2) nonhuman terrestrial species of living things (animals and plants); (3) nonhuman extraterrestrial species of living things (should there be any); (4) artificial "life forms" (androids, robots, computers); (5) grossly defective human beings (the severely and permanently retarded or deranged); (6) human beings at the end of life (especially the severely and permanently senile or comatose); (7) human beings at the beginning of life (fetuses, infants, and children). Since the last context is the one in which we wish to apply a criterion, it will here be set aside. This will enable us to settle on a criterion without tailoring it specially for the problem of abortion. Once a criterion has established its credentials in other domains, we will be able to trace out its implications for the case of the fetus.

The first candidate for a criterion takes a direction rather different from that of the remaining three. It is a commonplace in moral philosophy to attribute to (normal adult) human beings a special worth or value or dignity in virtue of which they possess (among other rights) a full right to life. This position implies that (some degree of) moral standing extends just as far as (some degree of) this intrinsic value, a higher degree of the latter entailing a higher degree of the former. We cannot know which things have moral standing without being told which things have intrinsic worth (and why)—without, that is, being offered a theory of intrinsic value. What is unique about this criterion, however, is that it is quite capable in principle of extending moral standing beyond the class of living beings, thus embracing such inanimate objects as rocks and lakes, entire landscapes (or indeed worlds), and artifacts. Of course, nonliving things cannot literally have a right to *life*, but it would be simple enough to generalize to a right to (continued) *existence*, where this might include both a right not to be destroyed and a right to such support as is necessary for that existence. A criterion that invokes intrinsic value is thus able to define a much more capacious moral sphere than is any of the other candidates.

Such a criterion is undeniably attractive in certain respects; how else are we to explain why it is wrong to destroy priceless icons or litter the moon even when doing so will never affect any living, sentient, or rational being? But it is clear that it cannot serve our present purpose. A criterion must connect moral standing with some property of things whose presence or absence can be confirmed by a settled, objective, and public method of investigation. The property of being intrinsically valuable is not subject to such verification. A criterion based on intrinsic value cannot be applied without a theory of intrinsic value. But if things have moral standing in virtue of having intrinsic value, and if they have intrinsic value in virtue of having some natural property, then it is that natural property which is serving as the real criterion of moral standing, and the middle term of intrinsic value is eliminable without loss. A theory of intrinsic value may thus entail a criterion of moral standing, but intrinsic value cannot itself serve as that criterion.

There is a further problem confronting any attempt to ground moral rights in the intrinsic worth of creatures. One must first be certain that this is not merely a verbal exercise in which attributing intrinsic value to things is just another way of attributing intrinsic moral standing to them. Assuming that the relation between value and rights is synthetic, there are then two possibilities: the value in question is moral or it is nonmoral. If it is moral, the criterion plainly fails to break out of the circle of moral properties to connect them with the nonmoral properties of things. But if it is nonmoral, it is unclear what it has to do with moral rights. If there are realms of value, some case must be made for deriving moral duties toward things from the nonmoral value of these things.

The remaining three candidates for a criterion of moral standing (life, sentience, rationality) all satisfy the verification requirement since they all rest standing on empirical properties of things. They may be ordered in terms of the breadth of the moral spheres they define. Since rational beings are a proper subset of sentient beings, which are a proper subset of living beings, the first candidate is the weakest and will define the broadest sphere, whereas the third is the strongest and will define the narrowest sphere. In an interesting recent discussion, Kenneth Goodpaster (1978) has urged that moral standing be accorded to all living things, simply in virtue of the fact that they are alive. Although much of his argument is negative, being directed against more restrictive criteria, he does provide a positive case for including all forms of life within the moral sphere.

Let us assume that the usual signs of life—nutrition, metabolism, spontaneous growth, reproduction—enable us to draw a tolerably sharp distinction between animate and inanimate beings, so that all plant and animal species, however primitive, are collected together in the former category. All such creatures share the property of being *teleological systems*; they have functions, ends, directions, natural tendencies, and so forth. In virtue of their teleology such creatures have needs, in a nonmetaphorical sense—conditions that must be satisfied if they are to thrive or flourish. Creatures with needs can be benefited or harmed, they are benefited when their essential needs are satisfied and harmed when they are not. It also makes sense to say that such creatures have a good: the conditions that promote their life and health are good for them, whereas those that impair their normal functioning are bad for them. But it is common to construe morality as having essentially to do with benefits and harms or with the good of creatures. So

doing will lead us to extend moral standing to all creatures capable of being benefited and harmed, that is, all creatures with a good. But this condition will include all organisms (and systems of organisms), and so life is the only reasonable criterion of moral standing.

This extension of moral standing to plants and to the simpler animals is of course highly counterintuitive, since most of us accord the lives of such creatures no weight whatever in our practical deliberations. How could we conduct our affairs if we were to grant protection of life to every plant and animal species? Some of the more extreme implications of his view are, however, forestalled by Goodpaster's distinction between a criterion of inclusion and a criterion of comparison.[2] The former determines which creatures have (some) moral standing and thus locates the boundary of the moral sphere; it is Goodpaster's contention that life is the proper inclusion criterion. The latter is operative entirely within the moral sphere and enables us to assign different grades of moral standing to different creatures in virtue of some natural property that they may possess in different degrees. Since all living beings are (it seems) equally alive, life cannot serve as a comparison criterion. Goodpaster does not provide such a criterion, though he recognizes its necessity. Thus his view enables him to affirm that all living creatures have (some) moral standing but to deny that all such creatures have equal standing. Though the lives of all animate beings deserve consideration, some deserve more than others. Thus, for instance, higher animals might count for more than lower ones, and all animals might count for more than plants.

In the absence of a criterion of comparison, it is difficult to ascertain just what reforms Goodpaster's view would require in our moral practice. How much weight must human beings accord to the lives of lichen or grass or bacteria or insects? When are such lives more important than some benefit for a higher form of life? How should we modify our eating habits, for example? There is a problem here that extends beyond the incompleteness and indeterminacy of Goodpaster's position. Suppose that we have settled on a comparison criterion; let it be sentience (assuming that sentience admits of degrees in some relevant respect). Then a creature's ranking in the hierarchy of moral standing will be determined by the extent of its sentience: nonsentient (living) beings will have minimal standing, whereas the most sentient beings (human beings, perhaps) will have maximal standing. But then we are faced with the obvious question: if sentience is to serve as the comparison criterion, why should it not also serve as the inclusion criterion? Conversely, if life is the inclusion criterion, does it not follow that nothing else can serve as the comparison criterion, in which case all living beings have equal standing? It is difficult to imagine an argument in favor of sentience as a comparison criterion that would not also be an argument in favor of it as an inclusion criterion. Since the same will hold for any other comparison criterion, Goodpaster's view can avoid its extreme implications only at the price of inconsistency.

Goodpaster's view also faces consistency problems in its claim that life is necessary for moral standing. Beings need not be organisms in order to be teleological systems, and therefore to have needs, a good, and the capacity to be benefited and harmed. If these conditions are satisfied by a tree (as they surely are), then they are equally satisfied by a car. In order to function properly most machines need periodic maintenance; such maintenance is good for them, they are benefited by it, and they are harmed by its neglect. Why then is being alive a necessary condition of moral standing? Life is but an (imperfect) indicator of teleology and the capacity to be benefited and harmed. But Goodpaster's argument then commits him to treating these deeper characteristics as the criterion of moral standing, and thus to according standing to many (perhaps most) inanimate objects.[3]

This inclusion of (at least some) nonliving things should incline us to re-examine Goodpaster's argument—if the inclusion of all living things has not already done so. The connection between morality and the capacity to be benefited and harmed appears plausible, so what has gone wrong? We may form a conjecture if we again consider our paradigm bearer of moral standing. In the case of a fully normal adult human being, it does appear that moral questions are pertinent whenever the actions of another agent promise to benefit or threaten to harm such a being. Both duties and rights are intimately connected with benefits and harms. The kinds of acts that we have a (strict) duty not to do are those that typically cause harm, whereas positive duties are duties to confer benefits. Liberty-rights protect autonomy, which is usually thought of as one of the chief goods for human beings, and the connection between welfare-rights and benefits is obvious. But if we ask what counts as a benefit or a harm for a human being, the usual answers take one or both of the following directions:

(1) *The desire model.* Human beings are benefited to the extent that their desires (or perhaps their considered and informed desires) are satisfied; they are harmed to the extent that these desires are frustrated.

(2) *The experience model.* Human beings are benefited to the extent that they are brought to have experiences that they like or find agreeable; they are harmed to the extent that they are brought to have experiences that they dislike or find disagreeable.

We need not worry at this stage whether one of these models is more satisfactory than the other. On both models benefits and harms for particular persons are interpreted in terms of the psychological states of those persons, in terms, that is, of their interests or welfare. Such states are possibly only for beings who are conscious or sentient. Thus, if morality has to do with the promotion and protection of interests or welfare, morality can concern itself only with beings who are conscious or sentient.[4] No other beings can be beneficiaries or victims *in the morally relevant way.* Goodpaster is not mistaken in suggesting that nonsentient beings can be benefited and harmed. But he is mistaken in suggesting that morality has to do with benefits and harms as such, rather than with a particular category of them. And that can be seen the more clearly when we realize that the broadest capacity to be benefited and harmed extends not only out to but beyond the frontier of life. Leaving my lawn mower out in the rain is bad for the mower, pulling weeds is bad for the weeds, and swatting mosquitoes is bad for the mosquitoes; but there are no moral dimensions to any of these acts unless the interests or welfare of some sentient creature is at stake. Morality requires the existence of sentience in order to obtain a purchase on our actions.

The failure of Goodpaster's view has thus given us some reason to look into sentience as a criterion of moral standing. Before considering this possibility directly, it will be helpful to turn to the much narrower criterion of rationality.[5] The rational/nonrational boundary is more difficult to locate with certainty than the animate/inanimate boundary, since rationality (or intelligence) embraces a number of distinct but related capacities for thought, memory, foresight, language, self-consciousness, objectivity, planning, reasoning, judgment, deliberation, and the like.[6] It is perhaps possible for a being to possess some of these capacities and entirely lack others, but for simplicity we will assume that the higher-order cognitive processes are typically owned as a bundle. The bundle is possessed to one extent or another by normal adult human beings, by adolescents and older children, by persons suffering from the milder cognitive disorders, and by some other animal species (some primates and cetaceans for example). It is not possessed to any appreciable extent by fetuses and infants, by the severely retarded or disordered, by the irreversibly comatose, and by most other animal species. To base moral standing on rationality is thus to deny it alike to most non-human beings and to many human beings. Since the implications for fetuses and infants have already been examined, they will be ignored in the present discussion. Instead we will focus on why one might settle on rationality as a criterion in the first place.

That rationality is sufficient for moral standing is not controversial (though there are some interesting questions to be explored here about forms of artificial intelligence). As a necessary condition, however, rationality will exclude a good many sentient beings—just how many, and which ones, to be determined by the kind and the stringency of the standards employed. Many will find objectionable this constriction of the sphere of moral concern. Because moral standing has been defined in terms of the right to life, to lack moral standing is not necessarily to lack all rights. Thus one could hold that, although we have no duty to (nonrational) animals to respect their lives, we do have a duty to them not to cause them suffering. For the right not to suffer, one might choose a different (and broader) criterion—sentience, for example. (However, if this is the criterion appropriate for that right, why is it not also the criterion appropriate for the right to life?) But even if we focus strictly on the (painless) killing of animals, the implications of the criterion are harsh. Certainly we regularly kill nonhuman animals to satisfy our own needs or desires. But the justification usually offered for these practices is either that the satisfaction of those needs and desires outweighs the costs to the animals (livestock farming, hunting, fishing, trapping, experimentation) or that no decent life would have been available for them anyway (the killing of stray dogs and cats). Although some of these arguments doubtless are rationalizations, their common theme is that the lives of animals do have some weight (however slight) in the moral scales, which is why the practice of killing animals is one that requires

moral justification (raises moral issues). If rationality is the criterion of moral standing, and if (most) nonhuman animals are nonrational, killing such creatures could be morally questionable only when it impinges on the interests of rational beings (as where animals are items of property). In no case could killing an animal be a wrong against it. However callous and chauvinistic the common run of our treatment of animals may be, still the view that killing a dog or a horse is morally no more serious (ceteris paribus) than weeding a garden can be the considered judgment of only a small minority.

The standard we apply to other species we must in consistency apply to our own. The greater the number of animals who are excluded by that standard, the greater the number of human beings who will also be excluded. In the absence of a determinate criterion it is unclear just where the moral line will be drawn on the normal/abnormal spectrum: will a right to life be withheld from mongoloids, psychotics, the autistic, the senile, the profoundly retarded? If so, killing such persons will again be no wrong to them. Needless to say, most such persons (in company with many animals) are sentient and capable to some extent of enjoyable and satisfying lives. To kill them is to deprive them of lives that are of value to them. If such creatures are denied standing, this loss will be entirely discounted in our moral reasoning. Their lack of rationality may ensure that their lives are less full and rich than ours, that they consist of simpler pleasures and more basic enjoyments. But what could be the justification for treating their deaths as though they cost them nothing at all?

There is a tradition, extending back at least to Kant, that attempts just such a justification. One of its modern spokesmen is A. I. Melden (1977), who treats the capacity for moral agency as the criterion of moral standing. This capacity is manifested by participation in a moral community—a set of beings sharing allegiance to moral rules and recognition of one another's integrity. Rights can be attributed only to beings with whom we can have such moral intercourse, thus only to beings who have interests similar to ours, who show concern for the well-being of others, who are capable of uniting in cooperative endeavors, who regulate their activities by a sense of right and wrong, and who display the characteristically moral emotions of indignation, remorse, and guilt. Rationality is a necessary condition (thought not a sufficient one) for possessing this bundle of capacities. Melden believes that of all living creatures known to us only human beings are capable of moral agency.[7] Natural rights, including the right to life, are thus human rights.

We may pass over the obvious difficulty to extending moral standing to all human beings on this basis (including the immature and abnormal) and focus on the question of why the capacity for moral agency should be thought necessary for possession of a right to life. The notion of a moral community to which Melden appeals contains a crucial ambiguity. On the one hand it can be thought of as a community of moral agents—the bearers of moral duties. Clearly to be a member of such a community one must be capable of moral agency. On the other hand a moral community can be thought of as embracing all beings to whom moral agents owe duties—the bearers of moral rights. It cannot simply be assumed that the class of moral agents (duty-bearers) is co-extensive with the class of moral patients (right-bearers). It is quite conceivable that some beings (infants, nonhuman animals) might have rights though they lack duties (because incapable of moral agency). The capacity for moral agency is (trivially) a condition of having moral duties. It is not obviously also a condition of having moral rights. The claim that the criterion for rights is the same as the criterion for duties is substantive and controversial. The necessity of defending this claim is merely concealed by equivocating on the notion of a moral community.

Beings who acknowledge one another as moral agents can also acknowledge that (some) creatures who are not themselves capable of moral agency nonetheless merit (some) protection of life. The more we reflect on the function of rights, the stronger becomes the inclination to extend them to such creatures. Rights are securities for beings who are sufficiency autonomous to conduct their own lives but who are also vulnerable to the aggression of others and dependent upon these others for some of the necessaries of life. Rights protect the goods of their owners and shield them from evils. We ascribe rights to one another because we all alike satisfy these minimal conditions of autonomy, vulnerability, and dependence. In order to satisfy these conditions, a creature need not itself be capable of morality: it need only possess interest that can be protected by rights. A higher standard thus seems appropriate for possession of moral duties than for possession of moral rights. Rationality appears to be the right sort of criterion for the former, but something less demanding (such as sentience) is better suited to the latter.

The moral issues raised by early abortion are precisely those raised by contraception. It is for early abortions that the liberal view is appropriate. Since the fetus at this stage has no right to life, early abortion (like contraception) cannot violate its rights. But if it violates no one's rights, early abortion (like contraception) is a private act. There are of course significant differences between contraception and early abortion, since the former is generally less hazardous, less arduous, and less expensive. A woman has, therefore, good prudential reasons for relying on contraception as her primary means of birth control. But if she elects an early abortion, then, whatever the circumstances and whatever her reasons, she does nothing immoral.

The moral issues raised by late abortion are similar to those raised by infanticide. It is for late abortions (a weakened form of) the conservative view is appropriate. Since the fetus at this stage has a right to life, late abortion (like infanticide) may violate its rights. But if it may violate the fetus' rights, then late abortion (like infanticide) is a public act. There is, however, a morally significant difference between late abortion and infanticide. A fetus is parasitic upon a unique individual in a manner in which a newborn infant is not. That parasitic relation will justify late abortion more liberally than infanticide, for they do not occur under the same circumstances.

Since we have already explored the morality of abortion for those cases in which the fetus has moral standing, the general approach to late abortions is clear enough. Unlike the simple and uniform treatment of early abortion, only a case-by-case analysis will here suffice. We should expect a serious threat to the woman's life or health (physical or mental) to justify abortion, especially if that threat becomes apparent only late in pregnancy. We should also expect a risk of serious fetal deformity to justify abortion, again especially if that risk becomes apparent (as it usually does) only late in pregnancy. On the other hand, it should not be necessary to justify abortion on the ground that pregnancy was not consented to, since a woman will have ample opportunity to seek an abortion before the threshold stage. If a woman freely elects to continue a pregnancy past that stage, she will thereafter need a serious reason to end it.

A differential view of abortion is therefore liberal concerning early abortion and conservative (in an extended sense) concerning late abortion. The status of the borderline cases in the middle weeks of the second trimester is simply indeterminate. We cannot say of them with certainty either that the fetus has a right to life or that it does not. Therefore, we also cannot say either that a liberal approach to these abortions is suitable or that a conservative treatment of them is required. What we can say is that, from the moral point of view, the earlier an abortion is performed the better. There are thus good moral reasons, as well as good prudential ones, for women not to delay their abortions.

A liberal view of early abortion in effect extends a woman's deadline for deciding whether to have a child. If all abortion is immoral, her sovereignty over that decision ends at conception. Given the vicissitudes of contraception, a deadline drawn that early is an enormous practical burden. A deadline in the second trimester allows a woman enough time to discover that she is pregnant and to decide whether to continue the pregnancy. If she chooses not to continue it, her decision violates neither her duties nor any other being's rights. From the point of view of the fetus, the upshot of this treatment of early abortion is that its life is for a period merely probationary; only when it has passed the threshold will that life be accorded protection. If an abortion is elected before the threshold, it is as though from the moral point of view that individual had never existed.

Settling on sentience as a criterion of moral standing thus leads us to a view of the moral status of the fetus, and of the morality of abortion, which satisfies the constraints set out in Section 1. It is gradual, since it locates a threshold stage rather than a point, and allows moral standing to be acquired incrementally. It is differential, since it locates the threshold stage during gestation and thus distinguishes the moral status of newly conceived and full-term fetuses. It is developmental, since it grounds the acquisition of moral standing in one aspect of the normal development of the fetus. And it is moderate, since it distinguishes the moral status of early and late abortions and applies each of the established views to that range of cases for which it is appropriate.

Discussion Questions

1. Present and explain Professor Sumner's main criticisms of the conservative view on abortion. Do you think they are very strong? Why or why not?

2. Present and explain Professor Sumner's main criticisms of the liberal view on abortion. Do they think they are very strong? Why or why not?

3. Explain how Professor Sumner supports his moderate position by combining what he considers the better parts of the liberal and conservative positions. Do you think he succeeds? Why or why not?

4. What role does "sentience" play in Professor Sumner's view? How do you think liberals and conservatives would respond to this moderate view?

Notes

1. Both Tooley (1973) and Warren (1978) allow moral standing to be acquired gradually in the moral course of human development. But since both believe that such standing is only acquired after birth, neither attributes any importance to prenatal development—except as the groundwork of postnatal development.

2. These are my terms; Goodpaster distinguishes between a criterion of moral considerability and a criterion of moral significance (p. 311). It is odd that when Goodpaster addresses the practical problems created by treating life as an inclusion criterion (p. 324) he does not appeal to the inclusion/comparison distinction. Instead he invokes the quite different distinction between its being reasonable to attribute standing to a creature and its being (psychologically and causally) possible to act on that attribution. One would have thought the question is not what we can bring ourselves to do but what we *ought* to bring ourselves to do, and that the inclusion/comparison distinction is precisely designed to help us answer this question.

3. Tom Regan (1976), who argues that moral standing should be distributed on the basis of possession of a good (or the capacity to be benefited and harmed), explicitly accepts the implication that inanimate things may have standing. Regan sometimes fails to distinguish between "*x* has a good (can be benefited and harmed)" and "the existence of *x* is good (has intrinsic value)." Thus his apparent endorsement of both an intrinsic value and a benefit/harm criterion.

4. Goodpaster (1978) does not shrink from attributing interests to nonsentient organisms, and Regan (1976) does not shrink from attributing interests to both nonsentient organisms and artifacts. Both authors assume that if a being has needs, a good, and a capacity to be benefited and harmed, then that being has interests. There is much support for this assumption in the dictionary definitions of both "interest" and "welfare," though talk of protecting the interests or welfare of plants or machines seems contrived and strained. But philosophers and economists have evolved technical definitions of "interest" and "welfare" that clearly tie these notions to the psychological states of sentient beings. It is the existence of beings with interests or welfare *in this sense* that is a necessary condition of existence of moral issues.

5. Rationality is the basis of Kant's well-known distinction between persons (ends in themselves) and mere beings (means). It is also advanced as a criterion by Tooley (1973), Donagan (1977), and Warren (1978).

6. Possession of a capacity at a given time does not entail that the capacity is being manifested or displayed at that time. A person does not lose the capacity to use language, for instance, in virtue of remaining silent or being asleep. The capacity remains as long as the appropriate performance could be elicited by the appropriate stimuli. It is lost only when this performance can no longer be evoked (as when the person has become catatonic or comatose). Basing moral standing on the possession of some capacity or set of capacities does not therefore entail silly results, such as that persons lose their rights when they fall asleep. This applies of course, not only to rationality but also to other capacities, such as sentience.

7. Whether or not this is so will depend on how strong the conditions of moral agency are. Certainly many nonhuman species display altruism, if we mean by this a concern for the well-being of conspecifics and a willingness to accept personal sacrifices for their good. On p. 199 Melden enumerates a number of features of our lives that are to serve as the basis of our possession of rights; virtually all mammals display all of these features.

Works Cited

Donagan, Alan
1977   *The Theory of Morality.* Chicago and London: University of Chicago Press.

Melden, A. I.
1977   *Rights and Persons.* Oxford: Basil Blackwell.

Goodpaster, Kenneth E.
1978   "On Being Morally Considerable," *Journal of Philosophy* 75, 6 (June).

Regan, Tom
1976   "Feinberg on What Sorts of Beings Can Have Rights," *Southern Journal of Philosophy* 14, 4 (Winter).

Tooley, Michael
1973   "A Defense of Abortion and Infanticide," in Joel Feinberg, ed., *The Problem of Abortion.* Belmont, Calif: Wadsworth Publishing Company.

Warren, Mary Anne
1978   "On the Moral and Legal Status of Abortion," in Tom L. Beauchamp and LeRoy Walters, eds., *Contemporary Issues in Bioethics.* Encino and Belmont, Calif.: Dickenson Publishing Company, Inc.

SECTION B

Euthanasia

Introduction

The Hippocratic Oath, a minority viewpoint at the time of its origin in the 4th century B.C., would later become the guiding ethical light of Western medicine for nearly 20 centuries. One section of it, which deals with physician-assisted suicide and euthanasia, reads:

> I will not give poison to anyone though asked to do so, nor will I suggest such a plan. . . . But in purity and in holiness I will guard my life and my art.[1]

But within recent years there has come a serious challenge to the Hippocratic tradition. There are a number of reasons for this challenge. Some scholars say it is because there has been a philosophical shift in Western medicine from the Judeo-Christian view that human life is a gift of God and thus inherently sacred (which is consistent with the Hippocratic Oath, though it preceded Christianity by nearly 400 years) to a more secular view that sees the physician as the facilitator of the patient's autonomous choices (which may include physician-assisted suicide) based on the patient's own personal religious and philosophical views.[2]

Other scholars, though not entirely in disagreement with this assessment, see the rise of advanced medical technologies, especially those used to sustain life almost indefinitely, as making the greatest contribution to the waning influence of the Hippocratic Oath:

> People can be kept alive against their wishes or in states of pain and other forms of suffering, such as loss of control, fatigue, depression, hopelessness. It is also possible to keep people alive who are in a coma or a persistent vegetative state. . . . In cases like these, the use of medical technologies raises questions about the moral appropriateness of death.[3]

Involved in such cases are the following major life-sustaining interventions:

1. Cardiopulmonary resuscitation (CPR): This refers to a range of interventions that restore heartbeat and maintain blood flow and breathing following a cardiac or respiratory arrest, for example, mouth-to-mouth resuscitation and electric shock to restore the heart to its normal pacing.
2. Mechanical ventilation: The use of a machine to assist in breathing and in regulating the exchange of gases in the blood.
3. Renal dialysis: An artificial method of sustaining the chemical balance of the blood when the kidneys have failed.
4. Antibiotics: Any of a number of drugs used to protect a patient from various types of life-threatening infections.
5. Nutritional support and hydration: This refers to artificial methods of providing nourishment and fluids. This usually involves the insertion of a feeding tube that delivers nutrition directly into the bloodstream. . . .[4]

The traditional view, consistent with the Hippocratic Oath, maintains that it is always morally wrong to kill an innocent human being, but that sometimes it is morally permissible to allow a patient to die by withdrawing or withholding treatment (*withdrawing treatment* is ending treatment that has already begun; *withholding treatment* is not beginning the treatment at all). Recently a more radical view, espoused by groups such as the Hemlock Society and the Society for the Right to Die, has made some headway with the medical profession as well as the general public. This view maintains that physician-assisted suicide for terminally ill patients is morally justified. The controversial actions of physician Dr. Jack Kevorkian have forced a number of us to grapple with this view.

On June 4, 1990, Dr. Kevorkian, a Michigan pathologist, made headlines nationwide with the use of his "suicide machine" on a 54-year-old Oregon woman, Janet Adkins. Janet, who had been diagnosed with Alzheimer's disease a year earlier, had begun to experience the symptoms of the disease three years prior to her death. Alzheimer's disease is an irreversible degeneration of brain cells that can result in dementia, chronic and increasing memory loss, and death. In a 1968 Volkswagen van, Dr. Kevorkian attached Janet to his machine, which consisted of three bottles and an intravenous tube. When the button was pushed, the contents of each bottle was released into Janet. One bottle held saline solution, the second induced sleep and contained thiopental sodium, and the last held potassium chloride, which caused her heart to stop beating.

Calling his practice "medicide,"[5] Dr. Kevorkian engaged in a form of euthanasia that is rarely, if ever, approved by medical ethicists. Nevertheless, his actions have brought to the forefront the moral question of whether euthanasia of any sort is ever justified. The word *euthanasia* comes from two Greek words, *eu* and *thanatos*, which translated literally means "good death" or "happy death." Today euthanasia is defined as an act that brings about the death of a terminally ill person who is either suffering tremendously or near death. Death is brought about either by actively causing the patient's death, such as giving a lethal injection or removing oxygen from the patient's room, or by passively causing the patient's death, such as withdrawing or withholding treatment that is perceived as useless. The former is known as *active euthanasia*, the latter as *passive euthanasia*. In passive euthanasia the *intent* is not to kill but simply to relieve the patient of an unnecessary burden and to permit nature to take its course.

In decisions concerning the withdrawing or withholding of treatment, many ethicists argue that intentions are integral in judging the morality of the act. For example, if a man receiving chemotherapy that will extend his life only a few months chooses to withdraw treatment for the sake of not undergoing the physical pain, then he has chosen passive euthanasia, for his intention is not to die but to relieve pain (with the help of painkillers when the cancer gets more severe), although the decision to withdraw treatment will most certainly hasten death. On the other hand, suppose another man in a similar situation requests a lethal injection in addition to withdrawal of treatment. In this case, he has chosen death, and hence has chosen active euthanasia, for he intends to end his life prematurely rather than merely to relieve pain.

The difference between the first man and the second man is a difference between choosing life without pain (although the cancer will eventually kill the first man) and choosing death (i.e., it is the lethal injection and *not* the cancer that kills the second man). Although not all so-called cases of passive and active euthanasia are as clear-cut, the above clearly shows to most people's satisfaction that there is a fundamental moral difference between passive and active euthanasia.

The view of the American Medical Association (AMA) is based on this distinction. Consider the statement endorsed by the AMA's house of delegates on December 4, 1973:

> The intentional termination of life of one human being by another—mercy killing—is contrary to that for which the medical profession stands and is contrary to the policy of the American Medical Association.

The cessation of the employment of extraordinary means to prolong the life of the body when there is irrefutable evidence that biological death is imminent is the decision of the patient and/or his immediate family. The advice and judgment of the physician should be freely available to the patient and/or his immediate family.[6]

In 1982 the AMA's judicial council endorsed the following guidelines, which differ slightly from and are more detailed than the 1973 statement on euthanasia:

In the making of decisions for the treatment of seriously deformed newborns or persons who are severely deteriorated victims of injury, illness or advanced age, the primary consideration should be what is best for the individual patient and not the avoidance of a burden to the family or to society. Quality of life is a factor to be considered in determining what is best for the individual. Life should be cherished despite disabilities and handicaps, except when prolongation would be inhumane and unconscionable. Under these circumstances, withholding or removing life supporting means is ethical provided that the normal care given an individual who is ill is not discontinued. The social commitment of the physician is to prolong life and relieve suffering. Where the observance of one conflicts with the other, the physician, patient, and/or family of the patient have discretion to resolve the conflict.

For humane reasons, with informed consent a physician may do what is medically necessary to alleviate severe pain, or cease or omit treatment to let a terminally ill patient die, but should not intentionally cause death. In determining whether the administration of potentially life-prolonging medical treatment is in the best interest of the patient, the physician should consider what the possibility is for extending life under humane and comfortable conditions and what are the wishes and attitudes of the family or those who have responsibility for the custody of the patient.

Where a terminally ill patient's coma is beyond doubt irreversible and there are adequate safeguards to confirm the accuracy of the diagnosis, all means of life support may be discontinued. If death does not occur when life support systems are discontinued, the comfort and dignity of the patient should be maintained.[7]

Philosopher James Rachels disagrees with both the 1973 and 1982 statements. In Chapter 22 below, Rachels argues that there is no difference between active and passive euthanasia. He also argues that what makes life worth living is not merely biological life, but biographical life (one's hopes, life experiences, dreams, pursuits, interests, etc.). Thus, if one's biographical life has ended, we have no right to prevent a person from ending his or her biological life. J. P. Moreland responds to Rachels in Chapter 23 by defending the active/passive distinction as well as arguing that human beings are more than mere biological entities.

Ethicists who accept the passive/active distinction see each type of euthanasia as being either voluntary, involuntary, or nonvoluntary. *Voluntary* euthanasia occurs when a fully informed competent patient freely *consents* either to withdraw/withhold treatment (passive euthanasia) or to actively hasten death by any number of means, such as a lethal injection (active euthanasia). Euthanasia is *involuntary* when it is forced upon a patient (whether it is passive or active) *against* his or her request not to be euthanized. *Nonvoluntary* euthanasia, which can be either active or passive, is performed on a patient *without* but not against his request not to be euthanized. For example, a PVS (persistent vegetative state) patient is taken off life support by her physician even though the physician was given no prior indication by the patient of what her wishes concerning the withdrawing/withholding of treatment might be, such as through a living will. Hence, there are six types of euthanasia: (1) voluntary active euthanasia; (2) voluntary passive euthanasia; (3) nonvoluntary passive euthanasia; (4) nonvoluntary active euthanasia; (5) involuntary passive euthanasia; and (6) involuntary active euthanasia. Although types (1) and (2) are frequently defended by medical ethicists in the United States, with (2) being the only type supported by the AMA, it is difficult to find many proponents of types (3) and (4). Types (5) and (6) are associated by most people with the Nazi euthanasia programs.

Part 1 of this section ("The Law and Euthanasia") contains three contributions. The first (Chapter 19), by Victor Rosenblum and Clark Forsythe, is a brief legal history and critique of the right to assisted suicide. The other two contributions (Chapters 20 and 21) are abridged opinions in the court cases of Karen Ann Quinlan (New Jersey Supreme Court) and Nancy Cruzan (U.S. Supreme Court). In addition to the essays by Rachels and Moreland, Part 2 of this section ("Morality of Euthanasia") contains two other articles. The first (Chapter 24), written by physician Timothy Quill, originally appeared in 1991 in *The New England Journal of Medicine*. In this piece Dr. Quill defends his decision to give a patient diagnosed with leukemia a prescription for barbiturates, though knowing full well that she would commit suicide by taking an overdose in order to avoid dying of leukemia. In response to Dr. Quill (Chapter 25), psychiatrist Patricia Wesley argues that Dr. Quill's use of euphemisms in telling his story avoids confronting the important issue of physician responsibility to a despondent patient who is most likely suffering from clinical depression.

Notes

1. As quoted in Nigel M. DeS. Cameron, *The New Medicine: Life and Death after Hippocrates* (Wheaton, Ill.: Crossway Books, 1991), 25.

2. See Cameron in *The New Medicine* and Stanley Hauerwaus, *Suffering Presence: Theological Reflections on Medicine, the Mentally Handicapped, and the Church* (Notre Dame, Ind.: University of Notre Dame Press, 1986).

3. J. P. Moreland and Norman L. Geisler, *The Life and Death Debate: Moral Issues of Our Time* (New York: Praeger, 1990), 63.

4. This list is from Ibid., 63–64.

5. Jack Kevorkian, *Prescription: Medicide—The Goodness of Planned Death* (Buffalo, N.Y.: Prometheus Books, 1991).

6. As quoted in James Rachels, "Active and Passive Euthanasia," in *Ethical Theory and Social Issues: Historical Texts and Contemporary Readings*, ed. David Theo Goldberg (New York: Holt, Rinehart and Winston, 1989), 411–412.

7. From selections from "Opinions of the Judicial Council of the American Medical Association," John Burkhart, chairman, American Medical Association, Chicago (1982) at 9–10, as published in the President's Commission for the Study of Ethical Problems in Medicine and Biomedical and Behavioral Research, *Deciding to Forgo Life-Sustaining Treatment: A Report on the Ethical, Medical and Legal Issues of Treatment Decisions* (Washington, D.C.: GPO, 1983), 299–300.

For Further Reading

Nigel M. de S. Cameron, *The New Medicine: Life and Death after Hippocrates* (Wheaton, Ill.: Crossway, 1991).

Dennis J. Horan and David Mall, eds., *Death, Dying and Euthanasia* (Frederick, Md.: University Publications of America, 1980).

Jack Kevorkian, *Prescription: Medicide—The Goodness of Planned Death* (Buffalo, N.Y.: Prometheus Books, 1991).

J. P. Moreland and Norman L. Geisler, *The Life and Death Debate: Moral Issues of Our Time* (New York: Greenwood, 1990), Chapter 2.

President's Commission for the Study of Ethical Problems in Medicine and Biomedical and Behavioral Research, *Deciding to Forgo Life-Sustaining Treatment* (Washington, D.C.: GPO, 1983).

James Rachels, *The End of Life* (Oxford: Oxford University Press, 1986).

Paul Ramsey, *The Patient as Person* (New Haven, Conn.: Yale University Press, 1970).

David Schiedermayer, *Putting the Soul Back in Medicine: Reflections on Compassion and Ethics* (Grand Rapids, Mich.: Baker, 1994).

Sidney H. Wanzer, et al., "The Physician's Responsibility toward Hopelessly Ill Patients," *New England Journal of Medicine* 310 (1984): 955–959.

Robert Wennberg, *Terminal Choices: Euthanasia, Suicide, and the Right to Die* (Grand Rapids, Mich.: Eerdmans, 1989).

The Law and Euthanasia

19

The Right to Assisted Suicide: Protection of Autonomy or an Open Door to Social Killing?

Victor Rosenblum
Clark Forsythe

Victor G. Rosenblum is Nathaniel L. Nathanson Professor of Law, Northwestern University, Chicago. He served as counsel for intervening defendants in U.S. Supreme Court abortion funding cases, *Harris v. McRae* and *Williams v. Zbaraz*. Clark D. Forsythe is General Counsel, Americans United for Life Legal Defense Fund. Both Rosenblum and Forsythe have contributed to a number of law reviews and scholarly journals in the area of bioethics.

In this essay Professor Rosenblum and Mr. Forsythe present a brief overview of Anglo-American legal history on the right to suicide and euthanasia from the common law to the late 1980s. They conclude that "the current campaign for the legalization of assisted suicide runs directly counter to the long history of Anglo-American law." They argue that this was grounded directly in the common law's advocacy to protect vulnerable persons—including the mentally incompetent and older persons—through the criminal law. Citing the work of Cyril Means—a defender of abortion rights who concluded that "throughout its long history, the common law has always set its face against suicide"—Professor Rosenblum and Mr. Forsythe maintain that although the common law has supported a patient's right to refuse treatment (passive euthanasia), it has not supported a so-called right to die (active euthanasia). They also note a contemporary transition in the courts and in proposed legislation toward being more open to physician-assisted suicide. They take a strong stand against what they believe is a dangerous transition, maintaining that the legal basis (the right to privacy and/or the right to personal autonomy) for this is flawed and that there are a number of undesirable legal implications that will most likely result if a right to assisted suicide becomes the law of the land.

The status of assisted suicide as public policy in the United States is admittedly in a state of turmoil. This turmoil is reminiscent of the legal status of abortion in the few years preceding the Supreme Court's 1973 decision in *Roe v. Wade*. The parallel may be indicative of the future direction of law and public policy regarding suicide.

The call for legalized suicide has been increasing in several quarters, most loudly, of course, from suicide advocacy organizations like the Hemlock Society, the Society for the Right to Die, and Americans Against Human Suffering. Some have suggested that "the subject of assisted suicide deserves wide and open discussion."[1]

The Society for the Right to Die scored a publication victory earlier this year with the article "The Physician's Responsibility Toward Hopelessly Ill Patients" in the *New England Journal of Medicine*. The article supports assisted suicide for the "rational" patient who is hopelessly ill, dying, or in the end stages of an incurable disease. This article is merely one of many published in recent years that is sympathetic to active euthanasia or suicide.

At the same time, the attitude of Americans toward assisted suicide seems to be ambivalent. An

---

Reprinted with permission from *Issues in Law and Medicine* 6 (Summer 1990). Endnotes have been edited.

Associated Press–Media General poll in February 1985 reportedly found that 68% of the respondents believed that incurable patients ought to be permitted to end their lives by active means.

Conflicting legal decisions have added to the confusion. Cases such as those of Gary Weidner, Peter Rosier, Elizabeth Bouvia, and Roswell Gilbert are not based on identical premises and do not reach mutually reconcilable conclusions.

The rising incidence of suicide contributes to this turmoil. Suicide has been described as an "epidemic" in America in the 1980s. In 1985, 28,500 Americans committed suicide, making suicide the nation's eighth leading cause of death. Three years ago, the Metropolitan Life Insurance Company published a report that concluded that suicides among adolescents under age fifteen were hitting record numbers. At the same time, the suicide rate for older Americans is almost 50% above the rate for the general population and rising. Between 1948 and 1981, the suicide rate for older persons dropped from 28.1 to 17.1 per 100,000. But in the past several years, the rate has again risen, from 18.3 in 1982 to 19.2 in 1983 to 21.6 in 1986. In addition, it is generally believed that official suicide statistics underestimate the true rate of suicide.

All of these factors are converging to affect public opinion, to challenge the traditional opposition to suicide in Anglo-American law, medicine, and culture, and, potentially, to reshape public policy.

The Common Law and Assisted Suicide

The current campaign for the legalization of assisted suicide runs directly counter to the long history of Anglo-American common law. The traditional rejection of suicide in Anglo-American culture has been grounded in the common law's solicitousness toward vulnerable persons—including older persons, and persons who are mentally incompetent—through the criminal law. The treatment of vulnerable or incompetent persons by third parties has long been scrutinized through the law of guardians and wards. The Illinois guardianship statute commands: "Guardianship shall be utilized only as is necessary to promote the well-being of the disabled person, to protect him from neglect, exploitation, or abuse, and to encourage development of his maximum self-reliance and independence." Guardians have long been charged with the care of their wards and can be li-

able for negligent homicide if their wards die through their neglect. This includes neglecting to feed a disabled or incompetent ward.

Suicide, a felony at common law, was regarded as "self-murder." Cyril Means, among others, has concluded upon examination of its history at common law that suicide is not protected as a constitutional right: "Throughout its long history, the common law has always set its face against suicide. . . ."[2] The difficulty of penalizing the successful perpetrator was at the foundation of American law's failure to penalize suicide. However, even where the states failed to penalize suicide, many states penalized those who assisted suicide.

Did emergence of the right to privacy have any bearing on suicide? What is today called the right to privacy had its early development in the Brandeis-Warren *Harvard Law Review* article of 1890. In its original formulation, the Brandeis-Warren right to privacy was a right to informational family privacy. Viewed in the context of its relationship to the laws of homicide and suicide, the right to privacy did not encompass a right to suicide or to be free from interventions to prevent suicide.

The common law has protected a right to refuse medical treatment.[3] The so-called right to die is an unfortunate and inaccurate misnomer of very recent origin. As a phrase in increasingly common use, however, it reflects the abandonment of the traditional right to refuse medical treatment. That right of refusal connoted the right—not to seek death—but to avoid the imposition of a medical treatment that is simultaneously burdensome or painful and ineffective in averting imminent and inevitable death from a terminal illness. To transmute a right to refuse medical treatment into a "right to die," however, switches the focus from the burden of nonbeneficial medical treatment to the desire for death itself.

In applying the traditional right to refuse medical treatment, courts attempted to distinguish between ordinary and extraordinary medical treatment.[4] Some courts have failed to understand the distinction between extraordinary and ordinary treatment and have fostered the erroneous notion that the distinction relates to the frequency or novelty of the particular medical treatment. Rather the extraordinary/ordinary distinction has always been related to the *benefit* and *burden* of the particular treatment to the patient in the particular circumstances:

> Ordinary means are all medicines, treatments, and operations, which offer a reasonable hope of ben-

efit and which can be obtained and used without excessive expense, pain, or other inconvenience.

Extraordinary means are all medicines, treatments, and operations, which cannot be obtained or used without excessive expense, pain, or other inconvenience, or which if used, would not offer a reasonable hope of benefit.[5]

This balancing between the benefits and burdens of treatment inheres in traditional medical ethics and in the day to day practice of the clinician.

Maintenance of the distinction between ordinary and extraordinary treatment is essential to prevent the burgeoning of euthanasia and suicide. If, for example, the treatment will in fact entail excessive expense or pain *and* there is no reasonable hope of benefit, then the patient is not committing suicide but is merely acquiescing in imminent and inevitable death by avoiding a painful and nonbeneficial treatment. However, if the treatment involves no excessive pain, and a reasonable hope of benefit from the particular treatment exists, then the patient, in refusing the treatment, may rightly be seen as intending to cause death.

This distinction also highlights and preserves the physician's ethical duty. For moral agents, "ought" assumes "can." A physician is not obliged to do what he cannot do. If the treatment is truly "extraordinary," then the physician is not required to provide it, since the burden was excessive while there was no reasonable hope of benefit from it.

The earlier decisions in the development of the right to refuse medical treatment fostered this distinction. They eschewed quality of life criteria[6] and were resolvable under common law principles without resort to constitutional analysis.[7] In the 1980 *Eichner* decision, for example, the New York Supreme Court, Appellate Division, emphasized that the case involved the right of a *terminally ill* patient in a *comatose* state to refuse *extraordinary* medical treatment when he is *imminently dying*. After carefully defining the difference between "extraordinary" and "ordinary" treatment, the Appellate Division proceeded to use the term "extraordinary" treatment to define the right at issue no less than eight times. Likewise, the court emphasized that the right at stake was the right of those who are "terminally ill." More than once, the court emphasized that these were "[t]he necessary medical criteria for the activation of the patient's right . . . [t]he State's interest in protecting the sanctity of life will tolerate no less stringent medical standard than this. . . ." In summarizing New York law, the court stated: "[T]here seems to be no public policy

against permitting a terminally ill patient to choose not to delay the inevitable and imminent termination of his life. . . ." On appeal the New York Court of Appeals further narrowed the grounds for the *Eichner* decision, relying on common law, and declined to adopt the constitutional right of privacy rationale proffered by the Appellate Division.

Similarly, in *Storar*, the New York Court of Appeals held that blood transfusions could properly be continued to a patient with terminal cancer of the bladder, even though the patient found the transfusions "disagreeable."

> [T]he evidence convincingly shows that the transfusions did not involve excessive pain and that without them his mental and physical abilities would not be maintained at the usual level. With the transfusions, on the other hand, he was essentially the same as he was before except of course he had a fatal illness which would ultimately claim his life. Thus, on the record, we have concluded that the application for permission to continue the transfusions should have been granted . . . a court should not in the circumstances of this case allow an incompetent patient to bleed to death because someone, even someone as close as a parent or sibling, feels that this is best for one with an incurable disease.

In *Storar* the court of appeals recognized the distinction that must be drawn between invasive medical treatments, which are directed at pathologies, and ancillary forms of care that may be necessary to prevent the death of a patient. The court explicitly concluded that the "transfusions were *analogous to food*—they would not cure the cancer, but they could eliminate the risk of death from another treatable cause. With this analysis, the court recognized that the food could not be withdrawn on the premise that it would not cure the cancer—since that was not its intended function—but that the food would be effective in its essential function—sustaining the patient.

In *Quinlan* the New Jersey Supreme Court, addressing the issue of withdrawal of a respirator recognized "a real distinction between the self-infliction of deadly harm and a self-determination against artificial life support or radical surgery, for instance, in the face of irreversible, painful, and certain imminent death." The court distinguished between "extraordinary" and "ordinary" treatment.

In more recent years, the "treatment" at issue has been assisted feeding. The traditional view that food and water are not medical treatment was emphasized by the New Jersey Appellate Court in *Conroy:*

> The nasogastric tube was no more than a simple device which was part of Conroy's routine nursing care. It was not really 'medical treatment' at all.... Nourishment does not itself cure disease. Neither is it an artificial life-sustaining device. Rather it is a basic necessity of life whose withdrawal causes death and whose provision permits life to continue until the patient dies of his illness or injury.

It was only with the New Jersey Supreme Court's 1985 opinion in *Conroy* that New Jersey law abandoned the distinction between extraordinary and ordinary treatment and between food and water and medical treatment. The supreme court essentially said that the resistance to treating food and water as treatment is based merely on the "emotional symbolism" of food. As Daniel Callahan once wrote:

> There is reason enough to explain a spontaneous revulsion at the thought of cutting off food and water. We are being asked to do something that goes against our deepest social and moral instincts; that is why its importance is often called symbolic. Some issues are important because they are symbolic. Others are symbolic because they are important. I believe that is the case here.[8]

The so-called "symbolism" of feeding Mrs. Conroy derived from the importance of that act in meeting the fundamental moral and legal obligations of society and medicine to disabled persons.

Even if the contention is accepted that administering food and water should be redefined as "medical treatment," application of the extraordinary/ordinary distinction leaves food and water in the category of ordinary care. The provision of food and fluids generally does not involve undue expense or pain, and there is, generally, a reasonable hope that food and fluids will accomplish their natural and intended function—sustenance. Indeed, that is why the recent cases have been brought; the food and fluids have successfully sustained the patient. In virtually all of the recent food and fluid cases, there is little or no evidence that providing food and fluids to the patient will impose a physical or psychological burden to the patient. And the expense of sustaining these patients in secondary facilities is commensurate with sustaining competent, older patients at the same facilities. Withdrawing assisted feeding from incompetent patients on the basis of the expense would apply to many other incompetent patients with less extensive disabilities.

Accordingly, the common law's rejection of suicide on any grounds demonstrates that the common law has not protected the unfettered autonomy that serves as the rationale for the recent campaign for legalized suicide. The common law's solicitous protection of vulnerable patients reveals its protection for the sanctity of human life at all stages and its respect for the dignity of human life without regard to physical condition. And its regulation of guardians reflects the law's recognition that vulnerable patients need to be protected from the emotional, financial, or psychological burdens that often affect the persons to whose care they have been entrusted.

Recent Case Law and Assisted Suicide

If one were to look strictly at the state statutes presently on the books, it would not seem that the prospects for the legalization of assisted suicide in the near future are very good. At least twenty-six states by statute expressly prohibit the assistance of suicide. Moreover, living will statutes have been enacted in at least forty states, including Washington, D.C., but the statutes in no less than ten states, including Washington, D.C., expressly repudiate suicide and euthanasia, albeit with no penalties. No states expressly legalize suicide through either legislation or constitution.

This survey of legislation may be misleading, however. The introduction of assisted suicide into American law will more likely come through current judicial trends in the nontreatment of incompetent patients than through explicit legislative acceptance. There is an evident and increasing tension in judicial decisions of the past four years signaling efforts to transmute the right to refuse medical treatment into the "right to die." By abandoning the distinction between extraordinary and ordinary treatment, the focus of judicial inquiry has shifted from objective standards for evaluating the benefits and burdens of a treatment to the patient's subjective, allegedly autonomous desire for death. The judicial acceptance of assisted suicide may well be the logical development of the combination of judicial authorization for so-called substituted judgment and the withdrawal of life-sustaining food and fluids from patients who are profoundly disabled but neither terminally ill nor imminently dying.

Only the California Court of Appeals in the *Bouvia* case has gone so far as to permit suicide—

through the refusal of food and fluids—by a *competent*, nonterminally ill patient. But the *Bouvia* court opinion lends itself to emulation. The court held in *Bouvia* that a competent patient with cerebral palsy and quadriplegia—who was neither terminally ill nor imminently dying—had a right to refuse food and fluids through a nasogastric tube in order to bring about her death. The court denied any interest in preserving the life of a patient in the condition of Elizabeth Bouvia:

> We do not believe it is the policy of this State that all and every life must be preserved against the will of the sufferer. It is incongruous, if not monstrous, for medical practitioners to assert their right to preserve a life that someone else must live, or, more accurately, endure for '15 to 20 years.' We cannot conceive it to be the policy of this State to inflict such an ordeal upon anyone. It is, therefore, immaterial that the removal of the nasogastric tube will hasten or cause Bouvia's eventual death.

Justice Compton's concurring opinion more explicitly supported a right to *assisted* suicide. He concluded that the application of the California statute against assisted suicide to the case of Elizabeth Bouvia was "archaic and inhumane."

> Elizabeth apparently has made a conscious and informed choice that she prefers death to continued existence in her helpless and, to her, intolerable condition. I believe she has an absolute right to effectuate that decision. This state and the medical profession instead of frustrating her desire, should be attempting to relieve her suffering by permitting and in fact assisting her to die with ease and dignity. The fact that she is forced to suffer the ordeal of self-starvation to achieve her objective is in itself inhumane. . . .
>
> The right to die is an integral part of our right to control our own destinies so long as the rights of others are not affected. That right should, in my opinion, include the ability to enlist assistance from others, including the medical profession, in making death as painless and quick as possible.

Although the court of appeals vigorously agreed with the proposition that Bouvia's life was not worth living, at this time Elizabeth apparently has still not given up on herself.

Several courts in recent years have allowed the withdrawal of food and fluids from incompetent patients through substituted judgment.[9] The decision of the New York Supreme Court, Appellate Division,

in *Delio v. Westchester County Medical Center,* is a good example of the method by which courts have abandoned a distinction between extraordinary and ordinary treatment. *Delio* addressed the issue of the withdrawal of food and water through both a gastrostomy and jejunostomy tube from Daniel Delio, an individual in a "persistent" or "chronic vegetative state." The New York trial court denied the withdrawal of nutrition and hydration. The appellate division in *Delio* reversed the trial court, holding that all nutrition and hydration could be withdrawn from Delio. Creating new reasons for the court of appeals' decision in *Storar,* the Appellate Division found that *Storar* did not effectively distinguish food and water from medical treatment nor prevent its withdrawal from an incompetent patient. The court decided that the "primary focus" of *Storar* was "upon the patient's desires and his right to direct the course of his medical treatment rather than upon the specific treatment involved." The court emphasized that courts in other states (e.g., *Matter of Conroy, Brophy v. New England Sinai Hospital*) had found that "the emotional symbolism of food was without meaningful significance" and "refused to distinguish between types of treatment . . . or to base its decision on a distinction between extraordinary or ordinary treatment. . . ."

Based on *Conroy* and *Brophy,* the court concluded that food and water "should be evaluated in the same manner as any other medical procedure." "By parity of reasoning," the court concluded, *Storar* was stare decisis only "for the proposition that the dispositive issue is whether the [patient] demonstrate[s] by clear and convincing evidence that [he] had expressed a desire to discontinue life-prolonging treatment in these circumstances."

The subsequent extension of *Delio* by the same court to the recent case of Mary O'Connor demonstrates how the abandonment of the extraordinary/ordinary distinction inexorably leads down the slippery slope to decisionmaking based primarily on the patient's quality of life. The Appellate Division majority affirmed that clear and convincing evidence established that Mrs. O'Connor "expressed a desire, when she was competent, to exercise her common-law right to refuse all artificial life support systems, which would include nasogastric feeding and intravenous feeding." Ostensibly relying on precedent, the majority held that Mrs. O'Connor had a common-law right to refuse "life-sustaining medical treatment," which could be exercised by surrogates, when she became incompetent, that she expressed a desire while competent to deny all artificial means, that there is no difference between "feeding by artificial means" and any other medical procedures, and that the exercise of Mrs. O'Connor's right should not be "limited by reason of a person's age or medical condition."

Justice Balletta, dissenting, viewed the majority's decision as an unwarranted extension of the *Delio* decision:

> Neither the intravenous nor the nasogastric tube which is inserted in the throat is a highly invasive procedure, nor is Mrs. O'Connor's condition such as to require this court to override the State's interest in preserving human life. Where a non-terminally ill patient is being provided with nutrition in a relatively non-invasive and pain-free manner, the withdrawal of a feeding tube for the purpose of hastening his or her death ignores the legitimate and well-established interest of the State in preserving life and preventing suicide, exposes many members of our society to potential abuse, and should not be sanctioned.

The Maine Supreme Court in the *Gardner* case—citing John Stuart Mill's *On Liberty* and the principle of personal autonomy—allowed the withdrawal of food and fluids on the basis of the patient's prior expressed statements "that he would rather die than be maintained in a persistent vegetative state by artificial means." Thus, for the Maine Supreme Court, when a person is in a persistent vegetative state, there is "no reason" to disregard this desire and to sustain his life because of "the utter helplessness of the permanently comatose person, the wasting of a once strong body, and the submission of the most private bodily functions to the attention of others."

Likewise, the Massachusetts Supreme Court in the *Brophy* case allowed the withdrawal of food and fluids through a gastrostomy tube from a patient found to be in a persistent vegetative state but not terminally ill or imminently dying. There, the court held that the "interest in preserving life is very high when 'human life [can] be saved where the affliction is curable. . . .' That interest wanes when the underlying affliction is incurable and would 'soon cause death regardless of any medical treatment. . . .'"

> [W]e must recognize that the State's interest in life encompasses a broader interest than mere corporeal existence. In certain, thankfully rare, circumstances the burden of maintaining the corporeal existence degrades the very humanity it was meant to serve.

The Washington Supreme Court in the *Grant* case allowed the withdrawal of food and fluids from a patient with Batten's disease, an incurable neurological disorder. This precedent has recently been overturned, however, by the change in the vote of Justice Durham.

Not surprisingly, the abandonment by *Delio* and other recent decisions of the traditional contours of the right to refuse medical treatment, and the consequent permission of the withdrawal of assisted feeding, has been made only over the most vigorous dissent. Dissenting from the 4-3 decision in *Brophy v. New England Sinai Hospital*, in which the majority allowed the withdrawal of nutrition and hydration, Justice Nolan stated that he could "think of nothing more degrading to the human person than the balance which the court struck today in favor of death and against life." "Food and water are basic human needs," he wrote. "They are not medicines and feeding them to a patient is just not medical treatment." Justice Lynch, separately dissenting, charged the majority with "nullifying, if only in part, the law against suicide." "No case in this Commonwealth has ever construed the right to privacy and bodily integrity as more than the right to avoid invasive treatments and certain other bodily invasions under appropriate conditions." Justice O'Connor, separately dissenting, challenged the majority's sanctioning of the use of "substituted judgment" to withdraw food and water and the majority's implicit establishment of a right to suicide and euthanasia.

Dissenting in *In re Gardner*, Justice Clifford, joined by Justices Roberts and Wathen, argued that the 4-3 majority—in allowing a withdrawal of nutrition and hydration—had undervalued the state's "interest in preserving the life of Joseph Gardner as an individual and in preserving life in general." He noted that the majority had failed to properly distinguish between medical treatment and food and water. By allowing the withdrawal of food and water, the majority "ignore[d] the legitimate interest our society has in preventing such decisions from being based on the quality of life" and failed to defer to the Maine legislature's judgment in the Living Will Act that nutrition and hydration were different from medical treatment.

Dissenting in part in *In re Grant* from the court's 5-4 holding allowing nutrition and hydration to be withdrawn, Justice Andersen, joined by Justice Brachtenbach, wrote:

> Call it whatever the majority will, this is pure, unadorned euthanasia. It is a step upon a slippery slope, one that I would not take. If mores have changed to the extent that such conduct can now be sanctioned, I would let that change arrive through the moral judgment of the people as expressed through their duly elected legislators, not by the expedience of judicial fiat.

In separately dissenting, Justice Goodloe, joined by Justice Dore, argued that by authorizing "death by starvation and dehydration" and "passive euthanasia," the majority's decision was "in direct conflict with this court's duty to preserve life." He noted "that the potential for abuse is increased" because the court disregarded the dictates of the state's Natural Death Act, which required that death be imminent before even medical treatment could be withdrawn. By the recent switch in vote by Justice Durham, however, the majority opinion is no longer good law.

The adoption and particular application of the doctrine of substituted judgment in judicial decisions like these may serve to pave the way for the introduction of assisted suicide. Many of the recent cases involving nutrition and hydration have adopted the doctrine of substituted judgment. This has introduced a curious and pernicious fiction into the treatment of vulnerable patients—"a cruel charade," in the words of Massachusetts Justice Joseph Nolan. The doctrine of substituted judgment seeks to give the implementation of the incompetent patient's "right to choose" treatment to a third party, usually a family member or relative.

It must be recognized that a certain form of "substituted judgment" for incompetent patients is unavoidable. Medical personnel and family members must take some form of action toward incompetent patients who have lost the cognitive ability to decide for themselves. By their actions or omissions, they will have to make certain judgments, and these judgments will be "substituted" for the judgments that a competent patient would otherwise have the authority to make.

But while we must recognize that judgments are inevitably substituted for incompetent patients, it is something entirely different to think that third parties are merely implementing or capable of implementing what the patient himself would choose under the particular circumstances of the particular illness. The doctrine of substituted judgment, as formulated in recent years by the courts, is based on the reasoning that the patient's "right to choose" will be "lost" if a third party is not allowed to implement it.

This reasoning ignores what is self-evident in the context of other rights—namely, that the sine qua non of a right to "choose" anything is cognitive ability to choose. In the case of an incompetent patient, an illness—rather than any other person or state actor—has taken that capacity from the patient, and no amount of talk about "saving" that right makes a third party any more able to stand in the patient's shoes under the conditions of the particular case.

The substituted judgment doctrine fails to recognize that a competent patient makes a medical decision with respect to a particular treatment, at a particular time, with relation to how it affects his particular condition. This cannot be truly substituted by reliance on vague, usually remote, statements made by the person at a different time and place, in a different condition, without regard to any particular treatment. This is especially so with statements made in the peak of health. What is clear on a moment's reflection is that people change their minds about treatment, depending on the time and their condition and the treatment.

This is most clearly seen in the recent New York case of Carrie Coons. Judge Joseph Harris of the New York Supreme Court, Trial Division, entered an order on April 4, 1989, allowing a gastrostomy tube to be withdrawn from Mrs. Coons, an eighty-six-year-old patient at Albany Memorial Hospital, diagnosed to be in a "persistent vegetative state," since October 1988, nearly five and a half months. The order directed the hospital to perform "the procedure" if Coons was not transferred. Within days of the order, however, Coons "awoke." The order to withdraw the feeding tube was explained to Coons by Dr. Michael L. Wolff, her physician.

> 'At first she drew back from the question,' Wolff said. Eventually, he said she responded: 'That's a very difficult decision to make. . . .'
>
> . . . Later during the visit at Memorial Hospital in Albany, Wolff said he again brought up the subject of removing the tube and Coons replied, 'I never really thought of it in quite that way,' which Wolff explained meant in the 'context of life and death.'

The order was quickly revoked.

By both depreciating society's compelling interest in the sanctity of human life and in adopting substituted judgment, recent court decisions have laid the groundwork for the ultimate approval of suicide and assisted suicide.

Autonomy, Privacy, and Assisted Suicide

[handwritten annotation: claims that rt to suicide is protected under 5 & 14 Amend]

Beyond recent case law, there have been calls for the legalization of "rational suicide" through legislation. It is claimed that a right to suicide is protected under the liberty clauses of the fifth and fourteenth amendments to the Constitution. Derek Humphry, for example, has claimed that the case for legalized euthanasia and suicide stems from the privacy doctrine of *Roe v. Wade*. Short of constitutional protection, a right to "rational suicide" has been proposed as good public policy based on principles of autonomy and self-determination—the right to control one's body, destiny, and health care.

"Rational suicide" has as many different definitions as there are advocates. A "rational suicide" may be one undertaken by a patient "beyond all help and not merely suffering from a treatable depression of the sort common in people with terminal illnesses," or [i]f there is no treatable component to the depression and the patient's pain or suffering is refractory to treatment, then the wish for suicide may be rational."

Those who currently propose assisted suicide contend that life is only one among a number of goods, including individual autonomy, human dignity, intellectual capability, physical fitness, and other aspects that contribute to personal well-being. Life as a relative good must be compared with other goods, and suicide may become a "rational" choice if life has become "intolerable."

A second, but related, principle that is used to justify suicide is personal autonomy. The push for "patient autonomy" in medical ethics over the past twenty years has spurred the drive for euthanasia and suicide. Suicide is seen as a wholly individual act, a self-direct act, a "victimless crime." Whereas the traditional understanding has been that society has a compelling interest in preserving human life and preventing suicide, proponents of suicide contend that society has no legitimate interest in interfering in an act as personal as "rational" suicide.

The principle of the sanctity of human life, on the other hand, demands that human beings must always be treated as an end in themselves and should never be treated as a means to an end. The sanctity of human life is a paramount value; it is the denial of the sanctity of human life, rather than the denial of individual autonomy by prohibiting suicide, that violates human dignity. Human dignity is violated by failing to treat human beings as ends in themselves, by considering their physical or mental conditions as the measure of the value of their lives. In contrast, human dignity is protected by preserving a person's life, confirming the value of that person's life, and promoting that person's well-being, without regard to the physical or mental condition of the person.

Privacy is clearly a right that the American people cherish and enjoy. But the invocation of privacy or autonomy nearly always begs the question—privacy to do what? Autonomy to do what? More than one hundred years ago, during the Lincoln-Douglas Senate debates of 1858, Abraham Lincoln pointed out the boundaries of autonomy. Lincoln acknowledged that there were differences of opinion on the slavery question, but, to his mind, the "difference of opinion, reduced to its lowest terms, is no other than the difference between the men who think slavery a wrong and those who do not think it wrong."[10] Lincoln pointed out that it was logically impossible for Douglas to say both that slavery was wrong and that the people had a right to have slaves:

> When Judge Douglas says that whoever or whatever community wants slaves, they have a right to have them, he is perfectly logical if there is nothing wrong in the institution; but if you admit that it is wrong, he cannot logically say that any body has a right to do wrong.[11]

There is no "right" to do what is intrinsically wrong, and Anglo-American law and culture have always held suicide to be intrinsically wrong. It must be remembered that the Declaration of Independence refers to the right to life as an "unalienable" right and, thus, a right that cannot be waived or forfeited.

The location of an action alone does not shield the act from moral or legal scrutiny. Private actions are not shielded from scrutiny merely because the acts are committed in the home or between family members. The publicized outcry in recent years over child abuse and spousal abuse makes it clear that the American public understands this, at least in some cases.

The protection of human dignity involves more than simply implementing individual choice, especially when that choice is not really being voiced by the incompetent patient but is being articulated and implemented by a third party, who in many cases is feeling the full brunt of the emotional burden of the vulnerable patient's illness. Unfortunately, recent litigation involving food and fluids, under the guise of protecting "patient autonomy," has merely served to place the imprimatur of the law on the fears of dependence and frailty.

The case of Sidney Greenspan, currently pending before the Illinois Supreme Court, is representative. Mr. Greenspan has been diagnosed as being in a chronic vegetative state without any likely chance of recovery. He was first diagnosed in 1983 as having progressive dementia, which was a result of either Alzheimer's disease or a rare variant thereof, Pick's disease. He suffered a stroke in 1984. Doctors describe Sidney Greenspan as "a very active, dynamic man" who was extremely upset at his loss of memory and who felt useless. There was no testimony that Sidney Greenspan ever commented on the use or withdrawal of assisted feeding. Rather, the claim to withdraw assisted feeding was based on repeated statements that Sidney Greenspan would never want to reside in a nursing home or be placed on life support systems. He reportedly said, "Life is not worth living if you don't have the physical capacity to enjoy it." When he visited friends in a nursing home, he remarked that he never wanted to live that way. He said that he would prefer "to be shot" instead of being placed in a nursing home. His wife testified that he would never have wanted to live as a burden to someone else. Upon the basis of these statements, the Cook County Public Guardian has sought the authority to withdraw life-sustaining food and fluids. The Illinois Supreme Court's decision is expected in the near future. The approval of the withdrawal of assisted feeding teaches the public that fear of dependence and frailty can reasonably be acted upon to end one's life and serves to reinforce the feeling of the disabled persons that they are too much of a burden for family, friends, or society. By supporting such acts, the law teaches that this is true.

The notion of "rational suicide" is also belied by studies that have concluded that the desire for death, even among terminal patients, is the result of a preexisting mental illness and not a product of sober, rational calculation.[12] A general examination of recent suicides reveals that the typical suicide was motivated not by sober rational reasons, but by depression, a state of mind that is present in many older persons. Among the factors that motivate suicide in people of all ages are the same factors that result in depression generally—loss of a job through forced retirement, rapid urbanization and technological change, alcoholism, a universal fear of dependence and frailty, and illness. According to Daniel Plotkin, a geriatric psychiatrist at the University of California at Los Angeles, most suicides among older persons are caused not by terminal illness but by depression. Similarly, adolescent suicide is often a response to depression and feelings of hopelessness.

The call for legalized suicide based on autonomy, then, is not what it seems. The evidence suggests that "patient autonomy" is not truly autonomous.[13] This is most clearly seen in the courts' adoption in recent years of the doctrine of substituted judgment, the "cruel charade," in Justice Nolan's words. Even if we accept this autonomy at face value, it reflects exactly the desire for self-destruction that lies at the basis of the common law's long-held rejection of suicide and its corresponding devotion to the principle of the sanctity of human life. It is an autonomy that calls for the compassionate care and devotion of the physician who is committed to the welfare of his patient, not the destruction of the patient, either self-induced or assisted.

Legal Implications of a Right to Assisted Suicide

The Current Pressure to Introduce Direct Means of Killing

A right to assisted suicide may be a logical development of the current push for the withdrawal of assisted feeding from severely disabled patients. Judicial authorization of the withdrawal of life-sustaining food and fluids from patients who are not terminally ill nor imminently dying will inevitably create pressure in both law and medical practice to journey down the slippery slope toward use of lethal injections to hasten the death of a patient in a more "humane" manner.

By withdrawing nutrition and hydration from a patient who is not terminally ill or imminently dying—and who therefore will not die in the near future from any underlying illness—the physician sets in course an action that will inevitably and directly cause the death of the patient. However, death from starvation will take several days. This death may or may not create pain in the patient and may or may not produce a visible physiological change in the patient. This wait for a certain death that has been purposely induced will inevitably create a new kind of tension on the medical personnel and family. Since death is certain and has been purposely induced, the need for the patient to endure the starvation, and for the family and medical personnel to endure that wait, will be questioned. Those involved will inevitably desire that the time be shortened. If action is being *purposely* taken that will bring about *certain* death, merely waiting for the effect of that action will seem inhumane to patient and family. The pressure will mount for immediate action to end the patient's existence. A quick and easy death through lethal injection will seem more humane.

The pressure on clinical practice will, in turn, have an inevitable spillover in pressure for legal change to allow lethal injections when the patient is not terminally ill or imminently dying but death has been purposely induced through the withdrawal of nutrition and hydration. The law will be seen to be hypocritical if it allows action—the withdrawal of nutrition and hydration—that will purposely and certainly bring about the death of the patient but prohibits "humane" actions, such as lethal injections that merely hasten the direct, certain result that has been purposely set in motion.

If a lethal injection is seen as more humane, the withdrawal of nutrition and hydration will never be initiated. Once a patient is identified as one from whom nutrition and hydration could be withdrawn, a lethal injection will be recommended as a newer, quicker, more humane method of accomplishing the same desired effect. Withdrawing food and fluids will be remembered only as the old way of doing things. Once lethal injection is accepted for these people, its application will sweep as broadly as did the withdrawal of nutrition and hydration to encompass most incompetent patients.

A Fundamental Change in the Role of the Physician from Healer to Killer

The engagement of physicians in the introduction of assisted suicide would place "the very soul of medicine . . . on trial."[14] The fundamental distinction between the physician as healer and the physician as killer would be vaporized; morality would be severed from mortality. As Dr. Willard Gaylin and others have recently written:

[Direct killing] touches medicine at its very moral center; if this moral center collapses, if physicians become killers or are even merely licensed to kill, the profession—and, therewith, each physician—will never again be worthy of trust and respect as healer and comforter and protector of life in all its frailty. For if medicine's power over life may be used equally to heal or to kill, the doctor is no more a moral professional but rather a morally neutered technician.[15]

The Inability to Regulate "Rational Suicide"

The introduction of legalized suicide will induce two further problems: (1) an inability to limit "rational suicide" to "hard cases" and (2) the inability to enforce those limits that are imposed. Two historical scenarios and the current suicide literature provide support for this. First, the abortion parallel. In the 1960s, legalized abortion was proposed for the "hard cases," which were defined in different ways by different people. But, today, few can deny that, however defined, abortion is not limited to the "hard cases." In fact, rape, incest, gross genetic defect, and preservation of the mother's life make up less than 5% of the 1.5 million abortions performed annually in the United States.[16]

Second, in New Jersey in the aftermath of the *Conroy* decision, the ombudsman whose position was established by the state found widespread disregard of the regulations in the law for the withdrawal of food and fluids. Since then, the ombudsman has come under increasing criticism and pressure for intervening to do his assigned job of monitoring the conditions under which treatment is withdrawn. When the original, vital principle against direct killing is sacrificed, intermediate limitations and regulations will come to be viewed as arbitrary and not intellectually sustainable.

The recent article by Wanzer and others in the *New England Journal of Medicine* on "The Physician's Responsibility Toward Hopelessly Ill Patients" remarkably endorses actions traditionally considered irresponsible. The authors seem to concede that "rational suicide" is really born of distress, stating that "only the rare patient should be so distressed that he or she desires to commit suicide."[17] Ten of the twelve authors conclude that it *is* justifiable for the physician to assist suicide when "(1) [t]he doctor, the nurse, the family and the patient . . . have done everything possible to relieve the distress occasioned by a terminal illness, (2) and yet the patient perceives his or her situation as *intolerable* and seeks assistance. . . ."[18] They conclude that "[t]he physician . . . must determine first that the patient is indeed beyond all help and not merely suffering from a treatable depression of the sort common in people with terminal illnesses."[19] And, "[i]f there is no treatable component to the depression and the patient's pain or suffering is refractory to treatment, then the wish for suicide may be rational.[20] Is the author's message here a version of "If you can't beat 'em, join 'em"? If you can't cure the patient's desires, join him in fulfilling his desires? "Rational suicide," like the "hard cases" for abortion, has no secure semantic fence around it to prevent abuse. A 1986 note on "Criminal Liability for Assisting Suicide" in the *Columbia University Law Review* proposed a Model Suicide Assistance Statute that could allow assisted suicide for any "competent adult who was suffering from *permanent physical incapacitation*"—whatever that means. The inability to regulate "rational suicide" will quickly result in an unfettered "right" that is exercised by anyone, for "rational" or irrational motives.

Pressure on Persons with Disabilities to Forgo Care

Current living will and durable power of attorney legislation, along with current litigation involving the withdrawal of nutrition and hydration, have increased emotional, psychological, and social pressure on persons who are medically dependent and disabled to forgo medical care. Many, if not most, of the recent court decisions regarding the withdrawal of food and fluids have relied on vague but telling statements by patients that they would not want to be a burden or dependent on anyone. Patients like Sidney Greenspan, whose case awaits decision by the Illinois Supreme Court, are expressing little more than a universal fear of frailty and dependence. In effect, some courts have been saying, "Your fear is valid. You are a burden, and your desire not to be a burden or dependent is sufficient to justify the withdrawal of food and fluids."

The legalization of assisted suicide will only increase this pressure. If legalized, it will become available, and if available, it will become standard medical care. As standard medical care, it will become a "reasonable" option for anyone, and anyone who declines to take advantage of what is reasonably available to all will be seen as unreasonable.

"Wrongful Living" Suits against Doctors

The treatment of persons with disabilities involves questions of medical ethics that implicate the rights of conscience of medical personnel—doctors and nurses. For the skeptics, this scenario has a very recent antecedent—the aftermath of the legalization of abortion in *Roe v. Wade*. Medical personnel were repeatedly told that the new right to abortion was merely a matter between a doctor and his patient and that no doctors would be required to perform or counsel abortions.

In a few short years, however, wrongful birth and wrongful life causes of action—universally invalid before *Roe v. Wade*—arose in several states.[21] These are suits by parents or children against doctors for money damages for the failure to perform or facilitate—through information or referral—eugenic abortions. These suits are usually based on the reasoning that eugenic abortion is a legal right—a widely available legal option—and performed in the course of medical practice. This reasoning holds that any obstetrician/gynecologist is charged with a duty, at minimum, to inform a woman about her option of eugenic abortion. In approving these suits, the courts have largely ignored the conscience clauses in the majority of states that affirm that there is no duty to participate in abortion.

As in the late 1960s with abortion, current proponents of assisted suicide, like Don Shaw of Hemlock of Illinois, contend that the ethical objections of physicians will be respected. "The rights of physicians who cannot in good conscience perform aid-in-dying are to be fully respected," they say, "providing they in no way obstruct the practice of physicians who in good conscience give such aid."[22] But, if assisted suicide is a legal option, available in medical practice, then a physician could have a duty to inform his ill patient of this "option" for "treatment" as part of the doctrine of informed consent, and suit for what might be called "wrongful living" could result from his failure to do so. These suits have already been entertained in court and discussed in the academic literature.[23]

Application to a Wide Class of Disabled Persons

Another implication of a right to assisted suicide would be its inherent tendency to encompass a wide class of patients who are disabled or medically dependent, as we have seen with the withdrawal of nutrition and hydration. Many of the cases involving the withdrawal of food and fluids have involved patients in what is allegedly a persistent vegetative state (PVS). The courts have often examined this condition as though it established a discrete, distinct criterion that justified the withdrawal of nutrition and hydration.

In fact, the diagnosis of the persistent vegetative state is properly understood as part of a continuum of neurological deficit and interaction with the patient's environment. While PVS is at the extreme end of the neurological continuum, it is similar in physiology and phenomenology to related states such as multi-infarct dementia or other advanced dementing processes.

On this continuum, we can place Mary O'Connor, Dorothy Longeway, Sidney Greenspan, and Nancy Cruzan. The New York appellate division's decision in the *O'Connor* case is indicative of the tendency of these "right to die" cases to sweep in broadest class of patients. The appellate division's *O'Connor* decision was largely an extension to a broader class of patients of its previous decision in *Delio v. Westchester County Medical Center* that food and water are indistinguishable from medical treatment. Mary O'Connor is the seventy-seven-year-old incompetent patient at Westchester County Medical Center who was the subject of the New York Court of Appeals' decision in October 1988 allowing assisted feeding through a nasogastric tube. While Mrs. O'Connor is mentally disabled, she is not in a persistent vegetative state or in a coma, nor is she terminally ill or imminently dying. Mary O'Connor was diagnosed as having "multi-infarct dementia." According to the trial testimony, dementia "is a condition whereby someone becomes confused. They're [sic] cognitive ability becomes impaired."

Legalization of assisted suicide would be certain to have a disparate, deleterious impact on certain vulnerable segments of American society, especially on persons who are minors, poor, or mentally disabled.

Conclusion

The particular need for the legal and medical professions in responding to advocacy of assisted suicide was identified by Drs. Gaylin, Kass, Pellegrino, and Siegler:

Now is not the time for promoting neutral discussion. Rather, now is the time for the medical profession to rally in defense of its fundamental moral principles, to repudiate any and all acts of direct and intentional killing by physicians and their agents. We call on the profession and its leadership to obtain the best advice, regarding both theory and practice, about how to defend the profession's moral center and to resist growing pressures both from without and from within. We call on fellow physicians to say that we will not deliberately kill. We must say also to each of our fellow physicians that we will not tolerate killing of patients and that we shall take disciplinary action against doctors who kill. And we must say to the broader community that if it insists on tolerating or legalizing active euthanasia, it will have to find nonphysicians to do its killing.[24]

Dr. Kass echoed and reinforced these sentiments recently. No one has described our crisis and need more compellingly:

People who care for autonomy and dignity should try to reverse this dehumanization of the last stages of life, instead of giving dehumanization its final triumph by welcoming the desperate goodbye-to-all-that contained in one final plea for poison. . . .

. . . Should doctors cave in, should doctors become technical dispensers of death, they will not only be abandoning their posts, their patients, and their duty to care; they will set the worst sort of example for the community at large—teaching technicism and so-called humaneness where encouragement and humanity are both required and sorely lacking. On the other hand, should physicians hold fast . . . should doctors learn that finitude is no disgrace and that human wholeness can be cared for to the very end, medicine may serve not only the good of its patients, but also, by example, the failing moral health of modern times.[25]

Discussion Questions

1. What do Professor Rosenblum and Mr. Forsythe say that Anglo-American law, up until recently, has said about patients' rights and physician-assisted suicide?

2. How do Professor Rosenblum and Mr. Forsythe argue against the right to privacy being used to support a right to physician-assisted suicide? Do you find their argument compelling? Why or why not? Do you think that their appeal to the possible

legal implications of a right to assisted suicide has a bearing upon their critique of using the right to privacy? Explain.

3. Some may respond to Professor Rosenblum and Mr. Forsythe that their case, though intellectually persuasive, lacks compassion for the family and the patient whose employment of physician-assisted suicide would relieve them of additional suffering and economic burdens. How do you think Professor Rosenblum and Mr. Forsythe would reply to such a response?

Notes

1. Wanzer, Federman, Adelstein, Cassel, Cassem, Cranford, Hook, Lo, Moertel, Safar, Stone & VanEys, *The Physician's Responsibility Toward Hopelessly Ill Patients*, 320 New Eng J Med 844, 848 (1989) [hereinafter Wanzer].

2. Means, *The Phoenix of Abortional Freedom: Is a Penumbral or Ninth-Amendment Right About to Arise from the Nineteenth-Century Legislative Ashes of a Fourteenth-Century Common-Law Liberty?* 17 N.Y.L.F. 335, 374 (1971). The same is true with "mercy-killing." "In Anglo-American jurisprudence a 'mercy-killing' is murder. In theory, neither good motive nor consent of the victim is relevant." Kamisar, *Some Non-Religious Views Against Proposed "Mercy-Killing" Legislation*, 42 Minn. L. Rev. 969, 970 n. 9 (1958). *See* Gilbert v. State, 487 So. 2d 1185 (Fla. Dist. Ct. App. 1986); People v. Roberts, 211 Mich. 187, 178 N.W. 690 (1920). *See also* Louisell, *Euthanasia and Biathanasia: On Dying and Killing*, 22 Cath. U.L. Rev. 723, 731 n. 43 (1973).

3. *See generally* Byrn, *Compulsory Lifesaving Treatment for the Competent Adult*, 44 Fordham L. Rev. 1 (1975); Sharpe & Hargest, *Lifesaving Treatment for Unwilling Patients*, 36 Fordham L. Rev. 695 (1968); McCoid, *A Reappraisal of Liability for Unauthorized Medical Treatment*, 41 Minn. L. Rev. 381 (1957).

4. *In re* Severns, 425 A.2d 156, 159 (Del. Ch. 1980); *In re* P.V.W., 424 So. 2d 1015, 1018 (La. 182); *In re* Storar, 52 N.Y.2d 363, 380–83, 420 N.E.2d 64, 72–74, 438 N.Y.S.2d 266, 274–76 (1981); *In re* Quackenbush, 156 N.J. Super. 282, 383 A.2d 785 (1978); Superintendent of Belchertown State School v. Saikewicz, 373 Mass. 728, 370 N.E.2d 417 (1977); *In re* Quinlan, 70 N.J. 10, 355 A.2d 647 (1976), *cert. denied*, 429 U.S. 922 (1976), John F. Kennedy Memorial Hospital v. Heston, 58 N.J. 576, 279 A 2d 670 (1971).

5. Robertson, *Involuntary Euthanasia of Defective Newborns: A Legal Analysis*, 27 Stan. L. Rev. 213, 236 (1975) (footnote omitted).

6. *See* Superintendent of Belchertown State School v. Saikeweicz, 373 Mass. 728, 370 N.E.2d 417 (1977).

7. *See* Cruzan v. Harmon 760 S.W.2d 408 (Mo. 1988), *cert. granted sub. nom.*, Cruzan v. Director, Missouri Dep't of Health, 109 S.Ct. 3240 (1989) (no. 88-1503); *In re* Westchester County Medical Center *ex rel.* O'Connor, 72 N.Y.2d 517, 531 N.E.2d 607, 534 N.Y.S.2d 886 (1988), *In re* Storar, 52 N.Y.2d 363, 420 N.E.2d 64, 438 N.Y.S.2d 266, *cert. denied*, 454 U.S. 858 (1981).

8. Callahan, *Feeding the Dying Elderly*, 10 Generations 15–17 (Winter 1985).

9. Rasmussen v. Fleming, 154 Ariz. 207, 741 P.2d 674 (1987), *aff'g in part, rev'g in part*, 154 Ariz. 200, 741 P.2d 667 (1986); Bouvia v. Superior Court, 179 Cal. App. 3d 1127, 225 Cal. Rptr. 297 (1986); *In re* Hector Rodas, No. 87CV142 (D. Ct. Colo. filed Jan. 30, 1987); Corbett v. D'Alessandro, 487 So. 2d 368 (Fla. Dist. Ct. App.) *review denied*, 492 So. 2d 1331 (Fla. 1986); *In re* Gardner, 534 A.2d 947 (Me. 1987); Brophy v. New England Sinai Hosp., Inc., 398 Mass. 417, 497 N.E.2d 626 (1986); *In re* Jobes, 108 N.J. 394, 529 A.2d 434 (1987); *In re* Conroy, 98 N.J. 321, 486 A.2d 1209 (1985); Delio v. Westchester County Medical Center, 129 A.D.2d 1, 516 N.Y.S.2d 677 (1987), *rev'g*, 134 Misc. 2d 206, 510 N.Y.S.2d 415 (1986); *In re* Grant, 109 Wash. 2d 545, 747 P.2d 445 (1987), *vacated*, 757 P.2d 534 (Wash. 1988).

10. The Lincoln-Douglas Debates 254 (R. W. Johannsen ed. 1965).

11. *Id.* at 257.

12. Brown, Henteleff, Barakat & Rowe, *Is It Normal for Terminally Ill Patients to Desire Death?* 143 Am. J. Psych. 208 (1986).

13. Derr, *Nutrition and Hydration as Elective Therapy: Brophy and Jobes from an Ethical and Historical Perspective*, 2 Issues in Law & Med. 25 (1986):

> The preoccupation of so much contemporary academic work in medical ethics with the patient's 'autonomy' suggests a systematic ignorance of the clinical and census realities in modern teaching and community hospitals. For better or worse, few patients in such institutions resemble the rationally calculating, perfectly free, rights-asserting entities who populate so much of the academic literature. In the actual case, the clinician, who repeatedly and earnestly seeks the patient's direction, is likely to be told, just as repeatedly and just as earnestly, to '[d]o whatever you think is right, doctor.'

Id. at 30–31, n. 14.

14. Gaylin, Kass, Pellegrino & Siegler, *Doctors Must Not Kill* 259 JAMA 2139, 2159 (1988) [hereinafter Gaylin].

15. *Id.* at 2140.

16. Torres & Forrest, *Why Do Women Have Abortions?* 20 Fam. Plan. Persp. 169 (1988).

17. Wanzer, *supra* note 1, at 847.

18. *Id.* at 847–48 (emphasis added).

19. *Id.* at 848.

20. *Id.*

21. Causes of action for wrongful birth and wrongful life were uniformly rejected before Roe v. Wade. *See, e.g.,* Zepeda v. Zepeda, 41 Ill. App. 2d 240, 190 N.E. 2d 849 (1963), *cert. denied*, 379 U.S. 945 (1964). The contrast before and after *Roe* is most clearly seen in the New Jersey Supreme

Court's decision in Gleitman v. Cosgrove, 49 N.J. 22, 227 A.2d 689 (1967), rejecting a cause of action, which was overruled in part in Berman v. Allan, 80 N.J. 421, 404 A.2d 8 (1979), which adopted a cause of action. *See generally* Bopp, Bostrom & McKinney, *The "Rights" and "Wrongs" of Wrongful Birth and Wrongful Life: A Jurisprudential Analysis of Birth Related Torts,* 27 Duq. L. Rev. 461 (1989). After *Roe,* courts began to authorize such actions on the rationale that abortion was a legal medical service and that doctors, therefore, had a duty to provide information about such an option. *See, e.g.,* Speck v. Finegold, 497 Pa. 77, 85, 439 A.2d 110, 114 (1981) (per curiam) (Flaherty, J.). Wrongful birth and wrongful life claims against private practicing physicians cannot be predicated on the fact that abortion is a *constitutional* right, because the violation of such a right requires state action, and private physicians are not state actors. The rationale for wrongful birth and wrongful life, accordingly, has been simply that abortion is legal and doctors have a duty to provide information about a lawful medical service.

22. Shaw, *Letter to the Editor,* 259 JAMA 2096 (1988).

23. *See* Ross v. Hilltop Rehabilitation Hospital, 676 F. Supp. 1528 (D. Colo. 1987); Grant & Forsythe, *The Plight of the Last Friend: Legal Issues for Physicians and Nurses in Providing Nutrition and Hydration,* 2 Issues in Law & Med. 277 (1987); Oddi, *The Tort of Interference with the Right to Die: The Wrongful Living Cause of Action* 75 Geo. L. 625 (1986).

24. Gaylin, *supra* note 14, at 2140.

25. Kass, *Neither for Love nor Money: Why Doctors Must Not Kill.* Pub Interest, Winter 1989.

20

In the Matter of Karen Ann Quinlan, an Incompetent (1976)

New Jersey Supreme Court

Karen Ann Quinlan, at the age of 21, was left comatose and irreversibly brain-damaged (though not brain-dead) by two inexplicable seizures. Karen was being sustained by a respirator when the New Jersey Supreme Court, at the request of her father, ruled that there was no obligation to perpetuate her life by artificial means that are burdensome and provide no hope for recovery. After being removed from the respirator Karen lived for nearly ten years and died a natural death. Although some cite this case as an example of a court supporting a patient's "right to die" (active euthanasia), such an assessment is inaccurate. The Quinlan case seems more consistent with the right to withdraw or withhold burdensome treatment (or passive euthanasia), which is a right found in Anglo-American common law (see Chapter 19), rather than supporting a right to physician-assisted suicide. In the following excerpt from the majority opinion in the Quinlan case, Chief Justice Hughes bases his decision on the right to privacy, arguing that although the state has an interest in preserving the lives of its citizens, this interest "weakens and the individual's right to privacy grows as the degree of bodily invasion increases and the prognosis dims." Since Karen's treatment was highly invasive and there was no prognosis for recovery, she had the right to have treatment withdrawn based on her right to privacy. But since she was incompetent, the Chief Justice ruled that the right could be upheld by following Karen's wishes if she had expressed them in the past, but if these were not known, then the court would permit "the guardian and family of Karen to render their best judgment, subject to the qualifications hereinafter stated, as to whether she would exercise it in these circumstances" consistent with what the over-whelming majority in society would have chosen in similar circumstances.

Constitutional and Legal Issues

I. The Free Exercise of Religion

Simply stated, the right to religious beliefs is absolute but conduct in pursuance thereof is not wholly immune from governmental restraint. So it is that, for the sake of life, courts sometimes (but not always) order blood transfusions for Jehovah's Witnesses (whose religious beliefs abhor such procedure), forbid exposure to death from handling virulent snakes or ingesting poison (interfering with deeply held religious sentiments in such regard), and protect the public health as in the case of compulsory vaccination (over the strongest of religious objections). . . . The Public interest is thus considered paramount, without essential dissolution of respect for religious beliefs.

We think, without further examples, that, ranged against the State's interest in the preservation of life, the impingement of religious belief, much less religious "neutrality" as here, does not reflect a constitutional question, in the circumstances at least of the case presently before the Court. Moreover, like the trial court, we do not recognize an independent parental right of religious freedom to support the relief requested.

II. Cruel and Unusual Punishment

Similarly inapplicable to the case before us is the Constitution's Eighth Amendment protection against cruel and unusual punishment which, as held by the trial court, is not relevant to situations other than the imposition of penal sanctions. Historic in nature, it stemmed from punitive excesses in the infliction of criminal penalties. We find no precedent in law which would justify its extension to the correction of social injustice or hardship, such as, for instance, in the case of poverty. The latter often condemns the poor and deprived to horrendous living conditions which could certainly be described in the abstract as "cruel and unusual punishment." Yet the constitutional base of protection from "cruel and unusual punishment" is plainly irrelevant to such societal ills which must be remedied, if at all, under other concepts of constitutional and civil right.

So it is in the case of the unfortunate Karen Quinlan. Neither the State, nor the law, but the accident of fate and nature, has inflicted upon her conditions which though in essence cruel and most unusual, yet do not amount to "punishment" in any constitutional sense.

Neither the judgment of the court below, nor the medical decision which confronted it, nor the law and equity perceptions which impelled its action, nor the whole factual base upon which it was predicated, inflicted "cruel and unusual punishment" in the constitutional sense.

III. The Right of Privacy

It is the issue of the constitutional right of privacy that has given us most concern, in the exceptional circumstances of this case. Here a loving parent, *qua* parent and raising the rights of his incompetent and profoundly damaged daughter, probably irreversibly doomed to no more than a biologically vegetative remnant of life, is before the court. He seeks authorization to abandon specialized technological procedures which can only maintain for a time a body having no potential for resumption or continuance of other than a "vegetative" existence.

We have no doubt, in these unhappy circumstances, that if Karen were herself miraculously lucid for an interval (not altering the existing prognosis of the condition to which she would soon return) and perceptive of her irreversible condition, she could effectively decide upon discontinuance of the life-support apparatus, even if it meant the prospect of natural death. To this extent we may distinguish [a case] which concerned a severely injured young woman (Delores Heston), whose life depended on surgery and blood transfusion; and who was in such extreme shock that she was unable to express an informed choice (although the Court apparently considered the case as if the patient's own religious decision to resist transfusion were at stake), but most importantly a patient apparently salvable to long life and vibrant health;—a situation not at all like the present case.

We have no hesitancy in deciding, in the instant diametrically opposite case, that no external compelling interest of the State could compel Karen to endure the unendurable, only to vegetate a few measurable months with no realistic possibility of returning to any semblance of cognitive or sapient life. We perceive no thread of logic distinguishing between such a choice on Karen's part and a similar choice which, under the evidence in this case, could be made by a competent patient terminally ill, riddled by cancer and suffering great pain; such a patient would not be resuscitated or put on a respirator in the example described by Dr. Korein, and *a fortiori* would not be kept *against his will* on a respirator.

Although the constitution does not explicitly mention a right of privacy, Supreme Court decisions have recognized that a right of personal privacy exists and that certain areas of privacy are guaranteed under the Constitution. The Court has interdicted judicial intrusion into many aspects of personal decision, sometimes basing this restraint upon the conception of a limitation of judicial interest and responsibility, such as with regard to contraception and its relationship to family life and decision.

The Court in *Griswold* found the unwritten constitutional right of privacy to exist in the penumbra of specific guarantees of the Bill of Rights "formed by emanations from those guarantees that help give them life and substance." Presumably this right is broad enough to encompass a patient's decision to decline medical treatment under certain circumstances, in much the same way as it is broad enough to encompass a woman's decision to terminate pregnancy under certain conditions.

The claimed interests of the State in this case are essentially the preservation and sanctity of human life and defense to the right of the physician to administer medical treatment according to his best judgment. In this case the doctors say that removing Karen from the respirator will conflict with their professional judgment. The plaintiff answers that Karen's present treatment serves only a maintenance function; that the respirator cannot cure or improve her condition but at best can only prolong her inevitable slow deterioration and death; and that the interests of the patient, as seen by her surrogate, the guardian, must be evaluated by the court as predominant, even in the face of an option *contra* by the present attending physicians. Plaintiff's distinction is significant. The nature of Karen's care and the realistic chances of her recovery are quite unlike those of the patients discussed in many of the cases where treatments were ordered. In many of those cases the medical procedure required (usually a transfusion) constituted a minimal bodily invasion and the chances of recovery and return to functioning life were very good. We think that the State's interest *contra* weakens and the individual's right to privacy grows as the degree of bodily invasion increases and the prognosis dims. Ultimately there comes a point at which the individual's rights overcome the State interest. It is for that reason that we believe Karen's choice, if she were competent to make it, would be vindicated by the law. Her prognosis is extremely poor,—she will never resume cognitive life. And the bodily invasion is very great,—she requires 24-hour intensive nursing care, antibiotics, and the assistance of a respirator, a catheter and feeding tube.

Our affirmance of Karen's independent right of choice, however, would ordinarily be based upon her competency to assert it. The sad truth, however, is that she is grossly incompetent and we cannot discern her supposed choice based on the testimony of her previous conversation with friends, where such testimony is without sufficient probative weight. Nevertheless we have concluded that Karen's right of privacy may be asserted on her behalf by her guardian under the peculiar circumstances here present.

If a putative decision by Karen to permit this non-cognitive, vegetative existence to terminate by natural forces is regarded as a valuable incident of her right of privacy, as we believe it to be, then it should not be discarded solely on the basis that her condition prevents her conscious exercise of the choice. The only practical way to prevent destruction of the right is to permit the guardian and family of Karen to render their best judgment, subject to the qualifications hereinafter stated, as to whether she would exercise it in these circumstances. If their conclusion is in the affirmative this decision should be accepted by a society the overwhelming majority of whose members would, we think, in similar circumstances, exercise such a choice in the same way for themselves or for those closest to them. It is for this reason that we determine that Karen's right of privacy may be asserted in her behalf, in this respect, by her guardian and family under the particular circumstances presented by this record. [Sections IV (Medical Factors), V (Alleged Criminal Liability), and VI (Guardianship of the Person) omitted.]

Declaratory Relief

We thus arrive at the formulation of the declaratory relief which we have concluded is appropriate to this case. Some time has passed since Karen's physical and mental condition was described to the Court. At that time her continuing deterioration was plainly projected. Since the record has not been expanded we assume that she is now even more fragile and nearer to death than she was then. Since her present treating physicians may give reconsideration to her present posture in the light of this opinion, and since we are transferring to the plaintiff as guardian the choice of the attending physician and therefore other physicians may be in charge of the case who may take a different view from that of the present attending physicians, we herewith declare the following affirmative relief on behalf of the plaintiff. Upon the concurrence of the guardian and family of Karen, should the responsible attending physicians conclude that there is no reasonable possibility of Karen's ever emerging from her present comatose condition to a cognitive, sapient state and that the life-support apparatus now being administered to Karen should be discontinued, they shall consult with the hospital "Ethics Committee" or like body of the institution in which Karen is then hospitalized. If that consultative body agrees that there is no reasonable possibility of Karen's ever emerging from her present comatose condition to a cognitive, sapient state, the present life-support system may be withdrawn and said action shall be without any civil or criminal liability therefor on the part of any participant, whether guardian, physician, hospital or others. We herewith specifically so hold.

Discussion Questions

1. Present and explain Chief Justice Hughes's opinion in this case. To what constitutional right did he appeal? Do you find his arguments persuasive? Why or why not? Explain your answer.

2. Some people who defend active euthanasia for patients like Karen Ann Quinlan who are in a permanently vegetative state (PVS) argue that such patients are *not persons* since they no longer are capable of self-awareness or consciousness. If such patients are not persons, is it possible to sustain Chief Justice Hughes's opinion that they have a right to privacy, since only persons (according to *Roe v. Wade*) have constitutional rights? Or is there another way to justify passive euthanasia in such circumstances? Would it make a difference if a PVS patient had a living will instructing her physician to give her a lethal injection?

3. After Karen was removed from the respirator, she was able to breathe on her own, but was physically sustained for nearly a decade by the arti-

ficial administration of food and water. What if Karen's father had wanted the food and water to be withdrawn as well? Could the Chief Justice's opinion be applied to this action in the same way it was applied to removing Karen from the respirator? Is there a difference between artificial administration of food and water and artificial administration of oxygen (respirator)? Explain and defend your answer.

Oxygen — body dies naturally
food /water — body starves

21

Cruzan v. Harmon (1991)

U.S. Supreme Court

As a result of an accident on January 11, 1983, Nancy Beth Cruzan was in a persistent vegetative state (PVS), being fed through a tube inserted in her stomach. Someone who is PVS has lower brain functions (that is, the brain stem may be the only part of the brain that is functioning, the part that controls many normal bodily functions such as respiration and heartbeat) but no higher brain functions (that is, the cerebral cortex may not be functioning, the part of the brain whose function is associated with thought, intellect, and personality). Nancy Cruzan, like most PVS patients, was not hooked up to a machine, but was cared for by others in many ways (clothed, cleaned, fed via feeding tube, etc.). In this state she was awake but not aware, though she had been observed grimacing perhaps in recognition of ordinary painful stimuli and apparent response to sound. Nancy's parents asked her doctors to remove the feeding tube so that she could die. The case went to court. First a state trial court ruled in favor of withdrawal, saying that the feeding tube was "heroically invasive" or burdensome. But the Missouri Supreme Court ruled against that argument, declaring: "We choose to err on the side of life." The United States Supreme Court, in *Cruzan v. Harmon* (June 25, 1990), agreed with the state supreme court, concluding that if Nancy had a living will requesting the withdrawal of food and water, then termination would have been justified. Interestingly enough, several months later, the Cruzans obtained more evidence, which the lower court believed constituted a living will and was within the U.S. Supreme Court's parameters. In December 1990, physicians withdrew Nancy's feeding tubes. She died of starvation and dehydration several days later. The following is an abridged version of the majority opinion from *Cruzan v. Harmon*, written by Chief Justice William Rehnquist.

Petitioner Nancy Beth Cruzan was rendered incompetent as a result of severe injuries sustained during an automobile accident. Co-petitioners Lester and Joyce Cruzan, Nancy's parents and co-guardians, sought a court order directing the withdrawal of their daughter's artificial feeding and hydration equipment after it became apparent that she had virtually no chance of recovering her cognitive faculties. The Supreme Court of Missouri held that because there was no clear and convincing evidence of Nancy's desire to have life-sustaining treatment withdrawn under such circumstances, her parents lacked authority to effectuate such a request. . . .

After it had become apparent that Nancy Cruzan had virtually no chance of regaining her mental faculties her parents asked hospital employees to terminate the artificial nutrition and hydration procedures. All agree that such a removal would cause her death. The employees refused to honor the request without court approval. The parents then sought and received authorization from the state trial court for termination. The court found that a person in Nancy's condition had a fundamental right under the State and Federal Constitutions to refuse or direct the withdrawal of "death prolonging procedures." The court also found that Nancy's "expressed thoughts at age 25 in somewhat serious conversation with a housemate friend that if sick or injured she would not wish to continue her life unless she could live at least halfway normally" suggests that given her present condition she would not wish to continue on with her nutrition and hydration.

Missouri Court's Decision

The Supreme Court of Missouri reversed by a divided vote. The court recognized a right to refuse treatment embodied in the common-law doctrine of informed consent, but expressed skepticism about the application of that doctrine in the circumstances of this case. . . . The court also declined to read a broad right of privacy into the State Constitution which would "support the right of a person to refuse medical treatment in every circumstance," and expressed doubt as to whether such a right existed under the United States Constitution. It then decided that the Missouri Living Will statute embodied a state policy strongly favoring the preservation of life. The court found that Cruzan's statements to her roommate regarding her desire to live or die under certain conditions were "unreliable for the purpose of determining her intent," "and thus insufficient to support the co-guardians' claim to exercise substituted judgment on Nancy's behalf." . . .

We granted *certiorari* to consider the question of whether Cruzan has a right under the United States Constitution which would require the hospital to withdraw life-sustaining treatment from her under these circumstances.

At common law, even the touching of one person by another without consent and without legal justification was a battery.

The logical corollary of the doctrine of informed consent is that the patient generally possesses the right not to consent, that is, to refuse treatment. Until about 15 years ago and the seminal decision in *In re Quinlan*, 70 N.J. 10, the number of right-to-refuse-treatment decisions were relatively few. . . . More recently, however, with the advance of medical technology capable of sustaining life well past the point where natural forces would have brought certain death in earlier times, cases involving the right to refuse life-sustaining treatment have burgeoned. . . .

Doctrine of Informed Consent

As these cases demonstrate, the common-law doctrine of informed consent is viewed as generally encompassing the right of a competent individual to refuse medical treatment. Beyond that, these decisions demonstrate both similarity and diversity in their approach to decision of what all agree is a perplexing question with unusually strong moral and ethical overtones. State courts have available to them for decision a number of sources—state constitutions, statutes, and common law—which are not available to us.

In this Court, the question is simply and starkly whether the United States Constitution prohibits Missouri from choosing the rule of decision which it did. This is the first case in which we have been squarely presented with the issue of whether the United States Constitution grants what is in common parlance referred to as a "right to die."

The 14th Amendment provides that no state shall "deprive any person of life, liberty, or property, without due process of law." The principle that a competent person has a constitutionally protected liberty interest in refusing unwanted medical treatment may be inferred from our prior decisions. . . .

Just this term, in the course of holding that a state's procedures for administering antipsychotic

medication to prisoners were sufficient to satisfy due process concerns, we recognized that prisoners possess "a significant liberty interest in avoiding the unwanted administration of antipsychotic drugs under the Due Process Clause of the 14th Amendment." *Washington v. Harper* (1990) . . .

But determining that a person has a "liberty interest" under the Due Process Clause[1] does not end the inquiry; "whether respondent's constitutional rights have been violated must be determined by balancing his liberty interests against the relevant state interests."

Forced Medical Treatment

Petitioners insist that under the general holdings of our cases, the forced administration of life-sustaining medical treatment, and even of artificially delivered food and water essential to life, would implicate a competent person's liberty interest. Although we think the logic of the cases discussed above would embrace such a liberty interest, the dramatic consequences involved in refusal of such treatment would inform the inquiry as to whether the deprivation of that interest is constitutionally permissible. But for purposes of this case, we assume that the United States Constitution would grant a competent person a constitutionally protected right to refuse life-saving hydration and nutrition.

Petitioners go on to assert that an incompetent person should possess the same right in this respect as is possessed by a competent person. . . .

The difficulty with petitioners' claim is that in a sense it begs the question: an incompetent person is not able to make an informed and voluntary choice to exercise a hypothetical right to refuse treatment or any other right. Such a "right" must be exercised for her, if at all, by some sort of surrogate. Here, Missouri has in effect recognized that under certain circumstances a surrogate may act for the patient in electing to have hydration and nutrition withdrawn in such a way as to cause death, but it has established a procedural safeguard to assure that the action of the surrogate conforms as best it may to the wishes expressed by the patient while competent.

Missouri requires that evidence of the incompetent's wishes as to the withdrawal of treatment be proved by clear and convincing evidence. The question, then, is whether the United States Constitution forbids the establishment of this procedural requirement by the state. We hold that it does not.

Whether or not Missouri's clear and convincing evidence requirement comports with the United States Constitution depends in part on what interests the state may properly seek to protect in this situation. Missouri relies on its interest in the protection and preservation of human life, and there can be no gainsaying this interest. As a general matter, the states—indeed, all civilized nations—demonstrate their commitment to life by treating homicide as serious crime. Moreover, the majority of states in this country have laws imposing criminal penalties on one who assists another to commit suicide. We do not think a state is required to remain neutral in the face of an informed and voluntary decision by a physically able adult to starve to death.

Heightened Evidentiary Requirements

But in the context presented here, a state has more particular interests at stake. The choice between life and death is a deeply personal decision of obvious and overwhelming finality. We believe Missouri may legitimately seek to safeguard the personal element of this choice through the imposition of heightened evidentiary requirements. It cannot be disputed that the Due Process Clause protects an interest in life as well as an interest in refusing life-sustaining medical treatment. Not all incompetent patients will have loved ones available to serve as surrogate decision makers. . . .

In our view, Missouri has permissibly sought to advance these interests through the adoption of a "clear and convincing" standard of proof to govern such proceedings. . . .

In sum, we conclude that a state may apply a clear and convincing evidence standard in proceedings where a guardian seeks to discontinue nutrition and hydration of a person diagnosed to be in a persistent vegetative state. . . .

The Supreme Court of Missouri held that in this case the testimony adduced at trial did not amount to clear and convincing proof of the patient's desire to have hydration and nutrition withdrawn.

No doubt is engendered by anything in this record but that Nancy Cruzan's mother and father are loving and caring parents. If the state were required by the United States Constitution to repose a right of "substituted judgment" with anyone, the Cruzans would surely qualify. But we do not think the Due Process Clause requires the state to repose judgment on these matters with anyone but the patient herself. Close family members may have a strong feeling—a feeling not at all ignoble or unworthy, but not entirely disinterested, either—that they do not wish to witness the continuation of the life of a loved one which they regard as hopeless, meaningless and even degrading. But there is no automatic assurance that the view of close family members will necessarily be the same as the patient's would have been had she been confronted with the prospect of her situation while competent. All of the reasons previously discussed for allowing Missouri to require clear and convincing evidence of the patient's wishes lead us to conclude that the state may choose to defer only to those wishes, rather than confide the decision to close family members.

Discussion Questions

1. How did the Court justify its claim that Nancy Cruzan has a right under the U.S. Constitution to require the hospital to withdraw life-sustaining treatment from her? But why then did they reject her parents' wishes to require the hospital to withdraw food and water?

2. Why did the Court reject the testimony of Nancy Cruzan's housemate, who claimed that Nancy had told her a year before the accident that "she would not want to live should she face life as a 'vegetable,' and other observations to the same"?

3. The Court would have allowed Nancy Cruzan's parents to require the hospital to withdraw food and water if Nancy had made the r equest in a Living Will. On what legal basis did the Court justify this conclusion?

Notes

1. Although many state courts have held that a right to refuse treatment is encompassed by a generalized constitutional right of privacy, we have never so held. We believe this issue is more properly analyzed in terms of a 14th Amendment liberty interest.

The Morality of Euthanasia

22

A Defense of Active Euthanasia

James Rachels

But death of a dream is no reason to end a life

James Rachels is Professor of Philosophy at the University of Alabama, Birmingham. He is the author of numerous scholarly articles in ethics and moral philosophy. Among his published books are *The End of Life: Euthanasia and Morality* (1986) and *The Right Thing to Do: Basic Readings in Moral Philosophy* (1989).

In this essay Professor Rachels maintains that active euthanasia (i.e., killing a patient) is morally justified in some circumstances. First, he argues that a patient who has mere *biological* life and has lost his *biographical* life has a right to commit suicide. Professor Rachels believes that what makes life worth living is not mere biological life, but one's biographical life, one's hopes, life experiences, dreams, pursuits, interests, etc. Thus, if a person's biographical life has ended, we have no right to prevent that person from ending his or her biological life. Professor Rachels also argues that there is no essential moral difference between active (killing) and passive (letting-die) euthanasia. But then, he concludes, if passive euthanasia is morally acceptable, and there is no moral difference between passive and active euthanasia, then active euthanasia must also be morally acceptable. He defends this position by employing the fictional story of Jones and Smith, in which both seem to be

Reprinted by permission from "Active and Passive Euthanasia," *New England Journal of Medicine* 292 (January 9, 1975); and *The End of Life* (Oxford: Oxford University Press, 1986).

guilty of committing morally equivalent acts (i.e., murdering his six-year-old cousin), though Jones merely "let the boy die" whereas Smith "killed the boy."

The Traditional View

Consider the recent case of Hans Florian and his wife. They had been married for thirty-three years when he shot her dead. She was a victim of Alzheimer's disease, which attacks the brain, and for which there is no known cause or cure. The effects of the disease are devastating. The deterioration of the brain can be traced through several stages, as the victim loses all semblance of human personality.

Soon after the onset of the disease, Mrs. Florian began to lose the ability to do simple chores and, at the same time, began to develop abnormal fears. She could not drive or write, and would panic when her husband would leave the room. As the disease progressed, he would have to feed her by forcing her mouth open, and he would bathe her and change her clothes several times each day as she soiled them. Then her vocabulary shrank to two words: "fire" and "pain", screamed in her native German. Finally, she had to be placed in a nursing home for her own safety. Although her condition was irreversible, it was not "terminal"—she could have lived on, in this deranged state, indefinitely.

Was it wrong for Hans Florian to have killed his wife? He explained that he killed her because, being seventeen years older, he did not want to die first and leave her alone. Legally, of course, he had no right to do it. Under American law, he could have been found guilty of murder in the first degree—although no charges were brought, because the Florida grand jury refused to indict him. (As we shall see, juries often react this way in such cases.) But, legal questions aside, was his act *immoral*?

We may certainly feel sympathy for Hans Florian; he faced a terrible situation, and acted from honourable motives. Nevertheless, according to the dominant moral tradition of our culture, what he did was indefensible. He intentionally killed an innocent human being, and, according to our tradition, that is always wrong. This tradition is largely the product of Christian teaching. Christianity says, of course, that every human being is made in the image of God, and so all human life is sacred. Killing a person, even one so pitiable as Mrs. Florian, is therefore an offence against the Creator.

Most people in the Western world accept some such perspective as this. Even those who imagine themselves to have rejected this way of thinking continue, more often than not, to be influenced by it—it is not easy to shrug off the values of the culture in which one has been raised and educated. Thus, even those who reject the old theological ideas may continue to accept their secular equivalents—if one no longer believes that human life is "sacred", then one can at least believe that human life is "intrinsically valuable" or that "every human life has a special dignity and worth". And, on the strength of this, one may continue to doubt whether Mr. Florian acted correctly.

The traditional view is not, however, a simple view. Through the centuries various thinkers have contributed to its development, and a complex account of the morality of killing has resulted. This account appeals to a series of distinctions that, taken together, define a class of actions said to be absolutely forbidden. In deciding whether a particular killing is permissible, the method is to apply the distinctions to determine whether the act falls into the forbidden class.

Some of these distinctions have to do with the status of the victim: for example, the distinction between human and non-human is held to be crucial. At the heart of the traditional doctrine is the idea that the protection of *human* life—all human life—is immensely important. If one is human, and alive, then according to the traditional view one's life is sacred. At the same time, *non-human* life is given relatively little importance. So, in general, killing people is said to be gravely wrong, while killing other animals requires almost no justification at all.

But this does not mean that killing people can never be justified. Sometimes it is justified, and here it matters a great deal whether the human in question is "innocent". Capital punishment and killing in war are traditionally sanctioned, on the grounds that the people who are killed are not innocent. It is the killing of the *innocent*, such as Mrs. Florian, that is prohibited.

Other traditional distinctions focus on other qualities of the act; for example, it matters whether the killing would be *intentional*. (Like "innocent", "intentional" is something of a technical term, whose meaning we will have occasion to examine later.) It is *the intentional killing of innocent humans* that is absolutely forbidden.

But perhaps the most interesting of the traditional distinctions is between *killing people* and merely *letting people die*. On the traditional view, even though killing innocent people is forbidden, letting them die is sometimes permitted. This is especially important in considering what may or may not be done in medical treatment. The point is that we are not always required to use every available resource to prolong life, even if it is the life of an innocent human. When extraordinary means are required to keep someone alive, those means may be omitted. (The use of *ordinary* treatments is morally mandatory, but *extraordinary* treatments are optional—this is another of the distinctions the traditional view finds so important.)

The traditional theory must be taken seriously; not only has its influence been enormous, but from a philosophical point of view it is the only fully worked-out, systematically elaborated theory of the subject we have. Its development has been one of the great intellectual achievements of Western culture, accomplished by thinkers of great ingenuity and high moral purpose. However, I shall be mainly interested in the question of whether this theory is *true*—granted that it has history and tradition on its side, still we may ask whether there is good reason for a rational person to accept it.

If the traditional theory is not true, then in our society many decisions concerning life and death are being made on unsound grounds, and the law concerning such matters is badly in need of reform. I believe that the traditional view is mistaken at almost every point. The maze of distinctions on which it is based cannot withstand analysis. Much of this essay is a defence of that judgement.

An Alternative View

To replace the traditional view, I offer a different way of looking at such matters. The alternative view begins by pointing out that there is a deep difference between *having a life* and merely *being alive*. The point of the moral rule against killing is not to keep "innocent humans" alive. Being alive, in the biological sense, is relatively unimportant. One's *life*, by contrast, is immensely important; it is the sum of one's aspirations, decisions, activities, projects, and human relationships. The point of the rule against killing is the protection of *lives* and the interests that some beings, including ourselves, have in virtue of the fact that we are subjects of lives. Only by paying careful attention to the concept of a life can we understand the value of life and the evil of death.

The details of this account are strikingly different from the traditional approach. The distinction between human and non-human turns out to be less important than has been assumed. From a moral point of view, it is the protection of lives that is important, and so, because most humans have lives, killing them is objectionable. However, some unfortunate humans, such as Mrs. Florian, do not have lives, even though they are alive; and so killing *them* is a morally different matter. Moreover, some non-human animals also have lives, and so consistency requires that they also be protected by the rule against killing..

... And, I will argue, the distinction between killing and letting die is morally insignificant as well: the fact that one act is an act of killing (for example, "mercy-killing") while another act is an act of "merely" letting someone die (for example, "pulling the plug" of a life-sustaining medical device) is not in itself a reason for thinking one act morally better than the other.

The upshot is that this view is much simpler than the traditional view, in that not nearly so many things are considered important. In deciding questions of life and death, the crucial question is: Is a *life*, in the biographical sense, being destroyed or otherwise adversely affected? If not, the rule against killing offers no objection. The species of the subject of the life, and the means that are used, as well as the intention with which the act is done, are all more or less irrelevant.

As one might suspect, the implication for Mrs. Florian is different from the implication of the traditional view. Although this unfortunate woman was still alive, that fact has little significance. The critical fact is that, when her husband shot her, her life was already over. He was not destroying her life; it had already been destroyed by Alzheimer's disease. Thus he was not behaving immorally.

This approach assumes a certain conception of morality. The traditional theory is often presented in theological terms, but its partisans emphasize that the religious trappings are not necessary. It is meant to be a moral view, not a religious dogma, binding on moral agents regardless of their theological convictions or lack of them. My approach is secular in this sense, plus another. It sees being moral, not as a matter of faithfulness to abstract rules or divine laws, but as a matter of doing what is best for those who are affected by our conduct. If we should not kill, it is because in killing we are *harming someone.* That is the reason killing is wrong. The rule against killing has as its point the protection of the victims.

If this seems a truism, remember Mrs. Florian. This conception leads directly to the conclusion that her husband did no wrong. She was not harmed by her husband's killing her—indeed, if anything, it seems more likely that she was helped. But on the traditional view, this has little importance. Mrs. Florian was an innocent human, and so she could not intentionally be killed. Against the background of the traditional view, the alternative approach emerges not as a truism but as a radical idea. . . .

The Concept of a Life

Generally speaking, death is a misfortune for the person who dies because it puts an end to his life. Like many philosophical theses, this is more complicated than it first appears. Death is a misfortune, not because it puts an end to one's *being alive* (in the biological sense), but because it ends one's *life* (in the biographical sense). To explain the thesis— to show how the termination of one's life can be a bad thing—we need to examine some aspects of what it means to have a life.

Complete and Incomplete Lives

The contingencies of human existence determine the general shape of our lives. Because we are born physically weak and without knowledge or skills, the first part of our lives is a process of growth, learning, and general maturation. Because we will not live much longer than seventy-five years, and because in the last years we will decline mentally and physically, the projects and activities that will fill our lives cannot be planned for much longer than that. The forms of life within human society are adjusted to these dimensions: families care for children while they are small and are acquiring a basic understanding of the world; schools continue the educational process; careers last about forty years; and people normally retire some time between sixty and seventy.

A life can, therefore, be complete or incomplete; it can run its course, or be cut short. Bertrand Russell lived an extraordinarily full life. Born in 1872, he lived ninety-seven years, during which time he was twice married and raised a family; he travelled the world and enjoyed the friendship of such as George Bernard Shaw, H. G. Wells, and Ludwig Wittgenstein; he published seventy-one books and pamphlets, including many that made fundamental contributions to human thought, and was awarded the Nobel Prize; and he was internationally famous as a political and moral propagandist. Compare this with the life of another philosopher, Frank P. Ramsey, who died in 1930 at the age of twenty-six. Ramsey's life had hardly begun; he had achieved only a little of what he could have achieved. The two deaths were, therefore, very different. Ramsey's death was a tragedy, while Russell's death was only the occasion for solemn reflection on a life well lived.

The tragedy of Ramsey's death was threefold. First, there was the sense of *incompleteness*. It was as though a story was only half-told; we had the beginning, and intimations of the middle, but no idea of what the ending might be. Second, there was the sense of futility connected with the fact that Ramsey's life to that point had been *training* him for something that now could not take place. He had been educated and studied philosophy and the foundations of mathematics; prepared now for fundamental work in these fields, he died before he could do it. And third, there was the sense of unfulfilled promise: Ramsey *could have* done great things; but death prevented it. None of this could be said of Russell, whose life was complete, and so Russell's death was not comparably tragic.

This does not mean that Russell's death was not a bad thing in its own way, but we must be careful in describing how it was bad. Even Russell's personal friends, saddened by his passing, must have realized that his life was rich, successful, and in some important sense complete. If there was anything bad about the death, it is because we are able to view a life as in principle open-ended, as always having further possibilities that still might be realized, if only it could go on. There were still desires that Russell could have satisfied; there were still ambitions he might have accomplished. These thoughts make sense of seeing evil even in this death.

Our equanimity about his death, however, is due to our conception of life as bounded by the natural human contingencies. If those contingencies were different, our conception of a life's possibilities would be different. In reality, the possibilities for Russell's life had been exhausted by age and the feebleness it brings; thus thought about what he still might have done are largely fanciful. But suppose people lived to be a hundred and fifty, and at ninety-seven Russell was still vigorous and only half-done with the tasks he could naturally expect to accomplish. Then his death would be as tragic as Ramsey's; but then, too, our conception of what a life can contain would be changed, and so the reasons for judging the death tragic would be changed.

The Stages of a Life

The stages of a life are not isolated or self-contained parts. They bear relations to one another that must be understood if any part of the life is to be understood.

We cannot understand what a medical student is doing, for example, if we do not appreciate the way in which her present activity is preparation for the stages of her life which will come later. She wants to be a doctor, and live the kind of life that doctors have: apart from that, her present activity makes no sense. (Thus death at an early age renders this part of the life *pointless*.)

Moreover, the *evaluation* of one stage of a life may require reference to what came before. To be a doorkeeper, with a small but steady income sufficient to pay the rent on a modest apartment, might be a laudable achievement for one who previously was a homeless drunk; but for one who was a vice-president of the United States, caught taking bribes, the same existence might be a sign of failure and disgrace. (This is of course a fictitious example, since we know this is not what happens to American vice-presidents caught taking bribes.)

Thus the fact that people have memories, and are able to contemplate their futures, is important in explaining why they are able to have lives. Without these capacities, one could not see one's present condition as part of a larger, temporally extended existence; and one could have neither regrets nor aspirations.

Consider the plight of someone in whom the connections of memory have been severed. A striking example of this is described by Oliver Sacks, a professor of neurology at the Albert Einstein School of Medicine. Sacks has a patient, whom he calls Jimmie R., suffering from Korsakov's syndrome, which is associated with brain damage produced by alcohol. Jimmie remembers his life vividly up to 1945, when he was nineteen years old. After that, he remembers nothing. He is a bright, alert man who will talk to you intelligently when you are introduced; but two minutes later he will not remember having met you before and the conversation will start again. (Dr. Sacks has been "re-meeting" him regularly for nine years.) He believes he is still nineteen and that it is still 1945; but this is not because he is deluded in the way of someone who thinks he is Napoleon. He is rational enough; he simply has no memory of anything that has happened between then and now. When shown himself in the mirror he panics and thinks something terrible has happened to his face. Soon, though, he forgets having seen the mirror and the worry disappears.

Of course, Jimmie cannot have a normal life because he cannot do any of the things that constitute a life—he cannot relate normally to other people, hold a job, or even take care of his basic needs by shopping for food. (He is cared for in an institution.) But his lack of memory deprives him of a life in a deeper sense: without memory, he cannot conceive of his present state as connected with any other part of himself; plans, even intentional actions become impossible in any but a truncated sense. Without these connections, even the simplest feelings and attitudes lose their objects and meaning. Sacks recorded this conversation with Jimmie:

> "How do you feel?"
> "How do I feel," he repeated and scratched his head.
> "I cannot say I feel ill. But I cannot say I feel well. I cannot say I feel anything at all."
> "Are you miserable?" I continued.
> "Can't say I am."
> "Do you enjoy life?"
> "I can't say I do . . ."
> "You don't enjoy life," I repeated, hesitating somewhat. "How then *do* you feel about life?"
> "I can't say I feel anything at all."
> "You feel alive though?"
> "'Feel alive' . . . Not really. I haven't felt alive for a very long time."

After nine years of trying to deal with this case, Dr. Sacks's own conclusion is continuing bafflement about " . . . whether, indeed, one [can] speak of an 'existence,' given so absolute a privation of memory or continuity". We can, of course, speak of an "existence"—Jimmie R. exists. But Dr. Sacks's point is clear enough. Without the continuity that memory makes possible, a life, in any but the most rudimentary sense, is unattainable.

Multiple Lives

We sometimes speak of a person's having more than one life: a bigamist may be said to "lead two lives". This is not merely an idle way of speaking; it has a point. Lives are characterized by sets of interconnected projects, concerns, and relationships. A person may be said to "lead two lives" when there are two such sets, held rigidly separate, with little or no interaction between elements of the sets. The bigamist has two sets of relationships which must be kept absolutely apart—it is important that the members of one household not even know of the other's existence. Thus it is natural to speak of him as going back and forth between two lives.

Similarly, someone who moves to a distant city to start a new profession may be said to take up "a new life". Suppose a woman who was a prostitute in Miami moves to Los Angeles to become the proprietor of a clothing shop. She will spend her time on an entirely new set of activities, she will have a new set of friends—everything will be different. Like the bigamist, she may not even want her friends in Los Angeles to know about her life in Miami. Hence, a new life.

On some occasions, the effect of physical injury is to leave a patient alive and able to lead a life, but not the same life he had before. The famous "Texas burn case", often discussed in the literature of medical ethics, is a case of this type. In 1973 a young man known as "Donald C." was horribly burned over 68 percent of his body by an exploding gas line, and left blind, crippled, without fingers, and deformed in other ways as well. He was kept alive in the hospital for two years by a series of extraordinary and painful treatments; but all these treatments were against his will. Wanting to die, he continually demanded to be removed from the protective environment of the hospital. The doctors refused. He attempted to commit suicide, but was physically unable to bring it off. Finally, to justify keeping him in the hospital against his wishes, a psychiatrist was brought in to examine him, in the expectation that he would testify that Donald was incompetent. But, after interviewing him, the psychiatrist refused to do that, pronouncing—to the surprise of the physicians—that the patient was perfectly rational. So the young man was given the right to leave the hospital. But then, in a dramatic reversal, he changed his mind, and he is still alive today.

Now what could be said in defence of the judgement that this man's desire to die was rational? I believe focusing on the notion of his *life* (in the biographical sense) points us in the right direction. He was, among other things, a rodeo performer, a pilot, and what used to be called a 'ladies' man'. His life was not the life of a scholar or a solitary dreamer. What his injury had done, from his point of view, was to destroy his ability to lead the life that made him the distinctive individual he was. There could be no more rodeos, no more aeroplanes, no more dancing with the ladies, and a lot more. Donald's position was that if he could not lead *that* life, he didn't want to live.

Donald's physicians, in resisting his demand to die, argued in effect that he could take up a different sort of life, and that this different life might come to have some value for him. That is what he eventually did. The physicians may naturally think that these later developments vindicate their refusal to let Donald die, but Donald himself disagrees. Nine years after his ordeal, he appeared before a group of medical students to insist, with some bitterness, that the doctors had been wrong to refuse his demand. Although one may feel some sympathy with the doctors' view, it isn't hard to see Donald's point. We may applaud the courage he eventually showed in making a new life for himself, but we shouldn't miss noticing that his old life was gone. That is why his despair was not merely a temporary hysterical reaction to his situation.

The Temporal Boundaries of a Life

L. C. Morris was a 63-year-old Miami man who was shot in the head one night in 1970 when police mistook him for a roof-top sniper. The damage to his brain was extensive, but he did not die. He lived on, after a fashion, in a nursing home, where for more than three years he was fed through a tube running to his stomach and periodically turned to prevent bedsores. His body had private attendants round the clock; the cost of maintaining it alive was $2,600 per month. The emotional cost to Mrs. Morris cannot be calculated. Under the strain of daily visits to see him, her health deteriorated and she too had to be hospitalized. When told in 1972 that her husband might live for two more years, she replied, "He died back in 1970. We know that."

At the same time that Mr. Morris was in his coma, Miguel Martinez was also lying unconscious in a hospital. Martinez, a well-known Spanish athlete, had been injured in a soccer game in 1964 and remained in a coma until he died eight years later. When he died, his family announced, "Miguel died at the age of 34 after having lived 26 years."

Mrs. Morris's statement that her husband died in 1970 was simply false. The Martinez's melodramatic statement was paradoxical. Yet it is easy to see the point in both cases. The *lives* of these two men were over when they entered the comas, even though both remained alive for some time longer. Both families realized that being alive, in the absence of having a life, was not very important. . . .

Active and Passive Euthanasia

. . . The distinction between active and passive euthanasia is thought to be crucial for medical ethics. The idea is that it is permissible, at least in some cases, to withhold treatment and allow a patient to die, but it is never permissible to take any direct action designed to kill the patient. This doctrine seems to be accepted by most doctors, and it is endorsed in a statement adopted by the House of Delegates of the American Medical Association on December 4, 1973:

> The intentional termination of the life of one human being by another—mercy killing—is contrary to that for which the medical profession stands and is contrary to the policy of the American Medical Association.
>
> The cessation of the employment of extraordinary means to prolong the life of the body when there is irrefutable evidence that biological death is imminent is the decision of the patient and/or his immediate family. The advice and judgment of the physician should be freely available to the patient and/or his immediate family.

However, a strong case can be made against this doctrine. In what follows I will set out some of the relevant arguments, and urge doctors to reconsider their views on this matter.

To begin with a familiar type of situation, a patient who is dying of incurable cancer of the throat is in terrible pain, which can no longer be satisfactorily alleviated. He is certain to die within a few days, even if present treatment is continued, but he does not want to go on living for those days since the pain is unbearable. So he asks the doctor for an end to it, and his family joins in the request.

Suppose the doctor agrees to withhold treatment, as the conventional doctrine says he may. The justification for his doing so is that the patient is in terrible agony, and since he is going to die anyway, it would be wrong to prolong his suffering needlessly. But now notice this. If one simply withholds treatment, it may take the patient longer to die, and so he may suffer more than he would if more direct action were taken and a lethal injection given. This fact provides strong reason for thinking that, once the initial decision not to prolong his agony has been made, active euthanasia is actually preferable to passive euthanasia, rather than the reverse. To say otherwise is to endorse the option that leads to more suffering rather than less, and is contrary to the humanitarian impulse that prompts the decision not to prolong his life in the first place.

Part of my point is that the process of being "allowed to die" can be relatively slow and painful, whereas being given a lethal injection is relatively quick and painless. Let me give a different sort of example. In the United States about one in 600 babies is born with Down's syndrome. Most of these babies are otherwise healthy—that is, with only the usual pediatric care, they will proceed to an otherwise normal infancy. Some, however, are born with congenital defects such as intestinal obstructions that require operations if they are to live. Sometimes, the parents and the doctor will decide not to operate, and let the infant die. Anthony Shaw describes what happens then:

> . . . When surgery is denied [the doctor] must try to keep the infant from suffering while natural forces sap the baby's life away. As a surgeon whose natural inclination is to use the scalpel to fight off death, standing by and watching a salvageable baby die is the most emotionally exhausting experience I know. It is easy at a conference, in a theoretical discussion, to decide that such infants should be allowed to die. It is altogether *different* to stand by in the nursery and watch as dehydration and infection wither a tiny being over hours and days. This is a terrible for me and the hospital staff—much more so than for the parents who never set foot in the nursery.[1]

I can understand why some people are opposed to all euthanasia, and insist that such infants must be allowed to live. I think I can also understand why other people favor destroying these babies quickly and painlessly. But why should anyone favor letting "dehydration and infection wither a tiny being over hours and days"? The doctrine that says that a baby may be allowed to dehydrate and wither, but may not be given an injection that would end its life without suffering, seems so patently cruel as to require no further refutation. The strong language is not intended to offend, but only to put the point in the clearest possible way.

My second argument is that the conventional doctrine leads to decisions concerning life and death made on irrelevant grounds.

Consider again the case of the infants with Down's syndrome who need operations for congenital defects unrelated to the syndrome to live. Sometimes, there is no operation, and the baby dies, but when there is no such defect, the baby lives on. Now, an operation such as that to remove an intestinal obstruction is not prohibitively difficult. The reason why such operations are not performed in these cases is, clearly, that the child has Down's syndrome and the parents and doctor judge that because of that fact it is better for the child to die.

But notice that this situation is absurd, no matter what view one takes of the lives and potentials of such babies. If the life of such an infant is worth preserving, what does it matter if it needs a simple operation? Or, if one thinks it better that such a baby should not live on, what difference does it make that it happens to have an unobstructed intestinal tract? In either case, the matter of life and death is being decided on irrelevant grounds. It is the Down's syndrome, and not the intestines, that is the issue. The matter should be decided, if at all, on that basis, and not be allowed to depend on the essentially irrelevant question of whether the intestinal tract is blocked.

What makes this situation possible, of course, is the idea that when there is an intestinal blockage, one can "let the baby die," but when there is no such defect there is nothing that can be done, for one must not "kill" it. The fact that this idea leads to such results as deciding life or death on irrelevant grounds is another good reason why the doctrine should be rejected.

One reason why so many people think that there is an important moral difference between active and passive euthanasia is that they think killing someone is morally worse than letting someone die. But is it?

Is killing, in itself, worse than letting die? To investigate this issue, two cases may be considered that are exactly alike except that one involves killing whereas the other involves letting someone die. Then, it can be asked whether this difference makes any difference to the moral assessments. It is important that the cases be exactly alike, except for this one difference, since otherwise one cannot be confident that it is this difference and not some other that accounts for any variation in the assessments of the two cases. So, let us consider this pair of cases:

In the first, Smith stands to gain a large inheritance if anything should happen to his six-year-old cousin. One evening while the child is taking bath, Smith sneaks into the bathroom and drowns the child, and then arranges things so that it will look like an accident.

In the second, Jones also stands to gain if anything should happen to his six-year-old cousin. Like Smith, Jones sneaks in planning to drown the child in his bath. However, just as he enters the bathroom Jones sees the child slip and hit his head, and fall face down in the water. Jones is delighted; he stands by, ready to push the child's head back under if it is necessary, but it is not necessary. With only a little thrashing about, the child drowns all by himself, "accidentally," as Jones watches and does nothing.

Now Smith killed the child, whereas Jones "merely" let the child die. That is the only difference between them. Did either man behave better, from a moral point of view? If the difference between killing and letting die were in itself a morally important matter, one should say that Jones's behavior was less reprehensible than Smith's. But does one really want to say that? I think not. In the first place, both men acted from the same motive, personal gain, and both had exactly the same end in view when they acted. It may be inferred from Smith's conduct that he is a bad man, although that judgment may be withdrawn or modified if certain further facts are learned about him—for example, that he is mentally deranged. But would not the very same thing be inferred about Jones from his conduct? And would not the same further considerations also be relevant to any modification of this judgment? Moreover, suppose Jones pleaded, in his own defense, "After all, I didn't do anything except just stand there and watch the child drown. I didn't kill him; I only let him die." Again, if letting die were in itself less bad than killing, this defense should have at least some weight. But it does not. Such a "defense" can only be regarded as a

grotesque perversion of moral reasoning. Morally speaking, it is no defense at all.

Now, it may be pointed out, quite properly, that the cases of euthanasia with which doctors are concerned are not like this at all. They do not involve personal gain or the destruction of normal healthy children. Doctors are concerned only with cases in which the patient's life is of no further use to him, or in which the patient's life has become or will soon become a terrible burden. However, the point is the same in these cases: the bare difference between killing and letting die does not, in itself, make a moral difference. If a doctor lets a patient die, for humane reasons, he is in the same moral position as if he had given the patient a lethal injection for humane reasons. If his decision was wrong—if, for example, the patient's illness was in fact curable—the decision would be equally regrettable no matter which method was used to carry it out. And if the doctor's decision was the right one, the method used is not in itself important.

The AMA policy statement isolates the crucial issue very well; the crucial issue is "the intentional termination of the life of one human being by another." But after identifying this issue, and forbidding "mercy killing," the statement goes on to deny that the cessation of treatment is the intentional termination of a life. This is where the mistake comes in, for what is the cessation of treatment, in these circumstances, if it is not "the intentional termination of the life of one human being by another"? Of course, it is exactly that, and if it were not, there would be no point to it.

Many people will find this judgment hard to accept. One reason, I think, is that it is very easy to conflate the question of whether killing is, in itself, worse than letting die, with the very different question of whether most actual cases of killing are more reprehensible than most actual cases of letting die. Most actual cases of killing are clearly terrible (think, for example, of all the murders reported in the newspapers), and one hears of such cases every day. On the other hand, one hardly ever hears of a case of letting die, except for the actions of doctors who are motivated by humanitarian reasons. So one learns to think of killing in a much worse light than of letting die. But this does not mean that there is something about killing that makes it in itself worse than letting die, for it is not the bare difference between killing and letting die that makes the difference in these cases. Rather, the other factors—the murderer's motive of personal gain, for example, contrasted with the doctor's humanitarian motivation—account for different reactions to the different cases.

I have argued that killing is not in itself any worse than letting die; if my contention is right, it follows that active euthanasia is not any worse than passive euthanasia. What arguments can be given on the other side? The most common, I believe, is the following:

"The important difference between active and passive euthanasia is that, in passive euthanasia, the doctor does not do anything to bring about the patient's death. The doctor does nothing, and the patient dies of whatever ills already afflict him. In active euthanasia, however, the doctor does something to bring about the patient's death: he kills him. The doctor who gives the patient with cancer a lethal injection has himself caused his patient's death; whereas if he merely ceases treatment, the cancer is the cause of the death."

A number of points need to be made here. The first is that it is not exactly correct to say that in passive euthanasia the doctor does nothing, for he does do one thing that is very important: he lets the patient die. "Letting someone die" is certainly different, in some respects, from other types of action—mainly in that it is a kind of action that one may perform by way of not performing certain other actions. For example, one may let a patient die by way of not giving medication, just as one may insult someone by way of not shaking his hand. But for any purpose of moral assessment, it is a type of action nonetheless. The decision to let a patient die is subject to moral appraisal in the same way that a decision to kill him would be subject to moral appraisal; it may be assessed as wise or unwise, compassionate or sadistic, right or wrong. If a doctor deliberately let a patient die who was suffering from a routinely curable illness, the doctor would certainly be to blame if he had needlessly killed the patient. Charges against him would then be appropriate. If so, it would be no defense at all for him to insist that he didn't "do anything." He would have done something very serious indeed, for he let his patient die.

Fixing the cause of death may be very important from a legal point of view, for it may determine whether criminal charges are brought against the doctor. But I do not think that this notion can be used to show a moral difference between active and passive euthanasia. The reason why it is considered bad to be the cause of someone's death is that death is regarded as a great evil—and so it is. However, if it has been decided that euthanasia—even passive euthanasia—is desirable in a given case, it has also been decided that in this instance death is no greater an evil than the patient's continued existence. And if this is true, the usual reason for not wanting to be the cause of someone's death simply does not apply.

Finally, doctors may think that all of this is only of academic interest—the sort of thing that philosophers may worry about but that has no practical bearing on their own work. After all, doctors must be concerned about the legal consequences of what they do, and active euthanasia is clearly forbidden by the law. But even so, doctors should also be concerned with the fact that the law is forcing upon them a moral doctrine that may well be indefensible, and has a considerable effect on their practices. Of course, most doctors are not now in the position of being coerced in this matter, for they do not regard themselves as merely going along with what the law requires. Rather, in statements such as the AMA policy statement that I have quoted, they are endorsing this doctrine as a central point of medical ethics. In that statement, active euthanasia is condemned not merely as illegal but as "contrary to that for which the medical profession stands," whereas passive euthanasia is approved. However, the preceding considerations suggest that there is really no moral difference between the two, considered in themselves (there may be important moral differences in some cases in their *consequences*, but, as I pointed out, these differences may make active euthanasia, and not passive euthanasia, the morally preferable option). So whereas doctors may have to discriminate between active and passive euthanasia to satisfy the law, they should not do any more than that. In particular, they should not give the distinction any added authority and weight by writing it into official statements of medical ethics.

Discussion Questions

1. How does Professor Rachels distinguish between biographical and biological life? Why does he believe that biographical life is more important than biological life? And how does this distinction, according to Professor Rachels, justify active euthanasia? Do you agree with this? Why or why not?

2. Briefly tell the story of Jones and Smith. Why does Professor Rachels believe that this tale shows that there is no moral distinction between passive and active euthanasia? Do you agree that there is no distinction between active and passive euthanasia? Ex-

plain and defend your answer.

3. Imagine if a distraught teenager wants to commit suicide because he believes his biographical life has ended, e.g., his girlfriend has broken up with him and he has bad acne. Given the apparent subjective nature of what constitutes a biographically significant life, on what grounds could Professor Rachels argue that the teenager is morally wrong in committing suicide? If Professor Rachels says that it is an inappropriate choice for a human person to make, then isn't it possible that patients who want to end their biological lives because of what they perceive as the end of their biographical lives are making an inappropriate choice? How do you think Rachels would respond to this inquiry?

Notes

1. A. Shaw, "Doctor, Do We Have a Choice?" *The New York Times Magazine*, January 30, 1972, p. 54.

23

James Rachels and the Active Euthanasia Debate

J. P. Moreland

J. P. Moreland is Professor of Philosophy of Religion at the Talbot School of Theology, Biola University. He has contributed to numerous scholarly journals, in addition to writing several books, including *The Life and Death Debate: Moral Issues of Our Time* (1990), *Immortality* (1992), and *Scaling the Secular City* (1987).

In this essay Professor Moreland challenges both Professor Rachels' case for the biological/biographical distinction and his case against the active/passive distinction. Concerning the former, Professor Moreland argues that Professor Rachels' "understanding of biological life, far from rendering biological life morally insignificant, presupposes the importance of biological life." That is, "human being" is not merely a biological concept, but a metaphysical concept (a natural kind) that grounds both moral intuitions and biological functions. Concerning Professor Rachels' critique of the active/passive distinction, Professor Moreland argues that the "main difficulty with the bare-differences argument lies in its inadequate analysis of a human moral act." That is, the reason why Professor Rachels can find no moral distinction between the acts of Jones and Smith is because he ignores the important fact that each had the same *intention*: to kill his cousin for the sake of greed. What makes an act passive or active cannot be reduced to only the refraining or the moving of certain body parts, but must include the intention of the agent. Consequently, Jones and Smith were both engaged in an active deed of killing, since it was clearly their intention to commit the murder.

Reprinted by permission from *Journal of the Evangelical Theological Society* 31 (March 1988).

The rise of advanced medical technologies, especially life-sustaining ones, has brought to center stage the importance of bioethical issues that arise in acute and long-term care contexts. The recent avalanche of bioethics committees is a witness to the importance of bioethical issues.[1] Problems about the nature and permissibility of euthanasia have been especially pressing.[2]

Roughly speaking, there are two major views about euthanasia.[3] The traditional view holds that *prima facie* it is always wrong to intentionally kill an innocent human being, but that given certain circumstances it is permissible to withhold or withdraw treatment and allow a patient to die. A more radical view, embraced by groups like the Hemlock Society and the Society for the Right to Die, denies that there is a morally significant distinction between passive and active euthanasia that allows the former and forbids the latter. Accordingly this view argues that mercy killing, assisted suicide and the like are permissible. I want to argue against the radical view by criticizing the most articulate expression of it to date—that of James Rachels.[4]

I. Important Ethical Concepts

1. The Active/Passive Distinction

Passive euthanasia occurs when a person is allowed to die by withholding or withdrawing a life-sustaining treatment. Active euthanasia is the direct, intentional killing of a person either by himself (suicide) or another (assisted suicide or mercy killing).

2. Intentional Action and the Principle of Double Effect

The principle of double effect was given explicit formulation by moral philosophers and theologians of the nineteenth century, though its roots can be traced to Scripture itself.[5] The principle stated that when an action has good and bad consequences, then the act may be performed under the following conditions: (1) The act is good or at least indifferent by its object (where "object" means the directly intended thing one is doing); (2) the good and evil effects follow immediately from the act—that is, the good effect is not obtained by means of the evil effect; (3) one only intends the good effect and merely tolerates the bad one; (4) there is a proportion between the good and bad effects—that is the good must be at least equal to the bad.

The word "intends" has a technical meaning in condition (3). Sometimes we say that if someone intends something it was not an accident. An unintended action is one that is an accident or a mistake. This is not the meaning of the word here. Rather, it means "what one is aiming at or trying to accomplish by an action." Thus a patient in severe pain with no more than five days to live may be given an injection of morphine to relieve the pain, but due to the respiratory inhibition of morphine the patient may only live two days. The act of hastening the patient's death was intentional on the first definition but not on the second.

3. The Ordinary/Extraordinary Distinction

Ethicists frequently distinguish ordinary means of sustaining life from extraordinary means. Ordinary means are all medicines, treatments and operations that offer a reasonable hope of benefit for the patient and that can be obtained and used without excessive expense, pain, or other inconvenience. Extraordinary means are those that are not ordinary—that is, those that involve excessive expense, pain, or inconvenience and that do not offer reasonable hope of benefit. Terms like "reasonable hope" and "excessive" change as medicine changes. But this fact does not relativize the distinction morally because it continues to capture a balance between risks and benefits. Further, economic expense seems appropriate when considering macroallocation issues, but not microallocation issues focusing on specific patients. At that level patient advocacy should be in focus.

II. The Traditional View of Euthanasia

1. The Distinction between Active and Passive Euthanasia

Three reasons have been offered for the distinction between active and passive euthanasia. (1) The cause of death is different. In the former case it is the doctor or other human agent (e.g., the person himself in a suicide). In the latter case it is the disease or God himself. (2) The intent of the act is different. In active euthanasia it is the death of the patient. In passive euthanasia death is the (perhaps) foreseen consequence of an otherwise legitimate action whose intent may be to alleviate suffering, respect patient autonomy, cease interfering with the dying process, and so forth. (3) There is a distinction between negative and positive human (and, I would add, natural[6]) rights. The former state our obligation to refrain from harming another, and they form the basis of our correlative duty of nonmaleficence. The latter state our obligation to do something positive for another, and they form the basis of our correlative duty of beneficence.[7] Negative rights generally take precedence over positive rights. In passive euthanasia one refrains from benefiting a person, but in active euthanasia one directly harms another.

2. The Permissibility of Passive Euthanasia

The traditional view allows for withholding or withdrawing treatment in some cases where certain circumstances obtain. What are these circumstances? Two different cases arise. (1) Treatment may be withheld or withdrawn if such an action is requested by an autonomous, competent decision-maker. Thus if a person wishes to forego renal dialysis, it may be morally permissible to honor that request.[8] (2) Treatment may be withheld or withdrawn (assuming such an action is in keeping with patient autonomy) if the patient is terminal, death is imminent, treatment is judged extraordinary, and death is not directly intended.[9]

3. Active Euthanasia Is Morally Forbidden

The traditional view forbids active euthanasia—the direct, intentional killing of an innocent human being. At least six reasons have been offered for this position.

(1) Active euthanasia violates a person's negative right to be protected from harm, while passive euthanasia only violates a person's positive right to have a benefit—and the former usually has a higher degree of incumbency than the latter. Rachels denies the active/passive distinction, and as a result

he holds that failure to feed the hungry of the world is morally equivalent to killing them. We are, in short, murderers.

(2) A mistaken diagnosis can be reversed in passive euthanasia. If treatment is withdrawn or withheld and the patient was not as seriously ill as was thought, he will get well. But no such possibility exists if active euthanasia is allowed. Rachels agrees with this in principle, but he argues that there are some cases where we can know that death is imminent and irreversible. In those cases active euthanasia is permissible.

(3) Some (Rachels included) justify active euthanasia by an argument based on mercy. If one is going to die very soon but is in terrible pain, it is more merciful to kill the person. You may cut his life from five more days to one day but, given the horrible agony that the person is experiencing, mercy demands a quick death with dignity.

A defender of the traditional view can point out that there are very few cases where modern medicine cannot alleviate suffering in terminal cases, and it is wrong ethical methodology to build a major ethical doctrine on problem cases.[10] Further, even in cases where pain cannot be treated without a lethal injection the doctor can still intend to treat pain and not kill. Rachels rejects this suggestion because he does not think intentions are relevant to moral acts. We will analyze his reasoning later. Finally, though this can be abused, a Christian worldview implies that there can be a point to suffering.[11]

(4) Active euthanasia violates the special duty that physicians have to patients—namely, the preservation of life. Thus it violates the very nature of the health-care profession and the special duties that constitute that profession if we allow active euthanasia. Rachels counters this by arguing that we replace the profession of "medicine" with that of "smedicine," which is just like medicine except in cases where active euthanasia would be justified. His point is that if active euthanasia is justified, then the medical profession is built around the wrong set of duties.

(5) Active euthanasia weakens respect for human life and thus, even if it could be justified in a particular case, we could not adopt active euthanasia as a general policy. Such a move would destroy the confidence our society has in the medical profession and weaken the patient/professional relationship. This is a form of slippery-slope argument that can take one of two forms. A logical slippery-slope argument says that if a disputed act A cannot be logically distinguished from an act B, and we know that B is wrong, then A is wrong too. The logical version involves, among other things, a discussion of the significance of being a human being or a person. I will postpone discussion of this until later. A psychological slippery-slope argument says that even though a disputed act A is really different from a forbidden act B, nevertheless if we allow A it will contribute to causing people to do B, and so A should not be allowed. Rachels rightly points out that this is not a moral question but an empirical one. It is a factual question as to what effect a certain policy will have on society.[12]

Perhaps enough has been said about the first five arguments against active euthanasia to suggest the relevant lines of debate in defending or attacking them. There is, however, one more argument against active euthanasia that is the most important one.

(6) The intentional killing of an innocent human life is simply wrong. It is wrong because human life is sacred—or, to put the point less theistically, human life has intrinsic value as an end in itself. In active euthanasia one intends and causes directly the death of a human being, and such an act violates the deontological principle that such acts are wrong. This principle is knowable from special revelation, intuition into or inference from natural law, or by a criterion such as universalizability. This is the cornerstone of the traditional view, and it forms an appropriate transition to considering the radical position that seeks to provide an alternative vision of this principle.

III. The Radical View

According to Rachels, the distinctions used in the traditional view are inadequate. There is nothing sacred or morally significant about being a human being with biological life. Nor is there any moral difference between killing someone and letting him die. Thus if passive euthanasia is permitted in a given case, so is active euthanasia. Two distinctions are central for Rachels' position.

1. Biological Life versus Biographical Life

The mere fact that something has biological life, says Rachels, whether human or nonhuman, is relatively unimportant. What is important is that someone has biographical life. One's biographical life is "the sum of one's aspirations, decisions, activities, projects, and human relationships."[13] The facts of a person's biographical life are those of his history and character. They are the interests that are important and worthwhile from the point of view of the person him/herself. The value of one's biographical life is the value it has for that person, and something has value if its loss would harm that person.[14]

Two implications follow from Rachels' view. (1) Certain infants without a prospect for biographical life, and certain terminal patients (e.g., comatose patients, or those in a persistent vegetative state), have nothing to be concerned with from a moral point of view. They are not alive in the biographical sense, though they may be in the biological sense. But the former is what is relevant to morality. (2) Higher forms of animals do have lives in the biographical sense because they have thoughts, emotions, goals, cares, and so forth. Thus they should be given moral respect because of this. In fact a chimpanzee with a biographical life has more value than a human who only has biological life.

2. Killing and Letting Die

Rachels believes that there is no distinction between killing someone directly or letting that person die. There is no morally important difference between these. He calls this the "equivalence" thesis. His main argument for it is called the "bare difference" argument. Rachels sets up two cases that are supposed to be exactly alike except that one involves killing and the other involves letting die.[15]

> Smith stands to gain a large inheritance if anything should happen to his six-year-old cousin. One evening while the child is taking his bath, Smith sneaks into the bathroom and drowns the child, and then arranges things so that it will look like an accident. No one is the wiser, and Smith gets his inheritance. Jones also stands to gain if anything should happen to his six-year-old cousin. Like Smith, Jones sneaks in planning to drown the child in his bath. However, just as he enters the bathroom Jones sees the child slip, hit his head, and fall face-down in the water. Jones is delighted; he stands by, ready to push the child's head back under if necessary, but it is not necessary. With only a little thrashing about, the child drowns all by himself, "accidentally," as Jones watches and does nothing. No one is the wiser, and Jones gets his inheritance.

According to Rachels, neither man behaved better from a moral point of view even though Smith killed the child and Jones merely let the child die. Both acted from the same motive (personal gain) and the results were identical (death). Thus the only difference between the two cases is killing versus letting die, and since the cases are morally equivalent this distinction is morally irrelevant.

Two implications follow from the equivalence thesis. (1) Cases where passive euthanasia is permissible are also cases where active euthanasia is permissible. (2) Situations where we let people die—for example, when we let them starve in famine situations—are morally equivalent to killing them.

IV. Criticisms of the Radical View

1. The Biological/Biographical View of Life

There are at least three problems with Rachels' distinction between biological and biographical life.

(1) His understanding of biographical life, far from rendering biological life morally insignificant, presupposes the importance of biological human life. He describes biographical life as a unity of capacities, interests, and so forth, that a person freely chooses for himself and that unites the various stages of one's life. It is even possible for a bigamist, says Rachels, to lead two biographical lives.

Now it is precisely these (and other) features of life that the Aristotelian/Thomist notion of secondary substance (essence, natural kind) seeks to explain. It is because an entity has an essence and falls within a natural kind that it can possess a unity of dispositions, capacities, parts and properties at a given time and can maintain identity through change. And it is the natural kind that determines what kinds of activities are appropriate and natural for that entity.

Further, an organism *qua* essentially characterized particulars has second-order capacities to have first-order capacities that may or may not obtain (through some sort of lack). These second-order capacities are grounded in the nature of the organism. For example, a child may not have the first-order capacity to speak English due to a lack of education. But because the child has humanness it has the capacity to develop the capacity to speak English. The very idea of a defect presupposes these second-order capacities.

Now the natural kind "human being" or "human person" (I do not distinguish between these) is not to be understood as a mere biological concept. It is a metaphysical concept that grounds both biological functions and moral intuitions. In what is perhaps the most articulate modern defense of the doctrine of substance I am presenting, David Wiggins states:[16]

> If we ask what is so good, either absolutely or to me, about my mental life's flowing on from now into the future, the answer ... imports what makes me dear to myself—and with it my idea of myself as a continuant with certain moral or other qualities that make me fond of myself.

In sum, if we ask why biographical life is both possible and morally important, the answer will be that such a life is grounded in the kind of entity, a human person in this case, that typically can have that life.

2. Rachels' View Seems to Collapse into Subjectivism

According to him the importance of a biographical life is that a person has the capacity to set and achieve goals, plans and interests that are important from the point of view of the individual himself. But if this is true, then there is no objective moral difference in the different goals one chooses for himself. One can only be right or wrong about the best means to accomplish these goals.[17] To see this, consider Rachels' treatment of the 1973 "Texas burn case" where a man known as Donald C. was horribly burned but was kept alive for two years in the hospital against his will and is still alive today. Rachels believes his desire to die was rational because Donald C. had lost his biographical life. Says Rachels:[18]

> Now what could be said in defence of the judgement that this man's desire to die was rational? I believe focusing on the notion of his *life* (in the biographical sense) points us in the right direction. He was, among other things, a rodeo performer, a pilot, and what used to be called a "ladies' man." His life was not the life of a scholar or a solitary dreamer. What his injury had done, from his point of view, was to destroy his ability to lead the life that made him the distinctive individual he was. There could be no more rodeos, no more aeroplanes, no more dancing with the ladies, and a lot more. Donald's position was that

if he could not lead *that* life, he didn't want to live.

But surely some rational life plans are more valuable than others. In fact it is possible to choose goals and interests that are immoral and dehumanizing. Suppose there is a woman named Xavier. Her life plan is to become the best prostitute she can be. She enjoys bestiality, group sex, and certain forms of masochism. Her life has value from her point of view if and only if she can achieve these goals. Now suppose that she is in an accident that confines her to a wheelchair such that she is in no pain, she can lead a relatively productive life in various ways, but she can no longer pursue her desire to be the best prostitute ever. Does it make sense to say that she would be rational to desire to die? Does it make sense to say that her biographical life is what gave her life value? Rachels' view would seem to imply an affirmative answer to both of these questions. But is it not clear that Xavier was dehumanizing herself? Some forms of life are "appropriate" for humans, and others are not. The difference seems to be grounded in the fact that a human being is a creature of value, and a choice of life plans can be devaluing to the sort of creature one is. Without objective material grounds that constitute a morally appropriate life plan, subjectivism would seem to follow. But one can be wrong about one's point of view.

Rachels denies that his view is equivalent to moral subjectivism. He argues that it is objectively true that something has value for someone if its loss would harm that person. But this is a mere formal principle, and the material content one gives it—that is, what it is to be harmed—will depend in large degree on what interests constitute one's biographical life. The case of Donald C. illustrates this. But since a choice of interests is subjective, Rachels' view is subjectivist.

3. According to Rachels, People without Biographical Lives Are no Longer Morally Significant regarding the Rule not to Kill

This is because the point of the rule is to protect people with biographical lives. It would seem, then, that a person who no longer has such a life, who has no point of view, is no longer an object of a duty not to kill. There is not even a *prima facie* duty not to kill in this case. But if the person has lost the right not to be killed—for example, because he is in a persistent vegetative state—it would seem that he has lost other rights as well. It would seem that one could experiment on the person or kill him brutally if he so desired. Why? Because we are no longer dealing with an object that has relevant rights.

Rachels could respond that some other factor is relevant that would forbid killing the patient violently. Perhaps others would see the act, perhaps this would weaken respect for life, or perhaps such an act would foster hostility in the doctor's character. The difficulty with this response should be obvious. Cases can be set up where the other factors do not obtain: No one knows about the brutal killing of the patient, the doctor's psychologist has told him to express his aggression toward objects that remind him of his mother, and so on. In these cases there would seem to be no moral difference between a lethal injection or a more brutal means of killing. The patient has no life and is not an object of moral consideration and thus approaches thing-like status. If Rachels' views do in fact entail his conclusion, and if this conclusion is morally unacceptable, then Rachels' view must be mistaken.

2. The Killing/Letting-die Distinction

The "bare difference" argument involving the Smith and Jones cases was an attempt to show that two different actions—one killing and one letting die—can have the same intentions and results and thus are both morally forbidden in spite of the difference in actions. In fact, the cases are supposed to show that the mere difference between killing and letting die is irrelevant. But the cases fail to make the point. The cases have what some philosophers call a masking or sledge-hammer effect.[19] The fact that one cannot distinguish the taste of two wines when both are mixed with green persimmon juice fails to show that there is no difference between the wines. The taste of the persimmon juice is so strong that it overshadows the difference. Similarly, the intentions and motives of Smith and Jones are so atrocious, and both acts are so clearly unjustified, that it is not surprising that other features of their situation (killing versus letting die) are not perceived as the morally determinative factors in the cases.

But this observation, valid as it is, does not take us to the heart of the problem with Rachels' bare-difference argument. The main difficulty with the bare-difference argument lies in its inadequate analysis of a human moral act. Thomas Sullivan puts his finger on the difficulty when he argues that Rachels makes the distinction between the act of killing and the act of letting die be "a distinction that puts a moral premium on overt behavior—moving or not moving one's parts—while totally ignoring the intentions of the agent."[20] But is the proper analysis of a human action—especially a human moral action—one that merely treats that action as a physical event? I think not.

There is an alternative analysis of human action in general, and human moral action in particular, that finds its classic expression in Aquinas' *Summa Theologica* 1,2 qq. 6–20.[21] A human act, moral or otherwise, is a composite whole that contains various parts among which are these two: (1) the object, end, or intention of the act, and (2) the means-to-the-end of the act. As Richard M. Gula points out:

> The intention of the agent and the means-to-an-end form two structural elements of *one* composite action. To determine the morality of the human action, both of these elements must be taken together. The significance of this is that the physical action itself (the material event, or means-to-an-end) cannot be evaluated morally without considering the actor, especially the intention.[22]

To see this, consider the following case. Suppose a man named Jones is visited by the world's leading hypnotist. Jones is hypnotized, is told to hit the nose of the first person wearing a red shirt, and is causally determined to do so. Jones wakes up, leaves the office and strikes the first red-shirted person in the nose.

Now consider Smith. He hates his football coach because he is jealous of his good looks. His coach happens to be wearing a red shirt that day and Smith, out of hatred and jealousy and with an intent to hurt his coach, strikes him on the nose. It seems obvious that Smith's act was immoral and Jones' was not. In fact it does not seem that Jones really acted at all. What is the difference? Both acts have the same set of physical happenings or means to ends. The difference is that Smith intended an immoral end and Jones did not act out of intent at all.

Rachels' bare-difference cases differ in means-to-ends, but they have the same intent. Defenders of the active/passive distinction, however, do not ground the differences on mere physical happenings or means-to-ends. The acts of Smith and Jones drowning the two children differ only in physical properties. But that is just part of a human act, not the whole. Rachels leaves the intent of the two acts out of his analysis, but a defender of the traditional view would not allow such an analysis to stand.

Rachelss set up a different case to try to show that two acts can be the same with different intentions and thus intentions are not a part of an act.[23] Jack visits his sick and lonely grandmother, and his only intention is to cheer her up. Jill also visits the grandmother and provides her an afternoon of cheer. But Jill does it to influence the grandmother to put her in the grandmother's will. Both of them, says Rachels, did the same thing: They spent an afternoon cheering up the grandmother. Jill should be judged harshly and Jack praised—not because they did different acts, but because Jack's character is good and Jill's is faulty.

If my analysis of human action is correct, then Jack and Jill did not do the same actions. Their actions may be identical at the level of means-to-ends, but their intents were different. Jack's action was one of loving his grandmother and cheering her up by being with her. Jill's action was one of securing a place in the will by being with her.

The inseparability of intentions and means in human action can also be seen by asking how it is possible for an action to reveal one's character.[24] Character is a relatively stable unity or structure of moral virtues that underlies and expresses itself in the moral acts or conduct of the person. A moral virtue is an ingrained habit or disposition of the embodied will. A habit or disposition is a tendency to act in certain circumstances. Thus character is both formed by and an expression of intentional actions. That is why one's character is revealed by one's actions and why actions shape character. On Rachels' Humean analysis, actions are separate from intentions and vice versa. If that is the case, how is it that one can infer character from one's actions? It would seem that no necessary connection exists.

Discussion Questions

1. Present and explain in detail Professor Moreland's response to Professor Rachels' case for the biological/biographical distinction. Do you think he has adequately responded to the argument? Why or why not?

2. Present and explain in detail Professor Moreland's response to Professor Rachels' case against the active/passive distinction. What role does *intention* play in his response? Do you think Profes-

sor Moreland has adequately responded to the argument? Why or why not?

3. Although Professor Moreland may be correct that "human being" is a natural kind, could not someone sympathetic to Professor Rachels' position take a more moderate view and argue that when certain human characteristics are permanently missing, such as self-awareness and consciousness, the biological entity is no longer a "human being"? How do you think Professor Moreland would respond to this question? Explain your answer.

Notes

1. The development of bioethics committees is well advanced in acute-care facilities but not in long-term care. For more on the nature and function of bioethics committees see *Institutional Ethics Committees and Health Care Decision Making* (ed. R. E. Cranford and A. E. Doudera; Ann Arbor: Health Care, 1984); B. Hosford, *Bioethics Committees* (Rockville: Aspen, 1986).

2. For a survey of death and dying cases see R. M. Veatch, *Case Studies in Medical Ethics* (Cambridge: Harvard University, 1977) 317–347.

3. For a critique of voluntary active euthanasia see M. Erickson and I. Bowers, "Euthanasia and Christian Ethics," *JETS* 19 (1970) 15–24. Erickson and Bowers consider whether voluntary active euthanasia is ever right. But they assume—correctly, in my view—that active and passive euthanasia are distinct. The major burden of the present article is to justify that distinction.

4. See J. Rachels, "Active and Passive Euthanasia," *The New England Journal of Medicine* 292 (January 9, 1975) 78–80; *The End of Life* (Oxford: Oxford University, 1986).

5. For a helpful discussion of the doctrine of double effect see B. M. Ashley and K. D. O'Rourke, *Health Care Ethics* (St. Louis: Catholic Health Association of the United States, 1982) 187–191. For references that modify the double-effect principle but retain its substance see the President's Commission report entitled *Deciding to Forego Life-Sustaining Treatment* (Washington: U.S. Government Printing Office, 1983) 80.

6. On the difference between legal, human, and natural rights see J. Feinberg, *Social Philosophy* (Englewood Cliffs: Doubleday, 1973) 55–97. For a discussion of rights in general see J. W Montgomery, *Human Rights and Human Dignity* (Grand Rapids: Zondervan, 1986).

7. See T. L. Beauchamp and J. F. Childress, *Principles of Biomedical Ethics* (New York: Oxford University, 1983) 106–182.

8. Cases of this kind involve weighing conflicts between the principle of autonomy and the principles of beneficence or nonmaleficence, patient competence, and the quality of life. Quality-of-life considerations can be

especially perilous and abused. For different senses of the quality of life see A. R. Jonsen, M. Seigler and W. J. Winslade, *Clinical Ethics* (New York: Macmillan, 1986) 101–127.

9. For a brief survey of living-will provisions in various states see the report of the Special Committee on Biomedical Ethics entitled *Values in Conflict* (Chicago: American Hospital Association, 1985) 67–74.

10. In epistemology in general, one develops criteria for knowledge from clear cases of knowledge that are then used to judge borderline cases. See R. Chisholm, *The Problem of the Criterion* (Milwaukee: Marquette University, 1973).

11. See Ashley and O'Rourke, *Health* 199–205.

12. Rachels argues that active euthanasia will not have the effect of weakening respect for human life (*End* 171–180).

13. Ibid., p. 5; see also pp. 26, 33, 35, 38, 47, 49–59, 65, 76, 85.

14. Ibid., p. 38.

15. Ibid., p. 112.

16. D. Wiggins, *Sameness and Substance* (Cambridge: Harvard University, 1980) 152.

17. Rachels, *End* 46–47.

18. Ibid., p. 54.

19. See Beauchamp and Childress, *Principles* 117.

20. T. D. Sullivan, "Active and Passive Euthanasia: An Important Distinction?", reprinted in *Social Ethics* (ed. T. Mappes and J. Zembaty; New York: McGraw-Hill, 1982) 59.

21. For recent treatments of this view see R. M. Gula, *What Are They Saying About Moral Norms?* (New York: Paulist, 1982) 61–74; J. Finnis, *Fundamentals of Ethics* (Washington: Georgetown University, 1983) 37–48, 112–120; J. Fuchs, *Christian Ethics in a Secular Arena* (Washington: Georgetown University, 1984) 75–77. See also R.M. Chisholm, *Brentano and Intrinsic Value* (Cambridge: Cambridge University, 1986) 17–32.

22. Gula, *What* 27.

23. Rachels, *End* 93–94.

24. For a good but relatively unknown discussion of virtues and character see G. F. Thomas, *Christian Ethics and Moral Philosophy* (New York: Scribner's, 1955) 485–521.

24

Death and Dignity: A Case of Individualized Decision Making

Timothy E. Quill

Timothy E. Quill practices medicine at the Genesee Hospital in Rochester, N.Y. He is the author of *Death and Dignity: Making Choices and Taking Charge* (1993).

In this essay Dr. Quill tells the story of Diane, a patient of his who had been diagnosed with leukemia. Diane, who had overcome a number of obstacles throughout her life including vaginal cancer, depression, and alcoholism, chose not to undergo treatment that has a 25 percent success rate. Although the choice to refuse treatment is morally uncontroversial in most cases, it was his fulfillment of one of Diane's other requests that was morally problematic and caused Dr. Quill, in his own words, to explore the boundaries of the "spiritual, legal, professional, and personal." Several months before her death Diane told Dr. Quill that if toward the end of the illness she could no longer control herself and her dignity in the time remaining, she would want to die. In other words, Diane was requesting physician-assisted suicide. In order to facilitate her request, Dr. Quill told Diane that information was available from the Hemlock Society, a pro–active euthanasia activist group. Consistent with the society's protocol for suicide, Diane asked Dr. Quill for barbiturates for sleep. Knowing the real reason why she made the request, he wrote the prescription. Several months later in a hospice, after having called friends and family to say farewell, Diane killed herself with an overdose of barbiturates. However, in order to avoid criminal investigation, Dr. Quill told the medical examiner that she died from "acute leukemia."

Reprinted by permission from *New England Journal of Medicine* 324 (March 7, 1991).

Diane was feeling tired and had a rash. A common scenario, though there was something subliminally worrisome that prompted me to check her blood count. Her hematocrit was 22, and the white-cell count was 4.3 with some metamyelocytes and unusual white cells. I wanted it to be viral, trying to deny what was staring me in the face. Perhaps in a repeated count it would disappear. I called Diane and told her it might be more serious than I had initially thought—that the test needed to be repeated and that if she felt worse, we might have to move quickly. When she pressed for the possibilities, I reluctantly opened the door for leukemia. Hearing the word seemed to make it exist. "Oh, shit!" she said. "Don't tell me that." Oh, shit! I thought, I wish I didn't have to.

Diane was no ordinary person (although no one I have ever come to know has been really ordinary). She was raised in an alcoholic family and had felt alone for much of her life. She had vaginal cancer as a young woman. Through much of her adult life, she had struggled with depression and her own alcoholism. I had come to know, respect, and admire her over the previous eight years as she confronted these problems and gradually overcame them. She was an incredibly clear, at times brutally honest, thinker and communicator. As she took control of her life, she developed a strong sense of independence and confidence. In the previous 3½ years, her hard work had paid off. She was completely abstinent from alcohol, she had established much deeper connections with her husband, college-age son, and several friends, and her business and her artistic work were blossoming. She felt she was really living fully for the first time.

Not surprisingly, the repeated blood count was abnormal, and detailed examination of the peripheral-blood smear showed myelocytes. I advised her to come into the hospital, explaining that we needed to do a bone marrow biopsy and make some decisions relatively rapidly. She came to the hospital knowing what we would find. She was terrified, angry, and sad. Although we knew the odds, we both clung to the thread of possibility that it might be something else.

The bone marrow confirmed the worst: acute myelomonocytic leukemia. In the face of this tragedy, we looked for signs of hope. This is an area of medicine in which technological intervention has been successful, with cures 25 percent of the time—long-term cures. As I probed the costs of these cures, I heard about induction chemotherapy (three weeks in the hospital, prolonged neutropenia, probable infectious complications, and hair loss; 75 percent of patients respond, 25 percent do not). For the survivors, this is followed by consolidation chemotherapy (with similar side effects; another 25 percent die, for a net survival of 50 percent). Those still alive, to have a reasonable chance of long-term survival, then need bone marrow transplantation (hospitalization for two months and whole-body irradiation, with complete killing of the bone marrow, infectious complications, and the possibility for graft-versus-host disease—with a survival of approximately 50 percent, or 25 percent of the original group). Though hematologists may argue over the exact percentages, they don't argue about the outcome of no treatment—certain death in days, weeks, or at most a few months.

Believing that delay was dangerous, our oncologist broke the news to Diane and began making plans to insert a Hickman catheter and begin induction chemotherapy that afternoon. When I saw her shortly thereafter, she was enraged at this presumption that she would want treatment, and devastated by the finality of the diagnosis. All she wanted to do was go home and be with her family. She had no further questions about treatment and in fact had decided that she wanted none. Together we lamented her tragedy and the unfairness of life. Before she left, I felt the need to be sure that she and her husband understood that there was some risk in delay, that the problem was not going to go away, and that we needed to keep considering the options over the next several days. We agreed to meet in two days.

She returned in two days with her husband and son. They had talked extensively about the problem and the options. She remained very clear about her wish not to undergo chemotherapy and to live whatever time she had left outside the hospital. As we explored her thinking further, it became clear that she was convinced she would die during the period of treatment and would suffer unspeakably in the process (from hospitalization, from lack of control over her body, from the side effects of chemotherapy, and from pain and anguish). Although I could offer support and my best effort to minimize her suffering if she chose treatment, there was no way I could say any of this would not occur. In fact, the last four patients with acute leukemia at our hospital had died very painful deaths in the hospital during various stages of treatment (a fact I did not share with her). Her family wished she would choose treatment but sadly accepted her decision. She articulated very clearly that it was she who would be experiencing all the side effects of treatment and that odds of 25 percent were not good enough for her to undergo so toxic a course of therapy, given her expectations of chemotherapy and hospitalization and the absence of a closely matched bone marrow donor. I had her repeat her understanding of the treatment, the odds, and what to expect if there were no treatment. I clarified a few misunderstandings, but she had a remarkable grasp of the options and implications.

I have been a longtime advocate of active, informed patient choice of treatment or nontreatment and of a patient's right to die with as much control and dignity as possible. Yet there was something about her giving up a 25 percent chance of long-term survival in favor of almost certain death that disturbed me. I had seen Diane fight and use her considerable inner resources to overcome alcoholism and depression, and I half expected her to change her mind over the next week. Since the window of time in which effective treatment can be initiated is rather narrow, we met several times that week. We obtained a second hematology consultation and talked at length about the meaning and implications of treatment and nontreatment. She talked to a psychologist she had seen in the past. I gradually understood the decision from her perspective and became convinced that it was the right decision for her. We arranged for home hospice care (although at that time Diane felt reasonably well, was active, and looked healthy), left the door open for her to change her mind, and tried to anticipate how to keep her comfortable in the time she had left.

Just as I was adjusting to her decision, she opened up another area that would stretch me profoundly. It was extraordinarily important to Diane to maintain control of herself and her own dignity during the time remaining to her. When this was no longer possible, she clearly wanted to die. As a former director of a hospice program, I know how to use pain medicines to keep patients comfortable and lessen suffering. I explained the philosophy of comfort care, which I strongly believe in. Although Diane understood and appreciated this, she had known of people lingering in what was called relative comfort, and she wanted no part of it. When the time came, she wanted to take her life in the least painful way possible. Knowing of her desire for independence and her decision to stay in control, I thought this request made perfect sense. I acknowledged and explored this wish but also thought that it was out of the realm of currently accepted medical practice and that it was more than I could offer or promise. In our discussion, it became clear that preoccupation with her fear of a lingering death would interfere with Diane's getting the most out of the time she had left until she found a safe way to ensure her death. I feared the effects of a violent death on her family, the consequences of an ineffective suicide that would leave her lingering in precisely the state she dreaded so much, and the possibility that a family member would be forced to assist her, with all the legal and personal repercussions that would follow. She discussed this at length with her family. They believed that they should respect her choice. With this in mind, I told Diane that information was available from the Hemlock Society that might be helpful to her.

A week later she phoned me with a request for barbiturates for sleep. Since I knew that this was an essential ingredient in a Hemlock Society suicide, I asked her to come to the office to talk things over. She was more than wiling to protect me by participating in a superficial conversation about her insomnia, but it was important to me to know how she planned to use the drugs and to be sure that she was not in despair or overwhelmed in a way that might color her judgment. In our discussion, it was apparent that she was having trouble sleeping, but it was also evident that the security of having enough barbiturates available to commit suicide when and if the time came would leave her secure enough to live fully and concentrate on the present. It was clear that she was not despondent and that in fact she was making deep, personal connections with her family and close friends. I made sure that she knew how to use the barbiturates for sleep, and also that she knew the amount needed to commit suicide. We agreed to meet regularly, and she promised to meet with me before taking her life, to ensure that all other avenues had been exhausted. I wrote the prescription with an uneasy feeling about the boundaries I was exploring—spiritual, legal, professional, and personal. Yet I also felt strongly that I was setting her free to get the most out of the time she had left, and to maintain dignity and control on her own terms until her death.

The next several months were very intense and important for Diane. Her son stayed home from college, and they were able to be with one another and say much that had not been said earlier. Her husband did his work at home so that he and Diane could spend more time together. She spent time with her closest friends. I had her come into the hospital for a conference with our residents, at which she illustrated in a most profound and personal way the importance of informed decision making, the right to refuse treatment, and the extraordinarily personal effects of illness and interaction with the medical system. There were emotional and physical hardships as well. She had periods of intense sadness and anger. Several times she became very weak, but she received transfusions as an outpatient and responded with marked improvement of symptoms. She had two serious infections that responded surprisingly well to empirical courses of oral antibiotics. After three tumultuous months, there were two weeks of relative calm and well-being, and fantasies of a miracle began to surface.

Unfortunately, we had no miracle. Bone pain, weakness, fatigue, and fevers began to dominate her life. Although the hospice workers, family members, and I tried our best to minimize the suffering and promote comfort, it was clear that the end was approaching. Diane's immediate future held what she feared the most—increasing discomfort, dependence, and hard choices between pain and sedation. She called up her closest friends and asked them to come over to say goodbye, telling them that she would be even more terrified to stay and suffer. In our tearful goodbye, she promised a reunion in the future at her favorite spot on the edge of Lake Geneva, with dragons swimming in the sunset.

Two days later her husband called to say that Diane had died. She had said her final goodbyes to her husband and son that morning, and asked them to leave her alone for an hour. After an hour, which must have seemed an eternity, they found her on the couch, lying very still and covered by her favorite shawl. There was no sign of struggle. She seemed to be at peace. They called me for advice about how to proceed. When I arrived at their house, Diane indeed seemed peaceful. Her husband and son were quiet. We talked about what a remarkable person she had been. They seemed to have no doubts about the course she had chosen or about their cooperation, although the unfairness of her illness and the finality of her death were overwhelming to us all.

I called the medical examiner to inform him that a hospice patient had died. When asked about the cause of death, I said, "acute leukemia." He said that was fine and that we should call a funeral director. Although acute leukemia was the truth, it was not the whole story. Yet any mention of suicide would have given rise to a police investigation and probably brought the arrival of an ambulance crew for resuscitation. Diane would have become a "coroner's case," and the decision to perform an autopsy would have been made at the discretion of the medical examiner. The family or I could have been subject to criminal prosecution, and I to professional review, for our roles in support of Diane's choices. Although I truly believe that the family and I gave her the best care possible, allowing her to define her limits and directions as much as possible, I am not sure the law, society, or the medical profession would agree. So I said "acute leukemia" to protect all of us, to protect Diane from an invasion into her past and her body, and to continue to shield society from the knowledge of the degree of suffering that people often undergo in the process of dying. Suffering can be lessened to some extent, but in no way eliminated or made benign, by the careful intervention of a competent, caring physician, given current social constraints.

Diane taught me about the range of help I can provide if I know people well and if I allow them to say what they really want. She taught me about life, death, and honesty and about taking charge and facing tragedy squarely when it strikes. She taught me that I can take small risks for people that I really know and care about. Although I did not assist in her suicide directly, I helped indirectly to make it possible, successful, and relatively painless. Although I know we have measures to help control pain and lessen suffering, to think that people do not suffer in the process of dying is an illusion. Prolonged dying can occasionally be peaceful, but more often the role of the physician and family is limited to lessening but not eliminating severe suffering.

I wonder how many families and physicians secretly help patients over the edge into death in the face of such severe suffering. I wonder how many severely ill or dying patients secretly take their lives, dying alone in despair. I wonder whether the image of Diane's final aloneness will persist in the minds of her family, or if they will remember more the intense, meaningful months they had together before she died. I wonder whether Diane struggled in that last hour, and whether the Hemlock Society's way of death by suicide is the most benign. I wonder why Diane, who gave so much to so many of us, had to be alone for the last hour of her life. I wonder whether I will see Diane again, on the shore of Lake Geneva at sunset, with dragons swimming on the horizon.

Discussion Questions

1. Do you think it was morally right for Dr. Quill to lie to the medical examiner about the true cause of Diane's death? Explain and defend your answer.

2. Can you present and explain Dr. Quill's moral justification for assisting in Diane's suicide? Do you find this justification compelling? Why or why not?

3. Assuming Dr. Quill was morally justified in assisting with Diane's suicide, would he still be morally justified if Diane's chance of recovering after undergoing treatment was 80 percent rather than 25 percent? Explain and defend your answer.

25

Dying Safely: An Analysis of "A Case of Individualized Decision Making" by Timothy E. Quill, M.D.

Patricia Wesley

Patricia Wesley is Associate Professor of Psychiatry, School of Medicine, Yale University. She has contributed to a number of scholarly journals and has served as national president of University Faculty for Life.

Professor Wesley raises some serious moral and professional questions about the justification of Dr. Timothy Quill's assistance in the suicide of his patient, Diane (Chapter 24). In this essay Professor Wesley, employing her accomplished skills in literary analysis and psychiatry, asks us to read Dr. Quill's story "between the lines," to ask critical questions as to why Dr. Quill didn't make further inquiries about his patient's personal and medical background in order to better understand her reaction to being diagnosed with leukemia, to understand how Dr. Quill used euphemisms and emotive language to capture the reader's sympathy, and to notice how Dr. Quill's philosophical presuppositions about the morality of active euthanasia, and physician-assisted suicide in particular, influenced the interaction with his patient. Professor Wesley maintains that despite his claim of neutrality and respecting his patient's autonomy, Dr. Quill was a powerful actor in pushing Diane to commit suicide: "With his help, Diane dies a politically correct death, accompanied to her grave by all the rhetoric of patient autonomy and medical egalitarianism that litters our intellectual landscape today, and that so often distracts us

Published by permission from *Issues in Law & Medicine* 8, no. 4 (1993): 467–485. This is a revised version of Professor Wesley's keynote address at the first annual meeting of the University Faculty for Life, Georgetown University, Washington, D.C. (8–10 June 1991). The author wishes to thank UFL for the opportunity to deliver this paper.

from the difficult task of knowing, if we are lucky, the depths of human willing and acting, and of trying to preserve life while we do."

A rabbinical dictum has it that we should 'place fences around the law.' The idea that restraints and prohibitions should be in place to prevent us from reaching, or at least impede our progress toward, the point of absolute and damning transgression. There should at least be safety rails around the abyss. Perhaps the best that our culture can provide are signposts warning against the danger ahead.[1]

I wrote the prescription with an uneasy feeling about the boundaries I was exploring—spiritual, legal, professional, and personal.[2]

Tenderness leads to the gas chamber.[3]

Doctors like to tell stories. Sometimes the story is a brief clinical vignette one physician shares with another over coffee in the nurses' station. Sometimes the story is a literary masterpiece by a renowned physician-artist such as William Carlos Williams, Anton Chekhov, or Walker Percy. And sometimes doctors tell stories designed to revolutionize the heart and soul of medical practice. Such a story, "Death and Dignity: A Case of Individualized Decision Making," appeared in the March 7, 1991, issue of *The New England Journal of Medicine*.[4] Author Timothy E. Quill, M.D., a Rochester, New York, internist, tells us about his patient Diane, who developed acute leukemia, refused treatment for it, and ultimately asked for and got his aid in killing herself.[5] This story is no simple clinical anecdote, however. While never directly saying so, Dr. Quill offers it as evidence that under certain circumstances, like those in which he and Diane found themselves, physician-assisted suicide can be clinically and ethically "right," and our laws should be changed to permit it.[6]

This text invites examination precisely because of its revolutionary agenda. Yet this story is so disarmingly simple and moving, and its surface so smooth and opaque, that our inquiry seems to be barred. The euthanasia project is hidden here behind the mask of plain narrative and attractive metaphor. How can we get up close for a clear look at this encounter between Diane and Dr. Quill?

Any text speaks to us on many levels. Astute readers note *how* the author writes as well as *what* he writes about. Close attention is paid to such formal elements as language, tone of voice, point of view, genre, plot, and figures of speech. We note patterns in the narrative action. Who says or does what to whom, when? In addition to reading on the lines, readers should attend to the white space between the lines. What is not being said? Are there paradoxes or gaps in a seemingly unified text that, once explicated, can lead us to a more complete understanding of the story? What is the author trying to persuade us about? Are there contradictions in such authorial claims on us that might qualify our assent? In what social and cultural context does the text appear? What audience is it designed to reach? Who publishes it, and why? No work of art is ever simply the product of its time and place; nonetheless, attention to these more external factors provides another perspective for apprehending the text in its fullness.

Patients also tell physicians stories, to which physicians listen, although not always as patiently as they should. The patient's account of a developing illness is still the threshold at which the physician enters the patient's life. One group of specialists who are particularly likely to hear such stories are psychodynamically oriented psychiatrists. They use some of the same techniques to understand their patients' stories that a reader uses to understand a novel or a short story. Of course, no live patient is equivalent to a written text, or vice versa. Nonetheless, similar techniques of listening *do* characterize these two human activities. Let me first describe how the psychiatrist listens. Then, let us "listen" to Dr. Quill's story in the same way, and perhaps find a way into its interior.

At the beginning, the psychiatrist will hear the patient's story as it is told but, equally important, will note *how* the patient tells his story. What kind of language does the patient use, in what tone of voice and manner? Is the patient glib, humorous, vague, dramatic, or sarcastic? Is his mood anxious, angry, or sad? Discrepancies between what is said and the affect accompanying it are also noted; for example, the psychiatrist would be puzzled that whenever a particular patient says he's angry, he smiles or speaks so softly that he cannot heard.

What the patient doesn't say is important, too; the doctor/listener would observe that an elderly widow mentioned almost casually a few weeks ago that a much-loved, previously much-mentioned pet cat died, but since then she has said nothing further about this loss or her reactions to it.

Of particular interest are contradictions between what the patient says he wants and how he goes about getting it. For example, a patient may announce that he is bound and determined to succeed in the same family business his father failed at, yet repeatedly makes easily avoidable errors in management that bring the business to the brink of bankruptcy.

From a more historical perspective, the psychiatrist would want to know when a depression developed and what life events preceded it. Did the patient end a love affair, or make an important scientific discovery that brought acclaim? Did a decision to divorce follow a year or so after the death of a child in a car accident in which one of the parents was the driver? Did a loss of self-esteem follow the diagnosis of a serious illness? An investigation of the historical antecedents, near or remote, of any life event can often be illuminating.

Very crucially, the psychiatrist would try to help the patient become aware of how past experiences, from early childhood, adolescence, and adulthood, shape current reactions and decisions. When and in what human context did the patient develop certain views about herself? How might those views protect against the remembering of old traumas or the resurgence of old needs in new situations? Sometimes, even the patient may not be fully aware of how such views can influence current choices. As we will explore later in more detail, did Diane's view that she must be independent and in control, no matter what the cost, impair her ability to fully assess all her options as she faced a life-threatening illness?

For the psychiatrist to be of help to the patient, he must construct a safe, structured, and rule-bound therapeutic setting, in which the patient can articulate, perhaps for the first time, wishes, hopes, and fears from both past and present life dramas. The psychiatrist must attend not only to the patient, but to himself and his interaction with the patient as well. Psychiatric residents are admonished to keep the following question always in mind: Why is *this* patient saying *this* to *me* at *this* time? Does the patient want me to see her in a certain way, feel certain things about, or with, her? Is the patient trying to please me, enrage me, make me an ally or a judge, or test me in some way? Is the patient asking a question by enfolding it in a seemingly simple statement, one that might make "perfect sense," to use Dr. Quill's characterization of Diane's stated intention to take her own life?

The psychiatrist must also be constantly aware of how his own values and personality can shape what he says to the patient and how, in turn, this can influence the story the patient tells. Patients tend to tell stories they know, or imagine they know, their doctors like to hear.

The famous American psychiatrist Harry Stack Sullivan captured the complexities of the psychiatrist's tasks in his concept of the "participant-observer."[7] As he warned on many occasions, it is no easy job to simultaneously participate and observe. The psychiatrist, or any other doctor who listens to a patient, must resonate, judiciously, to the appeal and power of the story the patient tells. At the same time, she must meticulously avoid re-enacting past traumas, or joining in self-deluding scenarios, with the patient—especially those involving unlikely posthumous reunions along the shores of certain European bodies of water. The difficult balance required here is to remain inside *and* outside the story, empathic toward, but not misidentified with, the patient and the tale he tells.

To be such a listener and such a questioner, the physician must appreciate the complexity, ambiguity, and multiplicity in all human desire and action and in every human life, lived or told. However much we may speculate about their psychodynamic origins, or know about their neurophysiological correlates, human character and behavior remain resilient mysteries. Unhappily—and happily—no human being can ever be completely understood by someone else, even when the someone else is a skilled psychiatric professional. This is a chilly reminder of our essential aloneness, but it is also a helpful reminder to be chary about ever claiming, as Dr. Quill does, that we can know someone else "well."

When we, doctors and patients alike, acknowledge that we do not know, and can never know in any final sense, all the motivations for any human action, then we have paradoxically secured the only foundation for knowing what *can* be known, incomplete and tentative as that may be. We should be listening and asking questions, but we cannot expect any "right" answers or be assured, as Dr. Quill is, that our decisions or those of our patients are the "right" ones. The fences against euthanasia are there to remind us that when so much is unknown, we need to be aware of the dangers of false certainty. Even dragons cannot live in that abyss.

With this background in place, let us begin our confrontation of this most seductive text, "A Case of Individualized Decision Making."[8] As we do, keep in mind that we have no direct, unmediated knowledge about "Diane" herself, as she was in life or in death, or about her actual interactions with Dr. Quill.

We know her only through the filter of Dr. Quill's narrative. Absent actual clinical contact, we have no way of knowing if the questions I will raise about her psychological make-up were at all relevant to the actual person this account is based on. Too, either Dr. Quill himself or Diane's psychologist may have raised these questions with her, and others even far more pertinent.

What follows, then, is not so much a review of Dr. Quill's actual treatment of Diane as it is a critique of Dr. Quill's text and the rhetorical use he wishes to make of it. Dr. Quill wants us to believe that *what he tells us* about Diane and about his interactions with her constitutes sufficient evidence to support his claim that, at least in certain circumstances, physician-assisted suicide can be good medicine. Therefore, we are justified in taking this text itself as the object of our inquiry. What is the nature of the evidence it offers, and should we be persuaded by it?

Dr. Quill's account warrants scrutiny for a number of reasons. It is such an engaging and pretty story! We are made privy to an engrossing medical drama, in which Diane develops acute leukemia, refuses any specific treatment for it, and eventually requests and receives her physician's aid in taking her own life in the final—*presumably* final—days of her illness. Diane is an interesting and feisty woman, and Dr. Quill is a tenderhearted doctor who actually listens to and talks to his patients!

This story also deserves our attention because of where it was published. *The New England Journal of Medicine* is certainly the most respected medical journal in the United States and arguably in the world. Place of publication alone influenced how this report was received, and granted to assisted suicide a medical elitist cachet it might not otherwise have had. If you want to start the euthanasia train rolling, as at least some of medicine's best and brightest do, there is no better station to leave from than the editorial offices of *The New England Journal of Medicine*. Given its distinguished birthplace, this account is exactly what the Society for the Right to Die would love to hand out to voters considering the decriminalization of euthanasia. Dr. Kevorkian, with his rusty van and his macabre machinery, is one thing;[9] Dr. Quill and his dragons are quite another and deserve confrontation precisely because of the genteel but deadly power they wield.

The text awaits us.

Did Diane make an informed decision when she refused specific treatment for leukemia? Based on what we are told about her, and if we focus purely on her cognitive capacity, there is little question that she did. Diane is presented as an intelligent, intact woman, apparently free of any dementia or major mental illness that would impair her grasp of reality or her judgment. Moreover, Dr. Quill worked hard with her to be sure that she understood her illness and her options.

There is, however, another aspect of informed decision making that rarely gets the attention it deserves and certainly does not in Dr. Quill's story. All human willing and acting is imbued with complexities and ambiguities that can baffle our best efforts to sort them out. In life's drama, it is often not so easy to decide who does what to whom, when. Who is the actor, and who the acted-upon? Can we ever be sure we have teased apart the many densely intertwined strands of human motivation? Nowhere are these questions more relevant than in the human interaction between physician and patient. How do these questions play out with Diane and her doctors?

The skeptical reader spots the first gap in this seemingly seamless story in this passage:

> Believing that delay was dangerous, our oncologist broke the news to Diane and began to make plans to insert a Hickman catheter and begin induction chemotherapy that afternoon. When I saw her shortly thereafter, she was enraged at his presumption that she would want treatment, and devastated by the finality of the diagnosis. All she wanted to do was go home and be with her family. She had no further questions about treatment and in fact had decided that she wanted none. Together we lamented her tragedy and the unfairness of life.[10]

We are unsure here what news the oncologist broke to Diane—was it confirmation of the diagnosis, information about treatment, or both? Nonetheless, as the sequence of events is described, Diane makes her decision against treatment immediately after talking to the oncologist. By the time Dr. Quill sees her, her mind is already made up. Mutual lamentations about the unfairness of life can wait. What in heaven's name transpired between Diane and the oncologist during their meeting? We have no details, but we do know there was some clinical urgency about beginning treatment. Given this, was the oncologist possibly a bit pressing or peremptory with Diane? I do not raise this possibility to be critical of the oncologist; for all we know, he was the paragon of sensitivity. Nonetheless, physicians have an understandable, and even defensible, tendency to take action in urgent situations. The cost may be that

physicians appear pushy and arrogant and may evoke the patient's stormy "NO!" If people do not like the message, they may shoot the messenger; and if they do not like the way the messenger delivers the message, they may erase it, or they may reach some premature decision about it. Did something like this occur between Diane and the oncologist?

Often in discussions about patient decision making, the patient is presented as though she were an isolated individual, in a hermetically sealed room, getting information from a user-friendly computerized learning program. Unfortunately, and fortunately, that is not the case. The patient receives data in the context of a particular physician-patient relationship at a particular moment in time. Hopefully, the physician will temper the need to act with respect for the patient's ability to process the news that must be conveyed, but as in every profession, ideal and actual do not always meet. Medicine is a hands-on activity, and an "affect-on" activity as well. The affect—and the stress—can be found on both sides of the equation.

Here's the second series of gaps: Diane's rage at the oncologist, the fact that she had no further questions, and the rapidity of her decision against treatment. Why was she *so* mad, and why no further questions in a personal situation rife with questions of all sorts? Why the rush? Were there other, less obvious reasons for Diane's rage? Justified or not, did her rage at the oncologist influence her decision about treatment? Diane might have profited from a suggestion at this point that it's risky to make a life-and-death decision when one is in a rage. Anger is no friend of clear thinking and careful judgment.

Patients can and often do see their doctors as authority figures or parental stand-ins and may react to them in some ways similar to how they reacted to their own parents.[11] Indeed, some physicians have encouraged this view of themselves as presumably beneficent authorities as the only viable ethical basis for medical practice.[12] Doctor, like mother, knows best! Such an asymmetry in the doctor-patient relationship is not necessarily as evil as its critics charge, or as altruistic as its proponents believe, nor is it the only way or even the predominant way in which patients view their physicians. However, such tendencies do exist, particularly when a patient, like Diane, is facing a newly diagnosed, life-threatening illness. In such circumstances, when adult capacities to control fear and master stress are severely tested, patients tend to return to earlier models of interaction with others. They may wish for a benign and comforting authority who will tell them what to do and against whom they may then rebel. When people are seriously ill, the professional upon whose skill life depends becomes very important in many ways, some of them quite rational and some of them quite ancient.

We know very little about Diane, except that she was raised in an alcoholic family, had felt alone for much of her life, and had overcome her own alcoholism and depression.[13] Could this personal background have affected how Diane reacted to her illness and her doctors? Could it have shaped how she reached her decision to forgo treatment and ultimately end her own life?

While adult children of alcoholics have received much attention in the popular culture, and from researchers in the field of alcohol studies, there still is no scientific consensus on how parental alcoholism affects children. Some investigators have concluded that these children are at high risk for psychological and social problems;[14] others have concluded that no definitive conclusions can be drawn.[15] Still others have identified "resilient" offspring of alcoholic parents, who demonstrate good adaptation.[16]

Moreover, parental alcoholism and its alleged impact on children is not a unitary phenomenon; many variables affect how any particular child fares, including the severity and duration of parental alcoholism, the degree of conflict in the marital couple, the presence of violence in the home, the gender of the child vis-a-vis the affected parent, and the availability of alternative support systems.[17]

Given the complexity of these findings, any questions about how Diane might have been affected by her alcoholic family are tentative, especially since we know so little about her and her parents. Nonetheless, Dr. Quill's text virtually invites us to raise certain questions about this connection, precisely because he mentions nothing about it.

Throughout Dr. Quill's report, Diane's need to be "in control" is alluded to over and over again.[18] The wish to be responsible is an admirable trait of a mature individual; it makes "perfect sense," as Dr. Quill notes. However, at times we must surrender some control and tolerate a certain degree of dependence on others. Serious illness is such an occasion. Diane does accept some limited treatment from Dr. Quill, but her fear of losing that valued self-control and becoming dependent on others in a hospital setting is one of her reasons for refusing more aggressive therapy for her leukemia. Such reasoning may be fully compatible with Diane's adult character style,

but since it may have carried such a high price tag, we can also wonder about its origins in a more distant, and possibly more traumatic, childhood past as well.

Mental health professionals who treat adult children of alcoholics note that such individuals must always be "in control" and often cannot acknowledge their own needs or trust others to meet them when necessary. For example, Timmen Cermak and Stephanie Brown state:

> Our observations of the issues and dynamics that characterize group meetings [with adult children of alcoholics] could be condensed into one word, 'control.' Conflicts involving issues of control were pervasive and often were the context within which other issues concerning trust, acknowledgment of personal needs, responsibility, and feelings arose. . . . The concern with control was often the most significant source of anxiety.

* * *

> The other side of the issue of control—feelings of deprivation, depression, loss, and intense dependency needs—are well-disguised and hidden. The intense emphasis on control is a rigid defense to protect against acknowledging the overwhelming threat of that underlying neediness.[19]

Granting that further research is needed to confirm their clinical impressions, Cermak and Brown hypothesize as follows:

> Our experience to date does suggest the existence of a recognizable pattern of conflicts carried by the children of alcoholics into their adult lives. . . . Members recalled instructions from the nonalcoholic parent to help keep the family peace. . . . Those instructions result in the offspring's growing up in an atmosphere of arbitrariness and changing limits. . . . A unique poignancy seems to exist in the secondary gain that the adult children of alcoholics receive from their sense of control. Primarily, it is a gain in their sense of self-worth, which is greatly enhanced by feelings of having matters in control.[20]

Parents who are alcoholic may be unpredictable and unreliable; their actions toward their children may come out of the blue, without rhyme or reason. Was this Diane's experience? Did Diane's leukemia seem like a bolt from the blue? Did her oncologist's well-intentioned but perhaps too-quick decision to proceed with treatment seem like a replay of her parents' possibly unpredictable behavior and elicit her stormy "No" to try to regain control and predictability? When Diane was a child and got sick, how was she cared for? Did her parents muster their resources and do so properly—certainly a possibility—or was she neglected, humiliated, or made to feel alone? If Diane did have some unfortunate experiences with illness in the past, these may make her wary now about trusting Dr. Quill's assurances that he will do everything he can to alleviate her pain and discomfort during treatment or during her last days.

There is much in Dr. Quill's account to suggest that Diane's need to be in control was adaptive for her. Nonetheless, adaptive traits can have an origin in earlier trauma, as well as in autonomous ego capacities. We do not know if the observations made by Cermak and Brown, and others, about the adult children of alcoholics are at all applicable to Diane. Each patient can only be understood as an individual, with a unique history. Moreover, no adult decision can be explained away by possible—and here, quite hypothetical—childhood antecedents. However, each of us does begin life dependent on the adults around us for sheer survival; how those adults meet those needs early on shapes how much we trust others to meet similar needs later on.

This does not suggest that patients should blindly trust their physicians. It does suggest that physicians will enhance their patients' adult participation in their own medical care when they remember that old fears can affect how patients respond to new stressors.

Moving to the more recent past, we note that Diane had vaginal cancer as a young woman, although we are told nothing further about its etiology or treatment. Did this more recent experience echo in the conversations Diane had with herself and her doctors as she confronted a second malignancy? How was she treated then? Was she left with some disfigurement or dysfunction in a part of her body vital to her self-esteem? If her earlier treatment involved modalities other than surgery, could she secretly believe that it contributed to the development of her second malignancy, or that they were linked in some other way? How might such a belief affect her treatment decisions at this point?

According to Dr. Quill's history, Diane struggled with depression throughout most of her adult life.[21] If this depression was secondary to serious alcohol abuse, abstinence may have cured it. He presents little evidence that Diane was clinically depressed. Dr. Quill queries himself on this a number of times, as when he notes that she "was not in despair or overwhelmed"[22] or that she "was not despondent."[23] Nonetheless, Diane does have a history of chronic depression; could it be recurring? Moreover, serious physical illness can be accompanied by depression, either because of the impact of the patho-physiological processes on the central nervous system, or because of the psychological meaning of the illness to the afflicted person, or both.

Was Diane's refusal of treatment in itself a suicidal act, stemming from a depressive personality style, if not from an overt symptomatic depression? People can do highly self-destructive things without being overtly depressed; such individuals probably make up the majority of psychotherapy patients in any psychiatrist's practice. There are the noisy and public suicides, like jumps off a bridge, and there are the quiet and private suicides, like the single-car accidents in good weather, where determining if the death was intended is most difficult.

People with depressive tendencies often feel guilty and self-recriminatory and may seek punishments or limitations of various kinds.[24] Diane was "convinced" that she would die during treatment for her leukemia.[25] Why? True enough, the chances for cure are dicey, at best, but why is she "convinced" she won't make it? Like the word *control*, the word *conviction* also haunts this narrative. Did Diane become convinced she would die because she saw herself as deserving of punishment for some crime, real or fantasied? Did she feel that she did not deserve to survive a second bout with cancer? Skepticism about her treatment refusal is bolstered by the fact that in my experience, at least, very few patients forgo initial treatment for a *newly diagnosed*, nonterminal malignancy.

What role might Dr. Quill have played in Diane's conviction that she was doomed? Did his knowledge of those four patients who died painful deaths from similar disorders make it harder for him to keep in mind those who were cured? Was he thus less likely to probe Diane's conviction that she would perish, and did he instead mirror it with his own conviction that it was the "right" decision for her to refuse treatment?

There are no easy answers or neat resolutions to these questions. Childhood experience, personal history, and less than fully conscious motivation can influence any human decision, including the decision to accept a recommended treatment. It is all too easy to assume that the patient is acting rationally when he agrees with his physician and can only be acting irrationally when he disagrees.

Despite these salutary cautions, these questions about Diane emerge from the very text Dr. Quill offers as evidence that her decision to refuse treatment and to commit suicide was a fully conscious, autonomous human preference, not essentially different from a preference for country-western over classical. Indeed, Dr. Quill appeals to this type of characterization of Diane's wishes and actions to justify his own actions concerning her.[26] Dr. Quill wants us to leave his theater feeling reassured that no ambiguous plots or silent fears lurk in Diane's drama, at least.

But we remain troubled. The gaps in Dr. Quill's story challenge the simplistic notion that the psychological processes involved in patient choices are readily or completely apprehensible within the current emphasis, approaching obsession, on patient rationality and autonomy. The heart has reasons the ACLU knows nothing about.

When day is done and all the questions asked, it is the patient who decides to accept or reject treatment. That right is recognized in our law,[27] even though it has sometimes been ignored in the more paternalistic type of medical practice. Respecting a patient's right to decide about treatment does not necessarily mean, however, that we should become convinced that the decision is "right," as Dr. Quill did, despite his early reservations.

In this case, there was some chance that treatment would be effective and virtual certainty that no treatment would prove fatal.[28] The patient was initially in good enough physical condition to tolerate aggressive therapy and was not already terminally ill.[29] Too, Diane doesn't sound like someone who would pass up a good fight. Given all this, we are suspicious that much more is going on with the patient than Dr. Quill reveals and possibly more than Diane realized. Some blunt comments might be in order, such as: "While I respect your right to make decisions about your own medical care, I still have some reservations and questions about the decision you've made. I'm not convinced it is the right one, and I wonder if you might have some questions too, even now."

In medicine today, physicians are encouraged to be empathic towards patients, ascertain and respect their values, and support their choices.[30] There is much good in such an emphasis, but applied in a stereotyped fashion, without asking "Why?" "How come?" and "What makes you think that?" nothing can be more dangerous. The model of the beneficent, paternalistic physician, making choices in the patient's "best interest," was certainly not value-free. It had its own costly side effect, namely, the creation of passive and infantilized patients who end up bitterly disappointed and unable to trust any physician when magical expectations cannot be met. However,

it is frighteningly naive to assume that when our guide to medical practice is "doing what the patient wants," we will escape the imposition of the physician's values on the clinical encounter. Personal values can be sequestered in the question not asked, or the gentle challenge not posed, when both should have been.

Now let us turn to the far more controversial part of this story, Diane's suicidal wishes and Dr. Quill's series of responses to them. Far from being the neutral reflector and facilitator of Diane's desires that he believes himself to be, Dr. Quill in fact powerfully and directly shapes those desires.

> Just as I was adjusting to her decision, she opened up another area that would stretch me profoundly. It was extraordinarily important to Diane to maintain control of herself and her own dignity during the time remaining to her. When this was no longer possible, she clearly wanted to die. As a former director of a hospice program, I know how to use pain medicines to keep patients comfortable and lessen suffering. I explained the philosophy of comfort care, which I strongly believe in. Although Diane understood and appreciated this, she had known of people lingering in what was called relative comfort, and she wanted no part of it. When the time came, she wanted to take her life in the least painful way possible. Knowing of her desire for independence and her decision to stay in control, I thought this request made perfect sense.[31]

Note here again the icon words—control, dignity, and independence. Is this the new rhetoric of self-murder? Bear in mind that Diane's suicidal wishes came at a time when she was "reasonably well, was active, and looked healthy"[32] and when Dr. Quill was arranging supportive care, while still leaving "the door open for her to change her mind"[33] about treatment. Given what he was trying to accomplish, should Diane's statement just make "perfect sense" to Dr. Quill?

On one level, Diane's request for aid in killing herself does make some sense. Dr. Quill describes her as someone who wants to call the shots for many reasons, including the troubling one that she felt alone for much of her life;[34] perhaps someone like this sees little option but to be in lonely control at the end as well. Hearing of Diane's suicidal intentions, the skeptic might remember that advice I told you about earlier. Why is *this* patient saying *this* to *me* at *this* time? Is she asking a question in the guise of making a statement? Is a trial balloon being launched, some testing being done? Is Diane asking her doctor: When I become more ill, more dependent, and when I no longer have that control I prize so much—and that I suspect *you* prize so much—will you still see me as a person of value? What if I changed my mind and pursued treatment, with the need for hospital confinement and care by others, would you still see me as worthwhile even when I might seem worthless to myself?

At first, Dr. Quill keeps up the fences that might have made a fuller exploration of these hypotheses possible when he tells Diane that such assistance is more than he can give her. Then he wavers, takes down the fences, and clears the path to death: "In our discussion, it became clear that preoccupation with her fears of a lingering death would interfere with Diane's getting the most of the time she had left until she found a safe way to ensure her death."[35] If you feel a chill as you read this passage, it probably comes from the oxymoron "safe . . . death." Since when is death safe? This is classic doublespeak and reminiscent of the pro-abortion doublespeak that the only safe way to avoid being an unplanned child is to be destroyed before you're born.[36]

It is not clear if Diane actually threatened to take her own life by "violent means" or "force" a family member to kill her, or if these are solely Dr. Quill's fears. If Diane made these comments, then Dr. Quill allowed himself to be blackmailed when he gave in to them. No physician is responsible for every action a competent patient might take or persuade others to take. It is ironic that Dr. Quill, who so wants to enhance Diane's control, in effect takes control away from her by his own action. What might have happened if Dr. Quill had said, "I would be sorry to see you do that, or enlist someone else to do it, but I do not control you or everything you do. I have said I will not help you end your own life, and if I flip-flop on that now because of your threats, you'd never believe anything else I say, and you shouldn't." Such a statement would recognize Diane as the prime actor in her own play. Sometimes a "No" is a big relief to patients testing the waters and seeing just how tough their doctors can be when the going gets tough. Instead, Dr. Quill responds with a referral to the Hemlock Society.[37]

Those who favor assisted suicide and euthanasia often discuss the patient as though she were an isolated actor, totally divorced from any interpersonal or historical context. This is how Dr. Quill wants us to see Diane. He reassures us that he was only helping her to say and do what she "really wanted" and would do anyway, with or without his help. Dr. Quill wants us to see him as a kind of minimalist mirror or valueless facilitator of Diane's wishes. A close reading of the sequence of events indicates otherwise.

While this may be changing because of recent public discussion about euthanasia, it is still unlikely that most internists know what the Hemlock Society is, much less refer their seriously ill patients to it. More importantly, it is not clear that Diane had ever heard of the Hemlock Society—until Dr. Quill told her about it. In making this referral and describing it as "helpful,"[38] Dr. Quill once again powerfully shaped the clinical interaction between himself and his patient.

It is not a neutral act to refer a patient contemplating suicide to the Hemlock Society. It is putting a loaded gun into the hands of a desperate person. It renders utterly incoherent to us, as possibly it did to Diane, Dr. Quill's claim that he had left the door open for her to change her mind.[39] You cannot have it both ways, Dr. Quill! The Hemlock Society is about closing doors, not keeping them open.

What other messages might Diane have heard in this referral? Did she feel she had a physician who respected her as an autonomous person? Or did she feel that she had a doctor who shared her belief—forged in the heat of a troubled past—that if you cannot be fully independent, you are better off dead? Remember that Diane was in the midst of a profound crisis. In such circumstances any suggestion by the physician carries tremendous impact, often far more than the physician intends. When human beings are in such straits, they will grasp at anything that offers a way out. This anxious seeking for quick resolution, while understandable, must be mitigated and resisted by the physician. At the very least, doctors must be careful about any suggestions they might make, especially when their side effect is death. Would the endgame have been different if Dr. Quill had referred Diane to a self-help support group of cancer patients instead of the Hemlock Society?

Physicians' values affect how they deliver medical care and what they will or will not do for patients. Those who oppose assisted suicide are often reminded that they are imposing their own personal values and ignoring those of the dying patient who requests aid in committing suicide.[40] It seems that all those pesky "values" belong only to those of us who want to keep the fences intact, while those who favor taking them down costume themselves with the cloak of gray neutrality. Dr. Quill's own account shows how false this simplistic dichotomy is.

In providing Diane with a referral to the Hemlock Society, he interjects his own values into the clinical situation, just as his article disingenuously promotes the values of the Hemlock Society.

Dr. Quill knew that barbiturates are "an essential ingredient" in a Hemlock Society suicide.[41] If so, Dr. Quill's own act of referring Diane to the Hemlock Society brings him onto center stage to play a direct and material role in Diane's death. It is not a neutral act to advise a suicidal person how many barbiturate capsules are needed for sleep and how many are needed to commit suicide, and then provide the lethal quantity.

Throughout his story, and like many another skilled penman before him, Dr. Quill wants us to believe that he effaced himself as an actor, both in the story he lived and in the story he tells us. Diane is presented as someone who determined her own tragic fate, free of the imprisonment of medical paternalism and what Derek Humphry might call outmoded ideas about the sanctity of life. Closely observed, Dr. Quill's text itself reveals that he was a powerful actor in his story. With his help, Diane dies a politically correct death, accompanied to her grave by all the rhetoric of patient autonomy and medical egalitarianism that litters our intellectual landscape today, and that distracts us from the difficult task of knowing the depths of human willing and acting and of trying to preserve life while we do.

After Diane decides to take her own life, she and Dr. Quill meet for a final good-bye, in which she promises "a reunion in the future at her favorite spot on the edge of Lake Geneva, with dragons swimming in the sunset."[42] After her death, Dr. Quill mirrors her fantasy and wonders whether he "will see Diane again, on the shore of Lake Geneva at sunset, with dragons swimming on the horizon."[43]

This is a beautiful image. On one level we can hardly blame Dr. Quill for employing all the evocative metaphors he can to make his case. However, like all figurative language, this image is essentially a beautiful mistake, a transfer of elements from one realm of reference into another, where they literally do not belong. Does this shared image of a mystical afterlife, complete with mythical animals, signal a mistaken transfer between doctor and patient as well? Did Dr. Quill become so misidentified with Diane that he erased that disengagement so crucial in the doctor-patient relationship? Such disengagement might have permitted him to ask those literal and blunt questions that may have been needed but may not have been asked. Shared fantasies about drag-ons swimming in Lake Geneva do not make Diane's death less violent or less final, or lessen Dr. Quill's complicity in it. Charming figures of speech do not make her grave less of a grave.

If we follow them, Dr. Quill and his colleagues who promote assisted suicide will lead us not to the sunny shores of Lake Geneva, but rather into a very dark forest indeed, where we will wish we'd had those fences and warnings that Richard John Neuhaus told us to keep up. Dr. Quill's lakes and forests look sunny and bright in the daytime. Some in medicine and law find them alluring pieces of real estate. But anyone who grew up in the country knows that lakes can be deeper than they appear and that forests are inviting but dangerous places. Night falls quickly, and we can lose our way, and ourselves. Those fences will come in handy.

Discussion Questions

1. What does Professor Wesley mean when she says that we should "read between the lines" when reading Dr. Quill's report of his interaction with Diane? Provide some examples from Dr. Quill's essay of what she means.

2. Professor Wesley claims that Dr. Quill, far from being neutral on the issue of physician-assisted suicide, was a powerful actor in influencing Diane's decision to commit suicide. How does she draw this conclusion? Do you agree with her assessment? Why or why not? Explain your answer.

3. If you were Dr. Quill, how would you respond to Professor Wesley's critique? Explain and defend your answer. If as Dr. Quill you appeal to the autonomy of the patient to support your decision, reply in detail to Professor Wesley's claim that Diane may not have been truly autonomous.

Notes

1. Richard J. Neuhaus, *The Way They Were, the Way We Are: Bioethics and the Holocaust*, First Things, Mar. 1990, at 31, 34.

2. Timothy E. Quill, *Death and Dignity: A Case of Individualized Decision Making*, 324 New Eng. J. Med. 6791, 693 (1991).

3. Walker Percy, The Thanatos Syndrome 36 (1987).

4. Quill, *supra* note 2, at 691.

5. *See id.* at 693.

6. Dr. Quill has since directly advocated the legalization of physician-assisted suicide. *See* Timothy E. Quill et

al., *Care of the Hopelessly Ill: Proposed Clinical Criteria for Physician-Assisted Suicide,* 327 New Eng. J. Med. 1380 (1992).

7. *See* Harry S. Sullivan, The Psychiatric Interview 18–24 (Helen S. Perry & Mary L. Gawal, eds., 1954). *See also,* Donald P. Spence, Narrative Truth and Historical Truth 41 (1982). Spence identifies similarities between reading a text and listening to a patient in psychoanalysis, but also warns of the dangers in such similarities. In listening to the analysand's free associations, the analyst may impose narrative coherence and continuity where none exists, thereby distorting the very data (the patient's verbal productions) upon which interpretive hypotheses will be based. Moreover, the psychoanalytic concepts the analyst uses shape not only how the analyst listens, but also what the patient says. Thus, the analyst finds his hypotheses confirmed but, unaware of how the dice are loaded, believes that he is making "discoveries." Spence's masterful critique of psychoanalytic clinical theory reminds us that any communication between a doctor and a patient is not just a two-way street, but a complex tangle of verbal and cognitive traffic with the potential for many wrong exits and dead end streets. To some extent, the same cautions apply when we "listen" to a written text. In that case, however, we have a physical object (words printed on bound pieces of paper) that is relatively immutable and accessible to a more or less broad pubic. These facts impose some welcome constraints on textual criticism that are not present in the far more ambiguous oral milieu of the psychoanalytic situation, or in any doctor-patient exchange.

8. Quill, *supra* note 2, at 692.

9. *See* Lisa Belkin, *Doctor Tells of First Death Using His Suicide Device,* N.Y. Times, June 6, 1990, at A1 (describing how a woman, aided by Dr. Jack Kevorkian, committed suicide in an old Volkswagen van).

10. Quill, *supra* note 2, at 692.

11. Jay Katz, The Silent World of Doctor and Patient 142–47 (1984).

12. *See id.* at 2, 27.

13. Quill, *supra* note 2, at 691–92.

14. *See* M. Russell et al., Children of Alcoholics 17 (1985).

15. *See* Jeannette L. Johnson & Jon E. Rolf, *When Children Change: Research Perspectives on Children of Alcoholics, in* Alcohol and the Family 163 (R. Lorraine Collins et al., eds., 1990).

16. *See* Emmy E. Warner, *Resilient Offspring of Alcoholics: A Longitudinal Study from Birth to Age 18,* 47 J. Stud. on Alcohol 34, 39 (1986).

17. Johnson & Rolf, *supra* note 15, at 175.

18. Quill, *supra* note 2, at 692, 693.

19. Timmen L. Cermak & Stephanie Brown, *Interactional Group Therapy with the Adult Children of Alcoholics,* 32 Int'l. J. Group Psychotherapy 375, 377–78, 380 (1982).

20. *Id.* at 385–86.

21. Quill, *supra* note 2, at 692.

22. *Id.,* at 693.

23. *Id.*

24. American Psychiatric Association, Diagnostic and Statistical Manual of Mental Disorders 218–19 (3d ed. rev. 1987).

25. Quill, *supra* note 2, at 692.

26. *Id.* at 692, 693.

27. *See, e.g.,* Union Pac. Ry. Co. v. Botsford, 141 U.S. 250, 251 (1891) ("No right is held more sacred, or is more carefully guarded, by the common law, than the right of every individual to the possession and control of his own person, free from all restraint or interference of others, unless by clear and unquestionable authority of law"); Wall v. Brim, 138 F.2d 478, 481 (5th Cir. 1943) ("The law is well settled that an operation cannot be performed without the patient's consent . . . ."); Bouvia v. Superior Court, 225 Cal. Rptr. 197, 300 (Ct. App. 1986) ("[A] patient has the right to refuse *any* medical treatment, even that which may save or prolong her life"); Natanson v. Kline, 350 P.2d 1093, 1104 (Kan. 1960) ("[E]ach man is considered to be master of his own body, and he may, if he be of sound mind, expressly prohibit the performance of life-saving surgery, or other medical treatment"); *In re* Long Island Jewish Medical Ctr., 557 N.Y.S.2d 239, 242 (Sup. Ct. 1990) ("It is well-settled law in this, and most other jurisdictions, that a competent adult has a common law right to refuse medical treatment"); Scott v. Bradford, 606 P.2d 554, 558 (Okla. 1979) ("A patient's right to make up his mind whether to undergo treatment should not be delegated to the local medical group").

28. Quill, *supra* note 2, at 692.

29. *See id.* By "terminally ill," I mean suffering from an illness that will cause death within days or weeks, even if all appropriate treatment and supportive medical interventions are applied, including "artificially administered" food and water.

30. *See* Sidney H. Wanzer et al., *The Physician's Responsibility Toward Hopelessly Ill Patients: A Second Look,* 320 New Eng. J. Med. 844, 845 (1989).

31. Quill, *supra* note 2, at 693.

32. *Id.* at 692.

33. *Id.*

34. *Id.*

35. *Id.* at 693.

36. *See* Daniel Callahan, Abortion, Law, Choice, and Morality 451–60 (1970) (criticizing the assertion that one should abort a potential human being in the interests of that human being).

37. Quill, *supra* note 2, at 693.

38. *Id.*

39. *Id.* at 692.

40. A professor of nursing ethics at the University of California School of Nursing in San Francisco has written:

> Recently I had the clinical experience of caring for a dying patient who clearly said one week before she died, 'kill me.' She understood completely what she was asking for and the consequences of her request. I felt that we failed her and were less than faithful to her when we de-

nied this request. It seemed to me that, while we had said directly and indirectly all along that she was in charge, when it came to that moment, we said, No, we are in charge, and we won't do what you ask because it is not in our best interest.

Anne I. Davis, *Should Physicians Perform Euthanasia?* Am Med. News, Jan. 7, 1991, at 15.

41. Quill, *supra* note 2, at 693.
42. *Id.*
43. *Id.* at 694.

Fetal Tissue Transplantation and Embryo Experimentation

Introduction

Recently the use of fetal brain cells has shown some promise in improving the condition of some Parkinson's disease patients in whom the cells have been implanted. Consider the example of Don Nelson, a 52-year-old victim of Parkinson's disease, in whom surgeons at the University of Colorado Medical Center (on November 10, 1988) implanted the brain cells of a fetus. Soon after the surgery, Nelson noted improved walking and speaking ability. Should the technology be perfected on Parkinson's patients, "it shows promise for application to a number of other degenerative diseases such as Alzheimer's disease, Huntington's chorea, and spinal cord or other neural injuries. In addition, the use of fetal liver cells shows promise for treating bone marrow diseases and blood disorders, and fetal pancreatic cells have been shown to help treat diabetes."[1]

The ethical questions this research raises are numerous. Consider the following. If the fetus is not a human person, as abortion-rights supporters contend, why not encourage continued experimentation and research on the fetus so that those of us who *are* human persons can be helped? Why should we not permit women to purposely become pregnant so that we can use their fetal tissue for helping patients such as Mr. Nelson? But if the fetus is at least a *potential person* who is a human being, as almost all abortion-rights supporters affirm, does the fetus not have *some* right not to be treated as a thing we can take apart and on which we can experiment without any restrictions whatsoever? If fetal tissue transplantation becomes even more promising, will this not sway pregnant women ambivalent about undergoing an abortion in the direction of having one, since they will know that it is possible that some good for another person (such as Mr. Nelson) may come from their tragic decision? Will the pressure for fetal tissue transplantation provide a financial incentive for abortion clinics to sell fetal tissue either legally or on the black market? These and other questions will be the focus of the first two essays in this section. The latter two essays concern similar ethical questions raised by experimentation on the embryo within the first two weeks of its existence.

On January 22, 1993, on the twentieth anniversary of *Roe v. Wade* (1973), the decision that excluded fetuses from constitutional personhood, President Bill Clinton, with a stroke of his pen, lifted the Reagan and Bush administrations' moratorium on federal funding of fetal tissue experimentation and transplantation that uses the tissue of fetuses that result from elective abortions (that is, abortions that are not performed for therapeutic reasons, such as saving the pregnant woman's life). Thus, the moratorium did "not include research using fetal tissues from spontaneous abortions or stillbirths."[2]

The moratorium, which was declared by the assistant secretary of health in a March 22, 1988 memorandum to the director of the National Institutes of Health (NIH), was to be in effect "pending the outcome of the advisory committee(s)' assessment and" the NIH director's "subsequent review."[3] An advisory committee was created: the Human Fetal Tissue Transplantation Research (HFTTR) panel.

Members were appointed in the summer of 1988 by NIH and met later that fall. The panel, which included physicians, philosophers, theologians, and attorneys, was a philosophically diverse group of 21 members. However, prior to the first meeting of the panel, "the White House leaked a draft executive order that proposed a ban on transplantation research using human fetal tissue following elective abortions." Although over the next several weeks 50 members of Congress as well as several hundred physicians and others wrote to President Reagan urging him to sign the executive order, it never occurred.[4]

After interviewing a number of legal, ethical, and medical experts, the HFTTR panel made a number of recommendations. Although its final report consisted of majority conclusions as well as minority dissents, the panel made the following recommendations of what is considered ethically acceptable safeguards for research:

1. The decision to abort must be made prior to the discussion of the use of the tissue.
2. Anonymity is to be maintained between donor and recipient.
3. Timing and method of abortion is not to be influenced by the possibility of tissue use.
4. Consent of the pregnant woman is necessary and sufficient unless the husband objects (unless the pregnancy is the result of rape or incest).
5. No financial or other incentives are to be given to the woman who aborts and thus "donates" the tissue.[5]

The panel came to these conclusions based on a number of considerations, among which are the following: the volatile nature of the debate over abortion in the United States, the possibility of such research providing an altruistic and/or financial incentive for women to undergo abortions, the question of whether the dead fetus falls under the rubric of accepted protocols for organ donations and the use of adult human cadavers, and the need to morally separate the choice to abort from the choice to donate fetal tissue.[6] It should be noted, however, that the panel's recommendations were not set in stone. For example, in the last section of a concurring statement prepared by panel member John A. Robertson and signed by nine other panelists (the rest of the concurring statement was signed by a tenth who evidently did not agree with this section), it reads: "If the situation changes so that the supply of fetal tissue from family planning abortions proves inadequate, the ban on donor designation of recipients and aborting for transplant purposes should be reexamined. The ethical and legal arguments in favor of and against such a policy would then need careful scrutiny to determine whether such a policy remains justified."[7]

Despite the panel's recommendation to allow federal funding of fetal tissue research within certain parameters, the Bush administration maintained the moratorium. President Bush's Secretary of Health and Human Services, Louis Sullivan, in a November 2, 1989, letter to acting NIH director William F. Raub, expressed concern that "permitting the human fetal research at issue will increase the incidence of abortion across the country." Dr. Sullivan went on to say: "I am particularly convinced by those who point out that most women arrive at the abortion decision after much soul searching and uncertainty. Providing additional rationalization of directly advancing the cause of human therapeutics cannot help but tilt some already vulnerable women toward a decision to have an abortion."[8] Dr. Sullivan's letter provided several other reasons for continuing the moratorium.

According to bioethicist James Childress, critics challenged Secretary Sullivan's indefinite continuance of the moratorium:

Thirty-two medical research and education organizations, including the American Medical Association, the Association of American Medical Colleges, and the American Academy of Pediatrics, wrote Secretary Sullivan on January 4, 1990: "It is clear to us that the potential good to result from this research outweighs the concerns about the impact on the abortion rate in this country, concerns that are at best speculative. Continuing the moratorium ignores the suffering of millions of Americans". . . . After reviewing some documents and requesting others, Congressman Ted Weiss (D-N.Y.) contends that DHHS [Department of Health and Human Services] has offered no documentation that HFTTR would increase the number of abortions. . . . "The so-called indefinite moratorium," Congressman Weiss continues, "is a thinly veiled scheme to ban Federal funds for fetal tissue transplant research while avoiding the public outrage and scientific and legal scrutiny that would result from establishing a permanent ban. . . . I am hopeful Secretary Sullivan will be able to get beyond these abortion litmus tests to promote the crucial research that could be saving the lives of thousands of seriously ill Americans". . . . [9]

But simply because the Clinton administration has now lifted the moratorium it does not mean that the ethical questions raised by fetal tissue transplantation are any less compelling than when they were raised in 1988. The first two essays in this section answer these ethical questions in different ways, both taking positions that are opposed in general to the conclusions of the HFTTR panel. The first essay, "Rights, Symbolism, and Public Policy on Fetal Tissue Transplants" (Chapter 26), by John A. Robertson, argues for a position more liberal than the one taken by the HFTTR panel. The essay in Chapter 27 ("Spare Parts from the Unborn?: The Ethics of Fetal Tissue Transplantation"), authored by Scott B. Rae, takes a position more conservative than the one taken by the HFTTR panel.

On December 3, 1994, a National Institutes of Health "panel decided to accept a report recommending federal funding for research involving human embryos from conception to Day 14."[10] Chapter 28 is a summary of that report. Chapter 29 is a published statement by a group of scholars opposing the NIH report. The Clinton administration rejected the NIH's recommendations and continued the moratorium on federal funding of embryo experimentation.

Notes

1. Scott B. Rae, "Spare Parts from the Unborn?: The Ethics of Fetal Tissue Transplantation," *Christian Research Journal* 14 (Fall 1991), 29. Portions of this article are reprinted in this text as Chapter 27.

2. From a memorandum from the Assistant Secretary for Health, Robert E. Windom, to the Director of the National Institutes of Health (March 22, 1988), as reprinted in James F. Childress, "Deliberations of the Human Fetal Tissue Transplantation Research Panel," in *Biomedical Politics*, ed. Kathi E. Hanna (Washington, D.C.: National Academy Press, 1991), 244.

3. Ibid.

4. Ibid., 218–219.

5. From Rae, "Spare Parts from the Unborn?," 29–30.

6. Childress presents these and other considerations in greater detail in "Deliberations of the Human Fetal Tissue Transplantation Research Panel," op. cit., 220–234.

7. Ibid., 227.

8. Ibid., 235.

9. Ibid., 237–238.

10. Cheryl Wetzstein, "Activists Oppose Embryo Research," *The Washington Times* (December 6, 1994), A3.

For Further Reading

James Bopp and James Burtchaell, "Fetal Tissue Transplantation: The Fetus as Medical Commodity," *This World* 26 (Summer 1989).

James F. Childress, "Deliberations of the Human Fetal Tissue Transplantation Research Panel," in *Biomedical Politics*, ed. Kathi E. Hanna (Washington, D.C.: National Academy Press, 1991).

Alan Fine, "The Ethics of Fetal Tissue Transplants," *The Hastings Center Report* 18 (June/July 1988).

Henry T. Greely, et al., "The Ethical Use of Human Fetal Tissue in Medicine," *New England Journal of Medicine* 320 (April 20, 1989).

Dianne N. Irving, "'New Age' Embryology Text Books: 'Pre-Embryo,' 'Pregnancy' and Abortion Counseling; Implications for Fetal Research," *Linacre Quarterly* (May 1994).

National Institutes of Health, *Final Report of the Human Embryo Research Panel* (27 September 1994).

Paul Ramsey, *The Ethics of Fetal Research* (New Haven, Conn.: Yale University Press, 1975).

John A. Robertson, "Fetal Tissue Transplants," *Washington University Law Quarterly* 66 (1988).

Andrew Simons, "Brave New Harvest," *Christianity Today* (November 19, 1990).

LeRoy Walters, "Ethical Issues in Experimentation on the Human Fetus," *Journal of Religious Ethics* 2 (Spring 1974).

Mildred Washington, "Fetal Research: A Survey of State Law," *Congressional Research Service Report for Congress* (March 8, 1988).

26

Rights, Symbolism, and Public
Policy on Fetal Tissue Transplants

John A. Robertson

John A. Robertson is Baker & Botts Professor of
Law, University of Texas School of Law in Austin,
Texas. He was a member of the NIH Panel on Fetal
Tissue Transplantation Research. He has published
widely in the area of bioethics, law, and public
policy, including articles in *The Hastings Center
Report* and *Washington University Law Quarterly*. He
is author of the book *Children of Choice: Freedom and
the New Reproductive Technologies* (1994).

In this essay Professor Robertson defends a
liberal view of fetal tissue transplants, arguing that
it is morally justified to use fetal tissue for transplantation even if the fetus's death did result from
an elective nontherapeutic abortion. He begins his
essay with a clarification of the issues surrounding
fetal tissue transplantation. He then moves on to
respond to two arguments brought up by conservatives who oppose the use of fetal tissue from
elective abortions: (1) using such fetal tissue
involves moral complicity in the abortion, and (2)
using such fetal tissue will result in legitimizing,
entrenching, and encouraging abortion. In order to
articulate his position more clearly Professor
Robertson presents hypothetical scenarios that
concern the use of tissue in different situations
(e.g., a woman becoming pregnant with the intent
of donating the fetal tissue, a woman donating the
fetal tissue after she discovers she is pregnant). He
goes on to discuss recruiting unrelated fetal tissue
donors, the woman's right to dispose of fetal tissue,
the consent process and abortion, commercialization of fetal tissue, federal funding, and legal bans
on fetal tissue transplants. He concludes that
"ethical concerns should not bar research with fetal

Reprinted by permission from *The Hastings Center Report* 18
(December 1988).

tissue transplants as a therapy for serious illness."
Other than protecting women from possible
economic exploitation, he opposes nearly any
restriction on fetal tissue transplantation and
supports federal funding with a few caveats.

Clarifying the Issues

As with many issues in bioethics, careful analysis will
help elucidate the normative conflict, showing both
areas of agreement and irreducible conflict. An
essential distinction in the fetal tissue controversy is
between procuring tissue from family planning
abortions and procuring tissue from abortions
performed expressly to provide tissue for transplant.
Although opponents of fetal tissue transplants have
often conflated the two, tissue from family planning
abortions may be used without implying approval
of abortions to produce tissue. Indeed, with ample
tissue available from family planning abortions, the
latter scenario may never occur.

A second important distinction is that between
retrieving tissue for transplant from dead and from
live fetuses. Only the use of tissue from dead fetuses
is at issue. Researchers are not proposing to maintain
non-viable fetuses ex utero to procure tissue, or to
take tissue from them before they are dead, practices
that current regulations and law prohibit.[1]

A third set of issues concern tissue procurement
procedures. If fetal tissue transplants do occur,
questions about the timing, substance, and process
of consent must be addressed, as well as the role of
nonprofit and for-profit agencies in retrieving and
distributing fetal tissue. As with solid organ
transplantation, effective tissue procurement may
occur without buying and selling fetal tissue.

At present there are few legal barriers to research
or therapeutic use of donated fetal tissue for
transplant. The Uniform Anatomical Gift Act
(UAGA) in all states treats fetal remains like other
cadaveric remains and allows next of kin to donate
the tissue, though a few states have laws banning
experimental use of aborted fetuses.[2] Federal
regulations for fetal research, enacted in 1976 after
careful study by the National Commission for the
Protection of Human Subjects of Biomedical and
Behavioral Research, permit research activities
"involving the dead fetus, mascerated fetal material,
or cells, tissue, or organs excised from a dead fetus

. . . in accordance with any applicable state or local laws regarding such activities."[3]

The most immediate public policy question is whether these rules should be changed to prohibit experimental or therapeutic fetal tissue transplants, as the most extreme opponents urge. A second public policy issue is whether federal funding of fetal tissue research should occur. A third set of policy issues concerns the circumstances and procedures by which fetal tissue will be retrieved.

Tissue from Family Planning Abortions

Fetal tissue transplant research for Parkinson's disease, diabetes, and other disorders will use tissue retrieved from the one and a half million abortions performed annually in the United States to end unwanted pregnancies. Nearly 80 percent of induced abortions are performed between the sixth and eleventh weeks of gestation, at which time neural and other tissue is sufficiently developed to be retrieved and transplanted.[4] Abortions performed at fourteen to sixteen weeks provide pancreatic tissue used in diabetes research, but it may prove possible to use pancreases retrieved earlier.[5]

No need now or in the foreseeable future exists to have a family member conceive and abort to produce fetal tissue. The neural tissue to be transplanted in Parkinson's disease lacks antigenicity, thus obviating the need for a close match between donor and recipient. Fetal pancreas is more antigenetic, but processing can reduce this, also making family connection less important.

The key question is whether women who abort to end unwanted pregnancies may donate the aborted fetuses for use in medical research or therapy by persons who have no connection with or influence on the decision to terminate the pregnancy. One's views on abortion need not determine one's answer to this question, because the abortion and subsequent transplant use are clearly separated. But some opposed to abortion object that transplanting fetal tissue involves complicity in an immoral act and will legitimate and even encourage abortion. Analysis of these concerns will show that they are insufficient to justify a public policy that bans or refuses to fund research or therapy with fetal tissue from induced abortion.

Complicity in Abortion

Even proponents of the complicity argument recognize that not all situations of subsequent benefit make one morally complicitous in a prior evil act. For example, James Burtchaell claims that complicity occurs not merely from partaking of benefit but only when one enters into a "supportive alliance" with the underlying evil that makes the benefit possible. He distinguishes "a neutral or even an opponent and an ally" of the underlying evil by "the way in which one does or does not hold oneself apart from the enterprise and its purposes."[6]

On this analysis, a researcher using fetal tissue from an elective abortion is not necessarily an accomplice with the abortionist and woman choosing abortion. The researcher and recipient have no role in the abortion process. They will not have requested it, and may have no knowledge of who performed the abortion or where it occurred since a third-party intermediary will procure the tissue. They may be morally opposed to abortion, and surely are not compromised because they choose to salvage some good from an abortion that will occur regardless of their research or therapeutic goals.

A useful analogy is transplant of organs and tissue from homicide victims. Families of murder victims are often asked to donate organs and bodies for research, therapy, and education. If they consent, organ procurement agencies retrieve the organs and distribute them to recipients. No one would seriously argue that the surgeon who transplants the victim's kidneys, heart, liver, or corneas, or the recipient of the organs, becomes an accomplice in the homicide that made the organs available, even if aware of the source. Nor is the medical student who uses the cadaver of a murder victim to study anatomy.

If organs from murder victims may be used without complicity in the murder that makes the organs available, then fetal remains could also be used without complicity in the abortion. Burtchaell's approach to the problem of complicity assumes that researchers necessarily applaud the underlying act of abortion. But one may benefit from another's evil act without applauding or approving of that evil. X may disapprove of Y's murder of Z, even though X gains an inheritance or a promotion as a result. Indeed, one might even question Burtchaell's assumption that X becomes an accomplice in Y's prior act if he subsequently applauds it. Applauding Y's murder of Z might be insensitive or callous. But that alone would not make one morally responsible for, complicitous in, the murder that has already occurred. In any event, the willingness to derive benefit from another's wrongful death does not create complicity in that death because the beneficiary played no role in causing it.

The complicity argument against use of aborted fetuses often draws an analogy to a perceived reluctance to use the results of unethical medical research carried out by the Nazis. Burtchaell and others have claimed that it would make us retroactively accomplices in the Nazi horrors to use the results of their unethical and lethal research.[7] This ignores, however, the clear separation between the perpetrator and beneficiary of the immoral act that breaks the chain of moral complicity for that act.

Thus one could rely on Nazi-generated data while decrying the horrendous acts of Nazi doctors that produced the data. Nor would it necessarily dishonor those unfortunate victims. Indeed, it could reasonably be viewed as retrospectively honoring them by saving others. The Jewish doctors who made systematic studies of starvation in the Warsaw ghetto to reap some good from the evil being done to their brethren were not accomplices in that evil, nor are doctors and patients who now benefit from their studies.[8]

If the complicity claim is doubtful when the underlying immorality of the act is clear, as with Nazi-produced data or transplants from murder victims, it is considerably weakened when the act making the benefit possible is legal and its immorality vigorously debated, as is the case with abortion. Even persons opposed to abortion might agree that perceptions of complicity should not determine public policy on fetal tissue transplants.

Legitimizing, Entrenching, and Encouraging Abortion

A second objection is that salvaging tissue for transplant from aborted fetuses will make abortion less morally offensive and more easily tolerated both by individual pregnant women and by society, and perhaps transform it into a morally positive act. This will encourage abortions that would not otherwise occur, and dilute support for reversing the legal acceptability of abortion, in effect creating complicity in future abortions.[9]

But the feared impact on abortion practices and attitudes is highly speculative, particularly at a time when few fetal transplants have occurred. The main motivation for abortion is the desire to avoid the burdens of an unwanted pregnancy. The fact that fetal remains may be donated for transplant will continue to be of little significance in the total array of factors that lead a woman to abort a pregnancy.

Having decided to abort, a woman may feel better if she then donates the fetal remains. But this does not show that tissue donation will lead to a termination decision that would not otherwise have occurred, particularly if the decision to abort is made before the opportunity to donate the remains is offered. Perhaps a few more abortions will occur because of the general knowledge that tissue can be donated for transplant, but it is highly unlikely that donation— as opposed to contraceptive practices and sex education—will contribute significantly to the rate of abortion.[10]

Nor does the use of fetal remains for transplant mean that a public otherwise ready to outlaw abortion would refrain from doing so. Legal acceptance of abortion flows from the wide disagreement that exists over early fetal status. If a majority agreed that fetuses should be respected as persons despite the burdens placed on pregnant women, such possible secondary benefits of induced abortion as fetal tissue transplants would not prevent a change in the legality of abortion.

Indeed, one could make the same argument against organ transplants from homicide, suicide, and accident victims. The willingness to use their organs might be seen to encourage or legitimate such deaths, or at least make it harder to enact lower speed limits, seatbelt, gun control, and drunk driving laws to prevent them. After all, the need to prevent murder, suicide, and fatal accidents becomes less pressing if some good to others might come from use of victims' organs for transplant. In either case, the connection is too tenuous and speculative to ban organ or fetal tissue transplants.

In sum, fetal tissue transplants are practically and morally separate from decisions to end unwanted pregnancy. Given that abortion is legal and occurring on a large scale, the willingness to use resulting tissue for transplant neither creates complicity in past abortions nor appears significantly to encourage more future abortions. Such ethical concerns and speculations are not sufficient, given the possible good to others, to justify banning use of fetal tissue for research or therapy.

Aborting to Obtain Tissue for Transplant

Central to the argument for transplanting fetal tissue from family planning abortions has been the assumption that the abortion occurs independently of the need for tissue, and that permitting such transplants does not also entail pregnancy and abortion to produce fetal tissue.

But successful tissue transplants may create the need to abort to produce fetal tissue in two future situations. One situation would arise if histocompatibility between the fetus and recipient were necessary for effective fetal transplants. Female relatives, spouses, or even unrelated persons might then seek to conceive to provide properly matched fetal tissue for transplant.

The second situation would arise if fetal transplants were so successful that demand far outstripped supply, such as might occur if the treatment were advantageous to most patients with Parkinson's disease and diabetes, or if the number of surgical family planning abortions decreased. Pressure on supply might also occur if tissue from several aborted fetuses were needed to produce one viable transplant.

The hypothetical possibility of such situations is not a sufficient reason to ban all tissue transplants from family planning abortions. But should such abortions be banned if the imagined situations occurred? Most commentators assume that conception and abortion for tissue procurement is so clearly unethical that the prospect hardly merits discussion.[11] Accordingly, they would ban all tissue transplants from related persons and deny the donor the right to designate the recipient of a fetal tissue transplant.

Analysis will show, however, that the question is more ethically complicated than generally assumed, and should not be the driving force in setting policy for tissue transplants from family planning abortions.

A Hypothetical Situation

Consider first the situation where a woman pregnant with her husband's child learns that tissue from her fetus could cure severe neurologic disease in herself or a close relative, such as her husband, child, parent, father or mother-in-law, sibling, or brother or sister-in-law. May she ethically abort the pregnancy to obtain tissue for transplant to the relative? Or may a woman not yet pregnant, conceive a fetus that she will then abort to provide tissue for transplant to herself or to her relative?

To focus analysis on fetal welfare, assume in each case that no other viable tissue source exists, and that the advanced state of neurologic disease has become a major tragedy for the patient and family. The woman has broached the question of abortion to obtain tissue without any direct pressure or inducements from the family or others. Her husband accepts an abortion for transplant purposes if she is willing, but exerts no pressure on her to abort.

The woman is already pregnant. If the woman is already pregnant, the question is whether a first trimester fetus that would otherwise have been carried to term may be sacrificed to procure tissue for transplant to the woman herself or to a sick family member. The answer depends on the value placed on early fetuses and on the acceptable reasons for abortion. One may distinguish between fetuses that have developed the neurologic and cognitive capacity for sentience and interests in themselves, and those so neurologically immature that they cannot experience harm.[12] While aborting fetuses at that earlier stage prevents them from achieving their potential, it does not harm or wrong them, since they are insufficiently developed to experience harm.[13]

Although aborting the fetus at that early stage does not wrong the fetus, it may impose symbolic costs measurable in terms of the reduced respect for human life generally that a willingness to abort early fetuses connotes. Still, the abortion may be ethically acceptable if the good sought sufficiently outweighs the symbolic devaluation of life that occurs when fetuses that cannot be harmed in their own right are aborted. Many persons find that the burdens of unwanted pregnancy outweigh the symbolic devaluation of human life. Others would require a more compelling reason for abortion, such as protecting the mother's life or health, avoiding the birth of a handicapped child, or avoiding the burdens of a pregnancy due to rape or incest.

By comparison, abortion to obtain tissue to save one's own life or the life of a close relative seems equally, if not more compelling. If abortion in the case of an unwanted pregnancy is deemed permissible, surely abortion to obtain tissue to save another person's life is. Indeed, aborting to obtain tissue would seem as compelling as the most stringent reasons for permitting abortion. In fact, many would find this motive more compelling than the desire to end an unwanted pregnancy.

Of course, aborting a wanted pregnancy to prevent severe neurologic disease in oneself or a close relative will hardly be done joyfully, and will place the mother in an excruciating dilemma. A fetus that could be carried to term will have to be sacrificed to save a parent, spouse, sibling, or child who already exists. Such a tragic choice will induce fear and trembling, and engender loss or grief whatever the decision. Yet one cannot say that the choice to abort is ethically impermissible. There is no sound ethical basis for prohibiting *this* sacrifice of the fetus when its sacrifice to end an unwanted pregnancy or pursue other goals is permitted.

Public attitudes toward a woman aborting an otherwise wanted pregnancy to benefit a family member would most likely reflect attitudes toward abortion generally. Those who are against abortion in all circumstances will object to abortions done to treat severe neurologic disease in the mother or in a family member. Similarly, persons who accept family planning abortions should have no objection to abortion to procure tissue for transplant, since fetal status is no more compelling and the interest of the woman in controlling her body and reproductive capacity is similar.

Since neither group forms a majority, however, persons who object to family planning abortions but accept abortions necessary to protect the mother's health, in cases of rape or incest, or to prevent the birth of a handicapped child will determine whether a majority of people approve.[14] It is conceivable that many persons in this swing group would find abortion to produce tissue for transplant to a family member to be acceptable. The benefit of alleviating severe neurologic disease is arguably as great as the benefits in the cases they accept as justifiable abortion, and more compelling than abortions done for family planning purposes.

Conceiving and aborting for transplant purposes. What is the objection, then, when a woman not yet pregnant seeks to conceive in order to abort and provide tissue for transplant?

In terms of fetal welfare, no greater harm occurs to the fetus conceived to be aborted, as long as the abortion occurs at a stage at which the fetus is insufficiently developed to experience harm, such as during the first trimester. Of course, such deliberate creation may have greater symbolic significance, because it denotes a willingness to use fetuses as a means or object to serve other ends. However, aborting when already pregnant to procure tissue for transplant (or aborting for the more customary reasons) also denotes a willingness to use the fetus as a means to other ends.

As long as abortion of an existing pregnancy for transplant purposes is ethically accepted, conceiving in order to abort and procure tissue for transplant should also be ethically acceptable when necessary to alleviate great suffering in others.[15] People could reasonably find that the additional symbolic devaluation is negligible, or in any case, insufficient to outweigh the substantial gain to transplant recipients that deliberate creation provides.

Many people, no doubt, will resist this conclusion, even if they accept abortion to procure tissue when the woman is already pregnant. Whether rational or not, they assign moral or symbolic significance to deliberate creation, and are less ready to sanction such a practice. Others who accept abortion for tissue procurement when the woman is already pregnant will find an insufficient difference in deliberate creation to outweigh the resulting good. Public acceptability of such a practice thus depends on how the swing group that views abortion as acceptable only for very stringent reasons views the fact of deliberate creation for the purpose of abortion. If it would accept abortion to produce tissue when the pregnancy is unplanned, it might accept conception to produce fetal tissue as well.

In sum, deliberate creation of fetuses to be aborted for tissue procurement is more ethically complex, and more defensible, than its current widespread dismissal would suggest. Such a practice is, of course, not in itself desirable, but in a specific situation of strong personal or familial need may be more justified than previously thought. In any case, the fear that fetal tissue transplants will lead to abortions performed solely to obtain tissue for transplant should not prevent use of tissue from abortions not performed for that purpose.

Recruiting Unrelated Fetal Tissue Donors

The strongest case for conception and abortion to produce fetal tissue—if the need arose—is to save oneself or a close relative from death or serious harm. But many patients in need would lack a female relative willing to donate. May unrelated women be recruited for this purpose?

If the hypothetical need arose, a strong case for unrelated fetal tissue donors can be made. If a relative may provide tissue, why not a stranger who chooses to do so altruistically? At this point concerns about fetal status become less important, and the focus shifts toward the welfare of the donor. But the physical effects of pregnancy and abortion to produce fetal tissue are roughly comparable to the effects of kidney or bone marrow donation, though somewhat less since general anesthesia will not be involved. While few unrelated persons now act as kidney donors, there is a national registry for unrelated bone marrow donors. Even if fetal tissue donation were psychologically more complicated, the risks to the woman would appear to be within the boundaries of autonomous choice.

Some persons might object that this will turn women into "fetal tissue farms," thus denigrating their inherent worth as persons. This charge could also be made against any living donor, whether of kidney, bone marrow, blood, sperm, or egg. Insofar as persons donate body parts, they may be viewed as mere tissue or organ producers. Indeed, women who bear children are always in danger of being viewed as "breeders." But such views oversimplify the complex emotional reality of organ and tissue donation and of human reproduction. The risk of misperception does not justify barring women from freely choosing to be fetal tissue donors.

Special attention should be given to consent procedures that will protect the woman from coercion or undue pressure by prospective recipients and their families, just as occurs with living related kidney and marrow donors. Waiting periods, consent advisors and monitors, and other devices to guarantee free, informed consent are clearly justified.[16]

The Woman's Right to Dispose of Fetal Tissue

The UAGA and federal research regulations give the mother the right to make or withhold donations of fetal remains for research or therapy, subject to objection by the father.[17] Yet some ethicists claim that the decision to abort disqualifies the mother from playing any role in disposition of fetal remains.[18] If accepted, this argument would lead either to procuring fetal tissue without parental consent or to a total ban on fetal transplants. But the argument is mistaken on two grounds.

Its major premise is that the person disposing of cadaveric remains acts as a guardian or proxy for the deceased. Since the woman has chosen to kill the fetus by abortion, she is no longer qualified to act as proxy. But this premise is seriously flawed. Deceased persons or fetuses no longer have interests to be protected, as the notion of proxy implies. Control of human remains is assigned to next of kin because of their own interests and feelings about how cadaveric remains are treated, not because they are best situated to implement the deceased's prior wishes concerning disposition of his cadaver. The latter concern is particularly inappropriate in the case of an aborted fetus, which could have had no specific wishes concerning disposition of its remains.

A second mistake is the assumption that a woman has no interest in what happens to the fetus that she chooses to abort. As a product of her body and potential heir that she has for her own compelling reasons chosen to abort, she may care deeply about whether fetal remains are contributed to research or therapy to help others. Given that interest, there is good reason to respect her wishes, as current law does. Indeed, in cases of conflict between her and the father over disposition, one could argue that her interests control because the fetus was removed from her body.

An alternative policy requiring that fetal remains be used without parental consent or not at all is unacceptable. American public policy has vigorously rejected routine salvage of body parts without family consent as a way to increase the supply of organs for transplant.[19] Even presumed consent, which would take organs unless the family actually objects, has been largely rejected.[20] Depriving the mother (and father who agrees to the abortion) of the power to veto fetal tissue transplants would single out fetal tissue for transplant use without family consent. Such a radical change in tissue procurement practice is not needed to satisfy the demand for fetal tissue. It serves only to punish women who abort.

The alternative would be to ban fetal tissue transplants altogether. But this solution burns the house to roast the pig, in effect banning tissue transplants because the parent is not permitted to consent. As we have seen, however, a ban on all fetal transplants is not justified.

In short, the ethical case for denying the woman who aborts dispositional control of fetal remains is not persuasive. She cannot insist that fetal remains be used for transplant because no donor has the right to require that intended donees accept anatomical gifts, but she should retain the existing legal right to veto use of fetal remains for transplant research or therapy. Her consent to donation of fetal tissue should be routinely sought.

The Consent Process and Abortion

If the woman retains the right to determine whether fetal tissue is used for research or therapy, the main ethical concern is to assure that her choice about tissue donation and the abortion is free and informed. A clear separation of the two decisions will assure that tissue donation is not a prerequisite to performance of the abortion. Also, it will prevent the prospect of donating fetal remains from influencing the decision to abort, a preferable policy when sufficient tissue from family planning abortions is available.

To that end, the request to donate fetal tissue should be made only after the woman has consented to the abortion.[21] The alternative of waiting until the abortion has been performed would add little protection and not be practical. In addition, the person requesting consent to tissue donation and performing the abortion should not be the person using the donated tissue in research or therapy, a constraint widely followed in cadaveric organ procurement.

Federal regulations governing fetal research also state that "no procedural changes which may cause greater than minimal risk to the fetus or pregnant woman will be introduced into the procedure for terminating the pregnancy solely in the interest of the activity."[22] While this policy is partially intended to protect fetuses from later or more painful abortions, it also aims to protect women from prolonging pregnancy or undergoing more onerous abortion procedures to obtain tissue.

Some changes in abortion procedures to enhance tissue procurement pose little additional risk and should be permitted. For example, reductions in the amount of suction, use of a larger bore needle, and ultrasound-guided placement of the suction instrument in evacuation abortions would, without increasing risk, facilitate tissue retrieval by preventing masceration of the fetus.

More problematic would be changes such as substitution of prostaglandin-induced labor and delivery or hysterotomy for less risky methods, or postponement of abortion too late in the first trimester or to the second trimester. Apart from her desire to facilitate tissue donation, these changes would not appear to be in the woman's interest.

Asking a woman who is aborting to take on these extra burdens can be ethically justified only if necessary to obtain viable tissue. Because sufficient fetal tissue may now be obtained without increasing the burdens of abortion, the current federal regulations are sound.

A different policy should be considered if changes in timing or method of abortion became necessary to procure viable tissue for transplant. If the need were clearly shown, there is no objection in principle to asking a woman to assume some additional burdens for the sake of tissue procurement. If the woman is already pregnant and determined to have an abortion, the additional risks of postponing the abortion a few weeks or even changing to a prostaglandin abortion would be well within the range of risks that persons may voluntarily choose to benefit others. However, special procedures to protect the woman's autonomy would be in order.

Commercialization of Fetal Tissue

In addition to ethical concerns about fetal and maternal welfare, opponents of fetal tissue transplants have raised the specter of fetal tissue procurement leading to a commercial market in abortions and in fetal tissue.

Paying money to women to abort, or to donate once they abort, is generally perceived as damaging to human dignity, as would be commercial buying and selling of fetal tissue. Such market transactions risk exploiting women and their reproductive capacity and may denigrate the human dignity of aborted fetuses by treating them as market commodities.[23]

Most commentators and advisory bodies that have considered fetal tissue transplants recommend that market transactions in abortions and fetal tissue be prohibited.[24] The National Organ Transplant Act of 1984, which bans the payment of "valuable consideration" for the donation or distribution of solid organs, was amended in 1988 to ban sales of fetal organs and "subparts thereof."[25] Also, several states prohibit the sale of fetal tissue and organs.[26]

At present such policies are easily supported, for they would have little impact on the supply of fetal tissue. There is no reason to think that women who abort unwanted pregnancies would not donate fetal tissue altruistically. Indeed, many women who abort are likely to donate fetal remains in the hope that some additional good might result from the abortion. Paying them to donate—buying their aborted fetuses—is thus unnecessary.

But what if altruistic donations did not produce a sufficient supply of fetal tissue for transplant, or the need for histocompatible tissue required hiring women to be impregnated to produce a sufficient supply of fetal tissue? Would such payments be un-ethical? Should current legal policy still be maintained? Answering those questions would require balancing the risks of exploiting women and the symbolic costs of perceived commodification against the benefits to needy patients and the rights of women to determine use of their reproductive capacity.

No doubt many people would object to hiring women to become pregnant and abort. However, if pregnancy and abortion to produce fetal tissue is ethically defensible, then money payments in some circumstances may also be defensible, given obligations of beneficence and respect for persons, the lack of alternative tissue sources, and social practices in which some tissue donors are paid.[27] Legal policy might then be reconsidered to permit payments when essential to save the life or protect the health of transplant recipients who lack other alternatives. However, resolution of this difficult issue should await the actual occurrence of the need to pay to obtain fetal tissue for transplant. In the meantime, research and therapy with fetal tissue should proceed without payments to women to abort or to donate fetal tissue.

Current bans on buying and selling fetal tissue do not—and should not—prohibit making reasonable payments to recover the costs of retrieving fetal tissue. The law and ethics of organ procurement allow for payment of costs incurred in the acquisition of organs.[28] Organ donor families, for example, are not asked to pay for the costs of maintaining brain-dead cadavers or for surgically removing the organs that they donate. The same principle should apply to fetal tissue donations. Two related issues concern paying the donor's abortion expenses and paying other tissue retrieval costs.

Paying abortion expenses. Paying the cost of the abortion should occur only in those instances in which the abortion is performed solely to obtain tissue for transplant—a mere hypothetical possibility at present. In that case, paying for the abortion is not a fee to donate tissue, but payment of the costs of acquiring the donated tissue, comparable to paying the cost of the nephrectomy that makes a kidney donation possible. Other out-of-pocket costs incurred by the donor could also be reimbursed without violating federal law or ethical constraints.

In contrast, when the abortion is performed for reasons unrelated to tissue procurement, paying abortion expenses amounts to paying the women to donate the tissue. This payment would constitute a sale of fetal tissue and should not be permitted if fetal tissue sales are prohibited.[29] The willingness of

most women to donate without a fee should make payment of abortion expenses unnecessary.

Retrieval costs and for-profit agencies. In the past researchers have obtained fetal tissue through informal contacts with physicians doing abortions, often in the same institution. More recently, agencies that retrieve tissue from abortion facilities and distribute it to researchers have developed. In some cases for-profit firms that specialize in processing the tissue for transplant may enter the field.

What role will money payments play in the operation of retrieval agencies? Under existing law tissue procurement agencies will be unable to pay women to donate fetal tissue. However, they should be free to pay the costs of personnel directly involved in retrieval, whether employees of the procurement agency or of the facility performing the abortion. For example, a tissue retrieval agency may reimburse the abortion clinic for using its space and staff to obtain consent for tissue donations and to retrieve tissue from aborted fetuses.[30]

In distributing fetal tissue to researchers and physicians, retrieval agencies should be able to recoup the expenses of procuring the tissue, including overhead and other operating expenses of the agency itself. Such payment is consistent with heart and kidney transplant recipients (or their payors) paying for the analogous costs of organ procurement.

If the retrieval agency is a for-profit enterprise, some profit margin should also be recognized in the amount it charges the recipient of the tissue. While some persons might argue that allowing any profit amounts to a sale of fetal tissue that risks treating it as a market commodity, those who organize resources and invest capital to provide viable fetal tissue for transplant are performing a useful social activity. Fears about treating donors and fetuses as commodities might justify policies against buying tissue from donors and abortion facilities. But they should not prevent giving for-profit firms the incentives necessary to organize the resources required to obtain fetal tissue altruistically. Such a practice would be consistent with the role of for-profit physicians, hospitals, drug companies, and air transport services in organ transplantation.

Federal Funding

While existing federal regulations permit transplant research with tissue from aborted fetuses when state law permits, the question of whether the federal government should fund fetal tissue research nevertheless remains. A special panel was recently convened by the National Institutes of Health to advise the Assistant Secretary for Health on whether intramural and extramural research programs involving fetal tissue transplants should be supported.[31] The panel gave a positive recommendation, with restrictions on tissue procurement comparable to the existing federal regulations, but its approval does not guarantee that federal research funding will occur.[32]

Because funding decisions ordinarily do not infringe constitutional rights, the government is not obligated to fund fetal tissue research (or therapy), no matter how desirable it appears.[33] However, the arguments strongly favor supporting such research. Of overriding importance is the potential benefit to thousands of patients suffering from severe disease. Federal funding will also allow the government to play a more active oversight role than if it leaves the field entirely to private funding, as occurred with in vitro fertilization research.[34]

The arguments against federal research funding come from right-to-life groups that would remove the federal government entirely from any financial support of abortion in the United States. Research funding, however, does not subsidize the abortions making the tissue available. Nor, as we have seen, does it place an imprimatur of legitimacy on abortion, or encourage to any great extent abortions that would not otherwise have occurred.

If the politics of abortion lead to withdrawal of direct government funding of research with tissue from family planning abortions, the government should not penalize institutions that conduct such research with nonfederal funds by denying them other research assistance. The symbolic gains of refusing to fund other medical research in institutions doing nonfederally funded research with aborted fetuses are too few to justify the burden on researchers. Clearly at that point the link to abortion is too attenuated to claim complicity in or encouragement of it.

These same issues will be refought if fetal tissue transplants became a proven therapy for Parkinson's disease, diabetes, or other disorders. While the government is not constitutionally obligated to fund a given therapy, the case for federal funding of treatment is even stronger than for funding of research, because the benefits to patients are clearer. A policy of denying Medicare or Medicaid funding for safe and effective fetal tissue transplants would deprive needy patients of essential therapies simply to avoid speculative concerns about complicity and encouragement of abortion. A more prudent approach would be to fund all therapies that meet the general funding standards for these programs. Alternatively, the government's funding policies should distinguish between therapies dependent on tissue retrieved from family planning abortions and those dependent on tissue from abortions performed to provide tissue for transplant.

Legal Bans on Fetal Tissue Transplants

While the UAGA in every state permits the mother to donate fetal tissue for transplant research and therapy, eight states ban the experimental use of dead aborted fetuses.[35] None of these laws distinguish tissue from family planning abortions and abortions performed solely to obtain fetal tissue. Six of the eight states ban experimental but not unexperimental use of aborted fetuses. None ban similar uses of other cadaveric tissue, including cadavers that resulted from homicide.[36]

As a policy matter, the case for a legal ban on all research uses of dead fetal tissue is weak. Given that the use of fetal remains from lawful abortions is at issue, such laws are difficult to sustain. They purport to show the state's respect for prenatal life, but they do it in such an irrational way that they are clearly vulnerable to constitutional attack on several grounds, including vagueness, irrationality, and interference with the right to abort and the recipient's right to medical care.[37] A case invalidating the Louisiana law will be a potent precedent in future attacks on these laws.[38]

Even laws that prohibited intrafamilial donations or donor designation of recipients, which aim to prevent women from conceiving and aborting to produce fetal tissue, would be vulnerable if such practices were necessary to provide transplants to sick patients.[39] If the woman is already pregnant, such laws would prevent her from aborting to provide tissue. If not yet pregnant, they would arguably interfere with marital and procreative privacy or the recipient's right to life and medical care. A state's interest in preventing women from becoming "tissue farms," from abusing the reproductive process, or from being pressured to donate would not justify intrusion on such fundamental rights when the patient had no other alternative.[40]

Symbolic and Rights-Based Concerns

Ethical concerns should not bar research with fetal tissue transplants as a therapy for serious illness. Although many persons have ethical reservations about abortion, a wide range of opinion would likely support many research uses of fetal tissue, particularly when the abortions occur for reasons other than tissue procurement.

The use of fetal tissue inevitably implicates the strong feelings that abortion engenders. The disparate issues raised, however, can be treated separately, so that ethical concerns and the politics of abortion do not impede the progress of important research. For example, transplants with fetal tissue from family planning abortions do not necessarily entail approval of pregnancy and abortion undertaken to produce tissue for transplant. Nor will recognizing the woman's right to donate fetal tissue cause fetuses to be bought and sold, or women to be paid to abort.

In the final analysis, fetal tissue transplants raise symbolic questions as well as questions of rights. The symbolic issues raised by fetal tissue transplants cut in many directions. Sorting out symbolic and rights-based concerns will help to respect both important ethical values and the need for progress in medical science.

Discussion Questions

1. Briefly summarize the "complicity in abortion" as well as the "legitimizing, entrenching, and encouraging abortion" arguments against fetal transplantation. Present and explain Professor Robertson's responses to these arguments. Do you agree or disagree with his reasoning? Explain and defend your answer.

2. What is Professor Robertson's position on a woman intentionally becoming pregnant in order to donate fetal tissue to a relative or a nonrelative? How does he defend this position? Do you agree or disagree with his reasoning? Explain and defend your answer.

3. Many opponents of transplantation of fetal tissue from elective abortions argue that the woman has no parental right to dispose of the tissue as she wishes since she is the one who killed "her child." How does Professor Robertson respond to this argument? Do you find his case compelling? Why or why not?

4. Present and explain Professor Robertson's position on the commercialization of fetal tissue.

5. Present and explain Professor Robertson's position on the federal funding of fetal tissue transplantation.

Notes

1. 45 CFR 46.209; John A. Robertson, "Relaxing the Death Standard for Pediatric Organ Donations," in *Organ Substitution Technology: Ethical, Legal, and Public Policy Issues* (Boulder, CO: Westview Press, 1988), 69–77.

2. John A. Robertson, "Fetal Tissue Transplants," *Washington University Law Quarterly* 66:3 (November 1988).

3. 45 CFR 46.210.

4. Stanley K. Henshaw *et al.*, "A Portrait of American Women Who Obtain Abortions," *Family Planning Perspectives* 17:2 (1985), 90–96.

5. Kevin Lafferty, Statement to the Fetal Tissue Transplantation Research Panel, NIH, Sept. 15, 1988.

6. James Burtchaell, "Case Study: University Policy on Experimental Use of Aborted Fetal Tissue," *IRB: A Review of Human Subjects Research* 10:4 (July/August 1988), 7–11.

7. Burtchaell, "Case Study," 10; Phillip Shabecoff, "Head of E.P.A. Bars Nazi Data in Study in Gas," *New York Times*, March 23, 1988, 1.

8. Leonard Tushnet, *The Uses of Adversity: Studies of Starvation in the Warsaw Ghetto* (New York: Thomas Yoseloff, 1966); "Minnesota Scientist Plans to Publish a Nazi Study," *New York Times*, May 12, 1988, 9.

9. Tamar Lewin, "Medical Use of Fetal Tissue Spurs New Abortion Debate," *New York Times*, Aug. 16, 1987, A1.

10. John A. Robertson, "Fetal Tissue Transplants."

11. Mary B. Mahowald, Jerry Silver, and Robert A. Ratcheson, "The Ethical Options in Transplanting Fetal Tissue," *Hastings Center Report* 17:2 (February 1987), 9–15; Mark Danis, "Fetal Tissue Transplants: Restricting Recipient Designation," *Hastings Law Journal* 39:5 (July 1988), 1079–1107.

12. Clifford Grobstein, *Science and the Unborn* (New York: Basic Books, 1988).

13. John A. Robertson, "Gestational Burdens and Fetal Status: A Defense of *Roe v. Wade*," *American Journal of Law and Medicine* 13:2/3 (1988), 189–212; John Bigelow and Robert Pargetter, "Morality, Potential Persons, and Abortion," *American Philosophical Quarterly* 25 (1988), 173–81.

14. See, for example, "America's Abortion Dilemma," *Newsweek*, January 14, 1985, 22–26.

15. John A. Robertson, "Embryos, Families, and Procreative Liberty: The Legal Structure of the New Reproduction," *Southern California Law Review* 59 (1986), 939–1041.

16. John A. Robertson, "Taking Consent Seriously: IRB Interventions in the Consent Process," *IRB: A Review of Human Subjects Research* 4:5 (May 1982), 1–5.

17. Uniform Anatomical Gift Act, 8A U.L.A. 15–16 (West 1983 and Supp. 1987) (Table of Jurisdictions Wherein Act Has Been Adopted); 45 CFR 46.207(b).

18. Burtchaell, "Case Study," 8; Mary B. Mahowald, "Placing Wedges Along a Slippery Slope: Use of Fetal Neural Tissue for Transplantation," *Clinical Research* 36 (1988), 220–23.

19. John A. Robertson, "Supply and Distribution of Hearts for Transplantation: Legal, Ethical, and Policy Issues," *Circulation* 75 (1987), 77–88.

20. Robertson, "Supply and Distribution"; Department of Health and Human Services, *Organ Transplantation: Issues and Recommendations. Report of the Task Force on Organ Transplantation*, April 1986, 30.

21. 45 CFR 46.206(a).

22. 45 CFR 46.206(a)(4).

23. Margaret Radin, "Market Inalienability," *Harvard Law Review* 100 (1987), 1849–1931; Thomas H. Murray, "Gifts of the Body and the Needs of Strangers," *Hastings Center Report* 17:2 (April 1987), 30–38.

24. Alan Fine, "The Ethics of Fetal Tissue Transplants: *Hastings Center Report* 18:3 (June 1988): 5–8. Mahowald, Silver, and Ratcheson, "The Ethical Options."

25. 42 U.S.C.A. No. 247e (West Supp. 1985).

26. 28, Ark. Stat. Ann. §82-459 (Supp. 1985); Ill. Stat. Ann. ch. 38, §81.54(7) (Smith-Hurd 1983); La. Civ. Code Ann. art. 9:122 (Supp. 1987); Ohio Rev. Code Ann. §2919.14 (Page 1985); Okla. Stat. tit. 63, §1-753 (1987); Fla. Stat. Ann. §873.05 (West Supp. 1987); Mass. Gen. Laws Ann. ch. 112, §1593 (19640); Me. Rev. Stat. Ann. Tit. 22, §1593 (1964); Mich. Comp. Laws Ann. §333.2690 (West); Minn. Stat. Ann. §145.422 (West Supp. 1986); N.D. Cent. Code §14-022-02 (1981); Nev. Rev. Stat. §451.015 (1985); R.I. Gen. Laws §11-54-1(f) (Supp. 1987); Tenn. Code Ann. §39-4-208 (Supp. 1987); Tex. Penal Code Ann. §42.10, 48.02 (Vernon 1974 and Supp. 1988); Wyo. Stat. §35-6-115 (1986); 18 Pa. Cons. Stat. 3216 (Purdon 1983). See also "Note, Regulating the Sale of Human Organs," *Virginia Law Review* 71 (1985), 1015–38.

27. John A. Robertson, "Technology and Motherhood: Legal and Ethical Issues in Human Egg Donation," *Case Western Reserve Law Review* 39:1 (1988) (forthcoming).

28. National Organ Transplant Act, 42 U.S.C.A. 274e (West Supp. 1985).

29. National Organ Transplant Act.

30. National Organ Transplant Act.

31. G. Kolata, "Federal Agency Bars Implanting of Fetal Tissue," *New York Times*, April 16, 1988, 1.

32. "Fetal Tissue 'Acceptable' for Research," *Washington Post*, September 17, 1988, 1; Barbara Culliton, "White House Wants Fetal Research Ban," *Science* (Sept. 16, 1988), 1423.

33. *McCrae v. Harris*, 448 U.S. 297 (1980); *Beal v. Doe*, 432 U.S. 438 (1977); *Poelher v. Doe*, 432 U.S. 519 (1977) (*per curiam*).

34. John Fletcher and Kenneth Ryan, "Federal Regulations for Fetal Research: A Case for Reform," *Law, Medicine, and Health Care* 15:3 (Fall 1987), 126–28.

35. 37. Ark. Stat. Ann. §82-438 (Supp. 1985); Ariz. Rev. Stat. Ann. §36-2302 (1986); Ind. Code Ann. §35-1-58.5–6 (West 1986); Ill. Ann. Stat. ch. 38, §81-54(7) (Smith-Hurd 1983); La. Rev. Stat. Ann. §1299.35.13 (West 1986); Ohio Rev. Code Ann. §2919.14 (Page 1985); Okla. Stat. tit. 63, §1-735; N.M. Stat. Ann. §§24-9A-3, 24-9A-3, 24-9A-5 (1986).

36. A Missouri law bans use of fetal tissue produced for transplant purposes, but not fetal tissue from family planning abortions. Missouri HB No. 1479 (1988).

37. Robertson, "Fetal Tissue Transplants"; "Note: State Prohibition of Fetal Experimentation and the Fundamental Right of Privacy." *Columbia Law Review* 88 (1988), 1073–1109.

38. *Margaret S. v. Edwards*, 794 F.2d 944 (5th 1986).

39. Robertson, "Fetal Tissue Transplants."

40. Danis, "Fetal Tissue Transplants."

27

Spare Parts from the Unborn?: The Ethics of Fetal Tissue Transplantation

Scott B. Rae

Scott B. Rae is Associate Professor of Biblical Studies and Christian Ethics at Talbot School of Theology, Biola University (La Mirada, California). He has contributed to a number of scholarly journals as well as writing the books *The Ethics of Surrogate Motherhood: Brave New Families?* (1994) and *Moral Choices: An Introduction to Ethics*(1995).

In this essay Professor Rae maintains that it is morally wrong to use fetal tissue for experimentation if the fetus's death did not result from a spontaneous abortion, that is, a miscarriage. Professor Rae points out that proponents of using fetal tissue from elective abortions either imply or claim that their position is within the framework of the Uniform Anatomical Gift Act (UAGA), arguing that the dead fetus is parallel to the adult cadaver as an organ donor. Professor Rae claims that it is *not* parallel to adult organ transplants, since (1) the fetus's death is not accidental but caused intentionally, (2) it is impossible to receive valid consent from donor (fetus) or proxy (the mother), (3) the fetus is both donor and donation, and (4) the gift (the fetus) cannot at the same time be both worthless (under *Roe v. Wade*) and priceless (as an organ donation). Professor Rae also argues that proposed restrictions, such as banning financial inducements, are unenforceable, that fetal tissue donation will enhance abortion's image (which he considers a negative development), and that there are possibilities for serious abuse. He concludes with recommending an alternative: use only fetal tissue from spontaneous abortions and ectopic pregnancies (tubal pregnancies where abortion is necessary to save the mother's life).

Reprinted by permission from *Christian Research Journal* (Fall 1991).

The Ethics of Fetal Tissue Transplants

As we consider the ethical issues pertaining to fetal tissue transplants, three primary positions have emerged. The first not only justifies the use of the tissue from induced abortion; it also permits the conceiving woman to specify the person who receives the donated tissue. Thus, one may conceive *solely* for tissue donation (normally for a family member or relative), and even recruit unrelated women to conceive in order to donate the tissue.[1]

The idea of conceiving life solely to terminate it and use the remains strikes most people as morally repugnant since the fetus is overtly used as a means and not an end, treated as a thing and not a person or potential person. For example, a Southern California family recently acknowledged publicly that the mother had conceived solely to provide a bone marrow match for her teenage daughter suffering from leukemia.[2] There were significant ethical concerns raised, even though there was no intent at any point to terminate the pregnancy. The child would grow up to enjoy a normal life irrespective of donor compatibility. The strong reaction in a case where the pregnancy will continue helps one understand the discomfort many feel over terminating a pregnancy for the purpose of donating tissue. Even if one granted that the fetus may not have full personhood from the point of conception (an assumption that is clearly inconsistent with a biblical medical ethic), it would still have some interests and be entitled to certain protections under the law. It cannot be argued that the fetus is morally neutral in the same way an organ or a piece of tissue is. The fetus is at least a *potential* person not to be treated merely as a piece of tissue that is exclusively the property of the woman. To legitimate the use of fetal tissue to this degree makes a powerful statement that life in the womb can be used without any consideration for its *potential* to become a fully human being—let alone its *already realized* status, according to the pro-life position, as fully human.

The second position also justifies the use of the tissue, but prohibits the right of the conceiving mother to donate the tissue to whom she pleases. This is essentially the position recommended by the NIH Panel in their December 1988 report.

The third position prohibits the use of all fetal tissue obtained from induced abortions. Since abortion done for family planning purposes cannot in any sense be considered good, the use of fetal tissue obtained from abortion is morally tainted. In addition, this position points out the difficulty with which lines are drawn that restrict the use of the tissue, and argues that there is nothing to prevent one from ending up with the commercialization of organs and human tissue.[3]

Arguments against Fetal Tissue Transplants from Elective Abortion

Not Parallel to Adult Organ Transplants

Advocates of fetal tissue transplants either assume or explicitly invoke the framework of the Uniform Anatomical Gift Act (UAGA). The UAGA has governed adult organ transplants for some time, and recently—with the rise of fetal tissue transplant technology—the law was expanded to include the fetus as an organ donor. The relevant part of the UAGA framework is the parallel between the dead fetus and the adult cadaver as an organ donor.

In a recent article in *Christianity Today*, Dr. Billy Arant, Jr., of the University of Texas Southwestern Medical Center, makes this parallel when he compares the debate on fetal tissue transplants to the earlier debate on organ donations in general: "The ethical and moral concerns raised during the early years when human organ transplantation was considered experimental were not very different from the ones heard today regarding the use of fetal tissue."[4] Later he asks, "Where, then, is the difference in using tissue obtained from human fetuses to restore health or extend life, especially if the tissue is obtained from fetuses aborted spontaneously—which will occur unpredictably in many pregnancies—just as accidental deaths provide a source of donor organs?"[5] This is precisely the parallel that is appropriate, and there is no moral difficulty with using the tissue from spontaneous abortions. However, most fetal tissue used in transplants comes from induced, not spontaneous, abortions. There are enormous differences between fetal tissue transplants from induced abortions and adult organ transplantations from accidental deaths; these render this parallel highly invalid. The use of the tissue from induced abortion is inconsistent with the UAGA framework, since:

(1) The death of the fetus is intentionally caused, not accidental. Though a small amount of fetal tissue from miscarriages and ectopic pregnancies is useful for transplants, the great majority of fetal tissue becomes available when a woman agrees to end her pregnancy *intentionally*, thus killing the developing fetus. This is hardly the same as when organs are recovered from someone killed in a tragic accident, LeRoy Walters, the Chairman of the Ethical and Legal Issues of the NIH Panel, said in 1974 (when only experimentation with the fetus, not tissue transplants, was being deliberated): "Ought one to make experimental use of the products of an abortion system, when one would object on ethical grounds to many or most of the abortions performed within that system? If a particular hospital became the beneficiary of an organized homicide system which provided a fresh supply of cadavers, one would be justified in raising questions about the moral appropriateness of the hospital's continuing cooperation with the suppliers."[6]

A better parallel might be a banker who regards the drug trade as morally wrong, yet agrees to accept drug money at his bank in order to finance low income housing for the community. This banker would be involved in complicity with the drug trade, even though he is not involved with the actual sale of narcotics.

(2) Valid consent is impossible. To date, fetal tissue transplants have been treated as any other organ transplants under the UAGA, thus requiring consent of next of kin. The mother cannot give morally legitimate consent, since she initiated the termination of the pregnancy. Elimination of consent, however, would further turn the unborn child into an object; it would be inconsistent with the fact that, biologically, the developing fetus does not represent the woman's tissue.

The UAGA and the NIH Panel both fail to recognize the difference between normal organ transplants and the use of fetal tissue. In the case of fetal tissue, the mother is presumed to be the one who gives consent to the use of the tissue for the transplant (or for some other form of experimentation). According to the normal understanding of proxy consent, her role assumes that she is acting in the best interest of the unborn child. Yet, she is *also* the one who has initiated the termination of the pregnancy. The late ethicist Paul Ramsey concluded that it is morally outrageous and a charade to give the woman who aborts any right to proxy consent for the donation of or experimentation on the aborted fetus's body parts.[7] James Bopp and Father James Burtchaell conclude in their dissent from the NIH Panel Report, "We can think of no sound precedent for putting a living human into the power of such an estranged person, not for his or her own welfare, but for the 'interests' of the one in power."

Ironically, some who support fetal tissue transplants have argued that the aborted fetus would have "desired" to help those suffering from diseases that the tissue would benefit. This idea of fetal desire was first put forth in the attempt to justify research on living, nonviable fetuses. Case Western University ethicist Mary Mahowald and her team use this concept to justify not only fetal experiments but also tissue transplants, and appeal to Catholic ethicist Richard McCormick's concept that children, as members of the moral community, have a responsibility to be subjects in research that will benefit that community. (However, McCormick was arguing for the obligation of *children*, not *fetuses*, as research subjects.) When Mahowald and associates make this appeal, they are caught between affirming that the fetus has a responsibility as part of the moral community, and excluding it from the same community since it has no recognized right to life.[8]

One may object to the need for consent in the first place, if the fetus is not considered a person. Yet this fails to recognize why fetal tissue is so valuable: *precisely because it is human.* Biologically, the fetus is much more than an organ or a piece of tissue. It is a developing human being with *at least* the potential for full personhood and thus *at least* the potential for full membership in the moral community from the time of conception. (It is not necessary here to argue that the fetus has full personhood from the time of conception, only that its potential to assume personhood makes it qualitatively different from an organ or other piece of tissue. Though the only logical point during pregnancy in which to recognize the full personhood of the unborn child is at conception, one does not need to press this point in order to oppose fetal tissue transplants.) Since abortion is taking innocent human life, all use of fetal tissue for experiments and treatment is ethically troubling—it is doing evil to accomplish good. The notion of the fetus as the source of biological "spare parts" is uncomfortably reminiscent of Aldous Huxley's *Brave New World.*[9]

(3) There is an equation of the donor and the donation of the tissue. A more significant problem is encountered when one considers that the fetus is simultaneously both a *donation* and a *donor*. It is difficult to see how a fetus can be called a donor under the UAGA in parallel to an adult organ donor, if the personhood of the fetus is discounted. The fetus is a victim rather than a willing donor. When the donation of fetal tissue is described as a gift from the fetus

as a donor, only miscarriages and ectopic pregnancies can stand on a moral basis, since these fetuses were only *unable*, and not *unwelcome*, to join the human community.[10]

This is not a parallel to surrogate motherhood, where the mother is viewed as the donor and the tissue as the donation. Mahowald and associates equate the "moral problems thus raised [in fetal tissue transplants] to those that may occur in surrogate motherhood." However, they earlier acknowledge that "with fetal tissue transplantation (as with transplantation in general), a bad effect (loss of an organ or tissue) is suffered for the sake of the recipient, and there is no similarly bad effect in surrogacy." Their suggestion then that the parallel with surrogate motherhood helps provide some of the guidelines for fetal tissue transplantation ignores the obvious discontinuity, that the death of the fetus results from the transplants. This is hardly only a "bad effect," it is the destruction of the fetus.[11]

(4) The "gift" of the tissue transplant cannot be both priceless and worthless at the same time. The use of the term "gift" is, to say the least, inappropriate when induced abortion is the means by which the gift is made available. If the fetus has no value, how can the tissue be legitimately called a gift and the fetus a donor? Few seem prepared to reject the UAGA framework to govern the use of fetal tissue. Yet the inadequacy of the language to describe the "gift" of a fetus reflects a strange ambivalence about the nature of the fetus.

Kathleen Nolan of the Hastings Center describes the alternative if the UAGA framework is rejected: "If we reject the framework of the UAGA, we seem doomed to accept arguments that implicitly or explicitly equate fetuses with things or beings that they are not—among them kidneys, tumors and discarded surgical specimens. Yet biologically, the fetus is not a tissue or an organ but a body, and morally, the fetus is a developing being and potential member of the human community. Fetal remains accordingly ought to evoke emotions and protections beyond those given tumorous tissue or unwanted organs."[12]

Proposed Restrictions Are Unenforceable

Given the growing public awareness of medical technology and the increasing benefits that will be made available, *keeping the two distinct acts of consent (abor-*

tion and tissue donation) separate is virtually impossible.
All of the proposed guidelines treat this as one of the non-negotiable aspects of the transplants. It would not be difficult to imagine that, given separate consent forms, coercion to donate tissue would enter in, in view of potential transplant benefits, the likely scarcity of available tissue as the technology develops, and the vulnerability of women anticipating an abortion.

Given the potentially lucrative market for the transplants, keeping *financial inducements* from entering in would be difficult, and impossible to enforce. For example, Hana Biologics, one of the firms testifying before the NIH Panel, estimates the total market for using the fetal pancreatic tissue to treat diabetes amounts to approximately six billion dollars annually.[13] This obviously has the potential to become very big business.

Abortion clinics stand to reap a substantial increase in revenue simply from the small amount (on average, $25 per organ, multiplied by the hundreds of thousands of abortions performed annually) that the nonprofit acquisition organizations offer. The financial incentives to "recruit" fetal tissue donors would be significant. Moreover, there are numerous noncash inducements that are difficult to detect and impossible to adequately police that would be especially appealing to poor and minority women. For example, the clinic could offer a "discount" on the abortion procedure itself or promise to provide future medical care for a specified time following the donation of the tissue. With the anticipated profitability of the industry once the technology can alleviate a larger number of diseases, there will be increasing pressures to "share the wealth" produced by these transplants.

A recent California court decision may set a precedent that will make it more difficult to prevent women from obtaining compensation for the donation of fetal tissue. In Moore v. Regents of the University of California, an appeals court reversed a lower court decision, ruling that a person does have a property interest in his or her own cells.[14] In treatment for leukemia, doctors at the UCLA Medical Center removed the spleen of a Mr. Moore, and discovered that they could manufacture a cell line from that tissue that was effective in slowing certain types of leukemia. The medical center then sought out a commercial arrangement with a pharmaceutical company to market the cell line. When asked for his consent, Moore refused and sued the University for his share of any profit resulting from the cell line. Though the

court did not rule on his right to compensation, they did hold that individuals have a property interest in their own cells, and thus a right to control what becomes of their tissues. One can see how this could open the door not only to financial inducements but to a *right* to compensation for fetal tissue donation.

This potentially lucrative market will make it increasingly difficult to enforce another of the proponents' guidelines, *the separation of the transplant physician/researcher and the one who performs the abortion.* This is a key distinction for transplant proponents, even for those who are against abortion in most cases, who assume that the morality of abortion and transplants can be separated. Yet, clearly, the means as well as the end have moral significance.

For the best medical results there would need to be an institutional, symbiotic relationship with the abortion industry, thereby making the separation of abortion and tissue procurement very difficult. This partnership will also make it more complicated to isolate the timing and method of abortion from what is necessary to procure the best possible tissue. Mahowald and associates already propose that pregnancies be prolonged and the method of abortion be modified, if necessary, in order to procure the most fresh, and thus the most useful tissue.[15] In addition, some acknowledge the legitimate possibility of tissue being removed from live, nonviable fetuses.

Redeeming Abortion?

Fetal tissue transplants from induced abortions will serve to enhance abortion's image—to many it will at least seem morally neutral. At a minimum, donating tissue would offer relief from some of the guilt that many women feel when electing abortion, thus alleviating some of the ambivalence that usually accompanies it. Though our society tragically permits abortion, most do not view abortion itself as good. Even the most vocal pro-choice advocates acknowledge that it is the *right to choose* that is good, not the act of terminating a pregnancy itself.

The prospect of donating tissue is not likely to dramatically increase abortions unless the pregnant mother is allowed to designate who receives the tissue. But it would certainly *contribute* to the decision to abort and might push some women "over the line." The routine retrieval of the tissue would no doubt make the unborn's death seem less tragic. Nolan puts it this way: "Enhancing abortion's image could thus be expected to undermine efforts to make it as little needed and little used a procedure as possible."[16]

Even some tissue transplant advocates acknowledge that they may create a greater incentive to abortion, or may lead women to decide for abortion who would not otherwise.[17] This argument against the transplants distinguishes between abortion and the freedom to choose abortion. Many pro-choice advocates are increasingly uncomfortable with the number of abortions performed in this country. Many see the increased effectiveness of contraception as good because it prevents the occurrence of the trauma and tragedy of surgical abortion. Even support for RU 486 (the "abortion pill," currently sold in much of Europe and the Third World, but not available in the United States) is based on this same notion. Thus, anything that would increase surgical abortions can hardly be considered good by anyone. Though our society recognizes the *legality* of abortion, we have rarely seen fit to actively *encourage* it.

Research shows great ambivalence toward abortion among women considering it.[18] There is usually intense anxiety during the final 24 hours before the abortion is performed. Studies of pregnant women choosing abortion show that between one-third and 40 percent change their minds at least once, and around 30 percent do not finally make up their mind until just prior to the procedure. Thus, it is likely that the prospect of solace over the guilt that usually accompanies abortion will enter into the complex set of factors that are involved in the decision to abort. The possibility of "redeeming abortion" throws a powerful human motivation into the already complex situation that will affect those one-third to 40 percent who change their minds during the process. Bopp and Burtchaell, in their dissent from the NIH Panel Report, state, "It is willful fantasy to imagine that young pregnant women estranged from their families and their sexual partners, and torn by the knowledge that they are with child, will not be powerfully relieved at the prospect that the sad act of violence they are reluctant to accept can now have redemptive value."

One wonders if government sponsorship of fetal tissue transplants would have the same legitimizing influence on abortion that Roe v. Wade did. Though the justices in that decision clearly did not want to make a decision on the personhood of the fetus, it can be argued that by allowing abortion they did make a powerful statement that has "trickled down" to a significant part of society.

Possibilities for Abuse

Some of the abuses that the proponents' regulations are designed to prohibit are already being seriously proposed by more radical proponents. These primarily deal with recipient designation of the tissue. Though the "slide down the slippery slope" can likely be stopped in the short term, given the promise of the technology, it is doubtful that long-term pressures can be resisted to allow women to conceive in order to abort and thus donate the tissue. As interest groups—many of whom testified before the NIH Panel—become more dependent on this tissue, further complicating the ability of society to stop the descent down the slippery slope before it reaches a place that only the most extreme proponents advocate.

There are thus possibilities for abuse about which even the more moderate advocates are wary. Already there have been people not simply *willing* but eager to conceive just to donate the tissue.[19] Fetal tissue is currently being used to make cosmetics in Sweden, and fetal kidneys from Brazil and India are being sold in West Germany to physicians for transplant.[20] It is true that most advocates recommend some laws or voluntary guidelines to keep such abuses from taking place. These may be adequate for the short run, but there are no guarantees that these kinds of abuses can be prevented in the long run as the process becomes more acceptable. This opposition to the transplants is not "burning down the barn to roast the pig," but rather, stopping the descent down the slippery slope at the top. It is naive to think that the long-run pressure can be resisted, given the powerful incentives to donate the tissue that the advances in medical science promise to provide.

A Valid Alternative

One viable alternative is the combination of the use of tissue from spontaneous abortions and ectopic pregnancies for both transplants *and* the development of cell cultures from the most promising tissue. This is already being done for diabetes. Also, the development of neuroblastoma cells shows promise for treating Parkinson's disease. The American Paralysis Association's statement to the NIH Panel encouraged adequate funding to develop tissue cloning that will bypass the need for the fetus per se.

My opposition to fetal tissue transplants from induced abortion is essentially that of the British Medical Association in their interim guidelines.[21] The first of these guidelines is the most relevant for this section: "Tissue may be obtained only from dead foetuses [sic] resulting from therapeutic or spontaneous abortion." These guidelines reflect the statement of the Council of Europe, adopted in September, 1986. As of July, 1989, however, the British government had adopted the recommendation of the later Polkinghorne Report that fetal tissue transplants from induced abortions be allowed. Interestingly, the Committee suggested that the fetus does have the same moral status as a human being from the fourteenth day after conception. In contradiction to this, they denied that there is any inherent immorality involved in using the tissue from an induced abortion. If the fetus has such full personhood, the arguments favoring abortion as well as fetal tissue transplants are very difficult to maintain.

I wish there were not ethical difficulties with fetal tissue transplants, since they hold promise for treating various diseases. Because of the moral tensions involved, I support the continuation of the moratorium on research and transplants of fetal tissue from induced abortions. One hopes for the day when cell culture technology will have advanced to the point where fetal tissue from induced abortions. One hopes for the day when cell culture technology will have advanced to the point where fetal tissue from induced abortions will no longer be needed to achieve the same benefits.

Discussion Questions

1. Present and explain the four reasons why Professor Rae does not think the dead fetus is parallel to the adult cadaver as organ donor. Do you agree with his reasoning? Why or why not? Explain and defend your answer.

2. What are some of the abuses Professor Rae believes will occur if fetal tissue from elective abortions is allowed to be used for medical research? Do you agree with his concerns? Explain and defend your answer.

3. If the current law concerning fetal personhood (Roe v. Wade) states that fetuses are nonpersons, why should we worry about Professor's Rae's concerns if so much good for actual born persons may come from fetal tissue research? If you disagree with Professor Rae, do you think there should be any restrictions on

the use of fetal tissue? Explain and defend your answer. If you agree with Professor Rae, explain and defend his alternative to using fetuses who have died by elective abortions.

4. Why does Professor Rae hold that one does not have to be pro-life on abortion in order to oppose the transplantation of fetal tissue that results from elective abortions?

Notes

1. This position appears in the writing of John A. Robertson in two principal articles: "Fetal Tissue Transplants," *Washington University Law Quarterly* 66 (1988):443–98; and "Rights, Symbolism, and Public Policy in Fetal Tissue Transplants," *Hastings Center Report* 18 (December 1988): 5–12.

2. The intent of the family to conceive solely for the bone marrow donor is underscored by the fact that the father underwent surgery to reverse a vasectomy six months prior to conception of the child who will be the donor. See *Orange County Register*, Sect. B, 31 August 1990. The bone marrow transplant was performed in May , 1991.

3. This position is represented by James Bopp, Esq. and Father James Burtchaell in their dissent from the majority opinion of the NIH Panel.

4. Billy S. Arant, Jr., "Why the Government Should Lift the Moratorium," *Christianity Today*, 19 November 1990, 28.

5. *Ibid.*

6. LeRoy Walters, "Ethical Issues in Experimentation on the Human Fetus," *Journal of Religious Ethics* 2 (Spring 1974): 41, 48.

7. Paul Ramsey, *The Ethics of Fetal Research* (New Haven: Yale University Press, 1975): 89.

8. This point is made by Kathleen Nolan, "Genug Ist Genug: A Fetus Is Not a Kidney," *Hastings Center Report* 18 (Dec. 1988): 14. The reference to Mahowald and team is taken from Mary B. Mahowald, Jerry Silver, and Robert A. Ratcheson, "The Ethical Options in Transplanting Fetal Tissue," *Hastings Center Report* 17 (February 1987): 9–15.

9. Stuart Newman, "Statement on Proposed Uses of Human Fetal Tissue," *Panel Report*, vol. 2, D207.

10. Nolan, 18.

11. Mahowald, et al., 12, 15.

12. Nolan, 16.

13. Karen Southwick, "Fetal Tissue Market Draws Profits, Rebuke," *Health Week*, 12 October 1987, 1.

14. *Moore v. Regents of the University of California*, California Court of Appeal, 249 Cal. Rptr. 494 (1988). Review granted by California Supreme Court, 252 Cal. Rptr. 816 (10 November 1988).

15. Mahowald, et al., 7–15.

16. Nolan, 17.

17. Concern that the use of fetal tissue for transplantation in such cases could become an incentive for abortion

thus appears well grounded. Alan Fine, "The Ethics of Fetal Tissue Transplants," *Hastings Center Report* 18 (June/July 1988): 6.

18. Michael Bracken, Lorraine Klerman, and Mary Ann Bracken, "Abortion, Adoption or Motherhood: An Empirical Study of Decision-Making During Pregnancy," *American Journal of Obstetrics and Gynecology* 130 (1978): 256–57.

19. Tamar Lewin, "Medical Use of Fetal Tissue Spurs New Abortion Debate," *New York Times*, 16 August 1987, 1.

20. Debra McKenzie, "Third World Kidneys for Sale," *New Scientist*, 28 March 1985, 7; "Embryos to Lipsticks?" *New Scientist*, 10 October 1985, 21.

21. See David Dickson, "Fetal Tissue Transplants Win U.K. Approval," *Science* 245 (4 August 1989):464–65.

28

Executive Summary of the Final Report of the Human Embryo Research Panel

National Institutes of Health

The NIH Embryo Research Panel consisted of 19 members selected from a number of disciplines including biology, philosophy, theology, medicine, and public health. The panel's Overall Chair was Steven Muller (President Emeritus, the Johns Hopkins University). Patricia A. King (Professor of Law, Georgetown) was the panel's Co-Chair on Policy, and Brigid L. M. Hogan (Professor of Cell Biology, Vanderbilt) was the panel's Co-Chair on Science.

Formed in fall 1993, the NIH's Human Embryo Research Panel was commissioned to make recommendations about what types of research on the embryo prior to implantation and outside the woman's uterus (ex utero) are appropriate or inappropriate for federal funding. The main ethical concern for the panel was the moral permissibility of creating human embryos for the sole purpose of experimentation on them. After hearing thousands of hours of testimony by experts on all sides of the debate, in its final report the panel concluded that some research was acceptable for federal support, some warranted additional review, and some was unacceptable. The panel based its conclusions on ethical considerations as well as concern for promoting research that results in human benefit. Although the panel asserted that "it conducted its deliberations in terms that were independent of a particular religious or philosophical perspective," it nevertheless supported federal funding of research on the preimplanted embryo on the basis that "it does not have the same moral status as infants and children" because it lacks "develop-

From the National Institutes of Health, *Final Report of the Human Embryo Research Panel* (27 September 1994), 1–13.

mental individuation . . ., the lack of even the possibility of sentience and most other qualities considered relevant to the moral status of persons, and the very high rate of natural mortality at this stage" (i.e., the large number of preimplantation embryos that die before implantation). However, the panel did forbid federal funding of research on embryos after the fourteenth day after conception, because around that time it acquires the primitive streak, "an advancing groove that develops along the midline of the embryonic disc. . . . A milestone in embryo development, the primitive streak establishes and reveals the embryo's head-tail and left-right orientations" (from glossary of *Final Report*, 107).

Charge to the Panel

The mandate for the National Institutes of Health (NIH) Human Embryo Research Panel (the Panel) was to consider various areas of research involving the ex utero preimplantation human embryo and to provide advice as to those areas that: (1) are acceptable for Federal funding; (2) warrant additional review; and (3) are unacceptable for Federal support. For those areas of research considered acceptable for Federal funding, the Panel was asked to recommend specific guidelines for the review and conduct of this research.

The Panel's charge encompasses only research that involves extracorporeal human embryos produced by in vitro fertilization or other sources, or parthenogenetically activated oocytes. Research involving in utero human embryos, or fetuses, is not part of the charge since guidelines for such research are embodied in Federal laws and regulations governing human subjects research. Research involving human germ-line gene modification also is not within the Panel's scope. Therapeutic human fetal tissue transplantation research is also not a part of the panel's mandate, because guidelines are already in place to govern such research.

Throughout this report "ex utero preimplantation embryo" or "preimplantation embryo" refers to a fertilized ovum in vitro that has never been transferred to or implanted in a uterus. This includes a fertilized ovum that has been flushed from a woman before implantation in the uterus. This procedure, although infrequent and posing special risks, is included because it is one potential source of embryos.

Ethical Considerations

Throughout its deliberations, the Panel considered the wide range of views held by American citizens on the moral status of preimplantation embryos. In recommending public policy, the Panel was not called upon to decide which of these views is correct. Rather, its task was to propose guidelines for preimplantation human embryo research that would be acceptable public policy based on reasoning that takes account of generally held public views regarding the beginning and development of human life. The Panel weighed arguments for and against Federal funding of this research in light of the best available information and scientific knowledge and conducted its deliberations in terms that were independent of a particular religious or philosophical perspective.

The Panel received a considerable volume of public input which it carefully considered. The Panel heard from citizens who object to any research involving preimplantation embryos as well as those who support it and listened closely to the thinking underlying the various opinions expressed. In the process of receiving public input, the Panel realized that the scientific and policy issues involved in research on preimplantation embryos are complex and not easily comprehended. The Panel therefore recognizes that a special effort is required to enhance public understanding of the issues involved in research involving the preimplantation embryo. It is the Panel's hope that this report will in some measure contribute to a process of increasing public awareness, discussion, and understanding of these issues.

From the perspective of public policy, the Panel concludes that sufficient arguments exist to support the permissibility of certain areas of research involving the preimplantation human embryo within a framework of stringent guidelines. This conclusion is based on an assessment of the moral status of the preimplantation embryo from various viewpoints and not solely on its location ex utero. In addition, the Panel weighted the important human benefits that might be achieved if preimplantation embryo research were federally funded under stringent guidelines.

The Panel believes that certain areas of research are permissible based on three primary considerations, listed below. Different members of the Panel may have accorded different weight to each of these considerations in reaching a conclusion about the permissibility of certain areas of research.

- The promise of human benefit from research is significant, carrying great potential benefit to infertile couples, and to families with genetic conditions, and to individuals and families in need of effective therapies for a variety of diseases.
- Although the preimplantation human embryo warrants serious moral consideration as a developing form of human life, it does not have the same moral status as infants and children. This is because of the absence of developmental individuation in the preimplantation embryo, the lack of even the possibility of sentience and most other qualities considered relevant to the moral status of persons, and the very high rate of natural mortality at this stage.
- In the continued absence of Federal funding and regulation in this area, preimplantation human embryo research which has been and is being conducted without Federal funding and regulation would continue, without consistent ethical and scientific review. It is in the public interest that availability of Federal funding and regulation should provide consistent ethical and scientific review for this area of research. The Panel believes that because the preimplantation embryo possesses qualities requiring moral respect, research involving the preimplantation ex utero human embryo must be carefully regulated and consistently monitored.

Principles and Guidelines for Preimplantation Embryo Research

The Panel supports Federal funding of certain areas of preimplantation embryo research within the framework of the guidelines specified below. Any research conducted on the preimplantation ex utero human embryo or on gametes intended for fertilization should adhere to the following general principles as well as the more specific guidelines relevant to the nature of the particular research.

- The research must be conducted by scientifically qualified individuals in an appropriate research setting.
- The research must consist of a valid research design and promise significant scientific or clinical benefit.

- The research goals cannot be otherwise accomplished by using animals or unfertilized gametes. In addition, where applicable, adequate prior animal studies must have been conducted.
- The number of embryos required for the research must be kept to the minimum consistent with scientific criteria for validity.
- Donors of gametes or embryos must have given informed consent with regard to the nature and purpose of the specific research being undertaken.
- There must be no purchase or sale of gametes or embryos used in research. Reasonable compensation in clinical studies should be permissible to defray a subject's expenses, over and above the costs of drugs and procedures required for standard treatment, provided that no compensation or financial inducements of any sort are offered in exchange for the donation of gametes or embryos, and so long as the level of compensation is in accordance with Federal regulations governing human subjects research and that it is consistent with general compensation practice for other federally-funded experimental protocols.
- Research protocols and consent forms must be reviewed and approved by an appropriate institutional review board (IRB), and for the immediate future an ad hoc review process which extends beyond the existing review process to be established by NIH and operated for a period of at least three years.
- There must be equitable selection of donors of gametes and embryos and efforts must be made to ensure that benefits and risks are fairly distributed among subgroups of the population.
- Out of respect for the special character of the preimplantation human embryo, research involving preimplantation embryos should be limited to the shortest time period consistent with the goals of each research proposal, and for the present, research involving human embryos should not be permitted beyond the time of the usual appearance of the primitive streak in vivo (14 days). An exception to this is made for research protocols with the goal of reliably identifying in the laboratory the appearance of the primitive streak.

Fertilization of Oocytes Expressly for Research Purposes

One of the most difficult issues the Panel had to consider was whether it is ethically permissible to fertilize donated oocytes expressly for research purposes or whether researchers should be restricted to the use of embryos remaining from infertility treatments that are donated by women or couples. In developing its recommendation concerning this issue, the Panel considered both the deeply held moral concerns about the fertilization of oocytes for research as well as the potential clinical benefits to be gained from such research. The Panel concludes that studies that require the fertilization of oocytes are needed to answer crucial questions in reproductive medicine, and that it would therefore not be wise to prohibit altogether the fertilization and study of oocytes for research purposes. The Panel had to balance important issues regarding the health and safety of women, children, and men against the moral respect due the preimplantation embryo. Given the conclusions the Panel reached about the moral status of the preimplantation embryo, it concludes that the health needs of women, children, and men must be given priority.

The Panel recognizes, however, that the embryo merits respect as a developing form of human life and should be used in research only for the most serious and compelling reasons. There is also a possibility that if researchers had broad permission to develop embryos for research, more embryos might be created than is truly justified. The Panel believes that the use of oocytes fertilized expressly for research should be allowed only under two conditions. The first condition is when the research by its very nature cannot otherwise be validly conducted. Examples of studies that might meet this condition include oocyte maturation or oocyte freezing followed by fertilization and examination for subsequent developmental viability and chromosomal normalcy; and investigations into the process of fertilization itself (including the efficacy of new contraceptives). If oocyte maturation techniques were improved, eggs could be obtained without the reliance on stimulatory drugs, lessening some of the potential risks for both patients and egg donors.

The second condition under which the fertilization of oocytes would be allowed expressly for research is when a compelling case can be made that this is necessary for the validity of a study that is

potentially of outstanding scientific and therapeutic value. One member of the Panel dissented from the Panel conclusion that under this condition oocytes may be fertilized expressly for research purposes.
. . .

Panel members believe that special attention is warranted for such research because of their concern that attempts might be made to create embryos for reasons that relate solely to the scarcity of embryos remaining from infertility programs and because of their interest in preventing the creation of embryos for any but the most compelling reasons. An example of studies that might meet this second condition is research to ensure that specific drugs used in reproductive medicine, such as those for inducing ovulation, have no harmful effect on oocytes and their developmental potential and do not compromise the future reproductive health of women.

In another case, future discoveries might provide strong evidence that some forms of infertility, birth defects, or childhood cancer are due to chromosomal abnormalities, DNA modifications, or metabolic defects in embryos from gametes of men and women of a particular category; for example, those exposed to specific environmental agents or carrying specific genetic traits. In order to test or validate such hypotheses a compelling case might be made for comparing embryos from "at-risk" couples with "control" embryos from "normal" couples. While embryos from many infertile couples in in vitro fertilization (IVF) programs might be suitable for this control group, in specific cases a compelling argument might be made that gametes donated by fertile individuals carefully matched to those in the "at-risk" group for age and ethnic background are necessary for the most accurate and informative comparative scientific data.

Sources of Gametes and Embryos for Research

Having concluded that Federal funding of certain areas of preimplantation embryo research is acceptable within stringent guidelines, the Panel went on to address another set of ethical dilemmas raised by the issue of acceptability of various sources of gametes and embryos. In considering these issues the Panel identified four concerns that require special vigilance: the need for informed consent; limits on commercialization; equitable selection of donors for research; and, appropriate balancing of risks and benefits among subgroups of the population. These concerns parallel those addressed by well established ethical guidelines for all human research. The selection of sources of gametes and embryos for research must be consistent with these established guidelines and in addition must show respect for the special qualities of the human gamete and embryo.

The Panel gave careful consideration to the two distinct means by which a preimplantation human embryo can become available for research. The first occurs when embryos already fertilized for infertility treatments are not used for that purpose but are donated by the progenitors for research (these embryos are sometimes referred to as "spare" embryos). The second occurs when an oocyte is fertilized expressly for the purposes of research. The Panel also considered the ethical acceptability of the various donor sources of oocytes for research involving transfer, research without transfer, and research involving parthenogenesis. These possible donor sources include women in IVF programs, healthy volunteers, women undergoing pelvic surgery, women and girls who have died, and aborted fetuses.

In analyzing the acceptability of donor sources of gametes and embryos for research, the Panel emphasized that the risks of the research, including the risks of gamete procurement, must be in proportion to the anticipated benefits. Risks that occur at various stages of research and in the context of diverse protocols restrict the acceptable sources of research gametes and embryos. For example, the need to consider the well-being of the future child when embryos are transferred to the uterus mandates particular attention to the acceptability of gamete and embryo sources, including a requirement that the gamete donors approve of the research as well as the transfer.

In general, the Panel concludes that, provided all conditions regarding consent and limits on commercialization are met, embryos donated by couples in IVF programs are acceptable sources for basic research that does not involve transfer, as well as for clinical studies that may involve transfer. Women undergoing IVF treatment may also donate oocytes not needed for their own treatment, provided other guidelines are met. In this regard, the Panel believes it is right for women and couples undergoing infertility treatment to assume a fair share of the burden of advancing research in this area given that they, as a class, stand to benefit most from clinical applications that may result. However, the Panel also recognizes that infertility can cause great physical and psychological pain and that women and couples undergoing treatment may be more vulnerable as a result. For this reason one member of the Panel dissents from allowing women in IVF treatment the opportunity to donate oocytes for research that does not involve transfer. . . . In order that women and couples in IVF programs are not made to feel compelled to donate, great care must be taken to ensure that there is no undue, or even subtle, pressure to donate. The voluntary nature of such donations is essential, and under no circumstances should individuals who do not wish to donate their gametes ever feel pressured to do so.

Donation of oocytes for research purposes without intent to transfer raises special concerns regarding risks to women. Some of the methods used to procure eggs, especially hyperstimulation, involve the use of powerful drugs and invasive procedures that could pose risks to the health of women. Women undergoing treatment for infertility consent to these risks in return for potential therapeutic benefit and are an acceptable source of oocytes for basic research that does not involve transfer, as well as for clinical studies that may involve transfer.

Women undergoing scheduled pelvic surgery are an additional permissible source of oocytes for research, provided that other guidelines are met and that no additional risks are imposed. Researchers must explain any changes from standard surgical procedures and, if hormonal stimulation is used, the risks of such drugs.

Women who are not scheduled to undergo a surgical procedure are *not* a permissible source of oocytes for embryos developed for research at this time, even if they wish to volunteer to donate their oocytes. The Panel, however, is willing to allow such volunteers to donate oocytes if the intent is to transfer the resulting embryo for the purpose of establishing a pregnancy. This is because the risks to the donor undergoing oocyte retrieval may be justified by the potential direct benefit to the infertile couple who hope to become parents as a result of the procedure. Absent the goal of establishing a pregnancy for an infertile couple, the lack of direct therapeutic benefit to the donor and the dangers of commercial exploitation do not justify exposing women to such risks.

Women who have died are a permissible source of oocytes for research without transfer, provided that the woman had not expressly objected to such use of her oocytes and that appropriate consent is obtained. If the woman had expressed no objection to such use

of her oocytes, she must have either consented to donation before her death or, in the absence of explicit consent on her part, next of kin may give consent at the time of her death. One member of the Panel dissents from this recommendation based on the belief that consent must have been obtained from the woman prior to her death. . . . Care must be taken to ensure that the consenting donors, or their next of kin who would be providing proxy consent, be clearly and specifically aware that the organ being donated is the ovary and that it might be used in research that could involve the fertilization of any oocytes derived from it. It should also be made clear to donors and next of kin that transfer of any embryo created from such material to the uterus is prohibited.

Because of strong concerns about the importance of parenthood and the orderly sequence of generations, as well as the need for detailed medical histories, the Panel concluded that research involving the transfer of embryos created from oocytes obtained from cadaveric sources, including aborted fetuses, should be unacceptable for Federal funding. The Panel also felt that it would be unwise public policy at this time to support, without additional review, research involving the fertilization of fetal oocytes, even if not intended for transfer to the uterus. Such research should not be supported until the ethical implications are more fully explored and addressed by a national advisory body.

Transfer of Embryos to a Uterus

In addition to these general guidelines, the Panel developed specific guidelines for research on preimplantation embryos intended for transfer and for those not intended for transfer, as well as guidelines for research involving parthenogenesis.

It is important to recognize that when transfer to a uterus is intended, research on the preimplantation embryo can result in harm to the child who could be born, a research subject whose treatment raises distinct ethical issues. Both in law and ethics it is clear that fetuses who are brought to term are considered persons with full moral status and protectability. It would therefore be unacceptable to transfer an embryo if it is reasonable to believe that a child who might be born from these procedures will suffer harm as a result of the research. Even when research involves a diagnostic procedure, an embryo may not be transferred unless there is a reasonable confidence that any child born as a result of these procedures has not been harmed by them. This distinction in treatment between embryos that will be transferred and those that will not is warranted by the need to avoid harms to the child who could be born.

Parthenogenesis

In keeping with its mandate, the Panel also considered the acceptability of Federal funding of research involving the parthenogenetic activation of eggs. Parthenogenesis is the activation of eggs to begin cleavage and development without fertilization. It has been shown in research involving parthenogenesis in mammals that when such parthenotes are transferred to the uterus, few reach the stage of implantation. The few that do reach implantation develop to various stages of early cell differentiation but then lose capacity for further development and die. Parthenotes fail to develop further because they lack expression of essential genes contributed by the sperm. All evidence therefore suggests that human parthenotes intrinsically are not developmentally viable human embryos. Thus, they do *not* represent a form of asexual reproduction.

Research on parthenotes, or activated eggs, might provide information on the specific role of the egg mechanisms in activating and sustaining early development, without generating a human embryo. Parthenotes may have research utility nearly identical to the normal embryo up to the blastocyst stage. In addition, a certain type of ovarian tumor originates from eggs that develop as parthenotes while still in the ovary. Research on parthenotes may shed light on problems arising during oocyte development that promote this type of tumor formation.

The Panel recommends that research proposals involving parthenogenesis be considered ethically acceptable on condition that they adhere to the general principles and that under no circumstance is transfer of parthenogenetically activated oocytes permitted. The Panel wishes to allay fears expressed by the public who are concerned about the endpoint of research on parthenogenesis. To many, such research appears to represent a tampering with the natural order in unacceptable ways. Even though it is considered intrinsically impossible in humans, the Panel would preclude any attempts to develop a fetus or child without a paternal progenitor by prohibiting research involving the transfer of parthenotes.

Review and Oversight of Research

The Panel does not recommend that an Ethics Advisory Board (EAB) be reconstituted for the purpose of reviewing research protocols involving embryos and fertilized eggs. Although revisiting the EAB experience offers the potential for developing public consensus and a consistent application of the new guidelines, it nonetheless has significant disadvantages. These include the creation of an additional standing government board; the likelihood of a significant delay before embryo research could be funded in order to meet legal requirements for new rulemaking prior to the official creation of the government body; and further possibility for delay if all proposals for embryo research were required to be considered individually by an EAB-type board, despite appearing to be consistent with a developed consensus at NIH about acceptability for funding.

The Panel wishes to retain the strengths of the old EAB—such as its assurance of consistent application of guidelines—without creating a new regulatory body. Therefore, the Panel recommends that all research proposals involving preimplantation human embryo research that are submitted to NIH for funding or that are proposed for conduct in the NIH intramural research program be subject to an additional review at the national level by an ad hoc body created with discretionary authority of the Director of NIH. Two members of the Panel formally dissent from this recommendation, citing the adequacy of existing review through local IRBs and the possibility of such a review board being subject to undue pressures.

The purpose of the recommended review is to ensure that such research is conducted in accordance with guidelines established by NIH. This review is in addition to existing procedures and should occur after the standard reviews and approvals by study section and council have been completed. The additional review process should continue for a period of at least three years. If the NIH Director elects to dissolve this ad hoc review process after three years, a more decentralized review with certain additional oversight provisions, as specified further below, should begin.

When the ad hoc review body ceases to exist, the Panel recommends that all such research proposals continue to be specially monitored by the NIH councils and the NIH Office for Protection from Research Risks. This monitoring would include a commitment by the councils to pay particular attention to the protocols as they are presented for approval, in order to ensure that the local IRB and NIH study section have correctly applied the guidelines adopted by the NIH Director.

Categories of Research

Consistent with its mandate, the Panel considered specific areas of research in terms of acceptability for Federal funding. While it is clearly impossible to anticipate every type of research project that might be proposed, the Panel was charged to divide types of embryo research into three categories: (1) acceptable for Federal funding; (2) warranting additional review; and (3) unacceptable for Federal funding.

Acceptable for Federal Funding

A research proposal is presumed acceptable if it is in accordance with the guidelines described above and is not described below as warranting additional review or being unacceptable. A protocol not in the last two categories would be classified acceptable if it is scientifically valid and meritorious, relies on prior adequate animal studies and, where appropriate, studies on human embryos without transfer, uses a minimal number of embryos, documents that informed consent will be obtained from acceptable donor sources, involves no purchase or sale of gametes or embryos, does not continue beyond the time of the usual appearance of the primitive streak in vivo (14 days), and has passed the required review by a local IRB, appropriate NIH study section and council, and, for the immediate future, the additional review body at the national level established at the discretion of the NIH Director.

Proposals in the acceptable category must also meet the specific guidelines set forth in this report concerning types of research (i.e., transfer, no transfer, parthenogenesis) . . ., and acceptable sources of gametes and embryos. Examples of such proposals include, but are not limited to:

· Studies aimed at improving the likelihood of a successful outcome for a pregnancy.
· Research on the process of fertilization.
· Studies on egg activation and the relative role of paternally-derived and maternally-derived

genetic material in embryo development (parthenogenesis without transfer).
· Studies in oocyte maturation or freezing followed by fertilization to determine developmental and chromosomal normality.
· Research involving preimplantation genetic diagnosis, with and without transfer.
· Research involving the development of embryonic stem cells but only with embryos resulting from IVF for infertility treatment or clinical research that have been donated with the consent of the progenitors.
· Nuclear transplantation into an enucleated, fertilized or unfertilized (but activated) egg, without transfer, for research that aims to circumvent or correct an inherited cytoplasmic defect.

With regard to the last example, a narrow majority of the Panel believed such research should be acceptable for Federal funding. Nearly as many thought that the ethical implications of research involving the transplantation of a nucleus, whether transfer was contemplated or not, need further study before the research could be considered acceptable for Federal funding.

In addition to these examples, the Panel singled out two types of acceptable research for special consideration in the recommended ad hoc review process.

· Research involving the use of existing embryos where one of the progenitors was an anonymous gamete source who received monetary compensation. (This exception would apply only to embryos already in existence at the time at which this report is accepted by the Advisory Committee to the Director, NIH, should such acceptance occur.)
· A request to fertilize ova where this is necessary for the validity of a study that is potentially of outstanding scientific and therapeutic value.

In the first instance, for reasons explained in chapter 4 of this report, the Panel, with the exception of one member . . . would make an allowance for an interim period for research involving the use of existing embryos where one of the progenitors was anonymous and had received monetary compensation. However, the Panel believes that in order to determine whether the exception might apply, special attention must be given during the review process to ensure that payment has not been provided for the embryo itself and that all other proposed guidelines are met.

In the second instance, Panel members believe that special attention is warranted for such research because of concern that attempts might be made to create embryos for reasons that relate solely to the scarcity of embryos remaining from infertility programs and because of the Panel's interest in preventing the creation of embryos for any but the most compelling reasons.

Warrants Additional Review

The Panel places research of a particularly sensitive nature in this category. The Panel did not make a determination for the acceptability of these proposals, and therefore recommends that there be a presumption against Federal funding of such research for the foreseeable future. This presumption could be overcome only by an extraordinary showing of scientific or therapeutic merit, together with explicit consideration of the ethical issues and social consequences. Such research proposals could be funded only after review by a broad-based ad hoc body created at the discretion of the Director, NIH, or by some other formal review process.

Research that the Panel determined should be placed in a category warranting additional review includes:

- Research between the appearance of the primitive streak and the beginning of neural tube closure.
- Cloning by blastomere separation or blastocyst splitting without transfer.
- Nuclear transplantation into an enucleated, fertilized or unfertilized (but activated) egg, with transfer, with the aim of circumventing or correcting an inherited cytoplasmic defect.
- Research involving the development of embryonic stem cells from embryos fertilized expressly for this purpose. (One member of the panel dissents from this categorization. . . .)
- Research that uses fetal oocytes for fertilization without transfer.

The Panel wishes to note that it was extremely circumspect in its consideration of the appropriate classification of the last two research areas and that members were divided in their views about where

to place the research. For research involving the development of embryonic stem cells from deliberately fertilized oocytes, a narrow majority of members agreed such research warranted further review. A number of other members, however, felt that the research warranted further review. A number of other members, however, felt that the research was acceptable for Federal funding, while some believed that such research should be considered unacceptable for Federal funding. The Panel's deliberation about the use of fetal oocytes for research without transfer involved painstaking reflection about the ethical implications and public sensibilities. The decision to recommend that this research be placed in the further review category, rather than the unacceptable category, was made by a bare majority.

Unacceptable for Federal Funding

Four ethical considerations entered into the deliberations of the Panel as it determined what types of research were unacceptable for Federal funding: the potential adverse consequences of the research for children, women and men; the respect due the preimplantation embryo; concern for public sensitivities on highly controversial research proposals; and concern for the meaning of humanness, parenthood, and the succession of generations.

Throughout its report the Panel considered these concerns as well as the scientific promise and the clinical and therapeutic value of proposed research, particularly as it might contribute to the well-being of women, children, and men. Regarding the types of research considered unacceptable, the Panel determined that the scientific and therapeutic value was low or questionable, or that animal studies did not warrant progressing to human research.

Research proposals in the unacceptable category should not be funded for the foreseeable future. Even if claims were made for their scientific or therapeutic value, serious ethical concerns counsel against supporting such research. Such research includes:

- Cloning of human preimplantation embryos by separating blastomeres or dividing blastocysts (induced twinning), followed by transfer in utero.
- Studies designed to transplant embryonic or adult nuclei into an enucleated egg, including nuclear cloning, in order to duplicate a genome or to increase the number of embryos with the same genotype, with transfer.

- Research beyond the onset of closure of the neural tube.
- Research involving the fertilization of fetal oocytes with transfer.
- Preimplantation genetic diagnosis for sex selection except for sex-linked genetic diseases.
- Development of human-nonhuman and human-human chimeras with or without transfer.
- Cross-species fertilization except for clinical tests of the ability of sperm to penetrate eggs.
- Attempted transfer of parthenogenetically activated human eggs.
- Attempted transfer of human embryos into nonhuman animals for gestation.
- Transfer of human embryos for extrauterine or abdominal pregnancy.

Need for Public Education

Finally, the Panel believes that any successful efforts in preimplantation embryo research depend on improving public understanding of the nature of preimplantation embryo research and therefore recommends that NIH undertake efforts toward public education as it simultaneously educates the scientific community about guidelines for acceptable research.

Discussion Questions

1. Summarize the three main reasons why the NIH panel recommended allowing federal funding of embryo research. Do you find these reasons compelling? Why or why not?

2. Name and describe the categories of research that the panel concluded were acceptable for federal funding. Present and explain the panel's reasons why. Why do you agree or disagree with the panel's reasoning?

3. Name and describe the categories of research that warranted additional review. Present and explain the panel's reasons why. Why do you agree or disagree with the panel's reasoning?

4. Name and describe the categories of research that were unacceptable for federal funding. Present and explain the panel's reasons why. Why do you agree or disagree with the panel's reasoning?

5. The panel asserted that "it conducted its deliberations in terms that were independent of a particular religious or philosophical perspective." However, the panel supported federal funding of research on the preimplanted embryo on the basis that "it does not have the same moral status as infants and children" because it lacks "developmental individuation . . ., the lack of even the possibility of sentience and most other qualities considered relevant to the moral status of persons, and the very high rate of natural mortality at this stage." Do you think the panel is contradicting itself in these two sentences? Why or why not? Explain and defend your answer.

29

The Inhuman Use of Human Beings: A Statement on Embryo Research

The Ramsey Colloquium

The Ramsey Colloquium, which is sponsored by the Institute of Religion and Public Life, is a group of Jewish and Christian philosophers, theologians, and scholars that meets periodically to consider questions of ethics, religion, and public life. It is named after the distinguished ethicist Paul Ramsey (1913–1988).

In this essay the Ramsey Colloquium argues that the recommendation for federal funding by the NIH Human Embryo Research Panel (Chapter 28) is "morally repugnant, entails grave injustice to innocent human beings, and constitutes an assault upon the foundational ideas of human dignity and rights essential to a free and decent society." Moreover, the colloquium affirms that not only should the research not be funded, "it should not be done at all. It should be prohibited by law." The colloquium defends this position by first arguing that embryos are human beings who should not be created for the sole purpose of using them for experimentation to only discard them later. Second, the NIH panel's report is rejected because its reasoning is circular and its view of human personhood is flawed. Third, the colloquium maintains that the panel's distinction between research acceptable and research unacceptable for federal funding is unprincipled and buys into a crass utilitarianism. Fourth, according to the colloquium, the panel's claim that it has "established clear lines and clear time limits regarding what is permissible to do with human embryos . . . is false, and it seems that the panelists know it is false." Fifth, the colloquium accuses the panel of putting forth a particular philosophy though in its report the panel denies doing any such thing. This

Reprinted by permission from *First Things: A Monthly Journal of Religion and Public Life*, no. 49 (January 1995), 17–21.

essay concludes with citations from the Nuremberg Code and the 1975 Helsinki Declaration as well as a response to the argument that banning embryo experimentation is unenforceable.

A panel of nineteen experts appointed by the National Institutes of Health has recommended government funding for conceiving human embryos in the laboratory for the sole purpose of using them as materials for research. After carefully studying the Report of the Human Embryo Research Panel, we conclude that this recommendation is morally repugnant, entails grave injustice to innocent human beings, and constitutes an assault upon the foundational ideas of human dignity and rights essential to a free and decent society. The arguments offered by the Panel are more ideological and self-interested than scientific; the actions recommended by the Panel cross the threshold into a world of apparently limitless technological manipulation and manufacture of human life. The Panel claims to draw a "clear line" against experiments that almost everyone would deem abhorrent. In fact it does not draw such a line and, by virtue of its own logic, it cannot draw such a line. The recommendation, if adopted, will be a fateful step for humanity from which it may be impossible to turn back.

All of us have a stake in the questions raised. In a society such as ours, these questions cannot be, they must not be, decided by a committee of experts. We urge a comprehensive public debate and intense congressional scrutiny regarding the proposals emanating from the NIH. The research recommended by the Panel should not be funded by the government. It should not be done at all. It should be prohibited by law. In what follows we attempt to explain how we have reached this conclusion.

We are confident that most people, to the extent that they are aware of the Panel's recommendation, experience an immediate and strong revulsion. This is not to be dismissed as an irrational reaction. It signals a deep, intuitive awareness of lines that must not be crossed if we are to maintain our sometimes fragile hold upon our own humanity.

For instance, the *Washington Post*'s editorial response to the Panel's proposal declared flatly that "The creation of human embryos specifically for research that will destroy them is unconscionable." The acids of moral relativism have not advanced so far in our culture as to destroy completely the capacity to know and say that *some things are simply not to be countenanced*, much less approved and funded by the government. The editorial goes on to distinguish the present question from that of abortion. "To suggest that support for abortion rights equals support for such [embryo] experimentation is to buy abortion opponents' view that permitting abortion means erasing society's ability to make distinctions." The question of creating, using, and destroying human embryos cannot be separated entirely from the question of abortion, but the two questions can and should be distinguished. We hope that most people, whatever their views on the legalization of abortion, will be moved to take a stand at this new line that must not be crossed.

The ominously new thing in the Panel's Report is that embryonic human life should be treated simply as research material to be used and discarded—and should even be brought into being solely for that purpose. The Report readily acknowledges that the embryos to be used are instances of human life. It does not hesitate to answer the question of when a new human life begins. Indeed, indisputable scientific evidence leaves no choice: a new human life begins at conception (or, as the Report usually prefers, "fertilization"). The Report speaks of the embryo from the earliest moment as "developing human life." We are at various points told that the very early embryo deserves "serious moral consideration," "moral respect," "profound respect," and "some added measure of respect beyond that accorded animal subjects."

Honesty requires that we speak not simply of human life but of a human being. Skin and intestinal tissue, even eggs and sperm, are human life. But, unlike such instances of human life, the embryo from the earliest moment has the active capacity to articulate itself into what everyone acknowledges is a human being. The embryo is a being; that is to say, it is an integral whole with actual existence. The being is human; it will not articulate itself into some other kind of animal. Any being that is human is a human being. If it is objected that, at five days or fifteen days, the embryo does not look like a human being, it must be pointed out that this is precisely what a human being looks like—and what each of us looked like—at five or fifteen days of development. Clarity of language is essential to clarity of thought.

The question is whether the government should permit and fund the production of human beings—completely innocent and powerless human beings—to be used as material for scientific research. After answering that question in the affirmative, the Report then considers which human beings can be so used and which cannot. It is one of the most treasured maxims of our civilization that human beings are always to be treated as ends and never merely as means. In a partial dissent from the Report, Professor Patricia A. King, a member of the Panel, writes, "The fertilization of human oocytes [female eggs] for research purposes is unnerving because human life is being created solely for human *use*. I do not believe that this society has developed the conceptual frameworks necessary to guide us down this slope. . . . At the very least, we should proceed with extreme caution." The conclusion that properly follows from her fully justified anxiety is that we should proceed not at all. Regrettably, the other members of the Panel appear not to have shared even the anxiety.

In weighing the question of which human beings can be used as a means to the ends of scientific progress and which cannot, the Report says the decision must rest on a "multi-factorial" judgment. By this is meant that no one principle or line of reasoning will support the conclusion that the Panel reaches. The Report's use of "multi-factorial" judgment is tantamount to suggesting that an accumulation of doubtful arguments will produce a convincing conclusion. In the course of reaching its "multi-factorial" judgment, the Panel entangles itself in philosophical, moral, and even scientific confusions. We are sorry to report that, in some of its arguments, the Panel invites the charge of being more than a little disingenuous.

In order to decide which human embryos are usable and which are "protectable" from such use, the Report leans very heavily on the concept of "personhood." The question is switched from "When does the life of a human being begin?" to "When does a human being become a person?" Persons are protectable; nonpersons or those who are deemed to be something less than persons are not protectable. But the only reason they are not protectable is that they will not be protected. Although they are obviously protectable in the sense that we are capable of protecting them, they are designated "not protectable" because we have decided not to protect them. And we decide not to protect them because they are not persons. Whether they are persons, and therefore protectable, depends upon their possessing certain qualities that we associate with persons and think worth protecting. Here and elsewhere in the Report, the reader is struck by a large measure of circularity in the Panel's reasoning.

***

The question is not whether the embryo is protectable but whether it is in need of protection. The Report says that "the commencement of protectability is not an all or nothing matter, but results from a being's increasing possession of qualities that make respecting it (and hence limiting others' liberty in relation to it) more compelling." In other words, moral standing develops as the human being develops, and "personhood" is an award we bestow for performance. The principle espoused by the Report leads to the suggestion that our obligation to afford protection to a human being is in inverse proportion to his or her need for protection. Put differently, those who are fully and undoubtedly persons are protectable because they are, by and large, able to protect themselves.

It is not traditional in ethical discourse to discuss what "life" or "forms of life" or "developing forms of life" are entitled to respect and protection. Living human beings are so entitled. The classical conviction of our culture has been that, contrary to the Report, it is "an all or nothing matter." We are implicated in the fate of all; every human being is inviolable. It has taken society much blood and struggle to overcome what Professor King calls the "conceptual frameworks" whereby the powerful justified excluding various categories of the powerless from moral parity. The Panel's use of "personhood" is such a conceptual framework, and it applies to both the born and unborn.

The concept of personhood has a complicated history in theology, philosophy, and law. Personhood is certainly not a scientific concept. As used by the Panel, it is an ideological concept, an idea in the service of a program aimed at changing dramatically our civilization's understanding of human life and community. In this Report, personhood is a status that we bestow. We who have received that status decide who will be admitted to, and who will be excluded from, the circle of those who are recognized as persons and are therefore entitled to respect and protection. We are told that protectability increases with an "increasing possession of qualities" that we find compelling. It follows that protectability decreases with the decreasing possession of such qualities.

From their writings and public statements, we know that some members of the Panel do not flinch from the ominous implications of that principle for those who have lost their "compelling" qualities, especially at the end of the life spectrum. As a more complete explanation of its ethical reasoning, the Report cites an article by Professor Ronald Green, himself a member of the Panel, "Toward a Copernican Revolution in Our Thinking About Life's Beginning and Life's End." It is indeed a revolution that is proposed by Professor Green and by the Human Embryo Research Panel. The cited article asserts that there are no "qualities existing *out there*" in any human being requiring us to respect him or her as a person. Whether to grant or deny "personhood" (and hence the right not to be harmed or killed) is, we are told, "The outcome of a very active and complex process of decision on our part." In the current language of the academy, personhood is entirely a "social construct." Whether someone is too young or too old, too retarded or too sick, too troublesome or too useless to be entitled to personhood is determined by a "decision on our part." The American people have not been consulted about, and certainly have not consented to, this "Copernican Revolution" in our understanding of human dignity and human rights.

The revolution is necessary, however, in order to license, morally and legally, the research that the Panel recommends. The "conceptual frameworks" of the Report's extended ethical and philosophical reflection obscure rather than illumine the questions at hand. As already indicated, the question is not the difference between human beings and other animals. Similarly, the Report makes much of the "preimplantation embryo" (implantation in the womb usually begins with the sixth day and is completed by the fourteenth day after conception). A "greater measure of respect" is due the embryo after the fourteenth day, says the Panel. This is gravely misleading. In question are not preimplantation embryos but *unimplanted* embryos—embryos produced with the intention that they will *not* be implanted and can therefore be kept alive and experimented upon as long as they are scientifically useful.

There are additional obfuscations. The Report makes much of the "twinning" factor. An early embryo is said not to be "individuated" because in a very small minority of cases the embryo may "twin" into two or more human beings. The ethical significance of this possibility is elusive. The fact that in rare cases an embryo may divide is no justification whatever for deliberately producing human embryos for the purpose of experimentation that will destroy them. Moreover, the Report repeatedly points to the "potential" of the embryo for further development as an indicator of whether or not it is "protectable." Here the circularity of reasoning is particularly blatant: A human being is not protectable in the early stages of development because, the Report claims, it has no potential for further development. But in the case of the embryo produced in the laboratory it has no potential for further development for the sole reason that researchers will not protect it. Because they wish to use it, they do not protect it; because they do not protect it, its natural potential for development is destroyed; because it thus "has no potential," it is declared "not protectable."

The monumental questions raised by this Report—Who shall live and who shall die? Who belongs to the community of the commonly protected? How do we distinguish between human beings and laboratory animals?—demand much more serious thinking than is offered by the Human Embryo Research Panel.

The Panel claims to have established clear lines and clear time limits regarding what it is permissible to do with human embryos. That claim is false, and it seems that the panelists know that it is false. The Report says that research with these living human beings "should not be permitted beyond the time of the usual appearance of the primitive streak in vivo (14 days)." (The primitive streak is a groove that develops along the midline of the embryonic disc and its appearance is viewed as one of several milestones in the embryo's continuous development.) But this time limit is clearly arbitrary and chosen as a pragmatic compromise, as the transcript of the Panel's deliberations makes clear.

The panelists all know that development is continuous and it offers no such bright natural line to those who would "ascribe personhood." Moreover, this "time limit" is by no means firm, as is evident in the Report's assertion that it should serve "at the present time," and "for the foreseeable future." Some technically possible and scientifically interesting experiments "warrant additional review," while others are deemed "unacceptable for federal funding" because the desired experiments can at present be done with laboratory animals and because of "concern for public sensitivities on highly controversial research proposals." At the present time. For the foreseeable future.

For example, producing genetically identical individuals to be born at different times, freezing an embryonic human being who is genetically identical to a born child in order to serve as a later source for organ and tissue transplantation, cloning an existing human being, and making "carbon copies" of an existing embryo—these and other projects are declared to be "inappropriate." It is not clear that the Report opposes the doing of these things; it simply does not recommend, at present, federal funding for doing them. But in the logic of the Report, there is no reason *in principle* why these things should not be done or why they should not be funded by the government.

"Throughout its deliberations," we are told, "the Panel relied on the principle that research involving preimplantation embryos is acceptable public policy only if the research promises significant scientific and therapeutic benefits." But a principle that says something should not be done unless there are strong motives for doing it is no principle at all. The claim to have set limits is vitiated by the repeated assertion that exceptions can be made for "serious and compelling reasons," scientists can do whatever they decide to do with human beings who are declared to be "unprotectable." And they can get government funding for doing it, within the limits of "public sensitivities." There is no reason, in principle, why such license would be confined to very small and very young human beings.

Of course the Panel believes that its recommendations are supported by "serious and compelling reasons" having to do with gains in scientific knowledge and therapeutic benefits. We do not doubt that lethal experiments on powerless and unconsenting human beings might result in findings of scientific interest. As for therapeutic benefits, the Report holds out the promise of improved success with in vitro fertilization, new contraceptive techniques, new prospects for genetic screening, the production of cell lines for use in tissue transplantation, and, more vaguely, treatment of cancer and other diseases.

In fact, the Report seems too reticent in its discussion of possible "benefits" from the research it proposes. In a time when the entire human genome is being mapped, when the age is rising at which many women first become mothers, when, consequently, there is increased anxiety about the risk of genetic diseases, when harvesting parts from the embryo and fetus may have therapeutic uses for older human beings, when care for the handicapped and defective is viewed by many as excessively burdensome, and when it seems technically possible to produce custom-made babies—in such a time it is not surprising that people might be tempted to agree that the Panel's recommendations are supported by "serious and compelling reasons." The Report explicitly encourages funding for "preimplantation genetic screening," and the laboratory testing of artificially fertilized embryos before they are placed in the womb. The normalizing of in vitro fertilization and the universalizing of genetic screening in order to eliminate the unfit and advance eugenic goals are part of a "brave new world" clearly advanced by the proposals of the Human Embryo Research Panel.

Is this the future that we want? Who should decide? That brings us to the makeup and role of the Panel itself.

"Americans hold widely different views on the question of the moral value of prenatal life at its various stages," the Report notes. "It is not the role of those who help form public policy to decide which of these views is correct. Instead, public policy represents an effort to arrive at a reasonable accommodation to diverse interests." The Panel says it eschews the task of adopting a particular philosophy or settling arguments that it describes as "metaphysically complex and controverted." In fact, however, in order to legitimate morally what it recommends, the Panel does adopt a particular philosophy that it believes cuts through the complexities and controversies. That philosophy is ordinarily called utilitarianism. It is a primitive and unreflective version of utilitarianism, to be sure, but the message is unequivocal: the end justifies the means. If there are "serious and compelling reasons," it would seem that the end would justify any means. Certainly it justifies producing, using, and destroying human beings who are valued only for their utility as tools serving the purposes of scientific research. The Panel's is not a "multi-factorial" judgment. There is ultimately only one factor: scientific utility.

While claiming not to impose a moral judgment or philosophy, the Panel imposes a moral judgment and philosophy. At the same time, while apparently only offering advice to the NIH, the Panel has in effect arrogated to itself the work of our elected representatives. It is the task of politicians and legislatures "to arrive at a reasonable accommodation to diverse interests." A panel of experts might inform political deliberation by displaying the full range of facts, arguments, and considerations that legislators should take into account in making decisions. This Panel could not do that, however. While the Panel heard testimony from those who do not share its crassly utilitarian philosophy, such diversity was not included in the Panel itself. As explained by the chairman at the Panel's first meeting, it was thought inappropriate to include any members who oppose the research in question. Thus the Panel was able to arrive at a "reasonable accommodation" of the "widely different views" on the questions at hand by conveniently eliminating different views.

Additionally troubling is the fact that members of the Panel are themselves doing the very research for which they are recommending federal funding. An ethics advisory panel certainly must take testimony from scientists involved in the research under consideration. In this case, however, it would seem that members of an advisory panel are recommending federal grants for their own work. This is ordinarily not called advising but lobbying. Congress should examine closely the apparent conflict of interest involved.

Our concern is with the philosophy and moral reasoning embraced by the Panel. Our conviction—and, we are confident, the conviction of almost all Americans—is that the ominous questions engaged must not be decided by one-sided committees of the National Institutes of Health. What affects all should, through our representative process, be decided by all. The proposal that some human beings should be declared "not protectable" affects all of us. The proposal that human beings should be treated merely as means rather than ends is revolutionary, but it is not new. Such "conceptual frameworks" have a terrifying history, not least in this bloodiest of centuries.

The production of human beings for the purpose of experiments that will destroy them should be prohibited by law. The use of human beings for experiments that will do them harm and to which they have not given their consent should be prohibited by law. It matters not how young or how small, how old or how powerless, such human beings may be. Some nations ban or severely restrict the research proposed by the Panel (e.g., Norway, Germany, Austria, Australia). In the shadow of the unspeakable horror of Nazism, the Nuremberg Code declared, "No experiment should be conducted where there is an a priori reason to believe that death or disabling injury will occur." And the 1975 Helsinki Declaration of the World Medical Association affirms, "Concern for the interests of the subject must always prevail over the interest of science and society."

It is objected that a ban would not be enforceable. If so, how can anyone believe that the proposed regulation by NIH would be enforceable? The research recommended by the Panel is now being done under various auspices, with or without government funding. Driven by scientific curiosity and hubris, reinforced by the prospect of great commercial gain and a belief that it will produce benefits for society, such research probably cannot be stopped altogether. But the necessity of a law does not depend on its being universally effective. What must be made illegal and declared morally odious is any research that subjects human beings to scientific experimentation that will certainly result in their grave injury or death.

The shamelessly partisan and conceptually confused Report of the Human Embryo Research Panel should be unambiguously rejected. Limits that are "for the present time" and "for the foreseeable future" limit nothing. They are but unconvincing reassurances that scientists are going carefully where they should not be permitted to go at all. If the course recommended by the Panel is approved, the foreseeable future is ominously clear: it is a return to the past when people contrived "conceptual frameworks" for excluding categories of human beings, born and unborn, from our common humanity.

Hadley Arkes
Department of Political Science
Amherst College

Matthew Berke
First Things

Gerard V. Bradley
Notre Dame Law School

Fr. James T. Burtchaell
Congregation of Holy Cross

Fr. Francis Canavan
Department of Political Science
Fordham University

Rabbi David G. Dalin
West Hartford, CT

Midge Decter
Institute of Religion and Public Life

Thomas S. Derr
Department of Religion
Smith College

Fr. Ernest Fortin
Department of Theology
Boston College

Jorge Garcia
Department of Philosophy
Rutgers University

Rabbi Marc Gellman
Dix Hills, NY

Robert P. George
Department of Politics
Princeton University

Mary Ann Glendon
The Law School
Harvard University

Stanley Hauerwas
The Divinity School
Duke University

John Hittinger
Professor of Philosophy
Colorado Springs, CO

Russell Hittinger
School of Philosophy
Catholic University of America

The Rev. Robert W. Jenson
Department of Religion
St. Olaf College

Leon R. Kass, M.D.
Committee on Social Thought
The University of Chicago

Ralph McInerny
Maritain Center
University of Notre Dame

Fr. Richard John Neuhaus
Institute of Religion and Public Life

Rabbi David Novak
Department of Religious Studies
University of Virginia

Michael Novak
American Enterprise Institute

James Nuechterlein
First Things

David Singer
American Jewish Committee

George Weigel
Ethics and Public Policy Center

Robert L. Wilken
Department of Religious Studies
University of Virginia

Institutional affiliations given for identification purposes only.

Discussion Questions

1. Why does the Ramsey Colloquium maintain that the NIH panel accepts a crass utilitarian philosophy concerning embryo research? Why does the Ramsey Colloquium think that this is a bad thing?

2. How does the Ramsey Colloquium defend its main contention that the NIH panel's "recommendation is morally repugnant, entails grave injustice to innocent human beings, and constitutes an assault upon the foundational ideas of human dignity and rights essential to a free and decent society"? Do you think that the colloquium's defense of this position is flawed? Why or why not?

3. The Ramsey Colloquium claims that whatever one's views on the legalization of abortion, the NIH panel's conclusions should be opposed by all. But if someone believes that embryos are not morally persons, why should he or she oppose the NIH panel? Do you think that the colloquium responds to this question anywhere in its report?

4. According to the Ramsey colloquium, the NIH panel's claim that it has "established clear lines and clear time limits regarding what is permissible to do with human embryos . . . . is false, and it seems that the panelists know it is false." What does the colloquium mean by this and how does it defend it? Do you find its response compelling? Why or why not?

PART III

Issues of Social Justice and Personal Liberty

General Introduction

The following is from a *Wall Street Journal* editorial (December 13, 1993):

> Mrs. Schnell is a 50-year-old divorced woman who works part time. In October the state of Wisconsin found that she had engaged in sexual and religious discrimination by taking out the following ad in the local newspaper: *Apartment for rent, 1 bedroom, electric included, mature Christian handyman.*
>
> Initially, Mrs. Schnell was contacted by the Milwaukee Fair Housing Council, a nonprofit organization. The council said she had discriminated because her ad suggested that a "handyman" or male was preferred. And "Christian" implied that non-Christians wouldn't be welcome. . . . The Council offered to drop the case if Mrs. Schnell paid a $50 fine and $500 in attorney's fees.
>
> She refused, claiming she hadn't intended to discriminate. She says she merely wanted a tenant who could remodel her 100-year-old house in exchange for a lower rent. As a Christian, she also felt an obligation to help other Christians first. She never asked the religion of the emotionally disturbed man she ended up accepting as her tenant. . . .
>
> After Mrs. Schnell refused to settle with the Fair Housing Council, the next time she heard about her ad was last year, when she was notified that the Fair Housing Council had indeed filed a complaint with the state, as it is somehow empowered to do. After the state's Equal Rights Division found her guilty, she learned the fines and fees would total $8,000. She fears she may have to take out a second mortgage on her house if she loses her appeal to the local circuit court.

This real-life story raises some very important questions, such as the following: Does the state have a right to force its concepts of fairness and justice (nondiscrimination) so that Mrs. Schnell uses her property in a way that does not violate the state's concepts, or is such coercion a violation of Mrs. Schnell's personal liberty, privacy rights, and property rights? This sort of question brings out deeper philosophical questions of justice, fairness, liberty, privacy rights, and property rights as well as the role of the state and the "public good" in deciding such matters. This part of our text deals with issues that touch on these deeper philosophical questions: affirmative action (Section A), economic and social justice (Section B), freedom of expression (Section C), homosexuality (Section D), and family values and sex roles (Section E).

For Further Reading

Hadley Arkes, *First Things: An Inquiry into the First Principles of Morals and Justice* (Princeton, N.J.: Princeton University Press, 1986).

Ronald Dworkin, *Taking Rights Seriously* (Cambridge: Harvard University Press, 1977).

John Locke, *Two Treatises on Government,* a critical edition with an introduction and apparatus criticus by Peter Laslett, rev. ed. (New York: Cambridge University Press, 1963).

Karl Marx, *The Communist Manifesto,* ed. Frederic L. Bender (New York: W. W. Norton, 1988).

Michael Novak, *The Spirit of Democratic Capitalism* (New York: Simon & Schuster, 1982).

Robert Nozick, *Anarchy, State, and Utopia* (New York: Basic Books, 1974).

Susan Moller Okin, *Justice, Gender, and the Family* (New York: Basic Books, 1989).

John Rawls, *A Theory of Justice* (Cambridge: Belknap Press of the Harvard University Press, 1971).

Murray Rothbard, *For a New Liberty* (New York: Macmillan, 1973).

Jean-Jacques Rousseau, *The Social Contract* (London: Everyman's Library, 1947).

Michael Sandel, *Liberalism and the Limits of Justice* (Cambridge: Cambridge University Press, 1982).

Leo Strauss, *Natural Right and History* (Chicago: University of Chicago Press, 1950).

SECTION A

Affirmative Action

Introduction

In December 1988 someone I know attended the annual Eastern Division meeting of the American Philosophical Association (APA) in Washington, D.C. He was there not only to listen to some papers that were being read but to be interviewed for a job for which he was a finalist. While he was at the meeting he had the opportunity to meet a number of other candidates who were being interviewed for jobs at other institutions. He met several women who were among this group, some of whom were being interviewed for as many as 20 positions. None of the white male candidates he met were being interviewed for more than four. There was no doubt for the white male candidates at the meeting, many of whom had published more widely and had more teaching experience than most of the female candidates, that certain institutions were giving the female candidates *preferential treatment*.

The APA and almost every college and university in America has a policy of *affirmative action*, which some commentators see as having at least two different versions. The first, *weak affirmative action*, is the employment of "such measures as the elimination of segregation, widespread advertisement to groups not previously represented in certain privileged positions, special scholarships for the disadvantaged classes (e.g., all the poor), using underrepresentation or a history of past discrimination as a tie breaker when candidates are relatively equal, and the like."[1] This view stresses *equal opportunity* rather than equal results. In other words, an employer should in every case, except that of a tie, ignore the race or gender of the candidate; the candidate should be judged on the basis of his or her qualifications. If this results in a particular profession having a disproportionate number of a certain group in comparison to the percentage of the general population (e.g., 95 percent of the employees are white while only 78 percent of the general population is white), the result is not unfair because everyone was given an equal opportunity to excel.

On the other hand, *strong affirmative action* "involves more positive steps to eliminate past injustice, such as reverse discrimination, hiring candidates on the basis of race or gender in order to reach equal or near equal results, proportionate representation in each area of society."[2] That is to say, this view stresses *equal results* (or at least some goal or pattern of employment that ought to be achieved). It is evident from comparing the qualifications of the white male candidates with the female candidates at the 1988 APA meeting that a large number of the institutions interviewing at the meeting were practicing strong affirmative action, which entails preferential treatment.

Another example of strong affirmative action is what is called *race norming*, which is widely practiced though most people are unaware of it. Consider the following example:

> Imagine that four men came into a state employment office in order to apply for a job. One is black, one Hispanic, one Asian, and one white. They take the standard test (a version of the General Aptitude Test Battery or VG-GATB). All get a composite score of 300. None of them will ever see that score. Instead the numbers

will be fed into a computer and the applicant's percentile rank emerges. The scores are group-weighted. Blacks are measured against blacks, whites against whites, Hispanics against Hispanics. Since blacks characteristically do less well than other groups, the effect is to favor blacks. For example, a score of 300 as an accountant will give the black a percentile of 87, an Hispanic a percentile of 74 and a white or Oriental a score of 47. The black will get the job as the accountant.[3]

There is no doubt that minorities, especially blacks and women, have been discriminated against in American history. And many people maintain that this history of discrimination has resulted in white males dominating and controlling the network of social institutions that is the focus of power and authority in our society, including banks, universities, corporations, and governments (federal, state, and local). Thus, in order to truly achieve justice and fairness there must be a shift in the power base in these institutions. This can be achieved, according to the supporters of strong affirmative action, by preferential treatment programs with goals and timetables.

The Civil Rights Movement and Affirmative Action

The civil rights movement of late-twentieth-century America focused first on the predicament of African-Americans, who were denied full legal personhood under Southern slavery (prior to the adoption of the Thirteenth Amendment to the Constitution in 1865) and the U.S. Supreme Court's *Dred Scott* decision (*Scott v. Sandford*, 60 U.S. [19 How.] 393 [1857]). Although the Fourteenth Amendment was passed in 1868 granting black slaves full citizenship and Constitutional rights, for decades after, blacks were still denied their civil rights in many parts of the United States. They were forced to live in segregated areas, attend segregated schools, dine at segregated lunch counters, and sit at the back of the bus in deference to white passengers. On the basis of skin color only they were denied jobs and school entrance.

To remedy the denial of civil rights of not only blacks but women and other minorities, arguably the two most important events are the following: (1) the Supreme Court's *Brown v. the Board of Education* (347 U.S. 483 [1954]) in which the Court ruled racial segregation unconstitutional; and (2) passage of the Civil Rights Act of 1964.

The original goal of the civil rights movement was to eliminate barriers to advancement, such as segregation, laws that discriminated against blacks and other minorities, discrimination in employment, and policies that prevented black and other minorities from attending a number of educational institutions, including universities and colleges. The idea of strong affirmative action and/or preferential treatment was out of the question. In fact, Roy Wilkins, then executive director of the NAACP, testified before a congressional committee considering the 1964 Civil Rights Act: "Our association has never been in favor of a quota system. We believe the quota system is unfair whether it is used for [blacks] or against [blacks] . . . [We] feel people ought to be hired because of their ability, irrespective of their color . . . We want equality, equality of opportunity and employment on the basis of ability."[4] Consequently, the Civil Rights Act of 1964, which outlawed discrimination based on race or sex, states:

> . . . Nothing contained in this title shall be interpreted to require any employer . . . to grant preferential treatment to any individual or to any group . . . on account of an imbalance which may exist with respect to the total numbers of per-

centage of persons of any race . . . employed by any employer . . . in comparison with the total or percentage of persons of such race . . . in any community, State, section, or other area, or in the available work force in any community, State, section, or other area.[5]

In 1965 the U.S. Congress passed the Voting Rights Act. Jim Crow laws were overturned throughout the South, resulting in racially integrated schools and the opening of public accommodations to every citizen regardless of race. However, it became apparent that eradication of discriminatory laws did not result in the civil rights movement's vision of a completely unsegregated society. In pursuit of this vision, President Johnson in 1965 issued Executive Order 11246, in which the Department of Labor was required to award government contracts with construction companies while taking race into account. What occurred was a shift to the philosophy of affirmative action, justified by maintaining that it was necessary in order to make up for the centuries of the loathsome practice of racial discrimination that resulted in oppression. President Johnson used an analogy to make his point:

> Imagine a hundred-yard dash in which one of the two runners has his legs shackled together. He has progressed 10 yards, while the unshackled runner has gone 50 yards. How do they rectify the situation? Do they merely remove the shackles and allow the race to proceed? Then they could say that "equal opportunity" now prevailed. But one of the runners would still be forty yards ahead of the other. Would it not be the better part of justice to allow the previously shackled runner to make up the 40-yard gap; or to start the race all over again? That would be affirmative action towards equality. (President Lyndon Johnson, inaugurating the Affirmative Action Policy of Executive Order 11246 in 1965).[6]

President Johnson issued Executive Order 11375 so that affirmative action would be extended to women. In time affirmative action benefits were extended to Indians (or native Americans), Asians, Hispanics, and the handicapped. Although at this time affirmative action was interpreted by most to mean weak affirmative action (entailing equal opportunity, active recruitment of minorities, using race or gender as a tie breaker, etc.), eventually it evolved into strong affirmative action (entailing certain results of racial proportionality based on numerical quotas, goals, and timetables), because it was apparent to many supporters of affirmative action that the weak version of it was not producing the results they expected.

A number of courts have wrestled with the constitutionality of particular affirmative action programs, although in general the courts, including the U.S. Supreme Court, have concluded that certain programs are constitutional. Even though the Supreme Court ruled against particular preferential treatment programs in *University of California v. Bakke* (1978) and *City of Richmond v. Croson* (1989), it did not rule out such programs in general. In the case of *United Steelworkers v. Weber* (1979) the Supreme Court declared affirmative action programs constitutional.

Preferential treatment programs are defended in this section by Tom Beauchamp in Chapter 34 ("The Justification of Reverse Discrimination") and Richard Wasserstrom in Chapter 32 ("A Defense of Programs of Preferential Treatment"). There are two critiques of preferential treatment in this section, one in Chapter 33 by Louis P. Pojman ("The Moral Status of Affirmative Action"), and another in Chapter 35 by Thomas Sowell ("From Equal Opportunity to 'Affirmative Action'"). In Chapters 30 ("*University of California v. Bakke* [1978]") and 31 ("*City of Richmond v. Croson* [1989]") the U.S. Supreme Court upholds some, though not all, programs of preferential treatment as constitutional. In both decisions the Court establishes strict criteria to distinguish constitutional from unconstitutional forms of affirmative action.

Notes

1. Louis P. Pojman, "The Moral Status of Affirmative Action," *Public Affairs Quarterly* 6 (April 1992), 183.
2. Ibid.
3. Ibid., 188.
4. Quoted in Pojman, 184, which quoted from William Bradford Reynolds, "Affirmative Action Is Unjust," in *Social Justice*, ed. D. Bender and B. Lenore (St. Paul, Minn., 1984), 23.
5. 42 U.S.C.2000E-2(j)
6. Pojman, 185.

For Further Reading

Boris Bittker, *The Case for Black Reparations* (New York: Random House, 1973).

Norman E. Bowie, ed. *Equal Opportunity* (Boulder, Colo.; Westview, 1988).

Nicholas Capaldi, *Out of Order: Affirmative Action and the Crisis of Doctrinaire Liberalism* (Buffalo, N.Y.: Prometheus, 1985).

Marshall Cohen, Thomas Nagel, and Thomas Scanlon, eds., *Equality and Preferential Treatment* (Princeton, N.J.: Princeton University Press, 1976).

Joseph G. Conti and Brad Stetson, *Challenging the Civil Rights Establishment: Profiles of a New Black Vanguard* (Westport, Conn.: Praeger, 1993).

D. T. Goldberg, ed. *Anatomy of Racism* (Minneapolis: University of Minnesota Press, 1988).

Barry Gross, *Discrimination in Reverse: Is Turnabout Fair Play?* (New York: State University of New York Press, 1978).

Frederick R. Lynch, *Invisible Victims: White Males and the Crisis of Affirmative Action* (New York: Greenwood, 1989).

H. Remick, *Comparable Worth and Wage Dicrimination* (Philadelphia: Temple University Press, 1985).

Thomas Sowell, *Civil Rights: Rhetoric or Reality?* (New York: William Morrow, 1984).

Steven Yates, *Civil Wrongs: What Went Wrong with Affirmative Action* (San Francisco: Institute for Contemporary Studies, 1994).

The Law and Affirmative Action

30

University of California v. Bakke
(1978)

U.S. Supreme Court

The University of California, Davis Medical School had set aside 16 of its 100 first-year openings for minority students (Hispanics, Filipinos, and African-Americans), even though their qualifications for entrance were lower than those of white applicants. Although achieving better test scores than the scores of accepted minority applicants, Allan Bakke, a white candidate, was turned down twice by Davis. He subsequently filed suit against the university claiming that he was a victim of racial discrimination. The case eventually made it to the U.S. Supreme Court, which ruled that Bakke was indeed a victim of reverse racial discrimination. The Court argued that appeal to ethnic diversity *by itself* is not sufficient to justify racial quotas in admissions or hiring. In addition, the Court pointed out that it was unjust that minority applicants could compete for all 100 entry positions whereas nonminority applicants could only compete for 84. However, the Court did say that universities and colleges may employ "race" as part of their admission criteria as long as it is *one* of several criteria. Although the Court ruled against quotas in this case, it did claim that quotas could be justified constitutionally if they promote "a substantial state interest." The following is an abridged version of the majority opinion in *Bakke*, written by Justice Lewis F. Powell, Jr., who has since retired from the Court.

. . . Mr. Justice Powell announced the judgment of the court. . . .

I

The Medical School of the University of California at Davis opened in 1968 with an entering class of 50 students. In 1971, the size of the entering class was increased to 100 students, a level at which it remains. No admissions program for disadvantaged or minority students existed when the school opened, and the first class contained three Asians but no blacks, no Mexican-Americans, and no American Indians. Over the next two years, the faculty devised a special admissions program to increase the representation of "disadvantaged" students in each Medical School class. The special program consisted of a separate admissions system operating in coordination with the regular admissions process. . . .

The special admissions program operated with a separate committee, a majority of whom were members of minority groups. On the 1973 application form, candidates were asked to indicate whether they wished to be considered as "economically and/or educationally disadvantaged" applicants; on the 1974 form the question was whether they wished to be considered as members of a "minority group," which the Medical School apparently viewed as "Blacks," "Chicanos," "Asians," and "American Indians." If these questions were answered affirmatively, the application was forwarded to the special admissions committee. No formal definition of "disadvantaged" was ever produced, but the chairman of the special committee screened each application to see whether it reflected economic or educational deprivation. Having passed this initial hurdle, the applications then were rated by the special committee in a fashion similar to that used by the general admissions committee, except that special candidates did not have to meet the 2.5 grade point average cutoff applied to regular applicants. About one-fifth of the total number of special applicants were invited for interviews in 1973 and 1974. Following each interview, the special committee assigned each special applicant a benchmark score. The special committee then presented its top choices to the general admissions committee. The latter did not rate or compare the special candidates against the general applicants, but could reject recommended special candidates for failure to meet course requirements or other specific deficiencies. The special committee continued to recommend special applicants until a number prescribed by faculty vote were admitted. While the overall class size was still 50, the prescribed number was 8; in 1973 and 1974, when the class size had doubled to 100, the prescribed number of special admissions also doubled, to 16.

From the year of the increase in class size—1971—through 1974, the special program resulted in the admission of 21 black students, 30 Mexican-Americans, and 12 Asians, for a total of 63 minority students. Over the same period, the regular admissions program produced 1 black, 6 Mexican-Americans, and 37 Asians, for a total of 44 minority students. Although disadvantaged whites applied to the special program in large numbers, none received an offer of admission through that process. Indeed, in 1974, at least, the special committee explicitly considered only "disadvantaged" special applicants who were members of one of the designated minority groups.

Allan Bakke is a white male who applied to the Davis Medical School in both 1973 and 1974. In both years Bakke's application was considered under the general admissions program, and he received an interview. His 1973 interview was with Dr. Theodore C. West, who considered Bakke "a very desirable applicant to [the] medical school." Despite a strong benchmark score of 468 out of 500, Bakke was rejected. His application had come late in the year, and no applicants in the general admissions process with scores below 470 were accepted after Bakke's application was completed. There were four special admissions slots unfilled at the time however, for which Bakke was not considered. After his 1973 rejection, Bakke wrote to Dr. George H. Lowrey, Associate Dean and Chairman of the Admissions Committee, protesting that the special admissions program operated as a racial and ethnic quota.

Bakke's 1974 application was completed early in the year. His student interviewer gave him an overall rating of 94, finding him "friendly, well tempered, conscientious and delightful to speak with." His faculty interviewer was, by coincidence, the same Dr. Lowrey to whom he had written in protest of the special admissions program. Dr. Lowrey found Bakke "rather limited in his approach" to the problems of the medical profession and found disturbing Bakke's "very definite opinions which were based more on his personal viewpoints than upon a study of the total problem." Dr. Lowrey gave Bakke the lowest of his six ratings, an 86; his total was 549 out of 600. Again, Bakke's application was rejected. In neither year did the chairman of the admissions committee, Dr. Lowrey, exercise his discretion to place Bakke on the waiting list. In both years applicants were admitted under the special program with grade point averages, MCAT scores, and benchmark scores significantly lower than Bakke's. The table on page 309 compares Bakke's science grade point average, overall grade point average, and MCAT scores with the average scores of regular admittees and of special admittees in both 1973 and 1974.

After the second rejection, Bakke filed the instant suit in the Superior Court of California. He sought mandatory, injunctive, and declaratory relief compelling his admission to the Medical School. He alleged that the Medical School's special admissions program operated to exclude him from the school on the basis of his race, in violation of his rights under the Equal Protection Clause of the Fourteenth Amendment, Art. 1, § 21, of the California Constitution, and § 601 of Title VI of the Civil Rights Act of 1964. The University cross-complained for a declaration that its special admissions program was lawful. . . .

[II . . .]

III

A

. . . The guarantees of the Fourteenth Amendment extend to all persons. Its language is explicit: "No State shall . . . deny to any person within its jurisdiction the equal protection of the laws." It is settled beyond question that the "rights created by the first section of the Fourteenth Amendment are, by its terms, guaranteed to the individual. The rights established are personal rights." The guarantee of equal protection cannot mean one thing when applied to one individual and something else when applied to a person of another color. If both are not accorded the same protection, then it is not equal.

CLASS ENTERING IN 1973

	SGPA	OGPA	MCAT (Percentiles)			
			Verbal	Quantitative	Science	Gen Infor.
Bakke	3.44	3.46	96	94	97	72
Average of regular admittees	3.51	3.49	81	76	83	69
Average of special admittees	2.62	2.88	46	24	35	33

CLASS ENTERING IN 1974

	SGPA	OGPA	MCAT (Percentiles)			
			Verbal	Quantitative	Science	Gen Infor.
Bakke	3.44	3.46	96	94	97	72
Average of regular admittees	3.36	3.29	69	67	82	72
Average of special admittees	2.42	2.62	34	30	37	18

Applicants admitted under the special program also had benchmark scores significantly lower than many students, including Bakke, rejected under the general admissions program, even though the special rating system apparently gave credit for overcoming "disadvantage."

Nevertheless, petitioner argues that the court below erred in applying strict scrutiny to the special admissions program because white males, such as respondent, are not a "discrete and insular minority" requiring extraordinary protection from the majoritarian political process. This rationale, however, has never been invoked in our decisions as a prerequisite to subjecting racial or ethnic distinctions to strict scrutiny. Nor has this Court held that discreteness and insularity constitute necessary preconditions to a holding that a particular classification is invidious. These characteristics may be relevant in deciding whether or not to add new types of classifications to the list of "suspect" categories or whether a particular classification survives close examination. Racial and ethnic classifications, however, are subject to stringent examination without regard to these additional characteristics. We declared as much in the first cases explicitly to recognize racial distinctions as suspect:

> "Distinctions between citizens solely because of their ancestry are by their very nature odious to a free people whose institutions are founded upon the doctrine of equality."
> "[A]ll legal restrictions which curtail the civil rights of a single racial group are immediately suspect. That is not to say that all such restrictions are unconstitutional. It is to say that courts must subject them to the most rigid scrutiny."

The court has never questioned the validity of those pronouncements. Racial and ethnic distinctions of any sort are inherently suspect and thus call for the most exacting judicial examination.

B

This perception of racial and ethnic distinctions is rooted in our Nation's constitutional and demographic history. The Court's initial view of the Fourteenth Amendment was that in "one pervading purpose" was "the freedom of the slave race, the security and firm establishment of that freedom, and the protection of the newly-made freeman and citizen from the oppressions of those who had formerly exercised dominion over him." *Slaughter-House Cases* (1873). The Equal Protection Clause, however, was "[v]irtually strangled in infancy by post-civil-war judicial reactionism." It was relegated to decades of relative desuetude while the Due Process Clause of the Fourteenth Amendment, after a short germinal period, flourished as a cornerstone in the Court's defense of property and liberty of contract. In that cause, the Fourteenth Amendment's "one pervading purpose" was displaced. It was only as the era of substantive due process came to a close that the Equal Protection Clause began to attain a genuine measure of vitality.

By that time it was no longer possible to peg the guarantees of the Fourteenth Amendment to the struggle for equality of one racial minority. During the dormancy of the Equal Protection Clause, the United States had become a Nation of minorities. Each had to struggle—and to some extent struggles still—to overcome the prejudices not of a monolithic majority, but of a "majority" composed of various minority groups of whom it was said—perhaps unfairly in many cases—that a shared characteristic was a willingness to disadvantage other groups. As the Nation filled with the stock of many lands, the reach of the Clause was gradually extended to all ethnic groups seeking protection from official discrimination. The guarantees of equal protection, said the Court in *Yick Wo*, "are universal in their application, to all persons within the territorial jurisdiction, without regard to any differences of race, of color, or of nationality; and the equal protection of the laws is a pledge of the protection of equal laws."

Although many of the Framers of the Fourteenth Amendment conceived of its primary function as bridging the vast distance between members of the Negro race and the white "majority," the Amendment itself was framed in universal terms, without reference to color, ethnic origin, or condition of prior servitude. As this Court recently remarked in interpreting the 1866 Civil Rights Act to extend to claims of racial discrimination against white persons, "the 39th Congress was intent upon establishing in the federal law a broader principle than would have been necessary simply to meet the particular and immediate plight of the newly freed Negro slaves." And that legislation was specifically broadened in 1870 to ensure that "all persons," not merely "citizens," would enjoy equal rights under the law. Indeed, it is not unlikely that among the Framers were many who would have applauded a reading of the Equal Protection Clause that states a principle of universal application and is responsive to the racial, ethnic, and cultural diversity of the Nation.

Over the past 30 years, this Court has embarked upon the crucial mission of interpreting the Equal Protection Clause with the view of assuring to all persons "the protection of equal laws," in a Nation confronting a legacy of slavery and racial discrimination. Because the landmark decisions in this area arose in response to the continued exclusion of Negroes from the mainstream of American society, they could be characterized as involving discrimination by the "majority" white race against the Negro minority. But they need not be read as depending upon that characterization for their results. It suffices to say that "[o]ver the year, this Court has consistently repudiated '[d]istinctions between citizens solely because of their ancestry' as being 'odious to a free people whose institutions are founded upon the doctrine of equality.'"

Petitioner urges us to adopt for the first time a more restrictive view of the Equal Protection Clause and hold that discrimination against members of the white "majority" cannot be suspect if its purpose can be characterized as "benign."[1] The clock of our liberties, however, cannot be turned back to 1868. It is far too late to argue that the guarantee of equal protection to *all* persons permits the recognition of special wards entitled to a degree of protection greater than that accorded others.[2] "The Fourteenth Amendment is not directed solely against discrimination due to a 'two-class theory'—that is, based upon differences between 'white' and Negro."

Once the artificial line of a "two-class theory" of the Fourteenth Amendment is put aside, the difficulties entailed in varying the level of judicial review according to a perceived "preferred" status of a particular racial or ethnic minority are intractable. The concepts of "majority" and "minority" necessarily reflect temporary arrangements and political judgments. As observed above, the white "majority" itself is composed of various minority groups, most of which can lay claim to a history of prior discrimination at the hands of the State and private individuals. Not all of these groups can receive preferential treatment and corresponding judicial tolerance of distinctions drawn in terms of race and nationality, for then the only "majority" left would be a new minority of white Anglo-Saxon Protestants. There is no principled basis for deciding which groups would merit "heightened judicial solicitude" and which would not. Courts would be asked to evaluate the extent of the prejudice and consequent harm suffered by various minority groups. Those whose societal injury is thought to exceed some arbitrary level of tolerability then would be entitled to preferential classifications at the expense of individuals belonging to other groups. Those classifications would be free from exacting judicial scrutiny. As these preferences began to have their desired effect, and the consequences of past discrimination were undone, new judicial rankings would be necessary. The kind of variable sociological and political analysis necessary to produce such rankings simply does not lie within the judicial competence—even if they otherwise were politically feasible and socially desirable.

Moreover, there are serious problems of justice connected with the idea of preference itself. First, it may not always be clear that a so-called preference is in fact benign. Courts may be asked to validate burdens imposed upon individual members of a particular group in order to advance the group's general interest. Nothing in the Constitution supports the notion that individuals may be asked to suffer otherwise impermissible burdens in order to enhance the societal standing of their ethnic groups. Second, preferential programs may only reinforce common stereotypes holding that certain groups are unable to achieve success without special protection based on a factor having no relationship to individual worth. Third, there is a measure of inequality in forcing innocent persons in respondent's position to bear the burdens of redressing grievances not of their making.

By hitching the meaning of the Equal Protection Clause to these transitory considerations, we would be holding, as a constitutional principle, that judicial scrutiny of classifications touching on racial and ethnic background may vary with the ebb and flow of political forces. Disparate constitutional tolerance of such classifications well may serve to exacerbate racial and ethnic antagonisms rather than alleviate them. Also, the mutability of a constitutional principle, based upon shifting political and social judgments, undermines the chances for consistent application of the Constitution from one generation to the next, a critical feature of its coherent interpretation. In expounding the Constitution, the Court's role is to discern "principles sufficiently absolute to give them roots throughout the community and continuity over significant periods of time, and to lift them above the level of the pragmatic political judgments of a particular time and place."

If it is the individual who is entitled to judicial protection against classifications based upon his racial or ethnic background because such distinctions impinge upon personal rights, rather than the individual only because of his membership in a particular group, then constitutional standards may be applied consistently. Political judgments regarding the necessity for the particular classification may be weighed in the constitutional balance, but the standard of justification will remain constant. This is as it should be, since those political judgments are the product of rough compromise struck by contending groups within the democratic process. When they touch upon an individual's race or ethnic background, he is entitled to a judicial determination that the burden he is asked to bear on that basis is precisely tailored to serve a compelling governmental interest. The Constitution guarantees that right to every person regardless of his background. . . .

IV

We have held that in "order to justify the use of a suspect classification, a State must show that its purpose or interest is both constitutionally permissible and substantial, and that its use of the classification is 'necessary . . . to the accomplishment' of its purpose or the safeguarding of its interest." The special admissions program purports to serve the purposes of: (i) "reducing the historic deficit of traditionally disfavored minorities in medical schools and in the medical profession," (ii) countering the effects of societal discrimination; (iii) increasing the number of physicians who will practice in communities currently underserved; and (iv) obtaining the educational benefits that flow from an ethnically diverse student body. It is necessary to decide which, if any, of these purposes is substantial enough to support the use of a suspect classification.

A

If petitioner's purpose is to assure within its student body some specified percentage of a particular group merely because of its race or ethnic origin, such a preferential purpose must be rejected not as insubstantial but as facially invalid. Preferring members of any one group for no reason other than race or ethnic origin is discrimination for its own sake. This the Constitution forbids.

B

The State certainly has a legitimate and substantial interest in ameliorating, or eliminating where feasible, the disabling effects of identified discrimination. The line of school desegregation cases, commencing with *Brown*, attests to the importance of this state goal and the commitment of the judiciary to affirm all lawful means toward its attainment. In the school cases, the States were required by court order to redress the wrongs worked by specific instances of racial discrimination. That goal was far more focused than the remedying of the effects of "societal discrimination," an amorphous concept of injury that may be ageless in its reach into the past.

We have never approved a classification that aids persons perceived as members of relatively victimized groups at the expense of other innocent individuals in the absence of judicial, legislative, or administrative findings of constitutional or statutory violations. After such findings have been made, the governmental interest, in preferring members of the injured groups at the expense of others is substantial, since the legal rights of the victims must be vindicated. In such a case, the extent of the injury and the consequent remedy will have been judicially, legislatively, or administratively defined. Also, the remedial action usually remains subject to continuing oversight to assure that it will work the least harm possible to other innocent persons competing for the benefit. Without such findings of constitutional or statutory violations, it cannot be said that the government has any greater interest in helping one individual than in refraining from harming another. Thus, the government has no compelling justification for inflicting such harm. . . .

Hence, the purpose of helping certain groups whom the faculty of the Davis Medical School perceived as victims of "societal discrimination" does not justify a classification that imposes disadvantages upon persons like respondent, who bear no responsibility for whatever harm the beneficiaries of the special admissions program are thought to have suffered. To hold otherwise would be to convert a remedy heretofore reserved for violations of legal rights into a privilege that all institutions throughout the Nation could grant at their pleasure to whatever groups are perceived as victims of societal discrimination. That is a step we have never approved.

C

Petitioner identifies, as another purpose of its program, improving the delivery of health-care services to communities currently underserved. It may be assumed that in some situations a State's interest in facilitating the health care of its citizens is sufficiently compelling to support the use of a suspect classification. Btu there is virtually no evidence in the record indicating that petitioner's special admissions program is either needed or geared to promote that goal. The court below addressed this failure of proof:

"The University concedes it cannot assure that minority doctors who entered under the program, all of whom expressed an 'interest' in practicing in a disadvantaged community, will actually do so. It may be correct to assume that some of them will carry out this intention, and that it is more likely they will practice in minority communities than the average white doctor. Nevertheless, there are more precise and reliable ways to identify applicants who are genuinely interested in the medical problems of minorities than by race. An applicant of whatever race who has demonstrated his concern for disadvantaged minorities in the past and who declares that practice in such a community is his primary professional goal would be more likely to contribute to alleviation of the medical shortage than one who is chosen entirely on the basis of race and disadvantage. In short, there is no empirical data to demonstrate that any one race is more selflessly socially oriented or by contrast that another is more selfishly acquisitive."

Petitioner simply has not carried its burden of demonstrating that it must prefer members of particular ethnic groups over all other individuals in order to promote better health-care delivery to deprived citizens. Indeed, petitioner has not shown that its preferential classification is likely to have any significant effect on the problem.

D

The fourth goal asserted by petitioner is the attainment of a diverse student body. This clearly is a constitutionally permissible goal for an institution of higher education. Academic freedom, though not a specifically enumerated constitutional right, long has been viewed as a special concern of the First Amendment. The freedom of a university to make its own judgments as to education includes the selection of its student body. Mr. Justice Frankfurter summarized the "four essential freedoms" that constitute academic freedom:

"'It is the business of a university to provide that atmosphere which is most conducive to speculation, experiment and creation. It is an atmosphere in which there prevail "the four essential freedoms" of a university—to determine for itself on academic grounds who may teach, what may be taught, how it shall be taught, and who may be admitted to study.'"

Our national commitment to the safeguarding of these freedoms within university communities was emphasized in *Keyishian v. Board of Regents* (1967):

"Our Nation is deeply committed to safeguarding academic freedom which is of transcendent value to all of us and not merely to the teachers concerned. That freedom is therefore a special concern of the First Amendment. . . . The Nation's future depends upon leaders trained through wide exposure to that robust exchange of ideas which discovers truth out of a multitude of tongues, [rather] than through any kind of authoritative selection.'"

The atmosphere of "speculation, experiment and creation"—so essential to the quality of higher education—is widely believed to be promoted by a diverse student body. As the Court noted in *Keyishian*, it is not too much to say that the "nation's future depends upon leaders trained through wide exposure" to the ideas and mores of students as diverse as this Nation of many peoples.

Thus, in arguing that its universities must be accorded the right to select those students who will contribute the most to the "robust exchange of ideas," petitioner invokes a countervailing constitutional interest, that of the First Amendment. In this light, petitioner must be viewed as seeking to achieve a goal that is of paramount importance in the fulfillment of its mission.

It may be argued that there is a greater force to these views at the undergraduate level than in a medical school where the training is centered primarily on professional competency. But even at the graduate level, our tradition and experience lend support to the view that the contribution of diversity is substantial. In *Sweatt v. Painter*, the Court made a similar point with specific reference to legal education:

"The law school, the proving ground for legal learning and practice, cannot be effective in isolation from the individuals and institutions with which the law interacts. Few students and no one who has practiced law would choose to study in an academic vacuum, removed from the interplay of ideas and the exchange of views with which the law is concerned."

Physicians serve a heterogeneous population. An otherwise qualified medical student with a particular background—whether it be ethnic, geographic, culturally advantaged or disadvantaged—may bring to a professional school of medicine experiences, outlooks, and ideas that enrich the training of its student body and better equip its graduates to render with understanding their vital service to humanity.

Ethnic diversity, however, is only one element in a range of factors a university properly may consider in attaining the goal of a heterogeneous student body. Although a university must have wide discretion in making the sensitive judgments as to who should be admitted, constitutional limitations protecting individual rights may not be disregarded. Respondent urges—and the courts below have held—that petitioner's dual admissions program is a racial classification that impermissibly infringes his rights under the Fourteenth Amendment. As the interest of diversity is compelling in the context of a university's admissions program, the question remains whether the program's racial classification is necessary to promote this interest.

V

A

It may be assumed that the reservation of a specified number of seats in each class for individuals from the preferred ethnic groups would contribute to the attainment of considerable ethnic diversity in the student body. But petitioner's argument that this is the only effective means of serving the interest of diversity is seriously flawed. In a most fundamental sense the argument misconceives the nature of the state interest that would justify consideration of race or ethnic background. It is not an interest in simple ethnic diversity, in which a specified percentage of the student body is in effect guaranteed to be members of selected ethnic groups, with the remaining percentage an undifferentiated aggregation of students. The diversity that furthers a compelling state interest encompasses a far broader array of qualifications and characteristics of which racial or ethnic origin is but a single though important element. Petitioner's special admissions program, focused *solely* on ethnic diversity, would hinder rather than further attainment of genuine diversity.

Nor would the state interest in genuine diversity be served by expanding petitioner's two-track system into a multitrack program with a prescribed number of seats set aside for each identifiable category of applicants. Indeed, it is inconceivable that a university would thus pursue the logic of petitioner's two-track program to the illogical end of insulating each category of applicants with certain desired qualifications from competition with all other applicants. . . .

B

In summary, it is evident that the Davis special admissions program involves the use of an explicit racial classification never before countenanced by this Court. It tells applicants who are not Negro, Asian, or Chicano that they are totally excluded from a specific percentage of the seats in an entering class. No matter how strong their qualifications, quantitative and extracurricular, including their own potential for contribution to educational diversity, they are never afforded the chance to compete with applicants from the preferred groups for the special admissions seats. At the same time, the preferred applicants have the opportunity to compete for every seat in the class.

The fatal flaw in petitioner's preferential program is its disregard of individual rights as guaranteed by the Fourteenth Amendment. Such rights are not absolute. But when a State's distribution of benefits or imposition of burdens hinges on ancestry or the color of a person's skin, that individual is entitled to a demonstration that the challenged classification is necessary to promote a substantial state interest. Petitioner has failed to carry this burden. For this reason, that portion of the California court's judgment holding petitioner's special admissions program invalid under the Fourteenth Amendment must be affirmed. . . .

Discussion Questions

1. How does Justice Powell justify ruling in favor of Mr. Bakke? Do you agree or disagree with his decision? Explain and defend your answer.

2. Justice Powell claims that quotas could be justified constitutionally if it promotes "a substantial state interest." Think of a possible situation (either a fictional one or a real one) in which Justice Powell's standard for justification of quotas might be met. Do you agree with the Justice that in that situation racial quotas are justified? Why or why not? Explain and defend your answer.

3. A vast majority of public university faculty members in the humanities in the United States are politically to the Left. Do you think it is right in the name of "intellectual diversity" for universities to give preferential treatment to conservative job applicants? Do you think such a hiring scheme would fulfill the *Bakke* court's standard that it must promote "a substantial state interest"? Explain and defend your answer.

Notes

1. In the view of Mr. Justice Brennan, Mr. Justice White, Mr. Justice Marshall, and Mr. Justice Blackmun, the pliable notion of "stigma" is the crucial element in analyzing racial classifications. The Equal Protection Clause is not framed in terms of "stigma." Certainly the word has no clearly defined constitutional meaning. It reflects a subjective judgment that is standardless. *All* state-imposed classifications that rearrange burdens and benefits on the basis of race are likely to be viewed with deep resentment by the individuals burdened. The denial to innocent persons of equal rights and opportunities may outrage those so deprived and therefore may be perceived as invidious. These individuals are likely to find little comfort in the notion that the deprivation they are asked to endure is merely the price of membership in the dominant majority and that its imposition is inspired by the supposedly benign purpose of aiding others. One should not lightly dismiss the inherent unfairness of, and the perception of mistreatment that accompanies, a system of allocating benefits and privileges on the basis of skin color and ethnic origin. Moreover, Mr. Justice Brennan, Mr. Justice White, Mr. Justice Marshall, and Mr. Justice Blackmun offer no principle for deciding whether preferential classifications reflect a benign remedial purpose or a malevolent stigmatic classification, since they are willing in this case to accept mere *post hoc* declarations by an isolated state entity—a medical school faculty—unadorned by particularized findings of past discrimination, to establish such a remedial purpose.

2. Professor Bickel noted the self-contradiction of that view:

> "The lesson of the great decisions of the Supreme Court and the lesson of contemporary history have been the same for at least a generation: discrimination on the basis of race is illegal, immoral, unconstitutional, inherently wrong, and destructive of democratic society. Now this is to be unlearned and we are told that this is not a matter of fundamental principle but only a matter of whose ox is gored. Those for whom racial equality was demanded are to be more equal than others. Having found support in the Constitution for equality, they now claim support for inequality under the same Constitution." A. Bickel, The Morality of Consent 133 (1975).

31

City of Richmond v. Croson (1989)

U.S. Supreme Court

In this decision the U.S. Supreme Court ruled against the city of Richmond, Virginia, whose city council on April 11, 1983, adopted the Minority Business Utilization Plan. The plan obligated prime contractors who had been awarded contracts by the city to subcontract at least 30 percent of the contract's monetary amount to one or more minority business enterprises (MBEs). The plan did not require minority-owned prime contractors, who had been awarded city contracts, to abide by the same regulations. Writing for the majority, Justice Sandra Day O'Connor concluded that the plan was not a constitutionally justified form of preferential treatment. Some of the reasons she gave for this conclusion were the following: (1) statistical disparities in themselves do not prove racial discrimination; (2) there was no particular case of injury resulting from racial discrimination the plan was trying to rectify; and (3) there was no evidence that other minorities included in the plan (Spanish-speaking, Oriental, Indian, Eskimo, or Aleut) had been discriminated by Richmond's construction industry. This chapter also includes Justice Antonin Scalia's concurring judgment, in which he goes further than Justice O'Connor and argues that preferential treatment based on the race of the beneficiary is *never justified*. Only *identifiable victims* of discrimination, racial or otherwise, have a right to receive reparations from their *identifiable victimizers*, whether a government agency, a private individual, or an employer. Justice Scalia also maintains that a state can act to "'undo the effects of past discrimination' in many permissible ways that do not involve classification by race." He then cites some examples. Justice Thurgood Marshall's dissent ends this chapter. He provides a number of reasons why he believes that the majority decision is a "deliberate and giant step backward in this Court's affirmative action jurisprudence."

Justice O'Connor announced the judgment of the Court and delivered the opinion of the Court with respect to Parts I, III-B, and IV, an opinion with respect to Part II, in which the Chief Justice and Justice White join, and an opinion with respect to Parts III-A and V, in which the Chief Justice, Justice White and Justice Kennedy join.

In this case, we confront once again the tension between the Fourteenth Amendment's guarantee of equal treatment to all citizens, and the use of race-based measures to ameliorate the effects of past discrimination on the opportunities enjoyed by members of minority groups in our society. In *Fullilove v. Klutznick* (1980), we held that a congressional program requiring that 10% of certain federal construction grants be awarded to minority contractors did not violate the equal protection principles embodied in the Due Process Clause of the Fifth Amendment. Relying largely on our decision in *Fullilove*, some lower federal courts have applied a similar standard of review in assessing the constitutionality of state and local minority set-aside provisions under the Equal Protection Clause of the Fourteenth Amendment. . . .

I

On April 11, 1983, the Richmond City Council adopted the Minority Business Utilization Plan (the Plan). The Plan required prime contractors to whom the city awarded construction contracts to subcontract at least 30% of the dollar amount of the contract to one or more Minority Business Enterprises (MBEs). The 30% set-aside did not apply to city contracts awarded to minority-owned prime contractors.

The Plan defined an MBE as "[a] business at least fifty-one (51) percent of which is owned and controlled . . . by minority group members." "Minority group members" were defined as "[c]itizens of the United States who are Blacks, Spanish-speaking, Orientals, Indians, Eskimos, or Aleuts." There was no geographic limit to the Plan; an otherwise qualified MBE from anywhere in the United States could avail itself of the 30% set-aside. The Plan declared that it was "remedial" in nature, and enacted "for the purpose of promoting wider participation by minority business enterprises in the construction of public projects." The Plan expired on June 30, 1988, and was in effect for approximately five years. . . .

[II . . .]

III

A

The Equal Protection Clause of the Fourteenth Amendment provides that "[N]o State shall . . . deny to *any person* within its jurisdiction the equal protection of the laws" (emphasis added). As this Court has noted in the past, the "rights created by the first section of the Fourteenth Amendment are, by its terms, guaranteed to the individual. The rights established are personal rights." The Richmond Plan denies certain citizens the opportunity to compete for a fixed percentage of public contracts based solely upon their race. To whatever racial group these citizens belong, their "personal rights" to be treated with equal dignity and respect are implicated by a rigid rule erecting race as the sole criterion in an aspect of public decisionmaking.

Absent searching judicial inquiry into the justification for such race-based measures, there is simply no way of determining what classifications are "benign" or "remedial" and what classifications are in fact motivated by illegitimate notions of racial inferiority or simple racial politics. Indeed, the purpose of strict scrutiny is to "smoke out" illegitimate uses of race by assuring that the legislative body is pursuing a goal important enough to warrant use of a highly suspect tool. The test also ensures that the means chosen "fit" this compelling goal so closely that there is little or no possibility that the motive for the classification was illegitimate racial prejudice or stereotype.

Classifications based on race carry a danger of stigmatic harm. Unless they are strictly reserved for remedial settings, they may in fact promote notions of racial inferiority and lead to a politics of racial hostility. We thus reaffirm the view expressed by the plurality in *Wygant* that the standard of review under the Equal Protection Clause is not dependent on the race of those burdened or benefited by a particular classification.

Our continued adherence to the standard of review employed in *Wygant*, does not, as Justice Marshall's dissent suggests, indicate that we view "racial discrimination as largely a phenomenon of the past" or that "government bodies need no longer preoccupy themselves with rectifying racial injustice." As we indicate below States and their local subdivisions have many legislative weapons at their disposal both to punish and prevent present discrimination and to remove arbitrary barriers to minority advancement. Rather, our interpretation of § 1 stems from our agreement with the view expressed by Justice Powell in *Bakke*, that "[t]he guarantee of equal protection cannot mean one thing when applied to one individual and something else when applied to a person of another color."

Under the standard proposed by Justice Marshall's dissent, "[r]ace-conscious classifications designed to further remedial goals," are forthwith subject to a relaxed standard of review. How the dissent arrives at the legal conclusion that a racial classification is "designed to further remedial goals," without first engaging in an examination of the factual basis for its enactment and the nexus between its scope and that factual basis we are not told. However, once the "remedial" conclusion is reached, the dissent's standard is singularly deferential, and bears little resemblance to the close examination of legislative purpose we have engaged in when reviewing classifications based either on race or gender. The dissent's watered-down version of equal protection review effectively assures that race will always be relevant in American life, and that the "ultimate goal" of "eliminat[ing] entirely from governmental decisionmaking such irrelevant factors as a human being's race" will never be achieved.

Even were we to accept a reading of the guarantee of equal protection under which the level of scrutiny varies according to the ability of different groups to defend their interests in the representative process, heightened scrutiny would still be appropriate in the circumstances of this case. One of the central arguments for applying a less exacting standard to "benign" racial classifications is that such measures essentially involve a choice made by dominant racial groups to disadvantage themselves. If one aspect of the judiciary's role under the Equal Protection Clause is to protect "discrete and insular minorities" from majoritarian prejudice or indifference, some maintain that these concerns are not implicated when the "white majority" places burdens upon itself.

In this case, blacks comprise approximately 50% of the population of the city of Richmond. Five of the nine seats on the City Council are held by blacks. The concern that a political majority will more easily act to the disadvantage of a minority based on unwarranted assumptions or incomplete facts would seem to militate for, not against, the application of heightened judicial scrutiny in this case.

In *Bakke*, the Court confronted a racial quota employed by the University of California at Davis Medical School. Under the plan, 16 out of 100 seats in each entering class at the school were reserved exclusively for certain minority groups. Among the justifications offered in support of the plan were the desire to "reduc[e] the historic deficit of traditionally disfavored minorities in medical school and the medical profession" and the need to "counte[r] the effects of societal discrimination." Five Members of the Court determined that none of these interests could justify a plan that completely eliminated non-minorities from consideration for a specified percentage of opportunities.

Justice Powell's opinion applied heightened scrutiny under the Equal Protection Clause to the racial classification at issue. His opinion decisively rejected the first justification for the racially segregated admissions plan. The desire to have more black medical students or doctors, standing alone, was not merely insufficiently compelling to justify a racial classification, it was "discrimination for its own sake," forbidden by the Constitution. Nor could the second concern, the history of discrimination in society at large, justify a racial quota in medical school admissions. Justice Powell contrasted the "focused" goal of remedying "wrongs worked by specific instances of racial discrimination" with "the remedying of the effects of 'societal discrimination,' an amorphous concept of injury that may be ageless in its reach into the past." He indicated that for the governmental interest in remedying past discrimination to be triggered "judicial, legislative, or administrative findings of constitutional or statutory violations" must be made. Only then does the Government have a compelling interest in favoring one race over another.

In *Wygant* (1986), four Members of the Court applied heightened scrutiny to a race-based system of employee layoffs. Justice Powell, writing for the plurality, again drew the distinction between "societal discrimination" which is an inadequate basis for race-conscious classifications, and the type of identified discrimination that can support and define the scope of race-based relief. The challenged classification in that case tied the layoff of minority teachers to the percentage of minority students enrolled in the school district. The lower courts had upheld the scheme, based on the theory that minority students were in need of "role models" to alleviate the effects of prior discrimination in society. This Court reversed, with a plurality of four Justices reiterating the view expressed by Justice Powell in *Bakke* that "[s]ocietal discrimination, without more, is too amorphous a basis for imposing a racially classified remedy."

The role model theory employed by the lower courts failed for two reasons. First, the statistical disparity between students and teachers had no probative value in demonstrating the kind of prior discrimination in hiring or promotion that would justify race-based relief. Second, because the role model theory had no relation to some basis for believing a constitutional or statutory violation had occurred, it could be used to "justify" race-based decisionmaking essentially limitless in scope and duration.

B

We think it clear that the factual predicate offered in support of the Richmond Plan suffers from the same two defects identified as fatal in *Wygant*. The District Court found the city council's "findings sufficient to ensure that, in adopting the Plan, it was remedying the present effects of past discrimination in the *construction industry*" (emphasis added). Like the "role model" theory employed in *Wygant*, a generalized assertion that there has been past discrimination in an entire industry provides no guidance for a legislative body to determine the precise scope of the injury it seeks to remedy. It "has no logical stopping point." "Relief" for such an ill-defined wrong could extend until the percentage of public contracts awarded to MBEs in Richmond mirrored the percentage of minorities in the population as a whole.

Appellant argues that it is attempting to remedy various forms of past discrimination that are alleged to be responsible for the small number of minority businesses in the local contracting industry. Among these the city cites the exclusion of blacks from skilled construction trade unions and training programs. This past discrimination has prevented them "from following the traditional path from laborer to entrepreneur." The city also lists a host of nonracial factors which would seem to face a member of any racial group attempting to establish a new business enterprise, such as deficiencies in working capital, inability to meet bonding requirements, unfamiliarity with bidding procedures, and disability caused by an inadequate track record.

While there is no doubt that the sorry history of both private and public discrimination in this country has contributed to a lack of opportunities for black entrepreneurs, this observation, standing alone, cannot justify a rigid racial quota in the awarding of medical school admissions, an amorphous claim that there has been past discrimination in a particular industry cannot justify the use of an unyielding racial quota.

It is sheer speculation how many minority firms there would be in Richmond absent past societal discrimination, just as it was sheer speculation how many minority medical students would have been admitted to the medical school at Davis absent past discrimination in educational opportunities. Defining these sorts of injuries as "identified discrimination" would give local governments license to create a patchwork of racial preferences based on statistical generalizations about any particular field of endeavor.

These defects are readily apparent in this case. The 30% quota cannot in any realistic sense be tied to any injury suffered by anyone. The District Court relied upon five predicate "facts" in reaching its conclusion that there was an adequate basis for the 30% quota: (1) the ordinance declares itself to be remedial; (2) several proponents of the measure stated their views that there had been past discrimination in the construction industry; (3) minority businesses received .67% of prime contracts from the city while minorities constituted 50% of the city's population; (4) there were very few minority contractors in local and state contractors' associations; and (5) in 1977, Congress made a determination that the effects of past discrimination had stifled minority participation in the construction industry nationally.

None of these "findings," singly or together, provide the city of Richmond with a "strong basis in evidence for its conclusion that remedial action was necessary." There is nothing approaching a prima facie case of a constitutional or statutory violation by *anyone* in the Richmond construction industry.

The District Court accorded great weight to the fact that the city council designated the Plan as "remedial." But the mere recitation of a "benign" or legitimate purpose for a racial classification is entitled to little or no weight. Racial classifications are suspect, and that means that simple legislative assurances of good intention cannot suffice.

The District Court also relied on the highly conclusionary statement of a proponent of the Plan that there was racial discrimination in the construction industry "in this area, and the State, and around the nation." It also noted that the city manager had related his view that racial discrimination still

plagued the construction industry in his home city of Pittsburgh. These statements are of little probative value in establishing identified discrimination in the Richmond construction industry. The factfinding process of legislative bodies is generally entitled to a presumption of regularity and deferential review by the judiciary. But when a legislative body chooses to employ a suspect classification, it cannot rest upon a generalized assertion as to the classification's relevance to its goals. A governmental actor cannot render race a legitimate proxy for a particular condition merely by declaring that the condition exists. The history of racial classifications in this country suggests that blind judicial deference to legislative or executive pronouncements of necessity has no place in equal protection analysis.

Reliance on the disparity between the number of prime contracts awarded to minority firms and the minority population of the city of Richmond is similarly misplaced. There is no doubt that "[w]here gross statistical disparities can be shown, they alone in a proper case may constitute prima facie proof of a pattern or practice of discrimination" under Title VII. But it is equally clear that "[w]hen special qualifications are required to fill particular jobs, comparisons to the general population (rather than to the smaller group of individuals who possess the necessary qualifications) may have little probative value."

In the employment context, we have recognized that for certain entry level positions or positions requiring minimal training, statistical comparisons of the racial composition of the relevant population may be probative of a pattern of discrimination. But where special qualifications are necessary, the relevant statistical pool for purposes of demonstrating discriminatory exclusion must be the number of minorities qualified to undertake the particular task.

In this case, the city does not even know how many MBEs in the relevant market are qualified to undertake prime or subcontracting work in public construction projects. . . . Nor does the city know what percentage of total city construction dollars minority firms now receive as subcontractors on prime contracts let by the city.

To a large extent, the set-aside of subcontracting dollars seems to rest on the unsupported assumption that white prime contractors simply will not hire minority firms. Indeed, there is evidence in this record that overall minority participation in city contracts in Richmond is seven to eight percent, and that minority contractor participation in Community Block Development Grant *construction* projects is 17%

to 22%. Without any information on minority participation in subcontracting, it is quite simply impossible to evaluate overall minority representation in the city's construction expenditures.

The city and the District Court also relied on evidence that MBE membership in local contractors' associations was extremely low. Again, standing alone this evidence is not probative of any discrimination in the local construction industry. There are numerous explanations for this dearth of minority participation, including past societal discrimination in education and economic opportunities as well as both black and white career and entrepreneurial choices. Blacks may be disproportionately attracted to industries other than construction. The mere fact that black membership in these trade organizations is low, standing alone, cannot establish a prima facie case of discrimination.

For low minority membership in these associations to be relevant, the city would have to link it to the number of local MBEs eligible for membership. If the statistical disparity between eligible MBEs and MBE membership were great enough, an inference of discriminatory exclusion could arise. In such a case, the city would have a compelling interest in preventing its tax dollars from assisting these organizations in maintaining a racially segregated construction market.

Finally, the city and the District Court relied on Congress' finding in connection with the set-aside approved in *Fullilove* that there had been nationwide discrimination in the construction industry. The probative value of these findings for demonstrating the existence of discrimination in Richmond is extremely limited. By its inclusion of a waiver procedure in the national program addressed in *Fullilove*, Congress explicitly recognized that the scope of the problem would vary from market area to market area. . . .

In sum, none of the evidence presented by the city points to any identified discrimination in the Richmond construction industry. We, therefore, hold that the city has failed to demonstrate a compelling interest in apportioning public contracting opportunities on the basis of race. To accept Richmond's claim that past societal discrimination alone can serve as the basis for rigid racial preferences would be to open the door to competing claims for "remedial relief" for every disadvantaged group. The dream of a Nation of equal citizens in a society where race is irrelevant to personal opportunity and achievement would be lost in a mosaic of shifting preferences based on inherently unmeasurable claims of past wrongs. "Courts would be asked to evaluate the extent of the prejudice and consequent harm suffered by various minority groups. Those whose societal injury is thought to exceed some arbitrary level of tolerability then would be entitled to preferential classifications. . . ." We think such a result would be contrary to both the letter and spirit of a constitutional provision whose central command is equality.

The foregoing analysis applies only to the inclusion of blacks within the Richmond set-aside program. There is *absolutely no evidence* of past discrimination against Spanish-speaking, Oriental, Indian, Eskimo, or Aleut persons in any aspect of the Richmond construction industry. The District Court took judicial notice of the fact that the vast majority of "minority" persons in Richmond were black. It may well be that Richmond has never had an Aleut or Eskimo citizen. The random inclusion of racial groups that, as a practical matter, may never have suffered from discrimination in the construction industry in Richmond, suggests that perhaps the city's purpose was not in fact to remedy past discrimination.

If a 30% set-aside was "narrowly tailored" to compensate black contractors for past discrimination, one may legitimately ask why they are forced to share this "remedial relief" with an Aleut citizen who moves to Richmond tomorrow? The gross over-inclusiveness of Richmond's racial preference strongly impugns the city's claim of remedial motivation.

IV

As noted by the court below, it is almost impossible to assess whether the Richmond Plan is narrowly tailored to remedy prior discrimination since it is not linked to identified discrimination in any way. We limit ourselves to two observations in this regard.

First, there does not appear to have been any consideration of the use of race-neutral means to increase minority business participation in city contracting. Many of the barriers to minority participation in the construction industry relied upon by the city to justify a racial classification appear to be race neutral. If MBEs disproportionately lack capital or cannot meet bonding requirements, a race-neutral program of city financing for small firms would, *a fortiori*, lead to greater minority participation. The principal opinion in *Fullilove* found that Congress had carefully examined and rejected race-neutral alternatives before enacting the MBE set-aside. There is no evidence in this record that the Richmond City Council has considered any alternatives to a race-based quota.

Second, the 30% quota cannot be said to be narrowly tailored to any goal, except perhaps outright racial balancing. It rests upon the "completely unrealistic" assumption that minorities will choose a particular trade in lockstep proportion to their representation in the local population.

Since the city must already consider bids and waivers on a case-by-case basis, it is difficult to see the need for a rigid numerical quota. As noted above, the congressional scheme upheld in *Fullilove* allowed for a waiver of the set-aside provision where an MBE's higher price was not attributable to the effects of past discrimination. Based upon proper findings, such programs are less problematic from an equal protection standpoint because they treat all candidates individually, rather than making the color of an applicant's skin the sole relevant consideration. Unlike the program upheld in *Fullilove*, the Richmond Plan's waiver system focuses solely on the availability of MBEs; there is no inquiry into whether or not the particular MBE seeking a racial preference has suffered from the effects of past discrimination by the city or prime contractors.

Given the existence of an individualized procedure, the city's only interest in maintaining a quota system rather than investigating the need for remedial action in particular cases would seem to be simple administrative convenience. But the interest in avoiding the bureaucratic effort necessary to tailor remedial relief to those who truly have suffered the effects of prior discrimination cannot justify a rigid line drawn on the basis of a suspect classification. Under Richmond's scheme, a successful black, Hispanic, or Oriental entrepreneur from anywhere in the country enjoys an absolute preference over other citizens based solely on their race. We think it obvious that such a program is not narrowly tailored to remedy the effects of prior discrimination.

Justice Scalia, concurring in the judgment.

I agree with much of the Court's opinion, and, in particular, with its conclusion that strict scrutiny must be applied to all governmental classification by race, whether or not its asserted purpose is "remedial" or "benign." I do not agree, however, with the Court's dicta suggesting that, despite the Fourteenth Amendment, state and local governments may in some circumstances discriminate on the basis of race in order (in a broad sense) "to ameliorate the effects of past discrimination." The benign purpose of compensating for social disadvantages, whether they have been acquired by reason of prior discrimination or otherwise, can no more be pursued by the illegitimate means of racial discrimination than can other assertedly benign purposes we have repeatedly rejected. The difficulty of overcoming the effects of past discrimination is as nothing compared with the difficulty of eradicating from our society the source of those effects, which is the tendency—fatal to a nation such as ours—to classify and judge men and women on the basis of their country of origin or the color of their skin. A solution to the first problem that aggravates the second is no solution at all. I share the view expressed by Alexander Bickel that "[t]he lesson of the great decisions of the Supreme Court and the lesson of contemporary history have been the same for at least a generation: discrimination on the basis of race is illegal, immoral, unconstitutional, inherently wrong, and destructive of democratic society." At least where state or local action is at issue, only a social emergency rising to the level of imminent danger to life and limb—for example, a prison race riot, requiring temporary segregation of inmates—can justify an exception to the principle embodied in the Fourteenth Amendment that "[o]ur Constitution is color-blind, and neither knows nor tolerates classes among citizens." . . .

In my view there is only one circumstance in which the States may act *by race* to "undo the effects of past discrimination" where that is necessary to eliminate their own maintenance of a system of unlawful racial classification. If, for example, a state agency has a discriminatory pay scale compensating black employees in all positions at 20% less than their nonblack counterparts, it may assuredly promulgate an order raising the salaries of "all black employees" by 20%. This distinction explains our school desegregation cases, in which we have made plain that States and localities sometimes have an obligation to adopt race-conscious remedies. . . .

A State can, of course, act "to undo the effects of past discrimination" in many permissible ways that do not involve classification by race. In the particular field of state contracting, for example, it may adopt a preference for small businesses, or even for new businesses—which would make it easier for those previously excluded by discrimination to enter the field. Such programs may well have racially disproportionate impact, but they are not based on race.

And, of course, a State may "undo the effects of past discrimination" in the sense of giving the identified victim of state discrimination that which it wrongfully denied him—for example, giving to a previously rejected black applicant the job that, by reason of discrimination, had been awarded to a white applicant, even if this means terminating the latter's employment. In such a context, the white job-holder is not being selected for disadvantageous treatment because of his race, but because he was wrongfully awarded a job to which another is entitled. That is worlds apart from the system here, in which those to be disadvantaged are identified solely by race.

I agree with the Court's dictum that a fundamental distinction must be drawn between the effects of "societal" discrimination and the effects of "identified" discrimination, and that the situation would be different if Richmond's plan were "tailored" to identify those particular bidders who "suffered from the effects of past discrimination by the city or prime contractors." In my view, however, the reason that would make a difference is not, as the Court states, that it would justify race-conscious action, but rather that it would enable race-neutral remediation. Nothing prevents Richmond from according a contracting preference to identified victims of discrimination. While most of the beneficiaries might be black, neither the beneficiaries nor those disadvantaged by the preference would be identified *on the basis of their race*. In other words, far from justifying racial classification, identification of actual victims of discrimination makes it less supportable than ever, because more obviously unneeded.

In his final book, Professor Bickel wrote:

> "[A] racial quota derogates the human dignity and individuality of all to whom it is applied; it is invidious in principle as well as in practice. Moreover, it can easily be turned against those it purports to help. The history of the racial quota is a history of subjugation, not beneficence. Its evil lies not in its name, but in its effects: a quota is a divider of society, a creator of castes, and it is all the worse for its racial base, especially in a society desperately striving for an equality that will make race irrelevant."

Those statements are true and increasingly prophetic. Apart from their societal effects, however, which are "in the aggregate disastrous," it is important not to lose sight of the fact that even "benign" racial quotas have individual victims, whose very real injustice we ignore whenever we deny them enforcement of their right not to be disadvantaged on the basis of race. As Justice Douglas observed: "A DeFunis who is white is entitled to no advantage by virtue of that fact; nor is he subject to any disability, no matter what his race or color. Whatever his race, he had a constitutional right to have his application considered on its individual merits in a racially neutral manner." When we depart from this American principle we play with fire, and much more than an occasional DeFunis, Johnson, or Croson burns.

It is plainly true that in our society blacks have suffered discrimination immeasurably greater than any directed at other racial groups. But those who believe that racial preferences can help to "even the score" display, and reinforce, a manner of thinking by race that was the source of the injustice and that will, if it endures within our society, be the source of more injustice still. The relevant proposition is not that it was blacks, or Jews, or Irish who were discriminated against, but that it was individual men and women, "created equal," who were discriminated against. And the relevant resolve is that that should never happen again. Racial preferences appear to "even the score" (in some small degree) only if one embraces the proposition that our society is appropriately viewed as divided into races, making it right that an injustice rendered in the past to a black man should be compensated for by discriminating against a white. Nothing is worth that embrace. Since blacks have been disproportionately disadvantaged by racial discrimination, any race-neutral remedial program aimed at the disadvantaged *as such* will have a disproportionately beneficial impact on blacks. Only such a program, and not one that operates on the basis of race, is in accord with the letter and the spirit of our Constitution. . . .

Justice Marshall, with whom Justice Brennan and Justice Blackmun join, dissenting.

It is a welcome symbol of racial progress when the former capital of the Confederacy acts forthrightly to confront the effects of racial discrimination in its midst. In my view, nothing in the Constitution can be construed to prevent Richmond, Virginia, from allocating a portion of its contracting dollars for businesses owned or controlled by members of minority groups. Indeed, Richmond's set-aside program is distinguishable in all meaningful respects from—and in fact was patterned upon—the federal set-aside plan which this Court upheld in *Fullilove v. Klutznick* (1980).

A majority of this Court holds today, however, that the Equal Protection Clause of the Fourteenth Amendment blocks Richmond's initiative. The essence of the majority's position is that Richmond has failed to catalogue adequate findings to prove that past discrimination has impeded minorities from joining or participating fully in Richmond's construction contracting industry. I find deep irony in second-guessing Richmond's judgment on this point. As much as any municipality in the United States, Richmond knows what racial discrimination is; a century of decisions by this and other federal courts has richly documented the city's disgraceful history of public and private racial discrimination. In any event, the Richmond City Council *has* supported its determination that minorities have been wrongly excluded from local construction contracting. Its proof includes statistics showing that minority-owned businesses have received virtually no city contracting dollars and rarely if ever belonged to area trade associations; testimony by municipal officials that discrimination has been widespread in the local construction industry; and the same exhaustive and widely publicized federal studies relied on in *Fullilove*, studies which showed that pervasive discrimination in the Nation's tight-knit construction industry had operated to exclude minorities from public contracting. These are precisely the types of statistical and testimonial evidence which, until today, this Court had credited in cases approving of race-conscious measures designed to remedy past discrimination.

More fundamentally, today's decision marks a deliberate and giant step backward in this Court's affirmative action jurisprudence. Cynical of one municipality's attempt to redress the effects of past racial discrimination in a particular industry, the majority launches a grapeshot attack on race-conscious remedies in general. The majority's unnecessary pronouncements will inevitably discourage or prevent governmental entities, particularly States and localities, from acting to rectify the scourge of past discrimination. This is the harsh reality of the majority's decision, but it is not the Constitution's command.

[I . . .]

II

"Agreement upon a means for applying the Equal Protection Clause to an affirmative-action program has eluded this Court every time the issue has come before us." My view has long been that race-conscious classifications designed to further remedial goals "must serve important governmental objectives and must be substantially related to achievement of those objectives" in order to withstand constitutional scrutiny. Analyzed in terms of this two-prong standard, Richmond's set-aside, like the federal program on which it was modeled, is "plainly constitutional."

A

1

Turning first to the governmental interest inquiry, Richmond has two powerful interests in setting aside a portion of public contracting funds for minority-owned enterprises. The first is the city's interest in eradicating the effects of past racial discrimination. It is far too late in the day to doubt that remedying such discrimination is a compelling, let alone an important, interest. In *Fullilove*, six members of this Court deemed this interest sufficient to support a race-conscious set-aside program governing federal contract procurement. The decision, in holding that the federal set-aside provision satisfied the Equal Protection Clause under any level of scrutiny, recognized that the measure sought to remove "barriers to competitive access which had their roots in racial and ethnic discrimination, and which continue today, even absent any intentional discrimination or unlawful conduct." Indeed, we have repeatedly reaffirmed the government's interest in breaking down barriers erected by past racial discrimination, in cases involving access to public education, employment, and valuable government contracts.

Richmond has a second compelling interest in setting aside, where possible, a portion of its contracting dollars. That interest is the prospective one of preventing the city's own spending decisions from reinforcing and perpetuating the exclusionary effects of past discrimination.

The majority pays only lip service to this additional governmental interest. But our decisions have often emphasized the danger of the government tacitly adopting, encouraging, or furthering racial discrimination even by its own routine operations. In *Shelley v. Kraemer* (1948), this Court recognized this interest as a constitutional command, holding unanimously that the Equal Protection Clause forbids courts to enforce racially restrictive covenants even where such covenants satisfied all requirements of state law and where the State harbored no discriminatory intent. Similarly, in *Norwood v. Harrison* (1973), we invalidated a program in which a State purchased textbooks and loaned them to students in public and private schools, including private schools with racially discriminatory policies. We stated that the Constitution requires a State "to steer clear, not only of operating the old dual system of racially segregated schools, but also of giving significant aid to institutions that practice racial or other invidious discrimination."

The majority is wrong to trivialize the continuing impact of government acceptance or use of private institutions or structures once wrought by discrimination. When government channels all its contracting funds to a white-dominated community of established contractors whose racial homogeneity is the product of private discrimination, it does more than place its imprimatur on the practices which forged and which continue to define that community. It also provides a measurable boost to those economic entities that have thrived within it, while denying important economic benefits to those entities which, but for prior discrimination, might well be better qualified to receive valuable government contracts. In my view, the interest in ensuring that the government does not reflect and reinforce prior private discrimination in dispensing public contracts is every bit as strong as the interest in eliminating private discrimination—an interest which this court has repeatedly deemed compelling. The more government bestows its rewards on those persons or businesses that were positioned to thrive during a period of private racial discrimination, the tighter the dead-hand grip of prior discrimination becomes on the present and future. Cities like Richmond may not be constitutionally required to adopt set-aside plans. But there can be no doubt that when Richmond acted affirmatively to stem the perpetuation of patterns of discrimination through its own decisionmaking, it served an interest of the highest order.

[2 . . .]

B

In my judgment, Richmond's set-aside plan also comports with the second prong of the equal protection inquiry, for it is substantially related to the interests it seeks to serve in remedying past discrimination and in ensuring that municipal contract procurement does not perpetuate that discrimination. The most striking aspect of the city's ordinance is the similarity it bears to the "appropriately limited" federal set-aside provision upheld in *Fullilove*. Like the federal provision, Richmond's is limited to five years in duration and was not renewed when it came up for reconsideration in 1988. Like the federal provision, Richmond's contains a waiver provision freeing from its subcontracting requirements those nonminority firms that demonstrate that they cannot comply with its provisions. Like the federal provision, Richmond's has a minimal impact on innocent third parties. While the measure affects 30% of *public* contracting dollars, that translates to only 3% of overall Richmond area contracting.

Finally, like the federal provision, Richmond's does not interfere with any vested right of a contractor to a particular contract; instead it operates entirely prospectively. Richmond's initiative affects only future economic arrangements and imposes only a diffuse burden on nonminority competitors— here, businesses owned or controlled by nonminorities which seek subcontracting work on public construction projects. The plurality in *Wygant* emphasized the importance of this not disrupting the settled and legitimate expectations of innocent parties. "While hiring goals impose a diffuse burden, often foreclosing only one of several opportunities, layoffs impose the entire burden of achieving racial equality on particular individuals, often resulting in serious disruption of their lives. That burden is too intrusive."

These factors, far from "justify[ing] a preference of any size or duration," are precisely the factors to which this Court looked in *Fullilove*. The majority takes issue, however, with two aspects of Richmond's tailoring: the city's refusal to explore the use of race-neutral measures to increase minority business participation in contracting and the selection of a 30% set-aside figure. The majority's first criticism is flawed in two respects. First, the majority overlooks the fact that since 1975, Richmond has barred both discrimination by the city in awarding public contracts and discrimination by public contractors. The virtual absence of minority businesses from the city's contracting rolls, indicated by the fact that such businesses have received less than 1% of public contracting dollars, strongly suggests that this ban has not succeeded in redressing the impact of past discrimination or in preventing city contract procurement from reinforcing racial homogeneity. Second, the majority's suggestion that Richmond should have first undertaken such race-neutral measures as a program of city financing for small firms ignores the fact that such measures, while theoretically appealing, have been discredited by Congress as ineffectual in eradicating the effects of past discrimination in this very industry. For this reason, this Court in *Fullilove* refused to fault Congress for not undertaking race-neutral measures as precursors to its race-conscious set-aside. The Equal Protection Clause does not require Richmond to retrace Congress' steps when Congress has found that those steps lead nowhere. Given the well-exposed limitations of race-neutral measures, it was thus appropriate for a municipality like Richmond to conclude that, in the words of Justice Blackmun, "[i]n order to get beyond racism, we must first take account of race. There is no other way."

As for Richmond's 30% target, the majority states that this figure "cannot be said to be narrowly tailored to any goal, except perhaps outright racial balancing." The majority ignores two important facts. First, the set-aside measure affects only 3% of overall city contracting; thus, any imprecision in tailoring has far less impact than the majority suggests. But more important, the majority ignores the fact that Richmond's 30% figure was patterned directly on the *Fullilove* precedent. Congress' 10% figure fell "roughly halfway between the present percentage of minority contractors and the percentage of minority group members in the Nation." The Richmond city Council's 30% figure similarly falls roughly halfway between the present percentage of Richmond-based minority contractors (almost zero) and the percentage of minorities in Richmond (50%). In faulting Richmond for not presenting a different explanation for its choice of a set-aside figure, the majority honors *Fullilove* only in the breach.

III

I would ordinarily end my analysis at this point and conclude that Richmond's ordinance satisfies both the governmental interest and substantial relationship prongs of our Equal Protection Clause analysis. However, I am compelled to add more, for the majority has gone beyond the facts of this case to announce a set of principles which unnecessarily restrict the power of governmental entities to take race-conscious measures to redress the effects of prior discrimination.

A

Today, for the first time, a majority of this Court has adopted strict scrutiny as its standard of Equal Protection Clause review of race-conscious remedial measures. This is an unwelcome development. A profound difference separates governmental actions that themselves are racist, and governmental actions that seek to remedy the effects of prior racism or to prevent neutral governmental activity from perpetuating the effects of such racism.

Racial classifications "drawn on the presumption that one race is inferior to another or because they put the weight of government behind racial hatred and separatism" warrant the strictest judicial scrutiny because of the very irrelevance of these rationales. By contrast, racial classifications drawn for the purpose of remedying the effects of discrimination that itself was race-based have a highly pertinent basis: the tragic and indelible fact that discrimination against blacks and other racial minorities in this Nation has pervaded our Nation's history and continues to scar our society. As I stated in *Fullilove*: "Because the consideration of race is relevant to remedying the continuing effects of past racial discrimination, and because governmental programs employing racial classifications for remedial purposes can be crafted to avoid stigmatization, . . . such programs should not be subjected to conventional 'strict scrutiny'—scrutiny that is strict in theory, but fatal in fact."

In concluding that remedial classifications warrant no different standard of review under the Constitution than the most brute and repugnant forms of state-sponsored racism, a majority of this Court signals that it regards racial discrimination as largely a phenomenon of the past, and that government bodies need no longer preoccupy themselves with rectifying racial injustice. I, however, do not believe this Nation is anywhere close to eradicating racial discrimination or its vestiges. In constitutionalizing its wishful thinking, the majority today does a grave disservice not only to those victims of past and present racial discrimination in this Nation whom government has sought to assist, but also to this Court's long tradition of approaching issues of race with the utmost sensitivity.

Discussion Questions

1. Justice O'Connor believes that the city of Richmond's plan failed constitutional muster for a number of reasons. Present and explain those reasons. In his dissent, Justice Marshall challenges Justice O'Connor's position. Present and explain his case. Who do you think makes the better argument? Explain and defend our answer.

2. What are the grounds on which Justice Scalia objects to racial quotas that were not given in Justice O'Connor's opinion? Do you agree or disagree with these grounds? Explain and defend your answer.

3. Justice Marshall objects to the application of "strict scrutiny" in the majority opinion. Why does he think this way? Do you agree or disagree with his case? Explain and defend your answer.

The Moral Justification of Affirmative Action

32

A Defense of Programs of Preferential Treatment

Richard Wasserstrom

Richard Wasserstrom is Professor of Philosophy at the University of California at Santa Cruz. He has written extensively in professional journals in the areas of ethics and social philosophy. Among his books are *War and Morality* (1970) and *Philosophy and Social Issues* (1980).

In this essay Professor Wasserstrom presents a limited moral defense of affirmative action that entails preferential treatment of members of groups traditionally discriminated against (e.g., blacks, Hispanics, women) in hiring. Although he admits that he is not attempting to establish that preferential treatment programs are right and desirable, he is arguing that two of the arguments proposed by those who oppose preferential treatment do not work. The first argument is the argument from *intellectual inconsistency*: proponents of preferential treatment "programs are guilty of intellectual inconsistency," since they propose to use criteria (race and sex), in order to help minorities, that they condemn when used by bigots *against* minorities. Professor Wasserstrom responds to this argument by saying that what made and makes discrimination against minorities wrong is that it denies them

positions of social and political power in society; that is not happening to non-minorities when a job or an academic admission is given to a minority due to a preferential treatment program. The second argument is the argument from *an individual's qualifications*: "preferential treatment programs are wrong because they take race or sex into account rather than the only thing that does matter—that is, an individual's qualifications." Professor Wasserstrom provides three responses: (1) in jobs of substantial power and authority there is no serious "qualification requirement"; (2) if qualification is the same as "good consequences for the employer," then one must accept preferential treatment programs if they result in good consequences; and (3) nobody deserves or is entitled to a position simply because they are "qualified."

Many justifications of programs of preferential treatment depend upon the claim that in one respect or another such programs have good consequences or that they are effective means by which to bring about one desirable end, e.g., an integrated, equalitarian society. I mean by "programs of preferential treatment" to refer to programs such as those at issue in the *Bakke* case—programs which set aside a certain number of places (for example, in a law school) as to which members of minority groups (for example, persons who are non-white or female) who possess certain minimum qualifications (in terms of grades and test scores) may be preferred for admission to those places over some members of the majority group who possess higher qualifications (in terms of grades and test scores).

Many criticisms of programs of preferential treatment claim that such programs, even if effective, are unjustifiable because they are in some important sense unfair or unjust. In this paper I present a limited defense of such programs by showing that two of the chief arguments offered for the unfairness or injustice of these programs do not work in the way or to the degree supposed by critics of these programs.

Reprinted by permission from *National Forum: The Phi Kappa Phi Journal* 58 (Winter 1978). This originally appeared as Part II of "Racism, Sexism, and Preferential Treatment," *U.C.L.A. Law Review* 24 (1977), 581.

The first argument is this. Opponents of preferential treatment programs sometimes assert that proponents of these programs are guilty of intellectual inconsistency, if not racism or sexism. For, as is now readily acknowledged, at times past employers, universities, and many other social institutions did have racial or sexual quotas (when they did not practice overt racial or sexual exclusion), and many of those who were most concerned to bring about the eradication of those racial quotas are now untroubled by the new programs which reinstitute them. And this, it claimed, is inconsistent. If it was wrong to take race or sex into account when blacks and women were the objects of racial and sexual policies and practices of exclusion, then it is wrong to take race or sex into account when the objects of the policies have their race or sex reversed. Simple considerations of intellectual consistency—of what it means to give racism or sexism as a reason for condemning these social policies and practices—require that what was a good reason then is still a good reason now.

The problem with this argument is that despite appearances, there is no inconsistency involved in holding both views. Even if contemporary preferential treatment programs which contain quotas are wrong, they are not wrong for the reasons that made quotas against blacks and women pernicious. The reason why is that the social realities do make an enormous difference. The fundamental evil of programs that discriminated against blacks or women was that these programs were a part of a larger social universe which systematically maintained a network of institutions which unjustifiably concentrated power, authority, and goods in the hands of white male individuals, and which systematically consigned blacks and women to subordinate positions in the society.

Whatever may be wrong with today's affirmative action programs and quota systems, it should be clear that the evil, if any, is just not the same. Racial and sexual minorities do not constitute the dominant social group. Nor is the conception of who is a fully developed member of the moral and social community one of an individual who is either female or black. Quotas which prefer women or blacks do not add to an already relatively overabundant supply of resources and opportunities at the disposal of members of these groups in the way in which the quotas of the past did maintain and augment the overabundant supply of resources and opportunities already available to white males.

The same point can be made in a somewhat different way. Sometimes people say that what was wrong, for example, with the system of racial discrimination in the South was that it took an irrelevant characteristic, namely race, and used it systematically to allocate social benefits and burdens of various sorts. The defect was the irrelevance of the characteristic used—race—for that meant that individuals ended up being treated in a manner that was arbitrary and capricious.

I do not think that was the central flaw at all. Take, for instance, the most hideous of the practices, human slavery. The primary thing that was wrong with the institution was not that the particular individuals who were assigned the place of slaves were assigned there arbitrarily because the assignment was made in virtue of an irrelevant characteristic, their race. Rather, it seems to me that the primary thing that was and is wrong with slavery is the practice itself—the fact of some individuals being able to own other individuals and all that goes with that practice. It would not matter by what criterion individuals were assigned; human slavery would still be wrong. And the same can be said for most if not all of the other discrete practices and institutions which comprised the system of racial discrimination even after human slavery was abolished. The practices were unjustifiable—they were oppressive—and they would have been so no matter how the assignment of victims had been made. What made it worse, still, was that the institutions and the supporting ideology all interlocked to create a system of human oppression whose effects on those living under it were as devastating as they were unjustifiable.

Again, if there is anything wrong with the programs of preferential treatment that have begun to flourish within the past ten years, it should be evident that the social realities in respect to the distribution of resources and opportunities make the difference. Apart from everything else, there is simply no way in which all of these programs taken together could plausibly be viewed as capable of relegating white males to the kind of genuinely oppressive status characteristically bestowed upon women and blacks by the dominant social institutions and ideology.

The second objection is that preferential treatment programs are wrong because they take race or sex into account rather than the only thing that does matter—that is, an individual's qualification. What all such programs have in common and what makes them all objectionable, so this argument goes, is that they ignore the persons who are more qualified by bestowing a preference on those who are less qualified in virtue of their being black or female.

There are, I think, a number of things wrong with this objection based on qualifications, and not the least of them is that we do not live in a society in which there is even the serious pretense of a qualification requirement for many jobs of substantial power and authority. Would anyone claim, for example, that the persons who comprise the judiciary are there because they are the most qualified lawyers or the most qualified persons to be judges? Would anyone claim that Henry Ford II is the head of the Ford Motor Company because he is the most qualified person for the job? Part of what is wrong with even talking about qualifications and merit is that the argument derives some of its force from the erroneous notion that we would have a meritocracy were it not for programs of preferential treatment. In fact, the higher one goes in terms of prestige, power and the like, the less qualifications seem ever to be decisive. It is only for certain jobs and certain places that qualifications are used to do more than establish the possession of certain minimum competencies.

But difficulties such as these to one side, there are theoretical difficulties as well which cut much more deeply into the argument about qualifications. To begin with, it is important to see that there is a serious inconsistency present if the person who favors "pure qualifications" does so on the ground that the most qualified ought to be selected because this promotes maximum efficiency. Let us suppose that the argument is that if we have the most qualified performing the relevant tasks we will get those tasks done in the most economical and efficient manner. There is nothing wrong in principle with arguments based upon the good consequences that will flow from maintaining a social practice in a certain way. But it is inconsistent for the opponent of preferential treatment to attach much weight to qualifications on this ground, because it was an analogous appeal to the good consequences that the opponent of preferential treatment thought was wrong in the first place. That is to say, if the chief thing to be said in favor of strict qualifications and preferring the most qualified is that it is the most efficient way of getting things done, then we are right back to an assessment of the different consequences that will flow from different programs, and we are far removed from the considerations of justice or fairness that were thought to weigh so heavily against these programs.

It is important to note, too, that qualifications—at least in the educational context—are often not connected at all closely with any plausible conception of social effectiveness. To admit the most qualified students to law school, for example—given the way qualifications are now determined—is primarily to admit those who have the greatest chance of scoring the highest grades at law school. This says little about efficiency except perhaps that these students are the easiest for the faculty to teach. However, since we know so little about what constitutes being a good, or even successful lawyer, and even less about the correlation between being a very good law student and being a very good lawyer, we can hardly claim very confidently that the legal system will operate more efficiently if we admit only the most qualified students to law school.

To be at all decisive, the argument for qualifications must be that those who are the most qualified deserve to receive the benefits (the job, the place in law school, etc.) because they are the most qualified. The introduction of the concept of desert now makes it an objection as to justice or fairness of the sort promised by the original criticism of the programs. But now the problem is that there is no reason to think that there is any strong sense of "desert" in which it is correct that the most qualified deserve anything.

Let us consider more closely one case, that of preferential treatment in respect to admission to college or graduate school. There is a logical gap in the inference from the claim that a person is most qualified to perform a task, e.g., to be a good student, to the conclusion that he or she deserves to be admitted as a student. Of course, those who deserve to be admitted should be admitted. But why do the most qualified deserve anything? There is simply no necessary connection between academic merit (in the sense of being most qualified) and deserving to be a member of a student body. Suppose, for instance, that there is only one tennis court in the community. Is it clear that the two best tennis players ought to be the ones permitted to use it? Why not those who were there first? Or those who will enjoy playing the most? Or those who are the worst and, therefore, need the greatest opportunity to practice? Or those who have the chance to play least frequently?

We might, of course, have a rule that says that the best tennis players get to use the court before the others. Under such a rule the best players would deserve the court more than the poorer ones. But that is just to push the inquiry back one stage. Is there any reason to think that we ought to have a rule giving good tennis players such a preference? Indeed, the arguments that might be given for or against such a rule are many and varied. And few if any of the arguments that might support the rule would depend upon a connection between ability and desert.

Someone might reply, however, that the most able students deserve to be admitted to the university because all of their earlier schooling was a kind of competition, with university admission being the prize awarded to the winners. They deserve to be admitted because that is what the rule of the competition provides. In addition, it might be argued, it would be unfair now to exclude them in favor of others, given the reasonable expectations they developed about the way in which their industry and performance would be rewarded. Minority-admission programs, which inevitably prefer some who are less qualified over some who are more qualified, all possess this flaw.

There are several problems with this argument. The most substantial of them is that it is an empirically implausible picture of our social world. Most of what are regarded as the decisive characteristics for higher education have a great deal to do with things over which the individual has neither control nor responsibility; such things as home environment, socioeconomic class of parents, and, of course, the quality of the primary and secondary schools attended. Since individuals do not deserve having had any of these things vis-à-vis other individuals, they do not, for the most part, deserve their qualifications. And since they do not deserve their abilities they do not in any strong sense deserve to be admitted because of their abilities.

To be sure, if there has been a rule which connects, say, performance at high school with admission to college, then there is a weak sense in which those who do well at high school deserve, for that reason alone, to be admitted to college. In addition, if persons have built up or relied upon their reasonable expectations concerning performance and admission, they have a claim to be admitted on this ground as well. But it is certainly not obvious that these claims of desert are any stronger or more compelling than the competing claims based upon the needs of or advantages to women or blacks from programs of preferential treatment. And as I have indicated, all rule-based claims of desert are very weak unless and until the rule which creates the claim is itself shown to be a justified one. Unless one has a strong preference for the status quo, and unless one can defend that preference, the practice within a system of allocating places in a certain way does not go very far at all in

showing that this is the right or the just way to allocate those places in the future.

A proponent of programs of preferential treatment is not at all committed to the view that qualifications ought to be wholly irrelevant. He or she can agree that, given the existing structure of any institution, there is probably some minimal set of qualifications without which one cannot participate meaningfully within the institution. In addition, it can be granted that the qualifications of those involved will affect the way the institution works and the way it affects others in the society. And the consequences will vary depending upon the particular institution. But all of this only establishes that qualifications, in this sense, are relevant, not that they are decisive. This is wholly consistent with the claim that race or sex should today also be relevant when it comes to matters such as admission to college or law school. And that is all that any preferential treatment program—even one with the kind of quota used in the *Bakke* case—has ever tried to do.

I have not attempted to establish that programs of preferential treatment are right and desirable. There are empirical issues concerning the consequences of these programs that I have not discussed, and certainly not settled. Nor, for that matter, have I considered the argument that justice may permit, if not require, these programs as a way to provide compensation or reparation for injuries suffered in the recent as well as distant past, or as a way to remove benefits that are undeservedly enjoyed by those of the dominant group. What I have tried to do is show that it is wrong to think that programs of preferential treatment are objectionable in the centrally important sense in which many past and present discriminatory features of our society have been and are racist and sexist. The social realities as to power and opportunity do make a fundamental difference. It is also wrong to think that programs of preferential treatment could, therefore, plausibly rest both on the view that such programs are not unfair to white males (except in the weak, rule-dependent sense described above) and on the view that it is unfair to continue the present set of unjust—often racist and sexist—institutions that comprise the social reality. And the case for these programs could rest as well on the proposition that, given the distribution of power and influence in the United States today, such programs may reasonably be viewed as potentially valuable, effective means by which to achieve admirable and significant social ideals of equality and integration.

Discussion Questions

1. Professor Wasserstrom points out that opponents of preferential treatment claim that the supporters of preferential treatment are guilty of "intellectual inconsistency." How does Professor Wasserstrom attempt to refute this claim? Do you think he succeeds? Why or why not? Explain and defend your answer.

2. How does Professor Wasserstrom respond to the second argument against preferential treatment: "preferential treatment programs are wrong because they take race or sex into account rather than the only thing that does matter—that is, an individual's qualifications"? Do you think his response is convincing? Do you find his analogy with tennis to be a sound one? Explain and defend your answers.

3. Do you agree with Professor Wasserstrom's claim that there is no necessary connection between desert and qualifications? Explain and defend your answer.

33

The Moral Status of Affirmative Action

Louis P. Pojman

Louis P. Pojman is Professor of Philosophy at the U.S. Military Academy at West Point, N.Y. He has published widely in the areas of philosophy of religion, epistemology, and ethics. Among his many books are *Ethical Theory: Classical and Contemporary Readings* (1989), *Ethics: Discovering Right and Wrong* (1990), and *The Abortion Controversy: A Reader* (1994).

In this essay Professor Pojman makes a distinction between weak and strong versions of affirmative action and then argues that strong affirmative action is not morally justified. He defines *weak affirmative action* as the employment of "such measures as the elimination of segregation, widespread advertisement to groups not previously represented in certain privileged positions, special scholarships for the disadvantaged classes (e.g., all the poor), using underrepresentation or a history of past discrimination as a tie breaker when candidates are relatively equal, and the like." On the other hand, *strong affirmative action* "involves more positive steps to eliminate past injustice, such as reverse discrimination, hiring candidates on the basis of race or gender in order to reach equal or near equal results, proportionate representation in each area of society." In order to support his position, Professor Pojman critiques seven arguments for affirmative action and provides seven arguments against affirmative action. The seven arguments for affirmative action are (1) need for role models; (2) the need to break the stereotypes; (3) equal results argument; (4) the compensation argument; (5) compensation from those who have innocently benefited from past injustice; (6) the diversity argument; and (7) antimeritocratic (desert) argument to justify reverse discrimination: "no one deserves his talents." The seven arguments against affirmative action are (1) affirmative action requires discrimination against a different group; (2) affirmative action perpetuates victimization syndrome; (3) affirmative action encourages mediocrity and incompetence; (4) affirmative action policies unjustly shift the burden of proof; (5) an argument from merit; (6) the slippery slope; and (7) the mounting evidence against the success of affirmative action.

Reprinted by permission from *Public Affairs Quarterly* (1992).

A ruler who appoints any man to an office, when there is in his dominion another man better qualified for it, sins against God and against the State.
—The *Koran*

[Affirmative Action] is the meagerest recompense for centuries of unrelieved oppression.
—quoted by Shelby Steele as the justification for Affirmative Action

Hardly a week goes by but that the subject of Affirmative Action does not come up. Whether in the guise of reverse discrimination, preferential hiring, non-traditional casting, quotas, goals and time tables, minority scholarships, or race-norming, the issue confronts us as a terribly perplexing problem. Last summer's Actor's Equity debacle over the casting of the British actor, Jonathan Pryce, as a Eurasian in *Miss Saigon*; Assistant Secretary of Education Michael Williams' judgment that Minority Scholarships are unconstitutional; the "Civil Rights Bill of 1991," reversing recent decisions of the Supreme Court which constrain preferential hiring practices; the demand that Harvard Law School hire a black female professor; grade stipends for black students at Pennsylvania State University and other schools; the revelations of race norming in state employment agencies; as well as debates over quotas, underutilization guidelines, and diversity in employment; all testify to the importance of this subject for contemporary society.

There is something salutary as well as terribly tragic inherent in this problem. The salutary aspect is the fact that our society has shown itself committed to eliminating unjust discrimination. Even in the heart of Dixie there is a recognition of the injustice of racial discrimination. Both sides of the affirmative action debate have good will and appeal to moral principles. Both sides are attempting to bring about a better society, one which is color blind, but they differ profoundly on the morally proper means to accomplish that goal.

And this is just the tragedy of the situation: good people on both sides of the issue are ready to tear each other to pieces over a problem that has no easy or obvious solution. And so the voices become shrill and the rhetoric hyperbolic. The same spirit which divides the pro-choice movement from the right to life movement on abortion divides liberal pro–Affirmative Action advocates from liberal anti–Affirmative Action advocates. This problem, more than any other, threatens to destroy the traditional liberal consensus in our society. I have seen family members and close friends who until recently fought on the same side of the barricades against racial injustice divide in enmity over this issue. The anti-affirmative liberals ("liberals who've been mugged") have tended towards a form of neo-conservatism and the pro-affirmative liberals have tended to side with the radical left to form the "politically correct ideology" movement.

In this paper I will confine myself primarily to Affirmative Action policies with regard to race, but much of what I say can be applied to the areas of gender and ethnic minorities.

I. Definitions

First let me define my terms:

Discrimination is simply judging one thing to differ from another on the basis of some criterion. "Discrimination" is essentially a good quality, having reference to our ability to make distinctions. As rational and moral agents we need to make proper distinctions. To be rational is to discriminate between good and bad arguments, and to think morally is to discriminate between reasons based on valid principles and those based on invalid ones. What needs to be distinguished is the difference between rational and moral discrimination, on the one hand, and irrational and immoral discrimination, on the other hand.

Prejudice is a discrimination based on irrelevant grounds. It may simply be an attitude which never surfaces in action, or it may cause prejudicial actions. A prejudicial discrimination in action is immoral if it denies someone a fair deal. So discrimination on the basis of race or sex where these are not relevant for job performance is unfair. Likewise, one may act prejudicially in applying a relevant criterion on insufficient grounds, as in the case where I apply the criterion of being a hard worker but then assume, on insufficient evidence, that the black man who applies for the job is not a hard worker.

There is a difference between *prejudice* and *bias*. Bias signifies a tendency towards one thing rather than another where the evidence is incomplete or based on non-moral factors. For example, you may have a bias towards blondes and I towards red-heads. But prejudice is an attitude (or action) where unfairness is present—where one *should* know or do better, as in the case where I give people jobs simply because they are red-heads. Bias implies ignorance or incomplete knowledge, whereas prejudice is deeper, involving a moral failure—usually a failure to pay attention to the evidence. But note that calling people racist or sexist without good evidence is also an act of prejudice. I call this form of prejudice "defamism," for it unfairly defames the victim. It is a contemporary version of McCarthyism.

Equal Opportunity is offering everyone a fair chance at the best positions that society has at its disposal. Only native aptitude and effort should be decisive in the outcome, not factors of race, sex or special favors.

Affirmative Action is the effort to rectify the injustice of the past by special policies. Put this way, it is Janus-faced or ambiguous, having both a backward-looking and a forward-looking feature. The backward-looking feature is its attempt to correct and compensate for past injustice. This aspect of Affirmative Action is strictly deontological. The forward-looking feature is its implicit ideal of a society free from prejudice; this is both deontological and utilitarian.

When we look at a social problem from a backward-looking perspective we need to determine who has committed or benefited from a wrongful or prejudicial act and to determine who deserves compensation for that act.

When we look at a social problem from a forward-looking perspective we need to determine what a just society (one free from prejudice) would look like and how to obtain that kind of society. The forward-looking aspect of Affirmative Action is paradoxically race-conscious, since it uses race to bring about a society which is not race-conscious, which is color-blind (in the morally relevant sense of this term).

It is also useful to distinguish two versions of Affirmative Action. *Weak Affirmative Action* involves such measures as the elimination of segregation (namely the idea of "separate but equal"), widespread advertisement to groups not previously represented in certain privileged positions, special scholarships for the disadvantaged classes (e.g., all the poor), using underrepresentation or a history of past discrimination as a tie breaker when candidates are relatively equal, and the like.

Strong Affirmative Action involves more positive steps to eliminate past injustice, such as reverse discrimination, hiring candidates on the basis of race and gender in order to reach equal or near equal results, proportionate representation in each area of society. . . .

[II.] Arguments for Affirmative Action

Let us now survey the main arguments typically cited in the debate over Affirmative Action. I will briefly discuss seven arguments on each side of the issue.

1. Need for Role Models

This argument is straightforward. We all have need for role models, and it helps to know that others like us can be successful. We learn and are encouraged to strive for excellence by emulating our heroes and role models.

However, it is doubtful whether role models of one's own racial or sexual type are necessary for success. One of my heroes was Gandhi, an Indian Hindu, another was my grade school science teacher, one Miss DeVoe, and another was Martin Luther King. More important than having role models of one's own type is having genuinely good people, of whatever race or gender, to emulate. Furthermore, even if it is of some help to people with low self-esteem to gain encouragement from seeing others of their particular kind in leadership roles, it is doubtful whether this need is a sufficient condition to justify preferential hiring or reverse discrimination. What good is a role model who is inferior to other professors or business personnel? Excellence will rise to the top in a system of fair opportunity. Natural development of role models will come more slowly and more surely. Proponents of preferential policies simply lack the patience to let history take its own course.

2. The Need of Breaking the Stereotypes

Society may simply need to know that there are talented blacks and women, so that it does not automatically assign them lesser respect or status. We need to have unjustified stereotype beliefs replaced with more accurate ones about the talents of blacks and women. So we need to engage in preferential hiring of qualified minorities even when they are not the most qualified.

Again, the response is that hiring the less qualified is neither fair to those better qualified who are passed over nor an effective way of removing inaccurate stereotypes. If competence is accepted as the criterion for hiring, then it is unjust to override it for purposes of social engineering. Furthermore, if blacks or women are known to hold high positions simply because of reverse discrimination, then they will still lack the respect due to those of their rank. In New York City there is a saying among doctors, "Never go to a black physician under 40," referring to the fact that AA has affected the medical system during the past fifteen years. The police use "Quota Cops" and "Welfare Sergeants" to refer to those hired without passing the standardized tests. (In 1985 180 black and Hispanic policemen, who had failed a promotion test, were promoted anyway to the rank of sergeant.) The destruction of false stereotypes will come naturally as qualified blacks rise naturally in fair competition (or if it does not—then the stereotypes may be justified). Reverse discrimination sends the message home that the stereotypes are deserved—otherwise, why do these minorities need so much extra help?

3. Equal Results Argument

Some philosophers and social scientists hold that human nature is roughly identical, so that on a fair playing field the same proportion from every race and gender and ethnic group would attain to the highest positions in every area of endeavor. It would follow that any inequality of results itself is evidence for inequality of opportunity. John Arthur, in discussing an intelligence test, Test 21, puts the case this way.

> History is important when considering governmental rules like Test 21 because low scores by blacks can be traced in large measure to the legacy of slavery and racism: segregation, poor schooling, exclusion from trade unions, malnutrition,

and poverty have all played their roles. Unless one assumes that blacks are naturally less able to pass the test, the conclusion must be that the results are themselves socially and legally constructed, not a mere given for which law and society can claim no responsibility.

The conclusion seems to be that genuine equality eventually requires equal results. Obviously blacks have been treated unequally throughout US history, and just as obviously the economic and psychological effects of that inequality linger to this day, showing up in lower income and poorer performance in school and on tests than whites achieve. Since we have no reason to believe that differences in performance can be explained by factors other than history, equal results are a good benchmark by which to measure progress made toward genuine equality.[1]

The result of a just society should be equal numbers in proportion to each group in the work force.

However, Arthur fails even to consider studies that suggest that there are innate differences between races, sexes, and groups. If there are genetic differences in intelligence and temperament within families, why should we not expect such differences between racial groups and the two genders? Why should the evidence for this be completely discounted?

Perhaps some race or one gender is more intelligent in one way than another. At present we have only limited knowledge about genetic differences, but what we do have suggests some difference besides the obvious physiological traits.[2] The proper use of this evidence is not to promote discriminatory policies but to be *open* to the possibility that innate difference may have led to an over-representation of certain groups in certain areas of endeavor. It seems that on average blacks have genetic endowments favoring them in the development of skills necessary for excellence in basketball.

Furthermore, on Arthur's logic, we should take aggressive AA against Asians and Jews since they are over-represented in science, technology, and medicine. So that each group receives its fair share, we should ensure that 12% of the philosophers in the United States are Black, reduce the percentage of Jews from an estimated 15% to 2%—firing about 1,300 Jewish philosophers. The fact that Asians are producing 50% of Ph.D.'s in science and math and blacks less than 1% clearly shows, on this reasoning, that we are providing special secret advantages to Asians.

But why does society have to enter into this results game in the first place? Why do we have to decide whether all difference is environmental or genetic? Perhaps we should simply admit that we lack sufficient evidence to pronounce on these issues with any certainty—but if so, should we not be more modest in insisting on equal results? Here is a thought experiment. Take two families of different racial groups, Green and Blue. The Greens decide to have only two children, to spend all their resources on them, to give them the best education. The two Green kids respond well and end up with achievement test scores in the 99th percentile. The Blues fail to practice family planning. They have 15 children. They can only afford 2 children, but lack of ability or whatever prevents them from keeping their family down. Now they need help for their large family. Why does society have to step in and help them? Society did not force them to have 15 children. Suppose that the achievement test scores of the 15 children fall below the 25th percentile. They cannot compete with the Greens. But now enters AA. It says that it is society's fault that the Blue children are not as able as the Greens and that the Greens must pay extra taxes to enable the Blues to compete. No restraints are put on the Blues regarding family size. This seems unfair to the Greens. Should the Green children be made to bear responsibility for the consequences of the Blues' voluntary behavior?

My point is simply that Arthur needs to cast his net wider and recognize that demographics and childbearing and -rearing practices are crucial factors in achievement. People have to take some responsibility for their actions. The equal results argument (or axiom) misses a greater part of the picture.

4. The Compensation Argument

The argument goes like this: blacks have been wronged and severely harmed by whites. Therefore white society should compensate blacks for the injury caused them. Reverse discrimination in terms of preferential hiring, contracts, and scholarships is a fitting way to compensate for the past wrongs.

This argument actually involves a distorted notion of compensation. Normally, we think of compensation as owed by a specific person *A* to another person *B* whom *A* has wronged in a specific way *C*. For example, if I have stolen your car and used it for a period of time to make business profits that would have gone to you, it is not enough that I return your car. I must pay you an amount reflecting your loss and my ability to pay. If I have only made $5,000 and only have $10,000 in assets, it would not be possible for you to collect $20,000 in damages—even though that is the amount of loss you have incurred.

Sometimes compensation is extended to groups of people who have been unjustly harmed by the greater society. For example, the United States government has compensated the Japanese-Americans who were intenred during the Second World War, and the West German government has paid reparations to the survivors of Nazi concentration camps. But here a specific people have been identified who were wronged in an identifiable way by the government of the nation in question.

On the face of it the demand by blacks for compensation does not fit the usual pattern. Perhaps Southern States with Jim Crow laws could be accused of unjustly harming blacks, but it is hard to see that the United States government was involved in doing so. Furthermore, it is not clear that all blacks were harmed in the same way or whether some were *unjustly* harmed or harmed more than poor whites and others (e.g., short people). Finally, even if identifiable blacks were harmed by identifiable social practices, it is not clear that most forms of Affirmative Action are appropriate to restore the situation. The usual practice of a financial payment seems more appropriate than giving a high level job to someone unqualified or only minimally qualified, who, speculatively, might have been better qualified had he not been subject to racial discrimination. If John is the star tailback of our college team with a promising professional future and I accidentally (but culpably) drive my pick-up truck over his legs, and so cripple him, John may be due compensation, but he is not due the tailback spot on the football team.

Still, there may be something intuitively compelling about compensating members of an oppressed group who are minimally qualified. Suppose that the Hatfields and the McCoys are enemy clans and some youths from the Hatfields go over and steal diamonds and gold from the McCoys, distributing it within the Hatfield economy. Even though we do not know which Hatfield youths did the stealing, we would want to restore the wealth, as far as possible, to the McCoys. One way might be to tax the Hatfields, but another might be to give preferential treatment in terms of scholarships and training programs and hiring to the McCoys.[3]

This is perhaps the strongest argument for Affirmative Action, and it may well justify some weak versions of AA, but it is doubtful whether it is sufficient to justify strong versions with quotas and goals and time tables in skilled positions. There are at least two reasons for this. First, we have no way of knowing how many people of group G would have been at competence level L had the world been different. Secondly, the normal criterion of competence is a strong prima facie consideration when the most important positions are at stake. There are two reasons for this: (1) society has given people expectations that if they attain certain levels of excellence they will be awarded appropriately and (2) filling the most important positions with the best qualified is the best way to insure efficiency in job-related areas and in society in general. These reasons are not absolutes. They can be overridden. But there is a strong presumption in their favor so that a burden of proof rests with those who would override them.

At this point we get into the problem of whether innocent non-blacks should have to pay a penalty in terms of preferential hiring of blacks. We turn to that argument.

5. Compensation from Those Who Innocently Benefited from Past Injustice

White males as innocent beneficiaries of unjust discrimination of blacks and women have no grounds for complaint when society seeks to rectify the tilted field. White males may be innocent of oppressing blacks and minorities (and women), but they have unjustly benefited from that oppression or discrimination. So it is perfectly proper that less qualified women and blacks be hired before them.

The operative principle is: He who knowingly and willingly benefits from a wrong must help pay for the wrong. Judith Jarvis Thomson puts it this way. "Many [white males] have been direct beneficiaries of policies which have down-graded blacks and women . . . and even those who did not directly benefit . . . had, at any rate, the advantage in the competition which comes of the confidence in one's full membership [in the community], and of one's right being recognized as a matter of course."[4] That is, white males obtain advantages in self-respect and self-confidence deriving from a racist system which denies these to blacks and women.

Objection. As I noted in the previous section, compensation is normally individual and specific. If *A* harms *B* regarding *x*, *B* has a right to compensation from *A* in regards to *x*. If *A* steals *B*'s car and wrecks it, *A* has an obligation to compensate *B* for the stolen car, but *A*'s son has no obligation to compensate *B*. Furthermore, if *A* dies or disappears, *B* has no moral right to claim that society compensate him for the stolen car—though if he has insurance, he can make such a claim to the insurance company. Sometimes a wrong cannot be compensated, and we just have to make the best of an imperfect world.

Suppose my parents, divining that I would grow up to have an unsurpassable desire to be a basketball player, bought an expensive growth hormone for me. Unfortunately, a neighbor stole it and gave it to little Lew Alcindor, who gained the extra 18 inches—my 18 inches—and shot up to an enviable 7 feet 2 inches. Alias Kareem Abdul Jabbar, he excelled in basketball, as I would have done had I had my proper dose.

Do I have a right to the millions of dollars that Jabbar made as a professional basketball player—the unjustly innocent beneficiary of my growth hormone? I have a right to something from the neighbor who stole the hormone, and it might be kind of Jabbar to give me free tickets to the Laker basketball games, and perhaps I should be remembered in his will. As far as I can see, however, he does not *owe* me anything, either legally or morally.

Suppose further that Lew Alcindor and I are in high school together and we are both qualified to play basketball, only he is far better than I. Do I deserve to start in his position because I would have been as good as he is had someone not cheated me as a child? Again, I think not. But if being the lucky beneficiary of wrong-doing does not entail that Alcindor (or the coach) owes me anything in regards to basketball, why should it be a reason to engage in preferential hiring in academic positions or highly coveted jobs? If minimal qualifications are not adequate to override excellence in basketball, even when the minimality is a consequence of wrongdoing, why should they be adequate in other areas?

6. The Diversity Argument

It is important that we learn to live in a pluralistic world, learning to get along with those of other races and cultures, so we should have fully integrated schools and employment situations. Diversity is an important symbol and educative device. Thus preferential treatment is warranted to perform this role in society.

But, again, while we can admit the value of diversity, it hardly seems adequate to override considerations of merit and efficiency. Diversity for

diversity's sake is moral promiscuity, since it obfuscates rational distinctions, and unless those hired are highly qualified the diversity factor threatens to become a fetish. At least at the higher levels of business and the professions, competence far outweighs considerations of diversity. I do not care whether the group of surgeons operating on me reflect racial or gender balance, but I do care that they are highly qualified. And likewise with airplane pilots, military leaders, business executives, and, may I say it, teachers and professors. Moreover, there are other ways of learning about other cultures besides engaging in reverse discrimination.

7. Anti-Meritocratic (Desert) Argument to Justify Reverse Discrimination: "No One Deserves His Talents"

According to this argument, the competent do not deserve their intelligence, their superior character, their industriousness, or their discipline; therefore they have no right to the best positions in society; therefore society is not unjust in giving these positions to less (but still minimally) qualified blacks and women. In one form this argument holds that since no one deserves anything, society may use any criteria it pleases to distribute goods. The criterion most often designated is social utility. Versions of this argument are found in the writings of John Arthur, John Rawls, Bernard Boxill, Michael Kinsley, Ronald Dworkin, and Richard Wasserstrom. Rawls writes, "No one deserves his place in the distribution of native endowments, any more than one deserves one's initial starting place in society. The assertion that a man deserves the superior character that enables him to make the effort to cultivate his abilities is equally problematic; for his character depends in large part upon fortunate family and social circumstances for which he can claim no credit. The notion of desert seems not to apply to these cases."[5] Michael Kinsley is even more adamant:

> Opponents of affirmative action are hung up on a distinction that seems more profoundly irrelevant: treating individuals versus treating groups. What is the moral difference between dispensing favors to people on their "merits" as individuals and passing out society's benefits on the basis of group identification?
>
> Group identifications like race and sex are, of course, immutable. They have nothing to do with a person's moral worth. But the same is true of

most of what comes under the label "merit." The tools you need for getting ahead in a meritocratic society—not all of them but most: talent, education, instilled cultural values such as ambition—are distributed just as arbitrarily as skin color. They are fate. The notion that people somehow "deserve" the advantages of these characteristics in a way they don't "deserve" the advantage of their race is powerful, but illogical.[6]

It will help to put the argument in outline form.

1. Society may award jobs and positions as it sees fit as long as individuals have no claim to these positions.
2. To have a claim to something means that one has earned it or deserves it.
3. But no one has earned or deserves his intelligence, talent, education, or cultural values which produce superior qualifications.
4. If a person does not deserve what produces something, he does not deserve its products.
5. Therefore better qualified people do not deserve their qualifications.
6. Therefore, society may override their qualifications in awarding jobs and positions as it sees fit (for social utility or to compensate for previous wrongs).

So it is permissible if a minimally qualified black or woman is admitted to law or medical school ahead of a white male with excellent credentials or if a less qualified person from an "underutilized" group gets a professorship ahead of a far better qualified white male. Sufficiency and underutilization together outweigh excellence.

Objection. Premise 4 is false. To see this, reflect that just because I do not deserve the money that I have been given as a gift (for instance) does not mean that I am not entitled to what I get with that money. If you and I both get a gift of $100 and I bury mine in the sand for 5 years while you invest yours wisely and double its value at the end of five years, I cannot complain that you should split the increase 50/50 since neither of us deserved the original gift. If we accept the notion of responsibility at all, we must hold that persons deserve the fruits of their labor and conscious choices. Of course, we might want to distinguish moral from legal desert and argue that, morally speaking, effort is more important than outcome, whereas, legally speaking, outcome may be more important. Nevertheless, there are good reasons in terms of efficiency, motivation, and rough justice

for holding a strong prima facie principle of giving scarce high positions to those most competent.

The attack on moral desert is perhaps the most radical move that egalitarians like Rawls and company have made against meritocracy, but the ramifications of their attack are far reaching. The following are some of its implications. Since I do not deserve my two good eyes or two good kidneys, the social engineers may take one of each from me to give to those needing an eye or a kidney—even if they have damaged their organs by their own voluntary actions. Since no one deserves anything, we do not deserve pay for our labors or praise for a job well done or first prize in the race we win. The notion of moral responsibility vanishes in a system of levelling.

But there is no good reason to accept the argument against desert. We do act freely and, as such, we are responsible for our actions. We deserve the fruits of our labor, reward for our noble feats and punishment for our misbehavior.

We have considered seven arguments for Affirmative Action and have found no compelling case for Strong AA and only one plausible argument (a version of the compensation argument) for Weak AA. We must now turn to the arguments against Affirmative Action to see whether they fare any better.[7]

[III.] Arguments against Affirmative Action

1. Affirmative Action Requires Discrimination against a Different Group

Weak Affirmative Action weakly discriminates against new minorities, mostly innocent young white males, and Strong Affirmative Action strongly discriminates against these new minorities. As I argued in II.5, this discrimination is unwarranted, since, even if some compensation to blacks were indicated, it would be unfair to make innocent white males bear the whole brunt of the payments. In fact, it is poor white youth who become the new pariahs on the job market. The children of the wealthy have no trouble getting into the best private grammar schools and, on the basis of superior early education, into the best universities, graduate schools, managerial and professional positions. Affirmative Action simply shifts injustice, setting blacks and women against young white males, especially ethnic and poor white males. It does little to rectify the goal of providing equal opportunity to all. If the goal is a society where everyone has a fair chance, then it would be better to concentrate on support for families and early education and decide the matter of university admissions and job hiring on the basis of traditional standards of competence.

2. Affirmative Action Perpetuates the Victimization Syndrome

Shelby Steele admits that Affirmative Action may seem "the meagerest recompense for centuries of unrelieved oppression" and that it helps promote diversity. At the same time, though, notes Steele, Affirmative Action reinforces the spirit of victimization by telling blacks that they can gain more by emphasizing their suffering, degradation and helplessness than by discipline and work. This message holds the danger of blacks becoming permanently handicapped by a need for special treatment. It also sends to society at large the message that blacks cannot make it on their own.

Leon Wieseltier sums up the problem this way.

> The memory of oppression is a pillar and a strut of the identity of every people oppressed. It is no ordinary marker of difference. It is unusually stiffening. It instructs the individual and the group about what to expect of the world, imparts an isolating sense of aptness. . . . Don't be fooled, it teaches, there is only repetition. For that reason, the collective memory of an oppressed people is not only a treasure but a trap.
>
> In the memory of oppression, oppression outlives itself. The scar does the work of the wound. That is the real tragedy: that injustice retains the power to distort long after it has ceased to be real. It is a posthumous victory for the oppressors, when pain becomes a tradition. And yet the atrocities of the past must never be forgotten. This is the unfairly difficult dilemma of the newly emancipated and the newly enfranchised: an honorable life is not possible if they remember too little and a normal life is not possible if they remember too much.[8]

With the eye of recollection, which does not "remember too much," Steele recommends a policy which offers "educational and economic development of disadvantaged people regardless of race and the eradication from our society—through close monitoring and severe sanctions—of racial and gender discrimination."[9]

3. Affirmative Action Encourages Mediocrity and Incompetence

Last Spring Jesse Jackson joined protesters at Harvard Law School in demanding that the Law School faculty hire black women. Jackson dismissed Dean of the Law School, Robert C. Clark's standard of choosing the best qualified person for the job as "Cultural anemia." "We cannot just define who is qualified in the most narrow vertical academic terms," he said. "Most people in the world are yellow, brown, black, poor, non-Christian and don't speak English, and they can't wait for some White male with archaic rules to appraise them."[10] It might be noted that if Jackson is correct about the depth of cultural decadence at Harvard, blacks might be well advised to form and support their own more vital law schools and leave places like Harvard to their archaism.

At several universities, the administration has forced departments to hire members of minorities even when far superior candidates were available. Shortly after obtaining my Ph.D. in the late 70's I was mistakenly identified as a black philosopher (I had a civil rights record and was once a black studies major) and was flown to a major university, only to be rejected for a more qualified candidate when it discovered that I was white.

Stories of the bad effects of Affirmative Action abound. The philosopher Sidney Hook writes that "At one Ivy League university, representatives of the Regional HEW demanded an explanation of why there were no women or minority students in the Graduate Department of Religious Studies. They were told that a reading knowledge of Hebrew and Greek was presupposed. Whereupon the representatives of HEW advised orally: 'Then end those old fashioned programs that require irrelevant languages. And start up programs on relevant things which minority group students can study without learning languages.'"[11]

Nicholas Capaldi notes that the staff of HEW itself was one-half women, three-fifths members of minorities, and one-half black—a clear case of racial over-representation.

In 1972 officials at Stanford University discovered a proposal for the government to monitor curriculum in higher education: the "Summary Statement . . . Sex Discrimination Proposed HEW Regulation to Effectuate Title IX of the Education Amendment of 1972" to "establish and use internal procedure for reviewing curricula, designed both to ensure that they do not reflect discrimination on the basis of sex and to resolve complaints concerning allegations of such discrimination, pursuant to procedural standards to be prescribed by the Director of the office of Civil Rights." Fortunately, Secretary of HEW Caspar Weinberger, when alerted to the intrusion, assured Stanford University that he would never approve of it.[12]

Government programs of enforced preferential treatment tend to appeal to the lowest possible common denominator. Witness the 1974 HEW Revised Order No. 14 on Affirmative Action expectations for preferential hiring: "Neither minorities nor female employees should be required to possess higher qualifications than those of the lowest qualified incumbents."

Furthermore, no tests may be given to candidates unless it is *proved* to be relevant to the job.

> No standard or criteria which have, by intent or effect, worked to exclude women or minorities as a class can be utilized, unless the institution can demonstrate the necessity of such standard to the performance of the job in question.
>
> Whenever a validity study is called for . . . the user should include . . . an investigation of suitable alternative selection procedures and suitable alternative methods of using the selection procedure which have as little adverse impact as possible. . . . Whenever the user is shown an alternative selection procedure with evidence of less adverse impact and substantial evidence of validity for the same job in similar circumstances, the user should investigate it to determine the appropriateness of using or validating it in accord with these guidelines.[13]

At the same time Americans are wondering why standards in our country are falling and the Japanese are getting ahead. Affirmative Action with its twin idols, Sufficiency and Diversity, is the enemy of excellence. I will develop this thought below (IV.6).

4. Affirmative Action Policies Unjustly Shift the Burden of Proof

Affirmative Action legislation tends to place the burden of proof on the employer who does not have an "adequate" representation of "underutilized" groups in his work force. He is guilty until proven innocent.

I have already recounted how in the mid-eighties the Supreme Court shifted the burden of proof back onto the plaintiff, while Congress is now attempting to shift the burden back to the employer. Those in favor of deeming disproportional representation "guilty until proven innocent" argue that it is easy for employers to discriminate against minorities by various subterfuges, and I agree that steps should be taken to monitor against prejudicial treatment. But being prejudiced against employers is not the way to attain a just solution to discrimination. The principle: innocent until proven guilty, applies to employers as well as criminals. Indeed, it is clearly special pleading to reject this basic principle of Anglo-American law in this case of discrimination while adhering to it everywhere else.

5. An Argument from Merit

Traditionally, we have believed that the highest positions in society should be awarded to those who are best qualified—as the Koran states in the quotation at the beginning of this paper. Rewarding excellence both seems just to the individuals in the competition and makes for efficiency. Note that one of the most successful acts of integration, the recruitment of Jackie Robinson in the late 40s, was done in just this way, according to merit. If Robinson had been brought into the major league as a mediocre player or had batted .200 he would have been scorned and sent back to the minors where he belonged.

Merit is not an absolute value. There are times when it may be overridden for social goals, but there is a strong prima facie reason for awarding positions on its basis, and it should enjoy a weighty presumption in our social practices.

In a celebrated article Ronald Dworkin says that "Bakke had no case" because society did not owe Bakke anything. That may be, but then why does it owe anyone anything? Dworkin puts the matter in Utility terms, but if that is the case, society may owe Bakke a place at the University of California/Davis, for it seems a reasonable rule-utilitarian principle that achievement should be rewarded in society. We generally want the best to have the best positions, the best qualified candidate to win the political office, the most brilliant and competent scientist to be chosen for the most challenging research project, the best qualified pilots to become commercial pilots, only the best soldiers to become generals. Only when little is at stake do we weaken the standards and content ourselves with sufficiency (rather than excellence)—there are plenty of jobs where "sufficiency" rather than excellence is required. Perhaps we now feel that medicine or law or university professorships are so routine that they can be performed by minimally qualified people—in which case AA has a place.

But note, no one is calling for quotas or proportional representation of *underutilized* groups in the National Basketball Association where blacks make up 80% of the players. But if merit and merit alone reigns in sports, should it not be valued at least as much in education and industry?

6. The Slippery Slope

Even if Strong AA or Reverse Discrimination could meet the other objections, it would face a tough question: once you embark on this project, how do you limit it? Who should be excluded from reverse discrimination? Asians and Jews are overrepresented, so if we give blacks positive quotas, should we place negative quotas to these other groups? Since white males, "WMs," are a minority which is suffering from reverse discrimination, will we need a New Affirmative Action policy in the 21st century to compensate for the discrimination against WMs in the late 20th century?

Furthermore, Affirmative Action has stigmatized the *young* white male. Assuming that we accept reverse discrimination, the fair way to make sacrifices would be to retire *older* white males who are more likely to have benefited from a favored status. Probably the least guilty of any harm to minority groups is the young white male—usually a liberal who has been required to bear the brunt of ages of past injustice. Justice Brennan's announcement that the Civil Rights Act did not apply to discrimination against whites shows how the clearest language can be bent to serve the ideology of the moment.[14]

7. The Mounting Evidence against the Success of Affirmative Action

Thomas Sowell of the Hoover Institute has shown in his book *Preferential Policies: An International Perspective* that preferential hiring almost never solves social problems. It generally builds in mediocrity or incompetence and causes deep resentment. It is a short term solution which lacks serious grounding in social realities.

For instance, Sowell cites some disturbing statistics on education. Although twice as many blacks as Asian students took the nationwide Scholastic Aptitude Test in 1983, approximately fifteen times as many Asian students scored above 700 (out of a possible 800) on the mathematics half of the SAT. The percentage of Asians who scored above 700 in math was also more than six times higher than the percentage of American Indians and more than ten times higher than that of Mexican Americans—as well as more than double the percentage of whites. As Sowell points out, in all countries studied, "intergroup performance disparities are huge."

There are dozens of American colleges and universities where the median combined verbal SAT score and mathematics SAT score total 1200 or above. As of 1983 there were less than 600 black students in the entire US with combined SAT scores of 1200. This meant that, despite widespread attempts to get a black student "representation" comparable to the black percentage of the population (about 11%), there were not enough black students in the entire country for the Ivy League alone to have such a "representation" without going beyond this pool—even if the entire pool went to the eight Ivy League colleges.[15]

Often it is claimed that a cultural bias is the cause of the poor performance of blacks on SAT (or IQ tests), but Sowell shows that these test scores are actually a better predictor of college performance for blacks than for Asians and whites. He also shows the harmfulness of the effect on blacks of preferential acceptance. At the University of California, Berkeley, where the freshman class closely reflects the actual ethnic distribution of California high school students, more than 70% of blacks fail to graduate. All 312 black students entering Berkeley in 1987 were admitted under "Affirmative Action" criteria rather than by meeting standard academic criteria. So were 480 out of 507 Hispanic students. In 1986 the median SAT score for blacks at Berkeley was 952, for Mexican Americans 1014, for American Indians 1082 and for Asian Americans 1254. (The average SAT for all students was 1181.)

The result of this mismatching is that blacks who might do well if they went to a second tier or third tier school where their test scores would indicate they belong, actually are harmed by preferential treatment. They cannot compete in the institutions where high abilities are necessary.

Sowell also points out that Affirmative Action policies have mainly assisted the middle class black, those who have suffered least from discrimination. "Black couples in which both husband and wife are college-educated overtook white couples of the same description back in the early 1970's and continued to at least hold their own in the 1980's."

Sowell's conclusion is that similar patterns of results obtained from India to the USA wherever preferential policies exist. "In education, preferential admissions policies have led to high attrition rates and substandard performances for those preferred students . . . who survived to graduate." In all countries the preferred tended to concentrate in less difficult subjects which lead to less remunerative careers. "In the employment market, both blacks and untouchables at the higher levels have advanced substantially while those at the lower levels show no such advancement and even some signs of retrogression. These patterns are also broadly consistent with patterns found in countries in which majorities have created preferences for themselves. . . ."

The tendency has been to focus at the high level end of education and employment rather than on the lower level of family structure and early education. But if we really want to help the worst off improve, we need to concentrate on the family and early education. It is foolish to expect equal results when we begin with grossly unequal starting points—and discriminating against young white males is no more just than discriminating against women, blacks or anyone else.

Conclusion

Let me sum up. The goal of the Civil Rights movement and of moral people everywhere has been equal opportunity. The question is: how best to get there. Civil Rights legislation removed the legal barriers to equal opportunity, but did not tackle the deeper causes that produced differential results. Weak Affirmative Action aims at encouraging minorities in striving for the highest positions without unduly jeopardizing the rights of majorities, but the problem of Weak Affirmative Action is that it easily slides into Strong Affirmative Action where quotas, "goals," and equal results are forced into groups, thus promoting mediocrity, inefficiency, and resentment. Furthermore, Affirmative Action aims at the higher levels of society—universities and skilled jobs—yet if we want to improve our society, the best way to do it is to concentrate on families, children, early educa-

tion, and the like. Affirmative Action is, on the one hand, too much, too soon and on the other hand, too little, too late.

Martin Luther said that humanity is like a man mounting a horse who always tends to fall off on the other side of the horse. This seems to be the case with Affirmative Action. Attempting to redress the discriminatory iniquities of our history, our well-intentioned social engineers engage in new forms of discriminatory iniquity and thereby think that they have successfully mounted the horse of racial harmony. They have only fallen off on the other side of the issue.[16]

Discussion Questions

1. Present and explain the seven arguments for affirmative action that Professor Pojman critiques. Are there any aspects of his critiques with which you disagree and that you believe are flawed? Explain and defend your answer.

2. Present and explain the seven arguments against affirmative action that Professor Pojman supports. Are there any aspects of these arguments with which you disagree and that you believe are flawed? Explain and defend your answer.

3. Are there any arguments that Professor Pojman may have failed to mention that you believe either support or count against the morality of affirmative action? Explain and defend your answer.

Notes

1. John Arthur, *The Unfinished Constitution* (Belmont, CA, 1990), p. 238.

2. See Phillip E. Vernon's excellent summary of the literature in *Intelligence: Heredity and Environment* (New York, 1979) and Yves Christen "Sex Differences in the Human Brain" in Nicholas Davidson (ed.) *Gender Sanity* (Lanham, 1989) and T. Bouchard, *et al.*, "Sources of Human Psychological Differences: The Minnesota Studies of Twins Reared Apart," *Science*, vol. 250 (1990).

3. See Michael Levin, "Is Racial Discrimination Special?" *Policy Review*, Fall issue (1982).

4. Judith Jarvis Thomson, "Preferential Hiring" in Marshall Cohen, Thomas Nagel and Thomas Scanlon (eds.) *Equality and Preferential Treatment* (Princeton, 1977).

5. John Rawls, *A Theory of Justice* (Cambridge, 1971), p. 104; See Richard Wasserstrom "A Defense of Programs of Preferential Treatment," *National Forum* (Phi Kappa Phi Journal), vol. 58 (1978). See also Bernard Boxill, "The

Morality of Preferential Hiring," *Philosophy and Public Affairs*, vol. 7 (1978).

6. Michael Kinsley, "Equal Lack of Opportunity," *Harper's*, June issue (1983).

7. There is one other argument which I have omitted. It is from precedence and has been stated by Judith Jarvis Thomson in the article cited earlier:

> "Suppose two candidates for a civil service job have equally good test scores, but there is only one job available. We could decide between them by coin-tossing. But in fact we do allow for declaring for *A* straightaway, where *A* is a veteran, and *B* is not. It may be that *B* is a non-veteran through no fault of his own ... Yet the fact is that *B* is not a veteran and *A* is. On the assumption that the veteran has served his country, the country owes him something. And it is plain that giving him preference is not an unjust way in which part of that debt of gratitude can be paid" (p. 379f).

The two forms of preferential hiring are analogous. Veteran's preference is justified as a way of paying a debt of gratitude, preferential hiring is a way of paying a debt of compensation. In both cases innocent parties bear the burden of the community's debt, but it is justified.

My response to this argument is that veterans should not be hired in place of better qualified candidates, but that benefits like the GI scholarships are part of the contract with veterans who serve their country in the armed services. The notion of compensation only applies to individuals who have been injured by identifiable entities. So the analogy between veterans and minority groups seems weak.

8. Quoted in Jim Sleeper, *The Closest of Strangers* (New York, 1990), p. 209.

9. Shelby Steele, "A Negative Vote on Affirmative Action," *New York Times*, May 13, 1990 issue.

10. *New York Times*, May 10, 1990 issue.

11. Nicholas Capaldi, *Out of Order: Affirmative Action and the Crisis of Doctrinaire Liberalism* (Buffalo, NY: Prometheus, 1985), p. 85.

12. *Ibid.*, p. 95.

13. *Ibid.*

14. The extreme form of this New Speak is incarnate in the Politically Correct Movement ("PC" ideology) where a new orthodoxy has emerged, condemning white, European culture and seeing African culture as the new savior of us all. Perhaps the clearest example of this is Paula Rothenberg's book *Racism and Sexism* (New York, 1987) which asserts that there is no such thing as black racism; only whites are capable of racism (p. 6). Ms. Rothenberg's book has been scheduled as required reading for all freshmen at the University of Texas. See Joseph Salemi, "Lone Star Academic Politics," no. 87 (1990).

15. Thomas Sowell, *Preferential Policies: An International Perspective* (New York: Morrow, 1990), p. 108.

16. I am indebted to Jim Landesman, Michael Levin, and Abigail Rosenthal for comments on a previous draft of this paper. I am also indebted to Nicholas Capaldi's *Out of Order* for first making me aware of the extent of the problem of Affirmative Action.

34

The Justification of Reverse Discrimination

Tom Beauchamp

Tom Beauchamp is Professor of Philosophy at Georgetown University (Washington, D.C.) as well as Senior Research Scholar at Georgetown's Kennedy Institute of Ethics. One of America's leading ethicists, he is the author of numerous scholarly articles. His books include *Principles of Biomedical Ethics*, 4th ed. (1993), and *Medical Ethics* (1984).

In this essay Professor Beauchamp argues that some forms of reverse discrimination and preferential treatment are morally justified. Although he admits that reverse discrimination is prima facie unethical, just as taking a human life is prima facie unethical (my example), there may be situations in which certain moral principles and values justify reverse discrimination, just as there may be some situations in which certain moral principles and values justify taking a human life, such as in a just war or self-defense. Professor Beauchamp defends his position on two grounds: (1) there is overwhelming and wide-ranging statistical evidence, as well as testimonial evidence, that there is and has been unjust discrimination against minorities and women that cannot be overcome by weak affirmative action or equal opportunity policies, but only by policies that provide preferential treatment to members of discriminated groups with specified goals and timetables; (2) corporate interests as well as the public good are well served by goals and quotas, and Professor Beauchamp provides testimonial and

Reprinted by permission from *Ethical Theory and Business*, 3rd ed., ed. Tom Beauchamp (Princeton, N.J.:Prentice-Hall, 1988).

statistical evidence to support this. Even though there are counter-considerations against preferential treatment, they are "not strong enough to overcome the even more powerful case against" them.

During the past two decades, government and corporate policies aimed at hiring women and racial minorities by setting numerical goals have been sharply criticized on grounds that they discriminate in reverse, often against more qualified white males. My objective in this paper is to defend such policies. I agree with those critics who maintain that some policies have created situations of injustice. However, I do not agree with the presumption that when policies with numerical goals create *injustices* they are necessarily *unjustified*. Equal opportunity is but one principle of justice, and justice is but one demand of ethics. We need also to take account of principles of just compensation (compensatory justice) and the public interest (utility).

A policy can create or perpetuate injustices, such as violations of principles of equal opportunity, and yet be justified by other reasons. It would, for example, be an injustice in one respect for a bank to fire one of two branch managers with identical professional credentials while retaining the other; yet the financial condition of the bank or compensation owed the retained person might provide compelling reasons that justify the action. An established seniority system might justifiably be used to decide such a matter; indeed, a devoted employee with long service might be retained in preference to a younger person with better credentials and higher productivity. In some circumstances, when implementing schemes of hiring, promoting, and firing, equal opportunity and the blinded evaluations of persons will have to yield on the scales of justice to the weight of other principles.

I shall use this general line of argument in defense of numerical targets, goals, quotas, and timetables. I contend that goals and even quotas are congenial to management, not hostile to business, as academic and government agency officials generally seem to presume. I also believe that business' long-range interest and the public interest are best served by preferential hiring, advancement, and layoff policies.

Two Polar Positions

The U.S. Supreme Court and numerous scholars in ethics and legal theory have struggled with these problems of principle and balance in combatting discrimation, at least since President Lyndon Johnson's 1965 executive order that announced a toughened federal initiative by requiring specific goals and timetables for equal employment opportunity. This struggle has led to two primary competing schools of thought on the justifiability of preferential programs.

The first school locates justice in the claim that we are all entitled to an equal opportunity and to constitutional guarantees of equal protection in a color-blind, nonsexist society. An entitlement of this sort is an entitlement that only individuals possess. Civil rights laws therefore should offer protection not to aggregate groups but only to specific individuals who have been demonstrably victimized by racial, sexual, religious, or other forms of discrimination. Hiring goals, timetables, and quotas violate these laws as well as our moral sense of justice, because they create new victims of discrimination. The U.S. Department of Justice has spearheaded this view in recent years, but it has found adherents in many quarters as well.

The second school believes that mandated goals and enforced hiring measures are essential to ensure fairness in hiring and to achieve meaningful results in the attempt to eradicate discrimination. This group believes it is too onerous to require the actual identification of individual victims of discrimination—an assignment that is generally impossible because of secrecy (and sometimes even unintentional discrimination). Even the victims may not know they are victims. As the editors of the *New York Times* put it, finding actual victims as the means of ending discrimination would be the "project of a century and [would] leave most victims of discrimination with only empty legal rights. [Many] are still victims of the myths of racial superiority that once infused the law itself." The *Times* joined the Supreme Court in calling for the "adequate remedy" of "race-conscious relief" in the form of goals and timetables to the extent necessary to achieve the end of a nondiscriminatory society.[1] The second group thus tends to see the first group as construing "equal opportunity" and "civil rights" so narrowly that those affected by discrimination can receive no practical aid in overcoming the phenomenon of prejudice. That is, the noble ideal of equal opportunity is viewed as but a theoretical postulate that has no practical application in the real world under the first group's policies.

These two groups are perhaps not as far apart as they appear at first glance. Edwin Meese, Attorney General during the Reagan administration and the most publicly visible proponent of the first viewpoint in recent memory, dismissed the seemingly enormous gulf between his views and those of the U.S. Supreme Court—which has endorsed the second viewpoint—by saying that the Court *accepted* his views that racial preferences are wrong and merely "carved out various exceptions to that general rule, even while affirming the rule itself." There is something to be said for Meese's bold statement (although I think not quite what he intended): The second group need not disagree with the first group if legal enforcement were adequate to identify discriminatory treatment and to protect its victims. If we lived in such a society, then the second group could easily agree that the first group's policies are preferable for that society.

But there are two reasons why no member of the second group will agree to this solution at the present time. First, there is the unresolved issue whether those in contemporary society who have been advantaged by *past* discrimination deserve their advantages, and thus whether classes such as blacks and women deserve some of those advantages. This thorny issue is surpassed in importance, however, by the second reason, which is whether *present*, ongoing discrimination can be successfully, comprehensively, and fairly combatted by identifying and prosecuting the violators. I do not believe that the form of enforcement so essential to the first group's position is possible. But I do believe that the enforcement of goals and quotas is both possible and necessary. Two reasons now to be discussed lead me to the conclusion that the second position is preferable to the first.

The Data on Discrimination

My argument rests on the hypothesis that invidious discrimination that affects hiring and promotion is present in our society—not everywhere, of course, but pervasively. Such a claim requires empirical evidence; and like almost any broad generalization, the evidence is not entirely conclusive. However, I believe the claim can be adequately substantiated, as some representative samples of available data indicate.

Statistical imbalances in hiring and admission and promotion are often discounted because so many variables can be hypothesized to explain why, for nondiscriminatory reasons, an imbalance exists. We can all think of plausible nondiscriminatory reasons why almost half of the graduate students in the United States are women but the tenured Arts and Sciences graduate faculties often hover around 5 to 10 percent women—and in some of the most prestigious schools, even lower. Occasionally we are able to discover firm evidence supporting the claim that such skewed statistics are not random but are the result of discrimination. Quantities of such discriminatory findings, in turn, raise questions about the real reasons for suspicious statistics in those cases where we have not been able to determine these reasons.

An impressive body of statistics constituting prima facie evidence of discrimination has been assembled in recent years indicating that women with identical credentials are promoted at almost exactly one-half the rate of their male counterparts; that 69 percent or more of the white-collar positions in the United States are presently held by women, but only 10 percent or so of the management positions are held by women (and again their pay is significantly lower); that 8.7 percent of all professionals in the private business sector are Orientals, but they comprise only 1.3 percent of management; that in the population as a whole in the United States 3 out of 7 employees hold white-collar positions, but only 1 of 7 blacks holds such a position (and these positions are clustered in professions that have the fewest jobs to offer in top-paying positions); and that numerous major U.S. corporations have settled discrimination suits out of court for hundreds of millions of dollars.[2]

Such statistics are far from decisive indicators of discrimination. But further evidence concerning the reasons for the statistics can sometimes be discovered to prove a discriminatory influence.[3] Other facts support the general conclusion that racist and sexist biases have a powerful influence in the marketplace. For example, from 1965 to 1975 the number of blacks in college doubled, but from 1975 to 1985 it leveled off without increase. The number of blacks making more than $25,000 in constant-dollar salary also doubled from 1965 to 1975, but dropped from 1975 to 1985.[4] There is a ready reason for both statistics. Both the Grier Partnership and the Urban League produced separate studies completed in 1985 that show striking disparities in the employment levels of college-trained blacks and whites in the job market

in Washington, D.C.—one of the best markets for blacks. Both studies found that college-trained blacks find far more frustration in landing a position and that discrimination is a major underlying factor.[5]

Another example of prevailing biases in marketplace transactions is found in real estate rentals and sales. In a 1985 statement, Lucius McKelvey, president of a large Cleveland real estate firm, publicly proclaimed what numerous real estate agents had already privately reported: "You'd be surprised at the number of professional people, white-collar people, who ask us to discriminate—it's discouraging." Surveys have shown that blacks face an 85 percent probability of encountering discrimination in rental housing and almost 50 percent in buying a house.[6]

These studies and dozens that replicate their findings indicate that we live in a discriminatory society whose laws will make little difference in practice unless the laws are tough and are gauged to change the practices and underlying attitudes. The law cannot wait for evidence of abuse confined to demonstrable individual victims without permitting the continuation of present injustices.

Problems of Proof and Intention

The central problems of proof and enforcement in individual cases can best be captured in taking a particular case that illustrates the difficulty in determining whether discrimination—especially intentional discrimination—is occurring.

In December 1974 a decision was reached by the Commission against Discrimination of the Executive Department of the State of Massachusetts regarding a case at Smith College; the two complainants were women who were denied tenure and dismissed by the English Department.[7] The women claimed sex discrimination and based their case on the following: (1) Women at the full professor level in the college declined from 54 percent in 1958 to 21 percent in 1972 and in the English Department from 57 percent in 1960 to 11 percent in 1972. These statistics compare unfavorably at all levels with data from Mt. Holyoke, a comparable institution (since both have an all-female student body and are located in western Massachusetts). (2) Thirteen of the department's fifteen associate and full professorships at Smith belonged to men. (3) The two tenured women had obtained tenure under "distinctly peculiar experiences," including a stipulation that one be only part-time and that the other not be promoted when given tenure. (4) The department's faculty members conceded that tenure standards were applied subjectively, were vague, and lacked the kind of precision that would avoid discriminatory application. (5) The women denied tenure were at no time given advance warning that their work was deficient. Rather, they were given favorable evaluations of their teaching and were encouraged to believe that they would receive tenure. (6) Some of the stated reasons for the dismissals were later demonstrated to be rationalizations, and one letter from a senior member to the tenure and promotion committee contradicted his own appraisal of teaching ability filed with the department. (7) The court accepted expert testimony that any deficiencies in the women candidates were also found in male candidates promoted and given tenure in the same period and that the women's positive credentials were at least as good as the men's.[8]

The commissioner's opinion found that "the Complainants properly used statistics to demonstrate that the Respondents' practices operate with a discriminatory effect." Citing *Parham v. Southwestern Bell Telephone Co.*, the commissioner argued that "in such cases extreme statistics may establish discrimination as a matter of law, without additional supportive evidence." But in this case the commissioner found abundant additional evidence in the form of the "historical absence of women," "word-of-mouth recruitment policies" that operate discriminatorily, and a number of "subtle and not so subtle, societal patterns" existing at Smith.[9] On December 30, 1974, the commissioner ordered the two women reinstated with tenure and ordered the department to submit an affirmative action program within sixty days.

There is little in the way of clinching proof that the members of the English Department held discriminatory attitudes. Yet so consistent a pattern of *apparently* discriminatory results must be regarded, according to this decision, as de facto discrimination. The commissioner's ruling and other laws explicitly state that "intent or lack thereof is of no consequence." If a procedure constitutes discriminatory treatment, then the parties discriminated against must be recompensed. If irresistible statistics and other sociological evidence of "social exclusion" and "subtle societal patterns" provide compelling evidence that quotas, goals, or strong court-backed measures are necessary to overcome the discriminatory pattern (as the Respondents' testimony in the case

indicates),[10] I find this fact sufficient to justify the measures.

In early 1985 the U.S. Supreme Court came down with perhaps its clearest example of this general point in the case of *Alexander v. Choate*. The Court held unanimously—against the U.S. Justice Department and the state of Tennessee—that states may be held guilty of discriminating against the handicapped because such discrimination is "most often the product not of invidious animus, but rather of thoughtlessness and indifference—of benign neglect." The Court rightly held that discrimination would be "difficult if not impossible to ban if only *intentional* acts of discrimination qualified as discrimination."[11]

Problems of Enforcement

The protective camouflage surrounding discriminatory attitudes makes enforcement difficult in both the particular case and in the general case of monitoring nondiscriminatory guidelines. This problem is lessened by having specific goals and quotas, which are easier to meet and to enforce. In this section, I want to present two cases that show how difficult—indeed meaningless—enforcement can be in the absence of specified goals and tough-minded control.

The January 1975 Report of the United States Commission on Civil Rights contains a section of "compliance reviews" of various universities.[12] The commissioners reviewed four major campuses in the United States: Harvard, University of Michigan, University of Washington, and Berkeley. They concluded that there has been a pattern of inadequate compliance reviews, inordinate delays, and inexcusable failures to take enforcement action where there were clear violations of the executive order regulations.[13]

Consider the example of the "case history of compliance contracts at the University of California at Berkeley. When the Office for Civil Rights (OCR) of HHS determined to investigate Berkeley (April 1971), after several complaints, including a class action sex discrimination complaint, the university refused to permit access to its personnel files and refused to permit the interviewing of faculty members without an administrator present. Both refusals are, as the report points out, "direct violations of the Executive order's equal opportunity clause," under which Berkeley held contracts. A year and a half later, after negotiations and more complaints, the university was instructed to develop a written affirmative action plan to correct" documented deficiencies" of "pervasive discrimination." The plan was to include target goals and timetables wherever job underutilization had been identified.[14]

In January 1973 the university submitted a draft affirmative action plan that was judged "totally unacceptable." Throughout 1973 Berkeley received "extensive technical assistance" from the government to aid it in developing a better plan. No such plan emerged, and OCR at the end of the year began to question "the university's commitment to comply with the executive order." The university submitted other unacceptable plans, and finally in March 1974 a conciliation document was reached. However, the document was vague and the university and OCR continued for years to be in disagreement on the meaning of key provisions.

Berkeley is an instructive case study, because it was at the time among the most concerned institutions in the United States over issues of race and civil rights. If it and the other three universities studied by the Commission on Civil Rights have troubled histories in installing and monitoring antidiscrimination laws, one can imagine the problems found elsewhere. Consider, as a revealing example of far more egregious resistance, what is perhaps the most important Supreme Court case on the issues of quotas and reverse discrimination: the case of *Local 28 v. Equal Employment Opportunity Commission*, generally known as *Sheet Metal Workers*.[15] Although this case was decided in 1986, the discriminatory actions of Local 28 of the Sheet Metal Workers International had been in and out of court since 1963. The record, says the Supreme Court, was one of complete "foot-dragging resistance" to the idea of hiring from minority groups into the apprenticeship training programs that supply workers for construction in the New York City metropolitan area. In 1964 the New York Commission for Human Rights investigated the union and concluded that it excluded nonwhites through an impenetrable barrier of hiring by discriminatory selection. The state Supreme Court concurred and issued a "cease and desist" order. The union ignored it. Eventually, in a 1975 trial, the U.S. District Court found a record "replete with instances of bad faith" and ordered a "remedial racial goal" of 29 percent nonwhite membership (based on the percentage of

nonwhites in the local labor pool). Another court then found that the union had "consistently and egregiously violated" the law of the land (Title 7, in particular). In 1982 and 1983 court fines and civil contempt proceedings were issued. In 1981, virtually nothing had been done to modify the discriminatory hiring practices after twenty-two years of struggle.

The Supreme Court held that one need not produce "identified victims" of discrimination and that goals such as the 29 percent quota are justified when "an employer or a labor union has been engaged in persistent or egregious discrimination, or where necessary to dissipate the lingering effects of pervasive discrimination." I find the latter clause particularly suitable. Goals and quotas are needed where there are lingering effects of pervasive preference for particular groups (e.g., white male graduates of certain schools) or discriminatory attitudes that control hiring. Otherwise, goals and quotas are not needed, and no one should invoke them. But if these problems are not restricted to a few isolated cases involving Sheet Metal Workers Unions or Departments of English, then it makes sense to see goals and quotas as a basic tool for eradicating discriminatory practices.

The Supreme Court points out that the present laws in the United States were enacted by Congress to prevent "pervasive and systematic discrimination in employment." No one should expect that practices like those of the Sheet Metal Workers can easily be removed by exhortations or by finding "identified victims." The stronger the resistance, the tougher the rules must be.

I might add, however, that the Supreme Court has not said, nor have I, that there cannot be a case of reverse discrimination in which a white male has unjustifiably been excluded from consideration for employment and has a right to compensation. Certainly *unwarranted* discrimination in reverse is no better than unwarranted discrimination in forward speed. But the following should also be considered: There is an important distinction between real reverse discrimination and merely apparent reverse discrimination. Sometimes persons who appear to be displacing better applicants will be hired or admitted—on a quota basis, for example, but the appearance may be the result of discriminatory perceptions of the person's qualifications. In this case there will appear to be reverse discrimination, and this impression will be reinforced by knowledge that quotas were used. However, the allegation of reverse discrimination will be mistaken. On other occasions there will be genuine reverse discrimination, and on many occasions it will be impossible to determine whether this consequence occurs.

I have argued that real and not merely apparent reverse discrimination is justified. But it is justified only as a means to the end of ensuring nondiscriminatory treatment of all persons. If the use of goals and quotas functioned as a vindictive tool (and, let us suppose, the end of nondiscrimination had already been achieved), then no reverse discriminatory effects would be justified.

Why Corporations Should Welcome Goals and Quotas

Little has been said thus far about the relevance of these arguments to employment in business, largely because we have been concentrating on public policy affecting all institutions. In conclusion, I turn to corporate policy, which I believe would be aided by the use of goals and targets in the late 1980s and early 1990s. Here I shall discuss only policies voluntarily adopted by corporations—that is, voluntary programs using target goals and quotas. These programs stand in contrast to agency-ordered objectives featured in some previous examples.

Because of this shift to voluntary programs, my argument may seem a trivial addition to the problems mentioned above; a corporation can either accept or reject a program at its discretion. However, the issue of voluntary goals and quotas is far from trivial, for two reasons. First, the Justice Department has sought in recent years to ban voluntary corporate programs using goals and quotas, on grounds that these policies result in reverse discrimination. Many corporations and municipalities have resisted these government moves, and some have flatly refused to ease their affirmative action goals. Second, I believe that the active good will of corporations will prove to be more important than any other development (with the possible exception of activity in the U.S. Supreme Court) in ending discrimination and prejudice in the American workplace; and the workplace more than any other environment will serve as the melting pot of American society.

I offer four reasons why it is in the interest of responsible businesses to use aggressive plans involving goals and quotas. The judgment that such plans are fair and justified—as I have argued previously—could be appended as a reason, but it is not the type of reason needed in the present context.

(1) First, to the extent that a corporation either discriminates or fails to look at the full range of qualified persons in the market, to that extent it will eventually wind up with a larger percentage of second-best employees. Corporations continue to report that they find fewer qualified workers for available positions than they formerly did, and that they have profited from rules of nonracial, nonsexist hiring.[16] Hal Johnson, a senior vice-president at Travelers Companies, projects that, "In 1990 more of the work force is going to be minorities—Hispanics, blacks—and women. The companies that started building bridges back in the 1970s will be all right. Those that didn't won't."[17] The free market has its own way of eroding color and sexual barriers in the search for the best talent. No one would argue, for example, that baseball has poorer talent for dropping its color barrier. To find that talent in its best form, bridges had to be built that extended far into, for example, the population of Puerto Rico. Businesses will be analogously improved if they extend their boundaries and provide the proper training programs. Bill McEwen of Monsanto Corporation and spokesperson for the National Association of Manufacturers notes that this extension not only will happen but has been happening at NAM companies for twenty years:

> We have been utilizing affirmative action plans for over 20 years. We were brought into it kicking and screaming. But over the past 20 years we've learned that there's a reservoir of talent out there, of minorities and women that we hadn't been using before. We found that it works.[18]

Some corporations have found it difficult to find and keep these talented persons and therefore have developed incentives and special benefits, such as job-sharing, home work, flextime, extended maternity leave, and day-care centers in order to keep them. These companies include Gannett, General Foods, General Motors, IBM, Lotus Development, Mellon Bank, Mutual Life, Peat Marwick Mitchell, and Procter & Gamble.[19]

(2) A second reason is that pulling the foundations from beneath affirmative action hiring would open old sores, especially for municipalities and corporations who over a period of years have developed target goals and quotas either through a consent-decree process with courts or direct negotiations with representatives of minority groups

such as PUSH and the NAACP. These plans—which now cover over 20 million Americans employed by federal contractors alone—have been agonizingly difficult to develop in some cases and would be disintegrated by the principle that goals and timetables are impermissible. Removal might also stigmatize a business by signalling to minority groups a return to old patterns of discrimination.[20]

(3) Third, the risk of reverse discrimination suits would be minimized, not maximized, by the use of goals and quotas. This paradox has been explained by Peter Robertson of Organizational Resource Counselors:

> In a recent survey of chief executive officers by the management consulting firm for which I work, 95 percent indicated that they will use numbers as a management tool to measure corporate progress whether the government requires them or not. However, once the government requirements are gone, there would be a risk of so-called "reverse discrimination" suits alleging that employers have gone too far with affirmative action.[21]

Thus, government programs and court decisions that *allow* voluntary goals and quotas actually protect good-faith employers rather than undermining them. As Robertson points out, the president of the National Association of Manufacturers, Alexander Trowbridge, has been making exactly that point to affiliate manufacturers. It has also been reported that many corporations enthusiastically greeted the 1986 and 1987 pro-affirmative-action decisions in the U.S. Supreme Court, because they feared that if the Justice Department's argument had been victorious, then employers would have been exposed to reverse discrimination suits by white males because of the plans corporations already had in effect.[22]

(4) Finally, the editors of *Business Week* have offered the following general reason in favor of voluntary and negotiated goals and quotas: "over the years business and regulators have worked out rules and procedures for affirmative action, including numerical yardsticks for sizing up progress, that both sides understand. It has worked and should be left alone."[23] The reason why it has worked is intrinsic to a businesslike approach to problems: Managers set goals and timetables for almost everything they hope to achieve—from profits to salary bonuses. From a manager's point of view, setting goals and timetables is simply a basic way of measuring progress. One survey of 200 major American corporations found that over 75 percent already use "voluntary internal numerical objectives to assess [equal employment opportunity] performance."[24] A side benefit of the use of such numerical objectives is to create a ready defense of one's practices for government investigators, unions, or minority group representatives who inquire into the company's historical record. Many corporations have also promoted their record through public reports and recruiting brochures. Such reports and brochures have been developed, for example, by Schering-Plough, Philip Morris, Exxon, AT&T, IBM, Westinghouse, and Chemical Bank.[25]

Conclusion

Early in this paper I acknowledged that all racial and sexual discrimination, including reverse discrimination, is prima facie immoral, because a basic principle of justice creates a duty to abstain from such treatment of persons. But no absolute duty is created come what may. The thesis I have defended is that considerations of compensatory justice, equal opportunity, and utility are *conjointly* of sufficient weight to neutralize and overcome the quite proper presumption of immorality in the case of some policies productive of reverse discrimination.

My conclusion is premised on balancing several moral principles as well as on empirical judgments about the actual state of discrimination in American society. With some basic changes, the presumption might turn in a different direction, and thus my claims are contingent on the social circumstances. Moreover, I agree with critics of the position I have defended that the introduction of preferential treatment on a large scale might in some measure produce economic advantages to some who do not deserve them, protracted court battles, jockeying for favored position by other minorities, congressional lobbying by power groups, a lowering of admission and work standards in vital institutions, reduced social and economic efficiency, increased racial hostility, and continued suspicion that well-placed women and minority group members received their positions purely on the basis of quotas. Conjointly these reasons constitute a strong case against policies that use numerical goals and quotas in hiring, promotion, firing, and layoffs. However, this powerful case is not strong enough to overcome the even more powerful case against it.

Discussion Questions

1. Briefly summarize Professor Beauchamp's case for preferential treatment programs. What are the two grounds on which he bases his position? Present and explain each. Why does he believe that discrimination is pervasive and cannot be overcome except by preferential treatment programs? Do you consider his case persuasive? Why or why not?

2. What does Professor Beauchamp mean when he says that discrimination is prima facie immoral and that the burden of proof is on the person who supports preferential treatment programs? Explain his position. Do you agree or disagree with him? Explain and defend your position.

3. Why does Professor Beauchamp think that a policy of equal opportunity—under which protection is not provided to groups but only to individuals who have been discriminated against—will not work? Explain his position. Do you consider his case persuasive? Why or why not?

Notes

1. "Their Right to Remedy, Affirmed," *New York Times*, July 3, 1986, p. A30.

2. See the data and comments in the following sources: Kenneth M. Davidson, Ruth B. Ginsburg, and Herma H. Kay, eds., *Sex-Based Discrimination: Text, Cases and Materials* (Minneapolis: West Publishing Company, 1974), esp. Ch. 3. Hereafter *Sex-Based Discrimination;* Irene Pave, "A Woman's Place Is at GE, Federal Express, P&G . . . ," *Business Week*, June 23, 1986, pp. 75–76; Winifred Yu, "Asian Americans Charge Prejudice Slows Climb to Management Rank," *Wall Street Journal*, September 11, 1985, p. 35.

3. From *Discrimination Against Women: Congressional Hearings on Equal Rights in Education and Employment*, ed. Catharine R. Stimpson (New York: R. R. Bowker, 1973), 505–506.

4. See Juan Williams, "The Vast Gap Between Black and White Visions of Reality" and "Blacks Don't See It the Way Whites Do," *Washington Post*, March 31, 1985, pp. K1, K4.

5. As reported by Rudolf A. Pyatt, Jr., "Significant Job Studies," *Washington Post*, April 30, 1985, pp. D1–D2.

6. See "Business Bulletin," *Wall Street Journal*, February 28, 1985, p. 1.

7. *Maurianne Adams and Mary Schroeder v. Smith College*, Massachusetts Commission Against Discrimination, Nos. 72-S-53, 72-S-54 (December 30, 1974). Hereafter *The Smith College Case.*

8. 433 F.2d 421, 426 (8 cir. 1970).

9. *The Smith College Case*, pp. 23, 26.

10. *Ibid.*, pp. 26–27.

11. As reported by and quoted in Al Kamen, "Justices Attack Inadvertent Bias," *Washington Post*, January 10, 1985, p. A4.

12. *The Federal Civil Rights Enforcement Effort—1974*, 2: p. 276.

13. *Ibid.*, p. 281.

14. *Ibid.*, all the following text references are from pp. 281–286.

15. *Local 28 v. Equal Employment Opportunity Commission*, U.S. 84-1656. All the following quotations are from this case.

16. See Pave, "A Woman's Place," p. 76.

17. As quoted in Walter Kiechel, "Living with Human Resources," *Fortune*, August 18, 1986, p. 100.

18. As quoted in Peter Perl, "Rulings Provide Hiring Direction: Employers Welcome Move," *Washington Post*, July 3, 1986, pp. A1, A11.

19. See Alex Taylor, "Why Women Managers Are Bailing Out," *Fortune*, August 18, 1986, pp. 16–23 (cover story).

20. See Mary Thornton, "Justice Dept. Stance on Hiring Goals Resisted," *Washington Post*, May 25, 1985, p. A2; Linda Williams, "Minorities Find Pacts with Corporations Are Hard to Come By and Enforce," *Wall Street Journal*, August 23, 1985, p. 13; and Perl, "Rulings Provide Hiring Direction," pp. A1, A11.

21. Peter C. Robertson, "Why Bosses Like to Be Told to Hire Minorities," *Washington Post*, November 10, 1985, pp. D1–D2.

22. Perl, "Rulings Provide Hiring Direction," p. 1; Al Kamen, "Justice Dept. Surrenders in War on Hiring Goals," *Washington Post*, March 28, 1987, p. A4.

23. Editorial, "Don't Scuttle Affirmative Action," *Business Week*, April 5, 1985, p. 174.

24. Robertson, "Why Bosses Like to Be Told," p. 2.

25. *Ibid.*

35

From Equal Opportunity to "Affirmative Action"

Thomas Sowell

Thomas Sowell is a Senior Fellow at the Hoover Institution, Stanford University. He has been a professor of economics at a number of leading universities and colleges in America. He is the author of numerous articles and books including *The Economics and Politics of Race* (1983) and *Inside American Education* (1993).

In this essay Dr. Sowell challenges much of the reasoning found in Professor Beauchamp's article (Chapter 34), which attempted to prove pervasive discrimination against minorities and women on the basis of strong statistical disparities and then on that basis concluded that strong affirmative action programs are morally justified. Although he does not deny that discrimination exists, Dr. Sowell argues that one cannot prove that it is all-pervasive simply on the basis of statistical differences between racial, ethnic, and gender groups in society. He provides evidence to show that age, cultural differences, and other factors do a much better job (or at least as good a job) of accounting for disparities as does discrimination. He then goes on to make the controversial argument, by citing a number of statistical findings, that the civil rights movement and subsequent affirmative action policies have helped to advance highly qualified minorities but have resulted in harm to lower-class minorities. Dr. Sowell concludes by showing how statistics are manipulated in order to "prove" discrimination even if there is no concrete evidence.

Reprinted by permission from Thomas Sowell, *Civil Rights: Rhetoric or Reality?* (New York: William Morrow, 1984), 42–60.

The very meaning of the phrase "civil rights" has changed greatly since the *Brown* decision in 1954, or since the Civil Rights Act of 1964. Initially, civil rights meant, quite simply, that all individuals should be treated the same under the law, regardless of their race, religion, sex or other such social categories. For blacks, especially, this would have represented a dramatic improvement in those states where law and public policy mandated racially separate institutions and highly discriminatory treatment.

Many Americans who supported the initial thrust of civil rights, as represented by the *Brown v. Board of Education* decision and the Civil Rights Act of 1964, later felt betrayed as the original concept of equal individual *opportunity* evolved toward the concept of equal group *results*. The idea that statistical differences in results were weighty presumptive evidence of discriminatory processes was not initially an explicit part of civil rights law. But neither was it merely an inexplicable perversion, as many critics seem to think, for it followed logically from the civil rights *vision*.

If the causes of intergroup differences can be dichotomized into discrimination and innate ability, then non-racists and non-sexists must expect equal results from non-discrimination. Conversely, the persistence of highly disparate results must indicate that discrimination continues to be pervasive among recalcitrant employers, culturally biased tests, hypocritical educational institutions, etc. The early leaders and supporters of the civil rights movement did not advocate such corollaries, and many explicitly repudiated them, especially during the congressional debates that preceded passage of the Civil Rights Act of 1964.[1] But the corollaries were implicit in the vision—and in the long run that proved to be more decisive than the positions taken by the original leaders in the cause of civil rights. In the face of crying injustices, many Americans accepted a vision that promised to further a noble cause, without quibbling over its assumptions or verbal formulations. But visions have a momentum of their own, and those who accept their assumptions have entailed their corollaries, however surprised they may be when these corollaries emerge historically.

"Equal opportunity" laws and policies require that individuals be judged on their qualifications as individuals, *without regard* to race, sex, age, etc. "Affirmative action" requires that they be judged *with regard* to such group membership, receiving preferential or compensatory treatment in some cases to achieve a more proportional "representation" in various institutions and occupations. . . .

Those who carry the civil rights vision to its ultimate conclusion see no great difference between promoting equality of opportunity and equality of results. If there are not equal results among groups presumed to have equal genetic potential, then some inequality of opportunity must have intervened somewhere, and the question of precisely where is less important than the remedy of restoring the less fortunate to their just position. The fatal flaw in this kind of thinking is that there are many reasons, besides genes and discrimination, why groups differ in their economic performances and rewards. Groups differ by large amounts demographically, culturally, and geographically—and all of these differences have profound effects on incomes and occupations.

Age differences are quite large. Blacks are a decade younger than the Japanese. Jews are a quarter of a century older than Puerto Ricans. Polish Americans are twice as old as American Indians.[2] These represent major differences in the quantity of work experience, in an economy where income differences between age brackets are even greater than black-white income differences.[3] Even if the various racial and ethnic groups were identical in every other respect, their age differences alone would prevent their being equally represented in occupations requiring experience or higher education. Their very different age distributions likewise prevent their being equally represented in colleges, jails, homes for the elderly, the armed forces, sports and numerous other institutions and activities that tend to have more people from one age bracket than from another.

Cultural difference add to the age differences. . . . [Half] of all Mexican American wives were married in their teens, while only 10 percent of Japanese American wives married that young.[4] Such very different patterns imply not only different values but also very different future opportunities. Those who marry and begin having children earlier face more restricted options for future education and less geographic mobility for seeking their best career opportunities. Even among those young people who go on to colleges and universities, their opportunities to prepare themselves for the better paid professions are severely limited by their previous educational choices and performances, as well as by their selections of fields of study in the colleges and universities. All of these things vary enormously from one group to another.

For example, mathematics preparation and performance differ greatly from one ethnic group to another and between men and women. A study of high school students in northern California showed that four-fifths of Asian youngsters were enrolled in the sequence of mathematics courses that culminate in calculus, while only one-fifth of black youngsters were enrolled in such courses. Moreover, even among those who began this sequence in geometry, the percentage that persisted all the way through to calculus was several times higher among the Asian students.[5] Sex differences in mathematics preparation are comparably large. Among both black and white freshmen at the University of Maryland, the men had had four years of mathematics in high school more than twice as often as the women.[6]

Mathematics is of decisive importance for many more professions than that of mathematician. Whole ranges of fields of study and work are off-limits to those without the necessary mathematical foundation. Physicists, chemists, statisticians, and engineers are only some of the more obvious occupations. In some colleges, one cannot even be an undergraduate economics major without having had calculus, and to go on to graduate school and become a professional economist requires much more mathematics, as well as statistical analysis. Even in fields where mathematics is not an absolute prerequisite, its presence or absence makes a major difference in one's ability to rise in the profession. Mathematics is becoming an important factor in the social sciences and is even beginning to invade some of the humanities. To be mathematically illiterate is to carry an increasing burden into an increasing number of occupations. Even the ability to pass a civil service examination for modest clerical jobs is helped or hindered by one's facility in mathematics.

It is hardly surprising that test scores reflect these group differences in mathematics preparation. Nationwide results on the Scholastic Aptitude Test (SAT) for college applicants show Asians and whites consistently scoring higher on the quantitative test than Hispanics or blacks, and men scoring higher than women.[7] Nor are these differences merely the result of socioeconomic "disadvantage" caused by "society." Black, Mexican American, and American Indian youngsters from families with incomes of $50,000 and up score lower than Asians from families whose incomes are just $6,000 and under.[8] Moreover, Asians as a group score higher than whites as a group on the quantitative portion of the SAT and the Japanese in Japan specialize in mathematics, science and engineering to a far greater extent than do American students in the United States.[9] Cultural differences are real, and cannot be talked away by using pejorative terms such as "stereotypes" or "racism."

The racial, ethnic, and sex differences in mathematics that begin in high school (or earlier) continue on through to the Ph.D. level, affecting career choices and economic rewards. Hispanic Ph.D.'s outnumber Asian Ph.D.'s in the United States by three-to-one in history, but the Asians outnumber the Hispanics by ten-to-one in chemistry.[10] More than half of all Asian Ph.D.'s are in mathematics, science or engineering, and more than half the Asians who teach college teach in those fields. By contrast, more than half of all black doctorates are in the field of education, a notoriously undemanding and less remunerative field. So are half the doctorates received by American Indians, not one of whom received a Ph.D. in either mathematics or physics in 1980.[11] Female Ph.D.'s are in quantitatively-based fields only half as frequently as male Ph.D.'s.[12]

Important as mathematics is in itself, it is also a symptom of broader and deeper disparities in educational choices and performances in general. Those groups with smaller quantities of education tend also to have lower qualities of education, and these disparities follow them all the way through their educational careers and into the job market. The children of lower income racial and ethnic groups typically score lower on tests all through school and attend lower quality colleges when they go to college at all, as well as majoring in the easier courses in fields with the least economic promise. How much of this is due to the home environment and how much to the deficiencies of the public schools in their neighborhoods is a large question that cannot be answered here. But what is clear is that what is called the "same" education, measured in years of schooling, is not even remotely the same in reality.

The civil rights vision relies heavily on statistical "disparities" in income and employment between members of different groups to support its sweeping claims of rampant discrimination. The U.S. Civil Rights Commission, for example, considers itself to be "controlling for those factors"[13] when it examines people of the same age with the same number of years of schooling—resolutely ignoring the substance of that schooling.

Age and education do not begin to exhaust the differences between groups. They are simply more readily quantitative than some other differences. The geographic distributions of groups also vary greatly, with Mexican Americans being concentrated in the southwest, Puerto Ricans in the northeast, half of blacks in the south, and most Asians in California and Hawaii. Differences in income between the states are also larger than black-white income differences, so that these distributional differences affect national income differences. A number of past studies, for example, have shown black and Puerto Rican incomes to be very similar nationally, but blacks generally earn higher incomes than Puerto Ricans in New York and other places where Puerto Ricans are concentrated.[14] Their incomes nationally have shown up in the studies as similar, because there are very few Puerto Ricans living in low-income southern states.

One of the most important causes of differences in income and employment is the way people work— some diligently, carefully, persistently, cooperatively, and without requiring much supervision or warnings about absenteeism, tardiness, or drinking, and others requiring much such concern over such matters. Not only are such things inherently difficult to quantify; any suggestion that such differences even exist is sure to bring forth a storm of condemnation. In short, the civil rights vision has been hermetically sealed off from any such evidence. Both historical and contemporary observations on intergroup differences in work habits, discipline, reliability, sobriety, cleanliness, or cooperative attitude—anywhere in the world—or automatically dismissed as evidence only of the bias or bigotry of the observers. "Stereotypes" is the magic word that makes thinking about such things unnecessary. Yet despite this closed circle of reasoning that surrounds the civil rights vision, there is some evidence that cannot disposed of in that way.

Self-employed farmers, for example, do not depend for their rewards on the biases of employers or the stereotypes of observers. Yet self-employed farmers of different ethnicity have fared very differently on the same land, even in earlier pre-mechanization times, when the principal input was the farmer's own labor. German farmers, for example, had more prosperous farms than other farmers in colonial America[15]—and were more prosperous than Irish farmers in eighteenth-century Ireland,[16] as well as more prosperous than Brazilian farmers in Brazil,[17] Mexican farmers in Mexico,[18] Russian farmers in Russia,[19] and Chilean farmers in Chile.[20] We may ignore the forbidden testimony from these countries as to how hard the German farmers worked, how frugally they lived, or how sober they were. Still, the results speak for themselves.

That Jews earn far higher incomes than Hispanics in the United States might be taken as evidence that anti-Hispanic bias is stronger than anti-Semitism—if one followed the logic of the civil rights vision. But this explanation is considerably weakened by the greater prosperity of Jews than Hispanics in *Hispanic countries* throughout Latin America.[21] Again, even if one dismisses out of hand all the observers who see great differences in the way these two groups work, study, or save, major tangible differences in economic performance remain that cannot be explained in terms of the civil rights vision.

One of the commonly used indices of intergroup economic differences is family income. Yet families are of different sizes from group to group, reflecting differences in the incidence of broken homes. Female headed households are several times more common among blacks than among whites, and in both groups these are the lowest income families. Moreover, the proportion of people working differs greatly from group to group. More than three-fifths of all Japanese American families have multiple income earners while only about a third of Puerto Rican families do. Nor is this a purely socioeconomic phenomenon. Blacks have similar incomes to Puerto Ricans, but the proportion of black families with a woman working is nearly three times that among Puerto Ricans.[22]

None of this disproves the existence of discrimination, nor is that its purpose. What is at issue is whether statistical differences mean discrimination, or whether there are innumerable demographic, cultural, and geographic differences that make this crucial automatic inference highly questionable.

Effects versus Hopes

Thus far, we have not even considered the actual effects of the incentives and constraints created by affirmative action policies—as distinguished from the rationales, hopes or claims made for these policies. Because these policies are invoked on behalf of the most disadvantaged groups, and the most disadvantaged classes within these groups, it is especially important to scrutinize the factual record of what has happened to the economic position of such people under both equal opportunity and affirmative policies.

Before crediting either political policy with economic gains, it is worth considering what trends were already under way before they were instituted.

Much has been made of the number of blacks in high-level occupations before and after the Civil Rights Act of 1964. What has been almost totally ignored is the historical *trend* of black representation in such occupations before the Act was passed. In the period from 1954 to 1964, for example, the number of blacks in professional, technical, and similar high-level positions more than doubled.[23] In other kinds of occupations, the advance of blacks was even greater during the 1940s—when there was little or no civil rights policy—than during the 1950s when the civil rights revolution was in its heyday.[24]

The rise in the number of blacks in professional and technical occupations in the two years from 1964 to 1966 (after the Civil Rights Act) was in fact *less* than in the one year from 1961 to 1962 (before the Civil Rights Act).[25] If one takes into account the growing black population by looking at percentages instead of absolute numbers, it becomes even clearer that the Civil Rights Act of 1964 represented no acceleration in trends that had been going on for many years. The percentage of employed blacks who were professional and technical workers rose less in the five years following the Civil Rights Act of 1964 than in the five years preceding it. The percentage of employed blacks who were managers and administrators was the same in 1967 as in 1964—and in 1960. Nor did the institution of "goals and timetables" at the end of 1971 mark any acceleration in the long trend of rising black representation in these occupations. True, there was an appreciable increase in the percentage of blacks in professional and technical fields from 1971 to 1972, but almost entirely offset by a reduction in the percentage of blacks who were managers and administrators.[26]

The history of Asians and Hispanics likewise shows long-term upward trends that began years before the Civil Rights Act of 1964 and were not noticeably accelerated by the Act or by later "affirmative action" policies. The income of Mexican Americans rose relative to that of non-Hispanic whites between 1959 and 1969 (after the Civil Rights Act), but no more so than from 1949 to 1959 (before the Act).[27] Chinese and Japanese Americans overtook other Americans in income by 1959—five years before the Civil Rights Act.

Ignoring trends already in progress for years makes before-and-after comparisons completely misleading. Yet that is precisely the approach of supporters of the civil rights vision, who proceed as if "before" was a static situation. Yet the notion that the Civil Rights Act and "affirmative action" have had a dramatic impact on the economic progress of minorities has become part of the folklore of the land, established primarily through repetition and vehemence, rather than evidence.

The evidence of the *political* impact of civil rights changes in the 1960s is far more clear-cut. The number of black elected officials, especially in the South, increased many-fold in a relatively few years, including blacks elected to public office in some places for the first time since the Reconstruction era after the Civil War. Perhaps even more important, white elected officials in the South had to change both their policies and their rhetoric to accommodate the new political reality that blacks could vote.

What is truly surprising—and relatively ignored—is the economic impact of affirmative action on the disadvantaged, for whom it is most insistently invoked. The relative position of disadvantaged individuals within the groups singled out for preferential treatment has generally *declined* under affirmative action. This is particularly clear in data for individuals, as distinguished from families.

Family income data have too many pitfalls to be taken at face value. There are, for example, significant variations in what constitutes a family, both from time to time and from group to group. But since many people insist on using such data, these statistics cannot be passed over in silence. In 1969, *before* the federal imposition of numerical "goals and time-tables," Puerto Rican family income was 63 percent of the national average. By 1977, it was down to 50 percent. In 1969, Mexican American family income was 76 percent of the national average. By 1977 it was down to 73 percent. Black family income fell from 62 percent of the national average to 60 percent over the same span.[28]

There are many complex factors behind these numbers. The point here is simply that they do not support the civil rights vision. A finer breakdown of the data for blacks shows the most disadvantaged families—the female-headed, with no husband present—to be not only the poorest and with the slowest increase in money income during the 1970s (a decline in *real* income) but also with money incomes increasing even more slowly than among white, female-headed families. By contrast, black husband-wife families had money incomes that were rising faster than that of their white counterparts.[29] It is part of a more general pattern of the most disadvantaged falling farther behind during the affirmative action era, while the already advantaged forged ahead.

Individual data tell the same story, even more clearly. Those blacks with less education and less job experience—the truly disadvantaged—have been falling farther and farther behind their white counterparts under affirmative action, during the very same years when blacks with more education and more job experience have been advancing economically, both absolutely and relative to their white counterparts. First, the disadvantaged: Black male high school dropouts with less than six years of work experience earned 79 percent of the income of white male high school dropouts with less than six years of work experience in 1967 (before affirmative action quotas) and this *fell* to 69 percent by 1978 (after affirmative action quotas). Over these very same years, the income of black males who had completed college and had more than six years of work experience *rose* from 75 percent of the income of their white counterparts to 98 percent.[30] Some economic trends can be explained in terms of general conditions in the economy, but such diametrically opposite trends during the very same span of years obviously cannot.

There is additional evidence that the advantaged have benefited under affirmative action while the disadvantaged have fallen behind. Black faculty members with numerous publications and Ph.D.'s from top-rated institutions earned more than white faculty members with the same high qualifications, but black faculty members who lacked a doctorate or publications earned less than whites with the same low qualifications.[31] The pattern of diametrically opposite trends in economic well-being among advantaged and disadvantaged blacks is also shown by the general internal distribution of income among blacks. The top fifth of blacks have absorbed a growing proportion of all income received by blacks, while each of the bottom three fifths has received declining shares.[32] Black college-educated couples with husband and wife working had by 1980 achieved incomes higher than white couples of the same description.[33] Meanwhile, at the other end of the spectrum, the black female-headed household was receiving only 62 percent of the income of white, female-headed households—down from 70 percent in 1970.[34]

None of this is easily reconcilable with the civil rights vision's all-purpose explanation, racism and discrimination. To explain such diametrically opposite trends within the black community on the basis of whites' behavior would require us to believe that racism and discrimination were growing and declining at the same time. It is much more reconcilable with ordinary economic analysis.

Affirmative action hiring pressures make it costly to have no minority employees, but continuing affirmative action pressures at the promotion and discharge phases also make it costly to have minority employees who do not work out well. The net effect is to increase the demand for highly qualified minority employees while decreasing the demand for less qualified minority employees or for those without a sufficient track record to reassure employers.

Those who are most vocal about the need for affirmative action are of course the more articulate minority members—the advantaged who speak in the name of the disadvantaged. Their position on the issue may accord with their own personal experience, as well as their own self-interest. But that cannot dismiss the growing evidence that it is precisely the disadvantaged who suffer from affirmative action.

By the Numbers

Averages versus Variance

One of the remarkable aspects of affirmative action is that, while numbers—and *assumptions* about numbers—abound, proponents of the program are almost never challenged to produce positive numerical evidence for its effectiveness or to support their statistical presuppositions. The mere fact that some group is x percent of the population but only y percent of the employees is taken as weighty presumption of employer discrimination. There are serious statistical problems with this approach, quite aside from substantial group differences in age, education, and cultural values.

Even in a random world of identical things, to say that something happens a certain way *on the average* is not to say that it happens that way *every time*. But affirmative action deals with averages almost as if there were no variance. If Hispanics are 8 percent of the carpenters in a given town, it does not follow that *every* employer of carpenters in that town would have 8 percent Hispanics if there were no discrimination. Even if carpenters were assigned to employers by drawing lots (or by some other random process), there would be *variance* in the proportion of Hispanic carpenters from one employer to another. To convict those employers with fewer His-

panics of discrimination in hiring would be to make statistical variance a federal offense.

To illustrate the point, we can consider some process where racial, sexual, or ideological factors do not enter, such as the flipping of a coin. There is no reason to expect a persistent preponderance of heads over tails (or vice versa) on the *average*, but there is also no reason to expect exactly half heads and half tails every time we flip a coin a few times. That is, *variance* will exist.

To illustrate the effect of statistical variance, a coin was flipped ten times and then this experiment was repeated ten times. Here are the results.

Heads $\boxed{3}$ $\boxed{4}$ $\boxed{3}$ $\boxed{4}$ $\boxed{6}$ $\boxed{7}$ $\boxed{2}$ $\boxed{4}$ $\boxed{5}$ $\boxed{3}$

Tails $\boxed{7}$ $\boxed{6}$ $\boxed{7}$ $\boxed{6}$ $\boxed{4}$ $\boxed{3}$ $\boxed{8}$ $\boxed{6}$ $\boxed{5}$ $\boxed{7}$

At one extreme, there were seven heads and three tails, and at the other extreme eight tails and two heads. Statistics not only have averages, they have variance.

Translate this into employment decisions. Imagine that you are the employer who ends up with eight employees from one group and two from another, even though both groups are the same size and no different in qualifications, and even though you have been unbiased in selecting. Try explaining to EEOC and the courts that you ended up with four times as many employees from one group by random chance! You may be convicted of discrimination, even if you have only been guilty of statistical variance.

Of course some employers are biased, just as some coins are biased because of the way their weight is distributed on the design. This particular coin might have been biased; over all, it came up heads 41 percent of the time and tails 59 percent. But even if the coin was biased toward tails, it still came up heads seven times out of ten in one set of flips. If an employer were similarly biased in *favor* of a particular group, he could still be convicted of discrimination *against* that very group, if they ended up with less than half the "representation" of some other group.

No one needs to assume that this particular coin was unbiased or even that the results were accurately reported. Anyone can collect ten people and have them flip a coin ten times, to see the statistical variance for himself. Frivolous as this might seem, the results have deadly serious implications for the way people are convicted of violating federal laws, regulations, and guidelines. It might be especially instructive if this little experiment were performed by editorial writers for publications that fervently support affirmative action, or by clerks of the Supreme Court.

Even when conclusions are based only on differences that statisticians call "statistically significant," this by no means eliminates the basic problem. What is statistically significant depends upon the probability that such a result would have happened by random chance. A common litmus test used by statisticians is whether the event would occur more than 5 times out of a hundred by random chance. Applying this common test of statistical significance to affirmative action means that even in the most extreme case imaginable—zero dis-crimination and zero difference among racial, ethnic, and other groups—the EEOC could still run 10,000 employers' records through a computer and come up with about 500 "discriminators."

The illustration chosen is in fact too favorable to the proponents of affirmative action, because it shows the probability of incorrectly calling an employer a discriminator when there is only *one* group in question that might be discriminated against. Affirmative action has a number of groups whose statistical employment patterns can lead to charges of discrimination. To escape a false charge of discrimination, an employer must avoid being in the fatal 5 percent for *all* the groups in question simultaneously. That becomes progressively harder when there are more groups.

While there is a 95 percent chance for a non-discriminatory employer to escape when there is only one group, this falls to 86 percent when there are three separate groups and to 73 percent when there are six.[35] That is, even in a world of zero discrimination and zero differences among groups, more than one-fourth of all employers would be called "discriminators" by this common test of statistical significance, when there are six separate groups in question.

What this means is that the courts have sanctioned a procedure which insures that large-scale statistical "discrimination" will exist forever, regardless of what the actual facts may be. They have made statistical variance a federal offense.[36]

Shopping for Discrimination

Often the very same raw data point to different conclusions at different levels of aggregation. For example, statistics have shown that black faculty members earn less than white faculty members, but as these data are broken down by field of specialization, by number of publications, by possession (or non-possession) of a Ph.D. and by the ranking of the institution that issued it, then the black-white income difference not only shrinks but disappears, and in some fields reverses—with black faculty earning more than white faculty with the same characteristics.[37] For those who accept statistics as proof of discrimination, how much discrimination there is, and in what direction, depends upon how finely these data are broken down.

There is no "objective" or "scientific" way to decide at what level of aggregation to stop breaking the data down into finer categories. Nor have the laws or the courts specified in advance what will and will not be the accepted way to break down the statistics. Any individual or organization contemplating a lawsuit against an employer can arrange that employer's statistics in any number of possible ways and then go shopping among the possibilities for the one that will present the employment pattern in the worst light. This is a very effective strategy in a society in which groups differ enormously in their characteristics and choices, while the prevailing vision makes deviations from a random distribution evidence against the employer.

A discrimination case can depend entirely on what level of statistical breakdown the judge accepts, for different groups will be represented—or "under-represented"—differently according to how precisely occupations and qualifications are defined. While there were more black than Asian American "social scientists" receiving a Ph.D. in 1980, when social scientists were broken down further, there were nearly three times as many Asian as black *economists*.[38] While male recipients of Ph.D.'s in the social sciences outnumbered female recipients of Ph.D.'s by slightly less than two-to-one in 1980, men outnumbered women by more than four-to-one among doctorates in economics and by ten-to-one among doctorates in econometrics.[39] What is the employer hiring: social scientists, economists or econometricians? He may in fact be looking for an econometrician specializing in international trade—and there may be no statistics available on that. Nor can anyone infer the proportion of women or minority members available in that specialty from their distribution in broader categories, for the distribution changes at every level of aggregation.

The same principle applies in other fields as well. A computer manufacturer who is looking for an engineer is not looking for the same kind of engineer as a company that builds bridges. Nor is there the slightest reason to expect all groups to be distributed the same in these sub-specialties as they are among engineers in general. Even within a narrow occupational range such as mathematical specialists, blacks outnumber Asian Americans in gross numbers but Asian Americans outnumber blacks more than two-to-one among statisticians.[40]

When comparing any employer's work force with the available labor pool to determine "under-representation," everything depends on how that labor pool is defined—at what level of aggregation. Those who wish to argue for discrimination generally prefer broad, loose, heterogeneous categories. The concept of a "qualified" worker aids that approach. When the barely qualified is treated as being the same as the most highly skilled and experienced, it is the same as staying at a very general level of aggregation. Anything that creates or widens the disparity be-tween what the job requires and how the categories are defined increases the potential for statistical "discrimination."

An employer may be guilty or innocent according to what level of statistical aggregation a judge accepts, after the plaintiffs have shopped around among the many possibilities. But that is only part of the problem. A more fundamental problem is that *the burden of proof is on the accused* to prove his innocence, once suspicious numbers have been found. Shopping around for suspicious numbers is by no means difficult, especially for a federal agency, given statistical variance, multiple groups, multiple occupations, and wide-ranging differences in the characteristics and choices of the groups themselves.

Statistical aggregation is a major factor not only in courts of law but also in the court of public opinion. Many statistics from a very general level of aggregation are repeatedly presented in the media as demonstrating pervasive discrimination. The finer breakdowns are more likely to appear in specialized scholarly journals, read by a relative handful of people. Yet these finer breakdowns of statistics often tell a drastically different story, not only for black-white differences and male-female differences but for other groups as well.

For example, American Indian males earn significantly less than white males, and Asian males earn significantly more. Yet, as one holds a wide range of variables constant, these income differences shrink to the vanishing point. Asian Americans, for example, are distributed geographically in a very different pattern from whites. Asians are concentrated in higher income states, in more urban areas, and have more education. When all of this is held constant, their income advantage vanishes.[41] By the same token, when various demographic and cultural variables—notably proficiency in the English language—are held constant, the income disadvantages of Hispanic and American Indian males also disappear.[42]

It can hardly be expected that discrimination lawsuits and discrimination as a political issue will be correspondingly reduced any time soon. The methods by which it is measured in the courts and in politics insures that it will be a continuing source of controversy.

Poverty and huge intergroup differences in income are serious matters, whether or not discrimination is the cause—and whether or not affirmative action is the cure. Yet any attempt to deal with these very real disadvantages must first cut through the fog generated by a vision more powerful than its evidence—and, in fact, a vision shaping what courts will accept as evidence.

Discussion Questions

1. Dr. Sowell argues that one cannot prove that discrimination is all-pervasive simply on the basis of statistical differences between racial, ethnic, and gender groups in society. What evidence does he provide to support his claim that age, cultural differences, and other factors do a much better job (at least just as good a job) of accounting for disparities as does discrimination? Do you consider his case persuasive? Why or why not?

2. How does Dr. Sowell attempt to demonstrate his claim that the civil rights movement and subsequent affirmative action policies have helped to advance highly qualified minorities but have resulted in harm to lower-class minorities? What statistics does he cite in order to support his claim? Do you consider his case persuasive? Why or why not?

3. In the last section of his essay, Dr. Sowell argues that statistics are manipulated in order to "prove" discrimination even if there is no concrete evidence. How does he demonstrate this? What does he mean when he claims that current antidiscrimination policies make statistical variance a federal offense? Do you agree or disagree with Dr. Sowell's reasoning? Explain and defend your position.

Notes

1. U.S. Equal Employment Opportunity Commission, *Legislative History of Titles VII and XI of Civil Rights At of 1964* (Washington, D.C.: U.S. Government Printing Office, no date) pp. 1007–08, 1014, 3005, 3006, 3013, 3160, and *passim*.

2. Thomas Sowell, *Markets and Minorities* (New York: Basic Books, 1981), p. 11.

3. U.S. Bureau of the Census, *Social Indicators, 1976* (Washington, D.C.: U.S. Government Printing Office, 1977), pp. 454–456.

4. Peter Uhlenberg, "Demographic Correlates of Group Achievement: Contrasting Patterns of Mexican-Americans and Japanese-Americans," *Race, Creed, Color, or National Origin*, ed. Robert K. Yin (Itasca, Illinois: F. E. Peacock Publishers, 1973), p. 91.

5. Lucy W. Sells, "Leverage for Equal Opportunity Through Mastery of Mathematics," *Women and Minorities in Science*, ed. Sheila M. Humphreys (Boulder, Colorado: Westview Press, 1982), pp. 12, 16.

6. *Ibid.*, p. 11.

7. College Entrance Examination Board, *Profiles, College-Bound Seniors, 1981* (New York: College Entrance Examination Board, 1982), pp. 12, 22, 41, 51, 60, 65.

8. *Ibid.*, pp. 27, 36, 46, 55.

9. *Ibid.*, pp. 60, 79; Alexander Randall, "East Meets West," *Science*, November 1981, p. 72.

10. National Research Council, *Science, Engineering, and Humanities Doctorates in the United States* (Washington, D.C.: National Academy of Sciences, 1980), pp. 13, 39.

11. National Research Council, *Summary Report: 1980 Doctorate Recipients from United States Universities* (Washington, D.C.: National Academy Press, 1981), pp. 26, 29.

12. Sue E. Berryman, "Trends in and Causes of Minority and Female Representation Among Science and Mathematics Doctorates," mimeographed, The Rand Corporation, 1983, p. 13.

13. U.S. Commission on Civil Rights, *Unemployment and Underemployment Among Blacks, Hispanics, and Women* (Washington, D.C.: U.S. Commission on Civil Rights, 1982), p. 58.

14. Thomas Sowell, *Ethnic America* (New York: Basic Books, 1981), p. 222.

15. J. C. Furnas, *The Americans* (New York: G. P. Putnam's Sons, 1969), p. 86; Daniel Boorstin, *The Americans* (New York: Random House, 1958), Vol. I, p. 225.

16. Arthur Young, *A Tour in Ireland* (Shannon, Ireland: Irish University Press, 1970), Vol. I, pp. 377–379.

17. Thomas H. Holloway, *Immigrants on the Land* (Chapel Hill, N.C.: University of North Carolina Press, 1980), p. 151.

18. Harry Leonard Sawatzky, *They Sought a Country* (Berkeley: University of California Press, 1971), pp. 129, 244. Apparently Germans prospered in Honduras as well. *Ibid.*, pp. 361, 365.

19. Hattie Plum Williams, *The Czar's Germans* (Lincoln, Nebraska: American Historical Society of Germans from Russia, 1975), pp. 135, 159.

20. Carl Solberg, *Immigration and Nationalism* (Austin: University of Texas Press, 1970), pp. 27, 40.

21. Judith Laikin Elkin, *Jews of the Latin American Republics* (Chapel Hill, N.C.: University of North Carolina Press, 1980), pp. 214–237. See also Robert Weisbrot, *The Jews of Argentina* (Philadelphia: The Jewish Publication Society of America, 1979), pp. 175–184.

22. Thomas Sowell, *Ethnic America*, p. 238.

23. Daniel P. Moynihan, "Employment, Income, and the Ordeal of the Negro Family," *Daedalus*, Fall 1965, p. 752.

24. Daniel O. Price, *Changing Characteristics of the Negro Population* (Washington, D.C.: U.S. Government Printing Office, 1969), pp. 117, 118.

25. *Employment and Training Report of the President, 1981* (Washington, D.C.: U.S. Government Printing Office, 1981), p. 150.

26. *Ibid.*, p. 151.

27. Thomas Sowell, *Ethnic America*, p. 260.

28. Thomas Sowell, *The Economics and Politics of Race* (New York: William Morrow, 1983), p. 187.

29. U.S. Bureau of the Census, *Social Indicators III* (Washington, D.C.: U.S. Government Printing Office, 1980), p. 485.

30. Finis Welch, "Affirmative Action and Its Enforcement," *American Economic Review*, May 1981, p. 132.

31. Thomas Sowell, *Affirmative Action Reconsidered* (Washington, D.C.: American Enterprise Institute, 1975), pp. 16–22.

32. Martin Kilson, "Black Social Classes and Intergenerational Policy," *The Public Interest*, Summer 1981, p. 63.

33. U.S. Bureau of the Census, *Current Population Reports*, Series P-20, No. 366 (Washington, D.C.: U.S. Government Printing Office, 1981), pp. 182, 184.

34. U.S. Bureau of the Census, *Current Population Reports*, Series P-60, No. 80, p. 37; *Ibid.*, Series P-60, No. 132, pp. 41–42.

35. The probability that a non-discriminatory employer will escape a false charge of discrimination is 95 percent, when the standard of "statistical significance" is that his employment pattern would not occur more than 5 times out of 100 by random chance. But the probability of escaping the same false charge for three separate groups simultaneously is $(.95)^3$ or about 86 percent. When there are six separate groups, the probability is $(.95)^6$ or about 73 percent. Not all groups are separate; women and the aged, for example, overlap racial and ethnic groups. This complicates the calculation without changing the basic principle.

36. The greater ease of "proving" discrimination statistically, when there are multiple groups, multiple jobs, and substantial demographic, cultural and other differences between groups, may either take the form of finding more "discriminators" at a given level of statistical significance

(5 percent, for example) or using a more stringent standard of statistical significance (1 percent, for example) to produce a more impressive-looking case against a smaller number of "discriminators."

37. Thomas Sowell, *Affirmative Action Reconsidered* (Washington, D.C.: American Enterprise Institute, 1975), pp. 16–22.

38. Commission on Human Resources, National Research Council, *Summary Report: 1980 Doctorate Recipients from United States Universities* (National Academy Press, 1981), p. 27.

39. *Ibid.*, p. 25.

40. U.S. Bureau of the Census, *Current Population Reports*, Series P-23, No. 120 (Washington, D.C.: U.S. Government Printing Office, 1982), p. 5.

41. Barry R. Chiswick, "An Analysis of the Earnings and Employment of Asian-American Men," *Journal of Labor Economics*, April 1983, pp. 197–214.

42. Walter McManus, William Gould and Finis Welch, "Earnings of Hispanic Men: The Role of English Language Performance," *Ibid.*, pp. 101–130; Gary D. Sandefur, "Minority Group Status and the Wages of White, Black, and Indian Males," *Social Science Research*, March 1983, pp. 44–68.

SECTION B

Economic and Social Justice

Introduction

In today's world there are two primary forms by which the question of economic and social justice are manifested: (1) distributive justice, and (2) multiculturalism and justice.

I. Distributive Justice

On September 22, 1993, in an address on his Health Security Plan to a joint session of Congress and the nation, President Bill Clinton defended his plan by appealing to a number of principles, some of which apply to the issue debated in this section, *social justice*. Consider the following comments from the president's speech:

> [The principle of security] speaks to the human misery, to the costs, to the anxiety we hear about every day—all of us—when people talk about their problems with the present [health care] system. Security means that those who do not now have health care will have it; and for those who have it, it will never be taken away. We must achieve that security as soon as possible.
>
> Under our plan, every American would receive a health care security card that will guarantee a comprehensive package of benefits over the course of an entire lifetime, roughly comparable to the benefit package offered by most Fortune 500 companies. This health care security card will offer this package of benefits in a way that can never be taken away. . . .
>
> With this card, if you lose your job or you switch jobs, you're covered. If you leave your job to start a small business, you're covered. If you're an early retiree, you're covered. If someone in your family, unfortunately, had an illness that qualifies as a preexisting condition, you're still covered. If you get sick or a member of your family gets sick, even if it's a life-threatening illness, you're covered. And if your insurance company tries to drop you for any reason, you will still be covered, because that will be illegal. . . .
>
> And now, it is our turn to strike a blow for freedom in this country. The freedom of Americans to live without fear that their own nation's health care system won't be there for them when they need it.[1]

Although the President and the First Lady, Hillary Rodham Clinton, courageously took on the enormous task of reforming our health care system, their plan failed to make it through Congress. No one doubts that they should be applauded for their efforts, but a government program of universal health coverage raises some important philosophical questions concerning the meaning of *distributive justice*: What is the proper role of government in people's lives? What is the nature of private property? Do citizens have a right to receive certain positive benefits (such as health care) from their government? In other words, the president's health care plan raises questions about the meaning and application of such concepts as *liberty, justice,* and *ownership*.

There are a number of social philosophers, such as John Rawls (Chapter 36," A Theory of Justice") and Kai Nielsen (Chapter 37, "Radical Egalitarianism"), who would probably defend some type of universal health care plan as morally justifiable, because they agree with the president that Americans can only truly exercise *liberty* when they are "without fear that their own nation's health care system won't be there for them when they need it." That is, these philosophers believe that the principle of *justice* trumps property rights so that benefits (in this case, health care) can be distributed fairly to all, and, consequently, that it will lead to the greatest liberty for the greatest number. But it should be acknowledged that Professor Rawls and Professor Nielsen disagree as to how much redistribution is permissible. The latter's position is considered a defense of socialism.

On the other hand, there are other social philosophers, such as Murray N. Rothbard (Chapter 38, "Property, Exchange, and Libertarianism"), who see the president's plan as a violation of private property rights and personal liberty and as therefore unjust. That is to say, some social philosophers do not agree with the president's claim that a government-mandated universal health care plan will "strike a blow for freedom in this country"; rather, they argue that such a plan limits freedom because it entails the government confiscating the fairly acquired assets of employers and citizens so that it can redistribute these assets to those who are not entitled to them. It also requires all citizens to participate in the system without the consent of each individual who is forced to participate in it. Social philosophers who hold to this position see *property rights* and personal *liberty* as the means by which one evaluates the *justice* of an act. Thus, the president's health care plan is unjust since it violates property rights as well as personal liberty.

Of course, the philosophical dispute over distributive justice is much bigger than the issue of health care, but that issue, because it is paramount in the minds of most Americans, serves as an excellent way to introduce the dispute. Other issues, such as public education, welfare, food stamps, and government funding of public and private works, also raise the same questions about the meaning of distributive justice.

II. Multiculturalism and Justice

On university and college campuses today there is a movement popularly known as "political correctness." It is nearly impossible to define or to use the term without provoking vitriolic denunciations, accusations of either brutal caricature or false hysteria, or congratulations. So I offer, with great trepidation, the following definition.

"PC" can be loosely defined as a web of interconnected, though not mutually dependent, ideological beliefs that have challenged the traditional nature of the university as well as traditional curriculum, standards of excellence, and views about justice, truth, and the objectivity of knowledge, while accentuating our cultural, gender, class, and racial differences in the name of campus diversity. In some circles these beliefs have evolved into an unchallenged orthodoxy. Typically, PC is politically leftist, although some of its harshest critics are on the political left,[2] just as many critics of McCarthyism were on the political right.

Sensitivity to physical, racial, ethnic, and gender differences is also stressed. Although such a stress seems consistent with normal canons of politeness and respect, in some cases the silly has trivialized the serious. On one campus, for example, in the name of the noble goal of interpersonal sensitivity, students were told that short students should be called "vertically challenged."

Even the Las Vegas casino industry is not exempt. In summer 1993 Mirage Resorts Incorporated was building the hotel/casino resort, Treasure Island. On the north and east sides of the facility are replicas of old trading ships, resembling to some degree the Pirates of the Caribbean found in Disneyland. Each ship has a name inscribed on its side. One of the ships was named the Sir Francis Drake, after the great explorer and entrepreneur. Although Drake was the foremost British explorer and naval hero of the Elizabethan age, whose influence upon history is immeasurable, Drake also engaged in the slave trade. This fact upset a number of activists who argued that naming the ship after Drake is terribly insensitive to African-Americans. The name was eventually changed to the Royal Britannia.

The fact that the hotel at which this ship was built, Treasure Island, celebrates piracy, which entailed robbery, rape, and murder, did not seem to bother many people. Evidently, the ancestors of those victimized by pirates do not have a strong political lobby in southern Nevada. But why stop at Treasure Island? Caesar's Palace is named after the leader of an empire responsible for the brutal deaths of thousands of Christian martyrs. The Luxor, a hotel/casino built in the shape of a pyramid, extols the accomplishments of ancient Egypt. Of course, the pyramids were built with slave labor.

The reason why this seems so absurd is that history is much more complex than a series of unprosecuted crimes. Rather, it is a dynamic process of conflicting ideas, shaped by philosophy, geography, religion, and politics, resulting in everything from the grandeur of human genius, compassion, and love to the dehumanization of persons by means of gulag, gas chamber, crusade, and chains. If there is such a thing as original sin, it has been equitably distributed. But we must not forget: "Where sin abounded grace did abound more exceedingly."[3]

Whether rightly or wrongly, PC is often linked with *multiculturalism*, a philosophy of education that may be more difficult to define precisely than political correctness. In general it is probably fair to define multiculturalism as a philosophy of education that stresses the unique contributions of different cultures to the history of the world. According to this view, to emphasize "Western thought" at the expense of other types of thought is "Eurocentric" and consequently unjust. Thus, the defender of multiculturalism sees its incorporation into all levels of education and society as a means of achieving social justice.

Some multiculturalists argue that an African-American student who studies only Dead White European Males (DWEMs), such as Plato, Aristotle, and Galileo, will not do as well as he would studying the greats of "African" culture. This is why Afrocentric scholar Molefi Kete Asante claims that wherever people of African descent may live, "we respond to the same rhythms of the universe, the same cosmological sensibilities. . . . Our Africanity is our ultimate reality . . . . There exists an emotional, cultural, psychological connection . . . that spans the ocean."[4]

Philosopher Steven Yates argues that there are primarily two forms of multiculturalism, one *weak multiculturalism* and the other *strong multiculturalism*. The former sees the understanding, appreciation, and recognition of the accomplishments of those who have been ignored and oppressed as values grounded in our common humanity. That is to say, there are objective moral goods—such as justice and equality—for which we should strive.[5]

The latter form, strong multiculturalism, is much more closely aligned with PC. It makes a number of controversial claims, among them the following: (1) No one culture, thinker, or group has discovered the objective "truth" about anything, since there is no universal truth to be found in any culture. This is why the strong multiculturalist can say that all cultures have contributed "equally" to the history of the human race. Take, for example, the comments by the President's Task Force on Multicultural Education and Diversity (at Cal State, Long Beach): "The problem with 'exclusive curricula' is that they equate the value of a dominant group with 'universality,' and falsely present the experience of a dominant group as a formula for all other groups."[6]

(2) The ideas produced by members of one's own ethnic or racial group are easier to understand and comprehend.

(3) Every judgement can be reduced to a "cultural perspective." Barbara Herrnstein-Smith, Duke University English professor and former president of the Modern Language Association, seemed to support this claim when she remarked. "There is no knowledge, no standard, no choice that is objective. . . . Even Homer is a product of a specific culture, and it is possible to imagine cultures in which Homer would not be very interesting."[7]

The authors in this section address, each in his own way, these three controversial claims.

Chapter 39 ("The Challenge of Diversity and Multicultural Education"), put together by the President's Task Force on Multicultural Education at California State University at Long Beach, is a proposal for and defense of multicultural education at the university level. It is typical of proposals at hundreds of other colleges and universities throughout North America. In reply, Professor George Reisman ("Education and the Racist Road to Barbarism,"Chapter 40) argues that multicultural education like that proposed in Chapter 39, though employed to halt racism, makes certain assumptions that can only be described as racist. In Chapter 41, Mr. Jung Min Choi and Professor John W. Murphy present a philosophical defense of some of the concepts associated with multiculturalism and political correctness ("Skepticism, Nihilism, Amorality, and Anarchy: The Legacy of PC?"). A critique of Chapter 41 is the focus of Chapter 42 ("Two Philosophical Problems with Political Correctness"). In this chapter, I argue that Mr. Choi and Professor Murphy commit a number of mistakes in reasoning.

Notes

1. President Bill Clinton, "Address of the President to the Joint Session of Congress (September 22, 1993)," in *The President's Health Security Plan: The Complete Draft and Final Reports of the White House Domestic Policy Council* (New York: Random House, 1993), 108–109, 125.

2. See, for example, Irving Howe, "The Value of the Canon," in *Are You Politically Correct?: Debating America's Cultural Standards*, ed. Francis J. Beckwith and Michael Bauman (Buffalo, N.Y.: Prometheus, 1993), 133–146.

3. Romans 5:20 (ASB).

4. Molefi Kete Asante, *Afrocentricity*, rev. ed. (Trenton, 1988), as quoted in Arthur M. Schlesinger, Jr., *The Disuniting of America: Reflections on Multicultural Society* (New York: W. W. Norton, 1992), 65.

5. See Steven Yates, "Multiculturalism and Epistemology," *Public Affairs Quarterly* 6 (1992), 435–456.

6. From *Are You Politically Correct?*, 79.

7. As quoted in Dinesh D'Souza, *Illiberal Education: The Politics of Race and Sex on Campus* (New York: The Free Press, 1991), 157.

For Further Reading

Francis J. Beckwith and Michael E. Bauman, eds., *Are You Politically Correct?: Debating America's Cultural Standards* (Buffalo, N.Y.: Prometheus, 1993).

Kai Nielsen, *Equality and Liberty: A Defense of Radical Egalitarianism* (Totowa, N.J.: Rowman and Littlefield, 1985).

Michael Novak, *The Spirit of Democratic Capitalism* (New York: Simon and Schuster, 1982).

Robert Nozick, *Anarchy, State, and Utopia* (New York: Basic Books, 1974).

John Rawls, *A Theory of Justice* (Cambridge: Belknap Press of the Harvard University Press, 1971).

J. Reiman, "The Fallacy of Libertarian Capitalism," *Ethics* (October 1981).

Murray Rothbard, *For a New Liberty* (New York: Macmillan, 1973).

Arthur M. Schlesinger, Jr., *The Disuniting of America: Reflections on Multicultural Society* (New York: W. W. Norton, 1992).

Cornel West, "The New Cultural Politics of Difference," *October* 53 (Summer 1990).

Steven Yates, "Multiculturalism and Epistemology," *Public Affairs Quarterly* 6 (1992).

Distributive Justice

36

A Theory of Justice

John Rawls

John Rawls is Professor of Philosophy at Harvard University. He is one of the foremost political philosophers of the twentieth-century and is the author of numerous scholarly articles as well as a book that has become a contemporary classic, *A Theory of Justice* (1971). He is also the author of *Political Liberalism* (1993).

In this essay, Professor Rawls defends a theory of justice that most commentators have argued is consistent with the ideas of the liberal wing of the Democratic Party in the United States. In order to establish the rationality of this view, Professor Rawls asks us to use our imagination and pretend that each of us is behind a "veil of ignorance," that is, that we are unaware of our natural talents, age, appearance, social status, financial fortune or lack thereof, class, race, gender, etc. He then asks us to consider what principles of justice we would choose behind this veil of ignorance. Because there would be no bias behind the veil of ignorance (because one would not know who one really is or what one really has), Professor Rawls argues that the principles of justice arrived at by agreement behind that veil are most likely to be truly just and

rational. He suggests two principles, the first that "each person is to have an equal right to the most extensive basic liberty compatible with a similar liberty for others." The second principle is that "social and economic inequalities are to be arranged so that they are both (a) to the greatest benefit of the least advantaged, and (b) attached to offices and positions open to all under conditions of fair equality of opportunity. . . ." Professor Rawls then explains how these principles apply in society and government.

I shall begin by considering the role of the principles of justice. Let us assume, to fix ideas, that a society is a more or less self-sufficient association of persons who in their relations to one another recognize certain rules of conduct as binding and who for the most part act in accordance with them. Suppose further that these rules specify a system of cooperation designed to advance the good of those taking part in it. Then, although a society is a cooperative venture for mutual advantage, it is typically marked by a conflict as well as by an identity of interests. There is an identity of interests since social cooperation makes possible a better life for all than any would have if each were to live solely by his own efforts. There is a conflict of interests since persons are not indifferent as to how the greater benefits produced by their collaboration are distributed, for in order to pursue their ends they each prefer a larger to a lesser share. A set of principles is required for choosing among the various social arrangements which determine this division of advantages and for underwriting an agreement on the proper distributive shares. These principles are the principles of social justice: they provide a way of assigning rights and duties in the basic institutions of society and they define the appropriate distribution of the benefits and burdens of social cooperation. . . .

Men disagree about which principles should define the basic terms of their association. Yet we may still say, despite this disagreement, that they each have a conception of justice. That is, they understand the need for, and they are prepared to affirm, a characteristic set of principles for assigning basic rights and duties and for determining what they take to be the proper distribution of the benefits and burdens of social cooperation. Thus it seems natural to think of the concept of justice as distinct from the various conceptions of justice and as being specified by the role which these different sets of principles, these different conceptions, have in common. Those who hold different conceptions of justice can, then, still agree that institutions are just when no arbitrary distinctions are made between persons in the assigning of basic rights and duties and when the rules determine a proper balance between competing claims to the advantages of social life. . . .

Some measure of agreement in conceptions of justice is, however, not the only prerequisite for a viable human community. There are other fundamental social problems, in particular those of coordination, efficiency, and stability. Thus the plans of individuals need to be fitted together so that their activities are compatible with one another and they can all be carried through without anyone's legitimate expectations being severely disappointed. Moreover, the execution of these plans should lead to the achievement of social ends in ways that are efficient and consistent with justice. And finally the scheme of social cooperation must be stable; it must be more or less regularly complied with and its basic rules willingly acted upon; and when infractions occur, stabilizing forces should exist that prevent further violations and tend to restore the arrangement. Now it is evident that these three problems are connected with that of justice. In the absence of a certain measure of agreement on what is just and unjust, it is clearly more difficult for individuals to coordinate their plans efficiently in order to insure that mutually beneficial arrangements are maintained. Distrust and resentment corrode the ties of civility, and suspicion and hostility tempt men to act in ways they would otherwise avoid. So while the distinctive role of conceptions of justice is to specify basic rights and duties and to determine the appropriate distributive shares, the way in which a conception does this is bound to affect the problems of efficiency, coordination, and stability. We cannot, in general, assess a conception of justice by its distributive role alone, however useful this role may be in identifying the concept of justice. We must take into account its wider connections; for even though justice has a certain priority, being the most important

virtue of institutions, it is still true that, other things equal, one conception of justice is preferable to another when its broader consequences are more desirable. . . .

For us the primary subject of justice is the basic structure of society, or more exactly, the way in which the major social institutions distribute fundamental rights and duties and determine the division of advantages from social cooperation. By major institutions I understand the political constitution and the principal economic and social arrangements. Thus the legal protection of freedom of thought and liberty of conscience, competitive markets, private property in the means of production, and the monogamous family are examples of major social institutions. Taken together as one scheme, the major institutions define men's rights and duties and influence their life-prospects, what they can expect to be and how well they can hope to do. The basic structure is the primary subject of justice because its effects are so profound and present from the start. The intuitive notion here is that this structure contains various social positions and that men born into different positions have different expectations of life determined, in part, by the political system as well as by economic and social circumstances. In this way the institutions of society favor certain starting places over others. These are especially deep inequalities. Not only are they pervasive, but they affect men's initial chances in life; yet they cannot possibly be justified by an appeal to the notions of merit or desert. It is these inequalities, presumably inevitable in the basic structure of any society, to which the principles of social justice must in the first instance apply. These principles, then, regulate the choice of a political constitution and the main elements of the economic and social system. The justice of a social scheme depends essentially on how fundamental rights and duties are assigned and on the economic opportunities and social conditions in the various sectors of society. . . .

My aim is to present a conception of justice which generalizes and carries to a higher level of abstraction the familiar theory of the social contract as found, say, in Locke, Rousseau, and Kant. In order to do this we are not to think of the original contract as one to enter a particular society or to set up a particular form of government. Rather, the guiding idea is that the principles of justice for the basic structure of society are the object of the original agreement. They are the principles that free and rational persons concerned to further their own interests would accept in an initial position of equality as defining the fundamental terms of their association. These principles are to regulate all further agreements; they specify the kinds of social cooperation that can be entered into and the forms of government that can be established. This way of regarding the principles of justice I shall call justice as fairness.

Thus we are to imagine that those who engage in social cooperation choose together, in one joint act, the principles which are to assign basic rights and duties and to determine the division of social benefits. Men are to decide in advance how they are to regulate their claims against one another and what is to be the foundation charter of their society. Just as each person must decide by rational reflection what constitutes his good, that is, the system of ends which it is rational for him to pursue, so a group of persons must decide once and for all what is to count among them as just and unjust. The choice which rational men would make in this hypothetical situation of equal liberty, assuming for the present that this choice problem has a solution, determines the principles of justice.

In justice as fairness the original position of equality corresponds to the state of nature in the traditional theory of the social contract. This original position is not, of course, thought of as an actual historical state of affairs, much less as a primitive condition of culture. It is understood as a purely hypothetical situation characterized so as to lead to a certain conception of justice. Among the essential features of this situation is that no one knows his place in society, his class position or social status, nor does any one know his fortune in the distribution of natural assets and abilities, his intelligence, strength, and the like. I shall even assume that the parties do not know their conceptions of the good or their special psychological propensities. The principles of justice are chosen behind a veil of ignorance. This ensures that no one is advantaged or disadvantaged in the choice of principles by the outcome of natural chance or the contingency of social circumstances. Since all are similarly situated and no one is able to design principles to favor his particular condition, the principles of justice are the result of a fair agreement or bargain. For given the circumstances of the original position, the symmetry of everyone's relations to each other, this initial situation is fair between individuals as moral persons, that is, as rational beings with their own ends and capable, I shall assume, of a sense of justice. The original position is, one might say, the appropriate initial status quo, and thus the funda-mental agreements reached in it are fair. This explains the propriety of the name "justice as fairness": it conveys the idea that the principles of justice are agreed to in an initial situation that is fair. . . .

Justice as fairness begins, as I have said, with one of the most general of all choices which persons might make together, namely, with the choice of the first principles of a conception of justice which is to regulate all subsequent criticism and reform of institutions. Then, having chosen a conception of justice, we can suppose that they are to choose a constitution and a legislature to enact laws, and so on, all in accordance with the principles of justice initially agreed upon. Our social situation is just if it is such that by this sequence of hypothetical agreements we would have contracted into the general system of rules which defines it. Moreover, assuming that the original position does determine a set of principles (that is, that a particular conception of justice would be chosen), it will then be true that whenever social institutions satisfy these principles those engaged in them can say to one another that they are cooperating on terms to which they would agree if they were free and equal persons whose relations with respect to one another were fair. They could all view their arrangements as meeting the stipulations which they would acknowledge in an initial situation that embodies widely accepted and reasonable constraints on the choice of principles. The general recognition of this fact would provide the basis for a public acceptance of the corresponding principles of justice. No society can, of course, be a scheme of cooperation which men enter voluntarily in a literal sense; each person finds himself placed at birth in some particular position in some particular society, and the nature of this position materially affects his life prospects. Yet a society satisfying the principles of justice as fairness comes as close as a society can to being a voluntary scheme, for it meets the principles which free and equal persons would assent to under circumstances that are fair. In this sense its members are autonomous and the obligations they recognize self-imposed.

One feature of justice as fairness is to think of the parties in the initial situation as rational and mutually disinterested. This does not mean that the parties are egoists, that is, individuals with only certain kinds of interests, say in wealth, prestige, and domination. But they are conceived as not taking an interest in one another's interests. They are to presume that even their spiritual aims may be opposed, in the way that the aims of those of different religions may be opposed. Moreover, the concept of rationality must be interpreted as far as possible in the narrow sense, standard in economic theory, of taking the most effective means to given ends. . . .

In working out the conception of justice as fairness one main task clearly is to determine which principles of justice would be chosen in the original position. To do this we must describe this situation in some detail and formulate with care the problem of choice which it presents. . . . It may be observed, however, that once the principles of justice are thought of as arising from an original agreement in a situation of equality, it is an open question whether the principle of utility would be acknowledged. Offhand it hardly seems likely that persons who view themselves as equals, entitled to press their claims upon one another, would agree to a principle which may require lesser life prospects for some simply for the sake of a greater sum of advantages enjoyed by others. Since each desires to protect his interests, his capacity to advance his conception of the good, no one has a reason to acquiesce in an enduring loss for himself in order to bring about a greater net balance of satisfaction. In the absence of strong and lasting benevolent impulses, a rational man would not accept a basic structure merely because it maximized the algebraic sum of advantages irrespective of its permanent effects on his own basic rights and interests. Thus it seems that the principle of utility is incompatible with the conception of social cooperation among equals for mutual advantage. It appears to be inconsistent with the idea of reciprocity implicit in the notion of a well-ordered society. . . .

I shall maintain instead that the person in the initial situation would choose two rather different principles: the first requires equality in the assignment of basic rights and duties, while the second holds that social and economic inequalities, for example inequalities of wealth and authority, are just only if they result in compensating benefits for everyone, and in particular for the least advantaged members of society. These principles rule out justifying institutions on the grounds that the hardships of some are offset by a greater good in the aggregate. It may be expedient but it is not just that some should have less in order that others may prosper. But there is no injustice in the greater benefits earned by a few provided that the situation of persons not so fortunate is thereby improved. The intuitive idea is that since everyone's well-being depends upon a scheme of cooperation without which no one could have a satisfactory life, the division of advantages should be such

as to draw forth the willing cooperation of others when some workable scheme is a necessary condition of the welfare of all. Once we decide to look for a conception of justice that nullifies the accidents of natural endowment and the contingencies of social circumstance as counters in quest for political and economic advantage, we are led to these principles. They express the result of leaving aside those aspects of the social world that seem arbitrary from a moral point of view. . . .

Justice as fairness is an example of what I have called a contract theory. The merit of the contract terminology is that it conveys the idea that principles of justice may be conceived as principles that would be chosen by rational persons, and that in this way conceptions of justice may be explained and justified. . . . Furthermore, principles of justice deal with conflicting claims upon the advantages won by social cooperation; they apply to the relations among several persons or groups. The word "contract" suggests this plurality as well as the condition that the appropriate division of advantages must be in accordance with principles acceptable to all parties. The condition of publicity for principles of justice is also connoted by the contract phraseology. Thus, if these principles are the outcome of an agreement, citizens have a knowledge of the principles that others follow. . . .

I have said that the original position is the appropriate initial status quo which insures that the fundamental agreements reached in it are fair. This fact yields the name "justice as fairness." It is clear, then, that I want to say that one conception of justice is more reasonable than another, or justifiable with respect to it, if rational persons in the initial situation would choose its principles over those of the other for the role of justice. Conceptions of justice are to be ranked by their acceptability to persons so circumstanced. Understood in this way the question of justification is settled by working out a problem of deliberation: we have to ascertain which principles it would be rational to adopt given the contractual situation. This connects the theory of justice with the theory of rational choice. . . .

One should not be misled . . . by the somewhat unusual conditions which characterize the original position. The idea here is simply to make vivid to ourselves the restrictions that it seems reasonable to impose on arguments for principles of justice, and therefore on these principles themselves. Thus it seems reasonable and generally acceptable that no one should be advantaged or disadvantaged by natural fortune or social circumstances in the choice of principles. It also seems widely agreed that it should be impossible to tailor principles to the circumstances of one's own case. We should insure further that particular inclinations and aspirations, and persons' conceptions of their good do not affect the principles adopted. The aim is to rule out those principles that it would be rational to propose for acceptance, however little the chance of success, only if one knew certain things that are irrelevant from the standpoint of justice. For example, if a man knew that he was wealthy, he might find it rational to advance the principle that various taxes for welfare measures be counted unjust; if he knew that he was poor, he would most likely propose the contrary principle. To represent the desired restrictions one imagines a situation in which everyone is deprived of this sort of information. One excludes the knowledge of those contingencies which sets men at odds and allows them to be guided by their prejudices. In this manner the veil of ignorance is arrived at in a natural way. This concept should cause no difficulty if we keep in mind the constraints on arguments that it is meant to express. At any time we can enter the original position, so to speak, simply by following a certain procedure, namely, by arguing for principles of justice in accordance with these restrictions.

It seems reasonable to suppose that the parties in the original position are equal. That is, all have the same rights in the procedure for choosing principles; each can make proposals, submit reasons for their acceptance, and so on. Obviously the purpose of these conditions is to represent equality between human beings as moral persons, as creatures having a conception of their good and capable of a sense of justice. The basis of equality is taken to be similarity in these two respects. Systems of ends are not ranked in value; and each man is presumed to have the requisite ability to understand and to act upon whatever principles are adopted. Together with the veil of ignorance, these conditions define the principles of justice as those which rational persons concerned to advance their interests would consent to as equals when none are known to be advantaged or disadvantaged by social and natural contingencies.

There is, however, another side to justifying a particular description of the original position. This is to see if the principles which would be chosen match our considered convictions of justice or extend them in an acceptable way. We can note whether applying these principles would lead us to make the same judgments about the basic structure of society which we now make intuitively and in which we

have the greatest confidence; or whether, in cases where our present judgments are in doubt and given with hesitation, these principles offer a resolution which we can affirm on reflection. There are questions which we feel sure must be answered in a certain way. For example, we are confident that religious intolerance and racial discrimination are unjust. We think that we have examined these things with care and have reached what we believe is an impartial judgment not likely to be distorted by an excessive attention to our own interests. These convictions are provisional fixed points which we presume any conception of justice must fit. But we have much less assurance as to what is the correct distribution of wealth and authority. Here we may be looking for a way to remove our doubts. We can check an interpretation of the initial situation, then, by the capacity of its principles to accommodate our firmest convictions and to provide guidance where guidance is needed. . . .

I shall now state in a provisional form the two principles of justice that I believe would be chosen in the original position. . . .

The first statement of the two principles reads as follows.

First: each person is to have an equal right to the most extensive basic liberty compatible with a similar liberty for others.

Second: social and economic inequalities are to be arranged so that they are both (a) reasonably expected to be to everyone's advantage, and (b) attached to positions and offices open to all. . . .

By way of general comment, these principles primarily apply, as I have said, to the basic structure of society. They are to govern the assignment of rights and duties and to regulate the distribution of social and economic advantages. As their formulation suggests, these principles presuppose that the social structure can be divided into two more or less distinct parts, the first principle applying to the one, the second to the other. They distinguish between those aspects of the social system that define and secure the equal liberties of citizenship and those that specify and establish social and economic inequalities. The basic liberties of citizens are, roughly speaking, political liberty (the right to vote and to be eligible for public office) together with freedom of speech and assembly; liberty of conscience and freedom of thought; freedom of the person along with the right to hold (personal) property; and freedom from arbitrary arrest and seizure as defined by the concept of the rule of law. These liberties are all required to be equal by the first principle, since citizens of a just society are to have the same basic rights.

The second principle applies, in the first approximation, to the distribution of income and wealth and to the design of organizations that make use of differences in authority and responsibility, or chains of command. While the distribution of wealth and income need not be equal, it must be to everyone's advantage, and at the same time, positions of authority and offices of command must be accessible to all. One applies the second principle by holding positions open, and then, subject to this constraint, arranges social and economic inequalities so that everyone benefits.

These principles are to be arranged in a serial order with the first principle prior to the second. This ordering means that a departure from the institutions of equal liberty required by the first principle cannot be justified by, or compensated for, by greater social and economic advantages. The distribution of wealth and income, and the hierarchies of authority, must be consistent with both the liberties of equal citizenship and equality of opportunity.

Suppose that the basic structure of society distributes certain primary goods, that is, things that every rational man is presumed to want. These goods normally have a use whatever a person's rational plan of life. For simplicity, assume that the chief primary goods at the disposition of society are rights and liberties, powers and opportunities, income and wealth. . . . These are the social primary goods. Other primary goods such as health and vigor, intelligence and imagination, are natural goods; although their possession is influenced by the basic structure, they are not so directly under its control. Imagine, then a hypothetical initial arrangement in which all the social primary goods are equally distributed: everyone has similar rights and duties, and income and wealth are evenly shared. This state of affairs provides a benchmark for judging improvements. If certain inequalities of wealth and organizational powers would make everyone better off than in this hypothetical starting situation, then they accord with the general conception.

Now it is possible, at least theoretically, that by giving up some of their fundamental liberties men are sufficiently compensated by the resulting social and economic gains. The general conception of justice imposes no restrictions on what sort of inequalities are permissible; it only requires that everyone's position be improved. We need not suppose anything so drastic as consenting to a condition of slavery.

Imagine instead that men forego certain political rights when the economic returns are significant and their capacity to influence the course of policy by the exercise of these rights would be marginal in any case. It is this kind of exchange which the two principles as stated rule out; being arranged in serial order they do not permit exchanges between basic liberties and economic and social gains. The serial ordering of principles expresses an underlying preference among primary social goods. When this preference is rational so likewise is the choice of these principles in this order. . . .

The fact that the two principles apply to institutions has certain consequences. Several points illustrate this. First of all, the rights and liberties referred to by these principles are those which are defined by the public rules of the basic structure. Whether men are free is determined by the rights and duties established by the major institutions of society. Liberty is a certain pattern of social forms. The first principle simply requires that certain sorts of rules, those defining basic liberties, apply to everyone equally and that they allow the most extensive liberty compatible with a like liberty for all. The only reason for circumscribing the rights defining liberty and making men's freedom less extensive than it might otherwise be is that these equal rights as institutionally defined would interfere with one another.

. . .

Now the second principle insists that each person benefit from permissible inequalities in the basic structure. This means that it must be reasonable for each relevant representative man defined by this structure, when he views it as a going concern, to prefer his prospects with the inequality to his prospects without it. One is not allowed to justify differences in income or organizational powers on the ground that the disadvantages of those in one position are outweighed by the greater advantages of those in another. Much less can infringements of liberty be counterbalanced in this way. Applied to the basic structure, the principle of utility would have us maximize the sum of expectations of representative men (weighted by the number of persons they represent, on the classical view); and this would permit us to compensate for the losses of some by the gains of others. Instead, the two principles require that everyone benefit from economic and social inequalities. It is obvious, however, that there are indefinitely many ways in which all may be advantaged when the initial arrangement of equality is taken as a benchmark. How then are we to choose among these possibilities? The principles must be specified so that they yield a determinate conclusion. I now turn to this problem. . . .

In a basic structure with n relevant representatives, first maximize the welfare of the worst-off representative man; second, for equal welfare of the worst-off representative, maximize the welfare of the second worst-off representative man, and so on until the last case which is, for equal welfare of all the preceding n–1 representatives, maximize the welfare of the best-off representative man. We may think of this as the lexical difference principle. However, I shall always use the difference principle in the simpler form. And therefore. . . .

> the second principle is to read as follows. Social and economic inequalities are to be arranged so that they are both (a) to the greatest benefit of the least advantaged and (b) attached to offices and positions open to all under conditions of fair equality of opportunity. . . .

The idea of the original position is to set up a fair procedure so that any principles agreed to will be just. The aim is to use the notion of pure procedural justice as a basis of theory. Somehow we must nullify the effects of specific contingencies which put men at odds and tempt them to exploit social and natural circumstances to their own advantage. Now in order to do this I assume that the parties are situated behind a veil of ignorance. They do not know how the various alternatives will affect their own particular case and they are obliged to evaluate principles solely on the basis of general considerations.

It is assumed, then, that the parties do not know certain kinds of particular facts. First of all, no one knows his place in society, his class position or social status; nor does he know his fortune in the distribution of natural assets and abilities, his intelligence and strength, and the like. Nor, again, does anyone know his conception of the good, the particulars of his rational plan of life, or even the special features of his psychology such as his aversion to risk or liability to optimism or pessimism. More than this, I assume that the parties do not know the particular circumstances of their own society. That is, they do not know its economic or political situation, or the level of civilization and culture it has been able to achieve. The persons in the original position have no information as to which generation they belong. . . . In order to carry through the idea of the original position, the parties must not know the contingencies that set them in opposition. They must choose prin-

ciples the consequences of which they are prepared to live with whatever generation they turn out to belong to.

As far as possible, then, the only particular facts which the parties know is that their society is subject to the circumstances of justice and whatever this implies. It is taken for granted, however, that they know the general facts about human society. They understand political affairs and the principles of economic theory; they know the basis of social organization and the laws of human psychology. Indeed, the parties are presumed to know whatever general facts affect the choice of the principles of justice. There are no limitations on general information, that is, on general laws and theories, since conceptions of justice must be adjusted to the characteristics of the systems of social cooperation which they are to regulate, and there is no reason to rule out these facts. . . .

The original position is not to be thought of as a general assembly which includes at one moment everyone who will live at some time; or, much less, as an assembly of everyone who could live at some time. It is not a gathering of all actual or possible persons. To conceive of the original position in either of these ways is to stretch fantasy too far; the conception would cease to be a natural guide to intuition. In any case, it is important that the original position be interpreted so that one can at any time adopt its perspective. It must make no difference when one takes up its viewpoint, or who does so; the restrictions must be such that the same principles are always chosen. The veil of ignorance is a key condition in meeting this requirement. It insures not only that the information available is relevant, but that it is at all times the same. . . .

Thus there follows the very important consequence that the parties have no basis for bargaining in the usual sense. No one knows his situation in society nor his natural assets, and therefore no one is in a position to tailor principles to his advantage. We might imagine that one of the contractees threatens to hold out unless the others agree to principles favorable to him. But how does one know which principles are especially in his interests? . . .

I have assumed throughout that the persons in the original position are rational. In choosing between principles each tries as best he can to advance his interests. But I have also assumed that the parties do not know their conception of the good. This means that while they know that they have some rational plan of life, they do not know the details of this plan, the particular ends and interest which it is calculated to promote. How, then, can they decide which conceptions of justice are most to their advantage? Or must we suppose that they are reduced to mere guessing? To meet this difficulty, I postulate that . . . they assume that they would prefer more primary social goods rather than less. Of course, it may turn out, once the veil of ignorance is removed, that some of them for religious or other reasons may not, in fact, want more of these goods.

But from the standpoint of the original position, it is rational for the parties to suppose that they do want a larger share, since in any case they are not compelled to accept more if they do not wish to, nor does a person suffer from a greater liberty. Thus even though the parties are deprived of information about their particular ends, they have enough knowledge to rank the alternatives. They know that in general they must try to protect their liberties, widen their opportunities, and enlarge their means for promoting their aims whatever these are. . . .

The assumption of mutually disinterested rationality, then, comes to this: the persons in the original position try to acknowledge principles which advance their system of ends as far as possible. They do this by attempting to win for themselves the highest index of primary social goods, since this enables them to promote their conception of the good most effectively whatever it turns out to be. The parties do not seek to confer benefits or to impose injuries on one another; they are not moved by affection or rancor. Nor do they try to gain relative to each other; they are not envious or vain. . . .

It seems clear . . . that the two principles are at least a plausible conception of justice. The question, though, is how one is to argue for them more systematically. Now there are several things to do. One can work out their consequences for institutions and note their implications for fundamental social policy. In this way they are tested by a comparison with our considered judgments of justice. . . . But one can also try to find arguments in their favor that are decisive from the standpoint of the original position. In order to see how this might be done, it is useful as a heuristic device to think of the two principles and the maximin rule for choice under uncertainty. This is evident from the fact that the two principles are those a person would choose for the design of a society in which his enemy is to assign him his place. The maximin rule tells us to rank alternatives by their worst possible outcomes: we are to adopt the alternative the worst outcome of which is superior to the worst outcomes of the others. . . . The term "maximin" means the *maximum minimorum*; and the rule directs our attention to the worst that can happen under any proposed course of action, and to decide in the light of that. . . .

The veil of ignorance excludes all but the vaguest knowledge of likelihoods. The parties have no basis for determining the probable nature of their society, or their place in it. Thus they have strong reasons for being wary of probability calculations if any other course is open to them. They must also take into account the fact that their choice of principles should seem reasonable to others, in particular their descendants, whose rights will be deeply affected by it. . . .

In this section my aim is to use the conditions of publicity and finality to give some of the main arguments for the two principles of justice. I shall rely upon the fact that for an agreement to be valid, the parties must be able to honor it under all relevant and foreseeable circumstances. There must be a rational assurance that one can carry through. The arguments I shall adduce fit under the heuristic schema suggested by the reasons for following the maximin rule. That is, they help to show that the two principles are an adequate minimum conception of justice in a situation of great uncertainty. Any further advantages that might be won by the principle of utility, or whatever, are highly problematical, whereas the hardships if things turn out badly are intolerable. It is at this point that the concept of a contract has a definite role: it suggests the condition of publicity and sets limits upon what can be agreed to. Thus justice as fairness uses the concept of contract to a greater extent than the discussion so far might suggest.

The first confirming ground for the two principles can be explained in terms of what I earlier referred to as the strains of commitment. I said . . . that the parties have a capacity for justice in the sense that they can be assured that their undertaking is not in vain. Assuming that they have taken everything into account, including the general facts of moral psychology, they can rely on one another to adhere to the principles adopted. Thus they consider the strains of commitment. They cannot enter into agreements that may have consequences they cannot accept. They will avoid those that they can adhere to only with great difficulty. Since the original agreement is final and made in perpetuity, there is no second chance. In view of the serious nature of the possible consequences, the question of the burden of commitment is especially acute. A person is choosing once and for all the standards which are to govern his life prospects. Moreover, when we enter an agreement we must be able to honor it even should the worst possibilities prove to be the case. Otherwise we have not acted in good faith. Thus the parties must weigh with care whether they will be able to stick by their commitment in all circumstances. Of course, in answering this question they have only a general knowledge of human psychology to go on. But this information is enough to tell which conception of justice involves the greater stress.

In this respect the two principles of justice have a definite advantage. Not only do the parties protect their basic rights but they insure themselves against the worst eventualities. They run no chance of having to acquiesce in a loss of freedom over the course of their life for the sake of a greater good enjoyed by others, an undertaking that in actual circumstances they might not be able to keep. . . . The principle of utility seems to require a greater identification with the interests of others than the two principles of justice. Thus the latter will be a more stable conception to the extent that this identification is difficult to achieve. When the two principles are satisfied, each person's liberties are secured and there is a sense defined by the difference principle in which everyone is benefited by social cooperation. Therefore we can explain the acceptance of the social system and the principles it satisfies by the psychological law that persons tend to love, cherish, and support whatever affirms their own good. Since everyone's good is affirmed, all acquire inclinations to uphold the scheme.

When the principle of utility is satisfied, however, there is no such assurance that everyone benefits. Allegiance to the social system may demand that some should forgo advantages for the sake of the greater good of the whole. Thus the scheme will not be stable unless those who must make sacrifices strongly identify with interests broader than their own. . . .

A desirable feature of a conception of justice is that it should publicly express men's respect for one another. In this way they insure a sense of their own value. Now the two principles achieve this end. For when society follows these principles, everyone's good is included in a scheme of mutual benefit and this public affirmation in institutions of each man's endeavors supports men's self-esteem. The establishment of equal liberty and the operation of the difference principle are bound to have this effect. The two principles are equivalent, as I have remarked, to an undertaking to regard the distribution of natural abilities as a collective asset so that the more fortunate are to benefit only in ways that help those who have lost out. . . .

It is evident that some sort of framework is needed to simplify the application of the two principles of justice. For consider three kinds of judgments that a citizen has to make. First of all, he must judge the justice of legislation and social policies. But he also knows that his opinions will not always coincide with those of others, since men's judgments and beliefs are likely to differ especially when their interests are engaged. Therefore secondly, a citizen must decide which constitutional arrangements are just for reconciling conflicting opinions of justice. We may think of the political process as a machine which makes social decisions when the views of representatives and their constituents are fed into it. A citizen will regard some ways of designing this machine as more just than others. So a complete conception of justice is not only able to assess laws and policies but it can also rank procedures for selecting which political opinion is to be enacted into law. There is still a third problem. The citizen accepts a certain constitution as just, and he thinks that certain traditional procedures are appropriate, for example, the procedure of majority rule duly circumscribed. Yet since the political process is at best one of imperfect procedural justice, he must ascertain when the enactments of the majority are to be complied with and when they can be rejected as no longer binding. In short, he must be able to determine the grounds and limits of political duty and obligation. Thus a theory of justice has to deal with at least three types of questions, and this indicates that it may be useful to think of the principles as applied in a several-stage sequence. . . .

Thus I suppose that after the parties have adopted the principles of justice in the original position, they move to a constitutional convention. Here they are to decide upon the justice of political forms and choose a constitution; they are delegates, so to speak, to such a convention. Subject to the constraints of the principles of justice already chosen, they are to design a system for the constitutional powers of government and the basic rights of citizens. It is at this stage that they weigh the justice of procedures for coping with diverse political views. Since the appropriate conception of justice has been agreed upon, the veil of ignorance is partially lifted. The persons in the convention have, of course, no information about particular individuals; they do not know their own social position, their place in the distribution of natural attributes, or their conception of the good. But in addition to an understanding of the principles of social theory, they now know the relevant general facts about their society, that is, its natural circumstances and resources, its level of economic advance and political culture, and so on. They are no longer limited to the information implicit in the circumstances of justice. Given their theoretical knowledge and the appropriate general facts about their society, they are to choose the most effective just constitution, the constitution that satisfies the principles of justice and is best calculated to lead to just and effective legislation. . . .

The liberties of equal citizenship must be incorporated into and protected by the constitution. These liberties include those of liberty of conscience and freedom of thought, liberty of the person, and equal political rights. The political system, which I assume to be some form of constitutional democracy, would not be a just procedure if it did not embody these liberties.

Clearly any feasible political procedure may yield an unjust outcome. In fact, there is no scheme of procedural political rules which guarantees that unjust legislation will not be enacted. In the case of a constitutional regime, or indeed of any political form, the ideal of perfect procedural justice cannot be realized. The best attainable scheme is one of imperfect procedural justice. Nevertheless some schemes have a greater tendency than others to result in unjust laws. . . .

Now the question whether legislation is just or unjust, especially in connection with economic and social policies, is commonly subject to reasonable differences of opinion. In these cases judgment frequently depends upon speculative political and economic doctrines and upon social theory generally. Often the best that we can say of a law or policy is that it is at least not clearly unjust. The application of the difference principle in a precise way normally requires more information than we can expect to have and, in any case, more than the application of the first principle. It is often perfectly plain and evident when the equal liberties are violated. These violations are not only unjust but can be clearly seen to be unjust: the injustice is manifest in the public structure of institutions. But this state of affairs is comparatively rare with social and economic policies regulated by the difference principle.

I imagine then a division of labor between stages in which each deals with different questions of so-cial justice. This division roughly corresponds to the two parts of the basic structure. The first principle of equal liberty is the primary standard for the constitutional convention. Its main requirements are that the fundamental liberties of the person and liberty of conscience and freedom of thought be protected and that the political process as a whole be a just procedure. Thus the constitution establishes a secure common status of equal citizenship and realizes political justice. The second principle comes into play at the stage of the legislature. It dictates that social and economic policies be aimed at maximizing the long-term expectations of the least advantaged under conditions of fair equality of opportunity, subject to the equal liberties being maintained. At this point the full range of general economic and social facts is brought to bear. The second part of the basic structure contains the distinctions and hierarchies of political, economic, and social forms which are necessary for efficient and mutually beneficial social cooperation. Thus the priority of the first principle of justice to the second is reflected in the priority of the constitutional convention to the legislative stage.

The last stage is that of the application of rules to particular cases by judges and administrators, and the following of rules by citizens generally. At this stage everyone has complete access to all the facts. No limits on knowledge remain since the full system of rules has now been adopted and applies to persons in virtue of their characteristics and circumstances. . . .

The availability of knowledge in the four-stage sequence is roughly as follows. Let us distinguish between three kinds of facts: the first principles of social theory (and other theories when relevant) and their consequences; general facts about society, such as its size and level of economic advance, its institutional structure and natural environment, and so on; and finally, particular facts about individuals such as their social position, natural attributes, and peculiar interests. In the original position the only particular facts known to the parties are those that can be inferred from the circumstances of justice. While they know the first principles of social theory, the course of history is closed to them; they have no information about how often society has taken this or that form, or which kinds of societies presently exist. In the next stages, however, the general facts about their society are made available to them but not the particularities of their own condition. Limitations on knowledge can be relaxed since the principles of justice are already chosen. The flow of information is determined at each stage by what is required in order to apply these principles intelligently to the kind of question of justice at hand, while at the same time any knowledge that is likely to give rise to bias and distortion and to set men against one another is ruled out. The notion of the rational and impartial application of principles defines the kind of knowledge that is admissible. At the last stage, clearly, there are no reasons for the veil of ignorance in any form, and all restrictions are lifted.

It is essential to keep in mind that the four-stage sequence is a device for applying the principles of justice. This scheme is part of the theory of justice as fairness and not an account of how constitutional conventions and legislatures actually proceed. It sets out a series of points of view from which the different problems of justice are to be settled, each point of view inheriting the constraints adopted at the preceding stages. Thus a just constitution is one that rational delegates subject to the restrictions of the second stage would adopt for their society. And similarly just laws and policies are those that would be enacted at the legislative stage. Of course, this test is often indeterminate; it is not always clear which of several constitutions, or economic and social arrangements, would be chosen. But when this is so, justice is to that extent likewise indeterminate. Institutions within the permitted range are equally just, meaning that they could be chosen; they are compatible with all the constraints of the theory. Thus on many questions of social and economic policy we must fall back upon a notion of quasi-pure procedural justice: laws and policies are just provided that they lie within the allowed range, and the legislature, in ways authorized by a just constitution, has in fact enacted them. This indeterminacy in the theory of justice is not in itself a defect. It is what we should expect. Justice as fairness will prove a worthwhile theory if it defines the range of justice more in accordance with our considered judgments than do existing theories, and if it singles out with greater sharpness the graver wrongs a society should avoid. . . .

Political justice has two aspects arising from the fact that a just constitution is a case of imperfect procedural justice. First, the constitution is to be a just procedure satisfying the requirements of equal liberty; and second, it is to be framed so that of all the feasible just arrangements, it is the one more likely than any other to result in a just and effective system of legislation. The justice of the constitution is to be assessed under both headings in the light of what circumstances permit, these assessments being made from the standpoint of the constitutional convention.

The principle of equal liberty, when applied to the political procedure defined by the constitution, I shall refer to as the principle of (equal) participation. It requires that all citizens are to have an equal right to take part in, and to determine the outcome of, the constitutional process that establishes the laws with which they are to comply. Justice as fairness begins with the idea that where common principles are necessary and to everyone's advantage, they are to be worked out from the viewpoint of a suitably defined initial situation of equality in which each person is fairly represented. The principle of participation transfers this notion from the original position to the constitution as the highest-order system of social rules for making rules. If the state is to exercise a final and coercive authority over a certain territory, and if it is in this way to affect permanently men's prospects in life, then the constitutional process should preserve the equal representation of the original position to the degree that this is practicable. . . .

All sane adults, with certain generally recognized exceptions, have the right to take part in political affairs, and the precept one elector one vote is honored as far as possible. Elections are fair and free, and regularly held. Sporadic and unpredictable tests of public sentiment by plebiscite or other means, or at such times as may suit the convenience of those in office, do not suffice for a representative regime. There are firm constitutional protections for certain liberties, particularly freedom of speech and assembly, and liberty to form political associations. The principle of loyal opposition is recognized, the clash of political beliefs, and of the interests and attitudes that are likely to influence them, are accepted as a normal condition of human life. . . .

The principle of participation also holds that all citizens are to have an equal access, at least in the formal sense, to public office. Each is eligible to join political parties, to run for elective positions, and to hold places of authority. To be sure, there may be qualifications of age, residency, and so on. But these are to be reasonably related to the tasks of office; presumably these restrictions are in the common interest and do not discriminate unfairly among persons or groups in the sense that they fall evenly on everyone in the normal course of life.

The second point concerning equal political liberty is its extent. How broadly are these liberties to be defined? Offhand it is not clear what extent means here. Each of the political liberties can be more or less widely defined. Somewhat arbitrarily, but nevertheless in accordance with tradition, I shall assume that the main variation in the extent of equal political liberty lies in the degree to which the constitution is majoritarian. The definition of the other liberties I take to be more or less fixed. Thus the most extensive political liberty is established by a constitution that uses the procedure of so-called bare majority rule (the procedure in which a minority can neither override nor check a majority) for all significant political decisions unimpeded by any constitutional constraints. Whenever the constitution limits the scope and authority of majorities, either by requiring a greater plurality for certain types of measures, or by a bill of rights restricting the powers of the legislature, and the like, equal political liberty is less extensive. . . .

Turning now to the worth of political liberty, the constitution must take steps to enhance the value of the equal rights of participation for all members of society. It must underwrite a fair opportunity to take part in and to influence the political process. . . . Ideally, those similarly endowed and motivated should have roughly the same chance of attaining positions of political authority irrespective of their economic and social class. But how is this fair value of these liberties to be secured?

Compensating steps must . . . be taken to preserve the fair value for all of the equal political liberties. A variety of devices can be used. For example, in a society allowing private ownership of the means of production, property and wealth must be kept widely distributed and government monies provided on a regular basis to encourage free public discussion. In addition, political parties are to be made independent from private economic interests by allotting them sufficient tax revenues to play their part in the constitutional scheme. . . .

What is necessary is that political parties be autonomous with respect to private demands, that is, demands not expressed in the public forum and argued for openly by reference to a conception of the public good. If society does not bear the costs of organization, and party funds need to be solicited from the more advantaged social and economic interests, the pleadings of these groups are bound to receive excessive attention. And this is all the more likely when the less favored members of society, having been effectively prevented by their lack of means from exercising their fair degree of influence, withdraw into apathy and resentment.

Historically one of the main defects of constitutional government has been the failure to insure the fair value of political liberty. The necessary corrective steps have not been taken, indeed, they never seem to have been seriously entertained. Disparities in the distribution of property and wealth that far exceed what is compatible with political equality have generally been tolerated by the legal system. Public resources have not been devoted to maintaining the institutions required for the fair value of political liberty. Essentially the fault lies in the fact that the democratic political process is at best regulated rivalry; it does not even in theory have the desirable properties that price theory ascribes to truly competitive markets. Moreover, the effects of injustices in the political system are much more grave and long lasting than market imperfections. Political power rapidly accumulates and becomes unequal; and making use of the coercive apparatus of the state and its law, those who gain the advantage can often assure themselves of a favored position. Thus inequities in the economic and social system may soon undermine whatever political equality might have existed under fortunate historical conditions. Universal suffrage is an insufficient counterpoise; for when parties and elections are financed not by public funds but by private contributions, the political forum is so constrained by the wishes of the dominant interests that the basic measures needed to establish just constitutional rule are seldom properly presented. . . .

An economic system regulates what things are produced and by what means, who receives them and in return for which contributions, and how large a fraction of social resources is devoted to saving and to the provision of public goods. Ideally all of these matters should be arranged in ways that satisfy the two principles of justice. But we have to ask whether this is possible and what in particular these principles require. . . .

A . . . feature of the public sector is the proportion of total social resources devoted to public goods. . . . A public good has two characteristic features, indivisibility and publicness. That is, there are many individuals, a public so to speak, who want more or less of this good, but if they are to enjoy it at all must each enjoy the same amount. The quantity produced cannot be divided up as private goods can and purchased by individuals according to their preferences for more and less. . . .

Where the public is large and includes many individuals, there is a temptation for each person to try to avoid doing his share. This is because whatever one man does his action will not significantly affect the amount produced. He regards the collective action of others as already given one way or the other. If the public good is produced his enjoyment of it is not decreased by his not making a contribution. If it is not produced his action would not have changed the situation anyway. A citizen receives the same protection from foreign invasion regardless of whether he has paid his taxes. Therefore in the polar case trade and voluntary agreements cannot be expected to develop.

It follows that arranging for and financing public goods must be taken over by the state and some binding rule requiring payment must be enforced. Even if all citizens were willing to pay their share, they would presumably do so only when they are assured that others will pay theirs as well. Thus once citizens have agreed to act collectively and not as isolated individuals taking the actions of the others as given, there is still the task of tying down the agreement. The sense of justice leads us to promote just schemes and to do our share in them when we believe that others, or sufficiently many of them, will do theirs. But in normal circumstances a reasonable assurance in this regard can only be given if there is a binding rule effectively enforced. Assuming that the public good is to everyone's advantage, and one that all would agree to arrange for, the use of coercion is perfectly rational from each man's point of view. Many of the traditional activities of government, insofar as they can be justified, can be accounted for in this way.

I should like to conclude with a few comments about the extent to which economic arrangements may rely upon a system of markets in which prices are freely determined by supply and demand. Several cases need to be distinguished. All regimes will normally use the market to ration out the consumption goods actually produced. Any other procedure is administratively cumbersome, and rationing and other devices will be resorted to only in special cases. But in a free market system the output of commodities is also guided as to kind and quantity by the preferences of households as shown by their purchases on the market. Goods fetching a greater than normal profit will be produced in larger amounts until the excess is reduced. In a socialist regime planners' preferences or collective decisions often have a larger part in determining the direction of production. Both private-property and socialist systems normally allow for the free choice of occupation and of one's place of work. It is only under command systems of either kind that this freedom is overtly interfered with.

Finally, a basic feature is the extent to which the market is used to decide the rate of saving and the direction of investment, as well as the fraction of national wealth devoted to conservation and to the elimination of irremediable injuries to the welfare of future generations. Here there are a number of possibilities. A collective decision may determine the rate of saving while the direction of investment is left largely to individual firms competing for funds. In both a private-property as well as in a socialist society great concern may be expressed for preventing irreversible damages and for husbanding natural resources and preserving the environment. But again either one may do rather badly.

It is evident, then, that there is no essential tie between the use of free markets and private ownership of the instruments of production. The idea that competitive prices under normal conditions are just or fair goes back at least to medieval times. While the notion that a market economy is in some sense the best scheme has been most carefully investigated by so-called bourgeois economists, this connection is a historical contingency in that, theoretically at least, a socialist regime can avail itself of the advantages of this system. One of these advantages is efficiency. Under certain conditions competitive prices select the goods to be produced and allocate resources to their production in such a manner that there is no way to improve upon either the choice of productive methods by firms, or the distribution of goods that arises from the purchases of households. There exists no rearrangement of the resulting economic configuration that makes one household better off (in view of its preferences) without making another worse off. No further mutually advantageous trades are possible; nor are there any feasible productive processes that will yield more of some desired commodity without requiring a cutback in another. For if this were not so, the situation of some individuals could be made more advantageous without a loss for anyone else. The theory of general equilibrium explains how, given the appropriate conditions, the information supplied by prices leads economic agents to act in ways that sum up to achieve this outcome. Perfect competition is a perfect procedure with respect to efficiency. Of course, the requisite conditions are highly special ones and they are seldom if ever fully satisfied in the real world. Moreover, market failures and imperfections are often serious, and compensating adjustments must be made by the allocation branch. . . . Monopolistic restrictions, lack of information, external economies and diseconomies, and the like must be recognized and corrected. And the market fails altogether in the case of public goods. . . .

A further and more significant advantage of a market system is that, given the requisite background institutions, it is consistent with equal liberties and fair equality of opportunity. Citizens have a free choice of careers and occupations. There is no reason at all for the forced and central direction of labor. Indeed, in the absence of some differences in earnings as these arise in a competitive scheme, it is hard to see how, under ordinary circumstances anyway, certain aspects of a command society inconsistent with liberty can be avoided. Moreover, a system of markets decentralizes the exercise of economic power. Whatever the internal nature of firms, whether they are privately or state owned, or whether they are run by entrepreneurs or by managers elected by workers, they take the prices of outputs and inputs as given and draw up their plans accordingly. When markets are truly competitive, firms do not engage in price wars or other contests for market power. In conformity with political decisions reached democratically, the government regulates the economic climate by adjusting certain elements under its control, such as the overall amount of investment, the rate of interest, and the quantity of money, and so on. There is no necessity for comprehensive direct planning. Individual households and firms are free to make their decisions independently, subject to the general conditions of the economy. . . .

The main problem of distributive justice is the choice of a social system. The principles of justice apply to the basic structure and regulate how its major institutions are combined into one scheme. Now, as we have seen, the idea of justice as fairness is to use the notion of pure procedural justice to handle the contingencies of particular situations. The social system is to be designed so that the resulting distribution is just however things turn out. To achieve this end it is necessary to set the social and economic process within the surroundings of suitable political and legal institutions. Without an appropriate scheme of these background institutions the outcome of the distributive process will not be just.

I shall give a brief description of these supporting institutions as they might exist in a properly or-

ganized democratic state that allows private ownership of capital and natural resources. . . .

First of all, I assume that the basic structure is regulated by a just constitution that secures the liberties of equal citizenship (as described in the preceding chapter). Liberty of conscience and freedom of thought are taken for granted, and the fair value of political liberty is maintained. The political process is conducted, as far as circumstances permit, as a just procedure for choosing between governments and for enacting just legislation. I assume also that there is fair (as opposed to formal) equality of opportunity. This means that in addition to maintaining the usual kinds of social overhead capital, the government tries to insure equal chances of education and culture for persons similarly endowed and motivated either by subsidizing private schools or by establishing a public school system. It also enforces and underwrites equality of opportunity in economic activities and in the free choice of occupation. This is achieved by policing the conduct of firms and private associations and by preventing the establishment of monopolistic restrictions and barriers to the more desirable positions. Finally, the government guarantees a social minimum either by family allowances and special payments for sickness and employment, or more systematically by such devices as a graded income supplement (a so-called negative income tax).

In establishing these background institutions the government may be thought of as divided into four branches. Each branch consists of various agencies, or activities thereof, charged with preserving certain social and economic conditions. These divisions do not overlap with the usual organization of government but are to be understood as different functions. The allocation branch, for example, is to keep the price system workably competitive and to prevent the formation of unreasonable market power. Such power does not exist as long as markets cannot be made more competitive consistent with the requirements of efficiency and the facts of geography and the preferences of households. The allocation branch is also charged with identifying and correcting, say by suitable taxes and subsidies and by changes in the definition of property rights, the more obvious departures from efficiency caused by the failure of prices to measure accurately social benefits and costs. To this end suitable taxes and subsidies may be used, or the scope and definition of property rights may be revised. The stabilization branch, on the other hand, strives to bring about reasonably full employment in the sense that those who want work can find it and the free choice of occupation and the deployment of finance are supported by strong effective demand. These two branches together are to maintain the efficiency of the market economy generally.

The social minimum is the responsibility of the transfer branch.... The essential idea is that the workings of this branch take needs into account and assign them an appropriate weight with respect to other claims. A competitive price system gives no consideration to needs and therefore it cannot be the sole device of distribution. There must be a division of labor between the parts of the social system in answering to the common sense precepts of justice. Different institutions meet different claims. Competitive markets properly regulated secure free choice of occupation and lead to an efficient use of resources and allocation of commodities to households. They set a weight on the conventional precepts associated with wages and earning, whereas the transfer branch guarantees a certain level of well-being and honors the claims of need. ...

It is clear that the justice of distributive shares depends on the background institutions and how they allocate total income, wages and other income plus transfers. There is with reason strong objection to the competitive determination of total income, since this ignores the claims of need and an appropriate standard of life. From the standpoint of the legislative stage it is rational to insure oneself and one's descendants against these contingencies of the market. Indeed, the difference principle presumably requires this. But once a suitable minimum is provided by transfers, it may be perfectly fair that the rest of total income be settled by the price system, assuming that it is moderately efficient and free from monopolistic restrictions, and unreasonable externalities have been eliminated. Moreover, this way of dealing with the claims of need would appear to be more effective than trying to regulate income by minimum wage standards, and the like. It is better to assign to each branch only such tasks as are compatible with one another. Since the market is not suited to answer the claims of need, these should be met by a separate arrangement. Whether the prin-ciples of justice are satisfied, then, turns on whether the total income of the least advantaged (wages plus transfers) is such as to maximize their long-run expectations (consistent with the constraints of equal liberty and fair equality of opportunity).

Finally, there is a distribution branch. Its task is to preserve an approximate justice in distributive shares by means of taxation and the necessary adjustments in the rights of property. Two aspects of this branch may be distinguished. First of all, it imposes a number of inheritance and gift taxes, and sets restrictions on the rights of bequest. The purpose of these levies and regulations is not to raise revenue (release resources to government) but gradually and continually to correct the distribution of wealth and to prevent concentrations of power detrimental to the fair value of political liberty and fair equality of opportunity. ...

The unequal inheritance of wealth is no more inherently unjust than the unequal inheritance of intelligence. It is true that the former is presumably more easily subject to social control; but the essential thing is that as far as possible inequalities founded on either should satisfy the difference principle. Thus inheritance is permissible provided that the resulting inequalities are to the advantage of the least fortunate and compatible with liberty and fair equality of opportunity. As earlier defined, fair equality of opportunity means a certain set of institutions that assures similar chances of education and culture for persons similarly motivated and keeps positions and offices open to all on the basis of qualities and efforts reasonably related to the relevant duties and tasks. It is these institutions that are put in jeopardy when inequalities of wealth exceed a certain limit; and political liberty likewise tends to lose its value, and representative government to become such in appearance only. The taxes and enactments of the distribution branch are to prevent this limit from being exceeded. Naturally, where this limit lies is a matter of political judgment guided by theory, good sense, and plain hunch, at least within a wide range. On this sort of question the theory of justice has nothing specific to say. Its aim is to formulate the principles that are to regulate the background institutions.

The second part of the distribution branch is a scheme of taxation to raise the revenues that justice requires. Social resources must be released to the government so that it can provide for the public goods and make the transfer payments necessary to satisfy the difference principle. This problem belongs to the distribution branch since the burden of taxation is to be justly shared and it aims at establishing just arrangements. Leaving aside many complications, it is worth noting that a proportional expenditure tax may be part of the best tax scheme. For one thiing, it is preferable to an income tax (of any kind) at the level of common sense precepts of justice, since it imposes a levy according to how much a person takes out of the common store of goods and not according to how much he contributes (assuming here that income is fairly earned). Again, a proportional tax on total consumption (for each year say) can contain the usual exemptions for dependents, and so on; and it treats everyone in a uniform way (still assuming that income is fairly earned). It may be better, therefore, to use progressive rates only when they are necessary, and so to forestall accumulations of property and power likely to undermine the corresponding institutions. Following this rule might help to signal an important distinction in questions of policy. And if proportional taxes should also prove more efficient, say because they interfere less with incentives, this might make the case for them decisive if a feasible scheme could be worked out. . . .

The two parts of the distribution branch derive from the two principles of justice. The taxation of inheritance and income at progressive rates (when necessary), and the legal definition of property rights, are to secure the institutions of equal liberty in a property-owning democracy and the fair value of the rights they establish. Proportional expenditure (or income) taxes are to provide revenue for public goods, the transfer branch and the establishment of fair equality of opportunity in education, and the like, so as to carry out the second principle. No mention has been made at any point of the traditional criteria of taxation such as that taxes are to be levied according to benefits received or the ability to pay. . . .

So far I have assumed that the aim of the branches of government is to establish a democratic regime in which land and capital are widely though not presumably equally held. Society is not so divided that one fairly small sector controls the preponderance of productive resources. When this is achieved and distributive shares satisfy the principles of justice, many socialist criticisms of the market economy are met. But it is clear that, in theory anyway, a liberal socialist regime can also answer to the two prin-

ciples of justice. We have only to suppose that the means of production are publicly owned and that firms are managed by workers' councils say, or by agents appointed by them. Collective decisions made democratically under the constitution determine the general features of the economy, such as the rate of saving and the proportion of society's production devoted to essential public goods. Given the resulting economic environment, firms regulated by market forces conduct themselves much as before. Although the background institutions will take a different form, especially in the case of the distribution branch, there is no reason in principle why just distributive shares cannot be achieved. The theory of justice does not itself favor either form of regime. As we have seen, the decision as to which system is best for a given people depends upon their circumstances, institutions, and historical traditions. . . .

Discussion Questions

1. Define and explain what Professor Rawls means by "the original position." Why does he believe that it is the fairest and most rational way to arrive at principles of justice? Do you agree or disagree with his assessment? Explain and defend your answer.

2. What are the principles of justice at which Professor Rawls arrives? Do you agree or disagree with these principles and how Professor Rawls arrived at them? Explain and defend your answer.

3. In the second half of his essay Professor Rawls explains how the principles of justice may help us to make decisions about such public policy questions as economic policy, taxation, free markets, social welfare, and minimum wage. Present and explain at least two examples of public policies to which Professor Rawls applies the principles of justice. Explain why you agree or disagree that such applications are, or can be, successful.

37

Radical Egalitarianism

Kai Nielsen

Kai Nielsen is a Professor of Philosophy at the University of Calgary. He is the author of almost 400 scholarly articles as well as 25 books, among which are *Ethics without God* (1989, rev. ed.), *God and the Grounding of Morality* (1991), and *Equality and Liberty: A Defense of Radical Egalitarianism* (1985).

In this essay Professor Nielsen defends a position in social philosophy he calls *radical egalitarianism,* a view held by a great many social-ists and communists. This view holds that in a truly just society the needs and wants of its citizens should be met "as far as possible" and with "as fully as possible compatible with everyone else doing likewise." He clarifies and qualifies this position in response to possible objections to it. Professor Nielsen offers two moral principles on which he bases his philosophy: (1) "Each person is to have an equal right to the most extensive total system of equal basic liberties and opportunities . . . compatible with a similar treatment of all . . .," and (2) "After provisions are made for common . . . social values, for capital overhead to preserve the society's productive capacity, allowances made for differing unmanipulated needs and preferences, and due weight is given to the just entitlements of individuals, the income and wealth . . . is to be divided so that each person will have a right to an equal share . . . [and] necessary burdens requisite to enhance human well-being are equally shared, subject . . . to limitations by differing abilities and differing situations." According to Professor Nielsen, in an egalitarian society there would be no impoverished people, no useless products, no

Reprinted by permission from Kai Nielsen, *Equality and Liberty: A Defense of Radical Egalitarianism* (Totowa, N.J.: Rowman and Littlefield, 1985), 283–292, 302–306, 309.

waste, and the economic differences between people in affluent societies would be substantially, if not totally, reduced.

I

I have talked of equality as a right and of equality as a goal. And I have taken, as the principal thing, to be able to state that goal we are seeking when we say equality is a goal. When we are in a position actually to achieve that goal, then that same equality becomes a right. The goal we are seeking is an equality of basic condition for everyone. Let me say a bit what this is: everyone, as far as possible, should have equal life prospects, short of genetic engineering and the like and the rooting out any form of the family and the undermining of our basic freedoms. There should, where this is possible, be an equality of access to equal resources over each person's life as a whole, though this should be qualified by people's varying needs. Where psychiatrists are in short supply only people who are in need of psychiatric help should have equal access to such help. This equal access to resources should be such that it stands as a barrier to their being the sort of differences between people that allow some to be in a position to be in control and exploit others; such equal access to resources should also stand as a barrier to one adult person having power over other adult persons that does not rest on the revokable consent on the part of the persons over whom he comes to have power. Where, because of some remaining scarcity in a society of considerable productive abundance, we cannot reasonably distribute resources equally, we should at first, where considerations of desert are not at issue, distribute according to stringency of need, second according to the strength of unmanipulated preferences and third, and finally, by lottery. We should, in trying to attain equality of condition, aim at a condition of autonomy (the fuller and the more rational the better) for everyone and at a condition where everyone alike, to the fullest extent possible, has his or her needs satisfied. The limitations on the satisfaction of people's wants should be only where that satisfaction is incompatible with everyone getting the same treatment. Where we have conflicting wants, such as two persons want to marry the same person, the fair thing to do will vary with the circumstances. In the marriage case, freedom of choice is obviously the fair thing. But generally, what should be aimed at is having everyone have their wants satisfied as far as possible. To achieve equality of condition would be, as well, to achieve a condition where the necessary burdens of society are equally shared, where to do so is reasonable, and where each person has an equal voice in deciding what these burdens shall be. Moreover, everyone, as much as possible, should be in a position—and should be equally in that position—to control his own life. The goals of egalitarianism are to achieve such equalities.

Minimally, classlessness is something we should aim at if we are egalitarians. It is necessary for the stable achievement of equalities of the type discussed in the previous paragraph. Beyond that, we should also aim at a statusless society, though not at an undifferentiated society or a society which does not recognize merit. It is only in such a classless, statusless society that the ideals of equality (the conception of equality as a very general goal to be achieved) can be realized. In aiming for a statusless society, we are aiming for a society which, while remaining a society of material abundance, is a society in which there are to be no extensive differences in life prospects between people because some have far greater income, power, authority or prestige than others. This is the *via negativia* of the egalitarian way. The *via positiva* is to produce social conditions, where there is generally material abundance, where well-being and satisfaction are not only maximized (the utilitarian thing) but, as well, a society where this condition, as far as it is achievable, is sought equally for all (the egalitarian thing). This is the underlying conception of the egalitarian commitment to equality of condition.

II

Robert Nozick asks "How do we decide how much equality is enough?"[1] In the preceding section we gestured in the direction of an answer. I should now like to be somewhat more explicit. Too much equality, as we have been at pains to point out, would be to treat everyone identically, completely ignoring their differing needs. Various forms of "barracks equality" approximating that would also be too much. Too little equality would be to limit equality of condition, as did the old egalitarianism, to achieving equal legal and political rights, equal civil liberties, to equality of opportunity and to a redistribution of gross disparities in wealth sufficient to keep social peace,

the rationale for the latter being that such gross inequalities if allowed to stand would threaten social stability. This Hobbesist stance indicates that the old egalitarianism proceeds in a very pragmatic manner. Against the old egalitarianism I would argue that we must at least aim at an equality of whole life prospects, where that is not read simply as the right to compete for scarce positions of advantage, but where there is to be brought into being the kind of equality of condition that would provide everyone equally, as far as possible, with the resources and social conditions to satisfy their needs as fully as possible compatible with everyone else doing likewise. (Note that between people these needs will be partly the same but will still often be importantly different as well.) Ideally, as a kind of ideal limit for a society of wondrous abundance, a radical egalitarianism would go beyond that to a similar thing for wants. We should, that is, provide all people equally, as far as possible, with the resources and social conditions to satisfy their wants, as fully as possible with everyone else doing likewise. (I recognize that there is a slide between wants and needs. As the wealth of a society increases and its structure changes, things that started out as wants tend to become needs, e.g., someone in the Falkland Islands might merely reasonably want an auto while someone in Los Angeles might not only want it but need it as well. But this does not collapse the distinction between wants and needs. There are things in any society people need, if they are to survive at all in anything like a commodious condition, whether they want them or not, e.g., they need food, shelter, security, companionship and the like. An egalitarian starts with basic needs, or at least with what are taken in the cultural environment in which a given person lives to be basic needs, and moves out to other needs and finally to wants as the productive power of the society increases.)

I qualified my above formulations with "as far as possible" and with "as fully as possible compatible with everyone else doing likewise." These are essential qualifications. Where, as in societies that we know, there are scarcities, not everyone can have the resources or at least all the resources necessary to have their needs satisfied. Here we must first ensure that, again as far as possible, their basic needs are all satisfied and then we move on to other needs and finally to wants. But sometimes, to understate it, even in very affluent societies, everyone's needs cannot be met, or at least they cannot be equally met. In such circumstances we have to make some hard choices. I am thinking of a situation where there are not enough dialysis machines to go around so that everyone who needs one can have one. What then should we do? The thing to aim at, to try as far as possible to approximate, if only as a heuristic ideal, is the full and equal meeting of needs and wants of everyone. It is when we have that much equality that we have enough equality. But, of course, "ought implies can," and where we can't achieve it we can't achieve it. But where we reasonably can, we ought to do it. It is something that fairness requires.

The "reasonably can" is also an essential modification: we need situations of sufficient abundance so that we do not, in going for such an equality of condition, simply spread the misery around or spread very Spartan conditions around. Before we can rightly aim for the equality of condition I mentioned, we must first have the productive capacity and resource condition to support the institutional means that would make possible the equal satisfaction of basic needs and the equal satisfaction of other needs as well. Such achievements will often not be possible; perhaps they will never be fully possible, for, no doubt, the physically handicapped will always be with us. Consider, for example situations where our scarcities are such that we cannot, without causing considerable misery, create the institutions and mechanisms that would work to satisfy all needs, even all basic needs. Suppose we have the technology in place to develop all sorts of complicated life-sustaining machines all of which would predictably provide people with a quality of life that they, viewing the matter clearly, would rationally choose if they were simply choosing for themselves. But suppose, if we put such technologies in place, we will then not have the wherewithal to provide basic health care in outlying regions in the country or adequate educational services in such places. We should not, under those circumstances, put those technologies in place. But we should also recognize that where it becomes possible to put these technologies in place, without sacrificing other more pressing needs, we should do so. The underlying egalitarian rationale is evident enough: produce the conditions for the most extensive satisfaction of needs for everyone. Where A's need and B's need are equally important (equally stringent) but cannot both be satisfied, satisfy A's need rather than B's if the satisfaction of A's need would be more fecund for the satisfaction of the needs of others than B's, or less undermining of the satisfaction of the needs of others than B's. (I do not mean to say that that is our only criterion of choice but it is the criterion most relevant for us here.) We should

seek the satisfaction of the greatest compossible set of needs where the conditions for compossibilty are (a) that everyone's needs be considered, (b) that everyone's needs be *equally* considered and where two sets of needs cannot both be satisfied, the more stringent set of needs shall first be satisfied. (Do not say we have no working criteria for what they are. If you need food to keep you from starvation or debilitating malnutrition and I need a vacation to relax after a spate of hard work, your need is plainly more stringent than mine. There would, of course, be all sorts of disputable cases, but there are also a host of perfectly determinate cases indicating that we have working criteria.) The underlying rationale is to seek compossible sets of needs so that we approach as far as possible as great a satisfaction of needs as possible for everyone.

This might, it could be said, produce a situation in which very few people got those things that they needed the most, or at least wanted the most. Remember Nozick with his need for the resources of Widner Library in an annex to his house. People, some might argue, with expensive tastes and extravagant needs, say a need for really good wine, would never, with a stress on such compossibilia, get things they are really keen about.[2] Is that the kind of world we would reflectively want? Well, *if* their not getting them is the price we have to pay for everyone having their basic needs met, then it is a price we ought to pay. I am very fond of very good wines as well as fresh ripe mangos, but if the price of my having them is that people starve or suffer malnutrition in the Sahel, or indeed anywhere else, then plainly fairness, if not just plain human decency, requires that I forego them.

In talking about how much equality is enough, I have so far talked of the benefits that equality is meant to provide. But egalitarians also speak of an equal sharing of the necessary burdens of the society as well. Fairness requires a sharing of the burdens, and for a radical egalitarian this comes to an equal sharing of the burdens where people are equally capable of sharing them. Translated into the concrete this does *not* mean that a child or an old man or a pregnant woman are to be required to work in the mines or that they be required to collect garbage, but it would involve something like requiring every able-bodied person, say from nineteen to twenty, to take his or her turn at a fair portion of the necessary unpleasant jobs in the world. In that way we all, where we are able to do it, would share equally in these burdens— in doing the things that none of us want to do but that we, if we are at all reasonable, recognize the necessity of having done. (There are all kinds of variations and complications concerning this—what do we do with the youthful wonder at the violin? But, that notwithstanding, the general idea is clear enough.) And where we think this is reasonably feasible, it squares with our considered judgments about fairness.

I have given you, in effect appealing to my considered judgments but considered judgments I do not think are at all eccentric, a picture of what I would take to be enough equality, too little equality and not enough equality. But how can we know that my proportions are right? I do not think we can avoid or should indeed try to avoid an appeal to considered judgments here. But working with them there are some arguments we can appeal to to get them in wide reflective equilibrium. Suppose we go back to the formal principle of justice, namely that we must treat like cases alike. Because it does not tell us *what* are like cases, we cannot derive substantive criteria from it. But it may, indirectly, be of some help here. We all, if we are not utterly zany, want a life in which our needs are satisfied and in which we can live as we wish and do what we want to do. Though we differ in many ways, in our abilities, capacities for pleasure, determination to keep on with a job, we do not differ about wanting our needs satisfied or being able to live as we wish. Thus *ceterus paribus*, where questions of desert, entitlement and the like do not enter, it is only fair that all of us should have our needs equally considered and that we should, again *ceterus paribus*, all be able to do as we wish in a way that is compatible with others doing likewise. From the formal principle of justice and a few key facts about us, we get to the claim that *ceterus paribus* we should go for this much equality. But this is the core content of a radical egalitarianism.

However, how do we know that *ceterus* is *paribus* here? What about our entitlements and deserts? Suppose I have built my house with my own hands, from materials I have purchased and on land that I have purchased and that I have lived in it for years and have carefully cared for it. The house is mine and I am entitled to keep it even if by dividing the house into two apartments greater and more equal satisfaction of need would obtain for everyone. Justice requires that such an entitlement be respected here. (Again, there is an implicit *ceterus paribus* clause. In extreme situations, say after a war with housing in extremely short supply, that entitlement could be rightly overridden.)

There is a response on the egalitarian's part similar to a response utilitarians made to criticisms of a similar logical type made of utilitarianism by pluralistic deontologists. One of the things that people in fact need, or at least reflectively firmly want, is to have such entitlements respected. Where they are routinely overridden to satisfy other needs or wants, we would *not* in fact have a society in which the needs of everyone are being maximally met. To the reply, but what if more needs for everyone were met by ignoring or overriding such entitlements, the radical egalitarian should respond that that is, given the way we are, a thoroughly hypothetical situation and that theories of morality cannot be expected to give guidance for all logically possible worlds but only for worlds which are reasonably like what our actual world is or plausibly could come to be. Setting this argument aside for the moment, even if it did turn out that the need satisfaction linked with having other things—things that involved the overriding of those entitlements—was sufficient to make it the case that more need satisfaction all around for *everyone* would be achieved by overriding those entitlements, then, for reasonable people who clearly saw that, these entitlements would not have the weight presently given to them. They either would not have the importance presently attached to them or the need for the additional living space would be so great that their being overridden would seem, everything considered, the lesser of two evils (as in the example of the postwar housing situation).

There are without doubt genuine entitlements and a theory of justice must take them seriously, but they are not absolute. If the need is great enough we can see the merit in overriding them, just as in law as well as morality the right of eminent domain is recognized. Finally, while I have talked of entitlements here, parallel arguments will go through for desert.

III

I want now to relate this articulation of what equality comes to to my radically egalitarian principles of justice. My articulation of justice is a certain spelling out of the slogan proclaimed by Marx "From each according to his ability, to each according to his needs." The egalitarian conception of society argues for the desirability of bringing into existence a world, once the springs of social wealth flow freely, in which everyone's needs are as fully satisfied as possible and in which everyone gives according to his ability. Which means, among other things, that everyone, according to his ability, shares the burdens of society. There is an equal giving and equal responsibility here according to ability. It is here, with respect to giving according to ability and with respect to receiving according to need, that a complex equality of result, i.e., equality of condition, is being advocated by the radical egalitarian. What it comes to is this: each of us, where each is to count for one and none to count for more than one, is to give according to ability and receive according to need.

My radical egalitarian principles of justice, read as follows:

1. Each person is to have an equal right to the most extensive total system of equal basic liberties and opportunities (including equal opportunities for meaningful work, for self-determination and political and economic participation) compatible with a similar treatment of all. (This principle gives expression to a commitment to attain and/or sustain equal moral autonomy and equal self-respect.)

2. After provisions are made for common social (community) values, for capital overhead to preserve the society's productive capacity, allowances made for differing unmanipulated needs and preferences, and due weight is given to the just entitlements of individuals, the income and wealth (the common stock of means) is to be so divided that each person will have a right to an equal share. The necessary burdens requisite to enhance human well-being are also to be equally shared, subject, of course, to limitations by differing abilities and differing situations. (Here I refer to different natural environments and the like and not to class position and the like.)

Here we are talking about equality as a right rather than about equality as a goal as has previously been the subject matter of equality in this chapter. These principles of egalitarianism spell out rights people have and duties they have under *conditions of very considerable productive abundance*. We have a right to certain basic liberties and opportunities and we have, subject to certain limitations spelled out in the second principle, a right to an equal square of the income and wealth in the world. We also have a duty, again subject to the qualifications mentioned in the

principle, to do our equal share in shouldering the burdens necessary to protect us from ills and to enhance our well-being.

What is the relation between these rights and the ideal of equality of condition discussed earlier? That is a goal for which we can struggle now to bring about conditions which will some day make its achievement possible, while these rights only become rights when the goal is actually achievable. We have no such rights in slave, feudal or capitalist societies or such duties in those societies. In that important way they are not natural rights for they depend on certain social conditions and certain social structures (socialist ones) to be realizable. What we can say is that it is always desirable that socio-economic conditions come into being which would make it possible to achieve the goal of equality of condition so that these rights and duties I speak of could obtain. But that is a far cry from saying we have such rights and duties now.

It is a corollary of this, if these radical egalitarian principles of justice are correct, that capitalist societies (even capitalist welfare state societies such as Sweden) and statist societies such as the Soviet Union or the People's Republic of China cannot be just societies or at least they must be societies, structured as they are, which are defective in justice. (This is not to say that some of these societies are not juster than others. Sweden is juster than South Africa, Canada than the United States and Cuba and Nicaragua than Honduras and Guatemala.) But none of these statist or capitalist societies can satisfy these radical egalitarian principles of justice, for equal liberty, equal opportunity, equal wealth or equal sharing of burdens are not at all possible in societies having their social structure. So we do not have such rights now but we can take it as a goal that we bring such a society into being with a commitment to an equality of condition in which we would have these rights and duties. Here we require first the massive development of productive power.

The connection between equality as a goal and equality as a right spelled out in these principles of justice is this. The equality of condition appealed to in equality as a goal would, if it were actually to obtain, have to contain the rights and duties enunciated in those principles. There could be no equal life prospects between all people or anything approximating an equal satisfaction of needs if there were not in place something like the system of equal basic liberties referred to in the first principle. Furthermore, without the rough equality of wealth referred to in the second principle, there would be disparities in power and self-direction in society which would render impossible an equality of life prospects or the social conditions required for an equal satisfaction of needs. And plainly, without a roughly equal sharing of burdens, there cannot be a situation where everyone has equal life prospects or has the chance equally to satisfy his needs. The principles of radical egalitarian justice are implicated in its conception of an ideally adequate equality of condition.

IV

The principles of radical egalitarian justice I have articulated are meant to apply globally and not just to particular societies. But it is certainly fair to say that not a few would worry that such principles of radical egalitarian justice, if applied globally, would force the people in wealthier sections of the world to a kind of financial hari-kari. There are millions of desperately impoverished people. Indeed millions are starving or malnourished and things are not getting any better. People in the affluent societies cannot but worry about whether they face a bottomless pit. Many believe that meeting, even in the most minimal way, the needs of the impoverished is going to put an incredible burden on people—people of all classes—in the affluent societies. Indeed it will, if acted on non-evasively, bring about their impoverishment, and this is just too much to ask. Radical egalitarianism is forgetting Rawls' admonitions about "the strains of commitment"—the recognition that in any rational account of what is required of us, we must at least give a minimal healthy self-interest its due. We must construct our moral philosophy for human beings and not for saints. Human nature is less fixed than conservatives are wont to assume, but it is not so elastic that we can reasonably expect people to impoverish themselves to make the massive transfers between North and South—the industrialized world and the Third World—required to begin to approach a situation where even Rawls' principles would be in place on a global level, to say nothing of my radical egalitarian principles of justice.[3]

The first thing to say in response to this is that my radical egalitarian principles are meant actually to guide practice, to directly determine what we are to do, only in a world of extensive abundance where, as Marx put it, the springs of social wealth flow freely. If such a world cannot be attained with the under-mining of capitalism and the full putting into place, stabilizing and developing of socialist relations of production, then such radical egalitarian principles can only remain as heuristic ideals against which to measure the distance of our travel in the direction of what would be a perfectly just society.

Aside from a small capitalist class, along with those elites most directly and profitably beholden to it (together a group constituting not more than 5 percent of the world's population), there would, in taking my radical egalitarian principles as heuristic guides, be no impoverishment of people in the affluent societies, if we moved in a radically more egalitarian way to start to achieve a global fairness. There would be massive transfers of wealth between North and South, but this could be done in stages so that, for the people in the affluent societies (capitalist elites apart), there need be no undermining of the quality of their lives. Even what were once capitalist elites would not be impoverished or reduced to some kind of bleak life though they would, the incidental Spartan types aside, find their life styles altered. But their health and general well being, including their opportunities to do significant and innovative work, would, if anything, be enhanced. And while some of the sources of their enjoyment would be a thing of the past, there would still be a considerable range of enjoyments available to them sufficient to afford anyone a rich life that could be lived with verve and zest.

A fraction of what the United States spends on defense spending would take care of immediate problems of starvation and malnutrition for most of the world. For longer range problems such as bringing conditions of life in the Third World more in line with conditions of life in Sweden and Switzerland, what is necessary is the dismantling of the capitalist system and the creation of a socio-economic system with an underlying rationale directing it toward producing for needs—everyone's needs. With this altered productive mode, the irrationalities and waste of capitalist production would be cut. There would be no more built-in obsolescence, no more merely cosmetic changes in consumer durables, no more fashion roulette, no more useless products and the like. Moreover, the enormous expenditures that go into the war industry would be a thing of the past. There would be great transfers from North to South, but it would be from the North's capitalist fat and not from things people in the North really need. (There would, in other words, be no self-pauperization of people in the capitalist world.) . . .

VIII

It has been repeatedly argued that equality undermines liberty. Some would say that a society in which principles like my radical egalitarian principles were adopted, or even the liberal egalitarian principles of Rawls or Dworkin were adopted, would not be a free society. My arguments have been just the reverse. I have argued that it is only in an egalitarian society that full and extensive liberty is possible.

Perhaps the egalitarian and the anti-egalitarian are arguing at cross purposes? What we need to recognize, it has been argued, is that we have two kinds of rights both of which are important to freedom but to rather different freedoms and which are freedoms which not infrequently conflict.[4] We have rights to *fair terms of cooperation* but we also have rights to *non-interference*. If a right of either kind is overridden our freedom is diminished. The reason why it might be thought that the egalitarian and the anti-egalitarian may be arguing at cross purposes is that the egalitarian is pointing to the fact that rights to fair terms of cooperation and their associated liberties require equality while the anti-egalitarian is pointing to the fact that rights to non-interference and their associated liberties conflict with equality. They focus on different liberties.

What I have said above may not be crystal clear, so let me explain. People have a right to fair terms of cooperation. In political terms this comes to the equal right to all to effective participation in government and, in more broadly social terms, and for a society of economic wealth, it means people having a right to a roughly equal distribution of the benefits and burdens of the basic social arrangements that affect their lives and for them to stand in such relations to each other such that no one has the power to dominate the life of another. By contrast, rights to non-interference come to the equal right of all to be left alone by the government and more broadly to live in a society in which people have a right peacefully to pursue their interests without interference.

The conflict between equality and liberty comes down to, very essentially, the conflicts we get in modern societies between rights to fair terms of cooperation and rights to non-interference. As Joseph Schumpeter saw and J. S. Mill before him, one could have a thoroughly democratic society (at least in conventional terms) in which rights to non-interference might still be extensively violated. A central anti-egalitarian claim is that we cannot have an egalitarian society in which the very precious liberties that go with the rights to non-interference would not be violated.

Socialism and egalitarianism plainly protect rights to fair terms of cooperation. Without the social (collective) ownership and control of the means of production, involving with this, in the initial stages of socialism at least, a workers' state, economic power will be concentrated in the hands of a few who will in turn, as a result, dominate effective participation in government. Some right-wing libertarians blind themselves to that reality, but it is about as evident as can be. Only an utter turning away from the facts of social life could lead to any doubts about this at all. But then this means that in a workers' state, if some people have capitalistic impulses, that they would have their rights peacefully to pursue their own interests interfered with. They might wish to invest, retain and bequeath in economic domains. In a workers' state these capitalist acts in many circumstances would have to be forbidden, but that would be a violation of an individual's right to non-interference and the fact, if it was a fact, that we by democratic vote, even with vast majorities, had made such capitalist acts illegal would still not make any difference because individuals' rights to non-interference would still be violated.

We are indeed driven, by egalitarian impulses, of a perfectly understandable sort, to accept interference with laissez-faire capitalism to protect non-subordination and non-domination of people by protecting the egalitarian right to fair terms of cooperation and the enhanced liberty that that brings. Still, as things stand, this leads inevitably to violations of the right to non-interference and this brings with it a diminution of liberty. There will be people with capitalist impulses and they will be interfered with. It is no good denying, it will be said, that egalitarianism and particularly socialism will not lead to interference with very precious individual liberties, namely with our right peacefully to pursue our interests without interference.[5]

The proper response to this, as should be apparent from what I have argued throughout, is that to live in any society at all, capitalist, socialist, or whatever, is to live in a world in which there will be some restriction or other on our rights peacefully to pursue our interests without interference. I can't lecture in Albanian or even in French in a standard philosophy class at the University of Calgary. I can't jog naked on most beaches, borrow a book from your library without your permission, fish in your trout pond without your permission, take your dog for a walk without your say so and the like. At least some of these things have been thought to be things which I might peacefully pursue in my own interests. Stopping me from doing them is plainly interfering with my peaceful pursuit of my own interests. And indeed it is an infringement on liberty, an interference with my doing what I may want to do.

However, for at least many of these activities, and particularly the ones having to do with property, even right-wing libertarians think that such interference is perfectly justified. But, justified or not, they still plainly constitute a restriction on our individual freedom. However, what we must also recognize is that there will always be some such restrictions on freedom in any society whatsoever, just in virtue of the fact that a normless society, without the restrictions that having norms implies, is a contradiction in terms.[6] Many restrictions are hardly felt as restrictions, as in the attitudes of many people toward seatbelt legislation, but they are, all the same, plainly restrictions on our liberty. It is just that they are thought to be unproblematically justified.

To the question would a socialism with a radical egalitarianism restrict some liberties, including some liberties rooted in rights to noninterference, the answer is that it indeed would; but so would laissez-faire capitalism, aristocratic conceptions of justice, liberal conceptions or any social formations at all, with their associated conceptions of justice. The relevant question is which of these restrictions are justified.

The restrictions on liberty proffered by radical egalitarianism and socialism, I have argued, are justified for they, of the various alternatives, give us both the most extensive and the most abundant system of liberty possible in modern conditions with their thorough protection of the right to fair terms of cooperation. Radical egalitarianism will also, and this is central for us, protect our civil liberties and these liberties are, of course, our most basic liberties. These are the liberties which are the most vital for us to protect. What it will not do is to protect our unrestricted liberties to invest, retain and bequeath in the economic realm and it will not protect our unrestricted freedom to buy and sell. There is, however, no good reason to think that these restrictions are restrictions of anything like a basic liberty. Moreover, we are justified in restricting our freedom to buy and sell if such restrictions strengthen, rather than weaken, our total system of liberty. This is in this way justified, for only by such market restrictions can the

rights of the vast majority of people to effective participation in government and an equal role in the control of their social lives be protected. I say this because if we let the market run free in this way, power will pass into the hands of a few who will control the lives of the many and determine the fundamental design of the society. The actual liberties that are curtailed in a radically egalitarian social order are inessential liberties whose restriction in contemporary circumstances enhances human well-being and indeed makes for a firmer entrenchment of basic liberties and for their greater extension globally. That is to say, we here restrict some liberty in order to attain more liberty and a more equally distributed pattern of liberty. More people will be able to do what they want and have a greater control over their own lives than in a capitalist world order with its at least implicit inegalitarian commitments.

However, some might say I still have not faced the most central objection to radical egalitarianism, namely its statism. (I would prefer to say its putative statism.) The picture is this. The egalitarian state must be in the redistribution business. It has to make, or make sure there is made, an equal relative contribution to the welfare of every citizen. But this in effect means that the socialist state or, for that matter, the welfare state, will be deeply interventionist in our personal lives. It will be in the business, as one right-winger emotively put it, of cutting one person down to size in order to bring about that person's equality with another person who was in a previously disadvantageous position.[7] That is said to be morally objectionable and it would indeed be deeply morally objectionable in many circumstances. But it isn't in the circumstances in which the radical egalitarian presses for redistribution. (I am not speaking of what might be mere equalizing upwards.) The circumstances are these: Capitalist A gets his productive property confiscated so that he could not longer dominate and control the lives of proletarians B, C, D, E, F, and G. But what is wrong with it where this "cutting down to size"—in reality the confiscation of productive property or the taxation of the capitalist—involves no violation of A's civil liberties or the harming of his actual well-being (health, ability to work, to cultivate the arts, to have fruitful personal relations, to live in comfort and the like) and where B, C, D, E, F, and G will have their freedom and their well-being thoroughly enhanced if such confiscation or taxation occurs? Far from being morally objectional, it is precisely the sort of state of affairs that people ought to favor. It certainly protects more liberties and more significant liberties than it undermines.

There is another familiar anti-egalitarian argument designed to establish the liberty-undermining qualities of egalitarianism. It is an argument we have touched upon in discussing meritocracy. It turns on the fact that in any society there will be both talents and handicaps. Where they exist, what do we want to do about maintaining equal distribution? Egalitarians, radical or otherwise, certainly do not want to penalize people for talent. That being so, then surely people should be allowed to retain the benefits of superior talent. But this in some circumstances will lead to significant inequalities in resources and in the meeting of needs. To sustain equality there will have to be an ongoing redistribution in the direction of the less talented and less fortunate. But this redistribution from the more to the less talented does plainly penalize the talented for their talent. That, it will be said, is something which is both unfair and an undermining of liberty.

The following, it has been argued, makes the above evident enough. If people have talents they will tend to want to use them. And if they use them they are very likely to come out ahead. Must not egalitarians say they ought not be able to come out ahead no matter how well they use their talents and no matter how considerable these talents are? But that is intolerably restrictive and unfair.

The answer to the above anti-egalitarian argument is implicit in a number of things I have already said. But here let me confront this familiar argument directly. Part of the answer comes out in probing some of the ambiguities of "coming out ahead." Note, incidentally, that (1) not all reflective, morally sensitive people will be so concerned with that, and (2) that being very concerned with that is a mentality that capitalism inculcates. Be that as it may, to turn to the ambiguities, note that some take "coming out ahead" principally to mean "being paid well for the use of those talents" where "being paid well" is being paid sufficiently well so that it creates inequalities sufficient to disturb the preferred egalitarian patterns. (Without that, being paid well would give none no relative advantage.) But, as we have seen, "coming out ahead" need not take that form at all. Talents can be recognized and acknowledged in many ways. First, in just the respect and admiration of a fine employment of talents that would naturally come from people seeing them so displayed where these people were not twisted by envy; second, by having, because of these talents,

interesting and secure work that their talents fit them for and they merit in virtue of those talents. Moreover, having more money is not going to matter much—for familiar marginal utility reasons—where what in capitalist societies would be called the welfare floors are already very high, this being made feasible by the great productive wealth of the society. Recall that in such a society of abundance everyone will be well off and secure. In such a society people are not going to be very concerned about being a little better off than someone else. The talented are in no way, in such a situation, robbed to help the untalented and handicapped or penalized for their talents. They are only prevented from amassing wealth (most particularly productive wealth), which would enable them to dominate the untalented and the handicapped and to control the social life of the world of which they are both a part. . . .

Discussion Questions

1. What are the two moral principles on which Professor Nielsen grounds his egalitarian society? How does he apply them to concrete situations? How does Professor Nielsen morally justify his two moral principles? In other words, to what facts or principles does he appeal in order to make his case? Do you find his case persuasive? Why or why not? Explain and defend your answer.

2. Professor Nielsen argues that "it is only in an egalitarian society that full and extensive liberty is possible." What does he mean by that and how does he defend it?

3. How does Professor Nielsen respond to the objection that people are entitled to what they own, and thus, any redistribution scheme without the consent of the property owners from which the government confiscates assets is coercive and immoral?

Notes

1. See the debate between Robert Nozick, Daniel Bell and James Tobin, "If Inequality Is Inevitable What Can Be Done About It?" *The New York Times*, January 3, 1982, p. E5. The exchange between Bell and Nozick reveals the differences between the old egalitarianism and right-wing libertarianism. It is not only that the right and left clash but sometimes right clashes with right.

2. Amartya Sen, "Equality of What?" *The Tanner Lectures on Human Values*, vol. 1 (1980), ed. Sterling M.

McMurrin (Cambridge, England: Cambridge University Press, 1980), pp. 198–220.

3. Henry Shue, "The Burdens of Justice," *The Journal of Philosophy* 80, no. 10 (October 1983): 600–601; 606–8.

4. Richard W. Miller, "Marx and Morality," in *Marxism*, eds. J. R. Pennock and J. W. Chapman, Nomos 26 (New York: New York University Press, 1983), pp. 9–11.

5. Ibid., p. 10.

6. This has been argued from both the liberal center and the left. Ralf Dahrendorf, *Essays in the Theory of Society* (Stanford, Cal.: Stanford University Press, 1968), pp. 151–78; and G. A. Cohen, "Capitalism, Freedom and the Proletariat" in *The Idea of Freedom: Essays in Honour of Isaiah Berlin*, ed. Alan Ryan (Oxford: Oxford University Press, 1979).

7. The graphic language should be duly noted. Jan Narveson, "On Dworkinian Equality," *Social Philosophy and Policy* 1, no. 1 (autumn 1983): 4.

38

Property, Exchange, and Libertarianism

Murray N. Rothbard

Murray N. Rothbard, who died in January 1995, was the S. J. Hall Distinguished Professor of Economics at the University of Nevada, Las Vegas. One of the intellectual founders of the contemporary libertarian movement and arguably the leading spokesperson for Austrian Economics, Professor Rothbard is the author of numerous scholarly and popular articles. Among his books are *For a New Liberty* (1973) and his two-volume magnum opus, *Man, Economy, and State* (1962).

In this essay Professor Rothbard defends the political and economic philosophy of *libertarianism* (a view held by members of the Libertarian Party as well as the libertarian wing of the Republican Party in the United States), covering four issues: (1) property rights, (2) society and the individual, (3) free exchange and free contract, and (4) property rights and "human rights." In support of property rights—the right of the individual to own property—Professor Rothbard first dispenses with emotivism and utilitarianism as ways to ground these rights, but argues that "natural law" (or natural right) provides an adequate philosophical ground. He argues that human persons have a natural right to self-ownership as well as a right to private property. In response to the claim that individuals owe something to "society," or that society is to blame for crime and other ills, Professor Rothbard argues that "society" as such does not exist as an independent "person" or "identity" and that when people blame society they are blaming everyone *but* the perpetrator, which is absurd. He goes on to argue that people have a right to freely

Reprinted by permission from Murray N. Rothbard, *For a New Liberty* (New York: Macmillan, 1973), 23–46.

exchange what they own and to freely contract for goods and service. Professor Rothbard concludes by arguing that, contrary to what liberals generally think, there can be no "human rights" or personal liberty without property rights.

Property Rights

If the central axiom of the libertarian creed is nonaggression against anyone's person and property, how is this axiom arrived at? What is its groundwork or support? Here, libertarians, past and present, have differed considerably. Roughly, there are three broad types of foundation for the libertarian axiom, corresponding to three kinds of ethical philosophy: the emotivist, the utilitarian, and the natural rights viewpoint. The emotivists assert that they take liberty or nonaggression as their premise purely on subjective, emotional grounds. While their own intense emotion might seem a valid basis for their own political philosophy, this can scarcely serve to convince anyone else. By ultimately taking themselves outside the realm of rational discourse, the emotivists thereby insure the lack of general success of their own cherished doctrine.

The utilitarians declare, from their study of the consequences of liberty as opposed to alternative systems, that liberty will lead more surely to widely approved goals: harmony, peace, prosperity, etc. Now no one disputes that relative consequences should be studied in assessing the merits or demerits of respective creeds. But there are many problems in confining ourselves to a utilitarian ethic. For one thing, utilitarianism assumes that we can weight alternatives, and decide upon policies, on the basis of their good or bad *consequences*. But if it is legitimate to apply value judgments to the *consequences* of X, why is it not equally legitimate to apply such judgments to X *itself*? May there not be something about an act itself which, in its very nature, can be considered good or evil?

Another problem with the utilitarian is that he will rarely adopt a principle as an absolute and consistent yardstick to apply to the varied concrete situations of the real world. He will only use a principle, at best, as a vague guideline or aspiration, as a *tendency* which he may choose to override at any time. This was the major defect of the nineteenth-century English Radicals, who had adopted the laissez-faire view of the eighteenth-century liberals but had substituted a supposedly "scientific" utilitarianism for the supposedly "mystical" concept of natural rights as the groundwork for that philosophy. Hence the nineteenth-century laissez-faire liberals came to use laissez-faire as a vague tendency rather than as an unblemished yardstick, and therefore, increasingly and fatally compromised the libertarian creed. To say that a utilitarian cannot be "trusted" to maintain libertarian principle in every specific application may sound harsh, but it puts the case fairly. A notable contemporary example is the free market economist Professor Milton Friedman who, like his classical economics forebears, holds to freedom as against state intervention as a general tendency, but in practice allows a myriad of damaging exceptions, exceptions which serve to vitiate the principle almost completely, notably in the fields of police and military affairs, education, taxation, welfare, "neighborhood effects," antitrust laws, and money and banking.

Let us consider a stark example: Suppose a society which fervently considers all redheads to be agents of the Devil and therefore to be executed whenever found. Let us further assume that only a small number of redheads exist in any generation—so few as to be statistically insignificant. The utilitarian-libertarian might well reason: "While the murder of isolated redheads is deplorable, the executions are small in number; the vast majority of the public, as non-redheads, achieves enormous psychic satisfaction from the public execution of redheads. The social cost is negligible, the social, psychic benefit to the rest of society is great; therefore, it is right and proper for society to execute the redheads." The natural-rights libertarian, overwhelmingly concerned as he is for the *justice* of the act, will react in horror and staunchly and unequivocally oppose the executions as totally unjustified murder and aggression upon nonaggressive persons. The *consequence* of stopping the murders—depriving the bulk of society of great psychic pleasure—would not influence such a libertarian, the "absolutist" libertarian, in the slightest. Dedicated to justice and to logical consistency, the natural-rights libertarian cheerfully admits to being "doctrinaire," to being, in short, an unabashed follower of his own doctrines.

Let us turn then to the natural-rights basis for the libertarian creed, a basis which, in one form or another, has been adopted by most of the libertarians, past and resent. "Natural rights" is the cornerstone of a political philosophy which, in turn is embedded in a greater structure of "natural law." Natural law theory rests on the insight that we live in a world of more than one—in fact, a vast number—of entities, and that each entity has distinct and specific properties, a distinct "nature," which can be investigated by man's reason, by his sense perception and mental faculties. Copper has a distinct nature and behaves in a certain way, and so does iron, salt, etc. The species man, therefore, has a specifiable nature, as does the world around him and the ways of interaction between them. To put it with undue brevity, the activity of each inorganic and organic entity is determined by its own nature and by the nature of the other entities with which it comes in contact. Specifically, while the behavior of plants and at least the lower animals is determined by their biological nature or perhaps by their "instincts," the nature of man is such that each individual person must, in order to act, choose his own ends and employ his own means in order to attain them. Possessing no automatic instincts, each man must learn about himself and the world, use his mind to select values, learn about cause and effect, and act purposively to maintain himself and advance his life. Since men can think, feel, evaluate, and act only as individuals, it becomes vitally necessary for each man's survival and prosperity that he be free to learn, choose, develop his faculties, and act upon his knowledge and values. This is the necessary path of human nature; to interfere with and cripple this process by using violence goes profoundly against what is necessary by man's nature for his life and prosperity. Violent interference with a man's learning and choices is therefore profoundly "antihuman"; it violates the natural law of man's needs.

Individualists have always been accused by their enemies of being "atomistic"—of postulating that each individual lives in a kind of vacuum, thinking and choosing without relation to anyone else in society. This, however, is an authoritarian straw man; few, if any, individualists have ever been "atomists." On the contrary, it is evident that individuals always learn from each other, cooperate and interact with each other; and that this, too, is required for man's survival. But the point is that each individual makes the final choice of which influences to adopt and which to reject, or of which to adopt first and which afterwards. The libertarian welcomes the process of voluntary exchange and cooperation between freely acting individuals; what he abhors is the use of violence to cripple such voluntary cooperation and force someone to choose and act in ways different from what his own mind dictates.

The most viable method of elaborating the natural rights statement of the libertarian position is to divide it into parts, and to begin with the basic axiom of the "right to self-ownership." The right to self-ownership asserts the absolute right of each man, by virtue of his (or her) being a human being, to "own" his or her own body; that is, to control that body free of coercive interference. Since each individual must think, learn, value, and choose his or her ends and means in order to survive and flourish, the right to self-ownership gives man the right to perform these vital activities without being hampered and restricted by coercive molestation.

Consider, too, the consequences of denying each man the right to own his own person. There are then only two alternatives: either (1) a certain class of people, A, have the right to own another class, B; or (2) everyone has the right to own his own equal quotal share of everyone else. The first alternative implies that while Class A deserves the rights of being human, Class B is in reality subhuman and therefore deserves no such rights. But since they *are* indeed human beings, the first alternative contradicts itself in denying natural human rights to one set of humans. Moreover, as we shall see, allowing Class A to own Class B means that the former is allowed to exploit, and therefore to live parasitically, *at the expense* of the latter. But this parasitism itself violates the basic economic requirement for life: production and exchange.

The second alternative, what we might call "participatory communalism" or "communism," holds that every man should have the right to own his equal quotal share of everyone else. If there are two billion people in the world, then everyone has the right to own one two-billionth of every other person. In the first place, we can state that this ideal rests on an absurdity: proclaiming that every man is entitled to own a part of everyone else, yet is not entitled *to own himself.* Secondly, we can picture the viability of such a world: a world in which *no* man is free to take *any* action whatever without prior approval or indeed command by *everyone* else in society. It should be clear that in that sort of "communist" world, no one would be able to do anything, and the human race would quickly perish. But if a world of zero self-ownership and one hundred percent other ownership spells death for the human race, then any steps in that direction also contravene the natural law of what is best for man and his life on earth.

Finally, however, the participatory communist world *cannot* be put into practice. For it is physically impossible for everyone to keep continual tabs on everyone else, and thereby to exercise his equal quotal share of partial ownership over every other man. In practice, then, the concept of universal and equal other-ownership is utopian and impossible, and supervision and therefore control and ownership of others necessarily devolves upon a specialist group of people, who thereby become a ruling class. Hence, in practice, any attempt at communist rule will automatically become class rule, and we would be back at our first alternative.

The libertarian therefore rejects these alternatives and concludes by adopting as his primary axiom the universal right of self-ownership, a right held by everyone by virtue of being a human being. A more difficult task is to settle on a theory of property in nonhuman objects, in the things of this earth. It is comparatively easy to recognize the practice when someone is aggressing against the property right of another's person: If A assaults B, he is violating the property right of B in his own body. But with nonhuman objects the problem is more complex. If, for example, we see X seizing a watch in the possession of Y, we cannot automatically assume that X is aggressing against Y's right of property in the watch; for may not X have been the original, "true" owner of the watch who can therefore be said to be repossessing his own legitimate property? In order to decide, we need a theory of justice in property, a theory that will tell us whether X or Y or indeed someone else is the legitimate owner.

A great many libertarians, mostly those in the right wing of the libertarian spectrum, attempt to resolve the problem by asserting that whoever the existing government decrees has the property title should be considered the just owner of the property. At this point, we have not yet delved deeply into the nature of government, but the anomaly here should be glaring enough: it is surely odd to find a group eternally suspicious of virtually any and all functions of government suddenly leaving it to government to define and apply the precious concept of property, the base and groundwork of the entire social order. It is particularly the utilitarian laissez-fairists who believe it most feasible to begin the new libertarian world by confirming all existing property titles; that is, property titles and rights as decreed by the very government that is condemned as a chronic aggressor.

Let us illustrate with a hypothetical example. Suppose that libertarian agitation and pressure has escalated to such a point that the government and its various branches are ready to abdicate. But they engineer a cunning ruse. Just before the government of New York State abdicates it passes a law turning over the entire territorial area of New York to become the private property of the Rockefeller family. The Massachusetts legislature does the same for the Kennedy family. And so on for each state. The government could then abdicate and decree the abolition of taxes and coercive legislation, but the victorious libertarians would now be confronted with a dilemma. Do they recognize the new property titles as legitimately private property? The utilitarians, who have no theory of justice in property rights, would, if they were consistent with their acceptance of given property titles as decreed by government, have to accept a new social order in which 50 new satraps would be collecting taxes in the form of unilaterally imposed "rent." The point is that *only* natural-rights libertarians, only those libertarians who have a theory of justice in property titles that does not depend on government decree, could be in a position to scoff at the new rulers' claims to have private property in the territory of the country, and to rebuff these claims as invalid. As the great nineteenth-century liberal Lord Acton saw clearly, the natural law provides the only sure ground for a continuing critique of governmental laws and decrees.[1] What, specifically, the natural rights position on property titles may be is the question to which we now turn.

We have established each individual's right to self-ownership, to a property right in his own body and person. But people are not floating wraiths; they are not self-subsistent entities; they can only survive and flourish by grappling with the earth around them. They must, for example, *stand* on land areas; they must also, in order to survive and maintain themselves, transform the resources given by nature into "consumer goods," into objects more suitable for their use and consumption. Food must be grown and eaten; minerals must be mined and then transformed into capital and then useful consumer goods, etc. Man, in other words, must own not only his own person, but also material objects for his control and use. How, then, should the property titles in these objects be allocated?

Let us take, as our first example, a sculptor fashioning a work of art out of clay and other materials; and let us waive, for the moment, the question of original property rights in the clay and the sculptor's tools. The question then becomes: *who* owns the work of art as it emerges from the sculptor's fashioning? It is, in fact, the sculptor's "creation," not in the sense that he has created matter, but in the sense that he has transformed nature-given matter—the clay—into another form dictated by his own ideas and fashioned by his own hands and energy. Surely, it is a rare person who, with the case put thus, would say that the sculptor does *not* have the property right in his own product. Surely, if every man has the right to own his own body, and if he must grapple with the material objects of the world in order to survive, then the sculptor has the right to own the product he has made, by his energy and effort, a veritable *extension* of his own personality. He has placed the stamp of his person upon the raw material, by "mixing his labor" with the clay, in the phrase of the great property theorist John Locke. And the product transformed by his own energy has become the material embodiment of the sculptor's ideas and vision. John Locke put the case this way:

> . . . every man has a *property* in his own *person*. This nobody has any right to but himself. The *labour* of his body and the *work* of his hands, we may say, are properly his. Whatsoever, then, he removes out of the state that nature hath provided and left it in, he hath mixed his labour with it, and joined it to something that is his own, and thereby makes it his property. It being by him removed from the common state nature placed it in, it hath by this labour something annexed to it that excludes the common right of other men. For this labour being the unquestionable property of the labourer, no man but he can have a right to what that is once joined to . . .[2]

As in the case of the ownership of people's bodies, we again have three logical alternatives: (1) either the transformer, or "creator," has the property right in his creation; or (2) another man or set of men have the right in that creation, i.e., have the right to appropriate it by force without the sculptor's consent; or (3)—the "communal" solution—every individual in the world has an equal, quotal share in the ownership of the sculpture. Again, put baldly, there are very few who would not concede the monstrous injustice of confiscating the sculptor's property, either by one or more others, or on behalf of the world as a whole. By what right do they do so? By what right do they appropriate to themselves the product of the creator's mind and energy? In this clear-cut case, the right of the creator to own what he has mixed his person and labor with would be generally conceded. (Once again, as in the case of communal ownership of persons, the world communal solution would, in practice, be reduced to an oligarchy of a *few* other expropriating the creator's work in the *name* of "world public" ownership.)

The main point, however, is that the case of the sculptor is not qualitatively different from *all* cases of "production." The man or men who had extracted the clay from the ground and had sold it to the sculptor may not be as "creative" as the sculptor, but they too are "producers," they too have mixed their ideas and their technological know-how with the nature-given soil to emerge with a useful product. They, too, are "producers," and they too have mixed their labor with natural materials to transform those materials into more useful goods and services. These persons, too, are entitled to the ownership of their products. Where then does the process begin? Again, let us turn to Locke:

> He that is nourished by the acorns he picked up under an oak, or the apples he gathered from the trees in the wood, has certainly appropriated them to himself. Nobody can deny but the nourishment is his. I ask then, when did they begin to be his? When he digested? or when he ate? or when he boiled? or when he brought them home? or when he picked them up? and 'tis plain, if the first gathering made them not his, nothing else could. That labour put a distinction between them and common. That added something got them more than Nature, the common mother of all, had done, and so they became his private right. And will any one say he had no right to those acorns or apples he thus appropriated because he had not the consent of all mankind to make them his? Was it a robbery thus to assume to himself what belonged to all in common? If such a consent as that was necessary, man had starved, notwithstanding the plenty God had given him.... Thus, the grass my horse has bit, the turfs my servant has cut, and the ore I have digged in my place, where I have a right to them in common with others, become my property without the assignation or consent of anybody. The labour that was mine, removing them out of that common state they were in, hath fixed my property in them.
>
> By making an explicit consent of every commoner necessary to any one's appropriating to himself any part of what is given in common, children or servants could not cut the meat which their father or master had provided for them in common without assigning to every one his peculiar part. Though the water running in the fountain be every one's, yet who can doubt but that in the pitcher is his only who drew it out? His labour hath taken it out of the hands of Nature where it was common ... and hath thereby appropriated it to himself.
>
> Thus the law of reason makes the deer that Indian's who killed it; 'tis allowed to be his goods who hath bestowed his labour upon it, though, before, it was the common right of every one. And amongst those who are counted the civilized part of mankind ... this original law of nature for the beginning of property, in what was before common, still takes place, and by virtue thereof, what fish any one catches in the ocean, that great and still remaining common of mankind; or what ambergris any one takes up here is by the labour that removes it out of that common state nature left it in, made his property who takes that pains about it.[3]

If every man owns his own person and therefore his own labor, and if by extension he owns whatever property he has "created" or gathered out of the previously unused, unowned, "state of nature," then what of the last great question: the right to own or control the earth *itself*? In short, if the gatherer has the right to own the acorns or berries he picks, or the farmer the right to own his crop of wheat or peaches, *who* has the right to own the land on which these things have grown? It is at this point that Henry George and his followers, who have gone all the way so far with the libertarians, leave the track and deny the individual's right to own the piece of land itself, the ground on which these activities have taken place. The Georgists argue that, while every man should own the goods which he produces or creates, since Nature or God created the land itself, no individual has the right to assume ownership of that land. Yet, if the land is to be used at all as a resource in any sort of efficient manner, it must be owned or controlled by *someone* or some group, and we are again faced with our three alternatives: either the land belongs to the first user, the man who first brings it into production; or it begins to the world as a whole, with every individual owning a quotal part of every acre of land. George's option for the last solution hardly solves his moral problem: if the land itself should belong to God or Nature, then why is it more moral for every acre in the world to be owned by the world as a whole, than to concede individual ownership? In practice, again, it is obviously impossible for every person in the world to exercise effective ownership of his four-billionth portion (if the world population is, say, four billion) of every piece of the world's land surface. In practice, of course, a small oligarchy would do the controlling and owning, and not the world as a whole.

But apart from these difficulties in the Georgist position, the natural-rights justification for the ownership of ground land is the same as the justification for the original ownership of all other property. For, as we have seen, no producer *really* "creates" matter; he takes nature-given matter and transforms it by his labor energy in accordance with his ideas and vision. But *this* is precisely what the pioneer—the "homesteader"—does when he brings previously unused land into his own private ownership. Just as the man who makes steel out of iron ore transforms that ore out of his know-how and with his energy, and just as the man who takes the iron out of the ground does the same, so does the homesteader who clears, fences, cultivates or builds upon the land. The homesteader, too, has transformed the character of the nature-given soil by his labor and his personality. The homesteader is just as legitimately the owner of the property as the sculptor or the manufacturer; he is just as much a "producer" as the others.

Furthermore, if the original land is nature- or God-given then so are the people's talents, health, and beauty. And just as all these attributes are given to specific individuals and not to "society," so then are land and natural resources. All of these resources are given to individuals and not to "society," which is an abstraction that does not actually exist. There is no existing entity called "society"; there are only interacting individuals. To say that "society" should own land or any other property in common, then, must mean that a group of oligarchs—in practice, government bureaucrats—should own the property, and at the expense of expropriating the creator or the homesteader who had originally brought this product into existence.

Moreover, no one can produce *anything* without the cooperation of original land, if only as standing room. No man can produce or create anything by his labor alone; he must have the cooperation of land and other natural raw materials.

Man comes into the world with just himself and the world around him—the land and natural resources given him by nature. He takes these resources and transforms them by his labor and mind and energy into goods more useful to man. Therefore, if an individual cannot own original land, neither can he in the full sense own any of the fruits of his labor. The farmer cannot own his wheat crop if he cannot own the land on which the wheat grows. Now that his labor has been inextricably mixed with the land, he cannot be deprived of one without being deprived of the other.

Moreover, if a producer is *not* entitled to the fruits of his labor, who is? It is difficult to see why a newborn Pakistani baby should have a moral claim to a quotal share of ownership of a piece of Iowa land that someone has just transformed into a wheatfield—and vice versa of course for an Iowan baby and a Pakistani farm. Land in its original state is unused and unowned. Georgists and other land communalists may claim that the whole world population *really* "owns" it, but if no one has yet used it, it is in the real sense owned and controlled by no one. The pioneer, the homesteader, the first user and transformer of this land, is the man who first brings this simple valueless thing into production and social use. It is difficult to see the morality of depriving him of ownership in favor of people who have never gotten within a thousand miles of the land, and who may not even know of the existence of the property over which they are supposed to have a claim.

The moral, natural rights issue involved here is even clearer if we consider the case of animals. Animals are "economic land," since they are original nature-given resources. Yet will anyone deny full title to a horse to the man who finds and domesticates it—is this any different from the acorns and berries that are generally conceded to the gatherer? Yet in land, too, some homesteader takes the previously "wild," undomesticated land, and "tames" it by putting it to productive use. Mixing his labor with land sites should give him just as clear a title as in the case of animals. As Locke declared, "As much land as a man tills, plants, improves, cultivates, and can use the product of, so much is his property. He by his labour does, as it were, enclose it from the common."[4]

The libertarian theory of property was eloquently summed up by two nineteenth-century laissez-faire French economists:

> If man acquires rights over things, it is because he is at once active, intelligent and free; by his activity he spreads over external nature; by his intelligence he governs it, and bends it to his use; by his liberty, he establishes between himself and it the relation of cause and effect and makes it his own. . . .
>
> Where is there, in a civilized country, a clod of earth, a leaf, which does not bear this impress of the personality of man? In the town, we are surrounded by the works of man; we walk upon

a level pavement or a beaten road; it is man who made healthy the formerly muddy soil, who took from the side of a far-away hill the flint or stone which covers it. We live in houses; it is man who has dug the stone from the quarry, who has hewn it, who has planed the woods; it is the thought of man which has arranged the materials properly and made a building of what was before rock and wood. And in the country, the action of man is still everywhere present; men have cultivated the soil and generations of laborers have mellowed and enriched it; the works of man have dammed the rivers and created fertility where the waters had brought only desolation. . . . Everywhere a powerful hand is divined which has moulded matter, and an intelligent will which has adapted it . . . to the satisfaction of the wants of one same being. Nature has recognized her master, and man feels that he is at home in nature. Nature has been *appropriated* by him for his use; she has become his *own*; she is his *property*. This property is legitimate; it constitutes a right as sacred for man as is the free exercise of his faculties. It is his because it has come entirely from himself, and is in no way anything but an emanation from his being. Before him, there was scarcely anything but matter; since him, and by him, there is interchangeable wealth, that is to say, articles having acquired a value by some industry, by manufacture, by handling, by extraction, or simply by transportation. From the picture of a great master, which is perhaps of all material production that in which matter plays the smallest part, to the pail of water which the carrier draws from the river and takes to the consumer, wealth, whatever it may be, acquires its value only by communicated qualities, and these qualities are part of human activity, intelligence, strength. The producer has left a fragment of his own person in the thing which has thus become valuable, and may hence be regarded as a prolongation of the faculties of man acting upon external nature. As a free being he belongs to himself; now the cause, that is to say, the productive force is himself; the effect, that is to say, the wealth produced, is still himself. Who shall dare contest his title of ownership so clearly marked by the seal of his personality? . . .

It is then, to the human being, the creator of all wealth, that we must come back . . . it is by labor that man impresses his personality on matter. It is labor which cultivates the earth and makes of an unoccupied waste an appropriated field; it is labor which makes of an untrodden forest a regularly ordered wood; it is labor, or rather, a series of labors often executed by a very numerous succession of workmen, which brings hemp

from seed, thread from hemp, cloth from thread, clothing from cloth; which transforms the shapeless pyrite, picked up in the mine, into an elegant bronze which adorns some public place, and repeats to an entire people the thought of an artist. . . .

Property, made manifest by labor, participates in the rights of the person whose emanation it is; like him, it is inviolable so long as it does not extend so far as to come into collision with another right; like him, it is individual, because it has origin in the independence of the individual, and because, when several persons have cooperated in its formation, the latest possessor has purchased with a value, the fruit of his personal labor, the work of all the fellow-laborers who have preceded him; this is what is usually the case with manufactured articles. When property has passed, by sale or by inheritance, from one hand to another, its conditions have not changed; it is still the fruit of human liberty manifested by labor, and the holder has the rights as the producer who took possession of it by right.[5]

Society and the Individual

We have talked at length of individual rights; but what, it may be asked, of the "rights of society"? Don't they supersede the rights of the mere individual? The libertarian, however, is an individualist; he believes that one of the prime errors in social theory is to treat "society" as if it were an actual existing entity. "Society" is sometimes treated as a superior or quasi-divine figure with overriding "rights" of its own; at other times as an existing evil which can be blamed for all the ills of the world. The individualist holds that only individuals exist, think, feel, choose, and act; and that "society" is not a living entity but simply a label for a set of interacting individuals. Treating society as a thing that chooses and acts, then, serves to obscure the real forces at work. If, in a small community, ten people band together to rob and expropriate three others, then this is clearly and evidently a case of a group of individuals acting in concert against another group. In this situation, if the ten people presumed to refer to themselves as "society" acting in "its" interest, the rationale would be laughed out of court; even the ten robbers would probably be too shamefaced to use this sort of argument. But let their size increase, and this kind of obfuscation becomes rife and succeeds in duping the public.

The fallacious use of a collective noun like "nation," similar in this respect to "society," has been trenchantly pointed out by the historian Parker T. Moon:

> When one uses the simple monosyllable "France" one thinks of France as a unit, an entity. When . . . we say "France sent *her* troops to conquer Tunis"—we impute not only unity but personality to the country. The very words conceal the facts and make international relations a glamorous drama in which personalized nations are the actors, and all too easily we forget the flesh-and-blood men and women who are the true actors . . . if we had no such word as "France" . . . then we should more accurately describe the Tunis expedition in some such way as this: "A few of these thirty-eight million persons sent thirty thousand others to conquer Tunis." This way of putting the fact immediately suggests a question, or rather a series of questions. Who were the "few"? Why did they send the thirty thousand to Tunis? And why did these obey? Empire-building is done not by "nations," but by men. The problem before us is to discover the men, the active, interested minorities in each nation, who are directly interested in imperialism and then to analyze the reasons why the majorities pay the expense and fight the wars necessitated by imperialist expansion.[6]

The individualist view of "society" has been summed up in the phrase: *"Society" is everyone but yourself*. Put thus bluntly, this analysis can be used to consider those cases where "society" is treated, not only as a superhero with superrights, but as a supervillain on whose shoulders massive blame is placed. Consider the typical view that not the individual criminal, but "society," is responsible for his crime. Take, for example, the case where Smith robs or murders Jones. The "old-fashioned" view is that Smith is responsible for his act. The modern liberal counters that "society" is responsible. This sounds both sophisticated and humanitarian, until we apply the individualist perspective. Then we see that what liberals are *really* saying is that *everyone but* Smith, including of course the victim Jones, is responsible for the crime. Put this baldly, almost everyone would recognize the absurdity of this position. But conjuring up the fictive entity "society" obfuscates this process. As the sociologist Arnold W. Green puts it: "It would follow, then, that if society is responsible for crime, and criminals are not responsible for crime, only those members of society who do not commit crime can be held responsible for crime. Nonsense this ob-

vious can be circumvented only by conjuring up society as devil, as evil being apart from people and what they do."[7]

The great American libertarian writer Frank Chodorov stressed this view of society when he wrote that "Society Are People."

> Society is a collective concept and nothing else; it is a convenience for designating a number of people. So, too, is family or crowd or gang, or any other name we give to an agglomeration of persons. Society . . . is not an extra "person"; if the census totals a hundred million, that's all there are, not one more, for there cannot be any accretion to Society except by procreation. The concept of Society as a metaphysical person falls flat when we observe that Society disappears when the component parts disperse; as in the case of a "ghost town" or of a civilization we learn about by the artifacts they left behind. When the individuals disappear so does the whole. The whole has no separate existence. Using the collective noun with a singular verb leads into a trap of the imagination; we are prone to personalize the collectivity and to think of it as having a body and a psyche of its own.[8]

Free Exchange and Free Contract

The central core of the libertarian creed, then, is to establish the absolute right to private property of every man: first, in his own body, and second, in the previously unused natural resources which he first transforms by his labor. These two axioms, the right of self-ownership and the right to "homestead," establish the complete set of principles of the libertarian system. The entire libertarian doctrine then becomes the spinning out and the application of all the implications of this central doctrine. For example, a man, X, owns his own person and labor, and the farm he clears on which he grows wheat. Another man, Y, owns the fish he catches; A third man, Z, owns the cabbages he has grown and the land under it. But if a man owns anything, he then has the right to *give away* or *exchange* these property titles to someone else, after which point the other person also has absolute property title. From this corollary right to private property stems the basic justification for free contract and for the free-market economy. Thus, if X grows wheat, he may and probably will agree to exchange some of that wheat for some of the fish caught by Y or for some of the cabbages grown by Z. With both X and Y making voluntary agreements to exchange property titles (or Y and Z, or X and Z) the property then becomes with equal legitimacy the property of the other person. If X exchanges wheat for Y's fish, then that fish becomes X's property to do with as he wishes, and the wheat becomes Y's property in precisely the same way.

Further, a man may exchange not only the tangible objects he owns but also his own labor, which of course he owns as well. Thus, Z may sell his labor services of teaching farmer X's children in return for some of the farmer's produce.

It so happens that the free-market economy, and the specialization and division of labor it implies, is by far the most productive form of economy known to man, and has been responsible for industrialization and for the modern economy on which civilization has been built. This is a fortunate utilitarian result of the free market, but it is not, to the libertarian, the *prime* reason for his support of this system. That prime reason is moral, and is rooted in the natural rights defense of private property we have developed above. Even if a society of despotism and systematic invasion of rights could be shown to be more productive than what Adam Smith called "the system of natural liberty," the libertarian would support this system. Fortunately, as in so many other areas, the utilitarian and the moral, natural rights and general prosperity, go hand in hand.

The developed-market economy, as complex as the system appears to be on the surface, is nothing more than a vast network of voluntary and mutually agreed-upon two-person exchanges such as we have shown to occur between wheat and cabbage farmers, or between the farmer and the teacher. Thus, when I buy a newspaper for a dime, a mutually beneficial two-person exchange takes place: I transfer my ownership of the dime to the news dealer and he transfer ownership of the paper to me. We do this because, under the division of labor, I calculate that the paper is worth more to me than the dime, while the news dealer prefers the dime to keeping the paper. Or, when I teach at a university, I estimate that I prefer my salary to not expending my labor of teaching, while the university authorities calculate that they prefer gaining my teaching services to not paying me the money. If the newsdealer insisted on charging 50¢ for the paper, I might well decide that it isn't worth the price; similarly, if I should insist on triple my present salary, the university might well decide to dispense with my services.

Many people are willing to concede the justice and propriety of property rights and the free-market economy, to concede that the farmer should be able to charge whatever his wheat will bring from consumers or the worker to reap whatever others are willing to pay for his services. But they balk at one point: inheritance. If Willie Stargell is ten times as good and "productive" a ball player as Joe Jack, they are willing to concede the justice of Stargell's earning ten times the amount; but what, they ask, if the justification for someone whose only merit is being born a Rockefeller inheriting far more wealth than someone born a Rothbard? The libertarian answer is to concentrate *not* on the recipient, the child Rockefeller or the child Rothbard, but to concentrate on the *giver*, the man who bestows the inheritance. For if Smith and Jones and Stargell have the right to their labor and property and to exchange the titles to this property for the similar property of others, they also have the right to *give* their property to whomever they wish. And of course most such gifts consist of the gifts of the property owners to their children—in short, inheritance. If Willie Stargell owns his labor and the money he earns from it, then he has the right to give that money to the baby Stargell.

In the developed free-market economy, then, the farmer exchanges the wheat for money; the wheat is bought by the miller who processes and transforms the wheat into flour; the miller sells the flour to the baker who produces bread; the baker sells the bread to the wholesaler, who in turn sells it to the retailer, who finally sells it to the consumer. And at each step of the way, the producer may hire the labor services of the workers in exchange for money. How "money" enters the equation is a complex process; but it should be clear that *conceptually* the use of money is equivalent to any single or group of useful commodities that are exchanged for the wheat, flour, etc. Instead of money, the commodity exchanged could be cloth, iron, or whatever. At each step of the way, mutually beneficial exchanges of property titles are agreed upon and transacted.

We are now in the position to see how the libertarian defines the concept of "freedom" or "liberty." Freedom is a condition in which a person's ownership rights in his own body and his legitimate material property are *not* invaded, are not aggressed against. A man who steals another man's property is invading and restricting the victim's freedom, as does the man who beats another over the head. Freedom and unrestricted property right go hand in hand. On the other hand, to the libertarian, "crime" is an act of aggression against a man's property right, either in his own person or his materially owned objects. Crime is an invasion, by the use of violence, against a man's property and therefore against his liberty. "Slavery"—the opposite of freedom—is a condition in which the slave has little or no right of self-owner-ship; his person and his produce are systematically expropriated by his master by the use of violence.

The libertarian, then, is clearly an individualist but *not* an egalitarian. The only "equality" he would advocate is the equal right of every man to the prop-erty in his own person, to the property in the unused resources he "homesteads," and to the property of others he has acquired either through voluntary ex-change or gift.

Property Rights and "Human Rights"

Liberals will generally concede the right of every in-dividual to his "personal liberty," to his freedom to think, speak, write, and engage in such personal "ex-changes" as sexual activity between "consenting adults." In short, the liberal attempts to uphold the individual's right to the ownership of his own body, but then denies his right to "property," i.e., to the ownership of material objects. Hence, the typical lib-eral dichotomy between "human rights," which he upholds, and "property rights," which he rejects. Yet the two, according to the libertarian, are inextricably intertwined; they stand or fall together.

Take, for example, the liberal socialist who ad-vocates government ownership of all the "means of production" while upholding the "human" right of freedom of speech or press. How is this "human" right to be exercised if the individuals constituting the public are denied their right to ownership of prop-erty? If, for example, the government owns all the newsprint and all the printing shops, how is the right to a free press to be exercised? If the government owns all the newsprint, it then necessarily has the right and the power to allocate that newsprint, and someone's "right to a free press" becomes a mockery if the government decides not to allocate newsprint in his direction. And since the government must al-locate scarce newsprint in *some* way, the right to a free press of, say, minorities or "subversive" antisocialists will get short shrift indeed. The same

is true for the "right to free speech" if the govern-ment owns all the assembly halls, and therefore allo-cates those halls as it sees fit. Or, for example, if the government of Soviet Russia, being atheistic, decides not to allocate many scarce resources to the produc-tion of matzohs, for Orthodox Jews the "freedom of religion" becomes a mockery; but again, the Soviet government can always rebut that Orthodox Jews are a small minority and that capital equipment should not be diverted to matzoh production.

The basic flaw in the liberal separation of "hu-man rights" and "property rights" is that people are treated as ethereal abstractions. If a man has the right to self-ownership, to the control of his life, then in the real world he must also have the right to sustain his life by grappling with and transforming resources; he must be able to own the ground and the resources on which he stands and which he must use. In short, to sustain his "human right"—or his property rights in his own person—he must also have the property right in the material world, in the objects which he produces. Property rights *are* human rights, and are essential to the human rights which liberals attempt to maintain. The human right of a free press depends upon the human right of private property in news-print.

In fact, there *are* no human rights that are sepa-rable from property rights. The human right of free speech is simply the property right to hire an assem-bly hall from the owners, or to own one oneself; the human right of a free press is the property right to buy materials and then print leaflets or books and to sell them to those who are willing to buy. There is no extra "right of free speech" or free press beyond the property rights we can enumerate in any given case. And furthermore, discovering and identifying the property rights involved will resolve any apparent conflicts of rights that may crop up.

Consider, for example, the classic example where liberals generally concede that a person's "right of freedom of speech" must be curbed in the name of the "public interest": Justice Holmes' famous dictum that no one has the right to cry "fire" falsely in a crowded theater. Holmes and his followers have used the illustration again and again to prove the supposed necessity for all rights to be relative and tentative rather than precise and absolute.

But the problem here is *not* that rights cannot be pushed too far, but that the whole case is discussed in terms of a vague and woolly "freedom of speech" rather than in terms of the rights of private property.

Suppose we analyze the problem under the aspect of property rights. The fellow who brings on a riot by falsely shouting "fire" in a crowded theater is, necessarily, either the owner of the theater (or the owner's agent) or a paying patron. If he is the owner, then he has committed fraud on his customers. He has taken their money in exchange for a promise to put on a movie or play; and now, instead, he disrupts the show by falsely shouting "fire" and breaking up the performance. He has thus welshed on his contractual obligation, and has thereby stolen the property—the money—of his patrons and has violated their property rights.

Suppose, on the other hand, that the shouter is a patron and not the owner. In that case, he is violating the property right of the owner—as well as of the other guests to their paid-for performance. As a guest, he has gained access to the property on certain terms, including an obligation not to violate the owner's property or to disrupt the performance the owner is putting on. His malicious act, therefore, violates the property rights of the theater owner and of all the other patrons.

There is no need, therefore, for individual rights to be restricted in the case of the false shouter of "fire." The rights of the individual are *still* absolute; but they are *property* rights. The fellow who maliciously cried "fire" in a crowded theater is indeed a criminal, but *not* because his so-called "right of free speech" must be pragmatically restricted on behalf of the "public good"; he is a criminal because he has clearly and obviously violated the property rights of another person.

Discussion Questions

1. Why does Professor Rothbard believe that utilitarianism and emotivism are inadequate in grounding property rights?

2. Central to Professor Rothbard's philosophy is the view that self-ownership and ownership of property are natural rights. How does he argue for this position? How does he morally justify the acquisition and ownership of natural resources and land by individuals? Present and explain in detail. Do you find Professor Rothbard's case persuasive? Explain and defend your answer.

3. Why does Professor Rothbard believe that one cannot have personal liberty (or "human rights") without property rights? Do you find his case persuasive? Explain and defend your answer.

Notes

1. See Gertrude Himmelfarb, *Lord Acton: A Study in Conscience and Politics* (Chicago: Phoenix Books, 1962), pp. 204–05. Compare also John Wild, *Plato's Modern Enemies and the Theory of Natural Law* (Chicago: University of Chicago Press, 1953), p. 176.

2. John Locke, *An Essay Concerning the True Original, Extent and End of Civil Government*, in E. Barker, ed., *Social Contract* (New York: Oxford University Press, 1948), pp. 17–18.

3. Locke, *Civil Government*, pp. 18–19. While Locke was a brilliant property theorist, we are not claiming that he developed and applied his theory with anything like complete consistency.

4. Locke, *Civil Government*, p. 20.

5. Leon Wolowski and Émile Levasseur, "Property," in *Lalor's Cyclopedia of Political Science . . .* (Chicago: M. B. Cary & Co., 1884), III, 392–93.

6. Parker Thomas Moon, *Imperialism and World Politics* (New York: Macmillan, 1930), p. 58.

7. Arnold W. Green, "The Reified Villain," *Social Research* (Winter, 1968), p. 656.

8. Frank Chodorov, *The Rise and Fall of Society* (New York: Devin-Adair, 1959), pp. 29–30.

Multiculturalism and Justice

39

The Challenge of Diversity and Multicultural Education

The President's Task Force
on Multicultural Education,
California State University at Long Beach

The following is a proposal written by the President's Task Force on Multicultural Education, California State University, Long Beach (CSULB). Typical of committees and task forces at other academic institutions, the purpose of the CSULB task force is to address how the university can best adapt to the needs of a more diverse and multicultural community, that is, how the institution can move from an exclusive (i.e., white, male, heterosexual, European) to a more inclusive community (i.e., to include gays, women, and ethnic minorities as part of the academic community). Established in the summer of 1990 by the Provost and Academic Vice President Karl Anatol in order to meet the challenge of then-President Curtis McCray (the new president is Robert Clinton Maxson) for the university "to identify and institute ways to recognize and respond creatively to diversity," this task force proposes certain changes in university curriculum, social climate, underrepresentation of certain minority groups in

Reprinted with permission by California State University, Long Beach. This essay was originally published in *Are You Politically Correct?: Debating America's Cultural Standards*, ed. Francis J. Beckwith and Michael A. Bauman (Buffalo, N.Y.: Prometheus, 1993), 73–89.

the university community, and community relations and service. Parts I through VI of this document consist of the task force's rationale and purpose for its proposals and recommendations. After explaining its concerns and challenges, the task force makes a number of recommendations in various areas, including affirmative action in hiring and sensitivity training for faculty and students.

I. Executive Summary

This document envisions and seeks to initiate a process which leads to a profound appreciation and celebration of our diversity as an academic community and nation, a process which is colla-borative and supportive of sustained discourse and exchange. In this context of appreciated and celebrated diversity, we can and must create and promote an environment in which: (a) all members have equal opportunity; (b) respect, mutual regard for cultural and gender differences, and full democratic participation and partnership are the norm; (c) the diversity of communities we serve are reflected, thus enhancing our ability to serve and teach in a collaborative process; and (d) the quality of campus life is intellectually nurtured by university policies and practices.

II. Introduction

The President's Task Force on Multicultural Education and Campus Diversity was established in the summer of 1990 by Provost and Academic Vice President Karl Anatol in response to President Curtis McCray's challenge to the university to identify and institute ways to recognize and respond creatively to its diversity. The general charge for the Task Force was to initiate a process leading to the establishment of a truly multicultural, democratic institution which cherishes, builds on, and celebrates its diversity. The Task Force envisioned its charge to:

A. explore the intellectual underpinnings of a multicultural university, including defining multiculturalism as an intellectual and practical project;

B. draw upon faculty resources in the exploration of the intellectual rationale and educational imperative of the multicultural university;

C. assess the institutional environment, analyzing that which is good and essential and that which needs to be improved;

D. identify related issues of concern for study and action;

E. collaborate with academic bodies, executive offices, faculty and staff organizations, and student groups to move with insight, commitment, and speed toward policies and practices to implement the charge;

F. create and nurture an environment which fosters a process of mutual engagement in and challenge to realize and expand the educational mission and enhance the quality of campus life; and

G. produce a document which provides both an intellectual framework and inspiration for the initiation and achievement of the above process and task.

III. Background to the Project

The formation of the Task Force responds to several basic developments in American higher education in general and to developments at California State University, Long Beach in particular. First, in recent years a major debate has emerged in American universities and colleges and in the larger society over the content and purpose of a liberal education and the need for curricula to reflect the realities of American culture and society. This essentially requires moving from a monocultural model of education to a multicultural one which stresses the rich complexity and diversity of social and human reality. Second, the multicultural project has its historical roots in the social and academic struggles of various racial and ethnic groups. Women and the many faculty members who have been historically sensitive to issues of race, ethnicity, gender, and class view a multicultural and inclusive curriculum as indispensable to educational excellence.

The University Mission Statement adopted in Spring 1990 recognizes the need for multicultural education, stating that "A fundamental goal of all the university's programs is to prepare students to function effectively in a culturally diverse society, by developing an understanding of our diverse heritage(s), including essential contributions of women and ethnic (groups)." President McCray has also emphasized repeatedly in various contexts that multiculturalism is a fundamental part of CSULB's educational mission.

Finally, the increasing diversity of the student body in terms of race, ethnicity, gender, language, and class has encouraged a search not only for ways of accommodation, but also for ways to utilize this diversity creatively to enhance and expand the educational experience. The increasing diversity among the students reflects an increasing diversity in society and, thus, requires a similar proactive response to the university's service communities.

IV. Rationale

The university poses for itself the project of becoming truly a multicultural community which embraces, builds on, and celebrates its diversity. This project is a morally, intellectually, and socially grounded one. Its moral justification is rooted first in its commitment to respect for the human person. This respect is and must be for the person not simply as an abstracted individual but also as a concrete person-in-community or a person in a defining group. Thus, the University Mission Statement is correct to state that "instruction emphasizes the ethical and social dimensions in all disciplines, as well as their applications to contemporary world issues." The hinge upon which the ethical and social turn(s), is the fundamental and inviolable respect for each person in all her/his diverse expressions. Without such a respect, the humanistic mission or the university is undermined and unfulfilled. Also, our constant historical concern and quest for a just and good society is informed and undergirded by moral concerns about the quality and meaning of human relations in the full sense of the word human, i.e., in its rich and complex diversity.

Multicultural education is intellectually grounded on several levels. It is a necessary corrective for the conceptual and content inadequacy of the exclusive curriculum which omits or diminishes the rich variety of human culture. Likewise, multicultural education is a necessary corrective for racist, sexist, classist, and chauvinist approaches to knowledge and education, again enriching and expanding the educational enterprise. Multicultural education envisions and encourages, moreover, a curriculum reflective of the society and world in which we live, thus providing an intellectual and social competence otherwise diminished or denied and is an effective response to the global economy as well as societal changes and demands.

Multicultural education is socially grounded in its role as a just response to current demographic changes. While the U.S. and California cultural landscape has always been diverse, with the recent increased arrivals of immigrants from Southeast Asia, Central and South America, and other countries, our campus and societal community have become more varied. Across all age groups in the state, the population of people of color is expected to become the majority shortly after the next century. Among the K–12 population, people of color are already the majority. Within the service area of CSU, Long Beach and, in particular, the population of Long Beach Unified School District, there has been a dramatic demographic shift during the past two decades. This shift requires an adequate multicultural educational response which prepares for a diverse society through a curriculum which teaches social and human diversity and is grounded in it.

Social grounds for multicultural education are also found in the related area of preparing a youthful population of color (Latino, Asian, African, Native American) for what David Hayes-Bautista calls the "burden of support" of an older Euro-American population. Such an anticipated burden of support requires not only knowledge of its imminence but the cultivation of a quality of relations which appreciates diversity, mutuality, and interdependence of ethnic and age groups. A multicultural education, moreover, is part and parcel of the thrust to create the just and good society, to avoid civil strife, and to enhance the quality of social life through cultivation of democratic values of and for civility, cooperativeness, mutuality, mutual respect, equality, justice, and interdependence.

V. Goals of a Multicultural Education

The goals of multiculturalism emerge from the diversity of our historical experience and expand to include appreciation of our global interdependence. They aim at an education grounded in a diversity more reflective of the reality of American life than the monochromatic and monocultural versions often projected. These goals also reach beyond the mistaken image of U.S. society as a melting-pot in which diversity is dissolved and beyond the common but erroneous view of society as color and gender blind. Multiculturalism does not deny, ignore, or demean such fundamental expressions of diversity. On the contrary, it recognizes and respects them and utilizes them creatively to enrich and enhance the educational experience. It realizes that respect for the human person requires respect for people in all the diversities in which they are encountered.

The goals of multicultural education are thus practical as well as moral. Such an education prepares students for present-day American society by equipping them with a variety of skills and attitudes that will be useful and necessary for living in and contributing to the present and the emerging future. An important task of the university, then, is to create an environment in which students can learn *to think critically* about their own lives, to view life around them with a measure of objectivity and reason, and *to assume responsibility* for the world in which they live, which they help to create, and hope to pass on to future generations. Multicultural education aims to educate citizens who are able *to recognize, respect, and appreciate* human diversity and the rights of others, including their right to be different from one another and from us. Such an education aims higher than mere toleration, but accepts the word in at least the minimum sense which does not tolerate intolerance.

A person who has profited from a multicultural education will be able *to communicate* with others in spite of the differences brought by diversity of culture, race, gender, etc., and *to negotiate* with others and *to interact* with them for mutual benefit and the common good. Among many more such skills to be cultivated, a primary one is the civility which enables people to live together with a minimum of friction and the maximum of harmony.

Understanding and respecting diverse groups in the U.S. helps prepare persons for understanding and respecting others in a global context. This too is a fundamental goal of multicultural education. Global interdependence is becoming an increasingly compelling reality, and students and citizens in general must be prepared to respond positively and effectively to this. An essential part of the university's mission is to facilitate such preparation as an intellectual and ethical priority.

Another essential goal of multicultural education is a correct and effective orientation toward our past and future. The past which, in our society, is transmitted by education must be our collective past which includes our history in all of its diversity and cultural uniqueness. To recognize and build on the diversity of our past and present is to prepare ourselves for our future and to face successfully the national and global multicultural challenges which await us. The culture we need to appropriate from the past, then, is one which is respectful of diversity, useful, forward-facing, and of ethical merit.

Finally, to cherish both individuality and interdependence at the same time, and to respect the rights as well as responsibilities of individuals and diverse groups, necessitates a mutual respect, tolerance for difference and ambiguity, and an ability to deal effectively with conflicting claims and needs. This, too, is a major goal of multicultural education. The challenge, then, is not to sacrifice *pluribus* to *unum* or vice versa, but to achieve a synthesis which preserves and builds on both. To pose and achieve such a model of multiculturalism can be a fundamental contribution to the university and society.

VI. Defining the Multicultural Project

Multiculturalism is a complex and multidimensional phenomenon and project. It is, thus, several things at once. It is, first of all, a *philosophy* or a framework and statement of understanding and commitment. It is also a *methodology*, a definite approach and perspective to achieve stated goals. It is a *process*, that is to say, a series of activities and interactions to achieve identified goals. Finally, it is a *product*, perceptible and definable results, which are open to ongoing refinement and expansion.

Given this many-sidedness, multiculturalism is best defined as an education generated and sustained by a campus environment which genuinely respects and self-consciously builds on the rich diversity of its members. Its definition of diversity is broad and inclusive, and includes defining factors such as race, ethnicity, gender, special need, class, sexual orientation, language, religion, age, and other distinctions historically used to fragment the campus, society, and the human community. Within this document this entire list is implied whenever we refer to human diversity. Limitations of our time and energy require that we give primary attention to the broadest categories, but this does not mean a lack of concern for

all. Special care should be taken that no groups be made scapegoats or be abused in any way.

Multicultural education supports the construction of a curriculum which: (1) affirms the concept of diversity as central and indispensable to understanding social reality; (2) provides fundamental grounding in diverse cultures and gender studies as essential to a serious and adequate education; (3) is committed to educational equity for students which translates as equal opportunity and maximum outcome; (4) is directed toward providing students with knowledge, skills, and attitudes necessary to succeed in and contribute to society and the human community; and (5) is committed to furthering the body of knowledge on diversity through research and scholarly debate (e.g., graduate research methods classes, student and faculty research projects).

While clearly dedicated to *educational excellence* in a diversity-respecting environment, multicultural education is also committed to *social responsibility* and *solidarity*. As an essential, even vanguard, institution in society, the university is positioned in a context for cultivating civic values contributive to a multicultural, just, and democratic culture. This means building on our best ideals and values of mutual respect and shared goals of a truly inclusive and diversity-respecting, just, and democratic society. This respect for diversity must not only respect individual difference, but also group difference and the value and right of the continuity of cultural diversity within a common civic culture.

VII. Concerns and Challenges

To achieve such a broad and inclusive process of multicultural education, it is necessary to address successfully the issues of: curriculum, research, social climate on campus, underrepresentation of ethnic groups and women, and community relations including contributing to our service communities.

Curriculum

Reassessment and recrafting of the curriculum to reflect the multicultural reality of the campus, community, and world is essential, indeed indispensable. There is no single model which stands in opposition to the existing curricula. What unites most is their goal of overcoming what may be called the "exclusive" curricula, whether these be Euro-centric, Anglo-centric, or male-centric. The problem with "exclusive" curricula is that they equate the values of a dominant group with "universality," and falsely present the experience of a dominant group as a formula for all other groups. Any exclusive curricula, moreover, masks the rationale for one group's dominance over others and the mechanisms of social control by which this is maintained. Mutual knowledge, opportunity, and understanding and appreciation of difference must now be the foundation for a multicultural campus and for a multicultural society.

Various scholars in multicultural education have noted the negative effects of exclusive curricula on all students. First, such curricula, in ignoring other groups, reinforce a false sense of superiority for European American students by keeping them ignorant of the history, values, and beliefs of other groups and ignorant of the diversity within the so-called majority experience. These students are also robbed of an outsider perspective, i.e., they are denied the opportunity to see themselves as others see them. They fail to develop strategies for communication with individuals from a variety of backgrounds. They fail, furthermore, to develop the skills, knowledge, and attitudes necessary to succeed and contribute to our diverse society. Students from other cultural backgrounds are short-changed too because their own experiences are either ignored or seen from only the dominant perspective. Similar concerns can be raised with respect to male-centric curricula.

At a recent Celebrating Diversity Conference, Carl Grant noted that if we truly want a multicultural society and want to reflect all groups in our curriculum, we are faced with some hard choices in redefining and reconceptualizing the existing curriculum—especially in areas which directly reflect cultural values. James Banks stated, in his address to the CSULB community, that this requires that definitions of multicultural transformation not be considered as "catering to special interests," while the interests of dominant groups are seen as being "universal." Respect for diversity requires that we move beyond the chauvinistic notion that the "exclusive" curricula are synonymous with universalism. As an alternative to the exclusive curricula, we must facilitate what Banks calls "multiple acculturation," that is to say, pursuing multiple models.

Multicultural transformation also requires a greater emphasis on the critical analysis of social problems and inequity. It requires helping students to identify options for decisions and to take actions which implement their decisions. In such a process, students learn to become social critics and reflective agents of change.

The multicultural curriculum requires: (1) respect for human rights and human diversity; (2) recognition of the strengths and values of cultural diversity; (3) support for social justice and equal opportunity for all people; (4) commitment to democratic values of mutual respect, civility, equality, and mutual interdependence; and (5) awareness of the fundamental importance of race, ethnicity, gender, class, special needs, sexual orientation, language, religion, and age in understanding social reality.

Multiculturalism thus requires a complete rethinking and adaptation of the curriculum to the cultural reality of our university and society. It is a more thorough-going challenge than can be met by a single course or specific requirement. There is presently a proposal under consideration to include multicultural education within the general education program; regardless of how this process develops, we point out that the creation of a multicultural university must be a broader, more radical task.

Social Climate

Another major concern in creating the truly multicultural university is the challenge of creating a social climate on campus where diversity is not simply tolerated, but is embraced and built on to create a rich complexity of educational and social exchanges. This is not possible when physical and verbal incidents of intolerance tear at the social and educational fabric. Insensitivity and lack of respect for cultural and national differences have been increasing in small towns and large cities. Our own university, like other colleges and universities across the nation, is greatly concerned not only with the increase in insensitivity and lack of respect, but also with the growing number of violent acts based on race and gender.

The Office of the Chancellor has directed the CSU system to develop policies that will respond to incidents of racial and sexual abuses in a prompt and just manner. Formal policies alone, however, will not stem the rise of violent incidents in the universities. The institutions must prepare students, faculty, staff, and administrators to live in a society that is increasingly multicultural and multiethnic. Although California is leading the country in demographic diversity, the states of Florida, Illinois, New York, Texas, and most of the nation's largest cities will be equally diverse by the turn of the century.

America has entered a new era in which its previously ignored cultural and national groups and its women are seeking recognition and political power. Universities are the institutions best equipped to study and understand, explain and facilitate this step in the nation's historical development. Indeed, universities throughout the land proclaim this boldly in their mission statements, but have too often failed to prepare their students for the responsibilities and challenges of the America of the twenty-first century.

Universities must begin to fulfill this mission if they are to fulfill their obligations to society. At CSULB, both students and faculty need to learn how to interact with each other, how to be sensitive to cultural, national, and gender differences and how to value this diversity as they value the quest for knowledge, freedom of thought and expression, and democratic principles and ideals.

Finally, to have a university that embraces diversity, a campus community that nurtures all members, requires strong leadership. Although leadership in this clearly rests with the administration and faculty, each person on campus must collaborate in creating a campus community that embraces and builds on diversity. It is, therefore, the responsibility of every person, whether administrator, faculty, student, or staff to avoid and condemn any acts of intolerance or disrespect.

Underrepresentation

Underrepresentation of students, faculty, and staff of diverse groups poses another concern and challenge in the thrust toward the truly multicultural university. This is especially true and difficult for students. Since our university is entrusted with the role of educating tomorrow's leaders, it must exercise leadership to ensure that it is admitting an equitable cross-section of all students in the state, and preparing all students with the knowledge and skills necessary to participate in a multicultural society.

As many multicultural educators have recently pointed out, it is a mistake to cast the problem of equity and the need for multicultural education in terms of a majority/minority of Black/White or Asian formula. Khmer (Cambodians), to cite one example, are broadly labeled "Asians," but they are grossly underrepresented (given their numbers in our state

population) at the University of California and within the California State University system. California's increasing diversity, however, is not limited to ethnicity and language background. Increasingly, the gap between rich and poor—in our state and in the nation as a whole—is also widening. The correlation between family income and performance on standardized measures such as the SAT is well documented.

Given the continuing challenge of promoting an equitable representation among all major groups in the state, there is a need for the CSU system to exercise leadership by coming to grips with lingering discrepancies based upon ethnicity, linguistic background, and social class.

Ethnic underrepresentation among the faculty is also a major concern. Our commitment to creating a truly multicultural university requires that we make an active effort to hire qualified faculty members from underrepresented groups. To build for the future, it is also important that the university take an active role in encouraging a more diverse group of students to pursue graduate education and teaching careers. Enhancing and enriching the educational experience requires dealing with the present reality, that the majority of those entering graduate programs and ultimately teaching in higher education, are Anglo- or European American, middle class, monocultural, and monolingual.

Regardless of a person's background, it is essential that all faculty members have some knowledge of techniques for teaching students from a wide range of backgrounds. It is necessary that they have some understanding of the major cultural groups among our students, and also strategies for learning about students who come from smaller and less familiar groups. Hiring a diverse staff is important to the multicultural project for similar reasons.

Community Relations and Service

The university has both an academic and a social mission. These are inextricably linked. At the heart of the educational mission is the preparation of students for full and effective participation in and contribution to society. As part of the community in which it is located, the university can and must establish collaborative relations with its surrounding communities, to assist them in various kinds of problem-solving and developmental projects. Linkages need to be strengthened with surrounding communities, through partnerships with schools and through field activities and community learning, that broaden learning from mere book knowledge to experiential study.

Some universities have begun to do this already. For example, in the UC system, San Diego and Santa Cruz now provide either general education or major credit through supervised undergraduate community study courses. In UCSD's Third College, undergraduate students with an interest in teaching take a three course field experience track which begins with a focus on a local community, followed by a field experience in a classroom of that school.

Such an approach allows prospective teachers the opportunity to gain a holistic picture of the relationship between community and school and the chance to determine whether they are truly interested in teaching. All too often, those interested in teaching have little exposure to its daily challenges until they fulfill observation and student teaching requirements as part of their postgraduate professional preparation. These requirements are performed—all too frequently—in schools which are not repre-sentative of those in which they are most likely to be hired. The UCSD Third College approach overcomes these problems by linking preprofessional with professional training and by linking the university with local communities.

Experiential links with the community should not be limited to teacher education. Within the past fifteen years, California communities have provided a remarkable laboratory for field study in social and demographic change. Immigrant communities have revitalized decaying inner cities and stagnant suburban economies across the state. The recent emergence of these communities recalls the role which immigrant towns have played throughout our history and reinforces the evidence that immigrants contribute to the larger economy by helping themselves. Students in social sciences, the arts, and humanities need to be trained in the rudimentary data collection techniques to chronicle the contributions and impact of the new Americans within our communities.

VIII. Anticipated Difficulties

In pursuit of our objectives, we will, as have other educational institutions, face formidable difficulties. As a community united and committed to creating the best possible educational environment, however, we can overcome these difficulties. Among the first challenges we face are systemic challenges which include: (1) finding and securing adequate funding for the project in a context of shrinking resources; (2) developing a process of rewards for multicultural initiative and innovation; (3) overcoming the conservative nature of the institution as institution, i.e., its slowness and resistance to change; (4) urging, cultivating, and sustaining faculty and administrative leadership who are critical to the formulation and success of the project; and (5) successfully combatting false efficiency of the bureaucratic process which results in marginalization, compartmentalization, and counterproductive packaging.

The Task Force is also sensitive to anticipated faculty concerns which include: (1) apprehension about dealing with unfamiliar issues; (2) concern about new requirements competing for FTE; (3) reluctance to change carefully developed courses; (4) concerns about demands on one's time and energy; (5) concerns that foundational curriculum not be undermined or damaged; (6) concerns about competence and areas of expertise; and (7) adequate attention to the demands of academic freedom.

We are also aware of attitudes which must be challenged and overcome if the project is to succeed. These include: (1) deeply held personal beliefs that are contrary to diversity concerns; (2) prejudices of race, gender, class, and other differences; (3) monocultural intellectual preferences; (4) negative assumptions about the value and quality of multicultural research and scholarship; and (5) incorrect belief that multicultural education is an ethnic or gender project rather than a collaborative and collective project involving and benefitting all.

These concerns are understandable, and we are confident the problems they pose can be overcome in the spirit of collegiality and in the process of collaboration and mutual engagement for the best possible educational environment.

IX. Recommendations

A. Actions by University-Level Administrators
  1. Faculty development
    Faculty development activities need to provide assistance to new and continuing faculty members, both full- and part-time, to enable them to meet the needs of the twenty-first century. Some suggestions:

a. include information on the importance of multiculturalism in new faculty orientation;

b. offer workshops in developing teaching strategies that are effective for students with a variety of learning styles reflective of gender and ethnic diversity;

c. offer, in workshops and various other forums, such as school or department faculty meetings, suggestions on sensitivity to classroom language, interactions, and instructional tools, that make all students feel included; and

d. assist newly hired faculty members, both full- and part-time, in understanding university functioning, understanding the expectations of faculty members in instruction, research and scholarly activity, committees and university service assignments, and planning one's work both during the academic year and during summer, to accomplish the tasks.

2. Staff development

A university that embraces diversity, that conveys a sense of inclusion of and respect for all people, must have diversity in the staff and administration as well as in students and faculty. All administrative offices, at all levels, need to continue to make a conscious effort to include diversity.

a. Assure that affirmative action guidelines are followed in recruiting and hiring, and women and members of diverse cultural, racial, and ethnic groups have equitable opportunities for advancement.

b. Offer suggestions and training on sensitivity to language and behavior that demonstrate respect for all individuals, for all people who interact with students.

3. Dissemination of information

a. Identify a location as a central repository for materials on diversity issues, especially for materials and references that can be used by faculty members seeking to modify courses.

b. Gather and publicize information about projects and activities at other campuses that have been effective in helping all students succeed in their education, with special attention to the needs of women and students from diverse cultural, racial, and ethnic groups.

c. Consider distributing a periodic newsletter on diversity issues and on projects intended to improve diversity and multicultural education.

4. Work with the Surrounding Community

Campus administrators should help to develop links between the university and all of its service communities, including the various ethnic communities.

a. Promote interactions in which the university assists the communities in the maintenance, articulation, and development of their respective cultures.

b. Establish an Action Research Center that would serve to match faculty research projects with community interests and needs.

5. Support

Assist faculty members to find support for activities that promote diversity and multicultural education.

a. Provide funding where possible.

b. Solicit outside funding.

c. Assist in finding sources for sponsored research.

B. Actions at the School Level

School deans (or equivalent, for programs that are not within Schools) should be held responsible for fostering diversity by assuring that departments carry out activities leading to inclusion of students and faculty from all groups. In addition to activities specific to the discipline, these should include:

1. recruiting and hiring practices that assure the largest possible pool of qualified candidates who are women and members of various ethnic groups;

2. RTP procedures and standards that reward faculty activities which serve to promote diversity and multicultural education as an essential aspect of educational excellence;

3. encouraging and supporting efforts of faculty to include multicultural content and viewpoints in their teaching and research;

4. encouraging and supporting activities that lead to recruitment and retention of students from groups underrepresented in the discipline; and

5. fostering classroom atmospheres that help all students succeed in meeting the goals of the course, including developing teaching

strategies that recognize diverse learning styles; maintaining courtesy to all groups in classroom interactions; including students usually called "nontraditional" in such activities as special projects, research, and others appropriate to the discipline.

C. Ongoing Projects by Departments and Faculty Members

The university should encourage all faculty members to make a conscious effort to include gender and diversity issues in curriculum planning, course content, teaching styles, and research when appropriate.

1. Examine existing courses, and, where appropriate, develop new courses to include diversity of viewpoints.

a. Incorporate consideration of racial, ethnic, gender, class, and language issues in course materials and discussions.

b. Recognize and use student diversity in the classroom; use teaching strategies that promote active participation by students from diverse backgrounds and cultures; encourage students to interact with those of different backgrounds in group activities, study sessions, or activities appropriate to the course.

2. Encourage students to develop skills in cooperative work that are essential for effective performance in employment, in social interactions, in participatory democracy, in local communities, and in the nation.

3. Recognizing that education of teachers is a responsibility of the entire university, all departments should be especially attentive to the need to prepare future teachers to work with students from a variety of backgrounds and cultures.

4. Share resource materials, teaching materials, and information relative to diversity issues with other faculty members by providing materials to the central repository, participating in workshops, and assisting faculty members trying to modify courses.

5. Integrate diversity perspectives into research projects.

6. Include work with the surrounding community in research projects and internships.

D. Miscellaneous Recommendations

Some recommendations need to be referred to various campus offices or to faculty policy bodies.

1. Recruiting

There should be a handbook on recruiting, to be used by all search committees. This handbook should include hiring criteria and procedures, policy on affirmative action, and guidelines for effective recruiting of women and members of various ethnic groups.

2. Student Retention

There needs to be better use of information on student retention in policy decisions.

a. Collect student data in a way that makes it possible to evaluate the effects of programs and policies on student retention.

b. Examine policies, such as arbitrarily established GPA requirements, to see if they are having an inappropriate effect on retention of various ethnic group students.

c. Establish an orientation and advisement program that can recognize and meet the needs of students from diverse backgrounds.

3. Program Review

The Program Review Self-Study questionnaire should be revised to include specific questions on:

a. The program's hiring plan to achieve diversity in faculty and staff composition; and

b. an evaluation of the program's success in achieving multicultural education.

Conclusion

To fulfill its mission, the university's goal must be to provide an education which, at its core, has a multicultural foundation. It must do this not simply to respond to current demographic changes but for even more profound and important reasons. First, it must be done because an intellectually and ethnically sound education requires a multicultural foundation; diversity is at the heart of the human experience and there is no adequate intellectual understanding of it or ethical appreciation of it without such a multicultural approach. Second, in doing what is intellectually and ethnically sound, we at the same time respect, retrieve, and utilize the best of our past. Our nation has always had a demography of diversity and due respect was always warranted for it. The current changes merely reaffirm and increase the urgency of such a respect.

The United States, at this critical juncture in its history, is in a position to make a unique contribution to the world in the twenty-first century. This contribution would be a multicultural democracy which recognizes and respects not simply the rights of the individual but also the needs and rights of groups, not simply the person as an ideal or abstract, but the concrete person-in-community and in group. This is the next step in the "great experiment" we call democracy.

In California, we find ourselves with a unique and rare opportunity to create a vision and model of education for effective citizenship and global exchange in a multicultural democracy. Multiculturality is an indisputable part of California history and can be built on to provide a microcosm of national possibility and promise. Our contribution to the value and viability of the multicultural university, a dynamic example of human diversity as human richness, productivity, and promise.

Discussion Questions

1. How does the President's Task Force morally justify multicultural education at the university level? Present and explain the task force's reasoning and the values to which it appeals. Do you agree with its reasoning? Why or why not? Explain and defend your answer.

2. What issues does the President's Task Force believe need to be addressed in order to achieve true multicultural education? List the issues and then explain the task force's suggestions of how these issues can be handled in order to achieve multicultural diversity. How does this tie in with the task force's recommendations to the university community (Part IX)? Do you agree or disagree with the task force's arguments? Explain and defend your answer.

3. The President's Task Force claims that "an important part of the university . . . is to create an environment in which students can learn to *think critically* about their lives." It claims elsewhere that part of the multicultural project is that the university should "reflect all groups in our curriculum." But what if thinking critically leads a student (or a faculty member) to the conclusion that the task force's conclusions are misguided? Would the task force embrace this result? And what if thinking critically about the claim that the university should "reflect all groups in the curriculum" leads one to the belief that it is wrong? That is to say, what if someone concludes that (1) some groups have contributed virtually nothing to human progress (e.g., hillbillies in the Ozarks) and thus ought not to be represented in the curriculum, and (2) connecting "ideas" to ethnic and gender groups, which the multicultural project seems to maintain, assumes that cognition is inexorably linked to one's race and/or gender, an implicitly racist and sexist assumption? How would the task force reconcile this apparent inconsistency, which may arise if their proposal is enacted and enforced?

40

Education and the Racist Road to Barbarism

George Reisman

George Reisman is Professor of Economics at Pepperdine University's School of Business and Management. He is the author of many scholarly works, including the book *The Government against the Economy* (1979).

In this essay Professor Reisman argues that the trends toward "multicultural education" and "diversity" as well as critiques of "Eurocentric or Western values" are misguided and ill-informed. For one thing, these trends imply that all cultures are in some way equal to each other in their contribution to human progress and knowledge. Professor Reisman argues that this is simply false: Western values–whether scientific, philosophical, economic, or moral—have proved vastly superior, as evidenced by the advancement of the societies that have embraced these values, whether they be geographically in the Far East (e.g., Japan, South Korea, Taiwan) or in the West (e.g., the United States). Second, Western civilization is open to everyone, since it constitutes a *body of knowledge and values* that is not linked inexorably to any race, nationality, or region of the globe. (In fact, a strong influence on the "West" has been the ideas produced by societies of the Near East: Egypt and Israel.) Third, Professor Reisman contends that multiculturalism is a new form of racism, because it reduces a matter of the intellect to a matter of racial or ethnic membership.

Reprinted by permission of the author from *Are You Politically Correct?: Debating America's Cultural Standards*, ed. Francis J. Beckwith and Michael A. Bauman (Buffalo, N.Y.: Prometheus, 1993), 205–216.

Major changes are taking place in the philosophy of American education, changes which are potentially capable of having an enormous impact on all aspects of American life. The changes are inspired by what the *New York Times* refers to as the "Eurocentrism critique." According to the *Times*, "Eurocentrism" is a pejorative term supposed to describe "a provincial outlook that focuses overwhelmingly on European and Western culture while giving short shrift to Asia, Africa, and Latin America."

A typical manifestation of "Eurocentrism," according to its critics, is the statement that Columbus discovered America. This statement, which most children in America may have learned as their very first fact of history, is now regarded as controversial. Indeed, it is held to be positively offensive because it implies that "there had been no other people on the continent" before Columbus arrived. Traditional American education in general is denounced for seeing non-Western civilization and the rest of the world "only through a Western lens." Only through that "lens," it is held, can, for example, African art be regarded as primitive.

In an effort to eliminate such alleged Western and European "bias," schools are altering the way in which history, literature, and the arts are being taught. Recent changes at Stanford University, where a course on Western civilization was replaced by one in which non-Western ideas had to be included, are only one case in point. The revisions in the history curriculum in California's public school system, to emphasize Indian and African cultures, is another. Curricula and textbooks are being widely rewritten, and, as evidence of the depth of the changes, the *Times* reports that efforts are underway "to reconstruct the history of African tribes, going beyond relying on accounts of Western travelers to examining indigenous sources, often oral, and adapting anthropological approaches."

The implications of these changes are enormous. The acceptance of the "Eurocentrism" critique and its denial of such propositions as Columbus discovered America speaks volumes about the state of the educational establishment in general.

In order to understand the implications, it is first necessary to remind oneself what Western civilization is. From a historical perspective, Western civilization embraces two main periods: the era of Greco-Roman civilization and the era of modern Western civilization, which latter encompasses the rediscovery of Greco-Roman civilization in the late Middle Ages, and the periods of the Renaissance, the Enlightenment, and the Industrial Revolution. Modern Western civilization continues down to the present moment, of course, as the dominant force in the culture of the countries of Western Europe and the United States and the other countries settled by the descendants of West Europeans. It is an increasingly powerful force in the rapidly progressing countries of the Far East, such as Japan, Taiwan, and South Korea, whose economies rest on "Western" foundations in every essential respect.

From the perspective of intellectual and cultural content, Western civilization represents an understanding and acceptance of the following: the laws of logic; the concept of causality and, consequently, a universe ruled by natural laws intelligible to man; on these foundations, the whole known corpus of the laws of mathematics and science; the individual's self-responsibility based on his free will to choose between good and evil; the value of man above all other species on the basis of his unique possession of the power of reason; the value and competence of the individual human being and his corollary possession of individual rights, among them the right to life, liberty, property, and the pursuit of happiness; the need for limited government and for the individual's freedom from the state; on this entire preceding foundation, the validity of capitalism, with its unprecedented and continuing economic development in terms of division of labor, technological capital accumulation, and rising living standards; in addition, the importance of visual arts and literature depicting man as capable of facing the world with confidence in his power to succeed, and music featuring harmony and melody.

Western Civilization Is Open to Everyone

Once one recalls what Western civilization is, the most important thing to realize about it is that *it is open to everyone.* Indeed, important elements of "Western" civilization did not even originate in the West. The civilization of the Greeks and Romans incorporated significant aspects of science that were handed down from Egypt and Babylon. Modern "Western" civilization includes contributions from people living in the Middle East and China during the Dark Ages, when Western Europe had reverted to virtual barbarism. Indeed, during the Dark Ages, "Western" civilization resided much more in the Middle East than in West-

ern Europe. (It is conceivable that if present trends continue, in another century it might reside more in the Far East than in the West.)

The truth is that just as one does not have to be from France to like French-fried potatoes or from New York to like a New York steak, one does not have to be born in Western Europe or be of West European descent to admire Western civilization, or, indeed, even to help build it. Western civilization is not a product of geography. *It is a body of knowledge and values.* Any individual, any society, is potentially capable of adopting it and thereby becoming "Westernized." The rapidly progressing economies of the Far East are all "Western" insofar as they rest on a foundation of logic, mathematics, science, technology, and capitalism that are essential features of "Western" civilization.

For the case of a Westernized individual, I must think of myself. I am not of West European descent. All four of my grandparents came to the United States from Russia, about a century ago. Modern Western civilization did not originate in Russia and hardly touched it. The only connection my more remote ancestors had with the civilization of Greece and Rome was probably to help in looting and plundering it. Nevertheless, I am thoroughly a Westerner. I am a Westerner because of the *ideas and values* I hold. I have thoroughly internalized all of the leading features of Western civilization. They are now *my* ideas and *my* values. Holding these ideas and values as I do, I would be a Westerner wherever I lived and whenever I was born. I identify with Greece and Rome, and not with my ancestors of that time, because I share the ideas and values of Greece and Rome, not those of my ancestors. To put it bluntly, my ancestors were savages—certainly up to about a thousand years ago, and, for all practical purposes, probably as recently as four or five generations ago.

I know nothing for certain about my great-grandparents, but if they lived in rural Russia in the middle of the nineteenth century, they were almost certainly totally illiterate, highly superstitious, and primitive in every way. On winter nights, they probably slept with farm animals in their hut to keep warm, as was once a common practice in Northern Europe, and were personally filthy and lice-infested. I see absolutely nothing of value in their "way of life," if it can be called a way of life, and I am immeasurably grateful that my grandparents had the good sense to abandon it and come to America, so that I could have the opportunity of becoming a "Westerner" and, better still, an American "Westerner," because, in most respects, since colonial times, the United States has always been, intellectually and culturally, the *most* Western of Western countries.

Thus, I am a descendant of savages who dwelt in Eastern Europe—and before that probably the steppes of Asia—who has been Westernized and now sees the world entirely through a Western "lens," to use the term of the critics of "Eurocentrism." Of course, it is not really a lens through which I see the world. It is much more fundamental than that. I have developed a Western *mind*, a mind enlightened and thoroughly transformed by the enormous body of knowledge that represents the substance of Western civilization, and I now see the world entirely on the basis of that knowledge.

For example, I see the world on the foundation of the laws of logic, mathematics, and science that I have learned. And whenever something new or unexpected happens, which I do not understand, I know that it must nevertheless have a cause which I am capable of discovering. In these respects, I differ profoundly from my savage ancestors, who lacked the knowledge to see the world from a scientific perspective and who probably felt helpless and terrified in the face of anything new or unknown because, lacking the principle of causality and knowledge of the laws of logic, they simply had no basis for expecting to be able to come to an understanding of it.

It is on the basis of the same foundation of knowledge that I regard the discoverer of the Western hemisphere to be Columbus, rather than the very first human beings to arrive on the North American continent (probably across a landbridge from Asia), and rather than the Norwegian Leif Ericson. I consider Columbus to be the discoverer not because of any such absurd reason as a preference for Europeans over Asiatics (Leif Ericson was as much a European as Columbus), but because it was Columbus who opened the Western hemisphere to the civilization I have made my own. Columbus was the man who made it possible to bring to these shores *my ideas and values*. It is not from the perspective of the residence of my ancestors, who were certainly not Italian or Spanish or even West European, that I regard Columbus as the discoverer of America, but from the perspective of the residence of my ideas and values. Just as at an earlier time, they resided in Greece and Rome rather than in the Russia of my ancestors, so in the fifteenth and sixteenth centuries, the home of my ideas and values was in Western Europe. I hold Columbus to have been the discoverer of America from

that perspective. This is the perspective that *any* educated person would hold.

There is no need for me to dwell any further on my own savage ancestors. The plain truth is that *everyone's* ancestors were savages—indeed, at least 99.5 percent of everyone's ancestors were savages, even in the case of descendants of the founders of the world's oldest civilizations. For mankind has existed on earth for a million years, yet the very oldest of civilizations—as judged by the criterion of having possessed a written language—did not appear until less than 5,000 years ago. The ancestors of those who today live in Britain or France or most of Spain were savages as recently as the time of Julius Caesar, slightly more than 2,000 years ago. Thus, on the scale of mankind's total presence on earth, today's Englishmen, Frenchmen, and Spaniards earn an ancestral savagery rating of 99.8 percent. The ancestors of present-day Germans and Scandinavians probably deserve an ancestral savagery rating of at least 99.9 percent.

It is important to stress these facts to be aware of how little significance is to be attached to the members of any race or linguistic group achieving civilization sooner rather than later. Between the descendants of the world's oldest civilizations and those who might first aspire to civilization at the present moment, there is a difference of at most one-half of one percent on the time scale of man's existence on earth.

These observations should confirm the fact that there is no reason for believing that civilization is in any way a property of any particular race or ethnic group. It is strictly an *intellectual matter*—ultimately, a matter of the presence or absence of certain fundamental ideas underlying the acquisition of further knowledge.

Those peoples who possess a written language may be called civilized, inasmuch as writing is an indispensable means for the transmission of substantial knowledge, and thus for the accumulation of knowledge from generation to generation. Those who possess not only a written language but also knowledge of the laws of logic and the principle of causality are in a position to accumulate and transmit incomparably more knowledge than people who possess merely the art of writing alone. On this basis, Greco-Roman civilization is on a higher plane than any that had preceded it.

Finally, a civilization which possesses still further fundamental applications of human reason, such as the far more extensive development and elaboration of the principles of mathematics and science, the existence of the freedoms of speech and press, and the development of a division of labor economy, is a higher civilization than even that of Greece and Rome. (The freedoms of speech and press are an essential guarantee of the individual's right to disseminate knowledge without being stopped by the fears or superstitions of any group backed by the coercive power of the state. A division of labor economy makes possible a corresponding multiplication of the amount of knowledge applied to production and to meeting the needs of human life, for such knowledge exists essentially in proportion to the number of separate occupations being practiced, each with its own specialized body of knowledge. Equally or even more important, a division of labor economy means that geniuses can devote their talents full time to such fields as science, education, invention, and business, with a corresponding progressive increase in knowledge and improvements in human life.)

Such a civilization, of course, *is our very own, modern Western civilization*—incomparably the greatest civilization which has ever existed, and which, until fairly recently, had repeatedly been carried to its very highest points in some respects right here in the United States.

Reference to an objective superiority of one civilization or culture over another, encounters the opposition of a profound, self-righteous hatred of the very idea. Thus, cultures may practice ritual sacrifice, cannibalism, mass expropriation, slavery, torture, and wholesale slaughter—all of this is accepted as somehow legitimate within the context of the culture concerned. The only alleged sin, the only alleged act of immorality in the world is to display contempt for such cultures, and to uphold as superior the values of Western culture. Then one is denounced as an imperialist, racist, and virtual Nazi.

It should be realized that those who take this view do not regard as the essential evil of Nazism its avowed irrationalism, its love of force and violence, and its acts of destruction and slaughter. All this they could accept, and do accept in the case of other cultures, such as that of primitive tribes, ancient Egypt, the civilization of the Aztecs and Incas, the Middle Ages, and Soviet Russia. What they hold to be the evil of Nazism was its assertion that Nazi culture was superior to other cultures. The claim of superiority of one culture over another is the one evil in their eyes. Needless to say, of course, it is only on the basis of the recognition of objective values that

one can seriously condemn Nazism—not for its absurd claims of superiority, but as a primitive, barbaric culture of the type one would expect to find among savages.

The fact that civilization is an intellectual matter is not known to the critics of "Eurocentrism." In their view, Western civilization is a matter not even so much of geography as it is of *racial membership*. It is, as they see it, the civilization of the *white man*. In reporting the changes in California's world history curriculum, the *Times* notes, significantly, that Hispanic, Asian, and black students now make up a majority of the 4.4 million pupils in the state. It quotes the co-author of the new curriculum as saying many educators believe that "people who have non-European backgrounds don't feel their antecedents lie in Europe." Another critic of "Eurocentrism," who is described as "heading an overhauling of the public school curriculum of Camden, N.J., to stress . . . a more 'Afrocentric and Latinocentric' approach," is quoted as saying, "We are not living in a Western country. The American project is not yet completed. It is only in the eyes of the Eurocentrists who see it as a Western project, which means to hell with the rest of the people who have yet to create the project."

In these statements, Western civilization is clearly identified with people of a certain type, namely, the West Europeans and their descendants, who are white. Students descended from Asiatics or Africans, it is assumed, can feel at home only to the extent that the curriculum is revised to give greater stress to "the ancient civilizations of China, India and Africa, the growth of Islam and the development of sub-Saharan Africa." The critics of "Eurocentrism" proclaim themselves to be opponents of racism. In fact, they accept exactly the same false premise they claim to oppose—namely, that civilization, or the lack of it, is racially determined.

In earlier centuries, men of European descent observed the marked cultural inferiority of the native populations of Africa, Asia, and the Western hemisphere, and assumed that the explanation lay in a racial inferiority of these peoples. In passing this judgment, they forgot the cultural state of their own ancestors, which was as much below their own as was that of any of these peoples. They also overlooked the very primitive cultural state of many Europeans then living in the eastern part of the continent, and of Caucasians living in the Middle East. Even more important, they failed to see how in accepting racism, they contradicted the essential "Western" doctrine of individual free will and individual responsibility for choices made. For in condemning people as inferior on the basis of their race, they were holding individuals morally responsible for circumstances over which they had absolutely no control. At the same time, they credited themselves with accomplishments which were hardly their creations, but those of a comparative handful of other individuals, most of whom had happened to be of the same race and who, ironically enough, had had to struggle against the indifference or even outright hostility of the great majority of the members of their own race in order to create civilization.

Today, the critics of "Eurocentrism" rightly refuse to accept any form of condemnation for their racial membership. They claim to hold that race is irrelevant to morality and therefore people of every race are as good as people of every other race. But then they assume that if people of all races are equally good, *all civilizations and cultures must be equally good.* They derive civilization and culture from race, just as the European racists did. And this is why they too must be called racists. They differ from the European racists only in that while the latter started with the judgment of an inferior civilization or culture and proceeded backwards to the conclusion of an inferior race, the former begin with the judgment of an equally good race and proceed forward to the conclusion of an equally good civilization or culture. The error of both sets of racists is the same: the belief that civilization and culture are racially determined.

The racism of these newer racists, which is now being imposed on the educational system, implies a radical devaluation of civilization, knowledge, and education. The new racists do not want students to study non-Western civilizations and the conditions of primitive peoples from the perspective of seeing how they lag behind Western civilization and what they might do to catch up. Study from that perspective would be denounced as seeing the world through a "Western lens." It would be considered offensive to people of non–West European origin.

No, what they want is to conduct the study of the various civilizations and even the state of outright savagery itself in a way that makes all appear *equal.* It is assumed, for example, that black students can feel the equal of white students only if their sub-Saharan ancestors are presented as, in a fundamental sense, culturally *equivalent* to modern West Europeans or Americans.

Now such a program means the explicit obliteration of distinctions between levels of civilization, and between civilization and savagery. It pre-

sents ignorance as the equivalent of knowledge, and superstition as the equivalent of science. Everything—logic, philosophy, science, law, technology—is to be ignored, and a culture limited to the level of making dugout canoes is to be presented as the equivalent of one capable of launching space ships. And all this is for the alleged sake of not offending anyone who supposedly must feel inferior if such a monumental fraud is not committed.

I believe, contrary to the expectations of the new racists, that their program must be grossly offensive to the very students it is designed to reassure. I know that I would be personally outraged if I were told that my intellectual capacities and personal values had been irrevocably defined for me by my ancestors and that now I was to think of myself in terms of the folkways of Russian peasants. I believe that if my ancestors had been Africans and, for example, I wanted to be an artist, I could readily accept the fact that art produced on the basis of a knowledge of perspective, geometry, human anatomy, and the refraction of light was a higher form of art than that produced in ignorance of such considerations. I would readily accept the fact that the latter type of art was, indeed, primitive. I would not feel that I was unable to learn these disciplines merely because my ancestors or other contemporary members of my race had not. I would feel the utmost contempt for the deliberate, chosen primitiveness of those "artists" (almost all white) who had reverted to the level of art of my (and their) primitive ancestors.

Race is not the determinant of culture. Not only is Western civilization open to the members of every race, but its present possessors are also potentially capable of losing it, just as the people of the Western Roman Empire once lost the high degree of civilization they had achieved. What makes the acceptance of the "Eurocentrism" critique so significant is that it so clearly reveals just how tenuous our ability to maintain Western civilization has become.

The preservation of Western civilization is not automatic. In the span of less than a century, virtually the entire population at the end consists of people who were not alive at the beginning. Western civilization, or any civilization, can continue only insofar as its intellectual substance lives on in the minds of new generations.

And it can do so only if it is imparted to young minds through education. *Education is the formal process of transmitting the intellectual substance of civilization from one generation to the next and thereby developing the uncultivated minds of children into those of civilized adults*. Western civilization is imparted to young minds in the teaching of Euclidean geometry and Newtonian physics, no less than in the teaching of the philosophy of Plato and Aristotle or the plays of Shakespeare. It is imparted in the teaching of every significant subject, from arithmetic to nuclear physics, from reading and writing to the causes of the rise and fall of civilizations. Wherever the intellectual substance of Western civilization is known, its transmission to the minds of students is virtually *coextensive with the process of education*. For the intellectual substance of Western civilization is nothing other than the highest level of knowledge attained anywhere on earth, in virtually every aspect of every field, and if the purpose of education is to impart knowledge, then its purpose is to impart Western civilization.

Thus, to the extent that the process of education is undermined, the whole of civilization must also be undermined, starting a generation later. These results will appear more and more striking as time goes on and as more and more defectively educated people take the place of those whose education was better. The worsening effects will likely be further intensified as those whose own education was defective become educators themselves and thus cause succeeding generations to be still more poorly educated.

Education in the United States has been in obvious decline for decades, and, in some ways that are critical but not obvious, perhaps for generations. The decline has become visible in such phenomena as the rewriting of college textbooks to conform with the more limited vocabularies of present-day students. It is visible in the functional illiteracy of large numbers of high school and even college graduates, in their inability to articulate their thoughts or to solve relatively simple problems in mathematics or even plain arithmetic, and in their profound lack of elementary knowledge of science and history.

I believe that the decline in education is probably responsible for the widespread use of drugs. To live in the midst of a civilized society with a level of knowledge closer perhaps to that of primitive man than to what a civilized adult requires (which, regrettably, is the intellectual state of many of today's students and graduates) must be a terrifying experi-ence, urgently calling for some kind of relief, and drugs may appear to many to be the solution.

I believe that this also accounts for the relatively recent phenomenon of the public's fear of science and technology. Science and technology are increasingly viewed in reality as they used to be humorously depicted in Boris Karloff or Bela Lugosi movies, namely, as frightening "experiments" going on in Frankenstein's castle, with large numbers of present-day American citizens casting themselves in the real-life role of terrified and angry Transylvanian peasants seeking to smash whatever emerges from such laboratories. This attitude is the result not only of lack of education in science, but more fundamentally, loss of the ability to think critically—an ability which contemporary education provides little or no basis for developing. Because of their growing lack of knowledge and ability to think, people are becoming increasingly credulous and quick to panic.

Thus the critique of "Eurocentrism"—and any changes in curricula that may result from it—can hardly be blamed for inaugurating the decline in American education. On the contrary, it is a product of that decline. The fact that it is being accepted almost without opposition is evidence of how far the decline has already gone.

The equivalence of all cultures, the equivalence of civilization and savagery, is the avowed claim of the doctrine of cultural relativism, which has long been accepted by practically the whole of the educational establishment. It in turn is a consequence of the still older, more fundamental doctrine that there is no objective foundation for values—that all value-judgments are arbitrary and subjective. The new racists are now merely cashing in on this view and attempting to apply it on the largest possible scale, in the process substantially altering the manner in which subjects are taught. Today's educational establishment has fewer compunctions about putting absurd ideas into practice probably because of the deteriorated state of its own education. (Many of its members were educated in the 1960s, in the environment of the "student rebellion.")

The fact that the educational and intellectual establishments are fully in agreement with the fundamental premises of the new racists helps to explain why even when their members are opposed to the "Eurocentrism" critique, they have nothing of substance to say against it. As reported by the *Times*, the objections raised amounted to nothing more than complaints about the difficulty of finding non-European writers, philosophers, and artists to replace the European ones dropped from the curricula, and grumblings about the lack of Americans able to teach authoritatively about non-European cultures.

In capitulating to the "Eurocentrism" critique, the educational establishment has reached the point of reducing education to a level below that of ordinary ward politics: education is now to be a matter of pressure-group politics based on the totally false assumptions of racism. If there are now more black, Hispanic, or Asian students than white students in an area, then that fact is to be allowed to determine the substance of education, in the belief that these groups somehow "secrete," as it were, a different kind of civilization and culture than do whites and require a correspondingly different kind of education.

Colleges in the United States have demonstrated such utter philosophical corruption in connection with this subject that if there were a group of students willing to assert with pride their descent from the Vandals or Huns and to demand courses on the cultural contributions of their ancestors, the schools would provide such courses. All that the students would have to do to get their way is to threaten to burn down the campus.

But what best sums up everything involved is this: from now on, in the state of California, a student is to go through twelve years of public school, and the explicit goal of his education is that at the end of it, if he envisions Columbus being greeted by spear-carrying savages, and he happens not to be white, he should identify with the savages—and if he does happen to be white, and therefore is allowed to identify with Columbus, he should not have any idea why it is any better to identify with Columbus than with the savages.

This is no longer an educational system. Its character has been completely transformed and it now clearly reveals itself to be what for many decades it has been in the process of becoming: an agency working for the *barbarization* of youth.

The value of education is derived from the value of civilization, whose guardian and perpetuator education is supposed to be. An educational system dedicated to the barbarization of youth is a self-contradictory monstrosity that must be cast out and replaced with a true educational system. But this can be done only by those who genuinely understand, and are able to defend, the *objective* value of Western civilization.[1]

Discussion Questions

1. How does Professor Reisman define "Western Civilization"? Why does he believe that this definition is necessary in order to undercut the multicultural criticism of Eurocentrism?

2. Explain in detail Professor Reisman's argument against the claim that all cultures are equal. Why does he believe that Western civilization is superior? Do you agree or disagree with his assessment? Defend your answer.

3. Why does Professor Reisman think that multiculturalism is inherently racist? Do you agree with this view? Why or why not? Also, is it possible to espouse a form of multiculturalism without falling prey to Professor Reisman's charge of racism? If so, explain how it could be done.

Notes

1. This article is available from the Jefferson School of Philosophy, Economics and Psychology, P.O. Box 2934, Laguna Hills, CA 92654.

41

Skepticism, Nihilism, Amorality, and Anarchy: The Legacy of PC?

Jung Min Choi
John W. Murphy

Jung Min Choi is a graduate research assistant in the Department of Sociology, York University, Toronto, Canada. John W. Murphy is a professor at the University of Miami. He is the author of *Postmodern Social Analysis and Criticism* (1989). Choi and Murphy co-authored *The Politics and Philosophy of Political Correctness* (1992).

Charges of espousing relativism, nihilism (literally "nothingness," a view that there is no objective ground for truth concerning morality or knowledge), and radical skepticism have been leveled against those who support radical multiculturalism and political correctness. Jung Min Choi and John W. Murphy respond to these charges and argue that conservative critics of political correctness are misrepresenting and/or misunderstanding the PC position. Choi and Murphy argue that simply because there is no one objective or universal perspective by which to judge behavior, culture, morality, or knowledge, it does not follow, as the critics of PC allege, that this will lead to moral and epistemological relativism, nihilism, or radical skepticism. Although they argue that "a priori conceptions of normativeness must be abandoned," we all live in interpretive communities within which objective norms are valid. Consequently, for the critics of PC to claim that PC will lead us to accept the idea that "anything goes" (i.e., relativism, nihilism, and skepticism) is simply ridiculous, because all norms do not have equal validity *within* an interpretive community.

Reprinted by permission from Jung Min Choi and John W. Murphy, *The Politics and Philosophy of Political Correctness* (Westport, Conn.: Praeger Books, 1992), 81–107.

There should be little doubt that conservatives are not fond of political correctness and consider this outlook to be dangerous. Given their penchant for achieving a synoptic vision, the conservatives' reaction to PC should not be surprising. After all, denied by PC is the possibility of ever reconciling the disparate viewpoints that comprise social life; complete harmony among these perspectives can never be achieved. The total integration of outlooks desired by conservatives is impossible, claim PC'ers, due to the absence of an all-encompassing founda-tion. In Hegelian terms, there is no final *Aufhebung*.

Without a reality *sui generis*, the assimilation of perspectives cannot be accomplished. For what norms are to guide this process? If all norms are me-diated by interpretation, like all other phenomena, the issue arises of whose standards should be fol-lowed. Also, conservatives argue that once this im-passe is reached, relativism is inevitable. Because one interpretation is as good as any other, positions pro-liferate and demand recognition. According to con-servatives this is a recipe for chaos, despite their pro-fessed advocacy of individual freedom. Nonetheless, if PC is taken seriously, conservative critics tend to agree that culture will be fragmented, driven apart, and eventually destroyed.

This is not a pretty picture. But regardless of their protestations to the contrary, conservatives limit op-tions to a fairly narrow range, because of their insis-tence that reality must be recognized and re-spected. As a result, conformity to a priori standards is the cornerstone of civility. These norms, rules, laws and so forth are accorded this status because of their natu-ral and cosmic significance. From the vantage point of PC, this portrayal of how order is maintained is quite restrictive.

According to conservatives, however, this is not the case. The reason for this difference of opinion is quite simple. Conservatives wonder how someone could possibly be repressed by the truth. Quite the opposite, persons are set free by the truth. Because truth is natural, this knowledge can never become anathema to the human condition. PC'ers, on the other hand, argue that truth is not a natural condi-tion but, instead, represents a modality of *praxis*. There-fore, any version of truth that is accorded a universal status is in danger of becoming repressive. But for conservatives truth, and presumably all valid and objective knowledge, is by definition omnipres-ent and not naturally aligned with any particular social class, political party, or policy agenda.

Readers might begin to wonder about the conservatives' verdict of PC, given the commitment to certain absolutes that is the hallmark of conservatism. Is PC as bad as the critics on the Right claim? Considering the demands they make with respect to securing truth and ensuring order, someone would not have to say much to be labeled a radical and become known as disruptive. Accordingly, the philosophy that accompanies PC may not lead to the dire consequences predicted by conservatives. Society may be plunged into the dark night of barbarism, simply because a few of conservatism's most prized axioms are violated. Conservatism, in other words, does not necessarily offer the last word on preserving knowledge and order. Such a view, in fact, would be quite presumptuous and dogmatic.

Undoubtedly PC is antithetical to the vast system building encouraged by conservatives. This is why exponents of PC are constantly talking about margins, boundaries, and peripheries. PC'ers agree with Derrida that all proposals are made from the margin, and that, in point of fact, achieving finality is impossible.[1] In other words, there is no grand organizing principle. Searching for that elusive final frontier is futile. Neither atomic nor genetic research, for example, will lead to a foundation that is more central than anything else.[2] With regard to PC, there is no maximal event or primal scene.

But contrary to what the opponents of PC assert, stressing the inability to achieve completeness is not necessarily destructive. Rather truth, facts, order, and other key aspects of culture exist at the margin. For conservatives, however, to talk about culture existing in the margin is contradictory. Traditionally, the periphery is a place where alienation, powerlessness, and disorganization reign. After all, the periphery is the location farthest away from norms and is the place where nomads roam unchecked. "Nomad thought" is at home on the periphery.[3]

Yet this image of the margin has changed, according to PC'ers. The periphery is orderly but is structured in a manner different from centered visions of culture. As should be gleaned from the discussion in the previous chapter, different knowledge bases are juxtaposed and joined at the intersection of their differences. Furthermore, moving from one boundary to another signals change but not necessarily disorder. And simply because the existence of numerous relations (peripheries) is recognized, none of them automatically lose validity. Rather, more options gain legitimacy, which does not

discredit the ones that existed first, unless some ultimate *telos* or grand purpose is thought to regulate knowledge and order.

From this brief description, readers should sense that conservatives may have overreacted and misrepresented the thrust of PC. In order to give PC a fair hearing, a more thorough investigation is needed than that conducted by D'Souza and his conservative comrades. Accordingly, the purpose of this chapter is to address, in an in-depth manner, what conservatives believe to be the most objectional implications of PC.

What conservative critics have done is to invoke a chic set of shibboleths to obscure the serious philosophical issues that are at the heart of PC. Nihilism, skepticism, and relativism, for example, conjure up all sorts of horrors. With little explanation, PC has been characterized in these terms. These designations, however, are inaccurate, although they may strike fear into the public.

Radical Skepticism

PC has been chided regularly for fostering radical skepticism.[4] For example, Edward Shils describes deconstruction, which is a vital facet of PC, as "preach[ing] a nihilistic skepticism of language."[5] He goes on to state that because of this confusion about truth, the humanities have been reduced to little more than "radical political propaganda." Jon Weiner is more specific and writes that presupposed by deconstruction is that "one must be resigned to the impossibility of truth."[6] Apparently the close association between language and reality prescribed by this philosophy undermines valid knowledge. According to Kimball, Fish revels in his skepticism; Fish takes pride in renouncing truth, merit, justice, and facts.[7] The problem with *au courant* criticism, summarizes Rene Wellek, is that the "entire question of meaning is bracketed."[8]

In this regard, D'Souza is appalled that much of modern literary theory is premised on the claim that poems, for example, do not "correspond to any specific 'reality,' either material or metaphysical."[9] But with this charge the weakness of the conservatives' claim that PC culminates in skepticism becomes apparent. Skepticism is a hoary topic, and unanimity does not necessarily exist about the meaning of this notion. What the early Greeks seemed to have in mind, however, is that the search for truth is never-ending. They did not relinquish hope of ever discovering truth but merely argued that a critical attitude is essential to this task. Simply put, the early Skeptics believed that persons have both a right and duty to question the validity of knowledge.

So what is wrong with skepticism? Skeptics appear to be flexible, open-minded, and opposed to dogmatism. These are all traits that D'Souza and his fellow conservatives supposedly champion. But PC'ers go too far in their enthusiasm for openness and violate a key epistemological principle related to conservatism. In a word, they overlook the metaphysical justification for truth that conservatives insist is necessary; they fail to state that language corresponds exactly to an objective referent. Therefore, conservatives conclude that any search for truth will prove to be fruitless. For in the absence of a metaphysical reality, referent, or force, the result of a critical inquiry can only be uncertainty. Skepticism, according to the anti-PC'ers, has come to mean the inability to know anything. This sentiment is expressed by D'Souza when he states that as a result of deconstruction "literary reality is an illusion" and "fact dissolves into fiction."[10]

But whoever said that knowledge is an illusion? This is not the position of those associated with PC. All PC'ers do is reject a metaphysical basis of knowledge; they refuse to admit that knowledge has any ultimate justification. Not searching for a base of knowledge that is beyond the influence of interpretation, however, does not mean that truth does not exist.

This negative reaction to PC by conservatives is prompted by their refusal to recognize that truth can exist within interpretation. Truth can be sustained, in other words, without the assistance of a referent that exists *sui generis*. Through the exercise of language, a linguistic anchor can be developed to sustain truth. As Fish writes, truth can be established by "persuasion, that is, in the course of argument and counter-argument on the basis of examples and evidence that are themselves cultural and contextual."[11] In this sense, language use is sufficient to outline the conditions for truth, preserve them, and convey these assumptions to various speakers. This *modus operandi* may not be as appealing as a metaphysical approach to securing reality, but, according to PC'ers, it is very effective.

Take the example of texts that conservatives are so fond of citing. To say that literary meaning is indeterminate, due to the fragility of interpretation, is not the same as saying that the meaning of a text cannot be discovered. The point PC'ers are making is that the original or intended meaning of a text is not obvious but interpretive. A book, argues Barthes, is not an objective ensemble of words but conveys a linguistic "world."[12] This world, furthermore, constitutes a story that reflects certain assumptions about what is accepted as real and necessary. The reality of a text is conveyed through storytelling, and therefore creating a text involves interpretation.

Because a text embodies interpretation, this facet of literature cannot be expected to be removed from reading. As a result, reading consists of interpreting an interpretation. The implication is that reading can proceed in any direction; the meaning of a text can be construed in any number of ways. But why would someone want to avoid hearing what an author is trying to say? Intentionally interpreting a text in a manner different from the way intended by an author makes no sense, if communication is the aim of reading. What PC'ers want to avert, in fact, is the distortion of texts that results from capricious analysis. But by becoming conversant with a text, the reality that is embodied in it can be known.

The truth of a text, therefore, is exposed through a proper interpretation of an author's use of language. The value of a work, notes Smith, is by "no means independent of *authorial* design, labor, and skill."[13] What she means is that simply because various interpretations of a text are possible, each one is not necessarily equally valid. Nonetheless, a correct interpretation is not objective in the dualistic sense. An independent referent is not encountered. But a correct interpretation is truthful because it corresponds to the author's mode of interpretation. Accordingly, PC'ers accept Barthes's suggestion that the tune sung by an author should be reproduced through reading.[14] Truth is *aletheia*, because it scurries between, around, and through the various manifolds of interpretation. Most significant is that an author's interpretation is always accessible, although it may not be readily apparent.

Conservative critics would be well advised to remember that simply because various interpretations *can* be generated, this strategy *should not* necessarily be followed. For writing is based on an epistemic event that readers should respect, or a correct interpretation will not occur.[15] Similar to historical settings, a text has an interpretive truth that may not be absolute but is certainly present. While a reader may want many things to happen in a text, an author's world will survive no matter how a work is read. In the interpretive world that underpins a text only certain occurrences are possible, although a *tour de force* carried out by a reader cannot be prevented.

Now back to the issue of skepticism. PC'ers do not doubt that truth exists but merely claim that this form of knowledge, along with all other forms, is based on interpretation that is linguistically supported. Although this information is not a priori universal, it can be known. Moreover, once a mode of interpretation is recognized as truthful, this rendition of knowledge can begin to have widespread appeal. Certain linguistic acts can be repeated enough that they appear to be stable, even possibly objective.[16] Consequently, truth does not have to be based on correspondence but can be defined in terms of use and disuse. Once particular interpretations are regularly used, they can serve as a standard of truth. This is what even Hirsch seems to be saying, before his position becomes convoluted by his search for a more firm foundation for texts than he believes can be provided by language.

This is not to say that interpretive truth cannot change, possibly without warning. Nonetheless, recognizing the interpretive character of knowledge does not end automatically in the inability to posit truth. Interpretations are publicly accessible, reasonably stable, and persuasive. Interpretation, therefore, is not necessarily antagonistic to understanding. Yet conservatives believe this scenario is insufficient to substantiate truth. Without metaphysical guarantees, they regard knowledge to be illusive.

Nihilism

According to conservative critics, PC is basically nihilistic. For instance, Kimball refers to Charles Jencks as a "happy nihilist," because Jencks "assumes that the modern secular world has lost any compelling foundation for shared meaning."[17] Because signifiers float and can be attached to objects in a random manner, claim conservatives, the result is circuitous prose and idiocy.[18] As is the case with skepticism, nihilism occurs because a transcendent ground of values is missing from PC. Therefore, in the absence of this absolute principle, any value can be enacted; nothing is available to specify correct values. If all values are equal, goes the argument, chaos is inevitable. In fact, nihilism is defined by Bloom as the "chaos of the instincts and passions" that accompanies the demise of tradition interrogated by PC'ers.[19]

The leveling of all values is clearly problematic for conservatives. With all values placed on the same plane, there is nothing to justify acts of evaluation but more values. As logicians might say, there are no reliable predicates. When this is the case, conservatives believe that all values are diminished. No values, in short, are soundly justified. Subsequently, life is meaningless, because no criteria can be relied on to judge meaning. Furthermore, nothing substantial is available to ensure the regularity, continuity, and discipline that are essential to maintaining a meaningful order.

In the void associated with this meaninglessness, persons are free to do whatever they please. Without unquestioned authority, conservatives charge, only bleakness can be expected.[20] All that can be anticipated are unprincipled actions, for all guiding principles have been devalued. Convictions, likewise, are nonsensical, for how would they be substantiated? Conservatives maintain that even subjectivity is thought to be emptied of meaning and content by deconstruction.[21] Such a condition of meaninglessness can only be considered absurd. As is revealed in the plays of authors such as Samuel Beckett and George Albee, when the world is absurd discussion seems to go nowhere. Talk is incessant but silly; persons are in pain but with no justification. There is no escape from this absurd situation, except via divine intervention that never arrives. Humans are thus both hapless and helpless.

But does PC lead to a condition where human action is bankrupt and incapable of generating meaning? Does PC leave persons without guidance and encourage unprincipled behavior? As a consequence of PC, is the world stripped of con-straints? Contrary to the dismal assessment made by conservatives, constraints—on interpretation or action—are not undermined by PC. Intelligible structures and purposes survive the critique proffered by PC'ers. Nonetheless, how "disciplining rules" operate must be rethought in the wake of PC.[22]

Simply put, PC is not nihilistic. The result of PC is not the destruction of all values, or the elimination of standards for judging appropriate interpretations or behavior. On the other hand, however, values are no longer thought to have "cosmic support," argue PC'ers.[23] Like knowledge, values are in the service of *praxis* rather than the other way around, as conservatives believe. Guiding values are still present, but the historical status allotted to them by conservatives has changed. Still, persons' actions are not founded on "nothing"; "nothing" is not at the basis of every situation.

Fish declares that "nihilism is impossible."[24] There is no possibility of completely unguided actions; values are always operative in every claim. He substantiates this position with his now infamous phrase "all preferences are principled."[25] Among all the statements made by PC'ers, critics on the right have found this one to be especially vacuous. Therefore, Fish has been lampooned more than usual for making this comment.

But what is Fish trying to say? It must be remembered that nihilism is supposed to result from the destruction of so-called higher values. Without these exalted beliefs, actions have no substance or *raison d'être*. Yet Fish contends that this is simply not the case.

What would an action be that is not informed by some values? Boundless, directionless, or completely disorganized![26] Yet even recognizing the absence of organization presupposes the presence of some format. Otherwise, the condition known as disorganization could not be described and discussed. Even disorganization, according to Fish, might be better understood as novel, unfamiliar, or, possibly, a disliked mode of organization. But pure disorganization would be incomprehensible.

This is where Fish's charge that actions are always principled becomes relevant. All actions are principled, he writes, because "they are intelligible and doable only by virtue of some principled articulation of the world and its possibilities."[27] Every action, even one that may initially appear to be bizarre, is guided by some understanding of the world. All actions are fundamentally principled or organized in some way. A completely disorganized action could not be known. Accordingly, persons do not simply act irrationally, and, following this, they are somehow given guidance by higher values. Values, as conservatives seem to believe, are not interjected into the world from an outside source. Furthermore, without these rarefied informing principles, persons are not directionless and capricious. To paraphrase Sartre, individuals are never merely useless energy; actions are never empty. Behavior, instead, is always fused with values, thereby providing demeanor with its form and significance. A completely uninformed act would be neither recognizable nor comprehensible.

What this finding means is that life is never wholly absent of value or meaning. Nihilism descending on society, following the advent of PC or any other movement, is simply a myth. Different values may appear and challenge the status quo, but these are not incomprehensible by their very nature. For as Fish rightly notes, nothing exists without some sort of rationale. A thoroughly empty thought, statement, or act cannot be imagined. Every phenomenon has meaning that may eventually be comprehended. Any apparent absence of values, accordingly, should be understood to represent particular claims rather than a vacuum.

Additionally, the dissolution of ultimate values does not mean that all constraints are defunct. Instead, constraints, in the form of value orientations, are part of any action. Each action, in short, is constrained by the way in which it is defined. Every linguistic act has parameters and thus is constrained. Moreover, anyone who works within a specific genre of interpretation is expected to behave in a specific manner. Hence in any situation persons are not free to do whatever they desire, without reprisals.

To make this point Fish cites the example of a judge who is trying a case.[28] Without a doubt a judge could do anything in a courtroom. But his or her demeanor is constrained by expectations that are defined as part of a judge's role. To survive within the community of professional jurists, judges are required to act in a particular way no matter how they may feel personally about a crime. To be considered competent, a judge's actions are supposed to be informed by the definitions, concepts, goals, and purposes that are accepted as valid by jurists. Any deviation from these principles may jeopardize a trial, not to mention a judge's reputation, as long as a society is committed to these particular interpretive constraints.

What more do conservatives want from Fish? He has acknowledged constraints, and admits that those who violate these rules can be punished. Nonetheless, conservatives seem to disagree with two aspects of Fish's discussion. First, the constraints are not metaphysically justified. Merely a commitment to certain values serves to limit actions. But this means that constraints are based on interpretation and vulnerable to criticism. Constraints are not as independent as conservatives would like. Prohibitions, however, are still viable and enforceable.[29]

Second, persons are free to shift their allegiances. This fact may bother conservatives more than anything else about how PC'ers view values. Persons are able to defy authority and take control of their lives. As opposed to what conservatives believe, this is a life-affirming activity rather than a nihilistic one.

Values may change, but this occurs only through the institution of new ones. Persons are thus never left without some sort of guidance. But this is insufficient, assert conservatives, to avert a slide into meaninglessness.

Relativism

Conservatives contend that another product of PC is relativism. This problem results from the indeterminacy PC'ers say is at the heart of knowledge. For example, D'Souza objects to using the term cultures to describe society, for implied by this tactic is the existence of several, equally valid sources of knowledge.[30] For similar reasons, he dislikes the term values. The result of this most recent desire for pluralism, writes D'Souza, is that "anything goes."[31] Numerous options exist, with each one carrying equal weight. As a result, a vicious struggle among norms will more than likely occur, which D'Souza refers to as "anomie."[32] Conservatives seem to believe that this support for relativism is a remnant of the 1960s, which is a period in American history that they would like to forget.

The conservatives' pet remedy for this condition is to search for the core or essential properties of everything that exists. Accordingly, there must be core values, institutions, and texts. "Back to the basics," therefore, has been the rallying cry of conservatives during the 1980s.[33] They believe arriving at this sacred core will reverse the present decline of culture. All the idiosyncratic claims that have arisen lately, and that have been very costly in terms of a reduction in efficiency and loss of morality, can be suppressed, because they do not conform to the strictures imposed by this foundation. Similarly, the distractions that have been created by the voices from the periphery, related to these persons' calls for the recognition of difference, can be sublimated into greater cultural goals. These different perspectives can then be treated legitimately as epiphenomenal and insignificant.

But PC'ers have foiled this ploy. According to them, there is no core that is not another perspective; there is no essential element that is not interpreted and treated as vital. As Fish phrases this claim, "a normal context is just the special context you happen to be in."[34] A core, in other words, is simply the position adopted by a particular individual or group. As a result, to paraphrase Fish, there will always be a normal context, but this situation may differ from

place to place. What is believed to be at the core of education in one locale, for instance, may be perceived as irrelevant in another. Because of Fish's view of normalcy, Kimball contends that Fish is not a benign relativist.[35] Instead, Fish is truly dangerous, because there is no justification remaining for making one choice rather than another, or for sanctioning behavior.

According to those on the Right, such relativism should be rejected for at least three reasons. First, all norms have an equal status. Second, this means that any choice is valid. Finally, no rationale exists for criticizing an act. As D'Souza says, the result of relativism is that in any situation anything is possible. As part of relativism there can be no measure of truth, morality, or progress, charge conservatives. A relativistic culture would thus be a contradiction. Such a society would also be impossible to sustain.

Do PC'ers promote this state of affairs? When they say absolutes are outmoded, does this mean that all standards for reading and acting are equally valid? The answer is no. In point of fact, PC'ers are trying to avoid the insensitivity that accompanies this sort of arbitrariness. What they call for, accordingly, is "rigorous truth-telling about the nature of language . . . and of major texts [even] in the Western tradition."[36] To accomplish this, however, a priori conceptions of normativeness must be abandoned. The interpretive world embodied in a text must be encountered in its own terms; as mentioned earlier, an author's deployment of language must be understood. But does bracketing the notion of normativeness in this way imply that any norm can be applied to a text and enhance comprehension? Does the relativist anthem that anything goes apply to reading texts, or any other endeavor, if the aim is accuracy? Fish answers these queries by saying that "an infinite plurality of meanings would be a fear only if sentences existed in a state in which they were not already embedded in, and had come into view as a function of some situation or another."[37] His point is that there are contextual guidelines for sensitive reading, albeit they are limited. In most contexts, all values are not necessarily relevant, for particular assumptions about reality are accepted.

Language may not have an ultimate ground, but it is never without an interpretive framework. Language is never devoid of interpretive guidelines. For this reason, interpretation is always possible. All language is thus translatable with regard to either present customs or intentions that have yet to be voiced.

Fish, therefore, is no relativist. If anything, to use the topology supplied by Mannheim, he is a relationist.[38] Specifically, he recognizes the existence of a myriad of norms, all of which exist side by side. A host of regions exist—remember, Fish believes that "values are regional"—with each one having its own normative structure.[39] Nonetheless, in terms of the usual definition of relativism, this description of society does not make him a relativist. This is because each region constitutes an interpretive community.

As a "public and conventional point of view," an interpretive community is not neutral.[40] Each community, accordingly, values certain norms. Therefore, some norms may be irrelevant in a specific community, because behavior is not random but is guided by expectations that are known by every competent member of a region. Exhibiting just any behavior would certainly result in a negative sanction. Within an interpretive community the idea that anything goes is simply ridiculous, for all norms do not have equal validity.

Sociologists of various hues verified a long time ago what Fish is saying. Symbolic interactionists, for example, have illustrated that persons evaluate their actions with regard to their respective "reference groups."[41] Therefore, in terms of a single city, very different pockets of norms may be operative. To understand what deviance means in each circumstance, for example, a priori definitions of normativeness must be set aside. For norms are embedded in symbols, signs, and gestures that may be very unique and restricted to a specific locale.

Upon crossing one of these relatively invisible boundaries, an individual quickly learns which behaviors are acceptable. This diversity, moreover, has not resulted in the disaster that conservatives predict. Yet navigating through this montage of norms requires interpretive skill, tolerance, and an appreciation of pluralism.

The apparent harmony that exists between these various regions, however, does not mean that interpersonal conflict is totally absent. For example, a newcomer may unknowingly violate a norm, flare-ups may occur at the boundaries that unite regions, or someone may decide to challenge the usual way of behaving. In a fairly diverse society, such as the United States, norms can never be completely sequestered from one another. Nevertheless, standards exist within each region, along with both overt and covert methods of adjudicating conflicts. Chaos is thus not as imminent as conservatives seem to think.

There may be no ultimate *arche*, but this does not mean that saturnalia is inevitable. While borrowing from Hubert Dreyfus, Fish states that human behavior is "orderly, but not rule governed."[42] What they mean is that rather than inherently universal, norms are enacted and enforced on a local level. As a result there may be a lot of debate, many disagreements, and various ad hoc modifications made along the way but not necessarily the melee conservatives envision. For a local order "will be in force," writes Fish, "so long as a community of read-ers or believers (it is very much an act of faith) continues to abide by it."[43] Hence the local nature of norms does not automatically spell the demise of culture. Until further notice, as Lyotard likes to say, the prevailing commitments that perpetuate order will continue.

Clearly, PC'ers recognize the legitimacy of community. In fact, they praise solidarity as an organizing principle.[44] In this respect, how can they be considered relativists? If this allegation were true, both solidarity and community would be impossible to imagine. Again, all that seems to be absent from PC are the universals conservatives believe are imperative to avert the tragedy of relativism. Yet giving primacy to universals can easily result in undermining community as a viable principle. For community may come to be viewed as antithetical to rational governance, due to the interpersonal and thus limited nature of reality in these enclaves.

In this regard, PC is capable of *Ideologiekritik*. This activity may not be important to conservatives, although it should be. That is, any viewpoint that becomes so encompassing as to curtail discussion should be seen as problematic, by those on both the Right and the Left. Knowledge that masquerades as absolute, and is thus able to sabotage other options because of this status, should be viewed with suspicion. Nonetheless, the usual claim is that PC does not allow for this type of insight and its accompanying critique, because questions about norms are precluded by relativism.[45] Who, in short, can claim to know for certain what is right and wrong? Accordingly, who has the ability or right to identify, critique, or eliminate ideology (or any other means of repression)?

Yet PC is not relativistic, and thus a justification for *Ideologiekritik* exists. Considering the version of language propagated by PC'ers, ideology cannot be understood to mask universal interests. Instead, but equally important, ideology can be seen as distorting the outlook of an interpretive community. It must be recalled that what is real is defined locally instead of universally. In this sense, any stock of knowledge that is identified as universal *sui generis* is a potential source of ideology. For this exalted information can be introduced as a means of terrorizing communities, which by definition are lower in stature, into complying with these imperious standards. Through this mystification, or ideology, local reality is inferiorized and supplanted by a higher principle.

The reference point of critique, accordingly, is not a set of norms that is assumed to be universally esteemed. Nonetheless, because each interpretive community has integrity, none has to tolerate inferiorization. The "practical consciousness" that Raymond Williams argues is operative in daily affairs can be assertive and can confront authority.[46] Each community, accordingly, can demand respect. Therefore, any distortion of a community's vision warrants attention and intervention. Simply stated, ideology can be identified and discredited. Hegemony—which is the product of "an ensemble of normalized knowledgeable practices . . . regarded as a practical paradigm of sovereign political subjectivity and conduct"—can be counteracted.[47] Only now this is done at the local level rather than in terms of grandiose historical, economic, or spiritual schemes. The focus of concern is the violation of communities rather than the defilement of religious or governmental dogmas. The question that remains, which will be addressed in the following section, is why should this policy of protecting locales be treated as a moral imperative?

A related issue that should be addressed at this juncture is reification, which goes to the heart of ideology. Due to the absence of dualism, the reification of a text, or any other facet of life, consists of nothing more than freezing in place a particular interpretation of reality. Reminiscent of Marx's remarks about dead labor preying on workers who are alive, a mode of cultural *praxis* may become encrusted as a result of the abuse of power or some other aberration.

Because interpretation is not immune to revision, reification does not pose an insurmountable problem. Dismantling a manifestation of reification does not require that a reality *sui generis* be altered, which would be a foreboding task, but merely that life be breathed back into interpretation. As a result, the products of reification become less imposing, because they are transformed into modes of interpretation that can be mastered or redeployed. In a manner of speaking, a type of foreign occupation will thus have ended.

Anarchy

PC is believed to elevate idiosyncrasy to the pinnacle of political principles. Most important, charge conservatives, is meeting the personal needs, with minimal regard for the wider implications of a person's behavior. As a result, what becomes paramount is a sense of amorality, which stems from a primary concern with self-indulgence. Responsibility to others, in short, is allegedly eschewed by PC'ers. According to conservatives, the description of society offered by PC'ers discourages social ties, along with a commitment to basic institutions.

While criticizing Paul de Man for his wartime journalism, Kimball claims that deconstructionists "willingly forsake the most basic moral distinctions in [their] pursuit of ever more clever rhetorical constructs."[48] Tying language to reality, as PC'ers do, absolves an individual of guilt, even for the most hideous crimes committed by the Nazis. In a now infamous passage from *Allegories of Reading*, de Man is interpreted as saying that a person's actions can never be understood for certain as either good or bad.[49] Actual harm is illusory, because the person is merely a rhetorical trope. De Man's apparent support for the Nazis, writes Kimball, was thus simply dismissed by his friends as a "kind of linguistic, not a moral, lapse."[50] Real persons do not exist for deconstructionists, claim the opponents of PC, but merely themes about identity that can be manipulated in any way imaginable. Hence crimes against persons are nearly impossible to detect.

This critique of what might be called the "mythical other" associated with PC is continued by D'Souza. He believes, like Kimball, that PC leads to total disregard for others, as was exhibited by the Nazis. In fact, D'Souza argues that the "balkanization" and "atomization" of society is encouraged by PC.[51] This fragmentation is likely to occur when norms are understood to be interpretive, because no rule can be extended automatically beyond the confines of a particular interpretive community. If this is the case, asks Kimball, what is to prevent Hitler from killing Jews? After all, within his Nazi community— which, by the way, is not supported by Jews—this policy is justified![52]

Critics of PC contend that the vision of a shared humanity is inimical to this philosophy. Racial or any other type of harmony, states D'Souza, cannot be forthcoming from a viewpoint that does not lay the foundation for concrete interaction, which, in turn, may lead to friendship and solidarity. But according to PC'ers, norms are embedded within language, particularly interpretive communities, and thus there are no grounds for discourse. For this reason, PC has been labeled anarchistic.[53]

In one respect, this designation may be correct. For as suggested by the term anarchy, there is no single *arche*. And given the monistic character of the Western tradition, the presence of multiple *archi* is assumed to be undesirable. There is no doubt that because society comprises a myriad of regions the principle of a single *arche* is somewhat outmoded. Coming to this conclusion, accordingly, would technically classify PC as anarchistic.

But the pluralism advanced by PC'ers does not result in the breakdown of society for a key reason. The organization of this mosaic is not accomplished in a dualistic manner. A boundary, for example, is understood both to separate and unite different components of society. Neither regions nor persons are ever isolated, self-contained, or totally independent. "No self is an island," writes Lyotard, for "each exists in a fabric of relations that is now more complex and mobile than ever before."[54] Likewise, Fish adds that the "self does not exist apart from the communal or convention categories of thought that enable its operations (of thinking, seeing, and reading)."[55] Neither of these statements sounds like a recommendation for anarchy, for their focus is not the atomization of society.

Clearly each social unit is always open to others. Hence the real other can be encountered at the boundary of a region; the other is not merely a myth that cannot be recognized from within a region. This is because regions reside at "nodal points" and are closely linked to surrounding locales.[56] This co-presence of regions is an inescapable condition. Additionally, Fish argues that personal freedom should be recognized to exist within a framework of constraint.[57] Specifically, because identity presupposes difference—for example, to say a person is unique presupposes the realm of the mundane—they must be viewed to exist together. As postmodernists claim, differences are comple-mentary. Every act of interpretation, including the constitution of a self, is implicated in others. According to Fish, any other vision of individualism is an abstraction and hence invalid. The idea of a completely autonomous, free, or independent unit is simply a fantasy. Hell, as Sartre says, may be others, but the presence of others is not an anomaly.

However, this inescapable condition of intersubjectivity is not fundamental, for it does not constitute a uniform, homogeneous, pristine, or singular realm. Contrary to the usual conception of foundations, this inescapable situation is replete with ambiguity, change and, possibly, conflict. This is not the calm, peaceful, and reliable plane envisioned by most foundationalists.

Yet imagining the social world to consist of a host of interpretive communities should not be seen as an invitation to anarchy. As opposed to what conservatives think, PC'ers are not saying that individuals are unable to escape from their respective situations. Despite D'Souza's misunderstanding of this issue, persons can rise above their circumstances; they are not trapped within separate regions of sexual, racial, or class identity.[58] There may be different viewpoints, but these are not severed from others; a community is not a "prison-house," to use Fredric Jameson's imagery.[59]

Similar to regions of interpretive difference, communities are also not isolated. In point of fact, Fish states that a person's "status as something or someone outside is conferred by the very community from which he is supposedly distinct."[60] In other words, what is defined as relevant for a community exists against a backdrop of norms and other cultural matters that are deemed to be inconsequential. In postmodern terms, Fish is describing a rhizome, for regions are interlocked without the aid of metaphysical reinforcements. Here again, differences are joined but not necessarily as a tightly knit package. Yet complementarity such as this is not usually thought to be characteristic of anarchy. How can anarchy be said to exist in view of this nexus of different communities? Regardless of how this condition diverges from usual foundations, or *archi*, order and morality can be sustained by this patchwork of communities.

At this juncture the claim should be addressed that PC, because of its anarchistic nature, also supports the hedonism that is prevalent today among America's youth. In general, Americans may be apathetic and self-absorbed. But these conditions are not a part of PC, for individual and collective *praxis* are understood to support reality. Likewise, the intersubjective character of order is stressed by PC. On the other hand, the cynicism, resignation, and disenchantment expressed by persons, according to some modern writers, may be a consequence of the realism promoted by conservatives.[61] The idea is that if reality is already completed, and not subject to human control, why should persons exhibit any initiative? Indeed, their action is inconsequential. The reality unveiled by realists does not need to be supplemented by human effort; this kind of reality is impermeable. Realism is disastrous, because its message is that the world need not respond to reforms. Therefore conservatives, rather than PC'ers, may be the culprits who have introduced the social imagery that encourages lassitude.

Nonetheless, morality is traditionally thought to mimic absolute foundations. In terms of PC, however, morality reflects the mosaic of differences that constitute existence. Most important is that what some contemporary writers call the *equilibrio* between differences be maintained.[62] Accordingly, this is the moral imperative of PC: Foster and protect the integrity of difference. As Lyotard states, "one must maximize as much as possible the multiplication of small narratives."[63] The interpretive schemes that constitute persons' identities, experiences, cultures, and relationships, for example, should be allowed to flourish.

No norm, belief, or viewpoint should be allowed to upset the balance between narratives.

In this way, morality emerges out of difference and is not introduced from outside of the nexus of differences. Difference is sufficient to justify a moral position, and thus an absolute is not needed for this purpose. The recognition of difference provides imagery that allows for integration but without the reductionism that accompanies monism. Accordingly, each region should be maintained in its symmetrical relationship with others; the aim is to ensure a sense of proportion. These regions may be very different, like those in a mobile, but none owes its existence to another. As a result, no region should be allowed to dominate or force another locale out of existence. Maintaining the symmetry of the social mosaic is thus the aim of PC morality.

Hans-Georg Gadamer calls this a "dialectical ethic."[64] The idea is that citizens, and communities, look for conversational partners. Rather than searching for a perfect principle to guide interaction, which can easily become the all-encompassing *Fuhrerprinzip*, persons engage others and create a mutually satisfying linguistic bond. Through a process of iteration others are addressed, embraced, and protected. Respect is exhibited for others; others are not things. Persons encounter one another as unique individuals, rather than as objects to be classified and regulated. The result of this conversation is what Gadamer calls fellowship (*Koinonia*): Persons and communities create reciprocal relationships with one another.[65] At the heart of this ethics is a conversation rather than abstractions that denigrate the human presence.

This ethic is "anti-metaphysical," according to Werner Marx, because the guiding principle is the other rather than some abstract rendition of good or evil.[66] The realm of ethics exists between action and the other, which is a sphere that subtends the distinctions usually made between realism and atomism, absolutism and relativism, and solipsism and abstract universalism. Out of this gap that is presupposed by interaction, evaluation criteria can emerge. An earthly measure of morality, writes Marx, is thus possible. A trans-cultural, but immanent, ethics is available. Persons may invent truth, but this is not done in isolation. Instead, all rules make sense only against this link between action and the other; the other is part of every action. Responsibility toward the other is not optional but assumed by every act, unless dualism is enforced.

What would convince the anti-PC hounds that Nazism or some other form of totalitarianism is not supported by this movement? Probably nothing! Nonetheless, look at what PC'ers have already said. They celebrate difference, support local rights, encourage multiculturalism, and critique hierarchy. In this vein, Fish contends that the other "is one of many instantiations or interpretations of human nature that is necessary for its full emergence."[67] With all this and more, PC is still viewed as repressive by conservatives. What would advocates of PC have to do to be seen as moral—adopt the conservative agenda?

But D'Souza and other critics on the Right hold to the dubious notion that PC is amoral and thus incapable of thwarting the growth of totalitarianism. Even if PC were relativistic, however, research undertaken by the members of the Frankfurt School and others suggests that totalitarianism is not sustained by relativism.[68] Indeed, quite the opposite is true. Nazis, for example, believed that everything should be subordinated to an overriding force. Furthermore, due to the absolute character of this power, Nazis felt justified in extinguishing all resistance to this system. Nazis were not guided by relativistic ideas but instead by imagery they considered to be apocalyptic. For example, claims that were relativistic could never have supported the type of authority necessary to create and rationalize the Holocaust.

Many of those identified with PC have argued against this sort of totalization. Ideologies of all kinds, remarks Miller, are subverted by the style of literary criticism associated with PC.[69] It also should be noted that the power required to sustain interpretive communities is not the same as that needed to organize the Nazi state. The former is self-critical and limited, while the latter is unreflective and all-encompassing. One must conclude, therefore, that the attempt by conservatives to link PC to Nazism is disingenuous and, possibly, a red herring.

Conclusion

Ostensibly conservatives desire the kind of spontaneous order discussed by Friedrich Hayek.[70] But apparently they believe the social imagery sponsored by PC encourages too much spontaneity. On the other hand, however, PC is understood to be totalitarian. Clearly such conflation strains political analysis.

Nonetheless, the problem with conservatives is that they require abstractions to ensure the viability of discourse. Any deviation from this premise, accordingly, is assumed to be calamitous. This is extremely dangerous, for very likely market forces or other rarefied notions will begin to regulate interaction. When this is the case, however, the original intent of conservatives is contravened. Order is guided by these abstractions rather than by spontaneity.

That conservatives should contradict themselves is not the major issue. Much more serious than the absence of a truly spontaneous market is the gradual diminution of social actors. For once the source of order is externalized, the human element can easily come to be seen as a threat to harmony. In short, discussion and critique can come to be viewed as a threat to the polity. This situation, moreover, can quickly deteriorate and culminate in the totalization of society, thereby compromising democracy. Democracy may come to mean adherence to a particular mode of thought and demeanor rather than the ability to strike out in new directions that ignore the prevailing power structure.

Discussion Questions

1. How do Choi and Murphy respond to the charge that political correctness is a form of relativism? What do they mean when they claim that norms are valid within interpretive communities? Do you think that answers the charge of relativism? Why or why not?

2. Choi and Murphy write that critics of PC assume that it will lead to totalitarianism. How do they respond to this charge? Do you agree with this response? Why or why not?

3. At one point in their essay Choi and Murphy maintain that "giving primacy to universals can easily result in undermining community as a viable principle." Yet in another place they write "this is the moral imperative of PC: Foster and protect the integrity of difference." In the first quote, they apparently deny that there are any universal principles or moral norms. Yet in the second quote they seem to be affirming a universal. How do you think Choi and Murphy would reconcile this apparent inconsistency? Defend your answer.

Notes

1. Jacques Derrida, *Margins of Philosophy*. Chicago: University of Chicago Press, 1982, pp. xvii–xviii.

2. Jean Baudrillard, *Fatal Strategies*. New York: Semiotext(e), 1991, pp. 16–24.

3. Gilles Deleuze, "Nomad Thought." In *The New Nietzsche*, edited by David B. Allison. New York: Delta, 1977, pp. 142–149.

4. Dinesh D'Souza, *Illiberal Education*. New York: The Free Press, 1991, p. 191.

5. Edward Shils, "The Sad State of Humanities in America," *The Wall Street Journal*, July 3, 1989, p. 5.

6. Jon Weiner, "Deconstructing de Man," *The Nation*, January 9, 1988, pp. 22–24.

7. Roger Kimball, *Tenured Radicals*. New York: Harper and Row, 1990, p. 154.

8. Rene Wellek, "Destroying Literary Studies," *The New Criterion* 2(4), 1983, p. 4.

9. D'Souza, *Illiberal Education*, p. 177.

10. Ibid., pp. 178–179.

11. Stanley Fish, *Doing What Comes Naturally*. Durham, N.C.: Duke University Press, 1989, p. 29.

12. Roland Barthes, *Criticism and Truth*. Minneapolis: University of Minnesota Press, 1987, p. 84.

13. Barbara Herrnstein Smith, *Contingencies of Value*. Cambridge, Mass.: Harvard University Press, 1988, p. 48. See also, Fish, *Doing What Comes Naturally*, p. 100.

14. Barthes, *Criticism and Truth*, p. 69.

15. Paul de Man, "Foreword." In *The Dissimulating Harmony*, by Carol Jacobs. Baltimore: Johns Hopkins University Press, 1978, p. xi.

16. Roland Barthes, *Roland Barthes*. New York: Hill and Wang, 1977, p. 58.

17. Kimball, *Tenured Radicals*, p. 164.

18. D'Souza, *Illiberal Education*, p. 175.

19. Allan Bloom, *The Closing of the American Mind*. New York: Simon and Schuster, 1987, p. 155.

20. Kimball, *Tenured Radicals*, p. 164.

21. Jane Flax, *Thinking Fragments: Psychoanalysis, Feminism, and Postmodernism in the Contemporary West*. Berkeley: University of California Press, 1990, p. 231.

22. Fish, *Doing What Comes Naturally*, p. 128.

23. Bloom, *The Closing of the American Mind*, p. 150.

24. Fish, *Doing What Comes Naturally*, p. 139.

25. Ibid., p. 11.

26. Stanley Fish, "There Is No Such Thing as Free Speech and It's a Good Thing, Too." In *Debating PC*, edited by Paul Berman. New York: Dell, 1992, p. 233.

27. Fish, *Doing What Comes Naturally*, p. 11.

28. Ibid., pp. 11–14. See also, Ibid., pp. 120–140.

29. Ibid., p. 12.

30. D'Souza, *Illiberal Education*, p. 67.

31. Dinesh D'Souza, "Illiberal Education," *The Atlantic*, March 1991, p. 58.

32. D'Souza, *Illiberal Education*, p. 190.

33. Bloom, *The Closing of the American Mind*, p. 342.

34. Stanley Fish, "Normal Circumstances, Literal Language, Direct Speech Acts, the Ordinary, Everyday, the Obvious, What Goes On without Saying, and Other Special Cases," *Critical Inquiry* 4(4), 1978, pp. 640–641.

35. Kimball, *Tenured Radicals*, p. 157.

36. J. Hillis Miller, "An Open Letter to Professor Jon Weiner." In *Theory Now and Then*, by J. Hillis Miller. Durham, N.C.: Duke University Press, 1991, p. 379.

37. Stanley Fish, *Is There a Text in This Class?* Cambridge, Mass.: Harvard University Press, 1980, p. 307.

38. Karl Mannheim, *Ideology and Utopia*. New York: Harcourt, Brace and World, 1936, p. 79.

39. Stanley Fish, "Canon Busting: The Basic Issues," *National Forum* 69(3), 1989, p. 15.

40. Fish, *Is There a Text in This Class?*, p. 14.

41. Howard Becker, *Outsiders*. New York: The Free Press, 1963, pp. 8–18.

42. Fish, *Is There a Text in This Class?*, p. 68.

43. Ibid., p. 109.

44. Richard Rorty, *Contingency, Irony, and Solidarity*. Cambridge: Cambridge University Press, 1989, pp. 44–69.

45. Terry Eagleton, *Ideology*. London: Verso, 1991, pp. 40–41.

46. Raymond Williams, *Marxism and Literature*. Oxford: Oxford University Press, 1977, p. 125.

47. Richard Ashley, "Imposing International Purpose: Notes on a Problematic of Governance." In *Global Changes and Theoretical Challenges: Approaches to World Politics for the 1990's*, edited by Ernst-Otto Czempiel and James N. Rosenau. Lexington, Mass.: Lexington Books, 1989, p. 269.

48. Kimball, *Tenured Radicals*, p. 113.

49. Paul de Man, *Allegories of Reading*. New Haven: Yale University Press, 1979, p. 209.

50. Kimball, *Tenured Radicals*, P. 115.

51. D'Souza, *Illiberal Education*, pp. 46, 186.

52. Kimball, *Tenured Radicals*, p. 156.

53. D'Souza, *Illiberal Education*, p. 190.

54. Jean-François Lyotard, *The Postmodern Condition*. Minneapolis: University of Minnesota Press, 1984, p. 15.

55. Fish, *Is There a Text in This Class?*, p. 335.

56. Ibid., p. 15.

57. Fish, *Doing What Comes Naturally*, p. 89.

58. D'Souza, *Illiberal Education*, p. 191.

59. Fredric Jameson, *The Prison-House of Language*. Princeton: Princeton University Press, 1972, e.g., pp. x, 128.

60. Fish, *Doing What Comes Naturally*, p. 148.

61. Martin Jay, *Permanent Exiles*. New York: Columbia University Press, 1986, p. 169.

62. Paul Fleckenstein, "Review of *We Build the Road as We Travel* by Roy Morrison," *Z Magazine*, January 1992, pp. 61–63.

63. Jean-François Lyotard and Jean-Loup Thebaud, *Just Gaming*. Minneapolis: University of Minnesota Press, 1985, p. 59.

64. Hans-Georg Gadamer, *Plato's Dialectical Ethic*. New Haven: Yale University Press, 1991, pp. 17–65.

65. Ibid., p. 92.

66. Werner Marx, *Is There a Measure on Earth?* Chicago: University of Chicago Press, 1987, pp. 4–8.

67. Fish, *Doing What Comes Naturally*, p. 410.

68. Martin Jay, *The Dialectical Imagination*. Boston: Little, Brown and Company, 1973, pp. 113–142.

69. J. Hillis Miller, "An Open Letter to Professor Jon Weiner," p. 382.

70. Friedrich A. Hayek, *The Constitution of Liberty*. Chicago: University of Chicago Press, 1960, p. 160.

42

Two Philosophical Problems with Political Correctness

Francis J. Beckwith

I am a Lecturer in Philosophy at the University of Nevada, Las Vegas as well as Professor at Large, Simon Greenleaf University (Anaheim, California) and Senior Research Fellow, Nevada Policy Research Institute. Some of my books include *Politically Correct Death: Answering the Arguments for Abortion Rights* (1993), *Are You Politically Correct?: Debating America's Cultural Standards* (1993), and *The Abortion Controversy: A Reader* (1994).

In this essay I argue that Choi and Murphy (in Chapter 41) are committed to two philosophical positions that are highly problematic: (1) epistemological relativism, and (2) value relativism. The former is embodied in the multiculturalist's assumption that "every judgment can be reduced to a 'cultural perspective.'" I argue that this view fails because it is self-refuting, inconsistent with other PC norms, and unjustifiably dogmatic. The latter philosophical commitment, value relativism, is the view that there are no objective moral values that transcend individual and culture. I argue that there are several problems with this view. First, value relativism is self-refuting because it undermines the moral strength of the PCer's entire enterprise. Second, some defenders of PC celebrate the normative value of tolerance as an integral part of their commitment to diversity even though it is inconsistent with value relativism. Third, some in the PC movement confuse disagreement between political interests with a proof of value relativism. I conclude with some remarks concerning the way in

which Choi and Murphy attack those who oppose political correctness.

There seem to be two philosophical perspectives that undergird the political correctness movement: (1) epistemological relativism, and (2) value relativism. In the previous essay by Jung Min Choi and John W. Murphy ("Skepticism, Nihilism, Amorality, and Anarchy: The Legacy of PC?") as well as in the book from which it is reprinted, *The Politics and Philosophy of Political Correctness*,[1] they argue that these two philosophical perspectives, as they understand them (that is, they are reticent to call either "relativism," even though that's the appropriate name), can withstand philosophical scrutiny. In this paper I will present a philosophical critique of both perspectives, concluding with some brief comments about the way in which Choi and Murphy in their book attack opponents of PC.

I. Two Philosophical Presuppositions of Political Correctness

A. Epistemological Relativism

This view is embodied in the multiculturalist's assumption that "every judgment can be reduced to a 'cultural perspective.'" But this assumption is self-refuting, for it is a judgment, and hence (on its own terms) merely a cultural perspective, something that cannot be objectively and universally true. But it is put forth as universally true (since it is claimed about *every* judgment). Thus, if it is objectively and universally true that "every judgment can be reduced to a 'cultural prospective,'" then this statement is false, because it asserts that "every judgment can be reduced to a 'cultural perspective.'"

More sophisticated defenders of the PC position deny that they espouse epistemological relativism. They argue that although "a priori conceptions of normativeness must be abandoned," there are interpretive communities within which objective norms are valid. "Each community, accordingly, values certain norms. Therefore, some norms may be irrelevant in a specific community, because behavior is not random but guided by expectations that are known by

Part II of this essay was written exclusively for this anthology. The rest, though revised significantly, originally appeared as part of "The Epistemology of Political Correctness," *Public Affairs Quarterly* (1994), and is reprinted by permission.

every competent member of a region. Exhibiting just any behavior would certainly result in a negative sanction. Within an interpretive community the idea that anything goes [i.e., relativism] is simply ridiculous, for all norms do not have equal validity."[2] Because "there is no external reality subject to participation and definition, then different viewpoints generate different understandings of events."[3]

This defense fails as well. First, it is self-refuting. The claim that "a priori conceptions of normativeness must be abandoned" is an a priori normative claim. It is a normative judgment that applies to *all possible* a priori conceptions, which would make it *a priori* and consequently, an a priori normative judgment. Thus, if it is the case that "a priori conceptions of nor-\mativeness must be abandoned," then we must abandon the claim that "a priori conceptions of normativeness must be abandoned," since it is an a priori normative claim. But let's suppose that the PCer retorts by saying that the claim that "a priori conceptions of normativeness must be abandoned" is not a normative claim but merely a description of the world, something like "a priori conceptions of normativeness are false." But unless he is willing to argue that one ought to believe in false things, the normativeness of his claim is merely disguised. In addition, to claim that a priori conceptions of normativeness are false is to make a claim about reality, which would deny the PCer's claim that one cannot know reality but can know only through the rubric of interpretive communities. But if the PCer argues that his claim that "a priori conceptions of normativeness must be abandoned" is something he asserts only from the perspective of his interpretive community, then he cannot criticize those who still choose to believe in a priori conceptions of normativeness.

What if the PCer argues that his claim that "a priori conceptions of normativeness must be abandoned" is normative but not a priori? Then his case totally collapses, because it is then not possible to exclude a priori every possible a priori conception of normativeness. Thus, a priori conceptions of normativeness are possible, and to request that they be abandoned without reason and without argument is irrational dogma.

It is interesting to note that the defenders of the PC position seem to *presuppose* the very positions they denounce. For example, Jung Min Choi and John W. Murphy, after arguing for the concept of interpretive communities, go on to defend Stanley Fish, by arguing as follows:

Sociologists of various hues have *verified a long time ago* what Fish is saying. Symbolic interactionists, for example, have illustrated that *persons* evaluate their actions with regard to their respective "reference groups." Therefore, in terms of a single city, very different pockets of norms may be operative. To understand what deviance means in each circumstance, *a priori definitions of normativeness must be set aside. For norms are embedded in symbols, signs, and gestures that may be very unique and restricted to a specific locale.*

Upon crossing one of these relatively invisible boundaries, an individual quickly learns which behaviors are acceptable. This diversity, moreover, has not resulted in the disaster that conservatives predict. Yet navigating through this montage of norms *requires interpretive skill, tolerance, and an appreciation for pluralism*[4] (emphasis mine).

We learn from the above that *sociologists verify* the PC hypothesis. Apparently sociologists, at least the sociologists that verify the PC hypothesis, are exempt from being epistemologically restricted by their interpretive communities. But if they are, they provide us with no evidence of the PC hypothesis, because that evidence is skewed, by the PCer's own admission, by the interpretive community in which the sociologists have been nurtured, which may be a politically correct community which accepts the PC view of interpretive communities. Thus, the appeal to sociologists who "verify" the PC view is either self-refuting or question-begging. Consequently, the norms and observations put forth by these sociologists as well as Choi and Murphy—such as "a priori definitions of normativeness must be set aside," "norms are embedded in symbols, signs, and gestures that may be very unique and restricted to a specific locale," and "navigating through this montage of norms requires interpretive skill, tolerance, and an appreciation for pluralism"—are also either self-refuting or question-begging, because they are either claims about the world (thus affirming that knowledge can be objective) or they are claims by people who cannot break out of their own interpretive community, which may be PC (thus affirming that their observations are skewed by their interpretive community and are not a universal perspective).

In addition, to put forth interpretive skill, tolerance, and appreciation for pluralism as virtues by which one navigates "through this montage of norms" is to offer a priori normative guidelines that apparently transcend any particular interpretive community since these virtues are to be used while navigating through *all* of the interpretive communities. But if this is not the case, then these virtues are not normative for the members of some interpretive communities (e.g., Nazi Germany, a skinhead commune, or a group of solipsists), since those of us who belong to an interpretive community that may accept these norms would have to tolerate the Nazis and skinheads in appreciation of pluralism.

Other examples of self-refutation abound. Consider this brief sampling. In one place, Choi and Murphy claim that "achieving finality is impossible,"[5] which I assume is the final word on the matter. But they maintain elsewhere that "conservativism . . . does not necessarily offer the last word on preserving knowledge and order," for "such a view . . . would be quite presumptuous and dogmatic."[6] Yet, we are told, with no benefit of argument and with all the brashness of presumption and dogmatism, that "searching for that elusive final frontier is futile,"[7] "there are no concealed places where absolutes can be cultivated,"[8] "nothing is hidden, but instead paths are presented that have yet to be travelled,"[9] and "reality is . . . a human invention or, more accurately, a linguistic habit."[10] We are told by Choi and Murphy that "facts are interpretive rather than value-free and objective,"[11] except of course this one, which would mean that not all facts are interpretive rather than value-free and objective. However, if Choi and Murphy want to maintain that this "fact" too is merely interpretive, then we have as good a reason as any to return to a belief that some form of objectivity is possible, since the claim that "facts are interpretive rather than value-free and objective" would itself be incapable of being value-free, objective and a true description of reality. Why should we believe some claim as true if the claim itself claims nothing is true?

In his important and influential work on the crisis in our universities, *The Closing of the American Mind*, Allan Bloom writes that "there is one thing a professor can be absolutely certain of: almost every student entering the university believes, or says he believes, that truth is relative. . . . The students, of course, cannot defend their opinion. It is something with which they have been indoctrinated."[12] By dogmatically asserting that there is no truth, the naive student and the PC advocate become close-minded to the possibility of knowing the truth if in fact it does exist. This is why the PCer's view of epistemological relativism differs significantly from classical philosophical skepticism and is much closer to so-

lipsism. The skeptics did not deny that truth existed, but rather that one could not be sure when and if one had the truth, or at least one was incapable of providing a rational justification for it. The PCer is *not* a skeptic. She is a dogmatist who simply asserts that the truth cannot be known. Unlike the classical skeptic, she is emboldened, not humbled, by her ignorance.

It seems then that the view of epistemological relativism put forth by PCers fails because it is self-refuting, inconsistent with other PC norms, and unjustifiably dogmatic.

B. Value Relativism

Value relativism is the view espoused by a great number of those who defend politically correct policies. This view logically follows from epistemological relativism: if knowledge is relative to interpretive communities and moral claims are knowledge-claims,[13] then moral claims are relative to interpretive communities. According to this view, no one particular moral perspective is universally binding. Consider Stanley Fish's claim that freedom of speech, as found in the First Amendment of the Constitution, has no inherent value:

> . . . I think . . . that people cling to First Amendment pieties because they do not wish to face what they correctly take to be the alternative. That alternative is *politics*, the realization . . . that decisions about what is and is not protected in the realm of expression will rest not on principle or firm doctrine, but on the ability of some persons, to interpret—recharacterize or rewrite—principle and doctrine in ways that lead to the protection of speech they want heard and the regulation of the speech they want silenced. . . . In short, the name of the game has always been politics, even when (indeed, especially when) it is played by stigmatizing politics as the area to be avoided.[14]

According to Fish, there are no moral principles that are binding upon all persons everywhere and in every place. There is simply *politics*, the cultural perspective of the elite who control the interpretive community.

But this fares no better than epistemological relativism. The value relativist, like the epistemological relativist (they could, of course, as in the case of Fish, easily be the same person), believes that value judgments, like knowledge claims, can be reduced to a cultural perspective. There are many problems with this view. Consider the following.

(1) Value relativism undermines the moral strength of the PCer's entire enterprise. That is to say, if value judgments are *merely* cultural, then the value of PC is *merely* cultural. But if this is the case, why then does the PCer judge as morally wrong institutions such as slavery and apartheid? After all, people in cultures and societies that practice slavery and apartheid believe that these practices are correct. Who is the PCer to judge, from the perspective of his culture, that these practices are morally wrong? Now, of course, I believe that apartheid and slavery are morally wrong, but I don't think that the PC perspective (and its view of multiculturalism, as currently defined) does the moral work sufficient for us to make such a judgment. Although space does not permit me to present an alternative moral perspective for grounding multiculturalism,[15] I believe that there are several. For example, a robust view of natural rights (such as the view defended by Martin Luther King, Jr., in his "Letter from the Birmingham Jail"[16]) can rescue PC and multiculturalism from the philosophical problems inherent in value relativism.

(2) Some defenders of PC, like Choi and Murphy, celebrate the normative value of tolerance as an integral part of the PC enterprise.[17] According to Choi and Murphy, the purpose of tolerance is to help us to navigate "through this montage of norms."[18] There are several problems with this view. For example, the value of tolerance, as presented by most defenders of PC (such as Choi and Murphy), presupposes the existence of at least one nonrelative, objective value that transcends the "montage of norms": tolerance. Tom Beauchamp observes:

> If we interpret normative relativism as *requiring* tolerance of other views, the whole theory is imperiled by inconsistency. The proposition that we ought to tolerate the views of others, or that it is right not to interfere with others, is precluded by the very strictures of the theory. Such a proposition bears all the marks of a *nonrelative* account of moral rightness, one based on, but not reducible to, the cross-cultural findings of anthropologists. . . . But if this moral principle [of tolerance] is recognized as valid, it can of course be employed as an instrument of criticizing such cultural practices as the denial of human rights to minorities and such beliefs as that of racial superiority. A moral commitment to tolerance of other practices and beliefs thus leads inexorably to the abandonment of normative relativism.[19]

Choi and Murphy seem to affirm other objective moral norms that apparently transcend interpretive communities, since they are employed as part of a justification for the entire PC enterprise:

> . . . this is the moral imperative of PC: Foster and protect the integrity of difference.[20]

> The interpretive schemes that constitute persons' identities, experiences, cultures, and relationships, for example, should be allowed to flourish.[21]

> No norm, belief, or viewpoint should be allowed to upset the balance between narratives.[22]

> In short, PC consists of theories and practices that are designed to end injustices based on sex, race, class, and other social variables.[23]

(3) Fish, like so many in the political correctness movement, confuses disagreement between political interests with a proof of value relativism. Fish accurately points out that people will defend, employ, and interpret certain principles in a particular way when those principles serve their interest. That is to say, many apparent moral disputes are in fact merely political disputes. But it does not logically follow from this observation that all moral disputes can be reduced to politics. Fish's argument can be put this way:

1. Some moral disputes can be reduced to political disputes.
Therefore,
2. There are no objective moral principles.

Since the conclusion can be false *and* the premise true, the conclusion does not follow from the premise. Hence, Fish's case for value relativism is based on an invalid argument. Even if Fish were to change his premise to assert the stronger claim that "*all* moral disputes can be reduced to political disputes," it still would not follow that there are no objective moral principles. Perhaps human beings are fundamentally selfish creatures who, though intuitively aware of objective moral principles, most often or always choose what is expedient or more likely to keep themselves in political power. After all, if every nation were ruled by a tyrant, it would not follow that tyranny is morally justified. Fish commits the fallacy of confusing the *is* with the *ought*.

In addition, by claiming that "*all* moral disputes can be reduced to political disputes" without having examined *every* moral dispute, Fish commits himself to an a priori normative conception, which must be objectively true (which would be inconsistent with his PC epistemology) for *all* interpretive communities, because it serves as the basis for *justifying* the claim that moral disputes can be reduced to disputes between the political interests of interpretive communities.

C. Conclusion

As I noted earlier, two philosophical perspectives seem to undergird political correctness: (1) epistemological relativism, and (2) value relativism. In this paper I presented a philosophical critique of these two perspectives. I concluded that these two perspectives fail philosophically. This being the case, the philosophical basis for political correctness collapses. Perhaps this collapse beckons us to follow the call of two of the most profound claims in human history: "the unexamined life is not worth living" (Socrates) and "you shall know the truth and that truth shall set you free" (Jesus).

II. On the Opponents of Political Correctness

In addition to the philosophical problems in the position defended by Choi and Murphy, there are two problems with the way they characterize their opponents.

(1) Choi and Murphy refer to all opponents of PC as "conservatives." This is simply not true. Arthur Schlesinger (liberal historian), Irving Howe (Marxist scholar), Catharine Stimpson (feminist educator), Christina Sommers (liberal feminist philosopher), Ira Glasser (national director, American Civil Liberties Union), and Nat Hentoff (*Village Voice* columnist) are among the harshest critics of PC, yet they are never mentioned in Choi and Murphy's book. Consequently, they falsely portray the PC debate as a battle between conservatives and liberals (or as a debate between Right and Left).

(2) Choi and Murphy throughout their book make dogmatic assertions without *arguing for* their position. For instance, in one place they point out that PC proponents "reject the traditional dualistic conception of knowledge and order,"[24] though this conception of knowledge is never defined and never argued against. In numerous places Choi and Murphy make negative psychological assessments of their opponents, assuming that sufficient for philo-

sophical argument. Consider the following: "Given the perceived threat posed by political correctness";[25] "For those who are constantly looking for an angle, which can be used to preserve privilege and promote exploitation";[26] "PC has been so scurrilously attacked lately by those who are clinging desperately to outmoded principles in order to maintain their hegemony";[27] "despite their expected defensiveness";[28] "PC is threatening to both those who have been traditionally on the Right and neo-conservatives"[29]; "Clearly, denying autonomy of knowledge and order has conservatives of all stripes worried";[30] "Behind this concern for upholding philosophical principles lurk political motives."[31]

Nearly every page of this book is littered with these sorts of assessments of the anti-PCer's psychological state, yet no proof of these assessments is provided and no reason is given to suppose why they are relevant to supporting the PC position. What Choi and Murphy are engaged in are ad hominem attacks rather than serious philosophical argumentation.

Discussion Questions

1. Define what is meant by "epistemological relativism." What does Professor Beckwith mean when he says that this position is self-refuting? Do you agree? Why or why not?

2. Much of the motivation behind political correctness is to help people become more sensitive to minority groups. Do you think that Professor Beckwith's critique attacks this motivation? Why or why not?

3. One criticism of Professor Beckwith's view could be "You are using Western logic to show that non-Western thinking is illogical. Aren't you being ethnocentric and racist in your critique?" How do you think Professor Beckwith would respond to such a criticism? Do you agree with the criticism? Why or why not?

Notes

1. Jung Min Choi and John W. Murphy, *The Politics and Philosophy of Political Correctness* (Westport, Conn.: Praeger, 1992).

2. Ibid., 93, 94.

3. Betty Jean Craige, *Reconnection: Dualism to Holism in Literary Study* (Athens: University of Georgia Press, 1988), 111, as quoted in Jerry L. Martin, "The University as Agent

of Social Transformation," *Academic Questions* 6 (Summer 1993), 59.

4. Choi and Murphy, *Political Correctness*, 94.

5. Ibid., 83.

6. Ibid., 82.

7. Ibid., 83.

8. Ibid., xiii.

9. Ibid.

10. Ibid., 4.

11. Ibid., 31.

12. Allan Bloom, *The Closing of the American Mind* (New York: Simon & Schuster, 1987), 25.

13. Certainly there are and have been a number of philosophers and ethicists who deny that moral claims are knowledge-claims (e.g., emotivists), yet they may not be epistemological relativists about other matters. However, if one is an epistemological relativist about knowledge in general and one believes that moral claims are either not knowledge-claims or they are knowledge-claims relative only to an interpretive community, one nevertheless denies that moral claims have objective ontological status. (For more on these metaethical issues, see J. P. Moreland, *Scaling the Secular City* [Grand Rapids, Mich.: Baker Book House, 1987], 105–132.) But it seems to me that those who defend the PC position are arguing that moral-claims are knowledge-claims but they are relative to an interpretive community.

14. Stanley Fish, "There's No Such Thing as Free Speech and It's a Good Thing, Too," in *Are You Politically Correct? Debating America's Cultural Standards*, ed. F. J. Beckwith and M. Bauman (Buffalo: Prometheus, 1993), p. 51.

15. See, for example, Francis J. Beckwith, *Politically Correct Death: Answering the Arguments for Abortion Rights* (Grand Rapids, Mich.: Baker Book House, 1993), 19–28; Donald S. Miller, "Multicultural Education: The Counselor's Prime Directive?" professional paper, Master of Science in Marriage and Family Counseling, Graduate College, University of Nevada, Las Vegas (December 1993); Moreland, *Scaling the Secular City*, 105–132; and Steven Yates, "Multiculturalism and Epistemology," *Public Affairs Quarterly* 6 (1992), 435–456.

16. Martin Luther King, Jr., "Letter from the Birmingham Jail," in *The Right Thing to Do: Basic Readings in Moral Philosophy*, ed. James Rachels (New York: McGraw-Hill, 1989), 236–253. See also James Q. Wilson, *The Moral Sense* (New York: The Free Press, 1993).

17. Choi and Murphy, *Political Correctness*, 94.

18. Ibid.

19. Tom L. Beauchamp, *Philosophical Ethics: An Introduction to Moral Philosophy* (New York: McGraw-Hill, 1982), 42.

20. Choi and Murphy, *Political Correctness*, 101.

21. Ibid.

22. Ibid.

23. Ibid., 2.

24. Ibid., ix.

25. Ibid., xii.

26. Ibid., xiii.

27. Ibid.

28. Ibid., 3.

29. Ibid., 3.

30. Ibid., 4.

31. Ibid., xi.

SECTION C

Freedom of Expression

Introduction

In America today moral questions regarding freedom of expressions are found in primarily two areas: (1) law, morality, and the censorship of pornography, and (2) speech codes on college campuses.

I. Law, Morality, and the Censorship of Pornography

Although the First Amendment of the U.S. Constitution states that "Congress shall make no law . . . abridging the freedom of speech, or the press," it is clear that it is not absolute. For one cannot in the name of the First Amendment engage with impunity in slander, malice, sexual harassment, or the writing of fraudulent checks. Consequently, the question of whether the government has a right to censor pornographic materials that are obscene cannot be dismissed by merely appealing to the First Amendment as an absolute prohibition of censorship.

I teach a course called "Contemporary Moral Issues." In that course we usually discuss the issue of censorship and pornography. In order to provoke my students to understand the moral and social conflicts that the issue entails, I make the following challenge to them:

> Every year the university library celebrates "Banned Book Month" by putting in glass cases books that have been banned or that people have tried to ban throughout American history, such as *Catcher in the Rye, The Adventures of Huckleberry Finn,* and *Tropic of Cancer.* Under each book is an index card on which is a brief history of the banning or attempted banning of the book and the reason or reasons why people did not want the book sold and/or permitted in their library. Notice that all the books in the cases are classics that no intelligent person would want banned. The message is clear: people who favor censorship of any sort are idiots. But I have a feeling that the library would have a much more difficult time with its absolutism against censorship if one of you did the following. In fact, I challenge you to do this, if you have the guts. During "Banned Book Month" go to an adult bookstore and purchase the raunchiest hardcore pornographic magazine you can find, maybe with a catchy title like "Anal Sex Orgasm." Then take that magazine to the local public library and try to donate it. My guess is that the library staff will look at you as if you were crazy, and then politely say, "No, thank you." Now take that same magazine to the university library and ask to see the person in charge of the banned book cases. Present this person with the magazine and tell her that she should put it in the glass case because it is now a banned book. I have no doubt, like her colleagues at the public library, she will politely say, "No, thank you." At that point you should demand your own glass case for books banned from the "Banned Book Month" case. Then you should leave before she calls security.

No student has yet to take my challenge. But the point is clear. The issue of censorship and pornography cannot be easily resolved by appealing to classic works that have been banned in the past as evidence that censorship is always a bad thing. For it seems obvious to many people that there are certain photographs, films, and even literature that are so obscene that they have no place in either public or university libraries or even in the marketplace. On the hand, many people who oppose the censorship of any materials, even obscene ones, appeal to the First Amendment to the Constitution. They argue that those who want to restrict or ban speech, the press, or expression—which would include pornography—must first prove that the materials in question will pose a clear and present danger and/or significant harm to society and/or individuals. This is the position of Fred R. Berger, who argues, among other things, in Chapter 46 ("Pornography, Sex, and Censorship") that the censor has the burden of providing convincing reasons to interfere with someone's consumption of pornography. On the other hand, in Chapter 47 ("The Question of Harm"), the Attorney General's Commission on Pornography believes that this burden has been met and that government restriction of some forms of pornography may be justified on the basis of harm, though some harmful speech is no doubt protected by the First Amendment. And some legally obscene materials that are not obviously harmful may be restricted in accordance with the First Amendment.

The issue of pornography and whether the government should be permitted to censor it is one of the most hotly contested issues of our day. In fact, the executive branch of the United States federal government has formed two commissions within the past three decades to study the issue, the first coming to a more liberal conclusion in its final report (*Report of the Commission on Obscenity and Pornography* [[1970]) and the second coming to a more conservative conclusion (*Final Report of the Attorney General's Commission on Pornography* [1986]). The 1986 commission's legal review of the First Amendment, obscenity, and censorship is the topic of Chapter 43. It concludes that censorship of obscenity, which includes many but not all forms of pornography, is consistent with the First Amendment. This is supported by a number of U.S. Supreme Court decisions. According to the Court in *Miller vs. California* (1973), something is obscene if it fulfills three conditions and therefore can legally be banned. The commission for the most part agrees with the Court.

Within the past several years, some feminists have come out strongly in support of laws that restrict pornography. Instead of arguing in the way that traditional opponents to pornography have argued (e.g., the material is obscene, sexually immoral), they contend that pornography is an activity that abuses women by violating their dignity as well as aiding and abetting a climate in society that results in the rape of and unjust discrimination against women. In Chapter 44 ("The Sexual Politics of the First Amendment"), Professor Catharine MacKinnon takes this position, maintaining that the First Amendment allows for such restrictions, though it has been and is used to perpetuate pornography and oppress women. In reply to Professor MacKinnon's position, the authors of the essay in Chapter 45 ("Feminist Antipornography Legislation: A Critical Analysis"), Professors Lisa Duggan, Nan Hunter, and Carole Vance contend among other things that feminist antipornography legislation is hopelessly vague and ambiguous, paints all pornography with a broad brush, and plays into the hands of conservatives who have an antifeminist agenda.

II. Speech Codes on College Campuses

In 1993 a student at the University of Pennsylvania was studying in his dorm room late one evening. A small group of women were making noise outside his window, evidently disturbing his ability to study. After a few minutes, the student shouted out of his window to the women, "Shut up, you water buffalos." The student did not realize at the time that the women were African-American, and for this reason, his comment was interpreted as a racial epithet. The student was soon brought up on charges of violating the University of Pennsylvania's speech code, though these charges were subsequently dropped.

Consider more academically serious incidents:

> Nobody in Professor Dolfman's class in legal studies at the University of Pennsylvania could identify where the term "servitude" could be found in the American Constitution, so Dolfman commented that there were "ex-slaves" in the class who should have an idea. "I don't know if I should have used the term," Dolfman recalled, "but it got students to think of the Thirteenth Amendment right away."
>
> Shortly afterwards, a few minority students came up to Dolfman and accused him of racial insensitivity. A second charge against Dolfman was that he had once told a black student to change his pronunciation from "de" to "the." Dolfman said that he met with the students, and apologized if they had taken offense. "I told them that I understood and shared their concerns, that I am Jewish and during *seder* we pray: When we were slaves unto Pharaoh." Dolfman also pointed out that it would be important for students, in courtroom arguments in later years, to speak in a clear and comprehensible manner.
>
> "They seemed to understand," Dolfman recalled, and the matter was dropped for a few months. But after that, during Black History Month, it was brought up again and again, Dolfman said, "to illustrate just how bad things are at Penn."
>
> The adrenalin generated by the Black History Month rhetoric brought about a demonstration by minority students, several dozen of whom occupied Dolfman's class and prevented him from teaching. "They read a document of indictment to my students," Dolfman said. President Sheldon Hackney met with Dolfman and asked him to refrain from public comment, even to abstain from defending himself against accusations. Then Hackney joined the ranks of the accusers, telling the campus newspaper that conduct such as Dolfman's was "absolutely intolerable." Dolfman was pressured to issue what he termed a "forced apology," and to attend "racial awareness" sessions on campus. The university subsequently decided not to renew Dolfman's teaching contract for a year.
>
> Dolfman is now back at Penn, a chastened man. "The message has been driven home very clearly," Dolfman said. "You can't open your mouth on these issues now without fear of being humiliated."[1]

Marietta College—A student wrote an article in the student newspaper in which he referred to lesbianism as "deviant." He was charged with "sexual harassment" by a campus lesbian. The administration intended to expel him from the private Ohio college. [The Individual Rights Foundation] interceded with a threat of litigation based upon his contractual rights under the student code as well as the First Amendment principles based on the college's acceptance of government funding. The Board of Trustees reconsidered the administration's action, and the student was allowed to remain without disciplinary action.[2]

Cohen v. San Bernardino Valley College—A professor of creative writing was accused of "sexual harassment" as a result of assigning his class to write on the subject of pornography and discussing Jonathan Swift's "A Modest Proposal." He has been threatened with loss of tenure and direct firing.[3]

A number of similar cases have been documented, in which students and faculty have been brought up on charges because of the words they had spoken,[4] though some believe that these incidents have been inflated and overrated.[5]

Many colleges and universities have instituted rules forbidding "racist," "sexist," or "antihomosexual" speech. At the law school of the State University of New York at Buffalo, the faculty adopted a resolution that cautioned students not to make "remarks directed at another's race, sex, religion, national origin, age or sexual preference," which includes "ethnically derogatory statements, as well as other remarks based on prejudice or group stereotype."[6] A policy at the University of Connecticut, which is typical of many throughout the United States, "interprets as 'harassment' all remarks that offend or stigmatize women or minorities. Examples of violations of the University President's Policy on Harassment, for which the penalty ranges from a reprimand to expulsion, include 'the use of derogatory names,' 'inconsiderate jokes,' and even 'misdirected laughter' and 'conspicuous exclusion from conversation.'"[7]

For those opposed to these codes the question is not whether academic institutions should forbid verbal harassment, but rather who is to define what is racist, sexist, or antihomosexual speech. Civil libertarians view these speech codes as an attempt to silence unpopular ideas in the name of limiting "harassment." Those who support the speech codes argue that students and faculty have a right not to be subject to offensive speech, speech that is mean-spirited, hurtful, oppressive, and inconsistent with the mission of the university as a haven of tolerance and openness. At some institutions, instructors have distributed to students a list of politically incorrect "isms." Take for example the following handout provided to students at Smith College, "Specific Manifestations of Oppression":

> [P]eople can be oppressed in many ways and for many reasons because they are perceived to be different. As groups begin the process of realizing that they are oppressed and why, new words tend to be created to express the concepts that the existing language cannot. Thus, some of the words below may be familiar to you while others may be new.
>
> Ableism: oppression of the differently abled, by the temporarily able.
>
> Ethnocentrism: oppression of cultures other than the dominant one in the belief that the dominant way of doing things is the superior way.
>
> Heterosexism: oppression of those of sexual orientations other than heterosexual, such as gays, lesbians, and bisexuals; this can take place by not acknowledging their existence. Homophobia is the fear of lesbians, gays, or bisexuals.
>
> Lookism: the belief that appearance is an indicator of a person's value; the construction of a standard for beauty/attractiveness; and oppression through stereotypes and generalizations of both those who do not fit that standard and those who do.
>
> Racism: the belief that one group of people [is] superior to another and therefore [has] the right to dominate, and the power to institute and enforce [its] prejudice and discriminations.[8]

This section contains two essays dealing with the issue of speech codes on college campuses. In the first Stanley Fish argues (Chapter 48, "There's No Such Thing as Free Speech, and It's a Good Thing, Too") that the ideal of freedom of speech is illusory. For Fish, freedom of speech is merely a political weapon defined by those who are in power. Consequently, Fish sees nothing inherently wrong with speech codes on college campuses if they further the interests of his political perspective. In Chapter 49, civil libertarian Nat Hentoff ("'Speech Codes' on the Campus and Problems of Free Speech") defends a robust view of freedom of speech that is in direct contrast to Fish's view.

Notes

1. Dinesh D'Souza, *Illiberal Education: The Politics of Race and Sex on Campus* (New York: The Free Press, 1991), 201–202.

2. From *The Defender* 1, no. 2 (May 1994): 10.

3. Ibid.

4. See the cases documented in *The Defender*, op. cit., and D'Souza, *Illiberal Education*.

5. This is the view of Rosa Ehrenreich, "What Campus Radicals?: The P.C. Undergrad Is Useful Specter," in *Are You Politically Correct?: Debating America's Cultural Standards*, ed. Francis J. Beckwith and Michael E. Bauman (Buffalo, N.Y.: Prometheus, 1993), 33–39.

6. "Faculty Statement Regarding Intellectual Freedom, Tolerance, and Prohibited Harassment," State University of New York at Buffalo, 1988, as quoted in D'Souza, *Illiberal Education*, 9.

7. As cited in D'Souza, *Illiberal Education*, 9.

8. A photograph of this list is found in John Taylor, "Are You Politically Correct?" *New York* magazine (January 21, 1991), 34. This article, without photographs, is reprinted in *Are You Politically Correct?*, 15–31.

For Further Reading

Fred Berger, *Freedom of Expression* (Belmont, Calif.: Wadsworth, 1980).

Varda Burstyn, ed., *Women against Censorship* (Vancouver: Groundwood Books/ Douglas & McIntyre, 1985).

David Copp and Susan L. Wendell, eds., *Pornography and Censorship* (Buffalo, N.Y.: Prometheus, 1983).

Dinesh D'Souza, "The New Censorship," in his *Illiberal Education: The Politics of Race and Sex on Campus* (New York: The Free Press, 1991), Chapter 5.

Final Report of the Attorney General's Commission on Pornography (Nashville, Tenn.: Rutledge Hill Press, 1986).

Stanley Fish, *There's No Such Thing as Free Speech, and It's a Good Thing, Too* (New York: Oxford University Press, 1994).

H. H. Hart, ed., *Censorship: For and Against* (New York: Hart Publishing, 1971).

Nat Hentoff, *Free Speech for Me—But Not for Thee: How the American Left and Right Censor Each Other* (New York: HarperCollins, 1992).

Catharine MacKinnon, *Only Words* (Cambridge: Harvard University Press, 1993).

Richard Perry and Patricia Williams, "Freedom from Hate Speech," in *Debating P.C.*, ed. Paul Berman (New York: Dell, 1992), 225–230.

Report of the Commission on Obscenity and Pornography (New York: Bantam Books, 1970).

Law, Morality, and the Censorship of Pornography

43

The Constraints of the First Amendment

Attorney General's
Commission on Pornography

The Attorney General's Commission on Pornography was formed in 1985 by President Ronald Reagan's Attorney General, Edwin Meese III. The commission consisted of 11 members: three liberals, four conservatives, and three middle-of-the-roaders. In 1986 the commission published a report, from which the following essay is excerpted.

In the following essay, the Attorney General's Commission is concerned with the foremost legal objection to regulating pornography: it violates the First Amendment right to freedom of expression. Although the First Amendment states that "Congress shall make no law . . . abridging the freedom of speech, or the press," it is clear that it is no absolute. For one cannot with impunity in the name of the First Amendment engage in slander, malice, sexual harassment, or the writing of fraudulent checks. However, the question before the commission was this: Does the First Amendment allow the restriction of pornographic materials? After reviewing the court cases concerning this question, the commission concluded that pornography can be restricted without violating the First

Reprinted by permission from *Final Report of the Attorney General's Commission on Pornography* (Nashville, Tenn.: Rutledge Hill Press, 1986).

Amendment if the material under scrutiny is legally obscene. Something is obscene, according to the U.S. Supreme Court in *Miller v. California* (1973), if it fulfills three conditions. The commission reviews these conditions and then draws the conclusion that the Court was for the most part correct. The commission also makes some observations about different interpretations of the meaning of the First Amendment, arguing in one place that some pornography may not be a First Amendment concern because the amendment was intended to protect cognitive expression and this pornography has none and is merely a masturbatory tool. The commission sums up its case by responding to the objection that any restrictions on obscenity, even if legally justified, can lead to abuse. It believes that such a concern, though legitimate, lacks evidence.

The Presumptive Relevance of the First Amendment

The subject of pornography is not coextensive with the subject of sex. Definitionally, pornography requires a portrayal, whether spoken, written, printed, photographed, sculpted, or drawn, and this essential feature of pornography necessarily implicates constitutional concerns that would not otherwise exist. The First Amendment to the Constitution of the United States provides quite simply that "Congress shall make no law . . . abridging the freedom of speech, or of the press." Longstanding judicial interpretations make it now clear that this mandate is, because of the Fourteenth Amendment, applicable to the states as well, and make it equally clear that the restrictions of the First Amendment are applicable to any form of governmental action, and not merely to statutes enacted by a legislative body.

To the extent, therefore, that regulation of pornography constitutes an abridgment of the freedom of speech, or an abridgment of the freedom of the press, it is at least presumptively unconstitutional. And even if some or all forms of regulation of pornography are seen ultimately not to constitute abridgments of the freedom of speech or the freedom of the press, the fact remains that the Constitution treats speaking and printing as special, and thus the regulation of anything spoken or printed must be examined with extraordinary care. For even when some forms of regulation of what is spoken or printed are not abridgments of the freedom of speech, or abridgments of the freedom of the press, such regulations are closer to constituting abridgments than other forms of governmental action. If nothing else, the barriers between permissible restrictions on what is said or printed and unconstitutional abridgments must be scrupulously guarded.

Thus, we start with the presumption that the First Amendment is germane to our inquiry, and we start as well with the presumption that, both as citizens and as governmental officials who have sworn an oath to uphold and defend the Constitution, we have independent responsibilities to consider constitutional issues in our deliberations and in our conclusions. Although we are not free to take actions that relevant Supreme Court interpretations of the Constitution tell us we cannot take, we do not consider Supreme Court opinions as relieving us of our own constitutional responsibilities. The view that constitutional concerns are only for the Supreme Court, or only for courts in general, is simply fallacious, and we do no service to the Constitution by adopting the view that the Constitution is someone else's responsibility. It is our responsibility, and we have treated it as such both in this Report and throughout our deliberation.

The First Amendment, the Supreme Court, and the Regulation of Obscenity

Although both speaking and printing are what the First Amendment is all about, closer examination reveals that the First Amendment cannot plausibly be taken to protect, or even to be relevant to, every act of speaking or writing. Government may plainly sanction the written acts of writing checks backed by insufficient funds, filing income tax returns that understate income or overstate deductions, and describing securities and consumer products in false or misleading terms. In none of these cases would First Amendment defenses even be taken seriously. The same can be said about sanctions against spoken acts such as lying while under oath, or committing most acts of criminal conspiracy. Although urging the public to rise up and overthrow the government is protected by the First Amendment, urging your brother to kill your father so that you can split the insurance money has never been considered the kind of spoken activity with which the First Amendment is concerned. Providing information to the public about the misdeeds of their political leaders is central to the First Amendment, but providing information to one's friends about the combination to the vault at the local bank is not a First Amendment matter at all.

The regulation of pornography, in light of the constraints of the First Amendment must thus be considered against this background—that not every use of words, pictures, or a printing press automatically triggers protection by the First Amendment. Indeed, as the examples above demonstrate, many uses of words, pictures, or a printing press do not even raise First Amendment concerns. As Justice Holmes stated the matter in 1919, "the First Amendment . . . cannot have been, and obviously was not, intended to give immunity for every possible use of language." As described in Chapter 2, both the states and the federal government have long regulated the trade in sexually explicit materials under the label of "obscenity" regulation. And until 1957, obscenity regulation was treated as one of those forms of regulation that was totally unrelated to the concerns or the constraints of the First Amendment. If the aim of the state or federal regulation was the control of obscenity, then the First Amendment did not restrict government action, without regard to what particular materials might be deemed obscene and thus prohibited. When, throughout the first half of this century, states would determine to be obscene such works as Theodore Dreiser's *An American Tragedy*, or D. H. Lawrence's *Lady Chatterley's Lover*, or Erskine Caldwell's *God's Little Acre*, or Radclyffe Hall's *The Well of Loneliness*, the First Amendment was not taken to constitute a significant barrier to such actions.

In 1957, however, in *Roth v. United States*, the Supreme Court confronted squarely the tension between the regulation of what was alleged to be obscene and the constraints of the First Amendment. After *Roth*, it is not simply the form of regulation that immunizes a prosecution from the First Amendment. The Court made clear in *Roth*, and even clearer in subsequent cases, that the simple designation of a prosecution as one for obscenity does not cause the First Amendment considerations to drop out. If the particular materials prosecuted are themselves protected by the First Amendment, the prosecution is impermissible. After *Roth* mere labels could not be used to justify restricting the protected, and mere labels could not justify circumventing the protections of the First Amendment.

But the Supreme Court also made clear in *Roth* that some materials were themselves outside of the coverage of the First Amendment, and that obscenity, carefully delineated, could be considered as "utterly without redeeming social importance." As a result, the Court concluded, obscene materials were not the kind of speech or press included within the First Amendment, and could thus be regulated without the kind of overwhelming evidence of harm that would be necessary if materials of this variety were included within the scope of the First Amendment. But to the Court in *Roth*, that scope was limited to material containing *ideas*. All ideas, even the unorthodox, even the controversial, and even the hateful, were within the scope of the First Amendment. But if there were no ideas with "even the slightest redeeming social importance," then such material could be taken to be not speech in the relevant sense at all, and therefore outside of the realm of the First Amendment.

The general *Roth* approach to obscenity regulation has been adhered to ever since 1957, and remains still today the foundation of the somewhat more complex but nevertheless fundamentally similar treatment of obscenity by the Supreme Court. This treatment involves two major principles. The first, reiterated repeatedly and explained most thoroughly in *Paris Adult Theatre I v. Slaton*, is the principle that legal obscenity is treated as being either not speech at all, or at least not the kind of speech that is within the purview of any of the diverse aims and principles of the First Amendment. As a result, legal obscenity may be regulated by the states and by the federal government without having to meet the especially stringent standards of justification, often generalized as a "clear and present danger," and occasionally as a "compelling interest," that would be applicable to speech, including a great deal of sexually oriented or sexually explicit speech, that is within the aims and principles of the First Amendment. Instead, legal obscenity may constitutionally be regulated as long as there exists merely a "rational basis" for the regulation, a standard undoubtedly drastically less stringent than the standard of "clear and present danger" or "compelling interest."

That legal obscenity *may* be regulated by the states and the federal government pursuant to *Roth* and *Paris* does not, of course, mean that the states *must* regulate it, or even that they necessarily *should* regulate it. It is in the nature of our constitutional system that most of what the Constitution does is to establish structures and to set up outer boundaries of permissible regulation, without in any way addressing what ought to be done within these outer boundaries. There is no doubt, for example, that the speed limits on the highways could be significantly reduced without offending the Constitution, that states could eliminate all penalties for burglary without violating the Constitution, and that the highest marginal income tax rate could be increased from fifty percent to ninety percent without creating a valid constitutional challenge. None of these proposals seems a particularly good idea, and that is precisely the point—that the fact that an action is constitutional does not mean that it is wise. Thus, although the regulation of obscenity is, as a result of *Roth*, *Paris*, and many other cases, constitutionally permissible, this does not answer the question whether such regulation is desirable. Wisdom or desirability are not primarily constitutional questions.

Thus the first major principle is the constitutional permissibility of the regulation of obscenity. The second major principle is that the *definition* of what is obscene, as well as the determination of what in particular cases is obscene, is itself a matter of constitutional law. If the underpinnings of the exclusion of obscenity from the scope of the First Amendment are that obscenity is not what the First Amendment is all about, then special care must be taken to ensure that materials, including materials dealing with sex, that are within what the First Amendment is all about are not subject to restriction. Although what is on the unprotected side of the line between the legally obscene and constitutionally protected speech is not protected by the First Amendment, the location of the line itself is a constitutional matter. That obscenity may be regulated consistent with the First Amendment does not mean that anything that is perceived by people or by legislatures as obscene may be so regulated.

As a result, the definition of obscenity is largely a question of constitutional law, and the current constitutionally permissible definition is found in another 1973 case, *Miller v. California*. According to *Miller*, material is obscene if all three of the following conditions are met:

1. The average person, applying contemporary community standards, would find that the work, taken as a whole, appeals to a prurient interest [in sex]; and
2. The work depicts or describes, in a patently offensive way, sexual conduct specifically defined by the applicable state [or federal] law; and
3. The work, taken as a whole, lacks serious literary, artistic, political, or scientific value.

It is not our function in this Report to provide an exposition of the law of obscenity. In a later part of this Report we do provide a much more detailed treatment of the current state of the law that we hope will be useful to those with a need to consider some of the details of obscenity law. But we do not wish our avoidance of extensive description of the law here to imply that the law is simple. Virtually every word or phrase in the *Miller* test has been the subject of extensive litigation and substantial commentary in the legal literature. The result of this is that there is now a large body of explanation and clarification of concepts such as "taken as a whole," "prurient interest," "patently offensive," "serious value," and "contemporary community standards." Moreover, there are many constitutionally mandated aspects of obscenity law that are not derived directly from the definition of obscenity. For example, no person may be prosecuted for an obscenity offense unless it can be shown that the person had knowledge of the general contents, character, and nature of the materials involved, for if the law were otherwise booksellers and others would avoid stocking anything even slightly sexually oriented for fear of being prosecuted on account of materials the content of which they were unaware. The procedures surrounding the initiation of a prosecution, including search and seizure, are also limited by constitutional considerations designed to prevent what would in effect be total suppression prior to a judicial determination of obscenity. And the entire subject of child pornography, which we discuss in Chapters 4 and 11, is governed by different principles and substantially different legal standards.

The constitutionally-based definition of obscenity is enforced not only by requiring that that definition be used in obscenity rials, but also, and more importantly, by close judicial scrutiny of materials determined to be obscene. This scrutiny, at both trial and appellate levels, is designed to ensure that nonobscene material is not erroneously determined to be obscene. The leading case here is the 1974 unanimous Supreme Court decision in *Jenkins v. Georgia*, which involved a conviction in Georgia of the Hollywood picture *Carnal Knowledge*. In reversing the conviction, the Supreme Court made clear that regardless of what the local community standards of that community may have been, the First Amendment prohibited *any* community, regardless of its standards, from finding that a motion picture such as this appealed to the prurient interest or was patently offensive. Thus, although appeal to the prurient interest and patent offensiveness are to be determined in the first instance by reference to local standards, it is clear after *Jenkins* that the range of local variation that the Supreme Court will permit consistent with the First Amendment is in fact quite limited.

In the final analysis, the effect of *Miller*, *Jenkins*, and a large number of other Supreme Court and lower court cases is to limit obscenity prosecutions to "hard core" material devoid of anything except the most explicit and offensive representations of sex. As we explained in our Introduction to this part, we believe that the late Justice Stewart was more perceptive than he has been given credit for having been in saying of hard-core pornography that he knew it when he saw it. Now that we have seen much of it, we are all confident that we too know it when we see it, but we also know that others have used this and other terms to encompass a range of materials wider than that which the Supreme Court permits to be restricted, and wider than that which most of us think ought to be restricted. But it should be plain both from the law, and from inspection of the kinds of material that the law has allowed to be prosecuted, that only the most thoroughly explicit materials, overwhelmingly devoted to patently offensive and explicit representations, and unmitigated by any significant amount of anything else, can be and are in fact determined to be legally obscene.

Is the Supreme Court Right?

We cannot ignore our own obligations not to recommend what we believe to be unconstitutional. Numerous people, in both oral and written evidence, have urged upon us the view that the Supreme Court's approach is a mistaken interpretation of the

First Amendment. They have argued that we should conclude that any criminal prosecution based on the distribution to consenting adults of sexually explicit material, no matter how offensive to some, and no matter how hard-core, and no matter how devoid of literary, artistic, political, or scientific value, is impermissible under the First Amendment.

We have taken these arguments seriously. In light of the facts that the Supreme Court did not in *Roth* or since unanimously conclude that obscenity is outside the coverage of the First Amendment, and that its 1973 rulings were all decided by a scant 5-4 majority on this issue, there is no doubt that the issue was debatable within the Supreme Court, and thus could hardly be without difficulty. Moreover, we recognize that the bulk of scholarly comment is of the opinion that the Supreme Court's resolution of and basic approach to the First Amendment issues is incorrect. With dissent existing even within the Supreme Court, and with disagreement with the Supreme Court majority's approach predominant among legal scholars, we could hardly ignore the possibility that the Supreme Court might be wrong on this issue, and that we would wish to find protected that which the Supreme Court found unprotected.

There are both less and more plausible challenges to the Supreme Court's approach to obscenity. Among the least plausible, and usually more rhetorical device than serious argument, is the view that the First Amendment is in some way an "absolute," protecting, quite simply, all speech. Even Justices Black and Douglas, commonly taken to be "absolutists," would hardly have protected all spoken or written acts under the First Amendment, and on closer inspection of all those accused of or confessing to "absolutism" would at the very least apply their absolutism to a range of spoken or written acts smaller than the universe of all spoken, written, or pictorial acts. This is not to deny that under the views of many, including Black and Douglas, what is now considered obscene should be within the universe of what is absolutely protected. But "absolutism" in unadulterated form seems largely a strawman, and we see no need to use it as a way of avoiding difficult questions.

Much more plausible is the view not that the First Amendment protects all spoken, written, or pictorial acts, but that all spoken, written, or pictorial acts are at least in some way covered, even if not ultimately protected, by the First Amendment. That is, even if the government may regulate some such acts, it may never do so unless it has a reason substantially better than the reasons that normally are sufficient to justify governmental action. Whether this heightened standard of justification is described as a "clear and present danger," or "compelling interest," or some standard less stringent than those, the view is still that regulating any spoken, written, or pictorial act requires a particularly good reason. And when applied to the regulation of obscenity, so the argument goes, the reasons supplied and the empirical evidence offered remain too speculative to meet this especially high burden of justification.

Other views accept the fact that not all spoken, written, or pictorial acts need meet this especially high burden of justification. Only those acts that in some way relate to the purposes or principles of the First Amendment are covered, but, it is argued, even the hardest-core pornographic item is within the First Amendment's coverage. To some this is because both the distribution and use of such items are significant aspects of self-expression. And while not all acts of self-expression are covered by the First Amendment, acts of self-expression that take the form of books, magazines, and films are, according to the argument, so covered. These, it is argued, are the traditional media of communication, and when those media are used to express a different world view, or even merely to achieve sexual satisfaction, they remain the kinds of things towards which the First Amendment is directed. As a result, regulation of the process by which an alternative sexual vision is communicated, or regulation of the process by which people use the traditional media of communication to experience and to understand a different sexual vision, is as much a part of the First Amendment as communicating and experiencing different visions about, for example, politics or morals. A variant on this last argument, which takes obscenity to be within the range of First Amendment coverage admittedly smaller than the universe of communicative acts, looks not so much to the act or to the communication but instead to the government's reasons for regulating. If, so the argument goes, government's action in restricting is based on its reaction to a particular point of view, then the action is impermissible. Because it is the purpose of the First Amendment to allow all points of view to be expressed, an attempt by government to treat one point of view less favorably than another is unconstitutional for that reason alone, no matter how dangerous, offensive, or otherwise reprehensible the disfavored point of view may be.

We have heard witnesses articulate these various views intelligently and forcefully, and we have read more extensive versions of these arguments. They are not implausible by any means, but in the final analysis we remain unpersuaded that the fundamental direction of *Roth* and *Paris* is misguided. Indeed, we are confident that it is correct. Although we do not subscribe to the view that only political speech is covered by the First Amendment, we do not believe that a totally expansive approach is reasonable for society or conducive to preserving the particular values embodied in the First Amendment. The special power of the First Amendment ought, in our opinion, to be reserved for the conveying of arguments and information in a way that surpasses some admittedly low threshold of cognitive appeal, whether that appeal be emotive, intellectual, aesthetic, or informational. We have no doubt that this low threshold will be surpassed by a wide range of sexually explicit material conveying unpopular ideas about sex in a manner that is offensive to most people, and we accept that this is properly part of a vision of the First Amendment that is designed substantially to protect unpopular ways of saying unpopular things. But we also have little doubt that most of what we have seen that to us qualifies as hard-core material falls below this minimal threshold of cognitive or similar appeal. Lines are of course not always easy to draw, but we find it difficult to understand how much of the material we have seen can be considered to be even remotely related to an exchange of views in the marketplace of ideas, to an attempt to articulate a point of view, to an attempt to persuade, or to an attempt seriously to convey through literary or artistic means a different vision of humanity or of the world. We do not deny that in a different context and presented in a different way, material as explicit as that which we have seen could be said to contain at least some of all of these characteristics. But we also have no doubt that these goals are remote from the goals of virtually all distributors or users of this material, and we also have no doubt that these values are present in most standard pornographic items to an extraordinarily limited degree.

In light of this, we are of the opinion that not only society at large but the First Amendment itself suffers if the essential appeal of the First Amendment is dissipated on arguments related to material so tenuously associated with any of the purposes or principles of the First Amendment. We believe it necessary that the plausibility of the First Amendment be protected, and we believe it equally necessary for this society to ensure that the First Amendment retains the strength it must have when it is most needed.

This strength cannot reside exclusively in the courts, but must reside as well in widespread acceptance of the importance of the First Amendment. We fear that this acceptance is jeopardized when the First Amendment too often becomes the rhetorical device by which the commercial trade in materials directed virtually exclusively to sexual arousal is defended. There is a risk that in that process public willingness to defend and to accept the First Amendment will be lost, and the likely losers will be those who would speak out harshly, provocatively, and often offensively against the prevailing order, including the prevailing order with respect to sex. The manner of presentation and distribution of most standard pornography confirms the view that at bottom the predominant use of such material is as a masturbatory aid. We do not say that there is anything necessarily wrong with that for that reason. But once the predominant use, and the appeal to that predominant use, becomes apparent, what emerges is that much of what this material involves is not so much a portrayal of sex, or discussion of sex, but simply sex itself. As sex itself, the arguments for or against restriction are serious, but they are arguments properly removed from the First Amendment questions that surround primarily materials whose overwhelming use is not as a short-term masturbatory aid. Whether the state should, for example, prohibit masturbation in certain establishments that are open to the public is a question that some would wish to debate, but it is certainly not a First Amendment question. Similarly, the extent to which sex itself is and under what circumstances constitutionally protected is again an interesting and important constitutional question, but it is not usefully seen as a First Amendment question.

We recognize, of course, that using a picture of sex as a masturbatory aid is different from the simple act of masturbation, or any other form of sex. The very fact that pictures and words are used compels us to take First Amendment arguments more seriously than would be the case if the debate were about prostitution. Still, when we look at the standard pornographic item in its standard context of distribution and use, we find it difficult to avoid the conclusion that this material is so far removed from any of the central purposes of the First Amendment, and so close to so much of the rest of the sex industry, that including such material within the coverage of the First Amendment seems highly attenuated.

Like any other act, the act of making, distributing, and using pornographic items contains and sends messages. For government to act against some of these items on account of the messages involved may appear as problematic under the First Amendment, but to hold that such governmental action violates the First Amendment is to preclude government from taking action in every case in which government fears that the restricted action will be copied, or proliferate because of its acceptance. Government may prosecute scofflaws because it fears the message that laws ought to be violated, and it may restrict the use of certain products in part because it does not wish the message that the product is desirable to be widely disseminated in perhaps its most effective form. So too with reference to the kind of material with which we deal here. If we are correct in our conclusion that this material is far removed from the cognitive, emotive, aesthetic, informational, persuasive, or intellectual core of the First Amendment, we are satisfied that a governmental desire to restrict the material for the messages its use sends out does not bring the material any closer to the center.

We thus conclude not that obscenity regulation creates no First Amendment concerns, nor even that the Supreme Court's approach is necessarily correct. But we do believe the Supreme Court's approach is most likely correct, and we believe as well that arguments against the Supreme Court's approach are becoming increasingly attenuated as we focus on the kind of material commonly sold in "adults only" establishments in this country. We may be wrong, but most of us can see no good reason at the moment for substituting a less persuasive approach for the Supreme Court's more persuasive one.

The Risks of Abuse

Although we are satisfied that there is a category of material so overwhelmingly preoccupied with sexual explicitness, and so overwhelming devoid of anything else, that its regulation does no violence to the principles underlying the First Amendment, we recognize that this cannot be the end of the First Amendment analysis. We must evaluate the possi-bility that in practice materials other than these will be restricted, and that the effect therefore will be the restriction of materials that are substantially closer to what the First Amendment ought to protect than the items in fact aimed at by the *Miller* definition of obscenity. We must also evaluate what is commonly

referred to as the "chilling effect," the possibility that, even absent actual restriction, creators of material that is not in fact legally obscene will refrain from those creative activities, or will steer further to the safe side of the line, for fear that their protected works will mistakenly be deemed obscene. And finally we must evaluate whether the fact or restriction of obscene material will act, symbolically, to foster a "censorship mentality" that will in less immediate ways encourage or lead to various restrictions, in other contexts, of material which ought not in a free society be restricted. We have heard in one form or another from numerous organizations of publishers, booksellers, actors, and librarians, as well as from a number of individual book and magazine publishers. Although most have urged general anticensorship sentiments upon us, their oral and written submissions have failed to provide us with evidence to support claims of excess suppression in the name of obscenity laws, and indeed the evidence is to the contrary. The president of the Association of American Publishers testified that to his knowledge none of his members had even been threatened with enforcement of the criminal law against obscenity, and the American Library Association could find no record of any prosecution of a librarian on obscenity charges. Other groups of people involved in publishing, bookselling, or theatrical organizations relied exclusively on examples of excess censorship from periods of time no more recent than the 1940s. And still others were even less helpful, telling us, for example, that censorship was impermissible because "This is the United States, not the Soviet Union." We know that, but we know as well that difficult issues do not become easy by the use of inflammatory rhetoric. We wish that many of these people or groups had been able to provide concrete examples to support their fears of excess censorship.

Throughout recent and not so recent history, excess censorship, although not necessarily prevalent, can hardly be said not to have occurred. As a result we have not been content to rest on the hollowness of the assertions of many of those who have reminded us of this theme. If there is a problem, we have our own obligations to identify it, even if witnesses before us have been unable to do so. Yet when we do our own researches, we discover that, with few exceptions, the period from 1974 to the present is marked by strikingly few actual or threatened prosecutions of material that is plainly not legally obscene. We do not say that there have been none. Attempted and unsuccessful actions against the film *Caligula* by the United States Custom Service, against *Playboy* magazine in Atlanta and several other places, and against some other plainly nonobscene publications indicate that mistakes can be made. But since 1974 such mistakes have been extremely rare, and the mistakes have all been remedied at some point in the process. While we wish there would be no mistakes, we are confident that application of *Miller* has been overwhelmingly limited to materials that would satisfy everyone's definition of "hard core."

Even without successful or seriously threatened prosecutions, it still may be the case that the very possibility of such an action deters filmmakers, photographers, and writers from exercising their creative abilities to the fullest. Once it appears that the likelihood of actual or seriously threatened prosecutions is almost completely illusory, however, we are in a quandary about how to respond to these claims of "chilling." We are in no position to deny the reality of someone's fears, but in almost every case those fears are unfounded. Where, as here, the fears seem to be fears of phantom dangers, we are hard pressed to say that the law is mistaken. It is those who are afraid who are mistaken. At least for the past ten years, not one remotely serious author, photographer, or filmmaker has had anything real to fear from the obscenity laws. The line between what is legally obscene and what is not is now so far away from their work that even substantially mistaken applications of current law would leave these individuals untouched. In light of that, we do not see their fears, however real to them, as a sufficient reason now to reconsider our views about the extent of First Amendment protection.

Much more serious, much more real, and much less in our control, is the extent to which nongovernmental or governmental but nonprohibitory actions may substantially influence what is published and what is not. What television scriptwriters write is in reality controlled by what television producers will buy, which is in turn controlled by what sponsors will sponsor and what viewers will view. Screenwriters may be effectively censored by the extent to which producers or studios desire to gain an "R" rating rather than an "X," or a "PG" rather than "R," or an "R" rather than a "PG." Book and magazine writers and publishers are restricted by what stores are willing to sell, and stores are restricted by what people are willing to buy. Writers of textbooks are in a sense censored by what school districts are willing

to buy, authors are censored by what both bookstores and librarians are willing to offer, and librarians are censored by what boards of trustees are willing to tolerate.

In all of these settings there have been excesses. But every one of these settings involves some inevitable choice based on content. We think it unfortunate when *Catcher in the Rye* is unavailable in a high school library, but none of us would criticize the decision to keep *Lady Chatterley's Lover*, plainly protected by the First Amendment, out of the junior high schools.

We regret that legitimate bookstores have been pressured to remove from their shelves legitimate and serious discussions of sexuality, but none of us would presume to tell a Catholic bookseller that in choosing books he should not discriminate against books favoring abortion. Motion picture studios are unable to support an infinite number of screenwriters, and their choice to support those who write about families rather than homosexuality, for instance, is not only permissible, but is indeed itself protected by the First Amendment.

Where there have been excesses, and we do not ignore the extent to which the number of those excesses seems to be increasing, they seem often attributable to the plainly mistaken notion that the idea of "community standards" is a carte blanche to communities to determine entirely for themselves what is obscene. As we have tried once again to make clear in this report, nothing could be further from the truth. Apart from this, however, the excesses that have been reported to us are excesses that can only remotely be attributed to the obscenity laws. In a world of choice and of scarce resources, every one of these excesses could take place even were there no obscenity laws at all. In a world without obscenity law, television producers, motion picture studios, public library trustees, boards of education, convenience stores, and bookstores could still all choose to avoid any mention or discussion of sex entirely. And in a world without obscenity laws, all of these institutions and others could and would still make censorious choices based on their own views about politics, morals, religion, or science. Thus, the link between obscenity law and the excess narrowness, at times, of the choices made by private industry as well as government is far from direct.

Although the link is not direct, we are in no position to deny that there may be some psychological connection between obscenity laws and their enforcement and a general perception that nongovernmental restriction of anything dealing with sex is justifiable. We find the connection unjustifiable, but that is not to say that it may not exist in the world. But just as vigorous and vocal enforcement of robbery laws may create the environment in which vigilantes feel justified in punishing offenders outside the legal process, so too may obscenity law create an environment in which discussions of sexuality are effectively stifled. But we cannot ignore the extent to which much of this stifling, to the extent it exists, is no more than the exercise by citizens of their First Amendment rights to buy what they want to buy, and the exercise by others of First Amendment rights to sell or make what they wish. Choices are not always exercised wisely, but the leap from some unwise choices to the unconstitutionality of criminal laws only remotely related to those unwise choices is too big a leap for us to make.

Discussion Questions

1. What are some of the examples the commission cites in order to show that the First Amendment is not absolute? Do you think it makes its point? Why or why not?

2. How does the commission differentiate between pornography and obscenity? Why is not all obscenity pornography and all pornography obscenity? Explain.

3. What is the importance of the U.S. Supreme Court's decision *Roth v. United States* (1957)? How did it change the way the law dealt with the issue of pornography and censorship?

4. According to the commission, what are the two major principles in justifying regulation of obscenity? Present and explain each principle. How does the commission defend each?

5. What is the U.S. Supreme Court's view on the right of the government to restrict pornography? Present and explain the Court's three-part standard to determine obscenity as found in *Miller v. California* (1973). Do you agree or disagree with the court? Explain and defend your answer.

6. Why does the commission believe that those who claim that restricting pornography will lead to abuse are wrong? Explain and present their case. Do you agree or disagree? Explain and defend your answer.

44

The Sexual Politics of the First Amendment

Catharine MacKinnon

Catharine MacKinnon is Professor of Law at the University of Michigan Law School in Ann Arbor, Michigan. She is known for her application of feminist theory to American jurisprudence, especially in the areas of reproductive rights and pornography. She has contributed to many scholarly journals and anthologies, as well as producing several books, including *Only Words* (1993) and *Feminism Unmodified* (1987).

In this essay Professor MacKinnon contends that the use of the First Amendment to defend pornography is illegitimate, since it is being used to support an activity that abuses women by violating their dignity as well as aiding and abetting a climate in society that results in the rape of and unjust discrimination against women. Professor MacKinnon is arguing against those she calls the First Amendment absolutists who, in her opinion, use the Constitution to maintain their power and dominance over women. She maintains that it is morally obligatory, in order to move toward a society in which men and women are equal, to forbid the trafficking of pornography as well as to pass legislation that allows women to file civil suits against pornographers, because pornography, she believes, violates the civil rights of women. In defending her position, Professor MacKinnon draws an analogy between the *Dred Scott* (1856) decision, in which the U.S. Supreme Court asserted that black slaves were mere property, and the Supreme Court's decision (106 S. Ct. 1172 [1986]) that struck down an antipornography ordinance she and Andrea Dworkin had helped

Reprinted by permission from Catharine MacKinnon, *Feminism Unmodified* (Cambridge: Harvard University Press, 1987).

draft: it reduced women to mere speech just as *Dred Scott* had reduced blacks to mere property.

[The Dred Scott case] was a law to be cited, a lesson to be learned, judicial vigor to be emulated, political imprudence to be regretted, but most of all, as time passed—it was an embarrassment—the Court's highly visible skeleton in a transparent closet.

> —Don E. Ferrenbacher, *The Dred Scott Case: Its Significance in American Law and Politics*

Frankfurter is said to have remarked that Dred Scott was never mentioned by the Supreme Court any more than ropes and scaffolds were mentioned by a family that had lost one of its number to the hangman.

> —Bruce Catton, in John A. Garraty, ed., *Quarrels That Have Shaped the Constitution*

The Constitution of the United States, contrary to any impression you may have received, is a piece of paper with words written on it. Because it is old, it is considered a document. When it is interpreted by particular people under particular conditions, it becomes a text. Because it is backed up by the power of the state, it is a law.

Feminism, by contrast, springs from the impulse to self-respect in every woman. From this have come some fairly elegant things: a metaphysics of mind, a theory of knowledge, an approach to ethics, and a concept of social action. Aspiring to the point of view of all women on social life as a whole, feminism has expressed itself as a political movement for civil equality.

Looking at the Constitution through the lens of feminism, initially one sees exclusion of women from the Constitution. This is simply to say that we had no voice in the constituting document of this state. From that one can suppose that those who did constitute it may not have had the realities of our situation in mind.

Next one notices that the Constitution as interpreted is structured around what can generically be called the public, or state action. This constituting document pervasively assumes that those guarantees of freedoms that must be secured to citizens begin where law begins, with the public order. This posture is exalted as "negative liberty"[1] and is a cornerstone of the liberal state. You notice this from the feminist standpoint because women are oppressed socially, prior to law, without express state acts, often in intimate contexts. For women this structure means that those domains in which women are distinctly subordinated are assumed by the Constitution to be the domain of freedom.

Finally, combining these first two observations, one sees that women are not given affirmative access to those rights we need most. Equality, for example. Equality, in the words of Andrea Dworkin, was tacked on to the Constitution with spit and a prayer. And, let me also say, late.

If we apply these observations to the First Amendment, our exclusion means that the First Amendment was conceived by white men from the point of view of their social position. Some of them owned slaves; most of them owned women.[2] They wrote it to guarantee their freedom to keep something they felt at risk of losing.[3] Namely—and this gets to my next point—speech which they did not want to lose through state action. They wrote the First Amendment so their speech would not be threatened by this powerful instrument they were creating, the federal government. You recall it reads, "Congress shall make no law abridging . . . the freedom of speech." They were *creating* that body. They were worried that it would abridge something they *did have*. You can tell that they had speech, because what they said was written down: it became a document, it has been interpreted, it is the law of the state.[4]

By contrast with those who wrote the First Amendment so they could keep what they had, those who didn't have it didn't get it. Those whose speech was silenced prior to law, prior to any operation of the state's prohibition of it, were not secured freedom of speech. Their speech was not regarded as something that had to be—and this gets to my next point—affirmatively guaranteed. Looking at the history of the First Amendment from this perspective, reprehensible examples of state attempts to suppress speech exist. But they constitute a history of comparative privilege in contrast with the history of silence of those whose speech has ever been able to exist for the state even to contemplate abridging it.

A few affirmative guarantees of access to speech do exist. The *Red Lion* decision is one, although it may be slated for extinction.[5] Because certain avenues of speech are inherently restricted—for instance, there are only so many broadcast frequencies—according to the *Red Lion* doctrine of fairness in access to broadcast media, some people's access has to be restricted in the interest of providing access to all. In other words, the speech of those who could buy up all the

speech there is, is restricted. Conceptually, this doctrine works exactly like affirmative action. The speech of those who might be the only ones there, is not there, so that others' can be.

With a few exceptions like that[6] we find no guarantees of access to speech. Take, for example, literacy. Even after it became clear that the Constitution applied to the states, nobody argued that the segregation of schools that created inferior conditions of access to literacy for Blacks violated their First Amendment rights. Or the slave codes that made it a crime to teach a slave to read and write or to advocate their freedom.[7] Some of those folks who struggled for civil rights for Black people must have thought of this, but I never heard their lawyers argue it. If access to the means of speech is effectively socially precluded on the basis of race or class or gender, freedom from state burdens on speech does not meaningfully guarantee the freedom to speak.

The First Amendment absolutism, the view that speech must be absolutely protected, is not the law of the First Amendment. It is the conscience, the superego of the First Amendment, the implicit standard from which all deviations must be justified. It is also an advocacy position typically presented in debate as if it were legal fact. Consider for example that First Amendment bog, the distinction between speech and conduct. Most conduct is expressive as well as active; words are as often tantamount to acts as they are vehicles for removed cerebration. Case law knows this.[8] But the first question, the great divide, the beginning and the end, is still the absolutist question, "Is it speech or isn't it?"

First Amendment absolutism was forged in the crucible of obscenity litigation. Probably its most inspired expositions, its most passionate defenses, are to be found in Justice Douglas's dissents in obscenity cases.[9] This is not coincidence. Believe him when he says that pornography is at the core of the First Amendment. Absolutism has developed through obscenity litigation, I think, because pornography's protection fits perfectly with the power relations embedded in the First Amendment structure and jurisprudence from the start. Pornography is exactly that speech of men that silences the speech of women. I take it seriously when Justice Douglas speaking on pornography and others preaching absolutism say that pornography has to be protected speech or else free expression will not mean what it has always meant in this country.

I must also say that the First Amendment has become a sexual fetish through years of absolutist writing in the melodrama mode in *Playboy* in particular. You know those superheated articles where freedom of speech is extolled and its imminent repression is invoked. Behaviorally, *Playboy*'s consumers are reading about the First Amendment, masturbating to the women, reading about the First Amendment, masturbating to the women, reading about the First Amendment, masturbating to the women. It makes subliminal seduction look subtle. What is conveyed is not only that using women is as legitimate as thinking about the Constitution, but also that if you don't support these views about the Constitution, you won't be able to use these women.

This general approach affects even religious groups. I love to go speaking against pornography when the sponsors dig up some religious types, thinking they will make me look bad because they will agree with me. Then the ministers come on and say, "This is the first time we've ever agreed with the ACLU about anything . . . why, what she's advocating would *violate the First Amendment*." This isn't their view universally, I guess, but it has been my experience repeatedly, and I have personally never had a minister support me on the air. One of them finally explained it. The First Amendment, he said, also guarantees the freedom of religion. So this is not only what we already know: regardless of one's politics and one's moral views, one is into using women largely. It is also that, consistent with this, First Amendment absolutism resonates historically in the context of the long-term collaboration in misogyny between church and state. Don't let them tell you they're "separate" in that.

In pursuit of absolute freedom of speech, the ACLU has been a major institution in defending, and now I describe their behavior, the Nazis, the Klan, and the pornographers. I am waiting for them to add the antiabortionists, including the expressive conduct of their violence. Think about one of their favorite metaphors, a capitalist metaphor, the marketplace of ideas. Think about whether the speech of the Nazis has historically enhanced the speech of the Jews. Has the speech of the Klan expanded the speech of Blacks? Has the so-called speech of the pornographers enlarged the speech of women? In this context, apply to what they call the marketplace of ideas the question we were asked to consider in the keynote speech by Winona LaDuke: Is there a relationship between our poverty in speech and their wealth?

As many of you know, Andrea Dworkin and I, with a lot of others, have been working to establish a law that recognizes pornography as a violation of the civil rights of women in particular. It recognizes that pornography is a form of sex discrimination. Recently, in a fairly unprecedented display of contempt, the U.S. Supreme Court found that the Indianapolis version of our law violates the First Amendment.[10] On a direct appeal, the Supreme Court invalidated a local ordinance by summary affirmance—no arguments, no briefs on the merits, no victims, no opinion, not so much as a single line of citation to controlling precedent. One is entitled to think that they would have put one there if they had had one.

The Court of Appeals opinion they affirmed[11] expressly concedes that pornography violates women in all the ways Indianapolis found it did. The opinion never questioned that pornography is sex discrimination. Interesting enough, the Seventh Circuit, in an opinion by Judge Frank Easterbrook, conceded the issue of objective causation. The only problem was, the harm didn't matter as much as the materials mattered. They are valuable. So the law that prohibited the harm the materials caused was held to be content-based and impermissible discrimination on the basis of viewpoint.

This is a law that gives victims a civil action when they are coerced into pornography, when pornography is forced upon them, when they are assaulted because of specific pornography, and when they are subordinated through the trafficking of pornography. Some of us thought that sex discrimination and sexual abuse were against public policy. We defined pornography as the sexually explicit subordination of women through pictures or words that also includes presentations of women being sexually abused. There is a list of the specific acts of sexual abuse. The law covers men, too. We were so careful that practices whose abusiveness some people publicly question—for example, submission, servility, and display—are not covered by the trafficking provision. So we're talking rape, torture, pain, humiliation: we're talking violence against women turned into sex.

Now we are told that pornography, which, granted, does the harm we say it does, this pornography as we define it is protected speech. It has speech value. You can tell it has value as speech because it is so effective in doing the harm that it does.[12] (The passion of this rendition is mine, but the opinion really does say this.) The more harm, the more protection. This is now apparently the law of the First Amendment, at least where harm to women is the rationale. Judge LaDoris Cordell spoke earlier about the different legal standards for high-value and low-value speech, a doctrine that feminists who oppose pornography have always been averse to. But at least it is now clear that whatever the value of pornography is—and it is universally conceded to be low—the value of women is lower.

It is a matter of real interest to me exactly what the viewpoint element in our law is, according to Easterbrook's opinion. My best guess is that our law takes the point of view that women do not enjoy and deserve rape, and he saw that as just one point of view among many. Where do you suppose he got that idea? Another possible rendering is that our law takes the position that women should not be subordinated to men on the basis of sex, that women are or should be equal, and he regards relief to that end as the enforcement of a prohibited view.

Just what is and is not valuable, is and is not a viewpoint, is and is not against public policy was made even clearer the day after the summary affirmance. In the *Renton* case the Supreme Court revealed the conditions under which pornography can be restricted: it can be zoned away beyond the city limits.[13] It can be regulated this way on the basis of its "secondary effects"—which are, guess what, property values. But it cannot be regulated on the basis of its primary effects on the bodies of the women who had to be ground up to make it.

Do you think it makes any difference to the woman who is coerced into pornography or who has just hit the end of this society's chances for women that the product of her exploitation is sold on the other side of the tracks? Does it matter to the molested child or the rape victim that the offender who used the pornography to get himself up or to plan what he would do or to decide what "type" to do it to had to drive across town to get it? It *does* matter to the women who live or work in the neighborhoods into which pornography is zoned. They pay in increased street harassment, in an atmosphere of terror and contempt for what other neighborhoods gain in keeping their property values up.

Reading the two decisions together, you see the Court doing what it has always done with pornography: making it available in private while decrying it in public. Pretending to be tough on pornography's effects, the *Renton* case still *gives it a place to exist*. Although obscenity is supposed to have such little value that it is not considered speech at all, *Renton* exposes the real bottom line of the First Amendment: the pornography stays. Anyone who doesn't think absolutism has made any progress, check that.

Why is it that obscenity law can exist and our trafficking provision cannot? Why can the law against child pornography exist and not our law against coercion? Why aren't obscenity[14] and child pornography[15] laws viewpoint laws? Obscenity, as Justice Brennan pointed out in his dissent in *Renton*, expresses a viewpoint: sexual mores should be more relaxed, and if they were, sex would look like pornography.[16] Child pornography also presents a viewpoint: sex between adults and children is liberating, fulfilling, fun, and natural for the child. If one is concerned about the government taking a point of view through law, the laws against these things express the state's opposition to these viewpoints, to the extent of making them crimes to express. Why is a time-place-manner distinction all right in *Renton*, and not our forcing provision, which is kind of time-and-place-like and does not provide actions against the pornographers at all? Why is it all right to make across-the-board, content-based distinctions like obscenity and child pornography, but not our trafficking provision, not our coercion provision?

When do you see a viewpoint as a viewpoint? When you don't agree with it. When is a viewpoint not a viewpoint? When it's yours.[17] What is and is not a viewpoint, much less a prohibited one, is a matter of individual values and social consensus. The reason Judge Easterbrook saw a viewpoint in our law was because he disagrees with it. (I don't mean to personify it, because it isn't at all personal; I mean it *is* him, personally, but it isn't him only or only him, as a person.) There is real social disagreement as to whether women are or should be subordinated to men. Especially in sex.

His approach obscured the fact that our law is not content-based at all; it is harm-based. A harm is an act, an activity. It is not just a mental event. Coercion is not an image. Force is not a representation. Assault is not a symbol. Trafficking is not simply advocacy. Subordination is an activity, not just a point of view. The problem is, pornography is both theory and practice, both a metaphor for and a means of the subordination of women. The Seventh Circuit allowed the fact that pornography has a theory to obscure the fact that it is a practice, the fact that it is a metaphor to obscure the fact that it is also a means.

I don't want you to misunderstand what I am about to say. Our law comes nowhere near anybody's speech rights,[18] and the literatures of other inequalities do not relate to those inequalities in the same way pornography relates to sexism. But I risk your misunderstanding on both of these points in order to say that there have been serious movements of liberation in this world. This is by contrast with liberal movements. In serious movements for human freedom, speech is serious, both the attempt to get some for those who do not have any and the recognition that the so-called speech of the other side is a form of the practice of the other side. In union struggles, yellow-dog presses are attacked.[19] Abolitionists attacked slave presses.[20] The monarchist press was not tolerated by the revolutionaries who founded this country.[21] When the White Circle League published a racist pamphlet, it was found to violate a criminal law against libeling groups.[22] After World War II the Nazi press was restricted in Germany by law under the aegis of the Allies.[23] Nicaragua considers it "immoral" and contrary to the progress of education and the cultural development of the people to publish, distribute, circulate, exhibit, transmit, or sell materials that, among other things, "stimulate viciousness," "lower human dignity," or to "use women as sexual or commercial objects."[24]

The analogy Norma Ramos mentioned between the fight against pornography to sex equality and the fight against segregation to race equality makes the analogy between the Indianapolis case and *Brown v. Board of Education*[25] evocative to me also. But I think we may be at an even prior point. The Supreme Court just told us that it is a constitutional right to traffic in our flesh, so long as it is done through pictures and words, and a legislature may not give us access to court to contest it. The Indianapolis case is the *Dred Scott*[26] of the women's movement. The Supreme Court told Dred Scott, to the Constitution, you are property. It told women, to the Constitution, you are speech. The struggle against pornography is an abolitionist struggle to establish that just as buying and selling human beings never was anyone's property right, buying and selling women and children is no one's civil liberty.

Discussion Questions

1. Professor MacKinnon maintains that pornography is an instance of sex discrimination, and thus a violation of the civil rights of women. How does she support this position? Do you agree or disagree with her case? Explain and defend your answer.

2. Professor MacKinnon draws an analogy between the *Dred Scott* decision and the Court decision that struck down an antipornography ordinance she and Andrea Dworkin had helped draft. How does she support this analogy? Do you think she succeeds? Why or why not? Explain and defend your answer.

3. Professor MacKinnon critiques the opinion of the U.S. Supreme Court that struck down an Indianapolis ordinance she helped draft. What court of appeals decision did the Supreme Court affirm? And what points and concessions in that decision, which Professor MacKinnon believes are germane to her case, were not considered by the Supreme Court? What are her main points against the Court's opinion? Do you think she succeeds in making her case? Why or why not? Explain and defend your answer.

Notes

1. Isaiah Berlin distinguishes negative from positive freedom. Negative freedom asks the question, "what is the area within which the subject—a person or group of persons—is or should be left to do or be what [he] is able to do or be, without interference from other persons?" Positive freedom asks the question, "what, or who, is the source of control or interference that can determine someone to do, or be, this rather than that?" "Two Concepts of Liberty," in *Four Essays on Liberty* 121–22 (1970). Is it not obvious that if one group is granted the positive freedom to do whatever they want to another group, to determine that the second group will be and do this rather than that, that no amount of negative freedom guaranteed to the second group will make it the equal of the first? The negative state is thus incapable of effective guarantees of rights in any but a just society, which is the society in which they are needed the least.

2. The analysis here is indebted to Andrea Dworkin, "For Men, Freedom of Speech, For Women, Silence Please" in *Take Back the Night: Women on Pornography* 255–58 (Laura Lederer ed. 1982).

3. *But cf.* the words of framer William Livingston, who said, "Liberty of the press means promoting the common good of society, it does not mean unrestraint in writing." Livingston, "Of the Use, Abuse and Liberty of the Press," *Independent Reflector* (1754), quoted in Richard Buel, *The Press and the American Revolution* 69 (1980). Livingston's press as founded "to oppose superstition, bigotry, priestcraft, tyranny, servitude, public mismanagement and dishonesty in office." Quoted in Leonard W. Levy, *Emergence of a Free Press* 138 (1985). Levy, an absolutist, finds the theory that gave rise to the *Independent Reflector* "in fact reactionary if not vicious . . . That a Framer could ever have held such views surprises" at 138.

4. There is a major controversy about the intent of the framers in relation to existing law and values of the colonial period. The controversy is discussed in T. Terrar, "The New Social History and Colonial America's Press Legacy: Tyranny or Freedom?" (1986) (unpublished manuscript).

5. Red Lion Broadcasting Co. v. F.C.C., 395 U.S. 367 (1969). In F.C.C. v. League of Women Voters, 468 U.S. 364 (1984), the Supreme Court hints that it would be receptive to a challenge to the fairness doctrine on the basis that it impedes rather than furthers the values of the First Amendment, 376 n. 11, 378 n. 12.

6. Schneider v. State, 308 U.S. 174 (1939) (restricting street circulars because of litter is invalid if it is possible to clean them up).

7. Slave codes prohibited teaching slaves or free Blacks to read, write, or spell and giving them reading materials and permitting meetings for schooling. Punishment for Blacks included whipping; whites caught in the act could be fined and imprisoned but never whipped. Alabama: *Clay's Digest* 543, Act of 1832, § 10 (crime to teach Black to spell, read, or write); North Carolina: *Revised Statutes* ch. 3, § 74 (1836–7) (crime to teach slave to read or write, except figures, to give or sell to a slave a book or pamphlet); ch. 3, § 27 (slave who receives instruction receives thirty-nine lashes); Georgia: 2 *Cobb's Digest* 1001 (1829) (crime to teach Black to read or write); Virginia: "Every assemblage of Negroes for the purpose of instruction in reading or writing shall be an unlawful assembly." *Virginia Code*, §§ 747–48 (1849); South Carolina: meetings including even one person of color "for the purpose of mental instruction in a confined or secret place are declared to be an unlawful meeting." Police can "break doors" and may lash participants sufficiently to deter them from future such acts. 7 *Statutes of South Carolina* 440 (1800). See *generally* George M. Stroud, *Sketch of the Laws Relating to Slavery* 58–63 (1856, 1968 ed.). The slaves understood that literacy was as fundamental to effective expression as it was to every other benefit of equality: "It seemed to me that if I could learn to read and write, the learning might—nay I really thought it would, point out to me the way to freedom, influence, and real, secure, happiness." Slave narrative quoted in Thomas L. Webber, *Deep Like the Rivers: Education in the Slave Quarter Community* 144 (1978). The Statutes of Louisiana 208 (1852) state: "Whosoever shall make use of language in any public discourse from the bar, the bench, the stage, the pulpit, or in any place whatsoever, or whoever shall make use of language in private discourses or conversations, or shall make use of signs or actions, having a tendency to produce discontent among the free colored population of this state, or to excite insubordination among the slaves, or whosoever shall knowingly be instrumental in bringing into this state any paper, pamphlet or book having such tendency as aforesaid, shall, on conviction thereof before any court of competent jurisdiction, suffer imprisonment at hard labour not less than three years nor more than twenty-one years, or DEATH, at the discretion of the court" at 208.

8. The best examples are the laws against treason, bribery, conspiracy, threats, blackmail, and libel. Acts can also be expression, but are not necessarily protected as such. See, *e.g.*, Gilboney v. Empire Storage & Ins. Co., 336 U.S. 490 (1946) (labor picketing can be enjoined on the ground the First Amendment does not cover "speech or writing used as an integral part of conduct in violation of a valid criminal statute"). Action "is often a method of expression and within the protection of the First Amendment . . ." but "picketing [is] 'free speech plus' [and] can be regulated when it comes to the 'plus' or 'action' side of the protest. Brandenburg v. Ohio, 395 U.S. 444, 455 (1969) (Douglas, J., concurring). *See also* United States v. O'Brien, 391 U.S. 367 (1968) (burning draft card not protected speech as symbolic protest); Street v. New York, 394 U.S. 576 (1969) (burning flag while speaking not punishable because speech is protected even though burning is crime); Spence v. Washington, 418 U.S. 407 (1974) (altering flag is protected speech despite flag desecration statute); Clark v. Committee for Creative Non-Violence, 468 U.S. 288 (1984) (sleeping in park to protest homelessness not protected as expressive conduct when it violates regulation against camping).

9. Roth v. U.S., 354 U.S. 476, 508–14 ("The first amendment, in prohibitions in terms absolute" at 514); Memoirs v. Massachusetts, 383 U.S. 413, 424–33 (concurring); Miller v. California, 413 U.S. 15, 37–47; Paris Adult Theatres v. Slaton, 413 U.S. 49, 70–73 (1973).

10. 106 S. Ct. 1172 (1986).

11. American Booksellers v. Hudnut, 771 F.2d 323 (7th Cir. 1985), aff'd 106 S. Ct. 1172 (1986).

12. 771 F.2d at 329.

13. Renton v. Playtime Theatres, 106 S.Ct. 925 (1986).

14. *E.g.*, Miller v. California, 413 U.S. 15 (1973).

15. *E.g.*, New York v. Ferber, 458 U.S. 747 (1982).

16. 106 S.Ct. at 933 n.1 (Brennan, J., dissenting).

17. Laws against rape also express the view that sexual subordination is impermissible, and this is not considered repressive of thought, although presumably some thought is involved.

18. An erection is not a thought either, unless one thinks with one's penis.

19. The most celebrated and equivocal example is the prosecution of unionist McNamara brothers for blowing up the virulently antiunion *Los Angeles Times*. The McNamaras pleaded guilty but doubt remains whether they did it. Although the bombing was criticized as inhumane (many people died), needlessly destructive, and instrategic, I found no argument within the movement that the *Times* should not have been attacked because it was "speech." See P. Foner, *History of the Labor Movement in the United States*, vol. 5: *The AFL in the Progressive Era, 1910–1915* ch. 1 (1980).

20. Abraham Lincoln ordered "copperhead" (northern pro-slavery) newspapers closed and editors jailed during the Civil War. The postmaster general barred some "copperhead" newspapers from the mail. Abolitionists "threatened, manhandled, or tarred editors, required changes in editorial policy, [and] burned print shops" of pro-slavery presses. Harold L. Nelson, *Freedom of the Press from Hamilton to the Warren Court* xxvi–xxvii, 236–237 (1967).

21. For example, the Sons of Liberty in 1775 issued the following ultimatum to New York printers: "Sir, if you bring, or suffer to be printed in your press anything against

the rights and liberties of America, or in favor or our inveterate foes, the King, the Ministry and Parliament of Great Britain, death and destruction, ruin and perdition shall be your portion. Signed by Order of the Committee of Tarring and Feathering." Thomas Jones, *History of New York During the Revolutionary War* (E. F. DeLancey ed. 1879), quoted in Levy, note 3 above, at 175.

22. Beauharnais v. Illinois, 343 U.S. 250 (1952).

23. This was particularly true of the American-occupied zone. German publishers were licensed, and those who published materials inconsistent with the American objectives had their licenses revoked. They were kept under surveillance. Americans also imposed school reform and curriculum changes to reeducate German youth against the Nazi ideology. John Gimbel, *The American Occupation of Germany: Politics and the Military* (1945–1949) 246–47 (1968). Positive steps were also taken. American propaganda efforts included radio and television campaigns against the harm of Nazism and attacks on neo-Nazis. Kurt P. Tauber, *Beyond Eagle and Swastika* 434 (1967). The British and American forces denied that they practiced censorship, but destructive criticism of the occupying forces was forbidden.

Clara Menck, *A Struggle for Democracy in Germany* 298–99 (Gabriel L. Almon ed. 1965).

24. *La Gaceta-Diario Oficial* 73–75 (Sept. 13, 1979), Ley General Provisional Sobre los Medios de Comunicacion Arto. 3o prohibits materials "que utilicen a la mujer como objeto sexual o comercial" ("that uses women as sexual or commercial objects") Decree No. 48, Aug. 17, 1979, at 74. I make this reference not to hold up this language or this effort as an ideal to be strictly followed, but rather to remind leftists in particular that some efforts that they otherwise take as admirable (even under conditions very different from those in the United States) consider that the use of women to sell things, as well as prostitution itself, is the opposite of the liberation of women as intended by their revolutions. It is also instructive to notice that an otherwise hard-headed revolutionary government with a lot to worry about does not regard the issue of sexual sale of women as either too unimportant to address or too moralistic for political concern.

25. Brown v. Board of Education, 347 U.S. 483 (1954).

26. Dred Scott v. Sandford, 60 U.S. (19 How.) 393 (1856).

45

Feminist Antipornography Legislation: A Critical Analysis

Lisa Duggan
Nan Hunter
Carole Vance

Lisa Duggan is Visiting Assistant Professor of American Civilization at Brown University. She has published a number of scholarly works on feminism and social philosophy, including ones published in *Signs: Journal of Women in Culture and Society* and *Socialist Review*. Nan Hunter is Associate Professor of Law at Brooklyn Law School as well as founder and former director of the American Civil Liberties Union Lesbian and Gay Rights Project and AIDS Project. She has had articles published in such journals as *The Nation* and *Harvard Civil Rights–Civil Liberties Law Review*. Carole S. Vance is an anthropologist at the Columbia University School of Public Health. She is the editor of *Pleasure and Danger: Exploring Female Sexuality* (2nd ed., 1992) and has published pieces that have appeared in such journals as *Art in America* and *SIECUS Report*.

Professors Duggan, Hunter, and Vance challenge the antipornography position defended by Professor MacKinnon in Chapter 44 and the versions of it that have been proposed as civil law in the cities of Minneapolis and Indianapolis. Professor MacKinnon's proposal has also found support in the U.S. Congress. The authors of this essay argue that the proposed legislation, though claimed to be supportive of feminist values, is quite antifeminist, because it contributes to the antifeminist crusade of conservatives and traditionalists. After presenting a brief history of the legislation,

Reprinted by permission from *Women against Censorship*, ed. Varda Burstyn (Vancouver: Groundwood Books/Douglas & McIntyre, 1985).

the authors expose what they believe is its central flaw: it is hopelessly vague and ambiguous, prohibiting nearly anything that is sexually explicit, though its supporters contend that they are trying to prohibit only materials that are violent, sexist, and sexually explicit. The authors also contend that Professor MacKinnon's proposal, which she created with feminist activist Andrea Dworkin, paints with a broad brush, interpreting pornographic depictions in only one way, degrading to women. They conclude by warning of the dangers of applying this antipornography legislation, and they questioning whether pornography is responsible for any more harm to women than much of nonprohibited activity that is sexist and has been around for a much longer time.

In the United States, after two decades of increasing community tolerance for dissenting or disturbing sexual or political materials, there is now growing momentum for retrenchment. In an atmosphere of increased conservatism, evidenced by a wave of book banning and antigay harassment, support for new repressive legislation of various kinds—from an Oklahoma law forbidding school teachers from advocating homosexuality to new antipornography laws passed in Minneapolis and Indianapolis—is growing.

The antipornography laws have mixed roots of support, however. Though they are popular with the conservative constituencies that traditionally favor legal restrictions on sexual expression of all kinds, they were drafted and endorsed by antipornography feminists who oppose traditional obscenity and censorship laws. The model law of this type, which is now being widely copied, was drawn up in the politically progressive city of Minneapolis by two radical feminists, author Andrea Dworkin and attorney Catharine MacKinnon. It was passed by the city council there, but vetoed by the mayor. A similar law was also passed in Indianapolis, but later declared unconstitutional in federal court, a ruling that the city will appeal. Other versions of the legislation are being considered in numerous cities, and Pennsylvania senator Arlen Specter has introduced legislation modeled on parts of the Dworkin-MacKinnon bill in the U.S. Congress.

Dworkin, MacKinnon and their feminist supporters believe that the new antipornography laws are not censorship laws. They also claim that the legislative effort behind them is based on feminist support. Both of these claims are dubious at best. Though the new laws are civil laws that allow individuals to sue the makers, sellers, distributors or exhibitors of pornography, and not criminal laws leading to arrest and imprisonment, their censoring impact would be substantially as severe as criminal obscenity laws. Materials could be removed from public availability by court injunction, and publishers and booksellers could be subject to potentially endless legal harassment. Passage of the laws was therefore achieved with the support of right-wing elements who expect the new laws to accomplish what censorship efforts are meant to accomplish. Ironically, many antifeminist conservatives backed these laws, while many feminists opposed them. In Indianapolis, the law was supported by extreme right-wing religious fundamentalists, including members of the Moral Majority, while there was *no* local feminist support. In other cities, traditional procensorship forces have expressed interest in the new approach to banning sexually explicit materials. Meanwhile, anticensorship feminists have become alarmed at these new developments and are seeking to galvanize feminist opposition to the new antipornography legislative strategy pioneered in Minneapolis.

One is tempted to ask in astonishment, how can this be happening? How can feminists be entrusting the patriarchal state with the task of legally distinguishing between permissible and impermissible sexual images? But in fact this new development is not as surprising as it at first seems. . . . [P]ornography has come to be seen as a central cause of women's oppression by a significant number of feminists. Some even argue that pornography is the root of virtually all forms of exploitation and discrimination against women. It is a short step from such a belief to the conviction that laws against pornography can end the inequality of the sexes. But this analysis takes feminists very close—indeed far too close— to measures that will ultimately support conservative, antisex, procensorship forces in American society, for it is with these forces that women have forged alliances in passing such legislation.

The first feminist-inspired antipornography law was passed in Minneapolis in 1983. Local legislators had been frustrated when their zoning restrictions on porn shops were struck down in the courts. Public hearings were held to discuss a new zoning ordinance. The Neighborhood Pornography Task Force of South and South Central Minneapolis invited Andrea Dworkin and Catharine MacKinnon, who were

teaching a course on pornography at the University of Minnesota, to testify. They proposed an alternative that, they claimed, would completely eliminate, rather than merely regulate, pornography. They suggested that pornography be defined as a form of sex discrimination, and that an amendment to the city's civil rights law be passed to proscribe it. City officials hired Dworkin and MacKinnon to develop their new approach and to organize another series of public hearings.

The initial debate over the legislation in Minneapolis was intense, and opinion was divided within nearly every political grouping. In contrast, the public hearings held before the city council were tightly controlled and carefully orchestrated; speakers invited by Dworkin and MacKinnon— sexual abuse victims, counselors, educators and social scientists—testified about the harm pornography does women. (Dworkin and MacKinnon's agenda was the compilation of a legislative record that would help the law stand up to its inevitable court challenges.) The legislation passed, supported by antipornography feminists, neighborhood groups concerned about the effects of porn shops on residential areas, and conservatives opposed to the availability of sexually explicit materials for "moral" reasons.

In Indianapolis, the alignment of forces was different. For the previous two years, conservative antipornography groups had grown in strength and public visibility, but they had been frustrated in their efforts. The police department could not convert its obscenity arrests into convictions; the city's zoning law was also tied up in court challenges. Then Mayor William Hudnutt III, a Republican and a Presbyterian minister, learned of the Minneapolis law. Mayor Hudnutt thought Minneapolis's approach to restricting pornography might be the solution to the Indianapolis problems. Beulah Coughenour, a conservative Republican stop-ERA activist, was recruited to sponsor the legislation in the city-county council.

Coughenour engaged MacKinnon as consultant to the city—Dworkin was not hired, but then, Dworkin's passionate radical feminist rhetoric would not have gone over well in Indianapolis. MacKinnon worked with the Indianapolis city prosecutor (a well-known anti-vice zealot), the city's legal department and Coughenour on the legislation. The law received the support of neighborhood groups, the Citizens for Decency and the Coalition for a Clean Community. There were no crowds of feminist supporters—in fact, there were no feminist supporters at all. The only feminists to make public statements opposed the legislation, which was nevertheless passed in a council meeting packed with 300 religious fundamentalists. All 24 Republicans voted for its passage; all five Democrats opposed it to no avail.

A group of publishers and booksellers challenged the law in Federal District Court, where they won the first round. This legal setback for the ordinance may cause some other cities considering similar legislation to hold off until the final resolution of the appeal of the Indianapolis decision; meanwhile, however, mutated versions of the Dworkin-MacKinnon bill have begun to appear. A version of the law introduced in Suffolk County on Long Island in New York emphasized its conservative potential—pornography was said to cause "sodomy" and "disruption" of the family unit, in addition to rape, incest, exploitation and other acts "inimical to the public good." In Suffolk, the law was put forward by a conservative, anti-ERA male legislator who wishes to "restore ladies to what they used to be." The Suffolk County bill clearly illustrates the repressive, antifeminist potential of the new antipornography legislation. The appearance of a federal bill, together with the possibility of a new, Reagan-appointed commission to study new antipornography legislation, indicates how widespread the repressive effects of the ordinances may become.

Yet it is true that some of the U.S. laws have been proposed and supported by antipornography feminists. This is therefore a critical moment in the feminist debate over sexual politics. As anticensorship feminists work to develop alternatives to antipornography campaigns, we also need to examine carefully the new laws and expose their underlying assumptions. We need to know why these laws, for all their apparent feminist rhetoric, actually appeal to conservative antifeminist forces, and why feminists should be preparing to move in a different direction.

Definitions: The Central Flaw

The antipornography ordinances passed in Minneapolis and Indianapolis were framed as amendments to municipal civil rights laws. They provide for complaints to be filed against pornography in the same manner that complaints are filed against employment discrimination. If enforced, these laws would make illegal public or private availability (except in libraries) of any materials deemed pornographic.

Such material could be the object of a lawsuit on several grounds. The ordinance would penalize four kinds of behavior associated with pornography: its production, sale, exhibition or distribution ("trafficking"); coercion into pornographic performance; forcing pornography on a person; and assault or physical attack due to pornography. . . .

Although proponents claim that the Minneapolis and Indianapolis ordinances represent a new way to regulate pornography, the strategy is still laden with our culture's old, repressive approach to sexuality. The implementation of such laws hinges on the definition of pornography as interpreted by the court. The definition provided in the Minneapolis legislation is vague, leaving critical phrases such as "the sexually explicit subordination of women," "postures of sexual submission" and "whores by nature" to the interpretation of the citizen who files a complaint and to the civil court judge who hears the case. The legislation does not prohibit just the images of gross sexual violence that most supporters claim to be its target, but instead drifts toward covering an increasingly wide range of sexually explicit material.

The most problematic feature of this approach, then, is a conceptual flaw embedded in the law itself. Supporters of this type of legislation say that the target of their efforts is misogynist, sexually explicit and violent representation, whether in pictures or words. Indeed, the feminist antipornography movement is fueled by women's anger at the most repugnant of pornography. But a close examination of the wording of the model legislative text, and examples of purportedly actionable material offered by proponents of the legislation in court briefs suggest that the law is actually aimed at a range of material considerably broader than what proponents claim is their target. The discrepancies between the law's explicit and implicit aims have been almost invisible to us, because these distortions are very similar to distortions about sexuality in the culture as a whole. The legislation and supporting texts deserve close reading. Hidden beneath illogical transformations, nonsequiturs, and highly permeable definitions are familiar sexual scripts drawn from mainstream, sexist culture that potentially could have very negative consequences for women.

The Venn diagram [on the next page] illustrates the three areas targeted by the law, and represents a scheme that classifies words or images that have any of three characteristics: violence, sexual explicitness or sexism.

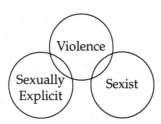

Clearly, a text or an image might have only one characteristic. Material can be violent but not sexually explicit or sexist: for example, a war movie in which both men and women suffer injury or death without regard to or because of their gender. Material can be sexist but not sexually explicit and violent. A vast number of materials from mainstream media—television, popular novels, magazines, newspapers—come to mind, all of which depict either distraught housewives or the "happy sexism" of the idealized family, with mom self-sacrificing, other-directed and content. Finally, material can be sexually explicit but not violent or sexist: for example the freely chosen sexual behavior depicted in sex education films or women's own explicit writing about sexuality.

As the diagram illustrates, areas can also intersect, reflecting a range of combinations of the three characteristics. Images can be violent and sexually explicit without being sexist—for example, a narrative about a rape in a men's prison, or a documentary about the effect of a rape on a woman. The latter example illustrates the importance of context in evaluating whether material that is sexually explicit and violent is also sexist. The intent of the maker, the context of the film and the perception of the viewer together render a depiction of a rape sympathetic, harrowing, even educational, rather than sensational, victim-blaming and laudatory.

Another possible overlap is between material that is violent and sexist but not sexually explicit. Films or books that describe violence directed against women by men in a way that clearly shows gender antagonism and inequality, and sometimes strong sexual tension, but no sexual explicitness fall into this category—for example, the popular genre of slasher films in which women are stalked, terrified and killed by men, or accounts of mass murder of women, fueled by male rage. Finally, a third point of overlap arises when material is sexually explicit and sexist without being violent—that is, when sex is consensual but still reflects themes of male superiority and female abjectness. Some sex education mate-

rials could be included in this category, as well as a great deal of regular pornography.

The remaining domain, the inner core, is one in which the material is simultaneously violent, sexually explicit and sexist—for example, an image of a naked woman being slashed by a knife-wielding rapist. The Minneapolis law, however, does not by any means confine itself to this material.

To be actionable under the law as pornography, material must be judged by the courts to be "the sexually explicit subordination of women, graphically depicted whether in pictures or in words that also includes at least one or more" of nine criteria. Of these, only four involve the intersection of violence, sexual explicitness and sexism, and then only arguably. . . . Even in these cases, many questions remain about whether images with all three characteristics do in fact cause violence against women. . . . And the task of evaluating material that is ostensibly the target of these criteria becomes complicated—indeed, hopeless—because most of the clauses that contain these criteria mix actions or qualities of violence with those that are not particularly associated with violence.

The section that comes closest to the stated purpose of the legislation is clause (iii): "women are presented as sexual objects who experience sexual pleasure in being raped." This clause is intended to cover depictions of rape that are sexually explicit and sexist; the act of rape itself signifies the violence. But other clauses are not so clearcut, because the list of characteristics often mixes signs or byproducts of violence with phenomena that are unrelated or irrelevant to judging violence. We might be willing to agree that clause (ii)—"women are presented as sexual objects who enjoy pain"—signifies the conjunction of all three characteristics, with violence the presumed cause of pain, but the presence of the words "and humiliation" at the end of the clause is problematic. Humiliation may be offensive or disagreeable, but it does not necessarily imply violence.

A similar problem occurs with clause (iv): "women are presented as sexual objects tied up or cut up or mutilated or bruised or physically hurt." All these except the first, "tied up," generally occur as a result of violence. "Tied up," if part of consensual sex, is not violent and, for some practitioners, not particularly sexist. Women who are tied up may be participants in nonviolent sex play involving bondage, a theme in both heterosexual and lesbian pornography. (See, for example *The Joy of Sex* and

Coming to Power.) Clause (ix) contains another mixed list, in which "injury," "torture, "bleeding," "bruised" and "hurt" are combined with words such as "degradation" and "shown as filthy and inferior," neither of which is violent. Depending on the presentation, "filthy" and "inferior" may constitute sexually explicit sexism, although not violence. "Degradation" is a sufficiently inclusive term to cover most acts of which a viewer disapproves.

Several other clauses have little to do with violence at all; they refer to material that is sexually explicit and sexist, thus falling outside the triad of characteristics at which the legislation is supposedly aimed. For example, movies in which "women are presented as dehumanized sexual objects, things, or commodities" may be infuriating and offensive to feminists, but they are not violent.

Finally, some clauses describe material that is neither violent nor necessarily sexist. Clause (v), "women . . . in postures of sexual submission or sexual servility, including by inviting penetration," and clause (viii), "women . . . being penetrated by objects or animals," are sexually explicit, but not violent and not obviously sexist unless one believes that penetration—whether heterosexual, lesbian, or autoerotic masturbation—is indicative of gender inequality and female oppression. Similarly problematic are clauses that invoke representations of "women . . . as whores by nature" and "women's body parts . . . such that women are reduced to those parts."

Texts filed in support of the Indianapolis law show how broadly it could be applied. In the amicus brief filed on behalf of Linda Marchiano ("Linda Lovelace," the female lead in *Deep Throat*) in Indianapolis, Catharine MacKinnon offered *Deep Throat* as an example of the kind of pornography covered by the law. *Deep Throat* served a complicated function in this brief, because the movie, supporters of the ordinance argue, would be actionable on two counts: coercion into pornographic performance, because Marchiano alleges that she was coerced into making the movie; and trafficking in pornography, because the content of the film falls within one of the categories in the Indianapolis ordinance's definition—that which prohibits presenting women as sexual objects "through postures or positions of servility or submission or display." Proponents of the law have counted on women's repugnance at allegations of coerced sexual acts to spill over and discredit the sexual acts themselves in this movie.

The aspects of *Deep Throat* that MacKinnon considered to be indicative of "sexual subordination" are of particular interest, since any movie that depicted similar acts could be banned under the law. MacKinnon explained in her brief that the film "subordinates women by using women . . . sexually, specifically as eager servicing receptacles for male genitalia and ejaculate. The majority of the film presents 'Linda Lovelace' in, minimally, postures of sexual submission and/or servility." In its brief, the City of Indianapolis concurred: "In the film *Deep Throat* a woman is being shown as being ever eager for oral penetration by a series of men's penises, often on her hands and knees. There are repeated scenes in which her genitalia are graphically displayed and she is shown as enjoying men ejaculating on her face."

These descriptions are very revealing, since they suggest that multiple partners, group sex and oral sex subordinate women and hence are sexist. The notion that the female character is "used" by men suggests that it is improbable that a woman would engage in fellatio of her own accord. *Deep Throat* does draw on several sexist conventions common in advertising and the entire visual culture—the woman as object of the male gaze, and the assumption of heterosexuality, for example. But it is hardly an unending paean to male dominance, since the movie contains many contrary themes. In it, the main female character is shown as both actively seeking her own pleasure and as trying to please men; a secondary female character is shown as actually directing encounters with multiple male partners. Both briefs described a movie quite different from the one viewers see.

At its heart, this analysis implies that heterosexual sex itself is sexist; that women do not engage in it of their own volition; and that behavior pleasurable to men is repugnant to women. In some contexts, for example, the representation of fellatio and multiple partners can be sexist, but are we willing to concede that they always are? If not, then what is proposed as actionable under the Indianapolis law includes merely sexually explicit representation (the traditional target of obscenity laws), which proponents of the legislation vociferously insist they are not interested in attacking.

Some other examples offered through exhibits submitted with the City of Indianapolis brief and also introduced in the public hearing further illustrate this point. Many of the exhibits are depictions of sadomasochism. The court briefs treat SM material as depicting violence and aggression, not consensual sex, in spite of avowals to the contrary by many SM practitioners. With this legislation, then, a major question for feminists that has only begun to develop would be closed for discussion. Instead, a simplistic reduction has been advanced as the definitive feminist position. The description of the material in the briefs focused on submissive women and implied male domination, highlighting the similarity proponents would like to find between all SM narratives and male/female inequality. The actual exhibits, however, illustrated plots and power relationships far more diverse than the descriptions provided by MacKinnon and the City of Indianapolis would suggest, including SM between women and female dominant/male submissive SM. For example, the Indianapolis brief stated that in the magazine *The Bitch Goddesses*, "women are shown in torture chambers with their nude body parts being tortured by their 'master' for 'even the slightest offense'. . . . The magazine shows a woman in a scenario of torture." But the brief failed to mention that the dominants in this magazine are all female, with one exception. This kind of discrepancy characterized many examples offered in the briefs.

This is not to say that such representations do not raise questions for feminists. The current lively discussion about lesbian SM clearly demonstrates that this issue is still unresolved. But in the Indianapolis briefs all SM material was assumed to be male dominant/female submissive, thereby squeezing a nonconforming reality into prepackaged, inadequate—and therefore dangerous—categories. This legislation would virtually eliminate all SM pornography by recasting it as violent, thereby attacking a sexual minority while masquerading as an attempt to end violence against women.

Analysis of clauses in the Minneapolis ordinance and several examples offered in court briefs filed in connection with the Indianapolis ordinance show that the law targets material that is sexually explicit and sexist, but ignores material that is violent and sexist, violent and sexually explicit, only violent or only sexist.

Certain troubling questions arise here, for if one claims, as some antipornography activists do, that there is a direct relationship between images and behavior, why should images of violence against women or scenarios of sexism in general not be similarly proscribed? Why is sexual explicitness singled out as the cause of women's oppression? For propo-

nents to exempt violent and sexist images, or even sexist images, from regulation is inconsistent, especially since they are so pervasive.

Even more difficulties arise from the vagueness of certain terms crucial in interpreting the ordinances. The term "subordination" is especially important, since pornography is defined as the "sexually explicit subordination of women." The authors of this legislation intend it to modify each of the clauses, and they appear to believe that it provides a definition of sexism that each example must meet. The term is never defined in the legislation, yet the Indianapolis brief, for example, suggests that the average viewer, on the basis of "his or her common understanding of what it means for one person to subordinate another" should be able to decide what is pornographic. But what kind of sexually explicit acts place a woman in an inferior status? To some, *any* graphic sexual act violates women's dignity and therefore subordinates them. To others, consensual heterosexual lovemaking within the boundaries of procreation and marriage is acceptable, but heterosexual acts that do not have reproduction as their aim lower women's status and hence subordinate them. Still others accept a wide range of nonprocreative, perhaps even nonmarital, heterosexuality but draw the line at lesbian sex, which they view as degrading.

The term "sex object" is also problematic. The City of Indianapolis's brief maintains that "the term sexual object, often shortened to sex object, has enjoyed a wide popularity in mainstream American culture in the past fifteen years, and is used to denote the objectification of a person on the basis of their sex or sex appeal. . . . People know what it means to disregard all aspects of personhood but sex, to reduce a person to a thing used for sex." But, indeed, people do not agree on this point. The definition of "sex object" is far from clear or uniform. For example, some feminist and liberal cultural critics have used the term to mean sex that occurs without strong emotional ties and experience. More conservative critics maintain that any detachment of women's sexuality from procreation, marriage and the family objectifies it, removing it from its "natural" web of associations and context. Unredeemed and unprotected by domesticity and family, women—and their sexuality—become things used by men. In both these views, women are never sexually autonomous agents who direct and enjoy their sexuality for their own purposes, but rather are victims. In the same vein, other problematic terms include "inviting penetration," "whores by nature" and "positions of display."

Through close analysis of the proposed legislation one sees how vague the boundaries of the definitions that contain the inner core of the Venn diagram really are. Their dissolution does not happen equally at all points, but only at some: the inner core begins to include sexually explicit and sexist material, and finally expands to include purely sexually explicit material. Thus "sexually explicit" becomes identified and equated with "violent" with no further definition or explanation.

It is also striking that so many feminists have failed to notice that the laws (as well as examples of actionable material) cover so much diverse work, not just that small and symbolic epicenter where many forms of opposition to women converge. It suggests that for us, as well as for others, sexuality remains a difficult area. We have no clearly developed framework in which to think about sex equivalent to the frameworks that are available for thinking about race, gender and class issues. Consequently, in sex, as in few other areas of human behavior, unexamined and unjustifiable prejudice passes itself off as considered opinion about what is desirable and normal. And finally, sex arouses considerable anxiety, stemming from both the meeting with individual difference and from the prospect—suggested by feminists themselves—that sexual behavior is constructed socially and is not simply natural.

The law takes advantage of everyone's relative ignorance and anxious ambivalence about sex, distorting and oversimplifying what confronts us in building a sexual politic. For example, antipornography feminists draw on several feminist theories about the role of violent, aggressive or sexist representations. The first is relatively straightforward: that these images trigger men into action. The second suggests that violent images act more subtly, to socialize men to act in sexist or violent ways by making this behavior seem commonplace and more acceptable, if not expected. The third assumption is that violent, sexually explicit or even sexist images are offensive to women, assaulting their sensibilities and sense of self. Although we have all used metaphor to exhort women to action or illustrate a point, antipornography proponents have frequently used these conventions of speech as if they were literal statements of fact. But these metaphors have gotten out of hand, as Julie Abraham has noted, for they fail to recognize that the assault committed by the wife beater is quite different from the visual "assault" of a sexist ad on TV. The nature of the differ-

ence is still being clarified in a complex debate within feminism that must continue; this law cuts off speculation, settling on a causal relationship between image and action that is starkly simple, if unpersuasive.

This metaphor also paves the way for reclassifying images that are merely sexist as also violent and aggressive. Thus, it is no accident that the briefs supporting the legislation first invoke violent images and rapidly move to include sexist and sexually explicit images without noting that they are different. The equation is made more easy by the constant shifts back to examples of depictions of real violence, almost to draw attention away from the sexually explicit or sexist material that in fact would be affected by the laws.

Most important, what underlies this legislation and the success of its analysis in blurring and exceeding boundaries is an appeal to a very traditional view of sex: sex is degrading to women. By this logic, any illustrations or descriptions of explicit sexual acts that involve women are in themselves affronts to women's dignity. In its brief, the City of Indianapolis was quite specific about this point: "The harms caused by pornography are by no means limited to acts of physical aggression. The mere existence of pornography in society degrades and demeans all women." Embedded in this view are several other familiar themes: that sex is degrading to women, but not to men; that men are raving beasts; that sex is dangerous for women; that sexuality is male, not female; that women are victims, not sexual actors; that men inflict "it" on women; that penetration is submission; that heterosexual sexuality, rather than the institution of heterosexuality, is sexist.

These assumptions, in part intended, in part unintended, lead us back to the traditional target of obscenity law: sexually explicit material. What initially appeared novel, then, is really the reappearance of a traditional theme. It's ironic that a feminist position on pornography incorporates most of the myths about sexuality that feminism has struggled to displace.

The Dangers of Application

The Minneapolis and Indianapolis ordinances embody a political view that holds pornography to be a central force in "creating and maintaining" the oppression of women. This view appears in summary form in the legislative findings section at the beginning of the Minneapolis bill, which describes a chain reaction of misogynistic acts generated by pornography. The legislation is based on the interweaving of several themes: that pornography constructs the meaning of sexuality for women and, as well, leads to discrete acts of violence against women; that sexuality is the primary cause of women's oppression; that explicitly sexual images, even if not violent or coerced, have the power to subordinate women; and that women's own accounts of force have been silenced because, as a universal and timeless rule, society credits pornographic constructions rather than women's experiences. Taking the silencing contention a step further, advocates of the ordinance effectively assume that women have been so conditioned by the pornographic world view that if their own experiences of the sexual acts identified in the definition are not subordinating, then they must simply be victims of false consciousness.

The heart of the ordinance is the "trafficking" section, which would allow almost anyone to seek the removal of any materials falling within the law's definition of pornography. Ordinance defenders strenuously protest that the issue is not censorship because the state, as such, is not authorized to initiate criminal prosecutions. But the prospect of having to defend a potentially infinite number of privately filed complaints creates at least as much of a chilling effect against pornographic or sexual speech as does a criminal law. And as long as representatives of the state—in this case, judges—have ultimate say over the interpretation, the distinction between this ordinance and "real" censorship will not hold.

In addition, three major problems should dissuade feminists from supporting this kind of law: first, the sexual images in question do not cause more harm than other aspects of misogynist culture; second, sexually explicit speech, even in male-dominated society, serves positive social functions for women; and third, the passage and enforcement of antipornography laws such as those supported in Minneapolis and Indianapolis are more likely to impede, rather than advance, feminist goals.

Ordinance proponents contend that pornography does cause violence because it conditions male sexual response to images of violence and thus provokes violence against women. The strongest research they offer is based on psychology experiments that employ films depicting a rape scene, toward the end of which the woman is shown to be enjoying the attack. The ordinances, by contrast, cover a much broader range of materials than this one specific het-

erosexual rape scenario. Further, the studies ordinance supporters cite do not support the theory that pornography causes violence against women. . . .

In addition, the argument that pornography itself plays a major role in the general oppression of women contradicts the evidence of history. It need hardly be said that pornography did not lead to the burning of witches or the English common law treatment of women as chattel property. If anything functioned then as the prime communication medium for woman-hating, it was probably religion. Nor can pornography be blamed for the enactment of laws from at least the eighteenth century that allowed a husband to rape or beat his wife with impunity. In any period, the causes of women's oppression have been many and complex, drawing on the fundamental social and economic structures of society. Ordinance proponents offer little evidence to explain how the mass production of pornography—a relatively recent phenomenon—could have become so potent a causative agent so quickly.

The silencing of women is another example of the harm attributed to pornography. Yet if this argument were correct, one would expect that as the social visibility of pornography has increased, the tendency to credit women's accounts of rape would have decreased. In fact, although the treatment of women complainants in rape cases is far from perfect, the last 15 years of work by the women's movement has resulted in marked improvements. In many places, the corroboration requirement has now been abolished; cross-examination of victims as to past sexual experiences has been prohibited; and a number of police forces have developed specially trained units and procedures to improve the handling of sexual assault cases. The presence of rape fantasies in pornography may in part reflect a backlash against these women's movement advances, but to argue that most people routinely disbelieve women who file charges of rape belittles the real improvements made in social consciousness and law.

The third type of harm suggested by the ordinance backers is a kind of libel: the maliciously false characterization of women as a group of sexual masochists. Like libel, the City of Indianapolis brief argues pornography is "a lie [which] once loosed" cannot be effectively rebutted by debate and further speech.

To claim that all pornography as defined by the ordinance is a lie is a false analogy. If truth is a defence to charges of libel, then surely depictions of consensual sex cannot be thought of as equivalent to a falsehood. For example, some women (and men) do enjoy being tied up or displaying themselves. The declaration by fiat that even sadomasochism is a "lie" about sexuality reflects an arrogance and moralism that feminists should combat, not engage in. When mutually desired sexual experiences are depicted, pornography is not "libelous." . . .

These laws, which would increase the state's regulation of sexual images, present many dangers for women. Although the ordinances draw much of their feminist support from women's anger at the market for images of sexual violence, they are aimed not at violence, but at sexual explicitness. Far-right elements recognize the possibility of using the full potential of the ordinances to enforce their sexually conservative world view, and have supported them for that reason. Feminists should therefore look carefully at the test of these "model" laws in order to understand why many believe them to be a useful tool in *anti*feminist moral crusades.

The proposed ordinances are also dangerous because they seek to embody in law an analysis of the role of sexuality and sexual images in the oppression of women with which even all feminists do not agree. Underlying virtually every section of the proposed laws there is an assumption that sexuality is a realm of unremitting, unequaled victimization for women. Pornography appears as the monster that made this so. The ordinances' authors seek to impose their analysis by putting state power behind it. But this analysis is not the only

feminist perspective on sexuality. Feminist theorists have also argued that the sexual terrain, however power-laden, is actively contested. Women are agents, and not merely victims, who make decisions and act on them, and who desire, seek out and enjoy sexuality.

Discussion Questions

1. Why do the authors believe that Dworkin-MacKinnon type legislation is ultimately antifeminist and lends support to conservative elements in society who do not agree with feminist goals?

2. What do the authors believe is the central flaw in the Dworkin-MacKinnon proposal? Present and explain their position. Do you agree or disagree with their assessment? Explain and defend your answer.

3. Why do the authors believe that the Dworkin-MacKinnon proposal is mistaken in thinking that all pornography is degrading to women? Provide some of the examples they use while presenting and explaining their answer. Do you agree or disagree with their view? Explain and defend your answer.

4. The authors question whether pornography is responsible for any more harm to women than much of nonprohibited activity that is sexist and has been around for a much longer time. Explain what they mean by this. Do you agree or disagree with their view? Explain and defend your answer.

46

Pornography, Sex, and Censorship

Fred R. Berger

Fred R. Berger, who died in 1988, was a Professor of Philosophy at the University of California, Davis. A social philosopher and civil libertarian, he published extensively in the areas of political philosophy, freedom of expression, and public policy in numerous journals including *Social Theory and Practice*. He is the author of *Freedom, Rights, and Pornography* (1991, edited by Bruce Russell) and *Happiness, Justice, and Freedom: The Moral and Political Philosophy of John Stuart Mill* (1984).

In this essay Professor Berger argues against the censorship of pornography. He begins by recognizing the difference between censorship and regulation, noting that he is arguing only against the former. He then moves to define pornography: "{P}ornography [is] art or literature which explicitly depicts sexual activity or arousal in a manner having little or no artistic or literary value." He goes on to outline three forms of argument employed by conservatives who favor censorship. Professor Berger is concerned only with the third form: "[P]ornography promotes or leads to certain kinds of socially harmful attitudes and/or behavior." In reply to this form of argument, he first rebuts versions of the argument presented by George Steiner and Irving Kristol. Professor Berger then presents several other reasons to reject the conservative argument, including the rather novel argument that censorship rather than pornography may result in socially harmful attitudes and/or behavior. He concludes his essay by arguing that the censor has the burden of providing convincing reasons to interfere with someone's consumption of pornography.

Reprinted by permission from *Social Theory and Practice* 4, no. 2 (1977).

An observer of American attitudes toward pornography faces a bewildering duality: on the one hand, we buy and read and view more of it than just about anyone else, while, on the other hand, we seek to suppress it as hard as anybody else. I presume that these facts do not merely reflect a judgment of social utilities, namely, that the best balance of goods is achieved by having it available, but under conditions of prohibition![1] I believe, in fact, that this state of things reflects aspects of our attitudes toward sex, and much of the current controversy has tended to obscure this fact, and to ignore the important issues concerning sex and freedom to which the pornography issue points.

There is an important reason why the pornography controversy in the American context has tended to be narrowly focused. Our First Amendment prohibits government from abridging freedom of speech and press. Whatever interpretation is to be given that amendment, it is, in fact, stated in absolutist terms, and carries no mention of definition of obscenity or pornography. This difficulty is exacerbated by the fact that in the common-law background of our legal system, there is very little litigation which established clear legal definitions and doctrines. Obscenity convictions in the form we know them seem very much an invention of the 1800s, and of the late 1800s at that.[2] Moreover, in our experience with obscenity litigation, we have discovered that an enormous array of serious, even important, literature and art has fallen to the censor's axe. Thus, liberals and conservatives alike have feared that the removal of pornography from the protections of the First Amendment can endanger materials the Constitution surely ought to protect. This has given the constitutional issue great urgency.

The upshot has been that much of the debate has centered on the question of definition, and, moreover, that question has been pursued with legal needs in mind.

In this paper, I want to put aside the First Amendment to ask if there are any justifiable grounds for rejecting the arguments offered for the censorship of pornography independent of First Amendment considerations. Moreover, I shall be concerned with the *censorship* of pornography, not its *regulation*. The regulation of speech often has the same effect as censorship, and that is an important danger; nevertheless, censorship and regulation differ radically in intention, and that is an important difference.[3] I should also indicate that I shall suppose that those who favor censorship (I shall refer to them as "the censors") are not *generally* in favor of censorship, and would not prohibit what they regard as "true" art or literature.

Moreover, to lend further clarity to my discussion I shall propose a definition which is useful for the purposes of this paper, and which picks out most of what is usually regarded as pornographic, and that is all I claim for it. I define pornography as art or literature which explicitly depicts sexual activity or arousal in a manner having little or no artistic or literary value.[4] (I am assuming that scientific and medical texts are a kind of literature, with appropriate criteria of acceptability.)

The definition does, I believe, make pornography a relatively objective classification, insofar as there are clear cases on both sides of the divide, and there are relatively standard literary and artistic criteria by which to judge disputed cases.[5] In this respect, I am somewhat sympathetic to the conservatives who chide those liberals who claim they are not able to recognize standard cases of pornography as such.[6]

1. Objections to Pornography: Conflicting Views on Sex

Generally speaking, there are three forms of argument employed by the conservatives in favor of censorship. First, they simply hold that pornography itself is immoral or evil, irrespective of ill-consequences which may flow from it.[7] Second, they sometimes assert that, irrespective of its morality, a practice which most people in a community find abhorrent and disgusting may be rightfully repressed. Finally, they sometimes contend that pornography promotes or leads to certain kinds of socially harmful attitudes and/or behavior.

In this paper, I wish to concentrate on this last form of argument. The proponents of the first kind of claim cannot, for the most part, meet Ronald Dworkin's challenge to specify some recognizable sense of morality according to which their claims are true.[8] Though I am aware of one form of this argument which I think *can* meet that challenge, it is dealt with obliquely in my responses to the other claims. The second form of argument has been widely debated in the literature, and I have little to add to that debate.[9] The arguments do not turn on the nature of pornography as such, and, moreover, it is fairly clear that in contemporary America there is not an overwhelming abhorrence of pornography as

such.[10] The last form of argument has been given new life, however, by claims based on analyses of pornographic materials as such. These new conservative arguments differ in important ways from the traditional views of the censors, and their arguments have been extremely influential. Each of the articles I shall discuss has been widely referred to; each has been reprinted a number of times, and all but one are cited in support of recent decisions in the courts.[11]

The traditional form of the claim can be labeled the "incitement to rape" theory. It holds that pornography arouses sexual desire, which seeks an outlet, often in antisocial forms such as rape. It is this version of the claim we are most familiar with, and the evidence which is available tends to refute it.[12] I shall have more to say about it later.

The conservative views I want to take up hold that the harms from pornography are somewhat long-range. These commentators maintain that the modes of sex depicted in pornography, and the manner of depiction, will result in altering our basic attitudes toward sex and to one another, so that in the end a climate of antisocial behavior will result. I have isolated four instances of such arguments in the literature of pornography.

The first claim I shall take up is put forth in an essay by George Steiner, entitled "Night Words," which has provoked considerable comment.[13] Though Steiner expressed disapproval of censorship because it is "stupid" and cannot work, his views have been taken as an argument supporting censorship. Steiner holds that pornography constitutes an invasion of privacy:

> Sexual relations are, or should be, one of the citadels of privacy, the night place where we must be allowed to gather the splintered, harried elements of our consciousness to some kind of inviolate order and repose. It is in sexual experience that a human being alone, and two human beings in that attempt at total communication which is also communion, can discover the unique bent of their identity. There we may find ourselves through imperfect striving and repeated failure, the words, the gestures, the mental images which set the blood to racing. In that dark and wonder ever renewed both the fumblings and the light must be our own.
>
> The new pornographers subvert this last, vital privacy; they do our imagining for us. They take away the words that were of the night and shout them over the rooftops, making them hollow. The images of our love-making, the stammerings we resort to in intimacy come pre-

packaged. . . . Natural selection tells of limbs and functions which atrophy through lack of use; the power to feel, to experience and realize the precarious uniqueness of each other's being, can also wither in a society.[14]

The second claim against pornography is made by Irving Kristol, in an article arguing for censorship. Kristol claims that pornography depersonalizes sex, reducing it to animal activity and thus debases it; that it essentially involves only the readers' or viewers' sexual arousal, and thus promotes an infantile sexuality which is dangerous to society:

> The basic psychological fact about pornography and obscenity is that it appeals to and provokes a kind of sexual regression. The sexual pleasure one gets from pornography and obscenity is autoerotic and infantile; put bluntly, it is a masturbatory exercise of the imagination, when it is not masturbation pure and simple. . . . Infantile sexuality is not only a permanent temptation for the adolescent or even the adult—it can quite easily become a permanent, self-reinforcing neurosis. It is because of an awareness of this possibility of regression toward the infantile condition, a regression which is always open to us, that all the codes of sexual conduct ever devised by the human race take such a dim view of autoerotic activities and try to discourage autoerotic fantasies. Masturbation is indeed a perfectly natural autoerotic activity. . . . And it is precisely because it is so perfectly natural that it can be so dangerous to the mature or maturing person, if it is not controlled or sublimated in some way.[15]

The danger is borne out, he thinks, in *Portnoy's Complaint*. Portnoy's sexuality is fixed in an infantile mode (he is a prolific and inventive masturbator), and he is incapable of an adult sexual relationship with a woman. The final consequences are quite dire, as Kristol concludes: "What is at stake is civilization and humanity, nothing less. The idea that 'everything is permitted,' as Nietzsche put it, rests on the premise of nihilism and has nihilistic implications."[16]

Professor Walter Berns, writing in the magazine *The Public Interest*, maintains that pornography breaks down the feelings of shame we associate with sex. This shame, he holds, is not merely a dictate of our society, it is natural in that it protects love, and promotes the self-restraint which is requisite for a democratic polity:

> Whereas sexual attraction brings man and woman together seeking a unity that culminates in the living being they together create, the voyeur maintains a distance; and because he maintains a distance he looks at, he does not communicate; and because he looks at he objectifies, he makes an object of that which it is natural to join; objectifying, he is incapable of uniting and is therefore incapable of love. The need to conceal voyeurism—the concealing shame—is corollary of the protective shame, the same that impels lovers to search for privacy and for an experience protected from the profane and the eyes of the stranger. . . . Shame, both concealing and protective, protects lovers and therefore love.[17]

The upshot, as we might have suspected, is catastrophic. Under the banner of "the forgotten argument," Bern writes:

> To live together requires rules and a governing of the passions, and those who are without shame will be unruly and unreliable; having lost the ability to restrain themselves by observing the rules they collectively give themselves, they will have to be ruled by others. Tyranny is the natural and inevitable mode of government for the shameless and the self-indulgent who have carried liberty beyond any restraint, natural and conventional.[18]

Finally, Professor Ernest van den Haag, in a series of articles, has argued for censorship on the grounds that pornography encourages "the pure libidinal principle," which leads to loss of empathy for others, and encourages violence and antisocial acts:

> By de-individualizing and dehumanizing sexual acts, which thus become impersonal, pornography reduces or removes the empathy and the mutual identification which restrain us from treating each other merely as objects or means. This empathy is an individual barrier to nonconsensual acts, such as rape, torture, and assaultive crimes in general. . . .
>
> By reducing life to varieties of sex, pornography invites us to regress to a premoral world, to return to, and to spin out, preadolescent fantasies—fantasies which reject reality and the burdens of individuation, of restraint, of tension, of conflict, of regarding others as more than objects of commitment, of thought, of consideration, and of love. These are the burdens which become heavy and hard to avoid in adolescence. By rejecting them, at least in fantasy, a return to the pure libidinal pleasure principle is achieved. And once launched by pornography, fantasy may regress to ever more infantile fears and wishes: people, together dehumanized, may be tortured, mutilated, and literally devoured.[19]

My response to these claims has two parts. First, I shall try to show that they reflect certain attitudes toward sex that are rejected by many, and that pornography will be judged differently by people with different attitudes toward sex. Second, I shall try to show why the gruesome results these writers foresee as the consequences of the state's failure to suppress dirty books and art are *not* likely consequences. Pornographic materials, *by their nature*, I shall contend, are an unlikely source or means of altering and influencing our basic attitudes toward one another.

Let us begin by noting certain features of pornography on which the conservative claims seem to hinge. First of all, by virtue of its lack of finesse, pornography is stark; it tends to remove those nuances of warmth and feeling which a more delicate approach is more apt to preserve. Second, there is some tendency of much pornography to assault our sensibilities and sense of the private, to estrange us somewhat. This is not difficult to understand, and it is not simply a result of our culture's attitudes toward sex. Sex, quite naturally, is associated with the notion of privacy because in sex we are in a vulnerable state, both emotionally and physically—we are very much in the control of our feelings and sensations, less aware of environmental factors, very much involved in and attending to our state of feeling and present activity.[20] Such vulnerability is the mark of private states—states on which we do not want others to intrude. This is reflected also in our attitudes toward grief and dying. Moreover, because we *want* to be totally taken with the activity itself, we do not usually want others present. So, we can concede that there is some truth to the conservative analyses of the nature of pornography.

These conservative arguments, however, involve and presuppose views on sex that many people reject. I think it is important to make these more explicit. Steiner, as we have seen, regards sex as a source of "inviolate order and repose," in which a sense of our identity is achieved by virtue of the private words, gestures, mental images which are shared with loved ones. (I envisage a hushed atmosphere.) For Van den Haag, sex, or mature sex, properly involves the burdens of "conflict, commitment, thought, consideration and love." And Kristol has distinguished mere "animal coupling" from making love, labeling the former "debased." Professor Berns's views about the nature of sex are, perhaps, clarified in a footnote:

It is easy to prove that shamefulness is not the only principle governing the question of what may properly be presented on the stage; shamefulness would not, for example, govern the case of a scene showing the copulating of a married

couple who love each other very much. That is not intrinsically shameful—on the contrary—yet it ought not to be shown. The principle here is, I think, an aesthetic one; such a scene is dramatically weak because the response of the audience would be characterized by prurience and not by a sympathy with what the scene is intended to portray, a beautiful love.[21]

The trouble with these views is that they see sex as normal or proper only within the context of deep commitment, shared responsibility, loving concern, and as involving restraint and repression of pure pleasure. Indeed, Professor Berns's footnote not only carries the suggestion that anything but married love is shameful, but also could be uncharitably interpreted as holding that "a beautiful love" is something which holds between disembodied souls, and in no way involves sexual communion, or the sharing of physical joy and pleasure. It seems to him that if we got some sense of the pleasure the couple take in one another physically, some hint of the physical forms of their communication and sense of mutuality, that this would somehow detract from our sympathy with their "beautiful love."

Now, many in our society reject these analyses of sex, either totally or partially. I want to sketch two possible views so that we might have a sense of the wider context of attitudes within which the pornography problem should be discussed. As many liberals share the conservative attitudes toward sex and many political conservatives do not, I shall label the views I discuss as "radical" or "radical-liberal," with no further political significance attached to them.

The radical maintains that the entire façade of sexual attitudes in contemporary society represents sham, hypocrisy, and unnecessary forms of social control. Sexual relations are governed by the notions of duty, shame, guilt. As such, there can be no honest sexuality, since mediating all sexual relations are feelings and associations which have nothing to do with our feelings *for* one another, and, often, little to do really with our sexual natures. The conservative picture of shared communication, in an aura of intimate connection, expressive of tender love, concern, commitment which are involved in mature (preferably married) sex, is an idealized, romanticized, unreal (perhaps even infantile) depiction of what really happens in sex. The fact is that most sex is routinized, dull, unfulfilling, a source of neurosis, precisely because its practice is governed by the restraints the conservatives insist on. Those constraints dictate with whom one has sex, *when* one has sex, how *often* one has sex, *where* one has sex, and so on. Moreover, the web of shame and guilt which is spun around sex tends to destroy its enjoyment, and thus to stunt our sexual natures—our capacity for joy and pleasure through sex. The result is a society which is highly neurotic in its attitudes toward and practice of sex—all of which interferes with honest communication and self-realization.

The radical solution to this perceived situation is to treat sex *as* a physical act, unencumbered with romanticized notions of love. Human sex just *is* a form of animal coupling, and to make more of it is to invite dishonesty and neurosis.

It seems to me that it is *this* sort of attitude which the conservative most fears. Though the conservative claims that such an attitude will result in devaluing humans, it is not clear why. He seems to infer that because the radical is willing to treat others as sources of pleasure, without the necessity of emotional commitment, he therefore perceives them as mere *instruments* of pleasure. This, of course, does not follow, either logically or as a matter of probability. Nor have I ever met a conservative who thought that correspondingly, if people are permitted to make profits from others in business dealings, they will come to view them as mere sources of profits. The point is that it is absurd to suppose that one who no longer thinks of *sex* in terms of shame and guilt must lose the sense of shame and guilt at harming others, either through sex, or in other ways.

I do not wish to dwell on the radical position, however, because there is a more widespread view which I have labeled the "radical-liberal" view which I wish to consider. This conception accepts a large part of the radical critique, in particular the notion that guilt and shame, duty and commitment, are not necessary to fully human sex. The radical-liberal agrees that much of our ordinary sexual relations are marred by the inhibitions these impose. He or she need not, however, reject sex as an element in loving relationships, and he or she may well insist that love does engender special commitments and concern with which sex is properly entangled. But, the radical-liberal does not reject physical sex for its own sake as something debased or wicked, or shorn of human qualities. Indeed, he or she may insist that greater concern with the physical aspects of sexuality is needed to break down those emotional connections with sex which stand as barriers to its enjoyment, and as barriers to free open communication with others, and to one's development of a sense of one's

sexual identity—a development in terms of one's own needs, desires, and life-style.

The intensity of such needs on the part of many people is, I believe, well-depicted in Erica Jong's contemporary novel, *Fear of Flying*. In the book, her heroine expresses her reaction to the attitude that a woman's identity is to be found in her relationship with a man. Female solitude is perceived as un-American and selfish. Thus, women live waiting to be half of something else, rather than being simply themselves. These American attitudes are perceived as inhibitions to the woman's self-discovery. . . .

The point is that to many people, the conservative's picture of sex, and the sorts of social relations in which he embeds it, has served to starve them of the unique development of their personali-ties, or an aspect of it. The antidote they see is a freer, more open attitude toward sex, removed from what they regard as a mystique of duty and guilt and shame.

People with the attitudes of the radical-liberal, or who see themselves as impeded in their full self-realization by the traditional views on sex, may well find pornography something of no consequence, or may even find it beneficial—a means of removing from their own psyches the associations which inhibit their sexual natures. The plain fact is that pornography is used for this effect by various therapists, who have thereby aided people to more fulfilled lives for themselves, and happier, healthier relations with loved ones.[22]

Will such a concern with physical pleasure result in nonattachment, in antihuman feelings, in the loss of loving relationships? It is at least as plausible that just the opposite is the probable result, that by virtue of lessened anxiety and guilt over sex, an important source of human communion is enhanced. In a Kinsey-type sex survey sponsored by *Playboy*, there was demonstrated a greatly heightened freedom in sex in America, and a greater emphasis on physical enjoyment, but this has not resulted in a significant lessening of the importance accorded to emotional ties.[23] Greater concern with pleasure has been used to *enhance* those relationships. Thus, it is no accident that among the millions who have lined up to see *Deep Throat*, *Behind the Green Door*, and *The Devil in Miss Jones*, have been a great many loving, married couples. Indeed, that there has come to be a body of "popular pornography"—porno for the millions—holds out some small hope that our culture will eventually develop a truly erotic artistic tradition, as explicitness becomes more natural, and tastes demand more of the productions.

We have seen that the conservative position presupposes attitudes toward sex which many reject, and that the alternative attitudes are consistent both with the acceptance of pornography and the values of care and concern for others. Let us turn now to the specific points the conservatives make concerning alleged harms.

2. The Response to Conservative Objections

I want to consider first the argument concerning privacy. It was Steiner's claim that pornography takes the "words of the night," and "by shouting them over the rooftops," robs us of the ability to use them or find them in private—sex becomes a matter in the public domain. Moreover, by dehumanizing the individual, people are treated as in concentration camps. As Steiner expressed it subsequent to the original publication of his essay: "Both pornography and totalitarianism seem to me to set up power relations which must necessarily violate privacy."[24]

If there is any plausibility to the first part of these claims, it must derive entirely from the metaphor of shouting the sacred night words over the rooftops. Were anyone to do such a thing with night words, day words, winter words, and so on, we would have a legitimate gripe concerning our privacy. But in what *way* is the voluntary perusal or viewing of pornography an invasion of privacy? His point *seems* to be that the constant consumption by the public of explicit sexual materials will come to make sex something "pre-packaged" for us, so that we will not discover how to do it ourselves, in our own ways. This is extraordinarily implausible, and if it were true, would constitute a reason for banning all literature dealing with human feelings and emotions, and ways of relating to one another. The evidence is that greater sexual explicitness is utilized as a means for people to have greater awareness of their sexuality and its possibilities, and to assimilate the experiences of others into their own lifestyles. The capacity to do this is *part* of what is involved in our being the unique individuals we are. At any rate, people who *want* the stimulation of erotic materials, who feel freer in expressing themselves through the influence of sexy art, who do not *want* an environment in which sex cannot be appreciated through explicit literature and art, will hardly be impressed with the manner in which the censor protects *their* privacy.

I want now to turn to Kristol's view that pornography is autoerotic, hence, infantile, and thus promotes a sexual regression which is a danger to civilization itself. The danger which this supposed form of infantilism poses is that it would destroy the capacity for an integral feature of mature relations (and ultimately civilized relations) if "not controlled or sublimated in some way."

Now the ultimate ground for censorship which the argument poses really has only secondary connections with the charges of autoeroticism and infantilism. Lots of things are "self-pleasing" without being thought infantile or dangerous on that account. Consider the pleasures of the gourmet, or wine aficionado, or devotees of Turkish baths.

Kristol believes that masturbation, and pornography which is its mental form, has an appeal to us as adults, and this is dangerous. Because it *is so* attractive, it is liable to draw us away from real love, and this is why it must be headed off at the pass. The charge of infantilism, then, is only Kristol's way of making us feel bad about masturbating. By virtue of his claiming to know the rationale underlying "all the codes of sexual conduct ever devised by the human race," we are made to feel beyond the pale of civilized adult society. The argument turns, really, on the supposed dangers of an *overly* autoeroticized society, which he thinks the legalization of pornography will help produce.

In criticizing pornography on these grounds, Kristol has surely overshot his mark; for, there is nothing more masturbatory than masturbation itself. If Kristol is right, then his concern with pornography is too tepid a treatment of the danger. What the argument would show is that we must stamp out masturbation itself!

Moreover, Kristol is mistaken if he thinks that censorship of pornography will make one whit of difference to the incidence of masturbation. This is because the masturbatory imagination is perfectly limitless; it does not *need* explicit sexual stimuli. Deprived of that, it can make do with virtually anything—the impassioned kisses of film lovers, a well-filled female's sweater, or male's crotch,[25] even, we are told, a neatly displayed ankle or bare shoulder. The enormity of the problem Kristol faces is shown in the revelation of the *Playboy* survey that: "a large majority of men and women in every age group say that while they masturbate, they fantasize about having intercourse with persons they love."[26] The implications for the censor are staggering!

There are two further reasons why reasonable

people will not take Kristol's view seriously. First, he underestimates the human capacity to assimilate varieties of sexual experience. People can enjoy pornography and intercourse without giving up one or the other.[27] Second, his entire argument grossly undervalues the appeal and attraction to us of the very thing he wants to preserve—mature sexual love which is fulfilling, rewarding, and integrated into the course of a loving relationship. Pornography may be in some sense autoerotic; it can be pleasant to be sexually stimulated. But it is rarely its own source of ultimate satisfaction; it usually stimulates to acquire further satisfactions. Indeed, this is presupposed by some of the conservative arguments. But there is no reason to assume that such satisfaction will be sought exclusively through masturbation, when a healthy sex relation is available with a loved one. I have *never* heard of anyone, male or female, complain that their love life had been ruined by their partner's turn to masturbation as a result of an excess of pornography. On the other hand, I have heard couples rave about sex had after viewing pornographic films.

Still, there does seem to be a lingering problem which the conservatives will regard as not adequately dealt with in anything said thus far. They think that literature and art *can* influence people's attitudes and beliefs, and also their behavior, and they cannot understand why the liberal, who believes this to be true in other cases, is unwilling to admit this with respect to pornography. Now, I believe the liberal *can* admit the possibility of a causal role for pornography with respect to people's attitudes and behavior. Such an admission does not, however, establish a case for censorship.

It would be quite extraordinary if literary and visual materials which are capable of arousing normal men and women did not also have some tendency to people already predisposed to harmful conduct, and especially people with an unstable psychological makeup. It is believable, even apart from any evidence, that such people might act from the fantasies such stimuli generate.

When the conservative is reasonable, however, he recognizes that the stimulation and consequent influence of pornography is a function not merely of the nature of the stimulus, but also of the person's background, upbringing, cultural environment, and his own genetic and personality structure and predispositions.[28] Put *this* way, the conservative has a somewhat plausible claim that pornography can sometimes be implicated as having some causal role in the etiology of social harms.

Put in its most reasonable form, however, the claim makes quite *un*reasonable the censorship of pornography. There are two primary reasons for this: (1) Pornography is not distinguishable from other materials in producing *direct* harms of this kind; it may, in fact, exert a counter-influence to other materials which are more likely to have these effects. (2) The *in*direct harms—those produced through the influence of altered attitudes and beliefs, are highly unlikely, and not of a kind a society which values freedom will allow to become the basis of suppression without strong evidence of probably causal connections. It will seek to counter such remote influences with noncoercive means.

Let us turn to the first point—that other materials which no one would dream of suppressing are as likely to produce harms. Earl Finbar Murphy, writing in the *Wayne Law Review*, has given some graphic illustrations. He beings by pointing out that "everything, every idea, is capable of being obscene if the personality perceiving it so apprehends it." He continues:

> It is for this reason that books, pictures, charades, ritual, the spoken word, *can* and *do* lead directly to conduct harmful to the self indulging in it and to others. Heinrich Pommerenke, who was a rapist, abuser, and mass slayer of women in Germany, was prompted to his series of ghastly deeds by Cecil B. DeMille's *The Ten Commandments*. During the scene of the Jewish women dancing about the Golden Calf, all the doubts of his life came clear: women were the source of the world's trouble and it was his mission both to punish them for this and to execute them. Leaving the theater, he slew his first victim in a park nearby. John George Haigh, the British vampire who sucked his victims' blood through soda straws and dissolved their drained bodies in acid baths, first had his murder-inciting dreams and vampire-longings from watching the "voluptuous" procedure of—an Anglican High Church Service!

The prohibition and effective suppression of what the average consensus would regard as pornographic would not have reached these two. Haigh, who drank his own urine as well as others' blood, was educated to regard "all forms of pleasure as sinful, and the reading of newspapers undesirable." Pommerenke found any reference to sex in a film, however oblique, made him feel so intense inside that, "I had to do something to a woman." Albert Fish, who has been called the most perverse case known to psychiatry, decided he had a mission to castrate small boys and offer them as human sacrifices to God as a result of reading the Old Testament. Each of these had the common quality of being beyond the reach of the conventionally pornographic. They had altered the range of the erotically stimulating, and each illustrates how impossible it is to predict what will precipitate or form psycho-neurotic conduct. . . . The scope of pornography, so far from being in any way uniform, is as wide as the peculiarities of the human psyche.[29]

These are extreme cases, but they do represent a pattern on the part of people disposed to deviant behavior, as is borne out by studies of the personalities and backgrounds of sex offenders. In their book, *Pornography and Sexual Deviance*, Michael J. Goldstein and Harold S. Kant report:

A problem that arises in studying reactions to pornography among sex offenders is that they appear to generate their own pornography from nonsexual stimuli. . . . The sex offenders deduced a significantly greater number of sexual activities from the drawings (children playing near a tree, figure petting a dog, and three people standing unrelated to each other) than did the nonsex offenders. They also were more prone to incorporate recently viewed sexual pictures into a series of gradually more explicit drawings. These results imply that the sex offender is highly receptive to sexual stimuli, and reads sexual meanings into images that would be devoid of erotic connotations for the normal person. Certainly, this finding was borne out by our study of institutionalized pedophiles (child molesters), who found the familiar suntan lotion ad showing a young child, with buttocks exposed to reveal his sunburn as a dog pulls at his bathing suit, to be one of the most erotic stimuli they had encountered.[30]

Indeed, their studies seem to yield the conclusion that pornography itself does not tend to produce antisocial behavior, and that, at least in the case of rapists, other materials are likely to do so:

We must consider that sex offenders are highly receptive to suggestions of sexual behavior congruent with their previously formed desires and will interpret the material at hand to fit their needs. It is true, however, that while few, if any, sex offenders suggest that erotica played a role in the commission of sex crimes, stimuli expressing brutality, with or without concomitant sexual behavior, were often mentioned as disturbing, by rapists in particular. This raises the question of whether the stimulus most likely to release antisocial sexual behavior is one representing sexuality, or one representing aggression.[31]

In summarizing the evidence they gathered, and which is supported by other studies, they conclude that pornography does not seem to be a significant factor in the behavior of sex offenders. Moreover, there is some evidence that "for rapists, exposure to erotica portraying 'normal' heterosexual relations can serve to ward off antisocial sexual impulses."[32]

The point is that if we take the conservative's "harm" claim in its most plausible form, we must conclude that while pornography *can* play a causal role of this type, the evidence is that many other ordinary visual and literary depictions are more likely to do so. If we take seriously the claim that having this kind of causal role is sufficient for a case of censorship, then we must do a much greater housecleaning of our media offerings than we had imagined. The problem is that while we know where to begin—with unalloyed portrayals of violence, we can hardly know where to end.

A further serious difficulty for the conservative "harm" argument arises when we ask just what *kinds* of backgrounds and attitudes *do* predispose to the unwanted behavior. The studies of Kant and Goldstein are of help here, especially with respect to rapists:

The rapists, who found it very difficult to talk about sex, said there was little nudity in their homes while they were growing up and that sex was never discussed. Only 18 percent of the rapists said their parents had caught them with erotic materials; in those instances the parents had become angry and had punished them. (In the control group, 37 percent reported that their parents know they read erotic materials, but only 7 percent reported being punished. Most said their parents had been indifferent, and some said their parents had explained the materials to them—an occurrence not reported by any other group.)[33]

For the *rapists*, the data suggest very repressive family backgrounds regarding sexuality.[34]

Moreover: "It appears that all our noncontrol groups, no matter what their ages, education, or occupations, share one common characteristic: they had little exposure to erotica when they were adolescents."[35]

These results at the very least carry the suggestion that the very attitudes toward sex which motivate the censor are part of the background and psychological information of the personality of sex offenders—backgrounds which include the repression of sexual feelings, repression of exposure to explicit sexual stimuli, an overly developed sense of shame and guilt related to sex. As we have seen, some of the censors advocate *just* this sort of model for all of society, wherein suppression of pornography is just *one* way of safeguarding society. It may well be that they are in the paradoxical position of isolating a possible evil of great extent, and then recommending and fostering a response which will help produce that very evil.[36]

There is, however, a more profound reason why the admission of a possible causal role for pornography in affecting attitudes and behavior need not support the conservative view, and why the traditional liberal may well have been right in not taking pornography seriously.

To begin with, I believe we have granted the conservatives too much in admitting that pornography depersonalizes sex. While there is a measure of truth in this claim, it is not literally true. By concentrating on physical aspects of sex, pornography does, somewhat, abstract from the web of feelings, emotions, and needs which are usually attendant on sexual experience in ordinary life. Nonetheless, people are not depicted as mere machines or animals. Indeed, where there is explicit pornographic purpose—the arousal of the reader or viewer—the end could not be accomplished were it not real fleshy people depicted. In addition, pornography almost always does have *some* human context within which sex takes place—a meeting in a bar, the bridegroom carrying his bride over the threshold, the window washer observing the inhabitant of an apartment. A study of pornography will reveal certain set patterns of such contexts: there is, indeed, a sort of orthodoxy among pornographers. And there is an obvious reason: pornography springs from and caters to sexual fantasies. This also explains why so little context is needed; the observer quickly identifies with the scene, and is able to elaborate it in his or her own mind to whatever extent he or she wishes or feels the need. That pornography is intimately tied to fantasy—*peopled* fantasy—also accounts for one of its worst features—its tendency to treat women in conventional male chauvinist ways. Pornography, as a matter of sociological fact, has been produced by and for men with such sexual attitudes.

There are further grounds for holding that pornography does not, by its nature, dehumanize sex in the feared ways. It usually depicts people as enjoying physical activity, that is, as mutually experiencing *pleasure*. Typical pornography displays sex as something people take fun in and enjoy. There is usually little doubt the persons involved are *liking* it. All

of the censors we have discussed treat *Fanny Hill* as pornographic, but it is obvious to anyone who has read the book that it absolutely resists the claim that the characters are not portrayed as real people with the usual hopes and fears, who desire not to be harmed, and desire a measure of respect as persons. The book concentrates on sex and sexual enjoyment, and *that* is why it is taken as pornographic.[37] Even sadistic pornography, it should be noted, depicts people as having enjoyment; and, it is usually sado-*masochistic* pleasures which are portrayed, with the resultant equalizing of the distribution of pleasure (if not of pain). In this respect, most pornography does not portray humans as *mere* instruments of whatever ends we have. And, in this respect, pornography does not express or evoke the genuinely immoral attitudes which a great deal of our movie, television, and literary materials cater to and reinforce.[38]

Indeed, much of what is found in the media *is* immoral in that it is expressive of, caters to, and fosters attitudes which *are* morally objectionable. People are treated as expendable units by international spies for whom *anything* is permitted in the name of national security; the typical laundry soap commercial treats women as idiotic house slaves; situation comedy typically portrays fathers as moronic bunglers who, nonetheless, rightfully rule their homes as dictators (albeit, benevolent ones); the various detective programs cater to the aggressive, dominating, *macho* image of male sexuality which is endemic within large portions of American society. Pornography cannot get off the hook merely by pointing out that it depicts *people*. On the other hand, most of it does not reflect or cater to attitudes as objectionable as one now finds dominating the output of television alone. And, where it does, it is not a result of the fact it is pornographic, but, rather, that it reflects conventional views widely expressed in other forms.[39]

There remains a final point to be made about the influence of pornography on attitudes. Pornography, when it does attract us, affect us, appeal to us, has a limited, narrowly focused appeal—to our sexual appetite. Such appeal tends toward short-lived enjoyments, rather than any far-reaching effects on the personality.[40] This is why pornography has essentially entertainment and recreational use and attraction; it is taken seriously by almost no one but the censors. It shows us people having sex, and that is it; we must do the rest. Serious literature and art, however, appeal to the whole person—to the entire range of his sensibilities, desires, needs, attitude patterns and beliefs and is thus far more likely to affect our ultimate behavior patterns. Even the limited re-action of sexual arousal is often better achieved through artistic technique. The conserva-tives deny this, but it is difficult to see on what grounds. Both in the essays of Van den Haag and of Walter Berns, there is the claim that aesthetic value would detract from the purely sexual appeal of a work.[41] I can only sup-pose that they think all people are possessed with, and exercise, the aesthetic sensibilities of literary and art critics, and thus readily separate out and analyze devices of technique in the experiencing of a work. This assuredly is not the case. Moreover, it is hardly plausible that artistic technique should enhance and further every *other* objective of an artist, and *not* be an accessory to the end of evoking sexual arousal. Real artistic value is unobtrusive in this respect.

Of course, television pap may well influence at-titudes without having significant artistic value, merely by its sheer preponderance on the airwaves. But it is not *this* sort of role we need envisage for pornography liberated from censorship. Moreover, it is not clear its influence would be worse than that of other materials which now hog the channels.

It seems to me, however, that we have yet to make the most important response to the conservative's claims. For, up to now, we have treated the issue as if it were merely a matter of weighing up possible harms from pornography against possible benefits, and the likelihood of the occurrence of the harms. Unfortunately, this is the form the debate usually takes, when it is not strictly concerned with the First Amendment. But, something important is lost if we think the issue resolves into these questions. The more important issue turns on the fact that a great many people *like* and *enjoy* pornography, and *want* it as part of their lives, either for its enjoyment, or for more serious psychological purposes. This fact means that censorship is an interference with the freedom and self-determination of a great many people, and it is on this ground that the conservative harm argument must ultimately be rejected. For a society which accepts freedom and self-determination as centrally significant values cannot allow interferences with freedom on such grounds as these.

To give a satisfactory argument for these claims would require another paper. Moreover, I believe (with certain reservations) this has been adequately done in Mill's *On Liberty*. As the conservatives do not regard *that* as enunciating a clear, defensible body of doctrine,[42] I cannot hope to present an entirely con-vincing argument here. I want at the very least, how-

ever, to outline a minimal set of claims which I think bear on the issue, and which can provide ground for further debate.

The idea of a self-determining individual in-volves a person developing his or her own mode of life according to the person's own needs, desires, personality, and perceptions of reality. This conception has at least three features: (1) the person's desires are (so far as possible) expressions of his or her own nature—not imposed from without; (2) the manner of the development of his or her character and the pattern of the person's life, are, in large measure, a resultant of his or her own judgment, choice, and personal experience; and (3) the person's unique capacities and potentialities have been developed, or at least tried out.[43] Now, *if* one regards this as a valuable manner of living, and freedom as of value, *both* because it is intrinsic to treating others *as* self-determining agents, *and* because it is requisite for the realization of self-determination, then I think one will accept the following propositions concerning freedom:

1. The burden of producing convincing reasons and evidence is always on the person who would interfere with people's freedom and life-styles.
2. The person who would interfere with freedom must show that the activity interfered with is likely to harm others or interfere with their rights as individuals.[44]
3. Those who would deny freedom must show that the harm or interference threatened is one from which others have a superior right to protection.

Though these propositions are subject to considerable interpretation, it seems to me that one who accepts them will, at the least, recognize that the burden of proof is not symmetric either in struc-ture or degree. The person who would deny freedom shoulders the burden, and, moreover, he or she does not succeed merely by showing *some* harms are likely to result. Accepting freedom and self-determination as central values entails accepting some risks, in or-der to *be* free. We do *not* presuppose that freedom will always produce good. And, insofar as the alleged harms are indirect and remote, we are committed to employing noncoercive means to combat them. Of course, we need not interpret this in a suicidal way—allowing interference only when the harm is inevita-bly upon us. But, at the least, we should require a strong showing of likely harms which are far from remote, and this is a burden which the censors of pornography *cannot* meet. Indeed, on this score, the conservative arguments are *many* times weaker than ones which can be made concerning many other kinds of communications, and such activities as hunting for sport, automobile racing, boxing, and so on.[45] If anyone wants a display of the extent to which our society allows recreation to instigate socially harmful attitudes and feelings, all he or she need do is sit in the stands during a hotly contested high school football or basketball game. And, of course these feelings quite often spill over into antisocial behavior.

Though I have defended pornography from criticisms based on its content or nature, I have certainly not shown that it is always unobjectionable. Insofar as it arises in a social context entirely infused with male sexism, much of it reflects the worst aspects of our society's approved conceptions of sexual relations. Too often, the scenes depicted involve male violence and aggression toward women, male dominance over women, and females as sexual ser-vants. Moreover, there are aspects of the commercial institutions which purvey it in the market which are quite objectionable. My argument is has been that this is not necessary to pornography as such; where it is true, this reflects social and sexual attitudes already fostered by other social forces. Moreover, I have maintained that by virtue of a feature which does seem to characterize pornography—its break with certain inhibiting conceptions of sexuality, pornography may well play a role in people determining for themselves the life-style which most suits them. A society which values self-determination will interfere with it only under circumstances which the censors of pornography cannot show to hold.

Of course, I have said almost nothing about the nature of the specific freedoms we incorporate in our notion of freedom of speech. It may well be that that set of rights imposes even stricter obligations on those who would suppress forms of its exercise.

Discussion Questions

1. How does Professor Berger define pornography? Do you agree or disagree with his definition? Explain and defend your answer.

2. What is the form of conservative argument to which Professor Berger is responding? Professor Berger cites two approaches to this argument, one by Steiner and one by Kristol. What are their arguments and how does Professor Berger respond to

them? Do you agree or disagree with his responses? Explain and defend your answer.

3. In addition to his responses to Steiner and Kristol, Professor Berger presents several other reasons to reject the conservative argument. What are those reasons? Present and explain them in detail. Do you consider them plausible? Explain and defend your answer.

4. Professor Berger makes the rather provocative argument that censorship rather than pornography may result in socially harmful attitudes and/or behavior. How does he defend this position? Do you agree or disagree with his defense? Explain and defend your answer.

5. Professor Berger concludes his essay by arguing that the censor has the burden of providing convincing reasons to interfere with someone's consumption of pornography. How does he argue for this point? Do you find his case compelling? Why or why not? Explain and defend your answer.

Notes

1. This proposition is argued for by one advocate of censorship. See Irving Kristol, "Pornography, Obscenity, and the Case for Censorship," *New York Times Magazine* (March 28, 1971): 23.

2. There are a number of brief summaries available on the development of the common-law approach to obscenity. See *The Report of the Commission on Obscenity and Pornography* (New York: Bantam, 1970), 348–54; Michael J. Goldstein and Harold S. Kant, *Pornography and Sexual Deviance* (Berkeley: University of California Press, 1973), 154–56; and an untitled essay by Charles Rembar in *Censorship: For and Against*, ed. Harold H. Hart (New York: Hart Publishing Co., 1971), 198–227. Apparently, the leading case prior to the 18th century involved Sir Charles Sedley, who, with some friends, had become drunk in a tavern, appeared naked on a balcony overlooking Covent Garden, and shouted profanities at the crowd which gathered below; then he urinated upon, and threw bottles of urine on, the bystanders.

3. Regulation of speech is one of the most pressing problems for free speech in our contemporary, mass society, in which the control of the media is in relatively few hands, primarily concerned with the use of that media to produce profits. Moreover, the spectre of nonlegal controls, which Mill feared, is very much with us. It is surprising that so little attention has been given to the issue of the principles properly governing regulation. An indication of various forms of control utilized by government for the suppression of pornography is found by studying the development of censorship in the United States. See James

C. N. Paul and Murray L. Schwartz, *Federal Censorship: Obscenity in the Mail* (New York: The Free Press, 1961).

4. I regard it as a serious drawback of the definition that it rules out by *fiat*, the claim that pornography *can* be, in and of itself, significant literature. This claim is convincingly argued for by Susan Sontag in her essay "The Pornographic Imagination," reprinted in *Perspectives on Pornography*, ed. Douglas A. Hughes (New York: St. Martin's Press, 1970), 131–69; also in her book *Styles of Radical Will* (New York: Farrar, Straus & Giroux, 1966). The argument for a broader, more inclusive definition is made convincingly by Morse Peckham in *Art and Pornography* (New York: Basic Books, 1969), chapter 1. Anyone with a serious interest in the subject of pornography will find this a most important work.

5. It is also clear that the definition would be a disaster in the legal context, since there is so great an area of *disagreement*. Moreover, there is a tremendous danger of a secondary form of censorship, in which literary critics come to watch closely how they criticize a work lest the critique be used by the censors. That this in fact has happened is testified to in an eye-opening note by the English critic Horace Judson, in *Encounter* 30 (March 1968): 57–60. To his dismay, a critical review he wrote of Selby's *Last Exit to Brooklyn* was read into the record and used in banning that book in England.

6. See, for example, Ernest van den Haag, writing in *Censorship: For and Against*, 158. Also, in "Is Pornography a Cause of Crime?" *Encounter* 29 (December 1967): 54.

7. I believe that the minority report of the Presidential Commission on Obscenity and Pornography reduces to such a view, when it is not concerned specifically with possible harms. See, for example the rationale given on 498–500 of the report, for their legislative recommendations. Sense can be made of these passages *only* on the assumption the commissioners believe pornography is itself immoral. I might also note that if one looks up "pornography" in the *Readers' Guide*, he is advised "See immoral literature and pictures."

8. Ronald Dworkin, "Lord Devlin and the Enforcement of Morals," *Yale Law Journal* 75 (1966): 986–1005; reprinted in *Morality and the Law*, ed. Richard Wasserstrom (Belmont, Calif.: Wadsworth, 1971), 55–72.

9. For starters, one might review the essays in Wasserstrom, *Morality and the Law*.

10. In surveys done for the Presidential Commission, it was found that a (slim) majority of adults would not object to the availability of pornography if it could be shown it was not harmful. While hardly a declaration of adoration for pornography, this is not a demonstration of utter, overwhelming intolerance for it, either.

11. See, for example, Paris Adult Theatre I v. Slaton, 431 U.S. 49 (1973).

12. Report of the Commission on Obscenity, 26–32, in which the effects are summarized. Also, Goldstein and Kant, *Pornography and Sexual Deviance*, 139–53.

13. George Steiner, "Night Words: High Pornography and Human Privacy," in *Perspectives on Pornography*, 96–108.

14. Ibid., 106–07.

15. Kristol, "Pornography, Obscenity and the Case for Censorship," 113.

16. Ibid.

17. Walter Berns, "Pornography vs. Democracy: The Case for Censorship," *The Public Interest* 22 (Winter 1971): 12.

18. Ibid., 13. Berns cites Washington, Jefferson, and Lincoln as holding that democracy requires citizens of good character and self-restraint, and he seems to think that somehow this is a "forgotten argument" against pornography.

19. Van den Haag, in *Censorship: For and Against*, 146–48.

20. The extent to which feelings of vulnerability can be involved in sex is testified to by the kinds of fears which can inhibit orgasmic response. In her book reporting on techniques she has used with non- or preorgasmic women, Dr. Lonnie Garfield Barbach reports that among the factors which inhibit these women from having orgasms is the fear of appearing ugly, of their partners being repulsed by them, of losing control, fainting, or screaming. See Lonnie Garfield Barbach, *For Yourself: The Fulfillment of Female Sexuality* (Garden City, N.J.: Doubleday, 1975), 11–12.

21. Berns, "Pornography vs. Democracy," 12.

22. In *For Yourself*, Dr. Lonnie Garfield Barbach recommends the use of pornography for preorgasmic women seeking increased sexual responsiveness and fulfillment. See *For Yourself*, 75, 77, 85, 86. Dr. Wardell B. Pomeroy, one of Kinsey's collaborators, wrote *Playboy*, in reaction to a 1973 Supreme Court ruling on pornography:

> As a psychotherapist and marriage counselor, I sometimes recommend various erotic films, books and pictures to my patients. Many of them report that erotica helps them to free them of their inhibitions and, thus, helps them function better with their spouses. Now they will have more difficulty in seeing and reading such seriously valuable material, and I am afraid I must enlarge my own library for their perusal. *Playboy* 20 (October 1973): 57.

23. This point is made at length in the report. One example: "Despite the extensive changes that the liberation has made in the feelings that most Americans have about their own bodies, about the legitimacy of maximizing sexual pleasure and about the acceptability and normality of a wide variety of techniques of foreplay and coitus, sexual liberation has not replaced the liberal-romantic concept of sex with the recreational one. The latter attitude toward sex now coexists with the former in our society, and in many a person's feeling, but the former remains the dominant ideal." *Playboy* 20 (October 1973): 204.

24. Steiner, "Night Words," in *Perspectives*, 97.

25. That women look at, and are excited by, the bulges in men's trousers is given ample testimony in Nancy Friday's book on women's sexual fantasies. See *My Secret Garden* (New York: Pocket Books, 1974), the section entitled "Women Do Look," 214–22.

26. *Playboy*, 202.

27. See, for example, *Report of the Commission on Obscenity*, 28–29; also, Goldstein and Kant, *Pornography and Sexual Deviance*, 30.

28. Van den Haag seems to recognize this point. See "Is Pornography a Cause of Crime?" in *Encounter*, 53.

29. Earl Finbar Murphy, "The Value of Pornography," *Wayne Law Review* (1964): 668–69.

30. Goldstein and Kant, *Pornography and Sexual Deviance*, 31.

31. Ibid., 108–09.

32. Ibid., 152.

33. Ibid., 143.

34. Ibid., 145.

35. Ibid., 147.

36. To compound the paradox, if being a remote cause of harms is a prima facie ground for censoring literature, then we have some evidence that the conservative arguments ought to be censored. This is *not* a view I advocate.

37. I do not appeal to its conventional format—girl meets boy, girl loses boy, girl reunites with boy in marriage.

38. Professor Van den Haag holds that pornography "nearly always leads to sadistic pornography." It is not clear what this means; moreover, his argument is that this results *because* pornography dehumanizes sex. Since we have grounds for doubting this, we have grounds for doubting the alleged result. Also, since I am denying that pornography significantly dehumanizes sex, I am implicitly rejecting a further conservative argument I have not taken up, namely, that pornography is itself expressive of immoral attitudes irrespective of any further harmful effects. Since some liberals seem to be willing to silence Nazis or racists on such grounds, some conservatives think this argument will appeal to such liberals. I believe that both Kristol and Van den Haag maintain this view. See also Richard Kuh, *Foolish Figleaves?* (New York: Macmillan, 1967), 280ff. A position of this sort is maintained by Susan Brownmiller in her book *Against Our Will: Men, Women and Rape* (New York: Simon and Schuster, 1975), 201. Brownmiller regards pornography as an invention designed to humiliate women. I have not responded to her arguments as she gives none. Moreover, she employs a curious "double standard." She gives great weight to law enforcement officials' opinions about pornography, but would hardly be willing to take these same persons' views on rape at face value.

39. In this paragraph I have attempted to bring to bear on the argument some points made by Professor Ann Garry, in her commentary on the paper at the meeting of the Society for Philosophy and Public Affairs in San Diego, March 18, 1975.

40. *Report of the Commission on Obscenity*, 28; and Goldstein and Kant, *Pornography and Sexual Deviance*, 151.

41. Berns, in *The Public Interest*, 12 footnote, and Van den Haag, in *Perspectives*, 129.

42. See, for example, Gertrude Himmelfarb's recent critical account of Mill, *On Liberty and Liberalism: The Case of John Stuart Mill* (New York: Alfred A. Knopf, 1974). It appears to me that she has not really understood Mill. Ronald Dworkin has picked out some of the most glaring of her errors in his review in *The New York Review of Books* 21 (October 31, 1974): 21.

43. I believe this is Mill's conception. See also Sharon Hill's essay, "Self-Determination and Autonomy," in *Today's Moral Problems*, ed. Richard Wasserstrom (New York: Macmillan, 1975), 171–86.

44. I want to note three points here. First, this view of freedom permits inferences for *moral* reasons; it does *not* insist on the moral neutrality of the law. It does, however, focus on the *kinds* of moral reasons allowed to count as grounds for the denial of freedom. Second, it does not rule out special legal recognition of modes of living which are central to the culture, for example, monogamous marriage. This will have indirect effects on freedom which a liberal theory would have to recognize and deal with, but it need not rule out such recognition out of hand. In addition, the notion of "harm" could be taken to include conduct or practices which are both intrusive on public consciousness, and offensive. This could provide a basis for *regulating* the sale and distribution of pornography, even if *prohibition* is not justified. Important discussion of the principles underlying the treatment of offensiveness in the law is to be found in an article by Joel Feinberg, "Harmless Immoralities and Offensive Nuisances," in *Issues in Law and Morality*, ed. Norman Care and Thomas Trelogan (Cleveland: Case Western Reserve University, 1973). Michael Bayles's commentary on that paper, also found in the same volume, is very useful. Third, valuing self-determination may entail a limited paternalism in circumstances where noninterference cannot possibly further autonomy. That it is at least possible for noninterference to promote self-determination seems to have been conceived by Mill as a presupposition for applications of the principle of liberty. This helps explain some of his "applications" at the end of the essay. Just how to incorporate limited paternalism in a liberal theory is a thorny issue. The pornography issue, however, does not appear to significantly involve that issue. A useful treatment of paternalism is in Gerald Dworkin, "Paternalism," in *Morality and the Law*, 107–26.

45. So far as I can judge, the most telling "evidence" the conservatives have thus far come up with is: (a) *some* reasonable criticisms of the studies which have been done, and the interpretations which have been given them; and (b) a few, isolated, contrary studies (which are, coincidentally, open to similar or stronger objections). See especially the criticisms of Victor B. Cline in the minority report of the Presidential Commission on Obscenity and Pornography, 463–89. While I do not think the conservatives need pro-

duce ironclad scientific data demonstrating their claims, we surely cannot allow the suppression of freedom when the reasons offered are poor, and the weight of available evidence is heavily *against* those claims. The minority report (it may be Dr. Cline writing in this instance—it is unclear) asserts that the "burden of proof" is on the one who would change current law. This is an indefensible imprimatur of existing law as such; and it is absolutely inconsistent with the recognition of freedom and self-determination as important moral values. The mere *existence* of law cannot be allowed as a ground for its continued existence, if freedom is to have anything but secondary importance.

47

The Question of Harm

Attorney General's
Commission on Pornography

A sketch of the commission is found at the beginning of Chapter 43.

One legal way to justify a government restriction on a fundamental right, such as the First Amendment right to freedom of expression, is to show that an unrestricted practice of this right in some circumstances results in significant social and/or individual harm. For example, restrictions on speech, such as a threat to the president's life, yelling "Fire!" in a crowded theatre, or sexually harassing a co-worker, are legally justified because of the harm that they are trying to prevent. In this essay, the Attorney General's Commission argues that some studies have clearly shown that some forms of pornography result in significant social and/or individual harm. For this reason, the government may have a right to restrict such pornography on that basis. On the other hand, the commission argues that although that may be a sufficient condition in some circumstances to restrict pornography, it is not a necessary condition. That is, there could be other reasons to restrict pornography that are consistent with the First Amendment and do not involve proving that the pornography in question causes significant social and/or individual harm (e.g., it is merely obscene). Also, there could be some circumstances in which harmful speech is protected by the First Amendment, such as in the cases of bigoted, racist, or hateful speech. For these reasons, the commission is not concerned so much in drawing legal lines—although it no doubt realizes the legal importance of proving harm—but rather with the evidence of

Reprinted by permission from *Final Report of the Attorney General's Commission on Pornography* (Nashville, Tenn.: Rutledge Hill Press, 1986).

whether pornography results in harm. After discussing what counts as harm as well as making a distinction between primary and secondary harms, the commission examines three different types of sexually explicit materials: (1) sexually violent material, (2) non-violent materials depicting degradation, domination, subordination, or humiliation, and (3) non-violent and non-degrading materials. The commission then critically evaluates the studies of those who consume each type, drawing several conclusions on the basis of the results of these studies.

Harm and Regulation— The Scope of Our Inquiry

A central part of our mission has been to examine the question of whether pornography is harmful. In attempting to answer this question, we have made a conscious decision not to allow our examination of the harm question to be constricted by the existing legal/constitutional definition of the legally obscene. We agree with that definition in principle and we believe that in most cases it allows criminal prosecution of what ought to be prosecuted and prohibits criminal prosecution of what most of us believe is material properly protected by the First Amendment. In light of this, our decision to look at the potential for harm in a range of material substantially broader than the legally obscene requires some explanation. One reason for this approach was the fact that in some respects existing constitutional decisions permit non-prohibitory restrictions of material other than the legally obscene. With respect to zoning, broadcast regulation, and liquor licensing, existing Supreme Court case law permits some control, short of total prohibition, of the time, place, and manner in which sexually explicit materials that are short of being legally obscene may be distributed. When these non-prohibitory techniques are used, the form of regulation is still constrained by constitutional considerations, but the regulation need not be limited only to that which has been or would be found legally obscene. To address fully the question of government regulation, therefore, requires that an examination of possible harm encompass a range of materials broader than the legally obscene.

Moreover, the range of techniques of social control is itself broader than the scope of any form of permissible or desirable governmental regulation. We discuss in Chapter 8 many of these techniques, including pervasive social condemnation, public protest, picketing, and boycotts, It is appropriate here, however, to emphasize that we do not see any necessary connection between what is protected by law (and therefore protected *from* law), on the one hand, and what citizens may justifiably object to and take non-governmental action against, on the other. And if it is appropriate for citizens justifiably to protest against some sexually explicit materials despite the fact that those materials are consti-tutionally protected, then it is appropriate for us to broaden the realm of our inquiry accordingly.

Most importantly, however, we categorically reject the idea that material cannot be constitutionally protected, and properly so, while still being harmful. All of us, for example, feel that the inflammatory utterances of Nazis, the Ku Klux Klan, and racists of other varieties are harmful both to the individuals to whom their epithets are directed as well as to society as a whole. Yet all of us acknowledge and most of us support the fact that the harmful speeches of these people are nevertheless constitutionally protected. That the same may hold true with respect to some sexually explicit materials was at least our working assumption in deciding to look at a range of materials broader than the legally obscene. There is no reason whatsoever to suppose that such material is necessarily harmless just because it is and should remain protected by the First Amendment. As a result, we reject the notion that an investigation of the question of harm must be restricted to material unprotected by the Constitution.

The converse of this is equally true. Just as there is no necessary connection between the constitutionally protected and the harmless, so too is there no necessary connection between the constitutionally unprotected and the harmful. We examine the harm question with respect to material that *is* legally obscene because even if material is therefore unprotected by the First Amendment, it does not follow that it is harmful. That some sexually explicit material is constitutionally regulable does not answer the question of whether anything justifies its regulation. Accordingly, we do not take our acceptance of the current constitutional approach to obscenity as diminishing the need to examine the harms purportedly associated with the distribution or use of such material.

We thus take as substantially dissimilar the question of constitutional protection and the question of harm. Even apart from constitutional issues, we also take to be separate the question of the advisability of governmental regulation, all things considered, and the question of the harmfulness of some or all sexually explicit materials. The upshot of all of this is that we feel it entirely proper to identify harms that may accompany certain sexually explicit material before and independent of an inquiry into the desirability and constitutionality of regulating even that sexually explicit material that may be harmful. As a result, our inquiry into harm encompasses much material that would not generally be considered "pornographic" as we use that term here.

What Counts as a Harm?

What is a harm? And why focus on harm at all? We do not wish in referring repeatedly to "harm" to burden ourselves with an unduly narrow conception of harm. To emphasize in different words what we said in the previous section, the scope of identifiable harms is broader than the scope of that with which government can or should deal. We refuse to truncate our consideration of the question of harm by defining harms in terms of possible government regulation. And we certainly reject the view that the only noticeable harm is one that causes physical or financial harm to identifiable individuals. An environment—physical, cultural, moral, or aesthetic—can be harmed, and so can a community, organization, or group be harmed independent of identifiable harms to members of that community.

Most importantly, although we have emphasized in our discussion of harms the kinds of harms that can most easily be observed and measured, the idea of harm is broader than that. To a number of us, the most important harms must be seen in moral terms, and the act of moral condemnation of that which is immoral is not merely important but essential. From this perspective there are acts that need be seen not only as causes of immorality but as manifestations of it. Issues of human dignity and human decency, no less real for their lack of scientific measurability, are for many of us central to thinking about the question of harm. And when we think about harm in this way, there are acts that must be condemned not because the evils of the world will thereby be eliminated, but because conscience demands it.

We believe it useful in thinking about harms to note the distinction between harm and offense. Although the line between the two is hardly clear, most people can nevertheless imagine things that offend them, or offend others, that still would be hard to describe as harms. . . .

In thinking about harms, it is useful to draw a rough distinction between primary and secondary harms. Primary harms are those in which the alleged harm is commonly taken to be intrinsically harmful, even though the precise way in which the harm is harmful might yet be further explored. Nevertheless, murder, rape, assault, and discrimination on the basis of race and gender are all examples of primary harms in this sense. We treat these acts as harms not because of where they will lead, but simply because of what they are.

In other instances, however, the alleged harm is secondary, not in the sense that it is in any way less important, but in the sense that the concern is not with what the act *is*, but where it will lead. Curfews are occasionally imposed not because there is anything wrong with people being out at night, but because in some circumstances it is thought that being out at night in large groups may cause people to commit other crimes. Possession of "burglar tools" is often prohibited because of what those tools may be used for. Thus, when it is urged that pornography is harmful because it causes some people to commit acts of sexual violence, because it causes promiscuity, because it encourages sexual relations outside of marriage, because it promotes so-called "unnatural" sexual practices, or because it leads men to treat women as existing solely for the sexual satisfaction of men, the alleged harms are secondary, again not in any sense suggesting that the harms are less important. The harms are secondary here because the allegation of harm presupposes a causal link that is superfluous if, as in the case of primary harms, the act quite simply *is* the harm.

Thus we think it important, with respect to every area of possible harm, to focus on whether the allegation relates to a harm that comes from the sexually explicit material itself, or whether it occurs *as a result* of something the material does. If it is the former, then the inquiry can focus directly on the nature of the alleged harm. But if it is the latter, then there must be a two-step inquiry. First it is necessary to determine if some hypothesized result is in fact harmful. In some cases, where the asserted consequent harm is unquestionably a harm, this step of the analysis is easy. With respect to claims that certain sexually explicit material increases the incidence of rape or other sexual violence, for example, no one could plausibly claim that such consequences were

not harmful, and the inquiry can then turn to whether the causal link exists. In other cases, however, the harmfulness of the alleged harm is often debated. With respect to claims, for example, that some sexually explicit material causes promiscuity, encourages homosexuality, or legitimizes sexual practices other than vaginal intercourse, there is serious societal debate about whether the consequences themselves are harmful.

Thus, the analysis of the hypothesis that pornography causes harm must start with the identification of hypothesized harms, proceed to the determination of whether those hypothesized harms are indeed harmful, and then conclude with the examination of whether a causal link exists between the material and the harm. When the consequences of exposure to sexually explicit material are not harmful, or when there is no causal relationship between exposure to sexually explicit material and some harmful consequence, then we cannot say that the sexually explicit material is harmful. But if sexually explicit material of some variety is causally related to, or increases the incidence of, some behavior that is harmful, then it is safe to conclude that the material is harmful.

The Standard of Proof

In dealing with these questions, the standard of proof is a recurrent problem. How much evidence is needed, or how convinced should we be, before reaching the conclusion that certain sexually explicit material *causes* harm? The extremes of this question are easy. Whenever a causal question is even worth asking, there will never be *conclusive* proof that such a causal connection exists, if "conclusive" means that no other possibility exists. We note that frequently, and all too often, the claim that there is no "conclusive" proof is a claim made by someone who disagrees with the implications of the conclusion.

Few if any judgments of causality or danger are ever conclusive, and a requirement of conclusiveness is much more rhetorical device than analytical method. We therefore reject the suggestion that a causal link must be proved "conclusively" before we can identify a harm.

The opposite extreme is also easily dismissed. The fact that someone makes an assertion of fact to us is not necessarily sufficient proof of that fact, even if the assertion remains uncontradicted. We do not operate as a judge sitting in a court of law, and we require more evidence to reach an affirmative conclusion than does a judge whose sole function might in some circumstances be to determine if there is sufficient evidence to send the case to the jury. That there is a bit of evidence for a proposition is not the same as saying that the proposition has been established, and we do not reach causal conclusions in every instance in which there has been some evidence of that proposition.

Between these extremes the issues are more difficult. The reason for this is that how much proof is required is largely a function of what is to be done with an affirmative finding, and what the consequences are of proceeding on the basis of an affirmative finding. As we deal with causal assertions short of conclusive but more than merely some trifle of evidence, we have felt free to rely on less proof merely to make assertions about harm than we have required to recommend legal restrictions, and similarly we have required greater confidence in our assertions if the result was to recommend criminal penalties for a given form of behavior than we did to recommend other forms of legal restriction. Were we to have recommended criminal sanctions against material now covered by the First Amendment, we would have required proof sufficient to satisfy some variant of the "clear and present danger" standard that serves to protect the communication lying at the center of the First Amendment's guarantees from government action resting on a less certain basis.

No government could survive, however, if all of its actions were required to satisfy a "clear and present danger" standard, and we openly acknowledge that in many areas we have reached conclusions that satisfy us for the purposes for which we draw them, but which would not satisfy us if they were to be used for other purposes. That we are satisfied that the vast majority of depictions of violence in a sexually explicit manner are likely to increase the incidence of sexual violence in this country, for example, does not mean that we have concluded that the evidence is sufficient to justify governmental prohibition of materials that both meet that description and are *not* legally obscene.

It would be ideal if we could put our evidentiary standards into simple formulas, but that has not been possible. The standards of proof applicable to the legal process—preponderance of the evidence, clear and convincing evidence, and proof beyond a reasonable doubt—are not easily transferred into a nonjudicial context. And the standards of justification of constitutional law—rational basis, compelling interest, and clear and present danger, for example—relate only to the constitutionality of governmental action, not to its advisability, nor to the standards necessary for mere warnings about harm. Thus we have felt it best to rely on the language that people ordinarily use, words like "convinced," "satisfied," and "concluded," but those words should be interpreted in light of the discussion in this section. . . .

Sexually Violent Material

The category of material on which most of the evidence is focused is the category of material featuring actual or unmistakably simulated or unmistakably threatened violence presented in sexually explicit fashion with predominant focus on the sexually explicit violence. Increasingly, the most prevalent forms of pornography, as well as an increasingly prevalent body of less sexually explicit material, fit this description. Some of this material involves sado-masochistic themes, with the standard accoutrements of the genre, including whips, chains, devices of torture, and so on. But another theme of some of this material is not sado-masochistic, but involves instead the recurrent theme of a man making some sort of sexual advance to a woman, being rebuffed, and then raping the woman or in some other way violently forcing himself on the woman. In almost all of this material, whether in magazine or motion picture form, the woman eventually becomes aroused and ecstatic about the initially forced sexual activity, and usually is portrayed as begging for more. There is also a large body of material, more "mainstream" in its availability, that portrays sexual activity or sexually suggestive nudity coupled with extreme violence, such as disfigurement or murder. The so-called "slasher" films fit this description, as does some material, both in film and magazines, that is less or more sexually explicit than the prototypical "slasher" film.

It is with respect to material of this variety that the scientific findings and ultimate conclusions of the 1970 Commission are least reliable for today, precisely because material of this variety was largely absent from that Commission's inquiries. It is not, however, absent from the contemporary world, and it is hardly surprising that conclusions about this material differ from conclusions about material not including violent themes.

Where clinical and experimental research has focused particularly on sexually violent material, the conclusions have been virtually unanimous. In both clinical and experimental settings, exposure to sexually violent materials has indicated an increase in the likelihood of aggression. More specifically, the research, which is described in much detail later in this Report, shows a causal relationship between exposure to material of this type and aggressive behavior towards women.

Finding a link between aggressive behavior towards women and sexual violence, whether lawful or unlawful, requires assumptions not found exclusively in the experimental evidence. We see no reason, however, not to make these assumptions. The assumption that increased aggressive behavior towards women is causally related, for an aggregate population, to increased sexual violence is significantly supported by the clinical evidence, as well as by much of the less scientific evidence. They are also to all of us assumptions that are plainly justified by our own common sense. This is not to say that all people with heightened levels of aggression will commit acts of sexual violence. But it is to say that over a sufficiently large number of cases we are confident in asserting that an increase in aggressive behavior directed at women will cause an increase in the level of sexual violence directed at women.

Thus we reach our conclusions by combining the results of the research with highly justifiable assumptions about the generalizability of more limited research results. Since the clinical and experimental evidence supports the conclusion that there is a causal relationship between exposure to sexually violent materials and an increase in aggressive behavior directed towards women, and since we believe that an increase in aggressive behavior towards women will in a population increase the incidence of sexual violence in that population, we have reached the conclusion, unanimously and confidently, that the available evidence strongly supports the hypotheses that substantial exposure to sexually violent materials as described here bears a causal relationship to antisocial acts of sexual violence and, for some subgroups, possibly to unlawful acts of sexual violence.

Although we rely for this conclusion on significant scientific empirical evidence, we feel it worthwhile to note the underlying logic of the conclusion. The evidence says simply that the images that people are exposed to bears a causal relationship to their behavior. This is hardly surprising. What would be surprising would be to find otherwise, and we have not so found. We have not, of course, found that the images people are exposed to are greater cause of sexual violence than all or even many other possible causes the investigation of which has been beyond our mandate. Nevertheless, it would be strange indeed if graphic representations of a form of behavior, especially in a form that almost exclusively portrays such behavior as desirable, did not have at least some effect on patterns of behavior.

Sexual violence is not the only negative effect reported in the research to result from substantial exposure to sexually violent materials. The evidence is also strongly supportive of significant attitudinal changes on the part of those with substantial exposure to violent pornography. These attitudinal changes are numerous. Victims of rape and other forms of sexual violence are likely to be perceived by people so exposed as more responsible for the assault, as having suffered less injury, and as having been less degraded as a result of the experience. Similarly, people with a substantial exposure to violent pornography are likely to see the rapist or other sexual offender as less responsible for the act and as deserving of less stringent punishment.

These attitudinal changes have been shown experimentally to include a larger range of attitudes than those just discussed. The evidence also strongly supports the conclusion that substantial exposure to violent sexually explicit material leads to a greater acceptance of the "rape myth" in its broader sense— that women enjoy being coerced into sexual activity, that they enjoy being physically hurt in sexual context, and that as a result a man who forces himself on a woman sexually is in fact merely acceding to the "real" wishes of the woman, regardless of the extent to which she seems to be resisting. The myth is that a woman who says "no" really means "yes," and that men are justified in acting on the assumption that the "no" answer is indeed the "yes" answer. We have little trouble concluding that this attitude is both pervasive and profoundly harmful, and that any stimulus reinforcing or increasing the incidence of this attitude is for that reason alone properly designated as harmful.

Two vitally important features of the evidence supporting the above conclusions must be mentioned here. The first is that all of the harms discussed here, including acceptance of the legitimacy of sexual violence against women but not limited to it, are more pronounced when the sexually violent materials depict the woman as experiencing arousal, orgasm, or other form of enjoyment as the ultimate result of the sexual assault. This theme, unfortunately very common in the materials we have examined, is likely to be the major, albeit not the only, component of what it is in the materials in this category that causes the consequences that have been identified.

The second important clarification of all of the above is that the evidence lends some support to the conclusion that the consequences we have identified here *do not vary with the extent of sexual explicitness so long as the violence is presented in an undeniably sexual context*. Once a threshold is passed at which sex and violence are plainly linked, increasing the sexual explicitness of the material, or the bizarreness of the sexual activity, seems to bear little relationship to the extent of the consequences discussed here. Although it is unclear whether sexually violent material makes a substantially greater causal contribution to sexual violence itself than does material containing violence alone, it appears that increasing the amount of violence after the threshold of connecting sex with violence is more related to increase in the incidence or severity of harmful consequences than is increasing the amount of sex. As a result, the so-called "slasher" films, which depict a great deal of violence connected with an undeniably sexual theme but less sexual explicitness than materials that are truly pornographic, are likely to produce the consequences discussed here to a greater extent than most of the materials available in "adults only" pornographic outlets.

Although we have based our findings about material in this category primarily on evidence presented by professionals in the behavioral sciences, we are confident that they are supported by the less scientific evidence we have consulted; and we are each personally confident on the basis of our own knowledge and experiences that the conclusions are justified. None of us has the least doubt that sexual violence is harmful, and that general acceptance of the view that "no" means "yes" is a consequence of the most serious proportions. We have found a causal relationship between sexually explicit materials featuring violence and these consequences, and thus conclude that the class of such materials, although not necessarily every individual member of that class, is on the whole harmful to society.

Non-Violent Materials Depicting Degradation, Domination, Subordination, or Humiliation

Current research has rather consistently separated out violent pornography, the class of materials we have just discussed, from other sexually explicit materials. With respect to further subdivision the process has been less consistent. A few researchers have made further distinctions, while most have merely classed everything else as "non-violent." We have concluded that more subdivision than that is necessary. Our examination of the variety of sexually explicit materials convinces us that once again the category of "non-violent" ignores significant distinctions within this category, and thus combines classes of material that are in fact substantially different.

The subdivision we adopt is one that has surfaced in some of the research. And it is also one that might explain a significant amount of what would otherwise seem to be conflicting research results. Some researchers have found negative effects from non-violent material, while others report no such negative effects. But when the stimulus material these researchers have used is considered, there is some suggestion that the presence or absence of negative effects from non-violent material might turn on the non-violent material being considered "degrading," a term we shall explain shortly. It appears that effects similar to, although not as extensive as that involved with violent material, can be identified with respect to such degrading material, but that these effects are likely absent when neither degradation nor violence is present.

An enormous amount of the most sexually explicit material available, as well as much of the material that is somewhat less sexually explicit, is material that we would characterize as "degrading," the term we use to encompass the undeniably linked characteristics of degradation, domination, subordination, and humiliation. The degradation we refer to is degradation of people, most often women, and here we are referring to material that, although not violent, depicts people, usually women, as existing solely for the sexual satisfaction of others, usually men, or that depicts people, usually women, in decidedly subordinate roles in their sexual relations with others, or that depicts people engaged in sexual practices that would to most people be considered humiliating. Indeed, forms of degradation represent the largely predominant proportion of commercially available pornography.

With respect to material of this variety, our conclusions are substantially similar to those with respect to violent material, although we make them with somewhat less assumption than was the case with respect to violent material. The evidence, scientific and otherwise, is more tentative, but supports the conclusion that the material we describe as degrading bears some causal relationship to the attitudinal changes we have previously identified. That is, substantial exposure to material of this variety is likely to increase the extent to which those exposed will view rape or other forms of sexual violence as less serious than they otherwise would have, will view the victims of rape and other forms of sexual violence as significantly more responsible, and will view the offenders as significantly less responsible. We also conclude that the evidence supports the conclusion that substantial exposure to material of this type will increase acceptance of the proposition that women like to be forced into sexual practices, and, once again, that the woman who says "no" really means "yes."

With respect to material of this type, there is less evidence causally linking the material with sexual aggression, but this may be because this is a category that has been isolated in only a few studies, albeit an increasing number. The absence of evidence should by no means be taken to deny the existence of the causal link. But because the causal link is less the subject of experimental studies, we have been required to think more carefully here about the assumptions necessary to causally connect increased acceptance of rape myths and other attitudinal changes with increased sexual aggression and sexual violence. And on the basis of all the evidence we have considered, from all sources, and on the basis of our own insights and experiences, we believe we are justified in drawing the following conclusion: Over a large enough sample of population that believes that many women like to be raped, that believes that sexual violence or sexual coercion is often desired or appropriate, and that believes that sex offenders are less responsible for their acts, will commit more acts of sexual violence or sexual coercion than would a population holding these beliefs to a lesser extent.

We should make clear what we have concluded here. We are not saying that everyone exposed to material of this type has his attitude about sexual violence changed. We are saying only that the evidence supports the conclusion that substantial

exposure to degrading material increases the likelihood for an individual and the incidence over a large population that these attitudinal changes will occur. And we are not saying that everyone with these attitudes will commit an act of sexual violence or sexual coercion. We are saying that such attitudes will increase the likelihood for an individual and the incidence for a population that acts of sexual violence, sexual coercion, or unwanted sexual aggression will occur. Thus, we conclude that substantial exposure to materials of this type bears some causal relationship to the level of sexual violence, sexual coercion, or unwanted sexual aggression in the population so exposed.

We need mention as well that our focus on these more violent or more coercive forms of actual subordination of women should not diminish what we take to be a necessarily incorporated conclusion: Substantial exposure to materials of this type bears some causal relationship to the incidence of various non-violent forms of discrimination against or subordination of women in our society. To the extent that these materials create or reinforce the view that women's function is disproportionately to satisfy the sexual needs of men, then the materials will have pervasive effects on the treatment of women in society far beyond the incidence of identifiable acts of rape or other sexual violence. We obviously cannot here explore fully all the forms in which women are discriminated against in contemporary society. Nor can we explore all of the causes of that discrimination against women. But we feel confident in concluding that the view of women as available for sexual domination is one cause of that discrimination, and we feel confident as well in concluding that degrading material bears a causal relationship to the view that women ought to subordinate their own desires and beings to the sexual satisfaction of men.

Although the category of the degrading is one that has only recently been isolated in some research, in the literature generally, and in public discussion of the issue, it is not a small category. If anything, it constitutes somewhere between the predominant and the overwhelming portion of what is currently standard fare heterosexual pornography, and is a significant theme in a broader range of materials not commonly taken to be sexually explicit enough to be pornographic. But as with sexually violent materials, the extent of the effect of these degrading materials may not turn substantially on the amount of sexual explicitness once a threshold of undeniable sexual content is surpassed. The category therefore includes a great deal of what would now be considered to be pornographic, and includes a great deal of what would now be held to be legally obscene, but it includes more than that. Since we are here identifying harms for a class, rather than identifying harms caused by every member of that class, and since we are here talking about the identification of harm rather than making recommendations for legal control, we are not reluctant to identify harms for a class of material considerably wider than what is or even should be regulated by law.

Non-Violent and Non-Degrading Materials

Our most controversial category has been the category of sexually explicit materials that are not violent and are not degrading as we have used that term. They are materials in which the participants appear to be fully willing participants occupying substantially equal roles in a setting devoid of actual or apparent violence or pain. This category is in fact quite small in terms of currently available materials. There is some, to be sure, and the amount may increase as the division between the degrading and the non-degrading becomes more accepted, but we are convinced that only a small amount of currently available highly sexually explicit material is neither violent nor degrading. We thus talk about a small category, but one that should not be ignored.

We have disagreed substantially about the effects of such materials, and that should come as no surprise. We are dealing in this category with "pure" sex, as to which there are widely divergent views in this society. That we have disagreed among ourselves does little more than reflect the extent to which we are representative of the population as a whole. In light of that disagreement, it is perhaps more appropriate to explain the various views rather than indicate a unanimity that does not exist, within this Commission or within society, or attempt the preposterous task of saying that some fundamental view about the role of sexuality and portrayals of sexuality was accepted or defeated by such-and-such vote. We do not wish to give easy answers to hard questions, and thus feel better with describing the diversity of opinion rather than suppressing part of it.

In examining the material in this category, we have not had the benefit of extensive evidence.

Research has only recently begun to distinguish the non-violent but degrading material from material that is neither violent nor degrading, and we have all relied on a combination of interpretation of existing studies that may not have drawn the same divisions, studies that did draw these distinctions, clinical evidence, interpretation of victim testimony, and our own perceptions of the effect of images on human behavior. Although the social science evidence is far from conclusive, we are, on the current state of the evidence, persuaded that material of this type does not bear a causal relationship to rape and other acts of sexual violence. We rely once again not only on scientific studies outlined later in the Report, and examined by each of us, but on the fact that the conclusions of these studies seem to most of us fully consistent with common sense. Just as materials depicting sexual violence seem intuitively to bear a causal relationship to sexual violence, materials containing no depictions or suggestions of sexual violence or sexual dominance seem to most of us intuitively unlikely to bear a causal relationship to sexual violence. The studies and clinical evidence to date are less persuasive on this lack of negative effect than they are persuasive for the presence of negative effect for the sexually violent material, but they seem to us of equal persuasive power as the studies and clinical evidence showing negative effects for the degrading materials. The fairest conclusion from the social science evidence is that there is no persuasive evidence to date supporting the connection between non-violent and non-degrading materials and acts of sexual violence, and that there is some, but very limited evidence, indicating that the connection does not exist. The totality of the social science evidence, therefore, is slightly against the hypothesis that non-violent and non-degrading materials bear a causal relationships to acts of sexual violence.

That there does not appear from the social science evidence to be a causal link with sexual violence, however, does not answer the question of whether such materials might not themselves simply for some other reason constitute a harm in themselves, or bear a causal link to consequences other than sexual violence but still be taken to be harmful. And it is here that we and society at large have the greatest differences in opinion.

One issue relates to materials that, although undoubtedly consensual and equal, depict sexual practices frequently condemned in this and other societies. In addition, level of societal condemnation varies for different activities; some activities are condemned by some people, but not by others. We have discovered that to some significant extent the assessment of the harmfulness of materials depicting such activities correlates directly with the assessment of the harmfulness of the activities themselves. Intuitively and not experimentally, we can hypothesize that materials portraying such an activity will either help to legitimize or will bear some causal relationship to that activity itself. With respect to these materials, therefore, it appears that a conclusion about the harmfulness of these materials turns on a conclusion about the harmfulness of the activity itself. As to this, we are unable to agree with respect to many of these activities. Our differences reflect differences now extant in society at large, and actively debated, and we can hardly resolve them here.

A larger issue is the very question of promiscuity. Even to the extent that the behavior depicted is not inherently condemned by some or any of us, the manner of presentation almost necessarily suggests that the activities are taking place outside the context of marriage, love, commitment, or even affection. Again, it is far from implausible to hypothesize that materials depicting sexual activity without marriage, love, commitment, or affection bear some causal relationship to sexual activity without marriage, love, commitment, or affection. There are undoubtedly many causes for what used to be called the "sexual revolution," but it is absurd to suppose that depictions or descriptions of uncommitted sexuality were not among them. Thus, once again our disagreements reflect disagreements in society at large, although not to as great an extent. Although there are many members of this society who can and have made affirmative cases for uncommitted sexuality, none of us believes it to be a good thing. A number of us, however, believe that the level of commitment in sexuality is a matter of choice among those who voluntarily engage in the activity. Others of us believe that uncommitted sexual activity is wrong for the individuals involved and harmful to society to the extent of its prevalence. Our view of the ultimate harmfulness of much of this material, therefore, is reflective of our individual views about the extent to whether sexual commitment is purely a matter of individual choice.

Even insofar as sexually explicit material of the variety being discussed here is not perceived as harmful for the messages it carries or the symbols it represents, the very publicness of what is commonly taken to be private is cause for concern. Even if we hypothesize a sexually explicit motion picture of a loving married couple engaged in mutually pleasurable and procreative vaginal intercourse, the depiction of that act on a screen or in a magazine may constitute harm in its own right (a "primary harm" in the terminology introduced earlier in this Chapter) solely by virtue of being shown. Here the concern is with the preservation of sex as an essentially private act, in conformity with the basic privateness of sex long recognized by this and all other societies. The alleged harm here, therefore, is that as soon as sex is put on a screen or put in a magazine it changes its character, regardless of what variety of sex is portrayed. And to the extent that the character of sex as public rather than private is the consequence here, then that to many would constitute a harm.

In considering the way in which making sex public may fundamentally transform the character of sex in all settings, it seems important to emphasize that the act of making sex public is as an empirical matter almost always coincident with the act of making sex a commercial enterprise. Whether the act of making sex public if done by a charitable institution would be harmful is an interesting academic exercise, but it is little more than that. For in the context we are discussing, taking the act of sex out of a private setting and making it public is invariably done for someone's commercial gain. To many of us, this fact of commercialization is vital to understanding the concern about sex and privacy.

We are again, along with the rest of society, unable to agree as to the extent to which making sex public and commercial should constitute a harm. We all agree for ourselves on the fundamental privateness of sex, but we disagree about the extent to which the privateness of sex is more than a matter of individual choice. And although we all to some extent think that sexuality may have in today's society become a bit too public, many of us are concerned that in the past it has been somewhat too private, being a subject that could not be talked about, could not constitute part of the discourse of society, and was treated in some ways as "dirty." To the extent that making sex more public has, while not without costs, alleviated some of these problems of the past, some of us would not take the increased publicness of sexuality as necessarily harmful, but here again we are quite understandably unable to agree.

The discussion of publicness in the previous paragraph was limited to the necessary publicness consequent in making a picture of a sexual act, regardless of whether the picture is made public in the broader sense. But to the extent that this occurs, we are once again in agreement. While some might argue that it is desirable for sexual explicitness to be publicly displayed to both willing and unwilling viewers, and while some might argue that this is either a positive advantage for the terrain of society or of no effect we unanimously reject those conclusions. We all agree that some large part of the privateness of sex is essential, and we would, for example, unanimously take to be harmful to society a proliferation of billboards displaying even the hypothesized highly explicit photograph of a loving married couple engaged in mutually pleasurable and procreative vaginal intercourse. Thus, to the extent that materials in this category are displayed truly publicly, we unanimously would take such a consequence to be harmful to society in addition to being harmful to individuals. Even if unwilling viewers are offended rather than harmed in any stronger sense, we take the large scale offending of the legitimate sensibilities of a large portion of the population to be harmful to society.

A number of witnesses have testified about the effects on their own sexual relations, usually with their spouses, of the depiction on the screen and in magazines of sexual practices in which they had not previously engaged. A number of these witnesses, *all women*, have testified that men in their lives have used such material to strongly encourage, or coerce, them into engaging in sexual practices in which they do not choose to engage. To the extent that such implicit or explicit coercion takes place as a result of these materials, we all agree that it is a harm. There has been other evidence, however, about the extent to which such material might for some be a way of revitalizing their sex lives, or, more commonly, simply constituting a part of a mutually pleasurable sexual experience for both partners. On this we could not agree. For reasons relating largely to the question of publicness in the first sense discussed above, some saw this kind of use as primarily harmful. Others saw it as harmless and possibly beneficial in contexts such as this. Some professional testimony supported this latter view, but we have little doubt that professional opinion is also divided on the issue.

Perhaps the most significant potential harm in this category exists with respect to children. We all agree that at least much, probably most, and maybe even all material in this category, regardless of whether it is harmful when used by adults only, is harmful when it falls into the hands of children. Exposure to sexuality is commonly taken, and properly so, to be primarily the responsibility of the family. Even those who would disagree with this statement would still prefer to have early exposure to sexuality be in the hands of a responsible professional in a controlled and guided setting. We have no hesitance in concluding that learning about sexuality from most of the material in this category is not the best way for children to learn about the subject. There are harms both to the children themselves and to notions of family control over a child's introduction to sexuality if children learn about sex from the kinds of sexually explicit materials that constitute the bulk of this category of materials.

We have little doubt that much of this material does find its way into the hands of children, and to the extent that it does we all agree that it is harmful. We may disagree about the extent to which people should, as adults, be tolerated in engaging in sexual practices that differ from the norm, but we all agree about the question of the desirability of exposing children to most of this material, and on that our unanimous agreement is that it is undesirable. For children to be taught by these materials that sex is public, that sex is commercial, and that sex can be divorced from any degree of affection, love, commitment, or marriage is for us the wrong message at the wrong time. We may disagree among ourselves about the extent to which the effect on children should justify large scale restrictions for that reason alone, but again we all agree that if the question is simply harm, and not the question of regulation by law, that material in this category is, with few exceptions, generally harmful to the extent it finds its way into the hands of children. Even those in society who would be least restrictive in sexually explicit materials tend, by and large, to limit their views to adults. The near unanimity in society about the effects on children and on all of society in exposing children to explicit sexuality in the form of even non-violent and non-degrading pornographic materials makes a strong statement about the potential harms of this material, and we confidently agree with that longstanding societal judgment.

Perhaps the largest question, and for that reason the question we can hardly touch here, is the question of harm as it relates to the moral environment of a society. There is no doubt that numerous laws, taboos, and other social practices all serve to enforce some forms of shared moral assessment. The extent to which this enforcement should be enlarged, the extent to which sexual morality is a necessary component of a society's moral environment, and the appropriate balance between recognition of individual choice and the necessity of maintaining some sense of community in a society are questions that have been debated for generations. The debates in the nineteenth century between John Stuart Mill and James Fitzjames Stephen, and in the twentieth century between Patrick Devlin and H. L. A. Hart, are merely among the more prominent examples of profound differences in opinion that can scarcely be the subject of a vote by this Commission. We all agree that some degree of individual choice is necessary in any free society, and we all agree that a society with no shared values, including moral values, is no society at all. We have numerous different views about the way in which these undeniably competing values should best be accommodated in this society at this time, or in any society at any time. We also have numerous different views about the extent to which, if at all, sexual morality is an essential part of the social glue of this or any other society. We have talked about these issues, but we have not even attempted to resolve our differences, because these differences are reflective of differences that are both fundamental and widespread in all societies. That we have been able to talk about them has been important to us, and there is no doubt that our views on these issues bear heavily on the views we hold about many of the more specific issues that have been within the scope of our mission.

Thus, with respect to the materials in this category, there are areas of agreement and areas of disagreement. We unanimously agree that the material in this category in some settings and when used for some purposes can be harmful. None of us think that the material in this category, individually or as a class, is in every instance harmless. And to the extent that some of the materials in this category are largely educational or undeniably artistic, we unanimously agree that they are little cause for concern if not made available to children or foisted on unwilling viewers. But most of the materials in this category would not now be taken to be explicitly educational or artistic, and as to this balance of materials our disagreements are substantial. Some of us think that some of the material at some times will be harmful, that some of the material at some times will be harmless, and that some of the material at times will be beneficial, espe-

cially when used for professional or nonprofessional therapeutic purposes. And some of us, while recognizing the occasional possibility of a harmless or beneficial use, nevertheless, for reasons stated in this section, feel that on balance it is appropriate to identify the class as harmful as a whole, if not in every instance. We have recorded this disagreement, and stated the various concerns. We can do little more except hope that the issues will continue to be discussed. But as it is discussed, we hope it will be recognized that the class of materials that is neither violent nor degrading, as it stands, is a small class, and many of these disagreements are more theoretical than real. Still, this class is not empty, and may at some point increase in size, and thus the theoretical disagreements may yet become germane to a larger class of materials actually available. . . .

Discussion Questions

1. How does the commission distinguish between primary and secondary harms and why is this distinction important?

2. What are the three types of sexually explicit materials the commission examined? Explain and describe each type.

3. What does the commission say about the harm resulting from the significant consumption of each one of these categories of materials? Explain and describe in detail the commission's arguments concerning each type.

4. Concerning non-violent, non-degrading pornography, do you agree with the commission's conclusions about its harm? Explain and defend your answer.

5. If the commission is correct about the harm resulting in the significant consumption of pornography, do you think that is a sufficient reason to allow governments to ban it? Or do you think that only certain types of pornography should be banned while other types are allowed? If so, on what basis do you make this distinction? Explain and defend your answers.

Speech Codes on College Campuses

48

There's No Such Thing as Free Speech, and It's a Good Thing, Too

Stanley Fish

Stanley Fish is Professor of English and Law at Duke University. A Milton scholar and literary theorist, he is the author of several works, including *Doing What Comes Naturally: Change, Rhetoric, and the Practice of Theory in Literary and Legal Studies* (1989) and *There's No Such Thing as Free Speech, and It's a Good Thing, Too* (1994).

In this essay Professor Fish argues that appeals to freedom of speech, by neoconservative and conservative critics of campus speech codes, mistakenly assume that "freedom of speech" has a neutral meaning outside of a political or social context. Professor Fish maintains that campus speech codes are justified because they forbid speech that assaults the core values of the institution's moral and intellectual foundation. Just as Canada's Charter of Rights and Freedoms forbids public hate speech because "every right and freedom herein granted can be trumped if its exercise is found to be in conflict with the principles that underwrite society," educational institutions have a right to forbid speech that the institution's community believes is harmful to its purpose and fundamental principles. Professor Fish points out that even a staunch conservative

Reprinted by permission from Stanley Fish, *There's No Such Thing as Free Speech, and It's a Good Thing, Too* (New York: Oxford, 1994).

critic of political correctness, Rep. Henry Hyde (R-Illinois), recognizes this. For Rep. Hyde exempted religious institutions from an anti-PC bill protecting "the free speech rights of college students," because, according to Hyde, religious institutions should not be forced to tolerate speech that conflicts with their purpose as well as their ethical and doctrinal beliefs. But why, asks Professor Fish, can't secular institutions have core beliefs, violations of which will not be tolerated? Professor Fish also responds to criticisms of his view.

Nowadays the First Amendment is the First Refuge of Scoundrels.

—S. Johnson and S. Fish

Lately, many on the liberal and progressive left have been disconcerted to find that words, phrases, and concepts thought to be their property and generative of their politics have been appropriated by the forces of neoconservatism. This is particularly true of the concept of free speech, for in recent years First Amendment rhetoric has been used to justify policies and actions the left finds problematical if not abhorrent: pornography, sexist language, campus hate speech. How has this happened? The answer I shall give in this essay is that abstract concepts like free speech do not have any "natural" content but are filled with whatever content and direction one can manage to put into them. "Free speech" is just the name we give to verbal behavior that serves the substantive agendas we wish to advance: and we give our preferred verbal behaviors *that* name when we can, when we have the power to do so, because in the rhetoric of American life, the label "free speech" is the one you want your favorites to wear. Free speech, in short, is not an independent value but a political prize, and if that prize has been captured by a politics opposed to yours, it can no longer be invoked in ways that further your purposes, for it is now an obstacle to those purposes. This is something that the liberal left has yet to understand, and what follows is an attempt to pry its members loose from a vocabulary that may now be a disservice to them.

Not far from the end of his *Areopagitica*, and after having celebrated the virtues of toleration and unregulated publication in passages that find their way into every discussion of free speech and the First Amendment, John Milton catches himself up short and says, of course I didn't mean Catholics, them we exterminate:

> I mean not tolerated popery, and open superstition, which as it extirpates all religious and civil supremacies, so itself should be extirpate . . . that also which is impious or evil absolutely against faith or manners no law can possibly permit that intends not to unlaw itself.

Notice that Milton is not stipulating a single exception to a rule generally in place; the kinds of utterance that might be regulated and even prohibited on pain of trial and punishment constitute an open set; popery is named only as a particularly perspicuous instance of the advocacy that cannot be tolerated. No doubt there are other forms of speech and action that might be categorized as "open superstitions" or as subversive of piety, faith, and manners, and presumably these too would be candidates for "extirpation." Nor would Milton think himself culpable for having failed to provide a list of unprotected utterances. The list would fill itself out as utterances are put to the test implied by his formulation: would this form of speech or advocacy, if permitted to flourish, tend to undermine the very purposes for which our society is constituted? One cannot answer this question with respect to a particular utterance in advance of its emergence on the world's stage; rather, one must wait and ask the question in the full context of its production and (possible) dissemination. It might appear that the result would be ad hoc and unprincipled, but for Milton the principle inheres in the core values in whose name individuals of like mind came together in the first place. Those values, which include the search for truth and the promotion of virtue, are capacious enough to accommodate a diversity of views. But at some point—again impossible of advance specification—capaciousness will threaten to become shapelessness, and at that point fidelity to the original values will demand acts of extirpation.

I want to say that all affirmations of freedom of expression are like Milton's, dependent for their force on an exception that literally carves out the space in which expression can then emerge. I do not mean that expression (saying something) is a realm whose integrity is sometimes compromised by certain restrictions but that restriction, in the form of an underlying articulation of the world that necessarily (if silently) negates alternatively possible articulations, is constitutive of expression. Without restriction, without an inbuilt sense of what it would be meaningless to say or wrong to say, there could be no assertion and no reason for asserting it. The exception to unregulated expression is not a negative restriction but a positive hollowing out of value— we are for *this*, which means we are against *that*—in relation to which meaningful assertion can then occur. It is in reference to that value—constituted as all values are by an act of exclusion—that some forms of speech will be heard as (quite literally) intolerable. Speech, in short, is never a value in and of itself but is always produced within the precincts of some assumed conception of the good to which it must yield in the event of conflict. When the pinch comes (and sooner or later it will always come) and the institution (be it church, state, or university) is confronted by behavior subversive of its core rationale, it will respond by declaring "of course we mean not tolerated ___, that we extirpate," not because an exception to a general freedom has suddenly and contradictorily been announced, but because the freedom has never been general and has always been understood against the background of an originary exclusion that gives it meaning.

This is a large thesis, but before tackling it directly I want to buttress my case with another example, taken not from the seventeenth century but from the charter and case law of Canada. Canadian thinking about freedom of expression departs from the line usually taken in the United States in ways that bring that country very close to the *Areopagitica* as I have expounded it. The differences are fully on display in a recent landmark case, *R. v. Keegstra*. James Keegstra was a high school teacher in Alberta who, it was established by evidence, "systematically denigrated Jews and Judaism in his classes." He described Jews as treacherous, subversive, sadistic, money loving, power hungry, and child killers. He declared them "responsible for depressions, anarchy, chaos, wars and revolution" and required his students "to regurgitate these notions in essays and examina-tions." Keegstra was indicted under Section 319(2) of the Criminal Code and convicted. The Court of Appeal reversed, and the Crown appealed to the Supreme Court, which reinstated the lower court's verdict.

Section 319(2) reads in part, "Every one who, by communicating statements other than in private conversation, willfully promotes hatred against any identifiable group is guilty of . . . an indictable offense and is liable to imprisonment for a term not exceeding two years." In the United States, this provision of the code would almost certainly be struck down because, under the First Amendment, restrictions on speech are prohibited without qualification. To be sure, the Canadian charter has its own version of the First Amendment, in Section 2(b): "Everyone has the following fundamental freedoms . . . (b) freedom of thought, belief, opinion, and expression, including freedom of the press and other media of communication." But Section 2(b), like every other section of the charter, is qualified by Section 1: "The Canadian Charter of Rights and Freedoms guarantees the rights and freedoms set out in it subject only to such reasonable limits prescribed by law as can be demonstrably justified in a free and democratic society." Or in other words, every right and freedom herein granted can be trumped if its exercise is found to be in conflict with the principles that underwrite the society.

This is what happens in *Keegstra* as the majority finds that Section 319(2) of the Criminal Code does in fact violate the right of freedom of expression guaranteed by the charter but is nevertheless a *permissible* restriction because it accords with the principles proclaimed in Section 1. There is, of course, a dissent that reaches the conclusion that would have been reached by most, if not all, U.S. courts; but even in dissent the minority is faithful to Canadian ways of reasoning. "The question," it declares, "is always one of balance," and thus even when a particular infringement of the charter's Section 2(b) has been declared unconstitutional, as it would have been by the minority, the question remains open with respect to the next case. In the United States the question is presumed closed and can only be pried open by special tools. In our legal culture as it is now constituted, if one yells "free speech" in a crowded courtroom and makes it stick, the case is over.

Of course, it is not that simple. Despite the apparent absoluteness of the First Amendment, there are any number of ways of getting around it, ways that are known to every student of the law. In general, the preferred strategy is to manipulate the distinction, essential to First Amendment jurisprudence, between speech and action. The distinction is essential because no one would think to frame a First Amendment that began, "Congress shall make no laws abridging free-dom of action," for that would amount to saying "Congress shall make no law," which would amount to saying, "There shall be no law," only actions uninhibited and unregulated. If the First Amendment is to make any sense, have any bite, speech must be declared not to be a species of action, or to be a special form of action lacking the aspects of action that cause it to be the object of regulation. The latter strategy is the favored one and usually involves the separation of speech from consequences. This is what Archibald Cox does when he assigns to the First Amendment the job of protecting "expressions separable from conduct harmful to other individuals and the community." The difficulty of managing this segregation is well known: speech always seems to be crossing the line into action, where it becomes, at least potentially, consequential. In the face of this categorical instability, First Amendment theorists and jurists fashion a distinction within the speech/action distinction: some forms of speech are not really speech because their purpose is to incite violence or they are, as the court declares in *Chaplinsky v. New Hampshire* (1942), "fighting words," words "likely to provoke the average person to retaliation, and thereby cause a breach of the peace."

The trouble with this definition is that it distinguishes not between fighting words and words that remain safely and merely expressive but between words that are provocative to one group (the group that falls under the rubric "average person") and the words that might be provocative to other groups, groups of persons not now considered average. And if you ask what words are likely to be provocative to those nonaverage groups, what are likely to be *their* fighting words, the answer is anything and everything, for as Justice Holmes said long ago (in *Gitlow v. New York*), every idea is an incitement to somebody, and since ideas come packaged in sentences, in words, every sentence is potentially, in some situation that might occur tomorrow, a fighting word and therefore a candidate for regulation.

This insight cuts two ways. One could conclude from it that the fighting words exception is a bad idea because there is no way to prevent clever and unscrupulous advocates from shoveling so many forms of speech into the excepted category that the zone of constitutionally protected speech shrinks to nothing and is finally without inhabitants. Or, alternatively, one could conclude that there was never anything in the zone in the first place and that the difficulty of limiting the fighting words exception is merely a particular instance of the general difficulty of separating speech from action. And if one opts for this second conclusion, as I do, then a further conclusion is inescapable: insofar as the point of the First Amendment is to identify speech separable from conduct and from the consequences that come in conduct's wake, there is no such speech and therefore nothing for the First Amendment to protect. Or, to make the point from the other direction, when a court invalidates legislation because it infringes on protected speech, it is not because the speech in question is without consequences but because the consequences have been discounted in relation to a good that is judged to outweigh them. Despite what they say, courts are never in the business of protecting speech per se, "mere" speech (a nonexistent animal); rather, they are in the business of classifying speech (as protected or regulatable) in relation to a value—the health of the republic, the vigor of the economy, the maintenance of the status quo, the undoing of the status quo—that is the true, if unacknowledged, object of their protection.

But if this is the case, a First Amendment purist might reply, why not drop the charade along with the malleable distinctions that make it possible, and declare up front that total freedom of speech is our primary value and trumps anything else, no matter what? The answer is that freedom of expression would only be a primary value if it didn't matter what was said, didn't matter in the sense that no one gave a damn but just liked to hear talk. There are contexts like that, a Hyde Park corner or a call-in talk show where people get to sound off for the sheer fun of it. These, however, are special contexts, artificially bounded spaces designed to assure that talking is not taken seriously. In ordinary contexts, talk is produced with the goal of trying to move the world in one direction rather than another. In these contexts—the contexts of everyday life—you go to the trouble of asserting that X is Y only because you suspect that some people are wrongly asserting that X is Z or that X doesn't exist. You assert, in short, because you give a damn, not about assertion—as if it were a value in and of itself—but about what your assertion is about. It may seem paradoxical, but free expression could only be a primary value if what you are valuing is the right to make noise; but if you are engaged in some purposive activity in the course of which speech happens to be produced, sooner or later you will come to a point when you decide that some forms of speech do not further but endanger that purpose.

Take the case of universities and colleges. Could it be the purpose of such places to encourage free expression? If the answer were "yes," it would be hard to say why there would be any need for classes, or examinations, or departments, or disciplines, or libraries, since freedom of expression requires nothing but a soapbox or an open telephone line. The very fact that the university's machinery—of the events, rituals, and procedures that fill its calendar—argues for some other, more substantive purpose. In relation to that purpose (which will be realized differently in different kinds of institutions), the flourishing of free expression will in almost all circumstances be an obvious good; but in some circumstances, freedom of expression may pose a threat to that purpose, and at that point it may be necessary to discipline or regulate speech, lest, to paraphrase Milton, the institution sacrifice itself to one of its *accidental* features.

Interestingly enough, the same conclusion is reached (inadvertently) by Congressman Henry Hyde, who is addressing these very issues in a recently offered amendment to Title VI of the Civil Rights Act. The first section of the amendment states its purpose, to protect "the free speech rights of college students" by prohibiting private as well as public educational institutions from "subjecting any student to disciplinary sanctions solely on the basis of conduct that is speech." The second section enumerates the remedies available to students whose speech rights may have been abridged; and the third, which is to my mind the nub of the matter, declares as an exception to the amendment's jurisdiction any "educational institution that is controlled by a religious organization," on the reasoning that the application of the amendment to such institutions "would not be consistent with the religious tenets of such organizations." In effect, what Congressman Hyde is saying is that at the heart of these colleges and universities is a set of beliefs, and it would be wrong to require them to tolerate behavior, including speech behavior, inimical to those beliefs. But insofar as this logic is persuasive, it applies across the board, for all educational institutions rest on some set of beliefs—no institution is "just there" independent of any purpose—and it is hard to see why the rights of an institution to protect and preserve its basic "tenets" should be restricted only to those that are religiously controlled. Read strongly, the third section of the amendment undoes sections one and two—the exception becomes, as it always was, the rule—and points us to a balancing test very much like that employed in Canadian law; given that any college or university is informed by a core rationale, an administrator faced with complaints about offensive speech should ask whether damage to the core would appear greater if the speech were tolerated or regulated.

The objection to this line of reasoning is well known and has recently been reformulated by Benno Schmidt, former president of Yale University. According to Schmidt, speech codes on campuses constitute "well intentioned but misguided efforts to give values of community and harmony a higher place than freedom" (*Wall Street Journal*, May 6, 1991). "When the goals of harmony collide with freedom of expression," he continues, "freedom must be the paramount obligation of an academic community." The flaw in this logic is on display in the phrase "academic community," for the phrase recognizes what Schmidt would deny, that expression only occurs in communities—if not in an academic community, then in a shopping mall community or a dinner party community or an airplane ride community or an office community. In these communities and in any others that could be imagined (with the possible exception of a community of major league baseball fans), limitations on speech in relation to a defining and deeply assumed purpose are inseparable from community membership.

Indeed, "limitations" is the wrong word because it suggests that expression, as an activity and a value, has a pure form that is always in danger of being compromised by the urgings of special interest communities; but independently of a community context informed by interest (that is, purpose), expression would be at once inconceivable and unintelligible. Rather than being a value that is threatened by limitations and constraints, expression, in any form worth worrying about, is a *product* of limitations and constraints, of the already-in-place presuppositions that give assertions their very particular point. Indeed, the very act of thinking of something to say (whether or not it is subsequently regulated) is already constrained—rendered impure, and because impure, communicable—by the background context within which the thought takes its shape. (The analysis holds too for "freedom," which in Schmidt's vision is an entirely empty concept referring to an urge without direction. But like expression, freedom is a coherent notion only in relation to a goal or good that limits and, by limiting, shapes its exercise.)

Arguments like Schmidt's only get their purchase by first imagining speech as occurring in no context whatsoever, and then stripping particular speech acts of the properties conferred on them by contexts. The trick is nicely illustrated when Schmidt urges protection for speech "no matter how obnoxious in content." "Obnoxious" at once acknowledges the reality of speech-related harms and trivializes them by suggesting that they are *surface* injuries that any large-minded ("liberated and humane") person should be able to bear. The possibility that speech-related injuries may be grievous and *deeply* wounding is carefully kept out of sight, and because it is kept out of sight, the fiction of a world of weightless verbal exchange can be maintained, at least within the confines of Schmidt's carefully denatured discourse.

To this Schmidt would no doubt reply, as he does in his essay, that harmful speech should be answered not by regulation but by more speech; but that would make sense only if the effects of speech could be canceled out by additional speech, only if the pain and humiliation caused by racial or religious epithets could be ameliorated by saying something like "So's your old man." What Schmidt fails to realize at every level of his argument is that expression is more than a matter of proffering and receiving propositions, that words do work in the world of a kind that cannot be confined to a purely cognitive realm of "mere" ideas.

It could be said, however, that I myself mistake the nature of the work done by freely tolerated speech because I am too focused on short-run outcomes and fail to understand the good effects of speech will be realized, not in the present, but in a future whose emergence regulation could only inhibit. This line of reasoning would also weaken one of my key points, that speech in and of itself cannot be a value and is only worth worrying about if it is in the service of something with which it cannot be identical. My mistake, one could argue, is to equate the something in whose service speech is with some locally espoused value (e.g., the end of racism, the empowerment of disadvantaged minorities), whereas in fact we should think of that something as a now-inchoate shape that will be given firm lines only by time's pencil. That is why the shape now receives such indeterminate characterizations (e.g., true self-fulfillment, a more perfect polity, a more capable citizenry, a less partial truth); we cannot now know it, and therefore we must not prematurely fix it in ways that will bind successive generations to error.

This forward-looking view of what the First Amendment protects has a great appeal, in part because it continues in a secular form the Puritan celebration of millenarian hopes, but it imposes a requirement so severe that one would except more justification for it than is usually provided. The requirement is that we endure whatever pain racist and hate speech inflicts for the sake of a future whose emergence we can only take on faith. In a specifically religious vision like Milton's, this makes perfect sense (it is indeed the whole of Christianity), but in the context of a politics that puts its trust in the world and not in the Holy Spirit, it raises more questions than it answers and could be seen as the second of two strategies designed to delegitimize the complaints of victimized groups. The first strategy, as I have noted, is to define speech in such a way as to render it inconsequential (on the model of "sticks and stones will break my bones, but . . ."); the second strategy is to acknowledge the (often grievous) consequences of speech but declare that we must suffer them in the name of something that cannot be named. The two strategies are denials from slightly different directions of the *present* effects of racist speech; one confines those effects to a closed and safe realm of pure mental activity; the other imagines the effects of speech spilling over into the world but only in an ever-receding future for whose sake we must forever defer taking action.

I find both strategies unpersuasive, but my own skepticism concerning them is less important than the fact that in general they seem to have worked; in the parlance of the marketplace (a parlance First Amendment commentators love), many in the society seemed to have bought them. Why? The answer, I think, is that people cling to the First Amendment pieties because they do not wish to face what they correctly take to be the alternative. That alternative is *politics*, the realization (at which I have already hinted) that decisions about what is and is not protected in the realm of expression will rest not on principle or firm doctrine but on the ability of some persons to interpret—recharacterize or rewrite—principle and doctrine in ways that lead to the protection of speech they want heard and the regulation of speech they want silenced. (That is how George Bush can argue *for* flag-burning statutes and *against* campus hate-speech codes.) When the First Amendment is successfully invoked, the result is not a victory for free speech in the face of a challenge from politics but a *political victory* won by the party that has managed to wrap its agenda in the mantle of free speech.

It is from just such a conclusion—a conclusion that would put politics *inside* the First Amendment—that commentators recoil, saying things like "This could render the First Amendment a dead letter," or "This would leave us with no normative guidance in

determining when and what speech to protect," or "This effaces the distinction between speech and action," or "This is incompatible with any viable notion of freedom of expression." To these statements (culled more or less at random from recent law review pieces) I would reply that the First Amendment has always been a dead letter if one understood its "liveness" to depend on the identification and protection of a realm of "mere" expression distinct from the realm of regulatable conduct; the distinction between speech and action has always been effaced in principle, although in practice it can take whatever form the prevailing political conditions mandate; we have never had any normative guidance for marking off protected from unprotected speech; rather, the guidance we have has been fashioned (and refashioned) in the very political struggles over which it then (for a time) presides. In short, the name of the game has always been politics, even when (indeed, especially when) it is played by stigmatizing politics as the area to be avoided.

In saying this, I would not be heard as arguing either for or against regulation and speech codes as a matter of general principle. Instead my argument turns away from general principle to the pragmatic (anti)principle of considering each situation as it emerges. The question of whether or not to regulate will always be a local one, and we can not rely on abstractions that are either empty of content or filled with the content of some partisan agenda to generate a "principled" answer. Instead we must consider in every case what is at stake and what are the risks and gains of alternative courses of action. In the course of this consideration many things will be of help, but among them will not be phrases like "freedom of speech" or "the gift of individual expression," because, as they are used now, these phrases tend to obscure rather than clarify our dilemmas. Once they are deprived of their talismanic force, once it is no longer strategically effective simply to invoke them in the act of walking away from a problem, the conversation could continue in directions that are now blocked by a First Amendment absolutism that has only been honored in the breach anyway. To the student reporter who complains that in the wake of the promulgation of a speech code at the University of Wisconsin there is now something in the back of his mind as he writes, one could reply, "There is always something in the back of your mind, and perhaps it might be better to have this code in the back of your mind than whatever was in there before." And when someone warns about the slippery slope and predicts mournfully that if you restrict one form of speech, you never know what will be restricted next, one could reply, "Some form of speech is always being restricted, else there could be no meaningful assertion; we have always and already slid down the slippery slope; someone is always going to be restricted next, and it is your job to make sure that the someone is not you." And when someone observes, as someone surely will, that antiharassment codes chill speech, one could reply that since speech only becomes intelligible against the background of what isn't being said, the background of what has already been silenced, the only question is the political one of which speech is going to be chilled, and, all things considered, it seems a good thing to chill speech like "nigger," "cunt," "kike," and "faggot." And if someone then says, "But what happened to free-speech principles?" one could say what I have now said a dozen times, free-speech principles don't exist except as a component in a bad argument in which such principles are invoked to mask motives that would not withstand close scrutiny.

An example of a wolf wrapped in First Amendment clothing is an advertisement that ran recently in the Duke University newspaper, the *Chronicle*. Signed by Bradley R. Smith, well known as a purveyor of anti-Semitic neo-Nazi propaganda, the ad is packaged as a scholarly treatise: four densely packed columns complete with "learned" references, undocumented statistics, and an array of so-called authorities. The message of the ad is that the Holocaust never occurred and that the German state never "had a policy to exterminate the Jewish people (or anyone else) by putting them to death in gas chambers." In a spectacular instance of the increasingly popular "blame the victim" strategy, the Holocaust "story" or "myth" is said to have been fabricated in order "to drum up world sympathy for Jewish causes." The "evidence" supporting these assertions is a slick blend of supposedly probative facts—"not a single autopsied body has been shown to be gassed"—and sly insinuations of a kind familiar to readers of *Mein Kampf* and *The Protocols of the Elders of Zion*. The slickest thing, however, is the representation of the argument as an exercise in free speech—the ad is subtitled "The Case for Open Debate"—that could be objected to only by "thought police" and censors. This strategy bore immediate fruit in the decision of the newspaper staff to accept the ad despite a long-standing (and historically honored) policy of refusing materials that contain ethnic

and racial slurs or are otherwise offensive. The reasoning of the staff (explained by the editor in a special column) was that under the First Amendment advertisers have the "right" to be published. "American newspapers are built on the principles of free speech and free press, so how can a newspaper deny these rights to anyone?" The answer to this question is that an advertiser is not denied his rights simply because a single media organ declines his copy so long as other avenues of publication are available and there has been no state suppression of his views. This is not to say that there could not be a case for printing the ad, only that the case cannot rest on a supposed First Amendment obligation. One might argue, for example, that printing the ad would foster healthy debate, or that lies are more likely to be shown up for what they are if they are brought to the light of day, but these are precisely the arguments the editor *disclaims* in her eagerness to take a "principled" free-speech stand.

What I find most distressing about this incident is not that the ad was printed but that it was printed by persons who believed it to be a lie and a distortion. If the editor and her staff were in agreement with Smith's views or harbored serious doubts about the reality of the Holocaust, I would still have a quarrel with them, but it would be a different quarrel; it would be a quarrel about evidence, credibility, documentation. But since on these matters the editors and I are in agreement, my quarrel is with the reasoning that led them to act in opposition to what they believed to be true. That reasoning, as I understand it, goes as follows: although we ourselves are certain that the Holocaust was a fact, facts are notoriously interpretable and disputable; therefore nothing is ever really settled, and we have no right to reject something just because we regard it as pernicious and false. But the fact—if I can use that word—that settled truths can always be upset, at least theoretically, does not mean that we cannot affirm and rely on truths that according to our present lights seem indisputable; rather, it means exactly the opposite; in the absence of absolute certainty of the kind that can only be provided by revelation (something I do not rule out but have not yet experienced), we must act on the basis of the certainty we have so far achieved. Truth may, as Milton said, always be in the course of emerging, and we must always be on guard against being so beguiled by its present shape that we ignore contrary evidence; but, by the same token, when it happens that the present shape of truth is compelling beyond a reasonable doubt, it is our moral obligation to act on it and not defer action in the name of an interpretive future that may never arrive. By running the First Amendment up the nearest flagpole and rushing to salute it, the student editors defaulted on that obligation and gave over their responsibility to a so-called principle that was not even to the point.

Let me be clear. I am not saying that the First Amendment principles are inherently bad (they are *inherently* nothing), only that they are not always the appropriate reference point for situations involving the production of speech, and that even when they are the appropriate reference point, they do not constitute a politics-free perspective because the shape in which they are invoked will always be political, will always, that is, be the result of having drawn the relevant line (between speech and action, or between high-value speech and low-value speech, or between words essential to the expression of ideas and fighting words) in a way that is favorable to some interests and indifferent or hostile to others. This having been said, the moral is not that the First Amendment talk should be abandoned, for even if the standard First Amendment formulas do not and could not perform the function expected of them (the elimination of political considerations in decisions about speech), they still serve a function that is not at all negligible: they slow down outcomes in an area in which the fear of overhasty outcomes is justified by a long record of abuses of power. It is often said that history shows (itself a formula) that even a minimal restriction on the right of expression too easily leads to ever-larger restrictions; and to the extent that this is an empirical fact (and it is a question one could debate), there is some comfort and protection to be found in a procedure that requires you to jump through hoops—do a lot of argumentative work—before a speech regulation will be allowed to stand.

I would not be misunderstood as offering the notion of "jumping through hoops" as a new version of the First Amendment claim to neutrality. A hoop must have a shape—in this case the shape of whatever binary distinction is representing First Amendment "interests"—and the shape of the hoop one is asked to jump through will in part determine what kinds of jumps can be regularly made. Even if they are only mechanisms for slowing down outcomes, First Amendment formulas by virtue of their substantive content (and it is impossible that they be without content) will slow down some outcomes more easily than others, and that means that the form they happen to have at the present moment will favor some interests more than others. Therefore, even with a reduced sense of the effectivity of First Amendment rhetoric (it can not assure any particular result), the counsel with which I began remains relevant: so long as so-called free-speech principles have been fashioned by your enemy (so long as it is *his* hoops you have to jump through), contest their relevance to the issue at hand; but if you manage to refashion them in line with your purposes, urge them with a vengeance.

It is a counsel that follows from the thesis that there is no such thing as free speech, which is not, after all, a thesis as startling or corrosive as may first have seemed. It merely says that there is no class of utterances separable from the world of conduct and that therefore the identification of some utterances as members of that nonexistent class will always be evidence that a political line has been drawn rather than a line that denies politics entry into the forum of public discourse. It is the job of the First Amendment to mark out an area in which competing views can be considered without state interference; but if the very marking out of that area is itself an interference (as it always will be), First Amendment jurisprudence is inevitably self-defeating and subversive of its own aspirations. That's the bad news. The good news is that precisely *because* speech is never "free" in the two senses required—free of consequences and free from state pressure—speech always matters, is always doing work; because everything we say impinges on the world in ways indistinguishable from the effects of physical action, we must take responsibility for our verbal performances—*all* of them—and not assume that they are being taken care of by a clause in the Constitution. Of course, with responsibility comes risks, but they have always been our risks, and no doctrine of free speech has ever insulated us from them. They are the risks, respectively, of permitting speech that does obvious harm and of shutting off speech in ways that might deny us the benefit of Joyce's *Ulysses* or Lawrence's *Lady Chatterley's Lover* or Titian's paintings. Nothing, I repeat, can insulate us from those risks. (If there is no normative guidance in determining when and what speech to protect, there is no normative guidance in determining what is art—like free speech a category that includes everything and nothing—and what is obscenity.) Moreover, nothing can provide us with the principle for deciding which risk in the long run is the best to take. I am persuaded that at the present moment, right now, the risk of not attending to hate speech is greater than the risk that by regulating it we will deprive ourselves of valuable voices and insights or slide down the slippery slope toward tyranny. This is a judgment for which I can offer reasons but no guarantees. All I am saying is that the judgments of those who would come down on the other side carry no guarantees either. They urge us to put our faith in apolitical abstractions, but the abstractions they invoke—the marketplace of ideas, speech alone, speech itself—only come in political guises, and therefore in trusting to them we fall (unwittingly) under the sway of the very forces we wish to keep at bay. It is not that there are no choices to make or means of making them; it is just that the choices as well as the means are inextricable from the din and confusion of partisan struggle. There is no safe place.

Discussion Questions

1. What does Professor Fish mean when he says that "there's no such thing as free speech, and it's a good thing, too"? What is his main argument for this view? Do you think it is flawed in any way? Why or why not?

2. Professor Fish claims that the First Amendment to the United States Constitution is not absolute. How does he argue for this point?

3. Professor Fish appears to be saying that all claims to moral or legal principle (e.g., "freedom of expression is a good thing") are really political claims: "free speech principles don't exist except as a component in a bad argument in which such principles are invoked to mask motives that would not withstand close scrutiny." If this is a principle by which Fish examines other people's claims, why can't we dismiss Fish's argument on the same grounds, because it evidently "masks motives" and is therefore "a component in a bad argument"? If it is not a principle, how then can Professor Fish say it applies to "all claims" since he obviously has not the time or the resources to examine *all* claims? How do you think Fish would respond to these questions?

49

"Speech Codes" on the Campus and Problems of Free Speech

Nat Hentoff

Nat Hentoff is a long-time defender of the First Amendment and civil liberties, having been affiliated for years with the American Civil Liberties Union (ACLU). He is a columnist for the *Village Voice* and *The Washington Post* as well as a staff writer for *The New Yorker*.

In this essay Mr. Hentoff, a political liberal, documents the actions of a number of politically liberal student groups on different college campuses throughout the United States who have called for, and in most cases have helped facilitate, the types of institutional speech codes supported by Professor Fish in the previous essay (Chapter 48). Mr. Hentoff argues that these speech codes are not justified for several reasons: (1) they squash legitimate intellectual discussion of important, though emotionally charged, social issues, such as abortion, affirmative action, and homosexuality; (2) they are based on an inappropriate appeal to the Fourteenth Amendment and the U.S. Supreme Court's decision on "fighting words"; and (3) they implicitly reinforce the racist notion that minorities are incapable of defending themselves intellectually against what they perceive as hostile speech. Mr. Hentoff is also disturbed by how the current climate on some college campuses has negatively affected fellow liberals who have traditionally been at the forefront of defending free speech, but some of whom now either support the speech codes or are intimidated into not resisting for fear of being called a racist, sexist, or homophobe.

Reprinted by permission from *Dissent* (Fall 1991).

During three years of reporting on anti-free-speech tendencies in higher education, I've been at more than twenty colleges and universities—from Washington and Lee and Columbia to Mesa State in Colorado and Stanford.

On this voyage of initially reverse expectations—with liberals fiercely advocating censorship of "offensive" speech and conservatives merrily taking the moral high ground as champions of free speech—the most dismaying moment of revelation took place at Stanford.

In the course of a two-year debate on whether Stanford, like many other universities, should have a speech code punishing language that might wound minorities, women, and gays, a letter appeared in the *Stanford Daily*. Signed by the African-American Law Students Association, the Asian-American Law Student Association, and the Jewish Law Students Association, the letter called for a harsh code. It reflected the letter and the spirit of an earlier declaration by Canetta Ivy, a black leader of student government at Stanford during the period of grand debate. "We don't put as many restrictions on freedom of speech," she said, "as we should."

Reading the letter by this rare ecumenical body of law students (so pressing was the situation that even Jews were allowed in), I thought of twenty, thirty years from now. From so bright a cadre of graduates, from so prestigious a law school would come some of the law professors, civic leaders, college presidents, and even maybe a Supreme Court Justice of the future. And many of them would have learned—like so many other university students in the land—that censorship is okay provided your motives are okay.

The debate at Stanford ended when the president, Donald Kennedy, following the prevailing winds, surrendered his previous position that once you start telling people what they can't say, you will end up telling them what they can't think. Stanford now has a speech code.

This is not to say that these gags on speech—every one of them so overboard and vague that a student can violate a code without knowing he or she has done so—are invariably imposed by student demand. At most colleges, it is the administration that sets up the code. Because there have been racist or sexist or homophobic taunts, anonymous notes or graffiti, the administration feels it must *do something*. The cheapest, quickest way to demonstrate that it cares is to appear to suppress racist, sexist, homophobic speech.

Usually, the leading opposition among the faculty consists of conservatives—when there is opposition. An exception at Stanford was law professor Gerald Gunther, arguably the nation's leading authority on constitutional law. But Gunther did not have much support among other faculty members, conservative or liberal.

At the University of Buffalo Law School, which has a code restricting speech, I could find just one faculty member who was against it. A liberal, he spoke only on condition that I not use his name. He did not want to be categorized as a racist.

On another campus, a political science professor for whom I had great respect after meeting and talking with him years ago, has been silent—students told me—on what Justice William Brennan once called "the pall of orthodoxy" that has fallen on his campus.

When I talked to him, the professor said, "It doesn't happen in my class. There's no 'politically correct' orthodoxy here. It may happen in other places at this university, but I don't know about that." He said no more.

One of the myths about the rise of P.C. (politically correct) is that, coming from the left, it is primarily intimidating conservatives on campus. Quite the contrary. At almost every college I've been, conservative students have their own newspaper, usually quite lively and fired by a muckraking glee at exposing "politically correct" follies on campus.

By and large, those most intimidated—not so much by the speech codes themselves but by the Madame Defarge-like spirit behind it—are liberal students and those who can be called politically moderate.

I've talked to many of them, and they no longer get involved in class discussions where their views would go against the grain of P.C. righteousness. Many, for instance, have questions about certain kinds of affirmative action. They are not partisans of Jesse Helms or David Duke, but they wonder whether progeny of middle-class black families should get scholarship preference. Others have a question about abortion. Most are not pro-life, but they believe that fathers should have a say in whether the fetus should be sent off to eternity.

Jeff Shesol, a recent graduate of Brown and now a Rhodes Scholar at Oxford, became nationally known while at Brown because of his comic strip, "Thatch," which, not too kindly, parodied P.C. students. At a forum on free speech at Brown before he left, Shesol said he wished he could tell the new students at Brown to have no fear of speaking freely. But he couldn't tell them that, he said, advising the new students to stay clear of talking critically about affirmative action or abortion, among other things, in public.

At that forum, Shesol told me, he said that those members of the left who regard dissent from their views as racist and sexist should realize that they are discrediting their goals. "They're honorable goals," said Shesol, "and I agree with them. I'm against racism and sexism. But these people's tactics are obscuring the goals. And they've resulted in Brown no longer being an open-minded place." There were hisses from the audience.

Students at New York University Law School have also told me that they censor themselves in class. The kind of chilling atmosphere they describe was exemplified last year as a case assigned for a moot court competition became subject to denunciation when a sizable number of law students said it was too "offensive" and would hurt the feelings of gay and lesbian students. The case concerned a divorced father's attempt to gain custody of his children on the grounds that their mother had become a lesbian. It was against P.C. to represent the father.

Although some of the faculty responded by insisting that you learn to be a lawyer by dealing with all kinds of cases, including those you personally find offensive, other faculty members supported the rebellious students, praising them for their sensitivity. There was little public opposition from the other students to the attempt to suppress the case. A leading dissenter was a member of the conservative Federalist Society.

What is P.C. to white students is not necessarily P.C. to black students. Most of the latter did not get involved in the N.Y.U. protest, but throughout the country many black students do support speech codes. A vigorous exception was a black Harvard law school student during a debate on whether the law school should start punishing speech. A white student got up and said that the codes are necessary because without them, black students would be driven away from colleges and thereby deprived of the equal opportunity to get an education.

A black student rose and said that the white student had a hell of a nerve to assume that he—in the face of racist speech—would pack up his books and go home. He's been familiar with that kind of speech all his life, and he had never felt the need to run away from it. He'd handled it before and he could again.

The black student then looked at his white colleague and said that it was condescending to say that blacks have to be "protected" from racist speech. "It is more racist and insulting," he emphasized, "to say that to me than to call me a nigger."

But that would appear to be a minority view among black students. Most are convinced they do need to be protected from wounding language. On the other hand, a good many black student organizations on campus do not feel that Jews have to protected from wounding language.

Though it's not much written about in reports of the language wars on campuses, there is a strong strain of anti-Semitism among some—not all, by any means—black students. They invite such speakers as Louis Farrakhan, the former Stokely Carmichael (now Kwame Touré), and such lesser but still burning bushes as Steve Cokely, the Chicago commentator who has declared that Jewish doctors inject the AIDS virus into black babies. That distinguished leader was invited to speak at the University of Michigan.

The black student organization at Columbia University brought to the campus Dr. Khallid Abdul Muhammad. He began his address by saying: "My leader, my teacher, my guide is the honorable Louis Farrakhan. I thought that should be said at Columbia Jewniversity."

Many Jewish students have not censored themselves in reacting to this form of political correctness among some blacks. A Columbia student, Rachel Stoll, wrote a letter to the *Columbia Spectator*: "I have an idea. As a white Jewish American, I'll just stand in the middle of a circle comprising . . . Khallid Abdul Muhammad and assorted members of the Black Students Organization and let them all hurl large stones at me. From recent events and statements made on this campus, I gather this will be a good cheap method of making these people feel good."

At UCLA, a black student magazine printed an article indicating there is considerable truth to the *Protocols of the Elders of Zion*. For months, the black faculty, when asked their reactions, preferred not to comment. One of them did say that the black students already considered the black faculty to be insufficiently militant, and the professors didn't want to make the gap any wider. Like white liberal faculty members on other campuses, they want to be liked—or at least not too disliked.

Along with quiet white liberal faculty members, most black professors have not opposed the speech codes. But unlike the white liberals, many honestly do believe that minority students have to be insulated from barbed language. They do not believe—as I have found out in a number of conversations—that an essential part of an education is to learn to demystify language, to strip it of its ability to demonize and stigmatize you. They do not believe that the way to deal with bigoted language is to answer it with more and better language of your own. This seems very elementary to me, but not to the defenders, black and white, of the speech codes.

Consider University of California president David Gardner. He has imposed a speech code on all the campuses in his university system. Students are to be punished—and this is characteristic of the other codes around the country—if they use "fighting words"—derogatory references to "race, sex, sexual orientation, or disability."

The term "fighting words" comes from a 1942 Supreme Court decision, *Chaplinsky v. New Hampshire*, which ruled that "fighting words" were not protected by the First Amendment. That decision, however, has been in disuse at the High Court for many years. But it is thriving on college campuses.

In the California code, a word becomes "fighting" if it is directly addressed to "any ordinary person" (presumably, extraordinary people are above all this). These are the kinds of words that are "inherently likely to provoke violent reaction, *whether or not they actually do*." (Emphasis added.)

Moreover, he or she who fires a fighting word at any ordinary person can be reprimanded or dismissed from the university because the perpetrator should "reasonably know" that what he or she has said will interfere with the "victim's ability to pursue effectively his or her education or otherwise participate fully in university programs and activities."

Asked Gary Murikami, chairman of the Gay and Lesbian Association at the University of California, Berkeley: "What does it mean?"

Among those—faculty, law professors, college administrators—who insist such codes are essential to the university's purpose of making *all* students feel at home and thereby able to concentrate on their work, there has been a celebratory resort to the Fourteenth Amendment.

That amendment guarantees "equal protection of the laws" to all, and that means to all students on campus. Accordingly, when the First Amendment rights of those engaging in offensive speech clash with the equality rights of their targets under the Fourteenth Amendment, the First Amendment must give way.

This is the thesis, by the way, of John Powell, legal director of the American Civil Liberties Union, even though that organization has formally opposed all college speech codes—after a considerable civil war among and within its affiliates.

The battle of the amendments continues, and when harsher codes are called for at some campuses, you can expect the Fourteenth Amendment—which was not intended to censor *speech*—will rise again.

A precedent has been set at, of all places, colleges and universities, that the principle of free speech is merely situational. As college administrators change, so will the extent of free speech on campus. And invariably, permissible speech will become more and more narrowly defined. Once speech can be limited in such subjective ways, more and more expression will be included in what is forbidden.

One of the exceedingly few college presidents who speaks out on the consequences of the anti-free-speech movement is Yale University's Benno Schmidt:

> Freedom of thought must be Yale's central commitment. It is not easy to embrace. It is, indeed, the effort of a lifetime. . . . Much expression that is free may deserve our contempt. We may well be moved to exercise our own freedom to counter it or to ignore it. But universities cannot censor or suppress speech, no matter how obnoxious in content, without violating their justification for existence. . . .
>
> On some other campuses in this country, values of civility and community have been offered by some as paramount values of the university, even to the extent of superseding freedom of expression.
>
> Such a view is wrong in principle and, if extended, is disastrous to freedom of thought. . . . The chilling effects on speech of the vagueness and open-ended nature of many universities' prohibitions . . . are compounded by the fact that these codes are typically enforced by faculty and students who commonly assert that vague notions of community are more important to the academy than freedom of thought and expression. . . .
>
> This is a flabby and uncertain time for freedom in the United States.

On the Public Broadcasting System in June, I was part of a Fred Friendly panel at Stanford University in a debate on speech codes versus freedom of expression. The three black panelists strongly supported the codes. So did the one Asian-American on the panel. But then so did Stanford law professor, Thomas Grey, who wrote the Stanford code, and Stanford president Donald Kennedy, who first opposed and then embraced the code. We have a new ecumenicism of those who would control speech for the greater good. It is hardly a new idea, but the mix of advocates is rather new.

But there are other voices. In the national board debate at the ACLU on college speech codes, the first speaker—and I think she had a lot to do with making the final vote against codes unanimous—was Gwen Thomas.

A black community college administrator from Colorado, she is a fiercely persistent exposer of racial discrimination.

She started by saying, "I have always felt as a minority person that we have to protect the rights of all because if we infringe on the rights of any persons, we'll be next."

"As for providing a nonintimidating educational environment, our young people have to learn to grow up on college campuses. We have to teach them how to deal with adversarial situations. They have to learn how to survive offensive speech they find wounding and hurtful."

Gwen Thomas is an educator—an endangered species in higher education.

Discussion Questions

1. Explain and present Mr. Hentoff's case against college speech codes. Do you agree or disagree with his assessment? Explain and defend your answer.

2. Many religious colleges and universities, which have a reputation for intellectual excellence, have speech and behavior codes for students and faculty that don't seem to negatively affect the quality of the graduates they produce. Why, then, should it matter at more secular institutions whether certain speech is forbidden? How do you think Mr. Hentoff would answer this question, and would you agree with his answer? Explain and defend your position.

3. In light of Mr. Hentoff's position, do you think there should be any limitations on speech on the college campus? If not, defend your answer and explain how you would deal with the problems of verbally abusive behavior, sexual harassment, and professors teaching false information (e.g., the earth is flat), all

of which are conveyed through speech. If you think there should be limitations on campus speech, where would you draw the line and why? How would you deal with speech that may appear offensive to some people but may raise legitimate intellectual questions, e.g., the moral status of homosexuality, inherent differences between men and women, the question of God's existence, inherent intellectual and physical differences between the races? Are alleged victims always correct about their perceptions?

SECTION D

Homosexuality

Introduction

One of the most controversial issues in the United States today is the rights of homosexuals, or what is called *gay rights*. Although no reasonable person denies that people who practice homosexuality have equal rights under the law, the gay rights movement raises the controversial question of whether the state has an obligation to treat homosexual behavior as fundamental to the nature of homosexuals, as salient a feature as race. If the state does not have such an obligation, does it have a right to favor certain forms of behavior and certain lifestyles, such as heterosexual monogamy, because the state perceives such practices as furthering the "public good" or the "good of the community"? As of the publication of this book, the individual 50 states of the United States officially sanction only heterosexual monogamy by recognizing traditional marriage in property law, tax law, family law, etc., and not recognizing other practices, such as polygamy, homosexual marriage, and bestiality. However, some jurisdictions allow for "domestic partnerships," in which homosexuals who cannot be legally married and heterosexuals who do not want to be married can have many of the same benefits allotted to partners in a heterosexual marriage, from health insurance to inheritance.

The gay rights movement asks whether the state's partiality toward heterosexual monogamy is consistent with our intuitions about justice, fairness, and personal autonomy. In fact, some of the changes in law called for by the gay rights movement assume that the latter intuitions along with mere individual consent are sufficient to invalidate as unethical the state's preference for heterosexual monogamy. Moreover, the state has an obligation to subsidize medical treatments and research in order to facilitate this equality. Consider the following demands taken from the "Platform of the 1993 March on Washington for Lesbian, Gay, and Bi Equal Rights and Liberation" (April 25, 1993):

> We demand passage of a Lesbian, Gay, Bisexual and Transgender civil rights bill. . . .; repeal of all sodomy laws and other laws that criminalize private sexual expression between consenting adults. . . .

> We demand legislation to prevent discrimination against Lesbians, Gays, Bisexuals and Transgendered people in the areas of family diversity, custody, adoption and foster care and that the definition of family includes the full diversity of all family structures.

> We demand full and equal inclusion of Lesbians, Gays, Bisexuals and Transgendered people in the educational system and inclusion of Lesbian, Gay, Bisexual and Transgender studies in multicultural curricula. . . .

> The implementation of laws that recognize sexual relationships among youth, between consenting peers.

There actually may be two issues in the question of gay rights. The first issue is whether the state should be forbidden to interfere with the private consensual sex of adults if no one outside the circle of consenters "gets hurt," even though such behavior violates the sensibilities of most people. The second issue is much more complex and is really at the heart of the above demands of the gay rights movement: Should the state be forbidden to give legal and social preference to heterosexual monogamy while denying such to alternative lifestyles, including homosexuality, polygamy, or adult incest? The first issue is not the same as the second. In fact, one can say "yes" to the privacy rights implied in the first issue and "no" to the sexual egalitarianism implied in the second. The differences between the first and second issues is not often appreciated or articulated in the popular debate over homosexual rights.

Many factions of the gay rights movement demand that homosexuals be given *minority status*, a status given by the federal government as well as state governments to groups whose members have suffered discrimination (e.g., African-Americans, women, Hispanics) and who have not, it is argued, advanced socially as far as they would have if they had not been discriminated against. Affirmative action policies, for example, apply only to members of groups that have minority status. Gay activists contend that homosexuals have suffered discrimination and therefore deserve minority status. Minority status for a group is established, according to the U.S. Supreme Court,[1] if the group fulfills at least three criteria:

Criterion 1: A history of discrimination evidenced by lack of ability to obtain economic mean income, adequate education, or cultural opportunity. . . .

Criterion 2: Specially protected classes should exhibit obvious, immutable, or distinguishing characteristics, like race, color, gender, or national origin, that define them as a discrete group. . . .

Criterion 3: "Protected classes" should clearly demonstrate political powerlessness.[2]

Opponents of applying minority status to homosexuals argue that the gay activists have failed to make a compelling case. For example, concerning the first criterion, it has been pointed out that "homosexuals have an average annual household income of $55,430 versus $32,144 for the general population and $12,166 for disadvantaged African-American households." In addition, "more than three times as many homosexuals as average Americans are college graduates (59.6 percent vs. 18 percent) . . ." and "more than three times as many homosexuals as average Americans hold professional or managerial positions (49 percent v. 15.9 percent."[3] Needless to say, criteria (2) and (3) have been challenged as well.[4]

The state of Colorado's controversial Amendment 2 concerned the issue of minority status. The amendment, as it appeared as a ballot question in 1992, read: "Shall there be an amendment to Article II of the Colorado Constitution to prohibit the state of Colorado and any of its political subdivisions from adopting or enforcing any law or policy that provides that homosexual, lesbian, or bisexual orientation or conduct, or relationships constitutes or entitles a person to claim any minority or protected status, quota preference or discrimination?" Passing in a referendum with 54 percent of the popular vote, Amendment 2 has been legally challenged in the courts by gay activists. As of the publication of this book, it has not been judicially resolved. For this reason, it has yet to become state law.

There are three parts to this section, each dealing with a different aspect of gay rights. Part one consists of one article (Chapter 50), excerpts from the Supreme Court's decision *Bowers v. Hardwick* (1986). In that decision the Court ruled that the state of Georgia's statute that made engaging in homosexual sodomy (anal sex) illegal does not violate the right to privacy and is in fact constitutional. The majority opinion as well as a concurring and a dissenting opinion are included. The second part concerns the question of whether homosexuality is immoral and how any conclusion on that question will translate into public policy. The first essay (Chapter 51) in this part ("Homosexuality, Public Health, and Civil Rights," by Daniel C. Palm) defends the view that homosexuals have equal rights under the law as citizens but not as homosexuals. Dr. Palm also argues against the view that homosexuals deserve protected minority status. In Chapter 52 ("Gay Basics: Some Questions, Facts, and Values"), Professor Richard Mohr defends the morality of homosexuality as well as the legal rights of homosexuals. He does this by covering four different moral and legal concerns. The third essay ("Sodomy and the Dissolution of Free Society," Chapter 55) in this part, by Professor Harry Jaffa, is a critical review of Professor Mohr's book (*Gays/Justice: A Study of Ethics, Society and Law* [1988]). Professor Jaffa defends the position that homosexuality is immoral and should neither be encouraged by society nor treated as equal to heterosexual monogamy. He argues for this position by appealing to "natural law." The concept of natural law and its application to homosexuality is the concern of Chapter 54 ("Is Homosexuality Unnatural?" by Burton M. Leiser). In this essay, Professor Leiser concludes that the opponents of homosexuality have not shown that homosexuality is unnatural in the sense of being immoral and/or impermissible.

The third part of this section deals with the volatile issue of homosexuals in the military. For quite some time the military has asked recruits if they are homosexuals. If the recruits answered "yes," they were forbidden to join any branch of the military. If the recruits answered "no," but later were discovered to be homosexual, then they would be formally discharged. According to this view, homosexuality is inconsistent with military service.

In early 1993 President Bill Clinton tried to lift this ban completely. However, after an outcry by military leaders, congressional hearings, and letters and phone calls of protest by a number of citizens, the White House and the Congress agreed on a compromise, which is known as the "don't ask, don't tell" policy. That is, recruiters and military personnel are required not to ask recruits about their sexual orientation but recruits are required not to tell their sexual orientation to recruiters or military personnel. Also, any military personnel discovered engaging in homosexual behavior while on active duty, on or off a military base, will be discharged.

Both essays in this part argue against this policy. In Chapter 55 ("Lifting the Gay Ban") Professor Charles L. Davis argues that the military's former policy of forbidding homosexuals in the military as well as President Clinton's "don't ask, don't tell" compromise are unjust to homosexual citizens who want to serve their country. In this part's second essay (Chapter 56, "Make War, Not Love: The Pentagon's Gay Ban Is Wise and Just"), John Luddy argues against both the position taken by Professor Davis in Chapter 51 as well as the "don't ask, don't tell" policy. Mr. Luddy supports the traditional position that "homosexuality is incompatible with military service."

Notes

1. The Court established these three criteria through a number of decisions with which civil rights experts are acquainted. See, for example, the affirmation of these criteria in *Jantz v. Muci* (March 29, 1991) 759 Fed. Supp. 1543.

2. Tony Marco, "Oppressed Minority, or Counterfeits?," *Citizen* 6 (April 20, 1992), 2, 3.

3. Ibid., 2. See *Statistical Abstract of the United States* (1990).

4. See Marco, "Oppressed Minority," 1–4.

For Further Reading

Paul Cameron, "A Case against Homosexuality," *Human Life Review* 4 (1978).

George Grant, ed., *Gays in the Military: The Moral and Strategic Crisis* (Franklin, Tenn.: Legacy, 1993).

George Grant and Mark A. Horne, *Legislating Immorality: The Homosexual Movement Comes Out of the Closet* (Chicago: Moody Press, 1993).

Harry V. Jaffa, *Homosexuality and the Natural Law* (Claremont, Calif.: The Claremont Institute for the Study of Statesmanship and Political Philosophy, 1990).

Marshall Kirk and Hunter Madsen, *After the Ball: How America Will Conquer Its Fear and Hatred of Gays in the 90s* (New York: Doubleday, 1989).

Roger J. Magnuson, *Are Gay Rights Right?: Making Sense of the Controversy* (Portland, Ore.: Multnomah, 1990).

Richard D. Mohr, *Gays/Justice: A Study of Ethics, Society, and the Law* (New York: Columbia University Press, 1988).

Michael Ruse, *Homosexuality: A Philosophical Inquiry* (Oxford: Basil Blackwell, 1988).

Randy Shilts, *And the Band Played On: Politics, People, and the AIDS Epidemic* (New York: St. Martin's, 1987).

———, *Conduct Unbecoming: Lesbians and Gays in the U.S. Military, Vietnam to the Persian Gulf* (New York: St. Martin's, 1993).

The Law and Homosexuality

50

Bowers v. Hardwick (1986)

U.S. Supreme Court

In the state of Georgia in August 1992, Michael Hardwick was charged with violating that state's criminal statute forbidding homosexual sodomy. Mr. Hardwick was discovered committing an act of sodomy with another male in the bedroom of his home. The question before the U.S. Supreme Court in this case was whether the Georgia statute violated the right to privacy, which in a number of cases the Court has ruled is found in the U.S. Constitution (e.g., *Griswold v. Connecticut* [1965], *Roe v. Wade* [1973]). In the majority opinion, Justice Byron White concluded, among other things, that the state of Georgia has the right, though not the obligation, to criminalize homosexual sodomy if it so chooses, since the right to privacy is not absolute, applying to such cases as the right to decide whether one wants to bear a child and a right to possess and read obscene material in the privacy of one's home. Homosexual sodomy is more akin to the possession and use of illegal drugs for which private consent does not invalidate laws prohibiting such activity. In his concurring opinion, former Chief Justice Warren Burger stresses the moral condemnation of homosexual sodomy throughout the history of Western Civilization, firmly rooted in the Judeo-Christian tradition, Roman law, the English Reformation, and common law. In his dissenting opinion, Justice Harry Blackmun chastises his brethren in the majority for not truly appreciating the constitutional right to privacy and how it applies to intimate personal decisions about one's own sexuality. He understands the right to privacy in previous decisions as grounded in the right to be let alone, which would make it unconstitutional to legally forbid consenting adults to engage in sodomy in the privacy of their own homes.

Justice White delivered the opinion of the Court.

In August 1982, respondent Hardwick. . . was charged with violating the Georgia statute criminalizing sodomy by committing that act with another adult male in the bedroom of respondent's home. After a preliminary hearing, the District Attorney decided not to present the matter to the grand jury unless further evidence developed.

Respondent then brought suit in the Federal District Court, challenging the constitutionality of the statute insofar as it criminalized consensual sodomy. He asserted that he was a practicing homosexual, that the Georgia sodomy statute, as administered by the defendants, placed him in imminent danger of arrest, and that the statute for several reasons violates the Federal Constitution. . . .

This case does not require a judgment on whether laws against sodomy between consenting adults in general, or between homosexuals in particular, are wise or desirable. It raises no question about the right or propriety of state legislative decisions to repeal their laws that criminalize homosexual sodomy, or of the state-court decisions invalidating those laws on state constitutional grounds. The issue presented is whether the Federal Constitution confers a fundamental right upon homosexuals to engage in sodomy and hence invalidates the laws of the many States that still make such conduct illegal and have done so for a very long time. The case also calls for some judgment about the limits of the Court's role in carrying out its constitutional mandate.

We first register our disagreement with the Court of Appeals and with respondent that the Court's prior cases have construed the Constitution to confer a right of privacy that extends to homosexual sodomy and for all intents and purposes have decided this case.... [Three] cases were interpreted as construing the Due Process Clause of the Fourteenth Amendment to confer a fundamental individual right to decide whether or not to beget or bear a child....

Accepting the decisions in these cases . . . we think it evident that none of the rights announced in those cases bears any resemblance to the claimed constitutional right of homosexuals to engage in acts of sodomy that is asserted in this case. No connection between family, marriage, or procreation on the one hand and homosexual activity on the other has been demonstrated, either by the Court of Appeals or by respondent. Moreover, any claim that these cases nevertheless stand for the proposition that any kind of private sexual conduct between consenting adults is constitutionally insulated from state proscription is unsupportable....

Precedent aside, however, respondent would have us announce, as the Court of Appeals did, the fundamental right to engage in homosexual sodomy. This we are quite unwilling to do. It is true that despite the language of the Due Process Clauses of the Fifth and Fourteenth Amendments, which appears to focus only on the processes by which life, liberty, or property is taken, the cases are legion in which those Clauses have been interpreted to have substantive content, subsuming rights that to a great extent are immune from federal or state regulation or proscription. Among such cases are those recognizing rights that have little or no textual support in the constitutional language....

Striving to assure itself and the public that announcing rights not readily identifiable in the Constitution's text involves much more than the imposition of the Justices' own choice of values on the States and the Federal Government, the Court has sought to identify the nature of the rights qualifying for heightened judicial protection. In *Palko v. Connecticut*, ... it was said that this category includes those fundamental liberties that are "implicit in the concept of ordered liberty," such that "neither liberty nor justice would exist if [they] were sacrificed." A different description of fundamental liberties appeared in *Moore v. East Cleveland*, ... where they are characterized as those liberties that are "deeply rooted in this Nation's history and tradition."...

It is obvious to us that neither of these formulations would extend a fundamental right to homosexuals to engage in acts of consensual sodomy. Proscriptions against that conduct have ancient roots.

. . . Sodomy was a criminal offense at common law and was forbidden by the laws of the original thirteen States when they ratified the Bill of Rights. In 1868, when the Fourteenth Amendment was ratified, all but 5 of the 37 States in the Union had criminal sodomy laws. In fact, until 1961, all 50 States outlawed sodomy, and today, 24 states and the District of Columbia continue to provide criminal penalties for sodomy performed in private and between consenting adults.... Against this background, to claim that a right to engage in such conduct is "deeply rooted in this Nation's history and tradition" or "implicit in the concept of ordered liberty" is, at best, facetious.

Nor are we included to take a more expansive view of our authority to discover new fundamental rights imbedded in the Due Process Clause. The Court is most vulnerable and comes nearest to illegitimacy when it deals with judge-made constitutional law having little or no cognizable roots in the language or design of the Constitution. That this is so was painfully demonstrated by the face-off between the Executive and the Court in the 1930's, which resulted in the repudiation of much of the substantive gloss that the Court had placed on the Due Process Clauses of the Fifth and Fourteenth Amendments. There should be, therefore, great resistance to expand the substantive reach of those Clauses, particularly if it requires redefining the category of rights deemed to be fundamental. Otherwise, the Judiciary necessarily takes to itself further authority to govern the country without express constitutional authority. The claimed right pressed on us today falls far short of overcoming this resistance.

Respondent, however, asserts that the result should be different where the homosexual conduct occurs in the privacy of the home. He relies on *Stanley v. Georgia*, ... where the court held that the First Amendment prevents conviction for possessing and reading obscene material in the privacy of one's home: "If the First Amendment means anything, it means that a State has no business telling a man, sitting alone in his house, what books he may read or what films he may watch." ...

Stanley did protect conduct that would not have been protected outside the home, and it partially prevented the enforcement of the state obscenity laws; but the decision was firmly grounded in the First Amendment. The right pressed upon us here has no similar support in the text of the Constitution, and it does not qualify for recognition under the prevailing principles of construing the Fourteenth

Amendment. Its limits are also difficult to discern. Plainly enough, otherwise illegal conduct is not always immunized whenever it occurs in the home. Victimless crimes, such as the possession and use of illegal drugs, do not escape the law where they are committed at home. *Stanley* itself recognized that its holding offered no protection for the possession in the home of drugs, firearms, or stolen goods. . . . And if respondent's submission is limited to the voluntary sexual conduct between consenting adults, it would be difficult, except by fiat, to limit the claimed right to homosexual conduct while leaving exposed to prosecution adultery, incest, and other sexual crimes even though they are committed in the home. We are unwilling to start down that road.

Even if the conduct at issue here is not a fundamental right, respondent asserts that there must be a rational basis for the law and that there is none in this case other than the presumed belief of a majority of the electorate in Georgia that homosexual sodomy is immoral and unacceptable. This is said to be an inadequate rationale to support the law. The law, however, is constantly based on notions of morality, and if all laws representing essentially moral choices are to be invalidated under the Due Process Clause, the courts will be very busy indeed. Even respondent makes no such claim, but insists that majority sentiments about the morality of homosexuality should be declared inadequate. We do not agree, and are unpersuaded that the sodomy laws of some 25 States should be invalidated on this basis.

Accordingly, the judgment of the Court of Appeals is
Reversed.

Chief Justice Burger, concurring.

I join the Court's opinion, but I write separately to underscore my view that in constitutional terms there is no such thing as a fundamental right to commit homosexual sodomy.

As the Court notes, . . . the proscriptions against sodomy have very "ancient roots." Decisions of individuals relating to homosexual conduct have been subject to state intervention throughout the history of Western civilization. Condemnation of those practices is firmly rooted in Judeo-Christian moral and ethical standards. Homosexual sodomy was a capital crime under Roman law. . . . During the English Reformation when powers of the ecclesiastical courts were transferred to the King's Courts, the first English statute criminalizing sodomy was passed. . . . Blackstone described "the infamous *crime against nature*" as an offense of "deeper malignity" than rape, a heinous act "the very mention of which is a disgrace to human nature," and "ac rime not fit to be named." . . . The common law of England, including its prohibition of sodomy, became the received law of Georgia and the other Colonies. In 1816 the Georgia Legislature passed the statute at issue here, and that statute has been continuously in force in one form or another since that time. To hold that the act of homosexual sodomy is somehow protected as a fundamental right would be to cast aside millennia of moral teaching.

This is essentially not a question of personal "preferences" but rather of the legislative authority of the State. I find nothing in the Constitution depriving a State of the power to enact the statute challenged here. . . .

Justice Blackmun, with whom Justice Brennan, Justice Marshall, and Justice Stevens join, dissenting.

This case is no more about a "fundamental right to engage in homosexual sodomy," as the Court purports to declare, . . . than *Stanley v. Georgia* . . . was about a fundamental right to watch obscene movies, or *Katz v. United States*, . . . was about a fundamental right to place interstate bets from a telephone booth. Rather, this case is about "the most comprehensive of rights and the right most valued by civilized men," namely, "the right to be let alone." . . .

The statute at issue, . . . denies individuals the right to decide for themselves whether to engage in particular forms of private, consensual sexual activity. The Court concludes that [the statute] is valid essentially because "the laws of . . . many States . . . still make such conduct illegal and have done so for a very long time." . . . But the fact that the moral judgments expressed by statutes like . . . [the Georgia statute] may be "'natural and familiar . . . ought not to conclude our judgment upon the question whether statutes embodying them conflict with the Constitution of the United States.'" . . . Like Justice Holmes, I believe that "[i]t is revolting to have no better reason for a rule of law than that so it was laid down in the time of Henry IV. It is still more revolting if the grounds upon which it was laid down have vanished long since, and the rule simply persists from blind imitation of the past." . . . I believe we must analyze Hardwick's claim in the light of the values that underlie the constitutional right to privacy. If that right means anything, it means that, before Georgia can prosecute its citizens for making choices about the most intimate aspects of their lives, it must do more than assert that the choice they have made is an "'abominable crime not fit to be named among Christians.'" . . .

In its haste to reverse the Court of Appeals and hold that the Constitution does not confe[r] a fundamental right upon homosexuals to engage in sodomy," . . . the Court relegates the actual statute being challenged to a footnote and ignores the procedural posture of the case before it. A fair reading of the statute and of the complaint clearly reveals that the majority has distorted the question this case presents.

. . . [T]he Court's almost obsessive focus on homosexual activity is particularly hard to justify in light of the broad language Georgia has used. Unlike the Court, the Georgia Legislature has not proceeded on the assumption that homosexuals are so different from other citizens that their lives may be controlled in a way that would not be tolerated if it limited the choices of those other citizens. . . . Rather, Georgia has provided that "[a] person commits the offense of sodomy when he performs or submits to any sexual act involving the sex organs of one person and the mouth or anus of another." . . . The sex or status of the persons who engage in the act is irrelevant as a matter of state law. In fact, to the extent I can discern a legislative purpose for Georgia's 1968 enactment . . . that purpose seems to have been to broaden the coverage of the law to reach heterosexual as well as homosexual activity. I therefore see no basis for the Court's decision to treat this case . . . solely on the grounds that it prohibits homosexual activity. Michael Hardwick's standing may rest in significant part on Georgia's apparent willingness to enforce against homosexuals a law it seems not to have any desire to enforce against heterosexuals. . . . But his claim that . . . [the Georgia statute] involves an unconstitutional intrusion into his privacy and his right of intimate association does not depend in any way on his sexual orientation. . . .

"Our cases long have recognized that the Constitution embodies a promise that a certain private sphere of individual liberty will be kept largely beyond the reach of government." . . . In construing the right to privacy, the Court has proceeded along two somewhat distinct, albeit complementary, lines. First, it has recognized a privacy interest with reference to certain *decisions* that are properly for the individual to make. . . . Second, it has recognized a privacy interest with reference to certain *places* without regard for the particular activities in which the

individuals who occupy them are engaged. . . . The case before us implicates both the decisional and the spatial aspects of the right to privacy.

The Court concludes today that none of our prior cases dealing with various decisions that individuals are entitled to make free of governmental interference "bears any resemblance to the claimed constitutional right of homosexuals to engage in acts of sodomy that is asserted in this case." . . . While it is true that these cases may be characterized by their connection to protection of the family, . . . the Court's conclusion that they extend no further than this boundary ignores the warning in *Moore v. East Cleveland*, . . . against "clos[ing] our eyes to the basic reasons why certain rights associated with the family have been accorded shelter under the Fourteenth Amendment's Due Process Clause." We protect those rights not because they contribute, in some direct and material way, to the general public welfare, but because they form so central a part of an individual's life. "[T]he concept of privacy embodies the 'moral fact that a person belongs to himself and not others nor to society as a whole.'" . . . And so we protect the decision whether to marry precisely because marriage "is an association that promotes a way of life, not causes; a harmony in living, not political faiths; a bilateral loyalty, not commercial or social projects." . . . We protect the decision whether to have a child because parenthood alters so dramatically an individual's self-definition, not because of demographic considerations or the Bible's command to be fruitful and multiply. . . . And we protect the family because it contributes so powerfully to the happiness of individuals, not because of a preference for stereotypical households. . . . The Court recognized in *Roberts* . . . that the "ability independently to define one's identity is central to any concept of liberty" cannot truly be exercised in a vacuum; we all depend on the "emotional enrichment from close ties with others."

Only the most willful blindness could obscure the fact that sexual intimacy is "a sensitive, key relationship of human existence, central to family life, community welfare, and the development of human personality," . . . The fact that individuals define themselves in a significant way through their intimate sexual relationships with others suggests, in a Nation as diverse as ours, that there may be many "right" ways of conducting those relationships, and that much of the richness of a relationship will come from the freedom an individual has to *choose* the form and nature of these intensely personal bonds. . . .

In a variety of circumstances we have recognized that a necessary corollary of giving individuals freedom to choose how to conduct their lives is acceptance of the fact that different individuals will make different choices. For example, in holding that the clearly important state interest in public education should give way to a competing claim by the Amish to the effect that extended formal schooling threatened their way of life, the Court declared: "There can be no assumption that today's majority is 'right' and the Amish and others like them are 'wrong.' A way of life that is odd or even erratic but interferes with no rights or interests of others is not to be condemned because it is different." . . . The Court claims that its decision today merely refuses to recognize a fundamental right to engage in homosexual sodomy; what the Court really has refused to recognize is the fundamental interest all individuals have in controlling the nature of their intimate associations with others.

The behavior for which Hardwick faces prosecution occurred in his own home, a place to which the Fourth Amendment attaches special significance. The Court's treatment of this aspect of the case is symptomatic of its overall refusal to consider the broad principles that have informed our treatment of privacy in specific cases. Just as the right to privacy is more than a mere aggregation of a number of entitlements to engage in specific behavior, so too, protecting the physical integrity of the home is more than merely a means of protecting specific activities that often take place there. Even when our understanding of the contours of the right to privacy depends on "reference to a 'place,'" . . . "the essence of a Fourth Amendment violation is 'not the breaking of [a person's] doors, and the rummaging of his drawers,' but rather is 'the invasion of his indefeasible right of personal security, personal liberty and private property.'" . . .

The Court's interpretation of the pivotal case of *Stanley v. Georgia*, . . . is entirely unconvincing. *Stanley* held that Georgia's undoubted power to punish the public distribution of constitutionally unprotected, obscene material did not permit the State to punish the private possession of such material. According to the majority here, *Stanley* relied entirely on the First Amendment, and thus, it is claimed, sheds no light on cases not involving printed materials. . . . But that is not what *Stanley* said. Rather, the *Stanley* Court anchored its holding in the Fourth Amendment's special protection for the individual in his home:

> "'The makers of our Constitution undertook to secure conditions favorable to the pursuit of happiness. They recognized the significance of man's spiritual nature, of his feelings and of his intellect. They knew that only a part of the pain, pleasure and satisfactions of life are to be found in material things. They sought to protect Americans in their beliefs, their thoughts, their emotions and their sensations.'

> "These are the rights that appellant is asserting in the case before us. He is asserting the right to read or observe what he pleases—the right to satisfy his intellectual and emotional needs in the privacy of his own home." . . . quoting *Olmstead v. United States* . . .

The central place that *Stanley* gives Justice Brandeis' dissent in *Olmstead*, a case raising *no* First Amendment claim, shows that *Stanley* rested as much on the Court's understanding of the Fourth Amendment as it did on the matter how uncomfortable a certain group may make the majority of this Court, we have held that "[m]ere public intolerance or animosity cannot constitutionally justify the deprivation of a person's physical liberty." . . .

. . . Reasonable people may differ about whether particular sexual acts are moral or immoral, but "we have ample evidence for believing that people will not abandon morality, will not think any better of murder, cruelty and dishonesty, merely because some private sexual practice which they abominate is not punished by the law." . . . Petitioner and the Court fail to see the difference between laws that protect public sensibilities and those that enforce private morality. Statutes banning public sexual activity are entirely consistent with protecting the individual's liberty interest in decisions concerning sexual relations: the same recognition that those decisions are intensely private which justifies protecting them from governmental interference can justify protecting individuals from unwilling exposure to the sexual activities of others. But the mere fact that intimate behavior may be punished when it takes place in public cannot dictate how States can regulate intimate behavior that occurs in intimate places. . . .

This case involves no real interference with the rights of others, for the mere knowledge that other individuals do not adhere to one's value system cannot be a legally cognizable interest, . . . let alone an interest that can justify invading the houses, hearts, and minds of citizens who choose to live their lives differently.

. . . I can only hope that . . . the Court soon will reconsider its analysis and conclude that depriving individuals of the right to choose for themselves how to conduct their intimate relationships poses a far greater threat to the values most deeply rooted in our Nation's history than tolerance of nonconformity could ever do. Because I think the Court today betrays those values, I dissent.

Discussion Questions

1. Present and explain Justice White's opinion that homosexual sodomy is not protected by the right to privacy. Do you agree or disagree with the case he supports? Explain and defend your answer.

2. Present and explain former Chief Justice Burger's concurring opinion. Do you agree with the former Chief Justice that millennia of moral condemnation of homosexual sodomy counts against its permissibility? Explain and defend your answer.

3. Present and explain Justice Blackmun's minority opinion. Do you agree with Justice Blackmun's claim that the right to privacy entails the right to do anything in the privacy of one's home as long as it does not interfere with another's freedom? Explain and defend your answer.

Social Policy, Morality, and Homosexual Rights

51

Homosexuality, Public Health, and Civil Rights

Daniel C. Palm

Daniel C. Palm is Director of the Center for the Study of Natural Law at the Claremont Institute (Claremont, California). He has published a number of articles and policy papers on political philosophy and public policy.

This essay begins with Dr. Palm quoting the demands of homosexuals as found in the 1972 Gay Rights Platform. Using that document as his point of departure Dr. Palm argues that although homosexuals *as citizens* deserve all the rights accorded to citizens of the United States, those who practice *homosexuality* should not be accorded specially protected minority status as traditional minority groups (e.g., African-Americans) have been and certainly not the privileges society grants to monogamous heterosexual marriage. In defense of this view he offers the following reasons: (1) The homosexual lifestyle is harmful to the public health and thus should not be encouraged; (2) sodomy (anal intercourse), which is the primary way male homosexuals have sex, "is unnatural and, as such, incompatible with any notion of human rights"; (3) homosexuals have failed to meet several legal tests

Reprinted by permission from *Moral Ideas for America*, ed. Larry P. Arnn and Douglas A. Jeffrey (Claremont, Calif.: The Claremont Institute for the Study of Statesmanship and Political Philosophy, 1993), 15–26.

to be considered a specially protected minority: (A) "its members must be identifiable by an unchanging physical condition—e.g., skin color, gender, handicap," (B) "they must be able to demonstrate that they suffered discrimination to the extent that they are unable to earn an average income, receive an adequate education, or enjoy a fulfilling cultural life," and (C) "they must show that their members are politically powerless to change their predicament."

The 1972 Gay Rights Platform[1] contained the following demands:

- Amend all federal Civil Rights Acts, other legislation and government controls to prohibit discrimination in employment, housing, public accommodations and public services.
- A presidential order prohibiting the military from excluding for reasons of their sexual orientation, persons who of their own volition desire entrance into the Armed Services; and from issuing less than fully-honorable discharges for homosexuality; and the upgrading to fully honorable all such discharges previously issued, with retroactive benefits.
- A presidential order prohibiting discrimination in the federal civil service because of sexual orientation, in hiring and promoting; and prohibiting discrimination against homosexuals in security clearances.
- Elimination of tax inequities [favoring traditional families].
- Elimination of bars to the entry, immigration and naturalization of homosexual aliens.
- Federal encouragement and support for sex education courses, prepared and taught by [homosexuals], presenting homosexuality as a valid, healthy preference and . . . a viable alternative to heterosexuality.

- Federal funding of aid programs of [homosexual] organizations designed to alleviate the problems encountered by [homosexuals].

The document made similar demands of states, including:

- Repeal of all state laws prohibiting solicitation for private voluntary sexual liaisons; and laws prohibiting prostitution, both male and female.
- [L]egislation prohibiting insurance companies and any other state-regulated enterprises from discriminating because of sexual orientation, in insurance and in bonding or any other prerequisite to employment or control of one's personal demesne.
- [L]egislation so that child custody, adoption, visitation rights, foster parenting, and the like shall not be denied because of sexual orientation or marital status.
- Repeal of all laws prohibiting transvestism and cross dressing.
- Repeal of all laws governing the age of sexual consent.
- Repeal of all legislative provisions that restrict the sex or number of persons entering into a marriage unit; and the extension of legal benefits to all persons who cohabit regardless of sex or numbers.

Two decades later, especially at the federal level, most of these demands have been met. Nor do signs look good for a quick reversal of this trend: The descriptive word "homosexual" has been replaced by the perfectly nondescriptive word "gay." Opponents of homosexuality are said to be afflicted with "homophobia." The media and academic elites are actively supporting the organized homosexual line. Politicians routinely court the "homosexual vote" in the same way theu court, for example, the votes of farmers. "The love that dare not speak its name" is fast becoming "the love that no one dares to question."

Defenders of morality have a tough row to hoe. They must begin by sensibly recasting the terms of the debate. This means, first, addressing sex-related diseases as health issues rather than civil rights issues. Second, it means distinguishing the civil rights of all Americans under the Constitution from the special rights demanded by organized homosexuals.

Homosexuality and the Public Health

While AIDS has destroyed the lives of non-homosexuals through intravenous drug use, blood transfusions, or promiscuity, until recently the disease has been primarily spread among homosexuals. The U.S. Department of Health and Human Services Centers for Disease Control reports that 65 percent of all adult/adolescent AIDS cases and 79 percent of AIDS cases among Caucasians in the U.S. were acquired through homosexual contact. Ninety-one percent of American AIDS cases have been traced to homosexual sex, intravenous drug use, or some combination of the two.[2]

Homosexuals also continue to contract and spread other diseases at rates significantly higher than the community at large. These include syphilis, gonorrhea, herpes, hepatitis A and B, a variety of intestinal parasites including amebiasis and giardiasis, and even typhoid fever.[3] This is because rectal intercourse or sodomy, typically practiced by homosexuals, is one of the most efficient methods of transmitting disease. Why? Because nature designed the human rectum for a single purpose: expelling waste from the body. It is built of a thin layer of columnar cells, different in structure than the plate cells that line the female reproductive tract. Because the wall of the rectum is so thin, it is easily ruptured during anal intercourse, allowing semen, blood, feces, and saliva to directly enter the bloodstream. The chances for infection increase further when multiple partners are involved, as is frequently the case: Surveys indicate that American male homosexuals average between 10 and 110 sex partners per year.[4]

Not surprisingly, these diseases shorten life expectancy. Social psychologist Paul Cameron compared over 6,200 obituaries from homosexual magazines and tabloids to a comparable number of obituaries from major American newspapers. He found that while the median age of death of married American males was 75, for sexually active homosexual American males it was 42. For homosexual males infected with the AIDS virus, it was 39. While 80 percent of married American men lived to 65 or older, less than two percent of the homosexual men covered in the survey lived as long.[5]

In the face of these facts, it is reprehensible that Americans, and especially American schoolchildren, are being told today that homosexual behavior can be safe. Condoms are no god-send: estimates of condom failure run from 15.7 to as high as 44 percent. Breakage is even more likely with rectal intercourse, where the wear and tear on condoms is obviously greater.

Because smokers don't live as long as non-smokers, society considers smoking harmful and discourages the use of tobacco. By the same logic, aren't homosexual practices deserving of social disapproval?

Civil Rights and Special Rights

The gay rights movement's main rhetorical ploy is to liken itself to the civil rights movement of the 1950s and '60s. The extent to which this line is successful reflects a confusion about the meaning of "rights" in the public mind.

The charter of the American liberty, the Declaration of Independence, explains that human beings are born with "certain unalienable rights, that among these are life, liberty, and the pursuit of happiness." These rights belong to people equally. No human being is so superior to another that he may treat the other as he would treat an irrational beast. This is the argument that Abraham Lincoln hearkened back to during the Civil War, and Martin Luther King, Jr. during the 1960s. Unlike people in most countries, Americans have been able to enjoy these rights, because the American Constitution sets up a government that is limited in what it can do.

Consider the claimed comparison between the gay rights movement and the civil rights movement in light of this. An obvious difference is that the former is centered around a type of behavior, namely sodomy. Is there a constitutional right to sodomy which can be deduced from our equal natural rights, such as there is, say, to practice our religion or speak our mind? No.

At the time of the American founding, and following the tradition of English common law, sodomy was a criminal or common law offense in each of the 13 states. Until 1961, all 50 states considered sodomy a punishable offense. It remains illegal today in 23 states and the District of Columbia, and in many of these stands as a felony offense. At the federal level, the question was dealt with in the Supreme Court's 1986 decision, *Bowers v. Hardwick*. The defendants in the case had asked the Court to proclaim, in effect, "a fundamental right to engage in homosexual sodomy." "This," wrote Justice Byron White in delivering the Court's decision, "we are quite unwilling to do."[6]

More deeply, sodomy is unnatural and, as such, incompatible with any notion of natural rights. We know that human beings are entitled to their liberty because they are, by nature, capable of reasoning and choosing. This is precisely the faculty that identifies a human being, among all the other beings in nature. We are entitled to civil rights, because we are the one creature equipped by nature to exercise them.

Human beings also have other aspects to their nature, aspects that are not unique to them and are not such noble features of their makeup. One is their method of sexual reproduction. And make no mistake: despite the astonishing denials of organized homosexuality, human beings, as surely as deer or elephants, come equipped with a natural method of reproduction. Unlike in other species, however, these lower aspects in man share in man's higher aspect, reason. The result is the virtue of temperance or self-control. The Founders of America understood that our rights stem from this capacity, the capacity for moral virtue.[7]

Homosexuals like to argue that, since people are by nature free to choose, the choice of sodomy should be protected, at least as much as any other choice. But the fact that people are free by nature to make choices does not mean that any choice they make is good or that all choices should be equal before the law. Some people choose to steal and lie. Some abandon their children or their wives or husbands. Some sink into the grip of drugs. Some evade the draft at their country's need, or abandon their duty in the face of battle. These are bad choices, and when they are made, the rest of us must bear part of the cost. These things are wrong in a democracy, as much as they are wrong anywhere else.

On the other hand, liberal societies recognize that all sins cannot be, and must not be, punished under the law. A state powerful enough to do that is too powerful to control. That is why we are cautious, in a free country, about telling others what to do. That is why our presidents often appeal to us to be upright, moral citizens, but they do not bring charges against us unless we break the law.

Still we must not forget that democracies have the greatest interest in the practice of virtue by citizens, because in democracy the citizens themselves are the rulers. So it is that George Washington, one of the greatest moral examples in history, said in his First Inaugural Address: "there is no truth more thoroughly established than that there exists an indissoluble union between virtue and happiness..."

A liberal society might, then, find it prudent to ignore homosexuality. It might well deem it unwise to peer into private bedrooms. But this is not the issue before us. Today the demand is not that people be allowed their privacy. The demand is that homosexuality be endorsed and promoted with the full power of the law. This would require us to abandon the standard of nature, the one standard that can teach us the difference between freedom and slavery, between right and wrong.

Once we abandon the standard of nature, what is to forbid us from resorting to any violation of nature that we may please? Why should we not return to slavery, if we find it convenient? Or the practices of incest or adultery or cannibalism? Without an understanding that there is a higher law that limits human will—whether divine law or a "law of Nature and Nature's God" which we can grasp through our reason—there is no basis to prohibit any activity. Anything becomes permissible.

In fact, the rights sought by homosexual activists are not natural or constitutional rights. They are the special rights granted ethnic minorities by affirmative action policies. These special rights would force businesses, schools, and virtually every institution in the land, public and private, to open their doors to homosexuals, and allow lawsuits to be brought against those that refuse.

To be considered a specially-protected minority under the law, a group must meet several tests, as determined by a series of Supreme Court decisions. Its members must be identifiable by an unchanging physical condition—e.g., skin color, gender, handicap. They must be able to demonstrate that they have suffered discrimination to the extent that they are unable to earn an average income, receive an adequate education, or enjoy a fulfilling cultural life. And they must show that their members are politically powerless to change their predicament.[8]

To date, the homosexual lobby has been unable to prove that its members meet these requirements. There is no evidence—statistical or otherwise—that homosexuals are suffering any practical or political disadvantages. They have never been denied the right to vote or other constitutional rights, nor have they suffered segregation under the law, nor have they been denied access to public facilities. Several U.S. Congressmen, Senators, and prominent state legislators are openly homosexual, as are high-level members of present and recent presidential administrations. Statistically, homosexuals enjoy higher economic status than average Americans. Any claim to political powerlessness is belied by how politicians today—especially Democratic politicians—court the "homosexual vote."

It is easy to see the difference between civil and constitutional rights and the special rights sought by homosexuals by considering the controversy over "gays" in the military. People are refused entrance for numerous reasons, e.g., age, intelligence, physical handicap, criminal record. Second: the racial integration of the armed forces (to which proponents of "sexual preference integration" like to point) was part of the proper expansion of *constitutional* rights because race was an irrational (hence unconstitutional) basis of discrimination. Those who thought blacks were different in behavior were simply prejudiced—they were wrong. Those who think homosexuals behave differently are self-evidently right. The word "homosexual," unlike the words "black" or "brown" or "yellow," denotes precisely a different behavior. In this case, those who deny a difference are being irrational.

As summed up by a veteran of the civil rights movement: "The road to Selma was not the road to Sodom."

Near-term Measures

There is no indication that the Supreme Court will strike down the remaining state anti-sodomy laws. Thus the organized homosexual offensive operates primarily in two areas: incorporating homosexual propaganda into public school curricula and promoting special "anti-discrimination laws" in states and cities.

In combatting this offensive, generally speaking, debates about Biblical doctrine, the percentage of the homosexual population, or whether homosexuality is genetic or psychological in origin, are fruitless and allow homosexual activists to obscure the main points on which the political battles will be won or lost: public health and civil rights.[10]

Champions for morality should really go on the offensive themselves on the issue of homosexuality as a public health hazard. A good place to do so is before the governing boards of public schools, where homosexuality (when practiced "safely") is often presented as an acceptable alternate lifestyle. The principle of the matter is simple: Parents must not tolerate anyone in a position of authority telling their children that anal intercourse is acceptable or can be safe.

The public must be educated to the fact that homosexuality is associated with higher rates of disease, and why. Then it must be mobilized to force the hand of school boards and state education commissions either to teach the benefits of traditional morality or to leave the job of sex education to families.

The best recent example of this sort of offensive campaign is the toppling of New York City's Chancellor Joseph Fernandez by an outraged public mobilized by a retired public school teacher from Brooklyn. Parents became incensed when they learned that the curriculum (entitled "Children of the Rainbow") portrayed homosexuality in a favorable light to children as young as eleven years.[11]

As for defense: A successful campaign against giving special rights to homosexuals was waged in Colorado in 1992.[12] Citizens were convinced to prohibit laws and ordinances requiring them to hire and accept homosexuals as tenants, teachers, employees, day-care providers, health care workers, ministers, etc. They were convinced primarily by arguments about fairness and equity. Pro-Amendment 2 campaign literature (often presented in myth/fact format) argued that while homosexuals ought to enjoy the same constitutional rights as other Americans, they ought not be granted rights and privileges above and beyond the rights of others.

Conclusion

The case against organized homosexuality is twofold. First, nature rewards healthy living habits with good health. It is abundantly clear that homosexual behavior is unnatural and unhealthy, and it is odd that such behavior is applauded in an age that worships nature and bodily good health, even to the exclusion of other good things.

Secondly, Americans are exceedingly tolerant. They are not as a rule inclined to dig around in each others' private lives. But they still believe that there is a right and wrong. They reject the absurd claim that the constitutional principle of equality before the law means that all behavior, no matter how heinous, is equally okay. And on the basis of this distinction, they can be mobilized against laws that give homosexuals special legal standing to bully the rest of us.

Discussion Questions

1. Present and explain the reasons why Dr. Palm thinks homosexuals have failed the legal tests necessary to be considered a specially protected minority. What are these tests? Is Dr. Palm correct in his assessment? Explain and defend your answer.

2. Dr. Palm claims that sodomy (anal intercourse), the primary way male homosexuals have sex, "is unnatural and, as such, incompatible with any notion of human rights." What does he mean by this and how does he defend it? Do you think he makes a persuasive case? Explain and defend your answer.

3. How does Dr. Palm defend his claim that the homosexual lifestyle is harmful to the public health and thus should not be encouraged? Do you think he makes a persuasive case? Explain and defend your answer.

4. How much of Dr. Palm's case applies to lesbians? Explain and defend your answer.

Notes

1. Drafted for the National Coalition of Gay Organizations at Chicago in 1972. See E.T. Rueda, *The Homosexual Network* (Greenwich, Connecticut: Devin-Adair, 1982).

2. Centers for Disease Control, *HIV/AIDS Surveillance*, February 1993, p. 11. See also "Acquired Immunodeficiency Syndrome—1991," *Journal of the American Medical Association*, August 12, 1992, p. 713; and Michael Fumento, *The Myth of Heterosexual AIDS* (Washington, D.C.: Regnery-Gateway Press, 1993).

3. David G. Ostrow, Terry Alan Sandholzer, and Yehudi M. Felman, eds., *Sexually Transmitted Diseases in Homosexual Men* (New York: Plenum Medical Book Company, 1983). See also Sevgi O. Aral and King K. Holmes, "Sexually Transmitted Diseases in the AIDS Era," *Scientific American*, February 1991, pp. 62–69.

4. L. Corey and K. K. Holmes, "Sexual Transmission of Hepatitis A in Homosexual Men," *New England Journal of Medicine*, Feb. 21, 1980, vol. 302, pp. 435–38; and Paul Cameron et al., "Sexual Orientation and Sexually Transmitted Disease," *Nebraska Medical Journal*, 1985, p. 292–299.

5. "The Lifespan of Homosexuals," *Family Research Report*, April–June 1991; and "Medical Consequences of What Homosexuals Do" (Washington, D.C.: Family Research Center, 1992).

6. *Bowers v. Hardwick*, 106 Sup. Ct. 2841 (1986).

7. By "lower," we do not mean "bad." The bliss of marriage consists in part in the sexual union of spouses. That union is, in the human species, elevated and inspired by the rational and moral union that married people enjoy.

A lifetime of commitment, chosen and not dictated by instinct, sustained by determination in the face of obstacles, is the specifically human satisfaction of human sexual relations. In that context, the human family is a reflection of the divine nature of man.

8. See Edward J. Erler, "Equal Protection and Personal Rights: The Regime of the 'Discrete and Insular Minority,'" *Georgia Law Review* 16: 407–444; and Kenneth L. Karst and Harold W. Horowitz, "Affirmative Action and Equal Protection," *Virginia Law Review* 60: 955–974.

9. A national marketing survey indicates that the average homosexual enjoys a household income of more than $55,400, a figure $23,000 higher than the average American household. Homosexuals are far more likely to hold a college degree, and far more likely to work in a professional or managerial position than average Americans. They are more than four times as likely to travel overseas, or to earn over $100,000 annually. See "Overcoming a Deep-Rooted Reluctance, More Firms Advertise to the Gay Community," in *The Wall Street Journal*, July 18, 1991, p. B-1.

10. On the other hand, for a brief clear response to homosexuals who try to bend the Bible to support their case, see Harry V. Jaffa, *Homosexuality and the Natural Law* (Claremont, California: The Claremont Institute, 1990), p. 31; for a summary of studies exploding the 10-percent myth, see "Homosexuals and the 10% Fallacy," *The Wall Street Journal*, March 31, 1993, p. A-14, and John Billy et al., "The Sexual Behavior of Men in the United States," *Family Planning Perspectives*, March/April 1993, pp. 52–60; for an argument that homosexuality is "curable" and not etched in genetic stone, see Mark Hartwig, "Is Homosexuality Destiny or Choice?" Focus on the Family *Citizen*, Nov. 16, 1992, pp. 12–14.

11. For a complete account, see William Tucker, "Revolt in Queens," *The American Spectator*, February 1993, pp. 26–31; and Midge Decter, "Homosexuality and the Schools," *Commentary*, March 1993, pp. 19–25.

12. Amendment 2, which received 54 percent of the popular vote, read as follows: "Shall there be an amendment to Article II of the Colorado Constitution to prohibit the state of Colorado and any of its political subdivisions from adopting or enforcing any law or policy which provides that homosexual, lesbian, or bisexual orientation or conduct, or relationships constitutes or entitles a person to claim any minority or protected status, quota preference or discrimination?"

52

Gay Basics: Some Questions, Facts, and Values

Richard D. Mohr

Richard D. Mohr is Associate Professor of Philosophy at the University of Illinois–Urbana, specializing in ancient Greek thought. He has published widely in scholarly publications on the issue of homosexual rights. He is the author of the book *Gays/Justice: A Study of Ethics, Society, and Law* (1988).

In this essay, Professor Mohr defends the morality of homosexuality as well as the legal rights of homosexuals. He does this by dealing with four different areas of concern: (1) the "immorality" of homosexuality, (2) the "unnaturalness" of homosexuality, (3) the question of whether homosexuals freely choose the way they are, and (4) how society at large would be changed if homosexuals were socially accepted. Concerning the first area, Professor Mohr concludes that those who oppose homosexuality, although persuasively showing that homosexuality has been condemned by certain religious people and societies throughout history, have not shown that it is immoral in a prescriptive or a normative sense. In answer to the question of whether homosexuality is "unnatural," Professor Mohr argues that the natural/unnatural distinction is ambiguous and in some cases presupposes a certain religious worldview, which would mean that such an opposition to homosexual behavior would be religiously based and a violation of the First Amendment if made law. Concerning the fourth area, Professor Mohr maintains that although evidence is inconclusive as to whether homosexuality has a genetic component, he does

Reprinted by permission of the author from *The Right Thing to Do: Basic Readings in Moral Philosophy*, ed. James Rachels (New York: Random House, 1989).

not believe that homosexuality is a matter of "choice." He argues that once one begins to act in accordance with one's orientation (either homosexual or heterosexual), then one is on the road to personal well-being, hardly an immoral goal. In response to the question of how society would be changed if homosexuality were socially accepted, Professor Mohr maintains that society would be richer, more open, and more just, extending its notion of family to include homosexual unions rather than threatening (as some detractors claim) the existence of the traditional family.

I. But Aren't They Immoral?

Many people think society's treatment of gays is justified because they think gays are extremely immoral. To evaluate this claim, different senses of "moral" must be distinguished. Sometimes by "morality" is meant the overall beliefs affecting behavior in a society—its mores, norms, and customs. On this understanding, gays certainly are not moral: lots of people hate them and social customs are designed to register widespread disapproval of gays. The problem here is that this sense of morality is merely a *descriptive* one. On this understanding *every* society has a morality—even Nazi society, which had racism and mob rule as central features of its "morality," understood in this sense. What is needed in order to use the notion of morality to praise or condemn behavior is a sense of morality that is *prescriptive* or *normative*—a sense of morality whereby, for instance, the descriptive morality of the Nazis is found wanting.

As the Nazi example makes clear, that something is descriptively moral is nowhere near enough to make it normatively moral. A lot of people in a society saying something is good, even over eons, does not make it so. Our rejection of the long history of socially approved and state-enforced slavery is another good example of this principle at work. Slavery would be wrong even if nearly everyone liked it. So consistency and fairness require that we abandon the belief that gays are immoral simply because most people dislike or disapprove of gays or gay acts, or even because gay sex acts are illegal.

Furthermore, recent historical and anthropological research has shown that opinion about gays has been by no means universally negative. Historically, it has varied widely even within the larger part of the Christian era and even within the church it-self.[1] There are even societies—current ones—where homosexuality is not only tolerated but a universal compulsory part of social maturation.[2] Within the last thirty years, American society has undergone a grand turnabout from deeply ingrained, near total condem-nation to near total acceptance on two emotionally charged "moral" or "family" issues: contraception and divorce. Society holds its current descriptive morality of gays not because it has to, but because it chooses to.

If popular opinion and custom are not enough to ground moral condemnation of homosexuality, perhaps religion can. Such argument proceeds along two lines. One claims that the condemnation is a direct revelation of God, usually through the Bible; the other claims to be able to detect condemnation in God's plan as manifested in nature.

One of the more remarkable discoveries of recent gay research is that the Bible may not be as univocal in its condemnation of homosexuality as has been usually believed.[3] Christ never mentions homosexu-ality. Recent interpreters of the Old Testament have pointed out that the story of Lot at Sodom is prob-ably intended to condemn inhospitality rather than homosexuality. Further, some of the Old Testament condemnations of homosexuality seem simply to be ways of tarring those of the Israelites' opponents who happened to accept homosexual practices when the Israelites themselves did not. If so, the condemna-tion is merely a quirk of history and rhetoric rather than a moral precept.

What does seem clear is that those who regularly cite the Bible to condemn an activity like homosexu-ality do so by reading it selectively. Do ministers who cite what they take to be condemnations of homo-sexuality in Leviticus maintain in their lives all the hygienic and dietary laws of Leviticus? If they cite the story of Lot at Sodom to condemn homosexual-ity, do they also cite the story of Lot in the cave to praise incestuous rape? It seems then not that the Bible is being used to ground condemnation of ho-mosexuality as much as society's dislike of homo-sexuality is being used to interpret the Bible.[4]

Even if a consistent portrait of condemnation could be gleaned from the Bible, what social signifi-cance should it be given? One of the guiding prin-ciples of society, enshrined in the Constitution as a check against the government, is that decisions af-fecting social policy are not made on religious grounds. If the real ground of the alleged immorality invoked by governments to discriminate against gays is religious (as it has explicitly been even in some recent court cases involving teachers and guardians), then one of the major commitments of our nation is violated.

II. But Aren't They Unnatural?

The most noteworthy feature of the accusation of something being unnatural (where a moral rather than an advertising point is being made) is that the plaint is so infrequently made. One used to hear the charge leveled against abortion, but that has pretty much faded as anti-abortionists have come to lay all their chips on the hope that people will come to view abortion as murder. Incest used to be considered unnatural but discourse now usually assimilates it to the moral machinery of rape and violated trust. The charge comes up now in ordinary discourse only against homosexuality. This suggests that the charge is highly idiosyncratic and has little, if any, explana-tory force. It fails to put homosexuality in a class with anything else so that one can learn by comparison with clear cases of the class just exactly what it is that is allegedly wrong with it.

Though the accusation of unnaturalness looks whimsical, in actual ordinary discourse when applied to homosexuality, it is usually delivered with venom aforethought. It carries a high emotional charge, usually expressing disgust and evincing queasiness. Probably it is nothing but an emotional charge. For people get equally disgusted and queasy at all sorts of things that are perfectly natural—to be expected in nature apart from artifice—and that could hardly be fit subjects for moral condemnation. Two typical examples in current American culture are some people's responses to mothers' suckling in public and to women who do not shave body hair. When people have strong emotional reactions, as they do in these cases, without being able to give good reasons for them, we think of them not as operating morally, but rather as being obsessed and manic. So the feelings of disgust that some people have to gays will hardly ground a charge of immorality. People fling the term "unnatural" against gays in the same breath and with the same force as when they call gays "sick" and "gross." When they do this, they give every appearance of being neurotically fearful and incapable of reasoned discourse.

When "nature" is taken in *technical* rather than ordinary usages, it looks like the notion also will not ground a charge of homosexual immorality. When unnatural means "by artifice" or "made by humans," it need only be pointed out that virtually everything that is good about life is unnatural in this sense, that the chief feature that distinguishes people from other animals is their very ability to make over the world to meet their needs and desires, and that their well-being depends upon these departures from nature. On this understanding of human nature and the natural, homosexuality is perfectly unobjectionable.

Another technical sense of natural is that something is natural and so, good, if it fulfills some function in nature. Homosexuality on this view is unnatural because it allegedly violates the function of genitals, which is to produce babies. One problem with this view is that lots of bodily parts have lots of functions and just because some one activity can be fulfilled by only one organ (say, the mouth for eating) this activity does not condemn other functions of the organ to immorality (say, the mouth for talking, licking stamps, blowing bubbles, or having sex). So the possible use of the genitals to produce children does not, without more, condemn the use of the genitals for other purposes, say, achieving ecstasy and intimacy.

The functional view of nature will only provide a morally condemnatory sense to the unnatural if a thing which might have many uses has but one proper function to the exclusion of other possible functions. But whether this is so cannot be established simply by looking at the thing. For what is seen is all its possible functions. The notion of function seemed like it might ground moral authority, but instead it turns out that moral authority is needed to define proper function. Some people try to fill in this moral authority by appeal to the "design" or "order" of an organ, saying, for instance, that the genitals are designed for the purpose of procreation. But these people cheat intellectually if they do not make explicit *who* the designer and orderer is. If it is God, we are back to square one—holding others accountable for religious beliefs.

Further, ordinary moral attitudes about childbearing will not provide the needed supplement which in conjunction with the natural function view of bodily parts would produce a positive obligation to use the genitals for procreation. Society's attitude toward a childless couple is that of pity not censure—even if the couple could have children. The pity may be an unsympathetic one, that is, not registering a course one would choose *for oneself*, but this does not make it a course one would *require* of others. The couple who discovers they cannot have children are viewed not as having thereby had a debt canceled, but rather as having to forgo some of the richness of life, just as a quadriplegic is viewed not as absolved from some moral obligation to hop, skip, and jump, but as missing some of the richness of life. Consistency requires then that, at most, gays who do not or cannot have children are to be pitied rather than condemned. What *is* immoral is the willful preventing of people from achieving the richness of life. Immorality in this regard lies with those social customs, regulations, and statutes that prevent lesbians and gay men from establishing blood or adoptive families, not with gays themselves.

Sometimes people attempt to establish authority for a moral obligation to use bodily parts in a certain fashion simply by claiming that moral laws are natural laws and vice versa. On this account, inanimate objects and plants are good in that they follow natural laws by necessity, animals by instinct, and persons by a rational will. People are special in that they must first discover the laws that govern them. Now, even if one believes the view—dubious in the post-Newtonian, post-Darwinian world—that natural laws in the usual sense ($E = mc^2$, for instance) have some moral content, it is not at all clear how one is to discover the laws in nature that apply to people.

On the one hand, if one looks to people themselves for a model—and looks hard enough—one finds amazing variety, including homosexuality as a social ideal (upper-class fifth-century Athens) and even as socially mandatory (Melanesia today). When one looks to people, one is simply unable to strip away the layers of social custom, history, and taboo in order to see what's really there to any degree more specific than that people are the creatures that make over their world and are capable of abstract thought. That this is so should raise doubts that neutral principles are to be found in human nature that will condemn homosexuality.

On the other hand, if one looks to nature apart from people for models, the possibilities are staggering. There are fish that change gender over their lifetimes: should we "follow nature" and be operative transsexuals? Orangutans, genetically our next of kin, live completely solitary lives without social organization of any kind: ought we to "follow nature" and be hermits? There are many species where only two members per generation reproduce: should we be bees? The search in nature for people's purpose, far from finding sure models for action, is likely to leave one morally rudderless.

III. But Aren't Gays Willfully the Way They Are?

It is generally conceded that if sexual orientation is something over which an individual—for whatever reason—has virtually no control, then discrimination against gays is especially deplorable, as it is against racial and ethnic classes, because it holds people accountable without regard for anything they themselves have done. And to hold a person accountable for that over which the person has no control is a central form of prejudice.

Attempts to answer the question whether or not sexual orientation is something that is reasonably thought to be within one's own control usually appeal simply to various claims of the biological or "mental" sciences. But the ensuing debate over genes, hormones, twins, early childhood development, and the like, is as unnecessary as it is currently inconclusive.[5] All that is needed to answer the question is to look at the actual experience of gays in current society and it becomes fairly clear that sexual orientation is not likely a matter of choice. For coming to have a homosexual identity simply does not have the same sort of structure that decision making has.

On the one hand, the "choice" of the gender of a sexual partner does not seem to express a trivial desire that might be as easily well fulfilled by a simple substitution of the desired object. Picking the gender of a sex partner is decidedly dissimilar, that is, to such activities as picking the flavor of ice cream. If an ice-cream parlor is out of one flavor, one simply picks another. And if people were persecuted, threatened with jail terms, shattered careers, loss of family and housing, and the like, for eating, say, rocky road ice cream, no one would ever eat it; everyone would pick another easily available flavor. That gay people abide in being gay even in the face of persecution shows that being gay is not a matter of easy choice.

On the other hand, even if establishing a sexual orientation is not like making a relatively trivial choice, perhaps it is nevertheless relevantly like making the central and serious life choices by which individuals try to establish themselves as being of some type. Again, if one examines gay experience, this seems not to be the case. For one never sees anyone setting out to become a homosexual, in the way one does see people setting out to become doctors, lawyers, and bricklayers. One does not find "gays-to-be" picking some end—"At some point in the future, I want to become a homosexual"—and then setting about planning and acquiring the ways and means to that end, in the way one does see people deciding that they want to become lawyers, and then sees them plan what courses to take and what sort of temperaments, habits, and skills to develop in order to become lawyers. Typically gays-to-be simply find themselves having homosexual encounters and yet initially resisting quite strongly the identification of being homosexual. Such a person even very likely resists having such encounters, but ends up having them anyway. Only with time, luck, and great personal effort, but sometimes never, does the person gradually come to accept her or his orientation, to view it as a given material condition of life, coming as materials do with certain capacities and limitations. The person begins to act in accordance with his or her orientation and its capacities, seeing its actualization as a requisite for an integrated personality and as a central component of personal well-being. As a result, the experience of coming out to oneself has for gays the basic structure of a discovery, not the structure of a choice. And far from signaling immorality, coming out to others affirms one of the few remaining opportunities in ever more bureaucratic, mechanistic, and socialistic societies to manifest courage.

IV. How Would Society at Large Be Changed If Gays Were Socially Accepted?

Suggestions to change social policy with regard to gays are invariably met with claims that to do so would invite the destruction of civilization itself: after all, isn't that what did Rome in? Actually Rome's decay paralleled not the flourishing of homosexuality but its repression under the later Christianized emperors.[6] Predictions of American civilization's imminent demise have been as premature as they have been frequent. Civilization has shown itself rather resilient here, in large part because of the country's traditional commitments to a respect for privacy, to individual liberties, and especially to people minding their own business. These all give society an open texture and the flexibility to try out things to see what works. And because of this one now need not speculate about what changes reforms in gay social policy might bring to society at large. For many reforms have already been tried.

Half the states have decriminalized homosexual acts. Can you guess which of the following states still have sodomy laws: Wisconsin, Minnesota; New Mexico, Arizona; Vermont, New Hampshire; Nebraska, Kansas. One from each pair does and one does not have sodomy laws. And yet one would be hard pressed to point out any substantial difference between the members of each pair. (If you're interested, it is the second of each pair with them.) Empirical studies have shown that there is no increase in other crimes in states that have decriminalized.[7] Further, sodomy laws are virtually never enforced. They remain on the books not to "protect society" but to insult gays, and for that reason need to be removed.

Neither has the passage of legislation barring discrimination against gays ushered in the end of civilization. Some 50 counties and municipalities, including some of the country's largest cities (like Los Angeles and Boston), have passed such statutes and among the states and colonies Wisconsin and the District of Columbia have model protective codes. Again, no more brimstone has fallen in these places than elsewhere. Staunchly anti-gay cities, like Miami and Houston, have not been spared the AIDS crisis.

Berkeley, California, has even passed domestic partner legislation giving gay couples the same rights to city benefits as married couples, and yet Berkeley has not become more weird than it already was.

Seemingly hysterical predictions that the American family would collapse if such reforms would pass proved false, just as the same dire predictions that the availability of divorce would lessen the ideal and desirability of marriage proved completely unfounded. Indeed if current discriminations, which drive gays into hiding and into anonymous relations, were lifted, far from seeing gays raze American families, one would see gays forming them.

Virtually all gays express a desire to have a permanent lover. Many would like to raise or foster children—perhaps those alarming numbers of gay kids who have been beaten up and thrown out of their "families" for being gay. But currently society makes gay coupling very difficult. A life of hiding is a pressure-cooker existence not easily shared with another. Members of non-gay couples are here asked to imagine what it would take to erase every trace of their own sexual orientation for even just one week.

Even against oppressive odds, gays have shown an amazing tendency to nest. And those gay couples who have survived the odds show that the structure of more usual couplings is not a matter of destiny but of personal responsibility. The so-called basic unit of society turns out not to be a unique immutable atom, but can adopt different parts, be adapted to different needs, and even be improved. Gays might even have a thing or two to teach others about division of labor, the relation of sensuality and intimacy, and stages of development in such relationships.

If discrimination ceased, gay men and lesbians would enter the mainstream of human community openly and with self-respect. The energies that the typical gay person wastes in the anxiety of leading a day-to-day existence of systematic disguise would be released for use in personal flourishing. From this release would be generated the many spinoff benefits that accrue to a society when its individual members thrive.

Society would be richer for acknowledging another aspect of human richness and diversity. Families with gay members would develop relations based on truth and trust rather than lies and fear. And the heterosexual majority would be better off for knowing that they are no longer trampling their gay friends and neighbors.

Finally and perhaps paradoxically, in extending to gays the rights and benefits it has reserved for its dominant culture, America would confirm its deeply held vision of itself as a morally progressive nation, a nation itself advancing and serving as a beacon for others—especially with regard to human rights. The words with which our national pledge ends—"with liberty and justice for all"—are not a description of the present but a call for the future. Ours is a nation given to a prophetic political rhetoric which acknowledges that morality is not arbitrary and that justice is not merely the expression of the current collective will. It is this vision that led the black civil rights movement to its successes. Those congressmen who opposed that movement and its centerpiece, the 1964 Civil Rights Act, on obscurantist grounds, but who lived long enough and were noble enough, came in time to express their heartfelt regret and shame at what they had done. It is to be hoped and someday to be expected that those who now grasp at anything to oppose the extension of that which is best about America to gays will one day feel the same.

Discussion Questions

1. Professor Mohr critiques the argument that homosexuality is immoral. Present and explain that argument, and then present and explain Professor Mohr's critique. Do you agree or disagree with his position? Explain and defend your answer.

2. Professor Mohr critiques the argument that homosexuality is unnatural. Present and explain that argument, and then present and explain Professor Mohr's critique. Do you agree or disagree with his position? Explain and defend your answer.

3. Professor Mohr maintains that picking the gender of one's sex partner is not something one "chooses" like a flavor of ice cream. Explain what he means by this analogy and how it ties into his view that homosexuality is not a choice. Also, why does Professor Mohr believe that if homosexuality is fully accepted by society, society will be better off? Do you agree or disagree with his assessment? Explain and defend your answer.

Notes

1. John Boswell, *Christianity, Social Tolerance and Homosexuality: Gay People in Western Europe from the Beginning of the Christian Era to the Fourteenth Century* (Chicago: University of Chicago Press, 1980).

2. See Gilbert Herdt, *Guardians of the Flute: Idioms of Masculinity* (New York: McGraw-Hill, 1981), pp. 232–239, 284–288; and see generally Gilbert Herdt, ed., *Ritualized Homosexuality in Melanesia* (Berkeley: University of California Press, 1984). For another eye-opener, see Walter L. Williams, *The Spirit and the Flesh: Sexual Diversity in American Indian Culture* (Boston: Beacon, 1986).

3. See especially Boswell, *Christianity*, ch. 4.

4. For Old Testament condemnations of homosexual acts, see Leviticus 18:22, 21:3. For hygienic and dietary codes, see, for example, Leviticus 15:19–27 (on the uncleanliness of women) and Leviticus 11:1–47 (on not eating rabbits, pigs, bats, finless water creatures, legless creeping creatures, etc.). For Lot at Sodom, see Genesis 19:1–25. For Lot in the cave, see Genesis 19:30–38.

5. The preponderance of the scientific evidence supports the view that homosexuality is either genetically determined or a permanent result of early childhood development. See the Kinsey Institute's study by Alan Bell, Martin Weinberg, and Sue Hammersmith, *Sexual Preference: Its Development in Men and Women* (Bloomington: Indiana University Press, 1981); Frederick Whitam and Robin Mathy, *Male Homosexuality in Four Societies* (New York: Praeger, 1986), ch. 7.

6. See Boswell, *Christianity*, ch. 3.

7. See Gilbert Geis, "Reported Consequences of Decriminalization of Consensual Adult Homosexuality in Seven American States," *Journal of Homosexuality* 1, no. 4 (1976): 419–426; Ken Sinclair and Michael Ross, "Consequences of Decriminalization of Homosexuality: A Study of Two Australian States," *Journal of Homosexuality* 12, no. 1 (1985): 119–127.

53

Sodomy and the Dissolution of Free Society

Harry V. Jaffa

Harry V. Jaffa is Professor Emeritus of Political Philosophy at Claremont McKenna College and a Senior Fellow at the Center for the Study of Natural Law. He has published widely in the areas of political philosophy, social ethics, and constitutional law, including the books *Crisis of the House Divided: An Interpretation of the Issues in the Lincoln-Douglas Debates* (1982) and *American Conservativism and the American Founding* (1984).

In this essay, which is a review of Richard Mohr's book *Gays/Justice: A Study of Ethics, Society, and the Law* (1988), Professor Jaffa defends the position that homosexuality is immoral and should neither be encouraged by society nor treated as equal to heterosexual monogamy. He argues for this position by appealing to "natural law," the view that human beings have a certain nature or essence that entails that certain behaviors, such as homosexuality, incest, cannibalism, and rape, are immoral. Professor Jaffa points out that Professor Mohr unwittingly appeals to this same natural law (though he does not use that term) when condemning racism and the Holocaust, ignoring the fact that if human beings have a particular nature that entails that it is morally wrong for them to be treated as less than human, then this nature may also have something to say about what is inappropriate and appropriate sexual behavior. Professor Jaffa argues that the natural law does provide us with that knowledge. He also argues that "consent" is not a sufficient or a necessary condition for declaring an act moral, arguing, among other

Reprinted by permission from Harry V. Jaffa, *Homosexuality and the Natural Law* (Claremont, Calif.: The Claremont Institute for the Study of Statesmanship and Political Philosophy, 1990), 27–39.

things, that "the consent of the German people" did not "legitimize the regime of Adolf Hitler." He concludes with some observations about the relationship between sexually transmitted diseases, the scientific search for cures, and sexual morality.

The author of *Gays/Justice*, an associate professor of philosophy at the University of Illinois–Urbana, is—we are told by the dust jacket—an "openly gay professor" who has turned his attention "to the lives of gay people in America and to the ethical issues raised by society's perception and treatment of gays." This "timely book," it is said,

> will prompt Americans to consider whether they have consistently applied their basic values to lesbians and gays.

It is precisely such an "application" that we propose herewith. We begin by rejecting the appropriation by sodomites of the ancient and honorable English word "gay." I do not know any dictionary that defines "gay" as a synonym for homosexual. (There may be a recent one that I do not know.) The word "gay," properly an adjective and not a noun, refers to something "festive," "merry," or "joyous." "Don we now our gay apparel . . ." trolls one of our most popular Christmas carols. Shall we allow this perversion of our language to queer the Spirit of Christmas? There is assuredly nothing gay about sodomy, the traditional word for anal intercourse between males.

Mohr invites us to recognize sodomy as belonging to that sphere of privacy recognized in the *Griswold* case as deserving of constitutional protection. There the Supreme Court declared unconstitutional a Connecticut statute that made it a felony for a physician to prescribe birth-control devices to a married couple. Mohr would have us place the innocent privacy of married couples on the same level as a homosexual relationship. He argues that homosexual liaisons ought to be offered the same legal footing as the marriage of a man and a woman.

Throughout his book Mohr rejects the morality inherent in those "laws of nature and of nature's God" which were the ground of the American Revolution, and are the moral foundation of our constitutional tradition. In fact, he denies that nature supplies any basis for distinguishing right and wrong. Yet he claims not to be a moral relativist. "[O]ne of our principles," he writes,

> is that simply a lot of people saying something is good [or bad!] . . . does not make it so. Our rejec-

tion of the long history of socially approved and state-enforced slavery is a good example of this principle at work. Slavery would be wrong even if nearly everyone liked it. So consistency and fairness requires that the culture abandon the belief that gays [sic] are immoral simply because most people dislike or disapprove of gays or gay acts, or even because gay sex acts are illegal. (p. 32)

What Mohr says here about morality being independent of opinion is common ground between us. In particular, we agree that slavery would be wrong even if everyone liked it. Unfortunately, Mohr never says why slavery is wrong. Had he ever examined the great historic arguments as to whether slavery was an evil—necessary or otherwise—or a "positive good," he would have concluded that there is no argument by which one can condemn slavery, that does not at the same time condemn homosexuality. The reason is that nature is the only ground upon which one can consistently condemn slavery. As we shall see, consistency and fairness require that Mohr either abandon the argument *against* slavery or the argument *for* homosexuality.

Lincoln at Gettysburg—with the Emancipation Proclamation in mind—said that the nation, at its birth, had been dedicated to the proposition that "all men are created equal." According to Lincoln, that proposition had been "the father of all moral principle" among us. Human equality was the foundation of morality, because the recognition of other human beings was a recognition of the nature that was common to us all, the nature in which all our rights and all our duties were grounded. The Gospel injunction to "do unto others what we would have others do unto us" refers to other human beings, but not to hogs or cattle. But it refers to *all* human beings, all those belonging to the human species, not Jews only, or white or black human beings. It is a self-evident truth that blacks and Jews and Moslems and Orientals and Arabs and Protestants and Catholics do not differ in respect to being human beings, and that the prohibitions against murder, theft, adultery and perjury a priori apply equally to them all. Morality is ineluctably grounded in the idea of species, of the distinction in nature between the human and the nonhuman. Morality depends upon distinguishing all nonessential intra-human differences from those that distinguish men from beasts on the one hand, and man from God on the other.

Why do we regard the slaughter by the Nazis of Jews and other "inferior" humans in the Holocaust as genocide, but not the slaughter of cattle? Why do we turn with horror from cannibalism—the eating of human flesh by human beings—but not the eating of beef or pork? Mohr notes the variety of human customs, as if that was an argument against identifying any moral customs as being more—or less—natural than any others. He mentions "Melanesia today" as a place where homosexual behavior is "socially mandatory" (p. 37). He might have mentioned other places where cannibalism was equally mandatory. (The late Michael Rockefeller is believed to have been eaten on an anthropological expedition.) But we remind him of what he himself said about slavery—its acceptance or nonacceptance by any particular culture or society in no way decides whether it is right or wrong. The reason slavery is wrong is that the slaves are members of the same species as ourselves. As rational, social, and political animals—for such are the identifying characteristics of *homo sapiens*—we see in every human being at least a potential friend and fellow-citizen. It is our natural interest to make potential friends into actual friends; it is against that same interest to make potential friends into actual enemies.

It is not murder or cannibalism to kill or eat cattle, and it is not theft to appropriate the labor of beasts, of horses or oxen, for example. Calling slaves chattels (which means cattle)—as they were in the antebellum United States—is unnatural, because the slaves were human beings, possessing rational wills, something that a chattel, properly so-called, cannot possess. As chattels, the slaves could not make contracts, especially that supremely important contract of marriage. Since there was no legal marriage among slaves, there was no ground in law for either chastity or fidelity. Intercourse between a master and his slave could not be rape, because by law (but not by nature) a chattel, having no power of consent, had no power to withhold consent. As a legal technicality, intercourse between a master and a slave was a form of bestiality rather than of fornication. This, notwithstanding the presence of many thousands of offspring of such liaisons, as biological proof of the equal humanity of the parents of these offspring. Hence slavery, be denying human equality, denied the slaves' nature as members of the human species, and therewith of their moral personality under "the laws of nature and of nature's God."

Although—as we have noted—Mohr says that slavery is wrong, he never says why. Had he done so he would have seen that sodomy is also wrong, no matter how many there are who (like himself) enjoy it and approve of it. Here we interject the observation that the condemnation of sodomy by the Bible is not—as Mohr supposes—to be compared with the prohibitions of the dietary laws (p. 33). No Jew, however orthodox, would say that the prohibition against eating pork is wrong for any reason other than that God has prohibited it. Nor would any Jew, however orthodox, say that murder, theft, and adultery were not wrong prior to and independently of being incorporated into the Laws of Moses. Abraham, Isaac, and Jacob recognized these moral prohibitions (including that of sodomy) long before Moses brought the Law down from Mt. Sinai. The story of Sodom is itself contemporaneous with Abraham. (Mohr follows the absurd interpretation of John Boswell in his *Christianity, Social Tolerance, and Homosexuality* [Chicago, 1980] in which it is claimed that the offense of the Sodomites is not sodomy, but inhospitality. Boswell—and Mohr—fail to see that what the men of Sodom attempted to do to the angels of the Lord was of the essence of inhospitality!) Later generations—both of Christians and Jews—would distinguish the divine law, which is binding only on those to whom it is promulgated, and the natural law, which is binding on man *qua* man. The prohibition upon sodomy, like that upon murder, theft, and adultery, belongs to the natural law. This is shown by the fact that Thomas Jefferson, in his "Bill for Proportioning Crimes and Punishments" of 1779—three years after the Declaration of Independence—unhesitatingly followed the common law in making sodomy "with man or woman" a felony subject to the same punishment as rape. Clearly, these were violations of natural law and, as such, deserving to be prohibited by the criminal law of any civilized society.

Why then is sodomy against the natural law? First of all, because man is a species-being and, as we have said, the species to which he belongs—the species that defines his nature—is both rational and social. Men cannot live at all—much less live well—except by the mutual protection and mutual support of other human beings. Morality refers to those rules that mankind has learned, both from reason and experience, are necessary for surviving and prospering. The inclination of many men—what we might call the inclination of their lower nature—to take their sex where they find it (whether their partners consent to it or not) and ignore the consequences, must be subordinated to their higher nature, which includes the interest of society (and the interest of nature in the species). For in no other species are the

young so helplessly dependent for so long. Hence the importance, even for survival, of both the moral and civil laws governing the institution of marriage and of the family. We know that the relaxation of these laws leads to disorder, disease, and death, no less surely in the most advanced cultures of modernity than in the most primitive. But the good of the family is not that only of self-preservation and survival, but of the higher good—the happiness—of all its members, including those whose original horizon may not have extended beyond immediate gratification.

Aristotle says that if a man had every good thing in the world, except friends, life would not be worth living. To be able to live without friends, one would have to be either a beast or a god. A friend is another self, someone one loves even as one loves one's self. Indeed, man is so constituted that he cannot know or love himself except by knowing and loving others. To understand that this is so, and why it is so, is the kernel of morality, as it is the kernel of humanity. This is the argument equally of the Sermon on the Mount and of the *Nicomachean Ethics*.

The foundation of all friendship, as it is the foundation of all community, is the first and most natural of all human associations, that beginning with a man and a woman, the family. The story of the Garden of Eden is not without its instruction here. When God saw that it was not good for the man to be alone, he provided him with a woman. As the Reverend Jerry Falwell put it, God created Adam and Eve, not Adam and Steve. All friendship, all society, indeed all of human existence, arises from the physical difference of male and female human beings. From this physical difference arises the ground and purpose of human life, because it is the ground and purpose of nature.

Morality comes to sight therefore as the relationship, first of all, of husband and wife, then of parents and children, and of brothers and sisters. From this it expands to include the extended family, the clan, tribe, city, country, and at last mankind. Mankind as a whole is recognized by its generations, like a river which is one and the same while the ever-renewed cycles of birth and death flow on. But the generations are constituted—and can only be constituted—by the acts of generation arising from the conjunction of male and female. It cannot be emphasized too often, however, that the root of all human relationships, the root of all morality, is nature, which is itself grounded in the generative distinction of male and female. Equally with rape and incest, homosexuality strikes at the authority and dignity of the family. The distinction between a man and a woman is a distinction as fundamental as any in nature, because it is the very distinction by which nature itself is constituted. It is the ability of two members of the same species to generate a third, that confirms them as members of the same species. It thereby confirms male and female members of the human species in that equality of rights to which they are entitled as members of that species.

Homosexuals like Mohr take the position that whatever is done by consenting adults is morally right. But why adults and why consent? We find this curious sentence in the book before us:

> Incest used to be considered unnatural [sic!] but discourse now usually assimilates it to the moral machinery of rape and violated trust. (p. 34)

Mohr seems reluctant to say candidly that the abhorrence of incest is just another superstition. But someone who cannot say that sodomy is unnatural cannot say that incest is unnatural. Mohr, like other sodomites, appears to make consent rather than nature the ground of morality, without regard to what is being consented to. But he forgets his own stricture against slavery. Is consent produced by force and fraud (or arising from mere ignorance) no different than the consent of a free and enlightened people? Could slavery have been legitimized by the consent of the slaves? Did the consent of the German people legitimize the regime of Adolf Hitler? Was the suicide of the 900 members of the Jonestown community—which included several hundred children—moral, because it had been agreed to in advance? And why should those who find forcible rape (whether homosexual or heterosexual) more gratifying than sex based upon consent, be denied their idiosyncratic pleasure? Why should violating trust—as for example, the ruses by which Ted Bundy lured his victims to their doom—be considered wrong? If Mohr were to think consistently about these questions, he would see that consent alone is no more a ground of morality than the doctrine of the right of the stronger. In the Declaration of Independence, the doctrine that the just powers of government arise from the consent of the governed is grounded in a series of truths held to be self-evident. Consent must then be rational and enlightened. It becomes part of morality only in the light of an intrinsic right and wrong. Rape, incest, adultery, and sodomy are wrong because they are inconsistent with the harmony and good order of the family, which is the foundation of all social harmony and social order, and thereby of all human happiness.

It is painful but unfortunately necessary to repeat the obvious. Adultery strikes at the good order of the family, because jealousy—properly understood—necessarily accompanies the passion by which and out of which the family is constituted. This jealousy is implanted by nature and serves the good ends of nature. It is acknowledged in the traditional marriage service, in which the partners promise to "renounce all others." A wife does not expect to be in sexual competition with other women, and a husband does not expect to be in such competition with other men. Nor does a wife expect to be in sexual competition with other men, or a man with other women. Where such competition exists, there can be no confidence and no love; in short, no family. Nor—odious as it is to say—does a wife expect to be in competition with her daughter, or a husband with his son. Sexual competition, whether from without or from within the family, destroys the friendship between man and wife, and thereby destroys the basis of all other forms of friendship. Confining sexual friendship to its proper sphere—between man and wife—is the very core of that morality by which civilization is constituted. It did not require Freud to instruct us in the fact that the sexual passion in its primal force is anarchic, and that the "discontents" of civilization may be traced to its imperfect sublimation. Nevertheless, without the control of the libido by the super ego, all the interests of civilized existence are at risk. Our contemporary moralists, whose categorical imperative is "If it feels good, do it," have forgotten the lessons of Freud no less than of Aristotle or Aquinas. In the training of infantry riflemen, the most intense male bonding is encouraged among members of a platoon. But if that bonding were to become homosexual, the discipline of the platoon would be disrupted, if not destroyed. The same observation would apply if a woman were substituted for a man among members of that platoon. There are many forms of human sociality whose effectiveness and intensity of purpose are incompatible with sexual friendship. What would happen to a Supreme Court, some of whose members became involved—whether homosexually or heterosexually—with other of its members? (Would a husband and wife, however distinguished, ever be appointed to sit on the same Court?) Suppose a sexual relationship arose between a Speaker and one (or more) committee (or subcommittee) chairmen (or chairwomen)? Indeed, we do not expect husband and wife to occupy any relationship outside the family in which honest diversity of interest or opinion may be expected. No wife can be compelled to testify against her husband in a criminal case. The interest of the family takes precedence over the criminal law. In despotic regimes, on the contrary, family members are both invited and compelled to spy on each other and to testify against each other. During the Civil War, President Lincoln was asked to approve a pass through Union lines of a Confederate wife. Lincoln said he would do so only on sufficient proof that she had already left her husband. He would not, he said, offer any wife an inducement to leave her husband.

The marriage bond is not only in the interest of marriage. It emancipates human friendship and love for their proper manifestations in the many other spheres of life. Where sexual love is so confined, or bounded, there is no confinement or boundary to the love of parents and children nor, indeed, to the lifelong attachments of relatives and friends or professional or political colleagues in all the walks of life, and throughout life.

The first case of AIDS—and the first isolation of the HIV virus in the United States—occurred in 1981. In its origins it was entirely a disease of sodomites, generated in and by anal intercourse. At the present time, according to the latest statistics I have seen, more than 85 percent of AIDS cases are sodomites. AIDS can be contracted by women from bisexual men, and they in turn may spread it to other men and thereby to other women. Infected women may transmit it to their unborn children. Intravenous drug users may contract it by sharing needles with infected persons. Innocent persons may contract it by transfusions of infected blood. While the proximate cause of AIDS may not now in every case be sodomy, the etiology of every case leads back to sodomy as its point of origin.

Why AIDS now? That the first case was diagnosed a little over a decade after the so-called "Gay Rights" and "Gay Pride" movement gained momentum and force can hardly be coincidental. That movement resulted in a quantum increase in sodomite activity. It was as if the numbers of smokers had increased by a factor of four or five, and the per capita consumption of cigarettes per smoker had gone from one to three or four packs a day. The result would have been a sudden jump in the incidence of lung cancer, emphysema, and heart disease. Homosexuality has always been with us. But in the last generation we have seen it "come out of the closet." We have seen growing public acceptance of the proposition that homosexuality and heterosexuality are simply alternative lifestyles. We have also seen growing acceptance of the doctrine that there is no moral distinction between promiscuity and chastity and that the only morality of sexual behavior is conformity with personal preference and personal choice. That nature itself seems to reward chastity with health, and punish promiscuity with disease, is seldom ever mentioned. For AIDS is a venereal disease, and as much the result of promiscuity as ever were syphilis or gonorrhea. The reigning assumption is that it is the function of science to emancipate human behavior from the restraints of nature. But it is by no means clear that in such matters this is either possible or desirable.

In all the public discussion of AIDS, and the present book is no exception, the connection between the movement of "Gay Liberation" and AIDS is never mentioned. Yet that connection is as evident as that between smoking and lung cancer. Why the same public officials—e.g., former Surgeon General C. Everett Koop—who tell people to stop smoking (or to "Just Say No" to drugs), will not tell them to stop sodomizing, is incomprehensible.

There was a time in the 1960s when antibiotics appeared to have conquered syphilis. Together with the birth control pill, this seems to have promoted an increase in heterosexual promiscuity. It was only a short time, however, before a new venereal disease, herpes, made its appearance, a virus immune to antibiotics. It would certainly seem that nature has an interest in the morality that is conducive to the family, and punishes behavior inimical to it. I would suggest therefore that the quest for a cure for AIDS, unaccompanied by any attempt to modify the behavior out of which AIDS was generated, is ultimately futile.

It is my impression, observing the propaganda of the homosexuals—and their gullible coadjutors—that their main reason for wanting a cure for AIDS, is to emancipate them for the unrestrained pursuit of sodomy and for the undiminished pleasures of what would now be called "unsafe sex." I would venture to suggest, however, that if a cure for AIDS was discovered tomorrow, it would not be very long before a new venereal disease would make its appearance, just as herpes did in the '60s and AIDS in the '80s. What is needed above all is not a medical miracle cure but a moral and behavioral change. Sodomites should be returned to the closet, where they were of relatively little danger to themselves or others.

We hear a great deal about how unfair it is to discriminate against sodomites and lesbians. But who in his right mind would put them in charge of troops of Boy Scouts or of Girl Scouts? Who in his right mind would put them in any positions within our educational system—from kindergarten to graduate school—where they might become role models of the young? Can anything destroy the possibility of happiness for a young person more than turning him or her away from traditional marriage and family life, to the dismal sewers of sodomy or lesbianism?

The dissolution of the family is at the root of nearly all the social problems afflicting contemporary American society. The high rate of divorce is making emotional cripples out of children at all levels of society. And the children of divorce become divorced themselves at much higher rates than others. Crime, drug abuse, alcoholism, mental illness, venereal disease, low educational achievement, lack of job-related skills, inability to function well on jobs, all of these things—and many more—can have their causes traced to the disintegration of the traditional family. And at the root of the disability of the contemporary American family is the ethic that says that sexual preference is, and should be, only a matter of personal preference and personal choice. The traditional family, the embodiment and expression of "the laws of nature and of nature's God," as the foundation of a free society, has become merely one of many "alternative lifestyles." But then a free society, as distinguished from a despotic one, itself becomes merely one of many "alternative lifestyles." A free people who succumbs to such teaching cannot long endure. Those who choose sodomy are already choos-ing slavery, because whoever is an indiscriminate slave to his own unreasoning passions will sooner or later become a slave to the passions of others.

Discussion Questions

1. Explain in detail how Professor Jaffa defends the view that Professor Mohr's moral condemnation of the Holocaust, slavery, and other past atrocities depends on the very assumptions that make homosexuality immoral. Do you agree or disagree with this view? Explain and defend your answer.

2. How does Professor Jaffa respond to Professor Mohr's claim that whatever an adult consents to do to himself (or herself) is morally permissible and ought to be legally permissible? Do you agree or disagree with this argument? Explain and defend your answer.

3. What are Professor Jaffa's observations about the relationship of AIDS and other venereal diseases to homosexuality and sexual promiscuity in general? What are his concerns about the possibility of scientists discovering a cure for these diseases? Do you agree or disagree with Professor Jaffa's observations and concerns? Explain and defend your answer.

54

Is Homosexuality Unnatural?

Burton M. Leiser

Burton M. Leiser is Professor of Philosophy at Pace University (New York). He is the author of numerous works in social ethics and political philosophy including the book *Liberty, Justice, and Morals*, 3rd ed. (1986).

In this essay Professor Leiser critically analyzes the claim of some philosophers and ethicists (such as Palm and Jaffa—see Chapters 51 and 53) that homosexuality is "unnatural" and therefore immoral. He begins his critical analysis by asking what is meant when people make the claim that something is "unnatural." Professor Leiser then goes on to examine two notions that could be employed to distinguish the "natural" from the "unnatural": (1) "the descriptive laws of nature" and (2) "the artificial as a form of the unnatural." He concludes that neither is adequate in evaluating the moral status of homosexuality. Professor Leiser continues his analysis by examining two other notions that may be employed by the opponent of homosexuality: (3) "anything uncommon or abnormal is unnatural," and (4) "any use of an organ or an instrument that is contrary to its principle purpose or function is unnatural." He finds these two as inadequate as the first two. He ends with an analysis of the claim that whatever is natural is good and whatever is unnatural is bad. He argues that this claim is problematic, because there are many artificial, or unnatural, things (such as cars, televisions, and homes) that are good, and even if something is unnatural in the sense of "harmful to human beings," it would not follow that it is immoral or evil, which is what the opponent of homosexuality wants to prove. Professor Leiser concludes that the opponents of

Reprinted by permission from Burton M. Leiser, *Liberty, Justice, and Morals* (New York: Macmillan, 1979).

homosexuality have not shown that homosexuality is unnatural in the sense of being immoral and/or impermissible.

Theologians and other moralists have said homosexual acts violate the "natural law," and that they are therefore immoral and ought to be prohibited by the state.

The word *nature* has a built-in ambiguity that can lead to serious misunderstandings. When something is said to be "natural" or in conformity with "natural law" or the "law of nature," this may mean either (1) that it is in conformity with the descriptive laws of nature, or (2) that it is not artificial, that man has not imposed his will or his devices upon events or conditions as they exist or would have existed without such interference.

1. *The descriptive laws of nature.* The laws of nature, as these are understood by the scientist, differ from the laws of man. The former are purely descriptive, where the latter are prescriptive. When a scientist says that water boils at 212° Fahrenheit and that as a matter of observed fact, the volume of a gas rises as it is heated and falls as pressure is applied to it. These "laws" merely *describe* the manner in which physical substances *actually behave.* They differ from municipal and federal laws in that they *do not prescribe behavior.* Unlike man-made laws, natural laws are not passed by any legislator or group of legislators; they are not proclaimed or announced; they impose no obligation upon anyone or anything; their violation entails no penalty, and there is no reward for following them or abiding by them. When a scientist says that the air in a tire obeys the laws of nature that govern gases, he does *not* mean that the air, having been informed that it *ought* to behave in a certain way, behaves appropriately under the right conditions. He means, rather, that as a matter of fact, the air in a tire *will* behave like all other gases. In saying that Boyle's law governs the behavior of gases, he means merely that gases do, as a matter of fact, behave in accordance with Boyle's law, and that Boyle's law enables one to predict accurately what will happen to a given quantity of a gas as its pressure is raised; he does *not* mean to suggest that some heavenly voice has proclaimed that all gases should henceforth behave in accordance with the terms of Boyle's law and that a ghostly policeman patrols the world, ready to mete out punishments to any gases that violate the heavenly decree. In fact, according to the scientist, it

does not make sense to speak of a natural law being violated. For if there were a true exception to a so-called law of nature, the exception would require a change in the description of those phenomena, and the law would have been shown to be no law at all. The laws of nature are revised as scientists discover new phenomena that require new refinements in their descriptions of the way things actually happen. In this respect they differ fundamentally from human laws, which are revised periodically by legislators who are not so interested in *describing* human behavior as they are in *prescribing* what human behavior *should* be.

2. *The artificial as a form of the unnatural.* On occasion when we say that something is not natural, we mean that it is a product of human artifice. A typewriter is not a natural object, in this sense, for the substances of which it is composed have been removed from their natural state—a state in which they existed before men came along—and have been transformed by a series of chemical and physical and mechanical processes into other substances. They have been rearranged into a whole that is quite different from anything found in nature. In short, a typewriter is an artificial object. In this sense, clothing is not natural, for it has been transformed considerably from the state in which it was found in nature; and wearing clothing is also not natural, in this sense, for in one's natural state, before the application of anything artificial, before any human interference with things as they are, one is quite naked. Human laws, being artificial conventions designed to exercise a degree of control over the natural inclinations and propensities of men, may in this sense be considered to be unnatural.

When theologians and moralists speak of homosexuality, contraception, abortion, and other forms of human behavior as being unnatural and say that for that reason such behavior must be considered to be wrong, in what sense are they using the word *unnatural*? Are they saying that homosexual behavior and the use of contraceptives are contrary to the scientific laws of nature, are they saying that they are artificial forms of behavior, or are they using the terms *natural* and *unnatural* in some third sense?

They cannot mean that homosexual behavior (to stick to the subject presently under discussion) violates the laws of nature in the first sense, for, as has been pointed out, in *that* sense it is impossible to violate the laws of nature. Those laws, being merely descriptive of what actually does happen, would have to *include* homosexual behavior if such behavior does

actually take place. Even if the defenders of the theological view that homosexuality is unnatural were to appeal to a statistical analysis by pointing out that such behavior is not normal from a statistical point of view, and therefore not what the laws of nature require, it would be open to their critics to reply that any descriptive law of nature must account for and incorporate all statistical deviations, and that the laws of nature, in this sense, do not *require* anything. These critics might also note that the best statistics available reveal that about half of all American males engage in homosexual activity at some time in their lives, and that a very large percentage of American males have exclusively homosexual relations for a fairly extensive period of time; from which it would follow that such behavior is natural, for them, at any rate, in this sense of the word *natural*.

If those who say that homosexual behavior is unnatural are using the term *unnatural* in the second sense of artificial, it is difficult to understand their objection. That which is artificial is often far better than what is natural. Artificial homes seem, at any rate, to be more suited to human habitation and more conducive to longer life and better health than are caves and other natural shelters. There are distinct advantages to the use of such unnatural (artificial) amenities as clothes, furniture, and books. Although we may dream of an idyllic return to nature in our more wistful moments, we would soon discover, as Thoreau did in his attempt to escape from the artificiality of civilization, that needles and thread, knives and matches, ploughs and anvils, and countless other products of human artifice are essential to human life. We would discover, as Plato pointed out in the *Republic*, that no man can be truly self-sufficient. Some of the by-products of industry are less than desirable, but neither industry nor the products of industry are intrinsically evil, even though both are unnatural in this sense of the word.

Interference with nature is not evil in itself. Nature, as some writers have put it, must be tamed. In some respects man must look upon it as an enemy to be conquered. If nature were left to its own devices, without the intervention of human artifice, men would be consumed by disease, they would be plagued by insects, they would be chained to the places where they were born with no means of swift communication or transport, and they would suffer the discomforts and the torments of wind and weather and flood and fire with no practical means of combating any of them. Interfering with nature, doing a battle with nature, using human will and reason and skill to thwart what might otherwise follow from the conditions that prevail in the world is a peculiarly human enterprise, one that can hardly be condemned merely because it does what is not natural.

Homosexual behavior can hardly be considered to be unnatural in this sense. There is nothing artificial about such behavior. On the contrary, it is quite natural, in this sense, to those who engage in it. And even if it were not, even if it were quite artificial, this is not in itself a ground for condemning it.

It would seem, then, that those who condemn homosexuality as an unnatural form of behavior must mean something else by the word *unnatural*, something not covered by either of the preceding definitions. A third possibility is this:

3. *Anything uncommon or abnormal is unnatural.* If this is what is meant by those who condemn homosexuality on the ground that it is unnatural, it is quite obvious that their condemnation cannot be accepted without further argument. The fact that a given form of behavior is uncommon provides no justification for condemning it. Playing viola in a string quartet may be an uncommon form of human behavior. Yet there is no reason to suppose that such uncommon behavior is, by virtue of its uncommonness, deserving of condemnation or ethically or morally wrong. On the contrary, many forms of behavior are praised precisely because they are so uncommon. Great artists, poets, musicians, and scientists are uncommon in this sense; but clearly the world is better off for having them, and it would be absurd to condemn them or their activities for their failure to be common and normal. If homosexual behavior is wrong, then, it must be for some reason other than its unnaturalness in this sense of the word.

4. *Any use of an organ or an instrument that is contrary to its principal function is unnatural.* Every organ and every instrument—perhaps even every creature—has a function to perform, one for which it is particularly designed. Any use of those instruments and organs that is consonant with their purposes is natural and proper, but any use that is inconsistent with their principal functions is unnatural and improper, and to that extent, evil or harmful. Human teeth, for example, are admirably designed for their principal functions—biting and chewing the kinds of food suitable for human consumption. But they are not particularly well suited for prying the caps from beer bottles. If they are used for that purpose, which is not natural to them, they are likely to crack and break under the strain. The abuse of one's teeth

leads to their destruction and to a consequent deterioration in one's overall health. If they are used only for their proper function, however, they may continue to serve well for many years. Similarly, a given drug may have a proper function. If used in the furtherance of that end, it can preserve life and restore health. But if it is abused and employed for purposes for which it was never intended, it may cause serious harm and even death. The natural uses of things are good and proper, but their unnatural uses are bad and harmful.

What we must do, then, is to find the proper use, or the true purpose, of each organ in our bodies. Once we have discovered that, we will know what constitutes the natural use of each organ and what constitutes an unnatural, abusive, and potentially harmful employment of the various parts of our bodies. If we are rational, we will be careful to confine behavior to the proper functions and to refrain from unnatural behavior. According to those philosophers who follow this line of reasoning, the way to discover the proper use of any organ is to determine what it is peculiarly suited to do. The eye is suited for seeing, the ear for hearing, the nerves for transmitting impulses from one part of the body to another, and so on.

What are the sex organs peculiarly suited to do? Obviously, they are peculiarly suited to enable men and women to reproduce their own kind. No other organ in the body is capable of fulfilling that function. It follows, according to those who follow the natural-law line, that the proper or natural function of the sex organs is reproduction, and that strictly speaking, any use of those organs for other purposes is unnatural, abusive, potentially harmful, and therefore wrong. The sex organs have been given to us in order to enable us to maintain the continued existence of mankind on this earth. All perversions—including masturbation, homosexual behavior, and heterosexual intercourse that deliberately frustrates the design of the sexual organs—are unnatural and bad. As Pope Pius XI once said, "Private individuals have no other power over the members of their bodies than that which pertains to their natural ends."

But the problem is not so easily resolved. Is it true that every organ has one and only one proper function? A hammer may have been designed to pound nails, and it may perform that particular job best. But it is not sinful to employ a hammer to crack nuts if you have no other suitable tool immediately available. The hammer, being a relatively versatile tool, may be employed in a number of ways. It has no one proper or natural function. A woman's eyes are well adapted to seeing, it is true. But they seem also to be well adapted to flirting. Is a woman's use of her eyes for the latter purpose sinful merely because she is not using them, at that moment, for their "primary" purpose of seeing? Our sexual organs are uniquely adapted for procreation, but that is obviously not the only function for which they are adapted. Human beings may—and do—use those organs for a great many other purposes, and it is difficult to see why any *one* use should be considered to be the only proper one. The sex organs seem to be particularly well adapted to give their owners and others intense sensations of pleasure. Unless one believes that pleasure itself is bad, there seems to be little reason to believe that the use of the sex organs for the production of pleasure in oneself or in others is evil. In view of the peculiar design of these organs, with their great concentration of nerve endings, it would seem that they were designed (if they *were* designed) with that very goal in mind, and that their use for such purposes would be no more unnatural than their use for the purpose of procreation.

Nor should we overlook the fact that human sex organs may be and are used to express, in the deepest and most intimate way open to man, the love of one person for another. Even the most ardent opponents of "unfruitful" intercourse admit that sex does serve this function. They have accordingly conceded that a man and his wife may have intercourse even though she is pregnant, or past the age of child bearing, or in the infertile period of her menstrual cycle.

Human beings are remarkably complex and adaptable creatures. Neither they nor their organs can properly be compared to hammers or to other tools. The analogy quickly breaks down. The generalization that a given organ or instrument has one and only one proper function does not hold up, even with regard to the simplest manufactured tools, for, as we have seen, a tool may be used for more than one purpose—less effectively than one especially designed for a given task, perhaps, but properly and certainly not *sinfully*. A woman may use her eyes not only to see and to flirt, but also to earn money—if she is, for example, an actress or a model. Though neither of the latter functions seems to have been a part of the original design, if one may speak sensibly of *design* in this context, of the eye, it is difficult to see why such a use of the eyes of a woman should be considered sinful, perverse, or unnatural. Her sex organs have the unique capacity of producing ova and nurturing human embryos, under the right conditions;

but why should any other use of those organs, including their use to bring pleasure to their owner or to someone else, or to manifest love to another person, or even, perhaps, to earn money, be regarded as perverse, sinful, or unnatural? Similarly, a man's sexual organs possess the unique capacity of causing the generation of another human being, but if a man chooses to use them for pleasure, or for the expression of love, or for some other purpose—so long as he does not interfere with the rights of some other person—the fact that his sex organs do have their unique capabilities does not constitute a convincing justification for condemning their other uses as being perverse, sinful, unnatural, or criminal. If a man "perverts" himself by wiggling his ears for the entertainment of his neighbors instead of using them exclusively for their "natural" function of hearing, no one thinks to consign him to prison. If he abuses his teeth by using them to pull staples from memos— a function for which teeth were clearly not designed—he is not accused of being immoral, degraded, or degenerate. The fact that people *are* condemned for using their sex organs for their own pleasure or profit, or for that of others, may be more revealing about the prejudices and taboos of our society than it is about our perception of the true nature or purpose of our bodies.

In this connection, it may be worthwhile to note that with the development of artificial means of reproduction (that is, test tube babies), the sex organs may become obsolete for reproductive purposes but would still contribute greatly to human pleasure. In addition, studies of animal behavior and anthropological reports indicate that such nonreproductive sex acts as masturbation, homosexual intercourse, and mutual fondling of genital organs are widespread, both among human beings and among lower animals. Under suitable circumstances, many animals reverse their sex roles, males assuming the posture of females and presenting themselves to others for intercourse, and females mounting other females and going through all the actions of a male engaged in intercourse. Many peoples all around the world have sanctioned and even ritualized homosexual relations. It would seem that an excessive readiness to insist that human sex organs are designed only for reproductive purposes and therefore ought to be used only for such purposes must be based upon a very narrow conception that is conditioned by our own society's peculiar history and taboos.

To sum up, then, the proposition that any use of an organ that is contrary to its principal purpose or function is unnatural assumes that organs *have* a principal purpose or function, but this may be denied on the ground that the purpose or function of a given organ may vary according to the needs and desires of its owner. It may be denied on the ground that a given organ may have more than one principal purpose or function, and any attempt to call one use or another the only natural one seems to be arbitrary, if not question-begging. Also, the proposition suggests that what is unnatural is evil or depraved. This goes beyond the pure description of things, and enters into the problem of the evaluation of human behavior, which leads us to the fifth meaning of *natural*.

5. *That which is natural is good, and whatever is unnatural is bad.* When one condemns homosexuality or masturbation or the use of contraceptives on the ground that it is unnatural, one implies that whatever is unnatural is bad, wrongful, or perverse. But as we have seen, in some senses of the word, the unnatural (the artificial) is often very good, whereas that which is natural (that which has not been subjected to human artifice or improvement) may be very bad indeed. Of course, interference with nature may be bad. Ecologists have made us more aware than we have ever been of the dangers of unplanned and uninformed interference with nature. But this is not to say that *all* interference with nature is bad. Every time a man cuts down a tree to make room for a home for himself, or catches a fish to feed himself or his family, he is interfering with nature. If men did not interfere with nature, they would have no homes, they could eat no fish, and, in fact, they could not survive. What, then, can be meant by those who say that whatever is natural is good and whatever is unnatural is bad? Clearly, they cannot have intended merely to reduce the word *natural* to a synonym of *good, right,* and *proper,* and *unnatural* to a synonym of *evil, wrong, improper, corrupt,* and *depraved.* If that were all they had intended to do, there would be very little to discuss as to whether a given form of behavior might be proper even though it is not in strict conformity with someone's views of what is natural; for *good* and *natural* being synonyms, it would follow inevitably that whatever is good must be natural, and vice versa, by definition. This is certainly not what the opponents of homosexuality have been saying when they claim that homosexuality, being unnatural, is evil. For if it were, their claim would be quite empty. They would be saying merely that homosexuality, being evil, is evil—a redundancy that could as easily be reduced to the simpler assertion that homosexuality

is evil. This assertion, however, is not an argument. Those who oppose homosexuality and other sexual "perversions" on the ground that they are "unnatural" are saying that there is some objectively identifiable quality in such behavior that is unnatural; and that that quality, once it has been identified by some kind of scientific observation, can be seen to be detrimental to those who engage in such behavior, or to those around them; and that *because* of the harm (physical, mental, moral, or spiritual) that results from engaging in any behavior possessing the attribute of unnaturalness, such behavior must be considered to be wrongful, and should be discouraged by society. "Unnaturalness" and "wrongfulness" are not synonyms, then, but different concepts. The problem with which we are wrestling is that we are unable to find a meaning for *unnatural* that enables us to arrive at the conclusion that homosexuality is unnatural or that if homosexuality is unnatural, it is therefore wrongful behavior. We have examined four common meanings of *natural* and *unnatural* and have seen that none of them performs the task that it must perform if the advocates of this argument are to prevail.

Discussion Questions

1. Present and explain the first two ways that Professor Leiser believes the terms "natural" and "unnatural" can be employed to condemn homosexuality as immoral. Why does he believe that neither is adequate for drawing the conclusion that homosexuality is immoral? Can you think of any possible objections to this position? Explain and defend your answer.

2. Present and explain the second two ways that Professor Leiser believes that terms "natural" and "unnatural" can be employed to condemn homosexuality as immoral. Why does he believe that neither is adequate for drawing the conclusion that homosexuality is immoral? Can you think of any possible objections to this position? Explain and defend your answer.

3. Professor Leiser ends his essay with an analysis of the claim that whatever is natural is good and whatever is unnatural bad. What conclusion does he draw concerning this claim? Present his defense of this position. Can you think of any possible objections to this position? Explain and defend your answer.

Homosexuals in the Military

55

Lifting the Gay Ban

Charles L. Davis

Charles L. Davis is Associate Professor of Political Science at the University of Kentucky, Lexington. He has written several articles on mass political behavior in Latin America as well as on political participation of soldiers in the United States military. He is the author of *Working-class Mobilization and Political Control: Venezuela and Mexico* (1989).

In this essay, Professor Davis argues that the military's former policy on homosexuals in the military and President Clinton's "Don't ask, don't tell" compromise are unjust to homosexual citizens who want to serve their country. Professor Davis maintains that if open homosexuals are allowed in the military, there would be little if no change in military effectiveness or discipline, contingent upon the military leadership not projecting antihomosexual attitudes and stereotypes. He draws this conclusion based on the fact that currently people in the military from diverse social, religious, cultural, political, and regional backgrounds work together interdependently, interact with each other, and, in many cases, live together. This, according to Professor Davis, shows that if homosexuals are integrated into the military correctly, group cohesion, unity, and effectiveness are unlikely to suffer (a common charge by those who do not want to lift

Reprinted by permission from *Society* (November/December 1993).

the ban). In addition, he compares military discrimination against homosexuals with the military's racial segregation policy that ended several decades ago, and points out that once white military personnel got to know black military personnel, stereotypes and prejudices vanished, making the armed forces one of the few places in contemporary society where the races work harmoniously. He believes that this may occur with homosexuals if the military handles their integration correctly.

Marine Colonel Fred Peck, who served as the military spokesman for the operation in Somalia, captured public attention recently in testimony before the Senate Armed Services Committee investigating the ban on homosexuals in the armed forces. Colonel Peck, a staunch foe of lifting the ban, revealed that one of his sons was a homosexual and that he would counsel all his sons to stay out of the military if the ban were lifted. He expressed particular concern for his homosexual son, whose life, the Colonel believed, would be in jeopardy were he to enter military service (*The New York Times*, May 12, 1993).

Underlying Colonel Peck's attitude toward the gay ban is a particular view of U.S. military community and its culture that seems to be widely shared by proponents of the gay ban. The military community is presumed to be less tolerant of social and cultural diversity than is civilian society. Intolerance is presumed to be rooted in both the institutional needs of the military and its social composition. Group cohesion and unity are paramount institutional needs for maintaining "discipline, good order, and morale." Cohesion and unity cannot be achieved if the boundaries of social diversity are extended to include "outgroups"—those whose values and behavior patterns conflict with those of the larger military community. Furthermore, the boundaries of acceptable behavior and values are more narrowly drawn in the military than in civilian society because of the social composition of the military.

The military is presumed to attract a relatively homogeneous group in terms of cultural values and perspectives. The social and political outlooks of the military community are characterized as narrow, parochial, conservative, and conventional. The boundaries of what is socially acceptable in military communities, therefore, is more narrowly drawn than in civilian society. The proponents of the gay ban, therefore, argue that the military cannot be "a laboratory for social experimentation" unless one were willing to sacrifice its group cohesion and unity and, thus, its effectiveness. Perhaps, Colonel Peck goes to the extreme in arguing that violence would result, but he shares the view that the military community will not accept declared homosexuals. That assumption is central to the thinking of the proponents of the ban.

Even those who, like Senator Sam Nunn and other senators, favor the "Don't ask, Don't tell" policy hold this view. This policy means that the military no longer asks recruits about their sexual orientation nor will it conduct investigations to identify homosexuals. However, gay men and women could not be open about their sexuality at the risk of being discharged from the military. Also a strict code of conduct would be imposed on overt behavior—same-sex dancing and the like would be prohibited. The underlying assumption is the same, open homosexuality is outside the norms of acceptable behavior in military communities. To protect legally the right to such behavior or even the right to declare one's sexual orientation would disrupt group cohesion and prevent the emotional bonding upon which the military so vitally depends for its effectiveness.

Such views are reflected in the Department of Defense policy that bans homosexuals from military service. According to the current department directive, as revised on February 12, 1986:

> Homosexuality is incompatible with military service.... The presence of such members adversely affects the ability of the Military Services to maintain discipline, good order, and morale; to foster mutual trust and confidence among service-members, to ensure the integrity of the system of rank and command, to facilitate assignment of worldwide deployment of service members who frequently must live and work under close conditions affording minimal privacy; to recruit and retain members of the Military Services; to maintain public acceptability of military services, and to prevent breaches of security.

While issues such as national security and privacy are invoked, the exclusionary policy is justified primarily in terms of the unacceptability of homosexuality to the military community and the general populace. Persuasive opinion data can be marshalled in support of this view. For example, one poll, completed in December 1992, found that 45 percent of the soldiers at two Texas Army bases indicated that they would resign if forced to serve with openly gay soldiers (*Lexington Herald-Leader*, April 30, 1993).

Other polls have also found widespread opposition within the military to lifting the ban. Within the general population, polls show the public has become more tolerant of gays, but even though, there is still substantial support for restricting the rights and opportunities of homosexuals. These data can be used to support the argument that recruitment, group cohesion, public support for the military, and so on would suffer as a consequence of lifting the ban.

An implicit assumption in this argument favoring the ban is that negative attitudes toward gays are not likely to change in the military community. Indeed, this assumption is central to much of the argument for retaining the ban. If it is granted that negative attitudes and stereotypes of gays could change, then one would have to grant that many of the dire consequences that are predicted need not occur. If the military community were to become tolerant of open gays in the ranks, there would be no threat to the "discipline, good order, and morale" of the military. The central issue is whether the large military community is capable of the attitude change needed to facilitate the integration of declared gays into the military service. My argument is that the military services may be far better able to adapt to such a policy change than proponents of the current ban claim.

No one can argue that attitude change on the gay issue is easily achieved. Homophobic attitudes are deeply rooted in the military culture as well as in the general American culture. Furthermore, negative attitudes toward gays tend to be more deeply rooted in emotions than for other "out-groups" in American society, as a recent empirical study has shown. Yet, attitude change in the military on the gay issue may not be so difficult as proponents of the ban suggest.

It would be unrealistic to expect homophobic elements in the military (or in civilian life) to condone homosexuality. But homophobic attitudes toward behavior need not change for attitudes to change about the rights of gay men and women. One need not like or approve of homosexuality in order to accept the premise that rights of consenting adults to privacy in their sexual conduct and to be free from discrimination based on sexual orientation ought to be respected. If such rights are accorded and respected, it is difficult to see why gay men and women would not be accepted in the work world of the military without disruption to "discipline, good order, and morale." The issue is not the acceptance of homosexual behavior, as General Colin Powell and other proponents of the gay ban argue, but acceptance of gay rights in accordance with American liberal culture.

But would acceptance of gay rights lead military personnel to accept gays in their ranks as colleagues? The nature of contact experiences would be partly determinative. Positive experience would contribute to reduction of prejudice and negative stereotyping, while negative experiences would reinforce existing prejudices and stereotypes. The nature of the work environment would seem to dictate what types of experiences would most likely occur. Positive experiences would seem more likely if harassment and intimidation of gays were not tolerated and existing norms about fraternization and intimacy in the military workplace respected. There is no reason to believe that such norms would be less respected by the entry of gays into the military. Allport's classic study of prejudice reduction suggests that close contact involving cooperative interdependence in the workplace helps to reduce prejudice and negative stereotyping of "out-groups"—not to increase hostility and conflict as suggested by proponents of the gay ban.

Racial integration of the military provides an instructive example. As Charles Moskos has made clear, conflict between black and white troops was common in the segregated armed forces. However, racial hostility disappeared among white and black troops who fought together in the Battle of the Bulge in 1944 in what was to be the first experiment in a racially integrated fighting force in American history. In "From Citizens' Army to Social Laboratory" (*The Wilson Quarterly*, Winter 1993), Moskos writes, "The soldiers who stepped forward performed exceptionally well in battle, gaining the respect of the white soldiers they fought next to and the high regard of the white officers under whom they served." The military has since become a model institution of racial harmony, Moskos notes. This case fully supports Allport's theory; it is not clear why integration of declared gays into the military would not also lead

to prejudice reduction rather than to conflict.

The case of racial integration—and more than simply integration, the high degree of racial harmony that Moskos notes—illustrates that attitudes toward "out-groups" can and do change in the military community. What is not clear is why a similar attitude change toward gays in the military could not also occur. Those who view the military community as incapable of integrating gays may be overlooking the highly diverse character of the military and its demonstrated capacity to integrate individuals from highly diverse social and cultural backgrounds.

The military imposes a high degree of unity and uniformity on its personnel through its hierarchical structure of authority. But at the same time it recruits from a very broad base of American society, though perhaps less so since compulsory military service has ended. Individuals from diverse backgrounds are placed in a close working situation of cooperative interdependence in which they must learn to interact with each other and, in many cases, live together.

Furthermore, military personnel frequently move to different places all over the world. With manpower cutbacks, the military has increasingly been able to recruit a more educated force (though not as educated as during compulsory military service) and it utilizes various incentives to encourage further education of its members once they are inducted into the services. In short, the contemporary U.S. military is comprised of individuals who have experienced considerable social and cultural diversity, who have traveled widely, and who tend to be relatively well educated. In many ways, the United States military is already a laboratory in social and cultural diversity by virtue of the fact that it draws recruits from all strata of an extremely diverse society. The American soldier may thus be better prepared to deal with the lifting of the gay ban than many expect.

Moskos recognizes that the era of compulsory universal military service promoted cultural and social diversity: "It brought together millions of Americans who otherwise would have lived their lives in relative social and geographic isolation. No other institution has accomplished such an intermingling of diverse classes, races, and ethnic groups."

My own experience with the military leads me to believe that an unusual degree of cultural and social diversity still exists in the post-draft military. What I encountered was a social and cultural diversity that was far greater than in other institutions, including institutions of higher learning. I was a college professor at the University of Kentucky Center at Fort Knox from 1977 to 1989 rather than a recruit or draftee. When I began teaching full-time at Fort Knox in the fall of 1977, I brought with me the full baggage of stereotypes about the United States military. I was not sure whether I would find an excessively deferential type of student or the narrow-minded, authoritarian type. I was also concerned about soldiers pulling rank in class discussions and the overall atmosphere of academic freedom. In short, I was afraid of pressures, both direct and subtle, to toe the line.

I do not wish to suggest that the University of Kentucky Center at Fort Knox was an academician's mecca. Our program was a very low priority with both the military and the University of Kentucky administration in Lexington. We were housed in an old WPA school building from the 1930s along with several other institutions of higher learning that offered programs at Fort Knox. Little of the elaborate and sophisticated equipment or modern facilities, used for military training, were available to us. Before the University of Kentucky program was pulled from Fort Knox, our offices were even shifted to an unused, run-down army barracks.

Whatever my reservations about the facilities and the priority of our program may have been, I soon began questioning my own negative stereotypes about the military community. Indeed, my experience is further confirmation of Allport's theory of prejudice reduction via social contact. Admittedly the student body at the Fort Knox Center was not a representative cross-section of the Fort Knox community, but I suspect that the social diversity of students reflected the diverse military community from which most of our students came. (It should be pointed out that students included civilian employees and spouses of military personnel as well as soldiers. Most students were connected to the military base at Fort Knox, even if not on active duty in the U.S. Army.) In any case, the diversity was far greater than what I have even experienced in conventional institutions of higher learning.

Not surprisingly, a significant number of students came from ethnic and racial minority groups, among them African-Americans, Koreans, and Hispanics. Minority groups were probably not proportionately represented in the student body, but their number was significantly greater than in more conventional institutions of higher learning. There was also a large number of students who did not come from the middle and upper-middle classes as do so many traditional college students. Many students represented the first generation in their families that attended college. In short, there was a higher degree of social and cultural diversity than one typically finds on most college or university campuses. Surprising too was the high degree of ideological diversity among the students—from one enlisted soldier who had joined a Democratic Socialist branch in nearby Louisville to a major who considered Milton Friedman too liberal.

What was particularly striking was the ability of these students to get along and to respect each other despite differences in social, cultural, or racial background, military rank, and even ideological orientation. Indeed, I suspect that informal norms that stress tolerance and mutual respect in the face of diversity were operative in this military community. Such norms may be vital for achieving the degree of cohesion and unity that the U.S. military needs to carry out its mission and may be the glue that holds military communities together.

My impressions of one military community are consistent with various sociological studies of the military with which I am familiar. While the available systematic research on the social and political attitudes of military personnel is still limited and not conclusive, there is nothing in that research to suggest that military personnel are more intolerant of "out-groups" or anti-democratic than their civilian counterparts.

Using a panel design for a larger study of political socialization of American youths, M. Kent Jennings and Gregory B. Markus compared attitude changes among respondents who had served in the military with those who had not. The panel consisted of a national probability sample of high school seniors, male and female, interviewed in 1956 and then reinterviewed in 1973 (N = 674 male respondents in the panel). These researchers found no evidence that prior military service results in a failure to acquire participatory skills and motivations, in spite of a time lag before many veterans become active voters. Nor did they uncover any evidence that military service is associated with heightened political intolerance. These findings are consistent with other research that shows that military service actually reduces authoritarian tendencies, as measured on Adorno's F-scale.

It might be objected that these findings are based on samples of inductees who served only briefly in the military and never acquired a syndrome of attitudes and beliefs more typical of the non-conscripted military. Furthermore, most respondents in the Jennings-Markus study had been reintegrated into civilian life. To account for these possibilities, Ronald D. Taylor and I conducted a study of students enrolled at the University of Kentucky Center at Fort Knox during the 1984/85 academic year (N = 116). The military sub-sample included non-conscripted soldiers currently serving in the U.S. Army, most of whom intended to remain in the service for an extended period of time. This sub-sample of active-duty soldiers was found to be more interested in politics, better informed about politics, and more politically tolerant than either the veteran or civilian sub-samples. These findings suggest that active military service might result in more democratic and tolerant behavior than proponents of the gay ban would lead one to believe.

It would be rash to conclude that, because of its social diversity, the U.S. military provides an ideal laboratory of social experimentation for integrating gays into the mainstream of American life. Homophobic attitudes are entrenched in military communities as elsewhere in American society. Certainly there are elements in the military that are not likely to change long-held beliefs about homosexuals, and there are no assurances that events like the murder of the gay sailor, Allen R. Schindler, in 1992 will not happen again. Nevertheless, there are reasons to believe that the United States military is much better able to manage the task without significant disruption of "discipline, good order, and morale" than proponents of the ban would grant.

It seems that successful integration of declared gay men and women into the military depends on leadership more than anything else. If the military leadership continues to project their own homophobic fears and to manipulate popular stereotypes about the U.S. military, homophobic attitudes are not likely to change in military communities. Indeed, the cues that are now emanating from some of the leaders suggest that to be pro–gay rights is to be anti-military. An implicit linkage to President Clinton and the views on the military he expressed during the Vietnam era is also being made. Some military leaders seem intent on creating a self-fulfilling prophecy that negative attitudes and stereotypes regarding gays are not going to change in military communities.

The official Department of Defense policy of excluding homosexuals might also reinforce and justify negative attitudes and stereotypes regarding gays. Similarly, any policy that does not recognize and protect the rights of gays to privacy and to non-discrimination because of sexual orientation is likely to reinforce and justify existing attitudes and stereotypes as well as to create an environment of distrust and suspicion toward gays in the military.

To accord less than full rights to gays who serve in the military, as the "Don't ask, Don't tell" policy does, is to continue to stigmatize the gay community and to justify continued distrust and suspicion. If attitude change is to occur within the heterosexual community in the miliary, it is essential that the official policy unambiguously protect the rights of gay military personnel and that the leadership be fully committed to implementation of those rights.

I grew up in a southern community in the 1950s where it was frequently asserted that "the southern way of life" would never change. Racial mores and attitudes were presumed to be too deeply ingrained to permit peaceful integration. As with Colonel Peck, the fear of violence was used to justify the status quo. It was amazing how peacefully and quickly racial integration came once federal and state civil rights laws were passed and the political leadership endorsed racial equality.

Integrating declared gays into the military may not follow as smooth a course, but the posture of the military leadership and the nature of the official policy will certainly make a difference. The basic problem facing the military is not that rank-and-file soldiers or sailors are inherently incapable of handling social and cultural diversity and change.

Discussion Questions

1. What is the "Don't ask, don't tell" policy and why does Professor Davis oppose it?

2. What are some of the reasons why Professor Davis is hopeful that homosexuals could be integrated into the military without loss of group cohesion, unity, or effectiveness? What part does military leadership play in this scenario? Do you agree or disagree with Professor Davis's position? Explain and defend your answer.

3. How does Professor Davis compare racial integration of the military with the integration of homosexuals in the military in order to support his position? Do you agree with this analogy? Why or why not? Explain and defend your answer.

56

Make War, Not Love:
The Pentagon's Gay Ban Is
Wise and Just

John Luddy

John Luddy, a former Marine infantry officer, is a defense policy analyst at the Heritage Foundation, a conservative think-tank in Washington, D.C.

In this essay, Mr. Luddy argues against both the position taken in the previous essay by Professor Charles L. Davis ("Lifting the Gay Ban"), who supports making sexual orientation irrelevant to military service, and the "Don't ask, don't tell" policy supported by President Clinton and recently approved by Congress. Mr. Luddy supports the traditional position that "Homosexuality is incompatible with military service." He stresses in this essay that his case against homosexuals in the military has nothing to do with the question of whether homosexuality is moral or immoral, but rather, his case rests on the power of sexual attraction and how it can work against military efficiency. Mr. Luddy rests his case on four points: (1) The military is not an ordinary workplace in which contemporary notions of equality apply (or as he puts it, "The Marine Corps is not Burger King"); (2) access to the military is *not* a constitutional right; (3) the analogy between racial minorities and homosexuals, which is used by those who want to lift the military ban, is unsound; and (4) if we assume that homosexuality is entirely natural, normal, and acceptable, the sexual tension, attraction, jealousy, and shame that will inevitably occur with open homosexuals in the military will have a negative result on decision-making, strategy, group cohesion, unity, and effectiveness. To deny this last

point, argues Mr. Luddy, is to deny the incredible power of human sexuality, which is clearly acknowledged and proudly affirmed by homosexual activists in nearly every context except when it comes to the question of the inclusion of open homosexuals in the military. He concludes by claiming that "the clearest and strongest reason for the ban is to remove the influence of sexuality . . . from the environment where the stakes are literally life and death."

The uproar over President Clinton's plan to end the Pentagon's policy banning open homosexuals from the military has subsided—for now. Both sides are braced for the next phase in the battle, to begin this spring with hearings before Senator Sam Nunn's Senate Armed Services Committee. The intensity of this debate should surprise no one, for few things get Americans so riled up as thinking about sex and talking about rights. It is unfortunate, however, that the controversy has focused more on the presumed rights of homosexuals than on the principles that are fundamental to a strong military.

The Pentagon's policy toward homosexuals is both wise and just. It is wise because it accounts for real people functioning in the real world, and recognizes that despite their best intentions, heterosexuals and homosexuals are above all human. It is just because it can be defended without recourse to any criticism of homosexuality on moral grounds; indeed, the only moral basis for the ban is the assertion that preventing unnecessary loss of life is more important than sexuality of any variety.

Those who would lift the ban have tried to dismiss the ensuing public outcry as a moral crusade orchestrated by the religious Right. But this underestimates the public's genuine concern. Senator Sam Nunn and Joint Chiefs of Staff Chairman Colin Powell are hardly right-wing fanatics. Nor are most other Americans, who view this as more than a discrimination issue; they may not condone hatred or intolerance toward homosexuals, but they see how sexuality in the ranks could endanger men in uniform.

The ban against homosexuals in the military is neither judgmental nor ideological. It is based on the recognition that military life cannot provide for different individual lifestyles, and that distractions in combat, sexual or otherwise, get people killed.

Reprinted by permission from *Policy Review* (Spring 1993).

The Marine Corps Is Not Burger King

The primary objective of the armed forces is to win battles with as few casualties as possible. For the president or any other leader to permit anything that detracts from this objective to influence military policy and training constitutes gross negligence and is truly immoral. While the military has been better at providing equal opportunity to women and minorities than any other part of society, this has until now been a fortuitous side benefit, not an objective or an obligation.

Combat is a team endeavor. To win in combat, individuals must be trained to subjugate their individual instinct for self-preservation to the needs of their unit. Since most people are not naturally inclined to do this, military training must break down an individual and recast him as part of a team. This is why recruits give up their first names, and why they look, act, dress, and train alike. To paraphrase an old drill instructor, the Marine Corps is not Burger King—you can't have it your way.

The purpose of this training, which is continually reinforced throughout the military culture, is to build unit cohesion. Unit cohesion—on an athletic team, in a family, in a marriage, and on the battlefield—hinges on trust. Military leaders gain the trust of their subordinates by demonstrating such attributes as character, courage, sound judgment, respect, and loyalty. Soldiers trust each other because of their shared values, objectives, training, and other experiences. To risk one's life willingly demands a degree of trust in one's comrades and one's com-manders not found in any other environment on earth. Although such demands occasionally may be made of firefighters or police, soldiers fight in wars, where such demands are routine.

It is difficult to foresee a time when homosexuals and heterosexuals no longer see each other as different in a fundamental way. With the slightest introspection, the reasonable person quickly realizes that bonds of trust will be difficult to create between men if there is sexuality beneath the surface. The thought that your comrade might have sexual feelings for you—even if he is suppressing those feelings—will make such trust impossible. The slightest inkling that a commander is influenced by his sexuality—even to the extent that he must resist that influence—will destroy his effectiveness as a leader. Soldiers must trust each other, and their command-ers, if they are to risk their lives in causes our nation deems appropriate. When trust is absent among civilians, society, although demeaned, still survives. But breaking trust within the military will cause our soldiers to die, our battles to be lost, and our interests to be threatened.

No Right to Serve

Access to the military is not a right enjoyed by all Americans. It is not guaranteed in the Constitution or anywhere else. Indeed, to build effective units, the armed forces routinely deny the privilege of military service to patriotic Americans who are too tall, too short, too fat, color blind, flat-footed, and mentally or physically handicapped in some way. Single parents are not allowed to enlist, nor are chronic bedwetters. This is not a judgment of the inherent worth of these people as human beings; indeed, each of these individuals properly enjoys numerous civil rights. It is simply a determination that they are not suited for military service.

In a recent decision in California, U.S. District Court Judge Terry Hatter ordered the Navy to reinstate an openly gay petty officer because, in his opinion, the Pentagon's policy on homosexuals is based merely on "cultural myths and false stereotypes." This language attempts to join the gay rights movement to the civil rights movement, and strikes a responsive chord among Americans who believe in civil rights and have yet to shake the burden of collective guilt over past injustices visited upon various racial and ethnic minorities. But logically, neither this language nor the linkage behind it make sense.

Skin color and sexual orientation are different. It is no irony that black Americans have strongly rejected attempts by homosexuals to cloak themselves in the civil rights movement. No clearer statement of this view can be found than General Colin Powell's response to a letter from Representative Pat Schroeder of Colorado. To Ms. Schroeder's patronizing assertion that "I am sure you are aware that your reasoning would have kept you from the mess hall a few decades ago, all in the name of good order and discipline and regardless of your dedication and conduct," General Powell responded:

> I am well aware of the attempts to draw parallels between this position and positions used years ago to deny opportunities to African-Americans.

... I can assure you I need no reminders concerning the history of African-Americans in the defense of their nation and the tribulations they faced. I am part of that history.

Skin color is a benign, non-behavioral characteristic. Sexual orientation is perhaps the most profound of human behavioral characteristics. Comparison of the two is a convenient but invalid argument. I believe the privacy rights of all Americans in uniform have to be considered, especially since those rights are often infringed upon by the conditions of military service.

As Chairman of the Joint Chiefs of Staff, as well as an African-American fully conversant with history, I believe the policy we have adopted is consistent with the necessary standards of good order and discipline required in the armed forces.

A lot of interesting things occur in bedrooms all across America. If minorities begin to be defined based on sexual behavior, there will soon be some fascinating civil rights cases. If the concept of "civil rights" is to continue to mean anything, it cannot be extended to various groups of people based on how they seek sexual pleasure. As for the president's assertion that in the absence of untoward behavior it is wrong to discriminate based on status alone, one notes that society discriminates on precisely this basis all the time. My behavior in a women's locker room might be above reproach, but I am still not allowed to enter one, simply because of my status as a male. Perhaps—to apply General Powell's standards to a civilian situation—my mere status might be threat to good order and discipline.

Consider Judge Hatter's reference to "cultural myths and false stereotypes." It is true that to accept racial integration of the armed forces, whites had to overcome what were truly false stereotypes and cultural myths. In the case of homosexuals, heterosexuals may likewise learn that homosexuals are not compulsive perverts, weaker or less masculine, or a physical threat of any kind. These are myths and stereotypes. But it is neither a myth nor a stereotype that homosexual men have sex with other men. It is this specific behavior to which people react.

Attraction, Jealousy, Hurt, Shame

What would be the effect of mixing homosexuals and heterosexuals in combat? Begin by making two assumptions: first, that homosexuality is viewed as entirely normal, natural, and otherwise acceptable throughout the population; and second, that the order has been given to admit open homosexuals, and that every military person attempts to execute it in good faith. Even under these highly unlikely conditions, the presence of homosexuals in a military unit would still be an invitation for disaster.

Military leaders are responsible for the training, morale, and physical well-being of each member of their unit. They must first mold a group of individuals into a cohesive team, and then lead them into battle. To their men, they must appear capable, physically and mentally tough, brave, and above all fair. Their typical responsibilities include, but are not limited to: planning a mission; navigating and otherwise controlling the movement of their troops; maintaining communication with their commander; directing aircraft and artillery fire to support their attack; arranging for resupply of food and ammunition; coordinating with other ground units; and seeing that casualties are treated and evacuated if necessary. They often do all of this in darkness, miserable weather, or both, and always with an enemy trying to kill them. They must continually make decisions that may cost one man's life and spare another's, such as choosing who is assigned a dangerous mission, and which of the wounded is treated and evacuated first. Should they be asked to contend with human sexual emotions as well?

One hopes that most people have enough common sense and experience to know that human sexuality is enormously complex. Even in the most civilized society, sexuality is never far from the surface. It can inspire attraction or revulsion, intimacy or objectification, trust or fear, jealousy, hurt, or shame. Any of these emotions can be enormously distracting and disruptive. Civilian employers recognize this and enact various policies that proscribe fraternization in the workplace. Still, as any woman—and some men—will attest, these rules are broken every day. Yet while the highest price a civilian will pay for sexual distractions will be some form of degradation, or the loss of a job, reputation, or career, distractions in the military cause people to suffer physical mutilation and often death. If this sounds extreme, consider the following:

A heterosexual lieutenant must order one of his squads to attack a machine gun position that has taken his platoon under fire. Two squads are in position to attack; one is led by a homosexual sergeant. The lieutenant must decide; if he sends the homosexual sergeant, and the sergeant is killed, will the platoon's other homosexual troops think that the lieutenant sent the sergeant because he dislikes homosexuals? Will they trust him with their lives in the future? If the lieutenant were homosexual, and found himself attracted to the sergeant—he is, of course, only human—would he spare that sergeant from dangerous missions and send the other squad instead? What would be the effect on the platoon's morale if he were even perceived as doing so? Above all, would weighing these issues cause him to hesitate while the lives of his men hang in the balance?

If every decision is made, and reacted to, with even the slightest chance that sexual attraction or revulsion played a part in it, how could those decisions be trusted? If a man does not trust his leaders or those around him, will he willingly put his life in their hands?

The Stakes Are Life and Death

In this scenario, no heterosexual is an irrational bigot, no homosexual is either compulsive or perverse, and no sexual advance or contact takes place; in short, no stereotypes are present. The reader will realize that, were the proportion of homosexuals and heterosexuals in society reversed, this argument rightly would be used to ban heterosexuals from the armed forces. The clearest and strongest reason for the ban is to remove the influence of sexuality—not heterosexuality, not homosexuality, just sexuality, period—from an environment where the stakes are literally life and death.

Discussion Questions

1. Mr. Luddy maintains that the military is not an ordinary workplace in which contemporary notions of equality apply. How does he argue for this position? Do you agree or disagree with his reasoning? Explain and defend your answer.

2. How does Mr. Luddy argue for his claim that access to the military is *not* a constitutional right? Also, how does he support his contention that the analogy between racial minorities and homosexuals, which is used by those who want to lift the military ban, is unsound? Do you agree or disagree with his reasoning? Explain and defend your answer.

3. Mr. Luddy claims that if we assume that homosexuality is entirely natural, normal, and acceptable, the sexual tension, attraction, jealousy, and shame that will inevitably occur with open homosexuals in the military will have a negative result on decision-making, strategy, group cohesion, unity, and effectiveness. How does he argue for this claim? Do you agree or disagree with his reasoning? Explain and defend your answer.

SECTION E

Family Values and Sex Roles

Introduction

In a speech delivered on May 19, 1992, in San Francisco, former Vice President Dan Quayle said the following words, which set off a firestorm of controversy:

> It doesn't help matters when prime-time TV has Murphy Brown—a character who supposedly epitomizes today's intelligent, highly paid, professional woman—mocking the importance of a father, bearing a child alone and calling it just another lifestyle choice.[1]

The former vice president was referring to the title character of the prime-time situation comedy, *Murphy Brown*. Ms. Brown, played by actress Candice Bergen, is an unmarried television anchorperson in her early forties who had a child out of wedlock and decides not to marry the child's father (though for some time the child's paternity was unknown to Ms. Brown).

This portion of the vice president's speech was replayed as a soundbite on news programs for several days afterwards. In some quarters he was praised for standing up for traditional values while in others he was vilified for being judgmental and insensitive to the plight of single parents.

However, all the hoopla generated by the Murphy Brown comment overshadowed the entirety of Mr. Quayle's speech, which raised some important social and moral questions about the nature of the family and sex roles. The following are some other excerpts from Mr. Quayle's speech:

> We are in large measure reaping the whirlwind of decades of changes in social mores. I was born in 1947. When we were young, it was fashionable to declare war against traditional values. Indulgence and self-gratification seemed to have no consequences. Many of our generation glamorized casual sex and drug use, evaded responsibility and trashed authority.
>
> The intergenerational poverty that troubles us so much today is predominantly a poverty of values. [It is a] testament to how quickly civilization falls apart when the family foundation cracks. Children need love and discipline. They need mothers and fathers. A welfare check is not a husband. The state is not a father. It is from parents that children learn how to behave in society; it is from parents, above all, that children come to understand values and themselves as men and women, mothers and fathers. . . .
>
> Ultimately, however, marriage is a moral issue that requires cultural consensus and the use of social sanctions. Bearing babies irresponsibly is, simply, wrong. Failing to support children one has fathered is wrong. We must be unequivocal about this. . . .
>
> It's time to talk again about family, hard work, integrity and personal responsibility. We cannot be embarrassed out of our belief that two parents, married to each other, are better in most cases for children than one. That homework is better than hand-outs—or crime. That we are our brother's keeper. That it's worth making an effort, even when the rewards aren't immediate.[2]

Two years after Mr. Quayle's speech, President Bill Clinton voiced his support for much of what the former vice president had said. And on July 14, 1994, Donna Shalala, Secretary of Health and Human Services, while testifying before a congressional committee on President Clinton's welfare plan, responded in the following way to Representative Richard Neal's (D-Mass.) inquiry as to whether the secretary believed the unwed Murphy Brown was right to have a child: "I don't think anyone in public life ought to condone children born out of wedlock. Even if the family is financially able."[3]

Apparently there is now bipartisan support for what was perceived in 1992 as a conservative-Republican point of view. But from the perspective of many social and moral philosophers Mr. Quayle's, President Clinton's, and Secretary Shalala's prescription for society's problems, a return to traditional family values, is entirely misguided. Although they do not disagree with the president, the former vice president, and the secretary of Health and Human Services that there are serious social problems, these philosophers argue that the solution cannot be the strengthening of an institution—the traditional family—that has been and is patriarchical and oppressive to women. Versions of this perspective are defended by Professor Richard Wasserstrom in Chapter 57 ("Sex Roles and the Ideal Society"), who believes that society should eliminate traditional sex roles, and Professor Marilyn Friedman in Chapter 59 ("They Lived Happily Ever After: Sommers on Women and Marriage"), who charges Professor Christina Sommers (in Chapter 60, "Philosophers against the Family," as well as in some of her other writings) with mistakenly blaming the problems of society on radical feminism. In Chapter 58 ("Biological Differences and the Perils of Androgyny"), George Gilder responds to the thinking found in Professor Wasserstrom's essay by arguing that androgyny is harmful to both men and women and consequently to society in general. In Chapter 61, Sommers responds to Friedman's critique. The last essay in this section, Chapter 62, by Susan Moller Okin, is a critique of the traditional family based on its failure to live up to fundamental principles of justice.

Notes

1. Excerpts of this speech were republished in Dan Quayle, "What Did Dan Quayle Really Say?," *Citizen* 6 (July 20, 1992), 6.

2. Ibid.

3. "Telling It Like It Is: Where's the Uproar over Donna Shalala's Murphy Brown Comments?," editorial, *Las Vegas Review-Journal* (18 July 1994), 6B.

For Further Reading

Brigitte Berger and Peter Berger, *The War over the Family: Capturing the Middle Ground* (New York: Doubleday, 1983).

Nicholas Davidson, *The Failure of Feminism* (Buffalo, N.Y.: Prometheus, 1988).

James Dobson and Gary Bauer, *Children at Risk* (Waco, Texas: Word Publishing, 1990).

Alison Jaggar, "On Sexual Equality," in *Sex Equality*, ed., Jane English (Englewood Cliffs, N.J.: Prentice-Hall, 1977).

Michael Levin, *Feminism and Freedom* (New Brunswick, N.J.: Transaction Books, 1987).

Susan Moller Okin, *Justice, Gender, and the Family* (New York: Basic Books, 1989).

Roger Scruton, *Sexual Desire: A Moral Philosophy of the Erotic* (New York: Macmillan, 1986).

Christina Hoff Sommers, *Who Stole Feminism?* (New York: Simon & Schuster, 1994).

Lenore Weitzman, *The Divorce Revolution: The Unexpected Social and Economic Consequences for Women and Children in America* (New York: The Free Press, 1985).

Mary Vetterling-Braggin, ed. *"Femininity," "Masculinity," and "Androgyny": A Modern Philosophical Discussion* (Totowa, N.J.: Rowman and Allanheld, 1982).

57

Sex Roles and the Ideal Society

Richard Wasserstrom

Richard Wasserstrom is Professor of Philosophy at the University of California at Santa Cruz. He has written extensively in professional journals in the areas of ethics and social philosophy. Among his books are *War and Morality* (1970) and *Philosophy and Social Issues* (1980).

In this essay Professor Wasserstrom argues against traditional gender roles and family life. He defends the position that society should strive to emulate what he calls the "assimilationist ideal." In such a society distinctions based on gender, sexual orientation, or family preference would have as much bearing as whether one is brown-eyed or blue-eyed. According to Professor Wasserstrom: "No political rights or social institutions, practices and norms would mark the physiological differences between males and females as important. . . . Bisexuality, not heterosexuality or homosexuality would be the typical intimate, sexual relationship in the ideal society that was assimilationist in respect to sex." He presents several arguments employed against this view: (1) gender differences are biologically determined; (2) the assimilationist ideal is "unnatural"; (3) sex roles are universal, which suggests that they are indispensable to human flourishing; and (4) children are better raised by women. He responds to each of these arguments and maintains that they all fail to overturn the assimilationist ideal.

Reprinted by permission from "Sex Roles and the Ideal Society," in *Philosophy and Social Issues* by Richard Wasserstrom (Notre Dame, Ind.: University of Notre Dame Press, 1980), 23–41.

. . . [O]ne conception of a nonracist society is that which is captured by what I shall call the assimilationist ideal: a nonracist society would be one in which the race of an individual would be the functional equivalent of the eye color of individuals in our society today. In our society no basic political rights and obligations are determined on the basis of eye color. No important institutional benefits and burdens are connected with eye color. Indeed, except for the mildest sort of aesthetic preferences, a person would be thought odd who even made private, social decisions by taking eye color into account. It would, of course, be unintelligible, and not just odd, were a person to say today that while he or she looked blue-eyed, he or she regarded himself or herself as really a brown-eyed person. Because eye color functions differently in our culture than does race, there is no analogue to passing for eye color. Were the assimilationist ideal to become a reality, the same would be true of one's race. In short, according to the assimilationist ideal, a nonracist society would be one in which an individual's race was of no more significance in any of these three areas than is eye color today.

What is a good deal less familiar is an analogous conception of the good society in respect to sexual differentiation—one in which an individual's sex were to become a comparably unimportant characteristic. An assimilationist society in respect to sex would be one in which an individual's sex was of no more significance in any of the three areas than is eye color today. There would be no analogue to transsexuality, and, while physiological or anatomical sex differences would remain, they would possess only the kind and degree of significance that today attaches to the physiologically distinct eye colors persons possess.

It is apparent that the assimilationist ideal in respect to sex does not seem to be as readily plausible and obviously attractive here as it is in the case of race. In fact, many persons invoke the possible realization of the assimilationist ideal as a reason for rejecting the Equal Rights Amendment and indeed the idea of women's liberation itself. The assimilationist ideal may be just as good and just as important an ideal in respect to sex as it is in respect to race, but it is important to realize at the outset that this appears to be a more far-reaching proposal when applied to sex rather than race and that many more persons think there are good reasons why an assimilationist society in respect to sex would not be desirable than is true for the comparable racial ideal. Before such a conception is assessed, however, it will be useful to provide a somewhat fuller characterization of its features.

To begin with, it must be acknowledged that to make the assimilationist ideal a reality in respect to sex would involve more profound and fundamental revisions of our institutions and our attitudes than would be the case in respect to race. On the institutional level we would, for instance, have to alter significantly our practices concerning marriage. If a nonsexist society is a society in which one's sex is no more significant than eye color in our society today, then laws which require the persons who are getting married to be of different sexes would clearly be sexist laws.

More importantly, given the significance of role differentiation and ideas abut the psychological differences in temperament that are tied to sexual identity, the assimilationist ideal would be incompatible with all psychological and sex-role differentiation. That is to say, in such a society the ideology of the society would contain no proposition asserting the inevitable or essential attributes of masculinity or femininity; it would never encourage or discourage the ideas of sisterhood or brotherhood; and it would be unintelligible to talk about the virtues or the disabilities of being a woman or a man. In addition, such a society would not have any norms concerning the appropriateness of different social behavior depending on whether one were male or female. There would be no conception of the existence of a set of social tasks that were more appropriately undertaken or performed by males or by females. And there would be no expectation that the family was composed of one adult male and one adult female, rather than, say, just two adults—if two adults seemed the appropriate number. To put it simply, in the assimilationist society in respect to sex, persons would not be socialized so as to see or understand themselves or others as essentially or significantly who they were or what their lives would be like because they were either male or female. And no political rights or social institutions, practices, and norms would mark the physiological differences between males and females as important.

Were sex like eye color, these kinds of distinctions would make no sense. Just as the normal, typical adult is virtually oblivious to the eye color of other persons for all significant interpersonal relationships, so, too, the normal, typical adult in this kind of nonsexist society would be equally as indifferent to the sexual, physiological differences of other persons for all significant interpersonal relationships. Bisexu-

ality, not heterosexuality or homosexuality, would be the typical intimate, sexual relationship in the ideal society that was assimilationist in respect to sex. . . .

. . . {T]here appear to be very few, if any, respects in which the ineradicable, naturally occurring differences between males and females *must* be taken into account. The industrial revolution has certainly made any of the general differences in strength between the sexes capable of being ignored by the good society for virtually all significant human activities. And even if it were true that women are naturally better suited than men to care for and nurture children, it is also surely the case that men can be taught to care for and nurture children well. Indeed, the one natural or biological fact that seems *required* to be taken into account is the fact that reproduction of the human species requires that the fetus develop *in utero* for a period of months. Sexual intercourse is not necessary, for artificial insemination is available. Neither marriage nor the nuclear family is necessary either for conception or child rearing. Given the present state of medical knowledge and what might be termed the natural realities of female pregnancy, it is difficult to see why any important institution or interpersonal arrangements are constrained to take the existing biological differences as to the phenomenon of *in utero* pregnancy into account.

But to say all this is still to leave it a wholly open question to what degree the good society *ought* to build upon any ineradicable biological differences, or to create ones in order to construct institutions and sex roles which would thereby maintain a substantial degree of sexual differentiation. . . .

The point that is involved here is a very general one that has application in contexts having nothing to do with the desirability or undesirability of maintaining substantial sexual differentiation. It has to do with the fact that humans possess the ability to alter their natural and social environment in distinctive, dramatic, and unique ways. An example from the nonsexual area can help bring out this too seldom recognized central feature. It is a fact that some persons born in human society are born with congenital features such that they cannot walk or walk well on their legs. They are born naturally crippled or lame. However, humans in our society certainly possess the capability to devise and construct mechanical devices and institutional arrangements which render this natural fact about some persons relatively unimportant in respect to the way they and others will live together. We can bring it about, and in fact are in the process of bringing it about, that persons who are confined to wheelchairs can move down sidewalks and across streets because the curb stones at corners of intersections have been shaped so as to accommodate the passage of wheelchairs. And we can construct and arrange buildings and events so that persons in wheelchairs can ride elevators, park cars, and be seated at movies, lectures, meetings, and the like. Much of the environment in which humans live is the result of their intentional choices and actions concerning what that environment shall be like. They can elect to construct an environment in which the natural incapacity of some persons to walk or walk well is a major difference or a difference that will be effectively nullified vis-à-vis the lives that they, too, will live.

Nonhuman animals cannot do this in anything like the way humans can. A fox or an ape born lame is stuck with the fact of lameness and the degree to which that will affect the life it will lead. The other foxes or apes cannot change things. This capacity of humans to act intentionally and thereby continuously create and construct the world in which they and others will live is at the heart of what makes studies of nonhuman behavior essentially irrelevant to and for most if not all of the normative questions of social, political, and moral theory. Humans can become aware of the nature of their natural and social environment and then act intentionally to alter the environment so as to change its impact upon or consequences for the individuals living within it. Nonhuman animals cannot do so. This difference is, therefore, one of fundamental theoretical importance. At the risk of belaboring the obvious, what is important to see is that the case against any picture of the good society of an assimilationist sort—if it is to be a defensible critique—ought to rest on arguments concerned to show why some other ideal would be preferable; it cannot plausibly rest in any significant respect upon the claim that the sorts of biological differences typically alluded to in contexts such as these require that the society not be assimilationist in character.

There are, though, several other arguments based upon nature, or the idea of the "natural" that also must be considered and assessed. First, it might be argued that if a way of doing something is natural, then it ought to be done that way. Here, what may be meant by "natural" is that this way of doing the thing is the way it would be done if culture did not direct or teach us to do it differently. It is not clear, however, that this sense of "natural" is wholly intelligible; it supposes that we can meaningfully talk about how humans would behave in the absence of culture. And few if any humans have ever lived in such a state. Moreover, even if this is an intelligible notion, the proposal that the natural way to behave is somehow the appropriate or desirable way to behave is strikingly implausible. It is, for example, almost surely natural, in this sense of "natural," that humans would eat their food with their hands, except for the fact that they are, almost always, socialized to eat food differently. Yet, the fact that humans would naturally eat this way, does not seem in any respect to be a reason for believing that that is thereby the desirable or appropriate way to eat food. And the same is equally true of any number of other distinctively human ways of behaving.

Second, someone might argue that substantial sexual differentiation is natural not in the sense that it is biologically determined nor in the sense that it would occur but for the effects of culture, but rather in the sense that substantial sexual differentiation is a virtually universal phenomenon in human culture. By itself, this claim of virtual universality, even if accurate, does not directly establish anything about the desirability or undesirability of any particular ideal. But it can be made into an argument by the addition of the proposition that where there is a widespread, virtually universal social practice or institution, there is probably some good or important purpose served by the practice or institution. Hence, given the fact of substantial sex-role differentiation in all, or almost all, cultures, there is on this view some reason to think that substantial sex-role differentiation serves some important purpose for and in human society.

This is an argument, but it is hard to see what is attractive about it. The premise which turns the fact of sex-role differentiation into any kind of a strong reason for sex-role differentiation is the premise of conservatism. And it is no more or less convincing here than elsewhere. There are any number of practices or institutions that are typical and yet upon reflection seem without significant social purpose. Slavery was once such an institution; war perhaps still is. . . .

To put it another way, the question that seems fundamentally to be at issue is whether it is desirable to have a society in which sex-role differences are to be retained in the way and to the degree they are today—or even at all. The straightforward way to think about the question is to ask what would be good and what would be bad about a society in which sex functioned like eye color does in our society; or alternatively, what would be good and what would be bad about a society in which sex functioned in the way in which religious identity does today; or alternatively, what would be good and what would be bad about a society in which sex functioned in the way in which it does today. We can imagine what such societies would look like and how they might work. It is hard to see how thinking about answers to this question is substantially advanced by reference to what has typically or always been the case. If it is true, for instance, that the sex-role-differentiated societies that have existed have tended to concentrate power and authority in the hands of males, have developed institutions and ideologies that have perpetuated that concentration, and have restricted and prevented women from living the kinds of lives that persons ought to be able to live for themselves, then this, it seems to me, says far more about what may be wrong with any strongly nonassimilationist ideal than does the conservative premise say what may be right about any strongly nonassimilationist ideal. . . .

One strong, affirmative moral argument on behalf of the assimilationist ideal is that it does provide for a kind of individual autonomy that a substantially nonassimilationist society cannot provide. The reason is because any substantially nonassimilationist society will have sex roles, and sex roles interfere in basic ways with autonomy. The argument for these two propositions proceeds as follows.

Any nonassimilationist society must have some institutions and some ideology that distinguishes between individuals in virtue of their sexual physiology, and any such society will necessarily be committed to teaching the desirability of doing so. That is what is implied by saying it is nonassimilationist rather than assimilationist. And any substantially nonassimilationist society will make one's sexual identity an important characteristic so that there will be substantial psychological, role, and status differences between persons who are male and those who are female. That is what is implied by saying that it is substantially nonassimilationist. Any such society will necessarily have sex roles, a conception of the places, characteristics, behaviors, etc., that are appropriate to one sex or the other but not to both. That is what makes it a *sex* role.

Now, sex roles are, I think, morally objectionable on two or three quite distinct grounds. One such ground is absolutely generic and applies to all sex roles. The other grounds are less generic and apply only to the kinds of sex roles with which we are fa-

miliar and which are a feature of patriarchal societies, such as our own. I begin with the more contingent, less generic objections.

We can certainly imagine, if we are not already familiar with, societies in which the sex roles will be such that the general place of women in that society can be described as that of the servers of men. In such a society individuals will be socialized in such a way that women will learn how properly to minister to the needs, desires, and interests of men; women and men will both be taught that it is right and proper that the concerns and affairs of men are more important than and take precedence over those of women; and the norms and supporting set of beliefs and attitudes will be such that this role will be deemed the basic and appropriate role for women to play and men to expect. Here, I submit, what is objectionable about the connected set of instructions, practices, and ideology—the structure of the prevailing sex role—is the role itself. It is analogous to a kind of human slavery. The fundamental moral defect—just as is the case with slavery—is not that women are being arbitrarily or capriciously assigned to the social role of server, but that such a role itself has no legitimate place in the decent or just society. As a result, just as in the case of slavery, the assignment on *any* basis of individuals to such a role is morally objectionable. A society arranged so that such a role is a prominent part of the structure of the social institutions can be properly characterized as an *oppressive* one. It consigns some individuals to lives which have no place in the good society, which restrict unduly the opportunities of these individuals, and which do so in order improperly to enhance the lives and opportunities of others.

But it may be thought possible to have sex roles and all that goes with them without having persons of either sex placed within a position of general, systemic dominance or subordination. Here, it would be claimed, the society would not be an oppressive one in this sense. Consider, for example, the kinds of sex roles with which we are familiar and which assign to women the primary responsibilities for child rearing and household maintenance. It might be argued first that the roles of child rearer and household maintainer are not in themselves roles that could readily or satisfactorily be eliminated from human society without the society itself being deficient in serious, unacceptable ways. It might be asserted, that is, that these are roles or tasks that simply must be filled if children are to be raised in a satisfactory way. Suppose this is correct, suppose it is granted that society would necessarily have it that these tasks would have to be done. Still, if it is also correct that, relatively speaking, these are unsatisfying and unfulfilling ways for humans to concentrate the bulk of their energies and talents, then, to the degree to which this is so, what is morally objectionable is that if this is to be a *sex* role, then women are unduly and unfairly allocated a disproportionate share of what is unpleasant, unsatisfying, unrewarding work. Here the objection is the degree to which the burden women are required to assume is excessive and unjustified vis-à-vis the rest of society, i.e., the men. Unsatisfactory roles and tasks, when they are substantial and pervasive, should surely be allocated and filled in the good society in a way which seeks to distribute the burdens involved in a roughly equal fashion.

Suppose, though, that even this feature were eliminated from sex roles, so that, for instance, men and women shared more equally in the dreary, unrewarding aspects of housework and child care, and that a society which maintained sex roles did not in any way have as a feature of that society the systemic dominance or superiority of one sex over the other, there would still be a generic moral defect that would remain. The defect would be that any set of sex roles would necessarily impair and retard an individual's ability to develop his or her own characteristics, talents, capacities, and potential life-plans to the extent to which he or she might desire and from which he or she might derive genuine satisfaction. Sex roles, by definition, constitute empirical and normative limits of varying degrees of strength—restrictions on what it is that one can expect to do, be, or become. As such, they are, I think, at least prima facie objectionable.

To some degree, all role-differentiated living is restrictive in this sense. Perhaps, therefore, all role differentiation in society is to some degree troublesome, and perhaps all strongly role-differentiated societies are objectionable. But the case against sex roles and the concomitant sexual differentiation they create and require need not rest upon this more controversial point. For one thing that distinguishes sex roles from many other roles is that they are wholly involuntarily assumed. One has no choice about whether one shall be born a male or female. And if it is a consequence of one's being born a male or a female that one's subsequent emotional, intellectual, and material development will be substantially controlled by this fact, then it is necessarily the case that

substantial, permanent, and involuntarily assumed restraints have been imposed on some of the most central factors concerning the way one will shape and live one's life. The point to be emphasized is that this would necessarily be the case, even in the unlikely event that substantial sexual differentiation could be maintained without one sex or the other becoming dominant and developing oppressive institutions and an ideology to support that dominance and oppression. Absent some far stronger showing than seems either reasonable or possible that potential talents, abilities, interests, and the like are inevitably and irretrievably distributed between the sexes in such a way that the sex roles of the society are genuinely congruent with and facilitative of the development of those talents, abilities, interests, and the like that individuals can and do possess, sex roles are to this degree incompatible with the kind of respect which the good or the just society would accord to each of the individual persons living within it. It seems to me, therefore, that there are persuasive reasons to believe that no society which maintained what I have been describing as *substantial* sexual differentiation could plausibly be viewed as a good or just society.

Discussion Questions

1. What does Professor Wasserstrom mean by the "assimilationist ideal" and what reasons does he provide for believing that such an ideal is the only basis for a truly just society? Do you agree with his assessment? Why or why not?

2. Explain and present the four arguments Professor Wasserstrom says are employed against the assimilationist ideal. Explain and present his responses to these arguments? Do you consider his responses persuasive? Explain and defend your position.

3. Professor Wasserstrom maintains that sex roles compromise individual autonomy and are therefore injurious to personal freedom. Thus, sex roles should be abolished. However, some have argued that male and female differences enrich and enhance our lives and make life worth living. If this is true, would not the institution of Professor Wasserstrom's assimilationist ideal coerce people into acting inconsistently with what they perceive to be the good life? Critically discuss this question, taking into consideration how we should define freedom and autonomy.

58

Biological Differences and the Perils of Androgyny

George Gilder

George Gilder writes regularly for *The Wall Street Journal, National Review, The American Spectator, Harper's,* and other publications. He has been a Fellow of the Kennedy School of Government at Harvard University as well as a speechwriter for Ronald Reagan and Nelson Rockefeller. He is the author of a number of books including *Men and Marriage* (1986) and *Wealth and Poverty* (1981).

In this essay Mr. Gilder argues against the assimilationist ideal supported by Professor Wasserstrom in the previous chapter. In the first part of his article, Mr. Gilder maintains, that although some differences between men and women can be accounted for by culture and environment, the universality of patriarchy and most differences in areas such as social behavior, relationships, sexuality, and aggression can be accounted for only by biology. In order to support this thesis, Mr. Gilder cites a number of studies, such as the one prepared by Steven Goldberg (*Inevitability of Patriarchy*), who "found no evidence that matriarchy had ever existed or is in any way emergent today," and George Murdock's comparison of "some 500 cultures [that] found that, in all of them, fighting and leadership were associated with men." In the second part of his article Mr. Gilder warns against enforcing the assimilationist ideal in society. Employing examples from education and athletics, he argues that androgyny is harmful to everyone, boys and girls and men and women.

Reprinted by permission from George Gilder, *Men and Marriage,* rev. ed. of *Sexual Suicide* (Gretna, La.: Pelican, 1986), 19–28, 115–125.

In recent years, a new professional has emerged in America: the sexologist. Usually a woman, conservative in dress and temperament, confident, with formidable credentials, she comes forth to utter the final word on contemporary sexual behavior. In this oracular role, though, she does not speak for herself. She represents an institution or an academy— some large and august first-personage plural—the learning of which looms up behind the speaker like a convocation of eminent ghosts, for which she is only a modest medium.

This would not matter necessarily. Her views are more significant if widely and prestigiously held. But what has this Delphic corporation learned about sex? Ask it any question and the answer is the same: "We don't know this"; "We have no evidence for that"; "Our experiments are inconclusive"; "Our knowledge is limited"; "We just don't know." In fact, if one presented in one place all the expressed opinions of these collective experts, one might suppose they were discussing some great mystery—the nature of God, perhaps—and one would have to conclude that all the "available data" from the "most knowledgeable sources" and most learned authorities, commanding all the "best experimental evidence," had as yet failed to substantiate widely heard rumors and superstitions concerning the existence of "sex." To be sure, *something* is going on out there, but as to what it is exactly . . . well, "we have very conflicting data on that point. We need more research."

The issue about which "we" are most assuredly and doggedly agnostic is the existence of two biologically different sexes. Dr. Babette Blackington, for example, a few years ago alerted a presumably perplexed television audience to the hitherto unknown possibilities of male breasts. "Men's breasts, you know, can be induced to lactate," she said, "and the woman's clitoris can be made to ejaculate." Thus she expressed in vivid terms the ultimate vision of the sexual liberationist: the two sexes are essentially identical, inessentially and arbitrarily divided.

To most people over the centuries this view would have seemed preposterous. And so it is today. For after all these years, scientists are finally affirming what nonexperts have always known: that there are profound and persistent biological differences between the sexes, with which every society must come to terms.

Some of the most formidable evidence comes from the studies of Dr. John Money and his colleagues at Johns Hopkins University in Baltimore, who for decades have been treating hermaphroditism and other sex anomalies.[1] Other persuasive material comes from the University of Wisconsin laboratories of the Harlows, who have long been examining the habits of Rhesus monkeys.[2] Further evidence comes from the studies of baboons, chimpanzees, and other primate cousins, both in captivity and in the wild. Then there are hundreds of interesting experiments with the hormonal systems of rats. Finally, there are scores of experiments and observations among humans from infancy to adulthood, in virtually every kind of society from the most primitive to the most advanced.[3] The evidence in fact is so hugely voluminous that our sexperts could be excused for their confusion—if all the material, without important exception, did not point in the same direction: that from conception to maturity, men and women are subjected to different hormonal influences that shape their bodies, brains, and temperaments in different ways.

The man is rendered more aggressive, exploratory, volatile, competitive and dominant, more visual, abstract, and impulsive, more muscular, appetitive, and tall. He is less nurturant, moral, domestic, stable, and peaceful, less auditory, verbal, and sympathetic, less durable, healthy, and dependable, less balanced, and less close to the ground. He is more compulsive sexually and less secure. Within his own sex, he is more inclined to affiliate upwards—toward authority—and less inclined to affiliate downward—toward children and toward the weak and needy.

Of course these tendencies are shaped by environment and culture, and are modified in crucial ways by the relations between men, women, and children in any society. But most of these propensities are substantiated by a large amount of cross-cultural material, combined with a growing body of physiological—particularly neuroendocrinological—data.

Among the many interesting cross-cultural comparisons is a study by B. Whiting of six separate cultures—one each in India, Okinawa, the Philippines, Mexico, Kenya, and New England. In all, the boys are more aggressive and violent than the girls and, in all, the girls are more nurturant and responsible with younger children.[4]

Steven Goldberg, in preparing his fine study, *The Inevitability of Patriarchy*,[5] examined most of the anthropological and sociological literature on the subject of political leadership and authority. In particular he scrutinized every report of an alleged matriarchy, where women were said to hold political power. He found no evidence that a matriarchy

had ever existed or is in any way emerging today. He found no society in which authority was associated chiefly with women in male-female relations. In a review, Margaret Mead agreed with these findings and described his presentation of the data as "faultless."[6] The degree to which women take power seems to depend on the extent to which the men are absent.[7] George Murdock compared some 500 cultures and found that, in all of them, fighting and leadership were associated with the men.[8]

Now there are two essential ways to deal with a pattern so universal. One can go to the thousands of human societies and find ingenious explanations for each incidence of masculinity and femininity. The men provide most of the food, so they dominate. Or they don't provide most of the food, but the women, feeling secure, allow them to dominate. The men are free from child-care responsibilities and can spend time competing for power. Or the men really have as much responsibility for the children as the women do, so the men create a pattern of dominance from generation to generation.

One can offer a similar catalogue of particular explanations for the other general patterns. One can find as many partial or apparent exceptions as possible. One can show how the general tendencies can be overcome by conditioning under some circumstances—as when a male Rhesus monkey grooms and fosters an infant put in its cage. One can write a lot about gibbons, beavers, marmosets, golden hamsters, and a few other animals that are less dimorphic than man, and in which the female is the same size as the male or larger.[9] One can assemble the various tests that fail to register differences between the sexes in humans. One can design and give new ones. Then if one wishes, one can say, "We just don't know." "The data on these points is very confusing." "We need more research."

It is simpler, however, to consult the existing research and arrive at a biological or physical explanation. The evidence is ample.

The sexes become significantly different, even in the very organization of their brains, during the time in the womb. There the presence or absence of a Y sex chromosome determines whether the embryo will be a boy or a girl. The fetus with a Y chromosome will develop testicles rather than ovaries. When the fetus develops male gonads, they will secrete small amounts of androgenic (from *andro*—male, and *genic*—creating) hormones, chiefly testosterone. The testosterone eventually acts on the brain, giving it a male form. So far, neuroendocrinologists have shown that the hypothalamus is measurably dimorphic, with different cell structure and weight for each sex. The hypothalamus is the part of the brain that governs such impulses as hunger, anger, and sex drive. In the man, it also ultimately controls the secretion of the androgens, chiefly testosterone, which themselves have a deep relationship to aggression and sexuality.

The female hypothalamus administers a more complex hormonal system, involving two major sex hormones, estrogen and progesterone, rather than essentially one, as in the male. It also ultimately governs the hormones involved in breast-feeding, both in causing lactation (prolactin) and in creating a desire to nurse and stimulating the flow of the milk (oxytocin). Oxytocin is also a tranquilizing hormone that encourages nurturant behavior.

The male neuroendocrinological system—chiefly the hypothalamus and the gonads—is thus less various and flexible than the woman's. The chief male hormone, testosterone, is very powerful, and small amounts of it given to a woman greatly stimulate her sex drive (her natural libidinal hormone is an androgen produced in the adrenal glands). But testosterone is almost the man's whole repertory, the only way he can respond hormonally to a sexual stimulus.

In a sense, sexual inequality begins in the fetus. The basic human form (template) is female. Even a male fetus will become a healthy *female* if, for some reason, the gonads do not secrete sufficient testosterone in the womb. The fetus becomes male only when it both has a Y chromosome and is acted upon by androgenic hormones. On the other hand, androgenic hormones cannot make a healthy male out of a female fetus, a fetus with X chromosomes. But the androgens can cause dramatic virilizing effects. By studying such accidents, one can learn much about the influence of the different hormonal and hypothalamic forms of males and females.

A hormonal accident or malfunction in the womb may cause a later sex confusion, or even a hermaphrodite, with the organs of both sexes. If one has a child of ambiguous sex, one may take it to the clinic conducted in Baltimore by Dr. Money and his colleagues. They have been treating and examining such patients for several decades and have become the world's leading authorities on the subject.

Many of their findings are presented in *Man and Woman, Boy and Girl* by Dr. Money and Anke Ehrhardt.[10] Described by the *New York Times* on publication in 1972 as the most important study published in the social sciences since the Kinsey reports, it is a fascinating exploration of the causes of sexual dimorphism or of its failure to occur.

In order to judge the impact of fetal masculinization on men, it is useful to appraise its effect on the female. Thus one can distinguish to some extent the impact of fetal testosterone on the brain from the continuing influence of testosterone secretions after birth.

Money and Ehrhardt compared a group of girls accidentally exposed as fetuses to an androgen with a group of girls suffering from a genetic disorder known as Turner's syndrome, in which they are born without sex hormones. Both groups—the androgenized girls and the girls without sex hormones—were raised as females and identified themselves as such. The results of the comparison are summarized succinctly by Corinne Hutt, an experimental psychologist at Oxford, in *Males and Females*, perhaps the most readable study of the biology of sex differences:

> Whereas none of the patients with Turner's syndrome showed "intense outdoor physical and athletic interest," all but one of the androgenized females did so; whereas none of the Turner cases regarded themselves or were considered by others to be a tomboy, most of the [androgenized] cases did, and were also regarded so by others. The majority of the androgenized girls preferred boys' toys to girls' toys, some of them playing *only* with boys' toys, while all the Turner girls preferred girls' toys to boys'. The same was true of clothes . . .[11]

Perhaps the most remarkable result, however, was the apparent influence of fetal experience on career and marriage priorities:

> No androgenized girls put marriage before a career, some put a career before marriage and many wanted both; of the girls with Turner's syndrome, some put marriage before career, more wanted both, but only one put a career before marriage and she wanted to be a nun.[12]

The point is that these genetic girls, exposed to a male hormone as fetuses, can develop a fully masculine childhood pattern as a result. They consider themselves girls, but they consistently reject most of the attempts of the culture to feminize them. One might plausibly conclude, therefore, that the similar biases in boys, massively reinforced at puberty, are not cultural fictions. In other words, boys are more aggressive, career-oriented, and physically exploratory chiefly because of the way they are born, not the way they are raised. Their brains are fetally masculinized. The major impact is on the hypothalamus as the center of appetites and emotion and the thalamus, which controls the erection, but some experts believe that the cortex is affected as well.

Many studies of small children indicate that the chief effect of masculinization is more roughhousing, aggressiveness, and competition, together with a tendency to affiliate upward, toward male leaders. The Harlows have demonstrated that, in monkeys, these effects are slightly diminished rather than heightened by maternal influence. Male monkeys raised in cages and fed artificially by simulated cloth "mothers" are more aggressive with their peers than normal monkeys (while females show just as much feminine "grooming" activity as normal monkeys and vastly more than the males).[13]

It is at puberty that the major hormonal crisis occurs in the lives of boys. Although they are not at that time significantly larger than girls, their bodies begin secreting testosterone in enormous quantities, ten to twenty times the amount of androgens received by girls. This has several effects beyond the obvious changes in external sexual characteristics. Testosterone promotes protein synthesis and thus greatly increases physical strength. By fifteen, the boys have shot ahead of the girls in all indices of athletic ability involving muscular strength, height, speed, and cardiorespiratory capacity. Testosterone vastly boosts sexual drive, to the extent that boys reach a peak at age sixteen or seventeen; such "peaking" does not happen to women. And, finally, testosterone fosters aggression and competition. Although the precise way testosterone works remains open to question, tests both on humans and monkeys have linked levels of testosterone with levels of aggressive or dominant behavior. Scientists have succeeded in changing the dominance order in groups of monkeys by injecting testosterone in the lower-ranking males.[14]

Although older men learn to "hold their hormones" to some degree, the young man is full of both aggression and sexual appetite. He wants to join with older boys and participate in highly charged group activity. He wants to define and fulfill his male sex drive. He is swept from day to day by waves of glandular emotion. The feminists who suppose that "the cortex has liberated men from hormonal influence" could not have much observed the behavior of young men.

It is not the exalted cortex that impels their passion for acceptance by the group, their eagerness to compete for a place, their obsessiveness in practic-

ing for the test. It is not cool passages of reason that govern the adolescent's sexual fears and compulsions—his pornographic curiosities, his masturbatory sieges, his ambivalent pursuit of girls. The boy is encountering in acute form the predicament of male sexual identity: a powerful group of drives that lack a specific shape or clear, ultimate resolution in modern society.

The adolescent girl, meanwhile, is often lethargic. Her hormonal surge may depress her. Her body is changing rapidly in ways that are initially uncomfortable. She is entering "the awkward age." But as her body fills out and she becomes a woman, a clear and important sexual role unfolds. Her breasts, her womb, her temperament—together with the increasing interest of boys—remind her of her possible future as wife and mother.

It is an identity of obvious importance to the society. It offers a variety of sensual rewards, from orgasmic sexual fulfillment to childbirth and on into the deep affirmations of breast-feeding and nurture. It is a sexual role that gives a nearly irrevocable value: one's own child. Needless to say, there are also conflicts and complications. Moreover, sexual identity in itself does not resolve all identity problems. But it is an indispensable beginning—a beginning directly related in women to specific and intelligible changes in their bodies and their lives.

It is hard to exaggerate how different is the adolescent boy's experience. His body is not evolving; it is launching an insurrection. It demands to be satisfied now, by external activity. Even in women and in male homosexuals, the injection of testosterone creates a desire for immediate but undefined sexual action.

The most obvious relief, masturbation, is a flight from sexual identity rather than an affirmation of it. Relations with girls, moreover, are ambiguous and complicated at this stage. Rejection of the overwrought male by the underripe female is frequent and deepens the boy's anxieties.

A sexual identity has to involve a role. In the past, there was a direct tie between the boy's growing strength and aggressiveness and his entry into adult male groups. In fact, he might be stronger and faster, a better hunter, than his elders. Like a woman's sexuality, his purpose in life was defined and fulfilled through the changes in his mind and body. But this is no longer true.

The relationship between virility and adult acceptance may even be negative in today's society. Not only do strength and aggression fail to provide a future, they are also likely to jeopardize one's present. Voluminous testing data indicate that "feminized" boys do best in school, while the strongest and most aggressive drop out.[15]

Despite all the blather to the contrary, it is obvious that virile men remain attractive to women. They can gain some sense of identity through sex and sports. The chief social problems are created by men of insecure sexual identity who cannot either find girls or excel them in "feminized" school and career competitions. Tests among prisoners indicate that it is the ones with the greatest sexual role anxieties who commit violent and predatory crimes.[16]

A man who cannot attain his manhood through an affirmative role resorts to the lowest terms of masculinity. What can he do that is exclusively male? He consults his body. He has a cock. But he is a failure and no woman wants it. He has greater physical strength and aggressiveness. He uses it.

The social and hormonal dilemma of young men was illuminated in a series of experiments with Rhesus monkeys in Atlanta.[17] The researchers found that when male monkeys compete, their testosterone levels rise. But when the contest is over, only the winner's remains high. He feels confident, dominant, and ready to pursue females. The loser, on the other hand, is dejected, and his hormone level plummets.

In modern society, sexual relations with women are becoming the chief way many men assert their sexual identity. But in most of the world's societies, sexual relations follow achievement of manhood, or accompany it. Male affirmation may lead to high testosterone levels, and to feelings of worth, that in turn lead to sexual fulfillment. In this society, it is very hard for many youths to qualify for the company of men on the job or elsewhere. They must validate themselves in sexual terms alone. Yet they lack the confidence and spirit to approach and win a woman.

Ford and Beach's study of nearly two hundred societies concluded that in virtually all of them sex is regarded as something the woman does for the man.[18] He needs it more urgently than she does. He has no alternative or extended sexual role.

Therefore in every human society the man has to bring something to the woman. He has to perform a service or give a gift. At the very least, he must offer more than his own urgency or he will not even be able to gratify the woman sexually.

Even when he cannot be the provider much of the time, he offers his success as a man, validated in a world of men inaccessible to her. Now, however, the man all too often comes to the woman seeking the very affirmation that he needs to have already if he is to win her. Nothing has occurred in the biology of love that significantly relieves him of this dilemma. The man still has to perform—still has to offer something beyond himself, and beyond her reach—if she is to receive him. To find the further sources of this male imperative, one must explore the realm of anthropology—the primal history of human societies.
. . .

To the sexual liberal, gender is a cage. Behind cruel bars of custom and tradition, men and women for centuries have looked longingly across forbidden spaces at one another and yearned to be free of sexual roles. The men dream of nurturing and consoling; the women want the right to be tough and child-free. Today it is widely believed that the dream of escape can come true at last.

This belief leads to a program of mixing the sexes in every possible way, at every stage of life. In nurseries and schools, in athletics and home economics, in sex education and social life, the sexes are thrown together in the continuing effort to create a unisex society. But the results are rarely as expected, and the policies are mostly founded on confusion.

Some of the confusions arise in the schools, where the androgynous agenda has made the greatest apparent headway and its effects can best be studied. It turns out that what seems elemental to many expert educationists is actually bizarre from the long perspective of history and anthropology.

Until recent years, for example, most American parochial schools have kept strict sexual segregation. The boys and girls joined chiefly on ceremonial occasions—assemblies and graduations. Even the playground was divided into male and female territories. The restrictions were lifted only during carefully supervised dances, when young couples made their way chastely around the floor of the gym under the watchful eyes of nuns. Any unseemly body contact brought a swift reprimand: "Leave six inches for the Holy Ghost."

There is no room for the Holy Ghost any longer at most of our schools. The bodies and minds rub together from kindergarten to graduate study. The result is perfectly predictable. Sexual activity occurs at an increasingly younger age. In communities where the family cannot impose discipline, illegitimate children are common. Classrooms become an intensely sexual arena, where girls and boys perform for the attention of the other sex and where unintellectual males quickly come to view schoolbooks as a menace to manhood.[19]

All of this happens at a time when education has become increasingly important and the distractions of early sex are increasingly subversive to one's future. Our society enforces an ever longer period of objective latency before full participation is allowed, and at the same time refuses to grant its children the "latency period" of sexual separation provided in societies where marriage comes at age fourteen.[20] Boys and girls, often forced to write before their hands can manage a pencil,[21] are later thrust into sexual contact before their minds and bodies can deal with sexual emotion.

But there is "no turning back the clock," as they say. The few remaining sex-segregated schools dwindle in an ideological void—as a species that survives the death of its philosophy and rationale. The issue today is not the desirability of coeducation. Coeducation is about as universal in American schools as dissatisfaction with their performance. The issue is whether the remaining male or female schools should rapidly open their doors to both sexes and whether coed schools should proceed with their apparent agenda of integrating all their activities, from sex-education classes to athletics.

The abandonment of separate education, peculiarly enough, has occurred without any visible national debate. Prestigious prep schools like Exeter and Groton, eminent women's colleges like Vassar and Sarah Lawrence, and male institutions like Yale and Princeton have all quietly adopted coeducation as if it were inevitable. New elementary schools are universally coed. Many coed schools provide excellent educations, but the reasons for the movement seem to be less academic than financial and ideological. No one seems to have been able to offer cogent answers to the question, "Why not?" The Holy Ghost, needless to say, is no longer much consulted.

Yet, regardless of whether one considers the trend as ultimately desirable, most of the assumptions that impel it are demonstrably fallacious. A shift to coeducation is in fact "unnatural" by most anthropological criteria. In the evolutionary scheme, it represents a radical change in the learning environment for both boys and girls, who mature in very different ways and phases.[22] Its effects in grade school are drastically different from its effects in college. And whatever the benefits, many of the problems of America's

schools—and disorders of the society—are attributable to the presumption, rare in all other human societies, that boys and girls should be thrown together whenever possible.

Let us begin with a few simple, crucial, and apparently unmentionable facts about a typical high-school classroom. First and most important, most of the boys and a good number of the girls are thinking about the opposite sex most of the time. If you do not believe this, you are a dreamer. The only thing about a classroom more important to adolescent boys than whether girls are present is whether or not it is on fire.

Imaginative advocates of coeducation will tell you that the boys are learning to regard the girls as "human beings" rather than as sexual objects. What in fact the boys are learning is that unless they are exceptionally "bright" and obedient, they will be excelled in their studies by most of the girls.[23] Unless you are imaginative, you will see that this is a further drag on their already faltering attention to Longfellow's *Evangeline*. Clearly in a losing game in masculine terms, the boys react in two ways: They put on a show for the girls and dominate the class anyway, or they drop out. Enough of them eventually drop out, in fact, to disguise the otherwise decided statistical superiority of the female performance in school.[24] But they do not drop out soon enough to suit educators for whom aggressive boys are the leading problem in every high school.

Adolescent boys are radically different from adolescent girls. The boys, for example, are at the pinnacle of sexual desire and aggressiveness. In school, what they chiefly need is male discipline and challenge, ideally without girls present to distract them. Girls, on the other hand, are less aggressive and sexually compulsive at this stage and are more willing to study without rigid policing and supervision. Thus a classroom that contains both boys and girls will hurt both. The boys will be excelled and demoralized by the girls; the girls will be distracted and demoralized by the boys. Both sexes will be damaged by the continuous disciplining that the rebellious and unsuccessful boys require.

The cost is a system which is experienced by many boys as oppressively feminine in spirit and in which, as Patricia Cayo Sexton has elaborately documented, the most "feminine" boys tend to excel. The problem begins in the first grade, where many of the boys are a full nine months behind the girls in digital coordination, and the emphasis is on penmanship.[25]

Mrs. Sexton believes that the striking aversion to writing shown by so many boys throughout their education may stem from their frustrations as six-year-olds when their hands are physically unready to write.[26] She contends that such patterns continue throughout a school career.

Mechanical and technical interests and skills, predominantly masculine, are downplayed in favor of the feminine realms of writing and high culture. The educational utility of the boys' preoccupation with sports and automobiles is universally neglected. The boys are not shown how to compute batting averages or taught the physical principles involved in a carburetor. Instead school consists almost exclusively of sitting down quietly for long periods among adolescent girls, at the behest of a female teacher, and reading and writing materials of little interest to most adolescent boys.

The result, according to Mrs. Sexton, who assembled reams of testing data to prove it, is that the most feminine boys prevail in school and tend to go on to college and into the best jobs. Meanwhile the most aggressive and masculine—the ones who cannot sit in one place for more than ten minutes without severe nervous strain, relieved only by dreams of cars and football games—these boys tend to drop out and take the lowest-paying work.

This pattern leads to tensions of sexuality and social class that are played out continually in the writings of sexual liberals. But their paradigms of victimization are no less valid when reversed. Some of the dropout males, for example, end up at construction sites whistling "oppressively" at upper-class feminist women as they amble by, their breasts jouncing loosely in their shirts. "Gee whiz, these brutes are treating us as *sex objects!*" say the feminists in their books and magazines, pamphlets and speeches. But a working man—committed to a lifetime of tough and relatively low-paid labor in support of his family—cannot feel himself the oppressor of women who seem to embody everything that world has denied him: options, money, style, easy sex, freedom.

The tensions also affect the men who remain in school and prevail under coeducation. Not only are they harassed as "grinds" and "apple-polishers" by the more masculine boys, but they are often alienated from their masculine natures and from technical experience. Their sexual anxieties sustain billion-dollar markets in porn and prostitution. Baffled by a car battery or blown fuse, disdainful of the blue-collar

life, and ignorant of the labor and business of the world, they tend to obsess themselves with odd resentments and conspiracy theories, abstract ideas and symbols.

As Mrs. Sexton writes, "In academic life, words are enshrined to the point that many feel all wars are settled, and all deeds accomplished, through arguments and speechmaking. The academy is often merely a repository of disembodied words . . . but there is hardly an act, deed or object in sight. That students should get restless about this condition and that they should be grossly inept at linking words with deeds should not startle us."[27]

Moreover, she explains, "If we block normal outlets of aggression, we may turn it inward. When we pacified the bopping gang of a decade ago, its members turned to narcotics and self-mutilation. And middle-class hippies (also without aggressive outlets) followed in the same path, adding their own variations."[28]

"We have much to overcome and destroy," Mrs. Sexton continues, " . . . floods and famine, illiteracy, anomie, unrewarding work, abuses of power, obsolete social institutions, the imminence of nuclear war. With so many enemies, we need a great deal of fighting spirit. It would seem wiser, both inside and outside our schools, to permit as much aggression as possible, but to direct it away from street fights and into combat with the real enemies of man."[29]

The mechanical interests that lead many boys to putter endlessly with automobiles, computers, and other technology represent no lesser intellectuality than the more verbal orientation of the others. But potentially valuable technical skills are lost and intellectual powers squandered or turned against society because the educational system does not know how to deal with masculinity.

Surprisingly, to imaginative educators, both the verbal and the mechanical boys have less trouble in all-male institutions. Contrary to the widespread notion, homosexuality is rare at most one-sex prep schools and military academies. Boys with masculinity problems are reinforced by an all-male environment, while less intellectually competent though virile students are not so estranged from education by their failures. Competition with females is destructive to males in any arena, but nowhere is it so damaging as among impressionable adolescents preoccupied with their intense but inchoate sexuality.

Nonetheless, enough boys are surviving school with their masculinity intact to deeply distress the liberationists. It has become clear that in order to extirpate "sexism," it is necessary to attack it at the root. Beyond the effects of coeducation itself, the educationists want to give boys a "head start" in emasculation. Thus the movement is striking at the early stages: nursery school, kindergarten, and the lower grades. Exploiting their great strength in the teaching professions, particularly at the elementary level, the feminists want to remove every vestige of sexual differentiation from textbooks and class activities. They are succeeding wildly, and, from Sesame Street to Main Street, few parents seem willing or able to resist.

The National Educational Association has adopted a militantly feminist position, and many teachers across the country are turning elementary school into an even more destructive experience for little boys than it long has been. The liberationists seem to imagine that the sexuality of children is some kind of ideological playground. They should recognize the terrible damage that sexual confusions can cause in young boys.

What is at stake, for example, in the frequent proposals for a qualified merger of male and female athletics in high schools is nothing less than the integrity of one vital remaining process of male socialization. Mrs. Sexton, among countless other observers, has described the vast importance of sports in the lives of many boys. "Fish like to swim, and boys like to play games," she writes. Speaking of Sioux Indian youths, she quotes an observer: "The unselfconscious devotion and ardor with which many of these young men play games must be witnessed to be appreciated even mildly."[30]

Sports are possibly the single most important male rite in modern society.

Whatever their detractors may say, sports embody for men a moral universe. On the team, the group learns to cooperate, learns the importance of loyalty, struggle, toughness, and self-sacrifice in pursuing a noble ideal. At a period of their lives when hormones of aggression are pouring through their bodies in unprecedented streams, boys learn that aggressiveness must be disciplined and regulated before it can be used in society. They learn the indispensable sensation of competition in solidarity.

The entrance of a large number of teenage girls, at a time in high school and junior high when they tend to be larger than boys, would be disastrous for all the slow developers. Leaders in Outward Bound physical programs for ghetto children, for example,

find that the best athletes perform as well—if in a different spirit—with females present. The smaller, shyer, and less developed boys, however, are completely daunted by the girls and refuse to make a resolute effort. In addition, the lessons of group morality are lost. The successful boys, those who work with and encourage others in all-male groups, simply show off for the females in mixed assemblages. Nor do the girls benefit. Some of them do quite well, but their performances seem directed more toward the boys than to the real values of the undertaking.

In joint athletics, girls subvert the masculinity of the weaker or slow-developing boys without gaining significant athletic reward themselves. The girls who could actually play on an integrated high-school team would be exceedingly rare. But the girls, nonetheless, would disrupt and deform the most precious rituals of young boys.

Athletics provide lessons relevant to many of the confusions and contradictions of American feminism. On the one hand, feminists make fervent demands for a separate realm for women, with prizes and other rewards equal to those received by far superior male athletes. In other words, for far inferior performances Martina Navratilova and Evelyn Ashford must receive prizes equal to John McEnroe and Carl Lewis— equal pay for unequal work. On the other hand, feminists make equally fervent appeals that exceptional girls—during the prepubescent stage when girls are as strong as boys—be admitted to boys' sports such as Little League baseball. High-school girls' teams, however, cannot be opened to the boys unable to make the first-string male teams, because by that route the girls' team would disappear. Yet scarce athletic moneys must be equally divided between male and female teams.

The victims of such practices are male athletes unable to make the men's teams in their early years but far superior to the women on the women's teams that are displacing men's junior varsities on many campuses. Lacking funds and required to increase spending for girls' sports under Title 9 of the Education Amendments of 1972, schools and colleges reduce spending on boys. In high schools in several progressive districts of California, for example, girls' participation rates have more than tripled—from 12 percent to 37 percent—but boys' participation has dropped from 76 percent to about 50 percent.[31] In other words, millions of potential male athletes are losing opportunities to athletically inferior women, exclusively by reason of sex. Some of the excluded boys, who might have had satisfying athletic careers as their bodies matured, instead turn to alcohol, drugs, and crime.

The women who succeed in sports, however, usually do not embody or dramatize the power of women or their athletic ability. Unlike men, who succeed in athletics largely in proportion to their manliness—by perfecting their male bodies—women succeed by suppressing their femininity and imitating men. The most extreme case is female bodybuilding, in which most of the women take male hormones and create bodies that parody the masculine ideal. But throughout track and field and in many other Olympic tests of speed and strength, women prevail chiefly by virilizing themselves.

The Eastern Europeans specialize in such transformations. By extinguishing every hint of femininity, for example, Jarmila Kratochvilova, the marvel of women's track, can run almost as fast as a male adolescent. But her achievement is flawed as an athletic performance because it is less a natural and beautiful fulfillment of the female body than a perversion of it. Through such perversions Communist nations usually "win" the Olympics. But in the past several of their female record-breakers have turned out later to be chromosomally male.

Many other sports, with greater stress on grace and timing, require much less physical or hormonal deformation. Female tennis players often display great feminine grace and appeal and bring a different dimension to the game. But however spectacular the performance of a Navratilova or a Billie Jean King, their lesbianism casts a pall on their skills as somehow unnatural and masculine in spirit.

Lionel Tiger and other anthropologists who emphasize the hunting origins of male *homo sapiens* offer plausible explanations for most of the specialized faculties of the male body. Its running and throwing skills, its ability to reach a pitch of violent activity for brief periods, all derive from the experience of the chase. The tendency to bond with other males in intensely purposeful and dangerous activities is said to come from the collective demands of pursuing large animals. The female body, on the other hand, more closely resembles the body of nonhunting primates. A woman throws, for example, like a male chimpanzee. She cannot run as well as men. But she has more long-range stamina and durability, particularly in the water, and, perhaps in compensation for limitations in pure strength, she has attained greater grace and beauty. Because her musculature is more internal, she can perform prodigious physical feats without breaking the aesthetic lines of her body with corrugations of bulging muscles. When she doesn't strain and struggle against her being to fulfill the standards of male physicality, she reaches greater kinesthetic perfection. She can achieve triumphs of her own at least the equal of male athletic exploits.

Consider, for example, women's gymnastics, a sport once obscure in the United States but universal in its appeal. The great performers achieve a synthesis of grace, agility, humor, beauty, flexibility, and stamina that reaches a level of sinuous poetry. Their dives and leaps and spins all fuse in a continuous calisthenic stream (in the true sense of the term—*kalos* and *sthenis*—beauty and strength).

Men, on the other hand, might leap higher, suspend themselves longer, and whirl faster. But they cannot touch the dazzling artistic integrity of the female performers. Their bodies seem less flexible and somehow excessively muscled, their effort too visible; and although they may do more, as often happens in aesthetics, even in athletics, more is less. In a pursuit of calisthenic grace, the men find themselves in a predicament suggestive of the female sprinter or weight lifter. They are working counter to their physical endowment. And when they assume a pose of elegance, it often seems narcissistic. All that male musculature burdens the terms of the art.

Like gymnasts, female divers and figure skaters have no apologies to make to the men in their fields— let alone to high-school freshmen in Keokuk. The female body, when trained calisthenically, attains a flexuous grace, a perfection of sensuous form and movement that finds no male counterpart.

Outside of the serious competitive arena, women can bring this kind of grace and style to a great many recreational sports. In general, women will do best by transforming athletics into calisthenics—by finding the aesthetic dimensions of a physical art and, by dint of the integrity of their performance, establishing it on their own terms.

In this sense athletics offer a metaphor of the entire dilemma of liberation. Jarmila Kratochvilova and her teammates enter the athletic realm on male terms. The sad irony is that, for all their effort, they gain not liberation but bondage to the male conditions of the activity. By submitting to male values, they symbolically affirm male superiority and betray the higher possibilities of their sex.

The lessons of athletics extend throughout the educational system. Boys and girls grow up in different ways and with overlapping but different potentials. Thus virtually every primitive society divides the children and teaches the sexes separately. Most provide the boys with dramatic initiatory rituals, needed because male lives lack distinct and dramatic stages like those found in the unfolding of female sexuality. In very few cases are the boys and girls thrown together more than two years before their marriages. These divisions may well promote the development of a confident masculinity and of a rich and successful later sex life.

In the United States and Western Europe girls and boys are expected to traffic together intimately for years before they marry. They are subjected to intense sexual distractions and competitions during the critical stages of their educations. They are brought up in a society where sex is continuously advertised and propagandized.

The result is that boys and girls are driven into periods of sexual experimentation and stress unparalleled in either length or intensity by any other societies. One aspect of sex is drastically downplayed, however, and that is the most important, fundamental, and sexually differentiated part—procreation.

Thus the American system of increasingly far-reaching sexual integration vividly teaches the lesson that boys and girls are sexually similar and that sex is a matter of exchanging pleasures between them in a reciprocal way. This approach is inimical to durable love and marriage. The boys do not learn to venerate the procreative powers of women, and the girls stunt their own consciousness of a more elaborate sexuality. Thus, in effect, despite the feminized regimen of many schools, in sex itself—the domain of women—masculine patterns prevail and both sexes are diminished.

The advocates of sexual integration, moreover, seem ready to stop at virtually nothing—not sex education classes, not even, so it seems, the ultimate male arena of military combat.

Notes

1. John Money and Anke A. Ehrhardt, *Man and Woman, Boy and Girl: The Differentiation and Dimorphism of Gender Identity from Conception to Maturity* (Baltimore, Md.: Johns Hopkins University Press, 1972).

2. Harry F. Harlow and Margaret Harlow, "Social Deviation in Monkeys," *Scientific American*, November 1962; Harry F. Harlow, "Sexual Behavior in the Rhesus Monkey," in Frank A. Beach, ed., *Sex and Behavior* (London: Wiley, 1965).

3. Eleanor Emmons Maccoby and Carol Nagy Jacklin, *The Psychology of Sex Differences* (Stanford, Calif.: Stanford University Press, 1974). Jacklin and Maccoby hedge their findings with the usual academic waffling. But their voluminous and authoritative study, based on analysis of some 2,000 research tests and experiments involving several hundred thousand subjects, explicitly confirms the biological origins of the male advantage in aggression and presents telling evidence on all the other points of difference cited between the sexes.

4. B. Whiting, *Six Cultures: Studies in Childrearing* (London: Wiley, 1963).

5. Steven Goldberg, *The Inevitability of Patriarchy* (New York: Morrow, 1973). As Goldberg points out in an unpublished recent paper answering his critics, "A society may have a titular queen or a powerful queen serving in an hereditary position when no appropriate male is available; there were more female heads-of-state in the monarchical world of the first two-thirds of the sixteenth century than in the first two-thirds of the twentieth. Occasionally a woman will attain the highest position in her society, but this is unusual in every such society; moreover, when this does occur . . . the vast majority of the other upper positions are filled by males. A government may claim an ideological commitment to hierarchical equality and even that this commitment is being met. But the reality is always that the claim is not true; in China, for example, sixty-seven of the ministers are male and the other five ministerial positions are vacant. One may choose any society that has ever existed anywhere and find the same thing."

See also Robin Fox, *Kinship and Marriage* (Baltimore, Md.: Penguin Books, 1967), p. 31 and passim. Fox maintains that no marriage system can endure with a male presence unless the men exercise control.

6. Margaret Mead, review of *The Inevitability of Patriarchy*, *Redbook*, October 1973. Although Mead objected to Goldberg's argument on inevitability (she thought new technologies might eventually overcome male dominance), she endorsed the persuasiveness and accuracy of his research. On his central empirical thesis, she wrote: "It is true, as Professor Goldberg points out, that all the claims so glibly made about societies ruled by women are nonsense. We have no reason to believe that they ever existed . . . Men have always been the leaders in public affairs and the final authorities in the home."

7. Clelland S. Ford and Frank A. Beach, *Patterns of Sexual Behavior* (New York: Harper & Row, 1951).

8. George P. Murdock, "World Ethnographic Sample," *American Anthropologist* 59 (1957).

9. Naomi Weisstein, "Tired of Arguing about Biological Inferiority" (*Ms.*, November 1982), is typical of this mode of denial. Ms. Weisstein ignores the fact that in size and sexuality humans are among the most dimorphic of primates. Men and women differ more in physique and hormonal makeup, and probably in psychology, than chimps, gibbons, macaques, and other monkeys that Weisstein cites; she stresses the few species of primates

with relatively large females. In addition, she implies that the critics of feminism deny virtually any influence of environment and culture. In fact, it is the thesis of this book that culture and environment are crucial to creating productive male roles, preventing male disruption of society, and inducing male submission to female values. If culture didn't matter, feminism and male chauvinism wouldn't matter either.

A recent presentation of evidence stressing the importance of the size advantage to male dominance and polygyny among primates is physiologist-anthropologist Jared Diamond's article on sexual differences in *Discover*, April 1985, p. 70 and passim.

10. Money and Ehrhardt, *Man and Woman*.

11. Corinne Hutt, *Males and Females* (Baltimore, Md.: Penguin Books, 1972). For a readable account of these and other studies, *see also* Maggie Scarf, *Body, Mind, Behavior* (Washington, D.C.: New Republic Book Co., 1976), pp. 19–35. For a more detailed explanation of the endocrinological material, see Seymour Levine, ed., *Hormones and Behavior* (New York: Academic Press, 1972), p. 73 and passim.

12. Hutt, *Males and Females*.

13. Ibid., pp. 52–56.

14. This is one of a long series of experiments and observations conducted at Yerkes Regional Primate Research Center, Lawrenceville, Georgia. Irwin S. Bernstein, "Spontaneous Reorganization of a Pigtail Monkey Group," *Studies of Social Behavior in (Large) Enclosures*. Proc. 2nd int. congr. primat., Atlanta, Ga., 1968, vol. 1 (New York: Karger, Basel, 1969), p. 111. *See also* Scarf, *Body, Mind, Behavior*.

15. Patricia Cayo Sexton, *The Feminized Male: White Collars and the Decline of Manliness* (New York: Random House, 1969; Vintage Books, 1970).

16. Thomas Pettigrew, *A Profile of the Negro American* (New York: Van Nostrand Reinhold, 1964), pp. 18, 20 (chart).

17. Robert M. Rose, Thomas R. Gordon, and Irwin S. Bernstein, "Plasma Testosterone Levels in the Male Rhesus: Influences of Sexual and Social Stimuli," *Science* 178 (10 November 1972), pp. 643–45. Rose has subsequently presented evidence that this phenomenon also applies to humans, with infantrymen in Vietnam, for example, registering very low testosterone levels under the stress of impending combat.

18. Ford and Beach, *Sexual Behavior*.

19. Sexton, *Feminized Male*.

20. Margaret Mead, *Male and Female: A Study of the Sexes in a Changing World* (New York: Morrow, 1949), quoted from the paperback (New York: Dell, 1968), p. 273.

21. Sexton, *Feminized Male*, p. 105.

22. Ibid., pp. 104–8.

23. Ibid., pp. 108–14.

24. Ibid., p. 8

25. Ibid., p. 105.

26. Ibid., p. 131.

27. Ibid., p. 130.

28. Ibid.

29. Ibid., p. 116.

30. Ibid.

31. Steve Fainaru, "Title IX Is So Effective, It's Forgotten," San Jose (Calif.) *Mercury-News*, 17 April 1985, p. 2-D.

Discussion Questions

1. What types of studies does Mr. Gilder cite in order to show that the biological differences between men and women result in behavioral, temperamental, and social differences? Do you find his arguments persuasive? Why or why not? If Mr. Gilder is correct, does it have *any* bearing on the view that men and women should be treated equally under the law? Explain and defend your answer.

2. Mr. Gilder warns against enforcing the assimilationist ideal in society, arguing that androgyny is harmful to everyone, boys and girls and men and women. What evidence does he cite to defend this viewpoint? Do you consider it persuasive? Why or why not?

3. Do you agree with Mr. Gilder's suggestion that separate gender schools ought to be reconsidered? If not, how would you argue against his position? If you agree with Mr. Gilder, how would you respond to the criticism that his suggestion is sexist (or sexually discriminatory)?

59

Philosophers against the Family

Christina Hoff Sommers

Christina Hoff Sommers is Associate Professor of Philosophy at Clark University in Worcester, Massachusetts. She has published widely in the areas of ethics, moral education, and feminist philosophy. Among her books are *Vice and Virtue in Everyday Life* (1993, 3rd ed.) and *Who Stole Feminism?* (1994).

In this essay Professor Sommers argues that the predominant views of moral obligation and family life are hostile to the family and traditional marriage. She believes that the attack is both direct and indirect. The direct attack on the family can be seen on two fronts: (1) leading social philosophers propose reforms of social arrangements (which are the foundation of family life) that they perceive as inequitable and an obstruction to individual freedom; and (2) these reformers, especially radical feminists, see the family as part of a "gender system" that results in oppression of women, and for this reason they call for androgyny and an assimilationist social framework that would abolish sex differences and any institution (such as the family and traditional marriage) that supports them. Professor Sommers criticizes these social philosophers who mount these direct attacks by arguing that they don't take into consideration what women actually want, they are ideologically inflexible, and they are irresponsible in not considering the possible cost in human suffering that may result from attempting to achieve their "ideal

Reprinted by permission from "Philosophers against the Family," in *Vice and Virtue in Everyday Life*, 3rd ed., ed. Christina Hoff Sommers and Fred Sommers (San Diego: Harcourt Brace Jovanovich, 1993), 804–829. This paper is part of a project funded by a National Endowment for the Humanities (NEH) Fellowship for College Teachers. An unabridged version of this paper is found in *Person to Person*, ed. Hugh LaFollette and George Graham (Philadelphia: Temple University Press, 1988).

society." Professor Sommers recommends a liberal feminism that she believes is more in line with the real needs of women. The indirect attack comes from those who suggest that there are no "special duties" but that the only obligations that one has are those for which one volunteers (the volunteerist thesis). Because family life entails duties to others to which one did not voluntarily choose to be related, the volunteerist thesis indirectly undermines the family. But Professor Sommers argues that the volunteerist thesis is a popular dogma that should be rejected because it is wholly inadequate in capturing most people's intuitions about the moral life. She concludes with some observations about the broken family.

Much of what commonly counts as personal morality is measured by how well we behave within family relationships. We live our moral lives as son or daughter to this mother and that father, as brother or sister to this sister or brother, as father or mother, grandfather, granddaughter to this boy or girl or that man or woman. These relationships and the moral duties defined by them were once popular topics of moral casuistry; but when we turn to the literature of recent moral philosophy, we find little discussion of what it means to be a good son or daughter, a good mother or father, a good husband or wife, a good brother or sister.

Modern ethical theory concentrates on more general topics. Perhaps the majority of us who involve ourselves with ethics accept some version of Kantianism or utilitarianism, yet these mainstream doctrines are better designed for telling us about what we should do as persons in general than about our special duties as parents or children or siblings. We believe, perhaps, that such universal theories can account fully for the morality of special relations. In any case, modern ethics is singularly silent on the bread and butter issues of personal morality in everyday life. However, silence is only part of it. With the exception of marriage itself, family relationships are a biological given. The contemporary philosopher is, on the whole, actively unsympathetic to the idea that we have *any* duties defined by relationships into which we have not voluntarily entered. We do not, after all, choose our parents or siblings. And even if we do choose to have children, this is not the same as choosing, say, our friends. Because the special relationships that constitute the family as a social arrangement are, in this sense, not voluntarily assumed, many moralists feel bound in principle to dismiss them altogether. The practical result is that philosophers are to be found among those who are contributing to an ongoing disintegration of the traditional family. In what follows I shall expose some of the philosophical roots of the current hostility to family morality. My own view that the ethical theses underlying this hostility are bad philosophy will be made evident throughout the discussion.

1. The Moral Vantage

Social criticism is a heady pastime to which philosophers are professionally addicted. One approach, Aristotelian in method and temperament, is antiradical, though it may be liberal, and approaches the task of needed reform with a prima facie respect for the norms of established morality. It is conservationist and cautious in its recommendations for change. It is, therefore, not given to such proposals as abolishing the family or abolishing private property and, indeed, does not look kindly on such proposals from other philosophers. The antiradicals I am concerned about are not those who would be called Burkean. I shall call them liberal but this use of "liberal" is somewhat perverse since, in my stipulative use of the term, a liberal is a philosopher who advocates social reform but always in a conservative spirit. My liberals share with Aristotle the conviction that the traditional arrangements have great moral weight and that common opinion is a primary source of moral truth. A good modern example is Henry Sidgwick with his constant appeal to Common Sense. But philosophers like John Stuart Mill, William James, and Bertrand Russell also can be cited. On the other hand, because no radical can be called a liberal in my sense, many so-called liberals could be excluded perversely. Thus when John Rawls toys with the possibility of abolishing the family because kinship bias is a force inimical to equality of opportunity, he is no liberal.

The more exciting genre of social criticism is not liberal-Aristotelian but radical and Platonist in spirit. Its vantage is external or even supernal to the social institutions it has placed under moral scrutiny. Plato was as aware as anyone could be that what he called the cave was social reality. One reason for calling it a cave was to emphasize the need, as he saw it, for an external, objective perspective on established morality. Another consideration in calling it a cave was his

conviction that common opinion was benighted, and that reform could not be accomplished except by substantial "consciousness raising" and enlightened social engineering. Plato's supernal vantage made it possible for him to look on social reality in somewhat the way the Army Corps of Engineers looks upon a river that must have its course changed and its waywardness tamed. In our own day much social criticism of a Marxist variety has taken this radical approach to social change. And, of course, much contemporary feminist philosophy is radical.

Some philosophers are easily classifiable as radical or liberal. John Locke is clearly a liberal. Leon Trotsky is clearly a radical. I remarked a moment ago that there is a radical strain in Rawls. But it is a strain only: Rawls's attitude to social reality is not, finally, condescending. On the other hand, much contemporary social criticism is radical in temper. In particular, I shall suggest that the prevailing attitude toward the family is radical and not liberal. And the inability of mainstream ethical theory to come to grips with the special obligations that family members bear to one another contributes to the current disregard of the commonsense morality of the family cave. We find, indeed, that family obligations are criticized and discounted precisely because they do not fit the standard theories of obligation. If I am right, contemporary ethics is at a loss when it comes to dealing with parochial morality; but few have acknowledged this as a defect to be repaired. Instead the common reaction has been: if the family does not fit my model of autonomy, rights, or obligations, then so much the worse for the family.

To illustrate this, I cite without comment recent views on some aspects of family morality.

1. Michael Slote[1] maintains that any child capable of supporting itself is "morally free to opt out of the family situation." To those who say that the child should be expected to help his needy parents for a year or two out of reciprocity or fair play, Slote responds:

   The duty of fair play presumably exists only where past benefits are voluntarily accepted . . . and we can hardly suppose that a child has voluntarily accepted his role in family . . . life.[2]

2. Virginia Held[3] wants traditional family roles to be abolished and she recommends that husbands and wives think of themselves as roommates of the same sex in assigning household and parental tasks. (She calls this

the "Roommate Test.") To the objection that such a restructuring might injure family life, she replies that similar objections were made when factory workers demanded overtime pay.

3. The late Jane English[4] defended the view that adult children owe their parents no more than they owe their good friends. "[A]fter friendship ends, the duties of friendship end." John Simmons[5] and Jeffrey Blustein[6] also look with suspicion upon the idea that there is a debt of gratitude to the parents for what, in any case, they were duty-bound to do.

4. Where Slote argues for the older child's right to leave, Howard Cohen[7] argues for granting that right to young children who still need parental care. He proposes that every child be assigned a "trusted advisor" or agent. If the child wants to leave his parents, his agent will be charged with finding alternative caretakers for him.

The philosophers I have cited are not atypical in their dismissive attitude to commonsense morality or in the readiness to replace the parochial norms of the family cave with practices that would better approximate the ideals of human rights and equality. A theory of rights and obligations that applies generally to moral agents is, in this way, applied to the family with the predictable result that the family system of special relations and non-contractual special obligations is judged to be grossly unfair to its members.

2. Feminism and the Family

I have said that the morality of the family has been relatively neglected. The glaring exception to this is, of course, the feminist movement. Although the movement is complex, I am confined primarily to its moral philosophers, of whom the most influential is Simone de Beauvoir. For de Beauvoir, a social arrangement that does not allow all its participants full autonomy is to be condemned. De Beauvoir criticizes the family as an unacceptable arrangement since, for women, marriage and childbearing are essentially incompatible with their subjectivity and freedom:

> The tragedy of marriage is not that it fails to assure woman the promised happiness . . . but that it mutilates her; it dooms her to repetition and

routine . . . At twenty or thereabouts mistress of a home, bound permanently to a man, a child in her arms, she stands with her life virtually finished forever.[8]

For de Beauvoir the tragedy goes deeper than marriage. The loss of subjectivity is unavoidable as long as human reproduction requires the woman's womb. De Beauvoir starkly describes the pregnant woman who ought to be a "free individual" as a "stockpile of colloids, an incubator, an egg."[9] And as recently as 1977 she compared childbearing and nurturing to slavery.[10]

It would be a mistake to say that de Beauvoir's criticism of the family is outside the mainstream of Anglo-American philosophy. Her criterion of moral adequacy may be formulated in continental existentialist terms, but its central contention is generally accepted: who would deny that an arrangement that systematically thwarts the freedom and autonomy of the individual is *eo ipso* defective? What is perhaps a bit odd to Anglo-American ears is that de Beauvoir makes such scant appeal to ideals of fairness and equality. For her, it is the loss of autonomy that is decisive.

De Beauvoir is more pessimistic than most feminists she has influenced about the prospects for technological and social solutions. But implicit in her critique is the ideal of a society in which sexual differences are minimal or nonexistent. This ideal is shared by many contemporary feminist philosophers. The views of Richard Wasserstrom, Ann Ferguson, Carol Gould, and Alison Jaggar are representative.

Wasserstrom's approach to social criticism is Platonist in its hypothetical use of a good society. The ideal society is nonsexist and "assimilationist."[11] Social reality is scrutinized for its approximation to this ideal and criticism is directed against all existing norms. Take the custom of having sexually segregated bathrooms: whether this is right or wrong "depends on what the good society would look like in respect to sexual differentiation." The key question in evaluating any law or arrangement in which sex difference figures is: "What would the good or just society make of (it)?"[12]

Thus the supernal light shines on the cave, revealing its moral defects. *There*, in the ideal society, gender in the choice of lover or spouse would be of no more significance than eye color. *There*, the family would consist of adults but not necessarily of different sexes and not necessarily in pairs. *There* we find equality ensured by a kind of affirmative action which compensates for disabilities. If women are somewhat weaker than men, or if they are subject to lunar disabilities, then this must be compensated for. (Wasserstrom compares women to persons with congenital defects for whom the good society makes special arrangements.) Such male-dominated sports as wrestling and football will there be eliminated and marriage, as we know it, will not exist. "Bisexuality, not heterosexuality or homosexuality, would be the typical intimate, sexual relationship in the ideal society that was assimilationist in respect to sex."[13]

Other feminist philosophers are equally confident about the need for sweeping change. Ann Ferguson wants a "radical reorganization of child rearing." She recommends communal living and a de-emphasis on biological parenting. In the ideal society "[l]ove relationships, and the sexual relationships developing out of them, would be based on the individual meshing-together of androgynous human beings."[14] Carol Gould argues for androgyny and for abolishing legal marriage. She favors single parenting, co-parenting and communal parenting. The only arrangement she opposes emphatically is the traditional one where the mother provides primary care for the children.[15] Alison Jaggar, arguing for a "socialist feminism," wants a society that is both classless and genderless. She looks to the day of a possible transformation of such biological functions as insemination, lactation, and gestation "so that one woman could inseminate another . . . and . . . fertilized ova could be transplanted into women's or even men's bodies." This idea is partly illustrated in a science fiction story that Jaggar praises in which "neither sex bears children, but both sexes, through hormone treatments, suckle them . . ."[16] To those of us who find this bizarre, Jaggar replies that this betrays the depth of our prejudice in favor of the "natural" family.

Though they differ in detail, the radical feminists hold to a common social ideal that is broadly assimilationist in character and inimical to the traditional family. Sometimes it seems as if the radical feminist simply takes the classical Marxist eschatology of the Communist Manifesto and substitutes "gender" for "class." Indeed, the feminist and the old-fashioned Marxist do have much in common. Both see their caves as politically divided into two warring factions: one oppressing, the other oppressed. Both see the need of raising the consciousness of the oppressed group to its predicament and to the possibility of removing its shackles. Both look forward to the day of a classless or genderless society. Both deny the value

and naturalness of tradition. Both believe that people and the institutions they inhabit are as malleable as Silly Putty. And both groups are zealots, paying little attention to the tragic personal costs to be paid for the revolution they wish to bring about. The feminists tell us little about that side of things. To begin with, how will the benighted myriads in the cave who do not wish to "mesh together" with other androgynous beings be reeducated? And how are children to be brought up in the genderless society? Plato took great pains to explain his methods: would the new methods be as thoroughgoing? Unless these questions can be given plausible answers, the supernal attack on the family must always be irresponsible. The appeal to the just society justifies nothing until it can be shown that the radical proposals do not have monstrous consequences. That has not been shown. Indeed, given the perennially dubious state of the social sciences, it is precisely what *cannot* be shown.

Any social arrangement that falls short of the assimilationist ideal is labeled "sexist." It should be noted that this characteristically feminist use of the term "sexist" differs significantly from its popular or literal sense. Literally, and popularly, "sexism" connotes unfair discrimination. But in its extended philosophical use it connotes discrimination, period. Wasserstrom and many feminists trade on the popular pejorative connotations of sexism when they invite us to be antisexist. Most liberals are antisexist in the popular sense. But to be antisexist in the technical, radical philosophical sense is not merely to be opposed to discrimination against women; it is to be *for* what Wasserstrom calls the assimilationist ideal. The antisexist philosopher opposes any social policy that is nonandrogynous, objecting, for example, to legislation that allows for maternity leave. As Alison Jaggar remarks: "We do not, after all, elevate 'prostate leave' into a special right of men."[17] From being liberally opposed to sexism, one may in this way be led insensibly to a radical critique of the family whose ideal is assimilationist and androgynous. For it is very clear that the realization of the androgynous ideal is incompatible with the survival of the family as we know it.

The neological extension of such labels as "sexism," "slavery," and "prostitution" is a feature of radical discourse. The liberal too sometimes calls for radical solutions to social problems. Some institutions are essentially unjust. To "reform" slavery or a totalitarian system of government is to eliminate them. Radicals trade on these extreme practices in characterizing other practices. They may, for example, characterize low wages as "slave" wages and the workers who are paid them as "slave" laborers. Taking these descriptions seriously may start one on the way to treating a free-labor market system as a "slave system" that, in simple justice, must be overthrown and replaced by an alternative system of production. The radical feminist typically explains that, "existentially," women, being treated by men as sex objects, are especially prone to bad faith and false consciousness. Marxist feminists see them as part of an unawakened and oppressed economic class. Clearly we cannot call on a deluded woman to cast off her bonds before we have made her aware of her bondage. So the first task of freeing the slave woman is dispelling the thrall of a false and deceptive consciousness. One must "raise" her consciousness to the "reality" of her situation. (Some feminists acknowledge that it may in fact be too late for many of the women who have fallen too far into the delusions of marriage and motherhood. But the educative process can save many from falling into the marriage and baby trap.)

In this sort of rhetorical climate nothing is what it seems. Prostitution is another term that has been subjected to a radical enlargement. Alison Jaggar believes that a feminist interpretation of the term "prostitution" is badly needed and asks for a "philosophical theory of prostitution." Observing that the average woman dresses for men, marries a man for protection, and so forth, she says, "For contemporary radical feminists, prostitution is the archetypal relationship of women to men."[18]

Of course, the housewife Jaggar has in mind might be offended at the suggestion that she herself is a prostitute, albeit less well paid and less aware of it than the professional street prostitute. To this the radical feminist reply is (quoting Jaggar):

> [I]ndividuals' intentions do not necessarily indicate the true nature of what is going on. Both men and women might be outraged at the description of their candlelit dinner as prostitution, but the radical feminist argues this outrage is due simply to the participants' failure or refusal to perceive the social context in which their dinner date occurs.[19]

Apparently this failure or refusal to perceive affects most women. Thus we may even suppose that the majority of women who have been treated to a candlelit dinner by a man prefer it to other dining alternatives they have experienced. To say that these preferences are misguided is a hard and condescending doctrine. It would seem that most feminist philosophers are not overly impressed with Mill's principle that there can be no appeal from a majority verdict of those who have experienced two alternatives.

The dismissive feminist attitude to the widespread preferences of women takes its human toll. Most women, for example, prefer to have children and those who have them rarely regret having them. It is no more than sensible, from a utilitarian standpoint, to take note of such widespread preferences and to take it seriously in planning one's own life. But a significant number of women discount this general verdict as benighted, taking more seriously the idea that the reported joys of motherhood are exaggerated and fleeting if not altogether illusory. These women tell themselves and others that having babies is a trap to be avoided. But for many women childlessness has become a trap of its own, somewhat lonelier than the more conventional traps of marriage and babies. Some come to find their childlessness regrettable; this sort of regret is common to those who flout Mill's reasonable maxim by putting the verdict of ideology over the verdict of human experience.

3. Feminists against Femininity

It is a serious defect of American feminism that it concentrates its zeal on impugning femininity and feminine culture at the expense of the grass roots fight against economic and social injustices to which women are subjected. As we have seen, the radical feminist attitude to the woman who enjoys her femininity is condescending or even contemptuous. Indeed, the contempt for femininity reminds one of misogynist biases in such philosophers as Kant, Rousseau, and Schopenhauer, who believed that femininity was charming but incompatible with full personhood and reasonableness. The feminists deny the charm, but they too accept the verdict that femininity is weakness. It goes without saying that an essential connection between femininity and powerlessness has not been established by *either* party.

By denigrating conventional feminine roles and holding to an assimilationist ideal in social policy, the feminist movement has lost its natural constituency. The actual concerns, beliefs, and aspirations of the majority of women are not taken seriously *except* as illustrations of bad faith, false consciousness, and successful brainwashing. What women actually want is discounted and reinterpreted as to what they (have been led to) *think* they want ("a man," "children"). What most women *enjoy* (male gallantry, candlelit dinners, sexy clothes, makeup) is treated as an obscenity (prostitution).

As the British feminist, Janet Radcliffe Richards, says:

> Most women still dream about beauty, dress, weddings, dashing lovers, domesticity and babies . . . but if feminists seem (as they do) to want to eliminate nearly all of these things—beauty, sex conventions, families and all—for most people that simply means the removal of everything in life which is worth living for."[20]

Radical feminism creates a false dichotomy between sexism and assimilation, as if there were nothing in between. This view ignores completely the middle ground in which a woman can be free of oppression and nevertheless feminine in the sense abhorred by many feminists. For women are simply not waiting to be freed from the particular chains the radical feminists are trying to sunder. The average woman enjoys her femininity. She wants a man, not a roommate. She wants children and the time to care for them. When she enters the work force, she wants fair opportunity and equal treatment. These are the goals that women actually have, and they are not easily attainable. But they will never be furthered by an elitist radical movement that views the actual aspirations of women as the product of a false consciousness. There is room for a liberal feminism that would work for reforms that would give women equal opportunity in the workplace and in politics, but would leave unimpugned the basic institutions that women want and support, i.e., marriage and motherhood. Such a feminism is already in operation in some European countries. But it has been obstructed here in the United States by the ideologues who now hold the seat of power in the feminist movement.[21]

In characterizing and criticizing American feminism, I have not taken into account the latest revisions and qualifications of a lively and variegated movement. There is a kind of "Feminism of the Week" that one cannot hope to keep abreast of short of divorcing all other concerns. The best one can do for present purposes is attend to central theses and arguments that bear on the feminist treatment of the family. Nevertheless, even for this limited purpose it would be wrong to omit discussion of an important turn taken by feminism in the past few years. I have in mind the recent literature on the theme that there is a specific female ethic that differs from the male ethic in being more "concrete," less rule oriented, more empathic and "caring," and more attentive to the demands of a particular context.[22] The kind of feminism that accepts the idea that women differ from men in approaching ethical dilemmas and social problems for a "care perspective" is not oriented to androgyny as a positive ideal. Rather it seeks to develop a special female ethic and to give it greater practical scope.

The stress on context might lead one to think that these feminists are more sympathetic to the family as the social arrangement that shapes the moral development of women since the family is the context for many of the moral dilemmas that women actually face. However, one sees as yet no attention being paid to the fact that feminism itself is a force working against the preservation of the family. Psychologists like Carol Gilligan and philosophers like Lawrence Blum concentrate their attention on the moral quality of caring relationships, yet these relationships themselves are not viewed in their concrete embedment in any formal social or institutional arrangement.

It should also be said that some feminists are moving away from the earlier hostility to motherhood.[23] Here, too, one sees the weakening of the positive assimilationist ideal in the acknowledgment of a primary gender role. However, childrearing is not seen primarily within the context of the family but as a special relationship between mother and daughter or (more awkwardly) between mother and son, a relationship that effectively excludes the male parent. And the new celebration of motherhood remains largely hostile to traditional familial arrangements.

It is too early to say whether a new style of nonassimilationist feminism will lead to a mitigation of the feminist assault on the family or even on femininity. In any case, the recognition of a female ethic of care and responsibility is hardly inconsistent with a social ethic that values the family as a vital (perhaps indispensable) institution. And the recognition that women have their own moral style may well be followed by a more accepting attitude toward the kind of femininity that some feminists currently reject. One may even hope to see the "holier than thou" aspects of feminism fade into a relaxed recognition that both sexes have their distinctive graces and virtues. Such a feminism would not be radical but liberal.

4. The Indirect Attack

The philosophers I shall now discuss do not criticize the family directly; in some cases they do not even mention the family. However, each one holds a view that subverts, ignores, or denies the special moral relations that characterize the family and are responsible for its functioning. And if they are right, family morality is a vacuous subject.

Judith Thomson maintains that an abortion may be permissible even if the fetus is deemed a person from the moment of conception,[24] for in that case being pregnant would be like having an adult surgically attached to one's body. And it is arguable that if one finds oneself attached to another person, one has the right to free oneself even if such freedom is obtained at the price of the other person's death by, say, kidney failure. I shall, for purposes of this discussion, refer to the fetus as a prenatal child. I myself do not think the fetus is a person from the moment of conception. Nor does Thomson. But here we are interested in her argument for the proposition that abortion of a prenatal child/person should be permissible.

Many have been repelled by Thomson's comparison of pregnancy to arbitrary attachment. Thomson herself is well aware that the comparison may be bizarre. She says:

> It may be said that what is important is not merely the fact that the fetus is a person, but that it is a person for whom the woman has a special kind of responsibility issuing from the fact that she is its mother.[25]

To this Thomson replies: "Surely we do not have any such 'special responsibility' for a person unless we have assumed it, explicitly or implicitly." If the mother does not try to prevent pregnancy, does not obtain an abortion, but instead gives birth to it and takes it home with her, then, at least implicitly, she has assumed responsibility for it.

One might object that although pregnancy is a state into which many women do not enter voluntarily, it is nevertheless a state in which one has some responsibility to care for the prenatal child. Many pregnant women do feel such a prenatal responsibility, and take measures to assure the prenatal child's survival and future health. But here one must be grateful to Professor Thomson for her clarity. A mother who has not sought pregnancy deliberately bears *no* special responsibility to her prenatal child. For she has neither implicitly nor explicitly taken on the responsibility of caring for it. For example, the act of taking the infant home from the hospital implies voluntary acceptance of such responsibility. By choosing to take it with her, the mother undertakes to care for the infant and no longer has the right to free herself of the burden of motherhood at the cost of the child's life.

The assumption, then, is that there are no noncontractual obligations or special duties defined by the kinship of mother to child. As for social expectations, none are legitimate in the morally binding sense unless they are underpinned by an implicit or explicit contract freely entered into. If this assumption is correct, sociological arrangements and norms have no moral force unless they are voluntarily accepted by the moral agent who is bound by them. I shall call this the "volunteer theory of moral obligation." It is a thesis that is so widely accepted today that Thomson saw no need to argue for it.

Michael Tooley's arguments in defense of infanticide provide another solid example of how a contemporary philosopher sidetracks and ultimately subverts the special relations that bind the family.[26] Tooley holds that being sentient confers the prima facie right not to be treated cruelly, and that possession of those characteristics that make one a person confers the *additional* right to life. Tooley then argues that infants lack these characteristics and so may be painlessly killed. In reaching this conclusion, Tooley's sole consideration is whether the infant intrinsically possesses the relevant "right-to-life-making characteristic" of personality—a consideration that abstracts from any right to care and protection that the infant's relation to its parents confers on it causally and institutionally. For Tooley, as for Thomson, the relations of family or motherhood are morally irrelevant. So it is perhaps not surprising that one finds nothing in the index under "family," "mother," or "father" in Tooley's book on abortion and infanticide.

Howard Cohen is concerned strictly with the rights of persons irrespective of the special relations they may bear to others.[27] Just as Thomson holds that the mother's right to the free unencumbered use of her body is not qualified by any special obligations to her child, so Cohen holds that the child's right to a no-fault divorce from its parents cannot be diminished because of the special relation it bears to them. Where Thomson is concerned with the overriding right of the mother, Cohen is concerned with the right of the child. Yet all three philosophers agree that the right of a child is not less strong than the right of any adult. Indeed, Thomson compares the unborn child to a fully grown adult and Tooley holds that any person—be it child, adult, or sapient nonhuman—is equal in rights.

Our three philosophers are typical in holding that any moral requirement is either a general duty incumbent on everyone or else a specific obligation voluntarily assumed. Let us call a requirement a *duty* if it devolves on the moral agents whether or not they have voluntarily assumed it. (It is, for example, a duty to refrain from murder.) And let us call a requirement an *obligation* only if it devolves on certain moral agents but not necessarily on all moral agents. (One is, for example, morally obligated to keep a promise.) According to our three philosophers, all duties are general in the sense of being requirements on all moral agents. Any moral requirement that is *specific* to a given moral agent must be grounded in his or her voluntary commitment. Thus, there is no room for any special requirement on a moral agent that has not been assumed voluntarily by that agent. In other words, *there are no special duties*. This is what I am calling the volunteer theory of obligation. According to the voluntaristic thesis, all duties are general and only those who volunteer for them have any obligations toward them.

This thesis underlies Cohen's view that the child can divorce its parents. For it is unnecessary to consider whether the child has any special duties to the parents that could conflict with the exercise of its right to leave them. It underlies Thomson's view that the woman who had not sought pregnancy has no special responsibility to her unborn child and that any such responsibility that she may later have is assumed implicitly by her voluntary act of taking it home with her. It underlies Tooley's psychobiological method for answering the moral question of infanticide by determining the right-making characteristics of personhood: all we need to know about the neonate is whether or not it possesses the psychological characteristics of personhood. If it does, then it has a right to life. If it does not, then it is not a person and thus may be killed painlessly. It is unnecessary to consider the question of whether the child has a special relation to anyone who may have a "special responsibility" to see to the child's survival.

What I am calling the volunteer thesis is a confidently held thesis of many contemporary Anglo-American philosophers. It is easy to see that the thesis is contrary to what Sidgwick called Common Sense. For it means that there is no such thing as filial duty per se, no such thing as the special duty of mother to child, and generally no such thing as a morality of special family or kinship relations. All of which is contrary to what people think. For most people think that we do owe special debts to our parents even though we have not voluntarily assumed our obligations to them. Most people think that what we owe to our own children does not have its origin in any voluntary undertaking, explicit or implicit, that we have made to them. And, "preanalytically," many people believe that we owe special consideration to our siblings even at times when we may not *feel* very friendly to them. But if there are no special duties, then most of these prima facie requirements are misplaced and without moral force, and should be looked upon as archaic survivals to be ignored in assessing our moral obligations.

The idea that to be committed to an individual is to have made a voluntarily implicit or explicit commitment to that individual is generally fatal to family morality. For it looks upon the network of felt obligation and expectation that binds family members as a sociological phenomenon that is without presumptive moral force. The social critics who hold this view of family obligation usually are aware that promoting it in public policy must further the disintegration of the traditional family as an institution. But whether they deplore the disintegration or welcome it, they are bound in principle to abet it.

It may be that so many philosophers have accepted the voluntaristic dogma because of an uncritical use of the model of promises as the paradigm for obligations. If all obligations are like the obligation to keep a promise, then indeed they could not be incumbent on anyone who did not undertake to perform in a specified way. But there is no reason to take promises as paradigmatic of obligation. Indeed, the moral force of the norm of promise-keeping must itself be grounded in a theory of obligations that moral philosophers have yet to work out.

A better defense of the special duties would require considerably more space than I can give it here.[28] However, I believe the defense of special duties is far more plausible than rival theories that reject special duties. My primary objective has been to raise the strong suspicion that the volunteer theory of obligation is a dogma that is very probably wrong and misconceived, a view that is certainly at odds with common opinion.

Once we reject the doctrine that a voluntary act by the person concerned is a necessary condition of special obligation, we are free to respect the commonsense views that attribute moral force to many obligations associated with kinship and other family relationships. We may then accept the family as an institution that defines many special duties but that is nevertheless imperfect in numerous respects. Nevertheless, we still face the choice of how, as social philosophers, we are to deal with these imperfections. That is, we have the choice of being liberal or conservative in our attitude toward reform.

Burkean conservatives would change little or nothing, believing that the historical development of an institution has its own wisdom. They oppose utopian social engineering, considering it altogether immoral in the profound sense of destroying the very foundations of the special duties. But Burkeans also oppose what Karl Popper called "piecemeal social engineering," which seeks to remedy unjust practices without destroying the institution that harbors them. For Burkeans believe, on empirical grounds, that reform is always dangerous: that reform usually has unforeseen consequences worse than the original injustices sought to be eliminated. Thus, conservatives are much like environmental conservationists in their attitude toward an ecological system: their general advice is extreme caution or hands off.

Liberals are more optimistic about the consequences of reform. Like conservatives, they believe that the norms of any tradition or institution not essentially unjust have prima facie moral force. All of which means we can rely on our commonsense beliefs that the system of expectations within the family is legitimate and should be respected. The liberal will acknowledge that a brother has the right to expect more help from a brother than from a stranger and not just because of what he has done for him lately. And the case is the same for all traditional expectations that characterize family members. On the other hand, there may be practices within the family that are systematically discriminatory and unfair to certain members. Unlike conservatives, liberals are prepared to do some piecemeal social engineering to eliminate injustice in the family.

It should be said that the appeal to common sense or common opinion is not final. For common sense often delivers conflicting verdicts on behavior. But a commonsense verdict is strongly presumptive. For example, there is the common belief that biological mothers have a special responsibility to care for their children, even their unwanted children. One *takes* this as a presumptive evidence of an *objective* moral responsibility on the part of the mother. Note that the "verdict" of common sense is not really a verdict at all. Rather, it is evidence of a moral consideration that *must* enter into the final verdict on what to do and how to behave. Thomson ignores common sense

when she asserts that the mother of a child, born or unborn, has no special responsibility to it unless she has in some way voluntarily assumed responsibility for it. Now, to say that a pregnant woman may have a moral responsibility to her unborn child does not entail that abortion is impermissible. For there are other commonsense considerations that enter here and other responsibilities that the mother may have (to her other children, to herself) that may conflict and override the responsibility to the fetus. So common sense is often not decisive. One may say that a commonsense opinion is symptomatic of a prima facie duty or liberty, as the case may be. Yet it still remains for the casuist to determine the *weight* of the duty in relation to other moral considerations that also may have the support of common sense. Politically and morally, lack of respect for common sense fosters illiberalism and elitism. Here we have the radical temper that often advocates actions and policies wildly at odds with common opinion—from infanticide to male lactation, from no-fault divorce on demand for children to the "roommate test" for marital relationships.

5. The Broken Family

In the final section we look at certain of the social consequences of applying radical theory to family obligation. I have suggested that, insofar as moral philosophers have any influence on the course of social history, their influence has recently been in aid of institutional disintegration. I shall now give some indication of how the principled philosophical disrespect for common sense in the area of family morality has weakened the family and how this affects the happiness of its members. Although much of what I say here is fairly well known, it is useful to say it in the context of an essay critical of the radical way of approaching moral philosophy. For there are periods in history when the radical way has great influence. And it is worth seeing what happens when Plato succeeds in Syracuse.

The most dramatic evidence of the progressive weakening of the family is found in the statistics on divorce. Almost all divorce is painful and most divorce affects children. Although divorce does not end but merely disrupts the life of a child, the life it disrupts is uncontroversially the life of a person who can be wronged directly by the actions of a moral agent. One might, therefore, expect that philosophers who carefully examine the morality of abortion also would carefully examine the moral ground for divorce. But here, too, the contemporary reluctance of philosophers to deal with the special casuistry of family relations is evidenced. For example, there are more articles on euthanasia or on recombinant DNA research than on divorce.

Each year there are another million and a quarter divorces in the United States affecting over one million children. The mother is granted custody in ninety percent of the cases, although legally it is no longer a matter of course. There is very persuasive evidence that children of divorced parents are affected seriously and adversely. Compared with children from intact families, they are referred more often to school psychologists, are more likely to have lower IQ and achievement test scores, are arrested more often, and need more remedial classes.[29] Moreover, these effects show little correlation to economic class. Children in the so-called latency period (between six and twelve) are the most seriously affected. In one study of children in this age group, one-half the subjects showed evidence of a "consolidation into troubled and conflicted depressive behavior patterns."[30] Their behavior patterns included "continuing depression and low self-esteem, combined with frequent school and peer difficulties."

One major cause for the difference between children from broken and intact families is the effective loss of the father. In the *majority* of cases the child has not seen the father within the past year. Only one child in six has seen his or her father in the past week; only 16 percent have seen their fathers in the past month; 15 percent see them once a year; the remaining 52 percent have had no contact at all for the past year. Although 57 percent of college educated fathers see their children at least once a month, their weekly contact is the same as for all other groups (one in six).[31]

It would be difficult to demonstrate that the dismissive attitude of most contemporary moral philosophers to the moral force of kinship ties and conventional family roles has been a serious factor in contributing to the growth in the divorce rate. But that is only because it is so difficult in general to demonstrate how much bread is baked by the dissemination of philosophical ideas. It is surely fair to say that the emphasis on autonomy and equality, when combined with the philosophical denigration of family ties, may have helped to make divorce both easy and respectable, thereby facilitating the rapid change from

fault-based to no-fault divorce. If contemporary moralists have not caused the tide of family disintegration, they are avidly riding it. On the other side, it is not difficult to demonstrate that there is very little in recent moral philosophy that could be cited as possibly contributing to *stemming* the tide.

In the past two decades there has been a celebrated resurgence of interest in applied or practical ethics. It would appear, however, that the new enthusiasm for getting down to normative cases does not extend to topics of personal morality defined by family relationships. Accordingly, the children who are being victimized by the breakdown of the family have not benefited from this. Indeed, we find far more concern about the effect of divorce on children from philosophers a generation or two ago when divorce was relatively rare than we find today. Thus, Bertrand Russell writes:

> [H]usband and wife, if they have any love for their children, will so regulate their conduct as to give their children the best chance of a happy and healthy development. This may involve, at times, very considerable self-repression. And it certainly requires that both should realize the superiority of the claims of children to the claims of their own romantic emotions.[32]

And while Russell is not opposed to divorce, he believes that children place great constraints on it.

> . . . parents who divorce each other, except for grave cause, appear to me to be failing their parental duty.[33]

Discerning and sensitive observers of a generation ago did not need masses of statistics to alert them to the effects of divorce on children. Nor did it take a professional philosopher (citing statistics gathered by a professional sociologist) to see that acting to dissolve a family must be evaluated morally primarily in terms of what such action means for the children.

Writing in the *London Daily Express* in 1930, Rebecca West says:

> The divorce of married people with children is nearly always an unspeakable calamity. It is only just being understood . . . how much a child depends for its healthy growth on the presence in the home of both its parents. . . . The point is that if a child is deprived of either its father or its mother it feels that it has been cheated out of a right."[34]

West describes the harmful effects of divorce on children as effects of "a radiating kind, likely to travel down and down through the generations, such as few would care to have on their consciences."

I have quoted West in some fullness because her remarks contrast sharply with what one typically finds in contemporary college texts. In a book called *Living Issues in Ethics*, the authors discuss unhappy parents and the moral questions they face in contemplating divorce.

> We believe that staying together for the sake of the children is worse than the feelings and adjustment of separation and divorce.[35]

Further on the authors give what they feel to be a decisive reason for this policy:

> Remaining together in an irreconcilable relationship violates the norm of interpersonal love.

One of the very few philosophers to discuss the question of divorce and its consequences for children is Jeffrey Blustein in his book, *Parents and Children*. Blustein looks with equanimity on the priority of personal commitment to parental responsibility, pointing out that

> The traditional view . . . that the central duties of husband and wife are the . . . duties of parenthood is giving way to a conception of marriage as essentially involving a serious commitment between two individuals as individuals.[36]

Blustein also tells us (without telling us how he knows it) that children whose parents are unhappily married are worse off than if their parents were divorced.

> Indeed it could be argued that precisely on account of the children the parents' unhappy marriage should be dissolved. . . .[37]

The suggestion that parents who are unhappy should get a divorce "for the sake of the children" is very contemporary.

To my knowledge, no reliable study has yet been made that compares children of divorced parents to children from intact families whose parents do not get on well together. So I have no way of knowing whether the claims of these authors are true or not. Moreover, because any such study would be compromised by certain arbitrary measures of parental incompatibility, one should probably place little reliance on them. It is, therefore, easy to see that contemporary philosophers are anxious to jump to conclusions that do not render implausible the interesting view that the overriding question in considering divorce is the compatibility of the parents, and that marital ties should be dissolved when they threaten or thwart the personal fulfillment of one or both the marital partners.

These philosophers set aside special duties and replace them with an emphasis on friendship, compatibility, and interpersonal love among family members. However, this has a disintegrative effect. That is to say, if what one owes to members of one's family is largely to be understood in terms of feelings of personal commitment, definite limits are placed on what one owes. For as feelings change, so may one's commitments. The result is a structure of responsibility within the family that is permanently unstable.

I have, in this final section, illustrated the indifference of contemporary philosophers to the family by dwelling on their indifference to the children affected by divorce. Nevertheless, I hope it is clear that nothing I have said is meant to convey that I oppose divorce. I do not. Neither Russell nor West nor any of the sane and compassionate liberal thinkers of the recent past opposed divorce. They simply did not play fast and loose with family mores, did not encourage divorce, and pointed out that moralists must insist that the system of family obligations is only partially severed by a divorce that cuts the marital tie. Morally, as well as legally, the obligations to the children remain as before. Legally, this is still recognized. But in a moral climate where the system of family obligation is given no more weight than can be justified in terms of popular theories of deontic volunteerism, the obligatory ties are too fragile to survive the personal estrangements that result from divorce. It is, therefore, to be expected that parents (especially fathers) will be off and away doing their own thing. And the law is largely helpless.

I have no special solutions to the tragedy of economic impoverishment and social deprivation that results fro the weakening of family ties. I believe in the right of divorce and do not even oppose no-fault divorce. I do not know how to get back to the good old days when moral philosophers had the common sense to acknowledge the moral in them—the days when, in consequence, the *climate* of moral approval and disapproval was quite different from what it is today. I do not know how to make fathers ashamed of their neglect and inadvertent cruelty. What I do know is that moral philosophers should be paying far more attention to the social consequences of their views than they are. It is as concrete as taking care that what one says will not affect adversely the students whom one is addressing. If what students learn from us encourages social disintegration, then we are responsible for the effects this may have on their lives and on the lives of their children. This then is a grave responsibility, even graver than the responsibility we take in being for or against something as serious as euthanasia or capital punishment—since most of our students will never face these questions in a practical way.

I believe then that responsible moral philosophers are liberal or conservative but not radical. They respect human relationships and traditions and the social environment in which they live as much as they respect the natural environment and its ecology. They respect the family. William James saw the rejection of radicalism as central to the pragmatist way of confronting moral questions.

> [Experience] has proved that the laws and usages of the land are what yield the maximum of satisfaction. . . . The presumption in cases of conflict must always be in favor of the conventionally recognized good. The philosopher must be a conservative, and in the construction of his casuistic scale must put things most in accordance with the customs of the community on top.[38]

A moral philosophy that does not give proper weight to the customs and opinions of the community is presumptuous in its attitude and pernicious in its consequences. In an important sense it is not a moral philosophy at all. For it is humanly irrelevant.

Discussion Questions

1. Explain and present what Professor Sommers believes are the direct attacks upon the family by social philosophers. Cite some of the examples to which she points. Do you share her concern? Do you find her arguments persuasive? Explain and defend your answer.

2. Explain and present what Professor Sommers believes is the indirect attack upon the family by social philosophers. Provide some examples of how Sommers believes the family is crippled by this indirect attack. Do you share her concern? Do you find her case persuasive? Explain and defend your answer.

3. Do you think Professor Sommers is correct in claiming that radical feminists are unsympathetic to femininity? Explain and defend your answer. What does she mean by "liberal feminisim" and how does it differ from radical feminism?

Notes

1. Michael Slote, "Obedience and Illusions," in Onora O'Neill and William Ruddick, eds., *Having Children* (New York: Oxford, 1979), p. 320.

2. Slote, p. 230.

3. Virginia Held, "The Obligations of Mothers and Fathers," in Joyce Trebilcot, ed., *Mothering: Essays in Feminist Theory* (Totowa, NJ: Rowman and Allanheld, 1983), pp. 7–20.

4. Jane English, "What Do Grown Children Owe Their Parents?" in O'Neill and Ruddick, *op. cit.*, pp. 351–56.

5. John Simmons, *Moral Principles and Political Obligation* (Princeton, NJ: Princeton University Press, 1979), p. 162.

6. Jeffrey Blustein, *Parents and Children: The Ethics of the Family* (New York: Oxford, 1982), p. 182.

7. Howard Cohen, *Equal Rights for Children* (Totowa, NJ: Rowman and Littlefield, 1980), p. 66.

8. Simone de Beauvoir, *The Second Sex*, tr. H. M. Parshley (New York: Random House, 1952), p. 534.

9. De Beauvoir, p. 553.

10. De Beauvoir, "Talking to De Beauvoir," *Spare Rib* (March 1977), p. 2.

11. Richard Wasserstrom, *Philosophy and Social Issues* (Notre Dame, IN: University of Notre Dame Press, 1980), p. 26.

12. Wasserstrom, p. 23.

13. Wasserstrom, p. 26.

14. Ann Ferguson, "Androgyny as an Ideal for Human Development," in *Feminism and Philosophy*, eds. M. Vetterling-Braggin, F. Elliston and J. English (Totowa, NJ: Rowman and Littlefield, 1977), pp. 45–69.

15. Carol Gould, "Private Rights and Public Virtues: Woman, the Family and Democracy," in *Beyond Domination*, ed. Carol Gould (Totowa, NJ: Rowman and Allanheld, 1983), pp. 3–18.

16. Alison Jaggar, "Human Biology in Feminist Theory: Sexual Equality Reconsidered," in Gould, *op. cit.*, p. 41. Jaggar is serious about the possibility and desirability of what she calls the "transformation of sexuality," which is elaborated in her book *Feminist Politics and Human Nature* (Totowa, NJ: Rowman and Allanheld, 1983), p. 132.

17. Alison Jaggar, "On Sex Equality," in *Sex Equality*, ed. Jane English (Englewood Cliffs, NJ: Prentice-Hall, 1977), p. 102.

18. Alison Jaggar, "Prostitution," in Marilyn Pearsell, ed., *Women and Values: Reading in Recent Feminist Philosophy* (Belmont, CA: Wadsworth, 1986), pp. 108–121.

19. Jaggar, "Prostitution," p. 117.

20. Janet Radcliffe Richards, *The Skeptical Feminist* (Middlesex, England: Penguin Books, 1980), pp. 341–42.

21. See Sylvia Ann Hewlett, *A Lesser Life: The Myth of Women's Liberation in America* (New York: William Morrow, 1986).

22. See, for example, Carol Gilligan, *In a Different Voice* (Cambridge, MA: Harvard University Press, 1982); Eva

Kittay and Diana Meyers, eds., *Women and Moral Theory* (Totowa, NJ: Rowman and Littlefield, 1987); Lawrence Blum, *Friendship, Altruism and Morality* (London: Routledge & Kegan Paul, 1980); Jean Grimshaw, *Philosophy and Feminist Thinking* (Minneapolis, MN: University of Minnesota Press, 1986); Nel Noddings, *Caring: A Feminine Approach to Ethics and Moral Education* (Berkeley, CA: University of California Press, 1984).

23. See, for example, Joyce Trebilcot, ed., *Mothering: Essays in Feminist Theory* (Totowa, NJ: Rowman and Allanheld, 1984).

24. Judith Thomson, "A Defense of Abortion," in *Philosophy and Public Affairs*, vol. 1, no. 1, 1972.

25. Thomson, p. 64.

26. Michael Tooley, "Abortion and Infanticide," in *Philosophy and Public Affairs*, vol. 2, no. 1, 1972.

27. Howard Cohen, *Equal Rights for Children*, chs. V and VI.

28. For a defense of the special duties not assumed voluntarily, see Christina Sommers, "Filial Morality," *The Journal of Philosophy*, no. 8, August 1986.

29. Lenore Weitzman, *The Divorce Revolution: The Unexpected Social and Economic Consequences for Women and Children in America* (New York: The Free Press, 1985).

30. A. Skolnick and J. Skolnick, eds., *Family in Transition* (Boston: Little, Brown, 1929), p. 452.

31. Weitzman, p. 259.

32. Bertrand Russell, *Marriage and Morals* (New York: Liveright, 1929), p. 236.

33. Russell, p. 238.

34. Rebecca West, *London Daily Express*, 1930.

35. R. Nolan and F. Kirkpatrick, eds., *Living Issues in Ethics* (Belmont, CA: Wadsworth, 1983), p. 147.

36. Blustein, *Parents and Children*, p. 230.

37. Blustein, p. 232.

38. William James, "The Moral Philosopher and the Moral Life," in *Essays in Pragmatism* (New York: Hafner, 1948), p. 80.

60

They Lived Happily Ever After: Sommers on Women and Marriage

Marilyn Friedman

Marilyn Friedman is Associate Professor of Philosophy at Washington University in St. Louis, Missouri. She has published widely in the areas of ethics, social philosophy, and feminist theory. She is the author of *What Are Friends for?: Feminist Perspectives on Personal Relationships and Moral Theory* (1993) and editor of *Feminism and Community* (1995).

In this article Professor Friedman replies to Professor Christina Hoff Sommers's critique of radical feminism, which is found in Chapter 59, as well as in some of her other publications. Professor Friedman first presents Professor Sommers's position and accuses her of blaming "feminists for contributing to the current divorce rate and the breakdown of the traditional family" in addition to repudiating "feminist critiques of traditional forms of marriage, family, and femininity." Professor Friedman claims that Professor Sommers advocates the "rape" of Scarlett O'Hara by Rhett Butler in the film *Gone with the Wind* as well as the sexist views of Arlene Dahl, a 1960s actress and model. Professor Friedman then critiques Professor Sommers on several points: (1) that she appeals naively to popular opinion and tradition, (2) that she claims to know what most women want although she cites no studies and ignores the wants of lesbians, (3) that her list of women's wants and values is internally inconsistent as well as woefully short, and (4) that she misuses John Stuart Mill's prin-

Reprinted by permission from *APA Newsletter on Feminism and Philosophy* 90, no. 2 (Winter 1991), 99–103. A slightly longer version of this paper was presented at a session of the Society for Women in Philosophy, Eastern Division, meeting in conjunction with the APA, Eastern Division, in Boston on December 28, 1990.

ciple that "there can be no appeal from a majority verdict of those who have experienced two alternatives," which ironically can be used effectively *against* Professor Sommers's position.

---

1. In a series of papers which has recently appeared in several philosophical and general academic publications, Christina Sommers (1988, 1989a, 1989b, 1990) mounts a campaign against feminist philosophers and "American feminism" in general. Sommers blames feminists for contributing to the current divorce rate and the breakdown of the traditional family, and she repudiates feminist critiques of traditional forms of marriage, family, and femininity. In this paper, I explore Sommers's views in some detail. My aim is not primarily to defend her feminist targets, but to ferret out Sommers's own views of traditional marriage, family, and femininity, and to see whether or not they have any philosophical merit.

2. In her writings, Sommers generally defends what she claims that feminists have challenged. Whether or not she is actually discussing the same things is often open to question since she fails to define the key terms behind which she rallies. Sommers, for example, endorses "the family," the "traditional family," and "the family as we know it" (1989a, 87–88). These are not equivalent expressions. The so-called "traditional family"—a nuclear family consisting of a legally married heterosexual couple and their children, in which the man is the sole breadwinner and "head" of the household, and the woman does the domestic work and childcare—comprised only 16% of all U.S. households in 1977, according to the U.S. Census Bureau (Thorne and Yalom, 1982, 5). Hence, the "traditional family" is no longer "*the* family" or "*the* family as we know it" (italics mine) but is only one sort of family that we know.

Sommers also rallies behind "femininity," "feminine culture," "conventional feminine roles," and "a primary gender role" (1989a, 90, 92). These expressions, as well, call for clarification; they do not necessarily refer to the same practices. In recent years, many feminists have defended various aspects of what might also be called "feminine culture." Sommers notes a few of these authors and works, but finds one reason or another for repudiating each one that she cites.[1]

3. To see what Sommers is promoting under the banner of "feminine culture," we should look to Sommers's claims about what women value, want,

and enjoy.[2] First, there are wants, values, and enjoyments pertaining to men. Sommers claims that women want "a man," "marriage," and "to marry good providers." (1989a, 90–91; 1990, 18) She asserts that "most women" enjoy "male gallantry," that the "majority of women" enjoy being "treated by a man to a candlelight dinner," and that "many women ... swoon at the sight of Rhett Butler carrying Scarlett O'Hara up the stairs to a fate undreamt of in feminist philosophy." (1989a, 89–90; 1989b, B3)

Second, there are wants, values and enjoyments having to do with children. Women, Sommers tells us, want children, motherhood, "conventional motherhood," "family," and "the time to care for children." (1989a, 90–91; 1989b; B2, 1990, 18) In a revealing turn of phrase, Sommers also asserts that women are "willing to pay the price" for family and motherhood. (1989b, B2). Sommers does not say, however, what she thinks the price is.

Third, there are wants, values, and enjoyments having to do with femininity. Women are said to enjoy their "femininity," makeup, "sexy clothes," and, even more specifically, "clothes that render them 'sex objects'." (1989a, 90; 1990, 18) On the topic of femininity, Sommers also quotes approvingly (1989a, 90–91) the words of Janet Radcliffe Richards who wrote that, "Most women still dream about beauty, dress, weddings, dashing lovers," and "domesticity," and that, for "most people," "beauty, sex conventions, family and all" comprise "everything in life which is worth living for." (1980, 341–42)

4. A very few of the wants which Sommers attributes to women do not fit into my three-part classification scheme (men, children, femininity). Sommers claims that women want "fair economic opportunities" (1989a, 91) and that they are "generally receptive to liberal feminist reforms that enhance their political and economic powers." (1989b, B2) Sommers, ironically, does not recognize that women's enhanced economic and political power makes them less needful of traditional marriage to a "good provider," and, when they are married, makes them less afraid to resort to divorce to solve marital and family problems.

Under traditional arrangements, most women did not merely want marriage; they needed it. It was by far a woman's most socially legitimated option for economic survival. Take away the need, as liberal feminism seeks to do, and at least some of the want also disappears. One otherwise very traditional aunt of mine became a wealthy widow in her late fifties when my rich uncle died. She never remarried.

Now a dynamic woman of 82 who travels widely and lives well, she confesses that no man has interested her enough to make it worthwhile to give up her freedom a second time. "I'm lucky," she confides, "I don't need a meal-ticket." Even a nonfeminist can understand what she is getting at.

5. Before assessing Sommers's overall views, let us rescue Scarlett O'Hara. Sommers's remark that Scarlett O'Hara's rape by Rhett Butler is a fate undreamt of in feminist philosophy is ... simply stunning. (Note that Sommers does not use the word 'rape' here—one of many omissions in her writings.) A passing knowledge of feminist philosophy reveals that rape is hardly undreamt of in it (cf. Vetterling-Braggin, et. al., 1977, T. VI). Rape, of course, is not a dream, it is a nightmare. Any form of sexual aggression can involve coercion, intimidation, degradation, physical abuse, battering, and in extreme cases, death.

The reality of rape is rendered invisible by the many novels and films, such as *Gone with the Wind*, which romanticize and mystify it. They portray the rapist as a handsome man whose domination is pleasurable in bed, and portray women as happy to have their own sexual choices and refusals crushed by such men. In a culture in which these sorts of portrayals are routine, it is no surprise that this scene arouses the sexual desire of some women. However, real rape is not the pleasurable fantasy intimated in *Gone with the Wind*. To put the point graphically: would "many women" still swoon over Butler's rape of O'Hara if they knew that he urinated on her? When you're the victim of rape, you don't have much choice over what goes on.

6. Let us move on to femininity. Sommers never spells out exactly what she means by femininity. For guidance on this topic, we could turn to literature in social psychology which identifies the important traits of femininity and which explores the social devaluation of the feminine. However, it might be more revealing to turn to a different sort of "authority," a 1965 book entitled, *Always Ask a Man: Arlene Dahl's Key to Femininity*, written by an actress and model of the 1960s, Arlene Dahl.

One guiding theme of this femininity manifesto is utter deference to the opinions of men. Dahl instructs the female reader: "Look at Yourself Objectively (try to see yourself through a man's eyes)." (p. 2) In Dahl's view, the "truly feminine" woman works "instinctively" at pleasing men and making men feel important. When [a man] speaks to her, she listens with rapt attention to every word" (p. 5). Dahl's book is laced with quotations from male celebrities who are treated as incontrovertible authorities on what women should be like. Yul Brynner, for example, wants women to be good listeners who are not particularly logical (p. 3). Richard Burton likes women who are "faintly giggly" (p. 3). Tony Perkins thinks that a "girl should act like a girl and not like the head of a corporation—even if she is" (p. 8). The most revealing observation comes from George Hamilton: "A woman is often like a strip of film—obliterated, insignificant—until a man puts the light behind her" (pp. 5–6).

Surprisingly, some of the traits advocated for women by male celebrities are valuable traits, for example, honesty, straightforwardness, maturity, ingenuity, understanding, dignity, generosity, and humor. These traits are not distinctively feminine, however, and that may be the reason why they quickly disappear from Dahl's discussion. The twin themes that resound throughout this femininity manual are that of cultivating one's physical attractiveness and slavishly deferring to men. The slavish deference to men is crucial, since the whole point of the enterprise is to get a man. Thus, Dahl explains in the introduction that this book is written to counteract a tendency for women to dress to please other women, and it also does not promote beauty for the sake of beauty itself (pp. x–xi).

The quintessential prohibition involved in femininity seems to be this: "NEVER upstage a man. Don't try to top his joke, even if you have to bite your tongue to keep from doing it. Never launch loudly into your own opinion on a subject—whether it's petunias or politics. Instead, draw out his ideas to which you can gracefully add your footnotes from time to time." (p. 12) Dahl is less sanguine than Sommers that the role of motherhood fits comfortably into a feminine life; she advises, ". . . don't get so involved with your role of MOTHER that you forget to play WIFE." (p. 9) Once married, your own interests should never outweigh your husband's interests, job, and hobbies, and the daily endeavor to be attractive and appealing to your husband should override even your "children's activities"! (p. 175)

Voila, femininity. Such servility shows the dubiousness of Sommers's claim that "a woman can be free of oppression and nevertheless feminine in the sense abhorred by many feminists" (1989a, 91).

7. Let us turn now to Sommers's *overall* defense of traditional marriage, family, and femininity. Having asserted that most women value or want all of these traditions, Sommers charges feminist views with a serious defect: they either dismiss or dispar-

age these popular feminine wants and values.[3] Sommers herself defers to these alleged views of most women as if they were as such reliable. It is important to note that Sommers does not argue that traditional marriage and so on, on balance, promote important moral values better than any feminist alternatives. No comprehensive comparisons appear in her writings. Her argument begins (and ends, as I will argue) with an appeal to popular opinion.

8. Is Sommers right about what "most women" think? She refers to no studies, no representative samples whatsoever to support her generalizations. Whole categories of women are patently excluded from her reference group and are invisible in her writings. This is a fitting moment to mention the "L" word—and I don't mean "liberal." Obviously, no lesbians, unless seriously closeted, are among Sommers's alleged majority of women who want "a man," conventional marriage, or a traditional family.

Even among nonlesbians, a goodly number of women these days do not want a *traditional* marriage or a *traditional* family. Some heterosexual women simply do not want to marry or to have children at all, and many others want *non*-traditional marriages and *non*-traditional families. Surveys show that *this* attitude, and not the preference for tradition alleged by Sommers, is actually in the majority. In one 1983 study, 63% of women surveyed expressed preferences for non-traditional family arrangements (Sapiro, 1990, 355). Sommers's factual claims are, thus, debatable.

Even apart from questions of popularity, the wants, values, and enjoyments which Sommers attributes to "most women" are frankly suspicious as an ensemble. Candlelight dinners do not combine easily with babies. Dashing lovers (extra-marital!) can be disastrous for a marriage. This lists of wants and values seems to show a failure to separate what is idealized and mythologized from what is (to put it very advisedly) authentic and genuinely possible in the daily reality of marital and family relationships over the long haul. To hear Sommers tell it, women are blandly unconcerned about wife-battering, incest, marital rape, or the profound economic vulnerability of the traditional non-income-earning wife. This is hard to believe. What is more likely is that, for many women, ". . . they got married and lived happily ever after," is only a fairy tale—especially for those who have been married for a while. Even the most traditional of women, I am convinced, has some sense of the risks involved in traditional heterosexual relationships. As an old saying goes, "When two hearts beat as one, someone is dead."

Sommers's list of women's wants and values is also woefully short. It suggests that this is *all* that "most women" want, that women's aspirations extend no farther than to being "feminine," getting a man—*any* man—and having babies. Many women want meaningful and fulfilling work apart from childcare and domestic labor. Many women aspire to making a social contribution, or they have artistic impulses seeking expression, spiritual callings, deep friendships with other women, and abiding concerns for moral value and their own integrity. One foundational motivation for feminism has always been the aim to overcome the *constraints* on women's genuinely wide-ranging aspirations posed by traditional marital and family arrangements.

9. What philosophical difference would it make if Sommers were right about women's wants and values in general? The popularity of an opinion is hardly an infallible measure of its empirical or moral credibility. Even popular opinions may be based on misinformation, unfounded rumor, and so on. Sommers ignores these possibilities and recommends that we defer to popular opinion on the basis of " . . . Mill's principle that there can be no appeal from a majority verdict of those who have experienced two alternatives" (1989a, 89–90). Sommers is evidently suggesting that feminist critiques of traditional family, marriage, and femininity should be judged by whether or not they conform to the "majority verdict of those who have experienced" the relevant alternatives. Now, carefully understood, this is actually not such a bad idea. However, rather than supporting Sommers's deference to popular opinion, this principle repudiates it.

First, there are more than just "two" feminist alternatives to any of the traditions in question. Feminist alternatives to traditional marriage and family include egalitarian heterosexual marriage, communal living, lesbian relationships, and single parenting when economic circumstances are favorable. To decide the value of traditional marriage and family, one would have to try all the relevant alternatives—or at least *some* of them. And on Mill's view, merely experiencing alternatives, is not enough; one must also be capable of "appreciating and enjoying" them (Mill, 1979, 9). If Sommers is right, however, most women want and choose only traditional marriage and family and, thus, do not either experience or enjoy living according to any feminist alternatives. Women such as these are not what Mill calls "competent judges"

of the value of those traditions since "they know only their own side of the question" (p. 10). And it is only from the verdict of *competent judges* that Mill believes that "there can be no appeal" (p. 11).

Second, of the "competent judges," in Mill's sense, that is, of the women who *have* experienced feminist alternatives to traditional marriage and family, most (I would wager) *prefer the feminist alternatives*. I am referring, among others, to women in lesbian relationships and women in genuinely egalitarian heterosexual relationships. If I am right about this, then on Mill's principle, we must reject "popular opinion" along with traditional marriage and the rest.

10. The truth of the matter is that, in the end, Sommers does not rest her case on Mill's principle. Apparently without realizing that she changes her argument, she ends by appealing to something less vaulted that the majority verdict of those who have experienced and enjoyed all the relevant alternatives. Her final court of appeal is simply to "what most people think," so-called "commonsense," and to "tradition" itself (1989a, 95, 97). Sommers urges simple deference to "the customs and opinions of the community" (1989a, 103). For her, "traditional arrangements have great moral weight and . . . common opinion is a primary source of moral truth" (1989a, 83).

Tradition, however, is a fickle husband. He is constantly changing his mind. On the grounds of tradition, eighty years ago, Sommers would have opposed women's suffrage. One hundred and fifty years ago, she would have opposed women speaking in public (she would have had to do so in private!), opposed the rights of married women to property in their own names, opposed the abolition of slavery, and so on. She would have supported wife-battering since it was permitted by legal tradition—so long as the rod was no bigger around than the size of the husband's thumb.

Not only is tradition ever-changing, it is also plural, both within our own society and globally. Which tradition shall we follow when there is more than one from which to choose? Islam is the world's most widely practiced religion. Shall we women in North America heed the most globally numerous of our sisters' voices and don the veil, retire from public life, and allow husbands to marry up to four wives? Within our own society, marital traditions also vary. Shall we follow the traditions of orthodox Jewish and orthodox Catholic women and avoid all contraceptives? My maternal grandmother did so; she had fourteen births. At nine months per gestation, she spent ten and a half years of her life being pregnant. Although she lingered on to the age of eighty-seven, she seemed even older than her age for the final sixteen, worn-out years of her life in which I knew her. Doubtless, that, too, was part of her tradition.

Why suppose that there is special merit to any of the alterative traditions that we happen to have at this historical moment in this particular geopolitical location? Why suppose that any of our current traditions are better or more deserving of loyalty and support than the traditions toward which we are evolving? And how will we ever evolve if we remain deadlocked in loyalty to all of the traditions we happen to have today?

11. Sommers allows that our traditions may need reform and even recommends "piecemeal social engineering" to deal with "imperfections" in the family (1989a, 97)—although it is noteworthy that she never specifies what these imperfections are, and, in a different passage, she inconsistently calls upon American feminism to leave marriage and motherhood simply "untouched and unimpugned" (1989a, 91). Nevertheless, she insists that her arguments are directed only against those radical feminists who seek the abolition of the family and the "radical reform" of preferences, values, and so on (1990, 20, 14).

A serious concern to reform the imperfections of the family should lead someone to consider the many reformist feminist criticisms of marital and family traditions (Thorne & Yalom, 1982; Okin, 1989). These approaches, however, are unmentioned in Sommers's writings. At any rate, this issue is a red herring. Disputes about the pace of reform do not show that radical feminist critiques of family traditions are wrong in substance. Most importantly, by allowing that change *is needed* in family traditions, Sommers effectively concedes that we should not automatically defer to tradition. To admit that reform of tradition is morally permissible is to reject tradition *per se* as an incontestable moral authority. The controversy can only be decided by directly evaluating the conditions of life established by marital and family traditions— and their alternatives.

12. Sommers has one final twist to her argument which we should consider. She notes briefly—all too briefly—that traditions "have a prima facie moral force" so long as they are not "essentially unjust" (1989a, 97). Sommers does not explain what she means by "essential injustice." Just how much injustice makes a traditional practice "essentially unjust"?

Despite its vagueness, this concession to injustice is critically important. It makes the merit of Sommers's own appeal to tradition contingent on the essential non-injustice of the particular traditions in question. Sommers, however, provides no argument to establish that traditional marriage practices and so forth are not essentially unjust. Nor does she respond substantively to those feminist arguments which claim to locate important injustices in these traditional practices. She rejects all feminist criticisms of the traditional family because they do not coincide with "popular opinion," "commonsense," or tradition.

We seem to have come full circle. Sommers rejects feminist critiques of traditional marriage and so on because they are inconsistent with popular opinion, commonsense, and tradition. Tradition is to be relied on, in turn, so long as it is not essentially unjust. But Sommers rejects feminist arguments to show injustices in marital and family traditions simply on the grounds that they are inconsistent with popular opinion, commonsense, and tradition itself. Sommers's defense of traditional marriage and family is, in the final analysis, circular and amounts to nothing more than simple *deference to tradition.*[4]

13. To conclude: My overall assessment of Sommers's views on marriage, family, and femininity is grim. Most importantly, Sommers rejects feminist views of marriage, family, and femininity ultimately on the basis of simple deference to (allegedly) popular opinion, commonsense, and tradition. This deference is defensible only if feminist views about the injustice of those traditions can be shown, on *independent* grounds, to be misguided—and Sommers never provides this independent argument.

Discussion Questions

1. Why does Professor Friedman accuse Professor Sommers of appealing to tradition and popular opinion? Explain why Professor Friedman thinks that these are inadequate ways to decide matters of social philosophy. Explain why you agree or disagree with Professor Friedman's critique. Do you think that Professor Friedman fairly assesses Professor Sommers's position? Explain and defend your answer.

2. In what ways does Professor Friedman challenge Professor Sommers's claim that radical feminists do not know what women really want? Do you think that Professor Friedman succeeds in her challenge? Why or why not?

3. Professor Friedman claims that Professor Sommers misuses John Stuart Mill's principle that

"there can be no appeal from a majority verdict of those who have experienced two alternatives." How does Professor Friedman support this claim and why does she think that Mill's principle can be used effectively *against* Professor Sommers's position? Do you agree with Professor Friedman? Explain and defend your answer.

Notes

1. Sommers repudiates the feminist literature which explores the value of mothering partly because it adopts a focus that "effectively excludes the male parent." (1989a, 92) Sommers forgets that in the traditional family the male parent plays a *negligible role* in day-to-day, primary childcare, especially in a child's early years. The comment also ignores the work of Nancy Chodorow (1978), which precisely urges *shared parenting* and, thus, a prominent role for the male parent. Chodorow's work has been extremely influential and widely cited among feminists.

2. Sommers complains that feminist philosophers have not been entrusted by ordinary women with a mission of speaking on behalf of those ordinary women (1989b, B3). Sommers, however, appears to think that she *is* thus entrusted, since she does not hesitate to make claims about what "most women . . . prefer," what "women actually want," and what "most women *enjoy*" (1989a, 90).

3. 1989a, 89–91. Sommers claims that "American feminism" has been attacking femininity at the expense of fighting "economic and social injustices to which women are subjected" (p. 90). American feminism has hardly neglected economic or social injustices against women. Ironically, Sommers herself seems to have published nothing on those injustices, and, in the essays reviewed here, does not even identify them.

4. Indeed, these particular traditions are no longer so pervasive or popular as Sommers thinks. If Sommers is right to blame feminists for contributing significantly to the growing divorce rate and the "disintegration of the traditional family," then it must be in virtue of the wide appeal of feminist criticisms of marriage and family.

Bibliography

Chodorow, Nancy. 1978. *The Reproduction of Mothering*. Berkeley: University of California Press.

Dahl, Arlene. 1965. *Always Ask a Man: Arlene Dahl's Key to Femininity*. Englewood Cliffs, N.J.: Prentice-Hall.

Mill, John Stuart. 1979. *Utilitarianism*. George Sher, ed. Indianapolis: Hackett.

Okin, Susan Moller. 1989. *Justice, Gender, and the Family*. New York: Basic Books.

Richards, Janet Radcliffe. 1980. *The Sceptical Feminist*. Harmondsworth: Penguin.

Sapiro, Virginia. 1990. *Women in American Society*. Mountain View, Calif.: Mayfield.

Sommers, Christina. 1988. "Should the Academy Support Academic Feminism." *Public Affairs Quarterly*, 2, 3 (July), 97–120

————. 1989a. "Philosophers against the Family." In: George Graham and Hugh LaFollette, eds. *Person to Person*. Philadelphia: Temple University Press, 82–105.

————. 1989b. "Feminist Philosophers Are Oddly Unsympathetic to the Women They Claim to Represent." *Chronicle of Higher Education*, October 11th, pp. B2–B3.

————. 1990. "The Feminist Revelation," presented at 1989 conference on Human Nature, Social Philosophy and Policy Center, Bowling Green State University (c. Basil Blackwell, 1990); page references are to typescript version.

Thorne, Barrie, with Marilyn Yalom, eds. 1982. *Rethinking the Family*. New York: Longman.

Vetterling-Braggin, Mary, Frederick A. Elliston, and Jane English, eds. 1977. *Feminism and Philosophy*. Totowa, N.J.: Littlefield, Adams & Co.

61

Do These Feminists Like Women?:
A Reply to Friedman's Response

Christina Hoff Sommers

A biographical sketch of Christina Hoff Sommers is found at the beginning of Chapter 59.

In this reply to Professor Marilyn Friedman, Professor Sommers clarifies her critique of radical feminism put forth in Chapter 59, "Philosophers against the Family," in addition to addressing specific criticisms in Professor Friedman's response. Professor Sommers argues that Professor Friedman gives the impression that Professor Sommers finds fault with all feminists. Rather, Professor Sommers distinguishes between *liberal* feminists and *gender* feminists and claims that her position is the former, and a legitimate feminist perspective. "The liberal feminist is not out to second guess what women want; if most women enjoy families, if they enjoy '*la différence*,' this is of no concern for them." On the other hand, "the gender feminist believes that women constitute an oppressed class within an oppressive system: what ails women cannot be cured by merely achieving equal opportunity." Consequently, the gender feminist, according to Professor Sommers, will never accept the testimonies of ordinary women, since the gender feminist believes that ordinary women have unconsciously bought into a system that oppresses them. Thus, without marshaling an argument (the very thing Professor Friedman accuses Professor Sommers of doing), the gender feminist simply presupposes her worldview and reinterprets all contrary facts as examples of false consciousness. Professor Sommers also addresses Professor Friedman's claims that Professor Sommers (1) defends a position indistinguishable from the view of women supported by 1960s

Reprinted by permission from *APA Newsletter on Feminism and Philosophy* 91, no. 1 (Spring 1992), 85–91.

actress and model Arlene Dahl, (2) misuses John Stuart Mill's principle, (3) naively and inadequately appeals to common opinion and tradition, and (4) fails to recognize that Rhett Butler raped Scarlett O'Hara in *Gone with the Wind*.

In presenting my views, Professor Friedman gives the impression that I find fault with all feminists.[1] But she well knows that I have made a plea for liberal feminism, and that my criticisms are directed to a popular school of thought to which she and all too many academic feminists belong, a school I call "gender feminism." Friedman says at the outset that it is not her primary purpose to defend feminism from my criticisms. Instead, she has assigned herself the not unpleasant chore of demonstrating that my views of family, motherhood and femininity are benighted and insensitive to feminist concerns. All the same, her failure to pay serious attention to my liberal criticisms of her own position effectively reduces her account of my views to an unfriendly caricature.

As I say, I am a liberal feminist. The liberal feminist is not out to second guess what women want; if most women enjoy families, if they enjoy "*la différence*," this is of no concern to them. It is no part of the agenda of the liberal feminist to change the desires and aspirations of women—especially when these desires and aspirations have been formed in an open and democratic society. The liberal feminist seeks legal equality for women and equality of opportunity in education and in the work place. I think it correct to say that liberal feminists, since Mary Wollstonecraft and John Stuart Mill, are more liberal than feminist; they want for women what any classical liberal wants for *anyone* who suffers bias: fair treatment.

By contrast, the gender feminist believes that women constitute an oppressed class within an oppressive system: what ails women cannot be cured by merely achieving equal opportunity. As a class women are seen to be politically at odds with the patriarchy that oppresses them. From the standpoint of gender feminism, the liberal's drive for parity and against discrimination misses the main point. The gender feminist has a radical perspective. She views social reality in terms of a patriarchal "sex/gender system" that, in the words of Sandra Harding, "organizes social life throughout most of recorded history and in every culture today."[2] Virginia Held considers the sex/gender system to be the controlling perspective of modern feminism. She tells us that feminists find it "intellectually gripping." And she reports: "Now that the sex/gender system has become visible to us, we can see it everywhere."[3]

For my part, I call anyone who adopts the sex/gender perspective on social reality a gender feminist. Their perspective has had a revolutionary effect on feminist theorizing and research. And of course the conviction that all culture and society is to be looked at in terms of a system of male domination informs the feminist struggle against the patriarchy and androcentricity in all aspects of life. On the intellectual side, it has led to demands for a "transformation of the academy" and to a search for a distinctively "woman's way of knowing." Those feminists who "see it everywhere" are convinced that the new perspective is introducing an intellectual revolution of historic dimensions. Says Elizabeth Minnich:

> What we [feminists] are doing, is comparable to Copernicus shattering our geocentricity, Darwin shattering our species-centricity. We are shattering andro-centricity, and the change is as fundamental, as dangerous, as exciting.[4]

The liberal feminist has little or no truck with this. I, for one, am embarrassed when I hear feminist theorists compare themselves to Copernicus or Darwin. I am saddened to see that gender feminism has proved to be so beguiling to so many feminist academics.

Friedman has chosen to discuss my views without focusing on my objections to gender feminism. But my views were formed in reaction to gender feminists who *reject* the family as we know it. These feminists present alternatives to the traditional family in which women no longer take primary responsibility for the rearing of children. For the gender feminist, the family is a bastion of the patriarchy, and many gender feminists propose new arrangements to replace it. It is in fact impossible to understand my use of the term "traditional family" without contrasting it to what some gender feminists would like to see in its place. Let me then quickly recite some of the proposals that have been made by some of the influential feminist philosophers that I criticize.

Ann Ferguson calls for a "radical reorganization of childrearing." She recommends the formation of "revolutionary family communities."[5] Carol Gould argues for androgyny and for abolishing legal marriage. She favors single parenting, co-parenting and communal parenting. The only arrangement she frowns upon is the traditional one where the mother provides primary care of the children.[6] Richard Wasserstrom argues for a sexually "assimilationist" society in which the gender system has been overthrown. "Bisexuality, not heterosexuality or homosexuality, would be the typical intimate, sexual relationship in the ideal society that was assimilationist in respect to sex."[7] Alison Jaggar defends a version of "socialist feminism" that envisions a society that is both classless and genderless. The socialist feminist utopia includes technological as well as sociological transformations of human nature. This ideal is partly illustrated in a science fiction story to which Jaggar calls our attention in which "Neither sex bears the children, but both sexes, through hormone treatments, suckle them. . . ."[8] To those who find this bizarre, Jaggar replies that this shows the depth of our prejudice regarding the "natural" basis of human social life. Some of the feminists I criticized are convinced that motherhood is demeaning to women. Here is Jeffner Allen telling us what being a mother really means:

> A mother is she whose body is used as a resource to reproduce men and the world of men. . . . Motherhood is dangerous to women because it continues the structure within which females must be women and mothers . . . It denies to females the creation of a . . . world that is open and free.[9]

Earlier, Simone de Beauvoir had described the pregnant women as a "stockpile of colloids, an incubator, an egg."[10] De Beauvoir was convinced that the modern family demeans women and she was fully prepared to use coercion to save women from the fate they unwittingly choose for themselves.

> No woman should be authorized to stay at home and raise her children . . . One should not have the choice precisely because if there is such a choice, too many women will make that one.[11]

Thus, my defense of the traditional family should be seen in the light of its gender feminist detractors. A word then about my use of "traditional family." Friedman treats it as synonymous with the "nuclear family," a technical term for families in which the man is the sole breadwinner. But that is not my usage: To me a traditional or natural family simply consists of two heterosexual parents and one or more children in which the mother plays a distinctive gender role in caring for the children. Moreover, if anyone wants some other arrangements, that is fine with me. Friedman would have you believe that I am *promoting* (that is her word) the traditional family, promoting motherhood, promoting femininity. As a liberal feminist all I do promote is the right and liberty to live under the arrangement of one's choice, be it traditional or nontraditional. But for that very reason I strongly object to those who find fault with women for being loyal to popular ideals of femininity, or to traditional norms of marriage and gender roles in the family.[12] Bluntly put: I dislike seeing women made to feel guilty because they choose to lead conventional lives. I particularly dislike it when *feminists*, in the name of a global struggle against male domination, make women feel that fidelity to conventional gender roles is tantamount to a betrayal of women.

I recently read a *New York Times* opinion piece that illustrates how quick the gender feminist is to condemn anything that smacks of conventional femininity. Amy Gelman, a New York editor and a feminist whose mother was a feminist before her, found that when she came to be married she wanted a traditional wedding, white dress, father walking her down the aisle and all. She wrote:

> More and more of my friends are surprising themselves and the people who know them by walking down the aisle in time-honored fashion. I know how strange they feel—but, in the end, I'll admit it was a wonderful walk to take.[13]

As you may imagine this did not sit well with the gender feminist. In a letter to the editor, S. T. Joshi of Hoboken, New Jersey, pointed out that Ms. Gelman's desire for a formal wedding "betrays how thoroughly and unconsciously she has been brainwashed into conventional social behavior. . . . Women will never get anywhere if they do not try to battle the systematic social indoctrination that is designed to keep them in a subordinate position."[14] And so it goes, on and on and on.

Note that it was not enough for Ms. Gelman to remind her audience of her impeccable credentials as a feminist activist. Where have we heard all of this before? The revolution devouring its own children, accusing them of final betrayal, of conscious or unconscious complicity, of joining forces with the enemy?

Let me now turn more directly to Friedman's discussion of my views. Friedman's tactic for discrediting my defense of the traditional family, motherhood and femininity consists mainly in casting doubt on what I and others take to be common knowledge. For example, she says that I *claim* most women want to marry, I claim they want children, I claim they enjoy feminine clothes, I claim they appreciate male gallantry and romantic weddings. Friedman reports

these claims suggesting they are all speculative and dubious. Thus she says, "Women, Sommers tells us, want children . . . and the time to care for children. . . . Sommers claims that women want marriage. . . . She asserts that 'most women' enjoy 'male gallantry,' that the 'majority of women' enjoy being 'treated by a man to a candlelight dinner,' and that 'many women . . . swoon at the sight of Rhett Butler carrying Scarlett up the stairs to a fate undreamt of in feminist philosophy.'"

One can just hear Friedman saying, "Now who in her right mind is going to believe that these things Sommers is telling us are true?" To which the only reasonable reply is "Who in her right mind *doubts* that these altogether commonplace things *are* true?"

Friedman, is, in fact, very careful not to come right out and say that any of the "claims" are false. Her tactic consists in insinuating that they are probably false or else not indicative of what women really want. Thus she tells us about her wealthy aunt who does not want to remarry, thereby casting doubt on the proposition that women tend to want to marry. Friedman knows very well that even the once bitten are not twice shy: most women who divorce or are widowed *do* remarry. But she discounts this commonplace fact. According to Friedman and other gender feminists, women differ from men in an important respect: what women *do* is no indicator of what women *want* to do. It is more an indicator of what they *have* to do.

But at other times, Friedman seems to acknowledge that many women *do* like dashing lovers, male gallantry, etc. She even seems to allow that most women want to be mothers and want conventional families. But then she falls back on discrediting my motives for calling *attention* to all these unpleasant truths about women. Not only do I announce these truths, I seem not to find them unpleasant and indeed I seem to be approving them. It is in this connection that she takes me to be promoting traditional lifestyles she considers harmful to women. Here she argues with me as one would argue with a person addicted to tobacco. Doesn't Sommers realize that some of the things women seem to want are bad for them, that wanting marriage, wanting a lot of children, angling for candlelight dinner-dates with a dashing lover, wanting to own that *wicked* pair of high heeled shoes, dreaming of being *swept off your feet by someone like Rhett Butler*?—does Sommers not see how degrading all this could be to a woman?

Well, as a liberal I am not in the business of second guessing the dreams and the passions of American women. Friedman and her sister gender feminists sit in judgment on the majority of American women, and they disapprove of what they see. They look upon most women as benighted in what they aspire to, incorrect in what they swoon at, complicitous and servile in their preferences. In all these respects the feminists find women sadly deficient and lacking in pride.

The gender feminists are of course keenly aware that what women want is at odds with what the feminists believe they *ought* to want. One of the busiest areas in feminist theory is speculation about why women are so resistant to their own emancipation.[15] In effect, Friedman does not have to deny the fact about what most women prefer: what really exercises her is that I have called attention to these facts without pointing out how *tragic* it all is. The fact that so many women fall into the marriage and baby trap, and seem to be enjoying many aspects of *la différence* is to be *deplored*. Why then is Sommers not lamenting them? Why does she recite these unfortunate truths without immediately following it by the obligatory incantation that women have been duped by the patriarchy, *conditioned* to want what they should not want?

To make matters worse, there are well known *correct* ways to talk of the unpleasant facts I talk about. Sandra Bartky, for example, in discussing women who like to dress in ways that feminists disapprove of, explains *why* women cling to those ways which so demean them. In her explanation, Bartky uses what she calls a "Foucauldian framework" to show that the "discipline" of popular femininity (make-up, skincare, haircare, feminine comportment, posture and gesture, clothing) is comparable to a penal colony from which women can never escape—since, as Ms. Bartky solemnly reports, "the ceaseless surveillance gets internalized as self-surveillance."[16]

It is thus possible to call attention to exactly the same facts but to do so in the proper way. When I say that most women want traditional families, children, etc., Friedman speaks snidely of "Sommers' alleged majority of women" who want those things. But when Alison Jaggar states that most women want to marry, Friedman does not object. For Jaggar knows *how* to state this unpleasant truth about women in terms acceptable to Friedman and other gender feminists.

Here's one way to do it right. Jaggar:

The ideology of romantic love has now become so pervasive that most women in contemporary capitalism probably believe they marry for love rather than for economic support.[17]

Now *that* is a paradigm of the acceptable way to state the very facts that I was pointing to. "Explain" that most women are in the thrall of a patriarchal capitalist culture that has rendered them incapable of distinguishing between love and economic necessity.

Friedman takes issue with me on my "claim," as she puts it, that many women prefer candlelight dinners to other dining alternatives. Here again she does not deny that they do prefer them, but she considers me, as it were, uncooperative for having brought it up. Well, as it happens, I am not the one who brought it up. I first came across the feminist discussion of the candlelight dinner in Alison Jaggar's influential article on prostitution. Jaggar had cited the feminist view that the average woman under patriarchy dresses for men, marries a man for protection, etc. Jaggar then tells us that "for the contemporary radical feminist prostitution is the archetypal relationship of women to men."[18]

Of course Jaggar, Friedman and other gender feminists are well aware that women do not think of themselves as prostitutes. They are even aware that women may well be offended at being so characterized. Here is the gender feminist reply. Again, I quote Jaggar:

Both man and woman might be outraged at the description of their candlelight dinner as prostitution, but the radical feminist argues this outrage is due simply to the participant's failure or refusal to perceive the social context in which their dinner date occurs.[19]

How patronizing and condescending this is! The "failure to perceive" afflicts most women except for the few elite feminists fitted with the gender feminist prism that enables them to see the sex/gender system "everywhere."

Friedman spends almost a fifth of her space telling us about the contents of a How-to-Get-a-Man-Book by Arlene Dahl, an actress I had not heard of before. It is not clear to me that 'servile' is the right word for the women who would practice the wiles Dahl describes. 'Manipulative' also comes to mind. And, of course, one could find books advising women to play distant and hard to get. But Friedman's thematic point is that we live in a patriarchal society in which femininity *means* obsequiousness. So Dahl's book is brought in evidence to show how women have interiorized their slavishness and become complicitous with the men that dominate them. Friedman sees the average woman as duped, as passive, as being in thrall to the patriarchy that shapes her values and even her fantasies. Here again we find Friedman looking at women as desperate and demoralized. "*Violà* femininity" as seen through the prism of gender feminism.

Friedman has throughout taken an anecdotal approach to my views and I have answered her in kind. Though the exchange between us is less than philosophical, it is instructive all the same. There are, however, two philosophical issues I should like to discuss. One concerns Mill and the other concerns the role of common opinion and tradition in morality. Both were hastily dealt with and again I answer in kind—hastily and sketchily.

I had expressed an admiration for Mill's empirical conception of happiness as defined by the actual preferences and desires of people. Friedman eagerly latches on to this, pointing out that it would deliver a verdict against the traditional family and for feminist alternatives. "Evidently," she says, "Sommers is suggesting that feminist critiques of the traditional family, marriage, and femininity should be judged by whether or not they conform to the 'majority verdict of those who have experienced' the relevant alternatives."

She goes on to say that getting the verdict of those women who have experienced both a traditional heterosexual family and various feminist alternatives is not at all a bad idea. Friedman is quite happy to point out that the verdict of *those* women will not favor the traditional family at all.

Note that Friedman is applying the dictum of preferential choice to whole lifestyles. But different lifestyles are often exclusive and not subject to comparison by a single person experiencing both and making a *preferential* choice.

Take the pivotal decision of whether to have children or never to have them. That is the case I discussed, and it is one that Friedman ignores. The choice of having or not having children is a choice between exclusive alternatives which, in the nature of the case, cannot be adjudicated by appealing to the verdict of those who have experienced both alternatives and have preferred one to the other. Though we cannot in such cases apply Mill's preferential principle, we still can and do appeal to common sense and common experience to help us choose wisely. Let us say, for the sake of argument, that of a thousand mothers taken at random, no more than

sixty regret having had children. On the other hand—again for the sake of argument (I have no statistical evidence)—assume that of a thousand childless women, now past the age of childbearing, more than two hundred express regret at never having had a child. Here we have nonpreferential evidence that is reasonable to attend to. This sort of appeal to common experience is valuable in considering how to live; and it is the kind of appeal that is entirely within the spirit of Mill's conception of happiness as defined by the desires of educated and informed persons. If, in fact, the feminists pay no heed to the regrets of women who chose not to have children, they do so at considerable risk to their happiness. They would be flouting Mill's wider principle that happiness is something empirically determined by common experience.

So not all verdicts of experience are preferential in the narrow sense. Moreover, even where Mill's narrow principle of preferential choice does apply, it is best to confine its application to simple cases like the candlelight dinner case. Choosing between two ways to dine is not like choosing between two ways to live. When the choice is between two lifestyles, the application of Mill's principle becomes dubious indeed. The other day I watched a television program featuring a guest who had been a man and was now a woman. She now says she prefers being a woman and that she is relieved at no longer having to be a man. Friedman believes that Millian verdicts of those who experience both apply to choices where the alternatives are whole lifestyles. She argues that women who experience feminist alternatives do prefer them to the traditional heterosexual arrangement they may have left, thereby delivering a Millian verdict against traditional marriage, family conventions, and femininity. But the case of the transsexual shows the risks of extending Mill's dictum to choosing between whole lifestyles. The transsexual case should give Friedman pause. The transsexual has experienced both and she prefers being a woman. Would Friedman be prepared to apply Mill's dictum here too, and would she then go on to argue that men who choose *not* to have their sex changed are flouting the utilitarian verdict from which there can be no appeal?

But in the end she does get *me* right at least, when she says, "Sommers does not rest her case on appealing to the majority verdict of those who have experienced and enjoyed both traditional and the various feminist alternatives." Quite right: I do not and for the reasons I just suggested. But now she faults me for speaking warmly of the Aristotelian and Sidgwickian appeals to common opinion as offering moral insight. Here Friedman charges me with simple deference to tradition, indeed to a devotion to particular traditions such as those governing wife beating in the nineteenth century.

That is unfair; my respect for tradition is not so fine grained, nor do I consider tradition and common sense to be final courts of appeal. When I defend the traditional family I mean to defend it as an institution from those who are attacking it as a bastion of the patriarchy and who want to replace it with what Friedman calls "feminist alternatives." I find it ironical that social philosophers like Friedman, who are generally respectful of the need for ecological caution in changing basic arrangements of nature, are so ready to play fast and loose with social arrangements and an institution like the family that have evolved over millennia. For me, a conservationist attitude in social philosophy and ethics is as important as a conservationist attitude in dealing with the natural environment. But, of course, I do not use tradition to block all reform. As Friedman reads me, I am the most callous of conservatives: I would even show what she calls simple deference to customs like wife battering, suttee or human sacrifice. But that is mere caricature: in one paper to which Friedman refers I distinguished between institutions and practices such as slavery and suttee that are essentially unjust and that cannot be reformed but must be *eliminated*, and institutions like the family that may have some unjust but corrigible elements.[20]

My appeal to common sense is qualified. Common sense considerations do often deliver conflicting verdicts. So an appeal to common opinion is never fully decisive. Rather it presents us with evidence that must figure importantly in the final verdict of what to do or how to live. Common sense opinion is symptomatic of a *prima facie* duty or liberty as the case may be. But though it is not decisive, it is strongly presumptive and may not be dismissed.

I have left my rejoinder to Friedman's reaction to the ever fascinating Rhett Butler for last. Friedman severely castigates me for saying "many women will continue to swoon at the sight of Rhett Butler carrying Scarlett up the stairs to a fate undreamt of in feminist philosophy." She finds that remark "simply stunning" and she pointedly reminds me that "a passing knowledge of feminist philosophy reveals that rape is hardly undreamt of in it." At the time I made the remark, I was unacquainted with a book that has since come into my hands called *Scarlett's Women: Gone with the Wind and Its Female Fans*.[21] The feminist author, Helen Taylor, actually did a *survey* of women who read *Gone with the Wind* or saw the movie asking them what they thought happened between Rhett and Scarlett on that memorable night. Here is the gist of what she learned:

> [T]he majority of my correspondents (and I agree) recognize the ambiguous nature of the encounter and interpret it as a scene of mutually pleasurable rough sex. . . . By far the majority of the women who responded to me saw the episode as erotically exciting, emotionally stirring and profoundly memorable. Few of them referred to it as 'rape.'[22]

Friedman objects to my failure to use the world 'rape—"one of the many omissions in [Sommers'] writings," she says. But Friedman is wrong to think of me as disingenuous. For I must confess: just as I am unable to see that most women under patriarchy are being prostituted, so too do I fail to see what is so evident to Friedman—that Scarlett was raped. Friedman *knows* Scarlett was raped, degraded, terrorized. (She actually compares Rhett Butler to the mass murderer/rapist Richard Speck.) So, once again, we have the gender feminist view that women are complicitously cooperating in their own degradation. Some of you might find Friedman's perverse insistence on rape simply stunning. Well, I too find it perverse, but I am not stunned. I read quite a lot of what the gender feminists write. And I have learned that they almost always interpret a text in a way that puts the most *humiliating* construction on women's experiences with men. The gender feminist "subtext" of almost everything written about men and women in the patriarchy is rape, prostitution, debasement of one kind or another.[23] For my part, I find such subtexts uniformly tiresome. But also I find them offensive. That gender feminists take a dim view of men is no news. I have been suggesting that they take an equally dim view of women: the gender feminist perspective on male-female relationships betrays a distinctly misogynist attitude to the women who persist in refusing to see themselves as the gender feminists see them.

A final word: Professor Friedman inveighs against me for appealing to common opinion and common sense, and she concludes that my kind of feminism is grim. She is right in one respect. *Her* kind of feminism is at odds with common opinion and *her* conclusions are admirably free of any *taint* of common sense. I won't call her feminist philosophy grim. On the other hand I must say I am quite unable to see anything cheerful in the way she looks upon us all.[24]

Discussion Questions

1. Why does Professor Sommers believe that gender feminists are wrong in not taking into consideration the wants and needs of ordinary women? How does Professor Sommers respond to the gender feminist charge that such women are suffering from "false consciousness"? Do you find her case persuasive? Explain and defend your answer.

2. How does Professor Sommers respond to Professor Friedman's charge that her appeals to common opinion and tradition are naive and inadequate? Do you think that Professor Sommers's response answers Professor Friedman's concerns? Explain and defend your answer.

3. How does Professor Sommers respond to Professor Friedman's critique of her use of John Stuart Mill's principle? Do you think Professor Sommers adequately responds to Professor Friedman? Explain and defend your answer.

Notes

1. The exchange between Professor Friedman and me was sponsored by the Society of Women in Philosophy. It took place at the Eastern Meetings of the American Philosophical Association on December 27, 1990.

2. Sandra Harding, "Why Has the Sex/Gender System Become Visible Only Now," in Sandra Harding and Merrill Hintikka, eds., *Discovering Reality: Feminist Perspectives on Science* (Dordrecht: D. Reidel, 1983), p. 312.

3. Virginia Held, "Feminism and Epistemology: Recent Work on the Connection Between Gender and Knowledge," *Philosophy and Public Affairs*, vol. 14, no. 3 (Summer 1985), pp. 296–307.

4. Elizabeth Minnich, "Friends and Critics: The Feminist Academy" (Keynote Address), Proceedings of the Fifth Annual GLCA Women's Studies Conference (November, 1979).

5. Ann Ferguson, "Androgyny as an Ideal for Human Development," in M. Vetterling-Braggin, F. Ellisten and J. English, ed., *Feminism and Philosophy* (Totowa, NJ: Rowman and Littlefield, 1977), p. 66.

6. Carol Gould, "Private Rights and Public Virtues: Women, the Family and Democracy," in Carol Gould, ed., *Beyond Domination* (Totowa, NJ: Rowman and Allanheld, 1983), pp. 3–18.

7. Richard Wasserstrom, "Racism and Sexism," in *Philosophy and Social Issues* (Notre Dame: University of Notre Dame Press, 1980), p. 26.

8. Alison Jaggar, "Human Biology in Feminist Theory: Sexual Equality Reconsidered," in Gould, *Beyond Domination*, p. 41.

9. Jeffner Allen, "Motherhood: The Annihilation of Women," in Joyce Trebilcot, ed., *Mothering: Essays in Feminist Theory* (Totowa, NJ: Rowman and Allanheld, 1984), p. 315.

10. Simone de Beauvoir, *The Second Sex*, tr. H. M. Priestly (New York: Random House, 1952), p. 553.

11. From "Sex, Society and the Female Dilemma: A Dialogue between Simone de Beauvoir and Betty Friedan," *Saturday Review* (June 14, 1975); quoted in Nicholas Davidson, *The Failure of Feminism* (Buffalo: Prometheus Books, 1988), p. 17.

12. Reports on the demise of the conventional "Ozzie and Harriet" family are exaggerated. Here are figures from the U.S. Government Bureau of Labor Statistics of families with pre-school children: (1) Father working full-time outside the home, mother at home 33.3%, (2) Father full-time, mother part-time 15.8%, (3) both mother and father working full-time outside the home 28.8%, (4) Single mother in labor force 10.1%, (5) Single mother not in labor force 7.3%, (6) Mother working full-time, father at home 2.7%, (7) Single father in labor force 2%. Figures for *all* women with children under 18: 40% in the work force full-time, 40% at home, 20% in work force part-time.

13. Amy Gelman, "Down the Aisle, Surprised," *New York Times* October 24, 1990.

14. S. T. Joshi, letter to the editor, *New York Times*, November 2, 1990.

15. See, for example, Alison Jaggar on "false consciousness," in Jaggar, *Feminist Politics and Human Nature* (Totowa: Rowman and Allanheld, 1983), pp. 150–151; or Catharine MacKinnon on why women fear sex equality in *Feminism Unmodified* (Cambridge: Harvard University Press, 1989), p. 226.

16. Sandra Bartky, "Women, Bodies and Power: A Research Agenda for Philosophy," in *APA Newsletter on Feminism and Philosophy*, Fall 1989, vol. 89:1, pp. 78–81.

17. Jaggar, *Feminist Politics and Human Nature*, p. 219.

18. Alison Jaggar, "Prostitution," in Marilyn Pearsell, ed., *Women and Values: Reading in Recent Feminist Philosophy* (Belmont, CA: Wadsworth, 1986), pp. 108–121.

19. Jaggar, "Prostitution," p. 117.

20. See "Philosophers Against the Family," in Hugh LaFollette and George Graham, eds., *Person to Person* (Philadelphia: Temple University Press); or "Filial Morality," in the *Journal of Philosophy*, no. 8 (August 1986).

21. Helen Taylor, *Scarlett's Women: Gone with the Wind and Its Female Fans* (New Brunswick, NJ: Rutgers University Press, 1989).

22. *Scarlett's Women*, p. 130 and p. 133.

23. From where Friedman stands, to discuss marriage and the family without highlighting marital rape and bat-

tering is to render the raped and battered women 'invisible.' Friedman, secure in her possession of the high moral ground, repeatedly accuses me of this offense. My only defense is that I do not identify marriage with being battered or raped, any more than I identify parenting with child abuse.

24. For further criticism of gender feminism see Christina Sommers, "The Feminist Revelation," *Social Philosophy and Public Policy*, vol. 8, Issue 1, Fall 1990.

62

Justice, Gender, and the Family

Susan Moller Okin

Susan Moller Okin is Professor of Political Science and Director of the Ethics in Society Program at Stanford University. She is the author of numerous works in social and political philosophy, including the books *Justice, Gender, and the Family* (1989) and *Women in Western Political Thought* (1979).

In this essay Professor Okin argues that the "traditional family" and the cultural assumptions entailed by it are inherently unjust. She defines the traditional family as father, mother, and children, in which the father is the primary income resource and the mother is the chief caretaker of the home and children. The reason why these roles exist, according to Okin, has nothing to do with their being essential to each gender (e.g., women are naturally better at nurturing children). Rather they are the result of social construction. That is, gender role differences are largely socially produced. Professor Okin calls this "the construction of gender." Consequently, if the traditional unjust gender roles have been socially constructed, then just gender roles can be socially constructed as well. Even though our society prides itself on its democratic values, Professor Okin maintains that there are "substantial inequalities between the sexes in our society today." She argues that such inequalities are the result of our culture's acceptance of the traditional family; at the same time she calls for more equality for women in society at large. Professor Okin believes that contemporary theories of justice (see Section B of Part III of this text) have not adequately addressed the issue of what constitutes a just family structure. Although there are a number of reasons for this, she believes, the primary reason is that most works of contem-

porary political theory do not discuss the family because it is assumed that the family is "nonpolitical." She gives three reasons why this is unacceptable.

We as a society pride ourselves on our democratic values. We don't believe people should be constrained by innate differences from being able to achieve desired positions of influence or to improve their well-being; equality of opportunity is our professed aim. The Preamble to our Constitution stresses the importance of justice, as well as the general welfare and the blessings of liberty. The Pledge of Allegiance asserts that our republic preserves "liberty and justice for all."

Yet substantial inequalities between the sexes still exist in our society. In economic terms, full-time working women (after some very recent improvement) earn on average 71 percent of the earnings of full-time working men. One-half of poor and three-fifths of chronically poor households with dependent children are maintained by a single female parent. The poverty rate for elderly women is nearly twice that for elderly men.[1] On the political front, [women are disproportionally unrepresented in the Congress and the courts]. . . . Underlying and intertwined with all these inequalities is the unequal distribution of the unpaid labor of the family.

An equal sharing between the sexes of family responsibilities, especially child care, is "the great revolution that has not happened."[2] Women, including mothers of young children, are, of course, working outside the household far more than their mothers did. And the small proportion of women who reach high-level positions in politics, business, and the professions command a vastly disproportionate amount of space in the media, compared with the millions of women who work at low-paying, dead-end jobs, the millions who do part-time work with its lack of benefits, and the millions of others who stay home performing for no pay what is frequently not even acknowledged as work. Certainly, the fact that women are doing more paid work does not imply that they are more equal. It is often said that we are living in a postfeminist era. This claim, due in part to the distorted emphasis on women who have "made it," is false, no matter which of its meanings is intended. It is certainly not true that feminism has been vanquished, and equally untrue that it is no

Reprinted by permission from Susan Moller Okin, *Justice, Gender, and the Family* (New York: Basic Books, 1989), 3–22.

longer needed because its aims have been fulfilled. Until there is justice within the family, women will not be able to gain equality in politics, at work, or in any other sphere.

. . . [T]he typical current practices of family life, structured to a large extent by gender, are not just. Both the expectation and the experience of the division of labor by sex make women vulnerable. . . . [A] cycle of power relations and decisions pervades both family and workplace, each reinforcing the inequalities between the sexes that already exist within the other. Not only women, but children of both sexes, too, are often made vulnerable by gender-structured marriage. One-quarter of children in the United States now live in families with only one parent—in almost 90 percent of cases, the mother. Contrary to common perceptions—in which the situation of never-married mothers looms largest—65 percent of single-parent families are a result of marital separation or divorce.[3] Recent research in a number of states has shown that, in the average case, the standard of living of divorced women and the children who live with them plummets after divorce, whereas the economic situation of divorced men tends to be better than when they were married.

A central source of injustice for women these days is that the law, most noticeably in the event of divorce, treats more or less as equals those whom custom, workplace discrimination, and the still conventional division of labor within the family have made very unequal. Central to this socially created inequality are two commonly made but inconsistent presumptions: that women are primarily responsible for the rearing of children; and that serious and committed members of the work force (regardless of class) do not have primary responsibility, or even shared responsibility, for the rearing of children. The old assumption of the workplace, still implicit, is that workers have wives at home. It is built not only into the structure and expectations of the workplace but into the other crucial social institutions, such as schools, which make no attempt to take account, in their scheduled hours or vacations, of the fact that parents are likely to hold jobs.

Now, of course, many wage workers do not have wives at home. Often, they *are* wives and mothers, or single, separated, or divorced mothers of small children. But neither the family nor the workplace has taken much account of this fact. Employed wives still do by far the greatest proportion of unpaid family work, such as child care and housework. Women are far more likely to take time out of the workplace or to work part-time because of family responsibilities than are their husbands or male partners. And they are much more likely to move because of their husbands' employment needs or opportunities than their own. All these tendencies, which are due to a number of factors, including the sex segregation and discrimination of the workplace itself, tend to be cyclical in their effects: wives advance more slowly than their husbands at work and thus gain less seniority, and the discrepancy between their wages increases over time. Then, because both the power structure of the family and what is regarded as consensual "rational" family decision making reflect the fact that the husband usually earns more, it will become even less likely as time goes on that the unpaid work of the family will be shared between the spouses. Thus the cycle of inequality is perpetuated. Often hidden from view within a marriage, it is in the increasingly likely event of marital breakdown that the socially constructed inequality of married women is at its most visible.

This is what I mean when I say that gender-structured marriage *makes* women vulnerable. These are not matters of natural necessity, as some people would believe. Surely nothing in our natures dictates that men should not be equal participants in the rearing of their children. Nothing in the nature of work makes it impossible to adjust it to the fact that people are parents as well as workers. That these things have not happened is part of the historically, socially constructed differentiation between the sexes that feminists have come to call *gender*. We live in a society that has over the years regarded the innate characteristic of sex as one of the clearest legitimizers of different rights and restrictions, both formal and informal. While the legal sanctions that uphold male dominance have begun to be eroded in the past century, and more rapidly in the last twenty years, the heavy weight of tradition, combined with the effects of socialization, still works powerfully to reinforce sex roles that are commonly regarded as of unequal prestige and worth. The sexual division of labor has not only been a fundamental part of the marriage contract, but so deeply influences us in our formative years that feminists of both sexes who try to reject it can find themselves struggling against it with varying degrees of ambivalence. Based on this linchpin, "gender"—by which I mean *the deeply entrenched institutionalization of sexual difference*—still permeates our society.

The Construction of Gender

Due to feminism and feminist theory, gender is coming to be recognized as a social factor of major importance. Indeed, the new meaning of the word reflects the fact that so much of what has traditionally been thought of as sexual difference is now considered by many to be largely socially produced.[4] Feminist scholars from many disciplines and with radically different points of view have contributed to the enterprise of making gender fully visible and comprehensible. At one end of the spectrum are those whose explanations of the subordination of women focus primarily on biological difference as causal in the construction of gender,[5] and at the other hand are those who argue that biological difference may not even lie at the core of the social construction that is gender[6]; the views of the vast majority of feminists fall between these extremes. The rejection of biological determinism and the corresponding emphasis on gender as a social construction characterize most current feminist scholarship. Of particular relevance is work in psychology, where scholars have investigated the importance of female primary parenting in the formation of our gendered identities,[7] and in history and anthropology,[8] where emphasis has been placed on the historical and cultural variability of gender. Some feminists have been criticized for developing theories of gender that do not take sufficient account of differences *among* women, especially race, class, religion, and ethnicity.[9] While such critiques should always inform our research and improve our arguments, it would be a mistake to allow them to detract our attention from gender itself as a factor of significance. Many injustices are experienced by women *as women*, whatever the differences among them and whatever other injustices they also suffer from. The past and present gendered nature of the family, and the ideology that surrounds it, affects virtually all women, whether or not they live or ever lived in traditional families. Recognizing this is not to deny or de-emphasize the fact that gender may affect different subgroups of women to a different extent and in different ways.

The potential significance of feminist discoveries and conclusions about gender for issues of social justice cannot be overemphasized. They undermine centuries of argument that started with the notion that not only the distinct differentiation of women and men but the domination of women by men, being natural, was therefore inevitable and not even to be considered in discussions of justice. . . . [D]espite the fact that such notions cannot stand up to rational scrutiny, they not only still survive but flourish in influential places.

During the same two decades in which feminists have been intensely thinking, researching, analyzing, disagreeing about, and rethinking the subject of gender, our political and legal institutions have been increasingly faced with issues concerning the injustices of gender and their effects. These issues are being decided within a fundamentally patriarchal system, founded in a tradition in which "individuals" were assumed to be male heads of households. Not surprisingly, the system has demonstrated a limited capacity for determining what is just, in many cases involving gender. Sex discrimination, sexual harassment, abortion, pregnancy in the workplace, parental leave, child care, and surrogate mothering have all become major and well-publicized issues of public policy, engaging both courts and legislatures. Issues of family justice, in particular—from child custody and terms of divorce to physical and sexual abuse of wives and children—have become increasingly visible and pressing, and are commanding increasing attention from the police and court systems. There is clearly a major "justice crisis" in contemporary society arising from issues of gender.

Theories of Justice and the Neglect of Gender

During these same two decades, there has been a great resurgence of theories of social justice. Political theory, which had been sparse for a period before the late 1960s except as an important branch of intellectual history, has become a flourishing field, with social justice as its central concern. Yet, remarkably, major contemporary theorists of justice have almost without exception ignored the situation I have just described. They have displayed little interest in or knowledge of the findings of feminism. They have largely bypassed the fact that the society to which their theories are supposed to pertain is heavily and deeply affected by gender, and faces difficult issues of justice stemming from its gendered past and present assumptions. Since theories of justice are centrally concerned with whether, how, and why persons should be treated differently from one another, this neglect seems inexplicable. These theories are *about* which initial or acquired characteristics or positions in society legitimize differential treatment of persons by social institutions, laws, and customs. They are *about* how and whether and to what extent beginnings should affect outcomes. The division of humanity into two sexes seems to provide an obvious subject for such inquiries. But, as we shall see, this does not strike most contemporary theorists of justice, and their theories suffer in both coherence and relevance because of it. . . .

Why is it that when we turn to contemporary theories of justice, we do not find illuminating and positive contributions to this question? How can theories of justice that are ostensibly about people in general neglect women, gender, and all the inequalities between the sexes? One reason is that most theorists *assume*, though they do not discuss, the traditional, gender-structured family. Another is that they often employ gender-neutral language in a false, hollow way. Let us examine [just the first point].

The Hidden Gender-Structured Family

In the past, political theorists often used to distinguish clearly between "private" domestic life and the "public" life of politics and the marketplace, claiming explicitly that the two spheres operated in accordance with different principles. They separated out the family from what they deemed the subject matter of politics, and they made closely related, explicit claims about the nature of women and the appropriateness of excluding them from civil and political life. Men, the subjects of the theories, were able to make the transition back and forth from domestic to public life with ease, largely because of the functions performed by women in the family.[10] When we turn to contemporary theories of justice, superficial appearances can easily lead to the impression that they are inclusive of women. In fact, they continue the same "separate spheres" tradition, by ignoring the family, its division of labor, and the related economic dependency and restricted opportunities of most women. The judgment that the family is "nonpolitical" is implicit in the fact that it is simply not discussed in most works of political theory today. In one way or another, as will become clear in the chapters that follow, almost all current theorists continue to assume that the "individual" who is the basic subject of their theories is the male head of a fairly traditional household. Thus the application of principles

of justice to relations between the sexes, or within the household, is frequently, though tacitly, ruled out from the start. In the most influential of all twentieth-century theories of justice, that of John Rawls, family life is not only assumed, but is assumed to be just—and yet the prevalent gendered division of labor within the family is neglected, along with the associated distribution of power, responsibility, and privilege. . . .

Moreover, this stance is typical of contemporary theories of justice. They persist, despite the wealth of feminist challenges to their assumptions, in their refusal even to discuss the family and its gender structure, much less to recognize the family as a political institution of primary importance. . . . For gender is one aspect of social life about which clearly, in the United States in the latter part of the twentieth century, there are no shared understandings.

What is the basis of my claim that the family, while neglected, is *assumed* by theorists of justice? One obvious indication is that they take mature, independent human beings as the subjects of their theories without any mention of how they got to be that way. We know, of course, that human beings develop and mature only as a result of a great deal of attention and hard work, by far the greater part of it done by women. But when theorists of justice talk about "work," they mean paid work performed in the marketplace. They must be assuming that women, in the gender-structured family, continue to do their unpaid work of nurturing and socializing the young and providing a haven of intimate relations—otherwise there would be no moral subjects for them to theorize about. But these activities apparently take place outside the scope of their theories. Typically, the family itself is not examined in the light of whatever standard of justice the theorist arrives at.[11]

The continued neglect of the family by theorists of justice flies in the face of a great deal of persuasive feminist argument. . . . Scholars have clearly revealed the interconnections between the gender structure inside and outside the family and the extent to which the personal is political. They have shown that the assignment of primary parenting to women is crucial, both in forming the gendered identities of men and women and in influencing their respective choices and opportunities in life. Yet, so far, the simultaneous assumption and neglect of the family has allowed the impact of these arguments to go unnoticed in major theories of justice. . . .

Gender as an Issue of Justice

For three major reasons, this state of affairs is unacceptable. The first is the obvious point that women must be fully included in any satisfactory theory of justice. The second is that equality of opportunity, not only for women but for children of both sexes, is seriously undermined by the current gender injustices of our society. And the third reason is that, as has already been suggested, the family—currently the linchpin of the gender structure—must be just if we are to have a just society, since it is within the family that we first come to have that sense of ourselves and our relations with others that is at the root of moral development.

Counting Women In

When we turn to the great tradition of Western political thought with questions about the justice of the treatment of the sexes in mind, it is to little avail. Bold feminists like Mary Astell, Mary Wollstonecraft, William Thompson, Harriet Taylor, and George Bernard Shaw have occasionally challenged the tradition, often using its own premises and arguments to overturn its explicit or implicit justification of the inequality of women. But John Stuart Mill is a rare exception to the rule that those who hold central positions in the tradition almost never question the justice of the subordination of women.[12] This phenomenon is undoubtedly due in part to the fact that Aristotle, whose theory of justice has been so influential, relegated women to a sphere of "household justice"—populated by persons who are not fundamentally equal to the free men who participate in political justice, but inferiors whose natural function is to serve those who are more fully human. The liberal tradition, despite its supposed foundation of individual rights and human equality, is more Aristotelian in this respect than is generally acknowledged.[13] In one way or another, almost all liberal theorists have assumed that the "individual" who is the basic subject of the theories is the male head of a patriarchal household.[14] Thus they have not usually considered applying the principles of justice to women or to relations between the sexes.

When we turn to contemporary theories of justice, however, we expect to find more illuminating and positive contributions to the subject of gender and justice. As the omission of the family and the falseness of their gender-neutral language suggest, however, mainstream contemporary theories of justice do not address the subject any better than those of the past. Theories of justice that apply to only half of us simply won't do; the inclusiveness falsely implied by the current use of gender-neutral terms must become real. Theories of justice must apply to all of us, and to all of human life, instead of *assuming* silently that half of us take care of whole areas of life that are considered outside the scope of social justice. In a just society, the structure and practices of families must afford women the same opportunities as men to develop their capacities, to participate in political power, to influence social choices, and to be economically as well as physically secure.

Unfortunately, much feminist intellectual energy in the 1980s has gone into the claim that "justice" and "rights" are masculinist ways of thinking about morality that feminists should eschew or radically revise, advocating a morality of care.[15] The emphasis is misplaced, I think, for several reasons. First, what is by now a vast literature on the subject shows that the evidence for differences in women's and men's ways of thinking about moral issues is not (at least yet) very clear; neither is the evidence about the source of whatever differences there might be.[16] It may well turn out that any differences can be readily explained in terms of roles, including female primary parenting, that are socially determined and therefore alterable. There is certainly no evidence—nor could there be, in such a gender-structured society—for concluding that women are somehow naturally more inclined toward contextuality and away from universalism in their moral thinking, a false concept that unfortunately reinforced the old stereotypes that justify separate spheres. The capacity of reactionary forces to capitalize on the "different moralities" strain in feminism is particularly evident in Pope John Paul II's recent Apostolic Letter, "On the Dignity of Women," in which he refers to women's special capacity to care for others in arguing for confining them to motherhood or celibacy.[17]

Second, . . . I think the distinction between an ethic of justice and an ethic of care has been overdrawn. The best theorizing about justice, I argue, has integral to it the notions of care and empathy, of thinking of the interests and well-being of others who may be very different from ourselves. It is, therefore, misleading to draw a dichotomy as though they were two contrasting ethics. The best theorizing about justice is not some abstract "view from nowhere," but results from the carefully attentive consideration of *everyone's* point of view. This means, of course, that the best theorizing about justice is not good enough if it does not, or cannot readily be adapted to, include women and their points of view as fully as men and their points of view.

Gender and Equality of Opportunity

The family is a crucial determinant of our opportunities in life, of what we "become." It has frequently been acknowledged by those concerned with real equality of opportunity that the family presents a problem.[18] But though they have discerned a serious problem, these theorists have underestimated it because they have seen only half of it. They have seen that the disparity among families in terms of the physical and emotional environment, motivation, and material advantages they can give their children has a tremendous effect upon children's opportunities in life. We are not born as isolated, equal individuals in our society, but into family situations; some in the social middle, some poor and homeless, and some superaffluent; some to a single or soon-to-be-separated parent, some to parents whose marriage is fraught with conflict, some to parents who will stay together in love and happiness. Any claims that equal opportunity exists are therefore completely unfounded. Decades of neglect of the poor, especially of poor black and Hispanic households . . . have brought us farther from the principles of equal opportunity. To come close to them would require, for example, a high and uniform standard of public education and the provision of equal social services—including health care, employment training, job opportunities, drug rehabilitation, and decent housing—for all who need them. In addition to redistributive taxation, only massive reallocations of resources from the military to social services could make these things possible.

But even if all these disparities were somehow eliminated, we would still not attain equal opportunity for all. This is because what has not been recognized as an equal opportunity problem, except in feminist literature and circles, is the disparity *within* the family, the fact that its gender structure is itself a major obstacle to equality of opportunity. This is very important in itself, since one of the factors with most influence on our opportunities in life is the social significance attributed to our sex. The opportunities of girls and women are centrally affected by the structure and practices of family life, particularly by the fact that women are almost invariably primary parents. What nonfeminists who see in the family an obstacle to equal opportunity have *not* seen is that the extent to which a family is gender-structured can make the sex we belong to a relatively insignificant aspect of our identity and our life prospects or an all-pervading one. This is because so much of the social construction of gender takes place in the family, and particularly in the institution of female parenting.

Moreover, especially in recent years, with the increased rates of single motherhood, separation, and divorce, the inequalities between the sexes have *compounded* the first part of the problem. The disparity among families has grown largely because of the impoverishment of many women and children after separation or divorce. The division of labor in the typical family leaves most women far less capable than men of supporting themselves, and this disparity is accentuated by the fact that children of separated or divorced parents usually live with their mothers. The inadequacy—and frequent nonpayment—of child support has become recognized as a major social problem. Thus the inequalities of gender are now directly harming many children of both sexes as well as women themselves. Enhancing equal opportunity for women, important as it is in itself, is also a crucial way of improving the opportunities of many of the most disadvantaged children.

As there is a connection among the parts of this problem, so is there a connection among some of the solutions: much of what needs to be done to end the inequalities of gender, and to work in the direction of ending gender itself, will also help to equalize opportunity from one family to another. Subsidized, high-quality day care is obviously one such thing; another is the adaptation of the workplace to the needs of parents. . . .

The Family as a School of Justice

One of the things that theorists who have argued that families need not or cannot be just, or who have simply neglected them, have failed to explain is how, within a formative social environment that is *not* founded upon principles of justice, children can learn to develop that sense of justice they will require as citizens of a just society. Rather than being one among many co-equal institutions of a just society, a just family is its essential foundation.

It may seem uncontroversial, even obvious, that families must be just because of the vast influence they have on the moral development of children. But this is clearly not the case. . . . [U]nless the first and most formative example of adult interaction usually experienced by children is one of justice and reciprocity, rather than one of domination and manipulation or of unequal altruism and one-sided self-sacrifice, and unless they themselves are treated with concern and respect, they are likely to be considerably hindered in becoming people who are guided by principles of justice. Moreover, . . . the sharing of roles by men and women, rather than the division of roles between them, would have a further positive impact because of the experience of *being* a physical and psychological nurturer—whether of a child or of another adult—would increase that capacity to identify with and fully comprehend the viewpoints of others that is important to a sense of justice. In a society that minimized gender this would be more likely to be the experience of all of us.

Almost every person in our society starts life in a family of some sort or other. Fewer of these families now fit the usual, though by no means universal, standard of previous generations, that is, wage-working father, homemaking mother, and children. More families these days are headed by a single parent; lesbian and gay parenting is no longer so rare; many children have two wage-working parents, and receive at least some of their early care outside the home. While its forms are varied, the family in which a child is raised, especially in the earliest years, is clearly a crucial place for early moral development and for the formation of our basic attitudes to others. It is, potentially, a place where we can *learn* to be just. It is especially important for the development of a sense of justice that grows from sharing the experiences of others and becoming aware of the points of view of others who are different in some respects from ourselves, but with whom we clearly have some interests in common.

The importance of the family for the moral development of individuals was far more often recognized by political theorists of the past than it is by those of the present. Hegel, Rousseau, Tocqueville, Mill, and Dewey are obvious examples that come to mind. Rousseau, for example, shocked by Plato's proposal to abolish the family, says that it is

> as though there were no need for a natural base on which to form conventional ties; as though the love of one's nearest were not the principle of the love one owes the state; as though it were not by means of the small fatherland which is the family that the heart attaches itself to the large one.[19]

Defenders of both autocratic and democratic regimes have recognized the political importance of different family forms for the formation of citizens. On the one hand, the nineteenth-century monarchist Louis de Bonald argued against the divorce reforms of the French Revolution, which he claimed had weakened the patriarchal family, on the grounds that "in order to keep the state out of the hands of the people, it is necessary to keep the family out of the hands of women and children."[20] Taking this same line of thought in the opposite direction, the U.S. Supreme Court decided in 1879 in *Reynolds v. Nebraska* that familial patriarchy fostered despotism and was therefore intolerable. Denying Mormon men the freedom to practice polygamy, the Court asserted that it was an offense "subversive of good order" that "leads to the patriarchal principles, . . . [and] when applied to large communities, fetters the people in stationary despotism, while that principle cannot long exist in connection with monogamy."[21]

However, while de Bonald was consistent in his adherence to an hierarchical family structure as necessary for an undemocratic political system, the Supreme Court was by no means consistent in promoting an egalitarian family as an essential underpinning for political democracy. For in other decisions of the same period—such as *Bradwell v. Illinois*, the famous 1872 case that upheld the exclusion of women from the practice of law—the Court rejected women's claims to legal equality, in the name of a thoroughly patriarchal, though monogamous, family that was held to require the dependence of women and their exclusion from civil and political life.[22] While bigamy was considered patriarchal, and as such a threat to republican, democratic government, the refusal to allow a married woman to employ her talents and to make use of her qualifications to earn an independent living was not considered patriarchal. It was so far from being a threat to the civil order, in fact, that it was deemed necessary for it, and as such was ordained by both God and nature. Clearly, in both *Reynolds* and *Bradwell*, "state authorities enforced family forms preferred by those in power and justified as necessary to stability and order."[23] The Court noticed the despotic potential of polygamy, but was blind to the despotic potential of patriarchal monogamy. This was perfectly acceptable to them as a training ground for citizens.

Most theorists of the past who stressed the importance of the family and its practices for the wider world of moral and political life by no means insisted on congruence between the structures or practices of the family and those of the outside world. Though concerned with moral development, they bifurcated public from private life to such an extent that they had no trouble reconciling inegalitarian, sometimes admittedly unjust, relations founded upon sentiment within the family with a more just, even egalitarian, social structure outside the family. Rousseau, Hegel, Tocqueville—all thought the family was centrally important for the development of morality in citizens, but all defended the hierarchy of the marital structure while spurning such a degree of hierarchy in institutions and practices outside the household. Preferring instead to rely on love, altruism, and generosity as the basis for family relations, none of these theorists argued for *just* family structures as necessary for socializing children into citizenship in a just society.

The position that justice within the family is irrelevant to the development of just citizens was not plausible even when only men were citizens. John Stuart Mill, in *The Subjection of Women*, takes an impassioned stand against it. He argues that the inequality of women within the family is deeply subversive of justice in general in the wider social world, because it subverts the moral potential of men. Mill's first answer to the question, "For whose good are all these changes in women's rights to be undertaken?" is: "the advantage of having the most universal and pervading of all human relations regulated by justice instead of injustice." Making marriage a relationship of equals, he argues, would transform this central part of daily life from "a school of despotism" into "a school of moral cultivation."[24] He goes on to discuss, in the strongest of terms, the noxious effect of growing up in a family not regulated by justice. Consider, he says, "the self-worship, the unjust self-preference," nourished in a boy growing up in a household in which "by the mere fact of being born a male he is by right the superior of all and every one of an entire half of the human race." Mill concludes that the example set by perpetuating a marital structure "contradictory to the first principles of social justice" must have such "a perverting influence" that it is hard even to imagine the good effects of changing it. All other attempts to educate people to respect and practice justice, Mill claims, will be superficial "as long as the citadel of the enemy is not attacked." Mill felt as much hope for what the family might be as he felt despair at what it was not. "The family, justly constituted, would be the real school of the virtues of freedom," primary among which was "justice, . . . grounded as before on equal, but now also on sympathetic association."[25] Mill both saw clearly and had the courage to address what so many other political philosophers either could not see, or saw and turned away from.

Despite the strength and fervor of his advocacy of women's rights, however, Mill's idea of a just family structure falls far short of that of many feminists even of his own time, including his wife, Harriet Taylor. In spite of the fact that Mill recognized both the empowering effect of earnings on one's position in the family and the limiting effect of domestic responsibility on women's opportunities, he balked at questioning the traditional division of labor between the sexes. For him, a woman's choice of marriage was parallel to a man's choice of a profession: unless and until she had fulfilled her obligations to her husband and children, she should not undertake anything else. But clearly, however equal the legal rights of husbands and wives, this position largely undermines Mill's own insistence upon the importance of marital equality for a just society. His acceptance of the traditional division of labor, without making any provision for wives who were thereby made economically dependent upon their husbands, largely undermines his insistence upon family justice as the necessary foundation for social justice.

Thus even those political theorists of the past who have perceived the family as an important school of moral development have rarely acknowledged the need for congruence between the family and the wide social order, which suggests that families themselves need to be just. Even when they have, as with Mill, they have been unwilling to push hard on the traditional division of labor within the family in the name of justice or equality.

Contemporary theorists of justice, with few exceptions, have paid little or no attention to the question of moral development—of how we are to *become* just. Most of them seem to think, to adapt slightly Hobbes's notable phrase, that just men spring like mushrooms from the earth.[26] Not surprisingly, then, it is far less often acknowledged in recent than in past theories that the family is important for moral development, and especially for instilling a sense of justice. As I have already noted, many theorists pay no attention at all to either the family or gender. In the rare case that the issue of justice within the family is given any sustained attention, the family is not viewed as a potential school of social justice.[27] In the rare case that a theorist pays any sustained attention to the development of a sense of justice or morality, little if any attention is likely to be paid to the family.[28] Even in the rare event that theorists pay considerably attention to the family *as* the first major locus of moral socialization, they do not refer to the fact that families are almost all still thoroughly gender-structured institutions.[29]

Among major contemporary theorists of justice, John Rawls alone treats the family seriously as the earliest school of moral development. He argues that a just, well-ordered society will be stable only if its members continue to develop a sense of justice. And he argues that families play a fundamental role in the stages by which this sense of justice is acquired. From the parents' love for their child, which comes to be reciprocated, comes the child's "sense of his own value and the desire to become the sort of person that they are."[30] The family, too, is the first of that series of "associations" in which we participate, from which we acquire the capacity, crucial for a sense of justice, to see things from the perspectives of others. . . . This capacity—the capacity for empathy—is essential for maintaining a sense of justice of the Rawlsian kind. For the perspective that is necessary for maintaining a sense of justice is not that of the egoistic or disembodied self, or of the dominant few who overdetermine "our" traditions or "shared understandings," or (to use Nagel's term) of "the view from nowhere," but rather the perspective of every person in the society for whom the principles of justice are being arrived at. . . . The problem with Rawls's rare and interesting discussion of moral development is that it rests on the unexplained *assumption* that family institutions are just. If gendered family institutions are *not* just, but are, rather, a relic of caste or feudal societies in which responsibilities, roles, and resources are distributed, not in accordance with the principles of justice he arrives at or with any other commonly respected values, but in accordance with innate differences that are imbued with enormous social significance, then Rawls's theory of moral development would seem to be built on uncertain ground. This problem is exacerbated by suggestions in some of Rawls's most recent work that families are "private institutions," to which it is not appropriate to apply standards of justice. But if families are to help form just individuals and citizens, surely they must be *just families*.

In a just society, the structure and practices of families must give women the same opportunities as men to develop their capacities, to participate in political power and influence social choices, and to be economically secure. But in addition to this, families must be just because of the vast influence that they have on the moral development of children. The family is the primary institution of formative and moral development. And the structure and practices of the family must parallel those of the larger society if the sense of justice is to be fostered and maintained. While many theorists of justice, both past and present, appear to have denied the importance of at least one of these factors, my own view is that both are absolutely crucial. A society that is committed to equal respect for all of its members, and to justice in social distributions of benefits and responsibilities, can neither neglect the family nor accept family structures and practices that violate these norms, as do current gender-based structures and practices. It is essential that children who are to develop into adults with a strong sense of justice and commitment to just institutions spend their earliest and most formative years in an environment in which they are loved and nurtured, *and* in which principles of justice are abided by and respected. What is a child of either sex to learn about fairness in the average household with two full-time working parents, where the mother does, at the very least, twice as much family work as the father? What is a child to learn about the value of nurturing and domestic work in a home with a traditional division of labor in which the father either subtly or not so subtly uses the fact that he is the wage earner to "pull rank" on or to abuse his wife? What is a child to learn about responsibility for others in a family in which, after many years of arranging her life around the needs of her husband and children, a woman is faced with having to provide for herself and her children but is totally ill-equipped for the task by the life she agreed to lead, has led, and expected to go on leading? . . .

Discussion Questions

1. What does Professor Okin mean by the "construction of gender"? Do you agree with her view of gender? Why or why not? Explain and defend your answer.

2. Professor Okin maintains that the traditional family and marriage (or "gendered structure of the family") are major obstacles to justice for women. What does she mean by this and how does she defend it?

3. Professor Okin claims that contemporary political theorists do not discuss the justice of family structures. How does she defend that claim? Present and explain the three reasons why she thinks the

current state of political theory is unacceptable.

4. How does Professor Okin suggest principles of justice should be used in judging family structures as just or unjust?

5. How does Professor Okin defend her assertion that there are "substantial inequalities between the sexes in our society today"? How does she think these inequalities have come about?

6. Professor Okin maintains that the traditional family teaches children injustice. How does she defend this position? Do you agree with her? Why or why not? Explain and defend your answer.

Notes

1. U.S. Department of Labor, *Employment and Earnings: July 1987* (Washington, D.C.: Government Printing Office, 1987); Ruth Sidel, *Women and Children Last: The Plight of Poor Women in Affluent America* (New York: Viking, 1986), pp. xvi, 158. See also David T. Ellwood, *Poor Support: Poverty in the American Family* (New York: Basic Books, 1988), pp. 84–85, on the chronicity of poverty in single-parent households. . . .

2. Shirley Williams, in Williams and Elizabeth Holtzman, "Women in the Political World: Observations," *Daedalus* 116, no. 4 (Fall 1987): 30.

3. Twenty-three percent of single parents have never been married and 12 percent are widowed. (U.S. Bureau of the Census, Current Population Reports, *Household and Family Characteristics: March 1987* [Washington, D.C.: Government Printing Office, 1987], p. 79). In 1987, 6.8 percent of children under eighteen were living with a never-married parent. ("Study Shows Growing Gap Between Rich and Poor," *New York Times*, March 23, 1989, p. A24). The proportions for the total population are very different from those for black families, of whom in 1984 half of those with adult members under thirty-five years of age were maintained by single, female parents, three-quarters of whom were never married. (Frank Levy, *Dollars and Dreams: The Changing American Income Distribution* [New York: Russell Sage, 1987], p. 156).

4. As Joan Scott has pointed out, *gender* was until recently used only as a grammatical term. See "Gender: A Useful Category of Historical Analysis," in Joan Wallach Scott, *Gender and the Politics of History* (New York: Columbia University Press, 1988), p. 28, citing Fowler's *Dictionary of Modern English Usage*.

5. Among Anglo-American feminists see, for example, Mary Daly, *Gyn/Ecology: The Metaethics of Radical Feminism* (Boston: Beacon Press, 1978); Susan Griffin, *Woman and Nature: The Roaring Inside Her* (New York: Harper & Row, 1978). For a good, succinct discussion of radical feminist biological determinism, see Alison Jaggar, *Feminist Politics and Human Nature* (Totowa, N.J.: Rowman and Allanheld, 1983).

6. See, for example, Sylvia Yanagisako and Jane Collier, "The Mode of Reproduction in Anthropology," in *Theoretical Perspectives on Sexual Difference*, ed. Deborah Rhode (New Haven: Yale University Press, in press).

7. Nancy Chodorow, *The Reproduction of Mothering: Psychoanalysis and the Sociology of Gender* (Berkeley: University of California Press, 1978); Dorothy Dinnerstein, *The Mermaid and the Minotaur: Sexual Arrangements and Human Malaise* (New York: Harper & Row, 1976). . . .

8. Linda Nichols, *Gender and History* (New York: Columbia University Press, 1986); Michelle Z. Rosaldo, "The Use and Abuse of Anthropology," *Signs* 5, no. 3 (1980); Joan Wallach Scott, *Gender and the Politics of History* (New York: Columbia University Press, 1986).

9. For such critiques, see Bell Hooks, *Ain't I a Woman: black women and feminism* (Boston: South End Press, 1981), and *Feminist Theory: from margin to center* (Boston: South End Press, 1984); Elizabeth V. Spelman, *Inessential Woman: Problems of Exclusion in Feminist Thought* (Boston: Beacon Press, 1989).

10. There is now an abundant literature on the subject of women, their exclusion from nondomestic life, and the reasons given to justify it, in Western political theory. See, for example, Lorenne J. Clark and Lynda Lange, eds., *The Sexism of Social and Political Thought* (Toronto: University of Toronto Press, 1979); Jean Bethke Elshtain, *Public Man, Private Woman: Woman in Social and Political Thought* (Princeton: Princeton University Press, 1981); Genevieve Lloyd, *The Man of Reason: "Male" and "Female" in Western Philosophy* (Minneapolis: University of Minnesota Press, 1984); Mary O'Brien, *The Politics of Reproduction* (London: Routledge & Kegan Paul, 1981); Susan Moller Okin, *Women in Western Political Thought* (Princeton: Princeton University Press, 1979); Carole Pateman, "Feminist Critiques of the Public/Private Dichotomy," in *Public and Private in Social Life*, ed. S. Benn and G. Gaus (London: Croom Helm, 1983); Carole Pateman and Elizabeth Gross, eds., *Feminist Challenges: Social and Political Theory* (Boston: Northeastern University Press, 1987); Carol Pateman, *The Sexual Contract* (Stanford: Stanford University Press, 1988); Carole Pateman and Mary L. Shanley, eds., *Feminist Critiques of Political Theory* (Oxford: Polity Press, in press).

11. This is commented on and questioned by Francis Schrag, "Justice and the Family," *Inquiry* 19 (1976): 200 and Michael Walzer, *Spheres of Justice* (New York: Basic Books, 1983), chap. 9.

12. I have analyzed some of the ways in which theorists in the tradition avoided considering the justice of gender in "Are Our Theories of Justice Gender-Neutral?" in *The Moral Foundations of Civil Rights*, ed. Robert Fullinwider and Claudia Mills (Totowa, N.J.: Rowman and Littlefield, 1986).

13. See Judith Hicks Stiehm, "The Unit of Political Analysis: Our Aristotelian Hangover," in *Discovering Reality: Feminist Perspectives on Epistemology, Metaphysics, Methodology, and Philosophy of Science*, ed. Sandra Harding and Merrill B. Hintikka (Dordrecht, Holland: Reidel, 1983).

14. See Carole Pateman and Theresa Brennan, "'Mere Auxiliaries to the Commonwealth': Women and the Origins of Liberalism," *Political Studies* 27, no. 2 (June 1979); also Susan Moller Okin, "Women and the Making of the Sentimental Family," *Philosophy and Public Affairs* 11, no. 1 (Winter 1982). This issue is treated at much greater length in Pateman, *The Sexual Contract.*

15. This claim, originating in the moral development literature, has significantly influenced recent feminist moral and political theory. Two central books are Carol Gilligan, *In a Different Voice* (Cambridge: Harvard University Press, 1982); and Nel Noddings, *Caring: A Feminine Approach to Ethics and Moral Education* (Berkeley: University of California Press, 1984). For the influence of Gilligan's work on feminist theory, see, for example, Seyla Benhabib, "The Generalized and the Concrete Other: The Kohlberg-Gilligan Controversy and Feminist Theory," in *Feminism as Critique,* ed. Benhabib and Drucilla Cornell (Minneapolis: University of Minnesota Press, 1987); Lawrence Blum, "Gilligan and Kohlberg: Implications for Moral Theory," *Ethics* 98, no. 3 (1988); and Eva Kittay and Diana Meyers, eds., *Women and Moral Theory* (Totowa, N.J.: Rowman and Allenheld, 1986). For a valuable alternative approach to the issues, and an excellent selective list of references to what has now become a vast literature, see Owen Flanagan and Kathryn Jackson, "Justice, Care and Gender: The Kohlberg-Gilligan Debate Revisited," *Ethics* 97, no. 3 (1987).

16. See, for example, John M. Broughton, "Women's Rationality and Men's Virtues: A Critique of Gender Dualism in Gilligan's Theory of Moral Development," *Social Research* 50, no. 3 (1983); Owen Flanagan, *Varieties of Moral Personality: Ethics and Psychological Realism* (Cambridge: Harvard University Press, forthcoming), ch. 8; Catherine G. Greeno and Eleanor E. Maccoby, "How Different Is the 'Different Voice'?" and Gilligan's reply, *Signs* 11, no. 2 (1986); Debra Nails, "Social-Scientific Sexism: Gilligan's Mismeasure of man," *Social Research* 50, no. 3 (1983); Joan Tronto, "'Women's Morality': Beyond Gender Difference to a Theory of Care," *Signs* 12, no. 4 (1987); Lawrence J. Walker, "Sex Differences in the Development of a Moral Reasoning: A Critical Review," *Child Development* 55 (1984).

17. See extracts from the Apostolic Letter in *New York Times,* October 1, 1988, pp. A1 and 6. On the reinforcement of the old stereotypes in general, see Susan Moller Okin, "Thinking like a Woman," in Rhode, ed., *Theoretical Perspectives.*

18. See esp. James Fishkin, *Justice, Equal Opportunity and the Family* (New Haven: Yale University Press, 1983); Derek L. Phillips, *Toward a Just Social Order* (Princeton, N.J.: Princeton University Press, 1986), esp. 346–49; John Rawls, *A Theory of Justice* (Cambridge, Mass.: Harvard University Press, 1971), pp. 74, 300–301, 511–12.

19. Jean-Jacques Rousseau, *Emile: or On Education,* trans. Allan Bloom (New York: Basic Books, 1979), p. 363.

20. Louis de Bonald, in *Archives Parlementaires,* 2e série (Paris, 1869), vol. 15, p. 612; cited and translated by Roderick Phillips, "Women and Family Breakdown in Eighteenth-Century France: Rouen 1780–1800," *Social History* 2 (1976): 217.

21. *Reynolds v. Nebraska,* 98 U.S. 145 (1879), 164, 166.

22. *Bradwell v. Illinois,* 83 U.S. 130 (1872).

23. Martha Minow, "We, the Family: Constitutional Rights and American Families," *The American Journal of History* 74, no. 3 (1987): 969, discussing *Reynolds* and other nineteenth-century cases.

24. John Stuart Mill, *The Subjection of Women* (1869), in *Collected Works,* ed. J. M. Robson (Toronto: University of Toronto Press, 1984), vol. 21, pp. 324, 293–95. At the time Mill wrote, women had no political rights and coverture deprived married women of most legal rights, too. He challenges all this in his essay.

25. Mill, *Subjection of Women,* pp. 324–25, 294–95.

26. Hobbes writes of "men . . . as if but even now sprung out of the earth . . . like mushrooms." "Philosophical Rudiments Concerning Government and Society," in *The English Works of Thomas Hobbes,* ed. Sir William Molesworth (London: John Bohn, 1966), vol. 2, p. 109.

27. For example, Walzer, *Spheres of Justice,* chap. 9, "Kinship and Love."

28. See Alan Gewirth, *Reason and Morality* (Chicago: University of Chicago Press, 1978). He discusses moral development from time to time, but places families within the broad category of "voluntary associations" and does not discuss gender roles within them.

29. This is the case with both Rawls's *Theory of Justice* and Phillips's sociologically oriented *Toward a Just Social Order,* as discussed above.

30. Rawls, *Theory,* p. 465.

APPENDIX

On Writing Philosophical Essays

Appendix

On Writing Philosophical Essays

Craig Walton

Craig Walton is Professor of Philosophy and Ethics and Policy Studies at the University of Nevada, Las Vegas. He is the author of numerous works in the areas of ethics, history of philosophy, and public policy that have appeared in such journals as *Southern Journal of Philosophy* and *The Journal of the History of Philosophy*. He is the translator of Nicholas Malebranche's (1638–1715) *Treatise on Ethics (1684)* (1993) as well as the author and/or editor of several books, including *De la recherche du bien: A Study of Malebranche's Science of Ethics* (1972) and *Hobbes's "Science of Natural Justice"* (1987).

We easily distinguish between puppy love and adult love, especially by the aid of hindsight. Aristotle tried to explain how love matures in us, by isolating three phases (in his *Ethics*, Book 8). But whether it is Aristotle or Pat Boone writing on love, we know that it must grow if it is to become serious, that if it does not grow it will lack roots, and that root-growing is damned hard to do. Now what has all that to do with writing philosophical essays?

"Essay" means an attempt. Philosophy is a love for wisdom, a love of a special sort, love of the self for conscious insight into ourselves, and what is going on around us. An essay in writing philosophically is an attempt to exercise a peculiar sort of love. If it is done well, it will be the occasion for growth of that sort of love. But what would that mean? Is there any rhyme or reason to such an essay? Are there ways to write, to put oneself forth, to test and probe oneself, that would be more fruitful than other ways? Couldn't we just get serious, or stay up late in the a.m., get a great idea and write like fury? Wouldn't that be writing a philosophical essay?

To a cynic, philosophers deal only with words. It is well known in our TV-screaming world that words are cheap. Humpty Dumpty is the archangel of mesmerology, and Marshall McLuhan is his prophet: "A word means exactly what I want it to mean." And that will depend on how I feel, or where I am, or who I want to hit with what emotion. So a word means everything, and anything. Those of us who felt fond emotions at Walt Disney's *Bambi* can only see Humpty Dumpty lurking in the background of the Pentagon when they develop a missile and call it BAMBI (Ballistic Antimissile Booster Intercept). A word means whatever its user wants it to mean? Then how do we know what we are talking about? We don't, until it is over and we decide what we wanted it all to mean. Madness? Ionesco's *Bald Soprano*? How could we say the word means anything at all, if its so-called meaning is one thing today and another tomorrow, or later tonight?

Such madness is rare, but the cynicism is popular. Usually most of us try to make sense to each other, even if we fail. We so communicate, if only on blunt issues. Philosophers deal with words, when they deal at all—but they do not deal with words that mean whatever they want them to mean. And their words are only the coin of their realm, not its natural resources or products. The coin may be used for dealing, for exchange, but trade is not *of* coin even if it does not occur *without* coin. Words are the coin of the mind's realm: we trade with them. If we fear, despise, or abandon that realm, its coin means anything and nothing. If we do not see or do not care about the consequences of debasing the coinage of the mind's realm, we cheapen it, drive it to bankruptcy. We convert communication into noise, entertainment into anesthesia, news into shock, and serious thought into slogans.

Puppy love is not "real" because it is based on feelings that come strongly and leave without a clue to their next destination; it is not "real" because it confuses my feeling and your feeling with my ability to feel what you need, and yours to feel what I need. These latter feelings can build into love, but the former are too private to build anything. And there is some analogy with the lover of wisdom; he begins someplace, as a student, and he begins with a puppy love for wisdom. He feels some words more strongly than others, he feels some truths and feels nothing about others. One semester he is up nights over civil disobedience, a year later political theory is useless and he must assess the status of ideas in

---

This essay is published here for the first time. Permission provided by the essay's author.

regard to the senses. He reads viscerally and reacts to words and phrases in his studies as he would react to TV or newspapers, to friends or enemies in conversation—that is to say, quickly, with great feeling, and with little awareness of whether or not there was an exact meaning there, much less what it was if it was. He is moving fast, and picks up only those parts of his reading that have large handles. And this is a way to start; sometime or other we must make our beginnings. We begin by becoming familiar with the coins of the realm of the mind, with words. Sometimes they mean what we feel them to mean, and that changes with our moods. Sometimes they mean what the face on the TV seems to feel they mean, or they mean what the color of the billboard makes you feel they mean.

But there is always that outside chance, that possibility that we might build love more solid and lasting than puppy love. And we might build meanings more solid and lasting than this season's commercials, this campaign's political harangue, or this morning's newspaper slogans. If there can be meanings, the words that communicate them must not be cheap or debased. If words can *mean*, if they can deal with and let us exchange labor with each other, they might fertilize and enrich us. There is the possibility of an adult love of wisdom that is hard to feel and hard to express, whose object is hard to find, but meaningful.

I have used the notion that words could help us exchange the fruits of our intellectual labors. This is a way of saying that words might carry freight, that they might communicate ideas. What do I mean by "ideas" here? By "idea" I mean a grip on a problem, a way of coming to grips with trouble, with some state of affairs unknown or poorly understood, grappling with it and in time achieving some kind of hold on its facets in a way that gets them all together in a working grip. It is a working-over and shaping of materials, of parts of a problem, until they break down into stages or bites that seem to fit the evidence, and then tying them to each other by patterns, priorities, or other relationships that link or constitute them all as the pieces of *this* problem, put together *this* way, in *this* intellectual grip. There aren't many ideas around, at least strong ones, and no one comes by a strong idea by sheer luck. Words might symbolize an idea, but only for purposes of memory: if an idea is to be communicated, its word must be uttered, but much more must be done. It must be seen in action, it must meet tests and show its stuff, it must be contrasted with other ideas better or worse than it, so as to show us what it *does* amount to. The fact that a person writes or utters a word does not mean he has sweated his intellectual way through the trouble and time it takes to build an idea for which that uttered word is a symbol. He may, like babies and parrots, be uttering it because he heard it, and has been conditioned to utter it in certain stimulus-response conditioning situations. There is no easy way out, here: a word might mean whatever he feels it means, it might mean only what society trained him to mean by it, or it might be in one of several stages of growth in his intellect: from public noise to philosophical sweat and blood to a grip on a tough issue. The latter I call an idea, a meaning with a record, with a relevance, a structure and tension and punch to it.

The labor of a philosopher is the application of intellect to problems. She attempts to grasp an issue: to break it into pieces big enough to keep in mind and small enough to allow for delicate observation. She watches and also experiments on those pieces, arranging them in various ways as a painter does with colors, to see what sense it makes to put them this way, or that; she hunts for the patterns of interrelationships that have the greatest scope, cover as much unity of complex aspects as she can achieve. Her mind is wrestling with real troubles, in real agonies and ecstasies, and its fruit, when it comes forth, gives understanding and comprehension, opens to others a new or fresh or stronger way of living with and working on that trouble. She creates grips on reality, with her mind—but not a dry mind. It is a mind full of passion, feeling, bloodied and frightened, lifted up and exhausted; it is her spirit. Socrates was not playing word-games when he called this search for wisdom a kind of love.

To "essay" into that arena is a difficult but beautiful labor. As with other, better advertised arenas, one is likely to fall on one's face quite often before getting very adept at the sort of wrestling that goes on in it. But whether one's love and quest for wisdom is in the puppy stage, or more mature, there are some identifiable features of that "essay" that build together to make it a work of tension, strength, coherence, and also—hopefully—meaning. I want to briefly comment on those identifiable features of a philosophical essay, as follows: (1) introduction, (2) interpretation; (3) critique, (4) reconstruction, and (5) conclusion.

(1) Introduction: Why is this essay being written? What is at stake here? If there is any serious issue to be handled, what is it, and what makes it serious? Presumably there could be evidence of widespread confusion about the problem; what difference does

that make? Some problems deserve to pass away, like the angel-seating capacity of the head of a pin. Presumably a piece of philosophical writing comes to grips with something of consequence, not with trivia. If on this subject on which you write there are two or three respected and well-known or easily available views that conflict with each other, tell us what they are, who said them, why they conflict and on what points. Help your readers at least get a bearing on where you are going and why this needs your work. Then, indicate briefly how you will go about that work, who you will consider as deserving of your attention, and where you intend to go after examining one or two of your predecessors in this problem area.

(2) *Interpretation:* Why should a philosopher spend time doing an interpretation of some dead philosopher? Why should he not read a few live ones, quote them a bit (for good manners), and then take off on his own? The question of dead versus living philosophers is not important at all; what matters is, why should a philosopher take seriously any previous philosopher? Why not read them and then go on to one's own modern and hopefully fresh thoughts? The answer cannot be given clearly in one sentence, but it can be given tersely: there is no solid achievement except on the shoulders of and out of sensitive response to the best that has been done so far. We may be eager to go farther than our predecessors, but in many ways we must admit that we at least start *behind* them. We need to see what they did and why, and how they did it; where it was solid and where weak; what skills they needed and which ones they lacked; if they fell into traps and, if so, whether those traps could be avoided. And most crucial of all, there is no greater guide to creative achievement than encounter with one who has sweated such greatness out of intercourse with life. The living power of such work, if we can but perceive it, arouses more response within us than a thousand of our isolated cries or resolutions of desire. We interpret not "dead" or "alive" predecessors, but the great ones, and we do it that we might find response within ourselves, at or near a point they reached. If we later have the strength to reach as high as their shoulders, though starting at their feet, then we might accept the advantage they thereby give us, and build a bit higher. But we begin by accepting the challenge, and that means the labor of interpretation.

There is here a trivial problem, and a damned nasty problem. The trivial one is this: What as a mat-

ter of textual fact did my challenger-predecessor have to say about the problem under study here? Not "what do people think he said?," or "what does the great textbook say he said?," but what did he say, where and in what context, in regard to the issue concerning which first he and now I have chosen to essay into philosophical labor?

That, I said, is trivial. But it is also poorly done too often. It is not difficult to see why that trivial problem of basic documentation and accurate quotation must be a foundation stone for any philosopher's work in interpreting and trying to reach up to the work of a great predecessor. But then comes the damned nasty problem, the guts of interpretation: In *view* of what he did in fact say about this issue, what did he *mean* by what he said? Was there an idea behind, symbolized by the words you are easily able to quote? Even if we graduate from textbook summaries to the level of presenting actual documented evidence that our predecessor said such-and-such, we still must realize that words take on freight. They become loaded with use. Our predecessor-philosopher started with words he learned in some language, and they had certain meanings or freight put on them by others, by custom, or by his own feelings or fantasies. But as he picked up these words and moved into the arena of wrestling with a serious problem, he unloaded other people's meanings and gradually developed and loaded on his own. He explores the problem and builds ideas, all behind the words we read. Ideas are symbolized by words, but unlike words or noises, ideas contain a nest of meanings. They are built up out of assertions here and restrictions or denials there, scope and limitations of definition or intent, all of which give them some sort of reach around the issue and some grip on it; that grip has power or weakness—maybe both, in different ways. If we are to find his meaning, we must interpret. That means we must hunt down that nest of meanings, we must go over and over his trail, following him through turmoil and repose, through great and small troubles, as he builds and shapes ideas in combat with a problem. How does he build, where and why does he deepen or shorten, expand or trim his ideas? What can they do? Interpretation of another thinker's work must be done before we can be challenged by it, and we must be challenged before we can respond. The quality of challenge has a great deal to do with the quality of our response. And if it begins with interpretation of the work of a great predecessor, that interpretation begins with love. It is an art, motivated by search for the greatness we need for our challenge, and it takes skill, time, sweat. It is the beginning of our essay into philosophical writing.

(3) Critique: Once we see not only that a selected predecessor wrote certain words, but what he meant by them, how they constituted ideas toward coming to grips with a problem we have chosen to tackle, our next need is to search out the ways in which he was strong and weak. If his ideas had solid features, which features were they, and what are your reasons for saying they were solid? If you see weaknesses in his grip on the problem, where are they, and what reasons are there for saying they are weak? If he communicated meanings, or if you found meanings he *never* knew he had discovered or created, what are they and what is their contribution? Did his ideas have consequences he never dreamed of, for good or for ill? If so, which ones and why? In short, what is your critical evaluation of his philosophical essay? Did he come to grips with the problem he thought he tackled? Or only some aspects of it? Did he get the problem wrong, taking three as one, or taking one third as the whole? Do the several meanings he built all hang together in a coherent and relevant whole or unit? Or is his approach to this problem a piecemeal one, with only glimmers of cohesiveness? Show us how and why he does or does not accomplish what he thought he accomplished.

In order to critique, we implicitly insert our own judgment, even more boldly than in interpretation. Now we begin to ask ourselves whether or not the problem our predecessor handled should be understood as he understood it, or perhaps in another way. We begin to assert our hunches, explore our own responses to his labor. When we give reasons why he was strong or weak, unified or scattered in this or that portion of his work, we are reaching for perspective—for his shoulders, as it were.

(4) Reconstruction: This is briefly described and tediously exemplified: here we begin to take our own steps. In view of the problem at stake, which we clarified in our introduction, and in view of one of our predecessors' ideas on the problem, and the ways he was strong and weak in his grip, what can we do to save his best and improve on his other work, so as to build a better idea? Let it be plainly said that this will take years. It may come forth as a hunch only; often our reconstruction is a solid achievement if we can restate the original problem, or open it up into three or four distinct problems, or show our readers clearly how one or two approaches do *not* work! There are many ways to build upon the best that has come along so far, and most of those ways are small bricks, hunches or even realizations of dead-ends never previously known to be dead.

(5) Conclusion: It is not merely for the reader's sake that we conclude by explaining why we embarked, where we went and in which ways the voyage hangs together. If there has been some fruit to this labor, if there has been a gutsy encounter with greatness and a response at the best level we have in us, all concerning a problem, what have we learned about the problem? Tie it up, pull it together, and show us how it all pulls together. Clashing cymbals are not needed, but if there is a germ discovered here and ready to grow, it can be simply offered.

I have said a great deal about skills, about the art of interpretation, the challenge of greatness, and the labor of the intellect over serious issues. I have not said much about syntax, grammar, or logic. The reason should be easy to guess: although our writing is not understandable without some grammar and our arguments will not tie together without training in logic, those two abilities are not at the gut of philosophy. Philosophical writing is the expression of the philosophical quest, sometimes of the fruit of that quest. It is not ever merely technique: no amount of validity will make it meaningful. Trivia can be explained with logical precision. This does not mean that disgust toward or ignorance of logic and precision automatically turns a novice into a philosopher. In fact they prevent that development as much as disgust for calisthenics would condemn a would-be athlete to the bench. We must strike for clarity, for care in analysis or in the construction of arguments, for sensitivity to the resources available in our native language. There could be a science, or at least a technology of good philosophical writing, and it would include grammar and logic. But when we come to the question of purpose, of seriousness, and of problems that we need to tackle and with which we and our fellows need to come to grips, technique must be assimilated and lifted up into art. Intellectual creativity requires several techniques, but only in the service of our reach, our need, our love for the possibility of putting together that which we find in pieces, of penetrating through our own and others' darkness to kindle some light. An essay is an attempt; those who make that attempt in philosophy are reaching out with feeling as well as with analytic precision, reaching for a solid grip on a problem for meaning where there was none, for ideas where there were slogans and noises. If a work is to mean what we want it to mean, it must mean something for others; therefore meaning must be built out of challenge, interpretation, and response to great achievement concerning serious human issues. We search the works of the best predecessors we can find, in order that we might then search ourselves for the best we can do. Today we have as much justification as anyone ever had for cursing the darkness. The tougher question, closer to home, is whether or not we have the nerve to chip away at the flint of an Aristotle or St. Augustine in order to build our own fires in today's dark regions, and commit our whole intellect, with passion and precision, to building ideas in response to the *presently* unmanageable problems of *our* times.

AUTHOR INDEX